The College Board
2009 Scholarship HANDBOOK

2009

The College Board

Scholarship
HANDBOOK

Twelfth Edition

The College Board, New York

The College Board: Connecting Students to College Success

The College Board is a not-for-profit membership association whose mission is to connect students to college success and opportunity. Founded in 1900, the association is composed of more than 5,400 schools, colleges, universities, and other educational organizations. Each year, the College Board serves seven million students and their parents, 23,000 high schools, and 3,500 colleges through major programs and services in college admissions, guidance, assessment, financial aid, enrollment, and teaching and learning. Among its best-known programs are the SAT®, the PSAT/NMSQT®, and the Advanced Placement Program® (AP®). The College Board is committed to the principles of excellence and equity, and that commitment is embodied in all of its programs, services, activities, and concerns.

For further information, visit www.collegeboard.com.

Editorial inquiries concerning this book should be directed to College Planning Services, The College Board, 45 Columbus Avenue, New York, NY 10023-6992; or telephone 212 713-8000.

Copies of this book are available from your local bookseller or may be ordered from College Board Publications, P.O. Box 869010, Plano, TX 75074-0998. The book may also be ordered online through the College Board Store at www.collegeboard.com. The price is $27.95.

© 2008 The College Board. All rights reserved. College Board, Advanced Placement Program, AP, CLEP, College-Level Examination Program, College Scholarship Service, CSS, CSS/Financial Aid PROFILE, SAT, and the acorn logo are registered trademarks of the College Board. connect to college success, My College QuickStart, MyRoad, SAT Preparation Booklet, SAT Preparation Center, SAT Reasoning Test, SAT Subject Tests, The Official SAT Online Course, The Official SAT Study Guide, and The Official Study Guide for all SAT Subject Tests are trademarks owned by the College Board. PSAT/NMSQT is a registered trademark of the College Board and National Merit Scholarship Corporation. All other products and services may be trademarks of their respective owners.

Library of Congress Catalog Number: 97-76451

ISBN-13: 978-0-87447-827-3

ISBN-10: 0-87447-827-8

Printed in the United States of America

Distributed by Macmillan

Contents

Preface vii

How to Use This Book 1

Understanding Financial Aid 5

Finding and Applying for Scholarships 11

Sources of Information About State Grant Programs 18

Glossary 21

Eligibility Indexes

    Corporate/Employer 27
    Disabilities 27
    Field of Study/Intended Career 27
    Gender 48
    International Student 49
    Military Participation 50
    Minority Status 50
    National/Ethnic Background 56
    Organization/Civic Affiliation 56
    Religious Affiliation 60
    Returning Adult 60
    State of Residence 61
    Study Abroad 73

Scholarships 75

Internships 527

Loans 577

Sponsor Index 595

Program Index 603

Preface

Searching for scholarships has often been described as looking for a needle in a haystack. There are thousands of award programs available, but the typical student can expect to qualify for only a small number of them. This book is designed to point you toward programs that match your own personal and academic qualifications.

Compiled within this book are detailed descriptions of national and state-level award programs for undergraduate students. Most are available to all undergraduates, but some are restricted to entering freshmen, and others are only for continuing students—sophomores, juniors, or seniors. Most awards are only available to U.S. citizens or permanent residents, but some are also available to students in other countries who plan to come to the United States for college.

The award program descriptions are based on information provided by the sponsors themselves, in response to the College Board's Annual Survey of Financial Aid Programs, conducted in the spring of 2008. A staff of editors verified the facts for every award program. While every effort was made to ensure that the information is correct and up to date, we urge you to confirm facts, especially deadline information, with the programs themselves. The award programs' Web sites are the best sources for current information.

We'd like to thank those who worked so hard to bring the *Scholarship Handbook 2009* to press: Andy Costello compiled and edited the data on the programs, with the assistance of James Greene Jr., Rachael Mason, C. LeMar McLean, and Jennifer Donato. Cathy Harlem and John Mullen at Content Data Solutions Inc., extracted the program data and turned it into composed pages. Kevin Iwano oversaw the production of the finished book.

Tom Vanderberg
Senior Editor, College Planning Services

Kevin Troy
Assistant Editor, College Planning Services

How to Use This Book

You may be tempted to go directly to the program descriptions and start browsing, but to get the most out of this book, start by reading the information and advice in the opening pages. They'll help you get a realistic perspective on financial aid and give you useful guidelines for understanding and taking advantage of your college funding options.

Your next step should be to complete the "Personal characteristics checklist" on page 13. This will help you think about all the ways you might qualify for scholarships, and give you an idea of where you might start looking for awards you can apply for.

Using the eligibility indexes

After your checklist is complete, use the eligibility indexes beginning on page 27 to find the award programs that correspond to your qualifications. You can also use the scholarship search program on www.collegeboard.com. This user-friendly program enables you to search with more criteria and with much greater speed than is possible with print indexes.

Please keep in mind that the eligibility indexes show programs for which *one* of the criteria is covered by the index. Most of these programs have additional requirements, such as financial need (as demonstrated on the FAFSA or CSS/Financial Aid PROFILE®), standardized test scores, or GPA.

Corporate/Employer: Listed here are the many companies and businesses that offer scholarships to employees and/or employees' family members. You should check out any company that employs a member of your immediate family.

Disabilities: This category covers students with hearing or visual impairments, physical handicaps, or learning disabilities.

Field of Study/Intended Career: This category, by far the longest, identifies broad major and career areas. If you don't see your specific area of interest, look for a more general area into which it might fit. In many cases, these awards require applicants to be already enrolled in college and to have declared a major in the relevant field.

> **KNOW THE LINGO**
>
> You'll find sidebars like this throughout the first part of this book highlighting and defining key terms. There's also a comprehensive glossary beginning on page 21.

Gender: Although the vast majority of awards are not gender-specific, there are over 100 awards in this book exclusively for women, and more than 20 for men only.

International Students: Most awards in this book are available only to U.S. citizens or permanent residents. The programs in this category, however, are open to students from outside the United States.

Military Participation: Many of the awards in this category are for the children, descendants, or spouses of members of the military, including the Reserves and National Guard, going back as far as the Civil War.

Minority Status: There are eight groups within this category, representing a wide range of awards.

National/Ethnic Background: The national/ethnic groups in this category are determined by the sponsoring organizations that responded to our annual survey.

Organization/Civic Affiliation: Many membership organizations and civic associations have generous higher education funding programs that are available for their members and/or their members' dependents or relatives. Check to see if any apply to your family.

Religious Affiliation: The 10 denominations in this category represent a broad range but, like the national/ethnic category, are determined by the respondents to our annual survey.

Returning Adult: This category includes awards for undergraduate, graduate, and nondegree study. The age qualification varies, but most often is for students 25 years or older.

State of Residence: Each state has several award programs exclusively for state residents. Be sure to examine closely all those listed under your state.

Study Abroad: While most award programs for study abroad are for graduate students, a few are geared for undergraduates, and you will find them listed here.

What's in the program descriptions

The scholarship programs in this book are organized alphabetically by sponsor within three sections.

The scholarships section covers public and private scholarships and research grants for undergraduates. To be included, a scholarship program must grant at least $250 for the purpose of financing some aspect of higher education: tuition and fees, research, study abroad, travel expenses, or other educational endeavors.

KEEP IN MIND

This book does not describe local award programs that are restricted to a single community or school. For information about local programs for which you might qualify, talk to your school counselor or contact your local chamber of commerce.

Also not included in this are scholarships offered by colleges to their own students. For these "inside" awards, you should consult the financial aid offices at the colleges you are considering. Detailed financial aid information for more than 3,000 colleges can also be found in the College Board book *Getting Financial Aid 2009*.

PLANNING AHEAD

Even if you qualify for a scholarship, you won't get it if you don't **apply on time**! Use the **planning worksheet on page 17** to keep track of deadlines, application requirements, and notification dates for the programs you've selected.

The internships section covers public and private internships, providing opportunities either to earn money for education or to gain academic credit. To be included, paid internships must pay at least $100 per week and provide a viable path toward a future career. (The General Motors internship is an example of this—the Oscar Mayer Wienermobile is not.)

The loans section covers public and private education loan programs. Many have loan forgiveness options, usually in exchange for public or community service for a certain period of time.

Each program description contains all of the information provided by the sponsor and verified for accuracy by a staff of editors at the College Board. A typical description includes:

Type of award: Whether the award is a scholarship, grant, internship, or loan; and whether it's renewable.

Intended use: Tells you the range and limitations of the award, such as level of study, full-time or part-time, at what kind of institution, and whether in the United States or abroad.

Eligibility: Indicates the characteristics you must have to be considered for an award—for example, U.S. citizenship, specific state of residence, disability, membership in a particular organization, or minority status.

Basis for selection: May include major or career interest; personal qualities such as seriousness of purpose, high academic achievement, depth of character; or financial need.

Application requirements: Outlines what you must provide in support of your application, such as recommendations, essay, transcript, interview, proof of eligibility, a résumé, or references.

Additional information: Gives you any facts or requirements not covered in the categories above—for example, which test scores to submit, GPA required, whether a particular type of student is given special consideration, when application forms are available, etc.

Amount of award: A single figure generally means the standard amount, but may indicate the maximum of a range of amounts. If a program awards different amounts, the range is provided.

Number of awards: Tells you how many awards are granted by the sponsor.

Number of applicants: Tells you how many students applied the previous year.

Application deadline: The date by which your application must be submitted; some scholarships have two deadlines for considering applications. Note: This information was obtained in spring 2008. Deadlines may have passed or changed. Check the sponsor's Web site for current deadlines.

Notification begins: The earliest date that an award notification is sent; in some cases, all go out on the same date, in others, notification is on a rolling basis; if there are two application deadlines, there are usually two notification dates.

GOOD TO KNOW

In addition to the eligibility indexes preceding the scholarship descriptions, there are two general indexes in the back of the book that list award programs by sponsor name and program name.

KNOW THE LINGO

Academic internship—An internship where you are not paid for your work, but rather earn college credit.

Paid internship—An internship where you are paid for your work.

Total amount awarded: Tells you how much money is disbursed in the current award year, including renewable awards.

Contact: Gives you all available information on where to get application forms and further information. Where the contact name and address are identical for several different scholarship programs sponsored by the same organization, this information will appear at the end of the last scholarship in that group.

While some descriptions don't include all these details because they were either not applicable or not supplied by the sponsor, in every case all essential information is provided. Readers are urged to verify all information (the sponsor's Web site is the best source) before submitting applications.

Understanding Financial Aid

You shouldn't count on "outside scholarships" and summer internships like the ones in this book to pay for college. Rather, you should treat them as one possible source of aid, along with federal student aid and the scholarships and work-study jobs offered by colleges. In fact, outside scholarships account for only 8 percent of total student financial aid each year.

In order to get the most out of this book, you should first understand how to apply for the other 92 percent of total aid.

What Is Financial Aid?

Financial aid is money given or loaned to you to help you pay for college. Different forms have different rules. The vast majority of aid comes from the federal government, and most of it consists of loans that you must pay back. However, some aid does not require repayment—which makes it the best kind.

If you qualify for financial aid, your college will put together an aid "package," usually with different types of aid bundled together. Most students qualify for some form of financial aid, so it makes sense to apply for it.

You'll apply for financial aid either at the same time or soon after you apply for admission. You may have to fill out more than one application. At the very least you will fill out the FAFSA, or federal government form, available on the Web at www.fafsa.ed.gov. You may also fill out another form, the CSS/Financial Aid PROFILE, which many colleges require. And some colleges and state aid agencies require their own financial aid forms, too. The colleges to which you apply will use the forms to figure out what your family can afford to pay and what your "need" is—that is, the difference between what you can pay and what the college actually costs. If the school wants you as a student but sees that you can't handle the whole bill, it will make you a financial aid offer to help you meet your need. If you accept, that financial aid package is your award.

KNOW THE LINGO

Merit aid—Aid awarded on the basis of academics, character, or talent.

Need-based aid—Aid awarded on the basis of a family's inability to pay the cost of attending a particular college.

Non-need-based aid—Aid awarded on some basis other than need or merit, such as grants with eligibility requirements related to field of study or state residence.

You will need to apply for financial aid every year that you are in college, mainly because your family's financial situation changes yearly. As a result, your financial aid package will probably be somewhat different from year to year.

Financial aid is a helping hand, not a free pass. In the United States, everyone has a right to a free public school education, but not to a free college education. The federal government and most colleges agree that students and their parents are the ones most responsible for paying for college. "The primary responsibility of paying for the student's education lies with the student and his or her parents," says Forrest M. Stuart, the director of financial aid at Rhodes College in Memphis, Tennessee. "Financial aid comes in to fill that gap, if you will, between what they can afford and what the college costs."

> **GOOD TO KNOW**
>
> For a more thorough explanation of student financial aid, read the College Board book *Getting Financial Aid 2009*, or read the articles in the "Pay for College" section of www.collegeboard.com.

Types of Aid

Financial aid may come in many forms. However, all forms can be grouped into two major categories: gift aid and self-help aid.

Gift Aid

Gift aid is free money, money that you don't have to pay back or work for. Naturally, this is the kind of aid most people want. It can take the form of grants or scholarships.

The terms "grant" and "scholarship" are often used interchangeably to mean free money. But here's the difference: A grant is usually given only on the basis of need, or your family's inability to pay the full cost of college. Scholarships are usually awarded only to those who have "merit," such as proven ability in academics, the arts, or athletics. Once you're in college, you may have to maintain a minimum GPA or take certain courses to continue receiving a scholarship.

Self-Help Aid

Self-help aid is money that requires a contribution from you. That can mean paying back the money (if the aid is a loan) or working for the money (if the aid is a work-study job).

The most common form of self-help aid is a loan. A loan is money that you have to pay back with interest. In light of that, you might not consider this aid at all. But it is—a loan means you don't have to pay the full price of college all at once: you can stretch the payments over time, as you would when buying a house or a car. Furthermore, some student loans are subsidized by the federal government, which means you don't have to pay the interest that comes due while you're in college.

Subsidized loans, which are awarded based on need and administered by the college, are the best kind. But you can also take out unsubsidized student loans and parent loans, which are not packaged by most colleges. However, be careful not to take on more debt than necessary. No matter what kind of loan you take out, you will have to pay it back.

Another form of self-help is work-study. This is financial aid in the form of a job. Since you earn the money through your work, this too may not seem like aid. But it is, because the federal work-study program pays most of your wages. And work-study jobs are usually available right on campus, with limits on your hours so that you won't be unduly distracted from studying.

Who Gets Aid?

Grants and loans are not just for the poorest of the poor, nor are scholarships only for the smartest of the smart. The truth about who gets financial aid is somewhat different from what many people think.

Those Who Need It

Most financial aid is based on need, not merit. There is money for merit, but since the 1950s most colleges in the United States have focused their financial aid packages on meeting financial need.

However, there is a lot of confusion about what "need" means. "A lot of people think that they either have to be on welfare or Social Security—really poor—to get financial aid, and that's not correct," says Mary San Agustin, director of financial aid and scholarships at Palomar College in San Marcos, California. On the other hand, some rich families mistakenly think they are needy because their high living expenses leave them little money for college. "It's this expectation of, I pay my taxes, so my kid should be entitled to some federal financial aid regardless of how much money I make," says Ms. San Agustin.

Need simply means that your family can't afford to pay the full cost of a particular college. The *amount* of your need will vary from college to college, because it depends on the cost of attending an individual college. Whether your family has need is determined not by whether you think you are rich or poor, but by the financial aid forms you fill out.

Those Who Don't

Despite the overall emphasis on need, many colleges do give away money on the basis of merit. They do this to attract the students they want most, and they may award this money even if it is more than the student needs. However, in many cases, the student both needs the money and has earned it on the basis of merit.

Don't think that only geniuses get merit aid. At many colleges a B average can put you in the running for merit money. Sometimes a separate application for merit aid is required to put you into consideration; sometimes your application for admission is enough. In either case, don't count yourself out by not applying; apply and let the college decide.

Grants are sometimes awarded based on neither need nor merit. For example, you may get a grant if you are in a certain field of study, are a resident of the state, or are a student from the same town as the college.

KNOW THE LINGO

EFC (Expected Family Contribution)—How much money a family is expected to pay for college, based on the family's ability to pay.

Need—The difference between your EFC and the cost of attending a particular college you've chosen. Financial aid is designed to meet your need, not your EFC.

Gap—The difference (if any) between the financial aid you need, and the amount offered by a particular college.

Part-Time Students

Some kinds of aid are only available to students enrolled in college full-time—usually 12 or more credit hours of courses per semester. But part-time students are eligible for some financial aid. For example, federal loan programs require only that students be enrolled at least half-time. Also, some employers offer tuition reimbursement benefits to students who work full-time and go to college part-time.

Where the Money Comes From

Financial aid comes from three basic sources: governments (both federal and state), colleges, and outside benefactors.

From the Government

The lion's share of total financial aid awarded to undergraduates comes from the federal government. Fully 58 percent of all such aid is sent from Washington. The largest chunk of that consists of federal loans, which total $39.1 billion a year and represent 40 percent of all student aid. The loans take multiple shapes. Perkins loans are subsidized, with the lowest interest rate of any education loan. Stafford loans may be subsidized or unsubsidized. Both Perkins and Stafford loans are for students, but parents may take out a PLUS loan, which is not subsidized, to help pay for their children's educations.

The federal government also funds several grants: the Pell Grant, the Supplemental Educational Opportunity Grant (SEOG), the Academic Competitiveness Grant, and the SMART Grant. The Pell and SEOG grants are strictly need based, while the last two are based on both need and academic criteria. The government also funds the federal work-study program.

A much smaller piece of the financial aid pie (8 percent) comes from individual state governments. This is available in the form of grants, scholarships, and loans. Most of this aid is for use only at colleges within the state, though a few states offer "portable" aid, which state residents can take with them to a college in another state.

From the College

A great deal of financial aid comes from individual colleges, using their own "institutional" funds. In fact, colleges award nearly half of all grants. Many, though not all, award merit scholarships as well as need-based grants. They may also offer on-campus job opportunities and loans.

Private colleges give more financial aid than public ones, but their tuition is usually higher as well. Public colleges award less aid, but taxpayer support keeps their tuition lower.

Outside Grants and Scholarships

Outside grants and scholarships come from sources other than the government or the college. These sources may include corporations like Coca-Cola or community groups like the Elks Club. Some are well known, such as National Merit Scholarship Corporation, but, altogether they are the smallest piece of the financial aid pie: only 8 percent of all student aid comes from outside sources. Pursue them, but don't expect them to outweigh the other aid you will get.

Bear in mind also that an outside scholarship is unlikely to expand the total aid you receive. If a college has already "met your full need"—that is, offered an aid package that covers the entire difference between what the college costs and what your family is expected to pay—it will not add an outside scholarship to that aid package. Rather, it will use your scholarship to substitute for some other piece of aid in the package. Think of your financial aid package as a barrel: when the barrel is full, no more can be added unless something is taken away. The last thing colleges will take away is whatever sum of money your family is expected to contribute.

How Outside Awards Can Help

Even though outside scholarships rarely decrease the amount that your family is expected to pay out-of-pocket, it's still very worthwhile to pursue them. Why? Simply put, they expand your options for where you can go to college.

At some colleges, the first things taken away from a full-need package to make room for an outside scholarship are loans. Since that reduces the total amount you will have to pay back later, it makes that college more affordable. (Colleges vary in their policies on how they adjust packages for outside scholarships; you should call or e-mail the financial aid offices at the colleges you're considering to learn about their policies.)

There are also colleges that can't afford to offer every admitted student a financial aid package that meets the student's full need. If, for example, your need is $25,000 at a particular university, and the university's aid office can only offer you a combined total of $23,000 in grants, scholarships, work-study, and subsidized federal loans, then there is a $2,000 "gap" in your aid package. Outside scholarships can help fill that gap.

Finally, there may be colleges where you don't have any financial need. For example, if your family's expected contribution to your college costs is $10,000, a state university that costs $10,000 a year to attend couldn't offer you any need-based aid. An outside merit scholarship, in this case, could decrease what your family pays below their expected contribution.

FINANCIAL AID APPLICATION CALENDAR

SOPHOMORE/JUNIOR YEARS

- Talk to your parents about college costs. Have realistic expectations, but understand how financial aid can expand your options.
- Take the PSAT/NMSQT® in October of each year. If you take it as a junior, you will be entered into the National Merit Scholarship Competition.
- Think about colleges you might want to apply to. If possible, visit some campuses in the spring of your junior year.
- Take the SAT® or ACT in the spring of your junior year.
- If you have a job, do your taxes each year (ask your parents for help). Knowing about tax forms and documents will be helpful when you have to fill out financial aid applications.

SENIOR YEAR

SEPTEMBER
- Create a list of colleges you want to apply to. Start a checklist of their financial aid requirements and deadlines.
- If you're thinking about applying Early Decision to a college, ask whether it offers an early estimate of financial aid eligibility, and if so, what forms are required to receive one.
- Begin searching for outside scholarship programs available to seniors. Ask your school counselor about local scholarships offered by groups and businesses in your community.

OCTOBER
- Ask your school counselor if there will be a family financial aid night at your school or elsewhere in your area this fall. If there is, be sure to attend; the event may be your single best source of information.
- Use the online calculators at www.collegeboard.com to estimate your family's expected family contribution (EFC).
- If you need to fill out the CSS/Financial Aid PROFILE®, you can register on the PROFILE Online Web site starting October 1.

NOVEMBER
- Finalize the list of colleges that you'll apply to regular decision. Make sure you have all the financial aid forms you need.
- Get PINs for the FAFSA for both yourself and one of your parents from www.pin.ed.gov.
- Starting November 1, you can visit the FAFSA on the Web and get a sense of how the site works and what the application will ask for. But remember, you can't file the FAFSA until January 1.

DECEMBER
- You and your parents should save all end-of-year pay stubs for the year. You can use these to estimate income on aid forms.
- Apply for scholarships in time to meet application deadlines.

JANUARY
- You can file the FAFSA starting January 1.
- If any colleges you're applying to have a financial aid priority date of February 1, fill out the FAFSA (and PROFILE, if necessary) using estimated income information from your end-of-year pay stubs and last year's tax returns.
- Submit any other financial aid forms that may be required. Keep copies.

FEBRUARY
- If you didn't file the FAFSA and other aid forms in January, do so now, using drafts of your family's income tax returns.
- Check your federal Student Aid Report (SAR) when you receive it, and correct it if necessary.
- If you filed the PROFILE and a college asks your family to complete the Business/Farm Supplement, download the form and send it to the college.
- You and your parents should consider filing your income tax returns early this year. Some colleges will request copies of your family's returns before finalizing offers.

MARCH
- If necessary, write to colleges alerting them to special circumstances that affect your family's ability to pay for college.
- As you begin to receive letters of acceptance, check with aid offices to see if additional documentation (such as tax forms) must be submitted.

APRIL
- Compare your financial aid award letters using the online tools at www.collegeboard.com.
- Write, e-mail, or call the colleges that have offered you aid if you have any questions about the packages they've offered you.
- If you don't get enough aid to be able to attend a college, consider your options, which include appealing the award.

MAY
- Be sure to accept the aid package from the college you want to attend by May 1.
- Be sure also to let other schools know you won't be attending.
- Consider applying for non-need-based loans to cover your family's out-of-pocket expenses.

Finding and Applying for Scholarships

While you're researching and applying for colleges, you should also use this book to find scholarships that you qualify for and apply for them. In this chapter you'll find advice, as well as a calendar and worksheets to help keep you on track.

When to Start Looking

It's never too early to start looking for scholarships. There are several programs that are open only to high school freshmen and sophomores, and some that are open only to juniors. There are other programs where you begin the work of applying up to a year before the final determination is made. For example, the National Merit Scholarship Competition begins when students take the PSAT/NMSQT® in October of their junior year, and the competition proceeds in several rounds until fall of their senior year. If you're already a senior, though, don't despair—there are plenty of programs for entering freshmen that you can apply for during your senior year.

No matter what grade level you're in, the best time of the year to research programs is in the summer or early fall. That way you can be sure to find programs before their deadlines have passed, and with enough advance time to prepare a complete, competitive application. Remember that many scholarship programs require you to submit an essay as part of your application, and essays take time to write. Many programs also require recommendations; as a general rule, you should ask for recommendations at least four weeks in advance, and preferably more. Some programs even require you to perform additional academic work outside of school, such as writing a research paper or competing in a science fair.

You should let your school counselor know as early as possible that you're interested in applying for scholarships. He or she can help you think about your strengths as a student, which will make it easier to narrow down your scholarship search. Your counselor will also be able to recommend some programs you should apply for. (See "Thinking Locally" on page 14.)

Playing Catch-Up

If it's already the middle of your senior year, you've probably missed a lot of opportunities to apply for scholarships with October, November, and December deadlines. But don't give up yet; there are plenty of scholarships with January, February, and March deadlines.

The key to playing catch-up is to start working now, today. Find scholarships where the deadline hasn't passed. Get applications from the sponsors' Web sites. Talk to your school counselor immediately. The longer you wait, the less likely you are to win any awards.

The good news: Since you're already far into the college application process, you're now a pro at describing yourself to admissions committees and scholarship review boards. You also have personal essays, academic writing samples, and teacher recommendations ready to go.

Choosing Where to Apply

There are so many scholarships, grants, fellowships, internships, fee waivers, work-study jobs, and low-interest loans available for college-level study that just looking at the options can be daunting. (This book alone describes 2,100 national and state-level programs.) Fortunately, there are some easy ways to narrow the field of potential programs down to the ones where you have a good chance of winning an award.

The personal characteristics checklist on the next page highlights some of the common eligibility criteria for scholarship programs. You're not likely to find a scholarship that's targeted to every one of your characteristics, but you can use your answers on the checklist as a starting point for finding programs. The eligibility indexes on pages 27 to 73 will help you quickly match your characteristics to programs.

You'll probably find a few scholarship programs that match your characteristics. If you find a lot, you should consider narrowing your search—applying for scholarships is a lot of work! It's far better to send in four high-quality applications to programs that closely match your characteristics and interests than to send 16 hurried applications to a wide variety of programs.

PLANNING AHEAD

If you haven't already started looking for scholarships, start now. Today. Use this book to find a program you qualify for, and make a note of its application deadline and requirements. Then go to the program's Web site and download an application.

PERSONAL CHARACTERISTICS
CHECKLIST

Are you **male** or **female**?

What is your **state of residence**?

Do you have a **learning or physical disability**? Many scholarships are offered to those who are disabled in any way, but some are for those with a specific disability.

Military service is the basis of many scholarships. Many of these awards are not just for those who have worn a uniform, but also for their spouses and children, or even descendants of a veteran. Talk to your family about its military history (was Grandpa in the Korean War?) Be sure to find out what branch of the military your family members served in, and, if possible, which unit(s) they served in.

List any family history of military service here:

You'll find scholarships for students with **minority status**, (e.g., African American, Alaskan Native), and also for students with a particular **nationality or ethnic background** (e.g., Chinese, Greek).

If you belong to a minority, list it here:

List your ethnic and/or national origin(s) here:

What, if any, is your **religious affiliation**?

Are you an **international student** (a citizen of a foreign country, including Canada, seeking to study in the United States)?

The largest category of scholarships and internships is for students planning to study a particular college major (e.g., math, English, a foreign language) or prepare for a particular career (e.g., law, education, aviation). Even if you are "undecided" at this point, you should list all the **majors/careers** you are leaning toward.

☐ Do you want to **study abroad**? There are scholarships to help you pay for it—check here to remind yourself to seek them out.

"**Returning adult**" refers to students who have been out of high school a year or more before entering college. If that's you, look for scholarships designed to encourage your pursuit.

Years out of high school:

Your age:

Do you or any members of your family belong to a **national or local organization** or **civic association** (e.g., Kiwanis, Rotary, Elks Club)? Many such groups offer scholarships to members and/or their families. List here any that apply:

Employers and corporations often offer scholarship benefits to employees and/or their families. List the companies that you or someone in your family works for here:

Narrowing Your Search

If you're having trouble narrowing down your scholarship search, consider the following:

How many applicants are there each year? Some of the better-known programs (such as the Coca-Cola Scholars Program) see hundreds of applicants for every award they give out! It can't hurt to apply for these programs, but you shouldn't invest so much effort in applying for them that you miss out on smaller programs where your chances may be better.

Is this really for me? If you couldn't get through *Atlas Shrugged* the first time, don't force yourself to read it and write an essay on its philosophical meaning for the Ayn Rand Institute contest—even if you're a great English student. Focus instead on programs that appeal to you or sound like fun.

Can I live with the strings attached? Many scholarship and internship programs have service requirements. Most notably, the Reserve Officers Training Corps (ROTC) program requires cadets to become military reserve officers upon graduation. And some summer internships will require you to move to another city.

Thinking Locally

This book contains national and statewide financial aid programs offered by government agencies, charitable foundations, and major corporations. But there are also thousands of small scholarship programs offered on a local level by civic clubs, parishes, memorial foundations, and small businesses.

In many cases, these programs award just a few hundred dollars—enough to buy a semester's worth of textbooks. But since they are offered on a local level, your chances of receiving an award are much higher than they are for the big national competitions. So it pays to look for local scholarships.

Your school counselor may have files of local scholarship programs. There may even be a scholarship designated for graduates of your high school—you'll never know until you ask. You should also check with employers (either your parents' or your own); your church, temple, or mosque; and any civic clubs that your family members are involved in.

Avoiding Scholarship Scams

The Federal Trade Commission (FTC) developed Project $cholar$cam to alert students and families about potential scams and how to recognize them. Here are the FTC's six basic warning signs:

- "This scholarship is guaranteed or your money back."
- "You can't get this information anywhere else."
- "May I have your credit card/bank account number to hold this scholarship?"
- "We'll do all the work for you."

> **KEEP IN MIND**
>
> **Don't let your scholarship search overshadow your other responsibilities** and application requirements. You still need to do well in school, get your college applications in on time, and submit the FAFSA and other financial aid forms by your colleges' priority dates.

GOOD TO KNOW

For more information about Project $cholar$cam, visit the FTC's Web site at **www.ftc.gov**.

- "The scholarship will cost some money."
- "You've been selected by a national foundation to receive a scholarship."
- "You're a finalist" in a competition you never entered.

Remember that no one can guarantee that you'll receive a grant or scholarship, and that you will have to do the work of submitting applications to be considered. Don't pay money for a service without a written document saying what you'll get for your money and what the company's refund policies are. And never, ever give your credit card number, Social Security number, or bank account information to someone who called you unsolicited.

Applying for Scholarships

This may mean not only filling out a form, but also compiling supporting documents, such as transcripts, recommendations, and an essay. Or, you might need to provide evidence of leadership, patriotism, depth of character, desire to serve, or financial need. Get to know the requirements of each scholarship as early as possible so you can do any necessary extra work on time.

A few pointers to remember:

Apply early! Apply as early as possible to scholarship programs. If you can, do it in the fall of your senior year, even if the deadlines aren't until February or March. Very often, scholarship programs will have awarded all their funds for the year on a first-come, first-served basis before their stated deadline.

Follow directions. Read instructions carefully and do what they say. Scholarship programs receive hundreds and even thousands of applications. Don't lose out because of failure to submit a typewritten essay versus a handwritten one if required, or to provide appropriate recommendations. If you have a question about your eligibility for a particular scholarship or how to complete the application, contact the scholarship sponsors.

Be organized. It's a good idea to create a separate file for each scholarship and sort them by their due dates. Track application deadlines and requirements. Store in one place the different supporting documents you may need, such as transcripts, standardized test scores, and letters of recommendation.

Check your work. Proofread your applications for spelling or grammar errors, fill in all blanks, and make sure your handwriting is legible.

Keep copies of everything. If application materials get lost, having copies on file will make it easier to resend the application quickly.

Reapply. Some programs only offer money for the first year of college, but others must be renewed each subsequent year.

SCHOLARSHIP APPLICATION PLANNER

	PROGRAM 1	PROGRAM 2	PROGRAM 3
PROGRAM/SPONSOR	National Merit Scholarship	Young Epidemiology Scholars	First Bank
ELIGIBILITY REQUIREMENTS	Academic merit	Academic merit	Need, local residency
TYPE OF AWARD	Scholarship	Scholarship	Internship
AMOUNT OF AWARD	$2,500	$1,000 or more	$2,500
CAN BE USED FOR	Tuition/fees	Any expense	Any expense
CAN BE USED AT	First-choice college	Any college	In-state colleges
DEADLINE	October 1 (give essay to English teacher for review)	February 1	April 1
FORMS REQUIRED	NMSC application	Web form	Application (includes need analysis)
TEST SCORES REQUIRED	PSAT/NMSQT (already took), SAT (by December)	None	SAT
ESSAY OR ACADEMIC SAMPLE	Personal statement, academic transcript	Essay, research project	None required
RECOMMENDATIONS	Principal	None	One teacher (Mr. Filmer), Local branch manager
NOTIFICATION BEGINS	February	Not sure	May 15
REQUIREMENTS TO KEEP AFTER FRESHMAN YEAR	Onetime payment only	Onetime payment only	Based on performance during internship

For a blank version of this worksheet that you can photocopy for your own use, see the next page.

SCHOLARSHIP APPLICATION PLANNER

	PROGRAM 1	PROGRAM 2	PROGRAM 3
PROGRAM/SPONSOR			
ELIGIBILITY REQUIREMENTS			
TYPE OF AWARD			
AMOUNT OF AWARD			
CAN BE USED FOR			
CAN BE USED AT			
DEADLINE			
FORMS REQUIRED			
TEST SCORES REQUIRED			
ESSAY OR ACADEMIC SAMPLE			
RECOMMENDATIONS			
NOTIFICATION BEGINS			
REQUIREMENTS TO KEEP AFTER FRESHMAN YEAR			

Sources of information about state grant programs

Alabama
Alabama Commission on Higher Education
P.O. Box 302000
Montgomery, AL 36130-2000
334 242-1998
www.ache.state.al.us

Alaska
Alaska Commission on Postsecondary Education
P.O. Box 110505
Juneau, AK 99811-0505
800 441-2962
www.state.ak.us/acpe

Arizona
Arizona Department of Education
1535 West Jefferson Street
Phoenix, AZ 85007
800 352-4558
www.ade.state.az.us

Arkansas
Arkansas Department of Higher Education
114 East Capitol Avenue
Little Rock, AR 72201
501 371-2000
www.arkansashighered.com

California
California Student Aid Commission
P.O. Box 419026
Rancho Cordova, CA 95741-9026
888 224-7268
www.csac.ca.gov

Colorado
Colorado Department of Education
201 East Colfax Avenue
Denver, CO 80203-1799
303 866-6600
www.cde.state.co.us

Connecticut
Connecticut Department of Higher Education
61 Woodland Street
Hartford, CT 06105-2326
860 947-1800
www.ctdhe.org

Delaware
Delaware Higher Education Commission
820 North French Street
Wilmington, DE 19801-3509
800 292-7935
www.doe.state.de.us/high-ed

District of Columbia
State Education Office
441 4th St., NW, Suite 350 North
Washington, DC 20001
202 727-6436
www.seo.dc.gov

Florida
Florida Department of Education
Office of Student Financial Aid
1940 North Monroe Street, Suite 70
Tallahassee, FL 32303-4759
888 827-2004
www.floridastudentfinancialaid.org

Georgia
Georgia Student Finance Commission
2082 East Exchange Place
Tucker, GA 30084
800 505-4732
www.gsfc.org

Hawaii
Hawaii State Department of Education
P.O. Box 2360
Honolulu, HI 96804
808 586-3230
www.doe.k12.hi.us

Idaho
Idaho State Department of Education
P.O. Box 83720
650 West State Street
Boise, ID 83720-0027
800 432-4601
www.sde.state.id.us

Illinois
Illinois Student Assistance Commission
1755 Lake Cook Road
Deerfield, IL 60015-5209
800 899-4722
www.collegezone.com

Indiana
State Student Assistance Commission of Indiana
150 West Market Street, Suite 500
Indianapolis, IN 46204
888 528-4719
www.in.gov/ssaci

Iowa
Iowa College Student Aid Commission
200 10th Street, Fourth Floor
Des Moines, IA 50309-3609
515 242-3344
www.iowacollegeaid.org

Kansas
Kansas Board of Regents
1000 SW Jackson Street, Suite 520
Topeka, KS 66612-1368
785 296-3421
www.kansasregents.org

Kentucky
KHEAA Student Aid Branch
P.O. Box 798
Frankfort, KY 40602
800 928-8926
www.kheaa.com

Louisiana
Louisiana Office of Student Financial Assistance
P.O. Box 91202
Baton Rouge, LA 70821-9202
800 259-5626
www.osfa.state.la.us

Maine
Finance Authority of Maine
Education Assistance Division
P.O. Box 949
5 Community Drive
Augusta, ME 04332
800 228-3734
www.famemaine.com

Maryland
Maryland Higher Education Commission
Office of Student Financial Assistance
839 Bestgate Road, Suite 400
Annapolis, MD 21401
800 974-0203
www.mhec.state.md.us

Massachusetts
Massachusetts Board of Higher Education
Office of Student Financial Assistance
454 Broadway, Suite 200
Revere, MA 02151-3034
617 727-9420
www.osfa.mass.edu

Michigan
Michigan Higher Education Assistance Authority
Office of Scholarships and Grants
P.O. Box 30462
Lansing, MI 48909-7962
888 447-2687
www.michigan.gov/mistudentaid

Minnesota
Minnesota Office of Higher Education
1450 Energy Park Drive, Suite 350
St. Paul, MN 55108-5227
800 657-3866
www.ohe.state.mn.us

Mississippi
Mississippi Office of Student Financial Aid
3825 Ridgewood Road
Jackson, MS 39211-6453
800 327-2980
www.ihl.state.ms.us/financialaid

Missouri
Missouri Department of Higher Education
3515 Amazonas Drive
Jefferson City, MO 65109-5717
800 473-6757
www.dhe.mo.gov

Montana
Montana Board of Regents
P.O. Box 203201
46 North Last Chance Gulch
Helena, MT 59620-3201
406 444-6570
www.bor.montana.edu

Nebraska
Nebraska Coordination Commission for Postsecondary Education
P.O. Box 95005
Lincoln, NE 68509-5005
402 471-2847
www.ccpe.state.ne.us

Nevada
Nevada Department of Education
700 East Fifth Street
Carson City, NV 89701
775 687-9228
www.doe.nv.gov

New Hampshire
New Hampshire Postsecondary Education Commission
3 Barrell Court, Suite 300
Concord, NH 03301-8543
603 271-2555
www.nh.gov/postsecondary

New Jersey
New Jersey Higher Education Student Assistance Authority
P.O. Box 540
Trenton, NJ 08625
800 792-8670
www.hesaa.org

New Mexico
New Mexico Higher Education Department
1068 Cerillos Road
Santa Fe, NM 87505
800 279-9777
www.hed.state.nm.us

New York
New York State Higher Education Services Corporation
99 Washington Avenue
Albany, NY 12255
888 697-4372
www.hesc.state.ny.us

North Carolina
North Carolina State Education Assistance Authority
P.O. Box 14103
Research Triangle Park, NC 27709
919 549-8614
www.ncseaa.edu

North Dakota
North Dakota University System
600 East Boulevard, Dept. 215
Bismarck, ND 58505-0230
701 328-2960
www.ndus.nodak.edu

Ohio
Ohio Board of Regents
30 East Broad Street, 36th floor
Columbus, OH 43215-3414
614 466-6000
www.regents.ohio.gov

Oklahoma
Oklahoma State Regents for Higher Education
Tuition Aid Grant Program
655 Research Parkway, Suite 200
Oklahoma City, OK 73104
405 225-9100
www.okhighered.org

Oregon
Oregon Student Assistance Commission
1500 Valley River Drive, Suite 100
Eugene, OR 97401
800 452-8807
www.osac.state.or.us

Pennsylvania

Pennsylvania Higher Education Assistance Agency
1200 North Seventh Street
Harrisburg, PA 17102-1444
800 692-7392
www.pheaa.org

Puerto Rico

Departmento de Educacion
P.O. Box 190759
San Juan, PR 00919-0759
787 759-2000
www.de.gobierno.pr

Rhode Island

Rhode Island Higher Education Assistance Authority
560 Jefferson Boulevard, Suite 100
Warwick, RI 02886
401 736-1100
www.riheaa.org

South Carolina

South Carolina Commission on Higher Education
1333 Main Street, Suite 200
Columbia, SC 29201
803 737-2260
www.che.sc.gov

South Dakota

South Dakota Department of Education
Office of Finance and Management
700 Governors Drive
Pierre, SD 57501
605 773-3134
http://doe.sd.gov/stateaid

Tennessee

Tennessee Student Assistance Corporation
404 James Robertson Parkway, Suite 1510, Parkway Towers
Nashville, TN 37243-0820
800 342-1663
www.state.tn.us/tsac

Texas

Texas Higher Education Coordinating Board
Division of Student Services
P.O. Box 12788, Capital Station
Austin, TX 78711
800 242-3062
www.collegefortexans.com

Utah

Utah Higher Education Assistance Authority
Board of Regents Building, The Gateway
60 South 400 West
Salt Lake City, UT 84101-1284
801 321-7200
www.uheaa.org

Vermont

Vermont Student Assistance Corporation
P.O. Box 999
Winooski, VT 05404
800 798-8722
www.vsac.org

Virginia

State Council of Higher Education for Virginia
101 North 14th Street
Richmond, VA 23219
804 225-2600
www.schev.edu

Washington

Washington Higher Education Coordination Board
917 Lakeridge Way
P.O. Box 43430
Olympia, WA 98504-3430
360 753-7800
www.hecb.wa.gov

West Virginia

West Virginia Higher Education Policy Commission
Central Office, Higher Education Grant Program
1018 Kanawha Boulevard East, Suite 700
Charleston, WV 25301-2800
304 558-4614
www.hepc.wvnet.edu

Wisconsin

Wisconsin Higher Educational Aids Board
131 West Wilson, Suite 902
Madison, WI 53707
608 267-2206
www.heab.state.wi.us

Wyoming

Wyoming Department of Education
2300 Capitol Avenue
Hathaway Building, Second Floor
Cheyenne, WY 82002-0050
307 777-7690
www.k12.wy.us

Guam

University of Guam
Student Financial Aid Office
UOG Station
Mangilao, GU 96923
671 735-2287
www.uog.edu

Virgin Islands

Financial Aid Office, Virgin Islands Board of Education
P.O. Box 11900
St. Thomas, VI 00801
340 774-4546

Glossary

Academic Competitiveness Grant. A federal financial aid award available to students in their first two years of undergraduate study who are eligible for a Pell Grant and have successfully completed a rigorous high school academic program, as determined by their state or local education agency. The maximum award is $750 for the first year of undergraduate study and $1,300 for the second year, both of which are in addition to the Pell Grant award.

ACT. A college entrance examination given at test centers in the United States and other countries on specified dates throughout the year. It includes tests in English, mathematics, reading, and science.

Award letter. A means of notifying admitted students of the financial aid being offered by the college or university. The award letter provides information on the types and amounts of aid offered, students' responsibilities, and the conditions that govern the awards. Generally, the award letter gives students the opportunity to accept or decline the aid offered, and a deadline by which to respond.

College Scholarship Service® (CSS®). *See* CSS/Financial Aid PROFILE®.

Competition. An award based upon superior performance in relation to others in the competition. This book lists competitions based upon artistic talent, writing ability, and other demonstrable talents.

Cooperative education (co-op). A career-oriented program in which students alternate between class attendance and employment in business, industry, or government. Co-op students usually receive both academic credit and payment for their work. Under a cooperative plan, five years are normally required for completion of a bachelor's degree, but graduates have the advantage of about a year's practical work experience in addition to their studies.

CSS code. A four-digit College Board number that students use to designate colleges or scholarship programs to receive their CSS/Financial Aid PROFILE information. A complete list of all CSS codes can be downloaded from the CSS/Financial Aid PROFILE section on collegeboard.com.

CSS/Financial Aid PROFILE®. A Web-based application service offered by the College Board and used by some colleges, universities, and private scholarship programs to award their private financial aid funds. Students register for and complete the PROFILE on collegeboard.com. PROFILE provides a customized application for each registrant, based on the student's registration information and the requirements of the colleges and programs to which she or he is applying. The PROFILE is not a federal form and may not be used to apply for federal student aid.

Curriculum Vitae (CV). A type of résumé, from the Latin for "the course of one's life." Typically, a CV is used by applicants for fellowships or grants, or jobs in higher education, the sciences, or in a research capacity. The CV is typically longer than a résumé, and provides details about papers published, research conducted, and more.

Dependent student. For financial aid purposes, the status that includes students who are under the age of 24, attend an undergraduate program, are not married, do not have children of their own, or are not orphans or wards of the court, or veterans of the active-duty armed services. The term is used to define eligibility for certain financial aid programs, regardless of whether the student lives with a parent, receives financial support from a parent, or is claimed on a parents' tax returns. If a student is defined as a dependent, parental financial information must be supplied on the Free Application for Federal Student Aid (FAFSA) and institutional aid applications.

Dependents. Generally speaking, people who are dependent upon others (parents, relatives, a spouse) for food, clothing, shelter, and other basics. For purposes of getting federal financial aid, students must meet strict criteria in order to be defined as dependents, as in the view of federal aid programs, the family is the primary source of support for college. College students may have dependents (children dependent on them), and this too is taken into account by the federal government. Federal forms ask a series of questions about age, marital status, etc., to determine whether applicants are dependent on others or independent.

Direct Loan Program. *See* Federal Direct Loan Program.

Expected family contribution (EFC). The total amount students and their families are expected to pay toward college costs from their income and assets for one academic year.

FAFSA. *See* Free Application for Federal Student Aid.

Federal code number. A six-digit number that identifies a specific college to which students want their Free Application for Federal Student Aid form submitted. Also known as Title IV number.

Federal Direct Loan Program. A program that allows participating schools to administer subsidized and unsubsidized Stafford and PLUS loans directly to student and parent borrowers. Direct loans have mostly the same terms and conditions as FFELP loans. Funds for these programs are provided by the federal government.

Federal Family Education Loan Program (FFELP). The subsidized and unsubsidized Federal Stafford Loan, PLUS Loan, and Federal Loan Consolidation programs. Funds for these programs are provided by lenders, and the loans are guaranteed by the federal government.

Federal Parent Loan for Undergraduate Students (PLUS). A program that permits parents of undergraduate students to borrow up to the full cost of education, less any other financial aid the student may have received.

Federal Pell Grant Program. A federally sponsored and administered program that provides need-based grants to undergraduate students. Eligibility for Pell Grants is based on a student's expected family contribution, the total cost of attendance at the college, and whether the student is attending the college full-time or part-time.

Federal Perkins Loan Program. A federally funded campus-based program that provides low-interest loans, based on need, for undergraduate study. The combined cumulative total of loan funds available to an individual for undergraduate and graduate education is $40,000. Repayment need not begin until completion of the student's education, and may be deferred for limited periods of service in the military, Peace Corps, or approved comparable organizations. The total debt may be forgiven by the federal government if the recipient enters a career of service as a public health nurse, law enforcement officer, public school teacher, or social worker.

Federal Stafford Loan. A program that allows students to borrow money for education expenses from banks and other lending institutions (and sometimes from the colleges themselves). Subsidized Stafford loans are offered by colleges based on need. The federal government pays the interest on subsidized loans while the borrower is in college. Unsubsidized Stafford loans are non-need-based; anyone may apply for one, regardless of their ability to pay for college. The interest on unsubsidized loans begins accumulating immediately. For both programs, the amounts that may be borrowed depend on the student's year in school.

Federal student aid. A number of programs sponsored by the federal government that award students loans, grants, or work-study jobs for the purpose of meeting their financial need. To receive any federal student aid, a student must demonstrate financial need by filing the Free Application for Federal Student Aid, be enrolled in college at least half-time, and meet certain other eligibility requirements.

Federal Supplemental Educational Opportunity Grant Program (SEOG). A federal campus-based program that provides need-based grants for undergraduate study. Each college is given a certain total amount of SEOG money each year to distribute amongst their financial aid applicants and determines the amount to which the student is entitled.

Federal Work-Study Program. A campus-based financial aid program that allows students to meet some of their financial need by working on or off campus while attending school. The wages earned are used to help pay the student's education costs for the academic year. Job opportunities vary from campus to campus. The time commitment for a work-study job is usually between 10 and 15 hours each week.

Financial aid. Money awarded to students to help them pay for college. Financial aid comes in the form of gifts (scholarships and grants) and self-help aid (loans and work-study opportunities). Most aid is awarded on the basis of financial need, but some awards are non-need-based. Both need-based and non-need-based aid may be offered on the additional basis of merit.

Financial aid award letter. *See* award letter.

Financial aid package. The total financial aid offered to a student by a college, including all loans, grants, scholarships, and work-study opportunities.

Financial Aid PROFILE. *See* CSS/Financial Aid PROFILE.

Financial need. The difference between the total cost of attending a college and a student's expected family contribution (EFC). Financial aid grants, loans, and work-study will be offered by each college to fill the student's need.

Free Application for Federal Student Aid (FAFSA). A form completed by all applicants for federal student aid. The FAFSA is available on the Web at www.fafsa.ed.gov. In many states, completion of the FAFSA is also sufficient to establish eligibility for state-sponsored aid programs. There is no charge to students for completing the FAFSA. The FAFSA may be filed any time after January 1 of the year for which one is seeking aid (e.g., after January 1, 2008, for the academic year 2008-09).

Full-time status. Enrollment at a college or university for 12 or more credit hours per semester. Students must be enrolled full-time to qualify for the maximum award available to them from federal grant programs.

General Educational Development (GED). A series of five tests that individuals who did not complete high school may take through their state education system to qualify for a high school equivalency certificate. The tests cover correctness and effectiveness of expression, interpretation of reading materials in the natural sciences and the social sciences, interpretation of literary materials, and general mathematics ability.

Gift. Financial aid in the form of scholarships or grants that do not have to be repaid.

Grade point average (GPA). A system used by many schools for evaluating the overall scholastic performance of students. Grade points are determined by first multiplying the number of hours given for a course by the numerical value of the grade and then dividing the sum of all grade points by the total number of hours carried. The most common system of numerical values for grades is A = 4, B = 3, C = 2, D = 1, and E or F = 0.

Grant. A financial aid award that is given to a student and does not have to be paid back. The terms "grant" and "scholarship" are often used interchangeably to refer to gift aid, but often grants are awarded solely on the basis of financial need, while scholarships may require the student to demonstrate merit.

Half-time status. Enrollment at a college or university for at least 6 credit hours per semester, but less than the 12 credit hours required to qualify as full-time. Students must be enrolled at least half-time to qualify for federal student aid loan programs.

High school transcript. A formal document that shows all classes taken and grades earned in high school. It needs to be sent from the school to the scholarship sponsor, not from the applicant.

Independent student. For financial aid purposes, the status that generally includes students who are either 24 years old, married, a veteran, an orphan, or have legal dependents (not including spouse). Independent students do not need to provide parental information to be considered for federal financial aid programs. However, private institutions may require independent students to provide parental information on their institutional forms in order to be considered for nonfederal sources of funding.

Internship. Any short-term, supervised work, usually related to a student's major, for which academic credit is earned. The work can be full- or part-time, on or off campus, paid or unpaid. Some majors require the student to complete an internship.

Loan. Money lent with interest for a specified period of time. This book includes several loan programs; some forgive the loan in exchange for public service, such as teaching in a rural area.

Major. The subject area in which students concentrate during their undergraduate study. At most colleges, students take a third to a half of their courses in the major; the rest of their course work is devoted to core requirements and electives. In liberal arts majors, students generally take a third of their courses in their chosen field, which they usually must choose by the beginning of their junior year. In career-related programs, such as nursing or engineering, students may take up to half of their courses in their major.

Merit aid. Financial aid awarded on the basis of academic qualifications, artistic or athletic talent, leadership qualities, or similar qualities. Most merit aid comes in the form of scholarships. Merit aid may be non-need-based, or the merit criteria may be in addition to a requirement that the student demonstrate financial need.

National Science and Mathematics Access to Retain Talent (SMART) Grant. A federal grant program for Pell Grant recipients who are in their third or fourth year of undergraduate study, have declared a major in the sciences, mathematics, engineering, technology, or certain foreign languages, and have maintained a GPA of at least 3.0 in that major. The maximum annual award is $4,000, in addition to the student's Pell Grant.

Need-based aid. Financial aid (scholarships, grants, loans, or work-study opportunities) given to students who have demonstrated financial need, calculated by subtracting the student's expected family contribution from a college's total cost of attendance. The largest source of need-based aid is the federal government, but colleges, states, and private foundations also award need-based aid to eligible students.

Nomination. Being named as a candidate for an award or scholarship. Some scholarship programs require that a teacher or principal nominate students as applicants, and do not invite applications from students.

Non-need-based aid. Financial aid awarded without regard to the student's demonstrated ability to pay for college. Unsubsidized loans and scholarships awarded solely on the basis of merit are both non-need-based. Some financial aid sponsors also offer non-need-based grants that are not tied to merit, but rather to other qualities, such as state of residence or participation in ROTC.

Outside resources. Student financial aid granted by a source other than the college that the college must take into account when assembling an aid package. Examples of common outside resources include scholarships from private foundations, employer tuition assistance, and veterans' educational benefits.

Parents' contribution. The amount a student's parents are expected to pay toward college costs from their income and assets. It is derived from need analysis of the parents' overall financial situation. The parents' contribution and the student's contribution together constitute the total expected family contribution (EFC).

Part-time status. Enrollment at a college or university for 11 or fewer credit hours per semester.

Pell Grant. *See* Federal Pell Grant Program.

Perkins Loan. *See* Federal Perkins Loan Program.

Permanent resident. A non-U.S. citizen who has been given permission to make his or her permanent home in the United States. All permanent residents hold a "green card" and all holders of a green card are permanent residents. Permanent residents are eligible for numerous award programs.

PLUS Loan. *See* Federal Parent Loan for Undergraduate Students.

Portfolio. A physical collection of a student's work that demonstrates their skills and accomplishments. Portfolios may be physical or electronic. There are academic portfolios that include student-written papers and projects, and also portfolios that include created objects—art, photography, fashion illustrations, and more. Some scholarship programs request a portfolio.

Priority date. The date by which applications for financial aid must be received to be given the strongest possible consideration. The college will consider the financial need of applicants who make the priority date before any other applicants. Qualified applicants who do not make the priority date are considered on a first-come, first-served basis, and are only offered financial aid if (and to the extent that) the college still has sufficient money left over after all the offers it has made.

PROFILE. *See* CSS/Financial Aid PROFILE.

PSAT/NMSQT® (Preliminary SAT/National Merit Scholarship Qualifying Test). A preparatory tool for the SAT that is administered by high schools to sophomores and juniors each year in October. The PSAT/NMSQT serves as the qualifying test for scholarships awarded by the National Merit Scholarship Corporation.

Renewable. A scholarship or loan that can be renewed after the first award. Typically students have to apply annually in order to receive the funds after the first year.

Renewal FAFSA. A simplified reapplication form for continuing students. The Renewal FAFSA allows the student to update the financial information and other items that have changed from the prior year's FAFSA, rather than completing the entire FAFSA for each award year.

Reserve Officers' Training Corps (ROTC). Programs conducted by certain colleges in cooperation with the United States Air Force, Army, and Navy reserves. Participating students may receive a merit scholarship while they are in college, and will enter the reserves of their service branch as an officer upon graduation. Naval ROTC includes the Marine Corps. (The Coast Guard and Merchant Marine do not sponsor ROTC programs.) Local recruiting offices of the services themselves can supply detailed information about these programs, as can participating colleges.

Residency requirements. The minimum amount of time a student is required to have lived in a particular state or community in order to be eligible for scholarship, internship, or loan programs offered to such residents. Can also refer to the minimum amount of time a student is required to have lived in a state to be eligible for in-state tuition at a public college or university.

SAR. *See* Student Aid Report.

SAT®. The College Board's test of critical reading, writing, and mathematical reasoning abilities, given on specified dates throughout the year at test centers in the United States and other countries. The SAT is required by many colleges and sponsors of financial aid programs, and many colleges use scores on the SAT as criteria for the awarding of merit scholarships.

SAT Subject Tests™. College Board tests in specific subjects that are given at test centers in the United States and other countries on specified dates throughout the year. The tests are used by colleges not only to help with decisions about admission but also in course placement and exemption of enrolled freshmen.

Scholarship. A type of financial aid that doesn't have to be repaid. Grants are often based on financial need. Scholarships may be based on need, on need combined with merit, or solely on the basis of merit or some other qualification, such as minority status.

Section 529 plans. State-sponsored college savings programs commonly referred to as "529 plans" after the section of the Internal Revenue Code that provides the plan's tax breaks. There are two kinds: Section 529 college savings plans and Section 529 prepaid tuition plans.

Self-help aid. Student financial aid, such as loans and jobs, that requires repayment or employment.

SEOG. *See* Federal Supplemental Educational Opportunity Grant.

SMART Grant. *See* National Science and Mathematics Access to Retain Talent Grant.

Stafford Loan. *See* Federal Stafford Loan Program.

Student Aid Report (SAR). A report produced by the U.S. Department of Education and sent to students in response to their having filed the Free Application for Federal Student Aid (FAFSA). The SAR contains information the student provided on the FAFSA as well as the federally calculated expected family contribution.

Student expense budget. A calculation of the annual cost of attending college that is used to determine your financial need. Student expense budgets usually include tuition and fees, books and supplies, room and board, personal expenses, and transportation. Sometimes additional expenses are included for students with special education needs, students who have a disability, or students who are married or have children.

Student's contribution. The amount you are expected to pay toward college costs from your income and assets. The amount is derived from need analysis of your resources. Your contribution and your parents' contribution together add up to the total expected family contribution.

Subsidized Federal Stafford Loan. *See* Federal Stafford Loan Program.

Subsidized loan. A loan awarded to a student on the basis of financial need. The federal government or the state awarding the loan pays the borrower's interest while they are in college at least half-time, thereby subsidizing the loan.

Supplemental Educational Opportunity Grant. *See* Federal Supplemental Educational Opportunity Grant.

Tuition. The price of instruction at a college. Tuition may be charged per term or per credit hour.

Undergraduate. A college student in the freshman, sophomore, junior, or senior year of study, as opposed to a graduate student who has earned an undergraduate degree and is pursuing a master's, doctoral, or professional degree.

Unmet need. The difference between a specific student's total available resources and the total cost for the student's attendance at a specific institution.

Unsubsidized Federal Stafford Loan. *See* Federal Stafford Loan Program.

Unsubsidized loan. An education loan that is non-need-based and therefore not subsidized by the federal government; the borrower is responsible for accrued interest throughout the life of the loan.

Verification. A procedure whereby a school checks the information that the student reported on the FAFSA, usually by requesting a copy of the tax returns filed by the student and, if applicable, the student's spouse and parent(s). Colleges are required by federal regulations to verify a minimum percentage of financial aid applications.

William D. Ford Federal Direct Loan Program. *See* Federal Direct Loan Program.

Work-study. An arrangement by which a student combines employment and college study. The employment may be an integral part of the academic program (as in cooperative education and internships) or simply a means of paying for college (as in the need-based Federal Work-Study Program).

Eligibility Indexes

Corporate/Employer

A. M. Castle & Co., 91
Alcoa Inc., 88
Aviation industry, 82
Bemis Company, 202
Butler Manufacturing Co. & subsidiaries, 209
Chesapeake Corporation, 218
Cone Mills Corporation, 223
Federal/U.S. Government, 245
Footwear/Leather Industry, 494
Oregon Department of Transportation/Parks and Recreation Dept., 413
Oregon Dungeness Crab Fishermen, 416
Oregon Refuse & Recycling Association, 417
Playtex Products, Inc. and subsidiaries, 427
Staples, 476
Tesoro Petroleum Companies, Inc., 266
United Parcel Service (UPS), 591
UPS Earn and Learn Program Grant, 504
Wal-Mart Stores, Inc., 514
Wal-Mart Associate Scholarship, 515
Walton Family Foundation Scholarship, 515
Waste Control Systems, Inc., 417
West Pharmaceutical Services, Inc., 518

Disabilities

Hearing impaired

AG Bell College Scholarship Awards, 88
New York State Readers Aid Program, 392
Scholarship for People with Disabilities, 230
Sertoma Scholarships for Hearing-Impaired Students, 442
Texas Tuition Exemption for Blind or Deaf Students, 488
Virginia Rehabilitative Services College Program, 514
Wisconsin Hearing & Visually Handicapped Student Grant, 522
Yellow Ribbon Scholarship, 491

Learning disabled

The Challenge Met Scholarship, 163
Marion Huber Learning Through Listening Award, 434
North Carolina Vocational Rehabilitation Award, 399
Virginia Rehabilitative Services College Program, 514

Physically challenged

ChairScholars Scholarship, 217
Microsoft Scholarship for Students with Disabilities, 338
New Mexico Teacher's Loan-for-Service, 587
North Carolina Vocational Rehabilitation Award, 399
Scholarship for People with Disabilities, 230
Virginia Rehabilitative Services College Program, 514
Yellow Ribbon Scholarship, 491

Visually impaired

Alabama Scholarship for Dependents of Blind Parents, 476
Arthur E. Copeland Scholarship for Males, 502
Charles and Melva T. Owen Memorial Scholarship, 371
Christian Record Services Scholarship, 219
Computer Science Scholarship, 371
Delta Gamma Foundation Memorial Scholarship, 104
E.U. Parker Memorial Scholarship, 372
Ferdinand Torres Scholarship, 104
Florida Educational Assistance for the Blind, 249
Floyd Qualls Memorial Scholarship, 100
Guide Dogs for the Blind Dorthea and Roland Bohde Personal Achievement Scholarship, 105
Hank LeBonne Scholarship, 372
Helen Copeland Scholarship for Females, 502
Hermione Grant Calhoun Scholarship, 372
Howard Brown Rickard Scholarship, 372
Jennica Ferguson Memorial Scholarship, 372
Kenneth Jernigan Memorial Scholarship, 373
Kuchler-Killian Memorial Scholarship, 373
Lighthouse College-Bound Award, 321
Lighthouse Graduate Award, 321
Lighthouse Undergraduate Award, 322
Mary P. Oenslager Scholastic Achievement Award, 434
Michael and Marie Marucci Scholarship, 373
National Federation of the Blind Educator of Tomorrow Award, 373
National Federation of the Blind Scholarships, 374
New York State Readers Aid Program, 392
Paul and Ellen Ruckes Scholarship, 105
R.L. Gillette Scholarship, 105
Rudolph Dillman Memorial Scholarship, 105
Scholarship for People with Disabilities, 230
Texas Tuition Exemption for Blind or Deaf Students, 488
Virginia Rehabilitative Services College Program, 514
Virginia Vocational Rehabilitation Program Education Sponsorship, 238
Wisconsin Hearing & Visually Handicapped Student Grant, 522
Yellow Ribbon Scholarship, 491

Field of Study/Intended Career

Agricultural science, business, and natural resources conservation

Abbie Sargent Memorial Scholarship, 75
Alaska Winn Brindle (W.B.) Memorial Education Loan Program, 577
Alpine Club A.K. Gilkey and Putnam/Bedayn Research Grant, 92
American Chemical Society Scholars Program, 95
AMHI Educational Scholarships, 158
AMHI van Schaik Dressage Scholarship, 158
Amtrol Scholarship, 106
Annie's Homegrown Sustainable Agriculture Scholarships, 186
Arboriculture Internship, 552
A.T. Anderson Memorial Scholarship, 109

Field of Study/Intended Career: Agricultural science, business, and natural resources conservation

Award in Desest Studies, 252
Baroid Scholarship, 106
Burlington Northern Santa Fe Foundation Scholarship, 109
California Farm Bureau Scholarship, 210
Caroline Thorn Kissel Summer Environmental Studies Scholarship, 252
Carville M. Akehurst Memorial Scholarship, 287
Charles (Tommy) Thomas Memorial Scholarship, 159
Dairy Product Marketing Scholarships, 369
Dairy Student Recognition Program, 370
Decommissioning, Decontamination and Reutilization Scholarship, 159
Denver Rescue Mission Center for Mission Studies Interns, 537
Disney College Program, 574
Donald A. Williams Soil Conservation Scholarship, 470
Dosatron International Scholarship, 102
Earl Dedman Memorial Scholarship, 102
Ed Markham International Scholarship, 102
Enology and Viticulture Scholarship, 170
Eos #1 Mother Lodge Chapter Award, 234
EPA National Network for Environmental Management Studies Fellowship, 506
Filoli Center Garden Internships and Apprenticeships, 542
Flora of Pennsylvania Internship, 552
Fran Johnson Non-Traditional Scholarship, 102
Garden Club of America Summer Environmental Awards, 253
GCA Internship in Garden History and Design, 543
Georgia-Pacific Internships and Co-ops, 544
Grange Denise Scholarship, 392
Greater Research Opportunities Undergraduate Student Fellowships, 507
Green Mountain Dog Club Scholarship, 510
Gulf Coast Research Laboratory Minority Summer Grant, 342
Harold Bettinger Memorial Scholarship, 102
Hopi Tribal Priority Award, 280
Horticultural Research Institute Spring Meadow Scholarship, 287
Jacob Van Namen Marketing Scholarship, 103
J.K. Rathmell, Jr., Memorial for Work/Study Abroad, 103
Katharine M. Grosscup Scholarship, 253
LAF/CLASS Fund Scholarship Ornamental Horticulture Program, 317
Leonard Bettinger Memorial Vocational Scholarship, 103
Lindbergh Grant, 218
Louisiana Rockefeller Wildlife Scholarship, 323
The Loy McCandless Marks Scholarship, 253
Maine Recreation and Parks Association Scholarship, 326
Maine Rural Rehabilitation Fund, 325
Marshall E. McCullough Undergraduate Scholarship, 370
Masonic Range Science Scholarship, 421
The Minority Scholarship, 535
Morris Arboretum Education Internship, 552
Morris Arboretum Horticulture Internship, 552
MTA Doug Slifka Memorial Scholarship, 348
National Dairy Shrine Kildee Scholarship, 370
National Dairy Shrine Klussendorf Scholarship, 370
National Dairy Shrine/Iager Dairy Scholarship, 370
National Limouselle Financial Assistance Grant, 397
National Oceanic and Atmospheric Administration Educational Partnership Program with Minority Serving Institutions Undergraduate Scholarship, 403
NDS/DMI Milk Marketing Scholarship, 231
NEHA/AAS Scholarship, 371
NPFDA Scholarship, 377
Oregon Dungeness Crab Commission, 416
Oregon Foundation for Blacktail Deer Outdoor & Wildlife Scholarship, 416
ORISE Community College Institute, 560
ORISE Higher Education Research Experiences at Oak Ridge National Laboratory, 561
ORISE Professional Internship Program for National Energy Technology Laboratory, 561
ORISE Student Environmental Management Participation at the U.S. Army Environmental Center, 561
ORISE Student Internship at the Office of Water, 562
ORISE Student Internship at the U.S. Army Center for Health Promotion and Preventive Medicine, 562
ORISE Student Research at the Centers for Disease Control and Prevention, 562
Paris Fracasso Production Floriculture Scholarship, 103
Phipps Conservatory and Botanical Gardens Internships, 565
Plant Propagation Internship, 552
Plant Protection Internship, 553
Rain Bird intelligent Use of Water Company Scholarship, 318
Rose and Flower Garden Internship, 553
Savannah River Site Professional Internship Program, 563
SCA Conservation Internships, 570
Science Undergraduate Laboratory Internships, 563
Siemens Competition in Math, Science and Technology, 444
Smithsonian Environmental Research Center Internship Program, 567
Smithsonian Minority Internship, 567
South Dakota Ardell Bjugstad Scholarship, 473
Southern Nursery Organization Sidney B. Meadows Scholarship, 475
Southern Progress Corporation Internship Program, 569
Southface Internship, 569
Student Research at the U.S. Army Edgewood Chemical Biological Center, 573
Timothy Bigelow Scholarship, 287
Truman D. Picard Scholarship, 298
Urban Forestry Internship, 553
U.S. National Arboretum Internship, 573
USDA/1890 National Scholars Program, 505
Usrey Family Scholarship, 287
Water Companies (NJ Chapter) Scholarship, 367
Women's Wildlife Management/Conservation Scholarship, 380

Architecture and design

AIA New Jersey Scholarship Foundation, Inc., 111
AIA/AAF Minority/Disadvantaged Scholarship, 92
Arboriculture Internship, 552
ASHRAE Region IV Benny Bootle Scholarship, 173
Award in Desest Studies, 252
Bechtel Foundation Scholarship, 460
BIA North County Division Scholarship, 208
Black & Veatch Internships, Co-op, and Summer Employment, 534
Carville M. Akehurst Memorial Scholarship, 287
Community Scholarship Fund, 264
Connecticut Building Congress Scholarship, 225
Courtland Paul Scholarship, 316
Dallas Architectural Foundation - Arch Swank, Jr. Fellowship in the Craft of Architecture, 231

David T. Woolsey Scholarship, 316
Delta Faucet Company Scholarship, 427
Disney Professional Internships, 574
Douglas Haskell Awards for Student Journalism, 111
The EDSA Minority Scholarship, 316
Elizabeth Dow Internship Program, 539
Elizabeth Dow Ltd. Internships, 532
Filoli Center Garden Internships and Apprenticeships, 542
Gabriel Prize, 519
GCA Internship in Garden History and Design, 543
GCSAA Scholars Competition, 259
GCSAA Student Essay Contest, 259
HKS/John Humphries Minority Scholarship, 231
Homestead Capital Housing Scholarship, 413
Honeywell International Inc. Scholarship, 465
Horticultural Research Institute Spring Meadow Scholarship, 287
Howard Brown Rickard Scholarship, 372
International Furnishings and Design Association Student Scholarships, 297
J.K. Rathmell, Jr., Memorial for Work/Study Abroad, 103
Joel Polsky Academic Achievement Award, 175
LAF/CLASS Fund (California Landscape Architectural Student Scholarship) University Scholarship Program, 316
LAF/CLASS Fund Internship Program, 549
LAF/CLASS Fund Landscape Architecture Program, 317
Landscape Forms Design for People Scholarship, 317
Multicultural Undergraduate Summer Internships at the Getty Center, 546
NASA Space Grant Wisconsin Consortium Undergraduate Research Program, 363
Part-Time Student Scholarship, 297
Peridian International Inc./Rae L. Price FASLA Scholarship, 317
Phipps Conservatory and Botanical Gardens Internships, 565
Plumbing-Heating-Cooling Contractors - National Association Educational Foundation Scholarship, 428
Rain Bird intelligent Use of Water Company Scholarship, 318
RTKL Traveling Fellowship, 92
Scotts Company Scholars Program, 259
Southern Progress Corporation Internship Program, 569
Southface Internship, 569

Steven G. King Play Environments Scholarship, 318
Timothy Bigelow Scholarship, 287
Urban Forestry Internship, 553
Usrey Family Scholarship, 287
Wendy Ella Guilford Scholarship Fund, 232
Women in Architecture Scholarship, 198
Women in Construction: Founders' Scholarship, 367
Women's Architectural Auxiliary Eleanor Allwork Scholarship Grants, 111
Yale R. Burge Competition, 175

Area and ethnic studies

Adele Filene Travel Award, 228
Blossom Kalama Evans Memorial Scholarship, 262
Elie Wiesel Prize in Ethics, 241
Goldman Family Fund: New Leader Scholarship, 327
Harriet Irsay Scholarship, 112
Jennifer C. Groot Fellowship, 95
Jerry Clark Memorial Scholarship, 101
Joseph S. Adams Scholarship, 445
King Olav V Norwegian-American Heritage Fund, 471
Kosciuszko Foundation Tuition Scholarships, 314
Kosciuszko Foundation Year Abroad Program, 314
Library of Congress Hispanic Division Junior Fellows Internship, 549
Shell Legislative Internship Program, 556
Smithsonian Native American Internship, 568
U.S. Department of Education Fulbright-Hays Project Abroad Scholarship for Programs in China, 229

Arts, visual and performing

AAJA/Chicago Tribune Internship Grant, 193
Abe Voron Scholarship, 206
Academy of Television Arts & Sciences Foundation Student Internship Program, 527
Adele Filene Travel Award, 228
Alexander M. Tanger Scholarship, 206
American College of Musicians $200 Scholarship, 96
American College of Musicians Piano Composition Contest, 97
American Conservatory Theater Production Internships, 528
American Legion Maryland Auxiliary Scholarship, 129
American Legion Music Scholarship, 125

Anna K. Meredith Fund Scholarship, 478
Anthropology Internship Program, 529
Applied Arts Internships, 532
Artistic and Administrative Internships, 528
ASCAP Morton Gould Young Composers Award, 193
Asian American Journalists Association Scholarships, 193
Associated Press/APTRA-CLETE Roberts Memorial Journalism Scholarship, 197
Association for Women in Communications Scholarship, 199
The Audria M. Edwards Scholarship Fund, 422
Bodie McDowell Scholarship, 420
Broadcast Internship Grant, 194
Carole Fielding Video Grant, 503
Carole Simpson Scholarship, 432
The CBC Spouse's Visual Arts Scholarship, 224
Charles & Lucille King Family Foundation Scholarships, 217
Clare Brett Smith Scholarship, 478
The Cloisters Summer Internship Program, 550
College Television Award, 75
Community Scholarship Fund, 264
Computer Science Scholarship, 371
CRT Internship Program, 536
David L. Stashower Scholarship, 321
Davidson Fellows Scholarship, 235
Doris & Clarence Glick Classical Music Scholarship, 265
Douglas Haskell Awards for Student Journalism, 111
Ed Bradley Scholarship, 432
Elizabeth A. Sackler Museum Educational Trust, 479
Elizabeth Dow Internship Program, 539
Elizabeth Dow Ltd. Internships, 532
The Elizabeth Greenshields Grant, 241
ESPN Internship, 540
Essence Summer Internship, 540
Esther Kanagawa Memorial Art Scholarship, 267
Eugene Bennet Visual Arts Scholarship, 412
Eugenia Vellner Fischer Award for the Performing Arts, 342
Executive Office Intern, 530
Fashion Group International of Portland Scholarship, 412
Feminist Web Internship, 541
Fisher Broadcasting Scholarship for Minorities, 246
Florence Lemcke Memorial Scholarship, 153
Franklin D. Roosevelt Library/Roosevelt Summer Internship, 543
The Fred Rogers Memorial Scholarship, 75

Field of Study/Intended Career: Arts, visual and performing

The General Fund Scholarships, 165
Gerrit R. Ludwig Scholarship, 268
Government and Public Affairs Internship, 530
Guggenheim Museum Internship, 568
Harold E. Fellows Scholarship, 207
Harriet Irsay Scholarship, 112
Hearst Journalism Award, 520
Helen J. Sioussat/Fay Wells Scholarship, 207
International Incentive Awards, 479
Janet Jackson Rhythm Nation Scholarships, 499
Japanese American Music Scholarship Competition, 306
John Lennon Scholarship, 204
John Lennon Scholarship Fund, 500
Jules Maidoff Scholarship, 479
Kennedy Library Archival Internship, 547
KIMT Weather/News Internships, 549
Lele Cassin Scholarship, 479
Leonard M. Perryman Communications Scholarship for Ethnic Minority Students, 497
Lou and Carole Prato Sports Reporting Scholarship, 433
Maryland Distinguished Scholar: Talent in the Arts, 329
MCC Theater Internships, 550
Michael Jackson Scholarships, 501
Mike Reynolds Scholarship, 433
Multicultural Undergraduate Summer Internships at the Getty Center, 546
Museum Coca-Cola Internship, 557
Museum of Modern Art Internship, 554
NABJ Scholarship, 366
NAMTA Foundation Visual Arts Major Scholarship, 365
Nancy Goodhue Lynch Scholarship, 233
National Museum of the American Indian Internship, 557
National Press Photographers Foundation Television News Scholarship, 378
NBA Internship Program, 556
New Dramatists Internship, 558
New York American Legion Press Association Scholarship, 144
Nissan Community College Transfer Scholarship, 279
Peggy Guggenheim Internship, 568
Pete Carpenter Fellowship, 534
PGA Tour Diversity Intern Program, 565
PGSF Annual Scholarship Competition, 431
Policy and Research Internship, 531
Presidents' $2,500 Scholarships, 433
Press Club of Houston Scholarship, 430
Princess Grace Award For Film, 430
Princess Grace Award For Playwriting, 431
Princess Grace Award For Theater, 431
Private-Sector Affairs Internship, 531
R.L. Gillette Scholarship, 105
Rudolf Nissim Prize, 193
SACI Consortium Scholarship, 479
Scholarships for Children of SACI Alumni, 480
Scholastic Art Portfolio Gold Award, 89
Scholastic Art Portfolio Silver Award, 89
Scholastic Photography Portfolio Gold Award, 90
Scholastic Photography Portfolio Silver Award, 90
Scholastic Writing Portfolio Gold Award, 90
Sculpture Society Scholarship, 380
Seventeen Magazine Internship, 566
Six-Month Internship, 551
Smithsonian Minority Internship, 567
Society for Technical Communication Scholarship Program, 446
Sony Credited Internship, 569
Southern California Council Endowed Internship, 557
Southern Progress Corporation Internship Program, 569
Spoleto Festival Apprenticeship Program, 570
Stanfield and D'Orlando Art Scholarship, 496
Stella Blum Research Grant, 228
Summer Internship Program, 551
Theodore Mazza Scholarship, 495
Twentieth Century Fox Internship, 571
Two Year Community College BEA Award, 207
United States Holocaust Memorial Museum Internship, 572
Vincent T. Wasilewski Scholarship, 207
Virgin Islands Music Scholarship, 513
Virginia Museum of Fine Arts Fellowship, 514
Walter S. Patterson Scholarship, 207
Web Challenge Contest, 482
Wilhelmina Models Internship, 575
Wolf Trap Foundation for the Performing Arts Internship, 575
Worldstudio AIGA Scholarship, 525
Xernona Clayton Scholarship, 200

Biological and biomedical sciences

American Foundation for Aging Research Fellowship, 104
American Legion Maryland Auxiliary Scholarship, 129

Biological and physical sciences

Adler Science and Math Scholarship, 129
Aerospace Undergraduate Research Scholarship Program, 362
AFCEA General Emmett Paige Scholarship, 190
AFCEA General John A. Wickham Scholarship, 190
AFCEA Professional Part-Time Scholarship, 190
AFCEA ROTC Scholarships, 190
AFCEA Scholarships for Math and Science Teachers, 80
AFCEA Sgt. Jeannette L. Winters, USMC Memorial Scholarship, 191
AFCEA/Lockheed Martin IT Scholarship, 191
AFPE "Gateway to Research" Scholarship, 104
Alfred R. Chisholm Memorial Scholarship, 498
Alpine Club A.K. Gilkey and Putnam/Bedayn Research Grant, 92
American Chemical Society Scholars Program, 95
American Electroplaters and Surface Finishers Foundation Scholarship, 101
American Foundation for Aging Research Fellowship, 104
American Heart Association Undergraduate Student Research Program, 106
American Legion Maryland Auxiliary Scholarship, 129
American Meteorological Society Undergraduate Scholarships, 157
American Meteorological Society/Industry Minority Scholarship, 157
Amtrol Scholarship, 106
Angelo S. Bisesti Scholarship, 159
ANS Undergraduate Scholarships, 159
Arthur and Doreen Parrett Scholarship, 193
A.T. Anderson Memorial Scholarship, 109
Award in Desert Studies, 252
Baroid Scholarship, 106
Barry M. Goldwater Scholarship, 202
Burlington Northern Santa Fe Foundation Scholarship, 109
Business and Professional Women's Career Advancement Scholarship, 209
Cargill Scholarship Program, 498
Castle & Cooke Mililani Technology Park Scholarship Fund, 263
Charles and Annette Hill Scholarship, 126
Charles (Tommy) Thomas Memorial Scholarship, 159
Chevron Internship Program, 535
Community College Graduates Scholarship Program, 356
Davidson Fellows Scholarship, 235
Delaware Space Grant Undergraduate Summer Scholarship, 352

Delaware Space Grant Undergraduate Tuition Scholarship, 352
Delayed Education Scholarship for Women, 159
Department of Commerce Internship for Postsecondary Students, 559
Department of Energy Special Emphasis Program, 560
Disney Professional Internships, 574
Distance-Learning/On-Line Programs Scholarship, 191
DOE Pre-Service Teacher Internships, 560
Dr. W. Wes Eckenfelder Jr. Scholarship, 208
DuPont Cooperative Education Program, 538
DuPont Internships, 538
Earl & Patricia Armstrong Scholarship, 499
Eastman Kodak Cooperative Internship Programs, 539
Energy Student Achievement Program, 560
The Entomological Foundation BioQuip Undergraduate Scholarship, 242
Eugene Borson Memorial Scholarship, 293
Explorers Club Youth Activity Fund, 245
Extrusion Division/Lew Erwin Memorial Scholarship, 456
Field Botany Scholarships, 253
Filoli Center Garden Internships and Apprenticeships, 542
Fleming/Blaszcak Scholarship, 456
Flora of Pennsylvania Internship, 552
Francis M. Peacock Native Bird Habitat Scholarship, 253
Freshman Undergraduate Scholarship Program, 157
Garden Club of America Summer Environmental Awards, 253
GCA Internship in Garden History and Design, 543
Genentech Internship Program, 543
George A. Hall/Harold F. Mayfield Award, 521
Great Lakes Colleges Association/Associated Colleges of the Midwest Oak Ridge Science Semester, 560
Greater Research Opportunities Undergraduate Student Fellowships, 507
Gulf Coast Research Laboratory Minority Summer Grant, 342
The Henry Broughton, K2AE Memorial Scholarship, 545
Historic Bok Sanctuary Conservation Program Internship, 545
Historically Black College and University Scholarship Fund, 349
Hoffman-La Roche Inc. Student Internship, 545

Horizons Scholarship of Women in Defense, 286
Howard Brown Rickard Scholarship, 372
Howard Vollum American Indian Scholarship, 413
Hubertus W.V. Willems Scholarship for Male Students, 349
Intel International Science and Engineering Fair, 446
Intel Science Talent Search, 446
Jacob Van Namen Marketing Scholarship, 103
Jennifer Ritzmann Scholarship for Studies in Tropical Biology, 228
Jeppesen Meterology Internship, 546
John and Muriel Landis Scholarship, 160
John R. Lamarsh Scholarship, 160
Joseph R. Dietrich Scholarship, 160
Kathleen S. Anderson Award, 327
Kathryn D. Sullivan Science and Engineering Fellowship, 361
KIMT Weather/News Internships, 549
Laurence R. Foster Memorial Scholarship, 415
Lockheed Martin Scholarship Program, 277
Louisiana Rockefeller Wildlife Scholarship, 323
The Loy McCandless Marks Scholarship, 253
Marathon Oil Corporation College Scholarship, 279
MESBEC Scholarships, 215
Meteorological Society Father James B. Macelwane Annual Award, 157
Microbiology Undergraduate Research Fellowship (MURF), 171
Microscopy Society of America Undergraduate Research Scholarship, 337
Microsoft General Scholarship, 337
Microsoft Minority Technical Scholarship, 338
Microsoft Scholarship for Students with Disabilities, 338
Microsoft Women's Technical Scholarship, 338
Morris Arboretum Education Internship, 552
MSGC Undergraduate Underrepresented Minority Fellowship Program, 355
MTA Doug Slifka Memorial Scholarship, 348
Nancy Lorraine Jensen Memorial Scholarship, 471
NASA Academy Internship, 555
NASA Connecticut Space Grant Undergraduate Fellowship, 351
NASA District of Columbia Undergraduate Scholarship, 352
NASA Hawaii Undergraduate Traineeship, 554
NASA Idaho Space Grant Undergraduate Scholarship, 353

NASA Indiana Space Grant Consortium Undergraduate Scholarships, 354
NASA Massachusetts Space Grant Summer Jobs for Students, 555
NASA Minnesota Space Grant Consortium Wide Scholarship, 355
NASA Missouri State Space Grant Undergraduate Scholarship, 356
NASA Ohio Space Grant Junior/Senior Scholarship Program, 359
NASA Pennsylvania Space Grant Undergraduate Scholarship, 359
NASA Rocky Mountain Space Grant Consortium Undergraduate Scholarship, 360
NASA Space Grant Arizona Undergraduate Research Internship, 554
NASA Space Grant Arkansas Undergraduate Scholarship, 351
NASA Space Grant Georgia Fellowship Program, 352
NASA Space Grant Hawaii Undergraduate Fellowship, 353
NASA Space Grant Kentucky Undergraduate Scholarship, 354
NASA Space Grant Maine Consortium Annual Scholarship and Fellowship Program, 354
NASA Space Grant Michigan Undergraduate Fellowship, 355
NASA Space Grant Mississippi Undergraduate Scholarship, 356
NASA Space Grant Montana Undergraduate Scholarship Program, 357
NASA Space Grant Nevada Undergraduate Scholarship, 357
NASA Space Grant New Mexico Undergraduate Scholarship, 357
NASA Space Grant North Dakota Consortium Lillian Goettler Scholarship, 358
NASA Space Grant North Dakota Undergraduate Scholarship, 358
NASA Space Grant Oregon Undergraduate Scholarship, 359
NASA Space Grant Rhode Island Summer Undergraduate Scholarship, 360
NASA Space Grant South Carolina Undergraduate Academic Year Research Program, 361
NASA Space Grant Teacher Education Scholarship, 362
NASA Space Grant Undergraduate Scholarship, 362
NASA Space Grant Vermont Consortium Undergraduate Scholarships, 362
NASA Space Grant Virginia Community College Scholarship, 362

Field of Study/Intended Career: Biological and physical sciences

NASA Space Grant Wisconsin Consortium Undergraduate Research Program, 363
NASA Space Grant Wisconsin Consortium Undergraduate Scholarship, 363
NASA West Virginia Space Grant Undergraduate Research Fellowship, 363
NASA Wyoming Space Grant Undergraduate Research Fellowships, 364
National Oceanic and Atmospheric Administration Educational Partnership Program with Minority Serving Institutions Undergraduate Scholarship, 403
Naval Engineers Scholarship, 179
Nick Van Pernis Scholarship, 273
North Carolina Student Loans for Health/Science/Mathematics, 588
Operations and Power Division Scholarship, 160
Oregon Foundation for Blacktail Deer Outdoor & Wildlife Scholarship, 416
ORISE Community College Institute, 560
ORISE Higher Education Research Experiences at Oak Ridge National Laboratory, 561
ORISE National Oceanic and Atmospheric Administration Faculty and Student Intern Research Participation, 561
ORISE Professional Internship Program for National Energy Technology Laboratory, 561
ORISE Student Environmental Management Participation at the U.S. Army Environmental Center, 561
ORISE Student Internship at the Office of Water, 562
ORISE Student Internship at the U.S. Army Center for Health Promotion and Preventive Medicine, 562
ORISE Student Research - National Center for Toxicological Research, 562
ORISE Student Research at the Centers for Disease Control and Prevention, 562
ORISE Student Research Participation at the U.S. Army Medical Research Institute of Chemical Defense, 562
ORISE Student Research Participation at U.S. Army Research Laboratory, 562
ORISE U.S. Nuclear Regulatory Commission Historically Black Colleges and Universities Student Research Participation, 563
Park Espenschade Memorial Scholarship, 294
Paul A. Stewart Award, 521
Paul and Ellen Ruckes Scholarship, 105
Payzer Scholarship, 245
Pearl I. Young Scholarship, 358
Phipps Conservatory and Botanical Gardens Internships, 565
Pittsburgh Local Section Scholarship, 160
Plant Propagation Internship, 552
Plant Protection Internship, 553
Plasma Physics National Undergraduate Fellowship Program, 565
Raymond DiSalvo Scholarship, 160
Research Experiences for Undergraduates - Maria Mitchell Observatory, 558
Research Experiences for Undergraduates in Systematics and Evolutionary Biology, 529
Research Experiences for Undergraduates in the Physical Sciences, 529
Robert G. Lacy Scholarship, 161
Robert N. Hancock Memorial Scholarship, 294
Robert Noyce Scholarship Program, 425
Robert T. (Bob) Liner Scholarship, 161
Rocky Mountain Coal Mining Scholarship, 435
Savannah River Site Professional Internship Program, 563
SCA Conservation Internships, 570
Scholarship for Minority Undergraduate Physics Majors, 161
Science Undergraduate Laboratory Internships, 563
SEG Foundation Scholarship, 441
Shuichi, Katsu and Itsuyo Suga Scholarship, 274
Siemens Competition in Math, Science and Technology, 444
Smithsonian Environmental Research Center Internship Program, 567
Smithsonian Minority Internship, 567
Society of Exploration Geophysicists Scholarship, 449
Society of Physics Students Leadership Scholarship, 456
Society of Physics Students Summer Internship Program, 568
Society of Plastics Engineers General Scholarships, 457
SPIE Educational Scholarship in Optical Science and Engineering, 475
Stan Beck Fellowship, 243
Student Research at the U.S. Army Edgewood Chemical Biological Center, 573
Student Research Participation at the Federal Bureau of Investigation Counterterrorism/Forensic Science Research Unit, 563
Technical Minority Scholarship, 525
Tennessee Student Assistance Corporation/Math And Science Teachers Loan Forgiveness Program, 590
Thermoforming Division Memorial Scholarships, 457
Thermoset Division/James I. MacKenzie Memorial Scholarship, 457
Thomas J. Bardos Science Education Awards for Undergraduate Students, 93
Toshiba/NSTA ExploraVision Award, 380
Undergraduate Fellowships in Engineering and Science, 555
Undergraduate Research Fellowship (URF), 171
Undergraduate Research Scholarship, 358, 360
Undergraduate Scholarship Program, 358
Urban Forestry Internship, 553
U.S. Department of Homeland Security Scholarship and Fellowship Program, 563
U.S. Department of State Internship, 573
U.S. National Arboretum Internship, 573
USDA/1890 National Scholars Program, 505
Vogt Radiochemistry Scholarship, 161
Water Companies (NJ Chapter) Scholarship, 367
West Virginia Engineering, Science and Technology Scholarship, 518
William James & Dorothy Bading Lanquist Fund, 276
William R. Goldfarb Memorial Scholarship, 168
The Yasme Foundation Scholarship, 169
Young Epidemiology Scholars Student Competition, 221
The Young Naturalist Awards Scholarship Program, 158
Zeller Summer Scholarship in Medicinal Botany, 254

Business/management/administration

Academic Scholarship for High School Seniors, 379
Academic Scholarship for Undergraduate Students, 379
Accuracy in Media Internships, 527
Advertising Internship (Summer Only), 533
AICP Heartland Chapter Scholarship, 199
AICP Scholarship, 199
Allstate Internships, 527
ALPFA Scholarship Program, 277
Alpha Beta Gamma International Scholarship, 90

Field of Study/Intended Career: Business/management/administration

Alumnae Panhellenic Association Women's Scholarship, 91
American Express Scholarship Competition, 107
American Hotel & Lodging Educational Foundation Incoming Freshman Scholarship Competition, 107
American Legion Maryland Auxiliary Scholarship, 129
American Savings Bank Scholars Program, 262
American Society of International Law Internships, 529
American Standard Scholarship, 427
A.O. Smith Water Heaters Scholarship, 427
Applied Arts Internships, 532
Applied Materials Internships and Co-ops, 532
Artistic and Administrative Internships, 528
Arts Action Fund Internship, 530
Arts Management Internship Program, 532
Association for Women in Communications Scholarship, 199
Baxter International Inc. Internships, 533
Bern Laxer Memorial Scholarship, 302
Best Teen Chef Culinary Scholarship Competition, 192
BIA North County Division Scholarship, 208
Bodie McDowell Scholarship, 420
Boeing Internship Program, 534
Bradford White Scholarship, 427
Burlington Northern Santa Fe Foundation Scholarship, 109
Business Achievement Awards, 256
Business and Professional Women's Career Advancement Scholarship, 209
Business Reporting Intern Program, 537
California Association of Realtors Scholarship, 210
Candon Consulting Group Scholarship Fund, 263
Cargill Scholarship Program, 498
Certified Public Accountants Minorities Scholarship, 111
Charles and Annette Hill Scholarship, 126
Chevron Internship Program, 535
CIA Undergraduate Scholarship, 216
CITE-NY Association Scholarship, 227
Colorado Society of CPAs General Scholarship, 222
Congressional Institute Internships, 536
Connecticut Building Congress Scholarship, 225
CRT Internship Program, 536

Dairy Product Marketing Scholarships, 369
David L. Stashower Scholarship, 321
Deloitte and Touche Internship Program, 536
Delta Faucet Company Scholarship, 427
Denver Rescue Mission Center for Mission Studies Interns, 537
Department of Commerce Internship for Postsecondary Students, 559
Department of Energy Special Emphasis Program, 560
Disney Professional Internships, 574
Dr. Alvin and Monica Saake Scholarship, 265
DuPont Cooperative Education Program, 538
DuPont Internships, 538
Earl G. Graves Scholarship, 349
Eastman Kodak Cooperative Internship Programs, 539
Ecolab Scholarship Competition, 107
Economic Research Division Project Internships, 534
Ed Markham International Scholarship, 102
Elizabeth Dow Internship Program, 539
Elizabeth Dow Ltd. Internships, 532
EMC Summer Internship Program and Co-ops, 539
Entergy Jumpstart Co-ops and Internships, 539
EPA National Network for Environmental Management Studies Fellowship, 506
The Erikka A. Hayes Foundation Scholarship, 331
ESPN Internship, 540
Essence Summer Internship, 540
Ethics in Business Scholarship, 247
Executive Office Intern, 530
fahrenHEIGHT 360 Intern Placement, 540
Federal Reserve Undergraduate Summer Analyst Program, 541
Feminism & Leadership Internship, 541
Feminist Web Internship, 541
Field Services Internship, 530
Finance Undergraduate Internships, 574
Financial Women International Scholarship, 267
Ford Motor Company/American Indian College Fund Corporate Scholars Program, 108
GE Business/Engineering Scholarship for Minority Students, 318
General Mills Summer Internship, 543
General Motors Corporation Talent Acquisition Internship, 544
George M. Brooker Collegiate Scholarship for Minorities, 295
George Mason Business Scholarship Fund, 268

Georgia-Pacific Internships and Co-ops, 544
Government and Public Affairs Internship, 530
Guggenheim Museum Internship, 568
Harold Bettinger Memorial Scholarship, 102
Harriet Irsay Scholarship, 112
Harry S. Truman Scholarship, 261
Henry A. Zuberano Scholarship, 268
Hoffman-La Roche Inc. Student Internship, 545
Homestead Capital Housing Scholarship, 413
Honors Internship Program, 540
Hopi Tribal Priority Award, 280
Horizons Scholarship of Women in Defense, 286
House Member Internships, 573
The Hyatt Hotels Fund for Minority Lodging Management Students Competition, 108
IBM Co-op and Intern Program, 545
IEHA Educational Foundation Scholarship, 296
INROADS Internship, 546
ISFA Education Foundation College Scholarship, 296
Jacob Van Namen Marketing Scholarship, 103
James A. Turner, Jr., Memorial Scholarship, 184
James Beard General Scholarships, 303
James E. Webb Internship Program for Minority Undergraduate Seniors and Graduate Students in Business and Public Administration, 567
Jean-Louis Palladin Memorial Scholarship, 304
Jebidiah Zabrosky Scholarship, 511
Jennifer Curtis Byler Scholarship Fund for the Study of Public Affairs, 383
John Deere Student Training Programs, 547
John F. Kennedy Scholars Award, 333
John Joseph Moakely Democratic Internship, 550
John Wiley and Sons, Inc. Internship Program, 548
Johnson Controls Co-op and Internship Programs, 548
Joint CAS/SOA Minority Scholarships for Actuarial Students, 447
J.W. Saxe Memorial Prize, 548
Kennedy Center Arts Management Internship, 547
KIMT Weather/News Internships, 549
Lagrant Scholarships, 315
Letitia B. Carter Scholarship, 332
Lockheed Martin Scholarship Program, 277
Lou and Carole Prato Sports Reporting Scholarship, 433
Louis Carr Summer Internship, 549

Eligibility Indexes

Field of Study/Intended Career: Business/management/administration

Maine Innkeepers Association Scholarship, 325
Marathon Oil Corporation College Scholarship, 279
Marcia S. Harris Legacy Fund Scholarship, 332
Mark J. Smith Scholarship, 223
Mayflower Tours Patrick Murphy Internship, 571
MCC Theater Internships, 550
MESBEC Scholarships, 215
Mexican American Grocers Association Scholarship, 335
Multicultural Advertising Intern Program, 527
Multicultural Undergraduate Summer Internships at the Getty Center, 546
Museum Coca-Cola Internship, 557
Museum of Modern Art Internship, 554
NABA National Scholarship Program, 365
NAMTA Foundation Visual Arts Major Scholarship, 365
NASA Space Grant Nevada Undergraduate Scholarship, 357
NASA Space Grant Wisconsin Consortium Undergraduate Research Program, 363
National Association of Women in Construction Scholarship, 511
National Society of Accountants Scholarship, 381
Native Daughters of the Golden West Scholarship, 384
NBA Internship Program, 556
NCR Summer Internships, 558
NDS/DMI Milk Marketing Scholarship, 231
NEEBC Scholarship, 386
New Dramatists Internship, 558
Nissan Community College Transfer Scholarship, 279
Oracle Scholars Internship Program, 572
ORISE National Oceanic and Atmospheric Administration Faculty and Student Intern Research Participation, 561
Oscar and Rosetta Fish Fund, 273
Owens Corning Internships, 564
Pat & Jim Host Internship/Scholarship, 571
PGA Tour Diversity Intern Program, 565
PHCC Educational Foundation Need-Based Scholarship, 428
Philip and Alice Angell Eastern Star Scholarship, 511
Plumbing-Heating-Cooling Contractors - National Association Educational Foundation Scholarship, 428
Policy and Research Internship, 531
Private-Sector Affairs Internship, 531
ProStart National Certificate of Achievement Scholarship, 379

PRSA-Hawaii/Roy Leffingwell Public Relations Scholarship, 273
Public Relations Internship, 550
Rhode Island State Government Internship Program, 566
Ritchie-Jennings Memorial Scholarship, 76
Sales and Marketing Internship, 531
Scarlett Family Foundation Scholarship, 440
SGI (Silicon Graphics) Internship/Co-op Program, 566
Shell Legislative Internship Program, 556
Shirley McKown Scholarship Fund, 274
Sony Credited Internship, 569
Southern California Council Endowed Internship, 557
Southern Progress Corporation Internship Program, 569
Southface Internship, 569
Spoleto Festival Apprenticeship Program, 570
Steve Hymans Extended Stay Scholarship, 108
Summer Internship Program, 551
Summer Research Diversity Fellowships in Law and Social Sciences for Undergraduate Students, 528
Sun Microsystems Student Intern and Co-op Program, 570
Taste America San Francisco Scholarship, 305
Texas Fifth-Year Accounting Student Scholarship Program, 487
Tribal Business Management Scholarship, 215
Trimmer Education Foundation ABC Student Chapter Scholarship Program, 196
Tri-State Surveying & Photogrammetry Kris M. Kunze Scholarship, 99
UBS/PaineWebber Scholarships, 501
United States Senate Member Internships, 572
U.S. Department of Education Fulbright-Hays Project Abroad Scholarship for Programs in China, 229
U.S. Department of State Internship, 573
USTA Scholarships, 508
Washington Crossing Foundation Scholarship, 515
Water Companies (NJ Chapter) Scholarship, 367
Wayne G. Failor Scholarship, 425
Web and Technology Internship, 531
William R. Goldfarb Memorial Scholarship, 168
Wilma D. Hoyal/Maxine Chilton Memorial Scholarship, 114
Wolf Trap Foundation for the Performing Arts Internship, 575

Women in Construction: Founders' Scholarship, 367
Women's Sports Foundation Internship, 576
Wooddy Scholarship, 76
Xernona Clayton Scholarship, 200
Yellow Ribbon Scholarship, 491

Communications

AAJA Texas Scholarship, 194
AAJA/Chicago Tribune Internship Grant, 193
Accuracy in Media Internships, 527
Advertising Internship (Summer Only), 533
Alexander M. Tanger Scholarship, 206
Allison E. Fisher Scholarship, 366
American Legion Press Club of New Jersey and Post 170--Arthur Dehardt Memorial Scholarship, 141
American Society of International Law Internships, 529
Arts Action Fund Internship, 530
Asian American Journalists Association Scholarships, 193
Aspiring Sports Journalist Internship, 570
Associated Press/APTRA-CLETE Roberts Memorial Journalism Scholarship, 197
Association for Women in Communications Scholarship, 199
Best Buy Scholarship Program, 203
Bill Farr Scholarship, 458
Bob Baxter Scholarship, 377
Bob East Scholarship Fund, 377
Bodie McDowell Scholarship, 420
Boston Globe Summer Internship, 535
Broadcast Internship Grant, 194
Business Reporting Intern Program, 537
Carl Greenberg Scholarship, 458
Carole Simpson Scholarship, 366, 432
CCNMA Scholarship, 216
Charles & Lucille King Family Foundation Scholarships, 217
Charles N. Fisher Memorial Scholarship, 163
CITE-NY Association Scholarship, 227
College Photographer of the Year Competition, 378
Congressional Institute Internships, 536
Dairy Product Marketing Scholarships, 369
Dana Campbell Memorial Scholarship, 303
David L. Stashower Scholarship, 321
Delaware Space Grant Undergraduate Tuition Scholarship, 352
Disney College Program, 574
Dr. James L. Lawson Memorial Scholarship, 164
Ed Bradley Scholarship, 432
Edward J. Nell Memorial Scholarship, 432

Field of Study/Intended Career: Computer and information sciences

Edward Payson and Bernice Pi'ilani Irwin Scholarship Trust Fund, 266
Entertainment Weekly Internship Program, 539
EPA National Network for Environmental Management Studies Fellowship, 506
ESPN Internship, 540
Essence Summer Internship, 540
Executive Office Intern, 530
fahrenHEIGHT 360 Intern Placement, 540
Fisher Broadcasting Scholarship for Minorities, 246
Foodservice Communicators Scholarship, 297
Fred R. McDaniel Memorial Scholarship, 164
The Freedom Forum/NCAA Sports Journalism Scholarship, 385
The General Fund Scholarships, 165
General Mills Summer Internship, 543
General News Copy Editing Internship, 537
The George Foreman Tribute to Lyndon B. Johnson Scholarship, 432
Georgia-Pacific Internships and Co-ops, 544
Harold K. Douthit Scholarship, 405
Harriet Irsay Scholarship, 112
Hearst Journalism Award, 520
Helen Johnson Scholarship, 458
House Member Internships, 573
INROADS Internship, 546
International Radio and Television Society Foundation, 546
Irving W. Cook, WAOCGS Scholarship, 165
Jackson Foundation Journalism Scholarship, 414
Janet Jackson Rhythm Nation Scholarships, 499
Jerry Clark Memorial Scholarship, 101
John Lennon Scholarship Fund, 500
John Wiley and Sons, Inc. Internship Program, 548
Kaplan/Newsweek "My Turn" Essay Contest, 310
Ken Inouye Scholarship, 458
Ken Kashiwahara Scholarship, 433
Kennedy Library Archival Internship, 547
KIMT Weather/News Internships, 549
L. Phil Wicker Scholarship, 166
Lagrant Scholarships, 315
Leonard M. Perryman Communications Scholarship, 497
Leonard M. Perryman Communications Scholarship for Ethnic Minority Students, 497
Lou and Carole Prato Sports Reporting Scholarship, 433
Louis Carr Summer Internship, 549
Marshall E. McCullough Undergraduate Scholarship, 370

Michael Jackson Scholarships, 501
Mike Reynolds Scholarship, 433
The Mississippi Scholarship, 166
Mother Jones Magazine Editorial Internship, 553
Mother JonesPhoto/Art Internship, 553
Multicultural Advertising Intern Program, 527
Multicultural Undergraduate Summer Internships at the Getty Center, 546
Museum Coca-Cola Internship, 557
NABJ Internships, 556
NABJ Scholarship, 366
NASA Space Grant Arizona Undergraduate Research Internship, 554
National Peace Essay Contest, 502
National Press Photographers Foundation Still Scholarship, 378
National Press Photographers Foundation Television News Scholarship, 378
National Speakers Association Scholarship, 383
The NEMAL Electronics Scholarship, 166
The New Republic Internship, 559
New York American Legion Press Association Scholarship, 144
New York Times James B. Reston Writing Portfolio Award, 89
New York Times Summer Internship Program, 559
Newhouse Foundation Scholarship, 556
Nissan Community College Transfer Scholarship, 279
Ohio Newspaper Association Publications/Public Relations Internship, 564
Ohio Newspaper Services, Inc. Advertising Internship, 564
Ohio Newspaper Women's Scholarship, 405
Ohio Newspapers Minority Scholarship, 405
Online Intern Program, 538
ORISE Student Research at the Centers for Disease Control and Prevention, 562
Owens Corning Internships, 564
Paul and Helen L. Grauer Scholarship, 167
Pete Wilson Journalism Scholarship, 312, 433
PGA Tour Diversity Intern Program, 565
PGSF Annual Scholarship Competition, 431
The PHD ARA Scholarship, 167
Presidents' $2,500 Scholarships, 433
Press Club of Houston Scholarship, 430
PRSA-Hawaii/Roy Leffingwell Public Relations Scholarship, 273
Public Relations Internship, 550

Pulliam Journalism Fellowship, 545
Random House Summer Internship Program, 566
Reader's Digest Foundation Scholarship Program, 501
Reid Blackburn Scholarship, 378
Sales and Marketing Internship, 531
SCA Conservation Internships, 570
Scholastic Writing Portfolio Gold Award, 90
Seventeen Magazine Internship, 566
Shirley McKown Scholarship Fund, 274
Siani Lee Broadcast Internship, 533
Simon and Schuster Summer Internship Program, 567
Society for Technical Communication Scholarship Program, 446
Southern Progress Corporation Internship Program, 569
Sports Copy Editing Program, 538
Stanford Chen Internship Grant, 533
Stoody-West Fellowship, 497
Twentieth Century Fox Internship, 571
United States Holocaust Memorial Museum Internship, 572
United States Senate Member Internships, 572
University Journalism Scholarship, 405
U.S. Department of State Internship, 573
Vincent T. Wasilewski Scholarship, 207
Wall Street Journal Internship, 574
Water Companies (NJ Chapter) Scholarship, 367
World Security Institute Internship, 576
Xernona Clayton Scholarship, 200

Computer and information sciences

Adobe Systems Computer Science Scholarships, 459
Aerospace Undergraduate Research Scholarship Program, 362
AFCEA General Emmett Paige Scholarship, 190
AFCEA General John A. Wickham Scholarship, 190
AFCEA Professional Part-Time Scholarship, 190
AFCEA ROTC Scholarships, 190
AFCEA Scholarships for Math and Science Teachers, 80
AFCEA Sgt. Jeannette L. Winters, USMC Memorial Scholarship, 191
AFCEA/Lockheed Martin IT Scholarship, 191
Albert E. Wischmeyer Memorial Scholarship Award, 449
Alfred R. Chisholm Memorial Scholarship, 498
Allstate Internships, 527
Alpha Beta Gamma International Scholarship, 90

Field of Study/Intended Career: Computer and information sciences

American Heart Association Undergraduate Student Research Program, 106
Barry M. Goldwater Scholarship, 202
Boeing Internship Program, 534
Boston Scientific Scholarship, 461
Business and Professional Women's Career Advancement Scholarship, 209
Cargill Scholarship Program, 498
Castle & Cooke Mililani Technology Park Scholarship Fund, 263
Chevron Corporation Scholarships, 462
Chevron Internship Program, 535
CIA Undergraduate Scholarship, 216
Cisco/UNCF Scholars Program, 499
CITE-NY Association Scholarship, 227
Community College Graduates Scholarship Program, 356
Computer Science Scholarship, 371
Davidson Fellows Scholarship, 235
Dell Inc. Scholarship, 462
Denver Rescue Mission Center for Mission Studies Interns, 537
Department of Commerce Internship for Postsecondary Students, 559
Department of Energy Special Emphasis Program, 560
Detroit Section SAE Technical Scholarship, 447
Disney Professional Internships, 574
Distance-Learning/On-Line Programs Scholarship, 191
DPMA/PC Scholarship, 232
DuPont Cooperative Education Program, 538
DuPont Internships, 538
Eastman Kodak Cooperative Internship Programs, 539
Economic Research Division Project Internships, 534
EMC Summer Internship Program and Co-ops, 539
Energy Student Achievement Program, 560
Entergy Jumpstart Co-ops and Internships, 539
EPA National Network for Environmental Management Studies Fellowship, 506
ESPN Internship, 540
fahrenHEIGHT 360 Intern Placement, 540
Federal Reserve Undergraduate Summer Analyst Program, 541
Feminist Web Internship, 541
Ford Motor Company/American Indian College Fund Corporate Scholars Program, 108
FORE Undergraduate Scholarship, 250
Franklin D. Roosevelt Library/Roosevelt Summer Internship, 543

GE Lloyd Trotter African American Forum Scholarship, 381
Genentech Internship Program, 543
Georgia-Pacific Internships and Co-ops, 544
Goldman, Sachs and Co. Scholarship, 465
Google Hispanic College Fund Scholarship Program, 277
Great Lakes Colleges Association/Associated Colleges of the Midwest Oak Ridge Science Semester, 560
Greater Research Opportunities Undergraduate Student Fellowships, 507
HENAAC Scholars Program, 278
Hoffman-La Roche Inc. Student Internship, 545
Honeywell International Inc. Scholarship, 465
Honors Internship Program, 540
Horizons Scholarship of Women in Defense, 286
Howard Vollum American Indian Scholarship, 413
IBM Co-op and Intern Program, 545
IBM Corporation Scholarship, 466
INROADS Internship, 546
John Deere Student Training Programs, 547
John Wiley and Sons, Inc. Internship Program, 548
Kawasaki-McGaha Scholarship Fund, 270
MESBEC Scholarships, 215
Microsoft Corporation Scholarships, 468
Microsoft General Scholarship, 337
Microsoft Minority Technical Scholarship, 338
Microsoft Scholarship for Students with Disabilities, 338
Microsoft Women's Technical Scholarship, 338
Nancy Goodhue Lynch Scholarship, 233
NASA Space Grant Georgia Fellowship Program, 352
NASA Space Grant Montana Undergraduate Scholarship Program, 357
NASA Space Grant Nevada Undergraduate Scholarship, 357
NASA Space Grant New Mexico Undergraduate Scholarship, 357
NASA Space Grant North Dakota Undergraduate Scholarship, 358
NASA Space Grant Teacher Education Scholarship, 362
NASA Space Grant Virginia Community College Scholarship, 362

National Oceanic and Atmospheric Administration Educational Partnership Program with Minority Serving Institutions Undergraduate Scholarship, 403
National Security Agency Stokes Educational Scholarship Program, 380
National Society of Black Engineers Golden Torch Awards, 382
NBA Internship Program, 556
NCR Summer Internships, 558
Northrop Grumman Corporation Scholarship, 468
Oracle Scholars Internship Program, 572
ORISE Community College Institute, 560
ORISE Higher Education Research Experiences at Oak Ridge National Laboratory, 561
ORISE National Oceanic and Atmospheric Administration Faculty and Student Intern Research Participation, 561
ORISE Professional Internship Program for National Energy Technology Laboratory, 561
ORISE Student Environmental Management Participation at the U.S. Army Environmental Center, 561
ORISE Student Research - National Center for Toxicological Research, 562
ORISE Student Research Participation at U.S. Army Research Laboratory, 562
ORISE U.S. Nuclear Regulatory Commission Historically Black Colleges and Universities Student Research Participation, 563
Owens Corning Internships, 564
Paul and Ellen Ruckes Scholarship, 105
Pearl I. Young Scholarship, 358
PGA Tour Diversity Intern Program, 565
The PHD ARA Scholarship, 167
Plasma Physics National Undergraduate Fellowship Program, 565
Robert Noyce Scholarship Program, 425
Rockwell Automation Scholarships, 469
Savannah River Site Professional Internship Program, 563
Science Undergraduate Laboratory Internships, 563
SGI (Silicon Graphics) Internship/Co-op Program, 566
Shuichi, Katsu and Itsuyo Suga Scholarship, 274
Siemens Competition in Math, Science and Technology, 444

Field of Study/Intended Career: Education

Society for Technical Communication Scholarship Program, 446
Sony Credited Internship, 569
Southern Progress Corporation Internship Program, 569
Student Research at the U.S. Army Edgewood Chemical Biological Center, 573
Sun Microsystems Student Intern and Co-op Program, 570
Technical Minority Scholarship, 525
TGS Scholarship, 482
Tyson Foods Intern Program, 571
Undergraduate Fellowships in Engineering and Science, 555
U.S. Department of Homeland Security Scholarship and Fellowship Program, 563
U.S. Department of State Internship, 573
Vice Admiral Jerry O. Tuttle, USN (Ret.), and Mrs. Barbara A. Tuttle Science and Technology Scholarship, 191
Washington Internships for Students of Engineering, 575
Water Companies (NJ Chapter) Scholarship, 367
Web and Technology Internship, 531
Web Challenge Contest, 482
West Virginia Engineering, Science and Technology Scholarship, 518
William R. Goldfarb Memorial Scholarship, 168
World Security Institute Internship, 576

Education

AFCEA Scholarships for Math and Science Teachers, 80
Alaska Teacher Education Loan, 577
Albert A. Marks Education Scholarship for Teacher Education, 341
Alma White-Delta Kappa Gamma Scholarship, 262
Alpha Delta Kappa/Harriet Simmons Scholarship, 409
American Legion Maryland Auxiliary Scholarship, 129
American Society for Training and Development -- Cascadia Chapter Scholarship, 410
Applied Arts Internships, 532
Arkansas Department of Higher Education Teacher Assistance Resource (STAR) Program, 579
Arkansas Minority Teachers Scholarship Program, 579
Averyl Elaine Keriakedes Memorial Scholarship, 138
Brown Foundation Academic Scholarships, 208
Business and Professional Women's Career Advancement Scholarship, 209

California Assumption Program of Loans for Education (APLE), 579
California Child Development Grant Program, 212
California Teachers Association Martin Luther King, Jr., Memorial Scholarship, 213
Christa McAuliffe Memorial Scholarship, 140
Christa McAuliffe Teacher Incentive Program, 580
Colorado Supplemental Leveraging Educational Assistance Partnership Program, 222
Community Scholarship Fund, 264
Connecticut Minority Teacher Incentive Grant, 226
Critical Needs Alternative Route Teacher Loan/Scholarship, 584
Critical Teacher Shortage Student Loan Forgiveness Program, 580
Crowley Family Scholarship, 412
CRT Internship Program, 536
CTA Scholarship for Dependent Children, 213
CTA Scholarships for Members, 213
Cushman School Internship, 536
Delta Gamma Foundation Memorial Scholarship, 104
Developmental Disability Scholastic Achievement Scholarship, 203
DOE Pre-Service Teacher Internships, 560
Dr. Alfred C. Fones Scholarship, 78
Dr. Hannah K. Vuolo Memorial Scholarship, 143
Dr. Hans & Clara Zimmerman Foundation Education Scholarship, 265
Early Childhood Development Scholarship, 311
Education Achievement Awards, 256
Erman W. Taylor Memorial Scholarship, 133
Franklin D. Roosevelt Library/Roosevelt Summer Internship, 543
The Fred Rogers Memorial Scholarship, 75
Future Teachers Scholarship, 406
Georgia Promise Teacher Scholarship, 581
Government and Public Affairs Internship, 530
Graduate Scholarship, 138
Grow Your Own Teacher Scholarship Program, 289
Harriet Hoffman Memorial Scholarship, 125
Harriet Irsay Scholarship, 112
Harry S. Truman Scholarship, 261
Hopi Tribal Priority Award, 280
Idaho Education Incentive Loan Forgiveness Program, 582
Illinois Future Teacher Corps, 291

Indiana Minority Teacher & Special Education Services Scholarship, 477
James Carlson Memorial Scholarship, 414
Jebidiah Zabrosky Scholarship, 511
Kansas Teacher Service Scholarship, 309
Kentucky Teacher Scholarship, 311
L. Gordon Bittle Memorial Scholarship for Student CTA, 214
Latin Honor Society Scholarship, 95
Lillian and Samuel Sutton Education Scholarship, 350
Lindbergh Grant, 218
Maureen V. O'Donnell Memorial Teacher Training Award, 96
McKinlay Summer Award, 96
MESBEC Scholarships, 215
Minority Teachers of Illinois Scholarship, 292
Mississippi Nursing Education Loan/Scholarship, 584
Mississippi William Winter Teacher Scholar Loan Program, 585
Missouri Minority Teaching Scholarship, 344
Missouri Teacher Education Scholarship, 344
Morris Arboretum Education Internship, 552
Museum Coca-Cola Internship, 557
NASA Pennsylvania Space Grant Undergraduate Scholarship, 359
NASA Space Grant Arizona Undergraduate Research Internship, 554
NASA Space Grant Georgia Fellowship Program, 352
NASA Space Grant Kentucky Undergraduate Scholarship, 354
NASA Space Grant Nevada Undergraduate Scholarship, 357
NASA Space Grant Teacher Education Scholarship, 362
National Federation of the Blind Educator of Tomorrow Award, 373
National Junior Classical League Scholarship, 96
Native American Leadership in Education Scholarship, 215
Native Daughters of the Golden West Scholarship, 384
New Mexico Teacher's Loan-for-Service, 587
Nick Van Pernis Scholarship, 273
PAGE Foundation Scholarships, 431
Phi Delta Kappa Scholarship for Prospective Educators, 426
Philip and Alice Angell Eastern Star Scholarship, 511
President's Parley Scholarship for Teachers of Exceptional Children, 143
Robert Noyce Scholarship Program, 425
Ron Bright Scholarship, 273

Field of Study/Intended Career: Education

Rudolph Dillman Memorial Scholarship, 105
SCA Conservation Internships, 570
Smithsonian Environmental Research Center Internship Program, 567
South Carolina Teacher Loans, 589
South Dakota Annis I. Fowler/Kaden Scholarship, 473
South Dakota Haines Memorial Scholarship, 474
Special Education Teacher Tuition Waiver, 293
Special Education Teaching Scholarships, 122
Teacher Assistant Scholarship Fund, 401
Tennessee Christa McAuliffe Scholarship Program, 483
Tennessee Teaching Scholars Program, 590
Urban Flight and Rural Needs Scholarship Program, 344
U.S. Department of Education Fulbright-Hays Project Abroad Scholarship for Programs in China, 229
Utah Career Teaching Scholarship/T.H. Bell Teaching Incentive Loan, 592
Weisman Scholarship, 227
West Virginia Underwood-Smith Teacher Scholarship, 593
Wilma D. Hoyal/Maxine Chilton Memorial Scholarship, 114
Wisconsin Minority Teacher Loan Program, 593
Workforce Incentive Program, 586

Engineering and engineering technology

Ada I. Pressman Memorial Scholarship, 459
ADC Communications and Foundation Scholarship, 459
Admiral Grace Murray Hopper Scholarship, 459
Aeronautics and Astronautics Undergraduate Scholarship, 110
Aerospace Undergraduate Research Scholarship Program, 362
AFCEA General Emmett Paige Scholarship, 190
AFCEA General John A. Wickham Scholarship, 190
AFCEA Professional Part-Time Scholarship, 190
AFCEA ROTC Scholarships, 190
AFCEA Sgt. Jeannette L. Winters, USMC Memorial Scholarship, 191
AFCEA/Lockheed Martin IT Scholarship, 191
AGC Education and Research Undergraduate Scholarship, 196
AGC of Maine Scholarship Program, 81
Agnes Malakate Kezios Scholarship, 178
Air Traffic Control Half- to Full-Time Student Scholarship, 82
Albert E. Wischmeyer Memorial Scholarship Award, 449
Alfred R. Chisholm Memorial Scholarship, 498
Allen J. Baldwin Scholarship, 178
Alwin B. Newton Scholarship, 172
American Chemical Society Scholars Program, 95
American Council of Engineering Companies of Oregon Scholarship, 409
American Council of Engineering Companies-Alaska Scholarship, 99
American Electroplaters and Surface Finishers Foundation Scholarship, 101
American Meteorological Society Undergraduate Scholarships, 157
American Meteorological Society/Industry Minority Scholarship, 157
American Society of Mechanical Engineers Foundation Scholarship, 175
American Standard Scholarship, 427
Amtrol Scholarship, 106
Angelo S. Bisesti Scholarship, 159
Anne Maureen Whitney Barrow Memorial, 460
ANS Undergraduate Scholarships, 159
A.O. Smith Water Heaters Scholarship, 427
AOPA Air Safety Foundation/McAllister Memorial Scholarship, 86
Applied Materials Internships and Co-ops, 532
ARRL Earl I. Anderson Scholarship, 162
Arthur and Doreen Parrett Scholarship, 193
Arthur and Gladys Cervenka Scholarship, 449
ASHRAE J. Richard Mehalick Scholarship, 172
ASHRAE Memorial Scholarship, 173
ASHRAE Region IV Benny Bootle Scholarship, 173
ASHRAE Region VIII Scholarship, 173
ASHRAE Scholarships, 173
ASM Outstanding Scholars Awards, 194
ASME Auxiliary Student Loan, 578
ASME Student Loan Program, 578
ASME/FIRST Robotics Competition Scholarship, 175
Associate Degree Engineering Technology Scholarship, 173
Associated General Contractors James L. Allhands Essay Competition, 197
A.T. Anderson Memorial Scholarship, 109
Aviation Maintenance Technician Scholarship Award, 276
B. J. Harrod Scholarships, 460
B. K. Krenzer Reentry Scholarship, 460
Bachelor Degree Engineering Technology Scholarship, 174
Baroid Scholarship, 106
Barry K. Wendt Commitment Award and Scholarship, 383
Barry M. Goldwater Scholarship, 202
Baxter International Inc. Internships, 533
Bechtel Foundation Scholarship, 460
Berna Lou Cartwright Scholarship, 178
Berntsen International Scholarship in Surveying Technology, 97
Bertha Lamme Memorial Scholarship, 461
BIA North County Division Scholarship, 208
Black & Veatch Internships, Co-op, and Summer Employment, 534
BMW/Society of Automotive Engineers (SAE) Engineering Scholarships, 447
Boeing Internship Program, 534
Boston Scientific Scholarship, 461
Bud Glover Memorial Scholarship, 83
Burlington Northern Santa Fe Foundation Scholarship, 109
Business and Professional Women's Career Advancement Scholarship, 209
Cady McDonnell Memorial Scholarship, 98
CaGIS Scholarship Award, 98
California Farm Bureau Scholarship, 210
Cargill Scholarship Program, 498
Castle & Cooke Mililani Technology Park Scholarship Fund, 263
Caterpillar Inc. Scholarship, 461
Caterpillar Scholars Award, 450
Central New Mexico Scholarship, 461
Chapter 17 St. Louis Scholarship, 450
Chapter 198 - Downriver Detroit Scholarship, 450
Chapter 4 - Lawrence A. Wacker Memorial Scholarship, 450
Chapter 52 - Wichita Scholarship, 451
Chapter 56 - Fort Wayne Scholarship, 451
Chapter 6 - Fairfield County Scholarship, 451
Chapter 67 - Phoenix Scholarship, 451
Charles and Annette Hill Scholarship, 126
Charles B. Scharp Scholarship, 178
Chevron Corporation Scholarships, 462
Chevron Internship Program, 535
ChevronTexaco Scholars Program, 498
CIA Undergraduate Scholarship, 216
Cisco/UNCF Scholars Program, 499
CITE-NY Association Scholarship, 227

Field of Study/Intended Career: Engineering and engineering technology

The Clarence & Josephine Myers Scholarship, 451
Clinton J. Helton Manufacturing Scholarship Award, 452
Community College Graduates Scholarship Program, 356
Computer Science Scholarship, 371
Connecticut Building Congress Scholarship, 225
Connie and Robert T. Gunter Scholarship, 452
DaimlerChrysler Corporation Fund Scholarships, 462
Dam Safety Officials Scholarship, 200
David Arver Memorial Scholarship, 83
Decommissioning, Decontamination and Reutilization Scholarship, 159
Delaware Space Grant Undergraduate Summer Scholarship, 352
Delaware Space Grant Undergraduate Tuition Scholarship, 352
Delayed Education Scholarship for Women, 159
Dell Inc. Scholarship, 462
Deloitte and Touche Internship Program, 536
Delta Faucet Company Scholarship, 427
Demonstration of Energy-Efficient Developments Program Scholarship, 236
Department of Commerce Internship for Postsecondary Students, 559
Department of Energy Special Emphasis Program, 560
Detroit Chapter One - Founding Chapter Scholarship Award, 452
Detroit Section SAE Technical Scholarship, 447
Disney Professional Internships, 574
Distance-Learning/On-Line Programs Scholarship, 191
Dorothy Lemke Howarth Scholarships, 462
Dorothy M. & Earl S. Hoffman Scholarships, 463
Dorothy P. Morris Scholarship, 463
Dr. W. Wes Eckenfelder Jr. Scholarship, 208
Duane Hanson Scholarship, 174
DuPont Company Scholarship, 463
DuPont Cooperative Education Program, 538
DuPont Internships, 538
E. Wayne Kay Co-op Scholarship, 453
E. Wayne Kay High School Scholarship, 453
E. Wayne Kay Scholarship, 453
Eastman Kodak Cooperative Internship Programs, 539
Edmond A. Metzger Scholarship, 164
Edward D. Hendrickson/SAE Scholarship, 447
Edward J. Brady Memorial Scholarship, 183
Edward J. Dulis Scholarship, 195

Edward S. Roth Manufacturing Engineering, 454
Electronics for Imaging Scholarship, 463
Elizabeth McLean Memorial Scholarship, 464
Ellison Onizuka Memorial Scholarship, 266
EMC Summer Internship Program and Co-ops, 539
Energy Student Achievement Program, 560
Engineering/Technology Achievement Awards, 257
Engineers Foundation of Ohio Scholarships, 242
Entergy Jumpstart Co-ops and Internships, 539
Eugene Borson Memorial Scholarship, 293
Eugene C. Figg Jr. Civil Engineering Scholarship, 171
Exelon Scholarship, 464
Extrusion Division/Lew Erwin Memorial Scholarship, 456
fahrenHEIGHT 360 Intern Placement, 540
Field Aviation Co., Inc. Scholarship, 83
Fleming/Blaszcak Scholarship, 456
Florida Power & Light Co-op Program, 542
Ford Motor Company Scholarship, 464
Ford Motor Company/American Indian College Fund Corporate Scholars Program, 108
Frank M. Coda Scholarship, 174
Frank William and Dorothy Given Miller Mechanical Engineering Scholarship, 176
Fred M. Young Sr./SAE Engineering Scholarship, 448
Freeman Fellowship, 171
Fulfilling the Legacy Scholarship, 381
Future Leaders of Manufacturing Scholarships, 454
F.W. "Beich" Beichley Scholarship, 176
Garland Duncan Mechanical Engineering Scholarship, 176
Garmin Scholarship, 84
GE Business/Engineering Scholarship for Minority Students, 318
GE Lloyd Trotter African American Forum Scholarship, 381
Genentech Internship Program, 543
General Electric Foundation Scholarship, 464
General Electric Women's Network Scholarship, 465
General Mills Summer Internship, 543
General Motors Corporation Talent Acquisition Internship, 544
General Motors Engineering Scholarship, 109

General Motors Foundation Scholarships, 465
Geography Students Internship, 557
George A. Roberts Scholarships, 195
Georgia Scholarship for Engineering Education, 581
Georgia-Pacific Internships and Co-ops, 544
Giuliano Mazzetti Scholarship, 454
GM Engineering Scholarship For Minority Students, 319
Goldman, Sachs and Co. Scholarship, 465
Google Hispanic College Fund Scholarship Program, 277
Great Lakes Colleges Association/Associated Colleges of the Midwest Oak Ridge Science Semester, 560
Greater Research Opportunities Undergraduate Student Fellowships, 507
Hansen Scholarship, 244
HENAAC Scholars Program, 278
Henry Adams Scholarship, 174
The Henry Broughton, K2AE Memorial Scholarship, 165
Historically Black College and University Scholarship Fund, 349
Hoffman-La Roche Inc. Student Internship, 545
Homestead Capital Housing Scholarship, 413
Honeywell Avionics Scholarship, 84
Honeywell International Inc. Scholarship, 465
Honors Internship Program, 540
Hopi Tribal Priority Award, 280
Horizons Scholarship of Women in Defense, 286
Howard Brown Rickard Scholarship, 372
Howard Vollum American Indian Scholarship, 413
Hubertus W.V. Willems Scholarship for Male Students, 349
IBM Co-op and Intern Program, 545
IBM Corporation Scholarship, 466
INROADS Internship, 546
Intel International Science and Engineering Fair, 446
Internship Program for Laboratory Technology, 560
Ivy Parker Memorial Scholarship, 466
Jere W. Thompson, Jr., Scholarship Fund, 232
Jill S. Tietjen P.E. Scholarship, 466
John and Elsa Gracik Mechanical Engineering Scholarship, 177
John and Muriel Landis Scholarship, 160
John Deere Student Training Programs, 547
John M. Haniak Scholarship, 195
John R. Lamarsh Scholarship, 160
Johnny Davis Memorial Scholarship, 84

Eligibility Indexes

Field of Study/Intended Career: Engineering and engineering technology

Johnson Controls Co-op and Internship Programs, 548
Joseph R. Dietrich Scholarship, 160
Judith Resnik Memorial Scholarship, 466
Kathryn D. Sullivan Science and Engineering Fellowship, 361
Kenneth Andrew Roe Mechanical Engineering Scholarship, 177
L-3 Avionics Systems Scholarship, 84
Laurence R. Foster Memorial Scholarship, 415
Lee Tarbox Memorial Scholarship, 84
Lillian Moller Gilbreth Scholarship, 467
Lockheed Martin Aeronautics Company Scholarships, 467
Lockheed Martin Foundation Scholarships, 467
Lockheed Martin Scholarship Program, 277
Lowell Gaylor Memorial Scholarship, 85
Lucile B. Kaufman Women's Scholarship, 454
Lucille & Charles A. Wert Scholarship, 195
Maine Metal Products Association Scholarship, 325
Maine Rural Rehabilitation Fund, 325
Maine Society of Professional Engineers Scholarship Program, 326
Marathon Oil Corporation College Scholarship, 279
MASWE Scholarships, 467
Matsuo Bridge Company Ltd of Japan Scholarship, 185
Melvin R. Green Scholarship, 177
Meridith Thoms Memorial Scholarships, 468
MESBEC Scholarships, 215
Meteorological Society Father James B. Macelwane Annual Award, 157
Michigan Society of Professional Engineers Scholarships, 337
Microscopy Society of America Undergraduate Research Scholarship, 337
Microsoft Corporation Scholarships, 468
Microsoft General Scholarship, 337
Microsoft Minority Technical Scholarship, 338
Microsoft Scholarship for Students with Disabilities, 338
Microsoft Women's Technical Scholarship, 338
The Minority Scholarship, 535
MSGC Undergraduate Underrepresented Minority Fellowship Program, 355
Myrtle and Earl Walker Scholarship, 454
Nancy Goodhue Lynch Scholarship, 233

Nancy Lorraine Jensen Memorial Scholarship, 471
NASA Academy Internship, 555
NASA Connecticut Space Grant Undergraduate Fellowship, 351
NASA District of Columbia Undergraduate Scholarship, 352
NASA Hawaii Undergraduate Traineeship, 554
NASA Idaho Space Grant Undergraduate Scholarship, 353
NASA Indiana Space Grant Consortium Undergraduate Scholarships, 354
NASA Massachusetts Space Grant Summer Jobs for Students, 555
NASA Minnesota Space Grant Consortium Wide Scholarship, 355
NASA Missouri State Space Grant Undergraduate Scholarship, 356
NASA Ohio Space Grant Junior/Senior Scholarship Program, 359
NASA Pennsylvania Space Grant Undergraduate Scholarship, 359
NASA Rocky Mountain Space Grant Consortium Undergraduate Scholarship, 360
NASA Space Grant Arizona Undergraduate Research Internship, 554
NASA Space Grant Arkansas Undergraduate Scholarship, 351
NASA Space Grant Georgia Fellowship Program, 352
NASA Space Grant Hawaii Undergraduate Fellowship, 353
NASA Space Grant Illinois Undergraduate Scholarship, 353
NASA Space Grant Kentucky Undergraduate Scholarship, 354
NASA Space Grant Maine Consortium Annual Scholarship and Fellowship Program, 354
NASA Space Grant Michigan Undergraduate Fellowship, 355
NASA Space Grant Mississippi Undergraduate Scholarship, 356
NASA Space Grant Montana Undergraduate Scholarship Program, 357
NASA Space Grant Nevada Undergraduate Scholarship, 357
NASA Space Grant New Mexico Undergraduate Scholarship, 357
NASA Space Grant North Dakota Consortium Lillian Goettler Scholarship, 358
NASA Space Grant North Dakota Undergraduate Scholarship, 358
NASA Space Grant Oregon Undergraduate Scholarship, 359
NASA Space Grant Rhode Island Summer Undergraduate Scholarship, 360

NASA Space Grant South Carolina Undergraduate Academic Year Research Program, 361
NASA Space Grant Undergraduate Scholarship, 351
NASA Space Grant Vermont Consortium Undergraduate Scholarships, 362
NASA Space Grant Virginia Community College Scholarship, 362
NASA Space Grant Wisconsin Consortium Undergraduate Research Program, 363
NASA Space Grant Wisconsin Consortium Undergraduate Scholarship, 363
NASA West Virginia Space Grant Undergraduate Research Fellowship, 363
NASA Wyoming Space Grant Undergraduate Research Fellowships, 364
National Oceanic and Atmospheric Administration Educational Partnership Program with Minority Serving Institutions Undergraduate Scholarship, 403
National Security Agency Stokes Educational Scholarship Program, 380
National Society of Black Engineers Corporate Scholarships Program, 382
National Society of Black Engineers Golden Torch Awards, 382
Naval Engineers Scholarship, 179
NCR Summer Internships, 558
New Jersey Scholarship, 468
Nicholas J. Grant Scholarship, 196
Nissan Community College Transfer Scholarship, 279
North Central Region Scholarship, 455
Northrop Grumman Corporation Scholarship, 468
NSBE Fellows Scholarship, 382
Oklahoma Engineering Foundation Scholarship, 406
Olive Lynn Salembier Reentry Scholarship, 469
Operations and Power Division Scholarship, 160
Oracle Scholars Internship Program, 572
ORISE Community College Institute, 560
ORISE Higher Education Research Experiences at Oak Ridge National Laboratory, 561
ORISE National Oceanic and Atmospheric Administration Faculty and Student Intern Research Participation, 561
ORISE Professional Internship Program for National Energy Technology Laboratory, 561

ORISE Student Environmental Management Participation at the U.S. Army Environmental Center, 561
ORISE Student Internship at the Office of Water, 562
ORISE Student Internship at the U.S. Army Center for Health Promotion and Preventive Medicine, 562
ORISE Student Research Participation at U.S. Army Research Laboratory, 562
ORISE U.S. Nuclear Regulatory Commission Historically Black Colleges and Universities Student Research Participation, 563
Owens Corning Internships, 564
Park Espenschade Memorial Scholarship, 294
Past Presidents Scholarship, 185
Past Presidents Scholarships, 469
Paul and Ellen Ruckes Scholarship, 105
Payzer Scholarship, 245
Pearl I. Young Scholarship, 358
PHCC Educational Foundation Need-Based Scholarship, 428
The PHD ARA Scholarship, 167
Phoenix Section Scholarship, 469
Pittsburgh Local Section Scholarship, 160
Plane & Pilot Magazine/Garmin Scholarship, 86
Plasma Physics National Undergraduate Fellowship Program, 565
Plumbing-Heating-Cooling Contractors - National Association Educational Foundation Scholarship, 428
Rain Bird intelligent Use of Water Company Scholarship, 318
Raymond DiSalvo Scholarship, 160
Reuben Trane Scholarships, 174
Robert G. Lacy Scholarship, 161
Robert N. Hancock Memorial Scholarship, 294
Robert Noyce Scholarship Program, 425
Robert T. (Bob) Liner Scholarship, 161
Rockwell Automation Scholarships, 469
Rocky Mountain Coal Mining Scholarship, 435
Rodney E. Powell Memorial Scholarship, 398
RWMA Scholarship, 186
Samuel Fletcher Tapman ASCE Student Chapter Scholarship, 172
Savannah River Site Professional Internship Program, 563
Scholarship Educational Assistance Program, 364
Science Undergraduate Laboratory Internships, 563

SGI (Silicon Graphics) Internship/Co-op Program, 566
Siemens Competition in Math, Science and Technology, 444
SME Education Foundation Family Scholarship, 455
Smithsonian Environmental Research Center Internship Program, 567
Society of Automotive Engineers (SAE) Longterm Member Sponsored Scholarship, 448
Society of Automotive Engineers (SAE) Yanmar Scholarship, 448
Society of Plastics Engineers General Scholarships, 457
Southface Internship, 569
The SPE Foundation Blow Molding Division Memorial Scholarships, 457
Spence Reese Scholarship, 206
SPIE Educational Scholarship in Optical Science and Engineering, 475
Student Research at the U.S. Army Edgewood Chemical Biological Center, 573
Sun Microsystems Student Intern and Co-op Program, 570
Susan Miszkowitz Memorial Scholarship, 470
Sylvia W. Farny Scholarship, 178
Tau Beta Pi/SAE Engineering Scholarship, 448
Technical Minority Scholarship, 525
TGS Scholarship, 482
Thermoforming Division Memorial Scholarships, 457
Thermoset Division/James I. MacKenzie Memorial Scholarship, 457
Thomas J. Bardos Science Education Awards for Undergraduate Students, 93
TMC/SAE Donald D. Dawson Technical Scholarship, 449
Tyson Foods Intern Program, 571
Undergraduate Fellowships in Engineering and Science, 555
Undergraduate Research Scholarship, 358, 360
Undergraduate Scholarship Program, 358
U.S. Department of Homeland Security Scholarship and Fellowship Program, 563
Vertical Flight Foundation Scholarship, 107
Vice Admiral Jerry O. Tuttle, USN (Ret.), and Mrs. Barbara A. Tuttle Science and Technology Scholarship, 191
Walt Bartram Memorial Education Award (Region 12 and Chapter 119), 455
Washington Internships for Students of Engineering, 575

Water Companies (NJ Chapter) Scholarship, 367
West Virginia Engineering, Science and Technology Scholarship, 518
William E. Weisel Scholarship, 455
William J. and Marijane E. Adams, Jr., Mechanical Engineering Scholarship, 177
William Park Woodside Founder's Scholarship, 196
William R. Goldfarb Memorial Scholarship, 168
Willis H. Carrier Scholarships, 175
Women in Architecture Scholarship, 198
Women in Construction: Founders' Scholarship, 367
The Yasme Foundation Scholarship, 169

English and literature

Ahmad-Sehar Saleha Ahmad and Abrahim Ekramullah Zafar Foundation, 409
Artistic and Administrative Internships, 528
Davidson Fellows Scholarship, 235
Gerrit R. Ludwig Scholarship, 268
Janet Jackson Rhythm Nation Scholarships, 499
Kennedy Library Archival Internship, 547
Latin Honor Society Scholarship, 95
Maureen V. O'Donnell Memorial Teacher Training Award, 96
McKinlay Summer Award, 96
Michael and Marie Marucci Scholarship, 373
Michael Jackson Scholarships, 501
National Junior Classical League Scholarship, 96
Reader's Digest Foundation Scholarship Program, 501
R.L. Gillette Scholarship, 105
Scholastic Writing Portfolio Gold Award, 90
Signet Classic Student Scholarship Essay Contest, 422
United States Holocaust Memorial Museum Internship, 572
Xernona Clayton Scholarship, 200

Foreign languages

Alpha Mu Gamma National Scholarship, 91
Cultural Ambassadorial Scholarship, 436
Honors Internship Program, 540
Joseph S. Adams Scholarship, 445
Michael and Marie Marucci Scholarship, 373
National Security Agency Stokes Educational Scholarship Program, 380
United States Holocaust Memorial Museum Internship, 572

Field of Study/Intended Career: Foreign languages

U.S. Department of Education Fulbright-Hays Project Abroad Scholarship for Programs in China, 229
U.S. Department of State Internship, 573
Workforce Incentive Program, 586

Health professions and allied services

Abbie Sargent Memorial Scholarship, 75
ADHA Institute for Oral Health Part-Time Scholarship, 77
ADHA Institute General Scholarships, 77
ADHA Institute Merit Scholarships, 78
AFPE "Gateway to Research" Scholarship, 104
Aiea General Hospital Association Scholarship, 261
Allied Dental Scholarship for Dental Assisting Students, 76
Allied Dental Scholarship for Dental Hygiene Students, 76
Allied Dental Scholarship for Dental Laboratory Technology Students, 77
Allman Medical Scholarships, 341
Aloha Scholarship, 135
Alton R. Higgins, MD, and Dorothy Higgins Scholarship, 498
AMBUCS Scholars-Scholarship for Therapists, 91
American Legion Arizona Auxiliary Health Care Occupation Scholarship, 114
American Legion Arizona Auxiliary Nurses' Scholarship, 114
American Legion Idaho Auxiliary Nurse's Scholarship, 120
American Legion Maryland Auxiliary Scholarship, 129
American Legion Ohio Auxiliary Past President's Parley Nurse's Scholarship, 145
American Legion Oregon Auxiliary Department Nurses Scholarship, 146
American Legion Puerto Rico Auxiliary Nursing Scholarships, 147
American Legion South Dakota Auxiliary Nurse's Scholarship, 148
American Legion Texas Auxiliary Medical Scholarship, 150
American Legion Wisconsin Auxiliary Past Presidents Parley Scholarship, 155
American Legion Wyoming Auxiliary Past Presidents' Parley Scholarship, 156
Arthur and Doreen Parrett Scholarship, 193
A.T. Anderson Memorial Scholarship, 109

Athletic Trainers' Entry Level Scholarship, 368
Athletic Trainers' Student Writing Contest, 368
Barry M. Goldwater Scholarship, 202
Behavioral Sciences Student Fellowship, 243
Bertha P. Singer Scholarship, 411
Black Nurses Scholarship, 368
Burlington Northern Santa Fe Foundation Scholarship, 109
Business and Professional Women's Career Advancement Scholarship, 209
Cadbury Adams Community Outreach Scholarships, 78
California Farm Bureau Scholarship, 210
Caroline Kark Scholarship, 392
Champlain Valley Kennel Club Scholarship, 510
Charles W. Riley Fire and Emergency Medical Services Tuition Reimbursement Program, 328
Chester Haddan Scholarship Program, 419
Clinique Nursing Scholarship, 220
Colgate "Bright Smiles, Bright Futures" Minority Scholarships, 78
Connecticut Nursing Scholarship, 227
Cora Aguda Manayan Fund, 264
Critical Care Nurses Education Advancement Scholarship, 94
The Cynthia E. Morgan Memorial Scholarship Fund, 230
Cystic Fibrosis Student Traineeship, 230
Dan McKeever Scholarship Program, 419
Delaware Nursing Incentive Program, 580
Delta Gamma Foundation Memorial Scholarship, 104
Denver Rescue Mission Center for Mission Studies Interns, 537
Developmental Disabilities Nursing Scholastic Achievement Scholarship, 203
Developmental Disability Scholastic Achievement Scholarship, 203
Dr. Alfred C. Fones Scholarship, 78
Dr. Alvin and Monica Saake Scholarship, 265
Dr. Hans and Clara Zimmerman Foundation Health Scholarship, 265
Dr. Harold Hillenbrand Scholarship, 78
Dr. Marie E. Zakrzewski Medical Scholarship, 314
Earl & Patricia Armstrong Scholarship, 499
Education Advancement Scholarship, 94
Edward and Norma Doty Scholarship, 266
Erby Young Scholarship, 346
Eva Vieira Memorial Scholarship, 324

fahrenHEIGHT 360 Intern Placement, 540
The Filipino Nurses' Organization of Hawaii Scholarship, 267
FORE Undergraduate Scholarship, 250
Foundation for Surgical Technology Scholarship Fund, 250
Goldman Family Fund: New Leader Scholarship, 327
Great Lakes Colleges Association/Associated Colleges of the Midwest Oak Ridge Science Semester, 560
Green Mountain Dog Club Scholarship, 510
The Grottos Scholarships, 480
Hannaford Internships, 544
Health Career Scholarship, 298
Hoffman-La Roche Inc. Student Internship, 545
Hopi Tribal Priority Award, 280
Howard Brown Rickard Scholarship, 372
Hu-Friedy/Esther Wilkins Instrument Scholarships, 79
Idaho Education Incentive Loan Forgiveness Program, 582
Indiana Minority Teacher & Special Education Services Scholarship, 477
Indiana Nursing Scholarship, 477
INROADS Internship, 546
Irene E. Newman Scholarship, 79
Jewish War Veterans of the United States of America Bernard Rotberg Memorial Scholarship, 307
Jewish War Veterans of the United States of America JWV Grant, 307
Jimmy A. Young Memorial Education Recognition Award, 169
John and Geraldine Hobble Licensed Practical Nursing Scholarship, 126
John Dawe Dental Education Fund, 269
John Deere Student Training Programs, 547
Juliette A. Southard/Oral B Laboratories Scholarship, 100
June Gill Nursing Scholarship, 393
Kaiser Permanente College to Caring Program, 277
Kaiser-Permanente Dental Assistant Scholarship, 415
Kansas Nursing Service Scholarship, 308
Ken Chagnon Scholarship, 420
Laura N. Dowsett Fund, 271
Laurence R. Foster Memorial Scholarship, 415
Lindbergh Grant, 218
Louis S. Silvey Grant, 308
Margaret E. Swanson Scholarship, 79
Margaret Jones Memorial Nursing Scholarship, 272
Margarite McAlpin Nurse's Scholarship, 153

Field of Study/Intended Career: Home economics

Mary Marshall Nursing Scholarship, 513
Mary Virginia Macrea Memorial Scholarship, 125
Maryland Tuition Reduction for Non-Resident Nursing Students, 331
McFarland Charitable Foundation Scholarship, 261
M.D. "Jack" Murphy Memorial Nurses Training Fund, 134
Medical Career Scholarships, 131
Medical Technologists Student Scholarship, 156
MESBEC Scholarships, 215
Michigan Nursing Scholarship, 336
Mississippi Health Care Professions Loan/Scholarship, 584
Mississippi Nursing Education Loan/Scholarship, 584
Missouri League for Nursing Scholarship, 346
Morton B. Duggan, Jr. Memorial Education Recognition Award, 169
Myasthenia Gravis Foundation Nursing Research Fellowship, 348
NASA District of Columbia Undergraduate Scholarship, 352
NASA Space Grant Arkansas Undergraduate Scholarship, 351
NASA Space Grant Maine Consortium Annual Scholarship and Fellowship Program, 354
NASA Space Grant Wisconsin Consortium Undergraduate Research Program, 363
National Amateur Baseball Federation Scholarship, 364
National Health Service Corps Scholarship, 506
National Student Nurses Association Scholarship, 250
Native Daughters of the Golden West Scholarship, 384
NBRC/AMP Robert M. Lawrence, MD Education Recognition Award, 170
NBRC/AMP William W. Burgin, Jr. MD Education Recognition Award, 170
NCAA Division I Degree-Completion Award Program, 385
NEHA/AAS Scholarship, 371
New Mexico Allied Health Student Loan-for-Service Program, 586
New Mexico Medical Student Loan-for-Service, 586
New Mexico Nursing Student Loan-for-Service, 587
Nick Van Pernis Scholarship, 273
Nicole Marie Goulart Memorial Scholarship, 324
North Carolina Nurse Scholars Program, 588
North Carolina Student Loans for Health/Science/Mathematics, 588

Nuclear Medicine Student Fellowship Award, 445
Nurse Gift Tuition Scholarships, 138
Nurse Praciticner Nurse Midwife Scholarship, 514
Ohio Nurse Education Assistance Loan Program, 588
OMNE/Nursing Leaders of Maine Scholarship, 408
Oncology Nursing Certification Corporation Bachelor's Scholarships, 408
Oral-B Laboratories Dental Hygiene Scholarship, 79
ORISE Student Internship at the U.S. Army Center for Health Promotion and Preventive Medicine, 562
ORISE Student Research - National Center for Toxicological Research, 562
ORISE Student Research at the Centers for Disease Control and Prevention, 562
ORISE Student Research Participation at the U.S. Army Medical Research Institute of Chemical Defense, 562
ORISE Student Research Participation at U.S. Army Research Laboratory, 562
ORISE U.S. Nuclear Regulatory Commission Historically Black Colleges and Universities Student Research Participation, 563
Past President's Parley Health Care Scholarship, 133
Past President's Parley Nurse's Scholarship, 117
Past President's Parley Nurses Scholarship, 120
Past President's Parley Nurses' Scholarship, 139, 141, 143
Past Presidents' Parley Nursing Scholarship, 116
Past President's Parley Nursing Scholarship, 118, 123
Past President's Parley Scholarship, 130, 134, 145
Past President's Parley Student Nurses Scholarship for Girls or Boys, 144
Paul Cole Scholarship, 445
Pfizer Inc. Scholarships, 80
Practical Nurse Scholarship, 138
President's Parley Nursing Scholarship, 128
Roberta Pierce Scofield Bachelor's Scholarships, 408
ROTC/Navy Nurse Corps Scholarship Program, 507
Rudolph Dillman Memorial Scholarship, 105
Science Undergraduate Laboratory Internships, 563
Siemens Competition in Math, Science and Technology, 444
Sigma Phi Alpha Undergraduate Scholarship, 80
Spence Reese Scholarship, 206

Student Nurse Scholarship, 122
Student Research Participation at the Federal Bureau of Investigation Counterterrorism/Forensic Science Research Unit, 563
Texas Scholarships for Nursing Students, 488
Thomas J. Bardos Science Education Awards for Undergraduate Students, 93
Thz Fo Farm Fund, 274
United States Army Four-Year Nursing Scholarship, 438
UNM Hospital Nursing Scholarship, 503
Viets Medical Student/Graduate Student Fellowship, 349
Walter and Marie Schmidt Scholarship, 418
William R. Goldfarb Memorial Scholarship, 168
Wilma Motley Memorial California Merit Scholarship, 80
Workforce Incentive Program, 586
Young Epidemiology Scholars Student Competition, 221

Home economics

Academic Scholarship for High School Seniors, 379
Academic Scholarship for Undergraduate Students, 379
Allen Susser Scholarship, 301
American Chemical Society Scholars Program, 95
Bern Laxer Memorial Scholarship, 302
Bryan Close Polo Grill Scholarship, 302
Chris Desens Scholarship, 302
Christian Wolffer Scholarship, 302
Clat Triplette Scholarship, 303
The Cynthia E. Morgan Memorial Scholarship Fund, 230
Dairy Product Marketing Scholarships, 369
Dairy Student Recognition Program, 370
Dana Campbell Memorial Scholarship, 303
Deseo at the Westin Scholarship, 303
Enology and Viticulture Scholarship, 170
Foodservice Communicators Scholarship, 297
Gene Hovis Memorial Scholarship, 303
General Mills Summer Internship, 543
Graduate, Baccalaureate or Coordinated Program Scholarships, 100
Institute of Food Technologists Freshman Scholarship, 294
Institute of Food Technologists Junior/Senior Scholarship, 294
Institute of Food Technologists Sophomore Scholarship, 295

43

Field of Study/Intended Career: Home economics

James Beard General Scholarships, 303
Jean-Louis Palladin Memorial Scholarship, 304
Marcia S. Harris Legacy Fund Scholarship, 332
National Dairy Shrine Kildee Scholarship, 370
National Dairy Shrine Klussendorf Scholarship, 370
National Dairy Shrine/Iager Dairy Scholarship, 370
NDS/DMI Milk Marketing Scholarship, 231
New Mexico Allied Health Student Loan-for-Service Program, 586
NPFDA Scholarship, 377
The Peter Cameron Scholarship, 304
Peter Kump Memorial Scholarship, 304
ProStart National Certificate of Achievement Scholarship, 379
Taste America San Francisco Scholarship, 305
Tyson Foods Intern Program, 571
USDA/1890 National Scholars Program, 505
Wally Joe (KC's) Scholarship, 305

Law

Alphonso Deal Scholarship, 368
American Society of International Law Internships, 529
BIA North County Division Scholarship, 208
Congressional Institute Internships, 536
Department of Energy Special Emphasis Program, 560
Energy Student Achievement Program, 560
EPA National Network for Environmental Management Studies Fellowship, 506
Feminism & Leadership Internship, 541
Honors Internship Program, 540
Hopi Tribal Priority Award, 280
Horizons Scholarship of Women in Defense, 286
Howard Brown Rickard Scholarship, 372
Johnson Controls Co-op and Internship Programs, 548
Leonard C. Horn Award for Legal Studies, 342
NASA Space Grant Wisconsin Consortium Undergraduate Research Program, 363
Sony Credited Internship, 569
Spence Reese Scholarship, 206
Summer Research Diversity Fellowships in Law and Social Sciences for Undergraduate Students, 528
United States Holocaust Memorial Museum Internship, 572

United States Senate Member Internships, 572
Water Companies (NJ Chapter) Scholarship, 367

Liberal arts and interdisciplinary studies

A. Patrick Charnon Memorial Scholarship, 216
Business and Professional Women's Career Advancement Scholarship, 209
Charles L. Hebner Memorial Scholarship, 236
Coca-Cola Two-Year Colleges Scholarship, 220
Community Scholarship Fund, 264
CRT Internship Program, 536
Feminism & Leadership Internship, 541
Feminist Web Internship, 541
Harriet Irsay Scholarship, 112
John M. Simpson Memorial Scholarship, 91
Multicultural Advertising Intern Program, 527
Multicultural Undergraduate Summer Internships at the Getty Center, 546
National Federation of the Blind Scholarships, 374
National Junior Classical League Scholarship, 96
Pulliam Journalism Fellowship, 545
Sid Richardson Scholarship, 443
Summer Research Diversity Fellowships in Law and Social Sciences for Undergraduate Students, 528
Wisconsin Indian Student Assistance Grant, 522
Wisconsin Talent Incentive Program Grant, 523

Library science

ALISE Bodhan S. Wynar Research Paper Competition, 197
ALISE Research Grant Award, 198
Dialog/ALISE Methodology Paper Competition, 198
Kennedy Library Archival Internship, 547
Library of Congress Hispanic Division Junior Fellows Internship, 549
Museum Coca-Cola Internship, 557

Mathematics

Adler Science and Math Scholarship, 129
Aerospace Undergraduate Research Scholarship Program, 362
AFCEA General Emmett Paige Scholarship, 190
AFCEA General John A. Wickham Scholarship, 190
AFCEA Professional Part-Time Scholarship, 190

AFCEA ROTC Scholarships, 190
AFCEA Scholarships for Math and Science Teachers, 80
AFCEA Sgt. Jeannette L. Winters, USMC Memorial Scholarship, 191
AFCEA/Lockheed Martin IT Scholarship, 191
AICP Heartland Chapter Scholarship, 199
AICP Scholarship, 199
Alfred R. Chisholm Memorial Scholarship, 498
Allstate Internships, 527
A.T. Anderson Memorial Scholarship, 109
Barry M. Goldwater Scholarship, 202
Boeing Internship Program, 534
Burlington Northern Santa Fe Foundation Scholarship, 109
Community College Graduates Scholarship Program, 356
Davidson Fellows Scholarship, 235
Department of Energy Special Emphasis Program, 560
Distance-Learning/On-Line Programs Scholarship, 191
DOE Pre-Service Teacher Internships, 560
Eastman Kodak Cooperative Internship Programs, 539
Economic Research Division Project Internships, 534
Energy Student Achievement Program, 560
Federal Reserve Undergraduate Summer Analyst Program, 541
Great Lakes Colleges Association/Associated Colleges of the Midwest Oak Ridge Science Semester, 560
Greater Research Opportunities Undergraduate Student Fellowships, 507
HENAAC Scholars Program, 278
Horizons Scholarship of Women in Defense, 286
Howard Vollum American Indian Scholarship, 413
Hubertus W.V. Willems Scholarship for Male Students, 349
Intel Science Talent Search, 446
Joint CAS/SOA Minority Scholarships for Actuarial Students, 447
Kathryn D. Sullivan Science and Engineering Fellowship, 361
MESBEC Scholarships, 215
Microsoft General Scholarship, 337
Microsoft Minority Technical Scholarship, 338
Microsoft Scholarship for Students with Disabilities, 338
Microsoft Women's Technical Scholarship, 338
MSGC Undergraduate Underrepresented Minority Fellowship Program, 355
NASA Academy Internship, 555

44

Field of Study/Intended Career: Social sciences and history

NASA District of Columbia Undergraduate Scholarship, 352
NASA Hawaii Undergraduate Traineeship, 554
NASA Idaho Space Grant Undergraduate Scholarship, 353
NASA Indiana Space Grant Consortium Undergraduate Scholarships, 354
NASA Minnesota Space Grant Consortium Wide Scholarship, 355
NASA Missouri State Space Grant Undergraduate Scholarship, 356
NASA Ohio Space Grant Junior/Senior Scholarship Program, 359
NASA Pennsylvania Space Grant Undergraduate Scholarship, 359
NASA Space Grant Michigan Undergraduate Fellowship, 355
NASA Space Grant Mississippi Undergraduate Scholarship, 356
NASA Space Grant Nevada Undergraduate Scholarship, 357
NASA Space Grant New Mexico Undergraduate Scholarship, 357
NASA Space Grant North Dakota Consortium Lillian Goettler Scholarship, 358
NASA Space Grant North Dakota Undergraduate Scholarship, 358
NASA Space Grant Oregon Undergraduate Scholarship, 359
NASA Space Grant South Carolina Undergraduate Academic Year Research Program, 361
NASA Space Grant Teacher Education Scholarship, 362
NASA Space Grant Vermont Consortium Undergraduate Scholarships, 362
NASA Space Grant Virginia Community College Scholarship, 362
NASA West Virginia Space Grant Undergraduate Research Fellowship, 363
NASA Wyoming Space Grant Undergraduate Research Fellowships, 364
National Oceanic and Atmospheric Administration Educational Partnership Program with Minority Serving Institutions Undergraduate Scholarship, 403
National Security Agency Stokes Educational Scholarship Program, 380
National Society of Black Engineers Golden Torch Awards, 382
North Carolina Student Loans for Health/Science/Mathematics, 588
ORISE Community College Institute, 560
ORISE Higher Education Research Experiences at Oak Ridge National Laboratory, 561

ORISE Professional Internship Program for National Energy Technology Laboratory, 561
ORISE Student Research - National Center for Toxicological Research, 562
ORISE U.S. Nuclear Regulatory Commission Historically Black Colleges and Universities Student Research Participation, 563
Payzer Scholarship, 245
Pearl I. Young Scholarship, 358
Plasma Physics National Undergraduate Fellowship Program, 565
Robert Noyce Scholarship Program, 425
Science Undergraduate Laboratory Internships, 563
SEG Foundation Scholarship, 441
SGI (Silicon Graphics) Internship/Co-op Program, 566
Shuichi, Katsu and Itsuyo Suga Scholarship, 274
Siemens Competition in Math, Science and Technology, 444
Smithsonian Environmental Research Center Internship Program, 567
Tennessee Student Assistance Corporation/Math And Science Teachers Loan Forgiveness Program, 590
U.S. Department of Homeland Security Scholarship and Fellowship Program, 563
Young Epidemiology Scholars Student Competition, 221

Military science

United States Army Four-Year Nursing Scholarship, 438
United States Army Four-Year Scholarship, 438
World Security Institute Internship, 576

Mortuary science

American Board of Funeral Service Education National Scholarship, 94

Multi/interdisciplinary studies

International Semester Scholarship, 110

Philosophy, religion, and theology

Davidson Fellows Scholarship, 235
Denver Rescue Mission Center for Mission Studies Interns, 537
Juliette M. Atherton Scholarship, 269
Leonard M. Perryman Communications Scholarship, 497

Leonard M. Perryman Communications Scholarship for Ethnic Minority Students, 497
Stoody-West Fellowship, 497

Protective services

Alphonso Deal Scholarship, 368
Charles W. Riley Fire and Emergency Medical Services Tuition Reimbursement Program, 328
Honors Internship Program, 540
National Technical Investigators' Captain James J. Regan Memorial Scholarship, 320
NC Sherrif's Association Criminal Justice Scholarship, 400
Ritchie-Jennings Memorial Scholarship, 76
Sheryl A. Horak Law Enforcement Explorer Scholarship, 320
Summer Research Diversity Fellowships in Law and Social Sciences for Undergraduate Students, 528
Troy Douglas Carr Scholarship for Criminal Justice, 494

Social sciences and history

A. Patrick Charnon Memorial Scholarship, 216
Adele Filene Travel Award, 228
AICP Scholarship, 199
American Society of International Law Internships, 529
Anne U. White Fund, 199
Anthropology Internship Program, 529
Arts Action Fund Internship, 530
Averyl Elaine Keriakedes Memorial Scholarship, 138
Behavioral Sciences Student Fellowship, 243
Business and Professional Women's Career Advancement Scholarship, 209
Charles L. Hebner Memorial Scholarship, 236
CIA Undergraduate Scholarship, 216
Citizens for Global Solutions Internship, 535
The Cloisters Summer Internship Program, 550
Community Scholarship Fund, 264
Congressional Institute Internships, 536
Delaware Space Grant Undergraduate Summer Scholarship, 352
Delaware Space Grant Undergraduate Tuition Scholarship, 352
Denver Rescue Mission Center for Mission Studies Interns, 537
Department of Energy Special Emphasis Program, 560
Developmental Disability Scholastic Achievement Scholarship, 203

Field of Study/Intended Career: Social sciences and history

The Donald Riebhoff Memorial Scholarship, 164
Douglas Haskell Awards for Student Journalism, 111
Economic Research Division Project Internships, 534
Elie Wiesel Prize in Ethics, 241
Energy Student Achievement Program, 560
Federal Reserve Undergraduate Summer Analyst Program, 541
Feminism & Leadership Internship, 541
Finance Undergraduate Internships, 574
Franklin D. Roosevelt Library/Roosevelt Summer Internship, 543
General Mills Summer Internship, 543
Geography Students Internship, 557
Goldman Family Fund: New Leader Scholarship, 327
Government and Public Affairs Internship, 530
Greater Research Opportunities Undergraduate Student Fellowships, 507
Harriet Irsay Scholarship, 112
Harry S. Truman Scholarship, 261
Henry A. Zuberano Scholarship, 268
Horizons Scholarship of Women in Defense, 286
House Member Internships, 573
International Semester Scholarship, 110
Jennifer C. Groot Fellowship, 95
Jeppesen Meterology Internship, 546
Jerry Clark Memorial Scholarship, 101
John F. Kennedy Scholars Award, 333
John Joseph Moakely Democratic Internship, 550
Kawasaki-McGaha Scholarship Fund, 270
Kennedy Library Archival Internship, 547
The Merchants Exhange Scholarship Fund, 334
Michael and Marie Marucci Scholarship, 373
Mississippi Health Care Professions Loan/Scholarship, 584
Mother Jones Magazine Editorial Internship, 553
NASA District of Columbia Undergraduate Scholarship, 352
NASA Space Grant Hawaii Undergraduate Fellowship, 353
NASA Space Grant Nevada Undergraduate Scholarship, 357
National Oceanic and Atmospheric Administration Educational Partnership Program with Minority Serving Institutions Undergraduate Scholarship, 403
National Peace Essay Contest, 502

Native Daughters of the Golden West Scholarship, 384
North Carolina Student Loans for Health/Science/Mathematics, 588
ORISE Student Environmental Management Participation at the U.S. Army Environmental Center, 561
ORISE Student Research at the Centers for Disease Control and Prevention, 562
Rain Bird intelligent Use of Water Company Scholarship, 318
Rhode Island State Government Internship Program, 566
Robert B. Bailey Scholarship, 229
SCA Conservation Internships, 570
Senior Scholarship, 316
Shell Legislative Internship Program, 556
Six-Month Internship, 551
Smithsonian Minority Internship, 567
Southface Internship, 569
Spence Reese Scholarship, 206
Stella Blum Research Grant, 228
Summer Research Diversity Fellowships in Law and Social Sciences for Undergraduate Students, 528
Thomas R. Pickering Foreign Affairs Fellowship, 524
Tribal Business Management Scholarship, 215
UBS/PaineWebber Scholarships, 501
United States Holocaust Memorial Museum Internship, 572
United States Senate Member Internships, 572
U.S. Department of Homeland Security Scholarship and Fellowship Program, 563
U.S. Department of State Internship, 573
Washington Crossing Foundation Scholarship, 515
Wilma D. Hoyal/Maxine Chilton Memorial Scholarship, 114
Women in Architecture Scholarship, 198
World Security Institute Internship, 576
Young Epidemiology Scholars Student Competition, 221

Trade and industry

AAGS Joseph F. Dracup Scholarship Award, 97
Academic Scholarship for High School Seniors, 379
Academic Scholarship for Undergraduate Students, 379
AFCEA General John A. Wickham Scholarship, 190
AFCEA ROTC Scholarships, 190
AFCEA/Lockheed Martin IT Scholarship, 191

AGC Education and Research Undergraduate Scholarship, 196
AGC of Maine Scholarship Program, 81
Air Traffic Control Full-Time Employee Student Scholarship, 82
Air Traffic Control Half- to Full-Time Student Scholarship, 82
Airgas-Jerry Baker Scholarship, 182
Airgas-Terry Jarvis Memorial Scholarship, 182
A.J. "Andy" Spielman Travel Agents Scholarship, 179
Albert E. Wischmeyer Memorial Scholarship Award, 449
Alice Glaisyer Warfield Memorial Scholarship, 491
Allen Susser Scholarship, 301
Alwin B. Newton Scholarship, 172
American Association of Airport Executives Foundation Scholarship, 93
American Association of Airport Executives Foundation Scholarship for Native Americans, 93
American Express Travel Scholarship, 179
American Welding Society District Scholarship, 183
AOPA Air Safety Foundation/McAllister Memorial Scholarship, 86
Arizona Chapter Gold Scholarship, 180
Arsham Amirikian Engineering Scholarship, 183
Arthur and Gladys Cervenka Scholarship, 449
ASHRAE J. Richard Mehalick Scholarship, 172
ASHRAE Memorial Scholarship, 173
ASHRAE Region IV Benny Bootle Scholarship, 173
ASHRAE Region VIII Scholarship, 173
ASHRAE Scholarships, 173
Associate Degree Engineering Technology Scholarship, 173
Associated General Contractors James L. Allhands Essay Competition, 197
Bachelor Degree Engineering Technology Scholarship, 174
Bern Laxer Memorial Scholarship, 302
Berntsen International Scholarship in Surveying, 97
Berntsen International Scholarship in Surveying Technology, 97
Best Teen Chef Culinary Scholarship Competition, 192
BIA North County Division Scholarship, 208
Black & Veatch Internships, Co-op, and Summer Employment, 534
Boeing Internship Program, 534
Bryan Close Polo Grill Scholarship, 302

Field of Study/Intended Career: Trade and industry

Bud Glover Memorial Scholarship, 83
Cady McDonnell Memorial Scholarship, 98
CaGIS Scholarship Award, 98
Canada Scholarship, 490
Caterpillar Scholars Award, 450
Chapter 17 St. Louis Scholarship, 450
Chapter 198 - Downriver Detroit Scholarship, 450
Chapter 4 - Lawrence A. Wacker Memorial Scholarship, 450
Chapter 6 - Fairfield County Scholarship, 451
Chapter 67 - Phoenix Scholarship, 451
Charles N. Fisher Memorial Scholarship, 163
Charlotte Woods Memorial Scholarship, 492
Chris Desens Scholarship, 302
Christian Wolffer Scholarship, 302
The Clarence & Josephine Myers Scholarship, 451
Clat Triplette Scholarship, 303
Clinton J. Helton Manufacturing Scholarship Award, 452
Connecticut Building Congress Scholarship, 225
Connie and Robert T. Gunter Scholarship, 452
Dairy Product Marketing Scholarships, 369
Dairy Student Recognition Program, 370
Dana Campbell Memorial Scholarship, 303
David Arver Memorial Scholarship, 83
Delta Faucet Company Scholarship, 427
Demonstration of Energy-Efficient Developments Program Scholarship, 236
Denny Lydic Scholarship, 492
Deseo at the Westin Scholarship, 303
Detroit Chapter One - Founding Chapter Scholarship Award, 452
Directors Scholarship, 452
Disney Professional Internships, 574
Donald and Shirley Hastings National Scholarship, 183
Donald Burnside Memorial Scholarship, 187
Donald F. Hastings Scholarship, 183
Dr. James L. Lawson Memorial Scholarship, 164
Duane Hanson Scholarship, 174
Dutch and Ginger Arver Scholarship, 83
E. Wayne Kay Community College Scholarship, 453
E. Wayne Kay Co-op Scholarship, 453
E. Wayne Kay High School Scholarship, 453
E. Wayne Kay Scholarship, 453
Eastman Kodak Cooperative Internship Programs, 539
Edward J. Brady Memorial Scholarship, 183
Edward S. Roth Manufacturing Engineering, 454
EMC Summer Internship Program and Co-ops, 539
Field Aviation Co., Inc. Scholarship, 83
Foodservice Communicators Scholarship, 297
Ford Motor Company Scholarship, 464
Frank M. Coda Scholarship, 174
Fred R. McDaniel Memorial Scholarship, 164
Future Leaders of Manufacturing Scholarships, 454
Gabriel A. Hartl Scholarship, 83
Garmin Scholarship, 84
Gene Hovis Memorial Scholarship, 303
General Motors Foundation Scholarships, 465
George Reinke Scholarships, 180
Ginger and Fred Deines Canada Scholarship, 492
Ginger and Fred Deines Mexico Scholarship, 492
Giuliano Mazzetti Scholarship, 454
Healy Scholarship, 180
Henry Adams Scholarship, 174
Holland America Line-Westours, Inc., Scholarship, 180
Honeywell Avionics Scholarship, 84
Honeywell International Inc. Scholarship, 465
Hooper Memorial Scholarship, 492
Howard E. and Wilma J. Adkins Memorial Scholarship, 184
INROADS Internship, 546
Irving W. Cook, WAOCGS Scholarship, 165
ITW Welding Companies Scholarship, 184
J. Desmond Slattery Award: Student, 493
Jack R. Barckhoff Welding Management Scholarship, 184
James A. Turner, Jr., Memorial Scholarship, 184
James Beard General Scholarships, 303
James Beard School Scholarships, 304
Jean-Louis Palladin Memorial Scholarship, 304
Jeppesen Meterology Internship, 546
Jerry Robinson-Inweld Corporation Scholarship, 184
John C. Lincoln Memorial Scholarship, 185
Johnny Davis Memorial Scholarship, 84
Johnson Controls Co-op and Internship Programs, 548
Joseph R. Stone Scholarship, 181
Kathy LeTarte Scholarship, 490
Kurt W. Schneider Memorial Scholarship Fund, 271
L. Phil Wicker Scholarship, 166
L-3 Avionics Systems Scholarship, 84
La Toque Scholarship in Wine Studies, 304
LaMacchia Family Scholarship, 491
Lee Tarbox Memorial Scholarship, 84
Leon Harris/Les Nichols Memorial to Spartan School of Aeronautics, 85
Lindbergh Grant, 218
Lowell Gaylor Memorial Scholarship, 85
Lucile B. Kaufman Women's Scholarship, 454
Maine Innkeepers Association Scholarship, 325
Maine Metal Products Association Scholarship, 325
Marcia S. Harris Legacy Fund Scholarship, 332
Mary Macey Scholarship, 523
Matsuo Bridge Company Ltd of Japan Scholarship, 185
Mayflower Tours Patrick Murphy Internship, 571
Mid-Continent Instrument Scholarship, 85
Miller Electric Manufacturing Company Ivic Scholarship, 185
The Mississippi Scholarship, 166
Monte R. Mitchell Global Scholarship, 85
Museum Coca-Cola Internship, 557
Myrtle and Earl Walker Scholarship, 454
Nancy Goodhue Lynch Scholarship, 233
NASA Space Grant Virginia Community College Scholarship, 362
National Association of Women in Construction Scholarship, 511
National Dairy Shrine Kildee Scholarship, 370
National Dairy Shrine Klussendorf Scholarship, 370
National Dairy Shrine/Iager Dairy Scholarship, 370
NDS/DMI Milk Marketing Scholarship, 231
The NEMAL Electronics Scholarship, 166
Nettie Dracup Memorial Scholarship, 98
North Carolina State Board of Refrigeration Examiners Scholarship, 399
North Central Region Scholarship, 455
Northern California Chapter/Richard Epping Scholarship, 181
NSPS Board of Governors Scholarship, 98
NSPS Scholarships, 99
Past Presidents Scholarship, 185

Eligibility Indexes

47

Field of Study/Intended Career: Trade and industry

Pat & Jim Host Internship/Scholarship, 571
Paul and Helen L. Grauer Scholarship, 167
The Peter Cameron Scholarship, 304
Peter Kump Memorial Scholarship, 304
PGSF Annual Scholarship Competition, 431
Plane & Pilot Magazine/Garmin Scholarship, 86
Plumbing-Heating-Cooling Contractors - National Association Educational Foundation Scholarship, 428
Praxair International Scholarship, 185
Princess Cruises and Princess Tours Scholarship, 181
Professional Land Surveyors of Oregon Scholarship, 417
ProStart National Certificate of Achievement Scholarship, 379
Quebec Scholarship, 491
Rene Campbell Memorial Scholarship, 491
Reuben Trane Scholarships, 174
Robert L. Peaslee-Detroit Brazing and Soldering Division Scholarship, 186
Rockwell Automation Scholarships, 469
Rocky Mountain Chapter-Donald Estey Scholarship Fund, 181
Rodney E. Powell Memorial Scholarship, 398
Russ Casey Scholarship, 326
RWMA Scholarship, 186
Schonstedt Scholarships in Surveying, 99
Southern California Chapter/Pleasant Hawaiian Holidays Scholarship, 182
Taste America San Francisco Scholarship, 305
Texas Transportation Scholarship, 492
Travel Research Grant, 493
Trimmer Education Foundation ABC Student Chapter Scholarship Program, 196
Tri-State Surveying & Photogrammetry Kris M. Kunze Scholarship, 99
Vertical Flight Foundation Scholarship, 107
Vice Admiral Jerry O. Tuttle, USN (Ret.), and Mrs. Barbara A. Tuttle Science and Technology Scholarship, 191
Vicki Willder Scholarship Fund, 275
Wally Joe (KC's) Scholarship, 305
Walt Bartram Memorial Education Award (Region 12 and Chapter 119), 455
William A. and Ann M. Brothers Scholarship, 186
William B. Howell Memorial Scholarship, 186
William E. Weisel Scholarship, 455
Willis H. Carrier Scholarships, 175
Women in Construction: Founders' Scholarship, 367
Yellow Ribbon Scholarship, 491

Gender

Female

Ada I. Pressman Memorial Scholarship, 459
ADC Communications and Foundation Scholarship, 459
Admiral Grace Murray Hopper Scholarship, 459
Adobe Systems Computer Science Scholarships, 459
Albert A. Marks Education Scholarship for Teacher Education, 341
Alexandra A. Sonenfeld Award, 233
Allman Medical Scholarships, 341
Alumnae Panhellenic Association Women's Scholarship, 91
American Legion Kentucky Auxiliary Mary Barrett Marshall Scholarship, 127
American Legion Maryland Auxiliary Scholarship, 129
American Legion Michigan Auxiliary Memorial Scholarship, 131
Anne Maureen Whitney Barrow Memorial, 460
Averyl Elaine Keriakedes Memorial Scholarship, 138
B. J. Harrod Scholarships, 460
B. K. Krenzer Reentry Scholarship, 460
Bechtel Foundation Scholarship, 460
Bertha Lamme Memorial Scholarship, 461
Boston Scientific Scholarship, 461
Business and Professional Women's Career Advancement Scholarship, 209
Cady McDonnell Memorial Scholarship, 98
California's Junior Miss Competition, 211
Caterpillar Inc. Scholarship, 461
Central New Mexico Scholarship, 461
Chevron Corporation Scholarships, 462
Cisco/UNCF Scholars Program, 499
DaimlerChrysler Corporation Fund Scholarships, 462
Daughters of Penelope Past Grand Presidents' Award, 234
Delayed Education Scholarship for Women, 159
Dell Inc. Scholarship, 462
Dorothy Campbell Memorial Scholarship, 412
Dorothy Lemke Howarth Scholarships, 462
Dorothy M. & Earl S. Hoffman Scholarships, 463
Dorothy P. Morris Scholarship, 463
Dr. Marie E. Zakrzewski Medical Scholarship, 314
DuPont Company Scholarship, 463
Electronics for Imaging Scholarship, 463
Elizabeth A. Sackler Museum Educational Trust, 479
Elizabeth McLean Memorial Scholarship, 464
Eos #1 Mother Lodge Chapter Award, 234
Eugenia Vellner Fischer Award for the Performing Arts, 342
Exelon Scholarship, 464
Financial Women International Scholarship, 267
Ford Motor Company Scholarship, 464
Gene Hovis Memorial Scholarship, 303
General Electric Foundation Scholarship, 464
General Electric Women's Network Scholarship, 465
General Motors Foundation Scholarships, 465
Girl Scout Achievement Award, 136
Goldman, Sachs and Co. Scholarship, 465
Grace S. High Memorial Child Welfare Scholarship Fund, 141
The Grottos Scholarships, 480
Helen Copeland Scholarship for Females, 502
Hermione Grant Calhoun Scholarship, 372
Honeywell International Inc. Scholarship, 465
IBM Corporation Scholarship, 466
Ivy Parker Memorial Scholarship, 466
Jean Fitzgerald Scholarship Fund, 268
Jeanette Rankin Foundation Scholarship, 307
Jill S. Tietjen P.E. Scholarship, 466
Judith Resnik Memorial Scholarship, 466
Junior Miss Scholarship, 92
Ka'iulani Home for Girls Trust Scholarship, 269
Kottis Family Award, 234
Laywomen Scholarships, 523
Leonard C. Horn Award for Legal Studies, 342
Lillian Moller Gilbreth Scholarship, 467
Lillie Lois Ford Girls' Scholarship, 134
Lockheed Martin Aeronautics Company Scholarships, 467
Lockheed Martin Foundation Scholarships, 467
Lucile B. Kaufman Women's Scholarship, 454
Margot Karle Scholarship, 200

Mary Barrett Marshall Student Loan Fund, 578
Mary M. Verges Award, 234
MASWE Scholarships, 467
Meridith Thoms Memorial Scholarships, 468
Microsoft Corporation Scholarships, 468
Microsoft Women's Technical Scholarship, 338
Miss America Competition Awards, 342
Nancy Lorraine Jensen Memorial Scholarship, 471
NASA Space Grant North Dakota Consortium Lillian Goettler Scholarship, 358
National Association of Women in Construction Scholarship, 511
New Jersey Scholarship, 468
Northrop Grumman Corporation Scholarship, 468
Olive Lynn Salembier Reentry Scholarship, 469
Past Grand Presidents' Memorial Award, 235
Past President's Parley Nurses Scholarship, 120
Past President's Parley Nursing Scholarship, 123
Past President's Parley Scholarship, 130
Past Presidents Scholarships, 469
Pearl I. Young Scholarship, 358
R.L. Gillette Scholarship, 105
Rockwell Automation Scholarships, 469
SAE Women Engineers Committee Scholarship, 448
Shannon Scholarship, 493
Student Aid Foundation Loan, 589
Supreme Guardian Council, International Order of Job's Daughters Scholarship, 481
Susan Burdett Scholarship, 153
Susan Miszkowitz Memorial Scholarship, 470
Susie Holmes Memorial Scholarship, 481
Top 10 College Women Competition, 256
Women in Architecture Scholarship, 198
Women's Western Golf Foundation Scholarship, 524
Women's Wildlife Management/Conservation Scholarship, 380

Male

American Legion Eagle Scout of the Year, 135, 151
American Legion Maryland Boys State Scholarship, 129
American Legion New Hampshire Boys State Scholarship, 140
American Legion Wisconsin Eagle Scout of the Year Scholarship, 154
Arthur E. Copeland Scholarship for Males, 502
Arthur M. and Berdena King Eagle Scout Scholarship, 383
Boy Scout of the Year Scholarship, 124
Chester M. Vernon Memorial Eagle Scout Scholarship, 376
Eagle Scout Academic Scholarships, 205
Eagle Scout of the Year, 119
Eagle Scout of the Year Scholarship, 123, 150
Frank D. Visceglia Memorial Scholarship, 205
Frank L. Weil Memorial Eagle Scout Scholarship, 376
Frank M. McHale Memorial Scholarship, 123
Hall/McElwain Merit Scholarships, 206
Hubertus W.V. Willems Scholarship for Male Students, 349
John McKee Scholarship, 334
Lillie Lois Ford Boys' Scholarship, 134
Outstanding Citizen of Boys State Scholarship, 124
Spence Reese Scholarship, 206

International Student

A. Patrick Charnon Memorial Scholarship, 216
ADC Communications and Foundation Scholarship, 459
Adele Filene Travel Award, 228
Akademos, Inc. TextbookX.com Scholarship, 86
Alexandra A. Sonenfeld Award, 233
Allison E. Fisher Scholarship, 366
ASCAP Morton Gould Young Composers Award, 193
ASM Outstanding Scholars Awards, 194
Automotive Educational Fund Scholarship, 200
Business Reporting Intern Program, 537
Carole Simpson Scholarship, 366
Caterpillar Inc. Scholarship, 461
Chevron Internship Program, 535
Clinique Nursing Scholarship, 220
Colorado Society of CPAs General Scholarship, 222
Colorado Student Grant, 222
Colorado Supplemental Leveraging Educational Assistance Partnership Program, 222
Colorado Work-Study Program, 222
Cushman School Internship, 536
Daughters of Penelope Past Grand Presidents' Award, 234
Deloitte and Touche Internship Program, 536
Disney College Program, 574
Disney Professional Internships, 574
Dosatron International Scholarship, 102
Earl Dedman Memorial Scholarship, 102
Ed Markham International Scholarship, 102
Eos #1 Mother Lodge Chapter Award, 234
ESA Foundation Scholarship Program, 244
Federal Reserve Undergraduate Summer Analyst Program, 541
Fran Johnson Non-Traditional Scholarship, 102
Genentech Internship Program, 543
General News Copy Editing Internship, 537
George A. Roberts Scholarships, 195
Guggenheim Museum Internship, 568
Hannaford Internships, 544
Harold Bettinger Memorial Scholarship, 102
Healy Scholarship, 180
Holland America Line-Westours, Inc., Scholarship, 180
IBM Corporation Scholarship, 466
Jacob Van Namen Marketing Scholarship, 103
J.K. Rathmell, Jr., Memorial for Work/Study Abroad, 103
Joint CAS/SOA Minority Scholarships for Actuarial Students, 447
Joseph R. Stone Scholarship, 181
Kenneth Andrew Roe Mechanical Engineering Scholarship, 177
Kottis Family Award, 234
Leonard Bettinger Memorial Vocational Scholarship, 103
Mark J. Smith Scholarship, 223
Mary M. Verges Award, 234
Newhouse Foundation Scholarship, 556
Nicholas J. Grant Scholarship, 196
Online Intern Program, 538
Paris Fracasso Production Floriculture Scholarship, 103
Past Grand Presidents' Memorial Award, 235
Playtex Scholarship, 427
Praxair International Scholarship, 185
Princess Cruises and Princess Tours Scholarship, 181
Rocky Mountain Chapter-Donald Estey Scholarship Fund, 181
Senior Citizen, 65 or Older, Free Tuition for Up to 6 Credit Hours, 486
Six-Month Internship, 551
Southface Internship, 569
Sports Copy Editing Program, 538
Stella Blum Research Grant, 228

International Student

Summer Internship Program, 551
Sun Microsystems Student Intern and Co-op Program, 570
Texas Highest Ranking High School Graduate Tuition Exemption, 488
Texas Public Educational Grant, 488
United States Holocaust Memorial Museum Internship, 572
William Park Woodside Founder's Scholarship, 196
Wolf Trap Foundation for the Performing Arts Internship, 575

Military Participation

Air Force

Air Force Aid Society Education Grant, 81
Air Force Sergeants Association, Airmen Memorial Foundation, and Chief Master Sergeants of the Air Force Scholarship Programs, 81
Katherine F. Gruber Scholarship Program, 204
Matthews/Swift Educational Trust - Military Dependants, 313
Military Dependents Scholarship Program, 189
MOAA Interest-Free Loan and Grant Program, 583
New Jersey War Orphans Tuition Credit Program, 387
North Carolina Scholarships for Children of War Veterans, 398
West Virginia War Orphans Educational Assistance, 518

Army

Katherine F. Gruber Scholarship Program, 204
Maryland Edward T. Conroy Memorial Scholarship Program, 330
Matthews/Swift Educational Trust - Military Dependants, 313
MG James Ursano Scholarship Fund, 192
Military Dependents Scholarship Program, 189
MOAA Interest-Free Loan and Grant Program, 583
Montgomery GI Bill (MGIB), 504
Montgomery GI Bill Plus Army College Fund, 504
New Jersey War Orphans Tuition Credit Program, 387
North Carolina Scholarships for Children of War Veterans, 398
Selected Reserve Montgomery GI Bill, 504
West Virginia War Orphans Educational Assistance, 518

Coast Guard

Katherine F. Gruber Scholarship Program, 204
Matthews/Swift Educational Trust - Military Dependants, 313
Military Dependents Scholarship Program, 189
MOAA Interest-Free Loan and Grant Program, 583
New Jersey War Orphans Tuition Credit Program, 387
North Carolina Scholarships for Children of War Veterans, 398
West Virginia War Orphans Educational Assistance, 518

Marines

AFCEA Sgt. Jeannette L. Winters, USMC Memorial Scholarship, 191
Dependents of Deceased Service Members Scholarship Program, 384
First Marine Division Association Scholarship, 246
Katherine F. Gruber Scholarship Program, 204
Marine Corps Scholarship, 328
Matthews/Swift Educational Trust - Military Dependants, 313
Military Dependents Scholarship Program, 189
MOAA Interest-Free Loan and Grant Program, 583
New Jersey War Orphans Tuition Credit Program, 387
North Carolina Scholarships for Children of War Veterans, 398
Second Marine Division Scholarship, 441
Vice Admiral E.P. Travers Loan, 585
West Virginia War Orphans Educational Assistance, 518

Navy

Dependents of Deceased Service Members Scholarship Program, 384
Dolphin Scholarship, 240
Katherine F. Gruber Scholarship Program, 204
Matthews/Swift Educational Trust - Military Dependants, 313
Military Dependents Scholarship Program, 189
MOAA Interest-Free Loan and Grant Program, 583
Navy Supply Corps Foundation Scholarship, 384
New Jersey War Orphans Tuition Credit Program, 387
North Carolina Scholarships for Children of War Veterans, 398
Seabee Memorial Scholarship, 441
Vice Admiral E.P. Travers Loan, 585
West Virginia War Orphans Educational Assistance, 518

Reserves/National Guard

Alabama National Guard Educational Assistance Award, 86
Illinois National Guard Grant, 291
Indiana National Guard Supplemental Grant, 477
Iowa National Guard Educational Assistance Program, 299
Matthews/Swift Educational Trust - Military Dependants, 313
Military Dependents Scholarship Program, 189
Minnesota GI Bill, 340
MOAA Interest-Free Loan and Grant Program, 583
National Guard Educational Assistance Program, 310
National Guard Tuition Waiver, 407
New Jersey War Orphans Tuition Credit Program, 387
Ohio National Guard Scholarship Program, 404
Selected Reserve Montgomery GI Bill, 504
Texas National Guard Tuition Assistance Program, 488
West Virginia War Orphans Educational Assistance, 518

Minority Status

African American

Abercrombie & Fitch Scholarship Program, 497
Alfred R. Chisholm Memorial Scholarship, 498
Alton R. Higgins, MD, and Dorothy Higgins Scholarship, 498
American Chemical Society Scholars Program, 95
American Meteorological Society/Industry Minority Scholarship, 157
Arkansas Minority Teachers Scholarship Program, 579
Berbeco Senior Research Fellowship, 498
Black Nurses Scholarship, 368
The BlackNews.com Scholarship, 204
Brown Foundation Academic Scholarships, 208
California Teachers Association Martin Luther King, Jr., Memorial Scholarship, 213
Cargill Scholarship Program, 498
Certified Public Accountants Minorities Scholarship, 111
ChevronTexaco Scholars Program, 498
Cisco/UNCF Scholars Program, 499
CITE-NY Association Scholarship, 227

Minority Status: Alaskan native

Colgate "Bright Smiles, Bright Futures" Minority Scholarships, 78
Connecticut Minority Teacher Incentive Grant, 226
Earl & Patricia Armstrong Scholarship, 499
The EDSA Minority Scholarship, 316
Education and Leadership Development Program, 301
Essence Summer Internship, 540
Fisher Broadcasting Scholarship for Minorities, 246
Foreign Study/Diversity Scholarship, 109
The Gates Millenium Scholarship, 203
Gates Millennium Scholars Program, 499
GE Lloyd Trotter African American Forum Scholarship, 381
Gene Hovis Memorial Scholarship, 303
George M. Brooker Collegiate Scholarship for Minorities, 295
GM Engineering Scholarship For Minority Students, 319
Gulf Coast Research Laboratory Minority Summer Grant, 342
Herbert Lehman Educational Fund, 350
Historically Black Colleges and Minority Institutions Scholarships, 205
HKS/John Humphries Minority Scholarship, 231
The Hyatt Hotels Fund for Minority Lodging Management Students Competition, 108
Indiana Minority Teacher & Special Education Services Scholarship, 477
INROADS Internship, 546
James E. Webb Internship Program for Minority Undergraduate Seniors and Graduate Students in Business and Public Administration, 567
Janet Jackson Rhythm Nation Scholarships, 499
Jimmy A. Young Memorial Education Recognition Award, 169
John Lennon Scholarship Fund, 500
John W. Anderson Foundation Scholarship, 500
Joint CAS/SOA Minority Scholarships for Actuarial Students, 447
Kansas Ethnic Minority Scholarship, 308
Ken Inouye Scholarship, 458
Ken Kashiwahara Scholarship, 433
Lagrant Scholarships, 315
Leonard M. Perryman Communications Scholarship for Ethnic Minority Students, 497
Louis Carr Summer Internship, 549
Malcolm X Scholarship for Exceptional Courage, 500
Marathon Oil Corporation College Scholarship, 279

Maya Angelou/Vivian Baxter Scholarship, 500
Michael Jackson Scholarships, 501
Microbiology Undergraduate Research Fellowship (MURF), 171
Microsoft Minority Technical Scholarship, 338
Mildred Towle Scholarship for African-Americans, 273
The Minority Scholarship, 535
Minority Teachers of Illinois Scholarship, 292
Missouri Minority Teaching Scholarship, 344
MSGC Undergraduate Underrepresented Minority Fellowship Program, 355
Multicultural Advertising Intern Program, 527
Multicultural Undergraduate Summer Internships at the Getty Center, 546
NABA National Scholarship Program, 365
NABJ Internships, 556
NABJ Scholarship, 366
National Achievement Scholarships, 376
National Society of Black Engineers Leroy Callendar Award Program, 382
Ohio Newspapers Minority Scholarship, 405
Oracle Scholars Internship Program, 572
"Writers of Passage" Essay Contest, 365
Reader's Digest Foundation Scholarship Program, 501
Richmond Scholarship, 501
The Ron Brown Scholar Program, 214
Rosewood Family Scholarship Program, 249
Sachs Foundation Undergraduate Grant, 439
Sallie Mae Fund American Dream Scholarship, 501
Scholarship for Minority Undergraduate Physics Majors, 161
Stan Beck Fellowship, 243
Technical Minority Scholarship, 525
Tennessee Minority Teaching Fellows Program, 590
UBS/PaineWebber Scholarships, 501
Weisman Scholarship, 227
Wisconsin Minority Teacher Loan Program, 593
Wisconsin Minority Undergraduate Retention Grant, 522
Xernona Clayton Scholarship, 200

Alaskan native

Abercrombie & Fitch Scholarship Program, 497
American Chemical Society Scholars Program, 95

American Meteorological Society/Industry Minority Scholarship, 157
A.T. Anderson Memorial Scholarship, 109
Berbeco Senior Research Fellowship, 498
Brown Foundation Academic Scholarships, 208
Burlington Northern Santa Fe Foundation Scholarship, 109
California Teachers Association Martin Luther King, Jr., Memorial Scholarship, 213
Cargill Scholarship Program, 498
Certified Public Accountants Minorities Scholarship, 111
ChevronTexaco Scholars Program, 498
Cisco/UNCF Scholars Program, 499
Connecticut Minority Teacher Incentive Grant, 226
Earl & Patricia Armstrong Scholarship, 499
Education and Leadership Development Program, 301
Fisher Broadcasting Scholarship for Minorities, 246
Ford Motor Company/American Indian College Fund Corporate Scholars Program, 108
The Gates Millenium Scholarship, 203
Gates Millennium Scholars Program, 499
General Motors Engineering Scholarship, 109
George M. Brooker Collegiate Scholarship for Minorities, 295
GM Engineering Scholarship For Minority Students, 319
Gulf Coast Research Laboratory Minority Summer Grant, 342
HKS/John Humphries Minority Scholarship, 231
The Hyatt Hotels Fund for Minority Lodging Management Students Competition, 108
Indians Higher Education Grant Program, 506
INROADS Internship, 546
Janet Jackson Rhythm Nation Scholarships, 499
Jimmy A. Young Memorial Education Recognition Award, 169
John Lennon Scholarship Fund, 500
John W. Anderson Foundation Scholarship, 500
Joint CAS/SOA Minority Scholarships for Actuarial Students, 447
Kansas Ethnic Minority Scholarship, 308
Ken Inouye Scholarship, 458
Ken Kashiwahara Scholarship, 433
Lagrant Scholarships, 315
Leonard M. Perryman Communications Scholarship for Ethnic Minority Students, 497

Minority Status: Alaskan native

Louis Carr Summer Internship, 549
Malcolm X Scholarship for Exceptional Courage, 500
Marathon Oil Corporation College Scholarship, 279
Maya Angelou/Vivian Baxter Scholarship, 500
MESBEC Scholarships, 215
Michael Jackson Scholarships, 501
Microbiology Undergraduate Research Fellowship (MURF), 171
The Minority Scholarship, 535
Minority Teachers of Illinois Scholarship, 292
Missouri Minority Teaching Scholarship, 344
NABA National Scholarship Program, 365
Ohio Newspapers Minority Scholarship, 405
Reader's Digest Foundation Scholarship Program, 501
Richmond Scholarship, 501
Rosewood Family Scholarship Program, 249
Stan Beck Fellowship, 243
Technical Minority Scholarship, 525
Tennessee Minority Teaching Fellows Program, 590
Tribal Business Management Scholarship, 215
Truman D. Picard Scholarship, 298
UBS/PaineWebber Scholarships, 501
Weisman Scholarship, 227

American Indian

Abercrombie & Fitch Scholarship Program, 497
American Association of Airport Executives Foundation Scholarship for Native Americans, 93
American Chemical Society Scholars Program, 95
American Meteorological Society/Industry Minority Scholarship, 157
Arkansas Minority Teachers Scholarship Program, 579
A.T. Anderson Memorial Scholarship, 109
Berbeco Senior Research Fellowship, 498
Brown Foundation Academic Scholarships, 208
Bureau of Indian Affairs-Osage Tribal Education Committee Award, 209
Burlington Northern Santa Fe Foundation Scholarship, 109
California Teachers Association Martin Luther King, Jr., Memorial Scholarship, 213
Cargill Scholarship Program, 498
ChevronTexaco Scholars Program, 498
Choctaw Nation Higher Education Program, 219
Cisco/UNCF Scholars Program, 499
Colgate "Bright Smiles, Bright Futures" Minority Scholarships, 78
Connecticut Minority Teacher Incentive Grant, 226
Earl & Patricia Armstrong Scholarship, 499
The EDSA Minority Scholarship, 316
Education and Leadership Development Program, 301
Fisher Broadcasting Scholarship for Minorities, 246
Ford Motor Company/American Indian College Fund Corporate Scholars Program, 108
Foreign Study/Diversity Scholarship, 109
The Gates Millenium Scholarship, 203
Gates Millennium Scholars Program, 499
General Motors Engineering Scholarship, 109
George M. Brooker Collegiate Scholarship for Minorities, 295
GM Engineering Scholarship For Minority Students, 319
Gulf Coast Research Laboratory Minority Summer Grant, 342
Higher Education Grant Program, 209
HKS/John Humphries Minority Scholarship, 231
Hopi BIA Higher Education Grant, 279
Hopi Education Award, 279
Hopi Tribal Priority Award, 280
Howard Vollum American Indian Scholarship, 413
The Hyatt Hotels Fund for Minority Lodging Management Students Competition, 108
Indians Higher Education Grant Program, 506
INROADS Internship, 546
James E. Webb Internship Program for Minority Undergraduate Seniors and Graduate Students in Business and Public Administration, 567
Janet Jackson Rhythm Nation Scholarships, 499
Jimmy A. Young Memorial Education Recognition Award, 169
John Lennon Scholarship Fund, 500
John W. Anderson Foundation Scholarship, 500
Joint CAS/SOA Minority Scholarships for Actuarial Students, 447
Kansas Ethnic Minority Scholarship, 308
Ken Inouye Scholarship, 458
Ken Kashiwahara Scholarship, 433
Lagrant Scholarships, 315
Leonard M. Perryman Communications Scholarship for Ethnic Minority Students, 497
Louis Carr Summer Internship, 549
Malcolm X Scholarship for Exceptional Courage, 500
Marathon Oil Corporation College Scholarship, 279
Maya Angelou/Vivian Baxter Scholarship, 500
Menominee Adult Vocational Training Grant, 334
Menominee Higher Education Grant, 334
MESBEC Scholarships, 215
Michael Jackson Scholarships, 501
Microbiology Undergraduate Research Fellowship (MURF), 171
Microsoft Minority Technical Scholarship, 338
Minnesota Indian Scholarship Program, 340
The Minority Scholarship, 535
Minority Teachers of Illinois Scholarship, 292
Missouri Minority Teaching Scholarship, 344
MSGC Undergraduate Underrepresented Minority Fellowship Program, 355
Multicultural Advertising Intern Program, 527
Multicultural Undergraduate Summer Internships at the Getty Center, 546
NABA National Scholarship Program, 365
Native American Leadership in Education Scholarship, 215
New York State Native American Student Aid Program, 396
North American Indian Scholarship, 298
North Dakota Indian Scholarship Program, 401
Northern Cheyenne Higher Education Program, 402
Ohio Newspapers Minority Scholarship, 405
Osage Tribal Education Scholarship, 420
Reader's Digest Foundation Scholarship Program, 501
Richmond Scholarship, 501
Rosewood Family Scholarship Program, 249
Scholarship for Minority Undergraduate Physics Majors, 161
Seneca Nation Higher Education Program, 442
Shoshone Tribal Scholarship, 443
Silver Eagle Indian Scholarship, 139
South Dakota Ardell Bjugstad Scholarship, 473
Stan Beck Fellowship, 243
Technical Minority Scholarship, 525
Tennessee Minority Teaching Fellows Program, 590
Tribal Business Management Scholarship, 215
Truman D. Picard Scholarship, 298
UBS/PaineWebber Scholarships, 501
Weisman Scholarship, 227

Wisconsin Indian Student Assistance Grant, 522
Wisconsin Minority Teacher Loan Program, 593
Wisconsin Minority Undergraduate Retention Grant, 522

Asian American

Abercrombie & Fitch Scholarship Program, 497
American Meteorological Society/Industry Minority Scholarship, 157
Arkansas Minority Teachers Scholarship Program, 579
Berbeco Senior Research Fellowship, 498
Brown Foundation Academic Scholarships, 208
California Teachers Association Martin Luther King, Jr., Memorial Scholarship, 213
Cargill Scholarship Program, 498
Certified Public Accountants Minorities Scholarship, 111
ChevronTexaco Scholars Program, 498
Cisco/UNCF Scholars Program, 499
Colgate "Bright Smiles, Bright Futures" Minority Scholarships, 78
Connecticut Minority Teacher Incentive Grant, 226
Earl & Patricia Armstrong Scholarship, 499
Education and Leadership Development Program, 301
Fisher Broadcasting Scholarship for Minorities, 246
Foreign Study/Diversity Scholarship, 109
Gates Millennium Scholars Program, 499
George M. Brooker Collegiate Scholarship for Minorities, 295
Gulf Coast Research Laboratory Minority Summer Grant, 342
HKS/John Humphries Minority Scholarship, 231
The Hyatt Hotels Fund for Minority Lodging Management Students Competition, 108
INROADS Internship, 546
Janet Jackson Rhythm Nation Scholarships, 499
Japanese American General Scholarship, 305
Japanese American Music Scholarship Competition, 306
Jimmy A. Young Memorial Education Recognition Award, 169
John Lennon Scholarship Fund, 500
John W. Anderson Foundation Scholarship, 500
Kansas Ethnic Minority Scholarship, 308
Ken Inouye Scholarship, 458
Ken Kashiwahara Scholarship, 433

Lagrant Scholarships, 315
Leonard M. Perryman Communications Scholarship for Ethnic Minority Students, 497
Louis Carr Summer Internship, 549
Malcolm X Scholarship for Exceptional Courage, 500
Maya Angelou/Vivian Baxter Scholarship, 500
Michael Jackson Scholarships, 501
The Minority Scholarship, 535
Minority Teachers of Illinois Scholarship, 292
Missouri Minority Teaching Scholarship, 344
Multicultural Advertising Intern Program, 527
Multicultural Undergraduate Summer Internships at the Getty Center, 546
NABA National Scholarship Program, 365
OCA-AXA Achievement Scholarship, 419
OCA/UPS Foundation Gold Mountain College Scholarship, 419
OCA/Verizon Foundation College Scholarship, 419
Ohio Newspapers Minority Scholarship, 405
Reader's Digest Foundation Scholarship Program, 501
Richmond Scholarship, 501
Rosewood Family Scholarship Program, 249
Stan Beck Fellowship, 243
Technical Minority Scholarship, 525
Tennessee Minority Teaching Fellows Program, 590
UBS/PaineWebber Scholarships, 501
Weisman Scholarship, 227
Wisconsin Minority Teacher Loan Program, 593

Hispanic American

Abercrombie & Fitch Scholarship Program, 497
ALPFA Scholarship Program, 277
American Chemical Society Scholars Program, 95
American Meteorological Society/Industry Minority Scholarship, 157
Arkansas Minority Teachers Scholarship Program, 579
Berbeco Senior Research Fellowship, 498
Brown Foundation Academic Scholarships, 208
California Teachers Association Martin Luther King, Jr., Memorial Scholarship, 213
Cargill Scholarship Program, 498
Certified Public Accountants Minorities Scholarship, 111
CHCI Congressional Internship Program, 535

ChevronTexaco Scholars Program, 498
Cisco/UNCF Scholars Program, 499
Colgate "Bright Smiles, Bright Futures" Minority Scholarships, 78
College Scholarship Fund, 278
Congressional Hispanic Caucus Institute Scholarship Awards, 224
Connecticut Minority Teacher Incentive Grant, 226
Earl & Patricia Armstrong Scholarship, 499
The EDSA Minority Scholarship, 316
Education and Leadership Development Program, 301
Fisher Broadcasting Scholarship for Minorities, 246
Foreign Study/Diversity Scholarship, 109
The Gates Millenium Scholarship, 203
Gates Millennium Scholars Program, 499
George M. Brooker Collegiate Scholarship for Minorities, 295
GM Engineering Scholarship For Minority Students, 319
Google Hispanic College Fund Scholarship Program, 277
Gulf Coast Research Laboratory Minority Summer Grant, 342
HCF Scholarship Program, 277
Hispanic Heritage Youth Awards Program, 278
Hispanic Youth Leaders Scholarship, 346
HKS/John Humphries Minority Scholarship, 231
The Hyatt Hotels Fund for Minority Lodging Management Students Competition, 108
Indiana Minority Teacher & Special Education Services Scholarship, 477
INROADS Internship, 546
Janet Jackson Rhythm Nation Scholarships, 499
Jimmy A. Young Memorial Education Recognition Award, 169
John Lennon Scholarship Fund, 500
John W. Anderson Foundation Scholarship, 500
Joint CAS/SOA Minority Scholarships for Actuarial Students, 447
Jose Marti Scholarship Challenge Grant, 248
Kaiser Permanente College to Caring Program, 277
Kansas Ethnic Minority Scholarship, 308
Ken Inouye Scholarship, 458
Ken Kashiwahara Scholarship, 433
Lagrant Scholarships, 315
Latin American Educational Scholarship, 318
Latino Diamante Scholarship Fund, 400

Minority Status: Hispanic American

Leonard M. Perryman Communications Scholarship for Ethnic Minority Students, 497
Lockheed Martin Scholarship Program, 277
Los Padres Foundation Scholarships, 322
Louis Carr Summer Internship, 549
LULAC National Scholarship Fund Honors Awards, 319
LULAC National Scholarship Fund National Scholastic Achievement Awards, 319
LULAC National Scholarshp Fund General Awards, 319
Malcolm X Scholarship for Exceptional Courage, 500
Marathon Oil Corporation College Scholarship, 279
Maya Angelou/Vivian Baxter Scholarship, 500
Mexican American Grocers Association Scholarship, 335
Michael Jackson Scholarships, 501
Microbiology Undergraduate Research Fellowship (MURF), 171
Microsoft Minority Technical Scholarship, 338
The Minority Scholarship, 535
Minority Teachers of Illinois Scholarship, 292
Missouri Minority Teaching Scholarship, 344
MSGC Undergraduate Underrepresented Minority Fellowship Program, 355
Multicultural Advertising Intern Program, 527
Multicultural Undergraduate Summer Internships at the Getty Center, 546
NABA National Scholarship Program, 365
Nissan Community College Transfer Scholarship, 279
Ohio Newspapers Minority Scholarship, 405
Reader's Digest Foundation Scholarship Program, 501
Richmond Scholarship, 501
Rosewood Family Scholarship Program, 249
Scholarship for Minority Undergraduate Physics Majors, 161
Shell Legislative Internship Program, 556
Stan Beck Fellowship, 243
Technical Minority Scholarship, 525
Tennessee Minority Teaching Fellows Program, 590
UBS/PaineWebber Scholarships, 501
Weisman Scholarship, 227
Wisconsin Minority Teacher Loan Program, 593
Wisconsin Minority Undergraduate Retention Grant, 522

Mexican American

Abercrombie & Fitch Scholarship Program, 497
American Chemical Society Scholars Program, 95
American Meteorological Society/Industry Minority Scholarship, 157
Arkansas Minority Teachers Scholarship Program, 579
Berbeco Senior Research Fellowship, 498
Brown Foundation Academic Scholarships, 208
California Teachers Association Martin Luther King, Jr., Memorial Scholarship, 213
Cargill Scholarship Program, 498
Certified Public Accountants Minorities Scholarship, 111
CHCI Congressional Internship Program, 535
ChevronTexaco Scholars Program, 498
Cisco/UNCF Scholars Program, 499
Colgate "Bright Smiles, Bright Futures" Minority Scholarships, 78
College Scholarship Fund, 278
Congressional Hispanic Caucus Institute Scholarship Awards, 224
Connecticut Minority Teacher Incentive Grant, 226
Earl & Patricia Armstrong Scholarship, 499
Education and Leadership Development Program, 301
Fisher Broadcasting Scholarship for Minorities, 246
Foreign Study/Diversity Scholarship, 109
Gates Millennium Scholars Program, 499
George M. Brooker Collegiate Scholarship for Minorities, 295
GM Engineering Scholarship For Minority Students, 319
Gulf Coast Research Laboratory Minority Summer Grant, 342
HKS/John Humphries Minority Scholarship, 231
The Hyatt Hotels Fund for Minority Lodging Management Students Competition, 108
Indiana Minority Teacher & Special Education Services Scholarship, 477
INROADS Internship, 546
Janet Jackson Rhythm Nation Scholarships, 499
Jimmy A. Young Memorial Education Recognition Award, 169
John Lennon Scholarship Fund, 500
John W. Anderson Foundation Scholarship, 500
Joint CAS/SOA Minority Scholarships for Actuarial Students, 447
Kansas Ethnic Minority Scholarship, 308
Ken Inouye Scholarship, 458
Ken Kashiwahara Scholarship, 433
Lagrant Scholarships, 315
Latin American Educational Scholarship, 318
Leonard M. Perryman Communications Scholarship for Ethnic Minority Students, 497
Louis Carr Summer Internship, 549
Malcolm X Scholarship for Exceptional Courage, 500
Maya Angelou/Vivian Baxter Scholarship, 500
Michael Jackson Scholarships, 501
Microbiology Undergraduate Research Fellowship (MURF), 171
Microsoft Minority Technical Scholarship, 338
The Minority Scholarship, 535
Minority Teachers of Illinois Scholarship, 292
Missouri Minority Teaching Scholarship, 344
Multicultural Advertising Intern Program, 527
Multicultural Undergraduate Summer Internships at the Getty Center, 546
NABA National Scholarship Program, 365
Nissan Community College Transfer Scholarship, 279
Ohio Newspapers Minority Scholarship, 405
Reader's Digest Foundation Scholarship Program, 501
Richmond Scholarship, 501
Rosewood Family Scholarship Program, 249
Scholarship for Minority Undergraduate Physics Majors, 161
Shell Legislative Internship Program, 556
Stan Beck Fellowship, 243
Technical Minority Scholarship, 525
UBS/PaineWebber Scholarships, 501
Weisman Scholarship, 227
Wisconsin Minority Teacher Loan Program, 593

Native Hawaiian/Pacific Islander

Abercrombie & Fitch Scholarship Program, 497
American Chemical Society Scholars Program, 95
Berbeco Senior Research Fellowship, 498
California Teachers Association Martin Luther King, Jr., Memorial Scholarship, 213
Cargill Scholarship Program, 498
Certified Public Accountants Minorities Scholarship, 111
ChevronTexaco Scholars Program, 498

Cisco/UNCF Scholars Program, 499
Connecticut Minority Teacher Incentive Grant, 226
Earl & Patricia Armstrong Scholarship, 499
Fisher Broadcasting Scholarship for Minorities, 246
Ford Motor Company/American Indian College Fund Corporate Scholars Program, 108
Foreign Study/Diversity Scholarship, 109
The Gates Millenium Scholarship, 203
Gates Millennium Scholars Program, 499
HKS/John Humphries Minority Scholarship, 231
The Hyatt Hotels Fund for Minority Lodging Management Students Competition, 108
Janet Jackson Rhythm Nation Scholarships, 499
Jimmy A. Young Memorial Education Recognition Award, 169
John Lennon Scholarship Fund, 500
John W. Anderson Foundation Scholarship, 500
Joint CAS/SOA Minority Scholarships for Actuarial Students, 447
Ka'iulani Home for Girls Trust Scholarship, 269
Ken Inouye Scholarship, 458
Ken Kashiwahara Scholarship, 433
Leonard M. Perryman Communications Scholarship for Ethnic Minority Students, 497
Louis Carr Summer Internship, 549
Malcolm X Scholarship for Exceptional Courage, 500
Marathon Oil Corporation College Scholarship, 279
Maya Angelou/Vivian Baxter Scholarship, 500
Michael Jackson Scholarships, 501
Microbiology Undergraduate Research Fellowship (MURF), 171
The Minority Scholarship, 535
MSGC Undergraduate Underrepresented Minority Fellowship Program, 355
Multicultural Advertising Intern Program, 527
Multicultural Undergraduate Summer Internships at the Getty Center, 546
OCA-AXA Achievement Scholarship, 419
Ohio Newspapers Minority Scholarship, 405
Richmond Scholarship, 501
Rosemary & Nellie Ebrie Fund, 274
Technical Minority Scholarship, 525
Tennessee Minority Teaching Fellows Program, 590
UBS/PaineWebber Scholarships, 501
Weisman Scholarship, 227

Puerto Rican

Abercrombie & Fitch Scholarship Program, 497
American Chemical Society Scholars Program, 95
American Meteorological Society/Industry Minority Scholarship, 157
Arkansas Minority Teachers Scholarship Program, 579
Berbeco Senior Research Fellowship, 498
Brown Foundation Academic Scholarships, 208
California Teachers Association Martin Luther King, Jr., Memorial Scholarship, 213
Cargill Scholarship Program, 498
Certified Public Accountants Minorities Scholarship, 111
CHCI Congressional Internship Program, 535
ChevronTexaco Scholars Program, 498
Cisco/UNCF Scholars Program, 499
Colgate "Bright Smiles, Bright Futures" Minority Scholarships, 78
College Scholarship Fund, 278
Congressional Hispanic Caucus Institute Scholarship Awards, 224
Connecticut Minority Teacher Incentive Grant, 226
Earl & Patricia Armstrong Scholarship, 499
Education and Leadership Development Program, 301
Fisher Broadcasting Scholarship for Minorities, 246
Foreign Study/Diversity Scholarship, 109
Gates Millennium Scholars Program, 499
George M. Brooker Collegiate Scholarship for Minorities, 295
GM Engineering Scholarship For Minority Students, 319
Gulf Coast Research Laboratory Minority Summer Grant, 342
Hispanic Youth Leaders Scholarship, 346
HKS/John Humphries Minority Scholarship, 231
The Hyatt Hotels Fund for Minority Lodging Management Students Competition, 108
Indiana Minority Teacher & Special Education Services Scholarship, 477
INROADS Internship, 546
James E. Webb Internship Program for Minority Undergraduate Seniors and Graduate Students in Business and Public Administration, 567
Janet Jackson Rhythm Nation Scholarships, 499
Jimmy A. Young Memorial Education Recognition Award, 169
John Lennon Scholarship Fund, 500
John W. Anderson Foundation Scholarship, 500
Joint CAS/SOA Minority Scholarships for Actuarial Students, 447
Kansas Ethnic Minority Scholarship, 308
Ken Inouye Scholarship, 458
Ken Kashiwahara Scholarship, 433
Lagrant Scholarships, 315
Latin American Educational Scholarship, 318
Leonard M. Perryman Communications Scholarship for Ethnic Minority Students, 497
Los Padres Foundation Scholarships, 322
Louis Carr Summer Internship, 549
Malcolm X Scholarship for Exceptional Courage, 500
Maya Angelou/Vivian Baxter Scholarship, 500
Michael Jackson Scholarships, 501
Microbiology Undergraduate Research Fellowship (MURF), 171
Microsoft Minority Technical Scholarship, 338
The Minority Scholarship, 535
Minority Teachers of Illinois Scholarship, 292
Missouri Minority Teaching Scholarship, 344
Multicultural Advertising Intern Program, 527
Multicultural Undergraduate Summer Internships at the Getty Center, 546
NABA National Scholarship Program, 365
Nissan Community College Transfer Scholarship, 279
Ohio Newspapers Minority Scholarship, 405
Reader's Digest Foundation Scholarship Program, 501
Richmond Scholarship, 501
Rosewood Family Scholarship Program, 249
Scholarship for Minority Undergraduate Physics Majors, 161
Shell Legislative Internship Program, 556
Stan Beck Fellowship, 243
Technical Minority Scholarship, 525
UBS/PaineWebber Scholarships, 501
Weisman Scholarship, 227
Wisconsin Minority Teacher Loan Program, 593

National/ethnic background

Armenian
Armenian General Benevolent Union International Scholarship Program, 192

Chinese
Thz Fo Farm Fund, 274

Danish
The Kaj Christensen Scholarship for Vocational Training, 402

Greek
Alexandra A. Sonenfeld Award, 233
Daughters of Penelope Past Grand Presidents' Award, 234
Eos #1 Mother Lodge Chapter Award, 234
Kottis Family Award, 234
Mary M. Verges Award, 234
Past Grand Presidents' Memorial Award, 235

Italian
Alphonse A. Miele Scholarship, 495
Columbus Citizens Foundation College Scholarship Program, 223
Henry Salvatori Scholarship, 470
Italian Catholic Federation Scholarship, 299
Major Don S. Gentile Scholarship, 495
Sons of Italy National Leadership Grant, 470
Theodore Mazza Scholarship, 495
William C. Davini Scholarship, 495

Japanese
Japanese American General Scholarship, 305
Japanese American Music Scholarship Competition, 306
Ventura County Japanese-American Citizens League Scholarships, 509

Jewish
Jewish War Veterans of the United States of America Bernard Rotberg Memorial Scholarship, 307
Jewish War Veterans of the United States of America JWV Grant, 307
Louis S. Silvey Grant, 308

Polish
Dr. Marie E. Zakrzewski Medical Scholarship, 314
Kosciuszko Foundation Tuition Scholarships, 314
Massachusetts Federation of Polish Women's Clubs Scholarships, 314
The Polish American Club of North Jersey Scholarships, 315
The Polish National Alliance of Brooklyn, USA, Inc. Scholarships, 315

Swiss
Sonia Streuli Maguire Outstanding Scholastic Achievement Award, 481
Swiss Benevolent Society Medicus Student Exchange, 481
Swiss Benevolent Society Pellegrini Scholarship, 482

Ukrainian
Eugene and Elinor Kotur Scholarship, 494
Ukrainian Fraternal Association Scholarship, 495

Welsh
Cymdeithas Gymreig (Welsh Society) Philadelphia Scholarship, 230
Welsh Heritage Scholarship, 517

Organization/civic affiliation

1199 National Benefit Fund
Joseph Tauber Scholarship, 75

Alpha Beta Gamma
Alpha Beta Gamma International Scholarship, 90

Alpha Mu Gamma
Alpha Mu Gamma National Scholarship, 91

American Academy of Physician Assistants
Physician Assistant Scholarship, 426

American Association of Critical Care Nurses
Education Advancement Scholarship, 94

American Classical League
Maureen V. O'Donnell Memorial Teacher Training Award, 96
McKinlay Summer Award, 96

American Congress of Surveying and Mapping
AAGS Joseph F. Dracup Scholarship Award, 97
Berntsen International Scholarship in Surveying, 97
Berntsen International Scholarship in Surveying Technology, 97
Cady McDonnell Memorial Scholarship, 98
CaGIS Scholarship Award, 98
Nettie Dracup Memorial Scholarship, 98
NSPS Board of Governors Scholarship, 98
NSPS Scholarships, 99
Schonstedt Scholarships in Surveying, 99

American Dental Assistants Association
Juliette A. Southard/Oral B Laboratories Scholarship, 100

American Dental Hygenists' Association
ADHA Institute General Scholarships, 77

American Fed. of State/County/Municipal Employees
Union Plus Scholarship, 101

American Health Information Management Association
FORE Undergraduate Scholarship, 250

American Hellenic Educational Progressive Association
AHEPA Educational Foundation Scholarships, 81

American Indian Science & Engineering Society
A.T. Anderson Memorial Scholarship, 109
Burlington Northern Santa Fe Foundation Scholarship, 109
General Motors Engineering Scholarship, 109

American Legion
Albert M. Lappin Scholarship, 125
Albert T. Marcoux Memorial Scholarship, 140
American Legion Alabama Oratorical Contest, 112

Organization/civic affiliation: American Legion, Boys State

American Legion Alabama Scholarship, 112
American Legion Alaska Oratorical Contest, 113
American Legion Arizona Oratorical Contest, 114
American Legion Arkansas Oratorical Contest, 115
American Legion Arkansas Scholarship, 115
American Legion California Oratorical Contest, 115
American Legion Family Scholarship, 122
American Legion Florida General Scholarship, 118
American Legion Idaho Scholarships, 120
American Legion Illinois Scholarships, 121
American Legion Massachusetts General and Nursing Scholarships, 130
American Legion Minnesota Legionnaire Insurance Trust Scholarship, 132
American Legion Nebraska Oratorical Contest, 137
American Legion New York Oratorical Contest, 143
American Legion North Dakota Oratorical Contest, 144
American Legion Ohio Scholarships, 145
American Legion Press Club of New Jersey and Post 170--Arthur Dehardt Memorial Scholarship, 141
American Legion Washington Scholarships, 152
American Legion Western District Postsecondary Scholarship, 113
American Legion Wyoming E.A. Blackmore Memorial Scholarship, 156
Charles and Annette Hill Scholarship, 126
Charles L. Bacon Memorial Scholarship, 133
Children and Youth Scholarships, 128
Christa McAuliffe Memorial Scholarship, 140
David C. Goodwin Scholarship, 142
Department of New Hampshire Scholarship, 140
Department Oratorical Awards, 145
Department Vocational Scholarship, 140
Dr. Hannah K. Vuolo Memorial Scholarship, 143
Eagle Scout of the Year, 119
Eagle Scout of the Year Scholarship, 123
Edgar J. Boschult Memorial Scholarship, 137
Hugh A. Smith Scholarship, 126
James V. Day Scholarship, 128
Joseph P. Gavenonis Scholarship, 147

Lawrence Luterman Memorial Scholarships, 142
Maynard Jensen American Legion Memorial Scholarship, 137
The Minnesota American Legion Memorial Scholarship, 132
New York American Legion Press Association Scholarship, 144
Rosedale Post 346 Scholarship, 126
Samsung American Legion Scholarship, 136
Stutz Memorial Scholarship, 142
Ted and Nora Anderson Scholarship, 126

American Legion Auxiliary

Aloha Scholarship, 135
American Legion Alabama Auxiliary Scholarship, 113
American Legion Alaska Auxiliary Scholarship, 113
American Legion Alaska Auxiliary Western District Scholarship, 113
American Legion Arizona Auxiliary Health Care Occupation Scholarship, 114
American Legion Arizona Auxiliary Nurses' Scholarship, 114
American Legion Arkansas Auxiliary Scholarships, 115
American Legion Auxiliary National President's Scholarship, 135
American Legion Florida Auxiliary Memorial Scholarship, 119
American Legion Florida Auxiliary Scholarships, 119
American Legion Georgia Auxiliary Scholarship, 119
American Legion Minnesota Auxiliary Department Scholarship, 133
American Legion New Jersey Auxiliary Department Scholarships, 142
American Legion New York Auxiliary Scholarship, 144
American Legion North Dakota Auxiliary Scholarships, 145
American Legion Ohio Auxiliary Past President's Parley Nurse's Scholarship, 145
American Legion Ohio Auxiliary Scholarship, 146
American Legion South Carolina Auxiliary Scholarship, 148
American Legion South Dakota Auxiliary Nurse's Scholarship, 148
American Legion South Dakota Auxiliary Scholarships, 149
American Legion Wisconsin Auxiliary Department President's Scholarship, 155
American Legion Wisconsin Auxiliary H.S. and Angeline Lewis Scholarships, 155

American Legion Wisconsin Auxiliary Merit and Memorial Scholarship, 155
American Legion Wisconsin Auxiliary Past Presidents Parley Scholarship, 155
Anna Gear Junior Scholarship, 152
Claire Oliphant Memorial Scholarship, 142
Della Van Deuren Memorial Scholarship, 155
Department President's Scholarship, 117
Department President's Scholarship for Junior Auxiliary Members, 117
Dr. Kate Waller Barrett Grant, 152
Girl Scout Achievement Award, 136
Grace S. High Memorial Child Welfare Scholarship Fund, 141
Marion J. Bagley Scholarship, 141
Memorial Education Grant, 117
National President's Scholarship, 146
Past Department Presidents' Junior Scholarship, 116
Past President's Parley Education Grant, 118
Past President's Parley Health Care Scholarship, 133
Past President's Parley Nurse's Scholarship, 117
Past President's Parley Nurses Scholarship, 120
Past President's Parley Nurses' Scholarship, 141, 143
Past President's Parley Nursing Scholarship, 118, 123
Past President's Parley Scholarship, 145
Past President's Parley Student Nurses Scholarship for Girls or Boys, 144
President's Parley Scholarship for Teachers of Exceptional Children, 143
Ruby Paul Campaign Fund Scholarship, 138
Scholarship for College or Vocational, 149
Spirit of Youth Scholarship, 146
Spirit of Youth Scholarship for Junior Members, 137
Thelma Foster Junior American Legion Auxiliary Members Scholarship, 149
Thelma Foster Senior American Legion Auxiliary Member Scholarship, 149
Wilma D. Hoyal/Maxine Chilton Memorial Scholarship, 114

American Legion, Boys State

American Legion Maryland Boys State Scholarship, 129
American Legion New Hampshire Boys State Scholarship, 140
Frank M. McHale Memorial Scholarship, 123

Eligibility Indexes

57

Organization/civic affiliation: American Legion, Boys State

Lillie Lois Ford Boys' Scholarship, 134
Outstanding Citizen of Boys State Scholarship, 124

American Legion/Boys Scouts of America

American Legion Wisconsin Eagle Scout of the Year Scholarship, 154

American Nuclear Society

Pittsburgh Local Section Scholarship, 160

American Radio Relay League

Albuquerque ARC/Toby Cross Scholarship, 162
ARRL Earl I. Anderson Scholarship, 162
The Donald Riebhoff Memorial Scholarship, 164
Edmond A. Metzger Scholarship, 164
"You've Got a Friend in Pennsylvania", 169

American Society of Civil Engineers

Eugene C. Figg Jr. Civil Engineering Scholarship, 171
Freeman Fellowship, 171
Samuel Fletcher Tapman ASCE Student Chapter Scholarship, 172

American Society of Mechanical Engineers

American Society of Mechanical Engineers Foundation Scholarship, 175
ASME Auxiliary Student Loan, 578
ASME Student Loan Program, 578
Frank William and Dorothy Given Miller Mechanical Engineering Scholarship, 176
F.W. "Beich" Beichley Scholarship, 176
Garland Duncan Mechanical Engineering Scholarship, 176
International Gas Turbine Institute Scholarship, 176
John and Elsa Gracik Mechanical Engineering Scholarship, 177
Kenneth Andrew Roe Mechanical Engineering Scholarship, 177
Melvin R. Green Scholarship, 177
William J. and Marijane E. Adams, Jr., Mechanical Engineering Scholarship, 177

Appaloosa Horse Club

Appaloosa Youth Foundation Educational Scholarships, 187

ASM International

ASM Outstanding Scholars Awards, 194
George A. Roberts Scholarships, 195
Nicholas J. Grant Scholarship, 196
William Park Woodside Founder's Scholarship, 196

Associated Builders and Contractors

Trimmer Education Foundation ABC Student Chapter Scholarship Program, 196

Association for Library/Information Science Education

ALISE Bodhan S. Wynar Research Paper Competition, 197
ALISE Research Grant Award, 198
Dialog/ALISE Methodology Paper Competition, 198

Association of American Geographers

Anne U. White Fund, 199

ASTA Arizona Chapter

Arizona Chapter Dependent Scholarship Fund, 179

Boy Scouts of America

American Legion Illinois Boy Scout Scholarship, 121

Boy Scouts of America, Eagle Scouts

American Legion Eagle Scout of the Year, 135, 151
Boy Scout of the Year Scholarship, 124
Chester M. Vernon Memorial Eagle Scout Scholarship, 376
Eagle Scout of the Year Scholarship, 150
Frank D. Visceglia Memorial Scholarship, 205
Frank L. Weil Memorial Eagle Scout Scholarship, 376
Hall/McElwain Merit Scholarships, 206

California Teachers Association

California Teachers Association Martin Luther King, Jr., Memorial Scholarship, 213
CTA Scholarship for Dependent Children, 213
CTA Scholarships for Members, 213
L. Gordon Bittle Memorial Scholarship for Student CTA, 214

Catholic Aid Association

Catholic Aid Association Scholarship, 216

Descendants of the Signers of the Declaration of Independence

Descendants of the Signers of the Declaration of Independence Scholarship, 238

Eagle Scouts

Arthur M. and Berdena King Eagle Scout Scholarship, 383

Elks

Elks National Foundation Legacy Awards, 242

First Catholic Slovak Ladies Association

CW Scholarships, 246
First Catholic Slovak Ladies Association Fraternal Scholarship, 246

Golden Key National Honor Society

Business Achievement Awards, 256
Education Achievement Awards, 256
Engineering/Technology Achievement Awards, 257
GEICO Life Scholarship, 257
Golden Key Research Grants, 257
Golden Key Service Award, 257
Golden Key Study Abroad Scholarships, 258
Literary Achievement Awards, 258
Student Leader Award, 258
Visual and Performing Arts Achievement Award, 258

Golf Course Superintendents Association of America

GCSAA Legacy Awards, 259
GCSAA Scholars Competition, 259
GCSAA Student Essay Contest, 259

Harness Racing Industry

Harness Tracks of America Scholarship Fund, 260

Hawaii Carpenter's Union Local 745

Walter H. Kupau Memorial Fund, 275

International Association of Fire Fighters

W.H. McClennan Scholarship, 296

Organization/civic affiliation: Reserve Officers Training Corps (ROTC)

International Buckskin Horse Association
Buckskin Horse Association Scholarship, 296

International Executive Housekeepers Association
IEHA Educational Foundation Scholarship, 296

International Order of Job's Daughters
The Grottos Scholarships, 480
Supreme Guardian Council, International Order of Job's Daughters Scholarship, 481
Susie Holmes Memorial Scholarship, 481

International Union of EESMF Workers, AFL-CIO
Bruce van Ess Scholarship, 300
David J. Fitzmaurice Scholarship, 300
James B. Carey Scholarship, 300
Paul Jennings Scholarship, 300
Robert L. Livingston Scholarship, 301
Sal Ingrassia Scholarship, 301
Willie Rudd Scholarship, 301

Jaycees
Charles R. Ford Scholarship, 306
Thomas Wood Baldridge Scholarship, 306

Kappa Kappa Gamma
Kappa Kappa Gamma Scholarship, 310

Knights of Columbus
Matthews/Swift Educational Trust - Military Dependants, 313
Matthews/Swift Educational Trust - Police/Firefighters, 313
Pro Deo/Pro Patria Scholarship, 313

Lambda Alpha
Senior Scholarship, 316

Learning for Life
National Technical Investigators' Captain James J. Regan Memorial Scholarship, 320
Sheryl A. Horak Law Enforcement Explorer Scholarship, 320

National Amateur Baseball Federation
National Amateur Baseball Federation Scholarship, 364

National Art Materials Trade Association
NAMTA Educational Assistance Award, 365
NAMTA Foundation Visual Arts Major Scholarship, 365

National Association for Advancement of Colored People
Agnes Jones Jackson Scholarship, 349
Hubertus W.V. Willems Scholarship for Male Students, 349
Lillian and Samuel Sutton Education Scholarship, 350
Roy Wilkins Scholarship, 350

National Association of Black Accountants
NABA National Scholarship Program, 365

National Association of Letter Carriers
Costas G. Lemonopoulos Scholarship, 366
William C. Doherty - John T. Donelson Scholarships, 367

National Athletic Trainers Association
Athletic Trainers' Entry Level Scholarship, 368
Athletic Trainers' Student Writing Contest, 368

National Black Nurses' Association
Black Nurses Scholarship, 368

National Foster Parent Association
Youth Scholarship, 374

National Junior Classical League
Latin Honor Society Scholarship, 95
National Junior Classical League Scholarship, 96

National Rifle Association
Jeanne E. Bray Law Enforcement Dependents Scholarship, 379

National Society of Black Engineers
Fulfilling the Legacy Scholarship, 381
GE Lloyd Trotter African American Forum Scholarship, 381
National Society of Black Engineers Corporate Scholarships Program, 382
National Society of Black Engineers Golden Torch Awards, 382
National Society of Black Engineers Leroy Callendar Award Program, 382
NSBE Fellows Scholarship, 382

Native Daughters of the Golden West
Native Daughters of the Golden West Scholarship, 384

New York State Grange
Grange Student Loan Fund, 587
Grange Susan W. Freestone Education Award, 393

North American Limousin Junior Association
Limouselle Scholarship, 397
National Limouselle Financial Assistance Grant, 397

Ohio National Guard
Ohio National Guard Scholarship Program, 404

Polish National Alliance of Brooklyn
The Polish National Alliance of Brooklyn, USA, Inc. Scholarships, 315

Portuguese Continental Union
Luso-American Education Foundation Scholarship, 324

Recording for the Blind & Dyslexic
Marion Huber Learning Through Listening Award, 434
Mary P. Oenslager Scholastic Achievement Award, 434

Reserve Officers Association or ROAL
Henry J. Reilly Memorial College Scholarship, 435

Reserve Officers Training Corps (ROTC)
AFCEA ROTC Scholarships, 190
Kansas ROTC Service Scholarship, 309
ROTC/Navy/Marine Two-Year Scholarship, 508

Screen Actor's Guild
John L. Dales Standard Scholarship, 440

Service Employees International Union
Charles Hardy Memorial Scholarship, 443

Slovak Gymnastic Union Sokol, USA
Milan Getting Scholarship, 444

Slovenian Women's Union of America
Slovenian Women's Union Scholarship, 444
Slovenian Women's Union Scholarship For Returning Adults, 445

Sociedad Honoraria Hispanica
Joseph S. Adams Scholarship, 445

Society of Automotive Engineers
Society of Automotive Engineers (SAE) Longterm Member Sponsored Scholarship, 448

Society of Manufacturing Engineers
Chapter 17 St. Louis Scholarship, 450
Detroit Chapter One - Founding Chapter Scholarship Award, 452
SME Education Foundation Family Scholarship, 455
Walt Bartram Memorial Education Award (Region 12 and Chapter 119), 455

Society of Physics Students
Society of Physics Students Leadership Scholarship, 456
Society of Physics Students Summer Internship Program, 568

Society of Women Engineers
Bechtel Foundation Scholarship, 460
Chevron Corporation Scholarships, 462
Goldman, Sachs and Co. Scholarship, 465
Judith Resnik Memorial Scholarship, 466

Sons of Norway
Astrid G. Cates Scholarship Fund and Myrtle Beinhauer Scholarship, 471
Nancy Lorraine Jensen Memorial Scholarship, 471

South Dakota National Guard
South Dakota National Guard Tuition Assistance, 474

Third Marine Division Association
Third Marine Division Memorial Scholarship Fund, 490

Transportation Clubs International
Charlotte Woods Memorial Scholarship, 492

Ukrainian Fraternal Association
Ukrainian Fraternal Association Scholarship, 495

United Food and Commerical Workers
United Food and Commercial Workers International Union Scholarship Program, 496

United States Association of Blind Athletes
Arthur E. Copeland Scholarship for Males, 502

United Transportation Union
United Transportation Union Insurance Association Scholarship, 503

Religious Affiliation

Eastern Orthodox
Boy and Girl Scouts Scholarship, 240

Episcopal
Shannon Scholarship, 493

Jewish
Chester M. Vernon Memorial Eagle Scout Scholarship, 376
Frank L. Weil Memorial Eagle Scout Scholarship, 376
JFCS Scholarship Fund, 582
JVS Jewish Community Scholarship Fund, 307
Taglit-Birthright Israel Gift, 482

Lutheran
Developmental Disabilities Nursing Scholastic Achievement Scholarship, 203
Developmental Disability Scholastic Achievement Scholarship, 203
Laywomen Scholarships, 523

Presbyterian
National Presbyterian Scholarship, 429
Presbyterian Student Opportunity Scholarship, 429
Presbyterian Undergraduate and Graduate Loan, 589
Samuel Robinson Award, 429

Protestant
Juliette M. Atherton Scholarship, 269

Roman Catholic
Italian Catholic Federation Scholarship, 299
Matthews/Swift Educational Trust - Military Dependants, 313
Matthews/Swift Educational Trust - Police/Firefighters, 313
Pro Deo/Pro Patria Scholarship, 313

Unitarian Universalist
Stanfield and D'Orlando Art Scholarship, 496

United Methodist
Leonard M. Perryman Communications Scholarship for Ethnic Minority Students, 497
United Methodist Loan Program, 591
United Methodist Scholarships, 496

Returning Adult

Air Traffic Control Full-Time Employee Student Scholarship, 82
A.J. "Andy" Spielman Travel Agents Scholarship, 179
American Legion Alaska Auxiliary Western District Scholarship, 113
B. K. Krenzer Reentry Scholarship, 460
Charles R. Ford Scholarship, 306
Connecticut Tuition Waiver for Senior Citizens, 226
Delayed Education Scholarship for Women, 159
Eight and Forty Lung and Respiratory Nursing Scholarship Fund, 136
Fran Johnson Non-Traditional Scholarship, 102
GEICO Life Scholarship, 257
Laywomen Scholarships, 523
Lighthouse Graduate Award, 321

Missouri Minority Teaching Scholarship, 344
Montgomery GI Bill Plus Army College Fund, 504
New York State Veterans Tuition Award, 395
Olive Lynn Salembier Reentry Scholarship, 469
Russ Griffith Memorial Scholarship, 233
Senior Citizen, 65 or Older, Free Tuition for Up to 6 Credit Hours, 486
Slovenian Women's Union Scholarship For Returning Adults, 445
Undergraduate Research Scholarship, 358
Urban Flight and Rural Needs Scholarship Program, 344
West Virginia Higher Education Adult Part-time Student (HEAPS) Grant Program, 519
Workforce Improvement Grant, 189

State of Residence

Alabama
Alabama GI Dependents Educational Benefit, 88
Alabama Junior/Community College Athletic Scholarship, 87
Alabama National Guard Educational Assistance Award, 86
Alabama Robert C. Byrd Honors Scholarship, 87
Alabama Scholarship for Dependents of Blind Parents, 476
Alabama Student Assistance Program, 87
Alabama Student Grant, 87
American Legion Alabama Auxiliary Scholarship, 113
American Legion Alabama Oratorical Contest, 112
American Legion Alabama Scholarship, 112
Charles Clarke Cordle Memorial Scholarship, 163
Dana Campbell Memorial Scholarship, 303
Horatio Alger Alabama Scholarship Program, 280
Institutional Scholarship Waivers, 88
NASA Space Grant Undergraduate Scholarship, 351
Police/Firefighters' Survivors Educational Assistance Program, 87

Alaska
Alaska Family Education Loan, 577
Alaska Teacher Education Loan, 577
Alaska Winn Brindle (W.B.) Memorial Education Loan Program, 577

American Council of Engineering Companies-Alaska Scholarship, 99
American Legion Alaska Auxiliary Scholarship, 113
American Legion Alaska Auxiliary Western District Scholarship, 113
American Legion Alaska Oratorical Contest, 113
American Legion Western District Postsecondary Scholarship, 113
Cady McDonnell Memorial Scholarship, 98
Carl N. & Margaret Karcher Founders' Scholarship, 214
Mary Lou Brown Scholarship, 166

Arizona
All-Arizona Academic Team, 187
American Legion Arizona Auxiliary Health Care Occupation Scholarship, 114
American Legion Arizona Auxiliary Nurses' Scholarship, 114
American Legion Arizona Oratorical Contest, 114
Arizona Chapter Dependent Scholarship Fund, 179
Arizona Chapter Gold Scholarship, 180
Arizona Tuition Scholarships for Children/Spouses of Slain Public Servants, 187
Arizona Tuition Scholarships for Residents, 188
A.W. Bodine Sunkist Memorial Scholarship, 480
Burlington Northern Santa Fe Foundation Scholarship, 109
Cady McDonnell Memorial Scholarship, 98
Carl N. & Margaret Karcher Founders' Scholarship, 214
Chapter 67 - Phoenix Scholarship, 451
Charles N. Fisher Memorial Scholarship, 163
Deseo at the Westin Scholarship, 303
High Honors Endorsement Tuition Scholarship, 188
Italian Catholic Federation Scholarship, 299
Legacy of Hope, 478
NASA Space Grant Arizona Undergraduate Research Internship, 554
Phoenix Section Scholarship, 469
Rocky Mountain Coal Mining Scholarship, 435
Shell Legislative Internship Program, 556
Walt Bartram Memorial Education Award (Region 12 and Chapter 119), 455
Wilma D. Hoyal/Maxine Chilton Memorial Scholarship, 114

Arkansas
Academic Challenge Scholarship, 188

American Legion Arkansas Auxiliary Scholarships, 115
American Legion Arkansas Oratorical Contest, 115
American Legion Arkansas Scholarship, 115
Arkansas Department of Higher Education Teacher Assistance Resource (STAR) Program, 579
Arkansas Law Enforcement Officers' Dependents Scholarship, 188
Arkansas Minority Teachers Scholarship Program, 579
Dana Campbell Memorial Scholarship, 303
Fred R. McDaniel Memorial Scholarship, 164
Governor's Scholars Program, 189
Military Dependents Scholarship Program, 189
NASA Space Grant Arkansas Undergraduate Scholarship, 351
Second Effort Scholarship, 189
Wally Joe (KC's) Scholarship, 305
Workforce Improvement Grant, 189

California
AFCEA/Lockheed Martin IT Scholarship, 191
American Legion California Auxiliary General Scholarships, 116
American Legion California Oratorical Contest, 115
Associated Press/APTRA-CLETE Roberts Memorial Journalism Scholarship, 197
A.W. Bodine Sunkist Memorial Scholarship, 480
Bay Area Council Scholarship Program, 202
BIA North County Division Scholarship, 208
Burlington Northern Santa Fe Foundation Scholarship, 109
Cady McDonnell Memorial Scholarship, 98
Cal Grant A & B Entitlement Award Program, 211
Cal Grant C Award Program, 211
California Association of Realtors Scholarship, 210
California Assumption Program of Loans for Education (APLE), 579
California Child Development Grant Program, 212
California Farm Bureau Scholarship, 210
California Law Enforcement Personnel Dependents Grant Program, 212
California Masonic Foundation Scholarship, 210
California Robert C. Byrd Honors Scholarship, 212
California's Junior Miss Competition, 211

State of Residence: California

Carl N. & Margaret Karcher Founders' Scholarship, 214
The CBC Spouses Education Scholarship, 224
Charles Hardy Memorial Scholarship, 443
Charles N. Fisher Memorial Scholarship, 163
Competitive Cal Grant A and B Award Programs, 212
Continuing or Re-entry Student Scholarship, 116
Dolores Nunes Lowry Scholarship, 323
Epilepsy Foundation of San Diego County Scholarship, 243
Eva Vieira Memorial Scholarship, 324
Fashion Group International of Portland Scholarship, 412
Goldman Family Fund: New Leader Scholarship, 327
Grange Insurance Scholarship, 260
Herbert Fernandes Scholarship, 324
Horatio Alger California Scholarship Program, 280
Italian Catholic Federation Scholarship, 299
JFCS Scholarship Fund, 582
JVS Jewish Community Scholarship Fund, 307
Kaiser Permanente College to Caring Program, 277
L. Gordon Bittle Memorial Scholarship for Student CTA, 214
LAF/CLASS Fund (California Landscape Architectural Student Scholarship) University Scholarship Program, 316
LAF/CLASS Fund Internship Program, 549
LAF/CLASS Fund Landscape Architecture Program, 317
LAF/CLASS Fund Scholarship Ornamental Horticulture Program, 317
Legacy of Hope, 478
Luso-American Education Foundation Scholarship, 324
Native Daughters of the Golden West Scholarship, 384
NCR Summer Internships, 558
Northern California Chapter/Richard Epping Scholarship, 181
Oracle Scholars Internship Program, 572
Past Department Presidents' Junior Scholarship, 116
Past Presidents' Parley Nursing Scholarship, 116
Pete Wilson Journalism Scholarship, 433
Shell Legislative Internship Program, 556
Southern California Council Endowed Internship, 557
Usrey Family Scholarship, 287
Ventura County Japanese-American Citizens League Scholarships, 509
Walt Bartram Memorial Education Award (Region 12 and Chapter 119), 455
William J. and Marijane E. Adams, Jr., Mechanical Engineering Scholarship, 177
Wilma Motley Memorial California Merit Scholarship, 80
Women in Architecture Scholarship, 198

Colorado

Burlington Northern Santa Fe Foundation Scholarship, 109
Cady McDonnell Memorial Scholarship, 98
Carl N. & Margaret Karcher Founders' Scholarship, 214
Charter Fund Scholarship, 218
Clinton J. Helton Manufacturing Scholarship Award, 452
Colorado Masons Scholarship, 222
Colorado Society of CPAs General Scholarship, 222
Colorado Student Grant, 222
Colorado Supplemental Leveraging Educational Assistance Partnership Program, 222
Colorado Work-Study Program, 222
Department President's Scholarship, 117
Department President's Scholarship for Junior Auxiliary Members, 117
Grange Insurance Scholarship, 260
Greenhouse Scholars, 260
Latin American Educational Scholarship, 318
Legacy of Hope, 478
Mark J. Smith Scholarship, 223
National High School Oratorical Contest, 116
Past President's Parley Nurse's Scholarship, 117
Rocky Mountain Coal Mining Scholarship, 435
Sachs Foundation Undergraduate Grant, 439
Shell Legislative Internship Program, 556

Connecticut

Columbus Citizens Foundation College Scholarship Program, 223
Connecticut Aid for Public College Students, 225
Connecticut Aid to Dependents of Deceased/Disabled/MIA Veterans, 225
Connecticut Building Congress Scholarship, 225
Connecticut Capitol Scholarship Program, 225
Connecticut Family Education Loan Program (CT FELP), 580
Connecticut Independent College Student Grant, 226
Connecticut Minority Teacher Incentive Grant, 226
Connecticut Nursing Scholarship, 227
Connecticut Robert C. Byrd Honors Scholarship, 226
Connecticut Tuition Set Aside Aid, 226
Connecticut Tuition Waiver for Senior Citizens, 226
Connecticut Tuition Waiver for Veterans, 227
Connecticut Tuition Waiver for Vietnam MIA/POW Dependents, 227
Dr. James L. Lawson Memorial Scholarship, 164
Japanese American General Scholarship, 305
Lighthouse College-Bound Award, 321
Lighthouse Graduate Award, 321
Lighthouse Undergraduate Award, 322
Massachusetts MASSgrant Program, 333
National High School Oratorical Contest, 117
New England Board of Higher Education's Regional Student Program, 386
The New England FEMARA Scholarship, 167
New Jersey STARS II, 388
New York Women in Communications Foundation Scholarship, 396
Sonia Streuli Maguire Outstanding Scholastic Achievement Award, 481
Swiss Benevolent Society Pellegrini Scholarship, 482
Timothy Bigelow Scholarship, 287
Weisman Scholarship, 227

Delaware

B. Bradford Barnes Scholarship, 236
Charles L. Hebner Memorial Scholarship, 236
Christa McAuliffe Teacher Incentive Program, 580
Columbus Citizens Foundation College Scholarship Program, 223
Cymdeithas Gymreig (Welsh Society) Philadelphia Scholarship, 230
Dana Campbell Memorial Scholarship, 303
Delaware Legislative Essay Scholarship, 236
Delaware Nursing Incentive Program, 580
Delaware Scholarship Incentive Program, 237
Diamond State Scholarship, 237
Educational Benefits for Children of Deceased Veterans and Others, 237
Herman M. Holloway, Sr., Memorial Scholarship, 237

Horatio Alger Delaware Scholarship Program, 280
Lighthouse College-Bound Award, 321
Lighthouse Graduate Award, 321
Lighthouse Undergraduate Award, 322
Past President's Parley Nursing Scholarship, 118
Robert C. Byrd Honors Scholarship, 238
Sonia Streuli Maguire Outstanding Scholastic Achievement Award, 481
Swiss Benevolent Society Pellegrini Scholarship, 482

District of Columbia

Alumnae Panhellenic Association Women's Scholarship, 91
The CBC Spouses Education Scholarship, 224
Columbus Citizens Foundation College Scholarship Program, 223
DC Adoption Scholarship, 239
DC Tuition Assistance Grant Program, 239
District of Columbia Leveraging Educational Assistance Partnership Program, 240
Horatio Alger District of Columbia, Maryland and Virgina Scholarship Program, 281
Lighthouse College-Bound Award, 321
Lighthouse Graduate Award, 321
Lighthouse Undergraduate Award, 322
Massachusetts MASSgrant Program, 333
National High School Oratorical Contest, 118
NCR Summer Internships, 558

Florida

Access to Better Learning and Education Grant Program (ABLE), 247
Allen Susser Scholarship, 301
American Legion Florida Auxiliary Memorial Scholarship, 119
American Legion Florida Auxiliary Scholarships, 119
American Legion Florida General Scholarship, 118
American Restaurant Scholarship, 302
ARRL Earl I. Anderson Scholarship, 162
Bern Laxer Memorial Scholarship, 302
Bob East Scholarship Fund, 377
The CBC Spouses Education Scholarship, 224
Critical Teacher Shortage Student Loan Forgiveness Program, 580
Dana Campbell Memorial Scholarship, 303
Eagle Scout of the Year, 119
Florida Academic Scholars Award, 247
Florida Educational Assistance for the Blind, 249
Florida Gold Seal Vocational Scholars Award, 247
Florida Medallion Scholars Award, 247
Florida Robert C. Byrd Honors Scholarship, 248
Florida Student Assistance Grant Program, 248
Florida Work Experience Program, 542
High School Oratorical Contest, 119
Horatio Alger Florida Scholarship Program, 281
Jose Marti Scholarship Challenge Grant, 248
Lighthouse College-Bound Award, 321
Lighthouse Graduate Award, 321
Lighthouse Undergraduate Award, 322
Mary McLeod Bethune Scholarship, 248
Rosewood Family Scholarship Program, 249
Salute to Education Scholarship, 439
Scholarships for Children and Spouses of Deceased or Disabled Veterans and Servicemembers, 249
Shell Legislative Internship Program, 556
William L. Boyd, IV, Florida Resident Access Grant, 249

Georgia

Accel Program Grant, 254
American Legion Georgia Auxiliary Scholarship, 119
The CBC Spouses Education Scholarship, 224
Charles Clarke Cordle Memorial Scholarship, 163
Dana Campbell Memorial Scholarship, 303
The Eugene "Gene" Sallee, W4YFR Memorial Scholarship, 164
Georgia Governor's Scholarship, 254
Georgia Hope Grant - GED Recipient, 254
Georgia Hope Grant - Public Technical Institution, 254
Georgia Hope Scholarship - Private Institution, 255
Georgia Hope Scholarship - Public College or University, 255
Georgia Law Enforcement Personnel Dependents Grant, 255
Georgia LEAP Grant, 255
Georgia Promise Teacher Scholarship, 581
Georgia Robert C. Byrd Scholarship, 255
Georgia Scholarship for Engineering Education, 581
Georgia Tuition Equalization Grant, 256
Horatio Alger Georgia Scholarship Program, 281
Lighthouse College-Bound Award, 321
Lighthouse Graduate Award, 321
Lighthouse Undergraduate Award, 322
NASA Space Grant Georgia Fellowship Program, 352
NCR Summer Internships, 558
PAGE Foundation Scholarships, 431
Past President's Parley Nurses Scholarship, 120
Student Aid Foundation Loan, 589
Web Challenge Contest, 482
Xernona Clayton Scholarship, 200

Hawaii

Aiea General Hospital Association Scholarship, 261
Alma White-Delta Kappa Gamma Scholarship, 262
Ambassador Minerva Jean Falcon Hawaii Scholarship, 262
American Legion Oratorical Contest, 120
American Savings Bank Scholars Program, 262
Associated Press/APTRA-CLETE Roberts Memorial Journalism Scholarship, 197
Bal Dasa Scholarship Fund, 262
Blossom Kalama Evans Memorial Scholarship, 262
Cady McDonnell Memorial Scholarship, 98
Camille C. Chidiac Fund, 263
Candon Consulting Group Scholarship Fund, 263
Carl N. & Margaret Karcher Founders' Scholarship, 214
Castle & Cooke Mililani Technology Park Scholarship Fund, 263
Cayetano Foundation Scholarship, 263
Community Scholarship Fund, 264
Cora Aguda Manayan Fund, 264
David L. Irons Memorial Scholarship Fund, 264
David T. Woolsey Scholarship, 316
Dolly Ching Scholarship Fund, 264
Doris & Clarence Glick Classical Music Scholarship, 265
Dr. Alvin and Monica Saake Scholarship, 265
Dr. Hans & Clara Zimmerman Foundation Education Scholarship, 265
Dr. Hans and Clara Zimmerman Foundation Health Scholarship, 265
Edward and Norma Doty Scholarship, 266
Edward Payson and Bernice Pi'ilani Irwin Scholarship Trust Fund, 266
E.E. Black Scholarship, 266
Ellison Onizuka Memorial Scholarship, 266
Esther Kanagawa Memorial Art Scholarship, 267

State of Residence: Hawaii

The Filipino Nurses' Organization of Hawaii Scholarship, 267
Financial Women International Scholarship, 267
Fletcher & Fritzi Hoffmann Education Fund, 267
Friends of Hawaii Public Housing Scholarship, 267
George Mason Business Scholarship Fund, 268
Gerrit R. Ludwig Scholarship, 268
Henry A. Zuberano Scholarship, 268
Jean Fitzgerald Scholarship Fund, 268
John Dawe Dental Education Fund, 269
John Ross Foundation, 269
Juliette M. Atherton Scholarship, 269
Ka'a'awa Community Fund, 270
Ka'iulani Home for Girls Trust Scholarship, 269
Kapolei Community & Business Scholarship, 270
Kawasaki-McGaha Scholarship Fund, 270
King Kekaulike High School Scholarship, 270
K.M. Hatano Scholarship, 270
Kohala Ditch Education Fund, 271
Koloa Scholarship, 271
Kurt W. Schneider Memorial Scholarship Fund, 271
Laura N. Dowsett Fund, 271
Margaret Jones Memorial Nursing Scholarship, 272
Marion Maccarrell Scott Scholarship, 272
Mary Josephine Bloder Scholarship, 272
Mildred Towle Scholarship - Study Abroad, 272
Mildred Towle Scholarship for African-Americans, 273
NASA Hawaii Undergraduate Traineeship, 554
NASA Space Grant Hawaii Undergraduate Fellowship, 353
Nick Van Pernis Scholarship, 273
Oscar and Rosetta Fish Fund, 273
PRSA-Hawaii/Roy Leffingwell Public Relations Scholarship, 273
Ron Bright Scholarship, 273
Rosemary & Nellie Ebrie Fund, 274
Shirley McKown Scholarship Fund, 274
Shuichi, Katsu and Itsuyo Suga Scholarship, 274
Thz Fo Farm Fund, 274
Tommy Lee Memorial Scholarship Fund, 274
Toraji & Toki Yoshinaga Scholarship, 275
Vicki Willder Scholarship Fund, 275
Walter H. Kupau Memorial Fund, 275
West Kauai Scholarship, 275
William J. and Marijane E. Adams, Jr., Mechanical Engineering Scholarship, 177
William James & Dorothy Bading Lanquist Fund, 276

Idaho

American Legion Idaho Auxiliary Nurse's Scholarship, 120
American Legion Idaho Scholarships, 120
Cady McDonnell Memorial Scholarship, 98
Carl N. & Margaret Karcher Founders' Scholarship, 214
Fashion Group International of Portland Scholarship, 412
Grange Insurance Scholarship, 260
Grow Your Own Teacher Scholarship Program, 289
Horatio Alger Idaho Scholarship Program, 282
Idaho Education Incentive Loan Forgiveness Program, 582
Idaho Governor's Cup Scholarship, 289
Idaho Minority/"At-Risk" Scholarship, 289
Idaho Robert C. Byrd Scholarship, 289
Idaho Robert R. Lee Category A Promise Scholarship, 289
Idaho Robert R. Lee Category B Promise Scholarship, 290
Mary Lou Brown Scholarship, 166
Oratorical Contest, 120
Treacy Company Scholarship, 493

Illinois

Ada Mucklestone Memorial Scholarship, 121
American Legion Illinois Boy Scout Scholarship, 121
American Legion Illinois Oratorical Contest, 121
American Legion Illinois Scholarships, 121
Americanism Essay Contest Scholarship, 121
ARRL Earl I. Anderson Scholarship, 162
Bonus Incentive Grant (BIG), 290
The CBC Spouses Education Scholarship, 224
The Chicago FM Club Scholarships, 163
College Bound Scholarship, 440
David Arver Memorial Scholarship, 83
Edmond A. Metzger Scholarship, 164
Grant Program for Dependents of Correctional Officers, 290
Grant Program for Dependents of Police or Fire Officers, 290
Horatio Alger Illinois Scholarship Program, 282
Illinois Future Teacher Corps, 291
Illinois National Guard Grant, 291
Illinois Veteran Grant (IVG) Program, 291
Italian Catholic Federation Scholarship, 299
Marie Sheehe Trade School Scholarship, 122
McFarland Charitable Foundation Scholarship, 261
Merit Recognition Scholarship, 291
Midwest Student Exchange Program, 338
Mildred R. Knoles Opportunity Scholarship, 122
Minority Teachers of Illinois Scholarship, 292
Monetary Award Program (MAP), 292
Robert C. Byrd Honors Scholarship Program, 292
Shell Legislative Internship Program, 556
Silas Purnell Illinois Incentive for Access, 292
The Six Meter Club of Chicago Scholarship, 168
Special Education Teacher Tuition Waiver, 293
Special Education Teaching Scholarships, 122
Student Nurse Scholarship, 122
Student-to-Student (STS) Program, 293

Indiana

American Legion Americanism and Government Test, 122
American Legion Family Scholarship, 122
American Legion Indiana Oratorical Contest, 123
American Legion Legacy Scholarship, 136
ARRL Earl I. Anderson Scholarship, 162
The CBC Spouses Education Scholarship, 224
Chapter 56 - Fort Wayne Scholarship, 451
The Chicago FM Club Scholarships, 163
The Clarence & Josephine Myers Scholarship, 451
David Arver Memorial Scholarship, 83
Eagle Scout of the Year Scholarship, 123
Edmond A. Metzger Scholarship, 164
Edna M. Barcus Memorial Scholarship and Hoosier Scholarship, 123
Frank M. McHale Memorial Scholarship, 123
Frank O'Bannon Grant, 477
Hoosier Scholar Award, 477
Horatio Alger Indiana Scholarship Program, 282
Indiana Minority Teacher & Special Education Services Scholarship, 477

State of Residence: Maine

Indiana National Guard Supplemental Grant, 477
Indiana Nursing Scholarship, 477
Indiana Robert C. Byrd Honors Scholarship, 478
Indiana Twenty-First Century Scholars Program, 478
John W. Anderson Foundation Scholarship, 500
Katharine M. Grosscup Scholarship, 253
NASA Indiana Space Grant Consortium Undergraduate Scholarships, 354
Past President's Parley Nursing Scholarship, 123
Young Survivor Scholarship, 95

Iowa

American Legion Iowa Oratorical Contest, 124
Boy Scout of the Year Scholarship, 124
David Arver Memorial Scholarship, 83
Department of Iowa Scholarships, 124
Harriet Hoffman Memorial Scholarship, 125
Horatio Alger Ak-Sar-Ben Scholarship Program, 280
Horatio Alger Iowa Scholarship Program, 282
Iowa Grant, 298
Iowa National Guard Educational Assistance Program, 299
Iowa Robert C. Byrd Honor Scholarship, 299
Iowa Tuition Grant, 299
Iowa Vocational-Technical Tuition Grant, 299
Mary Virginia Macrea Memorial Scholarship, 125
North Central Region Scholarship, 455
Outstanding Citizen of Boys State Scholarship, 124
Outstanding Senior Baseball Player Scholarship, 124
Past President's Scholarship, 125
Paul and Helen L. Grauer Scholarship, 167
The PHD ARA Scholarship, 167

Kansas

Albert M. Lappin Scholarship, 125
American Legion Kansas Auxiliary Department Scholarships, 127
American Legion Music Scholarship, 125
American Legion Oratorical Contest, 125
American Restaurant Scholarship, 302
Burlington Northern Santa Fe Foundation Scholarship, 109
Chapter 52 - Wichita Scholarship, 451
Charles and Annette Hill Scholarship, 126
David Arver Memorial Scholarship, 83
Dr. Click Cowger Scholarship, 126
Hugh A. Smith Scholarship, 126
Irving W. Cook, WAOCGS Scholarship, 165
John and Geraldine Hobble Licensed Practical Nursing Scholarship, 126
Kansas Comprehensive Grant, 308
Kansas Ethnic Minority Scholarship, 308
Kansas Nursing Service Scholarship, 308
Kansas ROTC Service Scholarship, 309
Kansas State Scholarship, 309
Kansas Teacher Service Scholarship, 309
Kansas Vocational Education Scholarship, 309
Midwest Student Exchange Program, 338
National Guard Educational Assistance Program, 310
Paul and Helen L. Grauer Scholarship, 167
The PHD ARA Scholarship, 167
Rosedale Post 346 Scholarship, 126
Ted and Nora Anderson Scholarship, 126

Kentucky

American Legion Department Oratorical Awards, 127
American Legion Kentucky Auxiliary Mary Barrett Marshall Scholarship, 127
Dana Campbell Memorial Scholarship, 303
Early Childhood Development Scholarship, 311
Horatio Alger Kentucky Scholarship Program, 282
Katharine M. Grosscup Scholarship, 253
Kentucky College Access Program Grant (CAP), 311
Kentucky Educational Excellence Scholarship (KEES), 311
Kentucky Teacher Scholarship, 311
Kentucky Tuition Grant, 312
Kentucky Work-Study Program, 548
Laura Blackburn Memorial Scholarship, 127
Mary Barrett Marshall Student Loan Fund, 578
Mary Jo Young Scholarship, 312
NASA Space Grant Kentucky Undergraduate Scholarship, 354
Pat & Jim Host Internship/Scholarship, 571
Robert C. Byrd Honors Scholarship, 312

Louisiana

The CBC Spouses Education Scholarship, 224
Dana Campbell Memorial Scholarship, 303
Fred R. McDaniel Memorial Scholarship, 164
Horatio Alger Louisiana Scholarship Program, 283
Louisiana Rockefeller Wildlife Scholarship, 323
Louisiana Tuition Opportunity Program for Students (TOPS) Award, 323
Louisiana Veterans Affairs Educational Assistance for Dependent Children, 322
Louisiana Veterans Affairs Educational Assistance for Surviving Spouse, 322
Robert C. Byrd Honors Scholarship, 323
Wally Joe (KC's) Scholarship, 305

Maine

AGC of Maine Scholarship Program, 81
American Legion Maine Auxiliary Scholarship, 128
Children and Youth Scholarships, 128
Columbus Citizens Foundation College Scholarship Program, 223
Daniel E. Lambert Memorial Scholarship, 128
Dr. James L. Lawson Memorial Scholarship, 164
James V. Day Scholarship, 128
Lighthouse College-Bound Award, 321
Lighthouse Graduate Award, 321
Lighthouse Undergraduate Award, 322
Maine Innkeepers Association Scholarship, 325
Maine Metal Products Association Scholarship, 325
Maine Robert C. Byrd Honors Scholarship, 245
Maine Rural Rehabilitation Fund, 325
Maine Society of Professional Engineers Scholarship Program, 326
Maine State Society of Washington, DC, Foundation Scholarship Program, 327
Maine Veterans Services Dependents Educational Benefits, 325
Massachusetts MASSgrant Program, 333
NASA Space Grant Maine Consortium Annual Scholarship and Fellowship Program, 354
New England Board of Higher Education's Regional Student Program, 386
The New England FEMARA Scholarship, 167
New Jersey STARS II, 388
OMNE/Nursing Leaders of Maine Scholarship, 408

Eligibility Indexes

65

State of Residence: Maine

President's Parley Nursing Scholarship, 128
Russ Casey Scholarship, 326
Senator George J. Mitchell Scholarship, 442
Senator Joel Abromson Memorial Scholarship Fund, 244
Timothy Bigelow Scholarship, 287

Maryland

Adler Science and Math Scholarship, 129
American Legion Maryland Auxiliary Scholarship, 129
American Legion Maryland Boys State Scholarship, 129
American Legion Maryland Oratorical Contest, 129
American Legion Maryland Scholarship, 129
Carville M. Akehurst Memorial Scholarship, 287
The CBC Spouses Education Scholarship, 224
Charles W. Riley Fire and Emergency Medical Services Tuition Reimbursement Program, 328
Columbus Citizens Foundation College Scholarship Program, 223
Cymdeithas Gymreig (Welsh Society) Philadelphia Scholarship, 230
The Cynthia E. Morgan Memorial Scholarship Fund, 230
Dana Campbell Memorial Scholarship, 303
The Erikka A. Hayes Foundation Scholarship, 331
Horatio Alger District of Columbia, Maryland and Virginia Scholarship Program, 281
Howard P. Rawlings Guaranteed Access Grant, 328
Letitia B. Carter Scholarship, 332
Lighthouse College-Bound Award, 321
Lighthouse Graduate Award, 321
Lighthouse Undergraduate Award, 322
Marcia S. Harris Legacy Fund Scholarship, 332
Maryland Delegate Scholarship, 328
Maryland Distinguished Scholar: Achievement, 329
Maryland Distinguished Scholar: National Merit and National Achievement Finalists, 329
Maryland Distinguished Scholar: Talent in the Arts, 329
Maryland Educational Assistance Grant, 329
Maryland Jack F. Tolbert Memorial Grant, 330
Maryland Part-Time Grant Program, 330
Maryland Senatorial Scholarship, 331
Maryland Tuition Reduction for Non-Resident Nursing Students, 331

Past President's Parley Scholarship, 130
Tuition Waiver for Foster Care Recipients, 331

Massachusetts

American Legion Massachusetts Auxiliary Scholarship, 130
American Legion Massachusetts General and Nursing Scholarships, 130
Columbus Citizens Foundation College Scholarship Program, 223
Department of Massachusetts Oratorical Contest, 130
Dr. James L. Lawson Memorial Scholarship, 164
Dr. Marie E. Zakrzewski Medical Scholarship, 314
Francis Ouimet Scholarship, 251
John F. Kennedy Scholars Award, 333
John Joseph Moakely Democratic Internship, 550
Lighthouse College-Bound Award, 321
Lighthouse Graduate Award, 321
Lighthouse Undergraduate Award, 322
Massachusetts Christian A. Herter Memorial Scholarship Program, 332
Massachusetts Gilbert Matching Student Grant, 332
Massachusetts MASSgrant Program, 333
Massachusetts No Interest Loan, 583
Massachusetts Public Service Grant Program, 333
Massachusetts Robert C. Byrd Honors Scholarship, 334
New England Board of Higher Education's Regional Student Program, 386
The New England FEMARA Scholarship, 167
New Jersey STARS II, 388
Past President's Parley Scholarship, 130
Paul Tsongas Scholarship Program, 333
PHCC Auxiliary of Massachusetts Scholarship, 428
Timothy Bigelow Scholarship, 287

Michigan

American Legion Michigan Auxiliary Memorial Scholarship, 131
American Legion Michigan Oratorical Contest, 131
ARRL Earl I. Anderson Scholarship, 162
The CBC Spouses Education Scholarship, 224
Children of Veterans Tuiton Grant, 335
David Arver Memorial Scholarship, 83
Guy M. Wilson Scholarship, 131

Katharine M. Grosscup Scholarship, 253
Kathy LeTarte Scholarship, 490
Medical Career Scholarships, 131
Michigan Adult Part-Time Grant, 335
Michigan Alternative Student Loan (MI-LOAN), 583
Michigan Competitive Scholarship, 336
Michigan Educational Opportunity Grant, 336
Michigan Nursing Scholarship, 336
Michigan Promise Scholarship, 336
Michigan Society of Professional Engineers Scholarships, 337
Michigan Tuition Grant, 336
Michigan Work-Study Program, 551
Midwest Student Exchange Program, 338
MSGC Undergraduate Underrepresented Minority Fellowship Program, 355
NASA Space Grant Michigan Undergraduate Fellowship, 355
National President's Scholarship, 132
North Central Region Scholarship, 455
Tuition Incentive Program, 336
William D. & Jewell W. Brewer Scholarship Trusts, 131
Young Survivor Scholarship, 95
The Zachary Taylor Stevens Memorial Scholarship, 169

Minnesota

American Legion Minnesota Auxiliary Department Scholarship, 133
American Legion Minnesota Legionnaire Insurance Trust Scholarship, 132
American Legion Minnesota Oratorical Contest, 132
Burlington Northern Santa Fe Foundation Scholarship, 109
David Arver Memorial Scholarship, 83
Horatio Alger Hormel Scholarship Program, 281
Horatio Alger Minnesota Scholarship Program, 283
Midwest Student Exchange Program, 338
The Minnesota American Legion Memorial Scholarship, 132
Minnesota Educational Assistance for Veterans, 340
Minnesota Educational Assistance for War Orphans, 340
Minnesota GI Bill, 340
Minnesota Post-Secondary Child Care Grant, 340
Minnesota Public Safety Officers Survivors Program, 341
Minnesota State Grant Program, 341
Minnesota Student Educational Loan Fund (SELF), 584
Minnesota Work-Study Program, 551

North Central Region Scholarship, 455
Past President's Parley Health Care Scholarship, 133
Scholarship for People with Disabilities, 230

Mississippi

American Legion Mississippi Auxiliary Scholarship, 133
The CBC Spouses Education Scholarship, 224
Community College Graduates Scholarship Program, 356
Critical Needs Alternative Route Teacher Loan/Scholarship, 584
Dana Campbell Memorial Scholarship, 303
Fred R. McDaniel Memorial Scholarship, 164
Gulf Coast Research Laboratory Minority Summer Grant, 342
Horatio Alger Mississippi Scholarship Program, 283
Leveraging Educational Assistance Partnership Program (LEAP), 342
Mississippi Eminent Scholars Grant, 343
Mississippi Health Care Professions Loan/Scholarship, 584
Mississippi Higher Education Legislative Plan, 343
Mississippi Law Enforcement Officers & Firemen Scholarship, 343
Mississippi Nursing Education Loan/Scholarship, 584
Mississippi Resident Tuition Assistance Grant, 343
The Mississippi Scholarship, 166
Mississippi William Winter Teacher Scholar Loan Program, 585
NASA Space Grant Mississippi Undergraduate Scholarship, 356
Nissan Scholarship, 343
Wally Joe (KC's) Scholarship, 305

Missouri

Access Missouri Financial Assistance Program, 345
American Legion Missouri Auxiliary Scholarship, 134
American Restaurant Scholarship, 302
The CBC Spouses Education Scholarship, 224
Chapter 52 - Wichita Scholarship, 451
Charles L. Bacon Memorial Scholarship, 133
Chris Desens Scholarship, 302
Dana Campbell Memorial Scholarship, 303
David Arver Memorial Scholarship, 83
Erby Young Scholarship, 346
Erman W. Taylor Memorial Scholarship, 133
Horatio Alger Missouri Scholarship Program, 283

Lillie Lois Ford Boys' Scholarship, 134
Lillie Lois Ford Girls' Scholarship, 134
Marguerite Ross Barnett Memorial Scholarship, 345
M.D. "Jack" Murphy Memorial Nurses Training Fund, 134
Midwest Student Exchange Program, 338
Missouri Department of Higher Education Vietnam Veteran's Survivor Grant Program, 345
Missouri Higher Education "Bright Flight" Academic Scholarship, 345
Missouri League for Nursing Scholarship, 346
Missouri Minority Teaching Scholarship, 344
Missouri Public Service Survivor Grant, 346
Missouri Robert C. Byrd Honors Scholarship, 344
Missouri Teacher Education Scholarship, 344
NASA Missouri State Space Grant Undergraduate Scholarship, 356
Past President's Parley Scholarship, 134
Paul and Helen L. Grauer Scholarship, 167
The PHD ARA Scholarship, 167
Urban Flight and Rural Needs Scholarship Program, 344

Montana

Aloha Scholarship, 135
American Legion Montana Auxiliary Scholarships (1), 135
American Legion Montana Auxiliary Scholarships (2), 135
Burlington Northern Santa Fe Foundation Scholarship, 109
Cady McDonnell Memorial Scholarship, 98
Governor's Postsecondary Scholarship, 347
Horatio Alger Montana Scholarship Program, 284
Legacy of Hope, 478
Mary Lou Brown Scholarship, 166
Montana Higher Education Grant, 347
Montana Tuition Fee Waiver for Veterans, 347
Montana University System Community College Honor Scholarship, 347
Montana University System Honor Scholarship, 348
MTA Doug Slifka Memorial Scholarship, 348
Rocky Mountain Coal Mining Scholarship, 435
Treacy Company Scholarship, 493

Nebraska

American Legion Nebraska Oratorical Contest, 137
American Legion Nebraska President's Scholarship, 137
Averyl Elaine Keriakedes Memorial Scholarship, 138
David Arver Memorial Scholarship, 83
Edgar J. Boschult Memorial Scholarship, 137
Graduate Scholarship, 138
Horatio Alger Ak-Sar-Ben Scholarship Program, 280
Junior Member Scholarship, 138
Maynard Jensen American Legion Memorial Scholarship, 137
Midwest Student Exchange Program, 338
Nebraska Robert C. Byrd Honors Scholarship, 385
North Central Region Scholarship, 455
Nurse Gift Tuition Scholarships, 138
Paul and Helen L. Grauer Scholarship, 167
The PHD ARA Scholarship, 167
Practical Nurse Scholarship, 138
The Richard W. Bendicksen Memorial Scholarship, 167
Roberta Marie Stretch Memorial Scholarship, 138
Ruby Paul Campaign Fund Scholarship, 138
Student Aid Grant or Vocational Technical Scholarship, 139

Nevada

American Legion Nevada Oratorical Contest, 139
Associated Press/APTRA-CLETE Roberts Memorial Journalism Scholarship, 197
Cady McDonnell Memorial Scholarship, 98
Carl N. & Margaret Karcher Founders' Scholarship, 214
Italian Catholic Federation Scholarship, 299
NASA Space Grant Nevada Undergraduate Scholarship, 357
Nevada Robert C. Byrd Honors Scholarship, 385
Nevada Student Incentive Grant, 386
Northern California Chapter/Richard Epping Scholarship, 181
Past President's Parley Nurses' Scholarship, 139
President's Scholarship and Junior Scholarship, 139
Silver Eagle Indian Scholarship, 139
William J. and Marijane E. Adams, Jr., Mechanical Engineering Scholarship, 177

67

New Hampshire

Abbie Sargent Memorial Scholarship, 75
Albert T. Marcoux Memorial Scholarship, 140
American Legion New Hampshire Boys State Scholarship, 140
American Legion New Hampshire Oratorical Contest, 140
Christa McAuliffe Memorial Scholarship, 140
Columbus Citizens Foundation College Scholarship Program, 223
Department of New Hampshire Scholarship, 140
Department Vocational Scholarship, 140
Dr. James L. Lawson Memorial Scholarship, 164
Grace S. High Memorial Child Welfare Scholarship Fund, 141
Leaf Loan Program, 585
Lighthouse College-Bound Award, 321
Lighthouse Graduate Award, 321
Lighthouse Undergraduate Award, 322
Marion J. Bagley Scholarship, 141
Massachusetts MASSgrant Program, 333
New England Board of Higher Education's Regional Student Program, 386
The New England FEMARA Scholarship, 167
New Hampshire Incentive Program, 386
New Hampshire Scholarship for Orphans of Veterans, 386
New Jersey STARS II, 388
Past President's Parley Nurses' Scholarship, 141
Timothy Bigelow Scholarship, 287
Workforce Incentive Program, 586

New Jersey

AIA New Jersey Scholarship Foundation, Inc., 111
Alfred R. Chisholm Memorial Scholarship, 498
American Legion New Jersey Auxiliary Department Scholarships, 142
American Legion New Jersey Oratorical Contest, 141
American Legion Press Club of New Jersey and Post 170--Arthur Dehardt Memorial Scholarship, 141
Caroline Thorn Kissel Summer Environmental Studies Scholarship, 252
The CBC Spouses Education Scholarship, 224
Claire Oliphant Memorial Scholarship, 142
Columbus Citizens Foundation College Scholarship Program, 223
Cymdeithas Gymreig (Welsh Society) Philadelphia Scholarship, 230
Dana Christmas Scholarship for Heroism, 388
David C. Goodwin Scholarship, 142
Educational Opportunity Fund (EOF), 388
Federal Family Education Loan Program, 586
Frank D. Visceglia Memorial Scholarship, 205
Horatio Alger New Jersey Scholarship Program, 284
Japanese American General Scholarship, 305
Jean Cebik Memorial Scholarship, 165
Lawrence Luterman Memorial Scholarships, 142
Lighthouse College-Bound Award, 321
Lighthouse Graduate Award, 321
Lighthouse Undergraduate Award, 322
New Jeresy Student Tuition Assistance Reward Scholarship (NJSTARS), 388
New Jersey Class Loan Program, 586
New Jersey Educational Opportunity Fund Grant, 387
New Jersey Edward J. Bloustein Distinguished Scholars, 388
New Jersey POW/MIA Program, 387
New Jersey Scholarship, 468
New Jersey Tuition Aid Grants (TAG), 389
New Jersey Urban Scholars, 389
New Jersey War Orphans Tuition Credit Program, 387
New Jersey World Trade Center Scholarship, 389
New York Women in Communications Foundation Scholarship, 396
Part-Time Tuition Aid Grant for County Colleges, 389
Past President's Parley Nurses' Scholarship, 143
Sonia Streuli Maguire Outstanding Scholastic Achievement Award, 481
Stutz Memorial Scholarship, 142
Swiss Benevolent Society Pellegrini Scholarship, 482
TGS Scholarship, 482
Water Companies (NJ Chapter) Scholarship, 367
Yankee Clipper Contest Club, Inc. Youth Scholarship, 168

New Mexico

Albuquerque ARC/Toby Cross Scholarship, 162
Burlington Northern Santa Fe Foundation Scholarship, 109
Cady McDonnell Memorial Scholarship, 98
Carl N. & Margaret Karcher Founders' Scholarship, 214
Central New Mexico Scholarship, 461
Fred R. McDaniel Memorial Scholarship, 164
NASA Space Grant New Mexico Undergraduate Scholarship, 357
New Mexico Allied Health Student Loan-for-Service Program, 586
New Mexico Competitive Scholarships, 390
New Mexico Legislative Endowment Program, 390
New Mexico Legislative Lottery Scholarship, 390
New Mexico Medical Student Loan-for-Service, 586
New Mexico Nursing Student Loan-for-Service, 587
New Mexico Scholars Program, 390
New Mexico Student Choice Program, 391
New Mexico Student Incentive Grant, 391
New Mexico Teacher's Loan-for-Service, 587
New Mexico Vietnam Veteran's Scholarship, 391
New Mexico Work-Study Program, 558
President's Parley Scholarship for Teachers of Exceptional Children, 143
Rocky Mountain Coal Mining Scholarship, 435
Shell Legislative Internship Program, 556
Walt Bartram Memorial Education Award (Region 12 and Chapter 119), 455

New York

Albert E. Wischmeyer Memorial Scholarship Award, 449
American Legion New York Auxiliary Scholarship, 144
American Legion New York Oratorical Contest, 143
Caroline Kark Scholarship, 392
The CBC Spouses Education Scholarship, 224
Christian Wolffer Scholarship, 302
CITE-NY Association Scholarship, 227
City University Seek/College Discovery Program, 393
Columbus Citizens Foundation College Scholarship Program, 223
Dr. James L. Lawson Memorial Scholarship, 164
Flight 587 Memorial Scholarships, 393
Grange Denise Scholarship, 392
Grange Student Loan Fund, 587
Grange Susan W. Freestone Education Award, 393
The Henry Broughton, K2AE Memorial Scholarship, 165
Hispanic Youth Leaders Scholarship, 346

State of Residence: Ohio

Horatio Alger New York Scholarship Program, 284
Japanese American General Scholarship, 305
June Gill Nursing Scholarship, 393
Leaders of Tomorrow Scholarship, 391
Lighthouse College-Bound Award, 321
Lighthouse Graduate Award, 321
Lighthouse Undergraduate Award, 322
MCC Theater Internships, 550
Military Service Recognition Scholarship (MSRS), 393
Moody's Mega Math "M3" Challenge, 348
The NCDXF Scholarship, 166
New York American Legion Press Association Scholarship, 144
New York State Aid for Part-time Study Program, 394
New York State Higher Education Opportunity Program (HEOP), 392
New York State Memorial Scholarship for Families of Deceased Police/Volunteer Firefighters/Peace Officers and Emergency Medical Service Workers, 394
New York State Native American Student Aid Program, 396
New York State Readers Aid Program, 392
New York State Regents Awards for Children of Deceased and Disabled Veterans, 394
New York State Robert C. Byrd Federal Honors Scholarship, 392
New York State Tuition Assistance Program, 394
New York State Veterans Tuition Award, 395
New York State Volunteer Recruitment Service Scholarship, 395
New York Women in Communications Foundation Scholarship, 396
Past President's Parley Student Nurses Scholarship for Girls or Boys, 144
Peter F. Vallone Academic Scholarship, 220
Quality of Life Research Competition, 524
Shell Legislative Internship Program, 556
Sonia Streuli Maguire Outstanding Scholastic Achievement Award, 481
Swiss Benevolent Society Pellegrini Scholarship, 482
Women's Architectural Auxiliary Eleanor Allwork Scholarship Grants, 111

North Carolina

The CBC Spouses Education Scholarship, 224
Community College Grant & Loan, 587
Dana Campbell Memorial Scholarship, 303
The Dayton Amateur Radio Association Scholarships, 163
GlaxoSmithKline Opportunity Scholarship, 399
Golden LEAF Scholars Program - Two-Year Colleges, 399
Golden LEAF Scholarship - Four-Year University Program, 399
Jagannathan Scholarship, 221
L. Phil Wicker Scholarship, 166
Latino Diamante Scholarship Fund, 400
Lighthouse College-Bound Award, 321
Lighthouse Graduate Award, 321
Lighthouse Undergraduate Award, 322
Maya Angelou/Vivian Baxter Scholarship, 500
NC Sherrif's Association Criminal Justice Scholarship, 400
North Carolina Aubrey Lee Brooks Scholarship, 400
North Carolina Community Colleges Wachovia Technical Scholarship, 398
North Carolina Legislative Tuition Grant, 400
North Carolina Nurse Scholars Program, 588
North Carolina Scholarships for Children of War Veterans, 398
North Carolina State Board of Refrigeration Examiners Scholarship, 399
North Carolina Student Incentive Grant, 221
North Carolina Student Loans for Health/Science/Mathematics, 588
North Carolina Vocational Rehabilitation Award, 399
Ray Jeffries Scholarship, 398
Rene Campbell Memorial Scholarship, 491
Rodney E. Powell Memorial Scholarship, 398
State Contractual Scholarship Fund, 401
Teacher Assistant Scholarship Fund, 401
Troy Douglas Carr Scholarship for Criminal Justice, 494
Undergraduate Research Scholarship, 358
Undergraduate Scholarship Program, 358

North Dakota

American Legion North Dakota Auxiliary Scholarships, 145
American Legion North Dakota Oratorical Contest, 144
Burlington Northern Santa Fe Foundation Scholarship, 109
David Arver Memorial Scholarship, 83
Horatio Alger North Dakota Scholarship Program, 284
Midwest Student Exchange Program, 338
NASA Space Grant North Dakota Consortium Lillian Goettler Scholarship, 358
NASA Space Grant North Dakota Undergraduate Scholarship, 358
North Central Region Scholarship, 455
North Dakota Indian Scholarship Program, 401
North Dakota Scholars Program, 401
North Dakota State Student Incentive Grant, 401
Past President's Parley Scholarship, 145
Pearl I. Young Scholarship, 358
Rocky Mountain Coal Mining Scholarship, 435
South Dakota Ardell Bjugstad Scholarship, 473
Treacy Company Scholarship, 493

Ohio

American Legion Ohio Auxiliary Past President's Parley Nurse's Scholarship, 145
American Legion Ohio Auxiliary Scholarship, 146
The CBC Spouses Education Scholarship, 224
David L. Stashower Scholarship, 321
Department Oratorical Awards, 145
Engineers Foundation of Ohio Scholarships, 242
Harold K. Douthit Scholarship, 405
Katharine M. Grosscup Scholarship, 253
NASA Ohio Space Grant Junior/Senior Scholarship Program, 359
NCR Summer Internships, 558
The NEMAL Electronics Scholarship, 166
Ohio Academic Scholarship, 403
Ohio College Opportunity Grant, 403
Ohio Instructional Grant, 403
Ohio National Guard Scholarship Program, 404
Ohio Newspaper Association Publications/Public Relations Internship, 564
Ohio Newspaper Services, Inc. Advertising Internship, 564
Ohio Newspaper Women's Scholarship, 405
Ohio Newspapers Minority Scholarship, 405
Ohio Nurse Education Assistance Loan Program, 588
Ohio Safety Officers College Memorial Fund, 403
Ohio Student Choice Grant, 404
Ohio War Orphans Scholarship, 404

69

State of Residence: Ohio

Part-time Student Instructional Grant Program, 404
University Journalism Scholarship, 405
The Zachary Taylor Stevens Memorial Scholarship, 169

Oklahoma

Academic Scholars Program, 406
Bryan Close Polo Grill Scholarship, 302
Burlington Northern Santa Fe Foundation Scholarship, 109
Carl N. & Margaret Karcher Founders' Scholarship, 214
Chapter 52 - Wichita Scholarship, 451
Dana Campbell Memorial Scholarship, 303
Fred R. McDaniel Memorial Scholarship, 164
Future Teachers Scholarship, 406
Heartland Scholarship Fund, 407
Independent Living Act (Department of Human Services Tuition Waiver), 407
National Guard Tuition Waiver, 407
Oklahoma Engineering Foundation Scholarship, 406
Oklahoma Tuition Aid Grant, 407
Oklahoma's Promise - OHLAP (Oklahoma Higher Learning Access Program), 407
Regional University Baccalaureate Scholarship, 407
Robert C. Byrd Honors Scholarship Program, 406
Tom and Judith Comstock Scholarship, 168

Oregon

Ahmad-Sehar Saleha Ahmad and Abrahim Ekramullah Zafar Foundation, 409
Albina Fuel Company Scholarship, 409
Allcott/Hunt Share It Now II Scholarship, 409
Alpha Delta Kappa/Harriet Simmons Scholarship, 409
American Council of Engineering Companies of Oregon Scholarship, 409
American Ex-Prisoner of War, Peter Connacher Memorial Scholarship, 410
American Federation of State, County, and Municipal Employees (AFSCME) Oregon Council # 75, 410
American Legion Department Oratorical Contest, 146
American Legion Oregon Auxiliary Department Nurses Scholarship, 146
American Society for Training and Development -- Cascadia Chapter Scholarship, 410

The Audria M. Edwards Scholarship Fund, 422
Bandon Submarine Cable Council Scholarship, 410
Bank of the Cascades Scholarship, 411
Ben Selling Scholarship, 411
Benjamin Franklin/Edith Green Scholarship, 411
Bertha P. Singer Scholarship, 411
Burlington Northern Santa Fe Foundation Scholarship, 109
Cady McDonnell Memorial Scholarship, 98
Carl N. & Margaret Karcher Founders' Scholarship, 214
Chafee Education and Training Scholarship, 411
Crowley Family Scholarship, 412
David Family Scholarship, 412
Dorothy Campbell Memorial Scholarship, 412
DPMA/PC Scholarship, 232
Eugene Bennet Visual Arts Scholarship, 412
Fashion Group International of Portland Scholarship, 412
Ford Opportunity Program, 413
Ford Scholars Program, 413
Glenn Jackson Scholars, 413
Grange Insurance Scholarship, 260
Homestead Capital Housing Scholarship, 413
Horatio Alger Oregon Scholarship Program, 285
Howard Vollum American Indian Scholarship, 413
Ida M. Crawford Scholarship, 414
Jackson Foundation Journalism Scholarship, 414
James Carlson Memorial Scholarship, 414
Jerome B. Steinbach Scholarship, 414
Jose D. Garcia Migrant Education Scholarship, 415
Kaiser-Permanente Dental Assistant Scholarship, 415
The Kaj Christensen Scholarship for Vocational Training, 402
Laurence R. Foster Memorial Scholarship, 415
Maria C. Jackson-General George A. White Scholarship, 415
Mary Lou Brown Scholarship, 166
NASA Space Grant Oregon Undergraduate Scholarship, 359
National President's Scholarship, 146
Oregon Collectors Association Bob Hasson Memorial Scholarship Fund Essay, 416
Oregon Dungeness Crab Commission, 416
Oregon Foundation for Blacktail Deer Outdoor & Wildlife Scholarship, 416
Oregon Occupational Safety and Health Division Workers Memorial Scholarship, 416

Oregon Robert C. Byrd Honors Scholarship, 417
Oregon Scholarship Fund Community College Student, 417
Professional Land Surveyors of Oregon Scholarship, 417
Richard F. Brentano Memorial Scholarship, 417
Roger W. Emmons Memorial Scholarship, 417
Spirit of Youth Scholarship, 146
Teamsters Clyde C. Crosby/Joseph M. Edgar Memorial Scholarship, 418
Teamsters Council #37 Federal Credit Union Scholarship, 418
Teamsters Local 305 Scholarship, 418
Walter and Marie Schmidt Scholarship, 418

Pennsylvania

American Restaurant Scholarship, 302
ASHRAE J. Richard Mehalick Scholarship, 172
The CBC Spouses Education Scholarship, 224
Columbus Citizens Foundation College Scholarship Program, 223
Cymdeithas Gymreig (Welsh Society) Philadelphia Scholarship, 230
Dr. & Mrs. Arthur William Phillips Scholarship, 424
George Griffiths/Ada Jakubic Scholarship, 424
Horatio Alger Franklin Scholarship, 281
Horatio Alger Pennsylvania Scholarship Program, 285
James Hughes Memorial Scholarship Fund, 424
John McKee Scholarship, 334
Joseph P. Gavenonis Scholarship, 147
Katharine M. Grosscup Scholarship, 253
Lighthouse College-Bound Award, 321
Lighthouse Graduate Award, 321
Lighthouse Undergraduate Award, 322
Massachusetts MASSgrant Program, 333
Minnie Patton Stayman Scholarship, 424
NASA Academy Internship, 555
NASA Pennsylvania Space Grant Undergraduate Scholarship, 359
New York Women in Communications Foundation Scholarship, 396
Pennsylvania Robert C. Byrd Honors Scholarship, 422
Pennsylvania State Grant Program, 423
Pennsylvania Work-Study Program, 423
PHEAA Academic Excellence Scholarship Award Program, 423
Rainbow Scholarship, 430
Robert Noyce Scholarship Program, 425

State of Residence: Texas

Robert W. Valimont Endowment Fund Scholarship, 147
Scholarship for Children of Deceased or Totally Disabled Veterans, 147
Scholarship for Children of Living Veterans, 147
SciTech Scholarship, 423
Shannon Scholarship, 493
Sonia Streuli Maguire Outstanding Scholastic Achievement Award, 481
Swiss Benevolent Society Pellegrini Scholarship, 482
Technology Scholarship, 423
Wayne G. Failor Scholarship, 425
West Virginia Higher Education Grant, 519

Puerto Rico

American Legion Puerto Rico Auxiliary Nursing Scholarships, 147

Rhode Island

College Bound Fund Academic Promise Scholarship, 435
Columbus Citizens Foundation College Scholarship Program, 223
Dr. James L. Lawson Memorial Scholarship, 164
Lighthouse College-Bound Award, 321
Lighthouse Graduate Award, 321
Lighthouse Undergraduate Award, 322
Massachusetts MASSgrant Program, 333
NASA Space Grant Rhode Island Summer Undergraduate Scholarship, 360
New England Board of Higher Education's Regional Student Program, 386
The New England FEMARA Scholarship, 167
New Jersey STARS II, 388
Rhode Island State Grant, 435
Timothy Bigelow Scholarship, 287
Undergraduate Research Scholarship, 360

South Carolina

American Legion South Carolina Auxiliary Scholarship, 148
American Legion South Carolina Department Oratorical Contest, 148
The CBC Spouses Education Scholarship, 224
C.G. Fuller Foundation Scholarship, 217
Charleston Women in International Trade Scholarship, 218
Dana Campbell Memorial Scholarship, 303
James F. Byrnes Scholarship, 305
Kathryn D. Sullivan Science and Engineering Fellowship, 361
L. Phil Wicker Scholarship, 166

LIFE Scholarship Program, 472
Lighthouse College-Bound Award, 321
Lighthouse Graduate Award, 321
Lighthouse Undergraduate Award, 322
Lottery Tuition Assistance Program, 472
NASA Space Grant South Carolina Undergraduate Academic Year Research Program, 361
NCR Summer Internships, 558
Palmetto Fellows Scholarship Program, 472
South Carolina HOPE Scholarships, 472
South Carolina Need-Based Grants Program, 472
South Carolina Teacher Loans, 589
South Carolina Tuition Grants, 473

South Dakota

American Legion South Dakota Auxiliary Nurse's Scholarship, 148
American Legion South Dakota Auxiliary Scholarships, 149
American Legion South Dakota Educational Loan, 578
American Legion South Dakota Oratorical Contest, 148
Burlington Northern Santa Fe Foundation Scholarship, 109
David Arver Memorial Scholarship, 83
Horatio Alger South Dakota Scholarship Program, 285
North Central Region Scholarship, 455
Scholarship for College or Vocational, 149
South Dakota Annis I. Fowler/Kaden Scholarship, 473
South Dakota Ardell Bjugstad Scholarship, 473
South Dakota Haines Memorial Scholarship, 474
South Dakota Marlin R. Scarborough Memorial Scholarship, 474
South Dakota National Guard Tuition Assistance, 474
South Dakota Robert C. Byrd Honors Scholarship, 474
Thelma Foster Junior American Legion Auxiliary Members Scholarship, 149
Thelma Foster Senior American Legion Auxiliary Member Scholarship, 149
Treacy Company Scholarship, 493

Tennessee

American Legion Tennessee Oratorical Contest, 149
Eagle Scout of the Year Scholarship, 150
HOPE-Aspire Award, 483
Hope-General Assembly Merit Scholarship, 483

Tennessee Christa McAuliffe Scholarship Program, 483
Tennessee Dependent Children Scholarship Program, 483
Tennessee HOPE Access Grant, 483
Tennessee HOPE Scholarship, 484
Tennessee Minority Teaching Fellows Program, 590
Tennessee Ned McWherter Scholars Program, 484
Tennessee Robert C. Byrd Honors Scholarship Program, 484
Tennessee Student Assistance Award Program, 484
Tennessee Student Assistance Corporation/Math And Science Teachers Loan Forgiveness Program, 590
Tennessee Teaching Scholars Program, 590
Vara Gray Scholarship Fund, 150
Wally Joe (KC's) Scholarship, 305
Wilder-Naifeh Technical Skills Grant, 484

Texas

American Legion Texas Auxiliary General Education Scholarship, 150
American Legion Texas Auxiliary Medical Scholarship, 150
Area Go Texan Scholarships, 288
Carl N. & Margaret Karcher Founders' Scholarship, 214
The CBC Spouses Education Scholarship, 224
Chuck Fulgham Scholarship Fund, 231
Dallas Architectural Foundation - Arch Swank, Jr. Fellowship in the Craft of Architecture, 231
Dana Campbell Memorial Scholarship, 303
Dr. Don and Rose Marie Benton Scholarship, 231
Educational Aide Exemption, 485
Exemption for Peace Officers Disabled in the Line of Duty, 485
Exemption for the Surviving Spouse and Dependent Children of Certain Deceased Public Servants (Employees), 485
Franklin Lindsay Student Aid Loan, 581
Fred R. McDaniel Memorial Scholarship, 164
The George Foreman Tribute to Lyndon B. Johnson Scholarship, 432
Hinson-Hazlewood College Access Loan (CAL), 590
HKS/John Humphries Minority Scholarship, 231
Horatio Alger Texas Ft. Worth Scholarship Program, 285
Horatio Alger Texas Scholarship Program, 285

71

State of Residence: Texas

Jere W. Thompson, Jr., Scholarship Fund, 232
Opportunity Scholarship, 288
Reduction in Tuition Charges for Students Taking 15 or More Semester Credit Hours Per Term, 485
Robert C. Byrd Honors Scholarship, 486
Rocky Mountain Coal Mining Scholarship, 435
RoyceBuilders.com Foundation for Youth Scholarship, 438
Shell Legislative Internship Program, 556
TANF (Temporary Assistance to Needy Families) Exemption, 486
Texas College Work-Study Program, 486
Texas Early High School Graduation Scholarship, 486
Texas Fifth-Year Accounting Student Scholarship Program, 487
Texas Foster Care Students Exemption, 487
Texas Good Neighbor Scholarship, 487
TEXAS Grant (Toward Excellence, Access, and Success), 487
Texas Hazlewood Act Tuition Exemption: Veterans, 487
Texas Highest Ranking High School Graduate Tuition Exemption, 488
Texas Legion Oratorical Contest, 150
Texas National Guard Tuition Assistance Program, 488
Texas Public Educational Grant, 488
Texas Scholarships for Nursing Students, 488
Texas Tuition Exemption for Blind or Deaf Students, 488
Tom and Judith Comstock Scholarship, 168
Tuition Equalization Grant (TEG), 489
Tuition Exemption for Children of Disabled or Deceased Firefighters, Peace Officers, Game Wardens, and Employees of Correctional Institutions, 489
Tuition Exemption for Children of U.S. Military POW/MIAs from Texas, 489
Tuition Rebate for Certain Undergraduates, 489
Wendy Ella Guilford Scholarship Fund, 232

U.S. Territories

National Co-op Scholarship, 369

Utah

American Legion Utah Auxiliary National President's Scholarship, 151
Cady McDonnell Memorial Scholarship, 98
Carl N. & Margaret Karcher Founders' Scholarship, 214
Horatio Alger Utah Scholarship Program, 286
Leveraging Educational Assistance Partnership (LEAP), 508
Rocky Mountain Coal Mining Scholarship, 435
UHEAA Grant, 508
Utah Career Teaching Scholarship/T.H. Bell Teaching Incentive Loan, 592
Utah Centennial Opportunity Program for Education (UCOPE), 508
Utah Robert C. Byrd Honors Scholarship, 509

Vermont

American Legion Eagle Scout of the Year, 151
American Legion Vermont Scholarship, 151
American Legion Vermont Scholarship Program, 151
Champlain Valley Kennel Club Scholarship, 510
Chittenden Bank Scholarship, 510
Columbus Citizens Foundation College Scholarship Program, 223
Dr. James L. Lawson Memorial Scholarship, 164
Emily Lester Vermont Opportunity Scholarship, 510
Green Mountain Dog Club Scholarship, 510
Jebidiah Zabrosky Scholarship, 511
Lighthouse College-Bound Award, 321
Lighthouse Graduate Award, 321
Lighthouse Undergraduate Award, 322
Massachusetts MASSgrant Program, 333
Michael and Deborah Weinberg Scholarship, 511
NASA Space Grant Vermont Consortium Undergraduate Scholarships, 362
National Association of Women in Construction Scholarship, 511
National High School Oratorical Contest, 151
New England Board of Higher Education's Regional Student Program, 386
The New England FEMARA Scholarship, 167
New Jersey STARS II, 388
Philip and Alice Angell Eastern Star Scholarship, 511
Samara Foundation of Vermont Scholarship, 511
Timothy Bigelow Scholarship, 287
Vermont Golf Association Scholarship, 509
Vermont Incentive Grant, 512
Vermont Non-Degree Program, 512
Vermont Part-Time Grant, 512
VSAC Advantage Loan, 592

Virgin Islands

The CBC Spouses Education Scholarship, 224
Virgin Islands Leveraging Educational Assistance Partnership Program, 513
Virgin Islands Music Scholarship, 513
Virgin Islands Territorial Grants/Loans Program, 592

Virginia

Aerospace Undergraduate Research Scholarship Program, 362
American Legion Virginia Oratorical Contest, 152
Anna Gear Junior Scholarship, 152
Carville M. Akehurst Memorial Scholarship, 287
The CBC Spouses Education Scholarship, 224
Dana Campbell Memorial Scholarship, 303
Dr. Kate Waller Barrett Grant, 152
Horatio Alger District of Columbia, Maryland and Virgina Scholarship Program, 281
L. Phil Wicker Scholarship, 166
Lighthouse College-Bound Award, 321
Lighthouse Graduate Award, 321
Lighthouse Undergraduate Award, 322
Mary Marshall Nursing Scholarship, 513
NASA Space Grant Virginia Community College Scholarship, 362
Nurse Practitioner Nurse Midwife Scholarship, 514
Oracle Scholars Internship Program, 572
Richmond Scholarship, 501
Virginia Academic Common Market, 476
Virginia Lee-Jackson Scholarship, 513
Virginia Museum of Fine Arts Fellowship, 514
Virginia Rehabilitative Services College Program, 514
Virginia Robert C. Byrd Honors Scholarship, 513
Virginia Tuition Assistance Grant, 476
Virginia Vocational Rehabilitation Program Education Sponsorship, 238

Washington

Albina Fuel Company Scholarship, 409
American Legion Department Oratorical Contest, 152
American Legion Washington Auxiliary Scholarships, 153
American Legion Washington Scholarships, 152

American Society for Training and Development -- Cascadia Chapter Scholarship, 410
Arthur and Doreen Parrett Scholarship, 193
Association for Women in Communications Scholarship, 199
The Audria M. Edwards Scholarship Fund, 422
Burlington Northern Santa Fe Foundation Scholarship, 109
Cady McDonnell Memorial Scholarship, 98
Carl N. & Margaret Karcher Founders' Scholarship, 214
DPMA/PC Scholarship, 232
Edmund F. Maxwell Foundation Scholarship, 241
Fashion Group International of Portland Scholarship, 412
Florence Lemcke Memorial Scholarship, 153
Fred G. Zahn Foundation Scholarship, 251
Grange Insurance Scholarship, 260
Homestead Capital Housing Scholarship, 413
Horatio Alger Washington Scholarship Program, 286
Howard Vollum American Indian Scholarship, 413
Kaiser-Permanente Dental Assistant Scholarship, 415
The Kaj Christensen Scholarship for Vocational Training, 402
Margarite McAlpin Nurse's Scholarship, 153
Mary Lou Brown Scholarship, 166
National Co-op Scholarship, 369
Seattle Jaycees Scholarship, 441
Susan Burdett Scholarship, 153
Washington State American Indian Endowed Scholarship, 516
Washington State Educational Opportunity Grant, 516
Washington State Need Grant, 516
Washington State PTA Financial Grant Program, 517
Washington State Scholars Program, 516

West Virginia

American Legion West Virginia Auxiliary Scholarship, 154
American Legion West Virginia Oratorical Contest, 153
Carville M. Akehurst Memorial Scholarship, 287
Dana Campbell Memorial Scholarship, 303
Greater Kanawha Valley Scholarship Program, 260
Herschel C. Price Educational Scholarship, 276
Katharine M. Grosscup Scholarship, 253
L. Phil Wicker Scholarship, 166
Lighthouse College-Bound Award, 321
Lighthouse Graduate Award, 321
Lighthouse Undergraduate Award, 322
NASA West Virginia Space Grant Undergraduate Research Fellowship, 363
PROMISE Scholarship, 518
West Virginia Engineering, Science and Technology Scholarship, 518
West Virginia Higher Education Adult Part-time Student (HEAPS) Grant Program, 519
West Virginia Higher Education Grant, 519
West Virginia Robert C. Byrd Honors Scholarship, 519
West Virginia Underwood-Smith Teacher Scholarship, 593
The Zachary Taylor Stevens Memorial Scholarship, 169

Wisconsin

American Legion Baseball Scholarship, 154
American Legion Wisconsin Auxiliary Department President's Scholarship, 155
American Legion Wisconsin Auxiliary H.S. and Angeline Lewis Scholarships, 155
American Legion Wisconsin Auxiliary Merit and Memorial Scholarship, 155
American Legion Wisconsin Auxiliary Past Presidents Parley Scholarship, 155
American Legion Wisconsin Eagle Scout of the Year Scholarship, 154
Chapter 4 - Lawrence A. Wacker Memorial Scholarship, 450
The Chicago FM Club Scholarships, 163
David Arver Memorial Scholarship, 83
Della Van Deuren Memorial Scholarship, 155
Edmond A. Metzger Scholarship, 164
LaMacchia Family Scholarship, 491
Midwest Student Exchange Program, 338
North Central Region Scholarship, 455
Oratorical Contest Scholarships, 154
West Virginia War Orphans Educational Assistance, 518
Wisconsin Academic Excellence Scholarship, 522
Wisconsin Hearing & Visually Handicapped Student Grant, 522
Wisconsin Higher Education Grant, 522
Wisconsin Indian Student Assistance Grant, 522
Wisconsin Minority Teacher Loan Program, 593
Wisconsin Minority Undergraduate Retention Grant, 522
Wisconsin Talent Incentive Program Grant, 523
Wisconsin Tuition Grant, 523
Wisconsin Veterans Affairs Personal Loan Program, 593
Wisconsin Veterans Affairs Retraining Grant, 521
Wisconsin Veterans Education Tuition and Fee Reimbursement Grant, 521

Wyoming

American Legion Wyoming Auxiliary Past Presidents' Parley Scholarship, 156
American Legion Wyoming E.A. Blackmore Memorial Scholarship, 156
American Legion Wyoming Oratorical Contest, 156
Cady McDonnell Memorial Scholarship, 98
Davis-Roberts Scholarship, 236
Grange Insurance Scholarship, 260
Horatio Alger Wyoming Scholarship Program, 286
Rocky Mountain Coal Mining Scholarship, 435

Study Abroad

Academic-Year Ambassadorial Scholarship, 436
Anna K. Meredith Fund Scholarship, 478
Clare Brett Smith Scholarship, 478
Cultural Ambassadorial Scholarship, 436
Foreign Study/Diversity Scholarship, 109
Freeman-ASIA Award Program, 295
International Incentive Awards, 479
International Semester Scholarship, 110
Jules Maidoff Scholarship, 479
Kosciuszko Foundation Year Abroad Program, 314
Lele Cassin Scholarship, 479
Multi-Year Ambassadorial Scholarship, 437
NSBE Fellows Scholarship, 382
SACI Consortium Scholarship, 479
Scholarships for Children of SACI Alumni, 480
Swiss Benevolent Society Medicus Student Exchange, 481

Scholarships

1199 National Benefit Fund

Joseph Tauber Scholarship

Type of award: Scholarship, renewable.
Intended use: For full-time undergraduate or non-degree study at accredited vocational, 2-year or 4-year institution in or outside United States.
Eligibility: Applicant or parent must be member/participant of 1199 National Benefit Fund.
Basis for selection: Applicant must demonstrate financial need.
Application requirements: Transcript, proof of eligibility.
Additional information: High school graduates, postsecondary school students and previous awardees whose parents have been in Benefit Fund Wage Class One for one year at time of application are eligible. Visit Website for updates.

Amount of award:	$750-$10,000
Number of awards:	2,000
Number of applicants:	3,000
Application deadline:	April 18
Notification begins:	November 1
Total amount awarded:	$9,747,197

Contact:
1199 National Benefit Fund
330 West 42nd Street, 12th floor
New York, NY 10036
Phone: 646-473-9200
Web: www.1199NBF.org

Abbie Sargent Memorial Scholarship Fund

Abbie Sargent Memorial Scholarship

Type of award: Scholarship, renewable.
Intended use: For undergraduate or graduate study at accredited 2-year or 4-year institution.
Eligibility: Applicant must be residing in New Hampshire.
Basis for selection: Major/career interest in agriculture or veterinary medicine. Applicant must demonstrate financial need, high academic achievement and depth of character.
Application requirements: Transcript.
Additional information: Recipient may attend out-of-state university. Send SASE for application or download from Website. Award amount tentatively set at $400, but may vary from year to year depending on funding. Number of awards varies.

Number of applicants:	18
Application deadline:	March 15
Notification begins:	June 1

Contact:
Abbie Sargent Memorial Scholarship Fund
295 Sheep Davis Road
Concord, NH 03301
Phone: 603-224-1934
Web: www.nhfarmbureau.org

Academy of Television Arts & Sciences Foundation

College Television Award

Type of award: Scholarship.
Intended use: For full-time undergraduate or graduate study in United States.
Basis for selection: Competition/talent/interest in visual arts, based on excellence of submitted film/video. Major/career interest in radio/television/film.
Application requirements: DVD, VHS, or beta of original film/video made for course credit within eligibility period. Piece must have been produced while registered in school and related to either a class or school club during the eligibility period. All works submitted online. Must be student producer of record. Composers may enter in best composition category.
Additional information: Award for student producer of student video, digital and film work in the following categories: Animation (all forms), Children's, Comedy, Comedy Series, Commercial, Documentary, Drama, Drama Series, magazine, Music (Best Composition), Music (Best Use), Newscast. Bricker Humanitarian award of $4000 is presented to the first or second place winner whose work best represents a humanitarian concern. Best directing award is presented for outstanding direction for a documentary, drama or comedy. Please visit Website for application. Yearly updated official entry form must be submitted.

Amount of award:	$500-$2,000
Number of awards:	25
Application deadline:	January 15
Notification begins:	February 15

Contact:
Academy of Television Arts & Sciences Foundation
College Television Awards
5220 Lankershim Boulevard
North Hollywood, CA 91601-3109
Phone: 818-754-2800
Fax: 818-509-2266
Web: www.emmysfoundation.org

The Fred Rogers Memorial Scholarship

Type of award: Scholarship.
Intended use: For junior, senior or graduate study.
Basis for selection: Major/career interest in education, early childhood; film/video or music.

Academy of Television Arts & Sciences Foundation: The Fred Rogers Memorial Scholarship

Application requirements: Two recommendations from faculty members in associated fields or professionals in children's media industry who have worked with applicant.
Additional information: Applicant must have ultimate goal of working in children's media and must have studied or have experience in at least two of the following fields: early childhood education, child development/child psychology, film/television production, music, or animation. Download application from Website.

Amount of award:	$10,000
Number of awards:	3
Number of applicants:	87
Application deadline:	February 15
Total amount awarded:	$10,000

Contact:
Academy of Television Arts & Sciences Foundation
Attention: Michele Fowble
5220 Lankershim Blvd.
North Hollywood, CA 91601-3109
Phone: 818-754-2802
Web: www.emmysfoundation.org

ACFE Foundation

Ritchie-Jennings Memorial Scholarship

Type of award: Scholarship.
Intended use: For full-time undergraduate or graduate study at 4-year or graduate institution.
Basis for selection: Major/career interest in criminal justice/law enforcement or accounting.
Application requirements: Recommendations, essay, transcript. Essay must be no more than 500 words and must explain why the applicant deserves scholarship and how the awareness of fraud will affect his or her professional career development. Three letters of recommendation, including at least one from Certified Fraud Examiner or local CFE chapter, plus additional recommendations from employer, faculty members or academic advisers.
Additional information: Visit Website for deadlines and additional information.

Amount of award:	$1,000
Number of awards:	30
Number of applicants:	150

Contact:
Association of Certified Fraud Examiners
The Gregor Building
716 West Avenue
Austin, TX 78701
Phone: 800-245-3321
Fax: 512-478-9297
Web: www.acfe.com/membership/rjennings.asp

The Actuarial Foundation

Wooddy Scholarship

Type of award: Scholarship.
Intended use: For full-time senior study at 4-year institution.
Eligibility: Applicant must be U.S. citizen or permanent resident.
Basis for selection: Major/career interest in insurance/actuarial science. Applicant must demonstrate high academic achievement and leadership.
Application requirements: Recommendations, essay, transcript.
Additional information: Applicant must have passed at least one actuarial examination and must rank in the top quarter of class. Application is available on Website. Immediate relatives of members of the Board of Trustees of the Actuarial Foundation or boards of affiliated organizations are not eligible to apply.

Amount of award:	$2,000
Number of awards:	4
Application deadline:	June 27
Notification begins:	August 29
Total amount awarded:	$8,000

Contact:
The Actuarial Foundation
475 N. Martingale Road, Suite 600
Schaumburg, IL 60173-2226
Phone: 847-706-3600
Fax: 847-706-3599
Web: www.actuarialfoundation.org/research_edu/prize_award.htm#wooddy

ADA Foundation

Allied Dental Scholarship for Dental Assisting Students

Type of award: Scholarship.
Intended use: For full-time freshman study in United States. Designated institutions: Institutions accredited by Commission on Dental Accreditation of the American Dental Association.
Eligibility: Applicant must be U.S. citizen.
Basis for selection: Major/career interest in dental assistant. Applicant must demonstrate financial need and high academic achievement.
Application requirements: Typed biographical questionnaire, two sealed references, copy of school's acceptance letter.
Additional information: Applicants must have minimum 3.0 GPA. Applicants must be entering students enrolled in dental assisting program. Full-time study equals no less than 12 credit hours. Must demonstrate minimum financial need of $1,000. Applicants must contact school's dental assisting program director for applications as ADA Foundation accepts only two applications from each program.

Amount of award:	$1,000
Number of awards:	10
Application deadline:	September 5
Notification begins:	November 5
Total amount awarded:	$10,000

Contact:
ADA Foundation Rose Famularo
Scholarship Coordinator
211 East Chicago Avenue
Chicago, IL 60611-2678
Phone: 312-440-2763
Fax: 312-440-3526
Web: www.adafoundation.org

Allied Dental Scholarship for Dental Hygiene Students

Type of award: Scholarship.
Intended use: For full-time undergraduate study in United States. Designated institutions: Institutions accredited by Commission on Dental Accreditation of the American Dental Association.
Eligibility: Applicant must be U.S. citizen.
Basis for selection: Major/career interest in dental hygiene. Applicant must demonstrate financial need and high academic achievement.
Application requirements: Typed biographical questionnaire, two sealed references.
Additional information: Minimum 3.0 GPA. Applicant must be entering last year of study. Full-time study equals no less than 12 credit hours. Must demonstrate minimum financial need of $1,000. Applicant must contact school's dental hygiene program director for application as ADA accepts only two applications from each program.

Amount of award:	$1,000
Number of awards:	15
Application deadline:	June 2
Notification begins:	August 2
Total amount awarded:	$15,000

Contact:
ADA Foundation Rose Famularo
Scholarship Coordinator
211 East Chicago Avenue
Chicago, IL 60611-2678
Phone: 312-440-2763
Fax: 312-440-3526
Web: www.adafoundation.org

Allied Dental Scholarship for Dental Laboratory Technology Students

Type of award: Scholarship.
Intended use: For full-time undergraduate study in United States. Designated institutions: Institutions accredited by Commission on Dental Accreditation of the American Dental Association.
Eligibility: Applicant must be U.S. citizen.
Basis for selection: Major/career interest in dental laboratory technology. Applicant must demonstrate financial need and high academic achievement.
Application requirements: Typed biographical questionnaire, two sealed references.
Additional information: Applicants must have minimum 3.0 GPA. Applicants must be entering last year of study. Full-time study equals no less than 12 credit hours. Must demonstrate minimum financial need of $1,000. Applicant must contact school's dental laboratory program director for application as the ADA Foundation accepts only two applications from each program.

Amount of award:	$1,000
Number of awards:	5
Application deadline:	September 5
Notification begins:	November 5
Total amount awarded:	$5,000

Contact:
ADA Foundation Rose Famularo
Scholarship Coordinator
211 East Chicago Avenue
Chicago, IL 60611-2678
Phone: 312-440-2763
Fax: 312-440-3526
Web: www.adafoundation.org

ADHA Institute for Oral Health

ADHA Institute for Oral Health Part-Time Scholarship

Type of award: Scholarship, renewable.
Intended use: For half-time sophomore, junior, senior or graduate study at accredited 4-year or graduate institution in United States.
Basis for selection: Major/career interest in dental hygiene. Applicant must demonstrate financial need.
Application requirements: Recommendations, essay. FAFSA.
Additional information: Applicant must be member of ADHA or Student ADHA and have completed a minimum of one year in dental hygiene program. Minimum 3.0 dental hygiene GPA. Download application from Website. Applicants may apply for only one ADHA scholarship, but those not selected may be eligible for general scholarship.

Amount of award:	$1,500
Number of awards:	1
Application deadline:	May 1

Contact:
ADHA Institute for Oral Health
444 N. Michigan Ave., Suite 3400
Chicago, IL 60611
Phone: 800-735-4916
Fax: 312-467-1806
Web: www.adha.org/institute

ADHA Institute General Scholarships

Type of award: Scholarship, renewable.
Intended use: For full-time undergraduate study at accredited postsecondary institution in United States.
Eligibility: Applicant or parent must be member/participant of American Dental Hygienists' Association.
Basis for selection: Major/career interest in dental hygiene. Applicant must demonstrate financial need.
Application requirements: Recommendations, essay. FAFSA and financial needs form. Program director verification.
Additional information: Download application from Website. Minimum 3.0 GPA required. Applicants must have completed at least one year in dental hygiene program. Applicant must be member of ADHA or Student ADHA. Number of awards varies based on funding. Applicants may apply for only one ADHA scholarship, but those not selected may be eligible for other general scholarships.

Amount of award:	$1,500
Application deadline:	May 1

Contact:
ADHA Institute for Oral Health
Scholarship Award Program
444 N. Michigan Ave. Suite 3400
Chicago, IL 60611-3980
Phone: 800-735-4916
Fax: 312-467-1806
Web: www.adha.org/institute

ADHA Institute Merit Scholarships

Type of award: Scholarship.
Intended use: For full-time undergraduate or graduate study.
Basis for selection: Major/career interest in dental hygiene. Applicant must demonstrate high academic achievement.
Application requirements: Recommendations. Goals statement. Program director verification form.
Additional information: Must have completed one year of dental hygiene curriculum by award year; may apply during first year. Must be active ADHA or Student ADHA member with minimum dental hygiene 3.0 GPA. Graduate applicants must have active dental hygiene license and hold at least baccalaureate. Download application from Website. Number of awards varies. Applicants may apply for only one ADHA scholarship, but those not selected may be eligible for general scholarship.
   Application deadline: May 1
Contact:
ADHA Institute for Oral Health
Scholarship Award Program
444 N. Michigan Ave., Ste. 3400
Chicago, IL 60611-3980
Phone: 800-735-4916
Web: www.adha.org/institute

Cadbury Adams Community Outreach Scholarships

Type of award: Scholarship.
Intended use: For full-time undergraduate study at accredited 2-year or 4-year institution.
Basis for selection: Major/career interest in dental hygiene. Applicant must demonstrate financial need and service orientation.
Application requirements: Recommendations, essay. FAFSA, goals statement, program director verification form.
Additional information: Must demonstrate need of at least $1,500. Must have completed one year of dental hygiene curriculum by award year; may apply during first year. May be studying for certificate. Must be active ADHA or Student ADHA member with minimum dental hygiene 3.0 GPA. Must display commitment to improving community's oral health. Download application from Website. Applicants may apply for only one ADHA scholarship, but those not selected may be eligible for general scholarship.
   Amount of award: $1,500
   Number of awards: 15
   Application deadline: May 1
Contact:
ADHA Institute for Oral Health
Scholarship Award Program
444 N. Michigan Ave. Ste. 3400
Chicago, IL 60611-3980
Phone: 800-735-4916
Web: www.adha.org/institute

Colgate "Bright Smiles, Bright Futures" Minority Scholarships

Type of award: Scholarship, renewable.
Intended use: For full-time undergraduate certificate study in United States.
Eligibility: Applicant must be Asian American, African American, Mexican American, Hispanic American, Puerto Rican or American Indian.
Basis for selection: Major/career interest in dental hygiene. Applicant must demonstrate financial need and high academic achievement.
Application requirements: Recommendations, essay. FAFSA.
Additional information: Applicant must be member of ADHA or Student ADHA. Men are considered a minority in this field and are encouraged to apply for this program. Applicant must have completed at least one year of certificate-level dental hygiene program. Minimum 3.0 dental hygiene GPA. Download application from Website. Applicants may apply for only one ADHA scholarship, but those not selected may be eligible for general scholarship.
   Amount of award: $1,250
   Number of awards: 2
   Application deadline: May 1
Contact:
ADHA Institute for Oral Health
Scholarship Award Program
444 N. Michigan Ave., Suite 3400
Chicago, IL 60611-3980
Phone: 800-735-4916
Fax: 312-467-1806
Web: www.adha.org/institute

Dr. Alfred C. Fones Scholarship

Type of award: Scholarship.
Intended use: For full-time undergraduate study at accredited 4-year or graduate institution.
Basis for selection: Major/career interest in dental hygiene or education. Applicant must demonstrate financial need.
Application requirements: Recommendations. Goals statement (graduate students must send specific goals statement). FAFSA, program director verification form.
Additional information: Must have completed one year of dental hygiene curriculum by award year; may apply during first year. Must be active ADHA or Student ADHA member with minimum dental hygiene 3.0 GPA. Graduate applicants must have active dental hygiene license and hold at least baccalaureate. Download application from Website. Must demonstrate at least $1,500 of financial need. Must intend to become dental hygiene educator. Applicants may apply for only one ADHA scholarship, but those not selected may be eligible for general scholarship.
   Amount of award: $1,500
   Number of awards: 1
   Application deadline: May 1
Contact:
ADHA Institute for Oral Health
Scholarship Award Program
444 N. Michigan Ave., Ste. 3400
Chicago 60611-3980
Phone: 800-735-4916
Web: www.adha.org/institute

Dr. Harold Hillenbrand Scholarship

Type of award: Scholarship, renewable.

Intended use: For full-time sophomore, junior, senior or graduate study at accredited 4-year institution in United States.
Basis for selection: Major/career interest in dental hygiene. Applicant must demonstrate financial need and high academic achievement.
Application requirements: Recommendations, essay. FAFSA.
Additional information: Applicant must have completed a minimum of one year of dental hygiene program, have outstanding clinical performance and minimum 3.5 GPA in dental hygiene. Applicant must be member of ADHA or Student ADHA. Download application from Website. Applicants may apply for only one ADHA scholarship, but those not selected may be eligible for general scholarship.
    Amount of award: $1,500
    Number of awards: 1
    Application deadline: May 1
Contact:
ADHA Institute for Oral Health
444 N. Michigan Ave., Suite 3400
Chicago, IL 60611
Phone: 800-735-4916
Fax: 312-467-1806
Web: www.adha.org/institute

Hu-Friedy/Esther Wilkins Instrument Scholarships

Type of award: Scholarship.
Intended use: For full-time undergraduate study at accredited 2-year or 4-year institution.
Basis for selection: Major/career interest in dental hygiene. Applicant must demonstrate financial need.
Application requirements: Recommendations. FAFSA. Program director verification form, goals statement.
Additional information: Must have completed one year of dental hygiene curriculum by award year; may apply during first year. May be pursuing certificate. Must be active ADHA or Student ADHA member with minimum dental hygiene 3.0 GPA. Download application from Website. Must demonstrate at least $1,500 of financial need. Award given as $1,000 worth of Hu-Friedy dental hygiene instruments. Applicants may apply for only one ADHA scholarship, but those not selected may be eligible for general scholarship.
    Amount of award: $1,000
    Number of awards: 5
    Application deadline: May 1
Contact:
ADHA Institute for Oral Health
Scholarship Award Program
444 N. Michigan Ave., Ste. 3400
Chicago, IL 60611-3980
Phone: 800-735-4916
Web: www.adha.org/institute

Irene E. Newman Scholarship

Type of award: Scholarship.
Intended use: For full-time undergraduate or graduate study at accredited 4-year or graduate institution.
Basis for selection: Major/career interest in dental hygiene or public health. Applicant must demonstrate financial need.
Application requirements: Recommendations. Goal statement (graduate applicants require specific goal statement). Program director verification form.
Additional information: Must demonstrate strong potential in public health or community dental health. Must demonstrate need of at least $1,500. Must have completed one year of dental hygiene curriculum by award year; may apply during first year. Graduate applicants must have active dental hygiene license and hold at least baccalaureate. Must be active ADHA or Student ADHA member with minimum dental hygiene 3.0 GPA. Download application from Website. Applicants may apply for only one ADHA scholarship, but those not selected may be eligible for general scholarship.
    Amount of award: $1,500
    Number of awards: 1
    Application deadline: May 1
Contact:
ADHA Institute for Oral Health
Scholarship Award Program
444 N. Michigan Ave., Ste. 3400
Chicago, IL 60611-3980
Phone: 800-735-4916
Web: www.adha.org/institute

Margaret E. Swanson Scholarship

Type of award: Scholarship.
Intended use: For full-time undergraduate certificate or post-bachelor's certificate study at accredited 4-year or graduate institution in United States.
Basis for selection: Major/career interest in dental hygiene. Applicant must demonstrate financial need, high academic achievement and leadership.
Application requirements: Recommendations, essay. FAFSA.
Additional information: Minimum 3.0 GPA in dental hygiene. Must be member of ADHA or Student ADHA, and have completed a minimum of one year in dental hygiene program. Download application from Website. Applicants may apply for only one ADHA scholarship, but those not selected may be eligible for general scholarship.
    Amount of award: $1,500
    Number of awards: 1
    Application deadline: May 1
Contact:
ADHA Institute for Oral Health
444 N. Michigan Ave., Suite 3400
Chicago, IL 60611
Phone: 800-735-4916
Fax: 312-467-1806
Web: www.adha.org/institute

Oral-B Laboratories Dental Hygiene Scholarship

Type of award: Scholarship.
Intended use: For full-time sophomore, junior or senior study at accredited 4-year institution in United States.
Basis for selection: Major/career interest in dental hygiene. Applicant must demonstrate financial need, high academic achievement, leadership and seriousness of purpose.
Application requirements: Recommendations, essay. FAFSA.
Additional information: Applicant must be enrolled in dental hygiene program and have completed a minimum of one year. Minimum 3.5 dental hygiene GPA. Must want to encourage professional excellence, scholarship, and quality research and to support dental hygiene through public and private education. Must be member of ADHA or Student ADHA. Download application from Website. Applicants may apply for only one ADHA scholarship, but those not selected may be eligible for general scholarship.
    Amount of award: $1,000
    Application deadline: May 1

Contact:
ADHA Institute for Oral Health
444 N. Michigan Ave., Suite 3400
Chicago, IL 60611
Phone: 800-735-4916
Fax: 312-467-1806
Web: www.adha.org/institute

Pfizer Inc. Scholarships

Type of award: Scholarship.
Intended use: For full-time undergraduate study at accredited 2-year or 4-year institution.
Basis for selection: Major/career interest in dental hygiene. Applicant must demonstrate financial need and high academic achievement.
Application requirements: Recommendations. FAFSA, program director verification form, goal statement.
Additional information: Must have completed one year of dental hygiene curriculum by award year; may apply during first year. May be studying for certificate. Must be active ADHA or Student ADHA member with minimum 3.5 dental hygiene GPA. Must demonstrate $1,500 financial need. Download application from Website. Applicants may apply for only one ADHA scholarship, but those not selected may be eligible for general scholarship.
    Amount of award: $1,500
    Number of awards: 5
    Application deadline: May 1
    Total amount awarded: $7,500
Contact:
ADHA Institute for Oral Health
Scholarship Award Program
444 N. Michigan Ave., Ste. 3400
Chicago, IL 60611-3980
Phone: 800-735-4916
Web: www.adha.org/institute

Sigma Phi Alpha Undergraduate Scholarship

Type of award: Scholarship.
Intended use: For full-time undergraduate certificate, sophomore, junior or senior study at accredited 4-year institution in United States. Designated institutions: Schools with active chapter of Sigma Phi Alpha Dental Hygiene Honor Society.
Basis for selection: Major/career interest in dental hygiene. Applicant must demonstrate financial need and high academic achievement.
Application requirements: Recommendations, essay. FAFSA.
Additional information: Minimum 3.5 GPA in dental hygiene. Must be member of ADHA or Student ADHA. Must have completed one year of study. Download application from Website. Applicants may apply for only one ADHA scholarship, but those not selected may be eligible for general scholarship.
    Amount of award: $1,000
    Number of awards: 1
    Application deadline: May 1
Contact:
ADHA Institute for Oral Health
Scholarship Award Program
444 N. Michigan Ave., Suite 3400
Chicago, IL 60611
Phone: 800-735-4916
Fax: 312-467-1806
Web: www.adha.org/institute

Wilma Motley Memorial California Merit Scholarship

Type of award: Scholarship.
Intended use: For full-time undergraduate study at accredited 2-year or 4-year institution.
Eligibility: Applicant must be residing in California.
Basis for selection: Major/career interest in dental hygiene. Applicant must demonstrate high academic achievement and leadership.
Application requirements: Recommendations. Specific goals statement. Program director verification form.
Additional information: Must have completed one year of dental hygiene curriculum by award year; may apply during first year. May be studying for certificate. Must be active ADHA or Student ADHA member with minimum 3.5 dental hygiene GPA. Download application from Website. Applicants may apply for only one ADHA scholarship, but those not selected may be eligible for general scholarship.
    Amount of award: $1,000
    Number of awards: 2
    Application deadline: May 1
    Total amount awarded: $2,000
Contact:
ADHA Institute for Oral Health
Scholarship Award Program
444 N. Michigan Ave., Ste. 3400
Chicago, IL 60611-3980
Phone: 800-735-4916
Web: www.adha.org/institute

AFCEA Educational Foundation

AFCEA Scholarships for Math and Science Teachers

Type of award: Scholarship.
Intended use: For sophomore or junior study in United States.
Eligibility: Applicant must be U.S. citizen or permanent resident.
Basis for selection: Major/career interest in education, teacher; science, general; mathematics or computer/information sciences. Applicant must demonstrate high academic achievement.
Additional information: For students pursuing an undergraduate degree education degree for the purpose of teaching science, mathematics or information technology at a U.S. secondary school. Minimum 3.0 GPA required.
    Amount of award: $2,000
    Application deadline: May 1
Contact:
AFCEA Professional Development Center
4400 Fair Lakes Court
Fairfax, VA 22033-3899
Phone: 703-631-6135
Fax: 703-631-6172
Web: www.afcea.org

AFSA Scholarship Programs

Air Force Sergeants Association, Airmen Memorial Foundation, and Chief Master Sergeants of the Air Force Scholarship Programs

Type of award: Scholarship.
Intended use: For full-time undergraduate study at accredited postsecondary institution in United States.
Eligibility: Applicant must be single, no older than 22. Applicant must be dependent of active service person or veteran in the Air Force. May be dependent of retired member as well. Dependents of members of the Air National Guard or Air Force Reserve also eligible.
Basis for selection: Applicant must demonstrate high academic achievement, depth of character and leadership.
Application requirements: Recommendations, essay, transcript, proof of eligibility.
Additional information: Applicant must be under 23 years of age as of August 1 of award year. Applications available November 1 to March 31. Amount and number of awards vary. See Website for application and eligibility requirements.

Amount of award:	$500-$3,000
Number of applicants:	154
Application deadline:	March 31
Notification begins:	August 1
Total amount awarded:	$358,800

Contact:
AFSA Scholarship Programs
P.O. Box 50
Temple Hills, MD 20757-0050
Phone: 800-638-0594
Fax: 301-899-8136
Web: www.afsahq.org

AGC of Maine Education Foundation

AGC of Maine Scholarship Program

Type of award: Scholarship.
Intended use: For full-time freshman, sophomore, junior or senior study at accredited 4-year institution in United States.
Eligibility: Applicant must be U.S. citizen residing in Maine.
Basis for selection: Major/career interest in construction or engineering, civil. Applicant must demonstrate financial need and high academic achievement.
Application requirements: Interview, recommendations, essay, transcript.
Additional information: Applicants must be interested in pursuing construction career. Priority will be given to students entering or enrolled in accredited Maine postsecondary institutions.

Amount of award:	$1,500-$4,000
Number of awards:	12
Number of applicants:	35
Application deadline:	March 17
Notification begins:	January 1
Total amount awarded:	$24,000

Contact:
AGC of Maine
P.O. Box 5519
Augusta, ME 04332
Phone: 207-622-4741
Web: www.agcmaine.org

AHEPA Educational Foundation

AHEPA Educational Foundation Scholarships

Type of award: Scholarship.
Intended use: For full-time undergraduate or graduate study at accredited postsecondary institution.
Eligibility: Applicant or parent must be member/participant of American Hellenic Educational Progressive Association. Must be of Hellenic heritage, although ancestry need not be 100 percent Greek.
Basis for selection: Applicant must demonstrate financial need, high academic achievement, depth of character, leadership, seriousness of purpose and service orientation.
Application requirements: Recommendations, essay, transcript, proof of eligibility.
Additional information: Applicant must be member, or child of member, in good standing of AHEPA, Daughters of Penelope, Sons of Pericles or Maids of Athena. High school seniors eligible to apply. Visit Website for details and application.

Amount of award:	$500-$2,000
Application deadline:	March 31

Contact:
AHEPA Educational Foundation
c/o AHEPA Headquarters
1909 Q Street, NW, Suite 500
Washington, DC 20009-1007
Phone: 202-232-6300
Web: www.ahepa.org/ahepa/

Air Force Aid Society

Air Force Aid Society Education Grant

Type of award: Scholarship.
Intended use: For full-time undergraduate study at accredited vocational, 2-year or 4-year institution in or outside United States.
Eligibility: Applicant must be dependent of active service person, veteran or deceased veteran; or spouse of active service person or deceased veteran who serves or served in the Air Force. Veteran status alone not eligible. Sponsoring member must be active duty, retired Reserve with 20-plus qualifying years, retired Air Force with 20-plus years active duty service, or deceased while on active duty or in retired status. Dependent children of Title 32 AGR performing full-time active duty service are also eligible.
Basis for selection: Applicant must demonstrate financial need.

Application requirements: Proof of eligibility.
Additional information: Minimum 2.0 GPA.
    Amount of award: $2,000
    Number of awards: 3,500
    Number of applicants: 7,000
    Application deadline: March 7
    Notification begins: June 1
    Total amount awarded: $7,000,000
Contact:
Air Force Aid Society
Education Assistance Department
241 18th Street South, Suite 202
Arlington, VA 22202
Phone: 800-429-9475
Web: www.afas.org

Air Traffic Control Association, Inc.

Air Traffic Control Children of Specialists Scholarship

Type of award: Scholarship.
Intended use: For undergraduate or graduate study at accredited 4-year or graduate institution.
Eligibility: Applicant must be U.S. citizen.
Basis for selection: Applicant must demonstrate financial need, depth of character and seriousness of purpose.
Application requirements: Recommendations, essay, transcript. Essay on "How My Education Efforts Will Enhance My Potential Contribution in My Chosen Career Field." Essay or application must address financial need and work or other experience that support goals.
Additional information: Applicant must be child of person serving, or having served, as air traffic control specialist. Must be at least half-time student. Must need to complete at least 30 semester or 45 quarter hours before graduating. Scholarship amount determined by ATCA Scholarship Program Board of Directors. Download application and terms of reference from Website.
    Number of awards: 2
    Number of applicants: 75
    Application deadline: May 1
Contact:
Air Traffic Control Association, Inc.
Attn: Scholarship Fund
1101 King Street, Suite 300
Arlington, VA 22314
Phone: 703-299-2430
Fax: 703-299-2437
Web: www.atca.org

Air Traffic Control Full-Time Employee Student Scholarship

Type of award: Scholarship.
Intended use: For undergraduate, graduate or non-degree study at postsecondary institution.
Eligibility: Applicant or parent must be employed by Aviation industry. Applicant must be returning adult student.
Basis for selection: Major/career interest in aviation. Applicant must demonstrate financial need, depth of character and seriousness of purpose.
Application requirements: Recommendations, transcript. Essay on "How My Education Efforts Will Enhance My Potential Contribution to Aviation." Essay or application must address financial need and work or other experience that support goals.
Additional information: Applicant must work full-time in aviation-related field, and coursework must enhance air traffic control or aviation skills. Scholarship must be used within four years of date awarded. Award amount determined by ATCA Scholarship Program Board of Directors. Application and terms of reference can be downloaded from Website.
    Number of awards: 1
    Number of applicants: 45
    Application deadline: May 1
Contact:
Air Traffic Control Association, Inc.
Attn: Scholarship Fund
1101 King Street, Suite 300
Alexandria, VA 22314
Phone: 703-299-2430
Fax: 703-299-2437
Web: www.atca.org

Air Traffic Control Half- to Full-Time Student Scholarship

Type of award: Scholarship.
Intended use: For undergraduate or graduate study at accredited 4-year or graduate institution in United States.
Basis for selection: Major/career interest in aviation or aerospace. Applicant must demonstrate financial need, depth of character and seriousness of purpose.
Application requirements: Recommendations, proof of eligibility. Four-hundred-word essay on "How My Education Efforts Will Enhance My Potential Contribution to Aviation." Essay or application must address financial need and work or other experience that supports goals. College transcript (high school transcript as well if under 30 college semester hours or 45 quarter hours completed).
Additional information: Must be enrolled at least half time. Must have minimum of 30 semester hours or 45 quarter hours still to be completed before graduation and attend at least half time (six hours). Application and terms of reference can be downloaded from Website.
    Amount of award: $1,500-$2,500
    Number of awards: 5
    Number of applicants: 300
    Application deadline: May 1
Contact:
Air Traffic Control Association, Inc.
Attn: Scholarship Fund
1101 King Street, Suite 300
Alexandria, VA 22314
Phone: 703-299-2430
Fax: 703-299-2437
Web: www.atca.org

Buckingham Memorial Scholarship

Type of award: Scholarship, renewable.
Intended use: For freshman, sophomore or graduate study in United States.
Eligibility: Applicant must be U.S. citizen.
Basis for selection: Applicant must demonstrate financial need.

Application requirements: Recommendations, essay, transcript. 400 word essay; high school and college transcripts; two letters of recommendation.
Additional information: Must be child of an air traffic control specialist. Must have minimum of 30 semester or 45 quarter hours to be completed before graduation.
   Application deadline: May 1
Contact:
Air Traffic Control Association, Inc. Attn: Scholarship Fund
1101 King Street, Suite 300
Alexandria, VA 22314
Phone: 703-299-2430
Fax: 703-299-2437
Web: www.atca.org

Gabriel A. Hartl Scholarship

Type of award: Scholarship, renewable.
Intended use: For freshman or sophomore study in United States. Designated institutions: FAA-approved institutions.
Basis for selection: Major/career interest in aviation. Applicant must demonstrate financial need.
Application requirements: Recommendations, essay, transcript. 400 word essay; high school and college transcripts; two letters of recommendation.
Additional information: Must have minimum of 30 semester or 45 quarter hours to be completed before graduation. Must be studying aviation science or be child of an air traffic control specialist.
   Application deadline: May 1
Contact:
Air Traffic Control Association, Inc. Attn: Scholarship Fund
1101 King Street, Suite 300
Alexandria, VA 22314
Phone: 703-299-2430
Fax: 703-299-2437
Web: www.atca.org

Aircraft Electronics Association Educational Foundation

Bud Glover Memorial Scholarship

Type of award: Scholarship, renewable.
Intended use: For full-time undergraduate study at accredited vocational, 2-year or 4-year institution.
Basis for selection: Major/career interest in aviation; aviation repair or electronics. Applicant must demonstrate depth of character and seriousness of purpose.
Application requirements: Recommendations, essay, transcript, proof of eligibility.
Additional information: Applicant may be high school senior or college student. Must have at least 2.5 GPA. Awards are announced at AEA Annual Convention and Trade Show each spring. Visit Website for more information.
   Amount of award: $1,000
   Number of awards: 1
   Application deadline: February 15
Contact:
Aircraft Electronics Association Educational Foundation
4217 S. Hocker Drive
Independence, MO 64055
Phone: 816-373-6565
Fax: 816-478-3100
Web: www.aea.net/educationalfoundation

David Arver Memorial Scholarship

Type of award: Scholarship, renewable.
Intended use: For full-time undergraduate study at accredited vocational or 2-year institution.
Eligibility: Applicant must be residing in Wisconsin, Michigan, Iowa, South Dakota, Minnesota, Kansas, Indiana, Nebraska, Illinois, North Dakota or Missouri.
Basis for selection: Major/career interest in aviation; aviation repair or electronics. Applicant must demonstrate depth of character and seriousness of purpose.
Application requirements: Recommendations, essay, transcript, proof of eligibility.
Additional information: Applicant may be high school senior or college student. Must have at least 2.5 GPA. Awards are announced at AEA Annual Convention and Trade Show each spring. Visit Website for more information.
   Amount of award: $1,000
   Number of awards: 1
   Application deadline: February 15
   Total amount awarded: $1,000
Contact:
Aircraft Electronics Association Educational Foundation
4217 S. Hocker Drive
Independence, MO 64055
Phone: 816-373-6565
Fax: 816-478-3100
Web: www.aea.net/educationalfoundation

Dutch and Ginger Arver Scholarship

Type of award: Scholarship, renewable.
Intended use: For full-time undergraduate study at accredited vocational, 2-year or 4-year institution.
Basis for selection: Major/career interest in aviation or electronics. Applicant must demonstrate depth of character and seriousness of purpose.
Application requirements: Recommendations, essay, transcript, proof of eligibility.
Additional information: Applicant must be high school senior or college student. Must have at least 2.5 GPA. Awards are announced at AEA Annual Convention and Trade Show. Visit Website for more information.
   Amount of award: $1,000
   Number of awards: 1
   Application deadline: February 15
   Total amount awarded: $1,000
Contact:
Aircraft Electronics Association Educational Foundation
4217 S. Hocker Drive
Independence, MO 64055
Phone: 816-373-6565
Fax: 816-478-3100
Web: www.aea.net/educationalfoundation

Field Aviation Co., Inc. Scholarship

Type of award: Scholarship, renewable.

Aircraft Electronics Association Educational Foundation: Field Aviation Co., Inc. Scholarship

Intended use: For full-time undergraduate study at accredited vocational, 2-year or 4-year institution.
Eligibility: Applicant must be high school senior.
Basis for selection: Major/career interest in aviation; aviation repair or electronics. Applicant must demonstrate depth of character and seriousness of purpose.
Application requirements: Recommendations, essay, transcript, proof of eligibility.
Additional information: Applicant may be high school senior or college student. Must have at least 2.5 GPA. Awards are announced at AEA Annual Convention and Trade Show each spring. Visit Website for more information.
    Amount of award: $1,000
    Number of awards: 1
    Application deadline: February 15
Contact:
Aircraft Electronics Association Educational Foundation
4217 S. Hocker Drive
Independence, MO 64055
Phone: 816-373-6565
Fax: 816-478-3100
Web: www.aea.net/educationalfoundation

Garmin Scholarship

Type of award: Scholarship, renewable.
Intended use: For full-time undergraduate study at accredited vocational, 2-year or 4-year institution.
Basis for selection: Major/career interest in aviation; aviation repair or electronics. Applicant must demonstrate depth of character and seriousness of purpose.
Application requirements: Recommendations, essay, transcript, proof of eligibility.
Additional information: Applicant may be high school senior or college student. Must have at least 2.5 GPA. Awards are announced at AEA Annual Convention and Trade Show each spring. For more information, visit Website.
    Amount of award: $2,000
    Number of awards: 1
    Application deadline: February 15
    Total amount awarded: $2,000
Contact:
Aircraft Electronics Association Educational Foundation
4217 S. Hocker Drive
Independence, MO 64055
Phone: 816-373-6565
Fax: 816-478-3100
Web: www.aea.net/educationalfoundation

Honeywell Avionics Scholarship

Type of award: Scholarship, renewable.
Intended use: For full-time undergraduate study at accredited vocational, 2-year or 4-year institution.
Basis for selection: Major/career interest in aviation; aviation repair or electronics.
Application requirements: Recommendations, essay, transcript, proof of eligibility.
Additional information: Applicant may be high school senior or college student. Must have at least 2.5 GPA. Awards are announced at AEA Annual Convention and Trade Show each spring. Visit Website for additional information.
    Amount of award: $1,000
    Number of awards: 1
    Application deadline: February 15
    Total amount awarded: $1,000

Contact:
Aircraft Electronics Association Educational Foundation
4217 S. Hocker Drive
Independence, MO 64055
Phone: 816-373-6565
Fax: 816-478-3100
Web: www.aea.net/educationalfoundation

Johnny Davis Memorial Scholarship

Type of award: Scholarship, renewable.
Intended use: For full-time undergraduate study at accredited vocational, 2-year or 4-year institution.
Basis for selection: Major/career interest in aviation; aviation repair or electronics. Applicant must demonstrate depth of character and seriousness of purpose.
Application requirements: Recommendations, essay, transcript, proof of eligibility.
Additional information: Applicant may be high school senior or college student. Must have at least 2.5 GPA. Awards are announced at AEA Annual Convention and Trade Show each spring. Visit Website for additional information.
    Amount of award: $1,000
    Number of awards: 1
    Application deadline: February 15
    Total amount awarded: $1,000
Contact:
Aircraft Electronics Association Educational Foundation
4217 S. Hocker Drive
Independence, MO 64055
Phone: 816-373-6565
Fax: 816-478-3100
Web: www.aea.net/educationalfoundation

L-3 Avionics Systems Scholarship

Type of award: Scholarship, renewable.
Intended use: For full-time undergraduate study at accredited vocational, 2-year or 4-year institution.
Basis for selection: Major/career interest in aviation; aviation repair or electronics. Applicant must demonstrate depth of character and seriousness of purpose.
Application requirements: Recommendations, essay, transcript, proof of eligibility.
Additional information: Applicant may be high school senior or college student. Must have at least 2.5 GPA. Awards are announced at AEA Annual Convention and Trade Show each spring. Visit Website for more information.
    Amount of award: $2,500
    Number of awards: 1
    Application deadline: February 15
    Total amount awarded: $2,500
Contact:
Aircraft Electronics Association Educational Foundation
4217 S. Hocker Drive
Independence, MO 64055
Phone: 816-373-6565
Fax: 816-478-3100
Web: www.aea.net/educationalfoundation

Lee Tarbox Memorial Scholarship

Type of award: Scholarship, renewable.
Intended use: For full-time undergraduate study at accredited vocational, 2-year or 4-year institution.
Eligibility: Applicant must be high school senior.

Basis for selection: Major/career interest in aviation; aviation repair or electronics. Applicant must demonstrate depth of character and seriousness of purpose.
Application requirements: Recommendations, essay, transcript, proof of eligibility.
Additional information: Applicant may be high school senior or college student. Must have at least 2.5 GPA. Scholarship given by Pacific Southwest Instruments. Awards are announced at AEA Annual Convention and Trade Show each spring. Visit Website for additional information.
- Amount of award: $2,500
- Number of awards: 1
- Application deadline: February 15
- Total amount awarded: $2,500

Contact:
Aircraft Electronics Association Educational Foundation
4217 S. Hocker Drive
Independence, MO 64055
Phone: 816-373-6565
Fax: 816-478-3100
Web: www.aea.net/educationalfoundation

Leon Harris/Les Nichols Memorial to Spartan School of Aeronautics

Type of award: Scholarship, renewable.
Intended use: For full-time undergraduate study at vocational or 2-year institution. Designated institutions: NEC Spartan School of Aeronautics in Tulsa, OK.
Basis for selection: Major/career interest in aviation or electronics. Applicant must demonstrate depth of character and seriousness of purpose.
Application requirements: Recommendations, essay, transcript, proof of eligibility.
Additional information: Applicant may be high school senior or college student. Must have at least 2.5 GPA. Applicant may not be currently enrolled in avionics program at Spartan. Award covers tuition for eight quarters or until associate's degree is completed, whichever comes first. All other costs (tools, living expenses and fees) must be covered by student. Awards are announced at AEA Annual Convention and Trade Show each spring. Visit Website for more information.
- Amount of award: Full tuition
- Number of awards: 1
- Application deadline: February 15

Contact:
Aircraft Electronics Association Educational Foundation
4217 S. Hocker Drive
Independence, MO 64055
Phone: 816-373-6565
Fax: 816-478-3100
Web: www.aea.net/educationalfoundation

Lowell Gaylor Memorial Scholarship

Type of award: Scholarship, renewable.
Intended use: For full-time undergraduate study at accredited vocational, 2-year or 4-year institution.
Basis for selection: Major/career interest in aviation; aviation repair or electronics. Applicant must demonstrate depth of character and seriousness of purpose.
Application requirements: Recommendations, essay, transcript, proof of eligibility.
Additional information: Applicant may be high school senior or college student. Must have at least 2.5 GPA. Awards are announced at AEA Annual Convention and Trade Show each year. Visit Website for more information.
- Amount of award: $1,000
- Number of awards: 1
- Application deadline: February 15

Contact:
Aircraft Electronics Association Educational Foundation
4217 S. Hocker Drive
Independence, MO 64055
Phone: 816-373-6565
Fax: 816-478-3100
Web: www.aea.net/educationalfoundation

Mid-Continent Instrument Scholarship

Type of award: Scholarship, renewable.
Intended use: For full-time undergraduate study at accredited vocational, 2-year or 4-year institution.
Basis for selection: Major/career interest in aviation or electronics. Applicant must demonstrate depth of character and seriousness of purpose.
Application requirements: Recommendations, essay, transcript, proof of eligibility.
Additional information: Applicant may be high school senior or college student. Must have at least 2.5 GPA. Awards are announced at AEA Annual Convention and Trade Show each spring. Visit Website for more information.
- Amount of award: $1,000
- Number of awards: 1
- Application deadline: February 15
- Total amount awarded: $1,000

Contact:
Aircraft Electronics Association Educational Foundation
4217 S. Hocker Drive
Independence, MO 64055
Phone: 816-373-6565
Fax: 816-478-3100
Web: www.aea.net/educationalfoundation

Monte R. Mitchell Global Scholarship

Type of award: Scholarship, renewable.
Intended use: For full-time undergraduate study at accredited postsecondary institution in or outside United States. Designated institutions: Institutions with aviation maintenance technology or avionics, programs, located in Europe, Australia, New Zealand, or the United States.
Eligibility: Applicant must be European, Australian or or New Zealand citizen.
Basis for selection: Major/career interest in aviation or electronics. Applicant must demonstrate depth of character and seriousness of purpose.
Application requirements: Recommendations, essay, transcript, proof of eligibility.
Additional information: Applicant must have finished secondary school. Scholarship given by Mid-Continent Instruments Co. Student must submit grade reports that show evidence of most recent academic marks. Awards are announced at AEA Annual Convention and Trade Show each spring.
- Amount of award: $1,000
- Number of awards: 1
- Application deadline: February 15
- Total amount awarded: $1,000

Aircraft Electronics Association Educational Foundation: Monte R. Mitchell Global Scholarship

Contact:
Aircraft Electronics Association Educational Foundation
4217 S. Hocker Drive
Independence, MO 64055
Phone: 816-373-6565
Fax: 816-478-3100
Web: www.aea.net/educationalfoundation

Plane & Pilot Magazine/Garmin Scholarship

Type of award: Scholarship, renewable.
Intended use: For full-time undergraduate study at accredited vocational institution. Designated institutions: Vocational and technical schools with avionics and aircraft repair programs.
Basis for selection: Major/career interest in aviation; aviation repair or electronics. Applicant must demonstrate depth of character and seriousness of purpose.
Application requirements: Recommendations, essay, transcript, proof of eligibility.
Additional information: Applicants may be high school, college, or vocational/technical school students. Must have at least 2.5 GPA. Awards are announced at AEA Annual Convention and Trade Show each spring. Visit Website for additional information.
    Amount of award: $2,000
    Number of awards: 1
    Application deadline: February 15
    Total amount awarded: $2,000
Contact:
Aircraft Electronic Association Educational Foundation
4217 S. Hocker Drive
Independence, MO 64055
Phone: 816-373-6565
Fax: 816-478-3100
Web: www.aea.net/educationalfoundation

Aircraft Owners and Pilots Association (AOPA)

AOPA Air Safety Foundation/McAllister Memorial Scholarship

Type of award: Scholarship.
Intended use: For full-time junior or senior study at accredited 4-year institution in United States.
Eligibility: Applicant must be U.S. citizen or permanent resident.
Basis for selection: Major/career interest in aviation or aviation repair. Applicant must demonstrate financial need and high academic achievement.
Application requirements: Essay, transcript, proof of eligibility. Essay of 250 words; essay topic changes every year.
Additional information: Applicant must be enrolled in aviation program at four-year institution. Applicant must have GPA of 3.25 or better. Application available online. Original and seven copies of entire application packet must be mailed to: Mark Sherman, Department of Aviation, 2000 University Ave, Dubuque, IA 52001.
    Amount of award: $1,000
    Number of awards: 1
    Application deadline: March 31
    Notification begins: July 1
    Total amount awarded: $1,000
Contact:
AOPA Air Safety Foundation
c/o Dr. Mark Sherman
2000 University Avnue
Dubuque, IA 52001
Phone: 301-695-2177
Fax: 301-695-2343
Web: www.aopa.org/asf/about/scholarship/mcallister.html

Akademos, Inc.

Akademos, Inc. TextbookX.com Scholarship

Type of award: Scholarship.
Intended use: For undergraduate or graduate study at accredited postsecondary institution in United States.
Eligibility: Applicant must be U.S. citizen or international student.
Basis for selection: Competition/talent/interest in writing/journalism.
Application requirements: 250- to 750-word essay based on question posted on Website.
Additional information: Awardees chosen based on essay. Scholarship awarded twice a year. Visit Website for essay guidelines and deadlines, and to apply. Applicant must be in good standing; cannot be relative or friend of Akademos employee. International students must have student visa.
    Amount of award: $250-$2,000
    Number of awards: 3
    Application deadline: October 31
    Notification begins: December 1
    Total amount awarded: $2,500
Contact:
Visit Website for more information.
Phone: 800-221-8480
Fax: 203-866-0199
Web: www.textbookx.com/scholarship

Alabama Commission on Higher Education

Alabama National Guard Educational Assistance Award

Type of award: Scholarship, renewable.
Intended use: For undergraduate or graduate study at 2-year or 4-year institution.
Eligibility: Applicant must be U.S. citizen residing in Alabama. Applicant must be in military service in the Reserves/National Guard. Must be active member in good standing with federally recognized unit of Alabama National Guard.
Application requirements: Proof of eligibility.
Additional information: Award to be used for tuition, books, fees, and supplies (minus any federal veterans' benefits).

Amount of award:	$25-$1,000
Number of applicants:	725
Total amount awarded:	$466,363

Contact:
Contact Alabama National Guard Unit.
Phone: 334-242-2273
Fax: 334-242-2269
Web: www.ache.state.al.us

Alabama Student Assistance Program

Type of award: Scholarship, renewable.
Intended use: For full-time undergraduate study at vocational, 2-year or 4-year institution. Designated institutions: Eligible Alabama institutions.
Eligibility: Applicant must be residing in Alabama.
Basis for selection: Applicant must demonstrate financial need.
Application requirements: Proof of eligibility. FAFSA.
Additional information: Students urged to apply early.

Amount of award:	$300-$2,500
Number of applicants:	3,742
Total amount awarded:	$2,077,150

Contact:
Applications available at high school or college financial aid office.
Phone: 334-242-2273
Fax: 334-242-2269
Web: www.ache.state.al.us

Alabama Student Grant

Type of award: Scholarship, renewable.
Intended use: For undergraduate study at 2-year or 4-year institution. Designated institutions: Birmingham-Southern College, Concordia College, Faulkner University, Huntingdon College, Judson College, Miles College, Oakwood College, Samford University, Southeastern Bible College, Spring Hill College, Stillman College, University of Mobile.
Eligibility: Applicant must be residing in Alabama.
Application requirements: Proof of Alabama residency.
Additional information: Award is not need-based. Deadlines printed on application form.

Amount of award:	$1,200
Number of applicants:	6,989
Total amount awarded:	$2,130,865

Contact:
Contact financial aid office of institution for application.
Phone: 334-242-2273
Fax: 334-242-2269
Web: www.ache.state.al.us

Police/Firefighters' Survivors Educational Assistance Program

Type of award: Scholarship, renewable.
Intended use: For undergraduate study at vocational, 2-year or 4-year institution.
Eligibility: Applicant must be residing in Alabama.
Application requirements: Proof of eligibility.
Additional information: Grant covers full tuition, mandatory fees, books, and supplies for dependents and eligible spouses of Alabama police officers and firefighters killed or totally disabled in line of duty.

Amount of award:	Full tuition
Number of applicants:	25
Total amount awarded:	$103,903

Contact:
Alabama Commission on Higher Education
P.O. Box 302000
Montgomery, AL 36130-2000
Phone: 334-242-2273
Fax: 334-242-2269
Web: www.ache.state.al.us

Alabama Department of Education

Alabama Robert C. Byrd Honors Scholarship

Type of award: Scholarship, renewable.
Intended use: For full-time undergraduate study at 2-year or 4-year institution in United States.
Eligibility: Applicant must be high school senior. Applicant must be U.S. citizen residing in Alabama.
Basis for selection: Applicant must demonstrate high academic achievement.
Application requirements: Nomination by high school guidance counselor. SAT/ACT scores.
Additional information: Contact high school guidance office or principal for information. Scholarship renewable for up to four years of undergraduate work. Award continues through senior year if qualifications are met. There are approximately 15 winners for each U.S. Congressional District, with seven districts in the state. Visit Website for deadline.

Amount of award:	$1,500
Number of awards:	105

Contact:
Robert C. Byrd Honors Scholarship Program
Alabama State Department of Education
3345 Gordon Persons Building, Box 302101
Montgomery, AL 36130-2101
Web: www.alsde.edu

Alabama Department of Postsecondary Education

Alabama Junior/Community College Athletic Scholarship

Type of award: Scholarship, renewable.
Intended use: For full-time freshman or sophomore study at 2-year institution.
Eligibility: Applicant must be U.S. citizen or permanent resident residing in Alabama.
Basis for selection: Competition/talent/interest in athletics/sports.
Additional information: Awards not need-based. Award covers tuition and books at Alabama two-year public institutions. Competitive tryout will be scheduled. Eligibility based on athletic ability determined through tryouts. Renewal

dependent on continued athletic participation. Award amount varies.
Contact:
401 Adams Avenue
P.O. Box 302130
Montgomery, AL 36130-2130
Phone: 334-242-2900
Fax: 334-353-5958
Web: www.ache.state.al.us

Institutional Scholarship Waivers

Type of award: Scholarship, renewable.
Intended use: For freshman or sophomore study at accredited 2-year institution.
Eligibility: Applicant must be U.S. citizen or permanent resident residing in Alabama.
Basis for selection: Applicant must demonstrate high academic achievement.
Application requirements: Transcript.
Additional information: Awards not need-based. Awards based on merit. Focus of scholarship is determined by each institution. Application deadlines printed on application forms. Award may be renewed if student demonstrates academic excellence. Amount and number of awards vary.
Contact:
401 Adams Avenue
P.O. Box 302130
Montgomery, AL 36130-2130
Phone: 334-242-2900
Fax: 334-353-5958
Web: www.ache.state.al.us

Alabama Department of Veterans Affairs

Alabama GI Dependents Educational Benefit

Type of award: Scholarship, renewable.
Intended use: For undergraduate or graduate study at postsecondary institution.
Eligibility: Applicant must be residing in Alabama. Applicant must be dependent of disabled veteran, deceased veteran or POW/MIA; or spouse of disabled veteran, deceased veteran or POW/MIA. Veteran must have been involved in active military duties for at least 90 days on continuous active duty. Disabled veterans must be rated at least 20% disabled due to service connected disabilities. Veteran parent/spouse must have been resident of Alabama at least one year prior to enlistment. Children of veterans must submit application before their 26th birthday. Spouses of veterans have no age limit.
Application requirements: Proof of eligibility.
Amount of award:	Full tuition
Number of awards:	967
Number of applicants:	2,417
Total amount awarded:	$15,827,191

Contact:
Alabama Department of Veterans Affairs
P.O. Box 1509
Montgomery, AL 36102-1509
Phone: 334-242-5077
Fax: 334-242-5102
Web: www.va.state.al.us/scholarship.htm

Alcoa Foundation

Alcoa Foundation Sons and Daughters Scholarship Program

Type of award: Scholarship.
Intended use: For undergraduate study at accredited postsecondary institution in United States.
Eligibility: Applicant or parent must be employed by Alcoa Inc. Applicant must be high school senior.
Basis for selection: Applicant must demonstrate high academic achievement, depth of character, leadership and service orientation.
Application requirements: Recommendations, essay, transcript, proof of eligibility. SAT/ACT scores if attending a four-year institution. Essay on one of two given topics.
Additional information: The four-year award is renewable for up to three years, the two-year award for up to one year.
Amount of award:	$1,500
Number of awards:	100
Number of applicants:	300
Application deadline:	January 16
Notification begins:	April 30

Contact:
Alcoa Foundation, Sons and Daughters Scholarship Program
P.O. Box 4030
Iowa City, IA 52243-4030
Phone: 800-525-6932
Fax: 319-337-1204
Web: www.act.org/alcoafoundation

Alexander Graham Bell Association for the Deaf and Hard of Hearing

AG Bell College Scholarship Awards

Type of award: Scholarship.
Intended use: For full-time undergraduate or graduate study at accredited 2-year, 4-year or graduate institution in or outside United States.
Eligibility: Applicant must be hearing impaired.
Basis for selection: Applicant must demonstrate financial need, high academic achievement and seriousness of purpose.
Application requirements: Recommendations, essay, transcript, proof of eligibility. Current audiogram.
Additional information: Applicant must have had a bilateral hearing loss since birth or before acquiring language, with 60db or greater loss in better ear in speech frequencies of 500, 1,000 and 2,000 Hz. Must use speech and residual hearing and/or speech-reading (lip-reading) as preferred form of communication. Must be accepted or enrolled in college/university program that primarily enrolls students with normal hearing. Number of awards granted varies. Application deadline and notification dates vary; see Website for details and application.
Amount of award:	$500-$2,000

Contact:
Alexander Graham Bell Association for the Deaf and Hard of Hearing
Scholarship Awards Committee
3417 Volta Place, NW
Washington, DC 20007-2778
Phone: 202-337-5220
Web: www.agbell.org/DesktopDefault.aspx?p=Awards

Alexia Foundation

Alexia Foundation Grant and Scholarship

Type of award: Scholarship.
Intended use: For full-time undergraduate or graduate study in United States or Canada.
Basis for selection: Competition/talent/interest in photography.
Application requirements: Resume, portfolio of six to twenty slides (digital formats also accepted), 750 word essay detailing proposed picture story.
Additional information: Open to all undergraduates. Grand prize of full tuition scholarship to study photojournalism during fall semester at Syracuse University in London, plus $1,000 grant for completion of photo-story proposal. Additional awards will be given. Students who have completed more than three internships or who have a year of full-time professional experience are not eligible. Visit Website for more information and application.

Amount of award:	$2,100-$10,000
Number of awards:	5
Number of applicants:	52
Application deadline:	February 1

Contact:
David Sutherland S.I. Newhouse Communications Center
Syracuse University
215 University Place
Syracuse, NY 13244
Phone: 800-235-3472
Web: www.alexiafounadation.org

All-Ink.com

All-Ink.com College Scholarship Program

Type of award: Scholarship.
Intended use: For undergraduate or graduate study at accredited 2-year, 4-year or graduate institution.
Eligibility: Applicant must be U.S. citizen or permanent resident.
Basis for selection: Applicant must demonstrate high academic achievement.
Application requirements: Essay (50-200 words) on the person who has had the greatest impact on your life. Essay (50-200 words) on what you hope to achieve in your personal and professional life after college.
Additional information: Applicants may be high school seniors up to graduate students. Must have minimum 2.5 GPA. Applications must be completed and submitted online at www.all-ink.com/scholarship.aspx. Winners will be notified by February 20.

Application deadline:	December 31
Total amount awarded:	$5,000

Contact:
Web: www.all-ink.com/scholarship.aspx

Alliance for Young Artists and Writers

New York Times James B. Reston Writing Portfolio Award

Type of award: Scholarship.
Intended use: For at postsecondary institution.
Eligibility: Applicant must be high school senior.
Basis for selection: Competition/talent/interest in writing/journalism, based on originality, level of technical proficiency, and emergence of personal voice or style. Major/career interest in journalism.
Application requirements: $10 application fee. Portfolio, recommendations, essay. Portfolio must contain three to eight works with table of contents listing title and category of each piece. Entry form must be signed by student's parent and teacher, counselor or principal.
Additional information: One scholarship awarded to most outstanding nonfiction portfolio. Submission must be collection of nonfiction works intended to instruct, inform, explain, persuade, or entertain (i.e. essays, journalistic articles or editorials). Deadlines vary, contact sponsor or visit Website for details.

Amount of award:	$10,000
Number of awards:	1

Contact:
The Scholastic Art & Writing Awards
557 Broadway
New York, NY 10012
Phone: 212-343-6493
Web: www.artandwriting.org

Scholastic Art Portfolio Gold Award

Type of award: Scholarship.
Intended use: For at postsecondary institution.
Eligibility: Applicant must be high school senior.
Basis for selection: Competition/talent/interest in visual arts, based on originality, level of technical proficiency, and emergence of personal style or vision. Major/career interest in arts, general.
Application requirements: Portfolio, recommendations, essay, transcript. Eight works, including at least three drawings.
Additional information: Five unrestricted scholarships awarded to exemplary works. Deadlines vary. Contact sponsor or visit Website for more information.

Amount of award:	$10,000
Number of awards:	5
Total amount awarded:	$50,000

Contact:
The Scholastic Art & Writing Awards
557 Broadway
New York, NY 10012
Phone: 212-343-6493
Web: www.artandwriting.org

Scholastic Art Portfolio Silver Award

Type of award: Scholarship.
Intended use: For at postsecondary institution.
Eligibility: Applicant must be high school senior.
Basis for selection: Competition/talent/interest in visual arts, based on originality, level of technical proficiency, and emergence of personal style or vision. Major/career interest in arts, general.
Application requirements: Portfolio, recommendations, essay, transcript. Eight works, including at least three drawings.
Additional information: Approximately 100 students nominated for scholarships offered by participating higher education institutions. Deadlines vary. Contact sponsor or visit Website for more information.
   Number of awards: 100
Contact:
The Scholastic Art & Writing Awards
557 Broadway
New York, NY 10012
Phone: 212-343-6493
Web: www.artandwriting.org

Scholastic Photography Portfolio Gold Award

Type of award: Scholarship.
Intended use: For at postsecondary institution.
Eligibility: Applicant must be high school senior.
Basis for selection: Competition/talent/interest in photography, based on originality, level of technical proficiency, and emergence of personal style or vision. Major/career interest in arts, general.
Application requirements: Portfolio, recommendations, essay, transcript. Eight works in form of prints.
Additional information: Two unrestricted scholarships awarded to most outstanding photography portfolio. Deadlines vary. Contact sponsor or visit Website for more information.
   Amount of award: $10,000
   Number of awards: 2
   Total amount awarded: $20,000
Contact:
The Scholastic Art & Writing Awards
557 Broadway
New York, NY 10012
Phone: 212-343-6493
Web: www.artandwriting.org

Scholastic Photography Portfolio Silver Award

Type of award: Scholarship.
Intended use: For at postsecondary institution.
Eligibility: Applicant must be high school senior.
Basis for selection: Competition/talent/interest in photography, based on originality, level of technical proficiency, and emergence of personal style or vision. Major/career interest in arts, general.
Application requirements: Portfolio, recommendations, essay, transcript. Eight works in form of prints.
Additional information: Approximately 50 students nominated for scholarships offered by participating higher education institutions. Deadlines vary. Contact sponsor or visit Website for more information.
   Number of awards: 50
Contact:
The Scholastic Art & Writing Awards
557 Broadway
New York, NY 10012
Phone: 212-343-6493
Web: www.artandwriting.org

Scholastic Writing Portfolio Gold Award

Type of award: Scholarship.
Intended use: For at postsecondary institution.
Eligibility: Applicant must be high school senior.
Basis for selection: Competition/talent/interest in writing/journalism, based on originality, level of technical proficiency, and emergence of personal voice or style. Major/career interest in English; journalism; literature or theater arts.
Application requirements: $10 application fee. Portfolio, recommendations, essay. Portfolio must contain three to eight works of narratives, individual poems or dramatic scripts demonstrating diversity and talent. Excerpts from longer works encouraged. Entry form must be signed by student's parent and teacher, counselor or principal.
Additional information: Four unrestricted scholarships awarded to exemplary works. Deadlines vary. Contact sponsor or visit Website for more information.
   Amount of award: $10,000
   Number of awards: 5
   Total amount awarded: $50,000
Contact:
The Scholastic Art & Writing Awards
557 Broadway
New York, NY 10012
Phone: 212-343-6493
Web: www.artandwriting.org

Alpha Beta Gamma International, Inc.

Alpha Beta Gamma International Scholarship

Type of award: Scholarship.
Intended use: For full-time junior or senior study at accredited 4-year institution.
Eligibility: Applicant or parent must be member/participant of Alpha Beta Gamma.
Basis for selection: Major/career interest in business; business, international; business/management/administration; accounting or computer/information sciences. Applicant must demonstrate high academic achievement and leadership.
Application requirements: Recommendations. Completed institutional financial forms.
Additional information: Must be initiated members of Alpha Beta Gamma. Awarded to enrollees of two-year schools who have been accepted at four-year schools to pursue baccalaureate degrees in business or related professions, including computer and information sciences. Amount of award varies by institution.
   Amount of award: $500-$10,000
   Number of awards: 300
   Number of applicants: 400
   Total amount awarded: $600,000

Contact:
Alpha Beta Gamma
Scholarship Committee
75 Grasslands Road
Valhalla, NY 10595
Web: www.abg.org

Alpha Mu Gamma, the National Collegiate Foreign Language Honor Society

Alpha Mu Gamma National Scholarship

Type of award: Scholarship.
Intended use: For full-time sophomore, junior, senior, master's, doctoral, first professional or postgraduate study at 2-year, 4-year or graduate institution.
Eligibility: Applicant or parent must be member/participant of Alpha Mu Gamma.
Basis for selection: Major/career interest in foreign languages. Applicant must demonstrate high academic achievement and seriousness of purpose.
Application requirements: Transcript. One-page essay discussing personal, academic, and career goals, and how academic and other experiences have prepared applicant to succeed. Three letters of recommendation. Four copies of essay, recommendations, and application. One photocopy of applicant's AMG full member certificate.
Additional information: Applicant must be full Alpha Mu Gamma member. Three $750 awards granted for study of any foreign language; one $400 award for expenses toward free, intensive one-month French course at Laval University, Quebec, Canada; and one $400 award for study of Esperanto or Spanish. May apply an unlimited number of times. National office will not acknowledge communications about applications. Must be requested from advisor of local AMG chapter.

Amount of award:	$400-$750
Number of awards:	5
Application deadline:	February 1
Notification begins:	April 1
Total amount awarded:	$2,100

Contact:
Sponsor/adviser of the local Alpha Mu Gamma chapter.
Web: www.lacitycollege.edu/academic/honor/amg/homepage.htm

Alumnae Panhellenic Association of Washington, DC

Alumnae Panhellenic Association Women's Scholarship

Type of award: Scholarship, renewable.
Intended use: For undergraduate or graduate study at 4-year or graduate institution.
Eligibility: Applicant must be female. Applicant must be residing in District of Columbia.
Basis for selection: Major/career interest in philanthropy. Applicant must demonstrate high academic achievement, depth of character and service orientation.
Application requirements: Recommendations, essay, transcript.
Additional information: Applicants must live or attend school in Washington, DC, area and have a demonstrated interest in philanthropic activities. Applications received after deadline will not be accepted. Send SASE with application request.

Amount of award:	$1,000
Number of awards:	3
Number of applicants:	45
Application deadline:	March 15
Notification begins:	April 1
Total amount awarded:	$3,000

Contact:
Alumnae Panhellenic Association of Washington, DC
c/o Tiffany Waddell
5704 Chapman Mill Drive #150
North Bethesda, MD 20852

A.M. Castle & Co.

John M. Simpson Memorial Scholarship

Type of award: Scholarship, renewable.
Intended use: For full-time undergraduate study.
Eligibility: Applicant or parent must be employed by A. M. Castle & Co. Applicant must be high school senior.
Basis for selection: Major/career interest in humanities/liberal arts.
Application requirements: Recommendations, essay, transcript.
Additional information: For children of A.M. Castle & Co. employees who have been with company for at least three years. Award is $3,000 per year for four years. Student must submit SAT or ACT scores.

Amount of award:	$3,000
Number of awards:	2
Application deadline:	January 1

Contact:
A.M. Castle & Co.
3400 North Wolf Road
Franklin Park, IL 60131
Phone: 847-455-7111

AMBUCS

AMBUCS Scholars-Scholarship for Therapists

Type of award: Scholarship.
Intended use: For full-time junior, senior or master's study at accredited 4-year or graduate institution in United States. Designated institutions: Schools with programs accredited by appropriate health therapy association.
Eligibility: Applicant must be U.S. citizen.
Basis for selection: Major/career interest in occupational therapy; physical therapy or speech pathology/audiology.

Applicant must demonstrate financial need, depth of character and service orientation.
Additional information: Award amount typically maximum $1,500, but one additional two-year award of $6,000 offered. Students must apply online; no paper applications accepted. Applicants may print online enrollment certificate. Additional documentation, including prior year's 1040 tax form, requested if applicant is selected as semifinalist.
    Amount of award: $500-$6,000
    Number of awards: 400
    Number of applicants: 2,188
    Application deadline: April 15
    Notification begins: June 20
    Total amount awarded: $165,150
Contact:
AMBUCS Resource Center
P.O. Box 5127
High Point, NC 27262
Phone: 800-838-1845
Fax: 336-852-6830
Web: www.ambucs.org

America's Junior Miss, Inc.

Junior Miss Scholarship

Type of award: Scholarship.
Intended use: For undergraduate or graduate study.
Eligibility: Applicant must be single, female, high school junior or senior. Applicant must be U.S. citizen.
Basis for selection: Competition/talent/interest in poise/talent/fitness, based on scholastic evaluation, skill in creative and performing arts, physical fitness, presence and composure, and panel interview.
Additional information: Must compete in state of legal residence. State winners expected to compete at higher levels. Must never have been married or pregnant. Only high school seniors can compete in finals but students are encouraged to begin application process during sophomore year. Scholarship funds can be used for undergraduate work or deferred for graduate and professional studies. Visit Website for application deadline information, as it varies from state to state.
    Amount of award: $100-$50,000
    Number of applicants: 6,000
Contact:
America's Junior Miss
Contestant Inquiry
P.O. Box 2786
Mobile, AL 36652-2786
Phone: 800-256-5435
Fax: 251-431-0063
Web: www.ajm.org

American Alpine Club

Alpine Club A.K. Gilkey and Putnam/Bedayn Research Grant

Type of award: Research grant.
Intended use: For undergraduate or graduate study.
Eligibility: Applicant must be U.S. citizen.
Basis for selection: Major/career interest in science, general; biology; environmental science; forestry or atmospheric sciences/meteorology.
Application requirements: Recommendations, research proposal. Curriculum vitae with all biographical information.
Additional information: Research proposals evaluated on scientific or technical quality and contribution to scientific endeavor germane to mountain regions. Applications available from Website.
    Amount of award: $200-$1,000
    Application deadline: March 1
Contact:
American Alpine Club
710 Tenth Street
Suite 100
Golden, CO 80401
Phone: 303-384-0110
Fax: 303-384-0111
Web: www.americanalpineclub.org

American Architectural Foundation

AIA/AAF Minority/Disadvantaged Scholarship

Type of award: Scholarship, renewable.
Intended use: For full-time undergraduate study in United States. Designated institutions: NAAB-accredited institutions.
Eligibility: Applicant must be U.S. citizen or permanent resident.
Basis for selection: Major/career interest in architecture. Applicant must demonstrate financial need.
Application requirements: Recommendations, essay, transcript, nomination by high school guidance counselor, architect, AIA component, or other individual who can speak to student's aptitude for architecture. Statement of disadvantaged circumstances. A drawing must also be included.
Additional information: Application sent to eligible students after nomination screening. Nomination form due early December; call between September 15 and December 1 to request form, or download from Website. Open to high school seniors and college freshmen who plan to enter programs leading to professional degree in architecture. Students who have completed full year of undergraduate course work not eligible. Renewable up to two years.
    Amount of award: $500-$2,000
    Number of awards: 20
    Number of applicants: 100
    Application deadline: January 15
    Notification begins: March 1
Contact:
American Institute of Architects
1735 New York Avenue, NW
Washington, DC 20006-5292
Phone: 202-626-7511
Fax: 202-626-7509
Web: www.archfoundation.org

RTKL Traveling Fellowship

Type of award: Research grant.
Intended use: For full-time senior, master's or first professional study at accredited 4-year or graduate institution in

United States. Designated institutions: NAAB-accredited institutions.
Basis for selection: Major/career interest in architecture.
Application requirements: Recommendations, transcript. Travel proposal budget outlining foreign itinerary directly relevant to applicant's educational goals.
Additional information: Must be in or be accepted to professional degree program in architecture. Award to be applied to travel. Application available from NAAB-accredited institutions, the AAF, or Website.

Amount of award:	$2,500
Number of awards:	1
Number of applicants:	50
Application deadline:	February 15
Total amount awarded:	$2,500

Contact:
American Architectural Foundation
Mary Felber
1735 New York Ave, NW
Washington, DC 20006-5292
Phone: 202-626-7511
Fax: 202-626-7509
Web: www.archfoundation.org

American Association for Cancer Research

Thomas J. Bardos Science Education Awards for Undergraduate Students

Type of award: Research grant.
Intended use: For full-time junior study at 4-year institution.
Basis for selection: Major/career interest in biochemistry; biology; chemistry; pharmacy/pharmaceutics/pharmacology; microbiology or engineering, chemical.
Application requirements: Cover letter, reference letters. Personal statement (no longer than two single-spaced pages in length).
Additional information: Two-year award consists of $1,500 per year and registration fee waiver for AACR annual meeting. Selection based on qualifications and interest in research, mentor references, and selection committee's evaluation of potential professional benefit. Applicants not yet committed to cancer research welcome; those studying molecular biology, genetics, pathology, or other related fields also eligible. Awardees must attend scientific sessions at AACR meeting for at least four days and participate in required activities. Must submit two comprehensive reports each year. For more information, contact AACR or visit Website. Application deadline in early December; notification begins in mid-January.

Amount of award:	$3,000

Contact:
American Association for Cancer Research
615 Chestnut Street, 17th Floor
Philadelphia, PA 19106-4404
Phone: 215-440-9300
Fax: 215-440-9412
Web: www.aacr.org

American Association of Airport Executives

American Association of Airport Executives Foundation Scholarship

Type of award: Scholarship.
Intended use: For full-time junior, senior or graduate study at accredited 4-year or graduate institution in United States.
Basis for selection: Major/career interest in aviation. Applicant must demonstrate financial need and high academic achievement.
Application requirements: Recommendations, transcript, nomination by school or aviation management department.
Additional information: Must have 3.0 GPA. Extracurricular and community activities important. Applicant must have reached at least junior year in an aviation/airport management program. Each school may submit only one student's application. Pick up applications at college scholarship office.

Amount of award:	$1,000
Number of awards:	10
Application deadline:	March 31
Total amount awarded:	$10,000

Contact:
The A.A.A.E. Foundation Scholarship Program
Scholarship Managers
P.O. Box 2810
Cherry Hill, NJ 08034
Phone: 856-573-9400
Fax: 856-573-9799
Web: www.aaae.org

American Association of Airport Executives Foundation Scholarship for Native Americans

Type of award: Scholarship.
Intended use: For full-time junior, senior or graduate study at accredited 4-year or graduate institution in United States.
Eligibility: Applicant must be American Indian.
Basis for selection: Major/career interest in aviation. Applicant must demonstrate financial need and high academic achievement.
Application requirements: Recommendations, transcript, nomination by school or aviation management department.
Additional information: Must have 3.0 GPA. Extracurricular and community activities important. Applicant must have reached at least junior year in an aviation/airport management program. Must apply through school scholarship or aviation management department. Only one recommendation per school. Pick up applications at college/university scholarship office.

Amount of award:	$1,000
Number of awards:	10
Application deadline:	March 31
Notification begins:	May 31

Contact:
The A.A.A.E. Scholarship Program for Native Americans
Scholarship Managers
P.O. Box 2810
Cherry Hill, NJ 08034
Phone: 856-573-9400
Fax: 856-573-9799
Web: www.aaae.org

American Association of Airport Executives Scholarship for Accredited Airport Executives (A.A.E.)

Type of award: Scholarship.
Intended use: For undergraduate or graduate study in United States.
Basis for selection: Applicant must demonstrate high academic achievement.
Application requirements: Recommendations, essay.
Additional information: Must be spouse or child of active, retired, or deceased A.A.E. Retired A.A.E.'s may also apply. Should demonstrate school and community activities and work experience.

Amount of award:	$900-$4,000
Application deadline:	March 31
Notification begins:	May 31

Contact:
The A.A.A.E. Foundation Scholarship Program for A.A.E.'s
Scholarship Managers
P.O. Box 2810
Cherry Hill, NJ 08034
Phone: 856-616-9311
Fax: 856-573-9799
Web: www.aaae.org

American Association of Critical Care Nurses

Critical Care Nurses Education Advancement Scholarship

Type of award: Scholarship.
Intended use: For junior, senior or graduate study.
Eligibility: Applicant must be U.S. citizen or permanent resident.
Basis for selection: Major/career interest in nursing or nurse practitioner. Applicant must demonstrate high academic achievement and seriousness of purpose.
Additional information: Intended for students who do not hold RN license (applicants may hold degrees in other nursing fields). Must be currently enrolled in NLN-accredited BSN or graduate program, and have cumulative 3.0 GPA or better. Applicant must be member of National Student Nurses Association or American Association of Critical Care Nurses. Program administered by NSNA. Application available on Website starting in August. Send SASE with all inquiries.

Amount of award:	$1,500
Number of awards:	100
Application deadline:	April 1
Notification begins:	July 31

Contact:
National Student Nurses Association
45 Main Street
Suite 606
Brooklyn, NY 11201
Phone: 718-210-0705
Web: www.nsna.org

Education Advancement Scholarship

Type of award: Scholarship, renewable.
Intended use: For junior or senior study at accredited 4-year institution in United States.
Eligibility: Applicant or parent must be member/participant of American Association of Critical Care Nurses. Applicant must be U.S. citizen or permanent resident.
Basis for selection: Major/career interest in nursing.
Application requirements: Essay, transcript, proof of eligibility.
Additional information: Minimum 3.0 GPA required. Must be licensed nurse (RN) and American Association of Critical Care Nurses member who works in critical care unit or has had one year's experience in last three years. Current enrollment in state-accredited nursing program. Recipients announced in summer for the fall academic term.

Amount of award:	$1,500
Application deadline:	April 1
Notification begins:	July 31

Contact:
American Association of Critical Care Nurses
101 Columbia
Aliso Viejo, CA 92656-4109
Phone: 800-899-2226
Fax: 949-362-2020
Web: www.aacn.org

American Board of Funeral Service Education

American Board of Funeral Service Education National Scholarship

Type of award: Scholarship.
Intended use: For full-time undergraduate study at 2-year or 4-year institution in United States.
Eligibility: Applicant must be U.S. citizen or permanent resident.
Basis for selection: Major/career interest in mortuary science. Applicant must demonstrate financial need, high academic achievement, depth of character, leadership and seriousness of purpose.
Application requirements: Recommendations, essay.
Additional information: Student must have completed at least one semester (or quarter) of study in funeral service or mortuary science education program accredited by American Board of Funeral Service Education. For more information and application, visit Website. Extracurricular activities are considered for eligibility.

Amount of award:	$250-$2,500
Number of awards:	30
Number of applicants:	80
Application deadline:	March 1, September 1

Contact:
American Board of Funeral Service Education
Attn: Scholarship Committee
3432 Ashland, Suite U
St. Joseph, MO 64506
Phone: 816-233-3747
Fax: 816-233-3793
Web: www.abfse.org

American Cancer Society Great Lakes Division Foundation

Young Survivor Scholarship

Type of award: Scholarship, renewable.
Intended use: For full-time undergraduate study at accredited postsecondary institution in United States.
Eligibility: Applicant must be no older than 20. Applicant must be U.S. citizen residing in Michigan or Indiana.
Basis for selection: Applicant must demonstrate financial need, depth of character, leadership and service orientation.
Application requirements: Recommendations, essay, transcript, proof of eligibility. FAFSA. Letter from doctor verifying diagnosis.
Additional information: American Cancer Society's college scholarships are Michigan and Indiana's first and only scholarship opportunities exclusively for students with history of cancer. Applicant must be cancer survivor, diagnosed before age 21.

Amount of award:	$2,500
Number of applicants:	115
Application deadline:	April 16

Contact:
American Cancer Society Great Lakes Division Foundation
Young Survivor Scholarship Program
1755 Abbey Road
East Lansing, MI 48823
Phone: 800-723-0360
Web: www.cancer.org/scholarships

American Center of Oriental Research

Jennifer C. Groot Fellowship

Type of award: Research grant.
Intended use: For undergraduate or graduate study at 4-year or graduate institution.
Eligibility: Applicant must be U.S. citizen or Canadian citizen.
Basis for selection: Major/career interest in archaeology; Middle Eastern studies; ancient near eastern studies or ethnic/cultural studies.
Application requirements: Proof of archaeological fieldwork in Jordan.
Additional information: Applicant must be accepted as staff member on archaeological project in Jordan with ASOR/CAP affiliation. Award used only for travel to project site in Jordan.

Amount of award:	$1,500
Number of awards:	3
Number of applicants:	15
Application deadline:	February 1
Notification begins:	April 15

Contact:
American Center of Oriental Research
Reseach Grant Coordinator
656 Beacon Street
Boston, MA 02215-2010
Phone: 617-353-6571
Fax: 617-353-6575
Web: www.bu.edu/acor

American Chemical Society

American Chemical Society Scholars Program

Type of award: Scholarship.
Intended use: For full-time freshman, sophomore, junior or senior study at accredited 2-year or 4-year institution in United States.
Eligibility: Applicant must be Alaskan native, African American, Mexican American, Hispanic American, Puerto Rican, American Indian or Native Hawaiian/Pacific Islander. Applicant must be U.S. citizen or permanent resident.
Basis for selection: Major/career interest in chemistry; biochemistry; engineering, chemical; materials science; environmental science; forensics or food science/technology. Applicant must demonstrate financial need, high academic achievement, seriousness of purpose and service orientation.
Application requirements: Recommendations, transcript. FAFSA.
Additional information: Majors/career interest may also be in toxicology. Must have minimum 3.0 GPA.

Amount of award:	$5,000
Number of awards:	125
Number of applicants:	600
Application deadline:	March 1
Notification begins:	June 1

Contact:
American Chemical Society
Scholars Program
1155 Sixteenth Street, NW
Washington, DC 20036
Phone: 800-227-5558 ext. 6250
Fax: 202-776-8003
Web: www.chemistry.org/scholars

American Classical League/ National Junior Classical League

Latin Honor Society Scholarship

Type of award: Scholarship.
Intended use: For full-time freshman study at 2-year or 4-year institution.
Eligibility: Applicant or parent must be member/participant of National Junior Classical League. Applicant must be high school senior.
Basis for selection: Major/career interest in Classics or education, teacher.

American Classical League/National Junior Classical League: Latin Honor Society Scholarship

Application requirements: Recommendations, essay, transcript.
Additional information: Must have been member of National Junior Classics League for at least three years and must be enrolled in National Junior Classics League Latin Honor Society for current academic year and at least one preceding year. Must be planning to teach Latin or Classics. Application available online.

Amount of award:	$1,500
Number of awards:	1
Application deadline:	May 1
Total amount awarded:	$1,500

Contact:
American Classical League
Miami University
422 Wells Mill Drive
Oxford, OH 45056
Phone: 513-529-7741
Fax: 513-529-7742
Web: www.aclclassics.org

Maureen V. O'Donnell Memorial Teacher Training Award

Type of award: Scholarship.
Intended use: For junior, senior or master's study at 4-year or graduate institution.
Eligibility: Applicant or parent must be member/participant of American Classical League.
Basis for selection: Major/career interest in education, teacher or Classics. Applicant must demonstrate financial need.
Application requirements: Recommendations, transcript.
Additional information: Must be training for certification to teach Latin and have completed a substantial number of these courses.

Amount of award:	$1,000
Application deadline:	December 1, March 1

Contact:
American Classical League
Miami University
422 Wells Mill Drive
Oxford, OH 45056
Phone: 513-529-7741
Fax: 513-529-7742
Web: www.aclclassics.org

McKinlay Summer Award

Type of award: Scholarship.
Intended use: For non-degree study.
Eligibility: Applicant or parent must be member/participant of American Classical League.
Basis for selection: Major/career interest in Classics or education, teacher. Applicant must demonstrate financial need.
Application requirements: Recommendations.
Additional information: Must have been member of American Classical League for three years preceding application. Must be planning to teach Classics in elementary or secondary school in upcoming school year. May apply for independent study program funding or support to attend American Classical League Institute for first time. Total amount awarded varies each year.

Amount of award:	$1,500
Application deadline:	January 15

Contact:
American Classical League
Miami University
422 Wells Mill Drive
Oxford, OH 45056
Phone: 513-529-7741
Fax: 513-529-7742
Web: www.aclclassics.org

National Junior Classical League Scholarship

Type of award: Scholarship.
Intended use: For full-time freshman study at 2-year or 4-year institution.
Eligibility: Applicant or parent must be member/participant of National Junior Classical League. Applicant must be high school senior.
Basis for selection: Major/career interest in Classics; humanities/liberal arts or education, teacher. Applicant must demonstrate financial need, high academic achievement, depth of character, leadership, patriotism, seriousness of purpose and service orientation.
Application requirements: Recommendations, transcript, proof of eligibility.
Additional information: Preference given to applicants who intend to teach Latin, Greek or classical humanities.

Amount of award:	$1,000-$2,000
Number of awards:	9
Application deadline:	May 1
Total amount awarded:	$11,200

Contact:
American Classical League
Miami University
422 Wells Mill Drive
Oxford, OH 45056
Phone: 513-529-7741
Fax: 513-529-7742
Web: www.aclclassics.org

American College of Musicians/National Guild of Piano Teachers

American College of Musicians $200 Scholarship

Type of award: Scholarship.
Intended use: For non-degree study.
Basis for selection: Major/career interest in music.
Application requirements: Nomination by piano teacher, who must be member of National Guild of Piano Teachers.
Additional information: Award to be used for piano study. Student must have been in national or international solo auditions for ten years, be Guild Paderewski winner, and be Guild High School diploma recipient.

Amount of award:	$200
Number of awards:	150
Application deadline:	September 15
Notification begins:	October 1

Contact:
National Guild of Piano Teachers
International Headquarters
P.O. Box 1807
Austin, TX 78767-1807
Phone: 512-478-5775
Web: www.pianoguild.com

American College of Musicians Piano Composition Contest

Type of award: Scholarship.
Intended use: For non-degree study.
Basis for selection: Competition/talent/interest in music performance/composition, based on compositions for solo keyboard and keyboard ensemble. Major/career interest in music.
Application requirements: Manuscript of composition.
Additional information: Teacher must be member of National Guild of Piano Teachers. Compositions rated on imagination, originality, and skill. Entry fees vary according to classification of students and length of composition. See Website for specific details.
    Amount of award: $50-$150
    Number of awards: 14
    Application deadline: November 8
Contact:
National Guild of Piano Teachers
International Headquarters
P.O. Box 1807
Austin, TX 78767-1807
Phone: 512-478-5775
Web: www.pianoguild.com

American Congress on Surveying and Mapping

AAGS Joseph F. Dracup Scholarship Award

Type of award: Scholarship, renewable.
Intended use: For undergraduate study at 4-year institution.
Eligibility: Applicant or parent must be member/participant of American Congress of Surveying and Mapping.
Basis for selection: Major/career interest in surveying/mapping. Applicant must demonstrate high academic achievement and seriousness of purpose.
Application requirements: Recommendations, essay, transcript, proof of eligibility.
Additional information: Preference will be given to applicants with significant focus on geodetic surveying. Visit Website for deadlines and additional information.
    Amount of award: $2,000
    Number of awards: 1
    Total amount awarded: $2,000
Contact:
American Congress on Surveying and Mapping
6 Montgomery Village Avenue
Suite 403
Gaithersburg, MD 20879
Phone: 240-632-9716 ext. 113
Fax: 240-632-1321
Web: www.acsm.net

ACSM Fellows Scholarship

Type of award: Scholarship.
Intended use: For junior or senior study at 4-year institution.
Additional information: May be student of any ACSM disciplines. Visit website for deadlines and additional information.
    Amount of award: $2,000
    Number of awards: 1
    Total amount awarded: $2,000
Contact:
American Congress on Surveying & Mapping
6 Montgomery Village Avenue
Suite 403
Gaithersburg, MD 20879
Phone: 240-632-9716 ext. 113
Fax: 240-632-1321
Web: www.acsm.net

Berntsen International Scholarship in Surveying

Type of award: Scholarship, renewable.
Intended use: For undergraduate study at 4-year institution.
Eligibility: Applicant or parent must be member/participant of American Congress of Surveying and Mapping.
Basis for selection: Major/career interest in surveying/mapping. Applicant must demonstrate high academic achievement and seriousness of purpose.
Application requirements: Recommendations, essay, transcript, proof of eligibility.
Additional information: Open to students in surveying or closely related programs such as geomatics or surveying engineering. Degree of financial need will be used, if necessary, to break ties after the primary criteria have been considered. Awarded by Berntsen International Inc. of Madison, Wisconsin. Visit website for deadlines and additional information.
    Amount of award: $1,500
    Number of awards: 1
    Total amount awarded: $1,500
Contact:
American Congress on Surveying and Mapping
6 Montgomery Village Avenue
Suite 403
Gaithersburg, MD 20879
Phone: 240-632-9716 ext. 113
Fax: 240-632-1321
Web: www.acsm.net

Berntsen International Scholarship in Surveying Technology

Type of award: Scholarship, renewable.
Intended use: For undergraduate certificate study at 2-year institution.
Eligibility: Applicant or parent must be member/participant of American Congress of Surveying and Mapping.
Basis for selection: Major/career interest in surveying/mapping or cartography. Applicant must demonstrate high academic achievement and seriousness of purpose.
Application requirements: Recommendations, essay, transcript, proof of eligibility.
Additional information: Award for programs in surveying technology. Awarded by Berntsen International Inc. of Madison, Wisconsin. Visit Website for deadlines and additional information.

Amount of award:	$500
Number of awards:	1

Contact:
American Congress on Surveying and Mapping
6 Montgomery Village Avenue
Suite 403
Gaithersburg, MD 20879
Phone: 240-632-9716 ext. 113
Fax: 240-632-1321
Web: www.acsm.net

Cady McDonnell Memorial Scholarship

Type of award: Scholarship, renewable.
Intended use: For undergraduate study at 2-year or 4-year institution.
Eligibility: Applicant or parent must be member/participant of American Congress of Surveying and Mapping. Applicant must be female. Applicant must be residing in Utah, Alaska, Washington, Arizona, Nevada, Wyoming, California, Montana, Oregon, New Mexico, Idaho, Colorado or Hawaii.
Basis for selection: Major/career interest in surveying/mapping or cartography. Applicant must demonstrate high academic achievement and seriousness of purpose.
Application requirements: Recommendations, essay, transcript, proof of eligibility. Proof of legal home residence.
Additional information: Degree of financial need will be used, if necessary, to break ties after the primary criteria have been considered. Visit Website for deadlines and additional information.

Amount of award:	$1,000
Number of awards:	1
Total amount awarded:	$1,000

Contact:
American Congress on Surveying and Mapping
6 Montgomery Village Avenue
Suite 403
Gaithersburg, MD 20879
Phone: 240-632-9716 ext. 113
Fax: 240-632-1321
Web: www.acsm.net

CaGIS Scholarship Award

Type of award: Scholarship, renewable.
Intended use: For full-time undergraduate or graduate study at 4-year or graduate institution.
Eligibility: Applicant or parent must be member/participant of American Congress of Surveying and Mapping.
Basis for selection: Major/career interest in cartography or surveying/mapping. Applicant must demonstrate high academic achievement and seriousness of purpose.
Application requirements: Recommendations, essay, transcript, proof of eligibility.
Additional information: Open to students of cartography, GIS or other mapping sciences. One award of $1,000 for Ph.D. student, $500 for one masters/undergraduate student. Undergraduates will compete with master's students. Preference will be given to undergraduates with junior or senior standing. Awarded by the Cartography and Geographic Information Society (CaGIS). Visit Website for deadlines and additional information.

Amount of award:	$500-$1,000
Number of awards:	2
Total amount awarded:	$1,500

Contact:
American Congress on Surveying and Mapping
6 Montgomery Village Avenue
Suite 403
Gaithersburg, MD 20879
Phone: 240-632-9716 ext. 113
Fax: 240-632-1321
Web: www.acsm.net

The Lowell H. and Dorothy Loving Undergraduate Scholarship

Type of award: Scholarship.
Intended use: For undergraduate study.
Additional information: Visit website for deadlines and additional information.

Amount of award:	$2,500
Number of awards:	1
Total amount awarded:	$2,500

Contact:
ACSM
6 Montgomery Village Avenue
Suite 403
Gaithersburg, MD 20879
Phone: 240-632-9716 ext. 113
Fax: 240-632-1321
Web: www.acsm.net

Nettie Dracup Memorial Scholarship

Type of award: Scholarship, renewable.
Intended use: For undergraduate study at accredited 4-year institution.
Eligibility: Applicant or parent must be member/participant of American Congress of Surveying and Mapping. Applicant must be U.S. citizen.
Basis for selection: Major/career interest in surveying/mapping. Applicant must demonstrate high academic achievement and seriousness of purpose.
Application requirements: Recommendations, essay, transcript, proof of eligibility.
Additional information: Intended for students enrolled in geodetic surveying. Degree of financial need will be used, if necessary, to break ties after primary criteria have been considered. Visit website for deadlines and additional information.

Amount of award:	$2,000
Number of awards:	1
Total amount awarded:	$2,000

Contact:
American Congress on Surveying and Mapping
6 Montgomery Village Avenue
Suite 403
Gaithersburg, MD 20879
Phone: 240-632-9716 ext. 113
Fax: 240-632-1321
Web: www.acsm.net

NSPS Board of Governors Scholarship

Type of award: Scholarship, renewable.
Intended use: For junior study at 4-year institution.
Eligibility: Applicant or parent must be member/participant of American Congress of Surveying and Mapping.

Basis for selection: Major/career interest in surveying/mapping. Applicant must demonstrate high academic achievement and seriousness of purpose.
Application requirements: Recommendations, essay, transcript, proof of eligibility.
Additional information: Minimum 3.0 GPA. Degree of financial need will be used, if necessary, to break ties after the primary criteria have been considered. Visit website for deadlines additional information.

Amount of award:	$1,000
Number of awards:	1
Total amount awarded:	$1,000

Contact:
American Congress on Surveying and Mapping
6 Montgomery Village Avenue
Suite 403
Gaithersburg, MD 20879
Phone: 240-632-9716 ext. 113
Fax: 240-632-1321
Web: www.acsm.net

NSPS Scholarships

Type of award: Scholarship, renewable.
Intended use: For full-time undergraduate study at 4-year institution.
Eligibility: Applicant or parent must be member/participant of American Congress of Surveying and Mapping.
Basis for selection: Major/career interest in surveying/mapping. Applicant must demonstrate high academic achievement and seriousness of purpose.
Application requirements: Recommendations, essay, transcript, proof of eligibility.
Additional information: Degree of financial need will be used, if necessary, to break ties after the primary criteria have been considered. Awarded by National Society of Professional Surveyors. Visit Website for deadlines additional information.

Amount of award:	$1,000
Number of awards:	2
Total amount awarded:	$2,000

Contact:
American Congress on Surveying and Mapping
6 Montgomery Village Avenue
Suite 403
Gaithersburg, MD 20879
Phone: 240-632-9716 ext. 113
Fax: 240-632-1321
Web: www.acsm.net

Schonstedt Scholarships in Surveying

Type of award: Scholarship, renewable.
Intended use: For undergraduate study at 4-year institution.
Eligibility: Applicant or parent must be member/participant of American Congress of Surveying and Mapping.
Basis for selection: Major/career interest in surveying/mapping. Applicant must demonstrate high academic achievement and seriousness of purpose.
Application requirements: Recommendations, essay, transcript, proof of eligibility.
Additional information: Preference given to applicants with junior or senior standing. Degree of financial need will be used, if necessary, to break ties after primary criteria have been considered. Awarded by Schonstedt Instrument Company of Kearneysville, West Virginia. Schonstedt donates magnetic locator to surveying program at each recipient's school. Visit website for deadlines and additional information.

Amount of award:	$1,500
Number of awards:	2
Total amount awarded:	$3,000

Contact:
American Congress on Surveying and Mapping
6 Montgomery Village Avenue
Suite 403
Gaithersburg, MD 20879
Phone: 240-632-9716 ext. 113
Fax: 240-632-1321
Web: www.acsm.net

Tri-State Surveying & Photogrammetry Kris M. Kunze Scholarship

Type of award: Scholarship.
Intended use: For undergraduate study at postsecondary institution.
Basis for selection: Major/career interest in business; business/management/administration or surveying/mapping.
Additional information: First priority: licensed professional land surveyors or certified photogrammetrists taking college business administration or management courses. Second priority: certified land survey interns taking college business administration or management courses. Third priority: full-time students in two or four-year surveying and mapping degree program and taking business administration or management courses. Visit website for deadlines and additional information.

Amount of award:	$1,000
Number of awards:	1
Total amount awarded:	$1,000

Contact:
ACSM
6 Montgomery Village Avenue
Suite 403
Gaithersburg, MD 20879
Phone: 240-632-9716 ext. 113
Fax: 240-632-1321
Web: www.acsm.net

American Council of Engineering Companies

American Council of Engineering Companies-Alaska Scholarship

Type of award: Scholarship, renewable.
Intended use: Designated institutions: ABET-accredited engineering programs.
Eligibility: Applicant must be residing in Alaska.
Basis for selection: Major/career interest in engineering.
Application requirements: Recommendations, essay, transcript.
Additional information: ACEC-Alaska accepts applications using the national format each late summer/fall. Preference is given to students in approved engineering fields entering junior, senior or post-graduate years. Applicants at all levels encouraged to apply. Winners of Alaska scholarship may be submitted to National for additional consideration.

Amount of award:	$1,000-$2,000
Number of awards:	2
Total amount awarded:	$2,000

Contact:
American Council of Engineering Companies
1015 15th Street NW
8th Floor
Washington, DC 20005-2605
Phone: 202-347-7474
Fax: 202-898-0068
Web: www.acec.org/awards/scholarships.cfm

American Council of the Blind

Floyd Qualls Memorial Scholarship

Type of award: Scholarship, renewable.
Intended use: For full-time undergraduate or graduate study at postsecondary institution in United States.
Eligibility: Applicant must be visually impaired.
Basis for selection: Applicant must demonstrate high academic achievement, depth of character and leadership.
Application requirements: Interview, recommendations, essay, transcript, proof of eligibility. Proof of legal blindness. Entering or transferring students must show proof of registration at accredited school.
Additional information: Applicant must be legally blind in both eyes. Must be in or currently under consideration for postsecondary program. Two awards for entering freshmen, two for other undergraduates, two for graduates, two for vocational students. Additional scholarships available: contact ACB for more information.

Amount of award:	$2,500
Number of awards:	15
Application deadline:	March 1
Notification begins:	May 15
Total amount awarded:	$37,500

Contact:
American Council of the Blind Scholarships
Attn: Patricia Castillo
1155 15 Street NW, Suite 1004
Washington, DC 20005
Phone: 800-424-8666
Fax: 202-467-5085
Web: www.acb.org

American Dental Assistants Association/Oral B Laboratories

Juliette A. Southard/Oral B Laboratories Scholarship

Type of award: Scholarship.
Intended use: For undergraduate study.
Eligibility: Applicant or parent must be member/participant of American Dental Assistants Association.
Basis for selection: Major/career interest in dental assistant. Applicant must demonstrate high academic achievement, depth of character and leadership.
Application requirements: Recommendations, transcript, proof of eligibility.
Additional information: Scholarship open to high school graduates and GED certificate holders. Must be American Dental Assistants Association member or American Dental Assistants Association student member. Applicants must be enrolled in dental assisting program or be taking courses applicable to furthering career in dental assisting.

Amount of award:	$500
Number of awards:	10
Number of applicants:	10
Application deadline:	March 1

Contact:
American Dental Assistants Association
Erek Armentrout
35 East Wacker Drive, Suite 1730
Chicago, IL 60601
Phone: 312-541-1550
Fax: 312-541-1496
Web: www.dentalassistant.org

American Dietetic Association Foundation

Graduate, Baccalaureate or Coordinated Program Scholarships

Type of award: Scholarship, renewable.
Intended use: For full-time junior, senior or graduate study at accredited 4-year institution. Designated institutions: CADE-accredited/approved dietetics education programs.
Eligibility: Applicant must be U.S. citizen or permanent resident.
Basis for selection: Major/career interest in dietetics/nutrition. Applicant must demonstrate high academic achievement and seriousness of purpose.
Application requirements: Recommendations, proof of eligibility. GPA documentation signed by academic advisor.
Additional information: Number and amount of awards vary; sponsor awarded about 210 scholarships to graduates and undergraduates in 2006-2007 school year. All scholarships require ADA membership. To be eligible, applicant must be enrolled in the approved program a minimum of four months during the academic year. Minority status considered. Must demonstrate or show promise of being a valuable, contributing member of the profession. See Website for more information and application.

Amount of award:	$500-$5,000
Number of awards:	200
Number of applicants:	500
Application deadline:	February 15
Total amount awarded:	$280,000

Contact:
American Dietetic Association
Education Programs
120 South Riverside Plaza, Suite 2000
Chicago, IL 60606-6995
Phone: 800-877-1600 ext. 5400
Web: www.eatright.org/scholelig.html

American Electroplaters and Surface Finishers Foundation

American Electroplaters and Surface Finishers Foundation Scholarship

Type of award: Scholarship, renewable.
Intended use: For full-time junior, senior or graduate study.
Basis for selection: Major/career interest in engineering, materials; engineering, chemical; engineering, environmental or chemistry.
Application requirements: Recommendations, essay, transcript. Resume.
Additional information: Undergrad applicants must have 3.0 GPA, graduates 3.3 GPA. May apply to any field of study or research related to plating and surface finishing technologies. Award notification occurs between late July and early August. Must reapply for renewal.

Amount of award:	$1,500
Number of applicants:	75
Application deadline:	April 15
Total amount awarded:	$10,500

Contact:
AESF Foundation
Attn: Scholarship
1155 Fifteenth Street, Suite 500
Washington, DC 20005
Phone: 202-457-8401
Fax: 202-530-0659
Web: www.nasf.org

American Federation of State, County and Municipal Employees

AFSCME Family Scholarship

Type of award: Scholarship, renewable.
Intended use: For full-time undergraduate study at accredited 4-year institution.
Eligibility: Applicant must be high school senior.
Application requirements: Recommendations, essay, transcript, proof of eligibility. SAT or ACT scores. Essay on subject: "What AFSCME means to our family." Copy of current AFSCME membership card.
Additional information: Scholarship open to children and grandchildren of AFSCME members.

Amount of award:	$2,000
Number of awards:	13
Number of applicants:	700
Application deadline:	December 31
Notification begins:	March 31

Contact:
American Federation of State, County and Municipal Employees
Education Department
1625 L Street NW
Washington, DC 20036
Web: www.afscme.org

Jerry Clark Memorial Scholarship

Type of award: Scholarship, renewable.
Intended use: For full-time junior or senior study at accredited 4-year institution.
Basis for selection: Major/career interest in political science/government; sociology; communications or ethnic/cultural studies. Applicant must demonstrate high academic achievement.
Application requirements: Proof of eligibility.
Additional information: Scholarship open to children and grandchildren of AFSCME members. Applicant must be a current college sophomore with a declared political science major. Winner given opportunity to intern at International Union Headquarters in Political Action department. Minimum 2.5 GPA required.

Amount of award:	$5,000
Number of awards:	2
Number of applicants:	30
Application deadline:	July 1
Notification begins:	August 1
Total amount awarded:	$10,000

Contact:
American Federation of State, County and Municipal Employees
Education Department
1625 L Street NW
Washington, DC 20036
Web: www.afscme.org

Union Plus Scholarship

Type of award: Scholarship.
Intended use: For undergraduate study at accredited vocational or 2-year institution.
Eligibility: Applicant or parent must be member/participant of American Fed. of State/County/Municipal Employees.
Basis for selection: Applicant must demonstrate financial need and high academic achievement.
Application requirements: Recommendations, essay, transcript, proof of eligibility.
Additional information: Members must have at least one year of continuous good-standing membership in AFSCME in order for spouses and children to be eligible.

Amount of award:	$500-$4,000
Application deadline:	January 31
Notification begins:	May 31

Contact:
American Federation of State, County and Municipal Employees
1625 L Street, N.W.
Washington, DC 20036-5687
Web: www.afscme.org

American Floral Endowment

Dosatron International Scholarship

Type of award: Scholarship.
Intended use: For junior, senior or graduate study at accredited 4-year or graduate institution in United States or Canada.
Eligibility: Applicant must be U.S. citizen, permanent resident or Canadian citizen.
Basis for selection: Major/career interest in horticulture. Applicant must demonstrate financial need and high academic achievement.
Application requirements: Recommendations, transcript. Statement of academic and professional intent.
Additional information: Minimum 3.0 GPA. Applicant must have interest in floriculture production, with a career goal of working in a greenhouse. Number and amount of scholarships vary.
    Amount of award: $500-$2,000
    Application deadline: June 1
    Notification begins: August 1
Contact:
American Floral Endowment
1 Horticultural Lane
P.O. Box 945
Edwardsville, IL 62025-0945
Phone: 618-692-0045
Fax: 618-692-4045
Web: www.endowment.org

Earl Dedman Memorial Scholarship

Type of award: Scholarship.
Intended use: For full-time sophomore, junior or senior study at accredited 4-year institution in United States or Canada.
Eligibility: Applicant must be U.S. citizen, permanent resident or Canadian citizen.
Basis for selection: Major/career interest in horticulture.
Application requirements: Recommendations, transcript. Statement of academic and professional intent.
Additional information: Minimum 3.0 GPA. Career interest in horticulture and becoming a grower required. To apply for this scholarship, applicant must have interest in greenhouse production and potted plants. Applicant must be from the Northwestern area of the U.S. Number and amount of scholarships vary.
    Amount of award: $500-$2,000
    Application deadline: June 1
    Notification begins: August 1
Contact:
American Floral Endowment
1 Horticultural Lane
P.O. Box 945
Edwardsville, IL 62025-0945
Phone: 618-692-0045
Fax: 618-692-4045
Web: www.endowment.org

Ed Markham International Scholarship

Type of award: Scholarship.
Intended use: For sophomore, junior, senior or graduate study at accredited 2-year, 4-year or graduate institution in United States or Canada.
Eligibility: Applicant must be U.S. citizen, permanent resident or Canadian citizen.
Basis for selection: Major/career interest in horticulture or marketing. Applicant must demonstrate financial need and high academic achievement.
Application requirements: Recommendations, transcript. Statement of academic and professional intent.
Additional information: Minimum 3.0 GPA. Must have interest in studying horticulture marketing through international travel. Number and amount of scholarships vary.
    Amount of award: $500-$2,000
    Application deadline: June 1
    Notification begins: August 1
Contact:
American Floral Endowment
1 Horticultural Lane
P.O. Box 945
Edwardsville, IL 62025-0945
Phone: 618-692-0045
Fax: 618-692-4045
Web: www.endowment.org

Fran Johnson Non-Traditional Scholarship

Type of award: Scholarship.
Intended use: For full-time undergraduate study at accredited 4-year or graduate institution in United States or Canada.
Eligibility: Applicant must be returning adult student. Applicant must be U.S. citizen, permanent resident or Canadian citizen.
Basis for selection: Major/career interest in horticulture. Applicant must demonstrate financial need and high academic achievement.
Application requirements: Recommendations, transcript. Statement of academic and professional intent.
Additional information: Study of horticulture or career interest in horticulture required. Specific interest in bedding plants or floral crops required. Must have been out of academic setting for at least five years and re-entering school. Number and amount of awards vary.
    Amount of award: $500-$2,000
    Application deadline: June 1
    Notification begins: August 1
Contact:
American Floral Endowment
1 Horticultural Lane
P.O. Box 945
Edwardsville, IL 62025-0945
Phone: 618-692-0045
Fax: 618-692-4045
Web: www.endowment.org

Harold Bettinger Memorial Scholarship

Type of award: Scholarship.
Intended use: For full-time sophomore, junior or senior study at accredited 4-year or graduate institution in United States or Canada.
Eligibility: Applicant must be U.S. citizen, permanent resident or Canadian citizen.

Basis for selection: Major/career interest in horticulture; business or marketing. Applicant must demonstrate financial need and high academic achievement.
Application requirements: Recommendations, transcript. Statement of academic and professional intent.
Additional information: Minimum 3.0 GPA. Study of horticulture or career interest in horticulture required. To apply for this scholarship, applicant's major or minor must be in business and/or marketing with intent to apply it to a horticulture-related business. Number and amount of awards vary.

Amount of award:	$500-$2,000
Number of awards:	1
Application deadline:	June 1
Notification begins:	August 1

Contact:
American Floral Endowment
1 Horticultural Lane
P.O. Box 945
Edwardsville, IL 62025-0945
Phone: 618-692-0045
Fax: 618-692-4045
Web: www.endowment.org

Jacob Van Namen Marketing Scholarship

Type of award: Scholarship.
Intended use: For sophomore, junior or senior study at accredited 2-year or 4-year institution in United States or Canada.
Eligibility: Applicant must be U.S. citizen, permanent resident or Canadian citizen/resident.
Basis for selection: Major/career interest in horticulture; agribusiness; marketing; botany or agriculture. Applicant must demonstrate financial need and high academic achievement.
Application requirements: Recommendations, transcript. Statement of academic and professional intent.
Additional information: Minimum 3.0 GPA. Applicant must have interest in agribusiness marketing and distribution of floral products. Number and amount of scholarships vary.

Amount of award:	$500-$2,000
Application deadline:	June 1
Notification begins:	August 1

Contact:
American Floral Endowment
1 Horticultural Lane
P.O. Box 945
Edwardsville, IL 62025-0945
Phone: 618-692-0045
Fax: 618-692-4045
Web: www.endowment.org

J.K. Rathmell, Jr., Memorial for Work/Study Abroad

Type of award: Scholarship.
Intended use: For full-time junior, senior or graduate study at accredited 4-year or graduate institution in or outside United States or Canada.
Eligibility: Applicant must be U.S. citizen, permanent resident or Canadian citizen.
Basis for selection: Competition/talent/interest in study abroad. Major/career interest in horticulture or landscape architecture. Applicant must demonstrate financial need, high academic achievement, depth of character and seriousness of purpose.
Application requirements: Recommendations, transcript. Statement of academic and professional intent.
Additional information: Minimum 3.0 GPA. Study of horticulture or career interest in horticulture required. Applicants must plan work/study abroad and submit specific plan for such. Preference given to those planning to work or study for six months or longer. Must have interest in floriculture, ornamental horticulture or landscape architecture. Must include letter of invitation from host institution abroad. Number and amount of awards vary.

Amount of award:	$500-$2,000
Application deadline:	June 1
Notification begins:	August 1

Contact:
American Floral Endowment
1 Horticultural Lane
P.O. Box 945
Edwardsville, IL 62025-0945
Phone: 618-692-0045
Fax: 618-692-4045
Web: www.endowment.org

Leonard Bettinger Memorial Vocational Scholarship

Type of award: Scholarship.
Intended use: For full-time undergraduate certificate, freshman, sophomore or non-degree study at accredited vocational or 2-year institution in United States or Canada.
Eligibility: Applicant must be U.S. citizen, permanent resident or Canadian citizen.
Basis for selection: Major/career interest in horticulture. Applicant must demonstrate financial need and high academic achievement.
Application requirements: Recommendations, transcript. Essay stating academic and professional intent.
Additional information: Minimum 3.0 GPA. Must intend to become floriculture grower or greenhouse manager. Number and amount of awards vary.

Amount of award:	$500-$2,000
Application deadline:	June 1
Notification begins:	August 1

Contact:
American Floral Endowment
1 Horticultural Lane
P.O. Box 945
Edwardsville, IL 62025-0945
Phone: 618-692-0045
Fax: 618-692-4045
Web: www.endowment.org

Paris Fracasso Production Floriculture Scholarship

Type of award: Scholarship.
Intended use: For junior or senior study at accredited 4-year institution in United States or Canada.
Eligibility: Applicant must be U.S. citizen, permanent resident or Canadian citizen/resident.
Basis for selection: Major/career interest in horticulture. Applicant must demonstrate financial need and high academic achievement.
Application requirements: Recommendations, transcript. Statement of academic and professional intent.
Additional information: Minimum 3.0 GPA. Applicant must have interest in career in floriculture production. Number and amount of scholarships vary.

Amount of award: $500-$2,000
Application deadline: June 1
Notification begins: August 1

Contact:
American Floral Endowment
1 Horticultural Lane
P.O. Box 945
Edwardsville, IL 62025-0945
Phone: 618-692-0045
Fax: 618-692-4045
Web: www.endowment.org

American Foundation for Aging Research

American Foundation for Aging Research Fellowship

Type of award: Research grant, renewable.
Intended use: For full-time undergraduate, master's, doctoral or first professional study in United States.
Basis for selection: Major/career interest in biochemistry or biomedical. Applicant must demonstrate high academic achievement.
Application requirements: Recommendations, transcript, proof of eligibility, research proposal.
Additional information: Applicants must be actively involved or planning active involvement in specific biomedical or biochemical research project in field of aging. AFAR areas of interest: cellular biology, immunobiology, cancer, neurobiology, biochemistry, molecular biophysics, genomics, and proteomics. Sociology, psychology, and health-related research (e.g., physical therapy/exercise physiology) not currently funded. Those granted awards utilize modern and innovative approaches/technologies. Also applicable toward Ph.D., MD, DVM, and DDS degrees. Number of awards varies. Call sponsor for information regarding deadline. Applicants must complete online preapplication in order to qualify for full application.

Amount of award: $1,000-$2,000
Number of awards: 12
Number of applicants: 50

Contact:
American Foundation for Aging Research
North Carolina State University
Biochem. Dept., Campus Box 7622
Raleigh, NC 27695-7622
Phone: 919-515-5679
Fax: 919-515-2047
Web: www.agingresearchfoundation.org

American Foundation for Pharmaceutical Education

AFPE "Gateway to Research" Scholarship

Type of award: Research grant.
Intended use: For sophomore, junior or senior study at accredited 4-year or graduate institution.
Eligibility: Applicant must be U.S. citizen or permanent resident.
Basis for selection: Major/career interest in pharmacy/pharmaceutics/pharmacology; biochemistry; chemistry or health sciences.
Application requirements: Recommendations, essay, transcript, research proposal. AFPE summary sheet, letter from faculty sponsor describing research.
Additional information: Awards intended to encourage undergraduates from any discipline to undertake mentored research experience and to consider pursuing Ph.D. in pharmaceutical science. At least $4,000 is provided as a student stipend for a research project done over the full calendar year. $500 is provided to recipient to attend AAPS annual meeting. Up to $1,000 may be used by sponsoring faculty member in direct support of research effort.

Amount of award: $5,000
Number of awards: 15
Application deadline: January 23
Notification begins: April 14
Total amount awarded: $30,000

Contact:
American Foundation for Pharmaceutical Education
One Church Street, Suite 202
Rockville, MD 20850
Phone: 301-738-2160
Fax: 301-738-2161
Web: www.afpenet.org

American Foundation for the Blind

Delta Gamma Foundation Memorial Scholarship

Type of award: Scholarship.
Intended use: For undergraduate or graduate study at accredited postsecondary institution in United States.
Eligibility: Applicant must be visually impaired. Applicant must be U.S. citizen.
Basis for selection: Major/career interest in health-related professions; rehabilitation/therapeutic services; education or education, special.
Application requirements: Recommendations, essay, transcript, proof of eligibility.
Additional information: Applicant must be legally blind and studying in the field of rehabilitation and/or the education of blind or visually impaired persons.

Amount of award: $1,000
Number of awards: 1
Application deadline: March 31
Total amount awarded: $1,000

Contact:
American Foundation for the Blind
Scholarship Committee
11 Penn Plaza, Suite 300
New York, NY 10001
Phone: 212-502-7661
Web: www.afb.org/scholarships.asp

Ferdinand Torres Scholarship

Type of award: Scholarship.
Intended use: For full-time undergraduate study at postsecondary institution in United States.
Eligibility: Applicant must be visually impaired. Applicant must be permanent resident.
Basis for selection: Applicant must demonstrate financial need, leadership, patriotism and seriousness of purpose.
Application requirements: Recommendations, essay, transcript, proof of eligibility.
Additional information: Applicant must be legally blind. Preference given to residents of New York City metropolitan area and new immigrants to the United States. New immigrants need to submit description of country of origin and reason for coming to the U.S.

Amount of award:	$2,000
Number of awards:	1
Application deadline:	March 31
Total amount awarded:	$2,000

Contact:
American Foundation for the Blind
Scholarship Committee
11 Penn Plaza, Suite 300
New York, NY 10001
Phone: 212-502-7661
Web: www.afb.org/scholarships.asp

Guide Dogs for the Blind Dorthea and Roland Bohde Personal Achievement Scholarship

Type of award: Scholarship, renewable.
Intended use: For full-time undergraduate study.
Eligibility: Applicant must be visually impaired. Applicant must be U.S. citizen.
Application requirements: Recommendations, essay, transcript. Proof of legal blindness, U.S. citizenship, and acceptance into a program.

Amount of award:	$1,000
Number of awards:	1
Application deadline:	March 31
Total amount awarded:	$1,000

Contact:
American Foundation for the Blind
Scholarship Committee
11 Penn Plaza, Suite 300
New York, NY 10001
Phone: 212-502-7661
Web: www.afb.org/scholarships.asp

Paul and Ellen Ruckes Scholarship

Type of award: Scholarship, renewable.
Intended use: For undergraduate or graduate study at accredited postsecondary institution in United States.
Eligibility: Applicant must be visually impaired. Applicant must be U.S. citizen.
Basis for selection: Major/career interest in engineering; computer/information sciences; physical sciences or life sciences.
Application requirements: Recommendations, essay, transcript, proof of eligibility.
Additional information: Applicant must be legally blind.

Amount of award:	$1,000
Number of awards:	1
Application deadline:	March 31
Total amount awarded:	$1,000

Contact:
American Foundation for the Blind
Scholarship Committee
11 Penn Plaza, Suite 300
New York, NY 10001
Phone: 212-502-7661
Web: www.afb.org/scholarships.asp

R.L. Gillette Scholarship

Type of award: Scholarship, renewable.
Intended use: For full-time undergraduate study at accredited postsecondary institution in United States.
Eligibility: Applicant must be visually impaired. Applicant must be female. Applicant must be U.S. citizen.
Basis for selection: Major/career interest in literature or music.
Application requirements: Recommendations, essay, transcript, proof of eligibility. Creative writing sample or performance tape not to exceed 30 minutes.
Additional information: Applicant must be legally blind.

Amount of award:	$1,000
Number of awards:	2
Application deadline:	March 31
Total amount awarded:	$2,000

Contact:
American Foundation for the Blind
Scholarship Committee
11 Penn Plaza, Suite 300
New York, NY 10001
Phone: 212-502-7661
Web: www.afb.org/scholarships.asp

Rudolph Dillman Memorial Scholarship

Type of award: Scholarship.
Intended use: For undergraduate or graduate study at accredited postsecondary institution in United States.
Eligibility: Applicant must be visually impaired. Applicant must be U.S. citizen.
Basis for selection: Major/career interest in health-related professions; rehabilitation/therapeutic services or education.
Application requirements: Recommendations, essay, transcript, proof of eligibility.
Additional information: Applicant must be legally blind and studying in the field of rehabilitation and/or the education of blind or visually impaired persons. One of these scholarships is specifically for a student who meets all requirements and submits evidence of economic need.

Amount of award:	$2,500
Number of awards:	4
Application deadline:	March 31
Total amount awarded:	$10,000

Contact:
American Foundation for the Blind
Scholarship Committee
11 Penn Plaza, Suite 300
New York, NY 10001
Phone: 212-502-7661
Web: www.afb.org/scholarships.asp

American Ground Water Trust

Amtrol Scholarship

Type of award: Scholarship.
Intended use: For full-time freshman study at 4-year institution.
Eligibility: Applicant must be high school senior. Applicant must be U.S. citizen or permanent resident.
Basis for selection: Major/career interest in geology/earth sciences; engineering, environmental; environmental science; natural resources/conservation or hydrology. Applicant must demonstrate high academic achievement, leadership, seriousness of purpose and service orientation.
Application requirements: Recommendations, essay, transcript. Description of completed high school science project involving ground water resources or of non-school work experience related to environment and natural resources.
Additional information: Applicant must be entering field related to ground water, e.g., geology, hydrology, environmental science, or hydrogeology. Minimum 3.0 GPA required. Visit Website for application procedure and forms.

Amount of award:	$1,000
Number of awards:	1
Number of applicants:	1
Application deadline:	June 1
Notification begins:	August 1

Contact:
American Ground Water Trust Scholarship
16 Centre Street
Concord, NH 03301
Phone: 603-228-5444
Web: www.agwt.org

Baroid Scholarship

Type of award: Scholarship.
Intended use: For full-time freshman study at accredited 4-year institution.
Eligibility: Applicant must be high school senior. Applicant must be U.S. citizen or permanent resident.
Basis for selection: Major/career interest in engineering, environmental; geology/earth sciences; environmental science or natural resources/conservation. Applicant must demonstrate high academic achievement, leadership, seriousness of purpose and service orientation.
Application requirements: Recommendations, essay, transcript. Description of previously completed high school science project involving ground water resources or of non-school work experience related to environment and natural resources.
Additional information: Must be entering field related to ground water, for example, hydrology or hydrogeology. Minimum 3.0 GPA. Visit Website for application procedure and forms.

Amount of award:	$2,000
Number of awards:	1
Number of applicants:	1
Application deadline:	June 1
Notification begins:	August 1

Contact:
American Ground Water Trust Scholarship
16 Centre Street
Concord, NH 03301
Phone: 603-228-5444
Fax: 603-228-6557
Web: www.agwt.org

Thomas M. Stetson Scholarship

Type of award: Scholarship.
Intended use: For full-time undergraduate study at 4-year institution. Designated institutions: Colleges and universities located west of the Mississippi River.
Eligibility: Applicant must be high school senior.
Basis for selection: Applicant must demonstrate high academic achievement.
Application requirements: Recommendations, essay, proof of eligibility.
Additional information: Applicant must attend a college west of the Mississippi River and must intend to pursue career in ground water related field. Minimum 3.0 GPA required. Visit Website for application procedure and forms.

Amount of award:	$1,500
Number of awards:	1
Number of applicants:	1
Application deadline:	June 1
Notification begins:	August 1

Contact:
American Ground Water Trust
P.O. Box 1796
Concord, NH 03302
Phone: 603-228-5444
Web: www.agwt.org

American Heart Association Western States Affiliate

American Heart Association Undergraduate Student Research Program

Type of award: Research grant.
Intended use: For full-time junior or senior study at 4-year institution. Designated institutions: Cardiovascular and cerebrovascular research laboratories in California, Nevada, and Utah.
Eligibility: Applicant must be U.S. citizen or permanent resident.
Basis for selection: Major/career interest in biology; chemistry; physics or computer/information sciences. Applicant must demonstrate high academic achievement, depth of character, seriousness of purpose and service orientation.
Application requirements: Recommendations, essay, transcript, proof of eligibility.
Additional information: Must be attending institution in or be resident of CA, UT, or NV. Women and minorities encouraged to apply. Must be college sophomore or junior and have completed at least four semesters or six quarters of biological sciences, physics or chemistry and at least one quarter of calculus, statistics, computational methods or computer science. Students assigned to scientist-supervised labs for ten weeks during summer, exploring careers in heart or

stroke research. Must participate in roundtable meetings in August to discuss research experience with supervisors and students.

Amount of award:	$4,000
Application deadline:	February 1
Notification begins:	March 30

Contact:
American Heart Association, Western States Affiliate
Research Department
1710 Gilbreth Road
Burlingame, CA 94010-1317
Phone: 650-259-6700
Fax: 650-259-6891
Web: www.americanheart.org/presenter.jhtml?identifier=3013196

American Helicopter Society, Inc.

Vertical Flight Foundation Scholarship

Type of award: Scholarship.
Intended use: For full-time junior, senior or graduate study at accredited postsecondary institution.
Basis for selection: Major/career interest in engineering; aerospace or aviation. Applicant must demonstrate high academic achievement, depth of character and seriousness of purpose.
Application requirements: Recommendations, essay, transcript. Academic endorsement by dean or professor.
Additional information: Must major in helicopter or vertical flight engineering industry. Minimum 3.0 GPA required, 3.5 recommended.

Amount of award:	$1,000-$4,000
Number of awards:	14
Number of applicants:	300
Application deadline:	February 1
Notification begins:	April 15

Contact:
Kay Brackins, VFF Scholarship Coordinator
American Helicopter Society
217 North Washington Street
Alexandria, VA 22314-2538
Phone: 703-684-6777
Fax: 703-739-9279
Web: www.vtol.org

American Hotel & Lodging Educational Foundation

American Express Scholarship Competition

Type of award: Scholarship, renewable.
Intended use: For undergraduate study at accredited 2-year or 4-year institution.
Basis for selection: Major/career interest in hotel/restaurant management or hospitality administration/management. Applicant must demonstrate financial need and high academic achievement.
Application requirements: Essay, transcript.
Additional information: Must work at hotel 20 hours a week and have 12 months of hotel experience. Hotel must be member of American Hotel & Lodging Association. Dependents of hotel employees may also apply. Award must be used in hospitality management degree program. Amount and number of awards vary. Visit Website to download application or apply online.

Amount of award:	$500-$2,000
Number of awards:	8
Number of applicants:	15
Application deadline:	May 1
Notification begins:	July 15
Total amount awarded:	$16,000

Contact:
American Hotel & Lodging Educational Foundation
1201 New York Avenue, NW 600
Washington, DC 20005-3931
Phone: 202-289-3188
Fax: 202-289-3199
Web: www.ahlef.org

American Hotel & Lodging Educational Foundation Incoming Freshman Scholarship Competition

Type of award: Scholarship.
Intended use: For full-time freshman study at 2-year or 4-year institution.
Eligibility: Applicant must be U.S. citizen or permanent resident.
Basis for selection: Major/career interest in hotel/restaurant management. Applicant must demonstrate financial need and high academic achievement.
Additional information: Applicant must have minimum 2.0 GPA. $1000 awards go to Associate majors, $2000 to Baccalaureate majors. Preference will be given to high school graduates of the Lodging Management Program (LMP).

Amount of award:	$1,000-$2,000
Number of awards:	9
Number of applicants:	1
Application deadline:	May 1
Notification begins:	July 15
Total amount awarded:	$19,500

Contact:
American Hotel & Lodging Educational Foundation
1201 New York Avenue, NW
Suite 600
Washington, DC 20005-3931
Phone: 202-289-3100
Fax: 202-289-3199
Web: www.ahlef.org

Ecolab Scholarship Competition

Type of award: Scholarship.
Intended use: For full-time undergraduate study at 2-year or 4-year institution in United States.
Basis for selection: Major/career interest in hotel/restaurant management. Applicant must demonstrate financial need and high academic achievement.
Application requirements: Essay, transcript.
Additional information: Applicant must maintain minimum of 12 credit hours. Amount and number of awards vary. Visit Website to download application or apply online.

time, $500. Apply online or download application from Website.

Amount of award:	$500-$2,000
Number of awards:	5
Number of applicants:	150
Application deadline:	May 1
Notification begins:	July 15
Total amount awarded:	$10,000

Contact:
American Hotel & Lodging Educational Foundation
1201 New York Avenue, N.W.
Suite 600
Washington, DC 20005-3931
Phone: 202-289-3188
Fax: 202-289-3199
Web: ahlef.org

The Hyatt Hotels Fund for Minority Lodging Management Students Competition

Type of award: Scholarship, renewable.
Intended use: For sophomore, junior or senior study at 4-year institution.
Eligibility: Applicant must be Alaskan native, Asian American, African American, Mexican American, Hispanic American, Puerto Rican, American Indian or Native Hawaiian/Pacific Islander. Applicant must be U.S. citizen or permanent resident.
Basis for selection: Major/career interest in hotel/restaurant management. Applicant must demonstrate financial need and high academic achievement.
Additional information: Must be enrolled in at least 12 credit hours for upcoming fall and spring semesters, or just the fall semester if graduating in December.

Amount of award:	$2,000
Number of awards:	18
Number of applicants:	19
Application deadline:	May 1
Notification begins:	July 15
Total amount awarded:	$38,000

Contact:
American Hotel & Lodging Educational Foundation
1201 New York Avenue, NW
Suite 600
Washington, DC 20005
Phone: 202-289-3188
Fax: 202-289-3199
Web: www.ahlef.org

Steve Hymans Extended Stay Scholarship

Type of award: Scholarship.
Intended use: For undergraduate study at 2-year or 4-year institution.
Eligibility: Applicant must be U.S. citizen or permanent resident.
Basis for selection: Major/career interest in hospitality administration/management or hotel/restaurant management. Applicant must demonstrate financial need and high academic achievement.
Application requirements: Recommendations, essay, transcript.
Additional information: Minimum 3.0 GPA. Must have experience working or interning at a lodging property; preference given to those with experience at an extended stay property. Full-time baccalaureate students receive $2,000; part time, $1,000. Full-time associates students receive $1,000; part

Amount of award:	$1,000-$2,000
Number of awards:	12
Number of applicants:	384
Application deadline:	May 1
Notification begins:	July 15
Total amount awarded:	$24,000

Contact:
American Hotel & Lodging Educational Foundation
1201 New York Avenue, NW
Suite 600
Washington, DC 20005-3931
Phone: 202-289-3188
Fax: 202-289-3199
Web: www.ahlef.org

American Indian College Fund

Ford Motor Company/American Indian College Fund Corporate Scholars Program

Type of award: Scholarship, renewable.
Intended use: For sophomore, junior or senior study at 4-year institution. Designated institutions: Participating colleges and universities.
Eligibility: Applicant must be Alaskan native, American Indian or Native Hawaiian/Pacific Islander. Must be American Indian or Alaska Native with proof of enrollment or descendancy. Applicant must be U.S. citizen.
Basis for selection: Major/career interest in computer/information sciences; engineering, electrical/electronic; accounting; finance/banking; information systems; marketing or business. Applicant must demonstrate financial need, high academic achievement, depth of character and leadership.
Application requirements: Recommendations, essay, transcript, proof of eligibility. Two letters of recommendation; 500 word essay; proof of tribal enrollment or descendancy; small color photo.
Additional information: Student must demonstrate leadership and commitment to the American Indian community and be attending a participating college or university. Award is up to $10,000 based on financial need. Applicant must have minimum 3.0 GPA.

Amount of award:	$10,000
Number of applicants:	40
Application deadline:	May 31

Contact:
American Indian College Fund
Corporate Scholars Program
8333 Greenwood Blvd
Denver, CO 80221
Phone: 800-776-3863
Fax: 303-426-1200
Web: www.collegefund.org

American Indian Science & Engineering Society

A.T. Anderson Memorial Scholarship

Type of award: Scholarship.
Intended use: For full-time undergraduate or graduate study at accredited 2-year, 4-year or graduate institution in United States or Canada.
Eligibility: Applicant or parent must be member/participant of American Indian Science & Engineering Society. Applicant must be Alaskan native or American Indian. Must be member of American Indian tribe or otherwise considered to be American Indian by tribe with which affiliation is claimed, or be at least 1/4 American Indian/Alaskan Native blood.
Basis for selection: Major/career interest in science, general; engineering; medicine; natural resources/conservation; mathematics or physical sciences. Applicant must demonstrate financial need, depth of character, leadership, seriousness of purpose and service orientation.
Application requirements: Recommendations, essay, transcript, proof of eligibility. Resume. Proof of tribal enrollment.
Additional information: Must be AISES member. Minimum 3.0 GPA. Undergraduate student award $1,000 per year; graduate student award $2,000. Membership and scholarship applications available on Website. Send SASE with information or application requests.
    Amount of award: $1,000-$2,000
    Application deadline: June 15
Contact:
AISES Scholarships
P.O. Box 9828
Albuquerque, NM 87119-9828
Phone: 505-765-1052
Fax: 505-765-5608
Web: www.aises.org/highered/scholarships

Burlington Northern Santa Fe Foundation Scholarship

Type of award: Scholarship, renewable.
Intended use: For full-time undergraduate study at accredited postsecondary institution in United States or Canada.
Eligibility: Applicant or parent must be member/participant of American Indian Science & Engineering Society. Applicant must be Alaskan native or American Indian. Must be member of American Indian tribe or otherwise considered to be American Indian by tribe with which affiliation is claimed, or be at least 1/4 American Indian/Alaskan Native blood. Applicant must be high school senior. Applicant must be U.S. citizen residing in South Dakota, Minnesota, Washington, Kansas, Arizona, Oklahoma, California, Oregon, Montana, New Mexico, Colorado or North Dakota.
Basis for selection: Major/career interest in science, general; engineering; mathematics; physical sciences; medicine; natural resources/conservation or business. Applicant must demonstrate financial need, depth of character, leadership, seriousness of purpose and service orientation.
Application requirements: Recommendations, essay, transcript, proof of eligibility. Resume. Proof of enrollment.
Additional information: Minimum 2.0 GPA. Award is renewable for four years (eight semesters) or until degree obtained, whichever comes first, assuming eligibility maintained. Membership and scholarship applications available on Website. Otherwise, include SASE with application or information requests.
    Amount of award: $2,500
    Number of awards: 5
    Application deadline: April 15
Contact:
AISES Scholarships
P.O. Box 9828
Albuquerque, NM 87119-9828
Phone: 505-765-1052
Fax: 505-765-5608
Web: www.aises.org/highered/scholarships

General Motors Engineering Scholarship

Type of award: Scholarship.
Intended use: For full-time undergraduate or graduate study at accredited 4-year or graduate institution in United States.
Eligibility: Applicant or parent must be member/participant of American Indian Science & Engineering Society. Applicant must be Alaskan native or American Indian. Must be member of American Indian tribe or otherwise considered to be American Indian by tribe with which affiliation is claimed, or be at least 1/4 American Indian/Alaskan Native blood. Applicant must be U.S. citizen or permanent resident.
Basis for selection: Major/career interest in engineering; engineering, electrical/electronic or engineering, mechanical. Applicant must demonstrate high academic achievement.
Application requirements: Recommendations, essay, transcript, proof of eligibility. Resume. Proof of tribal enrollment.
Additional information: Must be AISES member. Minimum 3.0 GPA. Applicant must be seeking engineering degree; preference given to those studying electrical, industrial or mechanical engineering. Eligible applicants will be required to complete inventory of skills administered by General Motors via the Internet. Scholarship includes mandatory paid eight- to ten-week internship at Bureau of Reclamation site, which must be completed prior to graduation. Membership and scholarship applications available on Website, or send SASE with information and application requests.
    Amount of award: $3,000
    Number of awards: 3
    Application deadline: June 15
Contact:
AISES Scholarships
P.O. Box 9828
Albuquerque, NM 87119-9828
Phone: 505-765-1052
Fax: 505-765-5608
Web: www.aises.org/highered/scholarships

American Institute For Foreign Study

Foreign Study/Diversity Scholarship

Type of award: Scholarship.
Intended use: For sophomore, junior or senior study in Argentina, Australia, Austria, China, Czech Republic, England, France, Hungary, Ireland, Italy, Russia, South Africa, Spain.

American Institute For Foreign Study: Foreign Study/Diversity Scholarship

Designated institutions: University of Belgrano, Buenos Aires; Macquarie University, Sydney; University of Salzburg, Austria; Nanjing University, Nanjing, China; Charles University, Prague; Richmond, The American International University in London; College International de Cannes, University of Grenoble, University of Paris IV (Sorbonne), France; Corvinus University, Budapest, Hungary; University of Limerick, Ireland; Richmond in Florence and Richmond in Rome, Italy; St. Petersburg State Polytechnic University, Russia; University of Stellenbosch, South Africa; University of Granada and University of Salamanca, Spain.
Eligibility: Applicant must be Asian American, African American, Mexican American, Hispanic American, Puerto Rican, American Indian or Native Hawaiian/Pacific Islander.
Basis for selection: Competition/talent/interest in study abroad. Applicant must demonstrate financial need, high academic achievement, depth of character, leadership, seriousness of purpose and service orientation.
Application requirements: $95 application fee. Recommendations, essay.
Additional information: Must have completed minimum 24 credits toward degree when program starts. Must be interested in multicultural/international issues and involved in multicultural/international activities. Three awards of $2,000 and two scholarships for 50% of program fee and round-trip airfare awarded each year. Award must be used for an AIFS program. Students who are unable to pay $95 application fee may submit fee waiver endorsed by their financial office or study-abroad advisor.

Number of awards:	5
Number of applicants:	70
Application deadline:	October 1, April 15

Contact:
AIFS College Division
River Plaza
9 West Broad Street
Stamford, CT 06902-3788
Phone: 800-727-2437
Fax: 203-399-5597
Web: www.aifsabroad.com

International Semester Scholarship

Type of award: Scholarship.
Intended use: For undergraduate study in Argentina, Australia, Austria, China, Czech Republic, England, France, Hungary, Ireland, Italy, Russia, South Africa, Spain. Designated institutions: University of Belgrano, Buenos Aires; Macquarie University, Sydney; University of Salzburg, Austria; Nanjing University, Nanjing, China; Charles University, Prague; Richmond, The American International University in London; College International de Cannes, University of Grenoble, University of Paris IV (Sorbonne), France; Corvinus University, Budapest, Hungary; University of Limerick; Richmond in Florence, Italy; Richmond in Rome, Italy; St. Petersburg State Polytechnic University, Russia; University of Stellenbosch, South Africa; University of Granada and University of Salamanca, Spain.
Basis for selection: Competition/talent/interest in study abroad. Major/career interest in international relations; social/behavioral sciences or multicultural studies. Applicant must demonstrate high academic achievement, leadership, seriousness of purpose and service orientation.
Application requirements: $95 application fee. Essay, transcript.
Additional information: Applicant must be currently enrolled college undergraduate with at least 3.0 cumulative GPA. Must be interested in multicultural/international issues and involved in multicultural/international activities. Minorities encouraged to apply. Award must be used in AIFS program. Award amount is per semester.

Amount of award:	$1,000
Number of awards:	40
Number of applicants:	300
Application deadline:	October 1, April 15
Total amount awarded:	$40,000

Contact:
AIFS College Division
River Plaza
9 West Broad Street
Stamford, CT 06902-3788
Phone: 800-727-2437
Fax: 203-399-5597
Web: www.aifsabroad.com

American Institute of Aeronautics and Astronautics

Aeronautics and Astronautics Undergraduate Scholarship

Type of award: Scholarship, renewable.
Intended use: For full-time sophomore, junior or senior study at accredited 4-year institution in United States. Designated institutions: ABET-accredited schools.
Basis for selection: Major/career interest in aerospace or engineering. Applicant must demonstrate high academic achievement.
Application requirements: Transcript, proof of eligibility. Three letters of recommendation. 500- to 1,000-word essay on how academic program supports career objectives.
Additional information: Must have completed at least two quarters or one semester of full-time college work. Minimum 3.3 GPA. Must join American Institute of Aeronautics and Astronautics before receiving award. Not open to members of any American Institute of Aeronautics and Astronautics national committees or subcommittees. Applications must be requested by January 15 if applying by mail. Online applications must be completed by January 31. Applicants must reapply for renewal.

Amount of award:	$2,000-$2,500
Number of awards:	30
Number of applicants:	60
Application deadline:	January 31
Notification begins:	June 15
Total amount awarded:	$60,000

Contact:
AIAA Foundation Undergraduate Scholarship Program
1801 Alexander Bell Drive
Suite 500
Reston, VA 20191-4344
Phone: 703-264-7564
Web: www.aiaa.org

American Institute of Architects New Jersey Scholarship Foundation, Inc.

AIA New Jersey Scholarship Foundation, Inc.

Type of award: Scholarship, renewable.
Intended use: For full-time sophomore, junior, senior, master's or first professional study at accredited postsecondary institution. Designated institutions: Architectural undergraduate or graduate schools.
Eligibility: Applicant must be residing in New Jersey.
Basis for selection: Major/career interest in architecture. Applicant must demonstrate financial need, high academic achievement and seriousness of purpose.
Application requirements: $5 application fee. Portfolio, recommendations, essay, transcript. FAFSA.
Additional information: Applicant must have completed one year at accredited architectural school. Application deadline in the end of May.
   Amount of award: $1,500-$5,000
   Number of awards: 7
   Number of applicants: 16
   Notification begins: July 15
Contact:
New Jersey Scholarship Foundation Inc.
c/o Robert Zaccone
212 White Avenue
Old Tappan, NJ 07675

American Institute of Architects New York Chapter

Douglas Haskell Awards for Student Journalism

Type of award: Scholarship.
Intended use: Designated institutions: NAAB-accredited schools.
Basis for selection: Competition/talent/interest in writing/journalism. Major/career interest in architecture; interior design; urban planning; landscape architecture or art/art history.
Application requirements: $15 application fee. Copy of publication or 12 copies of article if it has not yet been published with letter from editor stating intended date of publication; statement describing purpose of article, its intended audience and the school and degree program where entrant is enrolled; cover page with full contact information, including title of essay or story and title and date of publication.
Additional information: Applicants must be enrolled in an NAAB-accredited school of architecture or related program. Applicants must submit any article in a current publication, print or online, focused on design issues. Publications released before 2006 are ineligible. Visit Website for deadline information.

   Amount of award: $5,000
   Number of awards: 1
   Total amount awarded: $5,000
Contact:
Haskell Scholarship
Center for Architectural Foundation
536 LaGuardia Place
New York, NY 10012
Phone: 212-358-6133
Web: www.aiany.org/services/scholarship

Women's Architectural Auxiliary Eleanor Allwork Scholarship Grants

Type of award: Scholarship.
Intended use: For first professional study at postsecondary institution. Designated institutions: NAAB-accredited schools in the State of New York.
Eligibility: Applicant must be residing in New York.
Basis for selection: Major/career interest in architecture. Applicant must demonstrate financial need and high academic achievement.
Application requirements: Recommendations. Cover page with full contact information, two student projects as examples of work (no slides), resume or CV, SASE, recommendation from faculty member.
Additional information: Visit Website for deadline information.
   Amount of award: $10,000
   Number of awards: 3
   Total amount awarded: $30,000
Contact:
Allwork Scholarship
Center for Architecture Foundation
536 LaGuardia Place
New York, NY 10012
Phone: 212-358-6133
Web: www.aiany.org/services/scholarship

American Institute of Certified Public Accountants

Certified Public Accountants Minorities Scholarship

Type of award: Scholarship, renewable.
Intended use: For full-time undergraduate or graduate study at accredited 4-year or graduate institution in United States.
Eligibility: Applicant must be Alaskan native, Asian American, African American, Mexican American, Hispanic American, Puerto Rican or Native Hawaiian/Pacific Islander.
Basis for selection: Major/career interest in accounting. Applicant must demonstrate high academic achievement and seriousness of purpose.
Application requirements: Recommendations, transcript. Two essays.
Additional information: Scholarship provides competitive awards to encourage student's progress as accounting major, entry into accounting profession and, ultimately, achievement of the CPA designation. Undergraduate students must have completed at least 30 semester hours or equivalent of college

work, with at least six hours in accounting. Must have 3.3 GPA. Full-time graduate students (who are not CPAs) pursuing master's in accounting, taxation or business administration also eligible. MBA candidates must hold undergraduate degree in accounting. Notification begins in early August.

Amount of award:	$1,500-$5,000
Number of awards:	137
Number of applicants:	400
Application deadline:	June 1
Total amount awarded:	$423,000

Contact:
American Institute of Certified Public Accountants
Minority Scholarships Program
1211 Avenue of the Americas
New York, NY 10036-8775
Phone: 212-596-6270
Fax: 212-596-6292
Web: www.aicpa.org/members/div/career/mini/index.htm

American Institute of Polish Culture

Harriet Irsay Scholarship

Type of award: Scholarship.
Intended use: For full-time undergraduate or graduate study.
Eligibility: Applicant must be U.S. citizen or permanent resident.
Basis for selection: Major/career interest in journalism; communications; public relations; education; film/video; history; international relations; international studies; humanities/liberal arts or polish language/studies. Applicant must demonstrate financial need and high academic achievement.
Application requirements: $10 application fee. Transcript. Detailed resume. 200-400 word essay on "Why should I receive the scholarship." Three original, signed letters of recommendation on letterhead sent directly to institute. 700-word article on any subject about Poland.
Additional information: Send SASE with application request. Deadline for all application material is April 20, subject to extension. Preference given to American students of Polish heritage.

Amount of award:	$1,000
Number of awards:	15
Number of applicants:	55
Application deadline:	April 20
Notification begins:	June 15

Contact:
American Institute of Polish Culture
1440 79 Street Causeway, Suite 117
Miami, FL 33141-4135
Phone: 305-864-2349
Fax: 305-865-5150
Web: www.ampolinstitute.org

American Legion Alabama

American Legion Alabama Oratorical Contest

Type of award: Scholarship.
Intended use: For undergraduate study at postsecondary institution.
Eligibility: Applicant or parent must be member/participant of American Legion. Applicant must be enrolled in high school. Applicant must be U.S. citizen residing in Alabama.
Basis for selection: Competition/talent/interest in oratory/debate, based on language style, voice, diction, delivery, originality, logic, breadth of knowledge, application of knowledge about topic, and skill in selecting examples and analogies.
Application requirements: Proof of eligibility.
Additional information: Oratorical Scholarships: 1st place - $5,000; 2nd place - $3,000; 3rd place - $2,000. State finals held in March. Send business-size SASE for application.

Amount of award:	$2,000-$5,000
Number of awards:	3
Total amount awarded:	$10,000

Contact:
Department Adjutant
The American Legion
P.O. Box 1069
Montgomery, AL 36101-1069
Phone: 334-262-6638
Web: www.americanlegionalabama.org

American Legion Alabama Scholarship

Type of award: Scholarship, renewable.
Intended use: For undergraduate study at postsecondary institution.
Eligibility: Applicant or parent must be member/participant of American Legion. Applicant must be U.S. citizen or permanent resident residing in Alabama. Applicant must be descendant of veteran; or dependent of veteran during Korean War, Persian Gulf War, WW I, WW II or Vietnam.
Application requirements: Proof of eligibility.
Additional information: Four-year scholarships at Alabama colleges. Send business-size SASE for application.

Amount of award:	$850
Number of awards:	130
Application deadline:	May 1
Total amount awarded:	$110,500

Contact:
Department Adjutant
The American Legion
P.O. Box 1069
Montgomery, AL 36101-1069
Phone: 334-262-6638
Web: www.americanlegionalabama.org

American Legion Alabama Auxiliary

American Legion Alabama Auxiliary Scholarship

Type of award: Scholarship, renewable.
Intended use: For undergraduate study at postsecondary institution. Designated institutions: Alabama state-supported colleges.
Eligibility: Applicant or parent must be member/participant of American Legion Auxiliary. Applicant must be U.S. citizen or permanent resident residing in Alabama. Applicant must be descendant of veteran; or dependent of veteran during Grenada conflict, Korean War, Lebanon conflict, Panama conflict, Persian Gulf War, WW I, WW II or Vietnam.
Application requirements: Proof of eligibility.
Additional information: Four-year scholarships at Alabama colleges. Previous one-year scholarship recipients can reapply. Grandchildren of veterans also eligible. Send SASE for application.
    Amount of award: $850
    Number of awards: 40
    Application deadline: April 1
    Total amount awarded: $34,000
Contact:
American Legion Auxiliary, Department of Alabama
Department Headquarters
120 North Jackson Street
Montgomery, AL 36104
Phone: 334-262-1176

American Legion Alaska

American Legion Alaska Oratorical Contest

Type of award: Scholarship.
Eligibility: Applicant or parent must be member/participant of American Legion. Applicant must be enrolled in high school. Applicant must be U.S. citizen or permanent resident residing in Alaska.
Basis for selection: Competition/talent/interest in oratory/debate, based on language style, voice, diction, delivery, originality, logic, breadth of knowledge, application of knowledge about topic, and skill in selecting examples and analogies.
Application requirements: Proof of eligibility.
Additional information: Awards: 1st-$3,000; 2nd-$2,000; 3rd-$1,000. Must be high school student attending Alaska accredited institution. Must participate in local speech contests. Contest begins in November.
    Amount of award: $1,000-$3,000
    Number of awards: 3
    Total amount awarded: $6,000
Contact:
American Legion, Department of Alaska
Department Adjutant
1550 Charter Circle
Anchorage, AK 99508
Phone: 907-278-8598
Fax: 907-278-0041
Web: www.alaskalegion.org

American Legion Western District Postsecondary Scholarship

Type of award: Scholarship.
Intended use: For undergraduate study at postsecondary institution.
Eligibility: Applicant or parent must be member/participant of American Legion. Applicant must be high school senior. Applicant must be residing in Alaska.
Additional information: Minimum 2.0 GPA.
    Amount of award: $750
    Application deadline: February 15
Contact:
American Legion Western District Postsecondary Scholarship
Attn: Jim Scott
1124 Holmes Road
North Pole, AK 99705
Phone: 907-488-5310
Web: www.alaskalegion.org

American Legion Alaska Auxiliary

American Legion Alaska Auxiliary Scholarship

Type of award: Scholarship.
Intended use: For freshman study at postsecondary institution.
Eligibility: Applicant or parent must be member/participant of American Legion Auxiliary. Applicant must be at least 17, no older than 24, high school senior. Applicant must be U.S. citizen or permanent resident residing in Alaska. Applicant must be dependent of veteran during Grenada conflict, Korean War, Lebanon conflict, Panama conflict, Persian Gulf War, WW I, WW II or Vietnam.
Application requirements: Proof of eligibility.
Additional information: Scholarship to apply toward tuition, matriculation, laboratory, or similar fees. High school graduate must not have attended institution of higher education.
    Amount of award: $1,500
    Application deadline: March 15
Contact:
American Legion Auxiliary
Department of Alaska
1392 6th Avenue
Fairbanks, AK 99701

American Legion Alaska Auxiliary Western District Scholarship

Type of award: Scholarship.
Intended use: For at accredited postsecondary institution.

Eligibility: Applicant or parent must be member/participant of American Legion Auxiliary. Applicant must be returning adult student. Applicant must be residing in Alaska.
Additional information: For continuing education students who are furthering their education to enhance work skills in order to enter or re-enter the work field at a higher level.
  Amount of award: $1,000
  Application deadline: March 15
Contact:
American Legion Auxiliary
Department of Alaska
1392 6th Avenue
Fairbanks, AK 99701

American Legion Arizona

American Legion Arizona Oratorical Contest

Type of award: Scholarship.
Eligibility: Applicant or parent must be member/participant of American Legion. Applicant must be enrolled in high school. Applicant must be U.S. citizen or permanent resident residing in Arizona.
Basis for selection: Competition/talent/interest in oratory/debate, based on language style, voice, diction, delivery, originality, logic, breadth of knowledge, application of knowledge about topic, and skill in selecting examples and analogies.
Additional information: Awards: 1st-$1,500; 2nd-$800; 3rd-$500. For students enrolled in accredited Arizona high schools.
  Amount of award: $500-$1,500
  Number of awards: 3
  Application deadline: January 15
  Total amount awarded: $2,800
Contact:
American Legion Arizona, Oratorical Contest
4701 North 19th Avenue, Suite 200
Phoenix, AZ 85015-3727
Phone: 602-264-7706
Fax: 602-264-0029
Web: www.azlegion.org

American Legion Arizona Auxiliary

American Legion Arizona Auxiliary Health Care Occupation Scholarship

Type of award: Scholarship.
Intended use: For undergraduate study.
Eligibility: Applicant or parent must be member/participant of American Legion Auxiliary. Applicant must be U.S. citizen residing in Arizona.
Basis for selection: Major/career interest in health-related professions or health sciences.
Additional information: Must be resident of Arizona at least one year. Preference given to immediate family members of veterans.

  Amount of award: $400
  Application deadline: May 15
Contact:
American Legion Auxiliary Department of Arizona
4701 North 19th Avenue, Suite 100
Phoenix, AZ 85015-3727
Phone: 602-241-1080
Fax: 602-604-9640

American Legion Arizona Auxiliary Nurses' Scholarship

Type of award: Scholarship.
Intended use: For sophomore study.
Eligibility: Applicant or parent must be member/participant of American Legion Auxiliary. Applicant must be U.S. citizen residing in Arizona.
Basis for selection: Major/career interest in nursing.
Additional information: For second-year student nurses enrolled in accredited Arizona institutions awarding RN degrees. Must be Arizona resident for at least one year. Preference given to immediate family members of veterans.
  Amount of award: $500
  Application deadline: May 15
Contact:
American Legion Auxiliary, Department of Arizona
4701 North 19th Avenue, Suite 100
Phoenix, AZ 85015-3727
Phone: 602-241-1080
Fax: 602-604-9640

Wilma D. Hoyal/Maxine Chilton Memorial Scholarship

Type of award: Scholarship.
Intended use: For full-time. Designated institutions: University of Arizona, Arizona State University, Northern Arizona University.
Eligibility: Applicant or parent must be member/participant of American Legion Auxiliary. Applicant must be U.S. citizen residing in Arizona.
Basis for selection: Major/career interest in political science/government; education, special or public administration/service.
Additional information: For second-year or upper-division full-time students. Three $1,000 awards payable to three designated institutions in Arizona. Applicant must be state resident at least one year. Preference given to immediate family members of veterans.
  Amount of award: $1,000
  Number of awards: 3
  Application deadline: May 15
Contact:
American Legion Auxiliary, Department of Arizona
4701 North 19th Avenue, Suite 100
Phoenix, AZ 85015-3727
Phone: 602-241-1080
Fax: 602-604-9640

American Legion Arkansas

American Legion Arkansas Oratorical Contest

Type of award: Scholarship.
Intended use: For undergraduate study.
Eligibility: Applicant or parent must be member/participant of American Legion. Applicant must be residing in Arkansas.
Basis for selection: Competition/talent/interest in oratory/debate, based on language style, voice, diction, delivery, originality, logic, breadth of knowledge, application of knowledge about topic, and skill in selecting examples and analogies.
Application requirements: Proof of eligibility.
Additional information: Oratorical Contest, State Division: 1st-$1,000, 2nd-$750, 3rd-$500, 4th-$300. Must be state oratorical winner; contestant must compete in three contests before reaching state level.
    Amount of award: $300-$1,000
    Number of awards: 4
    Application deadline: March 15
    Total amount awarded: $2,550
Contact:
American Legion Arkansas
Department Adjutant
P.O. Box 3280
Little Rock, AR 72203
Phone: 501-375-1104
Fax: 501-375-4236
Web: www.arklegion.homestead.com

American Legion Arkansas Scholarship

Type of award: Scholarship.
Intended use: For undergraduate study.
Eligibility: Applicant or parent must be member/participant of American Legion. Applicant must be residing in Arkansas.
Application requirements: Proof of eligibility.
Additional information: Four scholarships: amount to be determined. Must be child, grandchild, or great-grandchild of American Legion member.
    Number of awards: 4
    Application deadline: March 15
Contact:
American Legion Arkansas
Department Adjutant
P.O. Box 3280
Little Rock, AR 72203
Phone: 501-375-1104
Fax: 501-375-4236
Web: www.arklegion.homestead.com

American Legion Arkansas Auxiliary

American Legion Arkansas Auxiliary Scholarships

Type of award: Scholarship.
Intended use: For undergraduate study.
Eligibility: Applicant or parent must be member/participant of American Legion Auxiliary. Applicant must be high school senior. Applicant must be U.S. citizen residing in Arkansas. Applicant must be dependent of veteran during Grenada conflict, Korean War, Lebanon conflict, Panama conflict, Persian Gulf War, WW I, WW II or Vietnam.
Application requirements: Proof of eligibility.
Additional information: Academic Scholarship: one $500; Nurse Scholarship: one $250. Awards paid half first semester, half second semester. Student must be Arkansas resident attending Arkansas school. Include name of high school and SASE with application request.
    Amount of award: $250-$500
    Number of awards: 2
    Application deadline: March 1
    Total amount awarded: $750
Contact:
American Legion Auxiliary Department of Arkansas
Department Secretary
1415 West 7th St.
Little Rock, AR 72201
Phone: 501-374-5836
Web: www.arklegion.homestead.com

American Legion California

American Legion California Oratorical Contest

Type of award: Scholarship.
Intended use: For undergraduate study.
Eligibility: Applicant or parent must be member/participant of American Legion. Applicant must be enrolled in high school. Applicant must be residing in California.
Basis for selection: Competition/talent/interest in oratory/debate, based on language style, voice, diction, delivery, originality, logic, breadth of knowledge, application of knowledge about topic, and skill in selecting examples and analogies.
Additional information: Students selected by schools to participate in district contests, followed by area and departmental finals. Awards: 1st-$1,200; 2nd-$1,000; 3rd to 6th-$700 each. See your local high school counselor for application.
    Amount of award: $700-$1,200
    Number of awards: 6
    Total amount awarded: $5,000
Contact:
American Legion California
401 Van Ness Avenue, Room 117
San Francisco, CA 94102-4587
Phone: 415-431-2400
Fax: 415-255-1571
Web: www.calegion.org

American Legion California Auxiliary

American Legion California Auxiliary General Scholarships

Type of award: Scholarship.
Intended use: For freshman study at postsecondary institution.
Eligibility: Applicant must be high school senior. Applicant must be residing in California. Applicant must be dependent of active service person or veteran during Grenada conflict, Korean War, Lebanon conflict, Panama conflict, Persian Gulf War, WW I, WW II or Vietnam.
Basis for selection: Applicant must demonstrate financial need.
Additional information: Annual scholarships: 1-$2,000 (payable at $1,000 per year); 4-$1,000; 3-$500. Must be high school senior or graduate who has not been able to begin college due to illness or financial circumstances. See Website for application. Applications must be submitted to local Unit.
    Amount of award: $500-$2,000
    Number of awards: 8
    Application deadline: March 16
    Total amount awarded: $7,500
Contact:
American Legion Auxiliary, Department of California
War Memorial Building
401 Van Ness Avenue, Room 113
San Francisco, CA 94102
Phone: 415-861-5092
Fax: 415-861-8365
Web: www.calegionaux.org

Continuing or Re-entry Student Scholarship

Type of award: Scholarship.
Intended use: For undergraduate study at postsecondary institution.
Eligibility: Applicant must be residing in California. Applicant must be dependent of active service person or veteran during Grenada conflict, Korean War, Lebanon conflict, Panama conflict, Persian Gulf War, WW I, WW II or Vietnam.
Additional information: Three $1,000 and two $500 scholarships for continuing or re-entering college students. See Website for application. Applications must be submitted to local Unit.
    Amount of award: $500-$1,000
    Number of awards: 5
    Application deadline: March 16
    Total amount awarded: $4,000
Contact:
American Legion Auxiliary, Department of California
War Memorial Building
401 Van Ness Avenue, Room 113
San Francisco, CA 94102
Phone: 415-861-5092
Fax: 415-861-8365
Web: www.calegionaux.org

Past Department Presidents' Junior Scholarship

Type of award: Scholarship.
Intended use: For undergraduate study.
Eligibility: Applicant or parent must be member/participant of American Legion Auxiliary. Applicant must be high school senior. Applicant must be residing in California. Applicant must be descendant of veteran; or dependent of veteran during Grenada conflict, Korean War, Lebanon conflict, Panama conflict, Persian Gulf War, WW I, WW II or Vietnam. Applicant must have consecutive membership as Junior for three years.
Additional information: See Website for application. Applications must be submitted to the Unit in which the Junior holds membership.
    Amount of award: $300-$1,000
    Number of awards: 1
    Application deadline: April 13
Contact:
American Legion Auxiliary, Department of California
War Memorial Building
401 Van Ness Avenue, Room 113
San Francisco, CA 94102
Phone: 415-861-5092
Fax: 415-861-8365
Web: www.calegionaux.org

Past Presidents' Parley Nursing Scholarship

Type of award: Scholarship.
Intended use: For undergraduate study at postsecondary institution.
Eligibility: Applicant must be residing in California. Applicant must be veteran; or dependent of veteran; or spouse of veteran or deceased veteran during Grenada conflict, Korean War, Lebanon conflict, Panama conflict, Persian Gulf War, WW I, WW II or Vietnam.
Basis for selection: Major/career interest in nursing.
Additional information: Applicant must be entering or continuing student in a nursing program. Amount and number of awards vary. See Website for application. Applications must be submitted to local Unit.
    Amount of award: $500-$1,500
    Application deadline: April 4
Contact:
American Legion Auxiliary, Department of California
War Memorial Building
401 Van Ness Avenue, Room 113
San Francisco, CA 94102
Phone: 415-861-5092
Fax: 415-861-8365
Web: www.calegionaux.org

American Legion Colorado

National High School Oratorical Contest

Type of award: Scholarship.
Intended use: For undergraduate study at accredited postsecondary institution.

Eligibility: Applicant must be enrolled in high school. Applicant must be residing in Colorado.
Basis for selection: Competition/talent/interest in oratory/debate, based on language style, voice, diction, delivery, originality, logic, breadth of knowledge, application of knowledge about topic, and skill in selecting examples and analogies.
Additional information: Awards: 1st-$2,500; 2nd-$2,000; 3rd-$1,500; 4th to 12th-$500.
   Amount of award: $500-$2,500
   Number of awards: 12
   Total amount awarded: $10,500
Contact:
American Legion, Department of Colorado
7465 E First Avenue, Suite D
Denver, CO 80230
Web: www.coloradolegion.org

American Legion Colorado Auxiliary

Department President's Scholarship

Type of award: Scholarship.
Intended use: For undergraduate study.
Eligibility: Applicant or parent must be member/participant of American Legion Auxiliary. Applicant must be residing in Colorado. Applicant must be dependent of veteran during Grenada conflict, Korean War, Lebanon conflict, Panama conflict, Persian Gulf War, WW I, WW II or Vietnam.
Additional information: Awards: 2-$500 and 1-$250.
   Amount of award: $250-$500
   Number of awards: 3
   Application deadline: March 12
   Total amount awarded: $1,250
Contact:
American Legion Colorado Auxiliary
Department Headquarters
7465 East First Avenue, Suite D
Denver, CO 80230
Phone: 303-367-5388

Department President's Scholarship for Junior Auxiliary Members

Type of award: Scholarship.
Intended use: For undergraduate study.
Eligibility: Applicant or parent must be member/participant of American Legion Auxiliary. Applicant must be residing in Colorado. Applicant must be Colorado Junior Auxiliary member.
   Amount of award: $500
   Number of awards: 1
   Application deadline: March 12
Contact:
American Legion Colorado Auxiliary
Department Headquarters
7465 East First Avenue, Suite D
Denver, CO 80230
Phone: 303-367-5388

Past President's Parley Nurse's Scholarship

Type of award: Scholarship.
Intended use: For undergraduate study at accredited 2-year or 4-year institution.
Eligibility: Applicant or parent must be member/participant of American Legion Auxiliary. Applicant must be residing in Colorado. Applicant must be veteran; or dependent of veteran; or spouse of veteran during Grenada conflict, Korean War, Lebanon conflict, Panama conflict, Persian Gulf War, WW I, WW II or Vietnam.
Basis for selection: Major/career interest in nursing.
Additional information: Number and amount of awards vary.
   Application deadline: April 15
Contact:
American Legion Colorado Auxiliary
Department Headquarters
7465 East First Avenue, Suite D
Denver, CO 80230
Phone: 303-367-5388

American Legion Connecticut

National High School Oratorical Contest

Type of award: Scholarship.
Eligibility: Applicant must be no older than 19. Applicant must be residing in Connecticut.
Basis for selection: Competition/talent/interest in oratory/debate, based on language style, voice, diction, delivery, originality, logic, breadth of knowledge, application of knowledge about topic, and skill in selecting examples and analogies.
Additional information: Awards: 1st-$2,000; 2nd-$1,000; 3rd to 7th-$500; all in Savings Bonds. Contest open only to students attending Connecticut high schools.
   Amount of award: $500-$2,000
   Number of awards: 7
   Total amount awarded: $5,500
Contact:
American Legion, Department of Connecticut
Department Oratorical Chairman
P.O. Box 208
Rocky Hill, CT 06067
Phone: 860-721-5942
Web: www.ct.legion.org

American Legion Connecticut Auxiliary

Memorial Education Grant

Type of award: Scholarship.
Intended use: For undergraduate study at postsecondary institution.

American Legion Connecticut Auxiliary: Memorial Education Grant

Eligibility: Applicant or parent must be member/participant of American Legion Auxiliary. Applicant must be at least 16, no older than 23.
Basis for selection: Applicant must demonstrate financial need.
Application requirements: Proof of eligibility.
Additional information: Half of grants awarded to child/grandchild of Connecticut AL/ALA member or to a member of Connecticut ALA/Sons of the AL. No residency requirement. Other half awarded to child of Connecticut resident veteran.

Amount of award:	$500
Number of awards:	4
Application deadline:	March 1
Total amount awarded:	$2,000

Contact:
American Legion Auxiliary
Department Headquarters
P.O. Box 266
Rocky Hill, CT 06067-0266
Phone: 860-721-5945
Fax: 860-721-5828
Web: www.ct.legion.org/auxiliary.htm

Past President's Parley Education Grant

Type of award: Scholarship, renewable.
Intended use: For undergraduate study at postsecondary institution.
Eligibility: Applicant or parent must be member/participant of American Legion Auxiliary. Applicant must be at least 16, no older than 23.
Basis for selection: Applicant must demonstrate financial need.
Application requirements: Proof of eligibility.
Additional information: Preference given to child or grandchild of ex-servicewoman who is a CT AL/ALA member of at least five years or who was a member for the five years prior to her death. Second preference to child or grandchild of CT AL/ALA member or to a member of CT ALA/Sons of AL at least five years.

Amount of award:	$500
Number of awards:	4
Application deadline:	March 1
Total amount awarded:	$2,000

Contact:
American Legion Auxiliary
Department Headquarters
P.O. Box 266
Rocky Hill, CT 06067-0266
Phone: 860-721-5945
Fax: 860-721-5828
Web: www.ct.legion.org/auxiliary.htm

American Legion Delaware Auxiliary

Past President's Parley Nursing Scholarship

Type of award: Scholarship.
Intended use: For undergraduate study.
Eligibility: Applicant or parent must be member/participant of American Legion Auxiliary. Applicant must be residing in Delaware. Applicant must be dependent of veteran.
Basis for selection: Major/career interest in nursing.

Amount of award:	$300
Number of awards:	1
Application deadline:	February 28
Total amount awarded:	$300

Contact:
American Legion Auxiliary, Department of Delaware
P.O. Box 156
Camden, DE 19934
Web: www.delegion.org

American Legion District of Columbia

National High School Oratorical Contest

Type of award: Scholarship.
Eligibility: Applicant must be no older than 20, enrolled in high school. Applicant must be U.S. citizen or permanent resident residing in District of Columbia.
Basis for selection: Competition/talent/interest in oratory/debate, based on language style, voice, diction, delivery, originality, logic, breadth of knowledge, application of knowledge about topic, and skill in selecting examples and analogies.
Application requirements: Proof of eligibility.
Additional information: All awards in U.S. Savings Bonds: 1st-$800, 2nd-$500, 3rd-$200, 4th-$100.

Amount of award:	$100-$800
Number of awards:	4
Total amount awarded:	$1,600

Contact:
The American Legion, Department of DC
3408 Wisconsin Avenue NW, Suite 218
Washington, DC 20016
Phone: 202-362-9151
Fax: 202-362-9152

American Legion Florida

American Legion Florida General Scholarship

Type of award: Scholarship.
Intended use: For undergraduate study at postsecondary institution.
Eligibility: Applicant or parent must be member/participant of American Legion. Applicant must be high school senior. Applicant must be residing in Florida. Must be child, grandchild, great-grandchild, or legally adopted child of member in good standing of American Legion Florida or a deceased U.S. veteran who would have been eligible for membership.
Additional information: Scholarships: 1st-$2,500; 2nd-$1,500; 3rd-$1,000; 4th to 7th-$500.

Amount of award:	$500-$2,500
Number of awards:	7
Application deadline:	March 1
Total amount awarded:	$7,000

Contact:
American Legion Florida, Department Headquarters
P.O. Box 547859
Orlando, FL 32854-7859
Phone: 407-295-2631 ext. 226
Web: www.floridalegion.org

Eagle Scout of the Year

Type of award: Scholarship.
Intended use: For undergraduate study at accredited postsecondary institution in United States.
Eligibility: Applicant or parent must be member/participant of American Legion. Applicant must be male, enrolled in high school. Applicant must be residing in Florida. Applicant must be in a troop chartered to an American Legion Post, be a son or grandson of Legion member, or have a parent eligible for membership into American Legion Florida.
Application requirements: Proof of eligibility.
Additional information: Awards: 1st-$2,500; 2nd-$1,500; 3rd-$1,000; 4th-$500. Must have earned Eagle Award and religious emblem.

Amount of award:	$500-$2,500
Number of awards:	4
Application deadline:	March 1
Total amount awarded:	$5,500

Contact:
American Legion Florida, Department Headquarters
P.O. Box 547859
Orlando, FL 32854-7859
Phone: 407-295-2631 ext. 226
Web: www.floridalegion.org

High School Oratorical Contest

Type of award: Scholarship.
Eligibility: Applicant must be enrolled in high school. Applicant must be residing in Florida.
Basis for selection: Competition/talent/interest in oratory/debate, based on language style, voice, diction, delivery, originality, logic, breadth of knowledge, application of knowledge about topic, and skill in selecting examples and analogies.
Additional information: Awards: 1st-$2,500; 2nd-$1,500; 3rd-$1,000; 4th to 6th-$500.

Amount of award:	$500-$2,500
Number of awards:	6
Application deadline:	December 1
Total amount awarded:	$6,500

Contact:
American Legion Florida, Department Headquarters
P.O. Box 547859
Orlando, FL 32854-7859
Phone: 407-295-2631 ext. 226
Web: www.floridalegion.org

American Legion Florida Auxiliary

American Legion Florida Auxiliary Memorial Scholarship

Type of award: Scholarship.
Intended use: For undergraduate study at vocational, 2-year or 4-year institution.
Eligibility: Applicant or parent must be member/participant of American Legion Auxiliary. Applicant must be residing in Florida. Members and daughters/granddaughters of members with at least three years' membership in FL unit.
Additional information: Up to $500 for junior colleges and vocational schools; $1,000 for four-year university. Send application request by January 1.

Amount of award:	$500-$1,000

Contact:
American Legion Auxiliary, Department of Florida
Department Secretary
P.O. Box 547917
Orlando, FL 32854-7917
Fax: 407-299-6522
Web: www.alafl.org

American Legion Florida Auxiliary Scholarships

Type of award: Scholarship.
Intended use: For undergraduate study at vocational, 2-year or 4-year institution.
Eligibility: Applicant or parent must be member/participant of American Legion Auxiliary. Applicant must be residing in Florida. Must be child of honorably discharged U.S. military veteran and sponsored by local Auxiliary Unit.
Application requirements: Proof of eligibility.
Additional information: Up to $500 for junior colleges and vocational schools; $1,000 for four-year university. Send application request by January 1.

Amount of award:	$500-$1,000

Contact:
American Legion Auxiliary, Department of Florida
Department Secretary
P.O. Box 547917
Orlando, FL 32854-7917
Fax: 407-299-6522
Web: www.alafl.org

American Legion Georgia Auxiliary

American Legion Georgia Auxiliary Scholarship

Type of award: Scholarship.
Intended use: For undergraduate study at postsecondary institution.
Eligibility: Applicant or parent must be member/participant of American Legion Auxiliary. Applicant must be high school senior. Applicant must be residing in Georgia. Applicant must

be dependent of veteran or deceased veteran. Must be sponsored by local Auxiliary Unit.
Additional information: Information and application materials available through local American Legion Auxiliary Unit.
   Amount of award: $1,000
   Number of awards: 2
   Total amount awarded: $2,000
Contact:
American Legion Georgia Auxiliary
Department Headquarters
3035 Mt. Zion Road
Stockbridge, GA 30281-4101
Web: www.galegion.org

Past President's Parley Nurses Scholarship

Type of award: Scholarship.
Intended use: For undergraduate study at 2-year or 4-year institution.
Eligibility: Applicant or parent must be member/participant of American Legion Auxiliary. Applicant must be female, high school senior. Applicant must be residing in Georgia. Applicant must be dependent of veteran or deceased veteran. Must be sponsored by local Auxiliary Unit.
Basis for selection: Major/career interest in nursing.
Application requirements: Proof of eligibility.
Additional information: Amount and number of scholarships determined by available funds.
Contact:
American Legion Georgia Auxiliary
Department Headquarters
3035 Mt. Zion Road
Stockbridge, GA 30281-4101
Web: www.galegion.org

American Legion Hawaii

American Legion Oratorical Contest

Type of award: Scholarship.
Eligibility: Applicant must be enrolled in high school. Applicant must be residing in Hawaii.
Basis for selection: Competition/talent/interest in oratory/debate, based on language style, voice, diction, delivery, originality, logic, breadth of knowledge, application of knowledge about topic, and skill in selecting examples and analogies.
Additional information: Awards: 1st-$500; 2nd-$300; 3rd-$100; 4th-$50. Contest normally held in February.
   Amount of award: $50-$500
   Number of awards: 4
   Total amount awarded: $950
Contact:
American Legion Hawaii, Department Headquarters
612 McCully Street
Honolulu, HI 96826
Phone: 808-946-6383
Fax: 808-947-3957
Web: www.50legion.org

American Legion Idaho

American Legion Idaho Scholarships

Type of award: Scholarship.
Intended use: For undergraduate study at postsecondary institution.
Eligibility: Applicant or parent must be member/participant of American Legion. Applicant must be residing in Idaho.
Application requirements: Proof of eligibility.
Additional information: Scholarships determined annually. See Website for more information.
   Application deadline: July 1
Contact:
American Legion Idaho, Department Headquarters
901 Warren Street
Boise, ID 83706
Phone: 208-342-7061
Fax: 208-342-1964
Web: idlegion.home.mindspring.com/

Oratorical Contest

Type of award: Scholarship.
Eligibility: Applicant must be enrolled in high school. Applicant must be residing in Idaho.
Basis for selection: Competition/talent/interest in oratory/debate, based on language style, voice, diction, delivery, originality, logic, breadth of knowledge, application of knowledge about topic, and skill in selecting examples and analogies.
Additional information: Awards: 1st-$750; 2nd-$500; 3rd-$250; 4th-$100. Visit Website for more information.
   Amount of award: $100-$750
   Number of awards: 4
   Total amount awarded: $1,600
Contact:
American Legion Idaho, Department Headquarters
901 Warren Street
Boise, ID 83706
Phone: 208-342-7061
Fax: 208-342-1964
Web: idlegion.home.mindspring.com/

American Legion Idaho Auxiliary

American Legion Idaho Auxiliary Nurse's Scholarship

Type of award: Scholarship.
Intended use: For undergraduate study at 2-year or 4-year institution.
Eligibility: Applicant must be residing in Idaho. Applicant must be veteran; or dependent of veteran.
Basis for selection: Major/career interest in nursing.
Additional information: Applicant must be Idaho resident five years prior to application.
   Amount of award: $750
   Application deadline: May 15

Contact:
American Legion Idaho Auxiliary
Department Headquarters
905 Warren Street
Boise, ID 83706-3825
Phone: 208-342-7066
Fax: 208-342-7066

American Legion Illinois

American Legion Illinois Boy Scout Scholarship

Type of award: Scholarship.
Intended use: For undergraduate study at postsecondary institution.
Eligibility: Applicant or parent must be member/participant of Boy Scouts of America. Applicant must be high school senior. Applicant must be residing in Illinois.
Basis for selection: Competition/talent/interest in writing/journalism.
Application requirements: Proof of eligibility. 500-word essay on Legion's Americanism and Boy Scout programs.
Additional information: Boy Scout Scholarship: $1,000. Four runner-up awards: $200 each.

Amount of award:	$200-$1,000
Number of awards:	5
Application deadline:	April 30
Total amount awarded:	$1,800

Contact:
American Legion, Department of Illinois
P.O. Box 2910
Bloomington, IL 61702-2910
Web: www.illegion.org

American Legion Illinois Oratorical Contest

Type of award: Scholarship.
Intended use: For undergraduate study.
Eligibility: Applicant must be enrolled in high school. Applicant must be U.S. citizen or permanent resident residing in Illinois.
Basis for selection: Competition/talent/interest in oratory/debate, based on language style, voice, diction, delivery, originality, logic, breadth of knowledge, application of knowledge about topic, and skill in selecting examples and analogies.
Application requirements: Proof of eligibility.
Additional information: Contest begins in January and starts at Post level, to District level, to Division level, to Department level, then to National Competition. Awards: 1st-$1,600, 2nd-$1,300, 3rd-$1,200, 4th-$1,000, 5th-$1,000; five awards for second place in each division at $150 each, 3rd-$100, 4th-$75; and three awards for each district: 1st-$125, 2nd-$100, 3rd-$75. Applications available in the fall. Contact local Post or Department Headquarters.

| Amount of award: | $75-$1,600 |

Contact:
American Legion, Department of Illinois
P.O. Box 2910
Bloomington, IL 61702-2910
Web: www.illegion.org

American Legion Illinois Scholarships

Type of award: Scholarship.
Intended use: For undergraduate study at accredited vocational, 2-year or 4-year institution.
Eligibility: Applicant or parent must be member/participant of American Legion. Applicant must be high school senior. Applicant must be residing in Illinois.
Basis for selection: Applicant must demonstrate financial need and high academic achievement.
Application requirements: Proof of eligibility.
Additional information: Applications available after December 15.

Amount of award:	$1,000
Number of awards:	20
Application deadline:	March 15
Total amount awarded:	$20,000

Contact:
American Legion, Department of Illinois
P.O. Box 2910
Bloomington, IL 61702
Phone: 309-663-0361
Web: www.illegion.org

Americanism Essay Contest Scholarship

Type of award: Scholarship.
Eligibility: Applicant must be enrolled in high school. Applicant must be residing in Illinois.
Application requirements: 500-word essay on selected topic.
Additional information: Awards: $50-$75 depending on grade level. Open to students grade 8-12 enrolled at accredited Illinois high schools.

| Amount of award: | $50-$75 |
| Application deadline: | February 2 |

Contact:
American Legion Illinois
P.O. Box 1426
Bloomington, IL 61702-1426
Web: www.illegion.org

American Legion Illinois Auxiliary

Ada Mucklestone Memorial Scholarship

Type of award: Scholarship.
Intended use: For undergraduate study at postsecondary institution.
Eligibility: Applicant must be high school senior. Applicant must be residing in Illinois. Applicant must be descendant of veteran; or dependent of veteran during Grenada conflict, Korean War, Lebanon conflict, Panama conflict, Persian Gulf War, WW I, WW II or Vietnam.
Additional information: Awards: 1st-$1,200; 2nd-$1,000; several $800. Unit sponsorship required. Contact local Unit for application.

| Amount of award: | $800-$1,200 |
| Application deadline: | March 15 |

American Legion Illinois Auxiliary: Ada Mucklestone Memorial Scholarship

Contact:
American Legion Auxiliary Department of Illinois
P.O. Box 1426
Bloomington, IL 61702-1426
Phone: 309-663-9366

Marie Sheehe Trade School Scholarship

Type of award: Scholarship.
Intended use: For undergraduate study at vocational institution.
Eligibility: Applicant must be residing in Illinois. Applicant must be descendant of veteran; or dependent of veteran during Grenada conflict, Korean War, Lebanon conflict, Panama conflict, Persian Gulf War, WW I, WW II or Vietnam.
Additional information: Unit sponsorship required. Contact local Unit for application.
    Amount of award: $800
    Number of awards: 1
    Application deadline: March 15
    Total amount awarded: $800
Contact:
American Legion Auxiliary Department of Illinois
P.O. Box 1426
Bloomington, IL 61702-1426
Phone: 309-663-9366

Mildred R. Knoles Opportunity Scholarship

Type of award: Scholarship.
Intended use: For undergraduate study at postsecondary institution.
Eligibility: Applicant must be residing in Illinois. Applicant must be veteran or descendant of veteran; or dependent of veteran during Grenada conflict, Korean War, Lebanon conflict, Panama conflict, Persian Gulf War, WW I, WW II or Vietnam.
Basis for selection: Applicant must demonstrate financial need.
Application requirements: Proof of eligibility.
Additional information: Awards: one $1,200; several $800. Unit sponsorship required. Contact local Unit for application.
    Amount of award: $800-$1,200
    Application deadline: March 15
Contact:
American Legion Auxiliary, Department of Illinois
P.O. Box 1426
Bloomington, IL 61702-1426
Phone: 309-663-9366

Special Education Teaching Scholarships

Type of award: Scholarship.
Intended use: For sophomore or junior study at 4-year institution.
Eligibility: Applicant must be residing in Illinois.
Basis for selection: Major/career interest in education, special.
Application requirements: Proof of eligibility.
Additional information: Unit sponsorship required. Contact local Unit for application.
    Amount of award: $1,000
    Application deadline: March 15
    Total amount awarded: $1,000

Contact:
American Legion Auxiliary, Department of Illinois
P.O. Box 1426
Bloomington, IL 61702-1426
Phone: 309-663-9366

Student Nurse Scholarship

Type of award: Scholarship.
Intended use: For undergraduate study at 2-year or 4-year institution.
Eligibility: Applicant must be residing in Illinois.
Basis for selection: Major/career interest in nursing.
Application requirements: Proof of eligibility.
Additional information: Unit sponsorship required. Contact local Unit for application.
    Amount of award: $1,000
    Number of awards: 1
    Application deadline: April 10
    Total amount awarded: $1,000
Contact:
American Legion Auxiliary, Department of Illinois
P.O. Box 1426
Bloomington, IL 61702-1426
Phone: 309-663-9366

American Legion Indiana

American Legion Americanism and Government Test

Type of award: Scholarship.
Eligibility: Applicant must be high school sophomore, junior or senior. Applicant must be residing in Indiana.
Additional information: Six state winners chosen annually (one male, one female in each grade). Test given during American Education Week in November.
    Amount of award: $500
    Number of awards: 6
    Total amount awarded: $3,000
Contact:
American Legion Indiana, Department Headquarters
Americanism Office
777 North Meridian Street
Indianapolis, IN 46204
Phone: 317-630-1264
Web: www.indlegion.org

American Legion Family Scholarship

Type of award: Scholarship.
Intended use: For undergraduate study at accredited postsecondary institution in United States.
Eligibility: Applicant or parent must be member/participant of American Legion. Applicant must be residing in Indiana. Applicant must be child or grandchild of current or deceased member of The American Legion Indiana, American Legion Indiana Auxiliary, or Sons of The American Legion.
Additional information: Three awards of approximately $700-$1,000 each.
    Amount of award: $700-$1,000
    Number of awards: 3
    Application deadline: April 1

Contact:
American Legion Indiana, Department Headquarters
Americanism Office
777 North Meridian Street
Indianapolis, IN 46204
Phone: 317-630-1264
Web: www.indlegion.org

American Legion Indiana Oratorical Contest

Type of award: Scholarship.
Eligibility: Applicant must be enrolled in high school. Applicant must be residing in Indiana.
Basis for selection: Competition/talent/interest in oratory/debate, based on language style, voice, diction, delivery, originality, logic, breadth of knowledge, application of knowledge about topic, and skill in selecting examples and analogies.
Application requirements: Proof of eligibility.
Additional information: State awards: 1st-$1,700, 2nd to 4th-$500. Zone: four awards, $350 each. Must participate in local contests.
    Amount of award: $350-$1,700
    Number of awards: 8
    Application deadline: December 1
    Total amount awarded: $4,600
Contact:
American Legion Indiana, Department Headquarters
Americanism Office
777 North Meridian Street
Indianapolis, IN 46204
Phone: 317-630-1264
Web: www.indlegion.org

Eagle Scout of the Year Scholarship

Type of award: Scholarship.
Intended use: For undergraduate study at accredited postsecondary institution in United States.
Eligibility: Applicant or parent must be member/participant of American Legion. Applicant must be male, enrolled in high school. Applicant must be residing in Indiana.
Additional information: For Indiana Eagle Scout of the Year winner. See Website for details.
Contact:
American Legion Indiana, Department Headquarters
Americanism Office
777 North Meridian Street
Indianapolis, IN 46204
Phone: 317-630-1264
Web: www.indlegion.org

Frank M. McHale Memorial Scholarship

Type of award: Scholarship.
Intended use: For undergraduate study.
Eligibility: Applicant or parent must be member/participant of American Legion, Boys State. Applicant must be male, high school junior. Applicant must be residing in Indiana.
Additional information: Only Hoosier Boys Staters the year they attend are eligible. Selected by staff at Hoosier Boys State.
    Number of awards: 3

Contact:
American Legion Indiana, Department Headquarters
Americanism Office
777 North Meridian Street
Indianapolis, IN 46204
Phone: 317-630-1264
Web: www.indlegion.org

American Legion Indiana Auxiliary

Edna M. Barcus Memorial Scholarship and Hoosier Scholarship

Type of award: Scholarship.
Intended use: For undergraduate study at postsecondary institution.
Eligibility: Applicant must be residing in Indiana. Applicant must be dependent of veteran.
Basis for selection: Applicant must demonstrate high academic achievement.
Application requirements: Send SASE for application.
    Amount of award: $500
    Application deadline: April 1
Contact:
American Legion Auxiliary, Department of Indiana
Department Secretary
777 North Meridian Street, Room 107
Indianapolis, IN 46204
Phone: 317-630-1390
Fax: 317-630-1277

Past President's Parley Nursing Scholarship

Type of award: Scholarship.
Intended use: For undergraduate study.
Eligibility: Applicant or parent must be member/participant of American Legion Auxiliary. Applicant must be female. Applicant must be residing in Indiana.
Basis for selection: Major/career interest in nursing.
Application requirements: Send SASE for application.
    Amount of award: $500
    Application deadline: April 1
    Total amount awarded: $500
Contact:
American Legion Auxiliary, Department of Indiana
Department Secretary
777 North Meridian Street, Room 107
Indianapolis, IN 46204
Phone: 317-630-1390
Fax: 317-630-1277

American Legion Iowa

American Legion Iowa Oratorical Contest

Type of award: Scholarship.
Eligibility: Applicant must be enrolled in high school. Applicant must be U.S. citizen or permanent resident residing in Iowa.
Basis for selection: Competition/talent/interest in oratory/debate, based on language style, voice, diction, delivery, originality, logic, breadth of knowledge, application of knowledge about topic, and skill in selecting examples and analogies.
Application requirements: Proof of eligibility.
Additional information: Awards: 1st-$2,000; 2nd-$1,500; 3rd-$1000. Must enter Oratorical Contest at Local level in September.
    Amount of award: $1,000-$2,000
    Number of awards: 3
    Total amount awarded: $4,500
Contact:
American Legion Iowa, Department Headquarters
720 Lyon Street
Des Moines, IA 50309
Phone: 515-282-5068
Fax: 515-282-7583
Web: www.ialegion.org

Boy Scout of the Year Scholarship

Type of award: Scholarship.
Intended use: For undergraduate study at postsecondary institution.
Eligibility: Applicant or parent must be member/participant of Boy Scouts of America, Eagle Scouts. Applicant must be male. Applicant must be residing in Iowa.
Basis for selection: Applicant must demonstrate service orientation.
Application requirements: Recommendations.
Additional information: Awards: 1st-$2,000; 2nd-$1,500; 3rd-$1,000. Awarded on recommendation of Boy Scout Committee to Boy Scout who demonstrates outstanding service to religious institution, school, and community. Must have received Eagle Scout Award.
    Amount of award: $1,000-$2,000
    Number of awards: 3
    Application deadline: February 1
    Total amount awarded: $4,500
Contact:
American Legion Iowa, Department Headquarters
720 Lyon Street
Des Moines, IA 50309
Phone: 515-282-5068
Fax: 515-282-7583
Web: www.ialegion.org

Outstanding Citizen of Boys State Scholarship

Type of award: Scholarship.
Intended use: For undergraduate study at postsecondary institution. Designated institutions: Eligible colleges and universities in Iowa.
Eligibility: Applicant or parent must be member/participant of American Legion, Boys State. Applicant must be male, high school senior. Applicant must be residing in Iowa.
Application requirements: Recommendations.
Additional information: Must have completed junior year in high school to attend Boys State. Awarded on recommendation of Boys State.
    Amount of award: $5,000
    Number of awards: 1
Contact:
American Legion Iowa, Department Headquarters
720 Lyon Street
Des Moines, IA 50309
Phone: 515-282-5068
Fax: 515-282-7583
Web: www.ialegion.org

Outstanding Senior Baseball Player Scholarship

Type of award: Scholarship.
Intended use: For undergraduate study at postsecondary institution.
Eligibility: Applicant must be high school senior. Applicant must be residing in Iowa.
Basis for selection: Competition/talent/interest in athletics/sports. Applicant must demonstrate high academic achievement.
Application requirements: Recommendations.
Additional information: Must be a participant in the Iowa American Legion Senior Baseball Program and display outstanding sportsmanship, team play, and athletic ability. Awarded on recommendation of State Baseball Committee.
    Amount of award: $1,500
    Number of awards: 1
    Total amount awarded: $1,500
Contact:
American Legion Iowa, Department Headquarters
720 Lyon Street
Des Moines, IA 50309
Phone: 515-282-5068
Fax: 515-282-7583
Web: www.ialegion.org

American Legion Iowa Auxiliary

Department of Iowa Scholarships

Type of award: Scholarship.
Intended use: For undergraduate study at postsecondary institution. Designated institutions: Eligible Iowa postsecondary institutions.
Eligibility: Applicant must be residing in Iowa. Applicant must be veteran or descendant of veteran; or dependent of veteran; or spouse of veteran or deceased veteran during Grenada conflict, Korean War, Lebanon conflict, Panama conflict, Persian Gulf War, WW I, WW II or Vietnam.
Application requirements: Send SASE with application request.
    Amount of award: $300
    Number of awards: 10
    Application deadline: June 1
    Total amount awarded: $3,000

Contact:
American Legion Auxiliary, Department of Iowa
720 Lyon Street
Des Moines, IA 50309
Phone: 515-282-7987
Fax: 515-282-7583

Harriet Hoffman Memorial Scholarship

Type of award: Scholarship.
Intended use: For undergraduate study at postsecondary institution. Designated institutions: Eligible Iowa postsecondary institutions.
Eligibility: Applicant must be residing in Iowa. Applicant must be veteran or descendant of veteran; or dependent of veteran or deceased veteran; or spouse of veteran or deceased veteran.
Basis for selection: Major/career interest in education or education, teacher.
Application requirements: Send SASE with application request.
    Amount of award: $400
    Number of awards: 1
    Application deadline: June 1
    Total amount awarded: $400
Contact:
American Legion Auxiliary, Department of Iowa
720 Lyon Street
Des Moines, IA 50309
Phone: 515-282-7987
Fax: 515-282-7583

Mary Virginia Macrea Memorial Scholarship

Type of award: Scholarship.
Intended use: For undergraduate study at postsecondary institution. Designated institutions: Eligible Iowa postsecondary institutions.
Eligibility: Applicant must be residing in Iowa. Applicant must be veteran or descendant of veteran; or dependent of veteran; or spouse of veteran or deceased veteran.
Basis for selection: Major/career interest in nursing.
Application requirements: Send SASE with application request.
    Amount of award: $400
    Number of awards: 1
    Application deadline: June 1
    Total amount awarded: $400
Contact:
American Legion Auxiliary, Department of Iowa
720 Lyon Street
Des Moines, IA 50309
Phone: 515-282-7987
Fax: 515-282-7583

Past President's Scholarship

Type of award: Scholarship.
Intended use: For undergraduate study at postsecondary institution.
Eligibility: Applicant must be residing in Iowa. Applicant must be veteran or descendant of veteran; or dependent of veteran or deceased veteran; or spouse of veteran or deceased veteran.
Application requirements: Proof of eligibility. SASE.
Additional information: Amount of award varies.
    Application deadline: June 1

Contact:
American Legion Iowa Auxiliary
720 Lyon Street
Des Moines, IA 50309
Phone: 515-282-7987
Fax: 515-282-7583

American Legion Kansas

Albert M. Lappin Scholarship

Type of award: Scholarship.
Intended use: For undergraduate study at accredited postsecondary institution. Designated institutions: Eligible colleges, universities, and trade schools in Kansas.
Eligibility: Applicant or parent must be member/participant of American Legion. Applicant must be high school senior. Applicant must be residing in Kansas.
Additional information: College-level freshman or sophomore also eligible to apply.
    Amount of award: $1,000
    Number of awards: 1
    Application deadline: February 15
    Total amount awarded: $1,000
Contact:
American Legion Kansas
1314 Southwest Topeka Boulevard
Topeka, KS 66612-1886
Phone: 785-232-9315
Web: www.ksamlegion.org

American Legion Music Scholarship

Type of award: Scholarship.
Intended use: For undergraduate study at accredited postsecondary institution. Designated institutions: Eligible Kansas colleges and universities.
Eligibility: Applicant must be high school senior. Applicant must be residing in Kansas.
Basis for selection: Major/career interest in music.
Application requirements: Proof of eligibility.
Additional information: College-level freshman or sophomore also eligible to apply.
    Amount of award: $1,000
    Number of awards: 1
    Application deadline: February 15
    Total amount awarded: $1,000
Contact:
American Legion Kansas
1314 Southwest Topeka Boulevard
Topeka, KS 66612-1886
Phone: 785-232-9315
Web: www.ksamlegion.org

American Legion Oratorical Contest

Type of award: Scholarship.
Intended use: For undergraduate study at postsecondary institution.
Eligibility: Applicant must be enrolled in high school. Applicant must be residing in Kansas.
Basis for selection: Competition/talent/interest in oratory/debate, based on language style, voice, diction, delivery, originality, logic, breadth of knowledge, application of

American Legion Kansas: American Legion Oratorical Contest

knowledge about topic, and skill in selecting examples and analogies.
Additional information: Awards: $1,500 provided by National Organization, 2nd-$500, 3rd-$250, 4th-$150. Additional awards: $1,500 provided by Emporia State University Foundation, 2nd-$500, 3rd-$250, 4th-$150 (renewable up to 4 years; must qualify for admission and attend Emporia State University).
   Amount of award: $150-$1,500
Contact:
American Legion Kansas
1314 Southwest Topeka Boulevard
Topeka, KS 66612-1886
Phone: 785-232-9315
Web: www.ksamlegion.org

Charles and Annette Hill Scholarship

Type of award: Scholarship.
Intended use: For undergraduate study at postsecondary institution.
Eligibility: Applicant or parent must be member/participant of American Legion. Applicant must be residing in Kansas.
Basis for selection: Major/career interest in science, general; engineering or business/management/administration.
Additional information: Must have 3.0 GPA.
   Amount of award: $1,000
   Number of awards: 1
   Application deadline: February 15
   Total amount awarded: $1,000
Contact:
American Legion Kansas
1314 SW Topeka Blvd.
Topeka, KS 66612-1886
Phone: 785-232-9315
Web: www.ksamlegion.org

Dr. Click Cowger Scholarship

Type of award: Scholarship.
Intended use: For undergraduate study at accredited postsecondary institution. Designated institutions: Eligible Kansas colleges, universities, and trade schools.
Eligibility: Applicant must be high school senior. Applicant must be residing in Kansas.
Basis for selection: Competition/talent/interest in athletics/sports.
Application requirements: Proof of eligibility.
Additional information: Must play or have played Kansas American Legion Baseball. College-level freshman or sophomore also eligible.
   Amount of award: $500
   Number of awards: 1
   Application deadline: July 15
   Total amount awarded: $500
Contact:
American Legion Kansas
1314 Southwest Topeka Boulevard
Topeka, KS 66612-1886
Phone: 785-232-9315
Web: www.ksamlegion.org

Hugh A. Smith Scholarship

Type of award: Scholarship.
Intended use: For undergraduate study at accredited postsecondary institution. Designated institutions: Eligible Kansas colleges, universities, and trade schools.
Eligibility: Applicant or parent must be member/participant of American Legion. Applicant must be high school senior. Applicant must be residing in Kansas.
Additional information: College-level freshman or sophomore also eligible to apply.
   Amount of award: $500
   Number of awards: 1
   Application deadline: February 15
   Total amount awarded: $500
Contact:
American Legion Kansas
1314 Southwest Topeka Boulevard
Topeka, KS 66612-1886
Phone: 785-232-9315
Web: www.ksamlegion.org

John and Geraldine Hobble Licensed Practical Nursing Scholarship

Type of award: Scholarship.
Intended use: For undergraduate study at accredited postsecondary institution. Designated institutions: Kansas accredited schools that award LPN diplomas.
Eligibility: Applicant must be at least 18. Applicant must be residing in Kansas.
Basis for selection: Major/career interest in nursing.
Application requirements: Proof of eligibility.
   Amount of award: $300
   Number of awards: 1
   Application deadline: February 15
   Total amount awarded: $300
Contact:
American Legion Kansas
1314 Southwest Topeka Boulevard
Topeka, KS 66612-1886
Phone: 785-232-9315
Web: www.ksamlegion.org

Rosedale Post 346 Scholarship

Type of award: Scholarship.
Intended use: For undergraduate study at postsecondary institution. Designated institutions: Approved junior colleges, colleges, universities, and trade schools.
Eligibility: Applicant or parent must be member/participant of American Legion. Applicant must be high school senior. Applicant must be residing in Kansas.
Additional information: College-level freshman or sophomore also eligible to apply.
   Amount of award: $1,500
   Number of awards: 2
   Application deadline: February 15
   Total amount awarded: $3,000
Contact:
American Legion Kansas
1314 SW Topeka Blvd.
Topeka, KS 66612-1886
Phone: 785-232-9315
Web: www.ksamlegion.org

Ted and Nora Anderson Scholarship

Type of award: Scholarship.

Intended use: For undergraduate study at accredited postsecondary institution. Designated institutions: Eligible colleges, universities, and trade schools in Kansas.
Eligibility: Applicant or parent must be member/participant of American Legion. Applicant must be high school senior. Applicant must be residing in Kansas.
Application requirements: Proof of eligibility.
Additional information: College-level freshman or sophomore also eligible to apply.
   Amount of award: $500
   Number of awards: 4
   Application deadline: February 15
   Total amount awarded: $2,000
Contact:
American Legion Kansas
1314 Southwest Topeka Boulevard
Topeka, KS 66612-1886
Phone: 785-232-9315
Web: www.ksamlegion.org

American Legion Kansas Auxiliary

American Legion Kansas Auxiliary Department Scholarships

Type of award: Scholarship.
Intended use: For freshman study at postsecondary institution.
Eligibility: Applicant must be residing in Kansas. Applicant must be dependent of veteran; or spouse of veteran or deceased veteran during Grenada conflict, Korean War, Lebanon conflict, Panama conflict, Persian Gulf War, WW I, WW II or Vietnam.
Additional information: Award: $500; payable at $250 per year for two years. Applicants must be entering college for the first time. Spouses of deceased veterans must not be remarried.
   Amount of award: $500
   Number of awards: 8
   Application deadline: April 1
   Total amount awarded: $4,000
Contact:
American Legion Kansas Auxiliary
Department Secretary
1314 SW Topeka Boulevard
Topeka, KS 66612-1886
Phone: 785-232-1396

American Legion Kentucky

American Legion Department Oratorical Awards

Type of award: Scholarship.
Intended use: For undergraduate study at postsecondary institution.
Eligibility: Applicant must be enrolled in high school. Applicant must be residing in Kentucky.
Basis for selection: Competition/talent/interest in oratory/debate, based on language style, voice, diction, delivery, originality, logic, breadth of knowledge, application of knowledge about topic, and skill in selecting examples and analogies.
Additional information: Awards: 1st-$1,000; 2nd-$800; 3rd-$600; plus 11-$100 for District winners. Must be Kentucky Department Oratorical Contest participant.
   Amount of award: $100-$1,000
   Number of awards: 14
   Total amount awarded: $3,500
Contact:
American Legion Kentucky, Department Headquarters
P.O. Box 2123
Louisville, KY 40201
Phone: 502-587-1414
Fax: 502-587-6356
Web: www.kylegion.org

American Legion Kentucky Auxiliary

American Legion Kentucky Auxiliary Mary Barrett Marshall Scholarship

Type of award: Scholarship.
Intended use: For undergraduate study at vocational, 2-year or 4-year institution. Designated institutions: Eligible postsecondary institutions in Kentucky.
Eligibility: Applicant must be female. Applicant must be residing in Kentucky. Applicant must be descendant of veteran; or dependent of veteran; or spouse of veteran or deceased veteran during Grenada conflict, Korean War, Lebanon conflict, Panama conflict, Persian Gulf War, WW I, WW II or Vietnam.
Application requirements: Proof of eligibility. SASE.
   Amount of award: $1,000
   Number of awards: 1
   Application deadline: April 1
   Total amount awarded: $1,000
Contact:
American Legion Auxiliary, Department of Kentucky
Chairman Velma Greenleaf
1448 Leafdale Road
Hodgenville, KY 42748-9379
Phone: 720-358-3341

Laura Blackburn Memorial Scholarship

Type of award: Scholarship.
Intended use: For undergraduate study at postsecondary institution.
Eligibility: Applicant must be high school senior. Applicant must be residing in Kentucky. Applicant must be descendant of veteran; or dependent of veteran during Grenada conflict, Korean War, Lebanon conflict, Panama conflict, Persian Gulf War, WW I, WW II or Vietnam.
Application requirements: Proof of eligibility.
   Amount of award: $1,000
   Number of awards: 1
   Application deadline: March 31
   Total amount awarded: $1,000

American Legion Maine

Children and Youth Scholarships

Type of award: Scholarship.
Intended use: For undergraduate study at postsecondary institution.
Eligibility: Applicant or parent must be member/participant of American Legion. Applicant must be high school senior. Applicant must be residing in Maine.
Basis for selection: Applicant must demonstrate financial need.
Additional information: High school seniors, college students, and veterans eligible.

Amount of award:	$500
Number of awards:	7
Number of applicants:	300
Application deadline:	May 1
Total amount awarded:	$3,500

Contact:
American Legion Maine
Department Adjutant, State Headquarters
P.O. Box 900
Waterville, ME 04903-0900
Phone: 207-873-3229
Fax: 207-872-0501
Web: www.mainelegion.org

Daniel E. Lambert Memorial Scholarship

Type of award: Scholarship.
Intended use: For undergraduate study at vocational, 2-year or 4-year institution.
Eligibility: Applicant must be high school senior. Applicant must be residing in Maine. Applicant must be dependent of veteran.
Basis for selection: Applicant must demonstrate financial need and depth of character.

Amount of award:	$1,000
Number of awards:	1
Application deadline:	May 1
Total amount awarded:	$1,000

Contact:
American Legion Maine
Department Adjutant, State Headquarters
P.O. Box 900
Waterville, ME 04903-0900
Phone: 207-873-3229
Fax: 207-872-0501
Web: www.mainelegion.org

James V. Day Scholarship

Type of award: Scholarship.
Intended use: For undergraduate study at vocational, 2-year or 4-year institution.
Eligibility: Applicant or parent must be member/participant of American Legion. Applicant must be high school senior. Applicant must be residing in Maine.
Basis for selection: Applicant must demonstrate financial need, high academic achievement and depth of character.
Additional information: Must be in top half of graduating class.

Amount of award:	$500
Number of awards:	2
Application deadline:	May 1
Total amount awarded:	$1,000

Contact:
American Legion Maine
Department Adjutant, State Headquarters
P.O. Box 900
Waterville, ME 04903-0900
Phone: 207-873-3229
Fax: 207-872-0501
Web: www.mainelegion.org

American Legion Maine Auxiliary

American Legion Maine Auxiliary Scholarship

Type of award: Scholarship.
Intended use: For undergraduate study at vocational, 2-year or 4-year institution.
Eligibility: Applicant must be high school senior. Applicant must be residing in Maine. Applicant must be dependent of veteran.
Basis for selection: Applicant must demonstrate financial need.
Application requirements: Send SASE with application request.
Additional information: Out-of-state applicants not considered.

Amount of award:	$300
Number of awards:	2
Application deadline:	April 5
Total amount awarded:	$600

Contact:
American Legion Auxiliary, Department of Maine
Department Secretary
P.O. Box 579
Union, ME 04862-0579

President's Parley Nursing Scholarship

Type of award: Scholarship.
Intended use: For undergraduate study.
Eligibility: Applicant must be residing in Maine. Applicant must be descendant of veteran; or dependent of veteran during WW I or WW II.
Basis for selection: Major/career interest in nursing.
Application requirements: Proof of eligibility.
Additional information: Must be graduate of accredited high school. Out-of-state applicants not considered.

Amount of award:	$300
Number of awards:	1
Application deadline:	April 5
Total amount awarded:	$300

Contact:
American Legion Auxiliary, Department of Maine
Department Secretary
P.O. Box 579
Union, ME 04862-0579

American Legion Maryland

Adler Science and Math Scholarship

Type of award: Scholarship.
Intended use: For undergraduate study at postsecondary institution.
Eligibility: Applicant must be at least 16, no older than 19. Applicant must be residing in Maryland. Applicant must be dependent of veteran.
Basis for selection: Major/career interest in science, general or mathematics.

Amount of award:	$500
Number of awards:	1
Application deadline:	March 31
Total amount awarded:	$500

Contact:
American Legion Maryland Attn: Department Adjutant
The War Memorial Building
101 N Gay St.
Baltimore, MD 21202
Phone: 410-752-1405
Web: www.mdlegion.org

American Legion Maryland Boys State Scholarship

Type of award: Scholarship.
Intended use: For undergraduate study at postsecondary institution.
Eligibility: Applicant or parent must be member/participant of American Legion, Boys State. Applicant must be male, at least 16, no older than 19. Applicant must be residing in Maryland.
Additional information: Applicant must be Maryland Boys State graduate.

Amount of award:	$500
Number of awards:	5
Application deadline:	May 1
Total amount awarded:	$2,500

Contact:
American Legion Maryland Attn: Department Adjutant
The War Memorial Building
101 N Gay St.
Baltimore, MD 21202-1405
Phone: 410-752-1405
Web: www.mdlegion.org

American Legion Maryland Oratorical Contest

Type of award: Scholarship.
Intended use: For undergraduate study at postsecondary institution.
Eligibility: Applicant must be at least 16, no older than 19. Applicant must be residing in Maryland.
Basis for selection: Competition/talent/interest in oratory/debate, based on language style, voice, diction, delivery, originality, logic, breadth of knowledge, application of knowledge about topic, and skill in selecting examples and analogies.
Additional information: Awards: 1st-$2,500; 2nd-$1,000; 3rd to 7th-$500 each. Must be an American Legion Oratorical Contest department winner. Apply to nearest American Legion Post.

Amount of award:	$500-$2,500
Number of awards:	7
Application deadline:	October 1
Total amount awarded:	$6,000

Contact:
American Legion Maryland
The War Memorial Building
101 N Gay St.
Baltimore, MD 21202-1405
Phone: 410-752-1405
Web: www.mdlegion.org

American Legion Maryland Scholarship

Type of award: Scholarship.
Intended use: For undergraduate study at postsecondary institution.
Eligibility: Applicant must be at least 16, no older than 19. Applicant must be residing in Maryland. Applicant must be dependent of veteran.
Additional information: Applicant must not have reached 20th birthday by January 1 of calendar year application is filed.

Amount of award:	$500
Number of awards:	11
Application deadline:	March 31
Total amount awarded:	$5,500

Contact:
American Legion Maryland Attn: Department Adjutant
The War Memorial Building
101 N Gay St.
Baltimore, MD 21202-1405
Phone: 410-752-1405
Web: www.mdlegion.org

American Legion Maryland Auxiliary

American Legion Maryland Auxiliary Scholarship

Type of award: Scholarship.
Intended use: For undergraduate study at 2-year or 4-year institution.
Eligibility: Applicant must be female, high school senior. Applicant must be residing in Maryland. Applicant must be dependent of veteran.
Basis for selection: Major/career interest in arts, general; science, general; business; public administration/service; education, teacher; biomedical or health-related professions.

Amount of award: $2,000
Number of awards: 1
Application deadline: May 1
Total amount awarded: $2,000

Contact:
American Legion Auxiliary, Department of Maryland
Department Secretary
1589 Sulphur Spring Road, Suite 105
Baltimore, MD 21227
Phone: 410-242-9519
Fax: 410-242-9553

Past President's Parley Scholarship

Type of award: Scholarship.
Intended use: For undergraduate study at 2-year or 4-year institution.
Eligibility: Applicant must be female, at least 16, no older than 22. Applicant must be residing in Maryland. Must be daughter/step-daughter, granddaughter/step-granddaughter, great-granddaughter/step-great-granddaughter of ex-servicewoman or ex-serviceman.
Basis for selection: Major/career interest in nursing. Applicant must demonstrate financial need.
Application requirements: Recommendations.
Additional information: For RN degree only.
Amount of award: $2,000
Number of awards: 1
Application deadline: May 1
Total amount awarded: $2,000

Contact:
American Legion Maryland Auxiliary
Chairman, Past President's Parley Scholarship
1589 Sulphur Spring Road, Suite 105
Baltimore, MD 21227
Phone: 410-242-9519
Fax: 410-242-9553

American Legion Massachusetts

American Legion Massachusetts General and Nursing Scholarships

Type of award: Scholarship.
Intended use: For freshman study at 2-year or 4-year institution.
Eligibility: Applicant or parent must be member/participant of American Legion. Applicant must be residing in Massachusetts. Applicant must be descendant of veteran; or dependent of veteran.
Additional information: General Scholarships: nine-$1,000; ten-$500. Nursing Scholarship: one-$1,000.
Amount of award: $500-$1,000
Number of awards: 20
Application deadline: April 1
Total amount awarded: $15,000

Contact:
American Legion Massachusetts
Department Adjutant
546-2 State House
Boston, MA 02133-1044
Web: www.masslegion.org

Department of Massachusetts Oratorical Contest

Type of award: Scholarship.
Intended use: For undergraduate study at postsecondary institution.
Eligibility: Applicant must be no older than 19. Applicant must be residing in Massachusetts.
Basis for selection: Competition/talent/interest in oratory/debate, based on language style, voice, diction, delivery, originality, logic, breadth of knowledge, application of knowledge about topic, and skill in selecting examples and analogies.
Application requirements: Proof of eligibility.
Additional information: Awards: 1st-$1,000; 2nd-$800; 3rd-$700; 4th-$600.
Amount of award: $600-$1,000
Number of awards: 4
Application deadline: December 15
Total amount awarded: $3,100

Contact:
American Legion Massachusetts
Department Oratorical Chair
State House, Room 546-2
Boston, MA 02133-1044
Web: www.masslegion.org

American Legion Massachusetts Auxiliary

American Legion Massachusetts Auxiliary Scholarship

Type of award: Scholarship.
Intended use: For undergraduate study at vocational, 2-year or 4-year institution.
Eligibility: Applicant must be at least 16, no older than 22. Applicant must be residing in Massachusetts. Applicant must be descendant of veteran; or dependent of veteran or deceased veteran during Grenada conflict, Korean War, Lebanon conflict, Panama conflict, Persian Gulf War, WW I, WW II or Vietnam.
Additional information: Awards: one-$750 and ten-$200.
Amount of award: $200-$750
Number of awards: 11
Application deadline: March 1
Total amount awarded: $2,750

Contact:
American Legion Auxiliary, Department of Massachusetts
Department Secretary
24 State House, Room 546-2
Boston, MA 02133-1044

Past President's Parley Scholarship

Type of award: Scholarship.
Intended use: For undergraduate study at postsecondary institution.
Eligibility: Applicant must be residing in Massachusetts. Applicant must be dependent of veteran or deceased veteran.
Basis for selection: Major/career interest in nursing.
Additional information: Must be child of living or deceased veteran not eligible for Federal or Commonwealth scholarships.

Amount of award: $200
Number of awards: 1
Application deadline: March 1
Total amount awarded: $200
Contact:
American Legion Massachusetts Auxiliary
Department Secretary
24 State House, Room 546-2
Boston, MA 02133-1044

American Legion Michigan

American Legion Michigan Oratorical Contest

Type of award: Scholarship.
Intended use: For undergraduate study at postsecondary institution.
Eligibility: Applicant must be enrolled in high school. Applicant must be residing in Michigan.
Basis for selection: Competition/talent/interest in oratory/debate, based on ability to deliver an 8- to 10-minute speech on the U.S. Constitution.
Additional information: Awards: $1,000, $800, $600. Local contest in early February. Must be finalist in Zone Oratorical Contest.
Amount of award: $600-$1,000
Number of awards: 3
Total amount awarded: $2,400
Contact:
Deanna Clark American Legion Michigan
212 North Verlinden Avenue
Lansing, MI 48915
Phone: 517-371-4720 ext. 25
Fax: 517-371-2401
Web: www.michiganlegion.org

Guy M. Wilson Scholarship

Type of award: Scholarship.
Intended use: For undergraduate study at 2-year or 4-year institution.
Eligibility: Applicant must be enrolled in high school. Applicant must be residing in Michigan. Applicant must be dependent of veteran or deceased veteran.
Basis for selection: Applicant must demonstrate financial need.
Application requirements: Transcript. Copy of living or deceased veteran's honorable discharge (DD-214). Also include copy of most recently filed federal tax form.
Additional information: GPA of 2.5 or higher. Application should be filed at local American Legion Post.
Amount of award: $500
Application deadline: January 1
Contact:
Deanna Clark American Legion Michigan
212 North Verlinden Avenue
Lansing, MI 48915
Phone: 517-371-4720 ext. 25
Fax: 517-371-2401
Web: www.michiganlegion.org

William D. & Jewell W. Brewer Scholarship Trusts

Type of award: Scholarship.
Intended use: For undergraduate study at 2-year or 4-year institution.
Eligibility: Applicant must be residing in Michigan. Applicant must be dependent of veteran or deceased veteran.
Basis for selection: Applicant must demonstrate financial need.
Application requirements: Transcript. Copy of deceased or living veteran's honorable discharge (DD-214). Also include copy of most recently filed federal tax form.
Additional information: GPA of 2.5 or higher. Application should be filed at local American Legion Post.
Amount of award: $500
Application deadline: January 1
Contact:
Deanna Clark American Legion Michigan
212 North Verlinden Avenue
Lansing, MI 48915
Phone: 517-371-4720 ext. 25
Fax: 517-371-2401
Web: www.michiganlegion.org

American Legion Michigan Auxiliary

American Legion Michigan Auxiliary Memorial Scholarship

Type of award: Scholarship, renewable.
Intended use: For undergraduate study at postsecondary institution.
Eligibility: Applicant must be female, at least 16, no older than 21. Applicant must be residing in Michigan. Applicant must be daughter, granddaughter, or great-granddaughter of honorably discharged or deceased veteran who served during eligible dates for membership in The American Legion.
Basis for selection: Applicant must demonstrate financial need and high academic achievement.
Application requirements: Recommendations, transcript, proof of eligibility.
Additional information: Visit Website for details and application.
Amount of award: $500
Application deadline: March 15
Contact:
American Legion Auxiliary, Department of Michigan
212 North Verlinden Avenue
Lansing, MI 48915
Phone: 517-371-4720 ext. 22
Fax: 517-371-2401
Web: www.michalaux.org

Medical Career Scholarships

Type of award: Scholarship.
Intended use: For freshman study at postsecondary institution.
Eligibility: Applicant must be high school senior. Applicant must be residing in Michigan. Applicant must be child, grandchild, great-grandchild, wife, or widow of honorably

discharged or deceased veteran who served during eligible dates for membership in The American Legion.
Basis for selection: Major/career interest in nursing; physical therapy or respiratory therapy. Applicant must demonstrate financial need.
Application requirements: Transcript, proof of eligibility.
Additional information: Applications available after November 15. Visit Website for details and application.
    Amount of award: $500
    Application deadline: April 1
Contact:
American Legion Auxiliary, Department of Michigan
212 North Verlinden Avenue
Lansing, MI 48915
Phone: 517-371-4720 ext. 22
Fax: 517-371-2401
Web: www.michalaux.org

National President's Scholarship

Type of award: Scholarship.
Intended use: For undergraduate study at postsecondary institution.
Eligibility: Applicant must be high school senior. Applicant must be residing in Michigan. Applicant must be dependent of veteran during Grenada conflict, Korean War, Middle East War, Lebanon conflict, Panama conflict, Persian Gulf War, WW I, WW II or Vietnam.
Application requirements: Applicant must have completed 50 hours of community service during high school.
    Amount of award: $1,000-$2,500
    Number of awards: 1
    Application deadline: March 1
Contact:
American Legion Auxiliary, Department of Michigan
212 North Verlinden Avenue
Lansing, MI 48915
Phone: 517-371-4720 ext. 22
Fax: 517-371-2401
Web: www.michalaux.org

American Legion Minnesota

American Legion Minnesota Legionnaire Insurance Trust Scholarship

Type of award: Scholarship.
Intended use: For undergraduate study at accredited postsecondary institution. Designated institutions: Minnesota colleges and universities and institutions in neighboring states with reciprocating agreements.
Eligibility: Applicant or parent must be member/participant of American Legion. Applicant must be residing in Minnesota. Applicant must be veteran or descendant of veteran; or dependent of veteran.
Basis for selection: Applicant must demonstrate high academic achievement.
Application requirements: Proof of eligibility.
    Amount of award: $500
    Number of awards: 3
    Application deadline: April 1
    Total amount awarded: $1,500
Contact:
American Legion Minnesota
Education Committee
20 West 12th Street, Room 300A
St. Paul, MN 55155-2000
Phone: 866-259-9163
Web: www.mnlegion.org

American Legion Minnesota Oratorical Contest

Type of award: Scholarship.
Intended use: For undergraduate study at accredited postsecondary institution.
Eligibility: Applicant must be enrolled in high school. Applicant must be residing in Minnesota.
Basis for selection: Competition/talent/interest in oratory/debate, based on language style, voice, diction, delivery, originality, logic, breadth of knowledge, application of knowledge about topic, and skill in selecting examples and analogies.
Additional information: Awards: $1,200, $900, $700, $500.
    Amount of award: $500-$1,200
    Number of awards: 4
    Application deadline: December 15
    Total amount awarded: $3,300
Contact:
American Legion Minnesota
Education Committee
20 West 12th Street, Room 300A
St. Paul, MN 55155-2000
Phone: 866-259-9163
Web: www.mnlegion.org

The Minnesota American Legion Memorial Scholarship

Type of award: Scholarship.
Intended use: For undergraduate study at accredited postsecondary institution. Designated institutions: Minnesota colleges and universities and institutions in neighboring states with reciprocating agreement.
Eligibility: Applicant or parent must be member/participant of American Legion. Applicant must be residing in Minnesota.
Basis for selection: Applicant must demonstrate financial need.
    Amount of award: $500
    Number of awards: 6
    Application deadline: April 1
    Total amount awarded: $3,000
Contact:
American Legion Minnesota
Education Committee
20 West 12th Street, Room 300A
St. Paul, MN 55155-2000
Phone: 866-259-9163
Web: www.mnlegion.org

American Legion Minnesota Auxiliary

American Legion Minnesota Auxiliary Department Scholarship

Type of award: Scholarship.
Intended use: For undergraduate study at accredited postsecondary institution.
Eligibility: Applicant or parent must be member/participant of American Legion Auxiliary. Applicant must be residing in Minnesota. Applicant must be descendant of veteran; or dependent of veteran.
    Amount of award: $1,000
    Number of awards: 7
    Application deadline: March 15
    Total amount awarded: $7,000
Contact:
American Legion Auxiliary, Department of Minnesota
State Veterans Service Building
20 W 12th Street, Room 314
St. Paul, MN 55155-2069
Phone: 651-224-7634
Fax: 651-224-5243

Past President's Parley Health Care Scholarship

Type of award: Scholarship.
Intended use: For undergraduate study at accredited postsecondary institution.
Eligibility: Applicant or parent must be member/participant of American Legion Auxiliary. Applicant must be residing in Minnesota.
Basis for selection: Major/career interest in health-related professions.
    Amount of award: $1,000
    Number of awards: 10
    Application deadline: March 15
    Total amount awarded: $10,000
Contact:
American Legion Auxiliary, Department of Minnesota
State Veterans Service Building
20 W. 12th Street, Room 314
St. Paul, MN 55155-2069
Phone: 651-224-7634
Fax: 651-224-5243

American Legion Mississippi Auxiliary

American Legion Mississippi Auxiliary Scholarship

Type of award: Scholarship.
Intended use: For undergraduate study at accredited postsecondary institution.
Eligibility: Applicant must be high school senior. Applicant must be residing in Mississippi. Applicant must be descendant of veteran; or dependent of veteran during Korean War, Lebanon conflict, Panama conflict, Persian Gulf War, WW I, WW II or Vietnam.
Basis for selection: Applicant must demonstrate financial need.
    Amount of award: $500
    Number of awards: 1
    Application deadline: March 1
    Total amount awarded: $500
Contact:
American Legion Mississippi Auxiliary
Department Headquarters
P.O. Box 1382
Jackson, MS 39215-1382
Phone: 601-353-3681
Fax: 601-353-3682

American Legion Missouri

Charles L. Bacon Memorial Scholarship

Type of award: Scholarship.
Intended use: For full-time undergraduate study at accredited 2-year or 4-year institution.
Eligibility: Applicant or parent must be member/participant of American Legion. Applicant must be single, no older than 20. Applicant must be U.S. citizen residing in Missouri. Applicants must be current member of American Legion, American Legion Auxiliary or the Sons of the American Legion, or descendent of any member.
    Amount of award: $500
    Number of awards: 2
    Application deadline: April 20
    Total amount awarded: $1,000
Contact:
American Legion Missouri Attn: Education and Scholarship Committee
P.O. Box 179
Jefferson City, MO 65102
Phone: 417-924-8186
Web: www.missourilegion.org

Erman W. Taylor Memorial Scholarship

Type of award: Scholarship.
Intended use: For full-time undergraduate study at accredited 2-year or 4-year institution.
Eligibility: Applicant must be U.S. citizen residing in Missouri. Applicant must be dependent of veteran. Must be dependent of veteran who served 90 or more days of active duty in the Armed Forces and have an honorable discharge.
Basis for selection: Major/career interest in education.
Application requirements: Copy of discharge certificate for veteran parent, grandparent; essay of 500 words or less on selected topic.
    Amount of award: $500
    Number of awards: 2
    Application deadline: April 20
    Total amount awarded: $1,000

Contact:
American Legion Missouri Attn: Education and Scholarship Committee
P.O. Box 179
Jefferson City, MO 65102
Phone: 417-924-8186
Web: www.missourilegion.org

Lillie Lois Ford Boys' Scholarship

Type of award: Scholarship.
Intended use: For undergraduate study at accredited postsecondary institution.
Eligibility: Applicant or parent must be member/participant of American Legion, Boys State. Applicant must be male. Applicant must be residing in Missouri.
Additional information: Must have attended complete session of Boys State or Cadet Patrol Academy.
    Amount of award: $1,000
    Number of awards: 1
    Application deadline: April 20
    Total amount awarded: $1,000
Contact:
American Legion Missouri Attn: Education and Scholarship Committee
P.O. Box 179
Jefferson City, MO 65102-0179
Phone: 417-924-8186
Web: www.missourilegion.org

Lillie Lois Ford Girls' Scholarship

Type of award: Scholarship.
Intended use: For undergraduate study at accredited postsecondary institution.
Eligibility: Applicant must be female. Applicant must be residing in Missouri.
Additional information: Must have attended complete session of Girls State or Cadet Patrol Academy.
    Amount of award: $1,000
    Number of awards: 1
    Application deadline: April 20
    Total amount awarded: $1,000
Contact:
American Legion Missouri Attn: Education and Scholarship Committee
P.O. Box 179
Jefferson City, MO 65102
Phone: 417-924-8186
Web: www.missourilegion.org

M.D. "Jack" Murphy Memorial Nurses Training Fund

Type of award: Scholarship, renewable.
Intended use: For full-time undergraduate study at 2-year or 4-year institution.
Eligibility: Applicant must be residing in Missouri.
Basis for selection: Major/career interest in nursing.
Additional information: Available to students training to be registered nurses. Applicant must have graduated in top 40% of high school class or have minimum "C" or equivalent standing in semester prior to applying for award. Award payment: $375 per semester.
    Number of awards: 1
    Application deadline: April 20
    Total amount awarded: $750

Contact:
American Legion Missouri Attn: Education and Scholarship Committee
P.O. Box 179
Jefferson City, MO 65102-0179
Phone: 417-924-8186
Web: www.missourilegion.org

American Legion Missouri Auxiliary

American Legion Missouri Auxiliary Scholarship

Type of award: Scholarship.
Intended use: For undergraduate study at postsecondary institution.
Eligibility: Applicant must be high school senior. Applicant must be residing in Missouri. Applicant must be descendant of veteran; or dependent of veteran during Korean War, Lebanon conflict, Panama conflict, Persian Gulf War, WW I, WW II or Vietnam.
Additional information: Applicant must not have previously attended institution of higher learning.
    Amount of award: $500
    Number of awards: 2
    Application deadline: March 15
    Total amount awarded: $1,000
Contact:
American Legion Missouri Auxiliary
Department Secretary
600 Ellis Blvd.
Jefferson City, MO 65101-2204
Phone: 573-636-9133
Fax: 573-635-3467

Past President's Parley Scholarship

Type of award: Scholarship.
Intended use: For undergraduate study at 2-year or 4-year institution.
Eligibility: Applicant must be high school senior. Applicant must be residing in Missouri. Applicant must be descendant of veteran; or dependent of veteran.
Basis for selection: Major/career interest in nursing.
Application requirements: Recommendations.
Additional information: Applicant must not have previously attended institution of higher learning.
    Amount of award: $500
    Number of awards: 1
    Application deadline: March 15
Contact:
American Legion Missouri Auxiliary
Department Secretary
600 Ellis Blvd
Jefferson City, MO 65101-2204
Phone: 573-636-9133
Fax: 573-635-3467

American Legion Montana Auxiliary

Aloha Scholarship

Type of award: Scholarship.
Intended use: For freshman study at postsecondary institution. Designated institutions: Accredited nursing schools.
Eligibility: Applicant or parent must be member/participant of American Legion Auxiliary. Applicant must be residing in Montana.
Basis for selection: Major/career interest in nursing.
Application requirements: Recommendations. Recommendations from local Auxiliary Unit, pastor, high school principal, and two local businesspeople.

Amount of award:	$400
Number of awards:	1
Application deadline:	April 1

Contact:
American Legion Montana Auxiliary Department Secretary
P.O. Box 40
Townsend, MT 59644
Phone: 406-266-4566
Fax: 406-266-4566

American Legion Montana Auxiliary Scholarships (1)

Type of award: Scholarship.
Intended use: For undergraduate study at postsecondary institution.
Eligibility: Applicant must be high school senior. Applicant must be residing in Montana. Applicant must be dependent of veteran.
Application requirements: Essay. 500-word essay on any topic.
Additional information: Applicant must be high school senior or graduate who has not attended college. Must be state resident for at least two years.

Amount of award:	$500
Number of awards:	2
Application deadline:	April 1
Total amount awarded:	$1,000

Contact:
American Legion Montana Auxiliary Department Secretary
P.O. Box 40
Townsend, MT 59644
Phone: 406-266-4566
Fax: 406-266-4566

American Legion Montana Auxiliary Scholarships (2)

Type of award: Scholarship.
Intended use: For junior study at postsecondary institution.
Eligibility: Applicant must be residing in Montana. Applicant must be dependent of veteran.
Application requirements: Essay stating interest in issues relating to children and youth.
Additional information: Must have completed sophomore year in college and be going into field relating to children and youth.

Amount of award:	$500
Number of awards:	2
Application deadline:	June 1
Total amount awarded:	$1,000

Contact:
American Legion Montana Auxiliary Department Secretary
P.O. Box 40
Townsend, MT 59644
Phone: 406-266-4566
Fax: 406-266-4566

American Legion National Headquarters

American Legion Auxiliary National President's Scholarship

Type of award: Scholarship.
Intended use: For undergraduate study at postsecondary institution.
Eligibility: Applicant or parent must be member/participant of American Legion Auxiliary. Applicant must be high school senior. Applicant must be dependent of veteran during Grenada conflict, Korean War, Lebanon conflict, Panama conflict, Persian Gulf War, WW I, WW II or Vietnam.
Basis for selection: Applicant must demonstrate financial need, high academic achievement, depth of character, leadership and patriotism.
Additional information: Scholarships: five-$2,500; five-$2,000; five-$1,000; awarded annually. Applications available online, from Unit President of Auxiliary in local community, from Department Secretary, or from National Headquarters. See Website for details.

Amount of award:	$1,000-$2,500
Number of awards:	15
Application deadline:	March 1
Total amount awarded:	$27,500

Contact:
American Legion Auxiliary
777 North Meridian Street, 3rd Floor
Indianapolis, IN 46204-1189
Phone: 317-955-3845
Web: www.legion-aux.org

American Legion Eagle Scout of the Year

Type of award: Scholarship.
Intended use: For undergraduate study at accredited postsecondary institution in United States.
Eligibility: Applicant or parent must be member/participant of Boy Scouts of America, Eagle Scouts. Applicant must be male, enrolled in high school. Applicant must be U.S. citizen.
Application requirements: Nomination.
Additional information: Applicant must be registered, active member of Boy Scout Troop, Varsity Scout Team or Venturing Crew AND either chartered to American Legion Post/Auxiliary Unit OR son or grandson of American Legion or Auxiliary member. Awards: One $10,000 Eagle Scout of the Year; three runners-up get $2,500. Scholarships available upon graduation from accredited high school and must be used within four years of graduation date. Request application from State Department Headquarters.

Amount of award: $2,500-$10,000
Number of awards: 4
Total amount awarded: $17,500
Contact:
The American Legion
Eagle Scout of the Year
P. O. Box 1055
Indianapolis, IN 46206-1055
Phone: 317-630-1249
Web: www.legion.org

American Legion Legacy Scholarship

Type of award: Scholarship, renewable.
Intended use: For undergraduate study at postsecondary institution in United States.
Eligibility: Applicant must be high school senior. Applicant must be residing in Indiana. Applicant must be child (dependent, legally adopted, or from a spouse of prior marriage) of active duty personnel of the U.S. military or National Guard or military reservists who were federalized and died on active duty on or after September 11, 2001.
Additional information: Amount and number of awards vary. Previous scholarship recipients may reapply. Visit Website for details.
Application deadline: April 15
Contact:
American Legion National Headquarters
Education Programs Chair
P.O. Box 1055
Indianapolis, IN 46206-1055
Web: www.legion.org

American Legion National High School Oratorical Contest

Type of award: Scholarship.
Intended use: For undergraduate study at postsecondary institution.
Eligibility: Applicant must be enrolled in high school. Applicant must be U.S. citizen or permanent resident.
Basis for selection: Competition/talent/interest in oratory/debate, based on language style, voice, diction, delivery, originality, logic, breadth of knowledge, application of knowledge about topic, and skill in selecting examples and analogies.
Additional information: Awards: State winners participating in regional level win $1,500; second-round participants not advancing to national finals receive additional $1,500. Finalists win $18,000 (first place), $16,000 (runner-up), and $14,000 (third place). Obtain oratorical contest rules from local Legion Post or state Department Headquarters.
Amount of award: $1,500-$18,000
Number of awards: 54
Contact:
American Legion National Headquarters
Education Programs Chair
P.O. Box 1055
Indianapolis, IN 46206-1055
Web: www.legion.org

Eight and Forty Lung and Respiratory Nursing Scholarship Fund

Type of award: Scholarship.
Intended use: For undergraduate, graduate or non-degree study.
Eligibility: Applicant must be returning adult student.
Application requirements: Proof of eligibility.
Additional information: Applicant must be registered nurse. Program assists registered nurses with advanced preparation for positions in supervision, administration, or teaching. On completion of education, must have full-time employment prospects related to lung and respiratory control in hospitals, clinics, or health departments. Contact Eight and Forty Scholarship Chairman or the American Legion Education Program for application.
Amount of award: $3,000
Application deadline: May 15
Notification begins: July 1
Total amount awarded: $3,000
Contact:
American Legion Education Program
Eight and Forty Scholarships
P.O. Box 1055
Indianapolis, IN 46206-1055
Web: www.legion.org

Girl Scout Achievement Award

Type of award: Scholarship.
Intended use: For freshman study at postsecondary institution.
Eligibility: Applicant or parent must be member/participant of American Legion Auxiliary. Applicant must be female, enrolled in high school.
Additional information: Applicant must be a Gold Award recipient and in 11th grade or higher. Must be an active member of religious institution and have received religious emblem. Must have demonstrated practical citizenship in church, school, scouting, and community. See Website for details.
Amount of award: $1,000
Number of awards: 1
Application deadline: February 11
Total amount awarded: $1,000
Contact:
American Legion Auxiliary
777 North Meridian Street, 3rd Floor
Indianapolis, IN 46204-1189
Phone: 317-955-3845
Web: www.legion-aux.org

Samsung American Legion Scholarship

Type of award: Scholarship.
Intended use: For undergraduate study at postsecondary institution in United States.
Eligibility: Applicant or parent must be member/participant of American Legion. Applicant must be high school junior. Applicant must be descendant of veteran; or dependent of veteran. Applicant must have completed American Legion Boys State or Girls State program.
Additional information: Amount and number of awards vary. In 2007, ten $20,000 and ninety $1,000 scholarships awarded. Visit Website for details.

Contact:
American Legion National Headquarters
Education Programs Chair
P.O. Box 1055
Indianapolis, IN 46206-1055
Web: www.legion.org

Spirit of Youth Scholarship for Junior Members

Type of award: Scholarship.
Intended use: For undergraduate study at postsecondary institution.
Eligibility: Applicant or parent must be member/participant of American Legion Auxiliary. Applicant must be high school senior. Applicant must be U.S. citizen.
Basis for selection: Applicant must demonstrate financial need, high academic achievement, depth of character, leadership and patriotism.
Application requirements: Proof of eligibility.
Additional information: Must be Junior member of three years' standing, holding current membership card. Applications available online, from Unit President of Auxiliary in local community, from Department Secretary, or from National Headquarters. See Website for details.
    Amount of award: $1,000
    Number of awards: 5
    Application deadline: March 1
    Total amount awarded: $5,000
Contact:
American Legion Auxiliary
777 North Meridian, 3rd Floor
Indianapolis, IN 46204-1189
Phone: 317-955-3845
Web: www.legion-aux.org

American Legion Nebraska

American Legion Nebraska Oratorical Contest

Type of award: Scholarship.
Intended use: For undergraduate study at postsecondary institution.
Eligibility: Applicant or parent must be member/participant of American Legion. Applicant must be enrolled in high school. Applicant must be residing in Nebraska.
Basis for selection: Competition/talent/interest in oratory/debate, based on language style, voice, diction, delivery, originality, logic, breadth of knowledge, application of knowledge about topic, and skill in selecting examples and analogies.
Application requirements: Proof of eligibility.
Additional information: Awards: 1st-$1,000, 2nd-$600, 3rd-$400, 4th-$200, plus one $100 award for 1st place in each District upon participation in area contest.
    Amount of award: $100-$1,000
    Application deadline: November 1

Contact:
American Legion Nebraska
Department Headquarters
P.O. Box 5205
Lincoln, NE 68505-0205
Phone: 402-464-6338
Web: www.ne.legion.org

Edgar J. Boschult Memorial Scholarship

Type of award: Scholarship.
Intended use: For undergraduate study. Designated institutions: University of Nebraska.
Eligibility: Applicant or parent must be member/participant of American Legion. Applicant must be residing in Nebraska.
Basis for selection: Applicant must demonstrate financial need and high academic achievement.
Additional information: Must be student at University of Nebraska with high academic and ROTC standing, or military veteran attending University of Nebraska with financial need and acceptable scholastic standing.
    Amount of award: $500
    Number of awards: 4
    Application deadline: March 1
Contact:
American Legion Nebraska, Department Headquarters
P.O. Box 5205
Lincoln, NE 68505-0205
Phone: 402-464-6338
Web: www.ne.legion.org

Maynard Jensen American Legion Memorial Scholarship

Type of award: Scholarship.
Intended use: For undergraduate study at 2-year or 4-year institution.
Eligibility: Applicant or parent must be member/participant of American Legion. Applicant must be residing in Nebraska. Applicant must be descendant of veteran; or dependent of veteran, deceased veteran or POW/MIA.
Basis for selection: Applicant must demonstrate financial need and high academic achievement.
    Amount of award: $500
    Number of awards: 10
    Application deadline: March 1
    Total amount awarded: $5,000
Contact:
American Legion Nebraska
Department Headquarters
P.O. Box 5205
Lincoln, NE 68505-0205
Phone: 402-464-6338
Web: www.ne.legion.org

American Legion Nebraska Auxiliary

American Legion Nebraska President's Scholarship

Type of award: Scholarship.

Intended use: For undergraduate study at postsecondary institution.
Eligibility: Applicant must be residing in Nebraska.
Additional information: Given to Nebraska's entry for National President's Scholarship in event applicant does not win same.
   Amount of award: $200
Contact:
American Legion Nebraska Auxiliary
Department Headquarters
P.O. Box 5227
Lincoln, NE 68505-0227
Phone: 402-464-1808
Web: www.ne.legion.org

Averyl Elaine Keriakedes Memorial Scholarship

Type of award: Scholarship.
Intended use: For undergraduate study. Designated institutions: University of Nebraska, Lincoln.
Eligibility: Applicant must be female. Applicant must be residing in Nebraska. Applicant must be descendant of veteran; or dependent of veteran; or spouse of veteran.
Basis for selection: Major/career interest in education or social/behavioral sciences.
Additional information: Applicant must plan to teach middle or junior high school social studies.
   Amount of award: $500
   Number of awards: 1
   Total amount awarded: $500
Contact:
American Legion Nebraska Auxiliary
Department Headquarters
P.O. Box 5227
Lincoln, NE 68505-0227
Web: www.ne.legion.org

Graduate Scholarship

Type of award: Scholarship.
Intended use: For graduate study.
Eligibility: Applicant must be residing in Nebraska. Applicant must be descendant of veteran; or dependent of veteran; or spouse of veteran.
Basis for selection: Major/career interest in education, special.
   Amount of award: $200
Contact:
American Legion Nebraska Auxiliary, Department Headquarters
P.O. Box 5227
Lincoln, NE 68505-0227
Web: www.ne.legion.org

Junior Member Scholarship

Type of award: Scholarship.
Intended use: For undergraduate study at postsecondary institution.
Eligibility: Applicant must be residing in Nebraska.
Additional information: Given to Nebraska's entry for Spirit of Youth Scholarship for Junior member, in event applicant does not win same.
   Amount of award: $200

Contact:
American Legion Nebraska Auxiliary
Department Education Chairman
P.O. Box 5227
Lincoln, NE 68505-0227
Phone: 402-466-1808
Web: www.ne.legion.org

Nurse Gift Tuition Scholarships

Type of award: Scholarship.
Intended use: For undergraduate study.
Eligibility: Applicant must be residing in Nebraska. Applicant must be descendant of veteran; or dependent of veteran; or spouse of veteran.
Basis for selection: Major/career interest in nursing. Applicant must demonstrate financial need.
Additional information: Awards given as funds permit.
   Amount of award: $200-$400
Contact:
American Legion Nebraska Auxiliary
Department Headquarters
P.O. Box 5227
Lincoln, NE 68505-0227
Phone: 402-466-1808
Web: www.ne.legion.org

Practical Nurse Scholarship

Type of award: Scholarship.
Intended use: For undergraduate study at 2-year or 4-year institution. Designated institutions: Schools of practical nursing.
Eligibility: Applicant must be residing in Nebraska. Applicant must be veteran or descendant of veteran; or dependent of veteran; or spouse of veteran.
Basis for selection: Major/career interest in nursing. Applicant must demonstrate financial need.
Additional information: Must be state resident for at least three years, be accepted at school of practical nursing, and be veteran-connected.
   Amount of award: $300
Contact:
American Legion Nebraska Auxiliary
Department Headquarters
P.O. Box 5227
Lincoln, NE 68505-0227
Phone: 402-466-1808
Web: www.ne.legion.org

Roberta Marie Stretch Memorial Scholarship

Type of award: Scholarship.
Intended use: For undergraduate or master's study at 4-year institution.
Eligibility: Applicant must be residing in Nebraska. Applicant must be descendant of veteran; or dependent of veteran; or spouse of veteran.
Additional information: Preference given to former Nebraska Girls State citizens.
   Amount of award: $400
Contact:
American Legion Nebraska Auxiliary
Department Headquarters
P.O. Box 5227
Lincoln, NE 68505-0227
Phone: 402-466-1808
Web: www.ne.legion.org

Ruby Paul Campaign Fund Scholarship

Type of award: Scholarship.
Intended use: For freshman study at accredited 2-year or 4-year institution.
Eligibility: Applicant or parent must be member/participant of American Legion Auxiliary. Applicant must be high school senior. Applicant must be residing in Nebraska. Must be Legion member, ALA member, Sons of the American Legion member of two years' standing, or child or grandchild of Legion or ALA member of two years' standing.
Basis for selection: Applicant must demonstrate high academic achievement.
Additional information: Award varies with availability of funds. Applicant must be state resident for three years. Must have maintained "B" or better during last two semesters of senior year in high school. Must be accepted for fall term at college or university. Cannot be nursing student.
   Amount of award: $100-$300
   Application deadline: April 1
Contact:
American Legion Nebraska Auxiliary
Department Headquarters
P.O. Box 5227
Lincoln, NE 68505
Phone: 402-466-1808
Web: www.ne.legion.org

Student Aid Grant or Vocational Technical Scholarship

Type of award: Scholarship.
Intended use: For undergraduate study at vocational or 2-year institution in United States.
Eligibility: Applicant must be residing in Nebraska. Applicant must be descendant of veteran; or dependent of veteran; or spouse of veteran.
   Amount of award: $200-$300
   Application deadline: April 1
Contact:
American Legion Nebraska Auxiliary
Department Headquarters
P.O. Box 5227
Lincoln, NE 68505-0227
Phone: 402-466-1808
Web: www.ne.legion.org

American Legion Nevada

American Legion Nevada Oratorical Contest

Type of award: Scholarship.
Intended use: For undergraduate study at postsecondary institution.
Eligibility: Applicant must be enrolled in high school. Applicant must be U.S. citizen or permanent resident residing in Nevada.
Basis for selection: Competition/talent/interest in oratory/debate, based on language style, voice, diction, delivery, originality, logic, breadth of knowledge, application of knowledge about topic, and skill in selecting examples and analogies.
Additional information: Awards: 1st-$500; 2nd-$300; 3rd-$200; all in promissory notes.
   Amount of award: $200-$500
   Number of awards: 3
   Application deadline: January 15
   Total amount awarded: $1,000
Contact:
American Legion Nevada Oratorical Contest
737 Veterans Memorial Drive
Las Vegas, NV 89101

American Legion Nevada Auxiliary

Past President's Parley Nurses' Scholarship

Type of award: Scholarship.
Intended use: For junior study at postsecondary institution.
Eligibility: Applicant must be residing in Nevada. Applicant must be veteran; or dependent of veteran.
Basis for selection: Major/career interest in nursing.
Additional information: $150 for each university. Applicant must have completed first two years of training.
   Amount of award: $150
Contact:
American Legion Nevada Auxiliary, Department Secretary
1549 Silver Point Avenue
Las Vegas, NV 89123

President's Scholarship and Junior Scholarship

Type of award: Scholarship.
Intended use: For undergraduate study at postsecondary institution.
Eligibility: Applicant must be residing in Nevada.
Additional information: President's Scholarship: $300 for winner of Department competition. Runner-ups: 1st-$200; 2nd-$100; 3rd-$100. Junior Scholarship: $100 for winner of National Competition.
   Amount of award: $100-$300
Contact:
American Legion Nevada Auxiliary, Department Secretary
1549 Silver Point Avenue
Las Vegas, NV 89123

Silver Eagle Indian Scholarship

Type of award: Scholarship.
Intended use: For undergraduate study at postsecondary institution.
Eligibility: Applicant must be American Indian. Applicant must be U.S. citizen residing in Nevada. Applicant must be child or grandchild of American Indian veteran.
   Amount of award: $200
Contact:
American Legion Nevada Auxiliary, Department Secretary
1549 Silver Point Avenue
Las Vegas, NV 89123

American Legion New Hampshire

Albert T. Marcoux Memorial Scholarship

Type of award: Scholarship.
Intended use: For undergraduate study at postsecondary institution.
Eligibility: Applicant or parent must be member/participant of American Legion. Applicant must be residing in New Hampshire.
Application requirements: Send SASE for application.
Additional information: Applicant must be child of living or deceased New Hampshire Legion or Auxiliary member; graduate of New Hampshire high school; and state resident for three years. Must be pursuing bachelor's degree.
    Amount of award: $2,000
    Number of awards: 1
    Application deadline: May 1
    Total amount awarded: $2,000
Contact:
American Legion New Hampshire
State House Annex
25 Capitol Street, Room 431
Concord, NH 03301-6312
Phone: 603-271-2211
Web: www.nhlegion.org

American Legion New Hampshire Boys State Scholarship

Type of award: Scholarship.
Intended use: For undergraduate study at postsecondary institution.
Eligibility: Applicant or parent must be member/participant of American Legion, Boys State. Applicant must be male. Applicant must be residing in New Hampshire.
Additional information: Award given to participants of Boys State during Boys State graduation. Award amount varies. Apply during Boys State session.
Contact:
American Legion New Hampshire
State House Annex
25 Capitol Street, Room 431
Concord, NH 03301-6312
Phone: 603-271-2211
Web: www.nhlegion.org

American Legion New Hampshire Oratorical Contest

Type of award: Scholarship.
Intended use: For undergraduate study at postsecondary institution.
Eligibility: Applicant must be enrolled in high school. Applicant must be residing in New Hampshire.
Basis for selection: Competition/talent/interest in oratory/debate, based on language style, voice, diction, delivery, originality, logic, breadth of knowledge, application of knowledge about topic, and skill in selecting examples and analogies.
Application requirements: Proof of eligibility.
Additional information: Awards: $1,000, $750, $500, $250, and four $100.
    Amount of award: $100-$1,000
    Number of awards: 8
    Total amount awarded: $2,900
Contact:
American Legion New Hampshire
State House Annex
25 Capitol Street, Room 431
Concord, NH 03301-6312
Phone: 603-271-2211
Web: www.nhlegion.org

Christa McAuliffe Memorial Scholarship

Type of award: Scholarship.
Intended use: For freshman study at postsecondary institution.
Eligibility: Applicant or parent must be member/participant of American Legion. Applicant must be residing in New Hampshire.
Basis for selection: Major/career interest in education.
Application requirements: Send SASE for application.
Additional information: Must be high school student or recent graduate of New Hampshire school entering first year of higher education; state resident for at least three years.
    Amount of award: $2,000
    Number of awards: 1
    Application deadline: May 1
    Total amount awarded: $2,000
Contact:
American Legion New Hampshire
State House Annex
25 Capitol Street, Room 431
Concord, NH 03301-6312
Phone: 603-271-2211
Web: www.nhlegion.org

Department of New Hampshire Scholarship

Type of award: Scholarship.
Intended use: For freshman study at postsecondary institution.
Eligibility: Applicant or parent must be member/participant of American Legion. Applicant must be enrolled in high school. Applicant must be residing in New Hampshire.
Application requirements: Send SASE for application.
Additional information: Must be high school student or graduate from New Hampshire school entering first year of higher education; state resident for at least three years.
    Amount of award: $2,000
    Number of awards: 2
    Application deadline: May 1
    Total amount awarded: $4,000
Contact:
American Legion New Hampshire
State House Annex
25 Capitol Street, Room 431
Concord, NH 03301-6312
Phone: 603-271-2211
Web: www.nhlegion.org

Department Vocational Scholarship

Type of award: Scholarship.
Intended use: For freshman study at vocational institution.

Eligibility: Applicant or parent must be member/participant of American Legion. Applicant must be enrolled in high school. Applicant must be residing in New Hampshire.
Application requirements: Send SASE for application.
Additional information: Must be high school student or graduate from New Hampshire school entering first year of higher education in specific vocation; state resident for at least three years.

Amount of award:	$2,000
Number of awards:	1
Total amount awarded:	$2,000

Contact:
American Legion New Hampshire
State House Annex
25 Capitol Street, Room 431
Concord, NH 03301-6312
Phone: 603-271-2211
Web: www.nhlegion.org

American Legion New Hampshire Auxiliary

Grace S. High Memorial Child Welfare Scholarship Fund

Type of award: Scholarship.
Intended use: For undergraduate study at postsecondary institution.
Eligibility: Applicant or parent must be member/participant of American Legion Auxiliary. Applicant must be female. Applicant must be residing in New Hampshire.
Basis for selection: Applicant must demonstrate financial need.
Application requirements: Send SASE for application.
Additional information: Applicant must be high school graduate and daughter of Legion or Auxiliary member.

Amount of award:	$300
Number of awards:	2
Application deadline:	April 15
Total amount awarded:	$600

Contact:
American Legion Auxiliary, Department of New Hampshire
Department Secretary
25 Capitol Street, Room 432
Concord, NH 03301-6312

Marion J. Bagley Scholarship

Type of award: Scholarship.
Intended use: For undergraduate study at postsecondary institution.
Eligibility: Applicant or parent must be member/participant of American Legion Auxiliary. Applicant must be residing in New Hampshire.
Application requirements: Send SASE for application.
Additional information: Applicant must be high school graduate (or equivalent) or attending school of higher learning.

Amount of award:	$1,000
Number of awards:	1
Application deadline:	May 1
Total amount awarded:	$1,000

Contact:
American Legion Auxiliary, Department of New Hampshire
Department Secretary
25 Capitol St., Room 432
Concord, NH 03301-6312

Past President's Parley Nurses' Scholarship

Type of award: Scholarship.
Intended use: For undergraduate study at postsecondary institution.
Eligibility: Applicant or parent must be member/participant of American Legion Auxiliary. Applicant must be residing in New Hampshire.
Basis for selection: Major/career interest in nursing. Applicant must demonstrate financial need.
Application requirements: Send SASE for application.
Additional information: Applicant must be high school graduate. Children of veteran given preference. One award to Registered Nurse study and one to Licensed Practical Nurse study.

Number of awards:	2
Application deadline:	May 10

Contact:
American Legion Auxiliary, Department of New Hampshire
Department Secretary
25 Capitol Street, Room 432
Concord, NH 03301-6312

American Legion New Jersey

American Legion New Jersey Oratorical Contest

Type of award: Scholarship.
Intended use: For undergraduate study at postsecondary institution.
Eligibility: Applicant must be enrolled in high school. Applicant must be residing in New Jersey.
Basis for selection: Competition/talent/interest in oratory/debate, based on language style, voice, diction, delivery, originality, logic, breadth of knowledge, application of knowledge about topic, and skill in selecting examples and analogies.
Application requirements: Proof of eligibility.
Additional information: Awards: 1st-$4,000; 2nd-$2,500; 3rd-$2,000; 4th-$1000; 5th-$1000. See high school counselor for application.

Amount of award:	$1,000-$4,000
Number of awards:	5
Total amount awarded:	$10,500

Contact:
American Legion New Jersey
135 West Hanover Street
Trenton, NJ 08618
Phone: 609-695-5418
Web: www.nj.legion.org

American Legion Press Club of New Jersey and Post 170--Arthur Dehardt Memorial Scholarship

Type of award: Scholarship.
Intended use: For freshman study at accredited 4-year institution.
Eligibility: Applicant or parent must be member/participant of American Legion. Applicant must be residing in New Jersey.
Basis for selection: Major/career interest in communications.
Application requirements: Send SASE to Education Chairman for application.
Additional information: Applicant must be child or grandchild of current member of Legion or Auxiliary, including Sons of American Legion and ALA Juniors. Graduates from either AL New Jersey Boys State or Auxiliary Girls State programs also eligible.
   Amount of award: $500
   Number of awards: 2
   Application deadline: July 15
   Total amount awarded: $1,000
Contact:
Jack W. Kuepfer, Education Chairman
American Legion Press Club of New Jersey
68 Merrill Road
Clifton, NJ 07012-1622
Phone: 973-473-5176
Web: www.nj.legion.org

David C. Goodwin Scholarship

Type of award: Scholarship.
Intended use: For undergraduate study at 4-year institution.
Eligibility: Applicant or parent must be member/participant of American Legion. Applicant must be high school junior. Applicant must be residing in New Jersey.
Additional information: Awards: $4,000 ($1,000/year for four years); $2,000 ($500/year for four years). Must be high school junior participating in New Jersey American Legion Baseball Program. Applications mailed to players.
   Amount of award: $2,000-$4,000
   Number of awards: 2
   Application deadline: October 15
   Total amount awarded: $6,000
Contact:
American Legion New Jersey
Baseball Committee
135 West Hanover St.
Trenton, NJ 08618
Phone: 609-695-5418
Web: www.nj.legion.org

Lawrence Luterman Memorial Scholarships

Type of award: Scholarship.
Intended use: For undergraduate study at 4-year institution.
Eligibility: Applicant or parent must be member/participant of American Legion. Applicant must be high school senior. Applicant must be residing in New Jersey.
Additional information: Awards: two-$4,000 ($1,000/year); three-$2,000; two-$1,000. Applicant must be natural or adopted descendant of member of American Legion, Department of New Jersey.
   Amount of award: $1,000-$4,000
   Number of awards: 7
   Application deadline: February 15
   Total amount awarded: $16,000
Contact:
American Legion New Jersey
Department Adjutant
135 West Hanover Street
Trenton, NJ 08618
Phone: 609-695-5418
Web: www.nj.legion.org

Stutz Memorial Scholarship

Type of award: Scholarship.
Intended use: For undergraduate study at 4-year institution.
Eligibility: Applicant or parent must be member/participant of American Legion. Applicant must be high school senior. Applicant must be residing in New Jersey.
Additional information: Applicant must be natural or adopted child of American Legion, Department of New Jersey member. Award is $4,000 ($1,000/year for four years).
   Amount of award: $4,000
   Number of awards: 1
   Total amount awarded: $4,000
Contact:
American Legion, Department of New Jersey
Department Adjutant
135 West Hanover Street
Trenton, NJ 08618
Phone: 609-695-5418
Web: www.nj.legion.org

American Legion New Jersey Auxiliary

American Legion New Jersey Auxiliary Department Scholarships

Type of award: Scholarship.
Intended use: For freshman study at 2-year or 4-year institution.
Eligibility: Applicant or parent must be member/participant of American Legion Auxiliary. Applicant must be high school senior. Applicant must be residing in New Jersey. Must be child or grandchild of honorably discharged veteran of U.S. Armed Forces.
Additional information: Several awards offered. Amount and number of awards vary. Rules and applications distributed to all New Jersey high school guidance departments.
   Application deadline: April 15
Contact:
American Legion Auxiliary, Department of New Jersey
Department Secretary
1540 Kuser Road, Suite A-8
Hamilton, NJ 08619
Phone: 609-581-9580
Fax: 609-581-8429

Claire Oliphant Memorial Scholarship

Type of award: Scholarship.

Intended use: For freshman study at 2-year or 4-year institution.
Eligibility: Applicant or parent must be member/participant of American Legion Auxiliary. Applicant must be high school senior. Applicant must be residing in New Jersey. Must be child of honorably discharged veteran of U.S. Armed Forces.
Additional information: Rules and applications distributed to all New Jersey high school guidance departments.

Amount of award:	$1,800
Number of awards:	1
Application deadline:	April 15
Total amount awarded:	$1,800

Contact:
American Legion Auxiliary, Department of New Jersey
Department Secretary
1540 Kuser Road, Suite A-8
Hamilton, NJ 08619
Phone: 609-581-9580
Fax: 609-581-8429

Past President's Parley Nurses' Scholarship

Type of award: Scholarship.
Intended use: For freshman study at 2-year or 4-year institution.
Eligibility: Applicant or parent must be member/participant of American Legion Auxiliary. Applicant must be high school senior. Applicant must be residing in New Jersey. Must be child or grandchild of honorably discharged veteran of U.S. Armed Forces.
Basis for selection: Major/career interest in nursing.
Additional information: Applicant must be enrolled in nursing program. Award amount varies. Rules and applications distributed to all New Jersey high school guidance departments.
   Application deadline: April 15

Contact:
American Legion Auxiliary, Department of New Jersey
Department Secretary
1540 Kuser Road, Suite A-8
Hamilton, NJ 08619
Phone: 609-581-9580
Fax: 609-581-8429

American Legion New Mexico Auxiliary

President's Parley Scholarship for Teachers of Exceptional Children

Type of award: Scholarship.
Intended use: For undergraduate or graduate study at postsecondary institution.
Eligibility: Applicant or parent must be member/participant of American Legion Auxiliary. Applicant must be residing in New Mexico.
Basis for selection: Major/career interest in education, special.
Additional information: Award for additional special education training to teach exceptional children in New Mexico for one year. Covers actual cost of tuition plus $50 travel; not to exceed $250.

Amount of award:	Full tuition
Number of awards:	1
Application deadline:	March 1

Contact:
American Legion Auxiliary, Department of New Mexico
Department Secretary
1215 Mountain Road, NE
Albuquerque, NM 87102
Phone: 505-242-9918

American Legion New York

American Legion New York Oratorical Contest

Type of award: Scholarship.
Intended use: For undergraduate study at postsecondary institution.
Eligibility: Applicant or parent must be member/participant of American Legion. Applicant must be no older than 20, enrolled in high school. Applicant must be residing in New York.
Basis for selection: Competition/talent/interest in oratory/debate, based on language style, voice, diction, delivery, originality, logic, breadth of knowledge, application of knowledge about topic, and skill in selecting examples and analogies.
Application requirements: Proof of eligibility.
Additional information: Awards: 1st-$6,000; 2nd-$4,000; 3rd-$2,500; 4th-$2,000; 5th-$2,000. Scholarship payments are made directly to student's college and are awarded over a four-year period.

Amount of award:	$2,000-$6,000
Number of awards:	5
Total amount awarded:	$16,500

Contact:
American Legion, Department of New York
Department Adjutant
112 State Street, Suite 1300
Albany, NY 12207
Phone: 518-463-2215
Web: www.ny.legion.org

Dr. Hannah K. Vuolo Memorial Scholarship

Type of award: Scholarship.
Intended use: For freshman study at accredited 2-year or 4-year institution.
Eligibility: Applicant or parent must be member/participant of American Legion. Applicant must be no older than 20, high school senior. Applicant must be descendant of veteran.
Basis for selection: Major/career interest in education, teacher.
Additional information: Applicant must be natural or adopted direct descendant of member or deceased member of American Legion, Department of New York.

Amount of award:	$250
Number of awards:	1
Application deadline:	May 1
Total amount awarded:	$250

Contact:
American Legion, Department of New York
Department Adjutant
112 State Street, Suite 1300
Albany, NY 12207
Phone: 518-463-2215
Web: www.ny.legion.org

New York American Legion Press Association Scholarship

Type of award: Scholarship.
Intended use: For full-time undergraduate study at accredited 4-year institution.
Eligibility: Applicant or parent must be member/participant of American Legion. Applicant must be residing in New York.
Basis for selection: Major/career interest in communications; journalism or graphic arts/design.
Additional information: Applicant must be child of New York Legion or Auxiliary member; Sons of American Legion or ALA Junior member; or graduate of New York American Legion Boys State or Girls State.
    Amount of award: $1,000
    Number of awards: 1
    Application deadline: April 15
Contact:
New York American Legion Press Association
Scholarship Chairman
P.O. Box 650
East Aurora, NY 14052
Web: www.ny.legion.org

American Legion New York Auxiliary

American Legion New York Auxiliary Scholarship

Type of award: Scholarship.
Intended use: For undergraduate study at postsecondary institution.
Eligibility: Applicant or parent must be member/participant of American Legion Auxiliary. Applicant must be residing in New York. Applicant must be descendant of veteran; or dependent of veteran or deceased veteran.
Additional information: Must be high school graduate. May use other scholarships. Obtain application from local American Legion Auxiliary Unit.
    Amount of award: $1,000
    Number of awards: 1
    Application deadline: March 1
    Total amount awarded: $1,000
Contact:
American Legion New York Auxiliary
112 State Street, Suite 409
Albany, NY 12207-0003
Web: www.deptny.org

Past President's Parley Student Nurses Scholarship for Girls or Boys

Type of award: Scholarship.
Intended use: For undergraduate study at 2-year or 4-year institution.
Eligibility: Applicant or parent must be member/participant of American Legion Auxiliary. Applicant must be no older than 19, high school senior. Applicant must be residing in New York. Applicant must be descendant of veteran; or dependent of veteran during Korean War, WW I, WW II or Vietnam.
Basis for selection: Major/career interest in nursing. Applicant must demonstrate financial need.
Additional information: Obtain application from local American Legion Auxiliary Unit.
    Amount of award: $1,000
    Number of awards: 1
    Application deadline: March 1
    Total amount awarded: $1,000
Contact:
American Legion New York Auxiliary
112 State Street, Suite 409
Albany, NY 12207-0003
Web: www.deptny.org

American Legion North Dakota

American Legion North Dakota Oratorical Contest

Type of award: Scholarship.
Intended use: For undergraduate study at postsecondary institution.
Eligibility: Applicant or parent must be member/participant of American Legion. Applicant must be high school freshman, sophomore, junior or senior. Applicant must be residing in North Dakota.
Basis for selection: Competition/talent/interest in oratory/debate, based on language style, voice, diction, delivery, originality, logic, breadth of knowledge, application of knowledge about topic, and skill in selecting examples and analogies.
Application requirements: Proof of eligibility. For application, contact local American Legion Post or Department Headquarters after start of school year.
Additional information: Awards: 1st-$400, 2nd-$300, 3rd-$200, 4th-$100; East and West Divisional Contests: 1st-$300, 2nd-$200 each; and 10 District Contests: 1st-$300, 2nd-$200, 3rd-$100. Local contests begin in the fall.
    Amount of award: $100-$400
Contact:
American Legion North Dakota
Department Headquarters
Box 2666
Fargo, ND 58108-2666
Phone: 701-293-3120
Fax: 701-293-9951
Web: www.ndlegion.org

American Legion North Dakota Auxiliary

American Legion North Dakota Auxiliary Scholarships

Type of award: Scholarship.
Intended use: For undergraduate study at postsecondary institution.
Eligibility: Applicant or parent must be member/participant of American Legion Auxiliary. Applicant must be residing in North Dakota.
Basis for selection: Applicant must demonstrate financial need.
Additional information: Obtain application from local American Legion Auxiliary Unit.
    Amount of award: $500
    Number of awards: 4
    Application deadline: January 15
Contact:
American Legion North Dakota Auxiliary
Department Education Chairman
P.O. Box 250
Beach, ND 58621
Phone: 701-253-5992

Past President's Parley Scholarship

Type of award: Scholarship.
Intended use: For undergraduate study at 2-year or 4-year institution. Designated institutions: North Dakota hospital and nursing schools.
Eligibility: Applicant or parent must be member/participant of American Legion Auxiliary. Applicant must be residing in North Dakota.
Basis for selection: Major/career interest in nursing.
Additional information: Children, grandchildren or great-grandchildren of American Legion or Auxiliary member in good standing. Must be graduate of North Dakota high school. Apply to local American Legion Auxiliary Unit.
    Amount of award: $350
    Application deadline: May 15
Contact:
American Legion Auxiliary, Department of North Dakota
Chair of Dept. Parley Scholarship Committee
P.O. Box 250
Beach, ND 58621
Phone: 701-872-3865

American Legion Ohio

American Legion Ohio Scholarships

Type of award: Scholarship.
Intended use: For undergraduate study at postsecondary institution.
Eligibility: Applicant or parent must be member/participant of American Legion. For Legion members; direct descendants of Legionnaires in good standing; direct descendants of deceased Legionnaires; spouses or children of deceased U.S. military persons who died on active duty or of injuries received on active duty.

Additional information: Number and amount of awards vary. Contact sponsor or visit Website for more information.
    Amount of award: $2,000
    Application deadline: April 15
Contact:
American Legion, Department of Ohio
Department Scholarship Committee
P.O. Box 8007
Delaware, OH 43015-8007
Web: www.ohiolegion.com

Department Oratorical Awards

Type of award: Scholarship.
Intended use: For undergraduate study at postsecondary institution.
Eligibility: Applicant or parent must be member/participant of American Legion. Applicant must be enrolled in high school. Applicant must be residing in Ohio.
Basis for selection: Competition/talent/interest in oratory/debate, based on language style, voice, diction, delivery, originality, logic, breadth of knowledge, application of knowledge about topic, and skill in selecting examples and analogies.
Additional information: Awards: 1st-$1,000; 2nd-$500; 3rd-$300; 4th-$200.
    Amount of award: $200-$1,000
    Number of awards: 4
    Total amount awarded: $2,000
Contact:
American Legion Ohio
Department Scholarship Committee
P.O. Box 8007
Delaware, OH 43015-8007
Phone: 740-362-7478
Fax: 740-362-1429
Web: www.ohiolegion.com

American Legion Ohio Auxiliary

American Legion Ohio Auxiliary Past President's Parley Nurse's Scholarship

Type of award: Scholarship.
Intended use: For undergraduate study at 2-year or 4-year institution.
Eligibility: Applicant or parent must be member/participant of American Legion Auxiliary. Applicant must be residing in Ohio. Applicant must be descendant of veteran; or dependent of veteran; or spouse of veteran.
Basis for selection: Major/career interest in nursing.
Additional information: Awards: 15-$300 and 2-$750 scholarships.
    Amount of award: $300-$750
    Number of awards: 17
    Application deadline: May 1
    Total amount awarded: $6,000

Contact:
American Legion Auxiliary
Department Secretary
P.O. Box 2760
Zanesville, OH 43702-2760
Phone: 740-452-8245
Fax: 740-452-2620

American Legion Ohio Auxiliary Scholarship

Type of award: Scholarship.
Intended use: For freshman study at postsecondary institution.
Eligibility: Applicant or parent must be member/participant of American Legion Auxiliary. Applicant must be high school senior. Applicant must be residing in Ohio. Applicant must be descendant of veteran; or dependent of veteran or deceased veteran during Grenada conflict, Korean War, Lebanon conflict, Persian Gulf War, WW I, WW II or Vietnam.
Additional information: Awards: one $1,500 and one $1,000.
    Amount of award: $1,000-$1,500
    Number of awards: 2
    Application deadline: March 1
    Total amount awarded: $2,500
Contact:
American Legion Ohio Auxiliary
Department Secretary
P.O. Box 2760
Zanesville, OH 43702-2760
Phone: 740-452-8245
Fax: 740-452-2620

American Legion Oregon

American Legion Department Oratorical Contest

Type of award: Scholarship.
Intended use: For undergraduate study at postsecondary institution.
Eligibility: Applicant must be enrolled in high school. Applicant must be U.S. citizen or permanent resident residing in Oregon.
Basis for selection: Competition/talent/interest in oratory/debate, based on language style, voice, diction, delivery, originality, logic, breadth of knowledge, application of knowledge about topic, and skill in selecting examples and analogies.
Application requirements: Proof of eligibility.
Additional information: Awards: 1st-$500; 2nd-$400; 3rd-$300; 4th-$200. Applications available at local high schools.
    Amount of award: $200-$500
    Number of awards: 4
    Application deadline: December 1
    Total amount awarded: $1,400
Contact:
American Legion Oregon
P.O. Box 1730
Wilsonville, OR 97070-1730
Phone: 503-685-5006
Fax: 503-685-5008

American Legion Oregon Auxiliary

American Legion Oregon Auxiliary Department Nurses Scholarship

Type of award: Scholarship.
Intended use: For undergraduate study at accredited 2-year or 4-year institution.
Eligibility: Applicant must be residing in Oregon. Applicant must be dependent of disabled veteran or deceased veteran; or spouse of disabled veteran or deceased veteran.
Basis for selection: Major/career interest in nursing. Applicant must demonstrate financial need, high academic achievement, depth of character, seriousness of purpose and service orientation.
Application requirements: Proof of eligibility.
    Amount of award: $1,500
    Number of awards: 1
    Application deadline: June 1
    Total amount awarded: $1,500
Contact:
American Legion Auxiliary, Department of Oregon
Chairman of Education
P.O. Box 1730
Wilsonville, OR 97070-1730

National President's Scholarship

Type of award: Scholarship.
Intended use: For undergraduate study at postsecondary institution.
Eligibility: Applicant or parent must be member/participant of American Legion Auxiliary. Applicant must be residing in Oregon. Applicant must be dependent of veteran during Grenada conflict, Korean War, Lebanon conflict, Panama conflict, Persian Gulf War, WW I, WW II or Vietnam.
Additional information: Three awards in each division of American Legion Auxiliary: 1st-$2,500, 2nd-$2,000, and 3rd-$1,000.
    Amount of award: $1,000-$2,500
    Number of awards: 10
    Application deadline: March 10
Contact:
American Legion Auxiliary, Department of Oregon
Chairman of Education
P.O. Box 1730
Wilsonville, OR 97070-1730

Spirit of Youth Scholarship

Type of award: Scholarship.
Intended use: For undergraduate study at accredited postsecondary institution.
Eligibility: Applicant or parent must be member/participant of American Legion Auxiliary. Applicant must be residing in Oregon. Applicant must be dependent of deceased veteran; or spouse of disabled veteran or deceased veteran.
    Amount of award: $1,000
    Application deadline: March 15
Contact:
American Legion Auxiliary, Department of Oregon
Chairman of Education
P.O. Box 1730
Wilsonville, OR 97070-1730

American Legion Pennsylvania

Joseph P. Gavenonis Scholarship

Type of award: Scholarship, renewable.
Intended use: For full-time undergraduate study at 4-year institution.
Eligibility: Applicant or parent must be member/participant of American Legion. Applicant must be high school senior. Applicant must be residing in Pennsylvania. Applicant must be child of living member in good standing of Pennsylvania American Legion, or child of deceased Pennsylvania American Legion member.
Application requirements: Proof of eligibility.
Additional information: Award is $1000 per year for four years; renewal based on grades.
    Amount of award: $1,000
    Number of awards: 1
    Application deadline: June 1
    Total amount awarded: $4,000
Contact:
American Legion Pennsylvania
Dept. Adjutant, Attn: Scholarship Secretary
P.O. Box 2324
Harrisburg, PA 17105-2324
Phone: 717-730-9100
Web: www.pa-legion.com

Robert W. Valimont Endowment Fund Scholarship

Type of award: Scholarship, renewable.
Intended use: For full-time undergraduate study at vocational or 2-year institution.
Eligibility: Applicant must be residing in Pennsylvania. Preference given in the following order: children of Legionnaires; children of veterans; children of disabled veterans; children of deceased veterans.
Application requirements: Proof of eligibility. Proof of Membership in Pennsylvania American Legion Post, if claimed.
Additional information: Award is $600 for first year; must reapply for second year.
    Amount of award: $600
    Total amount awarded: $600
Contact:
American Legion Pennsylvania
Dept. Adjutant, Attn: Scholarship Secretary
P.O. Box 2324
Harrisburg, PA 17105-2324
Phone: 717-730-9100
Web: www.pa-legion.com

American Legion Pennsylvania Auxiliary

Scholarship for Children of Deceased or Totally Disabled Veterans

Type of award: Scholarship.
Intended use: For undergraduate study at postsecondary institution.
Eligibility: Applicant must be high school senior. Applicant must be residing in Pennsylvania. Applicant must be dependent of disabled veteran or deceased veteran.
Basis for selection: Applicant must demonstrate financial need.
Additional information: Award is $600 per year for four years.
    Amount of award: $2,400
    Number of awards: 1
    Application deadline: March 15
    Total amount awarded: $2,400
Contact:
American Legion Auxiliary, Department of Pennsylvania
Department Education Chairman
P.O. Box 1285
Harrisburg, PA 17105
Phone: 717-763-7545
Fax: 717-763-0617

Scholarship for Children of Living Veterans

Type of award: Scholarship.
Intended use: For undergraduate study at postsecondary institution.
Eligibility: Applicant must be high school senior. Applicant must be residing in Pennsylvania. Applicant must be dependent of veteran.
Basis for selection: Applicant must demonstrate financial need.
Additional information: Award: $600 per year for four years.
    Amount of award: $2,400
    Number of awards: 1
    Application deadline: March 15
    Total amount awarded: $2,400
Contact:
American Legion Auxiliary, Department of Pennsylvania
Department Education Chairman
P.O. Box 1285
Harrisburg, PA 17105
Phone: 717-763-7545

American Legion Puerto Rico Auxiliary

American Legion Puerto Rico Auxiliary Nursing Scholarships

Type of award: Scholarship.

Intended use: For undergraduate study at 2-year or 4-year institution. Designated institutions: Eligible institutions in Puerto Rico.
Eligibility: Applicant must be residing in Puerto Rico.
Basis for selection: Major/career interest in nursing.
Application requirements: Interview.
Additional information: Two $250 awards for two consecutive years.
   Amount of award: $250
   Number of awards: 2
   Application deadline: March 15
Contact:
American Legion Auxiliary, Department of Puerto Rico
Education Chairman
P.O. Box 11424
Caparra Heights Station, PR 00922-1424

American Legion South Carolina

American Legion South Carolina Department Oratorical Contest

Type of award: Scholarship.
Intended use: For undergraduate study at postsecondary institution.
Eligibility: Applicant must be enrolled in high school. Applicant must be residing in South Carolina.
Basis for selection: Competition/talent/interest in oratory/debate.
Additional information: Awards: 1st-$1,600; 2nd-$1,000; 3rd and 4th-$500. Distributed over four-year period. Zone Contest winners: 4-$100.
   Amount of award: $100-$1,600
   Number of awards: 8
   Application deadline: January 15
   Total amount awarded: $4,000
Contact:
American Legion South Carolina, Department Adjutant
P.O. Box 11355
132 Pickens St.
Columbia, SC 29211
Phone: 803-799-1992
Fax: 803-771-9831
Web: www.scarolinalegion.org

American Legion South Carolina Auxiliary

American Legion South Carolina Auxiliary Scholarship

Type of award: Scholarship.
Intended use: For undergraduate study at postsecondary institution.
Eligibility: Applicant or parent must be member/participant of American Legion Auxiliary. Applicant must be high school senior. Applicant must be residing in South Carolina. Must be American Legion Auxiliary junior or senior member with at least three consecutive years' membership at time of application. Must have current membership card.
   Amount of award: $500
   Number of awards: 2
   Application deadline: April 15
   Total amount awarded: $1,000
Contact:
American Legion Auxiliary, Department of South Carolina
Department Secretary
132 Pickens Street
Columbia, SC 29205
Phone: 803-799-6695
Fax: 803-799-7907

American Legion South Dakota

American Legion South Dakota Oratorical Contest

Type of award: Scholarship.
Intended use: For undergraduate study at postsecondary institution.
Eligibility: Applicant must be enrolled in high school. Applicant must be residing in South Dakota.
Basis for selection: Competition/talent/interest in oratory/debate, based on language style, voice, diction, delivery, originality, logic, breadth of knowledge, application of knowledge about topic, and skill in selecting examples and analogies.
Application requirements: Proof of eligibility.
Additional information: Awards: 1st-$1,000; 2nd-$500; 3rd-$250; 4th and 5th-$100. Redeemable within five years of date of award.
   Amount of award: $100-$1,000
   Number of awards: 5
   Total amount awarded: $1,950
Contact:
American Legion, Department of South Dakota
Department Adjutant
P.O. Box 67
Watertown, SD 57201-0067
Phone: 605-886-3604

American Legion South Dakota Auxiliary

American Legion South Dakota Auxiliary Nurse's Scholarship

Type of award: Scholarship.
Intended use: For undergraduate study at postsecondary institution.
Eligibility: Applicant or parent must be member/participant of American Legion Auxiliary. Applicant must be at least 16, no older than 22. Applicant must be residing in South Dakota. Applicant must be dependent of veteran.
Basis for selection: Major/career interest in nursing.

Amount of award: $500
Number of awards: 2
Application deadline: March 1
Total amount awarded: $1,000

Contact:
American Legion South Dakota Auxiliary
Patricia Coyle, Department Secretary
P.O. Box 117
Huron, SD 57350-0117
Phone: 605-353-1793

American Legion South Dakota Auxiliary Scholarships

Type of award: Scholarship.
Intended use: For undergraduate study at vocational, 2-year or 4-year institution.
Eligibility: Applicant or parent must be member/participant of American Legion Auxiliary. Applicant must be at least 16, no older than 22. Applicant must be residing in South Dakota. Applicant must be dependent of veteran.
Additional information: College scholarships: two-$500; vocational scholarships: two-$500.

Amount of award: $500
Number of awards: 4
Application deadline: March 1
Total amount awarded: $2,000

Contact:
American Legion South Dakota Auxiliary
Patricia Coyle, Department Secretary
P.O. Box 117
Huron, SD 57350-0117
Phone: 605-353-1793

Scholarship for College or Vocational

Type of award: Scholarship.
Intended use: For undergraduate study at postsecondary institution.
Eligibility: Applicant or parent must be member/participant of American Legion Auxiliary. Applicant must be residing in South Dakota. Applicant must have been senior South Dakota American Legion Auxiliary member for three consecutive years including current year.

Amount of award: $400
Number of awards: 1
Application deadline: March 1
Total amount awarded: $400

Contact:
American Legion South Dakota Auxiliary
Patricia Coyle, Department Secretary
P.O. Box 117
Huron, SD 57350-0117
Phone: 605-353-1793

Thelma Foster Junior American Legion Auxiliary Members Scholarship

Type of award: Scholarship.
Intended use: For undergraduate study at postsecondary institution.
Eligibility: Applicant or parent must be member/participant of American Legion Auxiliary. Applicant must be high school senior. Applicant must be residing in South Dakota. Must be Junior American Legion member for at least three years, including current year.

Amount of award: $300
Number of awards: 1
Application deadline: March 1

Contact:
American Legion South Dakota Auxiliary
Patricia Coyle, Dept. Secretary
P.O. Box 117
Huron, SD 57350-0117
Phone: 605-353-1793

Thelma Foster Senior American Legion Auxiliary Member Scholarship

Type of award: Scholarship.
Intended use: For undergraduate study at postsecondary institution.
Eligibility: Applicant or parent must be member/participant of American Legion Auxiliary. Applicant must be residing in South Dakota. Must be senior South Dakota American Legion Auxiliary member for past three years, including current year.

Amount of award: $300
Number of awards: 1
Application deadline: March 1
Total amount awarded: $300

Contact:
American Legion South Dakota Auxiliary
Patricia Coyle, Department Secretary
P.O. Box 117
Huron, SD 57350-0117
Phone: 605-353-1793

American Legion Tennessee

American Legion Tennessee Oratorical Contest

Type of award: Scholarship, renewable.
Intended use: For undergraduate study at postsecondary institution in United States.
Eligibility: Applicant must be enrolled in high school. Applicant must be residing in Tennessee.
Basis for selection: Competition/talent/interest in oratory/debate, based on language style, voice, diction, delivery, originality, logic, breadth of knowledge, application of knowledge about topic, and skill in selecting examples and analogies.
Application requirements: Proof of eligibility.
Additional information: Awards: 1st-$3,000, 2nd-$2,000, 3rd-$1,000. First place winner eligible to enter National Contest. National winner receives $18,000 scholarship. Enter contest through local high school participating in Tennessee Oratorical Contest.

Amount of award: $1,000-$3,000
Number of awards: 3
Application deadline: January 1
Total amount awarded: $6,000

Contact:
American Legion Tennessee
215 8th Avenue North
Nashville, TN 37203-3583
Phone: 615-254-0568
Web: www.tennesseelegion.org

Eagle Scout of the Year Scholarship

Type of award: Scholarship.
Intended use: For undergraduate study at postsecondary institution in United States.
Eligibility: Applicant or parent must be member/participant of Boy Scouts of America, Eagle Scouts. Applicant must be male. Applicant must be residing in Tennessee.
Application requirements: Nomination by Tennessee American Legion.
    Amount of award: $1,500
    Number of awards: 1
    Application deadline: January 1
    Total amount awarded: $1,500
Contact:
American Legion Tennessee
215 8th Avenue North
Nashville, TN 37203-3583
Phone: 615-254-0568
Web: www.tennesseelegion.org

American Legion Tennessee Auxiliary

Vara Gray Scholarship Fund

Type of award: Scholarship.
Intended use: For undergraduate study at vocational, 2-year or 4-year institution.
Eligibility: Applicant must be high school senior. Applicant must be residing in Tennessee. Applicant must be dependent of veteran.
Application requirements: Recommendations, essay, nomination by local American Legion Auxiliary Unit. SAT/ACT report; proof of 50 hours of volunteer service.
    Amount of award: $500
    Number of awards: 3
    Application deadline: March 1
    Total amount awarded: $1,500
Contact:
American Legion Tennessee Auxiliary
Department Headquarters
104 Point East Drive
Nashville, TN 37216
Phone: 615-226-8648
Fax: 615-226-8649

American Legion Texas

Texas Legion Oratorical Contest

Type of award: Scholarship.
Intended use: For undergraduate study at postsecondary institution.
Eligibility: Applicant must be no older than 18, enrolled in high school. Applicant must be residing in Texas.
Basis for selection: Competition/talent/interest in oratory/debate, based on language style, voice, diction, delivery, originality, logic, breadth of knowledge, application of knowledge about topic, and skill in selecting examples and analogies. Applicant must demonstrate patriotism.
Application requirements: Proof of eligibility.
Additional information: Awards: 1st-$2,000, 2nd-$1,500, 3rd-$1,000, 4th-$500. First place winner eligible to enter national contest.
    Amount of award: $500-$2,000
    Number of awards: 4
    Application deadline: August 31
    Total amount awarded: $5,000
Contact:
American Legion, Department of Texas
Oratorical Contest
3401 Ed Bluestein Blvd, Suite 200
Austin, TX 78721-2902
Phone: 512-472-4138
Fax: 512-472-0603
Web: www.txlegion.org

American Legion Texas Auxiliary

American Legion Texas Auxiliary General Education Scholarship

Type of award: Scholarship.
Intended use: For undergraduate study at postsecondary institution.
Eligibility: Applicant must be residing in Texas. Applicant must be descendant of veteran; or dependent of veteran.
Application requirements: Nomination.
Additional information: Obtain application from local Unit. Unit sponsorship required.
    Amount of award: $500
    Application deadline: February 1
Contact:
American Legion Auxiliary
Department Headquarters
3401 Ed Bluestein Blvd, Suite 200
Austin, TX 78721-2902
Phone: 512-476-7278
Web: www.alatexas.org

American Legion Texas Auxiliary Medical Scholarship

Type of award: Scholarship.
Intended use: For undergraduate study at postsecondary institution.
Eligibility: Applicant must be residing in Texas. Applicant must be descendant of veteran; or dependent of veteran.
Basis for selection: Major/career interest in nursing; health sciences; health-related professions or medical assistant.
Application requirements: Nomination.
Additional information: Obtain application from local Unit. Unit sponsorship required.
    Amount of award: $500
    Application deadline: February 1

Contact:
American Legion Auxiliary
Department Headquarters
3401 Ed Bluestein Blvd, Suite 200
Austin, TX 78721-2902
Phone: 512-476-7278
Web: www.alatexas.org

American Legion Utah Auxiliary

American Legion Utah Auxiliary National President's Scholarship

Type of award: Scholarship.
Intended use: For undergraduate study at postsecondary institution.
Eligibility: Applicant must be high school senior. Applicant must be residing in Utah. Applicant must be dependent of veteran during Grenada conflict, Korean War, Lebanon conflict, Panama conflict, Persian Gulf War, WW I, WW II or Vietnam.
Additional information: Awards: one-$1,500.
- **Amount of award:** $1,500
- **Number of awards:** 1
- **Application deadline:** February 15
- **Total amount awarded:** $1,500

Contact:
American Legion Utah Auxiliary
Chesney Galindo
455 E 400 St., #50
Salt Lake City, UT 84119
Phone: 801-539-1015
Fax: 801-521-9191
Web: www.legion-aux.org

American Legion Vermont

American Legion Eagle Scout of the Year

Type of award: Scholarship.
Intended use: For undergraduate study.
Eligibility: Applicant or parent must be member/participant of Boy Scouts of America, Eagle Scouts. Applicant must be male, high school senior. Applicant must be residing in Vermont.
Additional information: Awarded to Boy Scout chosen for outstanding service to his religious institution, school and community. Applicant must have received Eagle Scout Award.
- **Amount of award:** $1,000
- **Number of awards:** 1
- **Application deadline:** March 1
- **Total amount awarded:** $1,000

Contact:
American Legion of Vermont
Education and Scholarship Committee
P.O. Box 192
Montpelier, VT 05601-0396
Phone: 802-223-7131
Fax: 802-223-7131
Web: www.legionvthq.com

American Legion Vermont Scholarship

Type of award: Scholarship.
Intended use: For undergraduate study at postsecondary institution.
Eligibility: Applicant must be high school senior. Applicant must be residing in Vermont.
Additional information: Awards: 1-$1,500; 1-$1,000; 10-$500. Applicant must be senior at Vermont secondary school; senior from adjacent state whose parents are legal Vermont residents; or senior from adjacent state attending Vermont school.
- **Amount of award:** $500-$1,500
- **Number of awards:** 12
- **Application deadline:** April 1
- **Total amount awarded:** $7,500

Contact:
American Legion of Vermont
Education and Scholarship Committee
P.O. Box 192
Montpelier, VT 05601-0396
Phone: 802-223-7131
Fax: 802-223-7131
Web: www.legionvthq.com

American Legion Vermont Scholarship Program

Type of award: Scholarship.
Intended use: For undergraduate study at postsecondary institution.
Eligibility: Applicant must be high school senior. Applicant must be residing in Vermont.
Basis for selection: Applicant must demonstrate financial need.
Additional information: Amount and number of awards vary. Contact local American Legion Post or American Legion Auxiliary Unit for application.

Contact:
American Legion of Vermont
Education and Scholarship Committee
P.O. Box 192
Montpelier, VT 05601-0396
Phone: 802-223-7131
Web: www.legionvthq.com

National High School Oratorical Contest

Type of award: Scholarship.
Intended use: For undergraduate study.
Eligibility: Applicant must be enrolled in high school. Applicant must be U.S. citizen or permanent resident residing in Vermont.
Basis for selection: Competition/talent/interest in oratory/debate, based on language style, voice, diction, delivery, originality, logic, breadth of knowledge, application of knowledge about topic, and skill in selecting examples and analogies.
Additional information: No applications required. Selection based on prepared oration. Request rules by January 1.
- **Amount of award:** $2,000
- **Number of awards:** 1
- **Total amount awarded:** $2,000

American Legion Vermont: National High School Oratorical Contest

Contact:
American Legion of Vermont
Education and Scholarship Committee
P.O. Box 192
Montpelier, VT 05601-0396
Phone: 802-223-7131
Web: www.legionvthq.com

American Legion Virginia

American Legion Virginia Oratorical Contest

Type of award: Scholarship.
Intended use: For undergraduate study at postsecondary institution.
Eligibility: Applicant must be enrolled in high school. Applicant must be residing in Virginia.
Basis for selection: Competition/talent/interest in oratory/debate, based on language style, voice, diction, delivery, originality, logic, breadth of knowledge, application of knowledge about topic, and skill in selecting examples and analogies.
Application requirements: Proof of eligibility.
Additional information: Awards: 1st-$1,100; 2nd-$600; 3rd-$600.

Amount of award:	$600-$1,100
Number of awards:	3
Application deadline:	December 1
Total amount awarded:	$2,300

Contact:
American Legion Virginia
Department Adjutant
1708 Commonwealth Ave.
Richmond, VA 23230
Phone: 804-353-6606
Fax: 804-358-1940
Web: www.valegion.org

American Legion Virginia Auxiliary

Anna Gear Junior Scholarship

Type of award: Scholarship.
Intended use: For undergraduate study at postsecondary institution.
Eligibility: Applicant or parent must be member/participant of American Legion Auxiliary. Applicant must be high school senior. Applicant must be residing in Virginia. Must be junior member of American Legion Auxiliary for three years.

Amount of award:	$1,000
Number of awards:	1
Application deadline:	April 1
Total amount awarded:	$1,000

Contact:
American Legion Auxiliary, Department of Virginia
Education Chairman
1708 Commonwealth Avenue
Richmond, VA 23230
Phone: 804-355-6410
Web: www.valegion.org

Dr. Kate Waller Barrett Grant

Type of award: Scholarship.
Intended use: For undergraduate study at accredited vocational, 2-year or 4-year institution.
Eligibility: Applicant or parent must be member/participant of American Legion Auxiliary. Applicant must be high school senior. Applicant must be residing in Virginia. Applicant must be dependent of veteran.
Basis for selection: Applicant must demonstrate financial need.

Amount of award:	$1,000
Number of awards:	1
Application deadline:	March 15
Total amount awarded:	$1,000

Contact:
American Legion Auxiliary, Department of Virginia
Education Chairman
1708 Commonwealth Avenue
Richmond, VA 23230
Phone: 804-355-6410
Web: www.valegion.org

American Legion Washington

American Legion Department Oratorical Contest

Type of award: Scholarship.
Intended use: For undergraduate study at postsecondary institution.
Eligibility: Applicant must be enrolled in high school. Applicant must be residing in Washington.
Basis for selection: Competition/talent/interest in oratory/debate, based on language style, voice, diction, delivery, originality, logic, breadth of knowledge, application of knowledge about topic, and skill in selecting examples and analogies.
Additional information: Student participates in Post, District, Area, and Department contests.

Application deadline:	April 1
Total amount awarded:	$7,800

Contact:
American Legion Washington
Chairman, Department of Child Welfare
P.O. Box 3917
Lacey, WA 98509-3917
Phone: 360-491-4373
Fax: 360-491-7442
Web: www.walegion.org

American Legion Washington Scholarships

Type of award: Scholarship.
Intended use: For undergraduate study at accredited vocational, 2-year or 4-year institution. Designated institutions: Eligible institutions in Washington State.
Eligibility: Applicant or parent must be member/participant of American Legion. Applicant must be residing in Washington. Must be child of living or deceased Washington Legionnaire or Auxiliary member.
Basis for selection: Applicant must demonstrate financial need.
Additional information: Awards: 1-$2,500 and 1-$1,500.
   Amount of award: $1,500-$2,500
   Number of awards: 2
   Application deadline: April 1
   Total amount awarded: $4,000
Contact:
American Legion Washington
Chairman, Department of Child Welfare
P.O. Box 3917
Lacey, WA 98509-3917
Phone: 360-491-4373
Fax: 360-491-7442
Web: www.walegion.org

American Legion Washington Auxiliary

American Legion Washington Auxiliary Scholarships

Type of award: Scholarship.
Intended use: For undergraduate study at postsecondary institution.
Eligibility: Applicant must be residing in Washington. Applicant must be dependent of disabled veteran or deceased veteran.
   Amount of award: $400
   Number of awards: 2
   Application deadline: March 15
   Total amount awarded: $800
Contact:
American Legion Washington Auxiliary
P.O. Box 5867
Lacey, WA 98509-5867

Florence Lemcke Memorial Scholarship

Type of award: Scholarship.
Intended use: For undergraduate study at 2-year or 4-year institution.
Eligibility: Applicant must be residing in Washington. Applicant must be dependent of veteran.
Basis for selection: Major/career interest in arts, general or art/art history.
Additional information: For use in field of fine arts.
   Amount of award: $300
   Number of awards: 1
   Application deadline: March 15
   Total amount awarded: $300
Contact:
American Legion Washington Auxiliary
P.O. Box 5867
Lacey, WA 98509-5867

Margarite McAlpin Nurse's Scholarship

Type of award: Scholarship.
Intended use: For undergraduate study at postsecondary institution.
Eligibility: Applicant must be residing in Washington. Applicant must be veteran or descendant of veteran; or dependent of veteran.
Basis for selection: Major/career interest in nursing.
   Amount of award: $300
   Number of awards: 1
   Application deadline: March 15
   Total amount awarded: $300
Contact:
American Legion Washington Auxiliary
P.O. Box 5867
Lacey, WA 98509-5867

Susan Burdett Scholarship

Type of award: Scholarship.
Intended use: For undergraduate study at postsecondary institution.
Eligibility: Applicant must be female. Applicant must be residing in Washington.
Additional information: Applicant must be former Evergreen Girls State Citizen (WA).
   Amount of award: $300
   Number of awards: 1
   Application deadline: March 15
   Total amount awarded: $300
Contact:
American Legion Washington Auxiliary
Education Scholarships
P.O. Box 5867
Lacey, WA 98509-5867

American Legion West Virginia

American Legion West Virginia Oratorical Contest

Type of award: Scholarship.
Intended use: For undergraduate study at postsecondary institution.
Eligibility: Applicant must be enrolled in high school. Applicant must be residing in West Virginia.
Basis for selection: Competition/talent/interest in oratory/debate, based on language style, voice, diction, delivery, originality, logic, breadth of knowledge, application of knowledge about topic, and skill in selecting examples and analogies.

Additional information: Nine district awards of $200; three section awards of $300. State winner receives $500 and four-year scholarship to West Virginia University or other state college under control of Board of Regents. Contest is held in January and February. Information may be obtained from local high school or American Legion Post.

   Amount of award: $200-$500

Contact:
American Legion West Virginia
State Adjutant
2016 Kanawha Blvd. E, Box 3191
Charleston, WV 25332-3191
Phone: 304-343-7591
Fax: 304-343-7592
Web: www.wvlegion.org

American Legion West Virginia Auxiliary

American Legion West Virginia Auxiliary Scholarship

Type of award: Scholarship.
Intended use: For undergraduate study at postsecondary institution.
Eligibility: Applicant must be no older than 22. Applicant must be residing in West Virginia. Applicant must be dependent of veteran.
Application requirements: Proof of eligibility.
Additional information: Four awarded annually.

   Number of awards: 4
   Application deadline: March 1

Contact:
American Legion West Virginia Auxiliary
Secretary/Treasurer Mary Rose Yoho
RR 1 Box 144A
Proctor, WV 26055-9616
Phone: 304-455-3449

American Legion Wisconsin

American Legion Baseball Scholarship

Type of award: Scholarship.
Intended use: For undergraduate study at postsecondary institution.
Eligibility: Applicant must be residing in Wisconsin.
Basis for selection: Competition/talent/interest in athletics/sports.
Application requirements: Nomination by Wisconsin American Baseball Board of Directors.
Additional information: Applicant must be current member of Wisconsin American Legion baseball team. Award rotates yearly from region to region and is awarded at State Convention.

   Amount of award: $500
   Number of awards: 1
   Total amount awarded: $500

Contact:
American Legion Wisconsin
Program Secretary
P.O. Box 388
Portage, WI 53901
Phone: 608-745-1090
Fax: 608-745-0179
Web: www.wilegion.org

American Legion Wisconsin Eagle Scout of the Year Scholarship

Type of award: Scholarship.
Intended use: For undergraduate study at postsecondary institution.
Eligibility: Applicant or parent must be member/participant of American Legion/Boys Scouts of America. Applicant must be male, high school senior. Applicant must be residing in Wisconsin.
Basis for selection: Applicant must demonstrate high academic achievement.
Additional information: Applicant must be Boy Scout, Varsity Scout or Explorer whose group is sponsored by Legion or Auxiliary Post, or whose father or grandfather is Legion or Auxiliary member. Award is $1,000 for state winner.

   Amount of award: $1,000
   Number of awards: 1
   Application deadline: March 1
   Total amount awarded: $1,000

Contact:
American Legion Wisconsin
Program Secretary
P.O. Box 388
Portage, WI 53901
Phone: 608-745-1090
Fax: 608-745-0179
Web: www.wilegion.org

Oratorical Contest Scholarships

Type of award: Scholarship.
Intended use: For undergraduate study at postsecondary institution.
Eligibility: Applicant must be enrolled in high school. Applicant must be residing in Wisconsin.
Basis for selection: Competition/talent/interest in oratory/debate, based on language style, voice, diction, delivery, originality, logic, breadth of knowledge, application of knowledge about topic, and skill in selecting examples and analogies.
Additional information: Awards: state winner - $2,000; three regional awards of $1,000 each; regional participants $600 each.

   Amount of award: $600-$2,000

Contact:
American Legion, Department of Wisconsin
Program Secretary
P.O. Box 388
Portage, WI 53901
Phone: 608-745-1090
Fax: 608-745-0179
Web: www.wilegion.org

American Legion Wisconsin Auxiliary

American Legion Wisconsin Auxiliary Department President's Scholarship

Type of award: Scholarship.
Intended use: For undergraduate study at accredited postsecondary institution.
Eligibility: Applicant or parent must be member/participant of American Legion Auxiliary. Applicant must be residing in Wisconsin. Applicant must be descendant of veteran; or dependent of veteran; or spouse of veteran or deceased veteran. Mother of applicant or applicant must be Auxiliary member. Grandchildren and great-grandchildren of veterans eligible if Auxiliary members.
Basis for selection: Applicant must demonstrate financial need.
Additional information: Minimum 3.5 GPA.
    Amount of award: $1,000
    Number of awards: 3
    Application deadline: March 15
    Total amount awarded: $3,000
Contact:
American Legion Wisconsin Auxiliary, Department Secretary
P.O. Box 140
Portage, WI 53901-0140
Phone: 608-745-0124
Fax: 608-745-1947
Web: www.amlegionauxwi.org

American Legion Wisconsin Auxiliary H.S. and Angeline Lewis Scholarships

Type of award: Scholarship.
Intended use: For undergraduate or graduate study at accredited postsecondary institution.
Eligibility: Applicant or parent must be member/participant of American Legion Auxiliary. Applicant must be residing in Wisconsin. Applicant must be descendant of veteran; or dependent of veteran; or spouse of veteran or deceased veteran. Grandchildren and great-grandchildren of veterans eligible if members of Auxiliary.
Basis for selection: Applicant must demonstrate financial need.
Additional information: Minimum 3.5 GPA. One award for graduate study; five awards for undergraduate study.
    Amount of award: $1,000
    Number of awards: 6
    Application deadline: March 15
    Total amount awarded: $6,000
Contact:
American Legion Wisconsin Auxiliary, Department Secretary
P.O. Box 140
Portage, WI 53901-0140
Phone: 608-745-0124
Fax: 608-745-1947
Web: www.amlegionauxwi.org

American Legion Wisconsin Auxiliary Merit and Memorial Scholarship

Type of award: Scholarship.
Intended use: For undergraduate study.
Eligibility: Applicant or parent must be member/participant of American Legion Auxiliary. Applicant must be residing in Wisconsin. Applicant must be descendant of veteran; or dependent of veteran; or spouse of veteran or deceased veteran. Grandchildren and great-grandchildren of veterans eligible if members of Auxiliary.
Basis for selection: Applicant must demonstrate financial need.
Additional information: Minimum 3.5 GPA.
    Amount of award: $1,000
    Number of awards: 6
    Application deadline: March 15
    Total amount awarded: $6,000
Contact:
American Legion Wisconsin Auxiliary, Department Secretary
P.O. Box 140
Portage, WI 53901-0140
Phone: 608-745-0124
Fax: 608-745-1947
Web: www.amlegionauxwi.org

American Legion Wisconsin Auxiliary Past Presidents Parley Scholarship

Type of award: Scholarship.
Intended use: For undergraduate study at accredited postsecondary institution.
Eligibility: Applicant or parent must be member/participant of American Legion Auxiliary. Applicant must be residing in Wisconsin. Applicant must be descendant of veteran; or dependent of veteran or deceased veteran; or spouse of veteran or deceased veteran. Grandchild or great-grandchild of veteran eligible if Auxiliary member.
Basis for selection: Major/career interest in nursing. Applicant must demonstrate financial need.
Additional information: Minimum 3.5 GPA. Must be in or accepted to accredited school of nursing, accredited hospital, or university registered nursing program. Course of study need not be a four-year program. Hospital, university, or technical school program acceptable.
    Amount of award: $1,000
    Number of awards: 5
    Application deadline: March 15
    Total amount awarded: $5,000
Contact:
American Legion Wisconsin Auxiliary, Department Secretary
P.O. Box 140
Portage, WI 53901-0140
Phone: 608-745-0124
Fax: 608-745-1947
Web: www.amlegionauxwi.org

Della Van Deuren Memorial Scholarship

Type of award: Scholarship.
Intended use: For undergraduate study.

Eligibility: Applicant or parent must be member/participant of American Legion Auxiliary. Applicant must be residing in Wisconsin. Applicant must be descendant of veteran; or dependent of veteran; or spouse of veteran or deceased veteran. Applicant's mother or applicant must be member of American Legion Auxiliary. Grandchildren and great-grandchildren of veterans are eligible if they are members of American Legion Auxiliary.
Basis for selection: Applicant must demonstrate financial need.
Additional information: Minimum 3.5 GPA. Applicant's school need not be in Wisconsin.

Amount of award:	$1,000
Number of awards:	2
Application deadline:	March 15
Total amount awarded:	$2,000

Contact:
American Legion Wisconsin Auxiliary, Department Secretary
P.O. Box 140
Portage, WI 53901-0140
Phone: 608-745-0124
Fax: 608-745-1947
Web: www.amlegionauxwi.org

American Legion Wyoming

American Legion Wyoming E.A. Blackmore Memorial Scholarship

Type of award: Scholarship.
Intended use: For undergraduate study at postsecondary institution.
Eligibility: Applicant or parent must be member/participant of American Legion. Applicant must be residing in Wyoming. Applicant must be veteran or descendant of veteran; or dependent of veteran.

Amount of award:	$1,000
Number of awards:	1
Application deadline:	May 15
Total amount awarded:	$1,000

Contact:
American Legion Wyoming
Department Adjutant
1320 Hugur Ave.
Cheyenne, WY 82001
Phone: 307-634-3035
Fax: 307-635-7093

American Legion Wyoming Oratorical Contest

Type of award: Scholarship.
Intended use: For undergraduate study at postsecondary institution.
Eligibility: Applicant must be enrolled in high school. Applicant must be residing in Wyoming.
Basis for selection: Competition/talent/interest in oratory/debate, based on language style, voice, diction, delivery, originality, logic, breadth of knowledge, application of knowledge about topic, and skill in selecting examples and analogies.
Application requirements: Proof of eligibility.

Amount of award:	$500
Number of awards:	1
Total amount awarded:	$500

Contact:
American Legion Wyoming
Department Adjutant
1320 Hugur Ave.
Cheyenne, WY 82001
Phone: 307-634-3035
Fax: 307-635-7093

American Legion Wyoming Auxiliary

American Legion Wyoming Auxiliary Past Presidents' Parley Scholarship

Type of award: Scholarship, renewable.
Intended use: For undergraduate study at 2-year or 4-year institution. Designated institutions: University of Wyoming or one of Wyoming community colleges.
Eligibility: Applicant must be residing in Wyoming. Preference given to nursing students who are children of veterans.
Basis for selection: Major/career interest in nursing or health-related professions. Applicant must demonstrate financial need and high academic achievement.
Application requirements: Recommendations.
Additional information: Must be in 3rd quarter of training and have minimum 3.0 GPA.

Amount of award:	$300
Number of awards:	2
Application deadline:	June 1
Total amount awarded:	$600

Contact:
American Legion Wyoming Auxiliary
Department Secretary
P.O. Box 2198
Gillette, WY 82717
Phone: 307-686-7137

American Medical Technologists

Medical Technologists Student Scholarship

Type of award: Scholarship.
Intended use: For full-time undergraduate or graduate study at accredited postsecondary institution in United States.
Eligibility: Applicant must be U.S. citizen or permanent resident.
Basis for selection: Major/career interest in medical assistant; dental assistant or health services administration. Applicant must demonstrate financial need and high academic achievement.
Application requirements: Essay, transcript, proof of eligibility. Two letters of recommendation. Typed statement on why applicant has chosen particular career.

Additional information: Scholarship is available only to high school graduates studying to become one of the following: medical assistant, dental assistant, medical administrative specialist, medical technologist, medical laboratory technician, office laboratory technician, or phlebotomy technician. Students pursuing careers in other medical, health or science fields do not qualify. Award may only be used to defray tuition costs and will be sent directly to the school of the recipient's choice. All applications and supporting documents become property of American Medical Technologists and cannot be returned.

    Amount of award: $500
    Number of awards: 5
    Application deadline: April 1
    Total amount awarded: $2,500

Contact:
American Medical Technologists
10700 West Higgins Road
Rosemont, IL 60018
Phone: 847-823-5169
Fax: 847-823-0458
Web: www.amt1.com

American Meteorological Society

American Meteorological Society Undergraduate Scholarships

Type of award: Scholarship.
Intended use: For full-time senior study at accredited 4-year institution in United States.
Eligibility: Applicant must be U.S. citizen or permanent resident.
Basis for selection: Major/career interest in atmospheric sciences/meteorology; oceanography/marine studies or hydrology. Applicant must demonstrate high academic achievement and seriousness of purpose.
Application requirements: Recommendations, essay, transcript, proof of eligibility. Three letters of recommendation.
Additional information: Minimum 3.25 GPA. Marine biology majors not eligible. Application deadline early February. Visit Website for exact date, for more information, and to download application. Number and amount of scholarships vary. Applicants must demonstrate financial need to be eligible for the Schroeder Scholarship. The Murphy Scholarship is awarded to students who, through curricular or extracurricular activities, have shown interest in weather forecasting or in the value and utilization of forecasts. The Glahn Scholarship is for a student who has shown strong interest in statistical meteorology. The Crow Scholarship is for a student who has shown strong interest in applied meteorology.

Contact:
American Meteorological Society
Fellowship/Scholarship Programs
45 Beacon Street
Boston, MA 02108-3693
Phone: 617-227-2425
Fax: 617-742-8718
Web: www.ametsoc.org/ams

American Meteorological Society/ Industry Minority Scholarship

Type of award: Scholarship.
Intended use: For full-time freshman study at accredited 4-year institution in United States.
Eligibility: Applicant must be Alaskan native, Asian American, African American, Mexican American, Hispanic American, Puerto Rican or American Indian. Applicant must be high school senior. Applicant must be U.S. citizen or permanent resident.
Basis for selection: Major/career interest in atmospheric sciences/meteorology; oceanography/marine studies or hydrology. Applicant must demonstrate high academic achievement.
Application requirements: Recommendations, essay, transcript, proof of eligibility. SAT scores.
Additional information: Minimum 3.25 GPA. Award is $3,000 each for freshman and sophomore years. Award is for minority students who have traditionally been underrepresented in the sciences, especially Hispanic, Native American, and African-American students. Marine biology majors ineligible. Deadline in early February. Visit Website for exact date and to download application.

    Amount of award: $3,000
    Total amount awarded: $3,000

Contact:
American Meteorological Society
Fellowship/Scholarship Programs
45 Beacon Street
Boston, MA 2108-3693
Phone: 617-227-2425
Fax: 617-742-8718
Web: www.ametsoc.org/ams

Freshman Undergraduate Scholarship Program

Type of award: Scholarship, renewable.
Intended use: For full-time freshman study at accredited 4-year institution in United States.
Eligibility: Applicant must be high school senior. Applicant must be U.S. citizen or permanent resident.
Basis for selection: Major/career interest in meteorology.
Additional information: Minimum 3.25 GPA. Scholarships are renewable for the sophomore year, providing recipient has plans to continue studies in the AMS related studies. Award $2,500 each for freshman and sophomore years. Applications accepted from September to February.

    Amount of award: $2,500

Contact:
American Meteorological Society
Fellowship/Scholarship Program
45 Beacon Street
Boston, MA 02108-3693
Phone: 617-227-2425
Fax: 617-742-8718
Web: www.ametsoc.org

Meteorological Society Father James B. Macelwane Annual Award

Type of award: Scholarship.
Intended use: For undergraduate study.
Eligibility: Applicant must be U.S. citizen or permanent resident.

Basis for selection: Major/career interest in atmospheric sciences/meteorology; oceanography/marine studies or hydrology.
Application requirements: Essay, transcript, proof of eligibility. Original paper plus four photocopies. Letter of application including contact information and stating paper's title and name of university where paper was written. Letter from university faculty stating author was undergraduate when paper was written and indicating elements of paper that are original contributions by the student. Abstract of maximum 250 words describing paper.
Additional information: Award intended to stimulate interest in meteorology among college students through encouragement of original papers concerned with some phase of atmospheric sciences. Student must be undergraduate when paper is written. Submissions from women, minorities and disabled students who are traditionally underrepresented in atmospheric and related oceanic and hydrologic sciences encouraged. No more than two students from any one institution may enter papers in any one contest. Application deadline in early June. Visit Website for exact date, application, and additional information.

Amount of award:	$1,000
Number of awards:	1
Total amount awarded:	$1,000

Contact:
American Meteorological Society
Fellowship/Scholarship Programs
45 Beacon Street
Boston, MA 02108-3693
Phone: 617-227-2425
Fax: 617-742-8718
Web: www.ametsoc.org/ams

American Morgan Horse Institute

AMHI Educational Scholarships

Type of award: Scholarship.
Intended use: For non-degree study at vocational, 2-year or 4-year institution.
Basis for selection: Major/career interest in equestrian/equine studies. Applicant must demonstrate financial need, high academic achievement, depth of character, leadership, seriousness of purpose and service orientation.
Application requirements: Recommendations, essay, transcript.
Additional information: Applicant must demonstrate achievement with registered Morgan horses. Send SASE for application or download from Website.

Amount of award:	$3,000
Number of awards:	5
Number of applicants:	100
Application deadline:	March 1
Notification begins:	June 1
Total amount awarded:	$15,000

Contact:
AMHI Scholarships
P.O. Box 837
Shelburne, VT 05482-0837
Web: www.morganhorse.com

AMHI van Schaik Dressage Scholarship

Type of award: Scholarship.
Intended use: For non-degree study.
Basis for selection: Major/career interest in dressage or equestrian/equine studies. Applicant must demonstrate seriousness of purpose.
Application requirements: Recommendations, essay.
Additional information: Must be dressage rider using a registered Morgan horse. For anyone competing in and interested in advancing through levels of dressage to Fourth level and above. Download application from Website.

Amount of award:	$1,000
Number of awards:	1
Number of applicants:	10
Application deadline:	November 30
Notification begins:	April 1
Total amount awarded:	$1,000

Contact:
AMHI Scholarships
P.O. Box 837
Shelburne, VT 05482-0837
Web: www.morganhorse.com

American Museum of Natural History

The Young Naturalist Awards Scholarship Program

Type of award: Scholarship, renewable.
Intended use: For freshman study.
Basis for selection: Competition/talent/interest in research paper. Major/career interest in science, general or natural sciences.
Application requirements: Essay for which students conduct their own research and which demonstrate independence and creativity. Include original artwork and/or photographs in essay. Word limits: grades 7 and 8, 500-2,000; grades 9 and 10, 750-2,500; grades 11 and 12, 1,000 to 3,000.
Additional information: For students in grades 7-12 in the U.S. and Canada to plan and conduct scientific investigations and report them in an illustrated essay. Children of Alcoa Corporation or American Museum of Natural History employees or consultants not eligible. Two winners per grade level receive the following: 7th grade, $500; 8th grade, $750; 9th grade, $1,000; 10th grade, $1,500; 11th grade, $2,000; 12th grade, $2,500. Also trip to New York City for award ceremony and tour at the Museum. Winners' teachers given classroom book collection. Up to 36 additional finalists receive $50 prize.

Amount of award:	$50-$2,500
Number of awards:	48
Application deadline:	March 1
Notification begins:	March 24
Total amount awarded:	$18,300

Contact:
American Museum of Natural History
Central Park West at 79th St.
New York, NY 10024
Web: www.amnh.org/youngnaturalistawards

American Nuclear Society

Angelo S. Bisesti Scholarship

Type of award: Scholarship.
Intended use: For full-time junior or senior study at 4-year institution in United States.
Eligibility: Applicant must be U.S. citizen or permanent resident.
Basis for selection: Major/career interest in nuclear science or engineering, nuclear.
Additional information: Applicant must be at least entering junior enrolled in program leading to degree in nuclear science, nuclear engineering, or nuclear-related field and pursuing a career in the field of commercial nuclear power. Visit Website to download application.
- **Amount of award:** $2,000
- **Number of awards:** 1
- **Application deadline:** February 1
- **Total amount awarded:** $2,000

Contact:
American Nuclear Society
555 North Kensington Avenue
La Grange Park, IL 60526
Phone: 708-352-6611
Fax: 708-352-0499
Web: www.ans.org

ANS Undergraduate Scholarships

Type of award: Scholarship.
Intended use: For sophomore, junior or senior study at accredited 4-year institution in United States.
Eligibility: Applicant must be U.S. citizen or permanent resident.
Basis for selection: Major/career interest in nuclear science or engineering, nuclear.
Additional information: Maximum of four scholarships for entering sophomores in study leading to degree in nuclear science, nuclear engineering, or nuclear-related field; maximum of 21 scholarships for students who will be entering junior or senior year.
- **Amount of award:** $2,000
- **Application deadline:** February 1

Contact:
American Nuclear Society
555 North Kensington Avenue
La Grange Park, IL 60526
Phone: 708-352-6611
Fax: 708-352-0499
Web: www.ans.org

Charles (Tommy) Thomas Memorial Scholarship

Type of award: Scholarship.
Intended use: For full-time junior or senior study at accredited 4-year institution in United States.
Eligibility: Applicant must be U.S. citizen or permanent resident.
Basis for selection: Major/career interest in nuclear science; environmental science; ecology or natural resources/conservation.
Additional information: Applicant must be undergraduate of at least junior status pursuing degree in discipline related to career in environmental aspects of nuclear science or nuclear engineering. See Website for application and requirements.
- **Amount of award:** $2,000
- **Number of awards:** 1
- **Application deadline:** February 1

Contact:
American Nuclear Society
555 North Kensington Avenue
La Grange Park, IL 60526
Phone: 708-352-6611
Fax: 708-352-0499
Web: www.ans.org

Decommissioning, Decontamination and Reutilization Scholarship

Type of award: Scholarship.
Intended use: For junior or senior study at accredited 4-year institution in United States.
Eligibility: Applicant must be U.S. citizen or permanent resident.
Basis for selection: Major/career interest in engineering, nuclear; environmental science or engineering, environmental.
Additional information: Applicants must be enrolled in curriculum of engineering or science associated with decommissioning/decontamination of nuclear facilities, management/characterization of nuclear waste, or restoration of environment. If awarded scholarship, student must join ANS and designate DDR Division as one professional division. Awardee must also provide student support to DDR Division at next ANS meeting after receiving award (funding provided for travel to meeting but does not include food and lodging).
- **Amount of award:** $2,000
- **Number of awards:** 1
- **Application deadline:** February 1

Contact:
American Nuclear Society
555 North Kensington Avenue
La Grange Park, IL 60526
Phone: 708-352-6611
Fax: 708-352-0499
Web: www.ans.org

Delayed Education Scholarship for Women

Type of award: Scholarship.
Intended use: For undergraduate study at accredited 4-year institution in United States.
Eligibility: Applicant must be female, returning adult student. Applicant must be U.S. citizen or permanent resident.
Basis for selection: Major/career interest in nuclear science or engineering, nuclear. Applicant must demonstrate financial need and high academic achievement.
Additional information: Award for mature women who have had delay in their education in field of nuclear science and engineering. One request and one application cover D.E.W.S. Award and John and Muriel Landis Award. Applicants must check appropriate box on Landis Scholarship form. Visit Website for application and requirements.
- **Amount of award:** $4,000
- **Number of awards:** 1
- **Application deadline:** February 1

American Nuclear Society: Delayed Education Scholarship for Women

Contact:
American Nuclear Society
555 North Kensington Avenue
La Grange Park, IL 60526
Phone: 708-352-6611
Fax: 708-352-0499
Web: www.ans.org

John and Muriel Landis Scholarship

Type of award: Scholarship.
Intended use: For undergraduate or graduate study at 4-year or graduate institution in United States.
Eligibility: Applicant must be U.S. citizen or permanent resident.
Basis for selection: Major/career interest in nuclear science or engineering, nuclear. Applicant must demonstrate financial need.
Additional information: Awarded to students with greater than average financial need. Consideration given to conditions or experiences that render student disadvantaged (poor high school/undergraduate preparation, etc.). Applicants should be planning career in nuclear science or nuclear engineering. Qualified high school seniors eligible to apply. Visit Website for application and requirements.
   Amount of award: $4,000
   Number of awards: 8
   Application deadline: February 1
Contact:
American Nuclear Society
555 North Kensington Avenue
La Grange Park, IL 60526
Phone: 708-352-6611
Fax: 708-352-0499
Web: www.ans.org

John R. Lamarsh Scholarship

Type of award: Scholarship.
Intended use: For full-time junior or senior study at accredited 4-year institution in United States.
Eligibility: Applicant must be U.S. citizen or permanent resident.
Basis for selection: Major/career interest in nuclear science or engineering, nuclear.
Additional information: Applicant must be at least an entering junior enrolled in program leading to degree in nuclear science or nuclear engineering. See Website for application and requirements.
   Amount of award: $2,000
   Number of awards: 1
   Application deadline: February 1
Contact:
American Nuclear Society
555 North Kensington Avenue
La Grange Park, IL 60526
Phone: 708-352-6611
Fax: 708-352-0499
Web: www.ans.org

Joseph R. Dietrich Scholarship

Type of award: Scholarship.
Intended use: For full-time junior or senior study at 4-year institution in United States.
Eligibility: Applicant must be U.S. citizen or permanent resident.
Basis for selection: Major/career interest in nuclear science; engineering, nuclear; chemistry or physics.
Additional information: Applicant must be at least an entering junior enrolled in program leading to degree in nuclear science, nuclear engineering, or nuclear-related field. See Website for application and requirements.
   Amount of award: $2,000
   Number of awards: 1
   Application deadline: February 1
Contact:
American Nuclear Society
555 North Kensington Avenue
La Grange Park, IL 60526
Phone: 708-352-6611
Fax: 708-352-0499
Web: www.ans.org

Operations and Power Division Scholarship

Type of award: Scholarship.
Intended use: For full-time junior or senior study at 4-year institution.
Eligibility: Applicant must be U.S. citizen or permanent resident.
Basis for selection: Major/career interest in nuclear science or engineering, nuclear.
Additional information: Applicant must be at least an entering junior enrolled in a program leading to a degree in nuclear science or nuclear engineering. Application available online.
   Amount of award: $2,500
   Number of awards: 1
   Application deadline: February 1
Contact:
American Nuclear Society
555 North Kensington Avenue
La Grange Park, IL 60526
Phone: 708-352-6611
Fax: 708-352-0499
Web: www.ans.org

Pittsburgh Local Section Scholarship

Type of award: Scholarship.
Intended use: For full-time junior, senior or graduate study at accredited 4-year or graduate institution in United States.
Eligibility: Applicant or parent must be member/participant of American Nuclear Society.
Basis for selection: Major/career interest in nuclear science or engineering, nuclear.
Application requirements: Transcript.
Additional information: Awards are $2,000 for undergraduates and $3,500 for graduate students. See Website for application and requirements.
   Amount of award: $2,000-$3,500
   Number of awards: 2
   Application deadline: February 1
Contact:
American Nuclear Society
555 North Kensington Avenue
La Grange Park, IL 60526
Phone: 708-352-6611
Fax: 708-352-0499
Web: www.ans.org

Raymond DiSalvo Scholarship

Type of award: Scholarship.
Intended use: For full-time junior or senior study at 4-year institution in United States.
Eligibility: Applicant must be U.S. citizen or permanent resident.
Basis for selection: Major/career interest in nuclear science or engineering, nuclear.
Additional information: Applicant must be at least an entering junior enrolled in program leading to degree in nuclear science or nuclear engineering. Application available online.
    Amount of award: $2,000
    Number of awards: 1
    Application deadline: February 1
Contact:
American Nuclear Society
555 North Kensington Avenue
La Grange Park, IL 60526
Phone: 708-352-6611
Fax: 708-352-0499
Web: www.ans.org

Robert G. Lacy Scholarship

Type of award: Scholarship.
Intended use: For full-time junior or senior study at 4-year institution in United States.
Eligibility: Applicant must be U.S. citizen or permanent resident.
Basis for selection: Major/career interest in nuclear science or engineering, nuclear.
Application requirements: Recommendations, transcript, proof of eligibility.
Additional information: Applicant must be at least an entering junior enrolled in a program leading to a degree in nuclear science or nuclear engineering. Application available online.
    Amount of award: $2,000
    Number of awards: 1
    Application deadline: February 1
    Notification begins: May 9
Contact:
American Nuclear Society
555 North Kensington Avenue
La Grange Park, IL 60526
Phone: 708-352-6611
Fax: 708-352-0499
Web: www.ans.org

Robert T. (Bob) Liner Scholarship

Type of award: Scholarship.
Intended use: For full-time junior or senior study at 4-year institution in United States.
Eligibility: Applicant must be U.S. citizen or permanent resident.
Basis for selection: Major/career interest in nuclear science or engineering, nuclear. Applicant must demonstrate depth of character, leadership, seriousness of purpose and service orientation.
Additional information: Applicant must be at least an entering junior enrolled in a program leading to a degree in nuclear science or nuclear engineering. Application available online.
    Amount of award: $2,000
    Number of awards: 1
    Application deadline: February 1
Contact:
American Nuclear Society
555 North Kensington Avenue
La Grange Park, IL 60526
Phone: 708-352-6611
Fax: 708-352-0499
Web: www.ans.org

Vogt Radiochemistry Scholarship

Type of award: Scholarship.
Intended use: For full-time undergraduate or graduate study at accredited 4-year or graduate institution.
Eligibility: Applicant must be U.S. citizen or permanent resident.
Basis for selection: Major/career interest in chemistry or nuclear science.
Additional information: Applicants must be enrolled in or proposing to undertake research in radioanalytical chemistry, analytical chemistry, or analytical applications of nuclear science. Awards are $2,000 for undergraduates and $3,000 for graduate students. See Website for application and requirements.
    Amount of award: $2,000-$3,000
    Number of awards: 1
    Application deadline: February 1
    Notification begins: May 9
Contact:
American Nuclear Society
555 North Kensington Avenue
La Grange Park, IL 60526
Phone: 708-352-6611
Fax: 708-352-0499
Web: www.ans.org

American Physical Society

Scholarship for Minority Undergraduate Physics Majors

Type of award: Scholarship, renewable.
Intended use: For full-time freshman, sophomore or junior study at 2-year or 4-year institution in United States.
Designated institutions: Institutions with physics department or provisions for procurement of physics degrees.
Eligibility: Applicant must be African American, Mexican American, Hispanic American, Puerto Rican or American Indian. Applicant must be U.S. citizen or permanent resident.
Basis for selection: Major/career interest in physics. Applicant must demonstrate high academic achievement.
Application requirements: Recommendations, essay, transcript, proof of eligibility. ACT/SAT scores.
Additional information: Must be high school senior or college freshman or sophomore to apply. Additional $500 awarded to physics department at eligible institution. Applications available early November. Visit Website for more information.
    Amount of award: $2,000-$3,000
    Number of awards: 25
    Number of applicants: 100
    Application deadline: February 6
    Notification begins: May 15
    Total amount awarded: $70,000

Contact:
American Physical Society
Minority Undergraduate Physics Scholarship
One Physics Ellipse
College Park, MD 20740
Phone: 301-209-3232
Fax: 301-209-0865
Web: www.aps.org/programs/minorities

American Quarter Horse Foundation

American Quarter Horse Foundation Scholarships

Type of award: Scholarship, renewable.
Intended use: For full-time undergraduate or first professional study in United States or Canada.
Eligibility: Applicant must be at least 17.
Basis for selection: Applicant must demonstrate financial need and high academic achievement.
Application requirements: Transcript, proof of eligibility. One-page essay on topic listed in application. Up to three reference letters. Financial tax forms.
Additional information: Minimum 2.5 GPA. Applicant may be high-school senior, undergraduate student, or veterinary student. Applicant must have been member of American Quarter Horse Youth Association or American Quarter Horse Association for at least three years. Notification begins May.

Amount of award:	$500-$25,000
Number of awards:	180
Number of applicants:	253
Application deadline:	January 2
Total amount awarded:	$380,000

Contact:
American Quarter Horse Foundation
Attn: Laura Owens
2601 East I-40
Amarillo, TX 79104
Phone: 806-378-5034
Fax: 806-376-1005
Web: www.aqha.com/foundation

American Radio Relay League (ARRL) Foundation, Inc.

Albuquerque ARC/Toby Cross Scholarship

Type of award: Scholarship.
Intended use: For undergraduate study at accredited 4-year or graduate institution in United States.
Eligibility: Applicant or parent must be member/participant of American Radio Relay League. Applicant must be residing in New Mexico.
Basis for selection: Competition/talent/interest in amateur radio. Applicant must demonstrate financial need.
Application requirements: Transcript, proof of eligibility. One-page essay on role amateur radio has played in applicant's life.
Additional information: Must be amateur radio operator holding any class license. Number of awards varies, but is usually one per year. Application may be obtained on Website, but no electronic submissions accepted.

Amount of award:	$500
Number of awards:	1
Application deadline:	February 1

Contact:
ARRL Foundation Inc.
225 Main Street
Newington, CT 06111
Phone: 860-594-0397
Fax: 860-594-0259
Web: www.arrlf.org

ARRL Earl I. Anderson Scholarship

Type of award: Scholarship.
Intended use: For undergraduate or graduate study at accredited 4-year or graduate institution.
Eligibility: Applicant or parent must be member/participant of American Radio Relay League. Applicant must be residing in Michigan, Indiana, Illinois or Florida.
Basis for selection: Competition/talent/interest in amateur radio. Major/career interest in engineering, electrical/electronic. Applicant must demonstrate financial need.
Application requirements: Transcript, proof of eligibility.
Additional information: Must be amateur radio operator holding any class license. Must be ARRL member. Major may be electronic engineering or other related technical field. Application may be obtained on Website, but no electronic submissions accepted.

Amount of award:	$1,250
Number of awards:	3
Application deadline:	February 1

Contact:
ARRL Foundation, Inc.
225 Main Street
Newington, CT 06111
Phone: 860-594-0397
Fax: 860-594-0259
Web: www.arrlf.org

ARRL Scholarship Honoring Senator Barry Goldwater, K7UGA

Type of award: Scholarship.
Intended use: For undergraduate or graduate study at accredited 4-year or graduate institution in United States.
Basis for selection: Competition/talent/interest in amateur radio. Applicant must demonstrate financial need.
Application requirements: Transcript, proof of eligibility.
Additional information: Must be amateur radio operator with novice license. Application may be obtained on Website, but no electronic submissions accepted.

Amount of award:	$5,000
Number of awards:	1
Application deadline:	February 1
Total amount awarded:	$5,000

Contact:
ARRL Foundation Inc.
225 Main Street
Newington, CT 06111
Phone: 860-594-0397
Fax: 860-594-0259
Web: www.arrlf.org

The Challenge Met Scholarship

Type of award: Scholarship.
Intended use: For undergraduate study at accredited vocational, 2-year, 4-year or graduate institution.
Eligibility: Applicant must be learning disabled.
Application requirements: Transcript.
Additional information: Must be amateur radio operator holding any class license. Preference given to those with documented learning disabilities who put forth effort regardless of resulting grades. Application may be obtained on Website, but no electronic submissions accepted. Number of awards varies.
   Amount of award: $500
   Application deadline: February 1
Contact:
The ARRL Foundation Scholarship Program
225 Main Street
Newington, CT 06111
Phone: 860-594-0347
Fax: 860-594-0259
Web: www.arrlf.org

Charles Clarke Cordle Memorial Scholarship

Type of award: Scholarship.
Intended use: For undergraduate or graduate study at accredited 4-year or graduate institution.
Eligibility: Applicant must be residing in Alabama or Georgia.
Basis for selection: Competition/talent/interest in amateur radio. Applicant must demonstrate financial need.
Application requirements: Transcript, proof of eligibility.
Additional information: Minimum 2.5 GPA. Must be amateur radio operator holding any class license. Application may be obtained from Website, but no electronic submissions accepted.
   Amount of award: $1,000
   Number of awards: 1
   Application deadline: February 1
   Total amount awarded: $1,000
Contact:
ARRL Foundation Inc.
225 Main Street
Newington, CT 06111
Phone: 860-594-0397
Fax: 860-594-0259
Web: www.arrlf.org

Charles N. Fisher Memorial Scholarship

Type of award: Scholarship.
Intended use: For undergraduate or graduate study at accredited 4-year or graduate institution in United States.
Eligibility: Applicant must be residing in California or Arizona.
Basis for selection: Competition/talent/interest in amateur radio. Major/career interest in communications or electronics. Applicant must demonstrate financial need.
Application requirements: Transcript, proof of eligibility.
Additional information: Must be amateur radio operator holding any class license. Major may be in other fields related to those listed. California candidates must reside in Los Angeles, Orange, San Diego and Santa Barbara areas. Application may be obtained on Website, but no electronic submissions accepted.
   Amount of award: $1,000
   Number of awards: 1
   Application deadline: February 1
   Total amount awarded: $1,000
Contact:
ARRL Foundation Inc.
225 Main Street
Newington, CT 06111
Phone: 860-594-0397
Fax: 860-594-0259
Web: www.arrlf.org

The Chicago FM Club Scholarships

Type of award: Scholarship.
Intended use: For undergraduate study at accredited vocational, 2-year or 4-year institution in United States.
Eligibility: Applicant must be residing in Wisconsin, Indiana or Illinois.
Basis for selection: Competition/talent/interest in amateur radio. Applicant must demonstrate financial need.
Application requirements: Transcript, proof of eligibility.
Additional information: Student must be U.S. citizen or within three months of becoming U.S. citizen. Must be amateur radio operator with technician license. Number of awards varies. Application may be obtained on Website, but no electronic submissions accepted.
   Amount of award: $500
   Application deadline: February 1
Contact:
ARRL Foundation Inc.
225 Main Street
Newington, CT 06111
Phone: 860-594-0397
Fax: 860-594-0259
Web: www.arrlf.org

The Dayton Amateur Radio Association Scholarships

Type of award: Scholarship.
Intended use: For undergraduate study at accredited 2-year, 4-year or graduate institution.
Eligibility: Applicant must be residing in North Carolina.
Basis for selection: Competition/talent/interest in amateur radio.
Application requirements: Transcript.
Additional information: Must be amateur radio operator holding any class license. Application may be obtained on Website, but no electronic submissions accepted.
   Amount of award: $1,000
   Number of awards: 4
   Application deadline: February 1

Contact:
The ARRL Foundation, Inc. Scholarship Program
225 Main Street
Newington, CT 06111
Phone: 860-594-0347
Fax: 860-594-0259
Web: www.arrlf.org

The Donald Riebhoff Memorial Scholarship

Type of award: Scholarship.
Intended use: For undergraduate or graduate study at accredited 4-year or graduate institution in United States.
Eligibility: Applicant or parent must be member/participant of American Radio Relay League.
Basis for selection: Competition/talent/interest in amateur radio. Major/career interest in international relations. Applicant must demonstrate financial need.
Application requirements: Transcript, proof of eligibility.
Additional information: Must be amateur radio operator with technician class license. Must be ARRL member. Application may be obtained on Website, but no electronic submissions accepted.
   Amount of award: $1,000
   Number of awards: 1
   Application deadline: February 1
Contact:
ARRL Foundation Inc.
225 Main Street
Newington, CT 06111
Phone: 860-594-0397
Fax: 860-594-0259
Web: www.arrlf.org

Dr. James L. Lawson Memorial Scholarship

Type of award: Scholarship.
Intended use: For undergraduate or graduate study at accredited 4-year or graduate institution.
Eligibility: Applicant must be residing in Vermont, Connecticut, New York, New Hampshire, Maine, Massachusetts or Rhode Island.
Basis for selection: Competition/talent/interest in amateur radio. Major/career interest in communications or electronics. Applicant must demonstrate financial need.
Application requirements: Transcript, proof of eligibility.
Additional information: Must be amateur radio operator holding general license. Major may be in other fields related to those listed. Application may be obtained on Website, but no electronic submissions accepted.
   Amount of award: $500
   Number of awards: 1
   Application deadline: February 1
   Total amount awarded: $500
Contact:
ARRL Foundation Inc.
225 Main Street
Newington, CT 06111
Phone: 860-594-0397
Fax: 860-594-0259
Web: www.arrlf.org

Edmond A. Metzger Scholarship

Type of award: Scholarship.
Intended use: For undergraduate, graduate or non-degree study at accredited 4-year or graduate institution.
Eligibility: Applicant or parent must be member/participant of American Radio Relay League. Applicant must be residing in Wisconsin, Indiana or Illinois.
Basis for selection: Competition/talent/interest in amateur radio. Major/career interest in engineering, electrical/electronic. Applicant must demonstrate financial need.
Application requirements: Transcript, proof of eligibility.
Additional information: Must be amateur radio operator with novice license. Must be electrical engineering student and member of ARRL. Application may be obtained on Website, but no electronic submissions accepted.
   Amount of award: $500
   Number of awards: 1
   Application deadline: February 1
   Total amount awarded: $500
Contact:
ARRL Foundation Inc.
225 Main Street
Newington, CT 06111
Phone: 860-594-0397
Fax: 860-594-0259
Web: www.arrlf.org

The Eugene "Gene" Sallee, W4YFR Memorial Scholarship

Type of award: Scholarship.
Intended use: For undergraduate or graduate study at accredited 4-year or graduate institution in United States.
Eligibility: Applicant must be residing in Georgia.
Basis for selection: Competition/talent/interest in amateur radio. Applicant must demonstrate financial need and high academic achievement.
Application requirements: Transcript, proof of eligibility.
Additional information: Must be amateur radio operator with technician plus class license. Minimum 3.0 GPA. Application may be obtained on Website, but no electronic submissions accepted.
   Amount of award: $500
   Number of awards: 1
   Application deadline: February 1
   Total amount awarded: $500
Contact:
ARRL Foundation Inc.
225 Main Street
Newington, CT 06111
Phone: 860-594-0397
Fax: 860-594-0259
Web: www.arrlf.org

Fred R. McDaniel Memorial Scholarship

Type of award: Scholarship.
Intended use: For undergraduate or graduate study at accredited 4-year or graduate institution in United States.
Eligibility: Applicant must be residing in Oklahoma, Texas, Mississippi, Arkansas, New Mexico or Louisiana.
Basis for selection: Competition/talent/interest in amateur radio. Major/career interest in electronics or communications. Applicant must demonstrate financial need.
Application requirements: Transcript, proof of eligibility.
Additional information: Preference for students with minimum 3.0 GPA. Must be amateur radio operator holding general license. Major may be in other fields related to those

listed. Application may be obtained from Website, but no electronic submissions accepted.

Amount of award:	$500
Number of awards:	1
Application deadline:	February 1
Total amount awarded:	$500

Contact:
ARRL Foundation Inc.
225 Main Street
Newington, CT 06111
Phone: 860-594-0397
Fax: 860-594-0259
Web: www.arrlf.org

The General Fund Scholarships

Type of award: Scholarship.
Intended use: For undergraduate or graduate study at accredited 4-year or graduate institution in United States.
Basis for selection: Competition/talent/interest in amateur radio. Major/career interest in radio/television/film or communications. Applicant must demonstrate financial need.
Application requirements: Transcript.
Additional information: Must be amateur radio operator holding any class license. Number of awards varies. Application may be obtained on Website, but no electronic submissions accepted.

Amount of award:	$1,000
Application deadline:	February 1

Contact:
ARRL Foundation Inc.
225 Main Street
Newington, CT 06111
Phone: 860-594-0397
Fax: 860-594-0259
Web: www.arrlf.org

The Henry Broughton, K2AE Memorial Scholarship

Type of award: Scholarship.
Intended use: For undergraduate or graduate study at accredited 4-year or graduate institution in United States.
Eligibility: Applicant must be residing in New York.
Basis for selection: Competition/talent/interest in amateur radio. Major/career interest in engineering or science, general. Applicant must demonstrate financial need.
Application requirements: Transcript, proof of eligibility.
Additional information: Applicant must live within 70-mile radius of Schenectady, New York. Must be amateur radio operator with general class license. Major may be in other fields similar to those listed. May offer additional awards if funding permits. Application may be obtained on Website, but no electronic submissions accepted.

Amount of award:	$1,000
Number of awards:	1
Application deadline:	February 1

Contact:
ARRL Foundation, Inc.
225 Main Street
Newington, CT 06111
Phone: 860-594-0397
Fax: 860-594-0259
Web: www.arrlf.org

Irving W. Cook, WAOCGS Scholarship

Type of award: Scholarship.
Intended use: For undergraduate or graduate study at accredited 4-year or graduate institution in United States.
Eligibility: Applicant must be residing in Kansas.
Basis for selection: Competition/talent/interest in amateur radio. Major/career interest in communications or electronics. Applicant must demonstrate financial need.
Application requirements: Transcript, proof of eligibility.
Additional information: Must be amateur radio operator holding any class license. Major may be in other fields related to those listed. Application may be obtained on Website, but no electronic submissions accepted.

Amount of award:	$1,000
Number of awards:	1
Application deadline:	February 1
Total amount awarded:	$1,000

Contact:
ARRL Foundation Inc.
225 Main Street
Newington, CT 06111
Phone: 860-594-0397
Fax: 860-594-0259
Web: www.arrlf.org

Jean Cebik Memorial Scholarship

Type of award: Scholarship.
Intended use: For undergraduate or graduate study at accredited 4-year or graduate institution.
Eligibility: Applicant must be residing in New Jersey.
Basis for selection: Competition/talent/interest in amateur radio.
Application requirements: Transcript.
Additional information: Must be amateur radio operator holding technician license or higher. Application may be obtained on Website, but no electronic submissions accepted.

Amount of award:	$1,000
Number of awards:	1
Application deadline:	February 1

Contact:
The ARRL Foundation, Inc. Scholarship Program
225 Main Street
Newington, CT 06111
Phone: 860-594-0347
Fax: 860-594-0259
Web: www.arrlf.org

The K2TEO Martin J. Green, Sr. Memorial Scholarship

Type of award: Scholarship.
Intended use: For undergraduate or graduate study at accredited 4-year or graduate institution in United States.
Basis for selection: Competition/talent/interest in amateur radio. Applicant must demonstrate financial need.
Application requirements: Transcript.
Additional information: Must be amateur radio operator with general license. Preference given to student from family of ham operators. Application may be obtained on Website, but no electronic submissions accepted.

Amount of award:	$1,000
Number of awards:	1
Application deadline:	February 1
Total amount awarded:	$1,000

American Radio Relay League (ARRL) Foundation, Inc.: The K2TEO Martin J. Green, Sr. Memorial Scholarship

Contact:
ARRL Foundation, Inc.
225 Main Street
Newington, CT 06111
Phone: 860-594-0397
Fax: 860-594-0259
Web: www.arrlf.org/

L. Phil Wicker Scholarship

Type of award: Scholarship.
Intended use: For undergraduate, graduate or non-degree study at accredited 4-year or graduate institution.
Eligibility: Applicant must be residing in Virginia, West Virginia, North Carolina or South Carolina.
Basis for selection: Competition/talent/interest in amateur radio. Major/career interest in communications or electronics. Applicant must demonstrate financial need.
Application requirements: Transcript, proof of eligibility.
Additional information: Must be amateur radio operator holding general license. Major may be in other fields related to those listed. Application may be obtained on Website, but no electronic submissions accepted.
    Amount of award: $1,000
    Number of awards: 1
    Application deadline: February 1
    Total amount awarded: $1,000
Contact:
ARRL Foundation Inc.
225 Main Street
Newington, CT 06111
Phone: 860-594-0397
Fax: 860-594-0259
Web: www.arrlf.org

The Louisiana Memorial Scholarship

Type of award: Scholarship.
Intended use: For undergraduate study at accredited 4-year or graduate institution.
Basis for selection: Competition/talent/interest in amateur radio.
Application requirements: Transcript.
Additional information: Must be resident of or student in LA. Must have 3.0 GPA. Must be amateur radio operator holding technician license or above. Application may be obtained on Website, but no electronic submissions accepted.
    Amount of award: $500
    Number of awards: 1
    Application deadline: February 1
Contact:
The ARRL Foundation, Inc. Scholarship Program
225 Main Street
Newington, CT 06111
Phone: 860-594-0347
Fax: 860-594-0259
Web: www.arrlf.org

Mary Lou Brown Scholarship

Type of award: Scholarship.
Intended use: For undergraduate or graduate study at accredited 4-year or graduate institution in United States.
Eligibility: Applicant must be residing in Oregon, Montana, Alaska, Idaho or Washington.
Basis for selection: Competition/talent/interest in amateur radio. Applicant must demonstrate financial need.
Application requirements: Transcript, proof of eligibility.
Additional information: Minimum 3.0 GPA with demonstrated interest in promoting Amateur Radio Service. Must be amateur radio operator with general license. Number of awards varies Application may be obtained on Website, but no electronic submissions accepted.
    Amount of award: $2,500
    Application deadline: February 1
Contact:
ARRL Foundation Inc.
225 Main Street
Newington, CT 06111
Phone: 860-594-0397
Fax: 860-594-0259
Web: www.arrlf.org

The Mississippi Scholarship

Type of award: Scholarship.
Intended use: For undergraduate or graduate study at accredited 4-year or graduate institution.
Eligibility: Applicant must be no older than 30. Applicant must be residing in Mississippi.
Basis for selection: Competition/talent/interest in amateur radio. Major/career interest in communications or electronics. Applicant must demonstrate financial need.
Application requirements: Transcript, proof of eligibility.
Additional information: Must be amateur radio operator with any class license. Major may be in other fields related to those listed. Application may be obtained on Website, but no electronic submissions accepted.
    Amount of award: $500
    Number of awards: 1
    Application deadline: February 1
    Total amount awarded: $500
Contact:
ARRL Foundation Inc.
225 Main Street
Newington, CT 06111
Phone: 860-594-0397
Fax: 860-594-0259
Web: www.arrlf.org

The NCDXF Scholarship

Type of award: Scholarship.
Intended use: For undergraduate study at accredited vocational, 2-year, 4-year or graduate institution in United States.
Eligibility: Applicant must be residing in New York.
Basis for selection: Competition/talent/interest in amateur radio.
Application requirements: Transcript.
Additional information: Must be amateur radio operator holding technician license or higher. Applicants demonstrating interest and activity in DX-ing preferred. Application may be obtained on Website, but no electronic submissions accepted.
    Amount of award: $1,500
    Number of awards: 2
    Application deadline: February 1
    Total amount awarded: $3,000
Contact:
The ARRL Foundation, Inc. Scholarship Program
225 Main Street
Newington, CT 06111
Phone: 860-594-0347
Fax: 860-594-0259
Web: www.arrlf.org

The NEMAL Electronics Scholarship

Type of award: Scholarship.
Intended use: For undergraduate study.
Eligibility: Applicant must be residing in Ohio.
Basis for selection: Competition/talent/interest in amateur radio. Major/career interest in electronics or communications. Applicant must demonstrate financial need and service orientation.
Application requirements: Transcript.
Additional information: Major may be in other fields related to those listed. Must have at least 3.0 GPA. Must be amateur radio operator holding general license or higher. Preference given to applicants residing in southeastern U.S. Application may be obtained on Website, but no electronic submissions accepted.
    Amount of award: $1,000
    Number of awards: 1
    Application deadline: February 1
Contact:
The ARRL Foundation, Inc. Scholarship Program
225 Main Street
Newington, CT 06111
Phone: 860-594-0347
Fax: 860-594-0259
Web: www.arrlf.org

The New England FEMARA Scholarship

Type of award: Scholarship.
Intended use: For undergraduate, graduate or non-degree study at accredited 4-year or graduate institution in United States.
Eligibility: Applicant must be residing in Vermont, Connecticut, New Hampshire, Maine, Massachusetts or Rhode Island.
Basis for selection: Competition/talent/interest in amateur radio. Applicant must demonstrate financial need.
Application requirements: Transcript, proof of eligibility.
Additional information: Must be amateur radio operator holding technician license. Number of awards varies. Application may be obtained on Website, but no electronic submissions accepted.
    Amount of award: $1,000
    Application deadline: February 1
Contact:
ARRL Foundation Inc.
225 Main Street
Newington, CT 06111
Phone: 860-594-0397
Fax: 860-594-0259
Web: www.arrlf.org

Paul and Helen L. Grauer Scholarship

Type of award: Scholarship.
Intended use: For undergraduate or graduate study at accredited 4-year or graduate institution in United States.
Eligibility: Applicant must be residing in Iowa, Nebraska, Kansas or Missouri.
Basis for selection: Competition/talent/interest in amateur radio. Major/career interest in communications or electronics. Applicant must demonstrate financial need.
Application requirements: Transcript, proof of eligibility.
Additional information: Must be amateur radio operator with novice license. Major may be in other fields related to those listed. Application may be obtained on Website, but no electronic submissions accepted.
    Amount of award: $1,000
    Number of awards: 1
    Application deadline: February 1
    Total amount awarded: $1,000
Contact:
ARRL Foundation Inc.
225 Main Street
Newington, CT 06111
Phone: 860-594-0397
Fax: 860-594-0259
Web: www.arrlf.org/

The PHD ARA Scholarship

Type of award: Scholarship.
Intended use: For undergraduate, graduate or non-degree study at accredited 4-year or graduate institution in United States.
Eligibility: Applicant must be residing in Iowa, Nebraska, Kansas or Missouri.
Basis for selection: Competition/talent/interest in amateur radio. Major/career interest in journalism; computer/information sciences or engineering, electrical/electronic. Applicant must demonstrate financial need.
Application requirements: Transcript, proof of eligibility.
Additional information: Must be amateur radio operator holding any class license. May be child of deceased radio amateur. Application may be obtained on Website, but no electronic submissions accepted.
    Amount of award: $1,000
    Number of awards: 1
    Application deadline: February 1
    Total amount awarded: $1,000
Contact:
ARRL Foundation Inc.
225 Main Street
Newington, CT 06111
Phone: 860-594-0397
Fax: 860-594-0259
Web: www.arrlf.org

The Richard W. Bendicksen Memorial Scholarship

Type of award: Scholarship.
Intended use: For undergraduate or graduate study at accredited 4-year or graduate institution.
Eligibility: Applicant must be residing in Nebraska.
Basis for selection: Competition/talent/interest in amateur radio.
Application requirements: Transcript.
Additional information: Must be amateur radio operator holding any class of active license. Application may be obtained on Website, but no electronic submissions accepted.
    Amount of award: $1,000
    Number of awards: 1
    Application deadline: February 1

American Radio Relay League (ARRL) Foundation, Inc.: The Richard W. Bendicksen Memorial Scholarship

Contact:
The ARRL Foundation, Inc. Scholarship Program
225 Main Street
Newington, CT 06111
Phone: 860-594-0347
Fax: 860-594-0259
Web: www.arrlf.org

Seth Horen, K1LOM, Memorial Scholarship

Type of award: Scholarship.
Intended use: For undergraduate study at accredited 4-year or graduate institution.
Application requirements: Transcript.
Additional information: Must be amateur radio operator holding any class active license. Application may be obtained on Website, but no electronic submissions accepted.
   Amount of award: $500
   Number of awards: 1
   Application deadline: February 1
Contact:
The ARRL Foundation Scholarship Program
225 Main Street
Newington, CT 06111
Phone: 860-594-0347
Fax: 860-594-0259
Web: www.arrlf.org

The Six Meter Club of Chicago Scholarship

Type of award: Scholarship.
Intended use: For undergraduate study at accredited vocational, 2-year or 4-year institution in United States.
Eligibility: Applicant must be residing in Illinois.
Basis for selection: Competition/talent/interest in amateur radio. Applicant must demonstrate financial need.
Application requirements: Transcript, proof of eligibility.
Additional information: Must be amateur radio operator holding any class license. Award open to remaining ARRL Central Division States (IN and WI) if no qualified Illinois student identified. Application may be obtained on Website, but no electronic submissions accepted.
   Amount of award: $500
   Number of awards: 1
   Application deadline: February 1
   Total amount awarded: $500
Contact:
ARRL Foundation Inc.
225 Main Street
Newington, CT 06111
Phone: 860-594-0397
Fax: 860-594-0259
Web: www.arrlf.org

Tom and Judith Comstock Scholarship

Type of award: Scholarship.
Intended use: For undergraduate study at accredited 2-year or 4-year institution in United States.
Eligibility: Applicant must be high school senior. Applicant must be residing in Oklahoma or Texas.
Basis for selection: Competition/talent/interest in amateur radio. Applicant must demonstrate financial need.
Application requirements: Transcript, proof of eligibility.

Additional information: Must be amateur radio operator holding any class license. Application may be obtained on Website, but no electronic submissions accepted.
   Amount of award: $2,000
   Number of awards: 1
   Application deadline: February 1
   Total amount awarded: $2,000
Contact:
ARRL Foundation Inc.
225 Main Street
Newington, CT 06111
Phone: 860-594-0397
Fax: 860-594-0259
Web: www.arrlf.org

William R. Goldfarb Memorial Scholarship

Type of award: Scholarship, renewable.
Intended use: For undergraduate study at accredited 4-year institution.
Eligibility: Applicant must be high school senior.
Basis for selection: Competition/talent/interest in amateur radio. Major/career interest in business; engineering; science, general; computer/information sciences; health-related professions or nursing. Applicant must demonstrate financial need.
Application requirements: Recommendations, transcript. FAFSA, Student Aid Report.
Additional information: Must be amateur radio operator holding any class license. Application may be obtained on Website, but no electronic submissions accepted.
   Amount of award: $10,000
   Number of awards: 1
   Application deadline: February 1
Contact:
The ARRL Foundation, Inc. Scholarship Program
225 Main Street
Newington, CT 06111
Phone: 860-594-0347
Fax: 860-594-0259
Web: www.arrlf.org

Yankee Clipper Contest Club, Inc. Youth Scholarship

Type of award: Scholarship.
Intended use: For undergraduate study at accredited 2-year or 4-year institution.
Eligibility: Applicant must be residing in New Jersey.
Basis for selection: Competition/talent/interest in amateur radio.
Application requirements: Transcript.
Additional information: Must be amateur radio operator holding general license or higher. Must be resident of or college/university student in area within 175-mile radius of YCCC center in Erving, MA. This includes MA; RI; CT; Long Island, NY; most of VT and NH; and parts of ME, eastern NY, and northeastern PA and NJ. Application may be obtained on Website, but no electronic submissions accepted.
   Amount of award: $1,000
   Number of awards: 1
   Application deadline: February 1

Contact:
The ARRL Foundation, Inc. Scholarship Program
225 Main Street
Newington, CT 06111
Phone: 860-594-0347
Fax: 860-594-0259
Web: www.arrlf.org

The Yasme Foundation Scholarship

Type of award: Scholarship.
Intended use: For undergraduate or graduate study at accredited 4-year or graduate institution.
Basis for selection: Competition/talent/interest in amateur radio. Major/career interest in science, general or engineering. Applicant must demonstrate service orientation.
Application requirements: Transcript.
Additional information: Must be amateur radio operator holding any class of active license. Two awards renewable up to three years or until undergraduate completion. Preference given to high school applicants in top 5 to 10 percent of class or college students in top 10 percent of class. Participation in local amateur radio club strongly preferred. Application may be obtained on Website, but no electronic submissions accepted.
   Amount of award: $2,000
   Number of awards: 5
   Application deadline: February 1
Contact:
The ARRL Foundation, Inc. Scholarship Program
225 Main Street
Newington, CT 06111
Phone: 860-594-0347
Fax: 860-594-0259
Web: www.arrlf.org

The Zachary Taylor Stevens Memorial Scholarship

Type of award: Scholarship.
Intended use: For undergraduate study at accredited vocational, 2-year, 4-year or graduate institution.
Eligibility: Applicant must be residing in Michigan, Ohio or West Virginia.
Basis for selection: Competition/talent/interest in amateur radio.
Application requirements: Transcript.
Additional information: Must be amateur radio operator holding technician license. Preference given to applicants residing in amateur radio call areas in MI, OH and WV. Application may be obtained on Website, but no electronic submissions accepted.
   Amount of award: $750
   Number of awards: 1
   Application deadline: February 1
Contact:
The ARRL Foundation, Inc. Scholarship Program
225 Main Street
Newington, CT 06111
Phone: 860-594-0347
Fax: 860-594-0259
Web: www.arrlf.org

"You've Got a Friend in Pennsylvania"

Type of award: Scholarship.
Intended use: For undergraduate, graduate or non-degree study at accredited 4-year or graduate institution.
Eligibility: Applicant or parent must be member/participant of American Radio Relay League.
Basis for selection: Competition/talent/interest in amateur radio. Applicant must demonstrate financial need.
Application requirements: Transcript, proof of eligibility.
Additional information: Resident of PA given preference. Must be amateur radio operator with general license. Must be member of ARRL. Application may be obtained from Website, but no electronic submissions accepted.
   Amount of award: $2,000
   Number of awards: 1
   Application deadline: February 1
   Total amount awarded: $2,000
Contact:
ARRL Foundation Inc.
225 Main Street
Newington, CT 06111
Phone: 860-594-0397
Fax: 860-594-0259
Web: www.arrlf.org

American Respiratory Care Foundation

Jimmy A. Young Memorial Education Recognition Award

Type of award: Scholarship, renewable.
Intended use: For sophomore, junior or senior study at accredited vocational, 2-year or 4-year institution.
Eligibility: Applicant must be Alaskan native, Asian American, African American, Mexican American, Hispanic American, Puerto Rican, American Indian or Native Hawaiian/Pacific Islander.
Basis for selection: Competition/talent/interest in research paper. Major/career interest in respiratory therapy. Applicant must demonstrate high academic achievement.
Application requirements: Recommendations, transcript, nomination by school or program representative. Student may initiate request for sponsorship in absence of nomination. Six copies of original referenced paper on some aspect of respiratory care. Letter of enrollment verification.
Additional information: Must be enrolled in respiratory care program. Minimum 3.0 GPA required. Award includes airfare, one night lodging, and registration for AARC International Respiratory Congress. Application and deadline available on Website. Application must be notarized.
   Amount of award: $1,000
   Number of awards: 1
   Number of applicants: 50
   Notification begins: September 15
   Total amount awarded: $1,000
Contact:
American Respiratory Care Foundation
Attn: Education Recognition Award
9425 North MacArthur Blvd., Suite 100
Irving, TX 75063-4706
Phone: 972-243-2272
Fax: 972-484-2720
Web: www.arcfoundation.org/awards

Morton B. Duggan, Jr. Memorial Education Recognition Award

Type of award: Scholarship, renewable.
Intended use: For sophomore, junior or senior study at accredited 2-year or 4-year institution in United States.
Basis for selection: Competition/talent/interest in research paper. Major/career interest in respiratory therapy. Applicant must demonstrate high academic achievement.
Application requirements: Recommendations, transcript. Six copies of original paper on some aspect of respiratory care. Letter of enrollment verification.
Additional information: Preference given to applicants from Georgia and South Carolina. Must be student in respiratory care training program with at least 3.0 GPA. Award includes airfare, one night lodging, and registration for the AARC International Respiratory Congress. Application and deadline available on Website. Application must be notarized.

Amount of award:	$1,000
Number of awards:	1
Number of applicants:	50
Notification begins:	September 15

Contact:
American Respiratory Care Foundation
Attn: Education Recogniton Award
9425 North MacArthur Blvd, Suite 100
Irving, TX 75063-4706
Phone: 972-243-2272
Fax: 972-484-2720
Web: www.arcfoundation.org/awards

NBRC/AMP Robert M. Lawrence, MD Education Recognition Award

Type of award: Scholarship.
Intended use: For full-time junior or senior study at accredited 4-year institution in United States.
Basis for selection: Competition/talent/interest in research paper. Major/career interest in respiratory therapy. Applicant must demonstrate high academic achievement and leadership.
Application requirements: Recommendations, transcript. Six copies each of original, referenced paper on some aspect of respiratory care and original essay of at least 1,200 words describing how award will help applicant reach degree and ultimate goals of health care leadership. Letter of enrollment verification.
Additional information: Must be student in bachelor-level respiratory care program. Must have at least 3.0 GPA. Award includes airfare, one night lodging, and registration for AARC International Respiratory Congress. Application and deadline on Website. Application must be notarized.

Amount of award:	$2,500
Number of awards:	1
Number of applicants:	50
Notification begins:	September 15

Contact:
American Respiratory Care Foundation
Attn: Education Recognition Award
9425 North MacArthur Blvd., Suite 100
Irving, TX 75063-4706
Phone: 972-243-2272
Fax: 972-484-2720
Web: www.arcfoundation.org/awards

NBRC/AMP William W. Burgin, Jr. MD Education Recognition Award

Type of award: Scholarship.
Intended use: For full-time sophomore study at accredited 2-year institution in United States.
Basis for selection: Competition/talent/interest in research paper. Major/career interest in respiratory therapy. Applicant must demonstrate high academic achievement and leadership.
Application requirements: Recommendations, transcript, nomination by school or educational program. May also apply without nomination. Six copies each of original referenced paper on some aspect of respiratory care and original essay of at least 1,200 words describing how award will help applicant reach degree and ultimate health care leadership goals. Letter of enrollment verification.
Additional information: Must be student in associate's respiratory therapy program. Must have at least 3.0 GPA. Award includes one night lodging and registration for AARC International Respiratory Congress. Application and deadline available on Website. Application must be notarized.

Amount of award:	$2,500
Number of awards:	1
Number of applicants:	10
Notification begins:	September 15

Contact:
American Respiratory Care Foundation
Attn: Education Recognition Award
9425 North MacArthur Blvd., Suite 100
Irving, TX 75063-4706
Phone: 972-243-2272
Fax: 972-484-2720
Web: www.arcfoundation.org/awards

American Society for Enology and Viticulture

Enology and Viticulture Scholarship

Type of award: Scholarship, renewable.
Intended use: For full-time junior, senior, master's or doctoral study at accredited 4-year or graduate institution.
Eligibility: Applicant must be U.S. citizen, permanent resident or resident of Canada or Mexico.
Basis for selection: Major/career interest in agriculture; food science/technology or horticulture. Applicant must demonstrate financial need and high academic achievement.
Application requirements: Essay, transcript, proof of eligibility. Student questionnaire; two letters of recommendation, at least one from academic advisor or recent instructor; written statement of intent relating to future career in wine or grape industry, interests in wine or grape industry or in related research; list of planned courses for the coming year.
Additional information: Minimum 3.0 GPA for undergraduate, 3.2 GPA for graduate students. Incomplete applications are not considered. Applicants must be enrolled in major or graduate program emphasizing enology or viticulture, or in curriculum emphasizing science basic to wine and grape industry. Awards vary. Previous applicants and recipients eligible to reapply each year in open competition with new applicants.

Amount of award:	$500-$5,000
Number of awards:	40
Application deadline:	March 1
Notification begins:	May 31
Total amount awarded:	$65,000

Contact:
American Society for Enology and Viticulture
P.O. Box 1855
Davis, CA 95617-1855
Phone: 530-753-3142
Fax: 530-753-3318
Web: www.asev.org

American Society for Microbiology

Microbiology Undergraduate Research Fellowship (MURF)

Type of award: Research grant.
Intended use: For full-time undergraduate study.
Eligibility: Applicant must be Alaskan native, African American, Mexican American, Hispanic American, Puerto Rican, American Indian or Native Hawaiian/Pacific Islander. Applicant must be U.S. citizen or permanent resident.
Basis for selection: Major/career interest in microbiology. Applicant must demonstrate high academic achievement, leadership and seriousness of purpose.
Application requirements: Recommendations, transcript. Personal statement.
Additional information: Applicant must demonstrate ability to pursue graduate career (PhD) in microbiology. Program provides opportunity for historically excluded and underrepresented undergraduate students to conduct summer research at selected institution for 10 to 12 weeks and present research results at ASM General Meeting and at Annual Biomedical Research Conference for Minority Students (ABRCMS) the following year. Fellowship offers $3,500 stipend plus housing expenses, travel, and one-year student membership to ASM. See Website for application and more details.

Amount of award:	$3,500-$5,850
Number of awards:	10
Number of applicants:	50
Application deadline:	February 1

Contact:
American Society for Microbiology
Microbiology Undergraduate Fellowship
1752 N Street NW
Washington, DC 20036
Phone: 202-942-9283
Fax: 202-942-9329
Web: www.asm.org/education

Undergraduate Research Fellowship (URF)

Type of award: Research grant.
Intended use: For full-time undergraduate study in United States.
Eligibility: Applicant must be U.S. citizen or permanent resident.
Basis for selection: Major/career interest in microbiology. Applicant must demonstrate high academic achievement and seriousness of purpose.
Application requirements: Recommendations, transcript. Program requires joint online application from student applicant and faculty member. Faculty member must have ongoing research project.
Additional information: Applicant must demonstrate strong interest to pursue graduate career (Ph.D. or M.D./Ph.D.) in microbiology. Students conduct research in summer and present results at ASM General Meeting the following year. Fellowship offers $4,000 stipend, travel funding and one-year student membership to ASM. Applicant must have ASM member at institution willing to serve as mentor. Students may not receive financial support for research from other scientific organization during fellowship. Faculty member's department head or dean must endorse project. Number of awards varies. See Website for application.

Amount of award:	$4,000-$5,000
Number of awards:	39
Number of applicants:	74
Application deadline:	February 1

Contact:
American Society for Microbiology
Undergraduate Research Fellowship
1752 N Street NW
Washington, DC 20036
Phone: 202-942-9283
Fax: 202-942-9329
Web: www.asm.org/education

American Society of Civil Engineers

Eugene C. Figg Jr. Civil Engineering Scholarship

Type of award: Scholarship.
Intended use: For junior or senior study. Designated institutions: ABET-accredited institutions.
Eligibility: Applicant or parent must be member/participant of American Society of Civil Engineers. Applicant must be U.S. citizen.
Basis for selection: Major/career interest in engineering, civil. Applicant must demonstrate financial need and high academic achievement.
Application requirements: Essay, transcript. Two letters of recommendation, resume and two 1,000-word essays.
Additional information: Must have passion for bridges. Visit Website for deadline.

Amount of award:	$3,000
Number of awards:	1
Total amount awarded:	$3,000

Contact:
American Society of Civil Engineers
Attn: Student Services
1801 Alexander Bell Drive
Reston, VA 20191-4400
Phone: 800-548-ASCE ext. 6106
Fax: 703-295-6222
Web: www.asce.org/student/scholarships.html

Freeman Fellowship

Type of award: Research grant.
Intended use: For undergraduate or graduate study in or outside United States or Canada.
Eligibility: Applicant or parent must be member/participant of American Society of Civil Engineers.
Basis for selection: Major/career interest in engineering, civil.
Application requirements: Recommendations, essay, transcript, research proposal. Resume. Detailed financial statement indicating how fellowship will finance applicant's research. Statement from institution where research will be conducted. Minimum of two recommendation letters; one must be from faculty member. Personal essay no longer than 500 words on why the applicant should receive the fellowship.
Additional information: Grants are made toward expenses for experiments, observations, and compilations to discover new and accurate data that will be useful in engineering. Grant may be in form of prize for most useful paper relating to science/art of hydraulic construction. Travel scholarships available to ASCE members under 45, in recognition of achievement or promise. Award is to be used for expenses for research and experiments. Visit Website for application and more information.

Amount of award:	$2,000-$5,000
Notification begins:	May 1

Contact:
American Society of Engineers
Attention: Student Services
1801 Alexander Bell Drive
Reston, VA 20191-4440
Phone: 800-548-ASCE ext. 6106
Web: www.asce.org/student/scholarships.html

Samuel Fletcher Tapman ASCE Student Chapter Scholarship

Type of award: Scholarship, renewable.
Intended use: For undergraduate study at accredited postsecondary institution.
Eligibility: Applicant or parent must be member/participant of American Society of Civil Engineers.
Basis for selection: Major/career interest in engineering, civil. Applicant must demonstrate financial need, high academic achievement, depth of character and leadership.
Application requirements: Recommendations, essay, transcript, proof of eligibility. Resume. Detailed financial statement indicating how scholarship will finance applicant's education. Minimum of two recommendation letters: one from student chapter/club faculty advisor; one from other faculty member. Personal essay no longer than 500 words on why the applicant wants to become a civil engineer.
Additional information: Any undergraduate who is ASCE student chapter member and ASCE national student member may apply for this scholarship, but must be in good standing at time of application. Membership applications may be submitted with scholarship application. Award is for undergraduate tuition. Visit Website for application and more information.

Amount of award:	$2,000
Number of awards:	12
Notification begins:	May 1
Total amount awarded:	$24,000

Contact:
American Society of Civil Engineers
Attention: Student Services
1801 Alexander Bell Drive
Reston, VA 20191-4440
Phone: 800-548-ASCE
Web: www.asce.org/student/scholarships.html

American Society of Heating, Refrigerating and Air-Conditioning Engineers

Alwin B. Newton Scholarship

Type of award: Scholarship, renewable.
Intended use: For full-time undergraduate study at 4-year institution. Designated institutions: Schools with ABET-accredited programs.
Basis for selection: Major/career interest in engineering or air conditioning/heating/refrigeration technology. Applicant must demonstrate financial need, depth of character and leadership.
Application requirements: Recommendations, transcript.
Additional information: For engineering students considering service to heating/ventilation/air-conditioning (HVAC) and/or refrigeration profession. Minimum 3.0 GPA.

Amount of award:	$3,000
Number of awards:	1
Application deadline:	December 1

Contact:
ASHRAE-Scholarship Program
1791 Tullie Circle NE
Atlanta, GA 30329-2305
Phone: 404-636-8400
Fax: 404-321-5478
Web: www.ashrae.org/students/page/1271

American Society of Heating, Refrigerating, and Air-Conditioning Engineers, Inc.

ASHRAE J. Richard Mehalick Scholarship

Type of award: Research grant, renewable.
Intended use: For full-time undergraduate study in United States. Designated institutions: University of Pittsburgh.
Eligibility: Applicant must be U.S. citizen residing in Pennsylvania.
Basis for selection: Major/career interest in engineering, mechanical or air conditioning/heating/refrigeration technology. Applicant must demonstrate financial need, depth of character and leadership.
Application requirements: Recommendations, transcript.
Additional information: Must have minimum 3.0 GPA. For mechanical engineering students considering service to heating/

ventilation/air-conditioning (HVAC) and/or refrigeration profession.
- **Number of awards:** 1
- **Application deadline:** December 1
- **Total amount awarded:** $3,000

Contact:
ASHRAE - Scholarship Program
1791 Tullie Circle NE
Atlanta, GA 30329
Phone: 404-636-8400
Fax: 404-312-5478
Web: www.ashrae.org/students/page/1271

ASHRAE Memorial Scholarship

Type of award: Scholarship, renewable.
Intended use: For full-time undergraduate study at 4-year institution. Designated institutions: Schools with ABET-accredited programs.
Basis for selection: Major/career interest in engineering or air conditioning/heating/refrigeration technology. Applicant must demonstrate financial need, depth of character and leadership.
Application requirements: Recommendations, transcript.
Additional information: For engineering students considering service to heating/ventilation/air-conditioning (HVAC) and/or refrigeration profession. Minimum 3.0 GPA.
- **Amount of award:** $3,000
- **Number of awards:** 1
- **Application deadline:** December 1

Contact:
ASHRAE-Scholarship Program
1791 Tullie Circle NE
Atlanta, GA 30329-2305
Phone: 404-636-8400
Fax: 404-321-5478
Web: www.ashrae.org/students/page/1271

ASHRAE Region IV Benny Bootle Scholarship

Type of award: Scholarship, renewable.
Intended use: For full-time undergraduate study. Designated institutions: Schools with NAAB or ABET-accredited program located within the geographic boundaries of ASHRAE's Region IV, currently NC, SC, and GA.
Basis for selection: Major/career interest in engineering; architecture or air conditioning/heating/refrigeration technology. Applicant must demonstrate financial need, high academic achievement, depth of character and leadership.
Application requirements: Recommendations, transcript.
Additional information: Minimum 3.0 GPA. For engineering or architecture students considering service to heating/ventilation/air-conditioning (HVAC) and/or refrigeration profession. Visit www.abet.org and www.naab.org for list of ABET- and NAAB-accredited programs within Region IV.
- **Amount of award:** $3,000
- **Number of awards:** 1
- **Application deadline:** December 1
- **Total amount awarded:** $3,000

Contact:
ASHRAE - Scholarship Programs
1791 Tullie Circle, NE
Atlanta, GA 30329-2305
Phone: 404-636-8400
Fax: 404-321-5478
Web: www.ashrae.org/students/page/1271

ASHRAE Region VIII Scholarship

Type of award: Scholarship, renewable.
Intended use: For full-time undergraduate study. Designated institutions: Schools with ABET-accredited programs located within the geographic boundaries of ASHRAE's Region VIII, currently Arkansas, Oklahoma, Mexico, and parts of Louisiana and Texas.
Basis for selection: Major/career interest in engineering or air conditioning/heating/refrigeration technology. Applicant must demonstrate financial need, high academic achievement, depth of character and leadership.
Application requirements: Recommendations, transcript.
Additional information: Minimum 3.0 GPA. For engineering students considering service to heating/ventilation/air-conditioning (HVAC) and/or refrigeration profession. Contact ASHRAE for information regarding Region VIII. Visit www.abet.org for ABET-accredited programs within the region.
- **Amount of award:** $3,000
- **Number of awards:** 1
- **Application deadline:** December 1
- **Total amount awarded:** $3,000

Contact:
ASHRAE - Scholarship Program
1791 Tullie Circle, NE
Atlanta, GA 30329-2305
Phone: 404-636-8400
Fax: 404-321-5478
Web: www.ashrae.org/students/page/1271

ASHRAE Scholarships

Type of award: Scholarship, renewable.
Intended use: For full-time undergraduate study at 4-year institution. Designated institutions: Schools with ABET-accredited programs.
Basis for selection: Major/career interest in engineering or air conditioning/heating/refrigeration technology. Applicant must demonstrate financial need, depth of character and leadership.
Application requirements: Recommendations, transcript.
Additional information: For engineering students considering service to heating/ventilation/air-conditioning (HVAC) and/or refrigeration profession. Minimum 3.0 GPA.
- **Amount of award:** $3,000
- **Number of awards:** 2
- **Application deadline:** December 1

Contact:
ASHRAE-Scholarship Program
1791 Tullie Circle NE
Atlanta, GA 30329-2305
Phone: 404-636-8400
Fax: 404-321-5478
Web: www.ashrae.org/students/page/1271

Associate Degree Engineering Technology Scholarship

Type of award: Scholarship, renewable.
Intended use: For full-time undergraduate study at accredited 2-year institution.
Basis for selection: Major/career interest in engineering or air conditioning/heating/refrigeration technology. Applicant must demonstrate financial need, high academic achievement, depth of character and leadership.
Application requirements: Recommendations, transcript.
Additional information: For students pursuing associate's degree in engineering technology and intending to pursue career

American Society of Heating, Refrigerating, and Air-Conditioning Engineers, Inc.: Associate Degree Engineering Technology Scholarship

in heating/ventilation/air conditioning (HVAC) and/or refrigeration. Minimum 3.0 GPA.
- Amount of award: $3,000
- Number of awards: 1
- Application deadline: May 1
- Total amount awarded: $3,000

Contact:
ASHRAE - Scholarship Program
1791 Tullie Circle, NE
Atlanta, GA 30329-2305
Phone: 404-636-8400
Fax: 404-321-5478
Web: www.ashrae.org/students/page/1271

Bachelor Degree Engineering Technology Scholarship

Type of award: Scholarship, renewable.
Intended use: For full-time undergraduate study at accredited 4-year institution. Designated institutions: Schools with ABET-accredited programs.
Basis for selection: Major/career interest in engineering or air conditioning/heating/refrigeration technology. Applicant must demonstrate financial need, high academic achievement, depth of character and leadership.
Application requirements: Recommendations, transcript.
Additional information: For students pursuing bachelor's degree in engineering technology and intending to pursue career in heating/ventilation/air-conditioning (HVAC) and/or refrigeration. Minimum 3.0 GPA.
- Amount of award: $3,000
- Number of awards: 1
- Application deadline: May 1
- Total amount awarded: $3,000

Contact:
ASHRAE - Scholarship Program
1791 Tullie Circle, NE
Atlanta, GA 30329-2305
Phone: 404-636-8400
Fax: 404-321-5478
Web: www.ashrae.org/students/page/1271

Duane Hanson Scholarship

Type of award: Scholarship, renewable.
Intended use: For full-time undergraduate study at 4-year institution. Designated institutions: Schools with ABET-accredited programs.
Basis for selection: Major/career interest in engineering or air conditioning/heating/refrigeration technology. Applicant must demonstrate financial need, depth of character and leadership.
Application requirements: Recommendations, transcript.
Additional information: For engineering students considering service to heating/ventilation/air-conditioning (HVAC) and/or refrigeration profession. Minimum 3.0 GPA.
- Amount of award: $3,000
- Number of awards: 1
- Application deadline: December 1

Contact:
ASHRAE-Scholarship Program
1791 Tullie Circle NE
Atlanta, GA 30329-2305
Phone: 404-636-8400
Fax: 404-321-5478
Web: www.ashrae.org/students/page/1271

Frank M. Coda Scholarship

Type of award: Scholarship, renewable.
Intended use: For full-time undergraduate study at 4-year institution. Designated institutions: Schools with ABET-accredited programs.
Basis for selection: Major/career interest in engineering or air conditioning/heating/refrigeration technology. Applicant must demonstrate financial need, depth of character and leadership.
Application requirements: Recommendations, transcript.
Additional information: For engineering students considering service to heating/ventilation/air-conditioning (HVAC) and/or refrigeration profession. Minimum 3.0 GPA.
- Amount of award: $5,000
- Number of awards: 1
- Application deadline: December 1

Contact:
ASHRAE-Scholarship Program
1791 Tullie Circle NE
Atlanta, GA 30329-2305
Phone: 404-636-2305
Fax: 404-321-5478
Web: www.ashrae.org/students/page/1271

Henry Adams Scholarship

Type of award: Scholarship, renewable.
Intended use: For full-time undergraduate study at 4-year institution. Designated institutions: Schools with ABET-accredited programs.
Basis for selection: Major/career interest in engineering or air conditioning/heating/refrigeration technology. Applicant must demonstrate financial need, depth of character and leadership.
Application requirements: Recommendations, transcript.
Additional information: For engineering students considering service to heating/ventilation/air-conditioning (HVAC) and/or refrigeration profession. Minimum 3.0 GPA.
- Amount of award: $3,000
- Number of awards: 1
- Application deadline: December 1

Contact:
ASHRAE-Scholarship Program
1791 Tullie Circle NE
Atlanta, GA 30329-2305
Phone: 404-636-8400
Fax: 404-321-5478
Web: www.ashrae.org/students/page/1271

Reuben Trane Scholarships

Type of award: Scholarship.
Intended use: For full-time junior or senior study at accredited 4-year institution. Designated institutions: Schools with ABET-accredited programs.
Basis for selection: Major/career interest in air conditioning/heating/refrigeration technology or engineering. Applicant must demonstrate financial need, high academic achievement, depth of character and leadership.
Application requirements: Recommendations, transcript.
Additional information: Minimum 3.0 GPA. Award is for two years, for engineering students with two years of undergraduate study remaining. Must be considering service to heating/ventilation/air-conditioning (HVAC) and/or refrigeration profession.
- Amount of award: $10,000
- Number of awards: 4
- Application deadline: December 1
- Total amount awarded: $40,000

Contact:
ASHRAE - Scholarship Program
1791 Tullie Circle NE
Atlanta, GA 30329-2305
Phone: 404-636-8400
Fax: 404-321-5478
Web: www.ashrae.org/students/page/1271

Willis H. Carrier Scholarships

Type of award: Scholarship, renewable.
Intended use: For full-time undergraduate study at 4-year institution. Designated institutions: ABET-accredited institutions.
Basis for selection: Major/career interest in engineering or air conditioning/heating/refrigeration technology. Applicant must demonstrate financial need, depth of character and leadership.
Application requirements: Recommendations, transcript.
Additional information: For engineering students considering service to heating/ventilation/air-conditioning (HVAC) and/or refrigeration profession. Minimum 3.0 GPA.
    Amount of award: $10,000
    Number of awards: 2
    Application deadline: December 1
Contact:
ASHRAE-Scholarship Program
1791 Tullie Circle NE
Atlanta, GA 30329-2305
Phone: 404-636-8400
Fax: 404-321-5478
Web: www.ashrae.org/students/page/1271

American Society of Interior Designers Foundation

Joel Polsky Academic Achievement Award

Type of award: Scholarship.
Intended use: For undergraduate or graduate study.
Basis for selection: Competition/talent/interest in research paper, based on content, breadth of material, comprehensive coverage of topic, innovative subject matter, bibliography and references. Major/career interest in interior design or architecture. Applicant must demonstrate high academic achievement.
Additional information: Award to recognize outstanding interior design research or thesis project addressing topics such as educational research, behavioral sciences, business practices, design process, theory or other technical subjects.
    Amount of award: $1,000
    Number of awards: 1
    Application deadline: April 30
    Total amount awarded: $1,000
Contact:
American Society of Interior Designers Foundation, Inc.
Joel Polsky Academic Achievement Award
608 Massachusetts Avenue, NE
Washington, DC 20002-6006
Phone: 202-546-3480
Fax: 202-546-3240
Web: www.asid.org/asidfoundation/projects

Yale R. Burge Competition

Type of award: Scholarship.
Intended use: For senior study at postsecondary institution.
Basis for selection: Competition/talent/interest in visual arts. Major/career interest in interior design.
Application requirements: Portfolio. At least eight but no more than twelve portfolio components submitted on slides, as PowerPoint presentation, or HTML saved on CD-ROM or floppy disk.
Additional information: Open to all interior design students in their final year of at least three-year undergraduate program. Awardees chosen based on quality of portfolio: presentation, design and planning, and conceptual creativity. Visit Website for application and more information.
    Amount of award: $750
    Number of awards: 1
    Application deadline: April 30
Contact:
ASID Foundation, Inc.
Yale R. Burge Competition
608 Massachusetts Avenue, NE
Washington, DC 20002-6006
Phone: 202-546-3480
Web: www.asid.org/asidfoundation/projects

American Society of Mechanical Engineers

American Society of Mechanical Engineers Foundation Scholarship

Type of award: Scholarship.
Intended use: For full-time sophomore, junior or senior study at accredited 4-year or graduate institution.
Eligibility: Applicant or parent must be member/participant of American Society of Mechanical Engineers.
Basis for selection: Major/career interest in engineering, mechanical. Applicant must demonstrate high academic achievement, depth of character and leadership.
Application requirements: Recommendations, essay, transcript.
Additional information: Applicant must be student member of ASME, enrolled in mechanical engineering or related field. Application is online.
    Amount of award: $1,500
    Number of awards: 16
    Application deadline: March 15
    Notification begins: June 15
    Total amount awarded: $24,000
Contact:
American Society of Mechanical Engineers
Three Park Avenue
New York, NY 10016-5990
Phone: 212-591-8131
Fax: 212-591-7856
Web: www.asme.org/education/college/financialaid

ASME/FIRST Robotics Competition Scholarship

Type of award: Scholarship.

American Society of Mechanical Engineers: ASME/FIRST Robotics Competition Scholarship

Intended use: For full-time freshman study at accredited 4-year institution. Designated institutions: Schools with ABET-accredited programs.
Eligibility: Applicant must be high school senior. Applicant must be U.S. citizen.
Basis for selection: Major/career interest in engineering, mechanical. Applicant must demonstrate financial need, high academic achievement and leadership.
Application requirements: Transcript, proof of eligibility, nomination by ASME member and student member active with FIRST.
Additional information: Applications are typically due on the first Monday in March. Applicant must be active on FIRST team. Students on same team must be nominated by separate ASME members. Applicant may also enroll in mechanical engineering technology program. Applicant must have an outstanding academic record. Recipient announced at FIRST National Championship. Visit Website for more information and to download forms.
- **Amount of award:** $5,000
- **Number of awards:** 10
- **Application deadline:** March 15
- **Notification begins:** April 1

Contact:
American Society of Mechanical Engineers
Three Park Avenue
New York, NY 10016-5990
Phone: 212-591-8131
Fax: 212-591-7856
Web: www.asme.org/education/college/financialaid

Frank William and Dorothy Given Miller Mechanical Engineering Scholarship

Type of award: Scholarship.
Intended use: For full-time sophomore, junior or senior study at accredited 4-year institution. Designated institutions: Schools with ABET-accredited programs.
Eligibility: Applicant or parent must be member/participant of American Society of Mechanical Engineers.
Basis for selection: Major/career interest in engineering, mechanical. Applicant must demonstrate high academic achievement, depth of character and leadership.
Application requirements: Recommendations, essay, transcript.
Additional information: Applicant must be member of ASME. Application is online. Applicant must be North American resident.
- **Amount of award:** $1,500
- **Number of awards:** 2
- **Application deadline:** March 15
- **Notification begins:** June 15
- **Total amount awarded:** $3,000

Contact:
American Society of Mechanical Engineers
Three Park Avenue
New York, NY 10016-5990
Phone: 212-591-8131
Fax: 212-591-7856
Web: www.asme.org/education/college/financialaid

F.W. "Beich" Beichley Scholarship

Type of award: Scholarship.
Intended use: For full-time junior or senior study.
Eligibility: Applicant or parent must be member/participant of American Society of Mechanical Engineers.
Basis for selection: Major/career interest in engineering, mechanical. Applicant must demonstrate financial need, high academic achievement, depth of character and leadership.
Application requirements: Recommendations, essay, transcript.
Additional information: Applicant must be member of ASME. Application is online.
- **Amount of award:** $2,000
- **Number of awards:** 1
- **Application deadline:** March 15
- **Notification begins:** June 15
- **Total amount awarded:** $2,000

Contact:
American Society of Mechanical Engineers
Three Park Avenue
New York, NY 10016-5990
Phone: 212-591-8131
Fax: 212-591-7856
Web: www.asme.org/education/college/financialaid

Garland Duncan Mechanical Engineering Scholarship

Type of award: Scholarship.
Intended use: For full-time junior or senior study at accredited 4-year institution. Designated institutions: Schools with ABET-accredited programs.
Eligibility: Applicant or parent must be member/participant of American Society of Mechanical Engineers.
Basis for selection: Major/career interest in engineering, mechanical. Applicant must demonstrate financial need, high academic achievement, depth of character and leadership.
Application requirements: Recommendations, essay, transcript.
Additional information: Applicant must be member of ASME. Application is online.
- **Amount of award:** $3,500
- **Number of awards:** 2
- **Application deadline:** March 15
- **Notification begins:** June 15
- **Total amount awarded:** $7,000

Contact:
American Society of Mechanical Engineers
Three Park Avenue
New York, NY 10016-5990
Phone: 212-591-8131
Fax: 212-591-7856
Web: www.asme.org/education/college/financialaid

International Gas Turbine Institute Scholarship

Type of award: Scholarship.
Intended use: Designated institutions: Schools with ABET-accredited programs.
Eligibility: Applicant or parent must be member/participant of American Society of Mechanical Engineers.
Additional information: Applicants must be ASME student members in good standing at the time of application. To join ASME, please visit https://members.asme.org/catalog/joinasme.cfm.
- **Amount of award:** $4,000
- **Number of awards:** 1
- **Application deadline:** March 15
- **Total amount awarded:** $4,000

Contact:
American Society of Mechanical Engineers
Three Park Avenue
New York, NY 10016-5990
Phone: 212-591-8131
Fax: 212-591-7856
Web: www.asme.org/education/college/financialaid/details_requirements.cfm

John and Elsa Gracik Mechanical Engineering Scholarship

Type of award: Scholarship.
Intended use: For full-time sophomore, junior or senior study at accredited 4-year institution. Designated institutions: Schools with ABET-accredited programs.
Eligibility: Applicant or parent must be member/participant of American Society of Mechanical Engineers. Applicant must be U.S. citizen.
Basis for selection: Major/career interest in engineering, mechanical. Applicant must demonstrate financial need, high academic achievement, depth of character and leadership.
Application requirements: Recommendations, essay, transcript, nomination by department head.
Additional information: Applicant must be member of ASME. Application is online.
    Amount of award: $1,500
    Number of awards: 18
    Application deadline: March 15
    Notification begins: June 15
    Total amount awarded: $27,000
Contact:
American Society of Mechanical Engineers
Three Park Avenue
New York, NY 10016-5990
Phone: 212-591-8131
Fax: 212-591-7856
Web: www.asme.org/education/college/financialaid

Kenneth Andrew Roe Mechanical Engineering Scholarship

Type of award: Scholarship.
Intended use: For full-time junior or senior study at accredited 4-year institution. Designated institutions: Schools with ABET-accredited program or equivalent.
Eligibility: Applicant or parent must be member/participant of American Society of Mechanical Engineers. Applicant must be U.S. citizen, permanent resident or resident of Canada or Mexico.
Basis for selection: Major/career interest in engineering, mechanical. Applicant must demonstrate financial need, high academic achievement, depth of character and leadership.
Application requirements: Recommendations, essay, transcript.
Additional information: Applicant must be member of ASME. Application is online.
    Amount of award: $10,000
    Number of awards: 1
    Application deadline: March 15
    Notification begins: June 15
    Total amount awarded: $10,000

Contact:
American Society of Mechanical Engineers
Three Park Avenue
New York, NY 10016-5990
Phone: 212-591-8131
Fax: 212-591-7856
Web: www.asme.org/education/college/financialaid

Melvin R. Green Scholarship

Type of award: Scholarship.
Intended use: For full-time junior or senior study at accredited 4-year institution in United States. Designated institutions: Schools with ABET-accredited programs.
Eligibility: Applicant or parent must be member/participant of American Society of Mechanical Engineers.
Basis for selection: Major/career interest in engineering, mechanical. Applicant must demonstrate high academic achievement, depth of character and leadership.
Application requirements: Recommendations, essay, transcript.
Additional information: Applicant must be student member of ASME. Application is online.
    Amount of award: $3,500
    Number of awards: 2
    Application deadline: March 15
    Notification begins: June 15
    Total amount awarded: $7,000
Contact:
American Society of Mechanical Engineers
Three Park Avenue
New York, NY 10016-5990
Phone: 212-591-8131
Fax: 212-591-7856
Web: www.asme.org/education/college/financialaid

William J. and Marijane E. Adams, Jr., Mechanical Engineering Scholarship

Type of award: Scholarship.
Intended use: For full-time sophomore, junior or senior study in United States. Designated institutions: Schools in ASME region IX: California, Nevada, Hawaii.
Eligibility: Applicant or parent must be member/participant of American Society of Mechanical Engineers. Applicant must be residing in California, Hawaii or Nevada.
Basis for selection: Major/career interest in engineering, mechanical. Applicant must demonstrate financial need, high academic achievement, depth of character and leadership.
Application requirements: Recommendations, essay, transcript.
Additional information: Minimum 2.5 GPA. Application must be endorsed by department head. Applicant must be member of ASME. Award designated for student with special interest in product development and design. Application is online.
    Amount of award: $3,000
    Number of awards: 1
    Application deadline: March 15
    Notification begins: June 15
    Total amount awarded: $3,000

American Society of Mechanical Engineers: William J. and Marijane E. Adams, Jr., Mechanical Engineering Scholarship

Contact:
American Society of Mechanical Engineers
Three Park Avenue
New York, NY 10016-5990
Phone: 212-591-8131
Fax: 212-591-7856
Web: www.asme.org/education/college/financialaid

American Society of Mechanical Engineers Auxiliary

Agnes Malakate Kezios Scholarship

Type of award: Scholarship.
Intended use: For senior study at 4-year institution in United States. Designated institutions: ABET-accredited mechanical engineering programs.
Eligibility: Applicant must be U.S. citizen.
Basis for selection: Major/career interest in engineering, mechanical. Applicant must demonstrate financial need, high academic achievement and depth of character.
Application requirements: Recommendations, transcript.
Additional information: For ASME student member in final year of undergraduate program in mechanical engineering. Download application from Website or send SASE or e-mail to request application.

Amount of award:	$2,000
Number of awards:	2
Number of applicants:	13
Application deadline:	March 15

Contact:
American Society of Mechanical Engineers Auxiliary, Inc.
Attn: Alverta Cover
5425 Caldwell Mill Road
Birmingham, AL 35242
Phone: 205-991-6109
Web: www.asme.org/auxiliary

Allen J. Baldwin Scholarship

Type of award: Scholarship.
Intended use: For senior study at 4-year institution in United States. Designated institutions: ABET-accredited mechanical engineering programs.
Eligibility: Applicant must be U.S. citizen.
Basis for selection: Major/career interest in engineering, mechanical. Applicant must demonstrate financial need, high academic achievement and depth of character.
Application requirements: Recommendations, transcript.
Additional information: For ASME student member in final year of undergraduate study in mechanical engineering. Download application from Website or send SASE or e-mail to request application.

Amount of award:	$2,000
Number of awards:	2
Number of applicants:	13
Application deadline:	March 15

Contact:
Alverta Cover Undergraduate Scholarships
5425 Caldwell Mill Road
Birmingham, AL 35242
Phone: 205-991-6109
Web: www.asme.org/auxiliary

Berna Lou Cartwright Scholarship

Type of award: Scholarship.
Intended use: For senior study at 4-year institution in United States. Designated institutions: ABET-accredited mechanical engineering programs.
Eligibility: Applicant must be U.S. citizen.
Basis for selection: Major/career interest in engineering, mechanical. Applicant must demonstrate financial need, high academic achievement and depth of character.
Application requirements: Recommendations, transcript.
Additional information: For ASME student member in final year of undergraduate program in mechanical engineering. Download application from Website or send SASE or email to request application.

Amount of award:	$2,000
Number of awards:	2
Number of applicants:	13
Application deadline:	March 15

Contact:
Alverta Cover Undergraduate Scholarships
5425 Caldwell Mill Road
Birmingham, AL 35242
Phone: 205-991-6109
Web: www.asme.org/auxiliary

Charles B. Scharp Scholarship

Type of award: Scholarship.
Intended use: For senior study at 4-year institution in United States. Designated institutions: ABET-accredited mechanical engineering programs.
Eligibility: Applicant must be U.S. citizen.
Basis for selection: Major/career interest in engineering, mechanical. Applicant must demonstrate financial need, high academic achievement and depth of character.
Application requirements: Recommendations, transcript.
Additional information: For ASME student member in final year of undergraduate program in mechanical engineering. Download application from Website or send SASE or email to request application.

Amount of award:	$2,000
Number of awards:	3
Number of applicants:	13
Application deadline:	March 15

Contact:
Alverta Cover Undergraduate Scholarships
5425 Caldwell Mill Road
Birmingham, AL 35242
Phone: 205-991-6109
Web: www.asme.org/auxiliary

Sylvia W. Farny Scholarship

Type of award: Scholarship.
Intended use: For senior study at 4-year institution in United States. Designated institutions: ABET-accredited mechanical engineering programs.
Eligibility: Applicant must be U.S. citizen.

Basis for selection: Major/career interest in engineering, mechanical. Applicant must demonstrate financial need, high academic achievement and depth of character.
Application requirements: Recommendations, transcript.
Additional information: For ASME student members in final year of undergraduate study in mechanical engineering. Download application from Website or send SASE or email to request application.

Amount of award:	$2,000
Number of awards:	3
Number of applicants:	13
Application deadline:	March 15

Contact:
Alverta Cover Undergraduate Scholarships
5425 Caldwell Mill Road
Birmingham, AL 35242
Phone: 205-991-6109
Web: www.asme.org/auxiliary

American Society of Naval Engineers

Naval Engineers Scholarship

Type of award: Scholarship, renewable.
Intended use: For full-time senior or master's study at accredited 4-year or graduate institution.
Eligibility: Applicant must be U.S. citizen.
Basis for selection: Major/career interest in engineering, marine; engineering, mechanical; engineering, electrical/electronic; physical sciences or engineering, civil. Applicant must demonstrate high academic achievement.
Application requirements: Recommendations, essay, transcript.
Additional information: Award for last year of undergraduate study or one year of graduate study. Applicants' major/career interests may also include naval architecture; aeronautical and ocean engineering; as well as other programs leading to careers with both military and civilian organizations. Financial need may be considered.

Amount of award:	$3,000-$4,000
Number of awards:	21
Number of applicants:	100
Application deadline:	February 15
Notification begins:	May 15
Total amount awarded:	$63,000

Contact:
American Society of Naval Engineers
1452 Duke Street
Alexandria, VA 22314
Phone: 703-836-6727
Fax: 703-836-7491
Web: www.navalengineers.org

American Society of Travel Agents Foundation

A.J. "Andy" Spielman Travel Agents Scholarship

Type of award: Scholarship, renewable.
Intended use: For undergraduate certificate or non-degree study at accredited vocational institution in United States or Canada. Designated institutions: Recognized proprietary travel schools.
Eligibility: Applicant must be returning adult student.
Basis for selection: Major/career interest in tourism/travel. Applicant must demonstrate high academic achievement and service orientation.
Application requirements: Recommendations, transcript, proof of eligibility. 500-word essay on "Why I Have Chosen the Travel Profession for My Reentry into the Workforce." Four copies of application and required materials.
Additional information: Visit Website for application and additional requirements.

Amount of award:	$2,500
Number of awards:	2
Number of applicants:	150
Application deadline:	June 15
Notification begins:	September 1

Contact:
American Society of Travel Agents Foundation
1101 King Street
Alexandria, VA 22314-2944
Phone: 703-739-2782
Fax: 703-684-8319
Web: www.astanet.com/education/edu_scholarships.asp

American Express Travel Scholarship

Type of award: Scholarship, renewable.
Intended use: For undergraduate study at accredited vocational, 2-year or 4-year institution in United States or Canada.
Eligibility: Applicant must be U.S. citizen, permanent resident or Canadian citizen/resident.
Basis for selection: Major/career interest in tourism/travel.
Application requirements: Recommendations, transcript, proof of eligibility. Five-hundred-word essay detailing student's plans in travel and tourism and view of the travel industry's future. Official curriculum description and statement of tuition amount. Four copies of application and required materials.
Additional information: Award also for students at proprietary travel schools. Minimum 2.5 GPA. Amount of award varies. Check Website for deadlines and to download application.

Application deadline:	June 15
Notification begins:	September 1

Contact:
American Society of Travel Agents Foundation
1101 King Street
Alexandria, VA 22314-2944
Phone: 703-739-2782
Fax: 703-684-8319
Web: www.astanet.com/education/edu_scholarships.asp

Arizona Chapter Dependent Scholarship Fund

Type of award: Scholarship, renewable.
Intended use: For sophomore, junior or senior study at accredited 2-year or 4-year institution.
Eligibility: Applicant or parent must be member/participant of ASTA Arizona Chapter. Applicant must be U.S. citizen or permanent resident residing in Arizona.
Basis for selection: Applicant must demonstrate high academic achievement.
Application requirements: Recommendations, transcript, proof of eligibility. 500-word essay on applicant's career goals. Four copies of application and required materials.
Additional information: Minimum 2.5 GPA. Applicant must be dependent of an ASTA Arizona Chapter Active or Active Associate member, or an employee of an Arizona ASTA member agency for minimum of six months. Open to applicants of all majors and fields of study; major in travel and tourism not required. Applicant must be enrolled in final year at two-year college or in junior or senior year at four-year university. Visit Website for application and additional requirements.
    Amount of award: $1,500
    Number of awards: 1
    Application deadline: June 15
    Notification begins: September 1
    Total amount awarded: $1,500
Contact:
American Society of Travel Agents Foundation
1101 King Street
Alexandria, VA 22314-2944
Phone: 703-739-2782
Fax: 703-684-8319
Web: www.astanet.com/education/edu_scholarships.asp

Arizona Chapter Gold Scholarship

Type of award: Scholarship, renewable.
Intended use: For sophomore, junior or senior study at accredited 4-year institution in United States.
Eligibility: Applicant must be U.S. citizen or permanent resident residing in Arizona.
Basis for selection: Major/career interest in tourism/travel. Applicant must demonstrate high academic achievement, seriousness of purpose and service orientation.
Application requirements: Recommendations, transcript, proof of eligibility. 500-word essay detailing applicant's plans in travel industry and interest in business of travel and tourism. Letter of recommendation must be from educator or employer regarding applicant's credentials. Include four copies of application and required materials.
Additional information: Minimum 2.5 GPA. Visit Website for application and additional requirements.
    Amount of award: $3,000
    Number of awards: 1
    Application deadline: June 15
    Notification begins: September 1
    Total amount awarded: $3,000
Contact:
American Society of Travel Agents Foundation
1101 King Street
Alexandria, VA 22314-2944
Phone: 703-739-2782 ext. 8721
Fax: 703-684-8319
Web: www.astanet.com/education/edu_scholarships.asp

George Reinke Scholarships

Type of award: Scholarship.
Intended use: For freshman or sophomore study.
Eligibility: Applicant must be U.S. citizen.
Basis for selection: Major/career interest in tourism/travel.
Application requirements: Recommendations, essay, transcript. 500-word essay on career goals in travel and tourism industry.
Additional information: Applicant must be enrolled in travel agent studies program. See Website for more information.
    Amount of award: $2,000
    Number of awards: 6
    Application deadline: June 15
    Notification begins: September 1
Contact:
American Society of Travel Agents (ASTA) Foundation
1101 King Street, Suite 200
Alexander, Va 22314-2187
Phone: 703-739-2782
Fax: 703-684-8319
Web: www.astanet.com/education/edu_scholarships.asp

Healy Scholarship

Type of award: Scholarship, renewable.
Intended use: For freshman, sophomore, junior or senior study at accredited 4-year institution in United States or Canada.
Eligibility: Applicant must be U.S. citizen, permanent resident or Canadian citizen/resident.
Basis for selection: Major/career interest in tourism/travel. Applicant must demonstrate high academic achievement and service orientation.
Application requirements: Recommendations, transcript, proof of eligibility. 500-word essay suggesting improvements in travel industry. Include four copies of application and required materials.
Additional information: Minimum 2.5 GPA. Visit Website for application and additional requirements.
    Amount of award: $2,000
    Number of awards: 1
    Application deadline: June 15
    Notification begins: September 1
    Total amount awarded: $2,000
Contact:
American Society of Travel Agents Foundation
1101 King Street
Alexandria, VA 22314-2944
Phone: 703-739-2782
Fax: 703-684-8319
Web: www.astanet.com/education/edu_scholarships.asp

Holland America Line-Westours, Inc., Scholarship

Type of award: Scholarship, renewable.
Intended use: For undergraduate study at accredited vocational, 2-year or 4-year institution in United States.
Eligibility: Applicant must be U.S. citizen, permanent resident or Canadian citizen/resident.
Basis for selection: Major/career interest in tourism/travel. Applicant must demonstrate high academic achievement, seriousness of purpose and service orientation.
Application requirements: Recommendations, transcript, proof of eligibility. 500-word essay on future of cruise industry. Four copies of application and required materials.

Additional information: Minimum 2.5 GPA. Visit Website for application and additional requirements.

Amount of award:	$3,000
Number of awards:	2
Application deadline:	June 15
Notification begins:	September 1

Contact:
American Society of Travel Agents Foundation
1101 King Street
Alexandria, VA 22314-2944
Phone: 703-739-2782
Fax: 703-684-8319
Web: www.astanet.com/education/edu_scholarships.asp

Joseph R. Stone Scholarship

Type of award: Scholarship, renewable.
Intended use: For freshman, sophomore, junior or senior study at accredited 2-year or 4-year institution in United States or Canada.
Eligibility: Applicant must be U.S. citizen, permanent resident or Canadian citizen/resident.
Basis for selection: Major/career interest in tourism/travel. Applicant must demonstrate high academic achievement.
Application requirements: Recommendations, transcript, proof of eligibility. 500-word essay on applicant's goals in travel industry. Four copies of application and required materials.
Additional information: Minimum 2.5 GPA. One parent must be employed by travel industry. Visit Website for application and additional requirements.

Amount of award:	$2,400
Number of awards:	1
Application deadline:	June 15
Notification begins:	September 1
Total amount awarded:	$2,400

Contact:
American Society of Travel Agents Foundation
1101 King Street
Alexandria, VA 22314-2944
Phone: 703-739-2782
Fax: 703-684-8319
Web: www.astanet.com/education/edu_scholarships.asp

Northern California Chapter/ Richard Epping Scholarship

Type of award: Scholarship, renewable.
Intended use: For undergraduate study at accredited vocational, 2-year or 4-year institution in United States. Designated institutions: Colleges, universities, and recognized proprietary travel and tourism schools in California and northern Nevada.
Eligibility: Applicant must be U.S. citizen or permanent resident residing in California or Nevada.
Basis for selection: Major/career interest in tourism/travel. Applicant must demonstrate high academic achievement, depth of character, seriousness of purpose and service orientation.
Application requirements: Recommendations, transcript, proof of eligibility. 500-word essay on why applicant desires profession in travel and tourism industry. Four copies of application and required materials.
Additional information: Minimum 2.5 GPA. Recipient must make presentation at NorCal ASTA chapter meeting within six months of receiving scholarship. Visit Website for application and additional information.

Amount of award:	$2,000
Number of awards:	1
Application deadline:	June 15
Notification begins:	September 1
Total amount awarded:	$2,000

Contact:
American Society of Travel Agents Foundation
1101 King Street
Alexandria, VA 22314-2944
Phone: 703-739-2782
Fax: 703-684-8319
Web: www.astanet.com/education/edu_scholarships.asp

Princess Cruises and Princess Tours Scholarship

Type of award: Scholarship, renewable.
Intended use: For undergraduate study at accredited vocational, 2-year or 4-year institution in United States or Canada.
Eligibility: Applicant must be U.S. citizen, permanent resident or Canadian citizen/resident.
Basis for selection: Major/career interest in tourism/travel. Applicant must demonstrate high academic achievement, seriousness of purpose and service orientation.
Application requirements: Recommendations, transcript, proof of eligibility. 300-word essay on two features cruise ships will need to offer passengers in next ten years. Four copies of application and required materials.
Additional information: Minimum 2.5 GPA. Visit Website for application and additional requirements.

Amount of award:	$2,000
Number of awards:	2
Application deadline:	June 15
Notification begins:	September 1

Contact:
American Society of Travel Agents Foundation
1101 King Street
Alexandria, VA 22314-2944
Phone: 703-739-2782
Fax: 703-684-8319
Web: www.astanet.com/education/edu_scholarships.asp

Rocky Mountain Chapter-Donald Estey Scholarship Fund

Type of award: Scholarship, renewable.
Intended use: For undergraduate study at 2-year or 4-year institution in United States.
Eligibility: Applicant must be U.S. citizen, permanent resident or Canadian citizen/resident.
Basis for selection: Major/career interest in tourism/travel.
Application requirements: Recommendations, transcript. Recommendation from official representative of ASTA Rocky Mountain Chapter. Statement indicating program's expected benefit. Eligibility for specific program applied for. Proof of enrollment, official curriculum description, and statement of tuition amount. Four copies of application and required materials.
Additional information: Applicants must be either enrolled at entry level in licensed preparatory travel program or active agent participating in ASTA-sponsored travel program, the Travel Institute Destination Specialist, or other industry training programs. Must have 2.5 GPA. Check Website for deadline.

Amount of award:	$1,000
Application deadline:	June 15
Notification begins:	September 1
Total amount awarded:	$3,000

Contact:
American Society of Travel Agents (ASTA) Foundation
1101 King Street, Suite 200
Alexandria, VA 22314-2187
Phone: 703-739-2782
Fax: 703-684-8319
Web: www.astanet.com/education/edu_scholarships.asp

Southern California Chapter/ Pleasant Hawaiian Holidays Scholarship

Type of award: Scholarship, renewable.
Intended use: For undergraduate study at accredited 4-year institution in United States.
Eligibility: Applicant must be U.S. citizen.
Basis for selection: Major/career interest in tourism/travel. Applicant must demonstrate high academic achievement, seriousness of purpose and service orientation.
Application requirements: Recommendations, transcript, proof of eligibility. 500-word essay on applicant's goals in travel industry and statement explaining why applicant should receive award. Four copies of application and required materials.
Additional information: Minimum 2.5 GPA. One award for student from Southern California region; one award for student from anywhere in the United States. Visit Website for application and more details.

Amount of award:	$2,500
Number of awards:	2
Application deadline:	June 15
Notification begins:	September 1

Contact:
American Society of Travel Agents Foundation
1101 King Street
Alexandria, VA 22314-2944
Phone: 703-739-2782
Fax: 703-684-8319
Web: www.astanet.com/education/edu_scholarships.asp

American Water Ski Educational Foundation

American Water Ski Educational Foundation Scholarship

Type of award: Scholarship.
Intended use: For full-time sophomore, junior or senior study at 2-year or 4-year institution.
Eligibility: Applicant must be U.S. citizen.
Basis for selection: Applicant must demonstrate financial need, high academic achievement, depth of character, leadership and seriousness of purpose.
Application requirements: Recommendations, essay, transcript. If applicant is college freshman, include both college and high school transcripts. Two letters of reference. Read the following mission statement of the American Water Ski Educational Foundation (AWSEF) and write a 500-word essay about what you would do to get more young people like yourself involved in activities, committees, and events sponsored by AWSEF.
Additional information: Must be member of USA Water Ski Association.

Amount of award:	$1,500
Number of awards:	6
Number of applicants:	26
Application deadline:	April 1
Notification begins:	September 1

Contact:
American Water Ski Educational Foundation
1251 Holy Cow Road
Polk City, FL 33868-8200
Phone: 863-324-2472
Fax: 863-324-3996
Web: www.waterskihalloffame.com

American Welding Society Foundation, Inc.

Airgas-Jerry Baker Scholarship

Type of award: Scholarship, renewable.
Intended use: For full-time undergraduate study.
Eligibility: Applicant must be at least 18. Applicant must be U.S. citizen.
Basis for selection: Major/career interest in welding.
Application requirements: Essay.
Additional information: Applicants must have minimum 2.8 overall GPA with 3.0 GPA in engineering courses. Priority will be given to those individuals residing or attending school in Alabama, Georgia, or Florida. Applicant must show interest in welding engineering or welding engineering technology.

Amount of award:	$2,500
Number of awards:	1
Number of applicants:	4
Application deadline:	January 15
Notification begins:	March 10
Total amount awarded:	$2,500

Contact:
American Welding Society Foundation, Inc.
550 N.W. LeJeune Road
Miami, FL 33126
Phone: 800-443-9353 ext. 461
Web: www.aws.org/foundation/scholarships/airgas_baker.html

Airgas-Terry Jarvis Memorial Scholarship

Type of award: Scholarship.
Intended use: For full-time sophomore, junior or senior study at 4-year institution in United States or Canada.
Eligibility: Applicant must be at least 18. Applicant must be U.S. citizen.
Basis for selection: Major/career interest in welding.
Application requirements: Recommendations, essay, transcript, proof of eligibility.
Additional information: Must have interest in pursuing a minimum four-year degree in welding engineering or welding engineering technology. Minimum 2.8 GPA overall, with 3.0 GPA in engineering courses. Priority given to residents of Florida, Alabama, and Georgia. Applicant does not have to be a member of the American Welding Society.

Amount of award:	$2,500
Number of awards:	1
Number of applicants:	4
Application deadline:	January 15
Notification begins:	March 10
Total amount awarded:	$2,500

Contact:
American Welding Society Foundation, Inc.
Attn: Scholarships
550 Northwest LeJeune Road
Miami, FL 33126
Phone: 800-443-9353
Web: www.aws.org

American Welding Society District Scholarship

Type of award: Scholarship.
Intended use: For undergraduate study at accredited vocational, 2-year or 4-year institution in United States.
Eligibility: Applicant must be U.S. citizen.
Basis for selection: Major/career interest in welding. Applicant must demonstrate financial need, high academic achievement, depth of character, leadership and seriousness of purpose.
Application requirements: Recommendations, transcript, proof of eligibility. Personal statement, biography, and photo.

Amount of award:	$200-$2,000
Number of awards:	150
Number of applicants:	270
Application deadline:	March 1
Notification begins:	July 1
Total amount awarded:	$110,000

Contact:
American Welding Society Foundation, Inc.
Attn: Scholarships
550 Northwest LeJeune Road
Miami, FL 33126
Phone: 800-443-9353

Arsham Amirikian Engineering Scholarship

Type of award: Scholarship, renewable.
Intended use: For undergraduate study at accredited 4-year institution.
Eligibility: Applicant must be at least 18. Applicant must be U.S. citizen.
Basis for selection: Major/career interest in welding. Applicant must demonstrate financial need.
Additional information: Applicant must have minimum 3.0 overall GPA. Must show interest in pursuing career in the application of the art of welding in civil and structural engineering.

Amount of award:	$2,500
Number of awards:	1
Number of applicants:	15
Application deadline:	January 15
Notification begins:	February 15
Total amount awarded:	$2,500

Contact:
American Welding Society Foundation, Inc.
550 Northwest LeJeune Road
Miami, FL 33126
Phone: 800-443-9353
Web: www.aws.org/foundation/scholarships/arsham.html

Donald and Shirley Hastings National Scholarship

Type of award: Scholarship, renewable.
Intended use: For undergraduate study at 4-year institution in United States.
Eligibility: Applicant must be at least 18. Applicant must be U.S. citizen.
Basis for selection: Major/career interest in welding. Applicant must demonstrate financial need.
Additional information: Applicant must have minimum 2.5 GPA. Must show interest in welding engineering or welding engineering technology. Priority for Iowa, Ohio, or California residents.

Amount of award:	$2,500
Number of awards:	1
Number of applicants:	13
Application deadline:	January 15
Notification begins:	February 15
Total amount awarded:	$2,500

Contact:
American Welding Society Foundation, Inc.
550 Northwest LeJeune Road
Miami, FL 33126
Phone: 800-443-9353

Donald F. Hastings Scholarship

Type of award: Scholarship, renewable.
Intended use: For sophomore, junior or senior study at 4-year institution in United States.
Eligibility: Applicant must be at least 18. Applicant must be U.S. citizen.
Basis for selection: Major/career interest in welding. Applicant must demonstrate financial need and seriousness of purpose.
Application requirements: Recommendations, transcript, proof of eligibility.
Additional information: Priority given to residents of Ohio and California. Minimum of 2.5 GPA.

Amount of award:	$2,500
Number of awards:	1
Number of applicants:	12
Application deadline:	January 15
Notification begins:	February 15
Total amount awarded:	$2,500

Contact:
American Welding Society Foundation, Inc.
Attn: Scholarships
550 Northwest LeJeune Road
Miami, FL 33126
Phone: 800-443-9353

Edward J. Brady Memorial Scholarship

Type of award: Scholarship, renewable.
Intended use: For sophomore, junior or senior study at 4-year institution.
Eligibility: Applicant must be at least 18. Applicant must be U.S. citizen or Canadian citizen.
Basis for selection: Major/career interest in welding or engineering. Applicant must demonstrate financial need and seriousness of purpose.
Application requirements: Recommendations, essay, transcript, proof of eligibility. Proposed curriculum; brief biography; proof of hands-on welding experience.

Additional information: Interest in pursuing minimum four-year degree in welding engineering or welding engineering technology. Minimum 2.5 GPA.
- **Amount of award:** $2,500
- **Number of awards:** 1
- **Number of applicants:** 6
- **Application deadline:** January 15
- **Notification begins:** February 15
- **Total amount awarded:** $2,500

Contact:
American Welding Society Foundation, Inc.
Attn: Scholarships
550 Northwest LeJeune Road
Miami, FL 33126
Phone: 800-443-9353

Howard E. and Wilma J. Adkins Memorial Scholarship

Type of award: Scholarship, renewable.
Intended use: For full-time junior or senior study at 4-year institution.
Eligibility: Applicant must be at least 18. Applicant must be U.S. citizen.
Basis for selection: Major/career interest in welding. Applicant must demonstrate high academic achievement and seriousness of purpose.
Application requirements: Recommendations, transcript, proof of eligibility.
Additional information: Applicant should have interest in pursuing four-year degree in welding engineering or welding engineering technology. Priority given to residents of Kentucky and Wisconsin. Minimum 3.2 GPA in engineering, scientific and technical subjects; minimum overall 2.8 GPA.
- **Amount of award:** $2,500
- **Number of awards:** 1
- **Number of applicants:** 17
- **Application deadline:** January 15
- **Notification begins:** March 10
- **Total amount awarded:** $2,500

Contact:
American Welding Society Foundation Inc.
Attn: Scholarships
550 Northwest LeJeune Road
Miami, FL 33126
Phone: 800-443-9353

ITW Welding Companies Scholarship

Type of award: Scholarship, renewable.
Intended use: For senior study at 4-year institution.
Eligibility: Applicant must be at least 18. Applicant must be U.S. citizen.
Basis for selection: Major/career interest in welding.
Additional information: Applicant must show interest in welding engineering or welding engineering technology, and have work experience in the welding equipment field. Applicant must have minimum 3.0 GPA.
- **Amount of award:** $3,000
- **Number of awards:** 2
- **Number of applicants:** 14
- **Application deadline:** January 15
- **Notification begins:** March 10
- **Total amount awarded:** $6,000

Contact:
American Welding Society Foundation, Inc.
550 Northwest LeJeune Road
Miami, FL 33126
Phone: 800-443-9353
Web: www.aws.org/foundation/scholarships/

Jack R. Barckhoff Welding Management Scholarship

Type of award: Scholarship.
Intended use: For junior study at 4-year institution.
Designated institutions: Ohio State University.
Eligibility: Applicant must be U.S. citizen.
Basis for selection: Major/career interest in welding. Applicant must demonstrate high academic achievement.
Additional information: Minimum 2.5 GPA.
- **Amount of award:** $2,500
- **Number of awards:** 2
- **Number of applicants:** 5
- **Application deadline:** January 15
- **Total amount awarded:** $5,000

Contact:
American Welding Society Foundation
550 NW LeJeune Road
Miami, FL 33126
Phone: 800-443-9353
Web: www.aws.org

James A. Turner, Jr., Memorial Scholarship

Type of award: Scholarship, renewable.
Intended use: For full-time sophomore, junior or senior study at accredited 4-year institution.
Eligibility: Applicant must be at least 18. Applicant must be U.S. citizen.
Basis for selection: Major/career interest in welding or business/management/administration. Applicant must demonstrate financial need and seriousness of purpose.
Application requirements: Recommendations, transcript, proof of eligibility. Verification of employment, brief biography, financial aid report, proposed curriculum.
Additional information: Must have interest in pursuing management career in welding. Must work minimum of 10 hours per week at welding store.
- **Amount of award:** $3,500
- **Number of awards:** 1
- **Number of applicants:** 2
- **Application deadline:** January 15
- **Notification begins:** March 10
- **Total amount awarded:** $3,500

Contact:
American Welding Society Foundation, Inc.
Attn: Scholarships
550 Northwest LeJeune Road
Miami, FL 33126
Phone: 800-443-9353

Jerry Robinson-Inweld Corporation Scholarship

Type of award: Scholarship, renewable.
Intended use: For full-time undergraduate study at accredited 4-year institution.
Eligibility: Applicant must be at least 18. Applicant must be U.S. citizen.

Basis for selection: Major/career interest in welding. Applicant must demonstrate financial need.
Application requirements: Essay, transcript.
Additional information: Applicant must have 2.5 overall GPA.
    Amount of award: $2,500
    Number of awards: 1
    Number of applicants: 4
    Application deadline: January 15
    Notification begins: February 15
    Total amount awarded: $2,500
Contact:
American Welding Society Foundation, Inc.
550 N.W. LeJeune Road
Miami, FL 33126
Phone: 800-443-9353 ext. 461
Web: www.aws.org/foundation/scholarships/robinson.html

John C. Lincoln Memorial Scholarship

Type of award: Scholarship, renewable.
Intended use: For sophomore, junior or senior study at 4-year institution.
Eligibility: Applicant must be at least 18. Applicant must be U.S. citizen.
Basis for selection: Major/career interest in welding. Applicant must demonstrate financial need and seriousness of purpose.
Application requirements: Recommendations, transcript, proof of eligibility.
Additional information: Minimum 2.5 GPA. Priority will be given to those individuals residing or attending school in Ohio or Arizona.
    Amount of award: $3,500
    Number of awards: 1
    Number of applicants: 11
    Application deadline: January 15
    Notification begins: February 15
    Total amount awarded: $3,500
Contact:
American Welding Society Foundation, Inc.
Attn: Scholarships
550 Northwest LeJeune Road
Miami, FL 33126
Phone: 800-443-9353

Matsuo Bridge Company Ltd of Japan Scholarship

Type of award: Scholarship.
Intended use: For junior, senior or graduate study at accredited 4-year or graduate institution in United States.
Eligibility: Applicant must be at least 18.
Basis for selection: Major/career interest in welding or engineering, civil.
Application requirements: Recommendations, transcript, proof of eligibility.
Additional information: Scholarship for a student interested in pursuing career in civil engineering, welding engineering, or welding engineering technology. Priority given to applicants residing in California, Texas, Oregon, or Washington. Applicant does not have to be member of American Welding Society but must agree to participate in AWS Foundation or Matsuo Bridge Company sponsored publicity. Minimum 3.0 GPA required.

    Amount of award: $2,500
    Number of awards: 1
    Number of applicants: 9
    Application deadline: January 15
    Notification begins: March 10
    Total amount awarded: $2,500
Contact:
American Welding Society Foundation, Inc.
Attn: Scholarships
550 Northwest LeJeune Road
Miami, FL 33126
Phone: 800-443-9353
Web: www.aws.org

Miller Electric Manufacturing Company Ivic Scholarship

Type of award: Scholarship, renewable.
Intended use: For undergraduate study at accredited vocational, 2-year or 4-year institution in United States.
Eligibility: Applicant must be U.S. citizen.
Basis for selection: Major/career interest in welding. Applicant must demonstrate depth of character, leadership and seriousness of purpose.
Additional information: Competition based on AWS National Welding Trials.
    Amount of award: $10,000
    Number of awards: 1
Contact:
American Welding Society Foundation, Inc.
Attn: Scholarships
550 Northwest LeJeune Road
Miami, FL 33126
Phone: 800-443-9353

Past Presidents Scholarship

Type of award: Scholarship.
Intended use: For junior, senior, master's or doctoral study at 4-year or graduate institution.
Basis for selection: Major/career interest in welding or engineering. Applicant must demonstrate financial need.
Application requirements: Essay. Essay should be 300-500 words.
    Amount of award: $2,500
    Number of awards: 1
    Application deadline: January 15
    Total amount awarded: $2,500
Contact:
American Welding Society Foundation, Inc.
550 LeJeune Road
Miami, FL 33126
Phone: 800-443-9353
Web: www.aws.org

Praxair International Scholarship

Type of award: Scholarship, renewable.
Intended use: For full-time sophomore, junior or senior study at 4-year institution.
Eligibility: Applicant must be at least 18. Applicant must be U.S. citizen or Canadian citizen/resident.
Basis for selection: Major/career interest in welding. Applicant must demonstrate financial need, leadership and service orientation.
Application requirements: Recommendations, transcript, proof of eligibility.

American Welding Society Foundation, Inc.: Praxair International Scholarship

Additional information: Applicant must have interest in pursuing minimum four-year degree in welding engineering or welding engineering technology. Minimum GPA of 2.5.

Amount of award:	$2,500
Number of awards:	1
Number of applicants:	23
Application deadline:	January 15
Notification begins:	March 10
Total amount awarded:	$2,500

Contact:
American Welding Society Foundation, Inc.
Praxair Scholarship
550 Northwest LeJeune Road
Miami, FL 33126
Phone: 800-443-9353

Robert L. Peaslee-Detroit Brazing and Soldering Division Scholarship

Type of award: Scholarship, renewable.
Intended use: For junior or senior study at 4-year institution.
Eligibility: Applicant must be at least 18. Applicant must be U.S. citizen.
Basis for selection: Major/career interest in welding.
Application requirements: Recommendations, essay, transcript.
Additional information: Applicant must have 3.0 GPA in engineering courses. Must show interest in pursuing degree in welding engineering or welding technology with emphasis on brazing and soldering application.

Amount of award:	$2,500
Number of awards:	1
Number of applicants:	13
Application deadline:	January 15
Notification begins:	March 10
Total amount awarded:	$2,500

Contact:
American Welding Society Foundation, Inc.
550 Northwest LeJeune Road
Miami, FL 33126
Phone: 800-443-9353
Web: www.aws.org/foundation

RWMA Scholarship

Type of award: Scholarship.
Intended use: For full-time junior study at 4-year institution.
Basis for selection: Major/career interest in welding or engineering. Applicant must demonstrate high academic achievement.
Additional information: Open to U.S. and Canadian citizens. Minimum 3.0 GPA.

Amount of award:	$2,500
Number of awards:	1
Number of applicants:	4
Application deadline:	January 15
Total amount awarded:	$2,500

Contact:
American Welding Society Foundation, Inc.
550 LeJeune Road
Miami, FL 33126
Phone: 800-443-9353
Web: www.aws.org

William A. and Ann M. Brothers Scholarship

Type of award: Scholarship, renewable.
Intended use: For full-time undergraduate study at accredited 4-year institution.
Eligibility: Applicant must be at least 18. Applicant must be U.S. citizen.
Basis for selection: Major/career interest in welding. Applicant must demonstrate financial need.
Additional information: Applicant must have minimum 2.5 GPA. Priority will be given to those individuals residing or attending schools in Ohio.

Amount of award:	$3,500
Number of awards:	1
Number of applicants:	12
Application deadline:	January 15
Notification begins:	February 15
Total amount awarded:	$3,500

Contact:
American Welding Society Foundation
550 N.W. LeJeune Road
Miami, FL 33126
Phone: 800-443-9353 ext. 461
Web: www.aws.org/foundation/scholarships/brothers.html

William B. Howell Memorial Scholarship

Type of award: Scholarship, renewable.
Intended use: For undergraduate study at accredited 4-year institution in United States.
Eligibility: Applicant must be at least 18. Applicant must be U.S. citizen.
Basis for selection: Major/career interest in welding. Applicant must demonstrate financial need.
Application requirements: Recommendations, transcript, proof of eligibility.
Additional information: Minimum 2.5 GPA required. Priority given to residents of Florida, Michigan, and Ohio. Applicant does not have to be a member of the American Welding Society.

Amount of award:	$2,500
Number of awards:	1
Number of applicants:	14
Application deadline:	January 15
Notification begins:	February 15
Total amount awarded:	$2,500

Contact:
American Welding Society Foundation, Inc.
Attn: Scholarships
550 Northwest LeJeune Road
Miami, FL 33126
Phone: 800-443-9353
Web: www.aws.org

Annie's Homegrown

Annie's Homegrown Sustainable Agriculture Scholarships

Type of award: Scholarship.

Intended use: For full-time undergraduate or graduate study in United States.
Basis for selection: Major/career interest in agriculture. Applicant must demonstrate high academic achievement, depth of character and seriousness of purpose.
Application requirements: Recommendations, essay, transcript.
Additional information: Application and more information available on Website.
  Number of applicants: 300
Contact:
Annie's Homegrown Scholarship
564 Gateway Drive
Napa, CA 94558
Phone: 707-254-3700
Web: www.annies.com/sustainable_agriculture_scholarship

AOPA Air Safety Foundation

Donald Burnside Memorial Scholarship

Type of award: Scholarship.
Intended use: For junior or senior study at 4-year institution.
Eligibility: Applicant must be U.S. citizen.
Basis for selection: Major/career interest in aviation.
Application requirements: Essay, transcript. Original and seven copies of application mailed to Mark Sherman.
Additional information: Applicant must have minimum 3.25 GPA. Application available on Website.
  Amount of award: $1,000
  Number of awards: 1
  Application deadline: March 31
  Notification begins: July 1
  Total amount awarded: $1,000
Contact:
Mark Sherman, Assistant Professor, Department of Aviation
2000 University Avenue
Dubuque, IA 52001
Phone: 301-695-2000
Fax: 301-695-2375
Web: www.aopa.org/asf/about/scholarship/burnside.html

Appaloosa Youth Foundation

Appaloosa Youth Foundation Educational Scholarships

Type of award: Scholarship, renewable.
Intended use: For full-time undergraduate or graduate study at accredited postsecondary institution in United States.
Eligibility: Applicant or parent must be member/participant of Appaloosa Horse Club. Applicant must be U.S. citizen or permanent resident.
Basis for selection: Competition/talent/interest in academics, based on scholastic aptitude, involvement in the Appaloosa industry, leadership potential, sportsmanship, community and civic responsibility, and general knowledge and accomplishments in horsemanship.
Application requirements: Recommendations, essay, transcript, proof of eligibility. Photo, SAT/ACT scores.
Additional information: Applicant must be member of Appaloosa Horse Club or Appaloosa Youth Association. One scholarship requires intent to pursue equine-related studies. GPA of 3.5 for one scholarship, GPA of 2.5 for other scholarships.
  Amount of award: $1,000-$2,000
  Number of awards: 9
  Number of applicants: 24
  Application deadline: June 10
  Notification begins: July 15
  Total amount awarded: $10,000
Contact:
Appaloosa Youth Foundation Scholarship Committee
2720 Pullman Road
Moscow, ID 83843
Phone: 208-882-5578
Fax: 208-882-8150
Web: www.appaloosa.com

Arizona Board of Regents

All-Arizona Academic Team

Type of award: Scholarship.
Intended use: For undergraduate study at postsecondary institution. Designated institutions: Arizona State University, Northern Arizona University, University of Arizona.
Eligibility: Applicant must be U.S. citizen or permanent resident residing in Arizona.
Application requirements: Proof of eligibility, nomination by Arizona community college.
Additional information: Award selection by an Arizona community college. Award is full tuition plus a stipend between $500 and $1,000.
  Amount of award: Full tuition
  Number of awards: 70
Contact:
Arizona Board of Regents
2020 North Central Ave.
Suite 230
Phoenix, AZ 85004
Phone: 602-229-2500
Fax: 602-229-2555
Web: www.azregents.edu

Arizona Tuition Scholarships for Children/Spouses of Slain Public Servants

Type of award: Scholarship, renewable.
Intended use: For undergraduate study at accredited postsecondary institution. Designated institutions: Arizona State University, Northern Arizona University, and University of Arizona.
Eligibility: Applicant must be U.S. citizen or permanent resident residing in Arizona.
Application requirements: Proof of eligibility. Documentation of eligibility by Arizona Peace Officers, Arizona Fire Fighters, or Arizona Emergency Paramedics.

Additional information: Applicant's parent or spouse must have been killed in work-related accident as AZ Fire Fighter, Peace Officer, or Emergency Paramedic. Students must meet university admissions criteria and maintain satisfactory academic progress to renew. Scholarship may also cover summer courses.
Contact:
Arizona Board of Regents
2020 North Central Avenue
Suite 230
Phoenix, AZ 85004-4593
Phone: 602-229-2500
Fax: 602-229-2555
Web: www.azregents.edu

Arizona Tuition Scholarships for Residents

Type of award: Scholarship, renewable.
Intended use: For undergraduate or graduate study at postsecondary institution. Designated institutions: Arizona State University, Northern Arizona University, and University of Arizona.
Eligibility: Applicant must be residing in Arizona.
Application requirements: Nomination by Arizona high schools or Arizona home-schooling families. FAFSA.
Additional information: Awarded to students who demonstrate financial need, merit, or both. Eligibility generally established one year prior to enrollment. Must meet university admissions criteria and maintain satisfactory academic progress to renew. Evidence for merit awards includes test scores, grades, and special talent. Additional Websites: ASU: www.asu.edu; NAU: www.nau.edu; UA: www.arizona.edu. Selection process and requirements may vary by institution.
    Amount of award: Full tuition
Contact:
Arizona high school counselor or institution's admissions office.
Phone: 602-229-2500
Fax: 602-229-2555
Web: www.azregents.edu

High Honors Endorsement Tuition Scholarship

Type of award: Scholarship, renewable.
Intended use: For undergraduate study at accredited postsecondary institution. Designated institutions: Arizona State University, Northern Arizona University, University of Arizona.
Eligibility: Applicant must be U.S. citizen or permanent resident residing in Arizona.
Application requirements: Proof of eligibility.
Additional information: Tuition scholarships are awarded to qualified AZ public high school graduates to attend an AZ university. Must have 3.5 GPA, complete 16 Core Competency courses with a B or better and exceed standards of all three Arizona Instrument Measuring Standards tests. Awardees selected by AZ high schools through the AZ Department of Education.
    Amount of award: Full tuition
    Number of awards: 2,500

Contact:
Arizona Board of Regents
2020 North Central Avenue
Suite 230
Phoenix, AZ 85004
Phone: 602-229-2500
Fax: 602-229-2555
Web: www.azregents.edu

Arkansas Department of Higher Education

Academic Challenge Scholarship

Type of award: Scholarship, renewable.
Intended use: For full-time undergraduate study at postsecondary institution. Designated institutions: Approved Arkansas colleges and universities.
Eligibility: Applicant must be high school senior. Applicant must be U.S. citizen or permanent resident residing in Arkansas.
Basis for selection: Applicant must demonstrate financial need and high academic achievement.
Application requirements: Transcript. ACT and FAFSA.
Additional information: Award is renewable annually up to four years, provided student maintains minimum cumulative GPA of 2.75 and at least 30 semester credit hours per academic year. Applications available online or from the Department of Higher Education.
    Amount of award: $2,500-$3,500
    Number of applicants: 6,821
    Application deadline: June 1
Contact:
Arkansas Department of Higher Education
114 E. Capitol Street
Little Rock, AR 72201-3818
Phone: 800-547-8839
Web: www.arkansaschallenge.com

Arkansas Law Enforcement Officers' Dependents Scholarship

Type of award: Scholarship, renewable.
Intended use: For undergraduate study at accredited vocational, 2-year or 4-year institution.
Eligibility: Applicant must be U.S. citizen or permanent resident residing in Arkansas.
Application requirements: Proof of eligibility.
Additional information: Applicant must be natural, adopted, or step child or spouse of one of the following who has been killed or permanently disabled in duty-related, non-self-inflicted incidents: law enforcement officer; firefighter; Department of Community Punishment employee; state highway, forestry, correction, or park employee; EMT; wildlife enforcement officer; or emergency services worker. Dependent child applicant may be no older than 23; no age restriction for spouse, but must not be remarried. Award is for tuition and room and is for up to 8 semesters. Applicant must be Arkansas resident for at least six months. Application deadlines are August 1 for fall; December 1 for spring/winter; May 1 for summer I; and July 1 for summer II. Visit Website for more information and application.
    Amount of award: Full tuition
    Application deadline: August 1, December 1

Contact:
Arkansas Department of Higher Education
114 E. Capitol Street
Little Rock, AR 72201-3818
Phone: 800-54-STUDY
Web: www.adhe.edu/lawenforcement.html

Governor's Scholars Program

Type of award: Scholarship, renewable.
Intended use: For full-time undergraduate study at postsecondary institution. Designated institutions: Approved Arkansas colleges and universities.
Eligibility: Applicant must be high school senior. Applicant must be U.S. citizen or permanent resident residing in Arkansas.
Basis for selection: Applicant must demonstrate high academic achievement and leadership.
Additional information: Governor's Distinguished Scholars must have at least 32 ACT or 1410 SAT or have been selected as National Merit or National Achievement Finalist. Governor's Distinguished Scholars receive award equal to tuition, fees, room and board up to $10,000 per year. One Governor's Scholarship award per county given to applicants who do not meet Governor's Distinguished Scholars criteria. Governor's Scholars must have minimum 3.5 GPA or 27 ACT or 1220 SAT and receive award of $4,000. Awards renewable up to four years if Distinguished Scholars maintain minimum 3.25 and Governor's Scholar minimum 3.0 GPA and at least 30 credit hours per year. Applications available from high school counselor's office. Visit Website for more information.

Amount of award:	$4,000-$10,000
Number of awards:	325
Application deadline:	February 1
Total amount awarded:	$7,480,950

Contact:
Arkansas Department of Higher Education
114 E. Capitol Street
Little Rock, AR 72201-3818
Phone: 800-547-8839
Web: http://gs.adhe.edu/ScholarshipInfo.aspx

Military Dependents Scholarship Program

Type of award: Scholarship, renewable.
Intended use: For full-time undergraduate, master's, first professional or non-degree study at 4-year or graduate institution.
Eligibility: Applicant must be U.S. citizen or permanent resident residing in Arkansas. Applicant must be dependent of disabled veteran or POW/MIA; or spouse of disabled veteran or POW/MIA who served in the Army, Air Force, Marines, Navy, Coast Guard or Reserves/National Guard. Parent/spouse may also have been killed in action or killed in active ordinance duty. All incidents must have occurred while on active duty after 1/1/60. Parent/spouse must be AR resident or must have been at time of enlistment. Dependent must have been born, adopted, or in legal custody of parent before and during incident.
Application requirements: Proof of eligibility. Graduate students only must submit transcripts.
Additional information: Award for tuition, fees, room and board. Renewable up to four years. Undergraduates must maintain 2.0 GPA, graduates 2.5. Graduate students must not have received any undergraduate education in AR. Application deadlines for summer sessions May 1 and July 1. Visit Website for more information and application.

Amount of award:	Full tuition
Application deadline:	August 1, December 1

Contact:
Arkansas Department of Higher Education
114 E. Capitol Street
Little Rock, AR 72201-3818
Phone: 800-547-8839
Web: www.adhe.edu/miakia.html

Second Effort Scholarship

Type of award: Scholarship, renewable.
Intended use: For undergraduate study at postsecondary institution.
Eligibility: Applicant must be at least 18. Applicant must be U.S. citizen or permanent resident residing in Arkansas.
Basis for selection: Applicant must demonstrate high academic achievement.
Additional information: Applicant must be either at least 18 or former member of high school class that has graduated. Must not have graduated from high school. Must have scored in top 25 of GED in year before application. Students apply for this award only after contacted directly by Arkansas Department of Higher Education. Must have resided in AR for at least 12 months before taking GED. Award renewable up to four years (or equivalent if student is enrolled part-time), provided student maintains minimum 2.5 GPA.

Amount of award:	$1,000
Number of awards:	10
Application deadline:	April 1

Contact:
Arkansas Department of Higher Education
114 E. Capitol Street
Little Rock, AR 72201-3818
Phone: 800-547-8839
Web: www.adhe.edu/secondeffort.html

Workforce Improvement Grant

Type of award: Scholarship.
Intended use: For undergraduate study at postsecondary institution. Designated institutions: Approved postsecondary institutions.
Eligibility: Applicant must be at least 24, returning adult student. Applicant must be U.S. citizen or permanent resident residing in Arkansas.
Basis for selection: Applicant must demonstrate financial need.
Application requirements: FAFSA.
Additional information: Must be AR resident at least six months before application. Students enrolled part time will have grants prorated. Must have unmet need after Pell Grant. Application deadlines determined by each institution for its students. Students apply by completing FAFSA. Must have graduated from high school or have GED.

Amount of award:	$2,000

Contact:
Arkansas Dept. of Higher Education
144 E. Capitol Street
Little Rock, AR 72201
Phone: 800-54-STUDY
Fax: 501-371-2001
Web: www.arscholarships.com

Armed Forces Communications and Electronics Association

AFCEA General Emmett Paige Scholarship

Type of award: Scholarship.
Intended use: For full-time sophomore, junior or senior study at accredited 4-year institution in United States.
Eligibility: Applicant must be U.S. citizen. Applicant must be in military service or veteran; or dependent of active service person, veteran or POW/MIA; or spouse of active service person, veteran or POW/MIA.
Basis for selection: Major/career interest in aerospace; computer/information sciences; engineering, computer; physics; mathematics or engineering, electrical/electronic. Applicant must demonstrate high academic achievement, depth of character, leadership, patriotism, seriousness of purpose and service orientation.
Application requirements: Recommendations, transcript, proof of eligibility. Freshman veteran students must have letters from employer or supervisor or copy of performance evaluation, fitness report or similar document. Copy of discharge form DD214, certificate of service, facsimile of applicant's current DOD, or Coast Guard identification card. At least two letters of recommendation printed on school stationery with signature will be required from field-of-study professors.
Additional information: Send SASE or visit Website for application. Must have minimum 3.4 GPA. Graduating high school seniors not eligible, but veterans enrolled as freshmen are eligible to apply.
   Amount of award: $2,000
   Number of awards: 10
   Application deadline: March 1
   Notification begins: June 1
   Total amount awarded: $20,000
Contact:
Armed Forces Communications and Electronics Association
Educational Foundation
4400 Fair Lakes Court
Fairfax, VA 22033-3899
Phone: 703-631-6149
Fax: 703-631-4693
Web: www.afcea.org/scholarships

AFCEA General John A. Wickham Scholarship

Type of award: Scholarship.
Intended use: For full-time sophomore or junior study at accredited 4-year institution in United States.
Eligibility: Applicant must be U.S. citizen.
Basis for selection: Major/career interest in aerospace; electronics; computer/information sciences; physics; mathematics or engineering, electrical/electronic. Applicant must demonstrate high academic achievement, depth of character, leadership, patriotism, seriousness of purpose and service orientation.
Application requirements: Transcript. At least two letters of recommendation printed on school stationery with signature will be required from field-of-study professors having personal knowledge of candidate's program, achievements and potential.
Additional information: Send SASE or visit Website for application. Student must be sophomore or junior enrolled full time at time of application. Minimum 3.5 GPA.
   Amount of award: $2,000
   Number of awards: 15
   Application deadline: May 1
   Notification begins: June 1
   Total amount awarded: $30,000
Contact:
Armed Forces Communications and Electronics Association
Educational Foundation
4400 Fair Lakes Court
Fairfax, VA 22033-3899
Phone: 800-336-4583 ext. 6149
Fax: 703-631-4693
Web: www.afcea.org/scholarships

AFCEA Professional Part-Time Scholarship

Type of award: Scholarship.
Intended use: For half-time sophomore, junior or senior study at accredited 2-year or 4-year institution in United States.
Eligibility: Applicant must be U.S. citizen.
Basis for selection: Major/career interest in engineering, electrical/electronic; aerospace; engineering, computer; information systems; physics or mathematics. Applicant must demonstrate high academic achievement.
Application requirements: Transcript, proof of eligibility.
Additional information: Scholarship awarded to part-time students pursuing eligible undergraduate program while currently employed in government or industry. Distance learning programs not eligible. Student must be enrolled in at least two classes per semester with major in science or technology degree program. Minimum 3.4 GPA required.
   Amount of award: $1,500
   Application deadline: September 1
Contact:
Armed Forces Communications and Electronics Association
Educational Foundation
4400 Fair Lakes Court
Fairfax, VA 22033-3899
Phone: 703-631-6149
Fax: 703-631-4693
Web: www.afcea.org

AFCEA ROTC Scholarships

Type of award: Scholarship.
Intended use: For full-time sophomore or junior study at accredited 4-year institution in United States.
Eligibility: Applicant or parent must be member/participant of Reserve Officers Training Corps (ROTC). Applicant must be U.S. citizen.
Basis for selection: Major/career interest in aerospace; engineering, electrical/electronic; computer/information sciences; engineering, computer; physics; mathematics; science, general or electronics. Applicant must demonstrate high academic achievement, depth of character, leadership, patriotism, seriousness of purpose and service orientation.
Application requirements: Transcript, nomination by professor of military science, naval science or aerospace studies. Recommendations from ROTC commander and professor in stated major.
Additional information: Applicant must be in ROTC. For application information, contact commander of ROTC unit.

Candidates must be enrolled as sophomores or juniors at time of application.

Amount of award:	$2,000
Number of awards:	60
Application deadline:	April 1
Notification begins:	June 1
Total amount awarded:	$120,000

Contact:
Armed Forces Communications and Electronics Association
Educational Foundation
4400 Fair Lakes Court
Fairfax, VA 22033-3899
Phone: 703-631-6149
Fax: 703-631-4693
Web: www.afcea.org/scholarships

AFCEA Sgt. Jeannette L. Winters, USMC Memorial Scholarship

Type of award: Scholarship.
Intended use: For sophomore, junior or senior study at accredited 4-year institution in United States.
Eligibility: Applicant must be U.S. citizen.
Basis for selection: Major/career interest in aerospace; computer/information sciences; mathematics; engineering or physics. Applicant must demonstrate high academic achievement, depth of character, leadership, patriotism, seriousness of purpose and service orientation.
Application requirements: Recommendations, transcript, proof of eligibility. Certificate of Service, Discharge Form DD214, or facsimile of a current Department of Defense Identification Card. At least two letters of recommendation printed on school stationery with signature will be required from field-of-study professors.
Additional information: For Marines on active duty or honorably discharged. Minimum 3.4 GPA. Qualified sophomore, junior or senior undergraduate students enrolled either part-time or full-time in an eligible degree program. Send SASE or visit Website for application.

Amount of award:	$2,000
Number of awards:	1
Application deadline:	September 1
Notification begins:	October 15
Total amount awarded:	$2,000

Contact:
Armed Forces Communications and Electronics Association
4400 Fair Lakes Court
Fairfax, VA 22033-3899
Phone: 800-336-4583 ext. 6149
Fax: 703-631-4693
Web: www.afcea.org/scholarships

AFCEA/Lockheed Martin IT Scholarship

Type of award: Scholarship.
Intended use: For full-time sophomore or junior study at accredited 4-year institution in United States. Designated institutions: Postsecondary institutions in the greater San Diego area.
Eligibility: Applicant must be U.S. citizen residing in California.
Basis for selection: Major/career interest in aerospace; electronics; computer/information sciences; physics; mathematics or engineering, electrical/electronic. Applicant must demonstrate high academic achievement, depth of character, leadership, patriotism, seriousness of purpose and service orientation.
Application requirements: Transcript. At least two letters of recommendation printed on school stationery with signature will be required from field-of-study professors.
Additional information: Minimum 3.5 GPA required.

Amount of award:	$3,000
Number of awards:	1
Application deadline:	May 1
Notification begins:	June 1

Contact:
Armed Forces Communications and Electronics Association
Educational Foundation
4400 Fair Lakes Court
Fairfax, VA 22033-3899
Phone: 800-336-4583 ext. 6149
Fax: 703-631-4693
Web: www.afcea.org

Distance-Learning/On-Line Programs Scholarship

Type of award: Scholarship.
Intended use: For full-time junior or senior study at accredited 4-year institution.
Eligibility: Applicant must be U.S. citizen.
Basis for selection: Major/career interest in mathematics; physics; engineering, electrical/electronic; engineering, chemical or computer/information sciences.
Application requirements: Transcript. At least two letters of recommendation printed on school stationery with signature will be required from field-of-study professors.

Amount of award:	$1,500
Number of awards:	1
Number of applicants:	10
Application deadline:	June 1
Total amount awarded:	$1,500

Contact:
Armed Forces Communications and Electronics Association
4400 Fair Lakes Court
Fairfax, VA 22033-3899
Phone: 703-631-6149
Fax: 703-631-4693
Web: www.afcea.org/scholarships

Vice Admiral Jerry O. Tuttle, USN (Ret.), and Mrs. Barbara A. Tuttle Science and Technology Scholarship

Type of award: Scholarship.
Intended use: For full-time sophomore, junior or senior study at accredited 4-year institution in United States. Designated institutions: Accredited technological institutes and accredited four-year colleges and universities with technology programs.
Eligibility: Applicant must be U.S. citizen.
Basis for selection: Major/career interest in computer/information sciences; engineering, computer or electronics. Applicant must demonstrate high academic achievement.
Application requirements: Recommendations, transcript. At least two letters of recommendation printed on school stationery with signature will be required from field-of-study professors.
Additional information: Student must be sophomore or junior enrolled full time in technology related field at time of application. Priority consideration will be given to military enlisted candidate.

Armed Forces Communications and Electronics Association: Vice Admiral Jerry O. Tuttle Science and Technology Scholarship

Amount of award: $2,000
Number of awards: 1
Application deadline: November 1
Contact:
Armed Forces Communications and Electronics Association
Educational Foundation
4400 Fair Lakes Court
Fairfax, VA 22033-3899
Phone: 703-631-6149
Fax: 703-631-4693
Web: www.afcea.org

Armenian General Benevolent Union

Armenian General Benevolent Union International Scholarship Program

Type of award: Scholarship, renewable.
Intended use: For full-time undergraduate or graduate study outside United States.
Eligibility: Applicant must be Armenian. Applicant must be U.S. citizen or permanent resident.
Basis for selection: Competition/talent/interest in study abroad. Applicant must demonstrate financial need, high academic achievement, depth of character, leadership, seriousness of purpose and service orientation.
Application requirements: Transcript, proof of eligibility. Two letters of recommendation, resume, copies of any published work, one small photograph.
Additional information: Students must provide verification of enrollment. Must be of Armenian descent. U.S. scholarship application deadline is April 1; international scholarship deadline is May 15. Applications may be downloaded from Website.

Amount of award: $2,500-$7,500
Application deadline: April 1, May 15
Notification begins: September 15
Contact:
Armenian General Benevolent Union
Mrs. Maral Achian
55 E. 59th Street, 7th Floor
New York, NY 10022-1112
Phone: 212-319-6383
Fax: 212-319-6507
Web: www.agbu.org

ARMY Emergency Relief

MG James Ursano Scholarship Fund

Type of award: Scholarship, renewable.
Intended use: For full-time freshman, sophomore, junior or senior study at accredited vocational, 2-year or 4-year institution.
Eligibility: Applicant must be single, at least 16, no older than 22. Applicant must be U.S. citizen or permanent resident. Applicant must be dependent of active service person, veteran or deceased veteran who serves or served in the Army.
Basis for selection: Applicant must demonstrate financial need, high academic achievement and leadership.
Application requirements: Transcript, proof of eligibility.
Additional information: Applicants must be enrolled, accepted or pending acceptance as full-time dependent students for entire academic year in postsecondary institutions approved by Department of Education for Title IV funds. For unmarried dependent children of army soldiers only. Applicants must maintain at least 2.0 GPA. Application may be downloaded from Website.

Amount of award: $1,000-$2,700
Number of awards: 2,338
Number of applicants: 3,300
Application deadline: March 1
Notification begins: June 1
Total amount awarded: $4,396,540
Contact:
ARMY Emergency Relief/MG James Ursano Scholarship Fund
200 Stovall Street
Room 5N13
Alexandria, VA 22332-0600
Phone: 703-428-0035
Fax: 703-325-7183
Web: www.aerhq.org

The Art Institutes

Best Teen Chef Culinary Scholarship Competition

Type of award: Scholarship.
Intended use: For undergraduate study at 2-year or 4-year institution in United States. Designated institutions: Art Institute schools offering culinary arts programs.
Eligibility: Applicant must be high school senior.
Basis for selection: Competition/talent/interest in culinary arts, based on meal preparation ability and originality. Major/career interest in culinary arts or hotel/restaurant management.
Application requirements: Essay, transcript. Plan for two-course menu, including original recipes.
Additional information: In addition to three full-tuition scholarships, the total of which exceeds $30,000, financial awards are given. Regional semifinalists notified on March 12, with first-place winner competing in national event slated for May. Minimum high school GPA of 2.0. For more information and deadline details, visit Website or contact nearest Art Institute.

Amount of award: Full tuition
Number of awards: 9
Number of applicants: 265
Application deadline: February 11
Notification begins: May 13
Contact:
The Art Institutes
210 Sixth Ave, 33rd Floor
Pittsburgh, PA 15222
Phone: 888-542-2600
Fax: 412-562-1732
Web: www.artinstitutes.edu/nc

Arthur and Doreen Parrett Scholarship Trust Fund

Arthur and Doreen Parrett Scholarship

Type of award: Scholarship, renewable.
Intended use: For full-time sophomore, junior, senior, master's, doctoral or first professional study.
Eligibility: Applicant must be residing in Washington.
Basis for selection: Major/career interest in science, general; engineering; dentistry or medicine. Applicant must demonstrate financial need and high academic achievement.
Application requirements: Recommendations, transcript.
Additional information: Applicants must have completed first year of college. Include SASE with inquiries, and information will be forwarded.
    Amount of award: $1,000-$3,500
    Number of awards: 15
    Number of applicants: 100
    Application deadline: January 31
Contact:
Arthur and Doreen Parrett Scholarship Trust Fund
c/o U.S. Bank of Washington - Trust Dept.
1420 5th Avenue, Suite 2100
Seattle, WA 98111-7206

The ASCAP Foundation

ASCAP Morton Gould Young Composers Award

Type of award: Scholarship, renewable.
Intended use: For non-degree study.
Eligibility: Applicant must be U.S. citizen, permanent resident or international student.
Basis for selection: Competition/talent/interest in music performance/composition. Major/career interest in music.
Application requirements: Reproduction of score or manuscript of one original concert music work, biographical information, list of compositions to date, and, if available, cd or tape of composition.
Additional information: Amount and number of awards vary. Applicant must not have reached 30th birthday by January 1. All applications must include SASE. Applicants may submit only one composition. International applicants must be enrolled students with student visa.
    Number of awards: 39
    Number of applicants: 570
    Application deadline: March 1
    Notification begins: May 1
    Total amount awarded: $30,000
Contact:
ASCAP Foundation Morton Gould Young Composers Awards
c/o Frances Richard, Concert Music
One Lincoln Plaza
New York, NY 10023
Phone: 212-621-6329
Fax: 212-595-3342
Web: www.ascapfoundation.org

Rudolf Nissim Prize

Type of award: Scholarship.
Intended use: For non-degree study.
Basis for selection: Competition/talent/interest in music performance/composition. Major/career interest in music.
Application requirements: Proof of eligibility. Bound copy of score of only one original music composition, which has not been professionally performed, for a large ensemble that requires a conductor.
Additional information: Applicant must be composer member of ASCAP. View Website for specific application requirements and details.
    Amount of award: $5,000
    Number of awards: 1
    Number of applicants: 250
    Application deadline: November 15
    Notification begins: January 15
    Total amount awarded: $5,000
Contact:
Fran Richard, Concert Music
The ASCAP Foundation
One Lincoln Plaza
New York, NY 10023
Phone: 212-621-6329
Web: www.ascapfoundation.org

Asian American Journalists Association

AAJA/Chicago Tribune Internship Grant

Type of award: Scholarship.
Intended use: For full-time undergraduate study.
Eligibility: Applicant must be at least 18.
Basis for selection: Major/career interest in journalism or radio/television/film. Applicant must demonstrate financial need.
Application requirements: Recommendations, essay. Resume, proof of age, and statement of financial need. Submit three copies of all material.
Additional information: Applicants may also be recent college graduates. Must have already secured summer broadcast internship at TV or radio network before applying. Application may be downloaded from Website. Must be serious about career in broadcast or online journalism. Must be 18 by May 15 of application year. One broadcast internship will also be given.
    Amount of award: $1,500
    Number of awards: 3
    Number of applicants: 24
    Application deadline: April 25
Contact:
AAJA/Chicago Tribune Internship Grant
Asian American Journalists Association
1182 Market Street, Suite 320
San Francisco, CA 94102
Phone: 415-346-2051 ext. 102
Fax: 415-346-6343
Web: www.aaja.org

Asian American Journalists Association Scholarships

Type of award: Scholarship.
Intended use: For full-time undergraduate or graduate study in United States.
Eligibility: Applicant must be high school senior.
Basis for selection: Major/career interest in journalism; film/video or radio/television/film. Applicant must demonstrate financial need, high academic achievement, depth of character, seriousness of purpose and service orientation.
Application requirements: Portfolio, recommendations, essay, transcript. Resume. Work samples according to emphasis (broadcast, photojournalism, or print). Submit three copies of all material.
Additional information: Asian heritage not required. Selection based on commitment to the field of journalism, sensitivity to Asian-American and Pacific Islander issues as demonstrated by community involvement, and journalistic ability. Visit Website for application and more information. AAJA membership is recommended for finalists and required for awardees. Must be taking or plan to take journalism courses and or/pursuing journalism career. One application for six named national scholarships as well as for local chapter scholarships. Some scholarships may have specific gender, major, or level-of-study requirement.
  Amount of award: $2,000-$25,000
  Number of awards: 18
  Number of applicants: 104
Contact:
Asian American Journalists Association
Scholarship Committee
1182 Market Street, Suite 320
San Francisco, CA 94102
Phone: 415-346-2051 ext. 102
Fax: 415-346-6343
Web: www.aaja.org

Broadcast Internship Grant

Type of award: Scholarship.
Intended use: For full-time undergraduate study at 4-year institution.
Eligibility: Applicant must be at least 18.
Basis for selection: Major/career interest in journalism or radio/television/film. Applicant must demonstrate financial need.
Application requirements: Recommendations, essay. Resume, proof of age, and statement of financial need. Submit three copies of all materials.
Additional information: Applicant must have already secured summer broadcast internship at TV or radio network. Must be 18 by May of application year. Application may be downloaded from Website. AAJA membership recommended for finalists and required for awardee.
  Amount of award: $2,500
  Number of awards: 1
  Number of applicants: 3
  Application deadline: April 25
Contact:
Asian American Journalists Association
1182 Market Street
Suite 320
San Francisco, CA 94102
Phone: 415-346-2051 ext. 102
Fax: 415-346-6343
Web: www.aaja.org

Asian American Journalists Association, Texas Chapter

AAJA Texas Scholarship

Type of award: Scholarship.
Intended use: For undergraduate or graduate study.
Basis for selection: Major/career interest in journalism.
Application requirements: Transcript. Resume, two letters of recommendation, work samples.
Additional information: The student must be a high school senior or college student, attending school in, or from, Texas, Oklahoma, or New Mexico. Application available on Website.
  Amount of award: $1,000
  Number of awards: 1
  Number of applicants: 2
  Application deadline: May 31
  Notification begins: June 30
  Total amount awarded: $1,000
Contact:
Asian American Journalists
Ft. Worth Star Telegram
P.O. Box 1870
Ft. Worth, TX 76110
Phone: 817-390-7695
Web: www.aajatexas.org

ASM Materials Education Foundation

ASM Outstanding Scholars Awards

Type of award: Scholarship, renewable.
Intended use: For full-time sophomore, junior or senior study at accredited 4-year institution in or outside United States.
Eligibility: Applicant or parent must be member/participant of ASM International. Applicant must be U.S. citizen, permanent resident or international student.
Basis for selection: Major/career interest in engineering or materials science. Applicant must demonstrate high academic achievement, depth of character and seriousness of purpose.
Application requirements: Recommendations, essay, transcript. Resume optional. List of complete and current courses. Photograph.
Additional information: May also major in metallurgy or related science or engineering disciplines if applicant demonstrates strong interest in materials science. Must be member of ASM International. International student members may apply. Limited to two years. Visit Website for application and full details.
  Amount of award: $2,000
  Number of awards: 3
  Application deadline: May 1
  Notification begins: July 15
  Total amount awarded: $6,000

Contact:
ASM Materials Education Foundation
Scholarship Program
9639 Kinsman Road
Materials Park, OH 44073-0002
Phone: 440-338-5151
Fax: 440-338-4634
Web: www.asminternational.org/foundation

Edward J. Dulis Scholarship

Type of award: Scholarship, renewable.
Intended use: For junior or senior study at accredited 4-year institution in United States or Canada.
Basis for selection: Major/career interest in engineering, materials. Applicant must demonstrate financial need, high academic achievement, depth of character and service orientation.
Application requirements: Recommendations, essay, transcript. Resume optional. List of complete and current courses. Photograph.
Additional information: Applicant may also major in metallurgy or related science or engineering field if has interest in materials science. Must be student member of ASM International. Visit Website for application and full details. Award limited to two years.

Amount of award:	$1,500
Number of awards:	1
Application deadline:	May 1
Notification begins:	July 15

Contact:
ASM Materials Education Foundation
Scholarship Program
9639 Kingman Road
Materials Park, OH 44073-0002
Phone: 440-338-5151
Fax: 440-338-4634
Web: www.asminternational.org/foundation

George A. Roberts Scholarships

Type of award: Scholarship, renewable.
Intended use: For full-time junior or senior study at accredited 4-year institution in United States or Canada.
Eligibility: Applicant or parent must be member/participant of ASM International. Applicant must be U.S. citizen, permanent resident or Canadian citizen or permanent resident.
Basis for selection: Major/career interest in engineering or materials science. Applicant must demonstrate financial need, high academic achievement, depth of character and seriousness of purpose.
Application requirements: Recommendations, essay, transcript. Resume optional. List of complete and current courses. Photograph.
Additional information: Applicant may also major in metallurgy or related science or engineering field if has interest in materials science. Must be student member of ASM International. Visit Website for application and full details. Award limited to two years.

Amount of award:	$6,000
Number of awards:	7
Application deadline:	May 1
Notification begins:	July 15
Total amount awarded:	$42,000

Contact:
ASM Materials Education Foundation
Scholarship Program
9639 Kinsman Road
Materials Park, OH 44073-0002
Phone: 440-388-5151
Fax: 440-388-4634
Web: www.asminternational.org/foundation

John M. Haniak Scholarship

Type of award: Scholarship, renewable.
Intended use: For junior or senior study at accredited 4-year institution in United States or Canada.
Basis for selection: Major/career interest in engineering, materials. Applicant must demonstrate financial need, high academic achievement, depth of character and service orientation.
Application requirements: Recommendations, essay, transcript. Resume optional. List of complete and current courses. Photograph.
Additional information: Applicant may also major in metallurgy or related science or engineering field if has interest in materials science. Must be student member of ASM International. Visit Website for application and full details. Award limited to two years.

Amount of award:	$1,500
Number of awards:	1
Application deadline:	May 1
Notification begins:	July 15

Contact:
ASM Materials Education Foundation
Scholarship Program
9639 Kingman Road
Materials Park, OH 44073-0002
Phone: 440-338-5151
Fax: 440-338-4634
Web: www.asminternational.org/foundation

Lucille & Charles A. Wert Scholarship

Type of award: Scholarship, renewable.
Intended use: For junior or senior study at accredited 4-year institution in United States or Canada.
Basis for selection: Major/career interest in engineering, materials. Applicant must demonstrate financial need, high academic achievement, depth of character and service orientation.
Application requirements: Recommendations, essay, transcript. Resume optional. List of complete and current courses. Photograph.
Additional information: Applicant may also major in metallurgy or related science or engineering field if has interest in materials science. Must be student member of ASM International. Scholarship provides recipient with one-year full tuition up to $10,000. Award limited to two years. Visit Website for application and full details.

Amount of award:	$10,000
Number of awards:	1
Application deadline:	May 1
Notification begins:	July 15

ASM Materials Education Foundation: Lucille & Charles A. Wert Scholarship

Contact:
ASM Materials Education Foundation
Scholarship Program
9639 Kingman Road
Materials Park, OH 44073-0002
Phone: 440-338-5151
Fax: 440-338-4634
Web: www.asminternational.org/foundation

Nicholas J. Grant Scholarship

Type of award: Scholarship, renewable.
Intended use: For full-time junior or senior study at accredited 4-year institution in United States or Canada.
Eligibility: Applicant or parent must be member/participant of ASM International. Applicant must be U.S. citizen, permanent resident or Canadian citizen or permanent resident.
Basis for selection: Major/career interest in engineering or materials science. Applicant must demonstrate financial need, high academic achievement, depth of character, leadership, seriousness of purpose and service orientation.
Application requirements: Recommendations, essay, transcript. Resume optional. List of complete and current courses. Photograph.
Additional information: Major may also be in metallurgy or related science or engineering disciplines if applicant demonstrates strong interest in materials science. Must be ASM International member. Award is one-year full tuition. Limited to two years. Visit Website for application and full details.

Amount of award:	Full tuition
Number of awards:	1
Application deadline:	May 1
Notification begins:	July 15

Contact:
ASM Materials Education Foundation
Scholarship Program
9639 Kinsman Road
Materials Park, OH 44073-0002
Phone: 440-338-5151
Fax: 440-338-4634
Web: www.asminternational.org/foundation

William Park Woodside Founder's Scholarship

Type of award: Scholarship, renewable.
Intended use: For full-time junior or senior study at accredited 4-year institution in United States or Canada.
Eligibility: Applicant or parent must be member/participant of ASM International. Applicant must be U.S. citizen, permanent resident or Canadian citizen or permanent resident.
Basis for selection: Major/career interest in engineering or materials science. Applicant must demonstrate financial need, high academic achievement, depth of character and seriousness of purpose.
Application requirements: Recommendations, essay, transcript. Resume optional. List of complete and current courses. Photograph.
Additional information: May also have major in metallurgy or related science or engineering disciplines if applicant demonstrates strong interest in materials science. Must be member of ASM International. Scholarship provides recipient with one-year full tuition, up to $10,000. Limited to two years. Visit Website for application and full details.

Amount of award:	$10,000
Number of awards:	1
Application deadline:	May 1
Notification begins:	July 15
Total amount awarded:	$10,000

Contact:
ASM Materials Education Foundation
Scholarship Program
9639 Kinsman Road
Materials Park, OH 44073-0002
Phone: 440-338-5151
Fax: 440-338-4634
Web: www.asminternational.org/foundation

Associated Builders and Contractors, Inc.

Trimmer Education Foundation ABC Student Chapter Scholarship Program

Type of award: Scholarship, renewable.
Intended use: For sophomore, junior or senior study at 2-year or 4-year institution.
Eligibility: Applicant or parent must be member/participant of Associated Builders and Contractors.
Basis for selection: Major/career interest in construction management or construction. Applicant must demonstrate financial need and high academic achievement.
Application requirements: Recommendations, transcript. Resume. Photocopy of first page of Student Aid Report.
Additional information: Minimum 3.0 GPA required in major; 2.85 minimum overall. Must be active member of Associated Builders and Contractors (ABC) student chapter or work for ABC member firm. Must have completed at least one year of construction-related associate or baccalaureate degree program, and have one full year remaining. Architecture and most engineering students excluded. See Website for application deadline.

Amount of award:	$5,000
Total amount awarded:	$50,000

Contact:
Trimmer Education Foundation Scholarship Program Attn: John Strock
c/o Associated Builders and Contractors
4250 North Fairfax Drive, 9th Floor
Arlington, VA 22203
Phone: 703-812-2000
Web: www.abc.org/

Associated General Contractors Education and Research Foundation

AGC Education and Research Undergraduate Scholarship

Type of award: Scholarship, renewable.

Intended use: For full-time sophomore or junior study at accredited 4-year institution.
Eligibility: Applicant must be U.S. citizen or permanent resident.
Basis for selection: Major/career interest in engineering, civil; engineering, construction or construction.
Application requirements: Recommendations, transcript.
Additional information: Must be enrolled in or planning to enroll in an ABET or ACCE accredited full-time, four- or five-year university program of construction or civil engineering. Applications are available September 1 from AGC office or Website. Seniors with one full academic year of course work remaining are eligible.

Amount of award:	$2,500-$7,500
Number of awards:	100
Number of applicants:	100
Application deadline:	November 1
Notification begins:	February 1

Contact:
Association of General Contractors Education and Research Foundation
Attn: Floretta Slade, Director of Programs
2300 Wilson Boulevard, Suite 400
Arlington, VA 22201
Phone: 703-837-5342
Fax: 703-837-5451
Web: www.agcfoundation.org

Associated General Contractors James L. Allhands Essay Competition

Type of award: Scholarship.
Intended use: For full-time senior study at accredited 4-year institution. Designated institutions: ABET- or ACCE-accredited universities with construction management or construction-related engineering programs.
Basis for selection: Competition/talent/interest in writing/journalism. Major/career interest in engineering, civil; engineering, construction or construction.
Application requirements: Essay. Essay abstract, letter from faculty sponsor.
Additional information: First prize is $1,000, plus all-expenses-paid trip to AGC convention; winner's sponsor/advisor receives $500, plus all-expenses-paid trip to convention. Second prize is $500. Third prize is $300. Application material must be emailed. See Website for essay topic and guidelines.

Amount of award:	$300-$1,000
Number of awards:	3
Number of applicants:	50
Application deadline:	November 1
Notification begins:	February 1
Total amount awarded:	$2,300

Contact:
Association of General Contractors Education and Research Foundation
Attn: Floretta Slade, Director of Programs
333 John Carlyle Street, Suite 200
Alexandria, VA 22314
Phone: 703-548-3118
Fax: 703-548-3119
Web: www.agcfoundation.org

Associated Press

Associated Press/APTRA-CLETE Roberts Memorial Journalism Scholarship

Type of award: Scholarship.
Intended use: For undergraduate or graduate study at 4-year or graduate institution in United States.
Eligibility: Applicant must be residing in California, Hawaii or Nevada.
Basis for selection: Major/career interest in journalism or radio/television/film.
Application requirements: Recommendations, essay. Examples of broadcast-related work.
Additional information: For study in broadcast journalism. Visit Website for more information and application.

Amount of award:	$1,500
Number of awards:	4
Application deadline:	December 10
Notification begins:	December 17
Total amount awarded:	$6,000

Contact:
APTRA
CBS 5 TV
855 Battery Street
San Francisco, CA 94111
Web: www.aptra.org

Association for Library and Information Science Foundation

ALISE Bodhan S. Wynar Research Paper Competition

Type of award: Scholarship.
Intended use: For undergraduate or graduate study.
Eligibility: Applicant or parent must be member/participant of Association for Library/Information Science Education.
Basis for selection: Competition/talent/interest in research paper, based on any aspect of library or information science using any methodology. Major/career interest in library science.
Application requirements: Proof of eligibility. Paper must not exceed 25 double-spaced pages with one-inch margins and 12-point font. Two title pages one with, one without, author and institution name. Must e-mail to Dr. Eileen G. Abels at eileen.abels@ischool.drexel.edu.
Additional information: Paper cannot have been published, though may be accepted for publication. Visit Website for detailed explanation of requirements. Research papers prepared by joint investigators eligible; at least one author must be member of ALISE by deadline date. Winners expected to present papers at ALISE Annual Conference. Can submit only one paper per competition and may not submit same paper to different ALISE competitions. Papers completed in pursuit of master and doctoral degrees ineligible, though data and spinoffs from such papers are eligible. Papers generated through other grants and funding are eligible.

Association for Library and Information Science Foundation: ALISE Bodhan S. Wynar Research Paper Competition

Amount of award: $2,500
Number of awards: 2
Application deadline: July 15
Total amount awarded: $5,000
Contact:
ALISE National Office
65 E. Wacker Place Suite 1900
Chicago, IL 60612
Phone: 312-795-0996
Fax: 312-419-8950
Web: www.alise.org

ALISE Research Grant Award

Type of award: Research grant.
Intended use: For undergraduate or graduate study.
Eligibility: Applicant or parent must be member/participant of Association for Library/Information Science Education.
Basis for selection: Major/career interest in library science. Applicant must demonstrate high academic achievement.
Application requirements: Proof of eligibility, research proposal. Proposal must not exceed 20 double-spaced pages. Submit via e-mail to Dr. Edie Rasmussen at edie@interchange.ubc.ca.
Additional information: Award to support research broadly related to education for library and information science. Visit Website for detailed explanation of proposal requirements. Must be member of ALISE as of deadline date. More than one grant may be awarded; however, total amount of funding for all grants not to exceed $5,000. Research grant award cannot be used to support doctoral dissertation. Awardee(s) must present preliminary report at ALISE Annual Conference.

Amount of award: $5,000
Number of awards: 1
Application deadline: July 15
Total amount awarded: $5,000
Contact:
ALISE National Office ALISE Awards
65 E. Wacker Place Suite 1900
Chicago, IL 60612
Phone: 312-795-0996
Fax: 312-419-8950
Web: www.alise.org

Dialog/ALISE Methodology Paper Competition

Type of award: Scholarship.
Intended use: For undergraduate or graduate study.
Eligibility: Applicant or parent must be member/participant of Association for Library/Information Science Education.
Basis for selection: Competition/talent/interest in research paper, based on description and discussion of a research method or technique, including discussion of method's or technique's relevance to library and information science. Major/career interest in library science.
Application requirements: Paper must not exceed 25 double-spaced pages with one-inch margins and 12-point font. Two title pages, one with and one without author name and institution. 200-word abstract. Must be e-mailed to Dr. Lisl Zach at lisl.zach@ischool.drexel.edu.
Additional information: Papers completed in pursuit of master's or doctoral degrees are eligible, as are papers generated as result of research grant or other source of funding. Papers prepared by joint authors eligible; at least one author must be member of ALISE. Papers that stress findings are ineligible. Winners expected to present papers at ALISE Annual Conference. May submit only one paper per competition and may not submit same paper to multiple ALISE competitions.

Amount of award: $500
Number of awards: 1
Application deadline: July 15
Total amount awarded: $500
Contact:
ALISE National Office ALISE Awards
65 E. Wacker Place Suite 1900
P.O. Box 4219
Chicago, IL 60612
Phone: 312-795-0996
Fax: 312-419-8950
Web: www.alise.org

Association for Women in Architecture Foundation

Women in Architecture Scholarship

Type of award: Scholarship, renewable.
Intended use: For full-time junior, senior, master's, doctoral or first professional study at 4-year or graduate institution.
Eligibility: Applicant must be female. Applicant must be residing in California.
Basis for selection: Major/career interest in architecture; interior design; engineering; landscape architecture; urban planning; engineering, civil; engineering, electrical/electronic; engineering, mechanical or engineering, structural. Applicant must demonstrate high academic achievement and seriousness of purpose.
Application requirements: Recommendations, essay, transcript. Portfolio. Essay giving reasons for studying chosen field, career objectives, and what you plan to be doing in 5 or 10 years. SASE.
Additional information: Must be California resident or attend California school to qualify. Students may also be studying in the following majors: land planning, environmental design, architectural rendering and illustrating. Student must have completed minimum of 18 units in major by application due date. Applications may be downloaded from Website. Applications due in mid-March; see Website for exact date.

Amount of award: $1,000
Number of awards: 5
Number of applicants: 60
Total amount awarded: $5,000
Contact:
Association for Women in Architecture Foundation
22815 Frampton Avenue
Torrence, CA 90501-5034
Phone: 310-534-8466
Fax: 310-257-6885
Web: www.awa-la.org

Association for Women in Communications

Association for Women in Communications Scholarship

Type of award: Scholarship.
Intended use: For full-time junior, senior or graduate study at accredited 4-year or graduate institution.
Eligibility: Applicant must be residing in Washington.
Basis for selection: Major/career interest in communications; journalism; radio/television/film; film/video; graphic arts/design; advertising; public relations or marketing. Applicant must demonstrate financial need, high academic achievement, depth of character and service orientation.
Application requirements: Transcript. Cover letter, resume. Two work samples.
Additional information: Additional major/career interests may include print or broadcast journalism, multimedia design, photography, or technical communication. Must attend or plan to attend accredited four-year college (applicant may be at community or junior college but be accepted to four-year college where scholarship will be used). Graduate students will be considered, however, if not about to graduate. Must demonstrate excellence in communications and positive contributions to communications on campus and in community.

Amount of award:	$1,500
Number of awards:	2
Application deadline:	March 16
Total amount awarded:	$3,000

Contact:
Scholarhip Chair Association for Women in Communications
Seattle Professional Chapter
P.O. Box 472
Mountlake, WA 98043
Phone: 206-654-2929
Web: www.seattleawc.org/scholarships.html

Association of American Geographers

Anne U. White Fund

Type of award: Research grant, renewable.
Intended use: For undergraduate, graduate or non-degree study at postsecondary institution.
Eligibility: Applicant or parent must be member/participant of Association of American Geographers.
Basis for selection: Major/career interest in geography.
Application requirements: Research proposal. Both spouses must complete background information forms. Digital submission required with limited exceptions.
Additional information: Fund enables AAG member to engage in useful field studies jointly with his/her spouse. Must have been member for at least two years at time of application. Report summarizing results and documenting expenses underwritten by grant must be submitted within 12 months after receiving award. Applicants may reapply but preference given to those who have not been awarded grants in the past.

Amount of award:	$1,500
Number of awards:	3
Number of applicants:	20
Application deadline:	December 31
Notification begins:	March 1
Total amount awarded:	$5,000

Contact:
Association of American Geographers
1710 16 Street, NW
Washington, DC 20009-3198
Phone: 202-234-1450
Web: www.aag.org

The Association of Insurance Compliance Professionals

AICP Heartland Chapter Scholarship

Type of award: Scholarship, renewable.
Intended use: For undergraduate or graduate study at postsecondary institution.
Basis for selection: Major/career interest in insurance/actuarial science; business or mathematics.
Application requirements: Recommendations, transcript. Resume, short narrative describing current and future interest to pursue education/career in the insurance field.
Additional information: Applicant or applicant's spouse (including domestic or civil union partner) parent, grandparent, or legal guardian must be current Heartland AICP member in good standing. Minimum 2.75 GPA.

Amount of award:	$500
Number of awards:	1
Application deadline:	April 1
Notification begins:	May 15

Contact:
Connie Doud, CPCU, CCP
Farmers Mutual Hail Ins. Co. of Iowa
6785 Westown Parkway
West Des Moines, IA 50266
Web: www.aicp.net

AICP Scholarship

Type of award: Scholarship, renewable.
Intended use: For full-time sophomore, junior, senior or master's study.
Basis for selection: Major/career interest in mathematics; insurance/actuarial science; business; economics or finance/banking.
Application requirements: Recommendations, transcript. Resume, short narrative describing current and future interest to pursue education/career in the insurance field.
Additional information: Minimum 2.75 GPA. Applicant must be at least a second-semester sophomore.

Amount of award:	$1,000
Number of awards:	3
Application deadline:	May 1
Notification begins:	July 1
Total amount awarded:	$3,000

The Association of Insurance Compliance Professionals: AICP Scholarship

Contact:
Association of Insurance Compliance Professionals
12100 Sunset Hills Road, Suite 130
Reston, VA 20190
Phone: 703-234-4074
Web: www.aicp.net

Association of State Dam Safety Officials

Dam Safety Officials Scholarship

Type of award: Scholarship.
Intended use: For senior study in United States.
Eligibility: Applicant must be U.S. citizen.
Basis for selection: Major/career interest in engineering, civil. Applicant must demonstrate financial need, high academic achievement, depth of character, leadership, seriousness of purpose and service orientation.
Application requirements: Recommendations, essay, transcript.
Additional information: Decisions based on grades, career goals, and extracurricular activities.
- **Amount of award:** $5,000
- **Number of awards:** 2
- **Number of applicants:** 50
- **Application deadline:** March 31
- **Notification begins:** July 1
- **Total amount awarded:** $10,000

Contact:
Association of State Dam Safety Officials
450 Old Vine Street, 2nd Floor
Lexington, KY 40507
Phone: 859-257-5140
Fax: 859-323-1958
Web: www.damsafety.org

Astraea Lesbian Foundation for Justice

Margot Karle Scholarship

Type of award: Scholarship.
Intended use: For full-time undergraduate study at 4-year institution in United States. Designated institutions: City University of New York (CUNY) schools.
Eligibility: Applicant must be female. Applicant must be U.S. citizen or permanent resident.
Basis for selection: Competition/talent/interest in gay/lesbian. Applicant must demonstrate depth of character, leadership and seriousness of purpose.
Application requirements: Recommendations, transcript. Two essays.
Additional information: Visit Website for deadline and more information. Application must be received by Astraea--not just postmarked--by deadline.
- **Amount of award:** $1,000
- **Number of awards:** 1
- **Application deadline:** November 15
- **Notification begins:** December 31

Contact:
Astraea National Lesbian Action Foundation
116 East 16th Street, 7th floor
New York, NY 10003
Phone: 212-529-8021
Fax: 212-982-3321
Web: www.astraeafoundation.org

Atlanta Association of Black Journalists

Xernona Clayton Scholarship

Type of award: Scholarship.
Intended use: For undergraduate study at accredited 4-year institution.
Eligibility: Applicant must be African American. Applicant must be U.S. citizen residing in Georgia.
Basis for selection: Major/career interest in communications; journalism; English; public relations or radio/television/film. Applicant must demonstrate depth of character and leadership.
Application requirements: Recommendations, essay, transcript.
Additional information: Minimum 3.0 GPA. Samples of published work may be submitted but are not required. Up to $10,000 in scholarships awarded depending on number of suitable applicants. Visit Website for details and application.
- **Amount of award:** $2,000-$5,000
- **Total amount awarded:** $10,000

Contact:
Atlanta Association of Black Journalists
P.O. Box 54128
Atlanta, GA 30308
Phone: 404-508-4612
Web: www.aabj.org

Automotive Hall of Fame

Automotive Educational Fund Scholarship

Type of award: Scholarship, renewable.
Intended use: For full-time undergraduate study at accredited 2-year, 4-year or graduate institution in United States.
Eligibility: Applicant must be U.S. citizen, permanent resident or international student.
Application requirements: Recommendations, transcript, proof of eligibility. High school seniors must have proof of acceptance to postsecondary institution and two letters of recommendation.
Additional information: Applicant must have interest in pursuing career in the automotive industry. SASE for application, or download from Website. All required materials must be submitted with application to be considered. Only award recipients will be notified. Minimum 3.0 GPA. High school seniors may also apply.
- **Amount of award:** $1,000-$2,000
- **Number of awards:** 20
- **Application deadline:** May 30
- **Notification begins:** July 31

Contact:
Automotive Hall of Fame
21400 Oakwood Blvd.
Dearborn, MI 48124-4078
Phone: 313-240-4000
Fax: 313-240-8641
Web: www.automotivehalloffame.org

AXA Achievement Scholarship

AXA Achievement Scholarship in Association with U.S. News & World Report

Type of award: Scholarship.
Intended use: For full-time undergraduate study at accredited 2-year or 4-year institution in United States.
Eligibility: Applicant must be high school senior. Applicant must be U.S. citizen.
Application requirements: Recommendations.
Additional information: Fifty-two students, to be known as AXA Achievers, will be selected to receive $10,000 scholarships, one from each state, the District of Columbia and Puerto Rico. From among the state recipients, ten students will be named national AXA Achievers. They will be selected to receive national awards at $15,000 each for a total of $25,000 per national recipient. Must demonstrate achievement in a non-academic activity or project. Consideration will also be given to other extracurricular activities in school and community, work experience, and the applicant's academic record over the past four years. Visit Website for more information or to download an application. Questions about the application process may be directed to Scholarship America's toll free number or by e-mail to axaachievement@scholarshipamerica.org.

Amount of award:	$10,000-$25,000
Number of awards:	52
Number of applicants:	52
Application deadline:	December 15
Notification begins:	March 15
Total amount awarded:	$670,000

Contact:
AXA Achievement Scholarship
Scholarship Management Services
One Scholarship Way, P.O. Box 297
Saint Peter, MN 56082
Phone: 800-537-4180
Web: www.axaonline.com/rs/axa/about-us/33b_axa_achievement.html

Ayn Rand Institute

Atlas Shrugged Essay Contest

Type of award: Scholarship.
Intended use: For undergraduate or graduate study at 2-year or 4-year institution.
Basis for selection: Competition/talent/interest in writing/journalism, based on an outstanding grasp of the philosophic meaning of "Atlas Shrugged."
Application requirements: Essay between 800 and 1,600 words, typewritten and double-spaced. Stapled cover sheet with entrant's name and address, e-mail address (if available), university and major, and the topic selected: Applicant chooses from three topic questions on "Atlas Shrugged."
Additional information: Student must be enrolled in full-time college degree program at time of entry.

Amount of award:	$50-$10,000
Number of awards:	49
Number of applicants:	1,415
Application deadline:	September 17
Notification begins:	November 27
Total amount awarded:	$24,000

Contact:
The Ayn Rand Institute
Atlas Shrugged Essay Contest
2121 Alton Parkway, Suite 250
Irvine, CA 92606
Phone: 949-222-6550
Fax: 949-222-6558
Web: www.aynrand.org/contests

The Fountainhead Essay Contest

Type of award: Scholarship.
Eligibility: Applicant must be high school junior or senior.
Additional information: Essay contest for eleventh and twelfth graders on Ayn Rand's novel, "The Fountainhead." Essays must be between 800 and 1600 words. Essays must demonstrate an outstanding grasp of the philosophic meaning of "The Fountainhead." Rules, guidelines and topic questions are on the Website.

Amount of award:	$50-$10,000
Number of awards:	236
Number of applicants:	6,000
Application deadline:	April 25
Total amount awarded:	$43,250

Contact:
Ayn Rand Institute
"The Fountainhead" Essay Contest
2121 Alton Parkway, Suite 250
Irvine, CA 92606
Phone: 949-222-6550
Fax: 949-222-6558
Web: www.aynrand.org/contests

"Anthem" Essay Contest

Type of award: Scholarship.
Eligibility: Applicant must be high school freshman or sophomore.
Additional information: Open to ninth and tenth graders worldwide. Essays must demonstrate an outstanding grasp of the philosophic meaning of "Anthem." Essays must be between 600 and 1200 words. Rules guidelines and topic questions are on Website.

Amount of award:	$30-$2,000
Number of awards:	236
Number of applicants:	14,000
Application deadline:	March 20
Total amount awarded:	$14,000

Ayn Rand Institute: "Anthem" Essay Contest

Contact:
Ayn Rand Institute
"Anthem" Essay Contest
2121 Alton Parkway, Suite 250
Irvine, CA 92606
Phone: 949-222-6550
Fax: 949-222-6558
Web: www.aynrand.org/contests

Barry M. Goldwater Scholarship and Excellence In Education Foundation

Barry M. Goldwater Scholarship

Type of award: Scholarship, renewable.
Intended use: For full-time sophomore or junior study at accredited 4-year institution in United States. Designated institutions: Schools listed in Directory of Postsecondary Institutions published by US Department of Education.
Eligibility: Applicant must be U.S. citizen or permanent resident.
Basis for selection: Major/career interest in engineering; mathematics; natural sciences; science, general; computer/information sciences; medical specialties/research; astronomy or geology/earth sciences. Applicant must demonstrate high academic achievement, depth of character, leadership and seriousness of purpose.
Application requirements: Recommendations, transcript, proof of eligibility, nomination by college faculty representative. Essay (600 words or less) relating to student's chosen career. Nominations of resident aliens must include letter of nominee's intent to obtain U.S. citizenship and photocopy of Alien Registration Card.
Additional information: Bulletin of information, nomination materials, application and list of faculty representatives available on Website. Students must be nominated by university's Goldwater Scholarship faculty representative. Applicants must be legal resident of state from which they are candidates. Residents of District of Columbia, Puerto Rico, Guam, American Samoa, Virgin Islands, and Commonwealth of North Mariana Islands also eligible. Minimum 3.0 GPA required.

Amount of award:	$7,500
Number of awards:	300
Number of applicants:	1,150
Application deadline:	January 31
Notification begins:	April 1

Contact:
Barry M. Goldwater/Excellence In Education Foundation
6225 Brandon Avenue, Suite 315
Springfield, VA 22150-2519
Phone: 703-756-6012
Fax: 703-756-6015
Web: www.act.org/goldwater

Bay Area Family of Funds

Bay Area Council Scholarship Program

Type of award: Scholarship.
Intended use: For full-time undergraduate study in United States. Designated institutions: Mills College, Santa Clara University, Stanford University, U.C. Berkeley, U.C. Davis, University of San Francisco.
Eligibility: Applicant must be high school senior. Applicant must be U.S. citizen or permanent resident residing in California.
Basis for selection: Applicant must demonstrate high academic achievement, leadership and service orientation.
Application requirements: Interview, recommendations, essay, transcript. Two letters of recommendation; FAFSA; SAR; copy of financial aid letter; photo.
Additional information: Available to current high school seniors who reside in underserved neighborhoods within the nine-county Bay Area, neighborhoods determined by census to be at 80% of Area Median Income or below. Visit Website for more information and application.

Amount of award:	$5,000-$10,000
Number of awards:	10
Number of applicants:	100
Application deadline:	March 23
Total amount awarded:	$81,000

Contact:
Bay Area Council Scholarship Program
Bay Area Family of Funds
201 California Street, Suite 1450
CA 94111
Phone: 415-946-8716
Fax: 415-981-6408
Web: www.bayareafamilyoffunds.org

Bemis Company Foundation

Bemis Company Foundation Scholarship

Type of award: Scholarship, renewable.
Intended use: For undergraduate study at accredited vocational, 2-year or 4-year institution.
Eligibility: Applicant or parent must be employed by Bemis Company.
Basis for selection: Applicant must demonstrate financial need, high academic achievement, depth of character, leadership, seriousness of purpose and service orientation.
Application requirements: Transcript, proof of eligibility.
Additional information: Award may be renewed up to three times if applicant is attending four-year school.

Amount of award:	$1,000-$5,000
Number of awards:	67
Number of applicants:	268
Total amount awarded:	$650,000

Contact:
Bemis Company Foundation
222 South Ninth Street
Suite 440
Minneapolis, MN 55402-3373
Phone: 612-376-3000
Web: www.bemis.com

Best Buy

Best Buy Scholarship Program

Type of award: Scholarship.
Intended use: For full-time undergraduate study at accredited vocational, 2-year or 4-year institution in United States.
Eligibility: Applicant must be high school senior.
Basis for selection: Major/career interest in advertising. Applicant must demonstrate high academic achievement, leadership and service orientation.
Additional information: Two $1,500 scholarships available to applicants within 75 miles of each Best Buy store in the country. One hundred scholarships awarded to online shoppers and students in remote areas. Fifty-one $10,000 scholarships also available. Employees and their children and relatives are eligible. Only online applications accepted. See Website for more information.

Amount of award:	$1,500-$10,000
Number of awards:	1,700
Application deadline:	February 15
Total amount awarded:	$2,700,000

Contact:
Phone: 507-931-1682
Fax: 507-931-9168
Web: www.bestbuy.com (click on "Community Relations" then "Making Learning Fun")

Bethesda Lutheran Homes and Services, Inc.

Developmental Disabilities Nursing Scholastic Achievement Scholarship

Type of award: Scholarship.
Intended use: For full-time junior or senior study at accredited 2-year or 4-year institution.
Eligibility: Applicant must be Lutheran.
Basis for selection: Major/career interest in nursing. Applicant must demonstrate high academic achievement, seriousness of purpose and service orientation.
Application requirements: Recommendations, essay, transcript, proof of eligibility.
Additional information: Minimum 3.0 GPA required. Must be working toward registered nurse (R.N.) degree. Preference given to those interested in working with developmentally disabled persons.

Amount of award:	$1,500
Number of awards:	2
Number of applicants:	1
Application deadline:	April 15
Notification begins:	June 1
Total amount awarded:	$3,000

Contact:
Bethesda Lutheran Homes and Services, Inc.
Coordinator, Outreach Programs
600 Hoffmann Drive
Watertown, WI 53094
Phone: 800-369-4636 ext. 4449
Fax: 920-262-6513
Web: www.blhs.org

Developmental Disability Scholastic Achievement Scholarship

Type of award: Scholarship.
Intended use: For full-time junior or senior study at accredited 4-year institution in United States.
Eligibility: Applicant must be Lutheran.
Basis for selection: Major/career interest in social work; education; psychology; mental health/therapy; education, special; education, early childhood; education, teacher; speech pathology/audiology; occupational therapy or health-related professions. Applicant must demonstrate financial need, high academic achievement, seriousness of purpose and service orientation.
Application requirements: Recommendations, essay, transcript, proof of eligibility.
Additional information: Preference given to those interested in working with persons with mental retardation. Minimum 3.0 GPA. Also available for students of Lutheran theology.

Amount of award:	$1,500
Number of awards:	3
Number of applicants:	3
Application deadline:	April 15
Notification begins:	June 1
Total amount awarded:	$4,500

Contact:
Bethesda Lutheran Homes and Services, Inc.
Coordinator, Outreach Programs
600 Hoffmann Drive
Watertown, WI 53094
Phone: 800-369-4636 ext. 4449
Fax: 920-262-6513
Web: www.blhs.org

Bill and Melinda Gates Foundation

The Gates Millenium Scholarship

Type of award: Scholarship.
Intended use: For undergraduate study in United States.
Eligibility: Applicant must be Alaskan native, African American, Hispanic American, American Indian or Native Hawaiian/Pacific Islander. Applicant must be high school senior. Applicant must be U.S. citizen or permanent resident.
Basis for selection: Applicant must demonstrate financial need, high academic achievement, leadership and service orientation.
Application requirements: Nomination. FAFSA.

Bill and Melinda Gates Foundation: The Gates Millenium Scholarship

Additional information: Minimum 3.3 GPA. Gates Millenium Scholars program works in conjunction with the American Indian Graduate Center, Hispanic Scholarship Fund, United Negro College Fund, and the Asian Pacific Islander Scholarship Fund.
    Application deadline: December 31
    Notification begins: May 1
Contact:
Bill and Melinda Gates Foundation
Fairfax, VA 22031-8044
Phone: 877-690-4677
Web: www.gmsp.org

Biocommunications Association, Inc.

Biocommunications Association Inc. Scholarship

Type of award: Scholarship.
Intended use: For full-time undergraduate or graduate study.
Application requirements: Portfolio, recommendations, essay, transcript. Proof of enrollment.
Additional information: For full time undergraduate or graduate student pursuing career in scientific/biomedical visual communications at an accredited school. Applicant must be enrolled in accredited college or technical school program as a second, third, or fourth year student, or working in the field and returning for graduate study.
    Number of awards: 1
    Application deadline: March 31
    Notification begins: June 1
    Total amount awarded: $1,000
Contact:
Phone: 520-626-0141
Web: www.bca.org

BlackNews.com

The BlackNews.com Scholarship

Type of award: Scholarship.
Intended use: For undergraduate or graduate study at 2-year or 4-year institution in United States.
Eligibility: Applicant must be African American. Applicant must be U.S. citizen.
Basis for selection: Competition/talent/interest in writing/journalism. Applicant must demonstrate depth of character, leadership and seriousness of purpose.
Application requirements: Two-page essay on why he or she thinks or does not think that racism still exists in the U.S. today.
Additional information: For additional information, visit the Website. Do not submit your essay through postal mail or e-mail as attachment.
    Amount of award: $500
    Number of awards: 3
    Number of applicants: 50,000
    Application deadline: April 15
    Notification begins: May 15
Contact:
Diversity City Media
750-Q Cross Pointe Road
Columbus, OH 43230
Phone: 866-910-6277
Web: www.blackstudents.com

Blinded Veterans Association

Katherine F. Gruber Scholarship Program

Type of award: Scholarship, renewable.
Intended use: For full-time undergraduate or graduate study at accredited postsecondary institution in United States.
Eligibility: Applicant must be U.S. citizen. Applicant must be dependent of disabled veteran; or spouse of disabled veteran who served in the Army, Air Force, Marines, Navy or Coast Guard.
Application requirements: Recommendations, essay, transcript.
Additional information: Dependent children and spouses of blinded U.S. Armed Forces veterans are eligible. Veteran must meet definition of blindness used by Blinded Veterans Association; blindness may be service-connected or non-service-connected. Katherine Gruber scholarships are awarded for one year only. The number of scholarships a recipient may receive under this program is limited to four.
    Amount of award: $2,000
    Number of awards: 6
    Number of applicants: 20
    Application deadline: April 14
    Notification begins: January 1
    Total amount awarded: $12,000
Contact:
Katherine F. Gruber Scholarship Program
Blinded Veterans Association
477 H Street NW
Washington, DC 20001-2694
Phone: 202-371-8880
Fax: 202-371-8258
Web: www.bva.org

BMI Foundation, Inc.

John Lennon Scholarship

Type of award: Scholarship.
Intended use: For undergraduate or graduate study.
Eligibility: Applicant must be at least 15, no older than 24.
Basis for selection: Competition/talent/interest in music performance/composition, based on best song of any genre with original music and lyrics. Major/career interest in music or performing arts.
Application requirements: Nomination by Music Educators National Conference (MENC) or select schools.
Additional information: Visit Website for application and more information.

Amount of award:	$5,000-$10,000
Number of awards:	3
Total amount awarded:	$20,000

Contact:
BMI Foundation, Inc.
320 W. 57th Street
New York, NY 10019
Web: www.bmifoundation.org

Boeing Company

The Boeing Company Undergraduate Scholarships

Type of award: Scholarship.
Intended use: For undergraduate study at 4-year institution in United States. Designated institutions: Boeing's partner colleges and universities.
Additional information: Scholarships are based upon merit and are made by the college with cooperation from Boeing. Available to students who attend one of Boeing's partner colleges and universities. Contact school adviser for more information.

Number of awards:	1

Contact:
Web: www.boeing.com/collegecareers

Historically Black Colleges and Minority Institutions Scholarships

Type of award: Scholarship.
Intended use: For undergraduate study at 4-year institution in United States. Designated institutions: Atlanta Consortium (Morehouse, Spelman, and Morris Brown colleges, and Clark Atlanta University), North Carolina A&T State University, Alabama A&M University, Florida A&M University, Howard University, Tuskegee University, University of Texas-El Paso, Prairie View A&M University, Southern University, University of Hawaii.
Eligibility: Applicant must be African American.
Additional information: Contact college adviser for application and more information.
Contact:
Web: www.boeing.com/collegecareers

Books and Scholarships LLC

Elwood Grimes Literary Scholarship

Type of award: Scholarship.
Intended use: For undergraduate study.

Amount of award:	$1,000-$5,000
Number of awards:	3
Number of applicants:	435
Application deadline:	October 31
Total amount awarded:	$7,500

Contact:
Books and Scholarships LLC
4525 Cherry Forest Circle
Louisville, KY 40245
Phone: 502-777-7504
Fax: 502-241-3827
Web: www.booksandscholarships.com

Boy Scouts of America

Eagle Scout Academic Scholarships

Type of award: Scholarship.
Intended use: For undergraduate study at accredited 4-year institution.
Eligibility: Applicant must be male, high school senior.
Basis for selection: Applicant must demonstrate financial need, high academic achievement and leadership.
Application requirements: Recommendations, transcript.
Additional information: Applicant must be Eagle Scout. Award may not be used at military institution. Must have SAT of at least 1090 or ACT of 26. Download form 58-702 from Website. Must be endorsed by professional or volunteer scout leader. Available awards: one nonrenewable $3,000 award; one Mabel and Lawrence S. Cooke scholarship of up to $12,000 per year for four years; and four $20,000 scholarships ($5,000 a year for four years) given annually.

Amount of award:	$3,000-$48,000
Number of applicants:	3,000
Application deadline:	January 31
Notification begins:	June 30
Total amount awarded:	$164,000

Contact:
Boy Scouts of America
1325 West Walnut Hill Lane
P.O. Box 152079
Irving, TX 75015-2079
Phone: 972-580-2032
Web: www.nesa.org

Frank D. Visceglia Memorial Scholarship

Type of award: Scholarship, renewable.
Intended use: For full-time freshman study at accredited 4-year institution.
Eligibility: Applicant or parent must be member/participant of Boy Scouts of America, Eagle Scouts. Applicant must be male, high school senior. Applicant must be U.S. citizen or permanent resident residing in New Jersey.
Additional information: Preference given to applicants whose service projects relate to the environment and/or economy.

Amount of award:	$1,000
Number of awards:	1
Number of applicants:	12
Application deadline:	June 1
Total amount awarded:	$1,000

Contact:
Frank D. Visceglia Memorial Scholarship Program
Dennis Kohl, Scout Executive
222 Columbia Turnpike
Florham Park, NJ 07932
Phone: 973-765-9322
Fax: 973-765-9142
Web: www.ppbsa.org

Hall/McElwain Merit Scholarships

Type of award: Scholarship.
Intended use: For undergraduate study.
Eligibility: Applicant or parent must be member/participant of Boy Scouts of America, Eagle Scouts. Applicant must be male, high school senior.
Basis for selection: Applicant must demonstrate leadership.
Application requirements: Recommendations, proof of eligibility. Proof of Eagle Scout rank. Recommendation must be from volunteer or professional Scout leader.
Additional information: Applicant may be senior in high school or freshman, sophomore, or junior in college. Only applications postmarked by January 31 will be considered. Amount of award varies; maximum is $1,000. Do not fax applications. Must have strong record of participation in activities outside of scouting. Visit Website for more information and to download application.

Number of applicants:	3,000
Application deadline:	January 31
Notification begins:	June 30

Contact:
Eagle Scout Service S220
Boy Scouts of America
1325 W. Walnut Hill Lane, P.O. Box 152079
Irving, TX 75015-2079
Phone: 972-580-2032
Web: www.nesa.org

Boys and Girls Clubs of Greater San Diego

Spence Reese Scholarship

Type of award: Scholarship, renewable.
Intended use: For full-time freshman, sophomore, junior or senior study at accredited 4-year institution in United States.
Eligibility: Applicant must be male, high school senior.
Basis for selection: Major/career interest in law; political science/government; engineering or medicine. Applicant must demonstrate financial need and high academic achievement.
Application requirements: Recommendations, essay, transcript. SAT scores.
Additional information: Award is renewable for four years of study. Send SASE with application request after January 1 of graduating year. Application also available on Website. Finalists interview in San Diego. Travel expenses will be reimbursed.

Amount of award:	$2,000
Number of awards:	4
Number of applicants:	200
Application deadline:	April 15
Notification begins:	May 1
Total amount awarded:	$32,000

Contact:
Boys and Girls Clubs of Greater San Diego
Attention: Jeff Miller
115 W. Woodward Ave.
Escondido, CA 92025-2638
Phone: 760-746-3315
Fax: 760-740-0242
Web: www.bgcsd.com

Broadcast Education Association

Abe Voron Scholarship

Type of award: Scholarship.
Intended use: For full-time junior, senior or graduate study at 4-year or graduate institution. Designated institutions: Schools where at least one department is BEA member.
Basis for selection: Major/career interest in radio/television/film. Applicant must demonstrate high academic achievement, depth of character and seriousness of purpose.
Application requirements: Recommendations, essay, transcript. Three references, waiver form.
Additional information: Award intended for study in radio only. Request printed application by late September; check Website for exact request deadline or to download forms and for additional information. Awards for tuition and fees. Current scholarship holders are not eligible for reappointment in year following award. Should be able to show evidence of potential.

Amount of award:	$5,000
Number of awards:	2
Application deadline:	October 10
Total amount awarded:	$10,000

Contact:
Broadcast Education Association
1771 N Street, N.W.
Washington, DC 20036-2891
Phone: 202-429-3935
Web: www.beaweb.org/AM/Template.cfm?Section=scholarships_and_grants

Alexander M. Tanger Scholarship

Type of award: Scholarship.
Intended use: For full-time junior, senior or graduate study at 4-year or graduate institution in United States. Designated institutions: Schools where at least one department is BEA member.
Basis for selection: Major/career interest in radio/television/film; communications or film/video. Applicant must demonstrate high academic achievement, depth of character and seriousness of purpose.
Application requirements: Recommendations, essay, transcript. Three references, waiver form.
Additional information: Request printed application by late September; check Website for exact request deadline or to download forms and for additional information. Awards for tuition and fees. Current scholarship holders are not eligible for reappointment in year following award. Must show evidence of potential in electronic media.

Amount of award:	$5,000
Number of awards:	1
Application deadline:	October 10

Contact:
Broadcast Education Association
1771 N Street, N.W.
Washington, DC 20036-2891
Phone: 202-429-3935
Web: www.beaweb.org/AM/
Template.cfm?Section=scholarships_and_grants

Harold E. Fellows Scholarship

Type of award: Scholarship.
Intended use: For full-time junior, senior or graduate study at 4-year or graduate institution. Designated institutions: Schools where at least one department is BEA member.
Basis for selection: Major/career interest in radio/television/film. Applicant must demonstrate high academic achievement, depth of character and seriousness of purpose.
Application requirements: Recommendations, essay, transcript. Three references. Waiver sheet. NAB station employment/internship affidavit.
Additional information: Request printed application by late September; check Website for exact request deadline or to download forms. Awards for tuition and fees. Current scholarship holders are not eligible for reappointment in year following award. Should be able to show evidence of potential in electronic media.

Amount of award:	$1,750
Number of awards:	4
Application deadline:	October 10
Total amount awarded:	$7,000

Contact:
Broadcast Education Association
1771 N Street, N.W.
Washington, DC 20036-2891
Phone: 202-429-3935
Web: www.beaweb.org/AM/
Template.cfm?Section=scholarships_and_grants

Helen J. Sioussat/Fay Wells Scholarship

Type of award: Scholarship.
Intended use: For full-time junior, senior or graduate study at 4-year or graduate institution. Designated institutions: Schools where at least one department is BEA member.
Basis for selection: Major/career interest in radio/television/film. Applicant must demonstrate high academic achievement, depth of character and seriousness of purpose.
Application requirements: Recommendations, essay, transcript. Three references. Waiver sheet.
Additional information: Request printed application by late September; check Website for exact request deadline, to download forms, and for additional information. Awards for tuition and fees. Current scholarship holders are not eligible for reappointment in year following award. Should be able to show evidence of potential in electronic media.

Amount of award:	$1,250
Number of awards:	2
Application deadline:	October 10
Total amount awarded:	$2,500

Contact:
Broadcast Education Association
1771 N Street, N.W.
Washington, DC 20036-2891
Phone: 202-429-3935
Web: www.beaweb.org/AM/
Template.cfm?Section=scholarships_and_grants

Two Year Community College BEA Award

Type of award: Scholarship.
Intended use: For full-time undergraduate study at 2-year or 4-year institution. Designated institutions: Schools where at least one department is BEA member.
Basis for selection: Major/career interest in radio/television/film. Applicant must demonstrate high academic achievement, depth of character and seriousness of purpose.
Application requirements: Recommendations, essay, transcript. Three references. Waiver form.
Additional information: Scholarship for use at two-year community college, or, if applicant has already graduated from two-year program, can be used at four-year institution. Request printed application by late September; check Website for exact request deadline or to download forms. Awards for tuition and fees. Current scholarship holders are not eligible for reappointment in year following award. Should show evidence of potential in electronic media.

Amount of award:	$1,500
Number of awards:	2
Application deadline:	October 10
Total amount awarded:	$3,000

Contact:
Broadcast Education Association
1771 N Street, N.W.
Washington, DC 20036-2891
Phone: 202-429-3935
Web: www.beaweb.org/AM/
Template.cfm?Section=scholarships_and_grants

Vincent T. Wasilewski Scholarship

Type of award: Scholarship.
Intended use: For full-time junior, senior or graduate study at 4-year or graduate institution in United States. Designated institutions: Schools where at least one department is BEA member.
Basis for selection: Major/career interest in radio/television/film; communications or film/video. Applicant must demonstrate high academic achievement, depth of character and seriousness of purpose.
Application requirements: Recommendations, essay, transcript. Waiver form.
Additional information: Must show evidence of potential in electronic media. Request printed application by late September; check Website for exact request deadline, to download forms, and for more information. May also obtain application from campus faculty. Award to be used for tuition and fees. Current scholarship holders not eligible for reappointment in following year.

Amount of award:	$5,000
Number of awards:	1
Application deadline:	October 10

Contact:
Broadcast Education Association
1771 N Street N.W.
Washington, DC 20036-2891
Phone: 202-429-3935
Web: www.beaweb.org/AM/
Template.cfm?Section=scholarships_and_grants

Walter S. Patterson Scholarship

Type of award: Scholarship.

Intended use: For full-time junior, senior or graduate study at 4-year or graduate institution. Designated institutions: Schools where at least one department is BEA member.
Basis for selection: Major/career interest in radio/television/film. Applicant must demonstrate high academic achievement, depth of character and seriousness of purpose.
Application requirements: Recommendations, essay, transcript. Three references, waiver sheet.
Additional information: Award intended for study in radio only. Request printed application by late September; check Website for exact request deadline or to download forms and for additional information. Awards for tuition and fees. Current scholarship holders are not eligible for reappointment in year following award. Should be able to show evidence of potential in electronic media.

Amount of award:	$1,750
Number of awards:	2
Application deadline:	October 10
Total amount awarded:	$3,500

Contact:
Broadcast Education Association
1771 N Street, N.W.
Washington, DC 20036-2891
Phone: 202-429-3935
Web: www.beaweb.org/AM/Template.cfm?Section=scholarships_and_grants

Brown and Caldwell

Dr. W. Wes Eckenfelder Jr. Scholarship

Type of award: Scholarship.
Intended use: For full-time junior, senior or graduate study at 4-year or graduate institution in United States.
Eligibility: Applicant must be U.S. citizen or permanent resident.
Basis for selection: Major/career interest in engineering, civil; engineering, chemical; engineering, environmental or geology/earth sciences. Applicant must demonstrate depth of character, leadership and seriousness of purpose.
Application requirements: Transcript. Essay (250 words) on the topic "My Future Career Goals in Environmental Science." Two written recommendations, at least one from university official. Academic advisor's contact information.
Additional information: Student must have minimum 3.5 GPA. Please visit Website for additional information.

Amount of award:	$3,000
Number of awards:	1
Application deadline:	January 31

Contact:
Brown and Caldwell
Attn: HR/Scholarship Programs
201 N. Civic Drive, Suite 115
Walnut Creek, CA 94598
Phone: 800-727-2224
Web: http://brownandcaldwell.com/EckenApp.pdf

Brown Foundation for Educational Equality, Excellence and Research

Brown Foundation Academic Scholarships

Type of award: Scholarship, renewable.
Intended use: For full-time junior or senior study at accredited 4-year institution.
Eligibility: Applicant must be Alaskan native, Asian American, African American, Mexican American, Hispanic American, Puerto Rican or American Indian.
Basis for selection: Major/career interest in education or education, teacher. Applicant must demonstrate high academic achievement, leadership and service orientation.
Application requirements: Two recommendations.
Additional information: Must have minimum 3.0 GPA, and be admitted to/enrolled in accredited program in teacher education. Application available on Website.

Amount of award:	$2,000
Number of awards:	4
Number of applicants:	30
Application deadline:	March 30
Notification begins:	May 17

Contact:
Brown Foundation Scholarship Program
P.O. Box 4862
Topeka, KS 66604
Phone: 785-235-3939
Fax: 785-235-1001
Web: www.brownvboard.org/foundation/scholarships

Building Industry Association

BIA North County Division Scholarship

Type of award: Scholarship.
Intended use: For undergraduate study.
Eligibility: Applicant must be high school senior. Applicant must be residing in California.
Basis for selection: Major/career interest in engineering, civil; real estate; construction; finance/banking; landscape architecture; engineering, construction; law; accounting; architecture or engineering, structural. Applicant must demonstrate high academic achievement.
Application requirements: Interview, essay, proof of eligibility.
Additional information: For high school seniors in California's North San Diego County interested in careers in the building industry. Also open to students pursuing major/career as developer, contractor, soils engineer, designer, land planner, framer, plumber, electrician or other related professions. Applications due in April. See Website for application and list of eligible high schools.

| Amount of award: | $500-$3,000 |
| Number of awards: | 15 |

Contact:
North County Building Industry Association
c/o Nancy Diamond
9201 Spectrum Center Blvd., Suite 110
San Diego, CA 92123
Phone: 858-450-1221
Fax: 858-558-1414
Web: www.biasandiego.org

Bureau of Indian Affairs

Higher Education Grant Program

Type of award: Scholarship, renewable.
Intended use: For full-time undergraduate study at accredited 2-year or 4-year institution in United States.
Eligibility: Applicant must be American Indian. Member or at least one-quarter degree descendent of member of federally recognized tribe.
Basis for selection: Applicant must demonstrate financial need.
Application requirements: Proof of eligibility. Proof of Native American Tribal Affiliation.
Additional information: Contacts or inquiries for these funds need to be directed to the tribal or prospective Education Line Office relative to the person's tribal headquarters. The Higher Education funds/scholarships are not awarded through the DC offices. In most circumstances, the awarding officials are the tribal program employees.

Number of awards:	12,000
Number of applicants:	16,000

Contact:
Office of Indian Education Programs
1849 C Street NW
MS 3609 MIB
Washington, DC 20240
Phone: 202-208-6123
Fax: 202-208-3312
Web: www.bia.edu

Bureau of Indian Affairs-Oklahoma Area Education Office

Bureau of Indian Affairs-Osage Tribal Education Committee Award

Type of award: Scholarship.
Intended use: For undergraduate or graduate study at postsecondary institution in United States.
Eligibility: Applicant must be American Indian. Must be member of Osage Tribe.
Application requirements: Recommendations, transcript, proof of eligibility.
Additional information: Minimum 2.0 GPA. Contact Bureau of Indian Affairs-Oklahoma Area Education Office for application and additional information.
   Application deadline: July 1, December 31

Contact:
Burea of Indian Affairs-Oklahoma Area Education Office
200 Northwest 4th Street
Suite 4049
Oklahoma City, OK 73102
Phone: 405-605-6051 ext. 304

Business and Professional Women's Foundation

Business and Professional Women's Career Advancement Scholarship

Type of award: Scholarship.
Intended use: For undergraduate, master's or first professional study at accredited 2-year, 4-year or graduate institution in United States.
Eligibility: Applicant must be female, at least 25. Applicant must be U.S. citizen or permanent resident.
Basis for selection: Major/career interest in science, general; education, teacher; engineering; computer/information sciences; humanities/liberal arts; social/behavioral sciences; business/management/administration; nursing or health-related professions. Applicant must demonstrate financial need.
Application requirements: Recommendations, transcript, proof of eligibility. If applicant selected as semifinalist, must submit more material by designated deadline. Tax forms, Student Aid Report.
Additional information: Must be within 24 months of receiving degree, demonstrate critical financial need (Estimated Family Contribution of $2,500 or less), and have definite career plan. Must be accepted into an accredited program (but must not be earning PhD, MD, DDS, DVM, JD, or other 'terminal' degree). Application available January 1 through April 15. Online applications only. First submit preliminary application online.

Amount of award:	$1,000-$2,500
Number of awards:	60
Number of applicants:	681
Application deadline:	April 15, May 18
Notification begins:	April 30, July 31
Total amount awarded:	$82,000

Contact:
Business and Professional Women's Foundation
Scholarship and Loan Programs
2012 Massachusetts Avenue NW
Washington, DC 20036
Phone: 800-525-3729
Fax: 202-861-0298
Web: www.bpwusa.org

Butler Manufacturing Company Foundation

Butler Manufacturing Company Foundation Scholarship

Type of award: Scholarship, renewable.

Intended use: For full-time undergraduate study at accredited 4-year institution.
Eligibility: Applicant or parent must be employed by Butler Manufacturing Co. & subsidiaries. Applicant must be high school senior.
Basis for selection: Applicant must demonstrate financial need, high academic achievement, depth of character, leadership and service orientation.
Application requirements: Recommendations, essay, transcript. SAT/ACT scores. Financial report.
Additional information: Applicant's parent must be employed by Butler Buildings or Blue Scope Steel Americas Groups. Contact human resources office at workplace for information and application. Renewable up to four years.

Amount of award:	$3,000
Number of awards:	8
Number of applicants:	36
Application deadline:	February 15
Notification begins:	May 1

Contact:
Butler Manufacturing Company Foundation
P.O. Box 419917
Kansas City, MO 64141-6917
Phone: 816-968-3208
Fax: 816-627-8993

California Association of Realtors Scholarship Foundation

California Association of Realtors Scholarship

Type of award: Scholarship, renewable.
Intended use: For undergraduate or graduate study at 2-year or 4-year institution.
Eligibility: Applicant must be U.S. citizen residing in California.
Basis for selection: Major/career interest in real estate. Applicant must demonstrate financial need.
Application requirements: Interview, recommendations, proof of eligibility. Minimum 300-word essay explaining why real estate is career goal. Enrollment verification. Photocopy of valid CA driver's license or ID card.
Additional information: Must be CA resident of at least one year before applying. Students attending two-year colleges eligible for $2,000 award; four-year college/university students eligible for $4,000 award. May receive one award per year, maximum two years. Rolling deadlines. Check Website for application, deadline and other information. Minimum 2.6 GPA. Must have completed minimum of 12 college-level course units within last four years. At least two courses must be in real estate or real estate related.

Amount of award:	$2,000-$4,000
Number of awards:	2

Contact:
California Association of Realtors Scholarship Foundation
525 South Virgil Avenue
Los Angeles, CA 90020
Phone: 213-739-8200
Fax: 213-739-7724
Web: www.car.org

California Farm Bureau

California Farm Bureau Scholarship

Type of award: Scholarship, renewable.
Intended use: For full-time freshman, sophomore, junior or senior study at accredited 4-year institution.
Eligibility: Applicant must be U.S. citizen residing in California.
Basis for selection: Major/career interest in agriculture; agribusiness; veterinary medicine or engineering, agricultural.
Application requirements: Recommendations, essay, transcript.
Additional information: Applications may be obtained from local County Farm Bureau office or Website. Applicant must be preparing for career in agricultural industry.

Amount of award:	$1,800-$5,000
Number of awards:	30
Application deadline:	March 1
Notification begins:	May 30

Contact:
California Farm Bureau Scholarship Foundation
2300 River Plaza Drive
Sacramento, CA 95833
Phone: 916-561-5520
Web: www.cfbf.com

California Masonic Foundation

California Masonic Foundation Scholarship

Type of award: Scholarship, renewable.
Intended use: For full-time undergraduate study at accredited 2-year or 4-year institution.
Eligibility: Applicant must be high school senior. Applicant must be U.S. citizen residing in California.
Basis for selection: Applicant must demonstrate financial need and high academic achievement.
Application requirements: Recommendations, essay, transcript, proof of eligibility. 1040 tax return, FAFSA.
Additional information: Minimum 3.0 GPA. Most awards are renewable. While not required, some preference is given to applicants with Masonic relationships and/or Masonic Youth Group membership. Number of awards granted is based on availability of funds. Visit Website for information and application.

Amount of award:	$500-$45,000
Number of applicants:	1,400
Application deadline:	February 15
Total amount awarded:	$918,316

Contact:
California Masonic Foundation
1111 California Street
San Francisco, CA 94108-2284
Web: www.freemason.org

California's Junior Miss Program

California's Junior Miss Competition

Type of award: Scholarship.
Intended use: For undergraduate study at accredited 2-year or 4-year institution in United States.
Eligibility: Applicant must be single, female, high school junior. Applicant must be U.S. citizen residing in California.
Basis for selection: Applicant must demonstrate high academic achievement.
Application requirements: Interview.
Additional information: Applications accepted anytime through Website, but must be received by January 1st of applicant's junior year of high school. Local competitions held from January to May; state competition held first half of August. Check Website for details. Awards not limited to state Junior Miss finalists; winners of various judged categories also receive awards. Winner of the state-level Junior Miss pageant will receive $10,000; other prizes of varying amounts may be awarded on the local level. Participants must never have been pregnant. Minimum 3.0 GPA required.

Number of awards:	20
Number of applicants:	60
Application deadline:	January 1
Total amount awarded:	$30,000

Contact:
California's Junior Miss
666 Park Glen Drive
Windsor, CA 95492
Web: new.ajm.org

California Student Aid Commission

Cal Grant A & B Entitlement Award Program

Type of award: Scholarship, renewable.
Intended use: For undergraduate study at postsecondary institution. Designated institutions: Cal Grant-qualifying California postsecondary schools.
Eligibility: Applicant must be high school senior. Applicant must be U.S. citizen or permanent resident residing in California.
Basis for selection: Applicant must demonstrate financial need and high academic achievement.
Application requirements: Applicants must submit FAFSA to federal processor and Cal Grant GPA Verification Form to California Student Aid Commission. Students with no available GPA may submit SAT, ACT, or GED.
Additional information: Applicants who graduated in the last year also eligible. Awards given to all eligible applicants. Applicants must have income and assets below established levels. Minimum 3.0 GPA for Cal Grant A; minimum 2.0 GPA for Cal Grant B. Cal Grant A provides tuition and fees. If awarded a Cal Grant A and attending a California community college, award can be reserved for up to two years until transfer to tuition/fee charging college, providing qualifications are still met. Cal Grant B awards up to $1,557 the first year and $1,557 plus tuition and fees for years two through four. Renewable if student maintains grades and continues to have financial need. Visit Website or contact CSAC for more details.

Amount of award:	$700-$9,700
Application deadline:	March 2
Total amount awarded:	$900,000,000

Contact:
California Student Aid Commission
Program Administration and Services Division
P.O. Box 419027
Rancho Cordova, CA 95741-9027
Phone: 888-224-7268
Web: www.calgrants.org

Cal Grant C Award Program

Type of award: Scholarship, renewable.
Intended use: For undergraduate study at postsecondary institution. Designated institutions: Cal Grant-qualifying California postsecondary and vocational institutions.
Eligibility: Applicant must be U.S. citizen or permanent resident residing in California.
Basis for selection: Applicant must demonstrate financial need.
Application requirements: FAFSA, Cal Grant GPA Verification Form. Students with no available GPA can submit SAT, ACT, or GED scores. All test scores must be submitted using the paper Cal Grant GPA Verification Form. Qualifying students will be sent a Cal C supplement form to complete and return to CSAC.
Additional information: Applicants must have income and assets below certain established levels. Funding is available for up to two years, and vocational program must be at least four months in length. Visit Website or contact CSAC for more details.

Amount of award:	$576-$2,592
Number of awards:	7,761
Number of applicants:	12,000
Application deadline:	March 2
Notification begins:	May 30
Total amount awarded:	$10,000,000

Contact:
California Student Aid Commission
Program Administration and Services Division
P.O. Box 419027
Rancho Cordova, CA 95741-9027
Phone: 888-224-7268
Web: www.calgrants.org

California Chafee Grant Program

Type of award: Scholarship, renewable.
Intended use: For undergraduate or graduate study. Designated institutions: Any participating Title IV college or career/technical school.
Eligibility: Applicant must be no older than 22.
Basis for selection: Applicant must demonstrate financial need.
Application requirements: FAFSA, Chafee Grant Application to California Student Aid Commission. Proof of enrollment in approved institution.
Additional information: Must be former foster youth from any state attending a CA college or current foster youth from CA attending any college. Must have been eligible for foster care between 16th and 18th birthdays. Must not have reached 22nd birthday by July 1st of award year. Must be enrolled at

least half time in course of study lasting at least one year. Renewable through 23rd birthday.
>Amount of award: $5,000

Contact:
California Student Aid Commission
Attn: Specialized Programs Operations Branch
P.O. Box 419029
Rancho Cordova, CA 95741-9029
Phone: 888-224-7268
Fax: 916-526-7977
Web: www.csac.ca.gov or www.chafee.csac.ca.gov

California Child Development Grant Program

Type of award: Scholarship.
Intended use: For undergraduate study at accredited 2-year or 4-year institution. Designated institutions: California public and private postsecondary institutions with approved child development classes.
Eligibility: Applicant must be U.S. citizen or permanent resident residing in California.
Basis for selection: Major/career interest in education, early childhood or education, teacher. Applicant must demonstrate financial need and high academic achievement.
Application requirements: Nomination by postsecondary institution or employing agency. Recommendations from institution faculty. FAFSA.
Additional information: Recipients attending two-year postsecondary institutions will receive up to $1,000 annually for up to two years. Recipients attending four-year institutions will receive up to $2,000 annually for up to two years. Applicants continuing beyond two years may reapply but cannot cumulatively receive more than $6,000 through the program. Recipients must maintain at least half-time enrollment in approved course of study leading to Child Development Permit; maintain satisfactory academic progress; meet federal Selective Service registration requirements; and commit to one year of full-time employment in licensed child care center for every year they receive the grant. Commission can award up to 100 new recipients each year. Points based on GPA, income, and EFC. Applicant must be pursuing permit to teach/supervise in field of child care and development. Applicant must select teaching area: Teacher, Site Supervisor, Master Teacher, Program Director. Deadlines and notification dates vary. Visit Website for application and information.
>Amount of award: $1,000-$2,000

Contact:
California Student Aid Commission
Specialized Programs; Attn: Child Development
P.O. Box 419029
Rancho Cordova, CA 95741-9029
Phone: 888-224-7268
Fax: 916-526-7977
Web: www.csac.ca.gov

California Law Enforcement Personnel Dependents Grant Program

Type of award: Scholarship, renewable.
Intended use: For undergraduate study at accredited 2-year or 4-year institution. Designated institutions: California postsecondary institutions accredited by Western Association of Schools and Colleges (WASC).
Eligibility: Applicant must be U.S. citizen residing in California. Applicant's parent must have been killed or disabled in work-related accident as firefighter, police officer or public safety officer.
Basis for selection: Applicant must demonstrate financial need.
Application requirements: Proof of eligibility. FAFSA and SAR. Birth certificate (not required for spouse).
Additional information: Additional application requirements: death certificate, coroner's report, police report, or any other documentation that shows evidence that the death or total disability was caused by external violence or physical force incurred in the line of duty (for peace, law enforcement, or public safety officers); that death, accident, or injury was caused by the direct action of an inmate (for officers and employees of the Department of Corrections and Rehabilitation); or that death or total disability was the result of accident or injury incurred in the performance of duty (for firefighters). All must include findings of Worker's Compensation Appeals Board or other evidence that fatality/disabling accident/injury is compensable under Division 4.0 and 4.5 of the Labor Code. Number of awards varies.
>Amount of award: $100-$11,259

Contact:
CA Student Aid Commission Specialized Programs Operations Branch
Attn: LEPD
P.O. Box 419029
Rancho Cordova, CA 95741-9029
Phone: 888-224-7268
Fax: 916-526-7977
Web: www.csac.ca.gov

California Robert C. Byrd Honors Scholarship

Type of award: Scholarship, renewable.
Intended use: For full-time undergraduate study at accredited 2-year or 4-year institution in United States.
Eligibility: Applicant must be high school senior. Applicant must be U.S. citizen residing in California.
Basis for selection: Applicant must demonstrate high academic achievement.
Application requirements: Nomination by high school.
Additional information: Students are awarded individually by their school based solely on merit. Students and parents should contact the principal or counselor at their high school for application instructions. GED students may apply directly. Renewable up to four years.
>Amount of award: $1,500
>Number of awards: 800
>Number of applicants: 1,700
>Application deadline: April 15
>Notification begins: May 15
>Total amount awarded: $5,000,000

Contact:
CA Student Aid Commission, Specialized Programs Operations Branch
Attn: Robert Byrd Honors Scholarship Program
P.O. Box 419029
Rancho Cordova, CA 95741-9029
Phone: 888-224-7268
Fax: 916-526-7977
Web: www.csac.ca.gov

Competitive Cal Grant A and B Award Programs

Type of award: Scholarship, renewable.
Intended use: For undergraduate study at postsecondary institution. Designated institutions: Qualifying California postsecondary schools.
Eligibility: Applicant must be U.S. citizen or permanent resident residing in California.
Basis for selection: Applicant must demonstrate financial need and high academic achievement.
Application requirements: Applicants must submit FAFSA to federal processor and Cal Grant GPA Verification Form to California Student Aid Commission. Both forms must be postmarked by March 2.
Additional information: Applicants must have income and assets below established levels. Minimum 3.0 GPA for Cal Grant A; minimum 2.0 GPA for Cal Grant B. Competitive grant program. Cal Grant A pays tuition and fees. Cal Grant B awards up to $1,551 first year and $1,551 plus tuition and fees for years two through four. Students with no available GPA can submit SAT, ACT or GED scores. Deadlines: March 2 for students not receiving an Entitlement award; September 2 for California Community College students only. Visit Websites or contact CSAC for more details.

Amount of award:	$700-$9,700
Number of awards:	22,500
Number of applicants:	140,000
Application deadline:	March 2, September 2
Notification begins:	April 1, October 1

Contact:
California Student Aid Commission
Program Administration Services Division
P.O. Box 419027
Rancho Cordova, CA 95741-9027
Phone: 888-224-7268
Web: www.calgrants.org

California Teachers Association

California Teachers Association Martin Luther King, Jr., Memorial Scholarship

Type of award: Scholarship.
Intended use: For undergraduate or graduate study at accredited postsecondary institution.
Eligibility: Applicant or parent must be member/participant of California Teachers Association. Applicant must be Alaskan native, Asian American, African American, Mexican American, Hispanic American, Puerto Rican, American Indian or Native Hawaiian/Pacific Islander.
Basis for selection: Major/career interest in education; education, teacher or education, special. Applicant must demonstrate financial need.
Application requirements: Recommendations, essay, transcript, proof of eligibility. CTA membership verification signed by chapter president.
Additional information: Must be active CTA member. If active student CTA member, must reside in CA. High school seniors may also apply. Amount of award varies. To receive funds, must show proof of registration in approved credential or degree program. Must pursue teaching-related career in public education. Application deadline between end of January and beginning of February. Check Website for exact dates and for more information.

Number of awards:	20
Number of applicants:	100

Contact:
CTA Martin Luther King, Jr. Scholarship
CTA Human Rights Department
P.O. Box 921
Burlingame, CA 94011-0921
Phone: 650-552-5446
Fax: 650-552-5001
Web: www.cta.org

CTA Scholarship for Dependent Children

Type of award: Scholarship, renewable.
Intended use: For full-time undergraduate or graduate study at accredited postsecondary institution.
Eligibility: Applicant or parent must be member/participant of California Teachers Association.
Basis for selection: Major/career interest in education. Applicant must demonstrate high academic achievement, depth of character, leadership, seriousness of purpose and service orientation.
Application requirements: Essay, transcript, proof of eligibility. Two letters of recommendation, one by educator, other by community member that separately address four categories specified on application. Membership verification signed by chapter president.
Additional information: Applicant must be dependent child of active, retired, or deceased member of CTA and claimed as dependent on current year's IRS tax forms. Must have high school GPA of at least 3.5. Awards based on overall achievement in four categories: 1) involvement in and sensitivity to human, social, and civic issues; 2) characteristics such as responsibility, reliability, and integrity; 3) academic and vocational potential; and 4) special and personal achievements. In order to receive funds, recipients must show proof of registration in approved credential or degree program. One scholarship set aside for student attending continuation high school. Application deadline between end of January and beginning of February; visit Website for exact dates and more information.

Amount of award:	$2,000
Number of awards:	25
Number of applicants:	900
Notification begins:	May 1

Contact:
CTA Scholarship Committee Human Rights Department
c/o Manuel Ayan
P.O. Box 921
Burlingame, CA 94011-0921
Phone: 650-552-5446
Fax: 650-552-5001
Web: www.cta.org

CTA Scholarships for Members

Type of award: Scholarship, renewable.
Intended use: For undergraduate or graduate study at accredited postsecondary institution.
Eligibility: Applicant or parent must be member/participant of California Teachers Association.

Basis for selection: Major/career interest in education, teacher. Applicant must demonstrate high academic achievement, depth of character, leadership, seriousness of purpose and service orientation.
Application requirements: Essay, transcript. Two letters of recommendation, one from an educator, other from community member. Each must separately address four categories specified on application. Membership verification signed by chapter president.
Additional information: Scholarships awarded based on overall achievement in four categories: 1) involvement in and sensitivity to human, social and civic issues; 2) characteristics such as responsibility, reliability and integrity; 3) academic and vocational potential; and 4) special and personal achievements. Applicant must be active member of CTA (including members working on emergency credential). In order to receive funds, recipients must show proof of registration in approved credential or degree program. Application deadline is between end of January and beginning of February; visit Website for exact dates and more information.

Amount of award:	$2,000
Number of awards:	5
Number of applicants:	150
Notification begins:	May 1
Total amount awarded:	$10,000

Contact:
CTA Scholarship Committee Human Rights Department
c/o Manuel Ayan
P.O. Box 921
Burlingame, CA 94011-0921
Phone: 650-552-5446
Fax: 650-552-5001
Web: www.cta.org

L. Gordon Bittle Memorial Scholarship for Student CTA

Type of award: Scholarship, renewable.
Intended use: For full-time undergraduate or graduate study at accredited postsecondary institution.
Eligibility: Applicant or parent must be member/participant of California Teachers Association. Applicant must be residing in California.
Basis for selection: Major/career interest in education; education, teacher or education, special. Applicant must demonstrate high academic achievement, depth of character and service orientation.
Application requirements: Essay, transcript. Membership verification signed by chapter president. Two letters of recommendation, one from educator, one from community member that separately address four categories listed on application.
Additional information: Must have high school GPA of at least 3.5. Must pursue career in public education. Scholarships are awarded based on overall achievement in four categories: 1) involvement in and sensitivity to human, social and civic issues; 2) characteristics such as responsibility, reliability and integrity; 3) academic and vocational potential; and 4) special and personal achievements. Applicant must be active member of Student CTA. Not available to CTA members currently working in public schools. In order to receive funds, recipients must show proof of registration in approved credential or degree program. May be teacher credential program at accredited postsecondary institution. Application deadline is between end of January and beginning of February; visit Website for exact dates and more information.

Amount of award:	$2,500
Number of awards:	3
Number of applicants:	20
Notification begins:	May 1
Total amount awarded:	$7,500

Contact:
CTA Scholarship Committee Human Rights Department
c/o Manuel Ayan
P.O. Box 921
Burlingame, CA 94011-0921
Phone: 650-552-5446
Fax: 650-552-5001
Web: www.cta.org

CAP Charitable Foundation

The Ron Brown Scholar Program

Type of award: Scholarship, renewable.
Intended use: For full-time undergraduate study at 4-year institution in United States.
Eligibility: Applicant must be African American. Applicant must be high school senior. Applicant must be U.S. citizen.
Basis for selection: Applicant must demonstrate financial need, high academic achievement, depth of character, leadership, seriousness of purpose and service orientation.
Application requirements: Recommendations, essay, transcript. Two essays.
Additional information: In addition to financial assistance, scholars get other benefits: summer internships, career guidance, placement opportunities, mentors, and leadership training. The scholarships are not limited to specific fields or career objectives and may be used to pursue any academic discipline. Funding is available for four years; a total of $40,000. Earlier deadline is for those who wish to apply and to have their information forwarded to select colleges and scholarship programs.

Amount of award:	$10,000-$40,000
Number of awards:	10
Number of applicants:	5,500
Application deadline:	November 1, January 9
Notification begins:	April 1

Contact:
Ron Brown Scholar Program
1160 Pepsi Place, Suite 206
Charlottesville, VA 22901
Phone: 434-964-1588
Fax: 434-964-1589
Web: www.ronbrown.org

Carl's Jr. Restaurants

Carl N. & Margaret Karcher Founders' Scholarship

Type of award: Scholarship.
Intended use: For full-time freshman study at accredited vocational, 2-year or 4-year institution.
Eligibility: Applicant must be no older than 21, high school senior. Applicant must be residing in Utah, Texas, Alaska,

Washington, Arizona, Nevada, Oklahoma, California, Oregon, Idaho, New Mexico, Colorado or Hawaii.
Application requirements: Transcript.
Additional information: High school graduates also eligible. Employees, affiliates, and franchisees of Carl Karcher Enterprises, Inc., Scholarship America, affiliated agencies and their immediate families are ineligible. Application available on Website.

Amount of award:	$1,000
Number of awards:	60
Number of applicants:	5,000
Application deadline:	February 1
Total amount awarded:	$60,000

Contact:
Carl N. & Margaret Karcher Founders' Scholarship
c/o Scholarship America
One Scholarship Way, PO Box 297
St. Peter, MN 56082
Phone: 507-931-1682
Web: www.carlsjr.com/promotions

Catching the Dream

MESBEC Scholarships

Type of award: Scholarship, renewable.
Intended use: For full-time undergraduate or graduate study at accredited postsecondary institution in United States.
Eligibility: Applicant must be Alaskan native or American Indian. Must be at least one-quarter Native American and enrolled member of federally recognized, state recognized, or terminated tribe. Applicant must be U.S. citizen or permanent resident.
Basis for selection: Major/career interest in mathematics; engineering; science, general; business; education; computer/information sciences; health sciences or medicine. Applicant must demonstrate high academic achievement, depth of character, leadership, seriousness of purpose and service orientation.
Application requirements: Recommendations, essay, transcript, proof of eligibility.
Additional information: Deadlines are March 15 for summer funding; April 15 for fall; September 15 for spring.

Amount of award:	$500-$5,000
Number of awards:	180
Number of applicants:	150
Total amount awarded:	$300,000

Contact:
Catching the Dream
8200 Mountain Road NE
Suite 203
Albuquerque, NM 87110
Phone: 505-262-2351
Fax: 505-262-0534
Web: www.catchingthedream.org

Native American Leadership in Education Scholarship

Type of award: Scholarship, renewable.
Intended use: For full-time undergraduate or graduate study at accredited postsecondary institution in United States.
Eligibility: Applicant must be American Indian. Must be at least one-quarter Native American and enrolled member of federally recognized, state recognized, or terminated tribe. Applicant must be U.S. citizen or permanent resident.
Basis for selection: Major/career interest in education. Applicant must demonstrate high academic achievement, depth of character, leadership, seriousness of purpose and service orientation.
Application requirements: Recommendations, essay, transcript, proof of eligibility.
Additional information: Deadlines are March 15 for summer funding; April 15 for fall; September 15 for spring.

Amount of award:	$500-$5,000
Number of awards:	30
Number of applicants:	40
Total amount awarded:	$100,000

Contact:
Catching the Dream
8200 Mountain Road NE
Suite 203
Albuquerque, NM 87110
Phone: 505-262-2351
Fax: 505-262-0534
Web: www.catchingthedream.org

Tribal Business Management Scholarship

Type of award: Scholarship, renewable.
Intended use: For full-time undergraduate, graduate or postgraduate study at accredited postsecondary institution in United States.
Eligibility: Applicant must be Alaskan native or American Indian. Must be at least one-quarter Native American and enrolled member of federally recognized, state recognized, or terminated tribe. Applicant must be U.S. citizen or permanent resident.
Basis for selection: Major/career interest in business; economics; finance/banking; hotel/restaurant management; accounting; marketing or business/management/administration. Applicant must demonstrate high academic achievement, depth of character, leadership, seriousness of purpose and service orientation.
Application requirements: Recommendations, essay, transcript, proof of eligibility.
Additional information: Scholarships are for fields of study directly related to tribal business development and management. Application deadlines are March 15 for summer semester; April 15 for fall semester; September 15 for spring semester.

Amount of award:	$500-$5,000
Number of awards:	15
Number of applicants:	30
Application deadline:	April 15, September 15
Total amount awarded:	$50,000

Contact:
Catching the Dream
8200 Mountain Road NE
Suite 203
Albuquerque, NM 87110
Phone: 505-262-2351
Fax: 505-262-0534
Web: www.catchingthedream.org

Catholic Aid Association

Catholic Aid Association Scholarship

Type of award: Scholarship.
Intended use: For full-time freshman or sophomore study at vocational, 2-year or 4-year institution in United States.
Eligibility: Applicant or parent must be member/participant of Catholic Aid Association.
Basis for selection: Applicant must demonstrate leadership and service orientation.
Application requirements: Essay, proof of eligibility.
Additional information: Open to college freshmen and high school seniors. Must have been member of Catholic Aid Association for two years prior to application deadline. Application forms change every year; $300 awards go to those who are or will be attending non-Catholic schools, while $500 awards go to those who are or will be attending Catholic universities. Applications can be downloaded from Website. Signed copy must be mailed in.

Amount of award:	$300-$500
Number of applicants:	415
Application deadline:	February 15
Notification begins:	April 1, May 1
Total amount awarded:	$120,000

Contact:
Catholic Aid Association Scholarship Program
3499 North Lexington Avenue
St. Paul, MN 55126
Phone: 651-490-0170
Web: www.catholicaid.org

CCNMA

CCNMA Scholarship

Type of award: Scholarship, renewable.
Intended use: For full-time undergraduate or graduate study at accredited postsecondary institution.
Basis for selection: Competition/talent/interest in writing/journalism. Major/career interest in journalism. Applicant must demonstrate financial need, high academic achievement, seriousness of purpose and service orientation.
Application requirements: Interview, recommendations, essay, transcript. Proof of full-time enrollment. Samples of work: newspaper clips, photographs, audio or television tapes. Two reference letters. Autobiographical essay (300 to 500 words) explaining family background, including any hardships experienced, why you want to be a journalist, and what you believe is the role, if any, of Latino journalists in the news media.
Additional information: Must be a Latino resident of California attending school in or out of state, or nonresident attending school in California.

Amount of award:	$500-$2,000
Number of awards:	15
Number of applicants:	100
Application deadline:	April 1
Notification begins:	June 1

Contact:
CCNMA
300 South Grand Avenue
Suite 3950
Los Angeles, CA 90071-3175
Phone: 213-437-4408
Fax: 213-437-4423
Web: www.ccnma.org

Center for Education Solutions

A. Patrick Charnon Memorial Scholarship

Type of award: Scholarship.
Intended use: For full-time undergraduate study at accredited 4-year institution in United States.
Eligibility: Applicant must be U.S. citizen, permanent resident or international student.
Basis for selection: Major/career interest in governmental public relations; humanities/liberal arts; social/behavioral sciences or sociology. Applicant must demonstrate seriousness of purpose and service orientation.
Application requirements: Transcript. Three letters of recommendation. Two- to four-page essay explaining how community services have shaped applicant's life and how he/she will use college education to build communities in a manner consistent with Pat Charnon's values of compassion, tolerance, generosity, and respect.
Additional information: Must demonstrate commitment to building communities, tolerance, compassion, and respect for all people. Non-traditional students may apply. See Website for application. Application may also be obtained by mailing SASE to address below. Relatives of selection committee ineligible for award. Renewable up to four years.

Amount of award:	$1,500
Number of awards:	1
Number of applicants:	549
Application deadline:	January 15, March 31
Notification begins:	August 1

Contact:
A. Patrick Charnon Memorial Scholarship
The Center for Education Solutions
P.O. Box 208
San Francisco, CA 94104-0208
Web: www.cesresources.org

Central Intelligence Agency

CIA Undergraduate Scholarship

Type of award: Scholarship, renewable.
Intended use: For full-time freshman, sophomore, junior or senior study at accredited 4-year institution in United States.
Eligibility: Applicant must be U.S. citizen.
Basis for selection: Major/career interest in engineering; computer/information sciences; economics; international relations; accounting or finance/banking. Applicant must demonstrate financial need, high academic achievement, depth

of character, leadership, patriotism, seriousness of purpose and service orientation.
Application requirements: Transcript. SAT/ACT scores. Resume.
Additional information: Applicants must be 18 by April of senior year in high school; if not, they can apply for the scholarship in freshman year of college. Award offers applicant chance to work at CIA during summer breaks. Minimum 3.0 GPA; 1000 SAT or 21 ACT required. Minority or disabled applicants given special consideration. Selected scholars are provided salary and up to $18,000 per school year for tuition, fees, books and supplies. Service commitment to CIA must be fulfilled or recipient must repay award. Applicants with family income over $80,000 not eligible. Applicants with family income between $70,000 and $80,000 accepted only if family has four or more dependents. Number of awards varies.

Amount of award:	$18,000
Application deadline:	November 1

Contact:
Central Intelligence Agency Recruitment Center
Attn: Student Programs
L100 L57
Washington, DC 20505
Phone: 800-368-3886
Web: www.cia.gov

C.G. Fuller Foundation

C.G. Fuller Foundation Scholarship

Type of award: Scholarship, renewable.
Intended use: For full-time undergraduate study at 4-year institution.
Eligibility: Applicant must be high school senior. Applicant must be residing in South Carolina.
Basis for selection: Applicant must demonstrate financial need and high academic achievement.
Application requirements: Interview, recommendations, transcript.
Additional information: Apply through financial aid office of university. Applications distributed between end of October and end of November. Applicant must have minimum 3.0 GPA and 1100 SAT. Amount awarded and number of awards vary with changes in funding. Parents' adjusted gross income must be $60,000 or less.

Amount of award:	$2,000
Number of awards:	15
Number of applicants:	200
Application deadline:	April 15
Notification begins:	August 1

Contact:
C.G. Fuller Foundation, c/o Bank of America
P.O. Box 448
SC3-240-04-17
Columbia, SC 29202-0448

ChairScholars Foundation, Inc.

ChairScholars Scholarship

Type of award: Scholarship, renewable.
Intended use: For full-time undergraduate study at postsecondary institution.
Eligibility: Applicant must be physically challenged. Applicant must be single, no older than 21. Applicant must be U.S. citizen.
Basis for selection: Applicant must demonstrate financial need, depth of character, leadership, seriousness of purpose and service orientation.
Application requirements: Recommendations, essay, transcript, proof of eligibility. Photograph. Essay (300-500 words) outlining how you became physically challenged, how your situation has affected your family, and what your goals are for the future. Include parent's or guardian's federal income tax return from last year. Send SAT and ACT scores.
Additional information: Twenty of the awardees for this scholarship receive four $5,000 awards, given yearly. Applicant must have a major physical challenge but does not have to be confined to a wheelchair. Applicant must be unable to attend college without financial aid. Applicant must have at least a B+ average. Applicant must be high school senior or college freshman. If applicant has obtained any other scholarships already, he or she must inform ChairScholars.

Amount of award:	$2,000-$25,000
Number of awards:	20
Number of applicants:	180
Application deadline:	February 28
Total amount awarded:	$800,000

Contact:
ChairScholars Foundation, Inc.
16101 Carencia Lane
Odessa, FL 33556
Phone: 813-920-1981
Fax: 813-920-7661
Web: www.chairscholars.org

Charles & Lucille King Family Foundation, Inc.

Charles & Lucille King Family Foundation Scholarships

Type of award: Scholarship, renewable.
Intended use: For full-time junior or senior study at accredited 4-year institution in United States.
Basis for selection: Major/career interest in communications or radio/television/film.
Application requirements: Recommendations, transcript. Personal statement. Application form with financial information.
Additional information: Download application from Website.

Amount of award:	$3,500
Number of awards:	21
Application deadline:	March 15
Total amount awarded:	$51,250

Contact:
Charles & Lucille King Family Foundation, Inc.
366 Madison Avenue, 10th Floor
New York, NY 10017
Phone: 212-682-2913
Fax: 212-949-0728
Web: www.kingfoundation.org

The Charles A. and Anne Morrow Lindbergh Foundation

Lindbergh Grant

Type of award: Research grant.
Intended use: For non-degree study.
Basis for selection: Major/career interest in environmental science; aviation; natural resources/conservation; education or health sciences.
Application requirements: Research proposal.
Additional information: Applicant research or educational project should address balance between technological advancement and environmental preservation. Project must address balance between technology and nature. Citizens of all countries are eligible. Deadline is second Thursday in June.

    Amount of award: $1,000-$10,580
    Number of awards: 8
    Number of applicants: 170
    Notification begins: April 15
    Total amount awarded: $100,000

Contact:
The Charles A. and Anne Morrow Lindbergh Foundation
2150 Third Avenue North
Suite 310
Anoka, MN 55303-2200
Phone: 763-576-1596
Fax: 763-576-1664
Web: www.lindberghfoundation.org

Charleston Women in International Trade

Charleston Women in International Trade Scholarship

Type of award: Scholarship.
Intended use: For undergraduate study at accredited postsecondary institution in United States.
Eligibility: Applicant must be U.S. citizen residing in South Carolina.
Basis for selection: Applicant must demonstrate financial need.
Application requirements: Essay, transcript. Provide a two-page (minimum length), double-spaced essay explaining the importance of international trade and state your goals for working in the international business environment. You must also explain why you believe you should be awarded this scholarship. Applicant must provide a listing of extra curricular activities, civic and community involvement and define accordingly.
Additional information: Applicant must be pursuing a degree in specific to international trade or related course of study. To apply, complete application on Website.

    Amount of award: $2,000
    Number of awards: 2
    Application deadline: February 26
    Total amount awarded: $4,000

Contact:
Joanne Fogg, CWIT Awards Chairperson
C/O Customs and Border Protection
200 East Bay St.
Charleston, SC 29401
Phone: 843-579-6508
Web: www.cwitsc.org

Charter Fund

Charter Fund Scholarship

Type of award: Scholarship.
Intended use: For full-time freshman study.
Eligibility: Applicant must be high school senior. Applicant must be U.S. citizen or permanent resident residing in Colorado.
Basis for selection: Applicant must demonstrate financial need.
Application requirements: Recommendations, transcript. Personal letter. ACT/SAT scores. College acceptance letter. Financial aid award info.
Additional information: Applicant must be senior in Colorado high school.

    Amount of award: $200-$2,500
    Number of awards: 64
    Number of applicants: 61
    Application deadline: May 2
    Notification begins: July 15
    Total amount awarded: $150,000

Contact:
Charter Fund- Jeanette Montoya
370 17th Street, Suite 5300
Denver, CO 80202
Phone: 303-572-1727
Fax: 303-628-3839
Web: www.piton.org/charterfund

Chesapeake Corporation Foundation

Chesapeake Corporation Scholarship

Type of award: Scholarship, renewable.
Intended use: For full-time undergraduate study.
Eligibility: Applicant or parent must be employed by Chesapeake Corporation. Applicant must be high school senior.
Basis for selection: Applicant must demonstrate high academic achievement.
Application requirements: SAT/ACT scores.

Additional information: Applicant or parent must be employed by Chesapeake Corporation.

Amount of award:	$4,000
Number of awards:	4
Application deadline:	November 15

Contact:
Chesapeake Corporation Foundation
James Center II
1021 East Cary Street, Box 2350
Richmond, VA 23218-2350
Web: www.cskcorp.com

Chesterfield Federal Credit Union

Charles R. Quaiff, Sr. Memorial Scholarship

Type of award: Scholarship.
Intended use: For freshman study.
Eligibility: Applicant must be high school senior.
Basis for selection: Applicant must demonstrate financial need and high academic achievement.
Application requirements: Essay, transcript.
Additional information: Applicant or a parent must be a member of Chesterfield Federal Credit Union.

Amount of award:	$1,000
Number of awards:	3
Application deadline:	March 31
Notification begins:	April 15

Contact:
Chesterfield Federal Credit Union
Attn: Chris Miller
P.O. Box 820
Chesterfield, VA 23832
Phone: 804-748-1417
Fax: 804-796-7813
Web: www.chesterfieldfcu.net/scholarships.html

Choctaw Nation of Oklahoma

Choctaw Nation Higher Education Program

Type of award: Scholarship, renewable.
Intended use: For undergraduate or graduate study at accredited 2-year, 4-year or graduate institution in United States.
Eligibility: Applicant must be American Indian. Must be enrolled member of Choctaw Tribe and have Certificate of Degree of Indian Blood (CDIB) and tribal membership card.
Application requirements: Transcript. Proof of Choctaw descent. FAFSA. School enrollment verification.
Additional information: Program made up of two awards: a grant and a scholarship. The $1,600 grant is based on financial need. The $2,000 scholarship is for applicants with minimum 2.5 GPA. Grant will assist with any unmet need up to award amount. Must reapply for renewal. Number of awards varies.

Amount of award:	$1,600-$2,000
Number of applicants:	5,000
Application deadline:	October 1
Notification begins:	July 15

Contact:
Choctaw Nation of Oklahoma
Higher Education Department
P.O. Box 1210
Durant, OK 74702-1210
Phone: 800-522-6170
Fax: 580-924-1267
Web: www.choctawnation.com

Christian Record Services

Christian Record Services Scholarship

Type of award: Scholarship, renewable.
Intended use: For full-time undergraduate study in United States.
Eligibility: Applicant must be visually impaired.
Basis for selection: Applicant must demonstrate financial need and high academic achievement.
Application requirements: Recommendations. Photo and bio.
Additional information: Applicants must be totally or legally blind. Awardees must reapply yearly.

Amount of award:	$500
Number of awards:	10
Number of applicants:	67
Application deadline:	April 1
Notification begins:	May 15
Total amount awarded:	$5,000

Contact:
Christian Record Services
4444 South 52 Street
Lincoln, NE 68516
Phone: 402-488-0981
Fax: 402-488-7582
Web: www.christianrecord.org

The Christophers

The Christophers Video Contest for College Students

Type of award: Scholarship.
Intended use: For undergraduate or graduate study at postsecondary institution.
Basis for selection: Competition/talent/interest in visual arts, based on video or film that captures theme, artistic and technical proficiency.
Application requirements: Entries must be submitted in NTSC format on standard, full-sized VHS tape or as a region 1 or regionless DVD. Entries over five minutes will not be considered.
Additional information: Video contest for college students. Preference given to students with a career interest or major in film and video, but all majors eligible. Visit Website for contest's annual theme and additional information. Winning

The Christophers: The Christophers Video Contest for College Students

entries aired internationally via Christopher Closeup television series.
- **Amount of award:** $100-$3,000
- **Application deadline:** June 6
- **Notification begins:** September 5

Contact:
The Christophers
5 Hanover Square
11th FL
New York, NY 10004
Phone: 212-759-4050 ext. 240
Fax: 212-838-5073
Web: www.christophers.org

City University of New York

Peter F. Vallone Academic Scholarship

Type of award: Scholarship, renewable.
Intended use: For full-time freshman study.
Eligibility: Applicant must be residing in New York.
Additional information: Students are considered as part of the admissions process. No separate application. Applicant must have a B average or better and successfully completed at least 12 College Preparatory Initiative (Regents level) year-long courses. Must be first-time college student. Must graduate from New York City high school. Award amount varies yearly.

Contact:
City University of New York
Office of Student Financial Assistance
1114 Avenue of the Americas FL15
New York, NY 10036
Phone: 212-220-1430
Web: www.bmcc.cuny.edu

Clinique Nursing Scholarship Program

Clinique Nursing Scholarship

Type of award: Scholarship, renewable.
Intended use: For undergraduate study in United States.
Designated institutions: Institutions accredited by the National League for Nursing Accrediting Commission (NLNAC) OR the Commission on Collegiate Nursing Education (CCNE).
Eligibility: Applicant must be U.S. citizen, permanent resident or international student.
Basis for selection: Major/career interest in nursing. Applicant must demonstrate financial need and seriousness of purpose.
Application requirements: Recommendations, essay, transcript. FAFSA, SAR, two 500-word essays.
Additional information: Minimum 3.0 GPA. Recipients must agree to work part-time as an Associate Clinique Consultant, earning hourly wage in addition to award. International students must be able to work in U.S. Visit Website for more information and application.

- **Amount of award:** $6,000
- **Number of awards:** 15
- **Application deadline:** May 2

Contact:
Clinique Nursing Scholarship Program
767 Fifth Ave, 37 Floor
New York, NY 10153
Web: www.cliniquescholar.com

The Coca-Cola Foundation

Coca-Cola Scholars Program

Type of award: Scholarship, renewable.
Intended use: For full-time undergraduate study at accredited 4-year institution in United States.
Eligibility: Applicant must be high school senior. Applicant must be U.S. citizen or permanent resident.
Basis for selection: Applicant must demonstrate high academic achievement, depth of character, leadership, seriousness of purpose and service orientation.
Additional information: Must be attending high school in United States or territories. Minimum 3.0 GPA required at the end of junior year high school. Award is for four years, $2,500 or $5,000 per year. Notification begins November 30 for semifinalists; end of February for finalists. Children of Coca-Cola employees not eligible.

- **Amount of award:** $10,000-$20,000
- **Number of awards:** 250
- **Application deadline:** October 31
- **Notification begins:** November 30
- **Total amount awarded:** $3,000,000

Contact:
Coca-Cola Scholars Foundation
P.O. Box 442
Atlanta, GA 30301-0442
Phone: 800-306-2653
Web: www.coca-colascholars.org

Coca-Cola Two-Year Colleges Scholarship

Type of award: Scholarship.
Intended use: For undergraduate study at 2-year institution in United States.
Eligibility: Applicant must be high school senior. Applicant must be U.S. citizen or permanent resident.
Basis for selection: Major/career interest in humanities/liberal arts. Applicant must demonstrate high academic achievement, depth of character and service orientation.
Application requirements: Nomination by college in which student is enrolled or planning to enroll.
Additional information: Applicant/nominee must have done community service within past 12 months. Minimum 2.5 GPA at time of nomination. Must be planning to enroll in at least two courses during next term. Children of Coca-Cola employees not eligible. Up to two nominations from each campus.

- **Amount of award:** $1,000
- **Number of awards:** 350
- **Application deadline:** May 31
- **Notification begins:** July 15
- **Total amount awarded:** $350,000

Contact:
Coca-Cola Two-Year Colleges Scholarship Program
P.O. Box 1615
Atlanta, GA 30301-1615
Phone: 800-306-2653
Web: www.coca-colascholars.org

First Generation Scholarship Program

Type of award: Scholarship, renewable.
Intended use: For full-time undergraduate study at accredited 2-year or 4-year institution in United States.
Eligibility: Applicant must be high school senior. Applicant must be U.S. citizen or permanent resident.
Basis for selection: Applicant must demonstrate financial need.
Application requirements: Proof of eligibility.
Additional information: Applicant must be first in immediate family to seek college education. Contact individual institution to see if scholarship is currently available. Contact Foundation for list of eligible institutions.
    Amount of award: $5,000
Contact:
The Coca-Cola Foundation
P.O. Drawer 1734
Atlanta, GA 30301

The College Board

Young Epidemiology Scholars Student Competition

Type of award: Scholarship.
Intended use: For undergraduate study at 4-year institution in United States.
Eligibility: Applicant must be high school junior or senior. Applicant must be U.S. citizen or permanent resident.
Basis for selection: Major/career interest in epidemiology; sociology; health sciences or mathematics.
Application requirements: An individual research project that applies epidemiological principles to health-related area is also required.
Additional information: YES research project should shed light on a health problem, using methods employed by epidemiologists. See Website for online registration and more information.
    Amount of award: $1,000-$50,000
    Number of awards: 120
    Number of applicants: 716
    Application deadline: February 2
    Notification begins: April 1
    Total amount awarded: $456,000
Contact:
The College Board
YES Program
11911 Freedom Drive, Suite 300
Reston, VA 20190-5602
Phone: 800-626-9795
Fax: 703-707-5599
Web: www.collegeboard.com/yes

College Foundation of North Carolina

Jagannathan Scholarship

Type of award: Scholarship, renewable.
Intended use: For full-time undergraduate study at 4-year institution in United States. Designated institutions: Constituent institutions of the University of North Carolina.
Eligibility: Applicant must be high school senior. Applicant must be U.S. citizen or permanent resident residing in North Carolina.
Basis for selection: Applicant must demonstrate financial need, high academic achievement and leadership.
Application requirements: Proof of eligibility, nomination by high school guidance counselor; financial office of UNC institution; or Tolaram Polymers, Cookson Fibers or related company. SAT scores, College Scholarship Service's PROFILE (register by January 26; file by February 7), and documented proof of financial need.
Additional information: Special consideration given to students whose parents are employees of Tolaram Polymers, Cookson Fibers and related companies. Applications available at all North Carolina public high schools. Students will be notified in May of their candidacy status. Check Website for specific details.
    Amount of award: $3,500
    Number of awards: 4
    Number of applicants: 4
    Total amount awarded: $14,000
Contact:
College Foundation of North Carolina
P.O. Box 12100
Raleigh, NC 27605-2100
Phone: 866-866-2362
Web: www.cfnc.org/jag

North Carolina Student Incentive Grant

Type of award: Scholarship, renewable.
Intended use: For full-time undergraduate study at postsecondary institution. Designated institutions: Approved institutions in North Carolina.
Eligibility: Applicant must be U.S. citizen residing in North Carolina.
Basis for selection: Applicant must demonstrate financial need.
    Amount of award: $700
    Number of awards: 8,110
    Number of applicants: 395,913
    Application deadline: March 15
    Total amount awarded: $5,101,881
Contact:
College Foundation of North Carolina
P.O. Box 12100
Raleigh, NC 27605-2100
Phone: 866-866-2362
Web: www.cfnc.org

Colorado Commission on Higher Education

Colorado Student Grant

Type of award: Scholarship.
Intended use: For undergraduate study at postsecondary institution.
Eligibility: Applicant must be U.S. citizen, permanent resident or permanent resident of Palau. Applicant must be residing in Colorado.
Basis for selection: Applicant must demonstrate financial need.
Application requirements: FAFSA.
Additional information: Contact college financial aid office or visit college Website for additional information. International students must be working toward becoming permanent resident of U.S.
   Amount of award: $250-$5,000
Contact:
Colorado Commission on Higher Education
1380 Lawrence Street
Suite 1200
Denver, CO 80204
Phone: 303-866-2723
Web: www.state.co.us/cche

Colorado Supplemental Leveraging Educational Assistance Partnership Program

Type of award: Scholarship.
Intended use: For undergraduate study at accredited postsecondary institution. Designated institutions: Four-year institutions in Colorado with a CCHE-authorized teacher education program. Institutions with post-baccalaureate licensing programs.
Eligibility: Applicant must be U.S. citizen, permanent resident or permanent resident of Palau. Applicant must be residing in Colorado.
Basis for selection: Major/career interest in education, teacher. Applicant must demonstrate financial need.
Application requirements: FAFSA.
Additional information: Priority given to applicants who will student teach during award year. Contact college financial aid office for information and application. International students must be working toward becoming permanent resident of U.S.
   Amount of award: $5,000
Contact:
Colorado Commission on Higher Education
1380 Lawrence Street
Suite 1200
Denver, CO 80204
Phone: 303-866-2723
Web: www.state.co.us/cche

Colorado Work-Study Program

Type of award: Scholarship.
Intended use: For undergraduate study at postsecondary institution. Designated institutions: Eligible postsecondary institutions in Colorado.
Eligibility: Applicant must be U.S. citizen, permanent resident or permanent resident of Palau. Applicant must be residing in Colorado.
Additional information: Part-time employment program for students who need work experience or who can prove financial need. International students must be working toward becoming permanent resident of U.S. Amount of award cannot exceed need. Contact college financial aid office or visit Website for additional information.
Contact:
Colorado Commission on Higher Education
1380 Lawrence Street
Suite 1200
Denver, CO 80204
Phone: 303-866-2723
Web: www.state.co.us/cche

Colorado Masons Benevolent Fund Association

Colorado Masons Scholarship

Type of award: Scholarship, renewable.
Intended use: For full-time undergraduate study at accredited vocational, 2-year or 4-year institution in United States.
Eligibility: Applicant must be high school senior. Applicant must be residing in Colorado.
Basis for selection: Applicant must demonstrate financial need, high academic achievement and depth of character.
Additional information: Applicant must be graduating senior at public high school within Colorado and attending an institution of higher learning within Colorado. Scholarship is renewable for up to four years. Contact high school counselor for application details. Do not contact association directly.
   Amount of award: $7,000
   Number of awards: 15
   Number of applicants: 456
   Application deadline: March 7
   Total amount awarded: $279,000
Contact:
Scholarship Administrator
1130 Panorama Drive
Colorado Springs, CO 80904
Phone: 800-482-4441 ext. 29
Fax: 800-440-3520
Web: www.coloradofreemasons.org

Colorado Society of CPAs Educational Foundation

Colorado Society of CPAs General Scholarship

Type of award: Scholarship, renewable.
Intended use: For junior, senior or graduate study at accredited 4-year or graduate institution in United States.
Eligibility: Applicant must be U.S. citizen, permanent resident or international student residing in Colorado.

Basis for selection: Major/career interest in accounting. Applicant must demonstrate high academic achievement.
Application requirements: Essay, transcript.
Additional information: Must have completed eight semester hours in accounting to be eligible to apply. Must be at least half-time student. Minimum 3.0 GPA required. International students must have work visa. Visit Website to download application.

Amount of award:	$2,500
Number of awards:	20
Number of applicants:	100
Application deadline:	June 30, November 30
Total amount awarded:	$50,000

Contact:
Colorado Society of CPAs Educational Foundation
7979 East Tufts Avenue, Suite 1000
Denver, CO 80237-2845
Phone: 800-523-9082 or 303-773-2877
Web: www.cocpa.org/student_faculty/scholarships.asp

Mark J. Smith Scholarship

Type of award: Scholarship, renewable.
Intended use: For junior, senior or graduate study at accredited 4-year or graduate institution in United States.
Eligibility: Applicant must be U.S. citizen, permanent resident or international student residing in Colorado.
Basis for selection: Major/career interest in accounting. Applicant must demonstrate financial need and high academic achievement.
Application requirements: Transcript.
Additional information: Must be student from a single-parent household. Must have completed eight semester hours in accounting. Must be at least half-time student. Minimum 3.0 GPA required. International students must have work visa. Visit Website to download application. Award given only once per year; contact organization to check which application deadline applies for given year.

Amount of award:	$2,500
Number of awards:	1
Number of applicants:	12
Application deadline:	June 30, November 30
Total amount awarded:	$2,500

Contact:
Colorado Society of CPAs Educational Foundation
7979 East Tufts Avenue, Suite 1000
Denver, CO 80237-2843
Phone: 800-523-9082 or 303-773-2877
Web: www.cocpa.org/student_faculty/scholarships.asp

Columbus Citizens Foundation, Inc.

Columbus Citizens Foundation College Scholarship Program

Type of award: Scholarship, renewable.
Intended use: For undergraduate study at accredited 4-year institution.
Eligibility: Applicant must be high school senior. Applicant must be Italian. Applicant must be residing in Vermont, New York, Maine, Delaware, Maryland, Pennsylvania, Massachusetts, District of Columbia, Connecticut, New Hampshire, New Jersey or Rhode Island.
Basis for selection: Applicant must demonstrate financial need, high academic achievement and service orientation.
Application requirements: Interview, transcript. Two recommendation letters: one from academic source and one from nonacademic source. Two essays: one outlining applicant's pride in Italian-American heritage and one about an Italian-American who has significantly impacted the applicant's life. Tax data verification.
Additional information: Applicants must be graduating high school seniors and have 85 average or higher (on scale of 100) or 3.0 GPA (on a scale of 4.0). Applicant's family per capita income must not exceed $30,000. Applicants who reach semifinalist round must travel to New York City for interview. Applications available on Website in December, when deadline for following year will also be posted.

Amount of award:	$500-$6,000
Number of awards:	96
Number of applicants:	273
Total amount awarded:	$244,250

Contact:
College Scholarship Program
Columbus Citizens Foundation
8 East 69th Street
New York, NY 10021-4906
Phone: 212-249-9923
Fax: 212-517-7619
Web: www.columbuscitizensfd.org

Cone Mills Corporation

Cone Mills Scholarship Program

Type of award: Scholarship, renewable.
Intended use: For full-time undergraduate study at accredited vocational, 2-year or 4-year institution in United States.
Eligibility: Applicant or parent must be employed by Cone Mills Corporation. Applicant must be high school senior. Applicant must be U.S. citizen.
Basis for selection: Applicant must demonstrate high academic achievement.
Application requirements: Essay, transcript, proof of eligibility.
Additional information: Applicant must be dependent child of Cone Mills Corporation employee. Applications accepted in mid-December. Application deadline at the end of January; see Website for exact date.

Amount of award:	$500-$2,500
Number of awards:	8
Number of applicants:	24
Notification begins:	April 30
Total amount awarded:	$41,000

Contact:
Cone Mills Corporation
Scholarship Program
P.O. Box 1465
Taylors, SC 29687-0031
Phone: 864-268-3363
Fax: 864-268-7160
Web: www.scholarshipprograms.org

Congressional Black Caucus Foundation, Inc.

The CBC Spouses Cheerios Brand Health Initiative Scholarship

Type of award: Scholarship, renewable.
Intended use: For full-time undergraduate study at accredited 4-year institution.
Eligibility: Applicant must be U.S. citizen or permanent resident.
Basis for selection: Applicant must demonstrate financial need.
Application requirements: Transcript.
Additional information: Applicant must have 2.5 GPA. All applicants must reside or attend school in congressional district represented by Congressional Black Caucus (CBC) Member. To find out more information about CBC districts, go to www.house.gov and enter ZIP Code. Award amount set annually. Submit application materials to CBC Member's Local Scholarship Selection Committee.
   Application deadline: May 1
Contact:
Contact CBC member for Local Scholarship Selection Committee address
Phone: 202-263-2800
Fax: 202-775-0773
Web: www.cbcfinc.org

The CBC Spouses Education Scholarship

Type of award: Scholarship, renewable.
Intended use: For full-time undergraduate or graduate study at accredited 4-year institution.
Eligibility: Applicant must be U.S. citizen or permanent resident residing in Ohio, New York, Louisiana, Virginia, California, Mississippi, Illinois, Missouri, Michigan, Texas, Maryland, Pennsylvania, South Carolina, Georgia, Florida, District of Columbia, Virgin Islands, Indiana, New Jersey or North Carolina.
Basis for selection: Applicant must demonstrate financial need.
Application requirements: Transcript.
Additional information: Applicant must have minimum 2.5 GPA and reside or attend school in Congressional Black Caucus district represented by Black Caucus member. To find out more information about CBC districts, go to www.house.gov and enter ZIP Code. Selection made at district level. Award amounts vary. List of eligible districts and members' addresses provided by national office. Employees or relatives of CBC members, CBC spouses, CBC Foundation, and/or General Mills not eligible for this program. For information about local contact, see Website. Submit application materials to CBC Member's Local Scholarship Selection Committee.
   Application deadline: May 1, September 15
Contact:
Contact CBC member for Local Scholarship Selection Committee address
Phone: 202-263-2800
Fax: 202-775-0773
Web: www.cbcfinc.org

The CBC Spouses Performing Arts Scholarship

Type of award: Scholarship, renewable.
Intended use: For full-time undergraduate study at accredited 4-year institution.
Eligibility: Applicant must be U.S. citizen or permanent resident.
Basis for selection: Applicant must demonstrate financial need.
Application requirements: Transcript. Videotape of performance.
Additional information: Applicant must have minimum 2.5 GPA and must reside or attend school in congressional district represented by Black Caucus member. To find out more information about a CBC district, go to www.house.gov and enter ZIP Code.
   Amount of award: $3,000
   Number of awards: 10
   Application deadline: May 1
Contact:
Congressional Black Caucus Foundation, Inc.
Phone: 202-263-2800
Fax: 202-775-0773
Web: www.cbcfinc.org

The CBC Spouse's Visual Arts Scholarship

Type of award: Scholarship.
Intended use: For undergraduate study at 4-year institution. Designated institutions: Colleges/universities in congressional districts represented by Congressional Black Caucus member.
Basis for selection: Major/career interest in arts, general or art/art history. Applicant must demonstrate financial need, leadership and service orientation.
Application requirements: Recommendations, essay, transcript. Photo of applicant. Submit video, DVD, or photograph of artwork. High school seniors must submit college acceptance letter.
Additional information: High school seniors and undergraduates pursuing career in visual arts may apply. Minimum 2.5 GPA.
   Amount of award: $3,000
   Number of awards: 5
   Application deadline: May 1
Contact:
Congressional Black Caucus Foundation
Phone: 202-263-2800
Fax: 202-775-0773
Web: www.cbcfinc.org

Congressional Hispanic Caucus Institute

Congressional Hispanic Caucus Institute Scholarship Awards

Type of award: Scholarship.
Intended use: For undergraduate or graduate study at 2-year, 4-year or graduate institution.

Eligibility: Applicant must be Mexican American, Hispanic American or Puerto Rican.
Basis for selection: Applicant must demonstrate leadership and service orientation.
Additional information: No GPA requirement. Community college students receive $1,000; students enrolled at four-year colleges or universities receive $2,500; students enrolled in two-year graduate programs receive $5,000. Undergraduate students also receive Dell Notebook Computer and Microsoft Package.
    Amount of award: $1,000-$5,000
    Number of awards: 103
    Application deadline: April 16
Contact:
Congressional Hispanic Caucus Institute
911 2nd Street NE
Washington, DC 20002
Phone: 202-543-1771
Fax: 202-546-2143
Web: www.chciyouth.org

Connecticut Building Congress Scholarship Fund

Connecticut Building Congress Scholarship

Type of award: Scholarship, renewable.
Intended use: For undergraduate study at 2-year or 4-year institution in United States.
Eligibility: Applicant must be residing in Connecticut.
Basis for selection: Major/career interest in engineering, construction; architecture; construction management; surveying/mapping or construction. Applicant must demonstrate financial need and high academic achievement.
Application requirements: Interview, transcript. Essay of no more than 500 words explaining how planned studies will relate to a career in the construction industry. Student Aid Report. SAT/ACT scores.
Additional information: Must give class standing. Recommendation letters optional. Must be involved in extracurricular activities and exhibit potential. Applicant may attend school outside of CT. Scholarships presented at CBC's Project Team Award Banquet. Number of awards and amount at discretion of Board of Directors. Renewable if student maintains 3.0 GPA and continues construction-related degree studies.
    Amount of award: $500-$2,000
    Number of awards: 4
    Number of applicants: 75
Contact:
Connecticut Building Congress Scholarship Fund
P.O. Box 185334
Hamden, CT 06518
Phone: 860-228-1387
Fax: 203-281-3631
Web: www.cbc-ct.org

Connecticut Department of Higher Education

Connecticut Aid for Public College Students

Type of award: Scholarship, renewable.
Intended use: For undergraduate study.
Eligibility: Applicant must be U.S. citizen residing in Connecticut.
Basis for selection: Applicant must demonstrate financial need.
Additional information: Awards up to amount of unmet financial need, determined by the college. Deadline based on financial aid deadline. Apply at financial aid office at Connecticut public college.
    Number of awards: 12,000
    Total amount awarded: $30,208,469
Contact:
Contact school's financial aid office, or:
Connecticut Department of Higher Education
61 Woodland Street
Hartford, CT 06105-2391
Phone: 800-842-0229
Fax: 860-947-1810
Web: www.ctdhe.org

Connecticut Aid to Dependents of Deceased/Disabled/MIA Veterans

Type of award: Scholarship.
Intended use: For undergraduate or graduate study.
Eligibility: Applicant must be U.S. citizen residing in Connecticut. Applicant must be dependent of disabled veteran, deceased veteran or POW/MIA; or spouse of disabled veteran, deceased veteran or POW/MIA. Death or disability must be service related. Parent/spouse must have been Connecticut resident prior to enlistment.
Basis for selection: Applicant must demonstrate financial need.
Application requirements: Proof of eligibility.
    Amount of award: $800
    Number of awards: 8
    Number of applicants: 3
    Total amount awarded: $1,200
Contact:
Connecticut Department of Higher Education
61 Woodland Street
Hartford, CT 06105-2391
Phone: 800-842-0229
Fax: 860-947-1311
Web: www.ctdhe.org

Connecticut Capitol Scholarship Program

Type of award: Scholarship, renewable.
Intended use: For undergraduate study.
Eligibility: Applicant must be high school senior. Applicant must be U.S. citizen or permanent resident residing in Connecticut.
Basis for selection: Applicant must demonstrate financial need and high academic achievement.

Additional information: Must rank in top 20 percent of class or have SAT score of at least 1800. May be used at institutions in Connecticut or at institutions in states with reciprocity agreements with Connecticut.
- **Amount of award:** $500-$3,000
- **Number of awards:** 5,684
- **Number of applicants:** 5,338
- **Application deadline:** February 15
- **Total amount awarded:** $10,170,096

Contact:
High school guidance office for application, or:
Connecticut Department of Higher Education
61 Woodlawn St.
Hartford, CT 06105-2391
Phone: 800-842-0229
Fax: 860-947-1313
Web: www.ctdhe.org

Connecticut Independent College Student Grant

Type of award: Scholarship, renewable.
Intended use: For undergraduate study in United States.
Designated institutions: Private institutions in Connecticut.
Eligibility: Applicant must be U.S. citizen residing in Connecticut.
Basis for selection: Applicant must demonstrate financial need.
Application requirements: FAFSA and any other financial aid forms required by the college.
Additional information: Award based on financial need. Deadline determined by financial aid deadline at each college.
- **Number of awards:** 4,800
- **Total amount awarded:** $23,913,860

Contact:
Contact school's financial office, or:
Connecticut Department of Higher Education
61 Woodland Street
Hartford, CT 06105-2391
Phone: 800-842-0229
Fax: 860-947-1810
Web: www.ctdhe.org

Connecticut Minority Teacher Incentive Grant

Type of award: Scholarship.
Intended use: For junior or senior study.
Eligibility: Applicant must be Alaskan native, Asian American, African American, Mexican American, Hispanic American, Puerto Rican, American Indian or Native Hawaiian/Pacific Islander. Applicant must be residing in Connecticut.
Basis for selection: Major/career interest in education.
Application requirements: Nomination.
Additional information: Award for minority juniors or seniors enrolled in Connecticut college or university teacher preparation program. Grants up to $5,000/year for two years; loan reimbursement of $2,500/year for up to four years of teaching in Connecticut public school. Visit Website for more information or contact Education Dean at Connecticut colleges and universities that offer teacher preparation programs by October 1.
- **Amount of award:** $2,500-$5,000
- **Number of awards:** 76
- **Application deadline:** October 1
- **Total amount awarded:** $334,667

Contact:
Education Dean at CT colleges with teacher preparation programs
Phone: 800-842-0229
Fax: 860-947-1810
Web: www.ctdhe.org

Connecticut Robert C. Byrd Honors Scholarship

Type of award: Scholarship, renewable.
Intended use: For undergraduate study.
Eligibility: Applicant must be high school senior. Applicant must be U.S. citizen residing in Connecticut.
Basis for selection: Applicant must demonstrate high academic achievement.
Additional information: Applicant must rank in top two percent of high school graduating class or have a combined SAT score above 2,100. File applications through high school guidance office by April 1.
- **Amount of award:** $1,500
- **Number of awards:** 314
- **Number of applicants:** 700
- **Application deadline:** April 1
- **Total amount awarded:** $502,370

Contact:
Connecticut Department of Higher Education
61 Woodland Street
Hartford, CT 06105-2391
Phone: 800-842-0229
Fax: 860-947-1311
Web: www.ctdhe.org

Connecticut Tuition Set Aside Aid

Type of award: Scholarship, renewable.
Intended use: For undergraduate study at 2-year or 4-year institution in United States.
Eligibility: Applicant must be U.S. citizen residing in Connecticut.
Basis for selection: Applicant must demonstrate financial need.
Additional information: Awards up to unmet financial need. Apply at financial aid office of institution. Scholarship awarded through Connecticut public colleges.
- **Total amount awarded:** $53,000,000

Contact:
Financial aid office of Connecticut public colleges, or:
Connecticut Department of Higher Education
61 Woodland St.
Hartford, CT 06105-2391
Phone: 800-842-0229
Fax: 860-947-1810
Web: www.ctdhe.org

Connecticut Tuition Waiver for Senior Citizens

Type of award: Scholarship.
Intended use: For undergraduate study.
Eligibility: Applicant must be returning adult student. Applicant must be U.S. citizen residing in Connecticut.
Application requirements: Proof of eligibility.
Additional information: Waivers approved on space available basis. Apply through financial aid office of institution.
- **Amount of award:** Full tuition

Contact:
Financial aid office of Connecticut public colleges, or:
Connecticut Department of Higher Education
61 Woodland St.
Hartford, CT 06105-2391
Phone: 800-842-0229
Fax: 860-947-1810
Web: www.ctdhe.org

Connecticut Tuition Waiver for Veterans

Type of award: Scholarship, renewable.
Intended use: For undergraduate study.
Eligibility: Applicant must be U.S. citizen residing in Connecticut. Applicant must be veteran. Must have served during time of conflict. Must have been Connecticut resident at time of enlistment.
Application requirements: Proof of eligibility.
   Amount of award: Full tuition
Contact:
Financial aid office of Connecticut public colleges, or:
Connecticut Department of Higher Education
61 Woodland St.
Hartford, CT 06105-2391
Phone: 800-842-0229
Fax: 860-947-1810
Web: www.ctdhe.org

Connecticut Tuition Waiver for Vietnam MIA/POW Dependents

Type of award: Scholarship.
Intended use: For undergraduate study.
Eligibility: Applicant must be U.S. citizen residing in Connecticut. Applicant must be dependent of POW/MIA; or spouse of POW/MIA during Vietnam.
Application requirements: Proof of eligibility.
Additional information: Apply at financial aid office of institution. Awarded through Connecticut public colleges.
Contact:
Connecticut public colleges, or:
Connecticut Department of Higher Education
61 Woodland St.
Hartford, CT 06105-0229
Phone: 800-842-0229
Fax: 860-842-1810
Web: www.ctdhe.org

Weisman Scholarship

Type of award: Scholarship, renewable.
Intended use: For junior or senior study.
Eligibility: Applicant must be Alaskan native, Asian American, African American, Mexican American, Hispanic American, Puerto Rican, American Indian or Native Hawaiian/Pacific Islander. Applicant must be residing in Connecticut.
Basis for selection: Major/career interest in education or education, teacher.
Application requirements: Nomination.
Additional information: Must intend to teach math or science in middle or high school. Loan reimbursement up to $2,500 per year for up to four years of teaching science or math in CT public middle or high school. Visit Website for more information or contact education dean at individual CT colleges/universities by October 1st.

   Amount of award: $2,500-$5,000
   Number of awards: 2
   Number of applicants: 31
   Application deadline: October 1
   Total amount awarded: $22,500
Contact:
Connecticut Department of Higher Education
61 Woodland Street
Hartford, CT 06105-2326
Phone: 800-842-0229
Fax: 860-947-1810
Web: www.ctdhe.org

Connecticut League for Nursing

Connecticut Nursing Scholarship

Type of award: Scholarship.
Intended use: For senior or graduate study at accredited postsecondary institution.
Eligibility: Applicant must be U.S. citizen residing in Connecticut.
Basis for selection: Major/career interest in nursing. Applicant must demonstrate financial need, high academic achievement, leadership and seriousness of purpose.
Application requirements: Recommendations, essay, transcript, proof of eligibility.
Additional information: At least one undergraduate and one graduate award given. Applicants must have 18 credits in nursing courses to be eligible for graduate scholarship; undergraduates must have completed one year of two-year program or three years of four-year program; RN students must be entering senior year in upper-division BSN program. Awardees notified in late November.
   Amount of award: $1,000-$1,500
   Number of applicants: 15
   Application deadline: October 14
   Notification begins: November 15
Contact:
Connecticut League for Nursing
51 N. Main St.
Suite 3D
Southington, CT 06489
Phone: 860-276-9621
Fax: 860-276-8798
Web: www.ctleaguefornursing.org

Consortium of Information and Telecommunication Executives, Inc.

CITE-NY Association Scholarship

Type of award: Scholarship.
Intended use: For undergraduate study in United States.
Eligibility: Applicant must be African American. Applicant must be high school senior. Applicant must be U.S. citizen or permanent resident residing in New York.

Basis for selection: Major/career interest in business; computer/information sciences; engineering or communications. Applicant must demonstrate financial need, high academic achievement, depth of character, leadership and service orientation.
Application requirements: Recommendations, essay, transcript, proof of eligibility.
Additional information: Recipient must be a New York State resident and must attend local CITE Scholarship awards dinner to accept award. Deadline is in March.
    Amount of award: $2,000
    Number of awards: 2
    Notification begins: April 1
Contact:
Verizon
Phone: 212-962-1730
Web: www.forcite.org

Costume Society of America

Adele Filene Travel Award

Type of award: Scholarship.
Intended use: For undergraduate or graduate study in United States.
Eligibility: Applicant must be U.S. citizen or international student.
Basis for selection: Major/career interest in ethnic/cultural studies; art/art history; arts, general; history or fashion/fashion design/modeling.
Application requirements: Two faculty recommendations, budget.
Additional information: Award only for those who have paper or research poster accepted for presentation at the national meeting. The award is for travel expenses to the meeting. Must be a student member of Costume Society of America. Major/career interests may include apparel design, historic costume, and fashion merchandising.
    Amount of award: $500
    Number of awards: 3
    Application deadline: March 1
Contact:
Costume Society of America National Office
203 Towne Center Drive
Hillsborough, NJ 08844
Phone: 800-CSA-9447 or 908-359-1471
Fax: 908-359-7619
Web: www.costumesocietyamerica.com/GrantsAwards/adelefilene.html

Stella Blum Research Grant

Type of award: Research grant.
Intended use: For undergraduate or graduate study at vocational, 2-year, 4-year or graduate institution in United States.
Eligibility: Applicant must be U.S. citizen, permanent resident or international student.
Basis for selection: Major/career interest in art/art history; arts, general; history; museum studies or performing arts.
Application requirements: Recommendations, transcript. References, recommendations, and written proposal researching North American costumes. The proposal should be typed double-spaced, no more than 1,000 words.
Additional information: Must be a member of Costume Society of America researching a North American costume topic as part of degree requirement. Award is $2,000 for research and $500 for expenses to present at national meeting.
    Amount of award: $2,500
    Number of awards: 1
    Application deadline: May 1
    Notification begins: August 1
    Total amount awarded: $2,500
Contact:
Costume Society of America
203 Towne Centre Drive
Hillsborough, NJ 08844
Phone: 800-272-9447
Web: www.costumesocietyamerica.com/GrantsAwards/stellablum.html

Council on International Educational Exchange

CIEE International Study Programs (CIEE-ISP) Scholarships

Type of award: Scholarship.
Intended use: For full-time undergraduate or graduate study at accredited 4-year or graduate institution. Designated institutions: CIEE Member or CIEE Academic Consortium member institutions.
Basis for selection: Applicant must demonstrate financial need and high academic achievement.
Application requirements: Financial aid administration form. Five-hundred word essay; guidelines on application.
Additional information: Available to CIEE study abroad program applicants only. Study Program Application is used in consideration of scholarship applicants. Visit Website for details and application.
    Amount of award: $500-$1,000
    Application deadline: April 1, November 1
Contact:
CIEE
Scholarship Committee
300 Fore Street
Portland, ME 04101
Phone: 800-40-STUDY ext. 2756
Fax: 207-553-4299
Web: www.ciee.org/study/scholarships.aspx

Jennifer Ritzmann Scholarship for Studies in Tropical Biology

Type of award: Scholarship.
Intended use: For undergraduate study.
Basis for selection: Major/career interest in biology. Applicant must demonstrate financial need and high academic achievement.
Application requirements: Essay.
Additional information: Applicant must have at least one semester of biology, plus an additional semester of biology, ecology, or environmental science. Minimum 2.75 GPA. Award is for students applying to the summer Monteverde program. Visit Website for more information.

Amount of award:	$1,000
Application deadline:	April 1
Notification begins:	May 1

Contact:
Council on International Educational Exchange
300 Fore Street
Portland, ME 04101
Phone: 800-40-STUDY ext. 2756
Fax: 207-553-4299
Web: www.ciee.org/study/scholarships.aspx

John E. Bowman Travel Grants

Type of award: Scholarship.
Intended use: For full-time undergraduate study at accredited 4-year institution. Designated institutions: CIEE Member or CIEE Academic Consortium member institutions.
Basis for selection: Applicant must demonstrate financial need and high academic achievement.
Application requirements: Recommendations, essay, transcript, proof of eligibility. Financial aid administrator form. Five-hundred word essay.
Additional information: Applicant must participate in CIEE study abroad program in Africa, Asia, Eastern Europe, or Latin America. Study Program Application is used in consideration of scholarship applicants. Visit Website for details and application.

Amount of award:	$500-$1,000
Application deadline:	April 1, November 1

Contact:
Council-International Educational Exchange
Attn: Scholarship Committee
300 Fore Street
Portland, ME 04101
Phone: 800-40-STUDY ext. 2756
Fax: 207-553-4299
Web: www.ciee.org/study/scholarships.aspx

Peter Wollitzer Scholarships for Study in Asia

Type of award: Scholarship.
Intended use: For undergraduate study. Designated institutions: CIEE Academic Consortium Board Member institutions: Arizona State University, Columbia University, Indiana University, Macalester College, Pacific Lutheran University, Scripps College, Smith College, University of Minnesota-Twin Cities, University of Nevada, Las Vegas, University of North Carolina, Charlotte, University of Texas at Austin, University of Washington, Yale University.
Basis for selection: Applicant must demonstrate financial need and high academic achievement.
Application requirements: Essay.
Additional information: Applicant must participate in a CIEE Study Center program in Asia. Award is $500 for summer semester, $2,000 for spring or fall.

Amount of award:	$500-$2,000
Application deadline:	April 1, November 1
Notification begins:	May 1, December 1

Contact:
Council on International Educational Exchange
300 Fore Street
Portland, ME 04101
Phone: 800-40-STUDY ext. 2756
Fax: 207-553-4299
Web: www.ciee.org/study/scholarships.aspx

Robert B. Bailey Scholarship

Type of award: Scholarship.
Intended use: For full-time undergraduate or graduate study at 2-year or 4-year institution.
Basis for selection: Major/career interest in international studies. Applicant must demonstrate financial need and high academic achievement.
Application requirements: Financial aid administrator form. Personal statement must specify what underrepresented group applicant belongs to and why applicant thinks it's been underrepresented in study abroad programs and how it's been a factor in applicant's decision to study abroad. Must address how plan to integrate international experience into future activities. Other essay guidelines on application.
Additional information: Must participate in a CIEE study abroad program. Study Program Application is used in consideration of scholarship applicants. Visit Website for details and application.

Amount of award:	$500
Application deadline:	April 1, November 1

Contact:
CIEE
Attn: Scholarship Committee
300 Fore Street
Portland, ME 04101
Phone: 800-40-STUDY ext. 2756
Fax: 207-553-4299
Web: www.ciee.org/study/scholarships.aspx

U.S. Department of Education Fulbright-Hays Project Abroad Scholarship for Programs in China

Type of award: Scholarship.
Intended use: For junior, senior, graduate or postgraduate study at 4-year or graduate institution. Designated institutions: CIEE Study Centers at Peking University (Beijing), Nanjing University, East China Normal University (Shanghai), or National Chengchi University (Taipei).
Eligibility: Applicant must be U.S. citizen or permanent resident.
Basis for selection: Major/career interest in asian studies; foreign languages; education or public administration/service. Applicant must demonstrate financial need and high academic achievement.
Application requirements: Financial aid administrator form. Five-hundred word essay including details of financial need and explaining how scholarship will help pursuit of advanced study or career related to China in areas of academia or public affairs.
Additional information: Must be applicant for CIEE programs in Beijing, Shanghai, Nanjing, or Taipei. Study Program Application taken into consideration for scholarship. Must have completed two years of college-level or equivalent Mandarin Chinese. Upon return, must submit brief report and evaluation. Visit Website for details and application.

Amount of award:	$1,000-$8,000
Application deadline:	April 1, November 1

Contact:
Council of International Educational Exchange
Attn: Scholarship Committee
300 Fore Street
Portland, ME 04101
Phone: 800-40-STUDY
Fax: 207-553-4299
Web: www.ciee.org/study/scholarships.aspx

Courage Center Vocational Services-United Way Organization

Scholarship for People with Disabilities

Type of award: Scholarship.
Intended use: For undergraduate study at accredited vocational, 2-year or 4-year institution.
Eligibility: Applicant must be visually impaired, hearing impaired or physically challenged. Applicant must be U.S. citizen residing in Minnesota.
Basis for selection: Applicant must demonstrate financial need, depth of character, leadership and seriousness of purpose.
Application requirements: Interview, essay, proof of eligibility.
Additional information: If not a Minnesota resident, student must be U.S. citizen who participated in Courage Center services.

Amount of award:	$500-$1,000
Number of awards:	21
Number of applicants:	43
Application deadline:	May 31
Notification begins:	July 31
Total amount awarded:	$14,000

Contact:
Courage Center (United Way Organization) Vocational Services Dept.
Leanne Jackson-Butala
3915 Golden Valley Rd.
Golden Valley, MN 55422-4298
Phone: 763-520-0553
Fax: 763-520-0577
Web: www.courage.org

Cymdeithas Gymreig/Philadelphia

Cymdeithas Gymreig (Welsh Society) Philadelphia Scholarship

Type of award: Scholarship.
Intended use: For full-time freshman, sophomore or junior study at accredited 2-year or 4-year institution in United States.
Eligibility: Applicant must be Welsh. Applicant must be residing in Delaware, New Jersey, Maryland or Pennsylvania.
Basis for selection: Applicant must demonstrate high academic achievement, leadership, seriousness of purpose and service orientation.
Application requirements: Recommendations, essay, transcript, proof of eligibility.
Additional information: If inquiry does not have proof of Welsh descent and evidence of participation in Welsh activities, sponsor will not reply. Applicant may study in Wales if primary residence is within 150 miles of Philadelphia. Must rank in top third of class. SASE is required or sponsor will not respond.

Amount of award:	$500-$1,000
Number of awards:	7
Number of applicants:	300
Application deadline:	March 1
Notification begins:	June 1
Total amount awarded:	$7,000

Contact:
Cymdeithas Gymreig/Philadelphia Scholarship Committee
c/o Dr. Donald Marcus
P.O. Box 7287
Saint Davids, PA 19087-7287
Phone: 610-256-3030
Web: www.welsh-society-phila.org

The Cynthia E. Morgan Memorial Scholarship Fund

The Cynthia E. Morgan Memorial Scholarship Fund

Type of award: Scholarship.
Intended use: For undergraduate or graduate study at accredited postsecondary institution.
Eligibility: Applicant must be high school junior or senior. Applicant must be residing in Maryland.
Basis for selection: Major/career interest in medicine; nursing; pharmacy/pharmaceutics/pharmacology or dietetics/nutrition. Applicant must demonstrate financial need and high academic achievement.
Application requirements: Essay, transcript.
Additional information: Must be first person in immediate family to attend college. Must be entering or planning on entering medical or medical-related field.

Amount of award:	$1,000
Application deadline:	February 25
Notification begins:	March 15

Contact:
The Cynthia E. Morgan Memorial Scholarship Fund
510 Sourghum Ct.
Joppa, MD 21085
Web: www.cemsfund.com

Cystic Fibrosis Foundation

Cystic Fibrosis Student Traineeship

Type of award: Research grant, renewable.
Intended use: For full-time senior, master's or doctoral study at accredited 4-year or graduate institution in United States.
Basis for selection: Major/career interest in medical specialties/research.
Application requirements: Recommendations, research proposal.
Additional information: Trainees must work with faculty sponsor on research project related to cystic fibrosis. Applications accepted throughout the year, but should be submitted at least two months prior to projected start date of project.

Amount of award:	$1,500

Contact:
Cystic Fibrosis Foundation
Office of Grants Management
6931 Arlington Road
Bethesda, MD 20814
Phone: 301-951-4422
Fax: 301-841-2605

Dairy Management, Inc.

NDS/DMI Milk Marketing Scholarship

Type of award: Scholarship, renewable.
Intended use: For full-time sophomore, junior or senior study at 4-year institution.
Basis for selection: Major/career interest in dairy; marketing; food production/management/services; food science/technology; agricultural education; agricultural economics or animal sciences. Applicant must demonstrate high academic achievement.
Application requirements: Proof of eligibility. Two letters of recommendation required: one must be from faculty member in applicant's major department.
Additional information: Applications available through food science department chairperson or financial aid officer of applicant's institution as well as online at Website. Must have commitment to career in dairy food-related disciplines. Top-rated applicant will receive $1,500 and several other winners receive $1,000 each.

Amount of award:	$1,000-$1,500
Number of applicants:	20
Application deadline:	March 15
Total amount awarded:	$7,500

Contact:
National Dairy Shrine
1224 Alton Darby Creek Road
Columbus, OH 43228-9792
Web: www.dairyshrine.org

The Dallas Foundation

Chuck Fulgham Scholarship Fund

Type of award: Scholarship.
Intended use: For undergraduate or graduate study at accredited 2-year, 4-year or graduate institution in United States.
Eligibility: Applicant must be residing in Texas.
Basis for selection: Applicant must demonstrate financial need.
Application requirements: Proof of eligibility.
Additional information: Applicant must be either a high school graduate with a demonstrated enthusiasm in the humanities and GPA of 3.0 or lower, or an adult graduate of a literacy program needing financial assistance to pursue a college education at a regionally accredited college/university. Award amount varies; maximum is $2,500. Preference given to residents of Dallas County.

Amount of award:	$2,500
Number of awards:	1
Number of applicants:	3
Application deadline:	April 1

Contact:
The Dallas Foundation
900 Jackson St., Suite 150
Dallas, TX 75202
Phone: 214-741-9898
Fax: 214-741-9848
Web: www.dallasfoundation.org

Dallas Architectural Foundation - Arch Swank, Jr. Fellowship in the Craft of Architecture

Type of award: Scholarship.
Intended use: For senior or graduate study.
Eligibility: Applicant must be U.S. citizen residing in Texas.
Basis for selection: Major/career interest in architecture.
Additional information: Established to assist architecture students or recent graduates to broaden the recipient's architectural knowledge. Funds must be used in same calendar year, and recipient must agree to present program of results to the Dallas Architectural Foundation board. Applicant must be permanent resident of the Dallas-Fort Worth area.

Amount of award:	$2,000
Number of awards:	1
Number of applicants:	5
Application deadline:	March 30

Contact:
Dallas Architectural Foundation
1444 Oak Lawn Ave., Suite 600
Dallas, TX 75207
Phone: 214-742-3242
Web: www.dallasfoundation.org

Dr. Don and Rose Marie Benton Scholarship

Type of award: Scholarship, renewable.
Intended use: For undergraduate or graduate study in United States.
Eligibility: Applicant must be residing in Texas.
Application requirements: Nomination by member of the Scholarship Committee at Trinity River Mission.
Additional information: Award amount varies; maximum is $1,500. Number of awards varies. Applicant or parent must be affiliated with Trinity River Mission. Applicant must be a resident of Dallas County.

Amount of award:	$1,500
Number of awards:	3
Number of applicants:	7
Application deadline:	April 1
Total amount awarded:	$4,500

Contact:
Trinity River Mission
1018 Gallagher
Dallas, TX 75212
Phone: 214-744-5648
Web: www.dallasfoundation.org

HKS/John Humphries Minority Scholarship

Type of award: Scholarship, renewable.

The Dallas Foundation: HKS/John Humphries Minority Scholarship

Intended use: For undergraduate study at 4-year institution in or outside United States.
Eligibility: Applicant must be Alaskan native, Asian American, African American, Mexican American, Hispanic American, Puerto Rican, American Indian or Native Hawaiian/Pacific Islander. Applicant must be high school senior. Applicant must be U.S. citizen residing in Texas.
Basis for selection: Major/career interest in architecture.
Application requirements: Nomination by dean of architecture school.
Additional information: Applicant must have been a resident of Dallas-Fort Worth metroplex and enrolled in the Skyline High School Architecture Cluster. Award amount varies.
    Amount of award: $2,000
    Number of awards: 1
    Application deadline: March 30
Contact:
The Dallas Architectural Foundation
1444 Oak Lawn Avenue
Suite 600
Dallas, TX 75207
Phone: 214-742-3242
Web: www.dallasfoundation.org

Jere W. Thompson, Jr., Scholarship Fund

Type of award: Scholarship, renewable.
Intended use: For full-time junior or senior study at accredited 4-year institution in United States.
Eligibility: Applicant must be U.S. citizen or permanent resident residing in Texas.
Basis for selection: Major/career interest in engineering, civil or engineering, construction. Applicant must demonstrate financial need and seriousness of purpose.
Application requirements: Recommendations, essay, transcript, proof of eligibility.
Additional information: Established by North Texas Tollway Authority and group of North Texas businesses to provide scholarships to disadvantaged students in civil engineering programs at public universities in Texas. Award amount varies; maximum is $2,000 per semester, renewable for three additional semesters if student maintains 2.5 GPA. Preference may be given to residents of Collin, Dallas, Denton, or Tarrant counties. Visit Website for program profiles and application.
    Amount of award: $2,000
    Number of awards: 1
    Number of applicants: 3
    Application deadline: April 1
Contact:
The Dallas Foundation Attn: Cathy McNally
900 Jackson Street
Suite 150
Dallas, TX 75202
Phone: 214-741-9898
Web: www.dallasfoundation.org

Wendy Ella Guilford Scholarship Fund

Type of award: Scholarship, renewable.
Intended use: For undergraduate study at 4-year institution.
Eligibility: Applicant must be high school senior. Applicant must be U.S. citizen or permanent resident residing in Texas.
Basis for selection: Major/career interest in architecture.
Application requirements: Interview.
Additional information: Must be a resident of Dallas-Fort Worth area.
    Amount of award: $2,000
    Number of awards: 1
    Application deadline: April 15
Contact:
Wendy Ella Guilford Scholarship Foundation
8300 Horseshoe Bend
Fort Worth, TX 76131
Phone: 214-741-9898
Web: www.dallasfoundation.org

Data Processing Management Association/Portland Chapter

DPMA/PC Scholarship

Type of award: Scholarship, renewable.
Intended use: For undergraduate study in United States.
Eligibility: Applicant must be high school senior. Applicant must be residing in Oregon or Washington.
Basis for selection: Major/career interest in computer/information sciences. Applicant must demonstrate financial need, high academic achievement and seriousness of purpose.
Application requirements: Recommendations, transcript. List and description of past and current IT-related activities, and of IT career goals. Explanation of reasons for applying for this scholarship.
Additional information: Applicants must be a resident of Oregon or of Clark County in Washington state. Up to three $500 follow-ups may be awarded.
    Amount of award: $1,000
    Number of applicants: 15
    Application deadline: May 1
    Notification begins: May 31
    Total amount awarded: $2,500
Contact:
DPMA/PC Scholarship
Attn: Scholarship Chair
P.O. Box 443
Portland, OR 97207
Web: www.dpmapc.com/scholarship.htm

Datatel Scholars Foundation

Angelfire Scholarship

Type of award: Scholarship.
Intended use: For undergraduate, graduate or non-degree study at accredited postsecondary institution. Designated institutions: Datatel client colleges/universities.
Eligibility: Applicant must be Vietnam veteran, spouse or child of Vietnam veteran, or refugee from Cambodia, Laos, or Vietnam during 1964-1975 time frame. Also open to U.S. military personnel involved in Operations Desert Storm, Enduring Freedom, or Iraqi Freedom.
Basis for selection: Applicant must demonstrate high academic achievement, depth of character and seriousness of purpose.

Application requirements: Recommendations, essay, transcript, proof of eligibility, nomination by Datatel client institution.
Additional information: Applicants evaluated on following scale: 40 percent personal essay; 30 percent academic merit; 20 percent achievements; 10 percent letters of recommendation. Visit Website to apply and for list of eligible institutions.

Amount of award:	$1,000-$2,400
Number of awards:	25
Number of applicants:	110
Application deadline:	January 31
Notification begins:	May 10
Total amount awarded:	$45,000

Contact:
Datatel Scholars Foundation
4375 Fair Lakes Court
Fairfax, VA 22033
Phone: 800-486-4332
Fax: 703-968-4625
Web: www.datatel.com

Datatel Scholars Foundation Scholarship

Type of award: Scholarship.
Intended use: For undergraduate, graduate or non-degree study at accredited postsecondary institution. Designated institutions: Datatel client colleges/universities.
Basis for selection: Applicant must demonstrate high academic achievement, depth of character and seriousness of purpose.
Application requirements: Recommendations, essay, transcript, proof of eligibility, nomination by Datatel client institution.
Additional information: Applicants evaluated on following scale: 40 percent personal essay; 30 percent academic merit; 20 percent achievements; 10 percent letters of recommendation. When requesting application, include institution name for determination of qualification. Visit Website to apply.

Amount of award:	$1,000-$2,400
Number of awards:	200
Number of applicants:	600
Application deadline:	January 31
Notification begins:	May 10
Total amount awarded:	$450,000

Contact:
Datatel Scholars Foundation
4375 Fair Lakes Court
Fairfax, VA 22033
Phone: 800-486-4332
Fax: 703-968-4625
Web: www.datatel.com

Nancy Goodhue Lynch Scholarship

Type of award: Scholarship.
Intended use: For undergraduate or non-degree study at accredited postsecondary institution. Designated institutions: Datatel client colleges/universities.
Basis for selection: Major/career interest in computer/information sciences; engineering, computer; engineering, electrical/electronic; information systems; electronics; computer graphics or robotics. Applicant must demonstrate high academic achievement, depth of character and seriousness of purpose.
Application requirements: Recommendations, essay, transcript, proof of eligibility, nomination by Datatel client institution.

Additional information: Scholarship for student enrolled in technology-related degree program. Applicants evaluated on following scale: 40 percent personal essay; 30 percent academic merit; 20 percent achievements; 10 percent letters of recommendation. Visit Website to apply and to find list of eligible institutions.

Amount of award:	$2,500
Number of awards:	2
Number of applicants:	90
Application deadline:	January 31
Notification begins:	May 10
Total amount awarded:	$5,000

Contact:
Datatel Scholars Foundation
4375 Fair Lakes Court
Fairfax, VA 22033
Phone: 800-486-4322
Fax: 703-968-4625
Web: www.datatel.com

Russ Griffith Memorial Scholarship

Type of award: Scholarship.
Intended use: For undergraduate, graduate or non-degree study at accredited postsecondary institution. Designated institutions: Datatel client colleges/universities.
Eligibility: Applicant must be returning adult student.
Application requirements: Recommendations, essay, transcript, proof of eligibility, nomination by Datatel client institution.
Additional information: Intended for any student returning to school after a five-year absence or more. Applicants evaluated on following scale: 40 percent personal essay; 30 percent academic merit; 20 percent achievements; 10 percent letters of recommendation. Visit Website to apply and for a list of eligible institutions.

Amount of award:	$2,000
Number of awards:	50
Number of applicants:	250
Application deadline:	January 31
Notification begins:	May 10
Total amount awarded:	$100,000

Contact:
Datatel Scholars Foundation
4375 Fair Lakes Court
Fairfax, VA 22033
Phone: 800-486-4322
Fax: 703-968-4625
Web: www.datatel.com

Daughters of Penelope

Alexandra A. Sonenfeld Award

Type of award: Scholarship.
Intended use: For undergraduate study at accredited vocational, 2-year or 4-year institution in United States.
Eligibility: Applicant must be female. Applicant must be Greek. Applicant must be U.S. citizen, permanent resident or Canadian citizen.
Basis for selection: Applicant must demonstrate financial need and high academic achievement.
Application requirements: Essay, transcript, proof of eligibility. Parents' IRS forms, federal aid forms, and SAT/ACT

scores. Letters of recommendation from faculty member and community source.
Additional information: Applicant must be a high school senior or recent graduate and have member of immediate family or court-appointed legal guardian in the Daughters of Penelope, Order of AHEPA, or Maids of Athena, and in good standing for at least two years. Applicant must not be past recipient of any undergraduate award from Daughters of Penelope National Scholarship program.

Amount of award:	$1,500
Number of awards:	1
Application deadline:	June 1
Total amount awarded:	$1,500

Contact:
Daughters of Penelope
1909 Q Street, NW
Suite 500
Washington, DC 20009
Phone: 202-234-9741
Fax: 202-483-6983

Daughters of Penelope Past Grand Presidents' Award

Type of award: Scholarship.
Intended use: For freshman study at vocational, 2-year or 4-year institution.
Eligibility: Applicant must be female. Applicant must be Greek. Applicant must be U.S. citizen, permanent resident or Canadian citizen.
Basis for selection: Applicant must demonstrate financial need and high academic achievement.
Application requirements: Essay, transcript, proof of eligibility. SAT/ACT scores, copy of parents' IRS forms, federal aid forms. Letters of recommendation from faculty member and community source.
Additional information: Applicant must be high school senior or recent graduate and have member of immediate family or court-appointed legal guardian in the Daughters of Penelope, Order of AHEPA, or Maids of Athena in good standing for minimum of two years. Applicant must not be past recipient of any undergraduate award from the Daughters of Penelope National Scholarship program.

Amount of award:	$1,500
Number of awards:	1
Application deadline:	June 1

Contact:
Daughters of Penelope
1909 Q Street NW
Suite 500
Washington, DC 20009
Phone: 202-234-9741
Fax: 202-483-6983

Eos #1 Mother Lodge Chapter Award

Type of award: Scholarship.
Intended use: For undergraduate study at accredited vocational, 2-year or 4-year institution in United States.
Eligibility: Applicant must be female. Applicant must be Greek. Applicant must be U.S. citizen, permanent resident or Canadian citizen.
Basis for selection: Major/career interest in agriculture. Applicant must demonstrate high academic achievement.

Application requirements: Essay, transcript, proof of eligibility. SAT/ACT scores. Letters of recommendation from faculty member and community source.
Additional information: Applicant must be high school senior or recent graduate, and have member of immediate family or court-appointed legal guardian in the Daughters of Penelope, Order of AHEPA, or Maids of Athena, and in good standing for at least two years. Applicant must not be past recipient of any undergraduate award from Daughters of Penelope National Scholarship program.

Amount of award:	$1,000
Number of awards:	1
Application deadline:	June 1

Contact:
Daughters of Penelope
1909 Q Street, NW
Suite 500
Washington, DC 20009
Phone: 202-234-9741
Fax: 202-483-6983

Kottis Family Award

Type of award: Scholarship.
Intended use: For freshman study at vocational, 2-year or 4-year institution.
Eligibility: Applicant must be female. Applicant must be Greek. Applicant must be U.S. citizen, permanent resident or Canadian citizen.
Basis for selection: Applicant must demonstrate high academic achievement.
Application requirements: Essay, transcript, proof of eligibility. SAT/ACT scores. Letters of recommendation from faculty member and community source.
Additional information: Applicant must be high school senior or recent graduate, and have member of immediate family or court-appointed legal guardian in the Daughters of Penelope, Order of AHEPA, or Maids of Athena in good standing for minimum of two years. Applicant must not be past recipient of any undergraduate award from Daughters of Penelope National Scholarship program.

Amount of award:	$1,000
Number of awards:	1
Application deadline:	June 1

Contact:
Daughters of Penelope
1909 Q Street, NW
Suite 500
Washington, DC 20009
Phone: 202-234-9741
Fax: 202-483-6983

Mary M. Verges Award

Type of award: Scholarship.
Intended use: For freshman study at vocational, 2-year or 4-year institution.
Eligibility: Applicant must be female. Applicant must be Greek. Applicant must be U.S. citizen, permanent resident or Canadian citizen.
Basis for selection: Applicant must demonstrate high academic achievement.
Application requirements: Essay, transcript, proof of eligibility. SAT/ACT scores. Letters of recommendation from faculty member and community source.
Additional information: Applicant must be high school senior or recent graduate and have member of immediate family in Daughters of Penelope, Order of AHEPA, or Maids of

Athena in good standing for minimum of two years. Applicant must not be past recipient of any undergraduate award from Daughters of Penelope National Scholarship program.
- Amount of award: $1,000
- Number of awards: 1
- Application deadline: June 1

Contact:
Daughters of Penelope
1909 Q Street, NW
Suite 500
Washington, DC 20009
Phone: 202-234-9741
Fax: 202-483-6983

Past Grand Presidents' Memorial Award

Type of award: Scholarship.
Intended use: For freshman study at vocational, 2-year or 4-year institution.
Eligibility: Applicant must be female. Applicant must be Greek. Applicant must be U.S. citizen, permanent resident or Canadian citizen.
Basis for selection: Applicant must demonstrate high academic achievement.
Application requirements: Essay, transcript, proof of eligibility. SAT/ACT scores. Letters of recommendation from faculty member and community source.
Additional information: Applicant must be high school senior or recent graduate and have member of immediate family or court-appointed legal guardian in the Daughters of Penelope, Order of AHEPA, or Maids of Athena in good standing for minimum of two years. Applicant must not be past recipient of any undergraduate award from Daughters of Penelope National Scholarship program.
- Amount of award: $1,000
- Number of awards: 1
- Application deadline: June 1

Contact:
Daughters of Penelope
1909 Q Street NW
Suite 500
Washington, DC 20009
Phone: 202-234-9741
Fax: 202-483-6983

Daughters of Union Veterans of the Civil War 1861-1865, Inc.

Grand Army of the Republic Living Memorial Scholarship

Type of award: Scholarship.
Intended use: For full-time junior, senior or graduate study at accredited 4-year institution in United States.
Eligibility: Applicant must be U.S. citizen. Applicant must be descendant of veteran during Civil War. Must be lineal descendant of Union Veteran of Civil War.
Basis for selection: Applicant must demonstrate high academic achievement, depth of character, leadership, patriotism, seriousness of purpose and service orientation.
Application requirements: Transcript. Two letters of reference, ancestor's military record.
Additional information: Must be of good moral character and have firm belief in US Government. Request for information and application honored only with SASE. Number of awards varies.
- Amount of award: $200
- Number of applicants: 8
- Application deadline: April 30
- Notification begins: August 30

Contact:
Daughters of Union Veterans of the Civil War 1861-1865, Inc.
503 South Walnut Street
Springfield, IL 62704-1932

Davidson Institute

Davidson Fellows Scholarship

Type of award: Scholarship.
Intended use: For undergraduate study in United States.
Eligibility: Applicant must be U.S. citizen or permanent resident.
Basis for selection: Major/career interest in literature; music; philosophy; mathematics; science, general or technology.
Application requirements: Three nominator forms, three copies of a 15-minute DVD or VHS videotape. Signed statement of commitment that, if named a Davidson Fellow, the applicant and a parent or guardian will attend the award reception in Washington, D.C.
Additional information: Applicants are awarded for accomplishment that is recognized as significant by experts in that field and has a positive contribution to society. Applicant must be under the age of 18 as of October 1 of the year of application. Applications are accepted in the following categories: science, technology, mathematics, music, literature, philosophy and "outside the box." Work may be exceptionally creative application of existing knowledge, new idea with high impact, innovative solution with broad-range implications, important advancement that can be replicated and built upon, interdisciplinary discovery, prodigious performance or another demonstration of extraordinary accomplishment. Deadline is the last Wednesday in March.
- Amount of award: $10,000-$50,000
- Number of awards: 20
- Application deadline: March 25
- Notification begins: July 1
- Total amount awarded: $400,000

Contact:
Davidson Institute for Talent Development
9665 Gateway Drive
Suite B
Reno, NV 89521
Phone: 775-852-3483
Fax: 775-852-2184
Web: www.davidsonfellows.org

Davis-Roberts Scholarship Fund

Davis-Roberts Scholarship

Type of award: Scholarship, renewable.
Intended use: For full-time undergraduate study at 2-year or 4-year institution.
Eligibility: Applicant must be U.S. citizen residing in Wyoming.
Basis for selection: Applicant must demonstrate financial need.
Application requirements: Recommendations, essay, transcript. Applicant's photograph.
Additional information: Applicant must be member of Wyoming Job's Daughters/DeMolay.
   Amount of award: $300-$1,000
   Number of awards: 10
   Number of applicants: 18
   Application deadline: June 15
   Notification begins: July 1
   Total amount awarded: $2,500
Contact:
Davis-Roberts Scholarship Fund
c/o Gary D. Skillern
P.O. Box 20645
Cheyenne, WY 82003
Phone: 307-632-0491

DEED

Demonstration of Energy-Efficient Developments Program Scholarship

Type of award: Scholarship.
Intended use: For undergraduate or graduate study at 2-year or 4-year institution in United States or Canada.
Eligibility: Applicant must be U.S. citizen.
Basis for selection: Major/career interest in electronics; engineering, electrical/electronic or engineering, mechanical.
Additional information: Applicants must complete a research project and must be members of the Demonstration of Energy-Efficient Developments Program.
   Amount of award: $4,000
   Number of awards: 10
   Application deadline: February 15, October 1
   Total amount awarded: $40,000
Contact:
DEED Administrator
American Public Power Association
1875 Connecticut Ave. NW, Suite 1200
Washington, DC 20009-5715
Phone: 202-467-2960
Fax: 202-467-2992
Web: www.appanet.org

Delaware Higher Education Commission

B. Bradford Barnes Scholarship

Type of award: Scholarship, renewable.
Intended use: For full-time freshman study. Designated institutions: University of Delaware.
Eligibility: Applicant must be high school senior. Applicant must be U.S. citizen or permanent resident residing in Delaware.
Basis for selection: Applicant must demonstrate high academic achievement.
Application requirements: Essay, transcript.
Additional information: Must rank in top 25 percent of high school class. Combined score of 1800 on the SAT required. Awards full tuition, fees, room, board and books. Visit Website for deadline information.
   Amount of award: Full tuition
   Number of awards: 1
   Number of applicants: 51
Contact:
Delaware Higher Education Commission
820 North French Street
Wilmington, DE 19801
Phone: 302-577-5240
Fax: 302-577-6765
Web: www.doe.k12.de.us/programs/dhec/how_to_apply/financial_aid

Charles L. Hebner Memorial Scholarship

Type of award: Scholarship, renewable.
Intended use: For full-time undergraduate study. Designated institutions: University of Delaware, Delaware State University.
Eligibility: Applicant must be high school senior. Applicant must be U.S. citizen or permanent resident residing in Delaware.
Basis for selection: Major/career interest in humanities/liberal arts; social/behavioral sciences or political science/government. Applicant must demonstrate high academic achievement.
Application requirements: Essay, transcript.
Additional information: Applicant must rank in top half of graduating class. Combined score of 1350 on the SAT. Preference given to political science majors. Award covers tuition, fees, room, board, and books. Visit Website for deadline information.
   Amount of award: Full tuition
   Number of awards: 2
   Number of applicants: 51
Contact:
Delaware Higher Education Commission
820 North French Street
Wilmington, DE 19801
Phone: 302-577-5240
Fax: 302-577-6765
Web: www.doe.k12.de.us/programs/dhec/how_to_apply/financial_aid

Delaware Legislative Essay Scholarship

Type of award: Scholarship.
Intended use: For undergraduate study.
Eligibility: Applicant must be high school senior. Applicant must be U.S. citizen or permanent resident residing in Delaware.
Application requirements: Essay on annually selected topic in American history from 1770 to 1860.
Additional information: Scholarship includes up to 62 nonrenewable $1,000 awards for each state senatorial and representative legislative district. District winners compete for three statewide nonrenewable awards: 1st place, $10,000; 2nd place, $7,500; 3rd place $5,000. Applicants may receive funds from one district only. Visit Website for deadline information.

Amount of award:	$1,000-$10,000
Number of awards:	65
Number of applicants:	162
Notification begins:	December 1

Contact:
Delaware Higher Education Commission
820 North French St
Wilmington, DE 19801
Phone: 302-577-5240
Fax: 302-577-6765
Web: www.doe.k12.de.us/programs/dhec/how_to_apply/financial_aid

Delaware Scholarship Incentive Program

Type of award: Scholarship.
Intended use: For full-time undergraduate study at accredited 2-year or 4-year institution. Designated institutions: Delaware or Pennsylvania nonprofit, regionally accredited colleges.
Eligibility: Applicant must be U.S. citizen or permanent resident residing in Delaware.
Basis for selection: Applicant must demonstrate financial need.
Application requirements: Transcript. FAFSA.
Additional information: Must have at least 2.5 GPA. Full-time undergraduate and graduate students whose major is not offered at a DE public college will be considered.

Amount of award:	$700-$2,200
Number of awards:	1,670
Number of applicants:	11,000
Application deadline:	April 15
Notification begins:	July 1
Total amount awarded:	$1,455,000

Contact:
Delaware Higher Education Commission
820 North French Street
Wilmington, DE 19801
Phone: 302-577-5240
Fax: 302-577-6765
Web: www.doe.k12.de.us/programs/dhec/how_to_apply/financial_aid

Diamond State Scholarship

Type of award: Scholarship, renewable.
Intended use: For full-time freshman study at accredited vocational, 2-year or 4-year institution in United States. Designated institutions: Nonprofit, regionally accredited colleges.
Eligibility: Applicant must be high school senior. Applicant must be permanent resident residing in Delaware.
Basis for selection: Applicant must demonstrate high academic achievement.
Application requirements: Essay, transcript.
Additional information: Must rank in top 25 percent of high school class. Combined score of at least 1800 on the SAT required. Visit Website for deadline information.

Amount of award:	$1,250
Number of awards:	50
Number of applicants:	275
Notification begins:	June 15
Total amount awarded:	$250,000

Contact:
Delaware Higher Education Commission
820 North French Street
Wilmington, DE 19801
Phone: 302-577-5240
Fax: 302-577-6765
Web: www.doe.k12.de.us/programs/dhec/how_to_apply/financial_aid

Educational Benefits for Children of Deceased Veterans and Others

Type of award: Scholarship, renewable.
Intended use: For undergraduate study.
Eligibility: Applicant must be at least 16, no older than 24. Applicant must be U.S. citizen or permanent resident residing in Delaware.
Additional information: Must live in DE for at least three years before applying. Must apply by four weeks before classes begin. Award prorated when major not available at a DE public college. Award for maximum of four years. Must be child of one of the following: member of armed forces whose death was service-related, who is or was a POW, or is officially MIA; state police officer whose death was service-related; or state employee of the Department of Transportation routinely employed in job-related activities on the state highway system whose death was job-related.

Amount of award:	Full tuition
Number of applicants:	2

Contact:
Delaware Higher Education Commission
820 North French Street
Wilmington, DE 19801
Phone: 302-577-5240
Fax: 302-577-6765
Web: www.doe.k12.de.us/high-ed

Herman M. Holloway, Sr., Memorial Scholarship

Type of award: Scholarship, renewable.
Intended use: For full-time freshman study. Designated institutions: Delaware State University.
Eligibility: Applicant must be high school senior. Applicant must be U.S. citizen or permanent resident residing in Delaware.
Basis for selection: Applicant must demonstrate high academic achievement.
Application requirements: Essay, transcript. FAFSA.
Additional information: Applicants must be high school seniors, be involved in extracurricular activities, rank in upper half of class and have combined score of at least 1350 on the SAT. Awards full tuition, fees, room, board and books. Visit Website for deadline information.

Delaware Higher Education Commission: Herman M. Holloway, Sr., Memorial Scholarship

Amount of award: Full tuition
Number of awards: 1
Number of applicants: 36
Notification begins: May 1
Contact:
Delaware Higher Education Commission
820 North French Street
Wilmington, DE 19801
Phone: 302-577-5240
Fax: 302-577-6765
Web: www.doe.k12.de.us/programs/dhec/how_to_apply/financial_aid

Robert C. Byrd Honors Scholarship

Type of award: Scholarship, renewable.
Intended use: For undergraduate study. Designated institutions: Nonprofit, regionally accredited schools.
Eligibility: Applicant must be high school senior. Applicant must be U.S. citizen or permanent resident residing in Delaware.
Basis for selection: Applicant must demonstrate high academic achievement.
Application requirements: Essay, transcript.
Additional information: Applicant must be high school senior in top 25 percent of graduating class or GED recipient with score of at least 300. Combined score of at least 1800 on the SAT. Program dependent on federal funding. Renewable up to three years. Visit Website for deadline information.

Amount of award: $1,500
Number of awards: 20
Number of applicants: 185
Contact:
Delaware Higher Education Commission
820 North French St
Wilmington, DE 19801
Phone: 302-577-5240
Fax: 302-577-6765
Web: www.doe.k12.de.us/programs/dhec/how_to_apply/financial_aid

Delta Delta Delta Foundation

Delta Delta Delta Undergraduate Scholarship

Type of award: Scholarship.
Intended use: For junior or senior study at 4-year institution.
Basis for selection: Applicant must demonstrate financial need, high academic achievement and service orientation.
Application requirements: Recommendations, essay, transcript.
Additional information: Campus, chapter and community involvement important. Applicants must be initiated members of Delta Delta Delta in good standing with chapter. Sophomores and juniors may apply, must be junior or senior during award year. Number of awards varies. Visit Website for more scholarship information.

Amount of award: $500-$1,500
Number of awards: 30
Number of applicants: 83
Application deadline: March 15
Notification begins: May 30
Total amount awarded: $40,000
Contact:
Delta Delta Delta Foundation
P.O. Box 5987
Arlington, TX 76005
Phone: 817-633-8001
Fax: 817-652-0212
Web: www.trideltafoundation.org

Department For The Blind & Vision Impaired

Virginia Vocational Rehabilitation Program Education Sponsorship

Type of award: Scholarship.
Intended use: For full-time undergraduate study at postsecondary institution.
Eligibility: Applicant must be visually impaired. Applicant must be residing in Virginia.
Basis for selection: Applicant must demonstrate financial need.
Application requirements: Vocational Rehab Application.
Additional information: Applicant must have been determined eligible for Vocational Rehabilitation Services. Sponsorship must be directly related to a specific vocational objective as developed through an individualized plan for employment. Available only when need exists after federal, state and private funding have been used. Full sponsorship only if student attends state school; sponsorship for private school will be calculated on most expensive state school.
Contact:
Susan Payne, Program Director for Vocational Rehabilitation Program
397 Azalea Avenue
Richmond, VA 23227
Phone: 804-371-3140
Web: www.vdbvi.org

Descendants of the Signers of the Declaration of Independence, Inc.

Descendants of the Signers of the Declaration of Independence Scholarship

Type of award: Scholarship, renewable.
Intended use: For full-time undergraduate or graduate study at accredited vocational, 2-year, 4-year or graduate institution.
Eligibility: Applicant or parent must be member/participant of Descendants of the Signers of the Declaration of Independence.

Basis for selection: Applicant must demonstrate high academic achievement, depth of character, leadership, patriotism, seriousness of purpose and service orientation.
Application requirements: Recommendations, essay, transcript, proof of eligibility. Resume.
Additional information: Applicant must be a direct lineal descendant of a signer of the Declaration of Independence. Preference given to persons involved in community, school activities, and volunteer work. Applicant must reapply for renewal. May be used world wide if institution accredited by local accreditation authority. See Website for more information.
   Application deadline: March 31
   Notification begins: May 1
Contact:
Descendants of the Signers of the Declaration of Independence, Inc.
Scholarship Committee
P.O. Box 8223
Savannah, GA 31412
Web: www.dsdi1776.com

Discover Financial Services, Inc.

Discover Scholarship Program

Type of award: Scholarship.
Intended use: For undergraduate study at accredited postsecondary institution.
Eligibility: Applicant must be high school junior. Applicant must be U.S. citizen or permanent resident.
Basis for selection: Applicant must demonstrate leadership and service orientation.
Application requirements: Transcript. Statement of obstacles overcome, leadership, and community service. Community service verification.
Additional information: Applicant must be high school junior enrolled in and graduating from public or accredited private school in U.S. (home school and U.S. Base High School students also eligible). Must have minimum cumulative GPA of 2.75 for 9th and 10th grades. Applicants must demonstrate leadership, community service, and obstacles overcome, as they will be judged on how well they address these in essay form. Application availability dates may vary each year, but typically in December or January. More information at and online applications available at www.discoverfinancial.com/community. Cannot be faxed or e-mailed. Check Website for application deadline. Notification dates may vary each year, but typically in April or May.
   Amount of award: $30,000
   Number of awards: 10
   Total amount awarded: $300,000
Contact:
Discover Scholarship Program
c/o Scholarship Program Administrators
Phone: 866-756-7932
Web: www.scholarshipadministrators.net/emailrequestform.asp
(Access key DISC)

District of Columbia Office of Post Secondar Education

DC Tuition Assistance Grant Program

Type of award: Scholarship, renewable.
Intended use: For undergraduate study at 4-year institution in United States.
Eligibility: Applicant must be U.S. citizen or permanent resident residing in District of Columbia.
Application requirements: Student Aid Report; DC Income Tax Returns or 12-month income/benefit history statement from TANF, SSI, SSDI, Child Support, Retirement Income, or Unemployment; copies of two current utility bills, bank statements, pay stubs, or mortgage statements no older than 45 days from date of application; Affirmation and Legal Disclaimer Statement; Copy of high school/GED diploma or Satisfactory Progress Toward Graduation form for recent high school graduates. Applicants who are Wards of DC Court must provide Ward of the Court verification letter.
Additional information: Applicant must be DC resident for 12 months prior to first year enrolled in college and through college career. Awards vary, visit Website for details. Awards do not cover summer term.
   Amount of award: $10,000
   Application deadline: June 30
Contact:
Higher Education Financial Services
51 N Street NW
7th Floor
Washington, DC 20002
Phone: 202-727-6436
Web: seo.dc.gov

District of Columbia Office of Postsecondary Education

DC Adoption Scholarship

Type of award: Scholarship, renewable.
Intended use: For undergraduate study. Designated institutions: Title IV-approved institutions.
Eligibility: Applicant must be no older than 24. Applicant must be U.S. citizen or permanent resident residing in District of Columbia.
Application requirements: All applicants: Student Aid Report, Satisfactory Academic Progress Toward Graduation form or copy of high school/GED diploma, affirmation and Legal Disclaimer Statement signed by guardian (if applicant is dependent). Adopted applicants: copy of final adoption decree. 9/11 applicants: copy of parent(s) death certificate; certified copy of DC Income Tax Return for most recent year or 12-month income/benefit history statement for previous year from Social Security Income, Social Security Disability Income, Retirement Income, Child Support, Unemployment, or Temporary Assistance for Needy Families; copies of two current utility bills, bank statements, pay stubs, or mortgage statements no older than 45 days from date of application submission.

Additional information: Award for District of Columbia children adopted on or after October 1, 2001, through the District of Columbia's Child and Family Services or foster care system, and/or children who lost one or both parents as a result of the events of September 11, 2001, while they were domiciled in the District of Columbia. Applicant must have graduated high school or have received GED. Must not be in default for any student loans. Awards do not cover summer term. Visit Website to apply.

Amount of award:	$10,000
Application deadline:	June 30

Contact:
Higher Education Financial Services
51 N Street NE
7th Floor
Washington, DC 20002
Phone: 202-727-6436
Web: seo.dc.gov

District of Columbia Leveraging Educational Assistance Partnership Program

Type of award: Scholarship, renewable.
Intended use: For undergraduate study at 2-year or 4-year institution in United States. Designated institutions: Postsecondary institutions certified to participate in Title IV Aid Programs.
Eligibility: Applicant must be U.S. citizen or permanent resident residing in District of Columbia.
Basis for selection: Applicant must demonstrate financial need and high academic achievement.
Application requirements: Proof of eligibility. Student Aid Report. Affirmation and Legal Disclaimer Statement with original signatures. DC Income Tax Return with Schedule S listing student as dependent; Office of Tax and Revenue Authorization Forms; or 12-month income/benefit history from TANF, SSI, SSDI, Retirement Income, Child Support, or Unemployment. Copies of two utility bills, bank statements, pay stubs, or mortgage statements no more than 45 days old. Wards of DC Court must provide additional documentation.
Additional information: Must be D.C. resident for 12 months prior to application and throughout college. Students are encouraged to apply online. $9,000 and six-year lifetime maximum.

Amount of award:	$1,500
Number of awards:	1,961
Number of applicants:	5,644
Application deadline:	June 30

Contact:
Higher Education Financial Services State Education Office
51 N Street, NE
7th Floor
Washington, DC 20002
Phone: 202-727-6436
Web: www.seo.dc.gov

Dolphin Scholarship Foundation

Dolphin Scholarship

Type of award: Scholarship, renewable.
Intended use: For full-time undergraduate study at accredited 4-year institution.
Eligibility: Applicant must be single, no older than 23. Applicant must be U.S. citizen. Applicant must be dependent of active service person in the Navy. Must be child/stepchild of member or former member of U.S. Navy who served in, or in support of, Submarine Force.
Basis for selection: Applicant must demonstrate financial need and high academic achievement.
Application requirements: Recommendations, essay, transcript, proof of eligibility. Three recommendations.
Additional information: Applicant must be high school senior or college student. Applicant must demonstrate commitment to community.

Amount of award:	$3,250
Number of awards:	137
Number of applicants:	208
Application deadline:	March 15
Notification begins:	April 15
Total amount awarded:	$445,250

Contact:
Dolphin Scholarship Foundation
5040 Virginia Beach Blvd., Suite 104A
Virginia Beach, VA 23462
Phone: 757-671-3200 ext. 111
Fax: 757-671-3330
Web: www.dolphinscholarship.org

Eastern Orthodox Committee on Scouting

Boy and Girl Scouts Scholarship

Type of award: Scholarship.
Intended use: For full-time freshman study at accredited 4-year institution in United States.
Eligibility: Applicant must be high school senior. Applicant must be Eastern Orthodox. Applicant must be U.S. citizen.
Basis for selection: Applicant must demonstrate depth of character and service orientation.
Application requirements: Four letters of recommendation with application, one from each of following groups: religious institution, school, community leader, and head of Scouting unit.
Additional information: Eligible applicant must be registered member of Boy or Girl Scouts unit; Eagle Scout or Gold Award recipient; active member of Eastern Orthodox Church; have received Alpha Omega Religious Scout Award; have demonstrated practical citizenship in his or her church, school, Scouting unit, and community. Offers one $1,000 scholarship and one $500 scholarship upon acceptance to four-year accredited college or university.

Amount of award:	$500-$1,000
Number of awards:	2
Number of applicants:	250
Application deadline:	May 1
Total amount awarded:	$1,500

Contact:
EOCS Scholarship Committee
862 Guy Lombardo Avenue
Freeport, NY 11520
Phone: 516-868-4050
Fax: 516-868-4052
Web: www.eocs.org

Edmund F. Maxwell Foundation

Edmund F. Maxwell Foundation Scholarship

Type of award: Scholarship, renewable.
Intended use: For full-time freshman study.
Eligibility: Applicant must be U.S. citizen or permanent resident residing in Washington.
Basis for selection: Applicant must demonstrate financial need, high academic achievement, depth of character, leadership, seriousness of purpose and service orientation.
Application requirements: Essay, transcript. Essay of about 500 words on one of the topics listed on application. Financial need assessment.
Additional information: Combined reading and math SAT scores must be greater than 1200. College or university must be independent. Only residents of western Washington are eligible. Applicants are encouraged to apply early in year. Visit Website for application and more information.
    Amount of award: $5,000
    Application deadline: April 30
    Notification begins: June 1
Contact:
Edmund F. Maxwell Foundation
P.O. Box 22537
Seattle, WA 98122-0537
Web: www.maxwell.org

Elder & Leemaur Publishers

University Writing Scholarship Program

Type of award: Scholarship.
Intended use: For undergraduate study at postsecondary institution.
Application requirements: Maximum 500-word essay on topic listed on Website--upload essay to Website. Three or four topics listed for each of the four deadlines.
Additional information: Deadlines for the four scholarship opportunities each year are March 1, July 1, September 30, and December 1.
    Application deadline: March 1, July 1
    Total amount awarded: $10,000
Contact:
Elder & Leemaur Publishers
115 Garfield Street
#5432
Sumas, WA 98295
Web: www.elpublishers.com

Elie Wiesel Foundation for Humanity

Elie Wiesel Prize in Ethics

Type of award: Scholarship.
Intended use: For full-time junior or senior study at accredited 4-year institution in United States.
Basis for selection: Competition/talent/interest in writing/journalism. Major/career interest in ethnic/cultural studies; social/behavioral sciences or governmental public relations.
Application requirements: Proof of eligibility. Letter from college/university verifying full-time junior or senior status. Sponsorship by faculty member. Submit three copies of essay concerning an ethical dilemma, issue, or question related to the contest's annual topic. In 3,000 to 4,000 words, students are encouraged to raise questions, single out issues, and identify dilemmas.
Additional information: First prize is $5,000; second prize is $2,500; third prize is $1,500; two honorable mentions are $500 each. Application deadline is first Friday in December. See Website for more information.
    Amount of award: $500-$5,000
    Number of awards: 5
    Number of applicants: 263
    Notification begins: May 31
    Total amount awarded: $10,000
Contact:
Elie Wiesel Prize in Ethics
The Elie Wiesel Foundation for Humanity
555 Madison Avenue, 20th Floor
New York, NY 10022
Phone: 212-490-7788
Fax: 212-490-6006
Web: www.eliewieselfoundation.org

Elizabeth Greenshields Foundation

The Elizabeth Greenshields Grant

Type of award: Scholarship, renewable.
Intended use: For undergraduate, graduate or non-degree study.
Basis for selection: Major/career interest in arts, general.
Application requirements: Jpeg on CD.
Additional information: For artists (fine arts) in the early stages of careers creating representational or figurative works through painting, drawing, printmaking, or sculpture. Must make a commitment to making art a lifetime career. Applications are welcome throughout the year. All award amounts are in Canadian dollars. Funds may be used for any art-related purpose.
    Amount of award: $12,500
    Number of awards: 50
    Number of applicants: 1,000

Elizabeth Greenshields Foundation: The Elizabeth Greenshields Grant

Contact:
Elizabeth Greenshields Foundation
1814 Sherbrooke Street West, Suite 1
Montreal
Quebec, Canada, H3H 1E4
Phone: 514-937-9225
Fax: 514-937-0141

Amount of award:	$1,000
Number of awards:	500
Notification begins:	April 30
Total amount awarded:	$500,000

Contact:
Elks National Foundation
2750 North Lakeview Avenue
Chicago, IL 60614-1889
Web: www.elks.org/enf

Elks National Foundation

Elks Most Valuable Student Scholarship

Type of award: Scholarship.
Intended use: For full-time undergraduate study in United States.
Eligibility: Applicant must be high school senior. Applicant must be U.S. citizen.
Basis for selection: Applicant must demonstrate financial need, high academic achievement and leadership.
Application requirements: Recommendations, essay, transcript. SAT or ACT scores.
Additional information: Applications available starting September 1 from local Benevolent and Protective Order of Elks Lodge; also available on Website or by sending SASE to foundation. Application deadline is in mid-January. Award is distributed over four years. Membership in Elks not required, but application must be endorsed by and submitted to local Elks Lodge for entry into competition. Judging occurs at lodge, district and state level before reaching national competition.

Amount of award:	$4,000-$60,000
Number of awards:	500
Notification begins:	May 15
Total amount awarded:	$2,296,000

Contact:
Elks National Foundation
2750 North Lakeview Avenue
Chicago, IL 60614-1889
Web: www.elks.org/enf

Elks National Foundation Legacy Awards

Type of award: Scholarship.
Intended use: For full-time freshman study at accredited postsecondary institution in United States.
Eligibility: Applicant or parent must be member/participant of Elks. Applicant must be high school senior. Applicant must be U.S. citizen.
Basis for selection: Applicant must demonstrate high academic achievement and leadership.
Application requirements: Recommendations, transcript. SAT/ACT scores, biographical questionnaire. Two sealed letters of recommendation.
Additional information: Application deadline in mid-January. Applicant must be child or grandchild of Elk who has been a paid-up member in good standing for two consecutive years. Application available on September 1 from local lodge's scholarship chairman, from Website or by sending SASE to foundation. Eligible applicants from Guam, Panama, Puerto Rico and the Philippines may attend schools in those countries. Visit Website for additional information.

Engineers Foundation of Ohio

Engineers Foundation of Ohio Scholarships

Type of award: Scholarship.
Intended use: For freshman study at accredited 4-year institution in United States. Designated institutions: ABET-accredited schools in Ohio and Notre Dame University.
Eligibility: Applicant must be U.S. citizen residing in Ohio.
Basis for selection: Major/career interest in engineering; engineering, civil; engineering, chemical; engineering, electrical/electronic; engineering, mechanical or engineering, structural. Applicant must demonstrate high academic achievement.
Application requirements: Essay, transcript.
Additional information: Minimum 3.0 GPA. Must have minimum 600 SAT (Math) and 500 SAT (Reading or Composition) or 29 ACT Math and 25 ACT English. EFO offers up to 12 scholarships per year with various requirements; see Website for specifics. Some awards renewable. For most scholarships applicant must be high school senior. Some awards require study of certain engineering branch. Some consider extracurricular activity, work experience, honors, memberships, dean evaluation, references, interview and/or financial need. Some are geographically restricted or school-specific.

Amount of award:	$500-$2,500
Number of awards:	25
Number of applicants:	200
Application deadline:	December 15

Contact:
Engineers Foundation of Ohio
400 South Fifth Street
Suite 300
Columbus, OH 43215-5430
Phone: 614-223-1177
Web: www.ohioengineer.com/info/Engineers.htm

The Entomological Foundation

The Entomological Foundation BioQuip Undergraduate Scholarship

Type of award: Scholarship.
Intended use: For full-time junior or senior study at 4-year institution in United States or Canada.
Eligibility: Applicant must be Mexican citizen.

Basis for selection: Competition/talent/interest in study abroad. Major/career interest in entomology; zoology; biology or science, general. Applicant must demonstrate financial need.
Application requirements: Recommendations, essay, transcript, nomination.
Additional information: Applicant must have been enrolled as undergraduate student in entomology in the fall prior to application deadline. If student's college or university does not offer a degree in entomology, student must be preparing to become an entomologist through his/her studies. By September 1 following application deadline, student must accumulate at least 90 credit hours and either complete two junior-level entomology courses or have a research project in entomology. See Website for more application information.

Amount of award:	$2,000
Number of awards:	1
Number of applicants:	72
Application deadline:	July 1
Notification begins:	September 30
Total amount awarded:	$2,000

Contact:
The Entomological Foundation
Undergraduate Scholarship
9332 Annapolis Road, Suite 210
Lanham, MD 20706-3115
Phone: 301-459-9082
Fax: 301-459-9084
Web: www.entfdn.org

Stan Beck Fellowship

Type of award: Scholarship, renewable.
Intended use: For undergraduate or graduate study at 4-year or graduate institution in United States or Canada. Designated institutions: Colleges or universities in the United States, Mexico, or Canada.
Eligibility: Applicant must be Alaskan native, Asian American, African American, Mexican American, Hispanic American, Puerto Rican or American Indian.
Basis for selection: Major/career interest in entomology. Applicant must demonstrate financial need.
Application requirements: Recommendations, essay, transcript, proof of eligibility, nomination.
Additional information: Award amount varies based on the earnings from the investment. Need is based on physical limitations or economic, minority, or environmental conditions. Applications must be submitted electronically. See Website for additional information.

Number of awards:	1
Application deadline:	July 1
Total amount awarded:	$1,000

Contact:
The Entomological Foundation
9332 Annapolis Road #210
Lanham, MD 20706
Phone: 301-459-9082
Fax: 301-459-9084
Web: www.entfdn.org

Epilepsy Foundation of America

Behavioral Sciences Student Fellowship

Type of award: Research grant.
Intended use: For undergraduate or graduate study in United States.
Basis for selection: Major/career interest in social/behavioral sciences; sociology; social work; psychology; anthropology; nursing; economics; rehabilitation/therapeutic services or political science/government.
Application requirements: Research proposal.
Additional information: Three-month fellowship for epilepsy study project. Professor or advisor must supervise student's project. Other appropriate fields include vocational rehabilitation, counseling, and subjects relevant to epilepsy research or practice. Women and minorities are especially encouraged to apply. Visit Website for application instructions and for more information.

Amount of award:	$3,000
Number of applicants:	4
Application deadline:	March 2

Contact:
Epilepsy Foundation National Office-Programs and Research
8301 Professional Place
Landover, MD 20785-2267
Phone: 301-459-3700
Fax: 301-577-2684
Web: www.epilepsyfoundation.org/grants

Epilepsy Foundation of San Diego County

Epilepsy Foundation of San Diego County Scholarship

Type of award: Scholarship.
Intended use: For undergraduate study at vocational, 2-year or 4-year institution.
Eligibility: Applicant must be residing in California.
Basis for selection: Applicant must demonstrate financial need and high academic achievement.
Additional information: Two categories of eligibility: 1) Student being treated for epilepsy who is or will be enrolled in a college, university, or trade school in the Fall. 2) Full-time college or university student involved in an epilepsy research project in health or social science with minimum 3.0 GPA. All applicants must be residents of San Diego or Imperial counties, but may be attending school outside the area.

Amount of award:	$250-$2,000
Number of awards:	6
Number of applicants:	8
Application deadline:	June 13
Total amount awarded:	$7,000

Contact:
Epilepsy Foundation of San Diego County
2055 El Cajon Boulevard
San Diego, CA 92104
Phone: 619-296-0161
Web: http://epilepsysandiego.org

EqualityMaine Foundation

Senator Joel Abromson Memorial Scholarship Fund

Type of award: Scholarship.
Intended use: For undergraduate study at postsecondary institution.
Eligibility: Applicant must be high school senior. Applicant must be U.S. citizen or permanent resident residing in Maine.
Basis for selection: Applicant must demonstrate depth of character and service orientation.
Application requirements: Recommendations, essay. Cover letter. Acceptance letter to chosen higher education institution.
Additional information: Awardees chosen based on involvement in, leadership in, and continued commitment to promoting lesbian, gay, bisexual, and transgender equality. Visit Website for essay question and additional information.
    Amount of award: $1,000
    Number of awards: 6
    Number of applicants: 50
    Application deadline: April 15
    Notification begins: May 15
Contact:
EqualityMaine Foundation
P.O. Box 1951
Portland, ME 04104
Phone: 207-761-3732
Fax: 207-761-3752
Web: www.equalitymaine.org

ESA Foundation

ESA Foundation Scholarship Program

Type of award: Scholarship, renewable.
Intended use: For undergraduate or graduate study at vocational, 2-year, 4-year or graduate institution.
Eligibility: Applicant must be U.S. citizen, permanent resident or international student.
Basis for selection: Applicant must demonstrate financial need, depth of character, leadership and service orientation.
Application requirements: $5 application fee. Recommendations, essay, transcript. Two letters of recommendation.
Additional information: Individual scholarships have specific requirements; visit Website for full details and application form.
    Amount of award: $300-$2,000
    Number of awards: 120
    Number of applicants: 7,000
    Total amount awarded: $145,000

Contact:
ESA Foundation
P.O. Box 270517
Fort Collins, CO 80527
Phone: 970-223-2824
Fax: 970-223-4456
Web: www.esaintl.com/esaf/

Executive Women International

Executive Women International Scholarship

Type of award: Scholarship, renewable.
Intended use: For full-time undergraduate study at accredited 4-year institution in United States.
Eligibility: Applicant must be high school junior.
Basis for selection: Applicant must demonstrate high academic achievement, depth of character, leadership, seriousness of purpose and service orientation.
Application requirements: Interview, recommendations, essay.
Additional information: Applicant must reside within boundaries of participating EWI chapter. Scholarship awarded each academic year, for up to five consecutive years, until student completes degree. Applicants must have sponsoring teacher at their school. Must have a major/career interest in a professional field.
    Amount of award: $1,000-$10,000
    Application deadline: March 1
    Notification begins: April 15
Contact:
Executive Women International
515 South 700 East
Suite 2A
Salt Lake City, UT 84102
Phone: 801-355-2800
Fax: 801-355-2852
Web: www.executivewomen.org

Experimental Aircraft Association, Inc.

Hansen Scholarship

Type of award: Scholarship, renewable.
Intended use: For undergraduate study.
Basis for selection: Major/career interest in aerospace or engineering. Applicant must demonstrate high academic achievement, depth of character, leadership and service orientation.
Additional information: Must be EAA member or recommended by an EAA member to apply. Student should be pursuing degree in aerospace engineering or aeronautical engineering. Financial need is a consideration. Visit Website for details and application.

Amount of award:	$1,000
Number of awards:	1
Application deadline:	March 1
Total amount awarded:	$1,000

Contact:
Scholarship Office
Phone: 920-426-6823
Web: www.youngeagles.org/programs/scholarships

Payzer Scholarship

Type of award: Scholarship.
Intended use: For undergraduate study at accredited postsecondary institution.
Basis for selection: Major/career interest in engineering; mathematics; physical sciences or biology. Applicant must demonstrate financial need, depth of character, leadership and service orientation.
Additional information: Must be EAA member or recommended by EAA member. Must complete application online.

Amount of award:	$5,000
Number of awards:	1
Application deadline:	March 1
Total amount awarded:	$5,000

Contact:
Scholarship Office
Phone: 902-426-6823
Web: www.youngeagles.org/programs/scholarships

Explorers Club

Explorers Club Youth Activity Fund

Type of award: Research grant.
Intended use: For undergraduate study.
Basis for selection: Competition/talent/interest in research paper, based on proposal's scientific and practical merit, investigator's competence, and budget's appropriateness. Major/career interest in natural sciences. Applicant must demonstrate seriousness of purpose.
Application requirements: Recommendations, research proposal. Physical release.
Additional information: For field research in the natural sciences under supervision of qualified scientist or institution. For full-time high school students or undergraduates only. Recipients of grants must provide one- to two-page report on their exploration or research within year of receiving the grant. Photographs are encouraged. Request application form from club. Application deadline in January. See Website for exact date and for more details.

Amount of award:	$500-$1,500
Number of applicants:	78
Application deadline:	January 15
Notification begins:	May 1

Contact:
The Explorers Club
46 East 70th Street
New York, NY 10021
Phone: 212-628-8383
Fax: 212-288-4449
Web: www.explorers.org

Federal Employee Education and Assistance Fund

Federal Employee Education and Assistance Fund Scholarship

Type of award: Scholarship.
Intended use: For undergraduate, master's or doctoral study at accredited 2-year, 4-year or graduate institution.
Eligibility: Applicant or parent must be employed by Federal/U.S. Government.
Basis for selection: Applicant must demonstrate high academic achievement.
Application requirements: Recommendations, essay, transcript.
Additional information: Current civilian federal and postal employees with minimum three years' service and their dependents are eligible. Applicant must have completed community service activities. Must have 3.0 GPA. Employee applicants eligible for part-time study; dependents must enroll full time. Send SASE for application materials or download from Website beginning mid-January.

Amount of award:	$300-$1,500
Number of applicants:	3,305
Application deadline:	March 30
Notification begins:	October 30

Contact:
Federal Employee Education and Assistance Fund
8441 West Bowles Avenue
Suite 200
Littleton, CO 80123-9501
Phone: 800-323-4140
Web: www.feea.org

Finance Authority of Maine

Maine Robert C. Byrd Honors Scholarship

Type of award: Scholarship, renewable.
Intended use: For full-time undergraduate study at 2-year or 4-year institution.
Eligibility: Applicant must be high school senior. Applicant must be U.S. citizen residing in Maine.
Basis for selection: Applicant must demonstrate high academic achievement.
Application requirements: Essay, transcript. High school profile from guidance office with SAT scores, list of scholastic achievements, awards and honors. FAFSA by May 1.
Additional information: Information available through Maine high school guidance offices and Finance Authority of Maine. See Website for further details.

Amount of award:	$1,500
Number of awards:	18
Number of applicants:	400
Application deadline:	May 1
Notification begins:	June 1

Finance Authority of Maine: Maine Robert C. Byrd Honors Scholarship

Contact:
Finance Authority of Maine
5 Community Drive
P.O. Box 949
Augusta, ME 04332-0949
Phone: 800-228-3734
Fax: 207-623-0095
Web: www.famemaine.com

First Catholic Slovak Ladies Association

CW Scholarships

Type of award: Scholarship, renewable.
Intended use: For undergraduate study.
Eligibility: Applicant or parent must be member/participant of First Catholic Slovak Ladies Association.
Additional information: Must have been a member of First Catholic Slovak Ladies Association for past three years.

Amount of award:	$1,250-$1,750
Number of awards:	133
Number of applicants:	427
Application deadline:	March 1
Notification begins:	May 1
Total amount awarded:	$174,250

Contact:
First Catholic Slovak Ladies Association
Director of Fraternal Scholarship Aid
24950 Chagrin Blvd.
Beachwood, OH 44122
Phone: 216-464-8015
Web: fcsla.org

First Catholic Slovak Ladies Association Fraternal Scholarship

Type of award: Scholarship, renewable.
Intended use: For full-time undergraduate, graduate or non-degree study at accredited postsecondary institution in United States.
Eligibility: Applicant or parent must be member/participant of First Catholic Slovak Ladies Association.
Basis for selection: Applicant must demonstrate high academic achievement, leadership and service orientation.
Application requirements: Recommendations, essay, transcript, proof of eligibility. SAT/ACT scores.
Additional information: Minimum 2.5 GPA. Visit Website for more information.

Amount of award:	$1,250-$1,750
Number of awards:	133
Application deadline:	March 1
Total amount awarded:	$248,250

Contact:
First Catholic Slovak Ladies Association
Director of Fraternal Scholarship
24950 Chagrin Boulevard
Beachwood, OH 44122
Phone: 800-464-4642
Fax: 216-464-9260
Web: www.fcsla.org

First Marine Division Association, Inc.

First Marine Division Association Scholarship

Type of award: Scholarship, renewable.
Intended use: For full-time undergraduate study at accredited vocational, 2-year or 4-year institution in United States.
Eligibility: Applicant must be high school senior. Applicant must be U.S. citizen. Applicant must be dependent of disabled veteran or deceased veteran who served in the Marines. Specifically in any unit part of, attached to, or in support of 1st Marine Division.
Basis for selection: Applicant must demonstrate depth of character and seriousness of purpose.
Application requirements: Essay, proof of eligibility. Veteran sponsor's DD214 if available (if not, applicant must complete Standard Form 180 and mail directly to National Personnel Records Center, GSA (Military Personnel Records) 9700 Page Blvd, St. Louis, MO 63132). Death certificate or affidavit proving veteran's 100 percent or permanent disability. Applicant's birth certificate. Photograph. See Website for other required information.
Additional information: Contact office by phone, fax, or mail for additional information and deadlines. Scholarship pays $1750 per academic year.

Amount of award:	$1,750-$7,000
Number of awards:	7
Number of applicants:	8

Contact:
First Marine Division Association
410 Pier View Way
Oceanside, CA 92054
Phone: 877-967-8561
Fax: 760-967-8567
Web: www.1stmarinedivisionassociation.org

Fisher Communications, Inc.

Fisher Broadcasting Scholarship for Minorities

Type of award: Scholarship.
Intended use: For full-time sophomore, junior or senior study at accredited vocational, 2-year or 4-year institution in United States.
Eligibility: Applicant must be Alaskan native, Asian American, African American, Mexican American, Hispanic American, Puerto Rican, American Indian or Native Hawaiian/Pacific Islander. Applicant must be U.S. citizen.
Basis for selection: Major/career interest in radio/television/film; journalism or communications. Applicant must demonstrate financial need, depth of character, seriousness of purpose and service orientation.
Application requirements: Interview, recommendations, essay, transcript, proof of eligibility. Proof of citizenship.
Additional information: Must have career interest in broadcast communications and coursework must be oriented to

broadcasting. Amount of award varies each year. Minimum 2.5 GPA. For schools in Washington, Oregon, Idaho and Montana or for students with permanent addresses in these states who attend school out of state. Only finalists will be interviewed.

    Number of awards: 4
    Number of applicants: 18
    Application deadline: April 30
    Notification begins: July 30
    Total amount awarded: $15,000

Contact:
Fisher Communications Inc.
100 Fourth Ave. N Ste 510
Seattle, WA 98109
Web: www.fsci.com/x100.xml

Florida Department of Education

Access to Better Learning and Education Grant Program (ABLE)

Type of award: Scholarship, renewable.
Intended use: For full-time undergraduate study at postsecondary institution in United States. Designated institutions: Eligible Florida public and private colleges and universities.
Eligibility: Applicant must be U.S. citizen or permanent resident residing in Florida.
Additional information: The amount of ABLE award plus all other scholarships and grants specifically designated for payment of tuition and fees cannot exceed the total amount of tuition and fees charged by the institution. May not be enrolled in program of study leading to degree in theology or divinity. The college or university will adjust the amount of the ABLE award to conform to this maximum.
Contact:
Florida Department of Education
1940 North Monroe Street
Suite 70
Tallahassee, FL 32303-4759
Phone: 888-827-2004
Fax: 850-488-3612
Web: www.floridastudentaid.org

Ethics in Business Scholarship

Type of award: Scholarship.
Intended use: For undergraduate study at 2-year or 4-year institution. Designated institutions: Florida community colleges and eligible private colleges and universities.
Basis for selection: Major/career interest in business.
Additional information: Scholarships funded by private and state contributions. Awards dependent on private matching funds. Contact financial aid office at participating institutions for more information.
Contact:
Florida Department of Education
1940 North Monroe Street
Suite 70
Tallahassee, FL 32303-4759
Phone: 888-827-2004
Web: www.FloridaStudentFinancialAid.org

Florida Academic Scholars Award

Type of award: Scholarship, renewable.
Intended use: For undergraduate study at postsecondary institution. Designated institutions: Eligible Florida postsecondary institutions.
Eligibility: Applicant must be high school senior. Applicant must be U.S. citizen or permanent resident residing in Florida.
Basis for selection: Applicant must demonstrate high academic achievement and service orientation.
Additional information: For public institutions scholarship covers full tuition and fees with up to $600 stipend; for private institutions it covers equivalent amount. Applicant should have 75 hours of community service experience. Must 1) be National Merit Scholarship finalist/Achievement Scholar/Finalist or National Hispanic Scholar; 2) be International Baccalaureate (IB) Diploma recipient or have completed IB curriculum with at least 1270/SAT or 28/ACT; or 3) have earned 3.5 GPA. GED Diplomas are also accepted. Two years of foreign language study necessary. In addition, high school senior with highest academic ranking in each county, based on GPA and SAT/ACT score, will receive annual Top Scholars Award of $1,500. Applications available from high school guidance office, office of financial assistance or online. Application must be completed before high school graduation. Check Website for additional information and requirements.

    Amount of award: Full tuition

Contact:
Florida Department of Education
Bright Futures Scholarship Program
1940 North Monore Street, Suite 70
Tallahassee, FL 32303-4759
Phone: 888-827-2004
Fax: 850-427-6244
Web: www.floridastudentfinancialaid.org/ssfad/home/uamain.htm

Florida Gold Seal Vocational Scholars Award

Type of award: Scholarship, renewable.
Intended use: For undergraduate study at vocational, 2-year or 4-year institution. Designated institutions: Eligible Florida postsecondary institutions.
Eligibility: Applicant must be high school senior. Applicant must be U.S. citizen or permanent resident residing in Florida.
Basis for selection: Applicant must demonstrate high academic achievement.
Additional information: At public institution, scholarship covers 75 percent of tuition and fees; at private institution, it covers equivalent amount. Applications available from high school guidance office, office of financial assistance or online. Application must be completed before high school graduation. CPT, SAT or ACT test scores required. Check Website for additional information and requirements.
Contact:
Florida Department of Education
Bright Futures Scholarship Program
1940 North Monroe Street, Suite 70
Tallahassee, FL 32303-4759
Phone: 888-827-2004
Fax: 850-487-6244
Web: www.floridastudentfinancialaid.org/ssfad/home/uamain.htm

Florida Medallion Scholars Award

Type of award: Scholarship, renewable.

Intended use: For undergraduate study at 2-year or 4-year institution. Designated institutions: Eligible Florida postsecondary institutions.
Eligibility: Applicant must be high school senior. Applicant must be U.S. citizen or permanent resident residing in Florida.
Basis for selection: Applicant must demonstrate high academic achievement.
Additional information: Minimum 2.75 GPA. At public institutions, scholarship covers 75 percent of tuition and fees; at private institutions, it covers equivalent amount. Applications available from high school guidance office, office of financial assistance or online. Minimum composite score of 970/SAT or 20/ACT. Two years of foreign language study necessary. Application must be completed before high school graduation. Check Website for additional information and requirements.
Contact:
Florida Department of Education
Bright Futures Scholarship Program
1940 North Monroe Street, Suite 70
Tallahassee, FL 32303-4759
Phone: 888-827-2004
Fax: 850-487-6244
Web: www.floridastudentfinancialaid.org

Florida Robert C. Byrd Honors Scholarship

Type of award: Scholarship, renewable.
Intended use: For full-time undergraduate study at 2-year, 4-year or graduate institution in United States. Designated institutions: Eligible Florida and non-Florida public and private nonprofit postsecondary institutions.
Eligibility: Applicant must be high school senior. Applicant must be U.S. citizen or permanent resident residing in Florida.
Basis for selection: Applicant must demonstrate high academic achievement.
Application requirements: Proof of eligibility, nomination by high school principal or adult education director.
Additional information: Application requires unweighted cumulative GPA and SAT/ACT scores. Applicants are ranked with members of designated geographical region. Number and award amount determined annually; maximum award $1,500. Applicant must meet registration requirements of Selective Service System.
   Amount of award: $1,500
   Application deadline: April 15
Contact:
Florida Department of Education
Office of Student Financial Assistance
1940 North Monroe Street, Suite 70
Tallahassee, FL 32303-4759
Phone: 888-827-2004
Web: www.FloridaStudentFinancialAid.org

Florida Student Assistance Grant Program

Type of award: Scholarship, renewable.
Intended use: For full-time undergraduate study at 2-year or 4-year institution. Designated institutions: Eligible Florida public and private postsecondary institutions.
Eligibility: Applicant must be U.S. citizen or permanent resident residing in Florida.
Basis for selection: Applicant must demonstrate financial need.
Application requirements: Proof of eligibility. FAFSA.
Additional information: Must be in top 20 percent of senior class. Each participating institution determines application deadlines, student eligibility, and award amounts. Applications available from high school guidance offices and participating schools' financial aid offices. FAFSA deadline determined by participating institution. Visit Website for more information.
   Amount of award: $200-$1,808
Contact:
Florida Department of Education
Office of Student Financial Assistance
1940 North Monroe Street, Suite 70
Tallahassee, FL 32303-4759
Phone: 888-827-2004
Web: www.FloridaStudentFinancialAid.org

Jose Marti Scholarship Challenge Grant

Type of award: Scholarship, renewable.
Intended use: For full-time undergraduate or graduate study at 2-year, 4-year or graduate institution in United States. Designated institutions: Eligible Florida postsecondary institutions.
Eligibility: Applicant must be Hispanic American. Applicant must be high school senior. Applicant must be U.S. citizen or permanent resident residing in Florida.
Basis for selection: Applicant must demonstrate financial need and high academic achievement.
Application requirements: FAFSA.
Additional information: Minimum 3.0 GPA. Must be of Spanish culture and born in Mexico or Spain or a Hispanic country of the Caribbean, Central America or South America, or child of same. Must meet Florida eligibility criteria for state student aid. Award number is limited to the amount of available funds; renewals take priority over new awards. Applications available from high school guidance office or college office of financial aid. Visit Website for more information.
   Amount of award: $2,000
   Application deadline: April 1
Contact:
Florida Department of Education
Office of Student Financial Assistance
1940 North Monroe Street, Suite 70
Tallahassee, FL 32303-4759
Phone: 888-827-2004
Web: www.FloridaStudentFinancialAid.org

Mary McLeod Bethune Scholarship

Type of award: Scholarship, renewable.
Intended use: For full-time undergraduate study at 4-year institution in United States. Designated institutions: Bethune-Cookman College, Edward Waters College, Florida A&M University, and Florida Memorial College.
Eligibility: Applicant must be high school senior. Applicant must be residing in Florida.
Basis for selection: Applicant must demonstrate financial need and high academic achievement.
Additional information: Minimum 3.0 high school GPA required. Applicant must maintain residency in Florida for purposes other than education for a minimum of 12 consecutive months prior to the first day of class of the academic term for which funds are requested. Deadlines established by participating institutions. Applicant must submit a renewal application. General award availability contingent on matching funds raised by the eligible institutions. Applications can be

obtained from any of four designated institutions' financial aid offices. Visit Website for more information.

Amount of award: $3,000
Contact:
Florida Department of Education
Office of Student Financial Assistance
1940 North Monroe Street, Suite 70
Tallahassee, FL 32303-4759
Phone: 888-827-2004
Web: www.FloridaStudentFinancialAid.org

Rosewood Family Scholarship Program

Type of award: Scholarship, renewable.
Intended use: For full-time undergraduate study at vocational, 2-year or 4-year institution in United States.
Eligibility: Applicant must be Alaskan native, Asian American, African American, Mexican American, Hispanic American, Puerto Rican or American Indian. Applicant must be U.S. citizen or permanent resident residing in Florida.
Basis for selection: Applicant must demonstrate financial need.
Application requirements: Transcript. FAFSA. If not Florida resident, copy of Student Aid Report (SAR) must be postmarked to Florida Bureau of Student Financial Assistance by May 15th (along with FAFSA).
Additional information: Descendants of African-American Rosewood families affected by the incidents of January 1923 given priority over other applicants. Award covers annual cost of tuition and fees up to $4,000 per semester for up to eight semesters. Visit Website for more information.

Amount of award: $4,000
Number of awards: 25
Application deadline: April 1
Total amount awarded: $100,000
Contact:
Florida Department of Education
Office of Student Financial Assistance
1940 North Monroe Street, 70
Tallahassee, FL 32303-4759
Phone: 888-827-2004
Web: www.FloridaStudentFinancialAid.org

Scholarships for Children and Spouses of Deceased or Disabled Veterans and Servicemembers

Type of award: Scholarship, renewable.
Intended use: For undergraduate study at postsecondary institution. Designated institutions: Eligible Florida postsecondary institutions.
Eligibility: Applicant must be at least 16, no older than 22. Applicant must be U.S. citizen or permanent resident residing in Florida. Applicant must be dependent of disabled veteran or deceased veteran; or spouse of disabled veteran or deceased veteran.
Basis for selection: Applicant must demonstrate financial need.
Application requirements: Proof of eligibility.
Additional information: Award amount covers tuition/fees at eligible Florida public postsecondary institution. Award for eligible private schools based on Florida public tuition/fees costs. Renewal applicant must maintain minimum 2.0 GPA. Must meet eligibility requirements for receipt of state aid. Visit Website for additional information and qualification specifications.

Amount of award: Full tuition
Application deadline: April 1
Contact:
Office of Student Financial Assistance
State Programs
1940 North Monroe Street, Suite 70
Tallahassee, FL 32303-4759
Phone: 888-827-2004
Web: www.floridastudentfinancialaid.org/ssfad/home/uamain.htm

William L. Boyd, IV, Florida Resident Access Grant

Type of award: Scholarship, renewable.
Intended use: For full-time undergraduate study at accredited 4-year institution. Designated institutions: Eligible private, nonprofit Florida colleges and universities.
Eligibility: Applicant must be U.S. citizen or permanent resident residing in Florida.
Application requirements: Proof of eligibility.
Additional information: Approximately $3,000; exact award amount determined by Florida legislature on yearly basis. Applicant must not have previously received bachelor's degree and may not use award for study of divinity or theology. Must enroll for minimum of 12 credit hours per term in bachelor's degree program. Renewal applicant must have minimum 2.0 GPA. Contact financial aid office for application and more information.

Amount of award: Full tuition
Contact:
Florida Department of Education
Office of Student Financial Assistance
1940 North Monroe Street, Suite 70
Tallahassee, FL 32303-4759
Phone: 888-827-2004
Web: www.FloridaStudentFinancialAid.org

Florida Division of Blind Services

Florida Educational Assistance for the Blind

Type of award: Scholarship, renewable.
Intended use: For full-time undergraduate, graduate or non-degree study at vocational, 2-year, 4-year or graduate institution in United States.
Eligibility: Applicant must be visually impaired. Applicant must be U.S. citizen or permanent resident residing in Florida.
Basis for selection: Applicant must demonstrate financial need and seriousness of purpose.
Application requirements: Transcript, proof of eligibility.
Additional information: Tuition, books, reader's service fees and maintenance awarded for out-of-state institutions. Only tuition paid for in-state institutions. Deadline dates vary. Applicants must be eligible for vocational rehabilitation services based on a bilateral visual impairment and require educational assistance for an employment outcome. Must be a client of State of Florida Division of Blind Services and eligible for vocational rehabilitation. Applicant must first secure federal or state scholarships/grants/loans.

Amount of award: Full tuition
Contact:
Florida State Division of Blind Services
325 West Gaines Street
Suite 1114
Tallahassee, FL 32399-0400
Phone: 850-245-0300
Fax: 850-245-0363

The Food Allergy & Anaphylaxis Network

The Food Allergy & Anaphylaxis Network College Scholarship Essay Contest

Type of award: Scholarship.
Intended use: For undergraduate or graduate study in United States.
Eligibility: Applicant must be U.S. citizen.
Basis for selection: Competition/talent/interest in writing/journalism.
Application requirements: Essay. Essay (500 words or less) on "How Food Allergy Has Made a Difference in My Life."
Additional information: Scholarship is open to all students who have a food allergy diagnosed by a physician. Applicants must be attending undergraduate or graduate program in the United States for the following school year.
  Amount of award: $1,500
  Number of awards: 3
  Number of applicants: 550
  Application deadline: February 15
  Notification begins: April 1
Contact:
The Food Allergy & Anaphylaxis Network
11781 Lee Jackson Highway
Suite 160
Fairfax, VA 22033-3309
Phone: 800-929-4040
Fax: 703-691-2713
Web: www.faanteen.org

Foundation for Surgical Technology

Foundation for Surgical Technology Scholarship Fund

Type of award: Scholarship.
Intended use: For undergraduate study at accredited vocational or 2-year institution in United States.
Basis for selection: Major/career interest in surgical technology. Applicant must demonstrate financial need and high academic achievement.
Application requirements: Recommendations, transcript, proof of eligibility. Recommendation from CAAHEP instructor.
Additional information: Applicant must be enrolled in surgical technology program accredited by CAAHEP and be eligible to sit for the NBSTSA national surgical technologist certifying examination. Interested students may visit Website for scholarship application.
  Amount of award: $500-$2,500
  Application deadline: April 1
  Notification begins: June 1
Contact:
Foundation for Surgical Technology
Scholarship Administrator
6 West Dry Creek Circle
Littleton, CO 80120
Phone: 303-694-9130
Fax: 303-694-9169
Web: www.ast.org

Foundation of Research and Education of the Am. Health Information Mgmt Assoc.

FORE Undergraduate Scholarship

Type of award: Scholarship.
Intended use: For full-time undergraduate study.
Eligibility: Applicant or parent must be member/participant of American Health Information Management Association.
Basis for selection: Major/career interest in information systems; health services administration or health-related professions. Applicant must demonstrate high academic achievement.
Application requirements: Recommendations, transcript, proof of eligibility. Verification of enrollment.
Additional information: Applicants must be members of AHIMA and accepted into accredited health information management or health information technology program with major/career interest in health information management. Must have 3.0 GPA (out of 4.0). Number of awards varies. Awardees notified no later than end of August.
  Amount of award: $1,000-$5,000
  Application deadline: April 25
Contact:
American Health Information Management Association
Foundation of Research and Education
233 North Michigan Avenue, 21st Floor
Chicago, IL 60601-5800
Phone: 312-233-1100
Fax: 312-233-1468
Web: www.ahima.org/fore/programs.asp

Foundation of the National Student Nurses Association, Inc.

National Student Nurses Association Scholarship

Type of award: Scholarship.

Intended use: For full-time undergraduate study at accredited 2-year or 4-year institution. Designated institutions: State-approved schools of nursing or pre-nursing.
Eligibility: Applicant must be U.S. citizen or permanent resident.
Basis for selection: Major/career interest in nursing or nurse practitioner. Applicant must demonstrate financial need, high academic achievement and service orientation.
Application requirements: $10 application fee. Recommendations, essay, transcript, proof of eligibility. National Student Nurses Association members must submit proof of membership.
Additional information: All applicants considered for following scholarships: General Scholarships, Career Mobility Scholarships, Breakthrough to Nursing Scholarships for Ethnic People of Color, Specialty Scholarships, and Promise of Nursing Scholarships. Applicants must be enrolled in nursing or pre-nursing program. Awards granted in spring for use in summer and following academic year. Applications available from August through January; see Website.

Amount of award:	$1,000-$5,000
Number of applicants:	222
Application deadline:	January 13
Notification begins:	February 28
Total amount awarded:	$120,000

Contact:
Foundation of the National Student Nurses Association, Inc.
45 Main Street
Suite 606
Brooklyn, NY 11201
Phone: 718-210-0705
Fax: 718-210-0710
Web: www.nsna.org

Francis Ouimet Scholarship Fund

Francis Ouimet Scholarship

Type of award: Scholarship, renewable.
Intended use: For full-time undergraduate study.
Eligibility: Applicant must be residing in Massachusetts.
Basis for selection: Competition/talent/interest in athletics/sports. Applicant must demonstrate financial need, high academic achievement and service orientation.
Application requirements: Interview, recommendations, essay, transcript, proof of eligibility. Three recommendations from club members, one from guidance counselor.
Additional information: Applicants should have worked on golf course for two years in Massachusetts; high school seniors may apply if they meet golf course criterion. Contact Marion Mackerwicz at the Ouimet Fund Office in midsummer to be put on application mailing list for awards for following school year. May also sign up for application online. Awards are announced in August.

Amount of award:	$1,500-$7,500
Number of awards:	362
Application deadline:	December 1
Notification begins:	August 1
Total amount awarded:	$1,150,000

Contact:
Francis Ouimet Scholarship Fund
Marion Mackerwicz, Scholarship Administrator
300 Arnold Palmer Blvd.
Norton, MA 02766
Phone: 774-430-9090
Fax: 774-430-9091
Web: www.ouimet.org

Fred G. Zahn Foundation

Fred G. Zahn Foundation Scholarship

Type of award: Scholarship, renewable.
Intended use: For undergraduate study at accredited 2-year, 4-year or graduate institution in United States.
Eligibility: Applicant must be residing in Washington.
Basis for selection: Applicant must demonstrate financial need and high academic achievement.
Application requirements: Transcript. Student Aid Report. Letter detailing cost of student's course of study; should also mention extracurricular activities; other financial resources available, including part-time employment, career plans, and work experience.
Additional information: Must have graduated from Washington state high school. Minimum 3.75 GPA. May obtain application and more information at eligible Washington state institution. Do not contact foundation.

Amount of award:	$1,500
Number of awards:	4
Number of applicants:	9
Application deadline:	April 15
Notification begins:	June 1

Contact:
Fred G. Zahn Foundation Scholarship; Bank of America Trust Services
GA 2-002-08-01
715 Peachtree Street, 8th Floor
Atlanta, GA 30308
Phone: 800-832-9071
Fax: 800-552-3182

Freedom From Religion Foundation

Blanche Fearn Memorial Award

Type of award: Scholarship.
Intended use: For undergraduate study.
Eligibility: Applicant must be high school senior.
Basis for selection: Competition/talent/interest in writing/journalism, based on best-written essays.
Application requirements: Essay, proof of eligibility. Essay should be three to four pages, double-spaced with standard margins. Include autobiographical paragraph giving permanent address, phone numbers, and e-mail. Identify high school and college/university to be attended. Include intended major and other interests.

Additional information: Applicant must be college-bound high school senior. Essay topics and requirements change annually and are announced in February. Check Website for current topic. Students are requested not to inquire before then. Send SASE or visit Website for more information. First place receives $2,000; second place, $1,000; third place, $500; honorable mention(s), $100.

    Amount of award: $100-$2,000
    Number of applicants: 200
    Application deadline: June 1
    Notification begins: August 1
    Total amount awarded: $3,500

Contact:
Freedom From Religion Foundation
High School Essay Competition
P.O. Box 750
Madison, WI 53701
Phone: 608-256-8900
Web: www.ffrf.org

FFRF Student Activist Award

Type of award: Scholarship.
Intended use: For undergraduate study at postsecondary institution.
Additional information: Given to students who have done something specific to separate church and state (e.g., stopped religious programs in public schools, been a plaintiff in a church-state lawsuit, etc.) or to promote nontheism. Nomination period varies but preference is to give award in person at foundation's fall national convention. Private nomination only.

    Amount of award: $1,000
    Number of awards: 2
    Total amount awarded: $2,000

Contact:
Freedom From Religion Foundation
P.O. Box 750
Madison, WI 53701
Phone: 608-256-8900
Web: www.ffrf.org

Michael Hakeem Memorial Award

Type of award: Scholarship.
Intended use: For full-time undergraduate or graduate study at postsecondary institution.
Eligibility: Applicant must be U.S. citizen.
Basis for selection: Competition/talent/interest in writing/journalism, based on best-written essays.
Application requirements: Essay. Essay should be four to five pages, typed and double-spaced with standard margins. Include autobiographical paragraph giving both campus and permanent addresses, phone numbers, and e-mail. Identify college/university, major, and interests. Essay on free thought concerning religion; essay most suitable for atheistic and agnostic student.
Additional information: Applicant must be currently enrolled college student. Essay topics and requirements change annually and are announced in February. Check Website for current topic. Students are requested not to inquire before then. Send SASE or visit Website for more information. First place receives $2,000; second place, $1,000; third place, $500; honorable mention(s), $100.

    Amount of award: $100-$2,000
    Number of applicants: 200
    Application deadline: July 1
    Notification begins: September 1
    Total amount awarded: $3,500

Contact:
Freedom From Religion Foundation
College Essay Competition
P.O. Box 750
Madison, WI 53701
Phone: 608-256-8900
Web: www.ffrf.org

The Gallup Organization

The Gallup Management Development Scholarship $2,500 Award

Type of award: Scholarship.
Intended use: For junior or senior study.
Basis for selection: Applicant must demonstrate depth of character, leadership and seriousness of purpose.
Additional information: Applicant must be interested in a management internship with The Gallup Organization or a full-time management position with Gallup. Apply online -- search for scholarship on Website.

    Amount of award: $2,500
    Number of awards: 10
    Application deadline: April 15
    Total amount awarded: $25,000

Contact:
Gallup World Headquarters
Attn: Sarah Van Allen
901 F Street NW
Washington, DC 20004
Phone: 877-242-5587
Web: www.gallup.com/Careers/

Garden Club of America

Award in Desest Studies

Type of award: Scholarship.
Intended use: For junior, senior or graduate study in United States.
Basis for selection: Major/career interest in horticulture; botany; environmental science or landscape architecture.
Application requirements: Recommendations, essay. Resume, itemized budget, 2-3 page essay describing proposed project.
Additional information: Only advanced undergraduate and graduate students eligible. Projects must pertain to arid environment, preference given to projects that generate scientifically sound and plant management.

    Amount of award: $4,000
    Application deadline: January 15
    Notification begins: March 31

Contact:
Garden Club of America Desert Botanical Garden
Attn: Cathy Babcock
1201 N. Galvin Parkway
Phoenix, AZ 85008
Phone: 480-481-8162
Web: www.gcamerica.org or www.desertbotanical.org

Caroline Thorn Kissel Summer Environmental Studies Scholarship

Type of award: Scholarship.
Intended use: For undergraduate or graduate study.
Eligibility: Applicant must be U.S. citizen residing in New Jersey.
Basis for selection: Major/career interest in environmental science.
Application requirements: Recommendations, essay. Two letters of recommendation.
Additional information: Applicants must be New Jersey residents or non-residents studying in New Jersey. All application elements must be mailed together in one envelope.
    Amount of award: $2,000
    Application deadline: February 10
Contact:
Garden Club of America
14 East 60th Street
New York, NY 10022
Phone: 212-753-8287
Fax: 212-753-0134
Web: www.gcamerica.org

Field Botany Scholarships

Type of award: Scholarship.
Intended use: For sophomore, junior, senior or master's study in United States.
Basis for selection: Major/career interest in botany.
Application requirements: Recommendations, essay, transcript. Two letters of recommendation (one from advisor, one from professor).
Additional information: One application for two awards: GCA Scholarship in Field Botany maybe used for study done in North, Central or South America (with preference given to studies done within the United States); Joan K. and Rachel M. Hunt Summer Scholarship in Field Botany must be used in United States.
    Amount of award: $1,500
    Application deadline: February 1
Contact:
Garden Club of America
14 East 60th Street
New York, NY 10022
Phone: 212-753-8287
Fax: 212-753-0134
Web: www.gcamerica.org

Francis M. Peacock Native Bird Habitat Scholarship

Type of award: Scholarship.
Intended use: For senior or graduate study at graduate institution.
Basis for selection: Major/career interest in ornithology.
Application requirements: Project proposal of no more than five pages.
Additional information: Grant for advanced study of U.S. winter/summer habitat of threatened or endangered native birds. Awarded in cooperation with the Cornell Lab of ornithology. No phone calls. For further information, send SASE. To apply, contact: www.birds.cornell.edu.
    Amount of award: $4,000
    Number of awards: 1
    Application deadline: January 15
    Total amount awarded: $4,000
Contact:
Cornell Lab of Ornithology
Scott Sutcliffe
159 Sapsucker Woods Road
Ithaca, NY 14850
Fax: 607-254-2415
Web: www.gcamerica.org

Garden Club of America Summer Environmental Awards

Type of award: Scholarship.
Intended use: For freshman, sophomore or junior study at 4-year institution.
Basis for selection: Major/career interest in environmental science or ecology.
Application requirements: Recommendations, essay, transcript.
Additional information: Three awards for summer study in field of ecology and environmental studies: The Mary T. Carothers Scholarship, The Clara Carter Higgins/GCA Scholarship, and The Elizabeth Gardner Norweb Scholarship.
    Amount of award: $2,000
    Number of awards: 3
    Application deadline: February 10
Contact:
Garden Club of America
Attn: Scholarship Committee Summer Studies
14 East 60th Street
New York, NY 10022
Phone: 212-753-8287
Fax: 212-753-0134
Web: www.gcamerica.org

Katharine M. Grosscup Scholarship

Type of award: Scholarship.
Intended use: For sophomore, junior, senior or graduate study at accredited 4-year or graduate institution in United States.
Eligibility: Applicant must be residing in Michigan, Ohio, West Virginia, Indiana, Kentucky or Pennsylvania.
Basis for selection: Major/career interest in horticulture. Applicant must demonstrate financial need and high academic achievement.
Application requirements: Interview, recommendations, transcript. Two recommendations (one academic, one work-related).
Additional information: Minimum 'B' GPA. Several scholarships available. Preference given to residents of Pennsylvania, Ohio, West Virginia, Michigan, Indiana and Kentucky. Please do not contact by phone. Application available on Website.
    Amount of award: $3,000
    Application deadline: January 25
Contact:
Grosscup Scholarship Committee/Cleveland Botanical Garden
Attn: Nancy Stevenson
11030 East Blvd, Attn: Mrs. Nancy Stevenson
Cleveland, OH 44106
Fax: 216-721-2056
Web: www.gcamerica.org

The Loy McCandless Marks Scholarship

Type of award: Scholarship.

Garden Club of America: The Loy McCandless Marks Scholarship

Intended use: For sophomore, junior, senior or graduate study at accredited 4-year or graduate institution in or outside United States.
Eligibility: Applicant must be U.S. citizen.
Basis for selection: Major/career interest in horticulture or botany.
Application requirements: Recommendations, essay, transcript. Two recommendations, expense budget.
Additional information: Complementary funding for science student to assist with tropical ornamental horticulture project. For graduate or advanced undergraduate students to study and do research at appropriate foreign institution specializing in study of tropical plants. Visit Website for application.
    Amount of award: $2,000
    Number of awards: 1
    Application deadline: January 15
Contact:
Garden Club of America
Attn: Scholarship Committee Summer Studies
14 East 60th Street
New York, NY 10022
Phone: 212-753-8287
Fax: 212-753-0134
Web: www.gcamerica.org

Zeller Summer Scholarship in Medicinal Botany

Type of award: Scholarship.
Intended use: For undergraduate study in United States.
Basis for selection: Major/career interest in botany.
Application requirements: Recommendations, essay, transcript. Two recommendations (one from advisor, one from professor).
Additional information: Mail all application materials together in one envelope.
    Amount of award: $1,500
    Application deadline: February 1
Contact:
Garden Club of America
14 East 60th Street
New York, NY 10022
Phone: 212-753-8287
Fax: 212-753-0134
Web: www.gcamerica.org

Georgia Student Finance Commission

Accel Program Grant

Type of award: Scholarship.
Intended use: For full-time undergraduate study at accredited postsecondary institution.
Eligibility: Applicant must be high school junior or senior. Applicant must be U.S. citizen or permanent resident residing in Georgia.
Additional information: Accel assistance for students enrolled at public college includes tuition, approved mandatory fees, and book allowance up to $150 per semester. For students enrolled at private college, Accel pays up to $1,500 per semester for full-time students. Awards are prorated for students taking less than 12 hours per semester.

Contact:
Georgia Student Finance Commission
2082 East Exchange Place
Suite 100
Tucker, GA 30084
Phone: 800-505-4732
Fax: 770-724-9004
Web: www.gacollege411.org

Georgia Governor's Scholarship

Type of award: Scholarship, renewable.
Intended use: For full-time undergraduate study at accredited 2-year or 4-year institution.
Eligibility: Applicant must be high school senior. Applicant must be U.S. citizen or permanent resident residing in Georgia.
Basis for selection: Applicant must demonstrate high academic achievement.
Additional information: Must be valedictorian or STAR Student. Must enroll at eligible Georgia school within nine months of high school graduation. Must maintain 3.0 GPA with 30 semester hours earned each year to renew.
    Amount of award: $900
    Number of awards: 2,828
    Total amount awarded: $2,709,516
Contact:
Georgia Student Finance Commission
2082 East Exchange Place
Suite 100
Tucker, GA 30084
Phone: 800-505-4732
Fax: 770-724-9004
Web: www.gacollege411.org

Georgia Hope Grant - GED Recipient

Type of award: Scholarship.
Intended use: For undergraduate study at accredited vocational, 2-year or 4-year institution. Designated institutions: Branches of University System of Georgia, Georgia Department of Technical and Adult Education, and HOPE-eligible private colleges and universities in Georgia.
Eligibility: Applicant must be U.S. citizen or permanent resident residing in Georgia.
Application requirements: Proof of eligibility.
Additional information: Must have received GED from Georgia Department of Technical and Adult Education after June 30, 1993. Submit HOPE voucher upon enrollment. Students receiving GED from DTAE receive voucher automatically.
    Amount of award: $500
    Number of awards: 4,947
    Total amount awarded: $2,467,836
Contact:
Georgia Student Finance Commission
2082 East Exchange Place, Suite 100
Tucker, GA 30084
Phone: 800-505-4732
Fax: 770-724-9004
Web: www.gacollege411.org

Georgia Hope Grant - Public Technical Institution

Type of award: Scholarship, renewable.

Intended use: For undergraduate certificate study at accredited vocational, 2-year or 4-year institution. Designated institutions: Branches and affiliates of the Georgia Department of Technical and Adult Education and branches of the University System of Georgia.
Eligibility: Applicant must be U.S. citizen or permanent resident residing in Georgia.
Application requirements: FAFSA or HOPE application.
Additional information: Scholarship covers tuition, mandatory fees plus book allowance up to $150 per semester for full-time students. Must be enrolled, matriculated technical certificate or diploma student.

Amount of award:	Full tuition
Number of awards:	104,707
Total amount awarded:	$86,910,529

Contact:
Georgia Student Finance Commission
2082 East Exchange Place
Suite 100
Tucker, GA 30084
Phone: 800-505-4732
Fax: 770-724-9004
Web: www.gacollege411.org

Georgia Hope Scholarship - Private Institution

Type of award: Scholarship, renewable.
Intended use: For undergraduate study at accredited 2-year or 4-year institution. Designated institutions: Georgia private colleges and universities.
Eligibility: Applicant must be U.S. citizen or permanent resident residing in Georgia.
Basis for selection: Applicant must demonstrate high academic achievement.
Application requirements: GSPAFFS or HOPE/Georgia Tuition Equalization Grant (TEG) Application.
Additional information: Award designed to help academically outstanding pupils. Must be attending eligible college or university in Georgia. Minimum 3.0 GPA required.

Amount of award:	$1,500-$3,000
Number of awards:	14,861
Total amount awarded:	$39,490,821

Contact:
Georgia Student Finance Commission
2082 East Exchange Place, Suite 100
Tucker, GA 30084
Phone: 800-505-4732
Fax: 770-724-9004
Web: www.gacollege411.org

Georgia Hope Scholarship - Public College or University

Type of award: Scholarship, renewable.
Intended use: For undergraduate study at accredited 2-year or 4-year institution. Designated institutions: Eligible Georgia public colleges and universities.
Eligibility: Applicant must be U.S. citizen or permanent resident residing in Georgia.
Basis for selection: Applicant must demonstrate high academic achievement.
Application requirements: Proof of eligibility. FAFSA, GSFAPPS, or HOPE application.
Additional information: Minimum 3.0 GPA. HOPE assistance includes any tuition, mandatory fees. Also includes book allowance for up to $150 per semester. Applicant must have graduated high school after 1993. Must be designated HOPE scholar.

Amount of award:	Full tuition
Number of awards:	76,692
Total amount awarded:	$189,979,288

Contact:
Georgia Student Finance Commission
2082 East Exchange Place
Suite 100
Tucker, GA 30084
Phone: 800-505-4732
Fax: 770-724-9004
Web: www.gacollege411.org

Georgia Law Enforcement Personnel Dependents Grant

Type of award: Scholarship, renewable.
Intended use: For full-time undergraduate study at accredited vocational, 2-year or 4-year institution. Designated institutions: Georgia private and public colleges and public technical institutes.
Eligibility: Applicant must be U.S. citizen or permanent resident residing in Georgia. Applicant's parent must have been killed or disabled in work-related accident as firefighter, police officer or public safety officer.
Application requirements: Proof of eligibility. GSFAPPS or LEPD Grant application.
Additional information: Must complete preliminary document that verifies claim with parent's former employer and doctors. Application deadline is last day of registration for school term. Parent must have been permanently disabled or killed in the line of duty as Georgia police officer, firefighter, emergency medical technician or corrections officer.

Amount of award:	$2,000
Total amount awarded:	$64,270

Contact:
Georgia Student Finance Commission
2082 East Exchange Place
Suite 100
Tucker, GA 30084
Phone: 800-505-4732
Fax: 770-724-9004
Web: www.gacollege411.org

Georgia LEAP Grant

Type of award: Scholarship, renewable.
Intended use: For undergraduate study.
Eligibility: Applicant must be residing in Georgia.
Basis for selection: Applicant must demonstrate financial need.
Application requirements: FAFSA.

Amount of award:	$300-$2,000
Number of awards:	3,135
Total amount awarded:	$1,475,500

Contact:
Georgia Student Finance Commission
2082 East Exchange Place
Suite 100
Tucker, GA 30084
Phone: 800-505-4732
Fax: 770-724-9004
Web: www.gacollege411.org

Georgia Robert C. Byrd Scholarship

Type of award: Scholarship, renewable.

Intended use: For full-time undergraduate study at accredited 2-year or 4-year institution in United States.
Eligibility: Applicant must be high school senior. Applicant must be U.S. citizen or permanent resident residing in Georgia.
Basis for selection: Applicant must demonstrate high academic achievement, depth of character, leadership, seriousness of purpose and service orientation.
Application requirements: Recommendations, essay, transcript, proof of eligibility.
Additional information: Application submitted to the Georgia Department of Education. Obtain application from high school guidance office.

Amount of award:	$1,500
Number of awards:	703
Total amount awarded:	$1,023,545

Contact:
Georgia Student Finance Commission
Grants and Scholarships Section
2082 East Exchange Place, Suite 100
Tucker, GA 30084
Phone: 800-505-4732
Fax: 770-724-9004
Web: www.gacollege411.org

Georgia Tuition Equalization Grant

Type of award: Scholarship, renewable.
Intended use: For full-time undergraduate study at accredited 2-year or 4-year institution. Designated institutions: Agnes Scott College, American Intercontinental University, Andrew College, Argosy University, Atlanta Christian College, Atlanta College of Art, Art Institute of Atlanta, Bauder College, Berry College, Brenau College, Brewton-Parker College, Clark Atlanta University, Covenant College, DeVry Institute, Embry-Riddle Aeronautical University, Emmanuel College, Emory University, Georgia Military College, Herzing College, LaGrange College, Life College, Mercer University, Morehouse College, Oglethorpe University, Oxford College, Paine College, Piedmont College, Reinhardt College, Saint Leo University, Savannah College of Art and Design, Shorter College, Spelman College, South University, Thomas College, Toccoa Falls College, Truett-McConnell College, Wesleyan College, Young Harris College. Also Clemson University, Florida A&M University, Florida State University, Troy State University at Dothan, University of Tennessee/Chattanooga.
Eligibility: Applicant must be U.S. citizen or permanent resident residing in Georgia.
Application requirements: Proof of eligibility. Mileage affidavit (for out-of-state schools only).
Additional information: Must be enrolled full-time at eligible private college or university in Georgia, or be a junior or senior with no Georgia public college within 50 miles of home and enrolled at eligible public college outside Georgia. Application deadlines set by schools.

Number of awards:	34,477
Total amount awarded:	$33,123,310

Contact:
Georgia Student Finance Commission
2082 East Exchange Place
Suite 100
Tucker, GA 30084
Phone: 800-505-4732
Fax: 770-724-9004
Web: www.gacollege411.org

Glamour Magazine

Top 10 College Women Competition

Type of award: Scholarship.
Intended use: For full-time junior study at accredited 4-year institution.
Eligibility: Applicant must be female.
Basis for selection: Applicant must demonstrate high academic achievement, depth of character, leadership, seriousness of purpose and service orientation.
Application requirements: Recommendations, essay, transcript. List of activities and organizations; black-and-white or color photograph.
Additional information: Selection based on meritorious attributes. Award includes trip to New York City. See Website for application.

Amount of award:	$3,000
Number of awards:	10
Number of applicants:	600
Application deadline:	November 30
Notification begins:	June 15

Contact:
Glamour Magazine
4 Times Square
16th Floor
New York, NY 10036-6593
Phone: 212-286-6667
Fax: 212-286-6922
Web: www.glamour.com

Golden Key International Honor Society

Business Achievement Awards

Type of award: Scholarship.
Intended use: For undergraduate or graduate study at accredited postsecondary institution.
Eligibility: Applicant or parent must be member/participant of Golden Key National Honor Society.
Basis for selection: Major/career interest in business. Applicant must demonstrate high academic achievement.
Application requirements: Recommendations, transcript. Business plan (must not exceed ten typed pages).
Additional information: Open to Golden Key members only. First-place winner receives $1,000; second place, $750; third place, $500. Visit Website for details and application.

Amount of award:	$500-$1,000
Number of awards:	3
Application deadline:	March 1
Total amount awarded:	$2,250

Contact:
Business Achievement Awards
Golden Key International Honor Society
P.O. Box 23737
Nashville, TN 37202-3737
Phone: 800-377-2401
Fax: 404-373-7033
Web: www.goldenkey.org

Education Achievement Awards

Type of award: Scholarship.
Intended use: For undergraduate or graduate study at accredited postsecondary institution.
Eligibility: Applicant or parent must be member/participant of Golden Key National Honor Society.
Basis for selection: Major/career interest in education. Applicant must demonstrate high academic achievement.
Application requirements: Recommendations, essay, transcript. An education related paper (no more than 10 pages); a two-page essay describing the assignment, the greatest challenge it presented, what lessons it taught, and what you would change, if you were to redo the report.
Additional information: Open to Golden Key members only. First-place winner receives $1,000; second place, $750; third place, $500. Visit Website for details and application.
    Amount of award: $500-$1,000
    Number of awards: 3
    Application deadline: March 1
    Total amount awarded: $2,250
Contact:
Education Achievement Awards
Golden Key International Honor Society
1189 Ponce de Leon Avenue
Atlanta, GA 30306-4624
Phone: 800-377-2401
Fax: 404-373-7033
Web: www.goldenkey.org

Engineering/Technology Achievement Awards

Type of award: Scholarship.
Intended use: For undergraduate or graduate study at accredited postsecondary institution.
Eligibility: Applicant or parent must be member/participant of Golden Key National Honor Society.
Basis for selection: Major/career interest in engineering.
Application requirements: Recommendations, essay, transcript. An engineering related paper (no more than 10 pages of text); a two-page essay describing the assignment, the greatest challenge it presented, what lessons it taught, and what you would change, if you were to redo the report.
Additional information: Open to Golden Key members only. First-place winner receives $1,000; second place, $750; third place, $500. Visit Website for details and application.
    Amount of award: $500-$1,000
    Number of awards: 3
    Application deadline: March 1
    Total amount awarded: $2,250
Contact:
Engineering/Technology Achievement Awards
Golden Key International Society
P.O. Box 23737
Nashville, TN 37202-3737
Phone: 800-377-2401
Fax: 404-373-7033
Web: www.goldenkey.org

GEICO Life Scholarship

Type of award: Scholarship.
Intended use: For undergraduate study at accredited postsecondary institution.
Eligibility: Applicant or parent must be member/participant of Golden Key National Honor Society. Applicant must be at least 25, returning adult student.
Basis for selection: Applicant must demonstrate high academic achievement.
Application requirements: Recommendations, essay, transcript. Personal essay of no more than 500 words and describe educational goals, other commitments, and obstacles overcome to achieve academic excellence.
Additional information: Only undergraduate Golden Key members 25 years of age or older are eligible to apply. Applicants must have completed at least 12 credit hours since returning to school. Visit Website for details and application.
    Amount of award: $1,000
    Number of awards: 10
    Number of applicants: 100
    Application deadline: April 1
    Total amount awarded: $10,000
Contact:
Golden Key International Honor Society
Attn: Scholarships
P.O. Box 23737
Nashville, TN 37202-3737
Phone: 800-377-2401
Fax: 404-373-7033
Web: www.goldenkey.org

Golden Key Research Grants

Type of award: Research grant.
Intended use: For undergraduate study.
Eligibility: Applicant or parent must be member/participant of Golden Key National Honor Society.
Basis for selection: Applicant must demonstrate high academic achievement.
Application requirements: Transcript. Budget summary and description of proposed research.
Additional information: Only undergraduate Golden Key members eligible to apply. Grant for members to travel to professional conferences and research symposia where they have been invited to present. Grants may also assist students who need funding to pursue field research related to honors thesis. Three awards will be presented for the October 15 deadline, seven for the April 15 deadline. Visit Website for details and application.
    Amount of award: $500
    Number of awards: 10
    Number of applicants: 75
    Application deadline: April 15, October 15
    Total amount awarded: $5,000
Contact:
Golden Key International Honor Society
Attn: Scholarships
P.O. Box 23737
Nashville, TN 37202-3737
Phone: 800-377-2401
Fax: 404-373-7033
Web: www.goldenkey.org

Golden Key Service Award

Type of award: Scholarship.
Intended use: For undergraduate or graduate study at accredited postsecondary institution.
Eligibility: Applicant or parent must be member/participant of Golden Key National Honor Society.
Basis for selection: Applicant must demonstrate service orientation.

Golden Key International Honor Society: Golden Key Service Award

Application requirements: Recommendations, essay. One recommendation from Golden Key chapter advisor, one from representative of selected charity; list of extracurricular activities.
Additional information: Only Golden Key members enrolled as students during previous academic year eligible to apply. Winner will receive $250; charity of winner's choice will receive $250. Visit Website for details and application.

Amount of award:	$500
Number of awards:	1
Application deadline:	March 1
Total amount awarded:	$500

Contact:
Golden Key International Honor Society
Attn: Scholarships
P.O. Box 23737
Nashville, TN 37202-3737
Phone: 800-377-2401
Fax: 404-373-7033
Web: www.goldenkey.org

Golden Key Study Abroad Scholarships

Type of award: Scholarship.
Intended use: For undergraduate study.
Eligibility: Applicant or parent must be member/participant of Golden Key National Honor Society.
Basis for selection: Competition/talent/interest in study abroad. Applicant must demonstrate high academic achievement.
Application requirements: Transcript. Details of Golden Key activities. Description of planned study program at host university. Statement of relevance of program to degree.
Additional information: Only undergraduate Golden Key members eligible to apply. Three awards presented for the October 15 deadline and seven for the April 15 deadline. Visit Website for details and application.

Amount of award:	$1,000
Number of awards:	10
Number of applicants:	200
Application deadline:	April 15, October 15
Total amount awarded:	$10,000

Contact:
Golden Key Study Abroad Scholarships
Golden Key National Honor Society
P.O. Box 23737
Nashville, TN 37202-3737
Phone: 800-377-2401
Fax: 404-373-7033
Web: www.goldenkey.org

Literary Achievement Awards

Type of award: Scholarship.
Intended use: For undergraduate or graduate study at accredited postsecondary institution.
Eligibility: Applicant or parent must be member/participant of Golden Key National Honor Society.
Basis for selection: Competition/talent/interest in writing/journalism.
Additional information: Open to Golden Key members only. $1,000 awarded to winners in each of four categories: fiction, non-fiction, poetry, and feature writing. Entry must be original composition; previously published works not accepted. Winning entries also published in CONCEPTS. Only one entry per member per category. Entry must not exceed 1,500 words. Visit Website for details and application.

Amount of award:	$1,000
Number of awards:	4
Application deadline:	April 1
Total amount awarded:	$4,000

Contact:
Golden Key International Honor Society
Attn: Scholarships
P.O. Box 23737
Nashville, TN 30202-3737
Phone: 800-377-2401
Web: www.goldenkey.org

Student Leader Award

Type of award: Scholarship.
Intended use: For undergraduate or graduate study at accredited postsecondary institution.
Eligibility: Applicant or parent must be member/participant of Golden Key National Honor Society.
Basis for selection: Applicant must demonstrate high academic achievement, leadership and service orientation.
Application requirements: Recommendations, essay, transcript. List of personal Golden Key involvement and extracurricular activities. A personal statement of no more than 1,000 words explaining why the applicant feels that he or she should receive a Student Leader Award.
Additional information: Open to Golden Key members only. Applicant must be active member in good standing. Must be currently enrolled in an undergraduate or graduate program in accredited college/university. Winners at regional level will be considered for International Student Leader Award. Application date varies by region; visit Website for details and application.

Amount of award:	$500-$1,500
Number of awards:	13
Total amount awarded:	$7,500

Contact:
International Student Leader Award
Student Leader Awards
621 North Avenue, NE, Suite C-100
Atlanta, GA 30308
Phone: 800-377-2401
Fax: 404-373-7033
Web: www.goldenkey.org

Visual and Performing Arts Achievement Award

Type of award: Scholarship.
Intended use: For undergraduate or graduate study at accredited postsecondary institution.
Eligibility: Applicant or parent must be member/participant of Golden Key National Honor Society.
Basis for selection: Based on artistic merit.
Application requirements: Slides of visual work; video or DVD of performance (10 minute maximum).
Additional information: Open to Golden Key members only. $500 awarded to winners in each of nine categories: painting, drawing, mixed media, sculpture, photography, computer-generated art/illustration/graphic design, instrumental performance, vocal performance and dance. Winning entries published in CONCEPTS and displayed at annual convention. One entry per member per category. Visit Website for details and application.

Amount of award:	$500
Number of awards:	9
Number of applicants:	600
Application deadline:	April 1
Total amount awarded:	$4,500

Contact:
Art International
Golden Key International Honor Society
P.O. Box 23737
Nashville, TN 37202-3737
Phone: 800-377-2401
Fax: 404-373-7033
Web: www.goldenkey.org

Golf Course Superintendents Association of America

GCSAA Legacy Awards

Type of award: Scholarship.
Intended use: For full-time undergraduate study at accredited 2-year, 4-year or graduate institution.
Eligibility: Applicant or parent must be member/participant of Golf Course Superintendents Association of America.
Application requirements: Recommendations, essay, transcript.
Additional information: Applicants must be child or grandchild of GCSAA members active for at least five years. Must be enrolled full-time at accredited postsecondary institution or, if high school senior, must be accepted for following academic year. Must be studying field unrelated to golf course management. Award is funded by Syngenta Professional Products. Visit Website or contact via e-mail (ahoward@gcsaa.org) for more information.

Amount of award:	$1,500
Number of awards:	20
Application deadline:	April 15
Notification begins:	June 15
Total amount awarded:	$30,000

Contact:
Senior Manager of Development
Attn: Mischia Wright
1421 Research Park Drive
Lawrence, KS 66049
Phone: 800-472-7878 ext. 4445
Fax: 785-832-3673
Web: www.gcsaa.org

GCSAA Scholars Competition

Type of award: Scholarship.
Intended use: For sophomore, junior or senior study at accredited 2-year or 4-year institution.
Eligibility: Applicant or parent must be member/participant of Golf Course Superintendents Association of America.
Basis for selection: Major/career interest in turf management. Applicant must demonstrate high academic achievement.
Application requirements: Recommendations, essay, transcript.
Additional information: Applicant must be GCSAA member. Must be planning career as golf course superintendent and have successfully completed at least one year of full-time study in golf course management program. Employees of GCSAA and their children are ineligible. Visit Website for more information.

Amount of award:	$500-$6,000
Number of awards:	24
Application deadline:	June 1

Contact:
Senior Manager of Development
Attn: Mischia Wright
1421 Research Park Drive
Lawrence, KS 66049-3859
Phone: 800-472-7878 ext. 4445
Fax: 785-832-3673
Web: www.gcsaa.org

GCSAA Student Essay Contest

Type of award: Scholarship.
Intended use: For undergraduate or graduate study at accredited 2-year, 4-year or graduate institution.
Eligibility: Applicant or parent must be member/participant of Golf Course Superintendents Association of America.
Basis for selection: Competition/talent/interest in writing/journalism, based on seven- to twelve-page essay focusing on golf-course management. Major/career interest in turf management.
Additional information: Applicant must be member of GCSAA. Applicant must be pursuing degree in turfgrass science, agronomy or other field related to golf-course management. First place award, $2,000; 2nd, $1,500; 3rd, $1,000. Visit Website or contact via e-mail (ahoward@gcsaa.org) for more information.

Amount of award:	$1,000-$2,000
Number of awards:	3
Application deadline:	March 31
Total amount awarded:	$4,500

Contact:
Senior Manager of Development
Attn: Mischia Wright
1421 Research Park Drive
Lawrence, KS 66049
Phone: 800-472-7878 ext. 4445
Fax: 785-832-3673
Web: www.gcsaa.org

Scotts Company Scholars Program

Type of award: Scholarship.
Intended use: For undergraduate study at accredited 2-year or 4-year institution.
Basis for selection: Major/career interest in turf management.
Application requirements: Recommendations, transcript. Two recommendations (academic or professional).
Additional information: Five finalists are selected for summer internships, and receive $500 award and chance to compete for two $2,500 scholarships. Applicants must be pursuing career in the green industry. Women, minorities, and persons with disabilities encouraged to apply. Visit Website or contact via e-mail (ahoward@gcsaa.org) for more information.

Amount of award:	$500-$2,500
Number of awards:	7
Application deadline:	March 1
Total amount awarded:	$7,500

Contact:
Senior Manager of Development
Attn: Mischia Wright
1421 Research Park Drive
Lawrence, KS 66049
Phone: 800-472-7878 ext. 4445
Fax: 785-832-3673
Web: www.gcsaa.org

Grange Insurance Association

Grange Insurance Scholarship

Type of award: Scholarship.
Intended use: For full-time undergraduate or graduate study at accredited vocational, 2-year, 4-year or graduate institution.
Eligibility: Applicant must be U.S. citizen or permanent resident residing in Wyoming, California, Oregon, Idaho, Washington or Colorado.
Basis for selection: Applicant must demonstrate financial need, high academic achievement, depth of character, leadership, patriotism, seriousness of purpose and service orientation.
Application requirements: Essay, transcript. Cover Letter.
Additional information: Applicant or parent must be permanent resident of the designated state and member of The Grange in that state. Applicant or parent need not have insurance with The Grange. Applicants must be GIG policyholders or children and grandchildren of GIG policyholders within the 6 states in which GIG operates: CA, CO, ID, OR, WA and WY, or children and grandchildren of Fraternal Grange members or the children and grandchildren of GIG company employees. Previous recipients also eligible to apply.
   Amount of award: $1,000-$1,500
   Number of awards: 25
   Number of applicants: 102
   Application deadline: April 15
   Notification begins: May 15
   Total amount awarded: $26,500
Contact:
Grange Insurance Association
Scholarship Committee
P.O. Box 21089
Seattle, WA 98111-3089
Phone: 800-247-2643 ext. 2200
Web: www.grange.com

Greater Kanawha Valley Foundation

Greater Kanawha Valley Scholarship Program

Type of award: Scholarship, renewable.
Intended use: For full-time undergraduate or graduate study at postsecondary institution.
Eligibility: Applicant must be residing in West Virginia.
Basis for selection: Applicant must demonstrate financial need, high academic achievement, depth of character and leadership.
Application requirements: Recommendations, essay, transcript.
Additional information: Greater Kanawha Valley Foundation offers several scholarships. Visit Website for complete listing. Student must have a minimum of 20 ACT.
   Amount of award: $1,000
   Number of applicants: 1,300
   Application deadline: January 15
   Notification begins: May 1
Contact:
Greater Kanawha Valley Foundation
P.O. Box 3041
Charleston, WV 25331
Phone: 304-346-3620
Web: www.tgkvf.org

Greenhouse Partners

Greenhouse Scholars

Type of award: Scholarship, renewable.
Intended use: For full-time undergraduate study at 4-year institution.
Eligibility: Applicant must be high school senior. Applicant must be U.S. citizen or permanent resident residing in Colorado.
Basis for selection: Applicant must demonstrate financial need, high academic achievement, depth of character, leadership, seriousness of purpose and service orientation.
Application requirements: Recommendations, essay, transcript.
Additional information: The Greenhouse Scholars Program is a scholarship and mentorship program for under-resourced, high-achieving students. The program uses a 'Whole Person' approach to address the intellectual, academic, professional, and financial needs of students. Minimum 3.5 GPA. Renewable for four years. Visit Website for application and more information.
   Amount of award: $1,000-$5,000
   Number of awards: 15
   Application deadline: February 11
   Total amount awarded: $25,000
Contact:
Greenhouse Scholars
1011 Walnut Street, Third Floor
Boulder, CO 80302
Phone: 303-464-7811
Fax: 303-464-7796
Web: www.greenhousescholars.org

Harness Tracks of America

Harness Tracks of America Scholarship Fund

Type of award: Scholarship.
Intended use: For full-time undergraduate or graduate study at accredited postsecondary institution.

Eligibility: Applicant or parent must be member/participant of Harness Racing Industry.
Basis for selection: Applicant must demonstrate financial need and high academic achievement.
Application requirements: Essay, transcript, proof of eligibility. FAFSA, and U.S. or Canadian tax return.
Additional information: Must be child of licensed driver, trainer, breeder, owner or caretaker of harness horses or be personally active in harness racing industry. Children of deceased industry members also eligible. Recommendations not required but considered if included with application. Awards based on financial need, academic excellence and active harness racing involvement. Visit Website for more information.

Amount of award:	$5,000
Number of awards:	5
Number of applicants:	38
Application deadline:	June 15
Notification begins:	September 15
Total amount awarded:	$25,000

Contact:
Harness Tracks of America
4640 East Sunrise Drive
Suite 200
Tucson, AZ 85718
Phone: 520-529-2525
Fax: 520-529-3235
Web: www.harnesstracks.com

Harry S. Truman Scholarship Foundation

Harry S. Truman Scholarship

Type of award: Scholarship.
Intended use: For junior study.
Eligibility: Applicant must be U.S. citizen.
Basis for selection: Major/career interest in public administration/service; governmental public relations; political science/government or education. Applicant must demonstrate high academic achievement, leadership, seriousness of purpose and service orientation.
Application requirements: Recommendations, transcript, nomination by Truman Scholarship Faculty Representative at applicant's school. Signed Institution Nomination Form, a signed Nominee Information Form, and an analysis of public policy issue.
Additional information: Award to be used for public service-related graduate study. Applicants must participate in Truman Scholars Leadership Week and Awards Ceremony at Harry S. Truman Library. Open to all fields of study as long as candidate plans to use degree in public service. Must be in upper third of class. United States nationals from American Samoa or the Commonwealth of the Northern Mariana Islands also eligible. Visit Website for application and important dates.

Amount of award:	$30,000
Number of awards:	65
Number of applicants:	600
Application deadline:	February 5
Notification begins:	February 20

Contact:
Harry Truman Scholarship Foundation
712 Jackson Place NW
Washington, DC 20006
Phone: 202-395-4831
Web: www.truman.gov

Havana National Bank

McFarland Charitable Foundation Scholarship

Type of award: Scholarship, renewable.
Intended use: For full-time undergraduate study at accredited vocational, 2-year or 4-year institution in United States.
Eligibility: Applicant must be residing in Illinois.
Basis for selection: Major/career interest in nursing. Applicant must demonstrate seriousness of purpose.
Application requirements: Interview, recommendations, transcript, proof of eligibility. Letter of acceptance to RN program, two letters of recommendation.
Additional information: Award recipients must contractually obligate themselves to return to Havana, Illinois, and work as registered nurses for two years for each year of funding. Reverts to loan if work obligation is not met. Two Cosigners are required. To fund RN programs only. Number of awards and amounts vary.

Amount of award:	$1,000-$20,000
Number of awards:	3
Number of applicants:	6
Application deadline:	May 1
Notification begins:	June 15
Total amount awarded:	$75,000

Contact:
Havana National Bank
112 South Orange
P.O. Box 200
Havana, IL 62644-0200
Phone: 309-543-3361
Web: www.havanabank.com

Hawaii Community Foundation

Aiea General Hospital Association Scholarship

Type of award: Scholarship, renewable.
Intended use: For full-time undergraduate or graduate study at accredited 2-year, 4-year or graduate institution in United States.
Eligibility: Applicant must be U.S. citizen or permanent resident residing in Hawaii.
Basis for selection: Major/career interest in health-related professions. Applicant must demonstrate financial need, high academic achievement and depth of character.
Application requirements: Recommendations, essay, transcript. FAFSA and SAR.
Additional information: Minimum 2.7 GPA required. Applicant must be resident of Leeward Oahu ZIP Codes:

96701, 96706, 96707, 96782, 96792, or 98797. Amount and number of awards vary and may change yearly.

Amount of award:	$1,000
Number of awards:	26
Application deadline:	March 1

Contact:
Hawaii Community Foundation Scholarships
1164 Bishop Street
Suite 800
Honolulu, HI 96813
Phone: 888-731-3863
Fax: 808-521-6286
Web: www.hawaiicommunityfoundation.org

Alma White-Delta Kappa Gamma Scholarship

Type of award: Scholarship.
Intended use: For full-time junior, senior or graduate study at accredited postsecondary institution in United States.
Eligibility: Applicant must be U.S. citizen or permanent resident residing in Hawaii.
Basis for selection: Major/career interest in education. Applicant must demonstrate financial need, high academic achievement and depth of character.
Application requirements: Recommendations, essay, transcript. FAFSA and SAR. Official letter confirming enrollment in education program.
Additional information: Minimum 2.7 GPA required. Applicants must have permanent address in Hawaii. Applicants taking up mainland residency must have relatives living in Hawaii. Amount and number of awards vary and may change yearly.

Amount of award:	$1,500
Number of awards:	10
Application deadline:	March 1

Contact:
Hawaii Community Foundation Scholarships
1164 Bishop Street
Suite 800
Honolulu, HI 96813
Phone: 888-731-3863
Fax: 808-521-6286
Web: www.hawaiicommunityfoundation.org

Ambassador Minerva Jean Falcon Hawaii Scholarship

Type of award: Scholarship.
Intended use: For full-time freshman study at accredited 2-year or 4-year institution.
Eligibility: Applicant must be of Filipino ancestry. Applicant must be U.S. citizen or permanent resident residing in Hawaii.
Basis for selection: Applicant must demonstrate financial need, high academic achievement, depth of character and service orientation.
Application requirements: Recommendations, essay, transcript. FAFSA and SAR.
Additional information: Minimum 2.7 GPA. Must be incoming college freshman. Amount of scholarship varies yearly. Applicants must have permanent address in Hawaii. Notifications mailed between April and June. Visit Website for details and application.

Amount of award:	$1,000
Number of awards:	1
Application deadline:	March 1

Contact:
Hawaii Community Foundation Scholarships
1164 Bishop Street
Suite 800
Honolulu, HI 96813
Phone: 888-731-3863
Fax: 808-521-6286
Web: www.hawaiicommunityfoundation.org

American Savings Bank Scholars Program

Type of award: Scholarship.
Intended use: For undergraduate study at 4-year institution in United States.
Eligibility: Applicant must be U.S. citizen residing in Hawaii.
Basis for selection: Major/career interest in business. Applicant must demonstrate service orientation.
Application requirements: Recommendations, essay, transcript. SAR, personal statement describing participation in community service projects.
Additional information: Minimum 3.0 GPA.

Amount of award:	$5,000
Number of awards:	3
Application deadline:	March 1
Total amount awarded:	$15,000

Contact:
Hawaii Community Foundation - Scholarships
1164 Bishop Street
Suite 800
Honolulu, HI 96813
Phone: 808-566-5570
Fax: 808-521-6286
Web: www.hawaiicommunityfoundation.org

Bal Dasa Scholarship Fund

Type of award: Scholarship.
Intended use: For full-time undergraduate study at accredited 2-year or 4-year institution in United States.
Eligibility: Applicant must be U.S. citizen or permanent resident residing in Hawaii.
Basis for selection: Applicant must demonstrate financial need, high academic achievement and depth of character.
Application requirements: Essay, transcript. FAFSA and SAR.
Additional information: Minimum 2.7 GPA required. Applicant must be a graduate of Waipahu High School. Amount of scholarship varies yearly. Applicants must have permanent address in Hawaii. Applicants taking up mainland residency must have relatives living in Hawaii.

Amount of award:	$2,000
Number of awards:	1
Application deadline:	March 1

Contact:
Hawaii Community Foundation Scholarships
1164 Bishop Street
Suite 800
Honolulu, HI 96813
Phone: 888-731-3863
Fax: 808-521-6286
Web: www.hawaiicommunityfoundation.org

Blossom Kalama Evans Memorial Scholarship

Type of award: Scholarship, renewable.

Intended use: For full-time junior, senior or graduate study at accredited 4-year or graduate institution in United States.
Eligibility: Applicant must be U.S. citizen or permanent resident residing in Hawaii.
Basis for selection: Major/career interest in hawaiian studies. Applicant must demonstrate financial need, high academic achievement and depth of character.
Application requirements: Essay, transcript. FAFSA and SAR. Essay must state how applicant's knowledge will be used to serve the needs of the Native Hawaiian community.
Additional information: Minimum 2.7 GPA required. Students must be of Hawaiian ancestry. Applicants must have permanent address in Hawaii. Applicants who take up mainland residency must have relatives living in Hawaii. Amount and number of awards vary.
    Amount of award: $1,166
    Number of awards: 9
    Application deadline: March 1
Contact:
Hawaii Community Foundation Scholarships
1164 Bishop Street
Suite 800
Honolulu, HI 96813
Phone: 888-731-3863
Fax: 808-521-6286
Web: www.hawaiicommunityfoundation.org

Camille C. Chidiac Fund

Type of award: Scholarship.
Intended use: For full-time undergraduate study at accredited 2-year or 4-year institution in United States.
Eligibility: Applicant must be high school senior. Applicant must be U.S. citizen or permanent resident residing in Hawaii.
Basis for selection: Applicant must demonstrate financial need, high academic achievement and depth of character.
Application requirements: Essay, transcript. FAFSA and SAR. Essay must state why it is important for Hawaii students to be internationally aware.
Additional information: Minimum 2.7 GPA required. Applicant must be student at Ka'u High School. Amount of scholarship varies yearly. Applicants taking up mainland residency must have relatives living in Hawaii.
    Amount of award: $800
    Number of awards: 1
    Application deadline: March 1
Contact:
Hawaii Community Foundation Scholarships
1164 Bishop Street
Suite 800
Honolulu, HI 96813
Phone: 888-731-3863
Fax: 808-521-6286
Web: www.hawaiicommunityfoundation.org

Candon Consulting Group Scholarship Fund

Type of award: Scholarship.
Intended use: For junior or senior study at 4-year institution in United States.
Eligibility: Applicant must be U.S. citizen residing in Hawaii.
Basis for selection: Major/career interest in accounting or finance/banking.
Application requirements: Recommendations, essay, transcript. SAR.
Additional information: Minimum 2.7 GPA.

    Amount of award: $500
    Number of awards: 1
    Application deadline: March 1
Contact:
Hawaii Community Foundation - Scholarships
1164 Bishop St
Suite 800
Honolulu, HI 96813
Phone: 808-566-5570
Fax: 808-521-6286
Web: www.hawaiicommunityfoundation.org

Castle & Cooke Mililani Technology Park Scholarship Fund

Type of award: Scholarship.
Intended use: For full-time freshman study at accredited 2-year or 4-year institution in United States.
Eligibility: Applicant must be high school senior. Applicant must be U.S. citizen or permanent resident residing in Hawaii.
Basis for selection: Major/career interest in science, general; engineering or computer/information sciences. Applicant must demonstrate financial need and high academic achievement.
Application requirements: Essay, transcript. FAFSA and SAR.
Additional information: Minimum 2.7 GPA required. Applicants must be graduating senior from Leilehua, Mililani, or Waialua high schools. Preference given to majors in technology fields. Applicants must have permanent address in Hawaii. Applicants taking up mainland residency must have relatives living in Hawaii. Amount and number of awards vary and may change yearly.
    Amount of award: $1,000
    Number of awards: 10
    Application deadline: March 1
Contact:
Hawaii Community Foundation Scholarships
1164 Bishop Street
Suite 800
Honolulu, HI 96813
Phone: 888-731-3863
Fax: 808-521-6286
Web: www.hawaiicommunityfoundation.org

Cayetano Foundation Scholarship

Type of award: Scholarship.
Intended use: For full-time undergraduate study at accredited 2-year or 4-year institution.
Eligibility: Applicant must be high school senior. Applicant must be residing in Hawaii.
Basis for selection: Applicant must demonstrate financial need, high academic achievement and depth of character.
Application requirements: Recommendations, essay, transcript. FAFSA and SAR. Personal statement should describe community service. In personal essay imagine yourself in your late 50s: Reflect on your adult life, list the major accomplishments in your life, and explain why you consider them to be significant.
Additional information: Minimum 3.5 GPA required. Preference given to students with greatest financial need. Applicants must have permanent Hawaii address. Applicants taking up mainland residency must have relatives living in Hawaii.
    Amount of award: $2,000
    Number of awards: 14
    Application deadline: March 1

Community Scholarship Fund

Type of award: Scholarship, renewable.
Intended use: For full-time undergraduate or graduate study at accredited 2-year or 4-year institution in United States.
Eligibility: Applicant must be U.S. citizen or permanent resident residing in Hawaii.
Basis for selection: Major/career interest in arts, general; architecture; education; humanities/liberal arts or social/behavioral sciences. Applicant must demonstrate financial need, high academic achievement, depth of character and service orientation.
Application requirements: Essay, transcript. FAFSA and SAR.
Additional information: Minimum 3.0 GPA required. Applicant must show potential for fulfilling a community need; demonstrate accomplishment, motivation, initiative, vision, and intention of returning to or staying in Hawaii to work. Applicants must have permanent address in Hawaii. Applicants taking up mainland residency must have relatives living in Hawaii. Amount and number of awards vary and may change yearly.

Amount of award:	$1,508
Number of awards:	61
Application deadline:	March 1

Contact:
Hawaii Community Foundation Scholarships
1164 Bishop Street
Suite 800
Honolulu, HI 96813
Phone: 888-731-3863
Fax: 808-521-6286
Web: www.hawaiicommunityfoundation.org

Cora Aguda Manayan Fund

Type of award: Scholarship, renewable.
Intended use: For full-time undergraduate or graduate study at accredited postsecondary institution in United States.
Eligibility: Applicant must be of Filipino ancestry. Applicant must be U.S. citizen or permanent resident residing in Hawaii.
Basis for selection: Major/career interest in health-related professions. Applicant must demonstrate financial need, high academic achievement and depth of character.
Application requirements: Essay, transcript. FAFSA and SAR.
Additional information: Minimum 2.7 GPA required. Preference given to students studying in Hawaii. Applicants must have permanent address in Hawaii. Applicants who take up mainland residency must have relatives living in Hawaii. Amount and number of awards vary and may change yearly.

Amount of award:	$1,000
Number of awards:	10
Application deadline:	March 1

David L. Irons Memorial Scholarship Fund

Type of award: Scholarship.
Intended use: For full-time undergraduate study at accredited 2-year or 4-year institution in United States.
Eligibility: Applicant must be high school senior. Applicant must be U.S. citizen or permanent resident residing in Hawaii.
Basis for selection: Applicant must demonstrate financial need, high academic achievement and depth of character.
Application requirements: Essay, transcript. FAFSA and SAR. Essay must respond to following questions: 1) What are your educational and career goals; 2) Why did you choose these goals; 3) How would you spend a free day; 4) Who is a hero of yours, and what is an overriding quality that makes this person your hero?
Additional information: Minimum 2.7 GPA required. Applicant must be student at Punahou School. Applicants taking up mainland residency must have relatives living in Hawaii. Amount of award may change yearly.

Amount of award:	$500
Number of awards:	1
Application deadline:	March 1

Contact:
Hawaii Community Foundation Scholarships
1164 Bishop Street
Suite 800
Honolulu, HI 96813
Phone: 888-731-3863
Fax: 808-521-6286
Web: www.hawaiicommunityfoundation.org

Dolly Ching Scholarship Fund

Type of award: Scholarship.
Intended use: For full-time undergraduate study at accredited postsecondary institution in United States. Designated institutions: Institutions in University of Hawaii system.
Eligibility: Applicant must be high school senior. Applicant must be U.S. citizen or permanent resident residing in Hawaii.
Basis for selection: Applicant must demonstrate financial need, high academic achievement, depth of character and service orientation.
Application requirements: Recommendations, essay, transcript. FAFSA and SAR.
Additional information: Minimum 2.7 GPA required. Amount and number of awards vary and may change yearly. Applicant must be a resident of Kauai.

Amount of award:	$3,000
Number of awards:	1
Application deadline:	March 1

Contact:
Hawaii Community Foundation Scholarships
1164 Bishop Street
Suite 800
Honolulu, HI 96813
Phone: 888-731-3863
Fax: 808-521-6286
Web: www.hawaiicommunityfoundation.org

Doris & Clarence Glick Classical Music Scholarship

Type of award: Scholarship.
Intended use: For full-time undergraduate study at accredited 2-year or 4-year institution in United States.
Eligibility: Applicant must be residing in Hawaii.
Basis for selection: Major/career interest in music. Applicant must demonstrate financial need, high academic achievement and depth of character.
Application requirements: Essay, transcript. FAFSA and SAR. Describe in personal statement how program of study relates to classical music.
Additional information: Minimum 2.7 GPA required. Must major in music, with emphasis on classical music. Applicants must have permanent address in Hawaii. Applicants taking up mainland residency must have relatives living in Hawaii. Amount and number of awards vary and may change yearly.

    Amount of award: $1,500
    Number of awards: 4
    Application deadline: March 1

Contact:
Hawaii Community Foundation Scholarships
1164 Bishop Street
Suite 800
Honolulu, HI 96813
Phone: 888-731-3863
Fax: 808-521-6286
Web: www.hawaiicommunityfoundation.org

Dr. Alvin and Monica Saake Scholarship

Type of award: Scholarship.
Intended use: For full-time junior, senior or graduate study at accredited 2-year, 4-year or graduate institution.
Eligibility: Applicant must be residing in Hawaii.
Basis for selection: Major/career interest in physical education; athletic training; sports/sports administration; physical therapy or occupational therapy. Applicant must demonstrate financial need, high academic achievement and depth of character.
Application requirements: Essay, transcript. FAFSA and SAR.
Additional information: Minimum 2.7 GPA required. Must be majoring in kinesiology, leisure science, physical education, athletic training, exercise science, sports medicine, physical therapy, or occupational therapy. Applicant must have permanent Hawaii address. Applicants taking up mainland residency must have relatives living in Hawaii.

    Amount of award: $1,750
    Number of awards: 12
    Application deadline: March 1

Contact:
Hawaii Community Foundation Scholarships
1164 Bishop Street
Suite 800
Honolulu, HI 96813
Phone: 888-731-3863
Fax: 808-521-6286
Web: www.hawaiicommunityfoundation.org

Dr. Hans & Clara Zimmerman Foundation Education Scholarship

Type of award: Scholarship.
Intended use: For full-time undergraduate or graduate study at accredited 2-year or 4-year institution in United States.
Eligibility: Applicant must be U.S. citizen or permanent resident residing in Hawaii.
Basis for selection: Major/career interest in education or education, teacher. Applicant must demonstrate financial need, high academic achievement, depth of character and leadership.
Application requirements: Recommendations, essay, transcript. FAFSA and SAR. Personal statement describing applicant's community service projects or activities. Essay must also answer question "What is your teaching philosophy and how is it applied in classroom today?" (with one example).
Additional information: Minimum 2.8 GPA required. Preference given to nontraditional students with at least two years of teaching experience. Preference given to students of Hawaiian ethnicity and those from neighboring islands who plan to teach in Hawaii. Applicants must have permanent address in Hawaii. Amount and number of awards vary and may change yearly.

    Amount of award: $2,825
    Number of awards: 28
    Application deadline: March 1

Contact:
Hawaii Community Foundation Scholarships
1164 Bishop Street
Suite 800
Honolulu, HI 96813
Phone: 888-731-3863
Fax: 808-521-6286
Web: www.hawaiicommunityfoundation.org

Dr. Hans and Clara Zimmerman Foundation Health Scholarship

Type of award: Scholarship, renewable.
Intended use: For full-time junior, senior or graduate study at accredited postsecondary institution in United States.
Eligibility: Applicant must be U.S. citizen or permanent resident residing in Hawaii.
Basis for selection: Major/career interest in health sciences; health-related professions or medicine. Applicant must demonstrate financial need, high academic achievement and depth of character.
Application requirements: Essay, transcript. FAFSA and SAR. Personal statement should include description of applicant's community service projects or activities.
Additional information: Minimum 3.0 GPA required. Applicants must have permanent address in Hawaii. Applicants who take up mainland residency must have relatives living in Hawaii. Sports medicine and some psychology majors ineligible. Amount and number of awards vary and may change yearly.

Amount of award:	$3,741
Number of awards:	190
Application deadline:	March 1

Contact:
Hawaii Community Foundation Scholarships
1164 Bishop Street
Suite 800
Honolulu, HI 96813
Phone: 888-731-3863
Fax: 808-521-6286
Web: www.hawaiicommunityfoundation.org

Edward and Norma Doty Scholarship

Type of award: Scholarship.
Intended use: For full-time junior, senior or graduate study at accredited 2-year or 4-year institution in United States.
Eligibility: Applicant must be U.S. citizen or permanent resident residing in Hawaii.
Basis for selection: Major/career interest in gerontology. Applicant must demonstrate financial need, high academic achievement and depth of character.
Application requirements: Essay, transcript. FAFSA and SAR.
Additional information: Minimum 2.7 GPA required. Preference given to dependents of former employees of Eagle Distributors. Applicants must have permanent address in Hawaii. Applicants taking up mainland residency must have relatives living in Hawaii. Amount of award may change yearly.

Amount of award:	$1,000
Number of awards:	1
Application deadline:	March 1

Contact:
Hawaii Community Foundation Scholarships
1164 Bishop Street
Suite 800
Honolulu, HI 96813
Phone: 888-731-3863
Fax: 808-521-6286
Web: www.hawaiicommunityfoundation.org

Edward Payson and Bernice Pi'ilani Irwin Scholarship Trust Fund

Type of award: Scholarship.
Intended use: For full-time junior, senior or graduate study at accredited 4-year institution in United States.
Eligibility: Applicant must be U.S. citizen or permanent resident residing in Hawaii.
Basis for selection: Major/career interest in journalism or communications. Applicant must demonstrate financial need, high academic achievement and depth of character.
Application requirements: Essay, transcript. FAFSA and SAR.
Additional information: Minimum 2.7 GPA required. Applicants must have permanent address in Hawaii. Applicants who take up mainland residency must have relatives living in Hawaii. Amount and number of awards vary and may change yearly.

Amount of award:	$1,894
Number of awards:	19
Application deadline:	March 1

Contact:
Hawaii Community Foundation Scholarships
1164 Bishop Street
Suite 800
Honolulu, HI 96813
Phone: 888-731-3863
Fax: 808-521-6286
Web: www.hawaiicommunityfoundation.org

E.E. Black Scholarship

Type of award: Scholarship, renewable.
Intended use: For full-time undergraduate study at accredited postsecondary institution in United States.
Eligibility: Applicant or parent must be employed by Tesoro Petroleum Companies, Inc. Applicant must be U.S. citizen or permanent resident residing in Hawaii.
Basis for selection: Applicant must demonstrate financial need, high academic achievement and depth of character.
Application requirements: Essay, transcript. FAFSA and SAR. Name of Tesoro employee and relationship.
Additional information: Minimum 3.0 GPA required. Applicants must have permanent address in Hawaii. Applicants who take up mainland residency must have relatives living in Hawaii. Amount and number of awards vary and may change yearly.

Amount of award:	$1,642
Number of awards:	11
Application deadline:	March 1

Contact:
Hawaii Community Foundation Scholarships
1164 Bishop Street
Suite 800
Honolulu, HI 96813
Phone: 888-731-3863
Fax: 808-521-6286
Web: www.hawaiicommunityfoundation.org

Ellison Onizuka Memorial Scholarship

Type of award: Scholarship.
Intended use: For full-time undergraduate study at accredited 2-year or 4-year institution in United States.
Eligibility: Applicant must be high school senior. Applicant must be U.S. citizen or permanent resident residing in Hawaii.
Basis for selection: Major/career interest in aerospace. Applicant must demonstrate financial need and depth of character.
Application requirements: Recommendations, transcript, nomination. SAT scores, FAFSA, SAR and personal statement describing extracurricular activities, club affiliations, and community service projects.
Additional information: Minimum 2.7 GPA required. Applicants must have permanent address in Hawaii. Applicants who take up mainland residency must have relatives living in Hawaii. Amount and number of awards vary and may change yearly.

Amount of award:	$2,500
Number of awards:	5
Application deadline:	March 1

Contact:
Hawaii Community Foundation Scholarships
1164 Bishop Street
Suite 800
Honolulu, HI 96813
Phone: 888-731-3863
Fax: 808-521-6286
Web: www.hawaiicommunityfoundation.org

Esther Kanagawa Memorial Art Scholarship

Type of award: Scholarship.
Intended use: For full-time undergraduate or graduate study at accredited 2-year or 4-year institution in United States.
Eligibility: Applicant must be U.S. citizen or permanent resident residing in Hawaii.
Basis for selection: Major/career interest in arts, general. Applicant must demonstrate financial need, high academic achievement and depth of character.
Application requirements: Essay, transcript. FAFSA and SAR.
Additional information: Minimum 2.7 GPA required. Must major in fine art, drawing, painting, sculpture, ceramics or photography. Applicants must have permanent address in Hawaii. Applicants taking up mainland residency must have relatives living in Hawaii. Amount of award varies yearly.
  Amount of award: $1,000
  Number of awards: 2
  Application deadline: March 1
Contact:
Hawaii Community Foundation Scholarships
1164 Bishop Street
Suite 800
Honolulu, HI 96813
Phone: 888-731-3863
Fax: 808-521-6286
Web: www.hawaiicommunityfoundation.org

The Filipino Nurses' Organization of Hawaii Scholarship

Type of award: Scholarship.
Intended use: For full-time undergraduate study at accredited 2-year or 4-year institution in United States.
Eligibility: Applicant must be of Filipino ancestry. Applicant must be U.S. citizen or permanent resident residing in Hawaii.
Basis for selection: Major/career interest in nursing. Applicant must demonstrate financial need, high academic achievement, depth of character and service orientation.
Application requirements: Essay, transcript. FAFSA and SAR.
Additional information: Minimum 2.7 GPA required. Applicants must have permanent address in Hawaii. Applicants taking up mainland residency must have relatives living in Hawaii. Amount of award may vary yearly.
  Amount of award: $1,000
  Number of awards: 2
  Application deadline: March 1
Contact:
Hawaii Community Foundation Scholarships
1164 Bishop Street
Suite 800
Honolulu, HI 96813
Phone: 888-731-3863
Fax: 808-521-6286
Web: www.hawaiicommunityfoundation.org

Financial Women International Scholarship

Type of award: Scholarship.
Intended use: For full-time junior, senior or graduate study at accredited 2-year or 4-year institution in United States.
Eligibility: Applicant must be female. Applicant must be U.S. citizen or permanent resident residing in Hawaii.
Basis for selection: Major/career interest in business. Applicant must demonstrate financial need, high academic achievement and depth of character.
Application requirements: Essay, transcript. FAFSA and SAR.
Additional information: Minimum 3.5 GPA. Applicant must have permanent address in Hawaii. Applicants taking up mainland residency must have relatives living in Hawaii. Amount of award may change yearly.
  Amount of award: $2,000
  Number of awards: 1
  Application deadline: March 1
Contact:
Hawaii Community Foundation Scholarships
1164 Bishop Street
Suite 800
Honolulu, HI 96813
Phone: 888-731-3863
Fax: 808-521-6286
Web: www.hawaiicommunityfoundation.org

Fletcher & Fritzi Hoffmann Education Fund

Type of award: Scholarship.
Intended use: For full-time undergraduate study at accredited vocational, 2-year or 4-year institution.
Eligibility: Applicant must be U.S. citizen or permanent resident residing in Hawaii.
Basis for selection: Applicant must demonstrate financial need, high academic achievement and depth of character.
Application requirements: Essay, transcript. FAFSA and SAR. Essay must include information on family's history and roots in the Hamakua area.
Additional information: Minimum 2.7 GPA required. Preference given to applicants whose families worked in sugar plantation industry. Must be longtime resident of Hamakua Coast in Hawaii. Amount of award may change yearly.
  Amount of award: $500
  Number of awards: 1
  Application deadline: March 1
Contact:
Hawaii Community Foundation Scholarships
1164 Bishop Street
Suite 800
Honolulu, HI 96813
Phone: 888-731-3863
Fax: 808-521-6286
Web: www.hawaiicommunityfoundation.org

Friends of Hawaii Public Housing Scholarship

Type of award: Scholarship.
Intended use: For full-time undergraduate or graduate study at accredited 2-year or 4-year institution in United States.
Eligibility: Applicant must be U.S. citizen or permanent resident residing in Hawaii.

Basis for selection: Applicant must demonstrate financial need, high academic achievement and depth of character.
Application requirements: Essay, transcript, proof of eligibility. FAFSA and SAR. Essay must include name of public housing complex in personal statement.
Additional information: Minimum 2.7 GPA required. Applicant must be resident of public housing unit in Hawaii. Amount and number of awards may change yearly.
   Amount of award: $500
   Number of awards: 6
   Application deadline: March 1
Contact:
Hawaii Community Foundation Scholarships
1164 Bishop Street
Suite 800
Honolulu, HI 96813
Phone: 888-731-3863
Fax: 808-521-6286
Web: www.hawaiicommunityfoundation.org

George Mason Business Scholarship Fund

Type of award: Scholarship.
Intended use: For full-time senior study at accredited 4-year institution.
Eligibility: Applicant must be residing in Hawaii.
Basis for selection: Major/career interest in business or business/management/administration. Applicant must demonstrate financial need, high academic achievement and depth of character.
Application requirements: Essay, transcript. FAFSA and SAR. Essay must state why you have chosen business as an intended career and how you expect to make a difference in the business world.
Additional information: Minimum 3.0 GPA required. Applicants must have permanent Hawaii address.
   Amount of award: $1,000
   Number of awards: 1
   Application deadline: March 1
Contact:
Hawaii Community Foundation Scholarships
1164 Bishop Street
Suite 800
Honolulu, HA 96813
Phone: 888-731-3863
Fax: 808-521-6286
Web: www.hawaiicommunityfoundation.org

Gerrit R. Ludwig Scholarship

Type of award: Scholarship.
Intended use: For full-time undergraduate or graduate study at accredited 2-year, 4-year or graduate institution.
Eligibility: Applicant must be residing in Hawaii.
Basis for selection: Major/career interest in Classics or arts, general. Applicant must demonstrate financial need, high academic achievement and depth of character.
Application requirements: Essay, transcript. FAFSA and SAR.
Additional information: Minimum 2.5 GPA required. Preference given to applicants pursuing a degree in fine arts or Classics. Must be graduate from East Hawaii public school: Hilo, Honoka'a, Kea'au, Laupahoehoe, Pahoa, and Waiakea. Applicants taking up mainland residency must have relatives living in Hawaii.

   Amount of award: $14,750
   Number of awards: 3
   Application deadline: March 1
Contact:
Hawaii Community Foundation Scholarship
1164 Bishop Street
Suite 800
Honolulu, HI 96813
Phone: 888-731-3863
Fax: 808-521-6286
Web: www.hawaiicommunityfoundation.org

Henry A. Zuberano Scholarship

Type of award: Scholarship.
Intended use: For full-time undergraduate study at accredited 2-year or 4-year institution.
Eligibility: Applicant must be residing in Hawaii.
Basis for selection: Major/career interest in political science/government; international relations; business, international or public administration/service. Applicant must demonstrate financial need, high academic achievement and depth of character.
Application requirements: Essay, transcript. FAFSA and SAR.
Additional information: Minimum 2.7 GPA required. Applicant must have permanent Hawaii address. Applicants taking up mainland residency must have relatives living in Hawaii.
   Amount of award: $1,000
   Number of awards: 9
   Application deadline: March 1
Contact:
Hawaii Community Foundation Scholarships
1164 Bishop Street
Suite 800
Honolulu, HI 96813
Phone: 888-731-3863
Fax: 808-521-6286
Web: www.hawaiicommunityfoundation.org

Jean Fitzgerald Scholarship Fund

Type of award: Scholarship, renewable.
Intended use: For full-time freshman study at accredited 2-year or 4-year institution in United States.
Eligibility: Applicant must be female. Applicant must be U.S. citizen or permanent resident residing in Hawaii.
Basis for selection: Applicant must demonstrate financial need, high academic achievement and depth of character.
Application requirements: Essay, transcript. FAFSA and SAR.
Additional information: Minimum 2.7 GPA required. Applicant must be active tennis player; preference may be given to USTA/Hawaii Pacific Section members. Applicants must have permanent address in Hawaii. Applicants who take up mainland residency must have relatives living in Hawaii. Amount and number of awards vary and may change yearly.
   Amount of award: $3,500
   Number of awards: 2
   Application deadline: March 1
   Total amount awarded: $7,000

Contact:
Hawaii Community Foundation Scholarships
1164 Bishop Street
Suite 800
Honolulu, HI 96813
Phone: 888-731-3863
Fax: 808-521-6286
Web: www.hawaiicommunityfoundation.org

John Dawe Dental Education Fund

Type of award: Scholarship, renewable.
Intended use: For full-time undergraduate or graduate study at accredited postsecondary institution in United States.
Eligibility: Applicant must be U.S. citizen or permanent resident residing in Hawaii.
Basis for selection: Major/career interest in dentistry; dental hygiene or dental assistant. Applicant must demonstrate financial need, high academic achievement and depth of character.
Application requirements: Recommendations, essay, transcript, proof of eligibility. FAFSA and SAR. Must submit Dawe Supplemental Financial Form (download from Website). Dental hygiene applicants must submit a letter from their school confirming enrollment in the dental hygiene program.
Additional information: Minimum 2.7 GPA required. Applicants must have permanent address in Hawaii. Applicants taking up mainland residency must have relatives living in Hawaii. Amount and number of awards vary and may change yearly.

Amount of award:	$3,000
Number of awards:	6
Application deadline:	March 1

Contact:
Hawaii Community Foundation Scholarships
1164 Bishop Street
Suite 800
Honolulu, HI 96813
Phone: 888-731-3863
Fax: 808-521-6286
Web: www.hawaiicommunityfoundation.org

John Ross Foundation

Type of award: Scholarship, renewable.
Intended use: For full-time undergraduate study at accredited postsecondary institution in United States.
Eligibility: Applicant must be U.S. citizen or permanent resident residing in Hawaii.
Basis for selection: Applicant must demonstrate financial need, high academic achievement and depth of character.
Application requirements: Essay, transcript. FAFSA and SAR. Personal statement should discuss applicant's plan to remain on or return to Hawaii after graduation.
Additional information: Minimum 2.7 GPA required. Applicant must be longtime resident of the island of Hawaii. Preference given to applicants born on the island with ancestors from that area. Applicants must have permanent address in Hawaii. Amount of award varies yearly.

Amount of award:	$1,206
Number of awards:	17

Contact:
Hawaii Community Foundation Scholarships
1164 Bishop Street
Suite 800
Honolulu, HI 96813
Phone: 888-731-3863
Fax: 808-521-6286
Web: www.hawaiicommunityfoundation.org

Juliette M. Atherton Scholarship

Type of award: Scholarship, renewable.
Intended use: For full-time undergraduate, graduate or non-degree study at accredited postsecondary institution in United States.
Eligibility: Applicant must be Protestant. Applicant must be U.S. citizen or permanent resident residing in Hawaii.
Basis for selection: Major/career interest in religion/theology. Applicant must demonstrate financial need, high academic achievement, depth of character, leadership, seriousness of purpose and service orientation.
Application requirements: Essay, transcript, proof of eligibility. FAFSA and SAR. Personal statement must include parent's current position, church/parish name, denomination, place and date of ordination, and name of seminary attended.
Additional information: Minimum 2.7 GPA required. Applicant must attend an accredited graduate school of theology with goal of becoming ordained in established Protestant denomination. Applicant must have permanent address in Hawaii. Applicants taking up mainland residency must have relatives living in Hawaii. Amount and number of awards vary and may change yearly.

Amount of award:	$2,285
Number of awards:	14
Application deadline:	March 1

Contact:
Hawaii Community Foundation Scholarships
1164 Bishop Street
Suite 800
Honolulu, HI 96813
Phone: 888-731-3863
Fax: 808-521-6286
Web: www.hawaiicommunityfoundation.org

Ka'iulani Home for Girls Trust Scholarship

Type of award: Scholarship, renewable.
Intended use: For full-time undergraduate study at accredited postsecondary institution in United States.
Eligibility: Applicant must be Native Hawaiian/Pacific Islander. Applicant must be female. Applicant must be U.S. citizen or permanent resident residing in Hawaii.
Basis for selection: Applicant must demonstrate financial need, high academic achievement and depth of character.
Application requirements: Essay, transcript, proof of eligibility. FAFSA and SAR. First-time applicants must be upcoming freshmen or sophomores, and must include birth certificate with application to verify ancestry.
Additional information: Minimum 3.0 GPA required. Must have permanent address in Hawaii. Applicants taking up mainland residency must have relatives living in Hawaii. Amount and number of awards vary and may change yearly.

Amount of award:	$739
Number of awards:	222
Application deadline:	March 1

Contact:
Hawaii Community Foundation Scholarships
1164 Bishop Street
Suite 800
Honolulu, HI 96813
Phone: 888-731-3863
Fax: 808-521-6286
Web: www.hawaiicommunityfoundation.org

Ka'a'awa Community Fund

Type of award: Scholarship.
Intended use: For full-time undergraduate or graduate study at accredited 2-year or 4-year institution in United States.
Eligibility: Applicant must be U.S. citizen or permanent resident residing in Hawaii.
Basis for selection: Applicant must demonstrate financial need, high academic achievement and depth of character.
Application requirements: Essay, transcript. FAFSA and SAR.
Additional information: Minimum 2.7 GPA required. Applicant must be resident of the Ka'a'awa area on Windward O'ahu. Preference given to long-time residents. Amount and number of awards vary and may change yearly.
  Amount of award: $600
  Number of awards: 7
  Application deadline: March 1
Contact:
Hawaii Community Foundation Scholarships
1164 Bishop Street
Suite 800
Honolulu, HI 96813
Phone: 888-731-3863
Fax: 808-521-6286
Web: www.hawaiicommunityfoundation.org

Kapolei Community & Business Scholarship

Type of award: Scholarship.
Intended use: For full-time undergraduate study at accredited 2-year or 4-year institution in United States.
Eligibility: Applicant must be high school senior. Applicant must be U.S. citizen or permanent resident residing in Hawaii.
Basis for selection: Applicant must demonstrate financial need, high academic achievement and depth of character.
Application requirements: Essay, transcript. FAFSA and SAR.
Additional information: Minimum 2.7 GPA required. Applicant must be a senior from Campbell, Nanakuli, or Waianae high schools. Applicants taking up mainland residency must have relatives living in Hawaii. Amount of award may vary yearly.
  Amount of award: $500
  Number of awards: 4
  Application deadline: March 1
Contact:
Hawaii Community Foundation Scholarships
1164 Bishop Street
Suite 800
Honolulu, HI 96813
Phone: 888-731-3863
Fax: 808-521-6286
Web: www.hawaiicommunityfoundation.org

Kawasaki-McGaha Scholarship Fund

Type of award: Scholarship.
Intended use: For full-time undergraduate study. Designated institutions: Hawaii Pacific University.
Eligibility: Applicant must be permanent resident residing in Hawaii.
Basis for selection: Major/career interest in computer/information sciences or international studies. Applicant must demonstrate financial need, high academic achievement and depth of character.
Application requirements: Essay, transcript. FAFSA and SAR.
Additional information: Minimum 2.7 GPA required. Applicants must have permanent address in Hawaii. Applicants taking up mainland residency must have relatives living in Hawaii. Amount and number of awards vary and may change yearly.
  Amount of award: $1,166
  Number of awards: 2
  Application deadline: March 1
Contact:
Hawaii Community Foundation Scholarships
1164 Bishop Street
Suite 800
Honolulu, HI 96813
Phone: 888-731-3863
Fax: 808-521-6286
Web: www.hawaiicommunityfoundaiton.org

King Kekaulike High School Scholarship

Type of award: Scholarship.
Intended use: For full-time undergraduate study at accredited 2-year or 4-year institution in United States.
Eligibility: Applicant must be high school senior. Applicant must be U.S. citizen or permanent resident residing in Hawaii.
Basis for selection: Applicant must demonstrate financial need, high academic achievement, depth of character and service orientation.
Application requirements: Essay, transcript. FAFSA and SAR. Additional 500-word essay on how well Na Alii 3 R's (Respect, Relevance, and Rigor) relate to your future goals.
Additional information: Minimum 2.8 GPA and three or more hours of community service. Applicant must be student at King Kekaulike High School. Children of KKHS staff members not eligible. Amount of award may change yearly. Applicants taking up mainland residency must have relatives living in Hawaii.
  Amount of award: $1,000
  Number of awards: 1
  Application deadline: March 1
Contact:
Hawaii Community Foundation Scholarships
1164 Biship Street
Suite 800
Honolulu, HI 96813
Phone: 888-731-3863
Fax: 808-521-6286
Web: www.hawaiicommunityfoundation.org

K.M. Hatano Scholarship

Type of award: Scholarship, renewable.

Intended use: For full-time undergraduate study at accredited 4-year institution in United States.
Eligibility: Applicant must be high school senior. Applicant must be U.S. citizen or permanent resident residing in Hawaii.
Basis for selection: Applicant must demonstrate financial need, high academic achievement and depth of character.
Application requirements: Essay, transcript. FAFSA and SAR.
Additional information: Minimum 2.7 GPA required. Applicant must be high school graduate of Maui, including Lanai or Molokai counties. Applicant must have permanent address in Hawaii. Applicants taking up mainland residency must have relatives living in Hawaii. Amount and number of awards vary and may change yearly.

    Amount of award: $1,500
    Number of awards: 8
    Application deadline: March 1

Contact:
Hawaii Community Foundation Scholarships
1164 Bishop Street
Suite 800
Honolulu, HI 96813
Phone: 888-731-3863
Fax: 808-521-6286
Web: www.hawaiicommunityfoundation.org

Kohala Ditch Education Fund

Type of award: Scholarship.
Intended use: For full-time undergraduate study at accredited 2-year or 4-year institution in United States.
Eligibility: Applicant must be high school senior. Applicant must be U.S. citizen or permanent resident residing in Hawaii.
Basis for selection: Applicant must demonstrate financial need, high academic achievement and depth of character.
Application requirements: Essay, transcript. FAFSA and SAR.
Additional information: Minimum 2.7 GPA required. Applicant must be student at Kohala High School. Amount of award may change yearly. Applicants taking up mainland residency must have relatives living in Hawaii.

    Amount of award: $1,000
    Number of awards: 3
    Application deadline: March 1

Contact:
Hawaii Community Foundation Scholarships
1164 Bishop Street
Suite 800
Honolulu, HI 96813
Phone: 888-731-3863
Fax: 808-521-6286
Web: www.hawaiicommunityfoundation.org

Koloa Scholarship

Type of award: Scholarship, renewable.
Intended use: For full-time undergraduate or graduate study at accredited vocational, 2-year or 4-year institution in United States.
Eligibility: Applicant must be U.S. citizen or permanent resident residing in Hawaii.
Basis for selection: Applicant must demonstrate financial need, high academic achievement and depth of character.
Application requirements: Recommendations, essay, transcript. FAFSA and SAR. Essay must explain personal understanding of meaning of "aloha," how it has played a part in personal development and how applicant hopes to use chosen field to further this meaning among family and community. Must include list of books or other publications read on Hawaii's history, and list of relatives born in Koloa District, including relationship to applicant, and place and approximate year of birth.
Additional information: Minimum 2.0 GPA required. Applicant must be resident of one of the following Kauai areas in Hawaii: Koloa, including Omao and Poipu (96756), Lawai (96765), or Kalaheo (96741). Applicants taking up mainland residency must have relatives living in Hawaii. Amount of award varies and may change yearly.

    Amount of award: $1,000
    Number of awards: 4
    Application deadline: March 1

Contact:
Hawaii Community Foundation Scholarships
1164 Bishop Street
Suite 800
Honolulu, HI 96813
Phone: 888-731-3863
Fax: 808-521-6286
Web: www.hawaiicommunityfoundation.org

Kurt W. Schneider Memorial Scholarship Fund

Type of award: Scholarship.
Intended use: For full-time undergraduate study at accredited 2-year or 4-year institution in United States.
Eligibility: Applicant must be high school senior. Applicant must be U.S. citizen or permanent resident residing in Hawaii.
Basis for selection: Major/career interest in tourism/travel. Applicant must demonstrate financial need, high academic achievement and depth of character.
Application requirements: Essay, transcript. FAFSA and SAR.
Additional information: Minimum 2.7 GPA required. Applicant must be student at Lanai High School. Preference given to travel industry management majors. Applicants taking up mainland residency must have relatives living in Hawaii. Amount of award may change yearly.

    Amount of award: $2,500
    Number of awards: 1
    Application deadline: March 1

Contact:
Hawaii Community Foundation Scholarships
1164 Bishop Street
Suite 800
Honolulu, HI 96813
Phone: 888-731-3863
Fax: 808-521-6286
Web: www.hawaiicommunityfoundation.org

Laura N. Dowsett Fund

Type of award: Scholarship, renewable.
Intended use: For full-time junior, senior or graduate study at accredited 2-year, 4-year or graduate institution in United States.
Eligibility: Applicant must be U.S. citizen or permanent resident residing in Hawaii.
Basis for selection: Major/career interest in occupational therapy. Applicant must demonstrate financial need, high academic achievement and depth of character.
Application requirements: Essay, transcript. FAFSA and SAR.
Additional information: Minimum 2.7 GPA required. Applicants must have permanent address in Hawaii. Applicants

who take up mainland residency must have relatives living in Hawaii. Amount and number of awards vary and may change yearly.

- Amount of award: $2,000
- Number of awards: 2
- Application deadline: March 1

Contact:
Hawaii Community Foundation Scholarships
1164 Bishop Street
Suite 800
Honolulu, HI 96813
Phone: 888-731-3863
Fax: 808-521-6286
Web: www.hawaiicommunityfoundation.org

Margaret Jones Memorial Nursing Scholarship

Type of award: Scholarship, renewable.
Intended use: For full-time junior, senior or graduate study at accredited 4-year or graduate institution in United States.
Eligibility: Applicant must be U.S. citizen or permanent resident residing in Hawaii.
Basis for selection: Major/career interest in nursing. Applicant must demonstrate financial need, high academic achievement and depth of character.
Application requirements: Essay, transcript. FAFSA and SAR.
Additional information: Minimum 3.0 GPA required. Applicants must be enrolled in BSN, MSN, or doctoral nursing program. Preference may be given to members of Hawaii Nurses Association. Applicants must have permanent address in Hawaii. Applicant taking up mainland residency must have relatives living in Hawaii. Amount and number of awards vary and change yearly.

- Amount of award: $888
- Number of awards: 13
- Application deadline: March 1

Contact:
Hawaii Community Foundation Scholarships
1164 Bishop Street
Suite 800
Honolulu, HI 96813
Phone: 888-731-3863
Fax: 808-521-6286
Web: www.hawaiicommunityfoundation.org

Marion Maccarrell Scott Scholarship

Type of award: Scholarship, renewable.
Intended use: For full-time undergraduate or graduate study at accredited postsecondary institution in United States.
Designated institutions: Institutions on U.S. mainland.
Eligibility: Applicant must be U.S. citizen or permanent resident residing in Hawaii.
Basis for selection: Applicant must demonstrate financial need, high academic achievement and depth of character.
Application requirements: Essay, transcript. FAFSA and SAR. Essay (2-3 typed pages, double-spaced) must demonstrate commitment to international understanding and world peace.
Additional information: Minimum 2.8 GPA required. Must be graduate of Hawaii public high school and attend accredited mainland U.S. college or university. Applicant must have permanent address in Hawaii. Applicants taking up mainland residency must have relatives living in Hawaii. Amount and number of awards vary and may change yearly.

- Amount of award: $1,384
- Number of awards: 331
- Application deadline: March 1

Contact:
Hawaii Community Foundation Scholarships
1164 Bishop Street
Suite 800
Honolulu, HI 96813
Phone: 888-731-3863
Fax: 808-521-6286
Web: www.hawaiicommunityfoundation.org

Mary Josephine Bloder Scholarship

Type of award: Scholarship.
Intended use: For full-time undergraduate study at accredited 2-year or 4-year institution in United States.
Eligibility: Applicant must be high school senior. Applicant must be U.S. citizen or permanent resident residing in Hawaii.
Basis for selection: Applicant must demonstrate financial need, high academic achievement and depth of character.
Application requirements: Recommendations, essay, transcript. FAFSA and SAR. One of the two letters of recommendation must be from Lahainaluna High School science teacher.
Additional information: Minimum 2.7 GPA required. Applicant must be student at Lahainaluna High School. Preference given to boarding students. Must have high GPA in sciences. Applicants taking up mainland residency must have relatives living in Hawaii. Amount and number of awards vary and may change yearly.

- Amount of award: $2,083
- Number of awards: 6
- Application deadline: March 1

Contact:
Hawaii Community Foundation Scholarships
1164 Bishop Street
Suite 800
Honolulu, HI 96813
Phone: 888-731-3863
Fax: 808-521-6286
Web: www.hawaiicommunityfoundation.org

Mildred Towle Scholarship - Study Abroad

Type of award: Scholarship, renewable.
Intended use: For full-time undergraduate or graduate study at accredited postsecondary institution outside United States.
Eligibility: Applicant must be residing in Hawaii.
Basis for selection: Applicant must demonstrate financial need, high academic achievement and depth of character.
Application requirements: Essay, transcript. FAFSA and SAR. Essay must include intended country and semester of study.
Additional information: Minimum 3.0 GPA required. Award for Hawaii residents studying abroad. Amount and number of awards vary and may change yearly.

- Amount of award: $1,000
- Number of awards: 6
- Application deadline: March 1

Contact:
Hawaii Community Foundation Scholarships
1164 Bishop Street
Suite 800
Honolulu, HI 96813
Phone: 888-731-3863
Fax: 808-521-6286
Web: www.hawaiicommunityfoundation.org

Mildred Towle Scholarship for African-Americans

Type of award: Scholarship.
Intended use: For undergraduate study.
Eligibility: Applicant must be African American. Applicant must be U.S. citizen residing in Hawaii.
Application requirements: Recommendations, essay, transcript. SAR.
Additional information: Minimum 3.0 GPA. Must attend school in Hawaii.
   Amount of award: $1,000
   Number of awards: 11
   Total amount awarded: $11,000
Contact:
Hawaii Community Foundation
1164 Bishop Street
Suite 800
Honolulu, HI 96813
Phone: 808-566-5570
Fax: 808-521-6286
Web: www.hawaiicommunityfoundation.org

Nick Van Pernis Scholarship

Type of award: Scholarship.
Intended use: For full-time undergraduate study at accredited 2-year or 4-year institution in United States.
Eligibility: Applicant must be U.S. citizen or permanent resident residing in Hawaii.
Basis for selection: Major/career interest in oceanography/marine studies; bioengineering; health sciences or education, early childhood. Applicant must demonstrate financial need, high academic achievement, depth of character and service orientation.
Application requirements: Essay, transcript. FAFSA and SAR. Essay must include record of community service and description of how student's education and career will benefit Hawaii residents.
Additional information: Minimum 2.7 GPA required. Applicant must be graduate of public or private school in the North Kona, South Kona, North Kohala, South Kohala, or Ka'u districts. Applicants taking up mainland residency must have relatives living in Hawaii. Amount and number of awards may vary yearly.
   Amount of award: $1,000
   Number of awards: 1
   Application deadline: March 1
Contact:
Hawaii Community Foundation Scholarships
1164 Bishop Street
Suite 800
Honolulu, HI 96813
Phone: 888-731-3863
Fax: 808-521-6286
Web: www.hawaiicommunityfoundation.org

Oscar and Rosetta Fish Fund

Type of award: Scholarship.
Intended use: For full-time undergraduate or graduate study. Designated institutions: Any University of Hawaii campus, excluding Manoa.
Eligibility: Applicant must be U.S. citizen or permanent resident residing in Hawaii.
Basis for selection: Major/career interest in business. Applicant must demonstrate financial need, high academic achievement and depth of character.
Application requirements: Essay, transcript. FAFSA and SAR.
Additional information: Minimum 2.7 GPA required. Applicants must have permanent address in Hawaii. Amount and number of awards vary and may change yearly.
   Amount of award: $1,814
   Number of awards: 13
   Application deadline: March 1
Contact:
Hawaii Community Foundation Scholarships
1164 Bishop Street
Suite 800
Honolulu, HI 96813
Phone: 888-731-3863
Fax: 808-521-6286
Web: www.hawaiicommunityfoundation.org

PRSA-Hawaii/Roy Leffingwell Public Relations Scholarship

Type of award: Scholarship.
Intended use: For full-time junior, senior or graduate study at accredited 2-year or 4-year institution in United States.
Eligibility: Applicant must be U.S. citizen or permanent resident residing in Hawaii.
Basis for selection: Major/career interest in public relations; communications or journalism. Applicant must demonstrate financial need, high academic achievement and depth of character.
Application requirements: Essay, transcript. FAFSA and SAR.
Additional information: Minimum 2.7 GPA, FAFSA and SAR required. Student must intend to pursue career in public relations.
   Amount of award: $1,000
   Number of awards: 1
   Application deadline: March 1
Contact:
Hawaii Community Foundation Scholarships
1164 Bishop Street
Suite 800
Honolulu, HI 96813
Phone: 888-731-3863
Fax: 808-521-6286
Web: www.hawaiicommunityfoundation.org

Ron Bright Scholarship

Type of award: Scholarship.
Intended use: For full-time undergraduate study at accredited 2-year or 4-year institution in United States.
Eligibility: Applicant must be high school senior. Applicant must be U.S. citizen or permanent resident residing in Hawaii.
Basis for selection: Major/career interest in education. Applicant must demonstrate financial need, high academic achievement and depth of character.

Hawaii Community Foundation: Ron Bright Scholarship

Application requirements: Essay, transcript. FAFSA and SAR. Submit grades from first semester of 12th grade.
Additional information: Minimum 2.7 GPA required. Applicant must be senior from one of these public Windward Oahu high schools: Castle, Kahuku, Kailua, Kalaheo, or Olomana. Preference given to students with extracurricular activities in the performing arts. Applicants must have permanent address in Hawaii. Applicants taking up mainland residency must have relatives living in Hawaii. Amount and number of awards vary and may change yearly.
   Amount of award: $2,000
   Number of awards: 1
   Application deadline: March 1
Contact:
Hawaii Community Foundation Scholarships
1164 Bishop Street
Suite 800
Honolulu, HI 96813
Phone: 888-731-3863
Fax: 808-521-6286
Web: www.hawaiicommunityfoundation.org

Rosemary & Nellie Ebrie Fund

Type of award: Scholarship.
Intended use: For full-time undergraduate or graduate study at accredited 2-year or 4-year institution in United States.
Eligibility: Applicant must be Native Hawaiian/Pacific Islander. Applicant must be U.S. citizen or permanent resident residing in Hawaii.
Basis for selection: Applicant must demonstrate financial need, high academic achievement and depth of character.
Application requirements: Essay, transcript. FAFSA and SAR.
Additional information: Minimum 2.7 GPA required. Must be long-term resident born and currently living on the island of Hawaii. Applicants taking up mainland residency must have relatives living in Hawaii. Amount of award may change yearly.
   Amount of award: $1,000
   Number of awards: 15
   Application deadline: March 1
Contact:
Hawaii Community Foundation Scholarships
1164 Bishop Street
Suite 800
Honolulu, HI 96813
Phone: 888-731-3863
Fax: 808-521-6286
Web: www.hawaiicommunityfoundation.org

Shirley McKown Scholarship Fund

Type of award: Scholarship.
Intended use: For full-time junior, senior or graduate study at accredited 4-year institution in United States.
Eligibility: Applicant must be U.S. citizen or permanent resident residing in Hawaii.
Basis for selection: Major/career interest in advertising; journalism or public relations. Applicant must demonstrate depth of character.
Application requirements: Essay, transcript. FAFSA and SAR.
Additional information: Minimum 3.0 GPA required. Applicants must have permanent address in Hawaii. Applicants taking up mainland residency must have relatives living in Hawaii.

   Amount of award: $1,000
   Number of awards: 1
   Application deadline: March 1
Contact:
Hawaii Community Foundation Scholarships
1164 Bishop Street
Suite 800
Honolulu, HI 96813
Phone: 888-731-3863
Fax: 808-521-6286
Web: www.hawaiicommunityfoundation.org

Shuichi, Katsu and Itsuyo Suga Scholarship

Type of award: Scholarship.
Intended use: For full-time undergraduate or graduate study at accredited 2-year or 4-year institution in United States.
Eligibility: Applicant must be U.S. citizen or permanent resident residing in Hawaii.
Basis for selection: Major/career interest in mathematics; physics; science, general or computer/information sciences. Applicant must demonstrate financial need, high academic achievement and depth of character.
Application requirements: Essay, transcript. FAFSA and SAR.
Additional information: Minimum 3.0 GPA required. Applicants must have permanent address in Hawaii. Applicants taking up mainland residency must have relatives living in Hawaii. Amount of award may change yearly.
   Amount of award: $1,000
   Number of awards: 9
   Application deadline: March 1
Contact:
Hawaii Community Foundation Scholarships
1164 Bishop Street
Suite 800
Honolulu, HI 96813
Phone: 888-731-3863
Fax: 808-521-6286
Web: www.hawaiicommunityfoundation.org

Thz Fo Farm Fund

Type of award: Scholarship.
Intended use: For full-time undergraduate or graduate study at accredited postsecondary institution in United States.
Eligibility: Applicant must be Chinese. Applicant must be U.S. citizen or permanent resident residing in Hawaii.
Basis for selection: Major/career interest in gerontology. Applicant must demonstrate financial need, high academic achievement and depth of character.
Application requirements: FAFSA and SAR.
Additional information: Minimum 2.7 GPA required. Applicants must have permanent address in Hawaii. Applicants who take up mainland residency must have relatives living in Hawaii. Amount of award may change yearly.
   Amount of award: $1,833
   Number of awards: 6
Contact:
Hawaii Community Foundation Scholarships
1164 Bishop Street
Suite 800
Honolulu, HI 96813
Phone: 888-731-3863
Fax: 808-521-6286
Web: www.hawaiicommunityfoundation.org

Tommy Lee Memorial Scholarship Fund

Type of award: Scholarship.
Intended use: For full-time undergraduate study at accredited 2-year or 4-year institution in United States.
Eligibility: Applicant must be high school senior. Applicant must be U.S. citizen or permanent resident residing in Hawaii.
Basis for selection: Applicant must demonstrate financial need, high academic achievement and depth of character.
Application requirements: Recommendations, essay, transcript. FAFSA and SAR.
Additional information: Minimum 2.7 GPA required. Must be a high school senior residing in the Waialua or Hale'iwa areas. Applicants taking up mainland residency must have relatives living in Hawaii. Amount of award may change yearly.

Amount of award:	$1,000
Number of awards:	4
Application deadline:	March 1

Contact:
Hawaii Community Foundation Scholarships
1164 Bishop Street
Suite 800
Honolulu, HI 96813
Phone: 888-731-3863
Fax: 808-521-6286
Web: www.hawaiicommunityfoundation.org

Toraji & Toki Yoshinaga Scholarship

Type of award: Scholarship.
Intended use: For full-time sophomore study at accredited 2-year or 4-year institution. Designated institutions: Brigham Young University-Hawaii, Chaminade University, Hawaii Pacific University and Heald College.
Eligibility: Applicant must be U.S. citizen or permanent resident residing in Hawaii.
Basis for selection: Applicant must demonstrate financial need, high academic achievement and depth of character.
Application requirements: Essay, transcript. FAFSA and SAR.
Additional information: Minimum 2.7 GPA required. Applicants must have permanent address in Hawaii. Applicants taking up mainland residency must have relatives living in Hawaii. Amount of award may change yearly.

Amount of award:	$1,500
Number of awards:	2
Application deadline:	March 1

Contact:
Hawaii Community Foundation Scholarships
1164 Bishop Street
Suite 800
Honolulu, HI 96813
Phone: 888-731-3863
Fax: 808-521-6286
Web: www.hawaiicommunityfoundation.org

Vicki Willder Scholarship Fund

Type of award: Scholarship.
Intended use: For full-time undergraduate study at accredited 2-year or 4-year institution in United States.
Eligibility: Applicant must be U.S. citizen or permanent resident residing in Hawaii.
Basis for selection: Major/career interest in culinary arts or tourism/travel. Applicant must demonstrate financial need, high academic achievement and depth of character.
Application requirements: Essay, transcript. FAFSA and SAR.
Additional information: Minimum 2.7 GPA required. Applicant must be employee or dependent of employee of Kamehameha Schools food services department or a graduate of Kamehameha Schools. Preference given to students majoring in culinary arts or travel industry management. Applicants taking up mainland residency must have relatives living in Hawaii. Amount and number of awards vary and may change yearly.

Amount of award:	$1,307
Number of awards:	13
Application deadline:	March 1

Contact:
Hawaii Community Foundation Scholarships
1164 Bishop Street
Suite 800
Honolulu, HI 96813
Phone: 888-731-3863
Fax: 808-521-6286
Web: www.hawaiicommunityfoundation.org

Walter H. Kupau Memorial Fund

Type of award: Scholarship.
Intended use: For full-time undergraduate study at accredited 2-year or 4-year institution in United States.
Eligibility: Applicant or parent must be member/participant of Hawaii Carpenter's Union Local 745. Applicant must be U.S. citizen or permanent resident residing in Hawaii.
Basis for selection: Applicant must demonstrate financial need, high academic achievement and depth of character.
Application requirements: Essay, transcript. FAFSA and SAR. Name and social security number of Local 745 member, along with relationship to applicant.
Additional information: Minimum 2.7 GPA required. Applicant must be descendant of Hawaii Carpenter's Union Local 745 member in good standing; preference given to descendants of retired members. Applicant must have permanent address in Hawaii. Applicants taking up mainland residency must have relatives living in Hawaii. Amount and number of awards vary.

Amount of award:	$1,000
Number of awards:	5
Application deadline:	March 1

Contact:
Hawaii Community Foundation Scholarships
1164 Bishop Street
Suite 800
Honolulu, HI 96813
Phone: 888-731-3863
Fax: 808-521-6286
Web: www.hawaiicommunityfoundation.org

West Kauai Scholarship

Type of award: Scholarship.
Intended use: For full-time undergraduate or graduate study at accredited 2-year or 4-year institution.
Eligibility: Applicant must be residing in Hawaii.
Basis for selection: Applicant must demonstrate financial need, high academic achievement and depth of character.
Application requirements: Essay, transcript. FAFSA and SAR. Personal statement should include description of family ties to West Kauai.

Additional information: Minimum 2.7 GPA required. Preference given to students from families who are long-time residents of West Kauai. Must be resident of one of the following West Kauai areas: Eleele (96705), Hanapepe (96716), Waimea (96796), Kekaha (96752), Makaweli (96769), or Kalaheo (96741). Applicants taking up mainland residency must have relatives living in Hawaii.
    Amount of award: $1,857
    Number of awards: 6
    Application deadline: March 1
Contact:
Hawaii Community Foundation Scholarship
1164 Bishop Street
Suite 800
Honolulu, HI 96813
Phone: 888-731-3863
Fax: 808-521-6286
Web: www.hawaiicommunityfoundation.org

William James & Dorothy Bading Lanquist Fund

Type of award: Scholarship.
Intended use: For full-time undergraduate or graduate study at accredited 2-year or 4-year institution in United States.
Eligibility: Applicant must be U.S. citizen or permanent resident residing in Hawaii.
Basis for selection: Major/career interest in physical sciences. Applicant must demonstrate financial need, high academic achievement and depth of character.
Application requirements: Essay, transcript. FAFSA and SAR.
Additional information: Minimum 2.7 GPA required. Must major in the physical sciences or related fields, excluding biological and social sciences. Applicants must have permanent address in Hawaii. Applicants taking up mainland residency must have relatives living in Hawaii. Amount and number of awards vary and may change yearly.
    Amount of award: $1,000
    Number of awards: 8
    Application deadline: March 1
Contact:
Hawaii Community Foundation Scholarships
1164 Bishop Street
Suite 800
Honolulu, HI 96813
Phone: 888-731-3863
Fax: 808-521-6286
Web: www.hawaiicommunityfoundation.org

Helicopter Association International

Aviation Maintenance Technician Scholarship Award

Type of award: Scholarship.
Intended use: For non-degree study. Designated institutions: U.S. helicopter airframe and engine manufacturers; Aviation maintenance schools.
Basis for selection: Major/career interest in aviation repair.
Application requirements: Recommendations.

Additional information: For students who wish to study helicopter maintenance. Award includes full tuition to aviation maintenance program and stipend of $1600. Applicant must be about to graduate from FAA-approved Aviation Maintenance Technician School, or a recent recipient of Airframe and Powerplant (A&P) certificate or international equivalent. Applications available on Website.
    Amount of award: Full tuition
    Number of awards: 5
    Number of applicants: 45
    Application deadline: January 18
Contact:
Aviation Maintenance Technician Scholarship
Helicopter Association International
1635 Prince Street
Alexandria, VA 22314-2818
Phone: 703-683-4646
Fax: 703-683-4745
Web: www.rotor.com

Henkel Corporation

Duck Brand Duct Tape Stuck at Prom Scholarship Contest

Type of award: Scholarship.
Intended use: For freshman study.
Additional information: Interested students can go to Website for official contest rules and registration form. Contest starts on March 3. Participants are required to submit entry form and photo of themselves wearing their duct tape prom formalwear. Applicant must sign release form.
    Amount of award: $1,000-$3,000
    Application deadline: June 11
    Notification begins: July 1
    Total amount awarded: $12,000
Contact:
Henkel Consumer Adhesives, Inc.
32150 Just Imagine Drive
Avon, OH 44011-1355
Web: www.stuckatprom.com

Herschel C. Price Educational Foundation

Herschel C. Price Educational Scholarship

Type of award: Scholarship, renewable.
Intended use: For undergraduate or graduate study at accredited 2-year, 4-year or graduate institution in United States.
Eligibility: Applicant must be U.S. citizen residing in West Virginia.
Basis for selection: Applicant must demonstrate financial need and high academic achievement.
Application requirements: Interview, transcript.
Additional information: Applicant must reside in West Virginia or attend West Virginia college/university. Achievement in community activities also considered. Preference shown to

undergraduates. Limited number of applications available by written request in January for fall term or August for spring term.

    Amount of award: $250-$5,000
    Number of awards: 175
    Number of applicants: 350
    Application deadline: April 1, October 1
    Notification begins: May 15, November 15
    Total amount awarded: $242,000
Contact:
Herschel C. Price Educational Foundation
P.O. Box 412
Huntington, WV 25708-0412
Phone: 304-529-3852

Hispanic College Fund

ALPFA Scholarship Program

Type of award: Scholarship.
Intended use: For full-time undergraduate or master's study. Designated institutions: Institutions in the United States and Puerto Rico.
Eligibility: Applicant must be Hispanic American. Applicant must be U.S. citizen or permanent resident.
Basis for selection: Major/career interest in accounting; business or finance/banking. Applicant must demonstrate financial need.
Application requirements: Recommendations, essay, transcript, proof of eligibility. Resume, proof of family income, proof of citizenship.
Additional information: Minimum 3.0 GPA. Must be pursuing degree in business, finance, or accounting.
    Amount of award: $1,250-$1,500
    Application deadline: March 15
    Total amount awarded: $150,000
Contact:
Hispanic College Fund
Scholarship Processing
1301 K St. NW, Ste. 450-A West
Washington, DC 20005
Phone: 800-644-4223
Web: www.hispanicfund.org

Google Hispanic College Fund Scholarship Program

Type of award: Scholarship.
Intended use: For junior, senior, master's or doctoral study in or outside United States.
Eligibility: Applicant must be Hispanic American. Applicant must be U.S. citizen or permanent resident.
Basis for selection: Major/career interest in computer/information sciences or engineering, computer. Applicant must demonstrate financial need.
Application requirements: Recommendations, essay, transcript, proof of eligibility. Official transcript, proof of family income, proof of citizenship status, resume, financial aid verification (if chosen as semi finalist only).
Additional information: Must attend school in the United States or Puerto Rico. Minimum 3.5 GPA. Visit Website for application and more information.

    Amount of award: $5,000
    Number of awards: 20
    Application deadline: March 15
    Total amount awarded: $100,000
Contact:
Hispanic College Fund
Scholarship Processing
1301 K St. NW, Ste. 450-A West
Washington, DC 20005
Phone: 800-644-4223
Web: www.hispanicfund.org

HCF Scholarship Program

Type of award: Scholarship.
Intended use: For full-time undergraduate study. Designated institutions: Institutions in the United States and Puerto Rico.
Eligibility: Applicant must be Hispanic American. Applicant must be U.S. citizen or permanent resident.
Basis for selection: Applicant must demonstrate financial need.
Application requirements: Recommendations, essay, transcript, proof of eligibility. Resume, proof of family income, proof of citizenship status.
Additional information: Minimum 3.0 GPA.
    Amount of award: $500-$5,000
    Application deadline: March 15
    Total amount awarded: $1,000,000
Contact:
Hispanic College Fund
Scholarship Processing
1717 Pennsylvania Avenue, NW
Washington, DC 20006
Phone: 800-644-4223
Web: www.hispanicfund.org

Kaiser Permanente College to Caring Program

Type of award: Scholarship, renewable.
Intended use: For junior or senior study in or outside United States.
Eligibility: Applicant must be Hispanic American. Applicant must be U.S. citizen or permanent resident residing in California.
Basis for selection: Major/career interest in nursing. Applicant must demonstrate financial need.
Application requirements: Recommendations, essay, transcript, proof of eligibility. Official transcript, proof of family income, proof of citizenship status, resume, financial aid verification (if chosen as semi finalist only).
Additional information: Must be a U.S. citizen or permanent resident residing in Northern California. Minimum 3.0 GPA. Must attend school in the United States or Puerto Rico. Visit Website for application and more information.
    Amount of award: $8,000
    Number of awards: 10
    Application deadline: March 15
    Total amount awarded: $50,000
Contact:
Hispanic College Fund
Scholarship Processing
1301 K St. NW, Ste. 450-A West
Washington, DC 20005
Phone: 800-644-4223
Web: www.hispanicfund.org

Lockheed Martin Scholarship Program

Type of award: Scholarship.
Intended use: For undergraduate study. Designated institutions: Institutions in the United States and Puerto Rico.
Eligibility: Applicant must be Hispanic American. Applicant must be U.S. citizen.
Basis for selection: Major/career interest in business; engineering or science, general. Applicant must demonstrate financial need.
Application requirements: Recommendations, essay, transcript, proof of eligibility. Resume, proof of family income, proof of citizenship.
Additional information: Minimum 3.0 GPA.
    Amount of award: $500-$5,000
    Application deadline: March 15
    Total amount awarded: $90,000
Contact:
Hispanic College Fund
Scholarship Processing
1301 K St. NW, Ste. 450-A West
Washington, DC 20005
Phone: 800-644-4223
Web: www.hispanicfund.org

Hispanic Engineer National Achievement Awards Conference

HENAAC Scholars Program

Type of award: Scholarship, renewable.
Intended use: For full-time undergraduate or graduate study at 2-year, 4-year or graduate institution.
Basis for selection: Major/career interest in engineering; computer/information sciences; materials science or mathematics. Applicant must demonstrate high academic achievement and leadership.
Application requirements: Recommendations, essay.
Additional information: All sciences except medicine eligible. Include SASE with application request, or download application from Website. Amount of award varies.
    Amount of award: $500-$5,000
    Number of awards: 78
    Number of applicants: 375
    Application deadline: April 30
    Notification begins: July 15
    Total amount awarded: $190,000
Contact:
HENAAC
Student Scholarship Committee
3900 Whiteside Street
Los Angeles, CA 90063
Phone: 323-262-0997
Web: www.henaac.org

Hispanic Heritage Foundation

Hispanic Heritage Youth Awards Program

Type of award: Scholarship.
Intended use: For full-time undergraduate study at postsecondary institution.
Eligibility: Applicant must be Hispanic American. Applicant must be high school senior. Applicant must be U.S. citizen or permanent resident.
Basis for selection: Applicant must demonstrate high academic achievement, depth of character, leadership and service orientation.
Application requirements: Recommendations, essay, transcript, proof of eligibility.
Additional information: Applicant must have at least one parent of Hispanic/Latino ancestry. Foundation offers regional and national awards in a number of categories; amount of award and application deadlines vary by year. Visit Website for application and updates regarding Youth Awards Program.
    Amount of award: $1,000-$8,000
    Number of awards: 252
    Number of applicants: 13,000
    Application deadline: March 14
    Notification begins: May 1
    Total amount awarded: $600,000
Contact:
Hispanic Heritage Foundation
Hispanic Heritage Youth Awards
2600 Virginia Avenue NW, Suite #406
Washington, DC 20037
Phone: 202-861-9797
Fax: 202-861-9799
Web: www.hispanicheritage.org

Hispanic Scholarship Fund

College Scholarship Fund

Type of award: Scholarship.
Intended use: For full-time undergraduate or graduate study at postsecondary institution in or outside United States. Designated institutions: Colleges in United States, Puerto Rico, U.S. Virgin Islands, and Guam.
Eligibility: Applicant must be Mexican American, Hispanic American or Puerto Rican. Applicant must be U.S. citizen or permanent resident.
Basis for selection: Applicant must demonstrate financial need, high academic achievement, seriousness of purpose and service orientation.
Application requirements: Recommendations, essay, transcript, proof of eligibility. FAFSA and SAR. Copy of permanent resident card or passport stamped I-551 (if applicable).
Additional information: Applicant must have earned minimum of 12 undergraduate units from accredited college or university. Minimum 3.0 GPA. Visit Website or contact via e-mail for more information and tips on how to apply.

Amount of award:	$1,000-$5,000
Application deadline:	March 15
Notification begins:	July 1

Contact:
General Selection Committee
Hispanic Scholarship Fund
55 Second St, Suite 1500
San Francisco, CA 94105
Phone: 415-808-2364
Fax: 415-808-2302
Web: www.hsf.net

Marathon Oil Corporation College Scholarship

Type of award: Scholarship, renewable.
Intended use: For sophomore, senior or master's study at 4-year institution.
Eligibility: Applicant must be Alaskan native, African American, Hispanic American, American Indian or Native Hawaiian/Pacific Islander. Applicant must be U.S. citizen or permanent resident.
Basis for selection: Major/career interest in engineering, chemical; engineering, civil; engineering, electrical/electronic; engineering, mechanical; engineering, petroleum; geology/earth sciences; geophysics; accounting or marketing. Applicant must demonstrate leadership and seriousness of purpose.
Application requirements: Recommendations, essay, transcript. Resume and FAFSA.
Additional information: Other acceptable fields of study are global procurement or supply chain management, environmental health and safety, energy management, petroleum land management, transportation and logistics, and geotechnical engineering. Must agree to participate in a possible paid summer internship. Minimum 3.0 GPA. See Website for application and further requirements.

Amount of award:	$10,000
Number of awards:	20
Application deadline:	November 1
Notification begins:	March 1

Contact:
HSF/ Marathon Oil Corporation Scholarship Committee
55 Second Street, Suite 1500
San Francisco, CA 94105
Phone: 415-808-2364
Web: apply.hsf.net/applications/

Nissan Community College Transfer Scholarship

Type of award: Scholarship.
Intended use: For full-time undergraduate study at accredited postsecondary institution in United States. Designated institutions: Accredited four-year postsecondary institutions in United States, Puerto Rico, U.S. Virgin Islands, and Guam.
Eligibility: Applicant must be Mexican American, Hispanic American or Puerto Rican. Applicant must be U.S. citizen or permanent resident.
Basis for selection: Major/career interest in business; engineering; communications or radio/television/film. Applicant must demonstrate financial need and high academic achievement.
Application requirements: Recommendations, essay, transcript, proof of eligibility. FAFSA and copy of permanent resident card or passport stamped I-551 (if applicable).
Additional information: Must reside in or transfer to school in one of the following locations: Atlanta, Georgia; Chicago, Illinois; Dallas/Fort Worth, Texas; Jackson/Canton, Mississippi; Los Angeles, California; Nashville, Tennessee; Northern California; New York City. Applicant must be enrolled part-time or full-time at community college and plan to transfer to four-year institution in fall or spring of next academic year. Minimum 3.0 GPA. Visit Website or contact via e-mail for more information.

Amount of award:	$2,500
Application deadline:	February 1
Notification begins:	June 1

Contact:
Community College Transfer Program
Hispanic Scholarship Fund
55 Second Street, Suite 1500
San Francisco, CA 94104
Phone: 415-808-2364
Fax: 415-808-2302
Web: www.hsf.net

Hopi Tribe Grants and Scholarship Program

Hopi BIA Higher Education Grant

Type of award: Scholarship, renewable.
Intended use: For undergraduate or graduate study at accredited 2-year, 4-year or graduate institution.
Eligibility: Applicant must be American Indian. Must be enrolled member of the Hopi Tribe.
Basis for selection: Applicant must demonstrate financial need.
Additional information: Entering freshmen must have 2.5 GPA for high school coursework or minimum composite score of 45% on GED Exam. Continuing students must have 2.5 GPA for all graduate coursework. Must reapply each academic year or semester.

Amount of award:	$2,500
Number of applicants:	150
Application deadline:	December 1, July 1

Contact:
Hopi Tribe Grants and Scholarship Program
P.O. Box 123
Kykotsmovi, AZ 86039
Phone: 800-762-9630
Fax: 928-734-9575

Hopi Education Award

Type of award: Scholarship, renewable.
Intended use: For undergraduate or graduate study at accredited 2-year, 4-year or graduate institution.
Eligibility: Applicant must be American Indian. Must be enrolled member of the Hopi Tribe.
Basis for selection: Applicant must demonstrate financial need.
Additional information: Entering freshmen must have 2.5 GPA for high school coursework or minimum composite score of 45 percent on the GED Exam. Continuing students must have 2.5 GPA for all college work. $2,500 may be awarded each semester. Must reapply each academic year or semester.

Amount of award:	$2,500
Number of applicants:	150
Application deadline:	December 1, July 1

Contact:
Hopi Tribe Grants and Scholarship Program
P.O. Box 123
Kykotsmovi, AZ 86039
Phone: 800-762-9630
Fax: 928-734-9575

Hopi Tribal Priority Award

Type of award: Scholarship, renewable.
Intended use: For full-time junior, senior or graduate study at accredited 4-year or graduate institution.
Eligibility: Applicant must be American Indian. Must be enrolled member of the Hopi Tribe.
Basis for selection: Major/career interest in law; natural resources/conservation; education; business; engineering; health-related professions or medical specialties/research. Applicant must demonstrate financial need, high academic achievement, depth of character, leadership and seriousness of purpose.
Application requirements: Recommendations, transcript.
Additional information: Applicant must show certification of Indian blood. Award is based on amount of college cost. Applicant must have college submit financial needs analysis to determine amount of award. Tuition, books, room and board covered until graduation.

Amount of award:	Full tuition
Number of awards:	5
Number of applicants:	3
Application deadline:	July 1

Contact:
Hopi Tribe Grants and Scholarship Program
P.O. Box 123
Kykotsmovi, AZ 86039
Phone: 800-762-9630
Fax: 928-734-9575

Horatio Alger Association

Horatio Alger Ak-Sar-Ben Scholarship Program

Type of award: Scholarship.
Intended use: For undergraduate study at accredited 2-year or 4-year institution.
Eligibility: Applicant must be high school senior. Applicant must be U.S. citizen residing in Iowa or Nebraska.
Basis for selection: Applicant must demonstrate financial need, seriousness of purpose and service orientation.
Application requirements: Essay.
Additional information: Minimum 2.0 GPA. Program assists high school seniors from Nebraska and specific counties in western Iowa who have faced and overcome great obstacles. Applicant should have strong commitment to use college degree in service to others. Must plan to pursue bachelor's degree. See Website for application.

Amount of award:	$5,000
Number of awards:	50
Application deadline:	October 30

Contact:
Horatio Alger Association
99 Canal Center Plaza
Alexandria, VA 22314
Phone: 703-684-9444
Fax: 703-684-9445
Web: www.horatioalger.org/scholarships

Horatio Alger Alabama Scholarship Program

Type of award: Scholarship.
Intended use: For undergraduate study at accredited 2-year or 4-year institution.
Eligibility: Applicant must be U.S. citizen residing in Alabama.
Basis for selection: Applicant must demonstrate financial need and seriousness of purpose.
Application requirements: Essay.
Additional information: Minimum 2.0 GPA. Program assists high school seniors who have faced and overcome great obstacles. Applicant should have strong commitment to use college degree in service to others. Must plan to pursue bachelor's degree. Visit Website for application.

Amount of award:	$5,000
Number of awards:	12
Application deadline:	October 30

Contact:
Horatio Alger Association
99 Canal Center Plaza
Alexandria, VA 22314
Phone: 703-684-9444
Fax: 703-684-9445
Web: www.horatioalger.org/scholarships

Horatio Alger California Scholarship Program

Type of award: Scholarship.
Intended use: For undergraduate study at accredited 2-year or 4-year institution.
Eligibility: Applicant must be high school senior. Applicant must be U.S. citizen residing in California.
Basis for selection: Applicant must demonstrate financial need, seriousness of purpose and service orientation.
Application requirements: Essay.
Additional information: Minimum 2.0 GPA. Program assists California high school seniors who have faced and overcome great obstacles. Applicant should have strong commitment to use college degree in service to others. Must plan to pursue bachelor's degree. See Website for application.

Amount of award:	$2,500
Number of awards:	100
Application deadline:	October 30

Contact:
Horatio Alger Association
99 Canal Center Plaza
Alexandria, VA 22314
Phone: 703-684-9444
Fax: 703-684-9445
Web: www.horatioalger.org/scholarships

Horatio Alger Delaware Scholarship Program

Type of award: Scholarship.

Intended use: For freshman study at accredited 2-year or 4-year institution.
Eligibility: Applicant must be high school senior. Applicant must be U.S. citizen residing in Delaware.
Basis for selection: Applicant must demonstrate financial need.
Application requirements: Essay.
Additional information: Minimum 2.0 GPA. Program assists Delaware high school seniors who have faced and overcome great obstacles. Applicants should have strong commitment to use college degree in service to others. Must plan to pursue bachelor's degree. See Website for application.
    Amount of award: $5,000
    Number of awards: 25
    Application deadline: October 30
Contact:
Horatio Alger Association
99 Canal Center Drive
Alexandria, VA 22314
Phone: 703-684-9444
Fax: 703-684-9445
Web: www.horatioalger.org/scholarships

Horatio Alger District of Columbia, Maryland and Virginia Scholarship Program

Type of award: Scholarship.
Intended use: For full-time undergraduate study at accredited 2-year or 4-year institution in United States.
Eligibility: Applicant must be high school senior. Applicant must be U.S. citizen residing in Virginia, District of Columbia or Maryland.
Basis for selection: Applicant must demonstrate financial need and service orientation.
Additional information: Minimum 2.0 GPA. Program assists Washington D.C. metro area high school seniors who have faced and overcome great obstacles. See Website for list of eligible counties. Applicant should have strong commitment to use college degree in service to others. Must plan to pursue bachelor's degree. See Website for application.
    Amount of award: $2,500
    Number of awards: 25
    Application deadline: October 30
Contact:
Horatio Alger Association
99 Canal Center Plaza
Alexandria, VA 22314
Phone: 703-684-9444
Fax: 703-684-9445
Web: www.horatioalger.com/scholarships/

Horatio Alger Florida Scholarship Program

Type of award: Scholarship.
Intended use: For undergraduate study at accredited 2-year or 4-year institution.
Eligibility: Applicant must be high school senior. Applicant must be U.S. citizen residing in Florida.
Basis for selection: Applicant must demonstrate financial need.
Application requirements: Essay.
Additional information: Minimum 2.0 GPA. Program assists Florida high school seniors who have faced and overcome great obstacles. Applicant should have strong commitment to use college degree in service to others and must be a resident of Broward, Martin, Miami-Dade, or St. Lucie counties. Must plan to pursue bachelor's degree. See Website for application.
    Amount of award: $5,000
    Number of awards: 50
    Application deadline: October 30
Contact:
Horatio Alger Association
99 Canal Center Plaza
Alexandria, VA 22314
Phone: 703-684-9444
Fax: 703-684-9445
Web: www.horatioalger.org/scholarships

Horatio Alger Franklin Scholarship

Type of award: Scholarship.
Intended use: For full-time undergraduate study at accredited 2-year or 4-year institution.
Eligibility: Applicant must be high school senior. Applicant must be U.S. citizen residing in Pennsylvania.
Basis for selection: Applicant must demonstrate financial need, seriousness of purpose and service orientation.
Application requirements: Essay.
Additional information: Minimum 2.0 GPA. Program assists high school seniors who have faced and overcome great obstacles. Applicant should have strong commitment to use college degree in service to others. Must plan to pursue bachelor's degree. Visit Website for application.
    Amount of award: $10,000
    Number of awards: 25
    Application deadline: October 30
Contact:
Horatio Alger Association
99 Canal Center Plaza
Alexandria, VA 22314
Phone: 703-684-9444
Fax: 703-684-9445
Web: www.horatioalger.org/scholarships

Horatio Alger Georgia Scholarship Program

Type of award: Scholarship.
Intended use: For undergraduate study at accredited 2-year or 4-year institution.
Eligibility: Applicant must be U.S. citizen residing in Georgia.
Basis for selection: Applicant must demonstrate financial need, seriousness of purpose and service orientation.
Application requirements: Essay.
Additional information: Minimum 2.0 GPA. Program assists high school seniors who have faced and overcome great obstacles. Applicant should have strong commitment to use college degree in service to others. Must plan to pursue bachelor's degree. Visit Website for application.
    Amount of award: $5,000
    Number of awards: 5
    Application deadline: October 30
Contact:
Horatio Alger Assocation
99 Canal Center Plaza
Alexandria, VA 22314
Phone: 703-684-9444
Fax: 703-684-9445
Web: www.horatioalger.org/scholarships

Horatio Alger Hormel Scholarship Program

Type of award: Scholarship.
Intended use: For undergraduate study at 2-year or 4-year institution.
Eligibility: Applicant must be high school senior. Applicant must be U.S. citizen residing in Minnesota.
Basis for selection: Applicant must demonstrate financial need, high academic achievement, depth of character and service orientation.
Additional information: Must be resident of Hormel, Minnesota.
    Number of awards: 4
    Application deadline: October 30
    Total amount awarded: $20,000
Contact:
Horatio Alger Association
99 Canal Center Plaza
Alexandria, VA 22314
Phone: 703-684-9444
Fax: 703-684-9445
Web: www.horatioalger.org/scholarships

Horatio Alger Idaho Scholarship Program

Type of award: Scholarship.
Intended use: For undergraduate study at 4-year institution in United States. Designated institutions: University of Idaho, North Idaho College, and Lewis-Clark State College (Coeur d'Alene or Lewiston).
Eligibility: Applicant must be high school senior. Applicant must be U.S. citizen residing in Idaho.
Basis for selection: Applicant must demonstrate financial need, high academic achievement, depth of character and service orientation.
Additional information: Program assists Idaho high school seniors who have faced and overcome great obstacles. Applicant should have strong commitment to use college degree in service to others. Must plan to pursue bachelor's degree. See Website for application, county eligibility, and additional information.
    Amount of award: $5,000
    Number of awards: 25
    Application deadline: October 30
Contact:
Horatio Alger Association
99 Canal Center Plaza
Alexandria, VA 22314
Phone: 703-684-9444
Fax: 703-684-9445
Web: www.horatioalger.org/scholarships

Horatio Alger Illinois Scholarship Program

Type of award: Scholarship.
Intended use: For undergraduate study at accredited 2-year or 4-year institution.
Eligibility: Applicant must be U.S. citizen residing in Illinois.
Basis for selection: Applicant must demonstrate financial need, seriousness of purpose and service orientation.
Application requirements: Essay.
Additional information: Minimum 2.0 GPA. Program assists high school seniors who have faced and overcome great obstacles. Applicant should have strong commitment to use college degree in service to others. Must plan to pursue bachelor's degree. Visit Website for application.
    Amount of award: $5,000
    Number of awards: 25
    Application deadline: October 30
Contact:
Horatio Alger Association
99 Canal Center Plaza
Alexandria, VA 22314
Phone: 703-684-9444
Fax: 703-684-9445
Web: www.horatioalger.org/scholarships

Horatio Alger Indiana Scholarship Program

Type of award: Scholarship.
Intended use: For undergraduate study at accredited 2-year or 4-year institution.
Eligibility: Applicant must be high school senior. Applicant must be U.S. citizen residing in Indiana.
Basis for selection: Applicant must demonstrate high academic achievement.
Application requirements: Essay.
Additional information: Minimum 2.0 GPA. Program assists Indiana high school seniors who have faced and overcome great obstacles. Applicant should have strong commitment to use college degree in service to others. Must plan to pursue bachelor's degree. See Website for application.
    Amount of award: $5,000
    Number of awards: 8
    Application deadline: October 30
Contact:
Horatio Alger Association
99 Canal Center Plaza
Alexandria, VA 22314
Phone: 703-684-9444
Fax: 703-684-9445
Web: www.horatioalger.org/scholarships

Horatio Alger Iowa Scholarship Program

Type of award: Scholarship.
Intended use: For undergraduate study at accredited 2-year or 4-year institution. Designated institutions: University of Iowa.
Eligibility: Applicant must be high school senior. Applicant must be residing in Iowa.
Basis for selection: Applicant must demonstrate financial need.
Application requirements: Essay.
Additional information: Minimum 2.0 GPA. Program assists Iowa high school seniors who have faced and overcome great obstacles. Applicant should have strong commitment to use college degree in service to others. Must plan to pursue bachelor's degree. See Website for application.
    Amount of award: $3,000
    Number of awards: 100
    Application deadline: October 30
Contact:
Horatio Alger Association
99 Canal Center Plaza
Alexandria, VA 22314
Phone: 703-684-9444
Fax: 703-684-9445
Web: www.horatioalger.org/scholarships

Horatio Alger Kentucky Scholarship Program

Type of award: Scholarship.
Intended use: For undergraduate study at accredited 2-year or 4-year institution.
Eligibility: Applicant must be high school senior. Applicant must be U.S. citizen residing in Kentucky.
Basis for selection: Applicant must demonstrate financial need.
Application requirements: Essay.
Additional information: Minimum 2.0 GPA. Program assists Kentucky high school seniors who have faced and overcome great obstacles. Applicant should have strong commitment to use college degree in service to others. Must plan to pursue bachelor's degree. See Website for application.

   Amount of award: $5,000
   Number of awards: 8
   Application deadline: October 30

Contact:
Horation Alger Association
99 Canal Center Plaza
Alexandria, VA 22314
Phone: 703-684-9444
Fax: 703-684-9445
Web: www.horatioalger.org/scholarships

Horatio Alger Louisiana Scholarship Program

Type of award: Scholarship.
Intended use: For undergraduate study at accredited 2-year or 4-year institution.
Eligibility: Applicant must be high school senior. Applicant must be U.S. citizen residing in Louisiana.
Basis for selection: Applicant must demonstrate financial need, seriousness of purpose and service orientation.
Application requirements: Essay.
Additional information: Minimum 2.0 GPA. Program assists Louisiana high school seniors who have faced and overcome great obstacles. Applicant should have strong commitment to use college degree in service to others. Must plan to pursue bachelor's degree. See Website for application.

   Amount of award: $10,500
   Number of awards: 50
   Application deadline: October 30

Contact:
Horatio Alger Association
99 Canal Center Plaza
Alexandria, VA 22314
Phone: 703-684-9444
Fax: 703-684-9445
Web: www.horatioalger.org/scholarships

Horatio Alger Minnesota Scholarship Program

Type of award: Scholarship.
Intended use: For undergraduate study at accredited 2-year or 4-year institution.
Eligibility: Applicant must be high school senior. Applicant must be U.S. citizen residing in Minnesota.
Basis for selection: Applicant must demonstrate financial need.
Application requirements: Essay.
Additional information: Minimum 2.0 GPA. Program assists Minnesota high school seniors who have faced and overcome great obstacles. Applicant should have strong commitment to use college degree in service to others. Must plan to pursue bachelor's degree. Applicant must be resident of Anoka, Carver, Dakota, Hennepin, Ramsey, Scott, or Washington counties. See Website for application.

   Amount of award: $4,000
   Number of awards: 42
   Application deadline: October 30

Contact:
Horatio Alger Association
99 Canal Center Plaza
Alexandria, VA
Phone: 703-684-9444
Fax: 703-684-9445
Web: www.horatioalger.org/scholarships

Horatio Alger Mississippi Scholarship Program

Type of award: Scholarship.
Intended use: For undergraduate study at accredited 2-year or 4-year institution.
Eligibility: Applicant must be U.S. citizen residing in Mississippi.
Basis for selection: Applicant must demonstrate financial need, seriousness of purpose and service orientation.
Application requirements: Essay.
Additional information: Minimum 2.0 GPA. Program assists high school seniors who have faced and overcome great obstacles. Applicant should have strong commitment to use college degree in service to others. Must plan to pursue bachelor's degree. Visit Website for application.

   Amount of award: $5,000
   Number of awards: 12
   Application deadline: October 30

Contact:
Horatio Alger Association
99 Canal Center Plaza
Alexandria, VA 22314
Phone: 703-684-9444
Fax: 703-684-9445
Web: www.horatioalger.org/scholarships

Horatio Alger Missouri Scholarship Program

Type of award: Scholarship.
Intended use: For undergraduate study at accredited 2-year or 4-year institution.
Eligibility: Applicant must be high school senior. Applicant must be U.S. citizen residing in Missouri.
Basis for selection: Applicant must demonstrate financial need.
Application requirements: Essay.
Additional information: Minimum 2.0 GPA. Program assists Missouri high school seniors who have faced and overcome great obstacles. Applicant should have strong commitment to use college degree in service to others. Must plan to pursue bachelor's degree. See Website for application.

   Amount of award: $5,000
   Number of awards: 50
   Application deadline: October 30

Horatio Alger Montana Scholarship Program

Type of award: Scholarship.
Intended use: For undergraduate study at accredited 2-year or 4-year institution. Designated institutions: University of Montana institutions.
Eligibility: Applicant must be high school senior. Applicant must be U.S. citizen residing in Montana.
Basis for selection: Applicant must demonstrate financial need.
Application requirements: Essay.
Additional information: Minimum 2.0 GPA. Program assists Montana high school seniors who have faced and overcome great obstacles. Applicant should have strong commitment to use college degree in service to others. Must plan to pursue bachelor's degree. See Website for application.

Amount of award:	$5,000
Number of awards:	50
Application deadline:	October 30

Contact:
Horatio Alger Association
99 Canal Center Plaza
Alexandria, VA 22314
Phone: 703-684-9444
Fax: 703-684-9445
Web: www.horatioalger.org/scholarships

Horatio Alger National Scholarship

Type of award: Scholarship.
Intended use: For undergraduate study at accredited 2-year or 4-year institution.
Eligibility: Applicant must be high school senior. Applicant must be U.S. citizen.
Basis for selection: Applicant must demonstrate financial need, seriousness of purpose and service orientation.
Application requirements: Essay.
Additional information: Minimum 2.0 GPA. Program assists high school seniors who have faced and overcome great obstacles. Applicant should have strong commitment to use college degree in service to others. Must plan to pursue bachelor's degree. Visit Website for application.

Amount of award:	$20,000
Number of awards:	106
Application deadline:	October 30

Contact:
Horatio Alger Association
99 Canal Center Plaza
Alexandria, VA 22314
Phone: 703-684-9444
Fax: 703-684-9445
Web: www.horatioalger.org/scholarships

Horatio Alger New Jersey Scholarship Program

Type of award: Scholarship.
Intended use: For undergraduate study at accredited 2-year or 4-year institution.
Eligibility: Applicant must be U.S. citizen residing in New Jersey.
Basis for selection: Applicant must demonstrate financial need, seriousness of purpose and service orientation.
Application requirements: Essay.
Additional information: Minimum 2.0 GPA. Program assists high school seniors who have faced and overcome great obstacles. Applicant should have strong commitment to use college degree in service to others. Must plan to pursue bachelor's degree. Visit Website for application.

Amount of award:	$5,000
Number of awards:	5
Application deadline:	October 30

Contact:
Horatio Alger Assocation
99 Canal Center Plaza
Alexandria, VA 22314
Phone: 703-684-9444
Fax: 703-684-9445
Web: www.horatioalger.org/scholarships

Horatio Alger New York Scholarship Program

Type of award: Scholarship.
Intended use: For undergraduate study at accredited 2-year or 4-year institution.
Eligibility: Applicant must be U.S. citizen residing in New York.
Basis for selection: Applicant must demonstrate financial need, seriousness of purpose and service orientation.
Application requirements: Essay.
Additional information: Minimum 2.0 GPA. Program assists high school seniors who have faced and overcome great obstacles. Applicant should have strong commitment to use college degree in service to others. Must plan to pursue bachelor's degree. Visit Website for application.

Amount of award:	$5,000
Number of awards:	5
Application deadline:	October 30

Contact:
Horatio Alger Association
99 Canal Center Plaza
Alexandria, VA 22314
Phone: 703-684-9444
Fax: 703-684-9445
Web: www.horatioalger.org/scholarships

Horatio Alger North Dakota Scholarship Program

Type of award: Scholarship.
Intended use: For undergraduate study at accredited 2-year or 4-year institution.
Eligibility: Applicant must be U.S. citizen residing in North Dakota.
Basis for selection: Applicant must demonstrate financial need, seriousness of purpose and service orientation.
Application requirements: Essay.
Additional information: Minimum 2.0 GPA. Program assists high school seniors who have faced and overcome great obstacles. Applicant should have strong commitment to use college degree in service to others. Must plan to pursue bachelor's degree. Visit Website for application.

Amount of award:	$5,000
Number of awards:	25
Application deadline:	October 30

Contact:
Horatio Alger Association
99 Canal Center Plaza
Alexandria, VA 22314
Phone: 703-684-9444
Fax: 703-684-9445
Web: www.horatioalger.org/scholarships

Horatio Alger Oregon Scholarship Program

Type of award: Scholarship.
Intended use: For undergraduate study at accredited 2-year or 4-year institution.
Eligibility: Applicant must be U.S. citizen residing in Oregon.
Basis for selection: Applicant must demonstrate financial need, seriousness of purpose and service orientation.
Application requirements: Essay.
Additional information: Minimum 2.0 GPA. Program assists high school seniors who have faced and overcome great obstacles. Applicant should have strong commitment to use college degree in service to others. Must plan to pursue bachelor's degree. Visit Website for application.

Amount of award:	$5,000
Number of awards:	5
Application deadline:	October 30

Contact:
Horatio Alger Association
99 Canal Center Plaza
Alexandria, VA 22314
Phone: 703-684-9444
Fax: 703-684-9445
Web: www.horatioalger.org/scholarships

Horatio Alger Pennsylvania Scholarship Program

Type of award: Scholarship.
Intended use: For undergraduate study at accredited 2-year or 4-year institution.
Eligibility: Applicant must be high school senior. Applicant must be U.S. citizen residing in Pennsylvania.
Basis for selection: Applicant must demonstrate financial need.
Application requirements: Essay.
Additional information: Minimum 2.0 GPA. Program assists Pennsylvania high school seniors who have faced and overcome great obstacles. Applicant should have strong commitment to use college degree in service to others. Must plan to pursue bachelor's degree. See Website for application.

Amount of award:	$5,000
Number of awards:	50
Application deadline:	October 30

Contact:
Horatio Alger Association
99 Canal Center Drive
Alexandria, VA 22314
Phone: 703-684-9444
Fax: 703-684-9445
Web: www.horatioalger.org/scholarships

Horatio Alger South Dakota Scholarship Program

Type of award: Scholarship.
Intended use: For full-time undergraduate study at accredited 2-year or 4-year institution in United States.
Eligibility: Applicant must be high school senior. Applicant must be U.S. citizen residing in South Dakota.
Basis for selection: Applicant must demonstrate financial need and service orientation.
Additional information: Minimum 2.0 GPA. Program assists South Dakota high school seniors who have faced and overcome great obstacles. Non-citizens in process of becoming citizens also eligible. Applicant should have strong commitment to use college degree in service to others. Must plan to pursue bachelor's degree. See Website for application and more information.

Amount of award:	$5,000
Number of awards:	25
Application deadline:	October 30

Contact:
The Horatio Alger Association
99 Canal Center Plaza
Alexandria, VA 22314
Phone: 703-684-9444
Fax: 703-684-9445
Web: www.horatioalger.org/scholarships

Horatio Alger Texas Ft. Worth Scholarship Program

Type of award: Scholarship.
Intended use: For undergraduate study at accredited 2-year or 4-year institution.
Eligibility: Applicant must be residing in Texas.
Basis for selection: Applicant must demonstrate financial need, seriousness of purpose and service orientation.
Application requirements: Essay.
Additional information: Minimum 2.0 GPA. Program assists high school seniors who have faced and overcome great obstacles. Applicant should have strong commitment to use college degree in service to others. Must plan to pursue bachelor's degree. Visit Website for application.

Amount of award:	$5,000
Number of awards:	12
Application deadline:	October 30

Contact:
Horatio Alger Assocation
99 Canal Center Plaza
Alexandria, VA 22314
Phone: 703-684-9444
Fax: 703-684-9445
Web: www.horatioalger.org/scholarships

Horatio Alger Texas Scholarship Program

Type of award: Scholarship.
Intended use: For undergraduate study at accredited 2-year or 4-year institution.
Eligibility: Applicant must be high school senior. Applicant must be U.S. citizen residing in Texas.
Basis for selection: Applicant must demonstrate financial need, high academic achievement, depth of character and service orientation.

Additional information: Program assists Texas high school seniors who have faced and overcome great obstacles. Applicant should have strong commitment to use college degree in service to others. Must plan to pursue bachelor's degree. See Website for application.

Amount of award:	$5,000
Number of awards:	40
Application deadline:	October 30

Contact:
Horatio Alger Association
99 Canal Center Plaza
Alexandria, VA 22314
Phone: 703-684-9444
Fax: 703-684-9445
Web: www.horatioalger.org/scholarships

Horatio Alger Utah Scholarship Program

Type of award: Scholarship.
Intended use: For undergraduate study at accredited 2-year or 4-year institution.
Eligibility: Applicant must be U.S. citizen residing in Utah.
Basis for selection: Applicant must demonstrate financial need and seriousness of purpose.
Application requirements: Essay.
Additional information: Minimum 2.0 GPA. Program assists high school seniors who have faced and overcome great obstacles. Applicant should have strong commitment to use college degree in service to others. Must plan to pursue bachelor's degree. Visit Website for application.

Amount of award:	$5,000
Number of awards:	25
Application deadline:	October 30

Contact:
Horatio Alger Association
99 Canal Center Plaza
Alexandria, VA 22314
Phone: 703-684-9444
Fax: 703-684-9445
Web: www.horatioalger.org/scholarships

Horatio Alger Washington Scholarship Program

Type of award: Scholarship.
Intended use: For undergraduate study at accredited 2-year or 4-year institution.
Eligibility: Applicant must be U.S. citizen residing in Washington.
Basis for selection: Applicant must demonstrate financial need, seriousness of purpose and service orientation.
Application requirements: Essay.
Additional information: Minimum 2.0 GPA. Program assists high school seniors who have faced and overcome great obstacles. Applicant should have strong commitment to use college degree in service to others. Must plan to pursue bachelor's degree. Visit Website for application.

Amount of award:	$5,000
Number of awards:	5
Application deadline:	October 30

Contact:
Horatio Alger Association
99 Canal Center Plaza
Alexandria, VA 22314
Phone: 703-684-9444
Fax: 703-684-9445
Web: www.horatioalger.org/scholarships

Horatio Alger Wyoming Scholarship Program

Type of award: Scholarship.
Intended use: For undergraduate study at accredited 2-year or 4-year institution.
Eligibility: Applicant must be U.S. citizen residing in Wyoming.
Basis for selection: Applicant must demonstrate financial need, seriousness of purpose and service orientation.
Application requirements: Essay.
Additional information: Minimum 2.0 GPA. Program assists high school seniors who have faced and overcome great obstacles. Applicant should have strong commitment to use college degree in service to others. Must plan to pursue bachelor's degree. Visit Website for application.

Amount of award:	$5,000
Number of awards:	25
Application deadline:	October 30

Contact:
Horatio Alger Association
99 Canal Center Plaza
Alexandria, VA 22314
Phone: 703-684-9444
Fax: 703-684-9445
Web: www.horatioalger.org/scholarships

Horizons Foundation

Horizons Scholarship of Women in Defense

Type of award: Scholarship.
Intended use: For junior, senior or graduate study at accredited 4-year institution in United States.
Eligibility: Applicant must be U.S. citizen.
Basis for selection: Major/career interest in science, general; engineering; mathematics; computer/information sciences; physics; business; law; international relations or political science/government. Applicant must demonstrate financial need and high academic achievement.
Application requirements: Recommendations, essay, transcript.
Additional information: Scholarship intended to provide financial assistance to individuals either employed or planning careers in defense or national security areas. Minimum 3.25 GPA. Studies must be aimed at national defense/national security. Visit Website for details and application (no phone calls).

Amount of award:	$500-$2,000
Number of awards:	5
Number of applicants:	40
Application deadline:	July 1
Total amount awarded:	$6,000

Contact:
Horizons/WID
2111 Wilson Blvd., Suite 400
Arlington, VA 22201-3061
Phone: 703-247-2552
Fax: 703-522-1885
Web: wid.ndia.org

Horticultural Research Institute

Carville M. Akehurst Memorial Scholarship

Type of award: Scholarship.
Intended use: For full-time junior or senior study at accredited postsecondary institution.
Eligibility: Applicant must be residing in Virginia, West Virginia or Maryland.
Basis for selection: Major/career interest in horticulture or landscape architecture. Applicant must demonstrate high academic achievement.
Application requirements: Recommendations, essay, transcript. Resume. Faculty Referral Form.
Additional information: Applicant must be resident of Maryland, Virginia or West Virginia. Minimum 2.7 overall GPA and minimum 3.0 in major. Must have junior standing in four-year curriculum or senior standing in two-year curriculum. Preference given to applicants who plan to work within industry following graduation. Previous winners eligible for additional funding. Visit Website for application and more information. Applications accepted all year. May submit application to hriresearch@anla.org.

Amount of award:	$4,000
Number of awards:	1
Number of applicants:	13
Application deadline:	April 1
Total amount awarded:	$4,000

Contact:
Horticultural Research Institute
1000 Vermont Avenue NW
Suite 300
Washington, DC 20005-4914
Phone: 202-789-2900
Fax: 202-789-1893
Web: www.hriresearch.org

Horticultural Research Institute Spring Meadow Scholarship

Type of award: Scholarship.
Intended use: For full-time undergraduate study at accredited postsecondary institution.
Basis for selection: Major/career interest in horticulture or landscape architecture.
Application requirements: Recommendations, essay, transcript. Resume. Faculty Referral Form.
Additional information: Must have minimum 2.25 overall GPA, and minimum 2.7 in major. Must be enrolled in accredited landscape/horticulture program. Preference given to those who plan to work in industry following graduation. Visit Website for application and more information. Applications may be submitted to hriresearch@anla.org.

Amount of award:	$2,500
Number of awards:	1
Number of applicants:	57
Application deadline:	April 1
Total amount awarded:	$2,500

Contact:
Horticultural Research Institute
1000 Vermont Avenue NW
Suite 300
Washington, DC 20005-4914
Phone: 202-789-2900
Fax: 202-789-1893
Web: www.hriresearch.org

Timothy Bigelow Scholarship

Type of award: Scholarship.
Intended use: For full-time undergraduate or graduate study at accredited 2-year, 4-year or graduate institution.
Eligibility: Applicant must be residing in Vermont, New Hampshire, Connecticut, Maine, Massachusetts or Rhode Island.
Basis for selection: Major/career interest in landscape architecture or horticulture. Applicant must demonstrate financial need, high academic achievement, depth of character and seriousness of purpose.
Application requirements: Recommendations, essay, transcript. Resume and cover letter.
Additional information: Minimum 2.25 GPA for undergraduates and 3.0 GPA for graduate students. Must be enrolled in accredited landscape or horticulture program. Applicant must have senior standing in two-year program, junior standing in four-year program, or graduate standing. Applicant must be resident of one of the six New England states, but need not attend institute there. Application may be submitted to hriresearch@anla.org.

Amount of award:	$3,500
Number of awards:	1
Number of applicants:	8
Application deadline:	April 1
Notification begins:	July 1
Total amount awarded:	$3,500

Contact:
Endowment Program Administrator
Horticultural Research Institute
1000 Vermont Ave. NW, Suite 300
Washington, DC 20005-4914
Phone: 202-789-2900 ext. 3014
Fax: 202-789-1893
Web: www.hriresearch.org

Usrey Family Scholarship

Type of award: Scholarship, renewable.
Intended use: For full-time undergraduate or graduate study at vocational, 2-year, 4-year or graduate institution in United States.
Eligibility: Applicant must be residing in California.
Basis for selection: Major/career interest in landscape architecture or horticulture.
Application requirements: Recommendations, essay, transcript. Cover letter and resume.
Additional information: Applicant must be student enrolled in California state college/university in undergraduate or graduate landscape or horticulture program. Non-resident applicants who attend California school are also eligible. Minimum 2.5 GPA overall; minimum 2.7 GPA in major. Visit Website for application. May submit application to hriresearch@anla.org.

Horticultural Research Institute: Usrey Family Scholarship

Amount of award: $1,500
Number of awards: 1
Number of applicants: 9
Application deadline: April 1
Total amount awarded: $1,500

Contact:
Endowment Program Administrator, Horticultural Research Institute
1000 Vermont Ave. NW
Suite 300
Washington, DC 20005-4914
Phone: 202-789-5980 ext. 3014
Fax: 202-789-1893
Web: www.hriresearch.org

Houston Livestock Show and Rodeo

Area Go Texan Scholarships

Type of award: Scholarship.
Intended use: For undergraduate study at postsecondary institution.
Eligibility: Applicant must be high school senior. Applicant must be U.S. citizen residing in Texas.
Basis for selection: Applicant must demonstrate financial need, high academic achievement, depth of character, leadership and service orientation.
Application requirements: Recommendations, essay, transcript, proof of eligibility. Class standing and photograph.
Additional information: Scholarships (payable at $1,500 over eight semesters) awarded to one eligible public high school student from each of 60 Area Go Texan counties. SAT score must be at least 1350 combined, and ACT score at least 19. Applicant must attend public high school and be in top third of graduating class. Applicant cannot receive more than $40,000 from financial aid or other scholarships. Contact sponsor or visit Website for details and application.

Amount of award: $15,000
Number of awards: 60
Application deadline: January 25

Contact:
Houston Livestock Show and Rodeo
Office of Education Programs
P.O. Box 20070
Houston, TX 77225
Phone: 832-667-1000
Web: www.hlsr.com/ed/s/s_agts.aspx

Opportunity Scholarship

Type of award: Scholarship, renewable.
Intended use: For full-time undergraduate study at postsecondary institution.
Eligibility: Applicant must be high school senior. Applicant must be U.S. citizen residing in Texas.
Basis for selection: Applicant must demonstrate financial need, high academic achievement, depth of character, leadership and service orientation.
Application requirements: Recommendations, essay, transcript, proof of eligibility. Up to three references. Two-page essay must describe importance of college and career goals. Class standing and photograph.

Additional information: Applicant must have minimum 1210 SAT or 17 ACT. Must be graduating in top half of class from specified Texas school districts in Brazoria, Chambers, Fort Bend, Galveston, Harris, Liberty, Montgomery, or Waller counties. Visit Website for list of eligible districts, application, and more information. For applications, contact guidance counselor or Office of Education Programs.

Amount of award: $15,000
Number of awards: 100
Application deadline: March 12
Total amount awarded: $1,500,000

Contact:
Houston Livestock Show and Rodeo
Office of Education Programs
P.O. Box 20070
Houston, TX 77225
Phone: 832-667-1000
Web: www.hlsr.com/ed/s/s_maos1.aspx

ICMA Retirement Corporation

Vantagepoint Public Employee Memorial Scholarship Fund

Type of award: Scholarship.
Intended use: For full-time undergraduate or graduate study at accredited postsecondary institution.
Basis for selection: Applicant must demonstrate financial need, high academic achievement, leadership and service orientation.
Application requirements: Recommendations, essay, transcript, proof of eligibility. Statement of goals and aspirations, official letter from deceased employee's place of work certifying employee died in line of duty.
Additional information: High school seniors and graduates, as well as current undergraduate or graduate students eligible. Must be dependent child or spouse of deceased public employees who have died in the line of duty. Awards available in following categories: fire and rescue, law enforcement, and general public employees. Work experience, goals and aspirations, and unusual personal or family circumstances also factored into selection. Award amount varies; maximum is $10,000 (tuition and fees only). Visit Website for complete information including downloadable application.

Amount of award: $10,000
Number of awards: 7
Application deadline: March 15
Total amount awarded: $40,000

Contact:
Vantagepoint Public Employee Memorial Scholarship Program
c/o Scholarship America
One Scholarship Way, PO Box 297
St. Peter, MN 56082
Phone: 507-931-1682
Web: www.vantagescholar.org

Idaho State Board of Education

Grow Your Own Teacher Scholarship Program

Type of award: Scholarship.
Intended use: For undergraduate study at 2-year or 4-year institution. Designated institutions: Boise State University, Idaho State University, Lewis-Clark State College, College of Southern Idaho.
Eligibility: Applicant must be residing in Idaho.
Basis for selection: Major/career interest in education.
Application requirements: FAFSA.
Additional information: Program established to aid students becoming bilingual education, ESL and Native American teachers. Minimum 3.0 GPA. Award for part-time students based on credit hours. Contact college of education at intended institution of matriculation for more information.
  Amount of award: $3,000
  Application deadline: February 15
Contact:
Idaho State Board of Education
650 West State Street
P.O. Box 83720
Boise, ID 83720-0037
Phone: 208-332-1574
Web: www.boardofed.idaho.gov/scholarships

Idaho Governor's Cup Scholarship

Type of award: Scholarship, renewable.
Intended use: For full-time undergraduate study at postsecondary institution.
Eligibility: Applicant must be high school senior. Applicant must be residing in Idaho.
Basis for selection: Applicant must demonstrate high academic achievement, leadership and service orientation.
Application requirements: Recommendations, essay, transcript. SAT/ACT scores. Documentation of volunteer work, leadership, and public service.
Additional information: Applicant must be senior at Idaho high school. Minimum 2.8 GPA. Must have demonstrated commitment to public service. For more information, contact high school guidance counselor or Idaho State Board of Education.
  Amount of award: $3,000
  Number of awards: 12
  Application deadline: January 15
Contact:
Idaho State Board of Education
650 State Street
P.O. Box 83720
Boise, ID 83720-0037
Phone: 208-332-1574
Web: www.boardofed.idaho.gov

Idaho Minority/"At-Risk" Scholarship

Type of award: Scholarship, renewable.
Intended use: For full-time undergraduate study. Designated institutions: Boise State University, Brigham Young University-Idaho, Idaho State University, North Idaho College, Eastern Idaho Technical College, Lewis-Clark State College, Northwest Nazarene University, University of Idaho, College of Southern Idaho, and Albertson College.
Eligibility: Applicant must be U.S. citizen residing in Idaho.
Basis for selection: Applicant must demonstrate financial need.
Additional information: Must be talented student at risk of failing to realize ambitions due to cultural, economic, or physical circumstances. Must be graduate of Idaho high school. Must meet three of the following criteria: be first-generation college student; be disabled; be a migrant worker or dependent of one; have substantial financial need; be member of ethnic minority historically underrepresented in higher education in Idaho. Award amount varies; maximum is $3,000. Contact high school counselor or financial aid office of participating postsecondary institutions for specific requirements and application.
  Amount of award: $3,000
  Number of awards: 45
  Total amount awarded: $120,000
Contact:
Financial aid office at designated institution.
Phone: 208-332-1574
Web: www.boardofed.idaho.gov

Idaho Robert C. Byrd Scholarship

Type of award: Scholarship, renewable.
Intended use: For full-time freshman study at 2-year or 4-year institution.
Eligibility: Applicant must be high school senior. Applicant must be U.S. citizen or permanent resident residing in Idaho.
Basis for selection: Applicant must demonstrate high academic achievement.
Application requirements: Transcript, proof of eligibility. Statement of Selective Service registration status.
Additional information: Award amount varies; maximum is $1,500 per year, renewable for up to four years. Visit Website or contact high school counselor for application, deadlines and more information.
  Amount of award: $1,500
Contact:
Dana Kelly, Idaho State Board of Education
650 West State Street
P.O. Box 83720
Boise, ID 83720-0037
Phone: 208-332-1574
Web: www.boardofed.idaho.gov

Idaho Robert R. Lee Category A Promise Scholarship

Type of award: Scholarship, renewable.
Intended use: For full-time freshman study at postsecondary institution.
Eligibility: Applicant must be high school senior. Applicant must be residing in Idaho.
Additional information: Applicant must have minimum 28 ACT and 3.5 GPA, and be in top ten percent of graduating class. Applicants for professional-technical programs must have minimum 2.8 GPA and take COMPASS exam. Apply online or contact Idaho State Board of Education for application.
  Amount of award: $3,000
  Number of awards: 25
  Number of applicants: 3,000
  Application deadline: December 15
  Total amount awarded: $75,000

Contact:
Dana Kelly, Idaho State Board of Education
650 West State Street
P.O. Box 83720
Boise, ID 83720-0037
Phone: 208-332-1574
Web: www.boardofed.idaho.gov

Idaho Robert R. Lee Category B Promise Scholarship

Type of award: Scholarship, renewable.
Intended use: For full-time freshman study at postsecondary institution. Designated institutions: Boise State University, College of Southern Idaho, Eastern Idaho Technical College, Idaho State University, Lewis-Clark State College, North Idaho College, University of Idaho, Albertson College of Idaho, Northwest Nazarene University, and BYU-Idaho.
Eligibility: Applicant must be no older than 21. Applicant must be residing in Idaho.
Additional information: Minimum 3.0 GPA or ACT score of 20. Must be younger than 22 on July 1 of academic term of award. Must have completed high school, or equivalent, in Idaho. For more information, contact college or university.

Amount of award:	$500

Contact:
Dana Kelly, Idaho State Board of Education
650 West State Street
P.O. Box 83720
Boise, ID 83720-0037
Phone: 208-332-1574
Web: www.boardofed.idaho.gov

Leveraging Educational Assistance State Partnership Program (LEAP)

Type of award: Scholarship, renewable.
Intended use: For undergraduate or graduate study at vocational, 2-year, 4-year or graduate institution. Designated institutions: Eligible Idaho public and private colleges and universities.
Eligibility: Applicant must be U.S. citizen or permanent resident.
Basis for selection: Applicant must demonstrate financial need.
Application requirements: FAFSA.
Additional information: Formerly the Idaho State Student Incentive Grant. Institution makes recommendations to Idaho State Board of Education. Contact financial aid office of Idaho public colleges and universities for materials or additional information.

Amount of award:	$400-$5,000
Number of awards:	2,000
Application deadline:	June 30
Total amount awarded:	$2,700,000

Contact:
Financial aid offices at Idaho colleges
Phone: 208-332-1574
Web: www.idahoboardofed.org/scholarships/leap.asp

Illinois Student Assistance Commission

Bonus Incentive Grant (BIG)

Type of award: Scholarship.
Intended use: For undergraduate study at 2-year or 4-year institution in United States. Designated institutions: Approved Illinois public and private colleges, universities, and hospital schools.
Eligibility: Applicant must be U.S. citizen or permanent resident residing in Illinois.
Additional information: Bonus Incentive Grants are non-need based grants available to beneficiaries of Illinois College Savings Bonds, if at least 70 percent of bond proceeds are used for costs at eligible institution. Must have owned bond for at least 12 consecutive months. Grant amounts range from $40 to $440 per bond. Grants can be used for educational purposes only. Not for use at religious institutions, for divinity programs, or for studies in preparation for the priesthood, regardless of denomination or faith. Contact sponsor for more information, or visit Website.

Number of awards:	399
Total amount awarded:	$219,000

Contact:
Illinois Student Assistance Commission
ISAC College Zone Counselor
1755 Lake Cook Road
Deerfield, IL 60015
Phone: 800-899-ISAC
Web: www.collegezone.com

Grant Program for Dependents of Correctional Officers

Type of award: Scholarship, renewable.
Intended use: For freshman study at 2-year or 4-year institution in United States. Designated institutions: ISAC-approved institutions in Illinois.
Eligibility: Applicant must be U.S. citizen or permanent resident residing in Illinois. Applicant's parent must have been killed or disabled in work-related accident as public safety officer.
Application requirements: Proof of eligibility.
Additional information: Must be child or spouse of Illinois corrections officer killed or at least 90 percent disabled in line of duty. Does not need to be Illinois resident at time of enrollment. Award is equal to full tuition and mandatory fees at public Illinois institutions; at private schools a corresponding amount is awarded. Applicant need not be Illinois resident at time of enrollment. Beneficiaries may receive the equivalent of eight semesters or 12 quarters of assistance. Contact ISAC or visit Website for additional information.

Number of awards:	69
Total amount awarded:	$349,576

Contact:
Illinois Student Assistance Commission
ISAC College Zone Counselor
1755 Lake Cook Road
Deerfield, IL 60015
Phone: 800-899-ISAC
Web: www.collegezone.com

Grant Program for Dependents of Police or Fire Officers

Type of award: Scholarship, renewable.
Intended use: For undergraduate or graduate study at 2-year, 4-year or graduate institution. Designated institutions: ISAC-approved institutions in Illinois.
Eligibility: Applicant must be U.S. citizen or permanent resident residing in Illinois. Applicant's parent must have been killed or disabled in work-related accident as firefighter or police officer.
Application requirements: Proof of eligibility.
Additional information: Grant for tuition and fees for spouse and children of Illinois policemen or firemen killed or at least 90 percent disabled in line of duty. Award amount adjusted annually. Applicant need not be Illinois resident at time of enrollment. Beneficiaries may receive the equivalent of eight semesters or 12 quarters of assistance. Contact ISAC or visit Website for additional information.

Amount of award:	Full tuition
Number of awards:	69
Application deadline:	October 1
Total amount awarded:	$349,997

Contact:
Illinois Student Assistance Commission
ISAC College Zone Counselor
1755 Lake Cook Road
Deerfield, IL 60015
Phone: 800-899-ISAC
Web: www.collegezone.com

Illinois Future Teacher Corps

Type of award: Scholarship, renewable.
Intended use: For junior, senior or graduate study at accredited 2-year or 4-year institution. Designated institutions: Approved Illinois public and private four-year colleges and universities offering teacher program, and certain other degree-granting institutions.
Eligibility: Applicant must be U.S. citizen or permanent resident residing in Illinois.
Basis for selection: Major/career interest in education; education, teacher or education, early childhood. Applicant must demonstrate financial need and high academic achievement.
Application requirements: FAFSA and Teacher Education Program Application.
Additional information: Scholarships for students planning to pursue careers as preschool, elementary school, and secondary school teachers in Illinois. Priority given to students with financial need, minority students, and students planning to teach in teacher shortage discipline and/or hard-to-staff school. Must fulfill teaching commitment or scholarship becomes loan. Minimum 2.5 GPA. See Website for application.

Amount of award:	$5,000-$15,000
Number of awards:	555
Application deadline:	March 1
Total amount awarded:	$3,770,517

Contact:
Illinois Student Assistance Commission
ISAC College Zone Counselor
1755 Lake Cook Road
Deerfield, IL 60015
Phone: 800-899-ISAC
Web: www.collegezone.com

Illinois National Guard Grant

Type of award: Scholarship, renewable.
Intended use: For undergraduate or graduate study at 2-year or 4-year institution.
Eligibility: Applicant must be residing in Illinois. Applicant must be in military service in the Reserves/National Guard. Must have served at least one year of active duty in Illinois National Guard or Naval Militia.
Application requirements: Proof of eligibility.
Additional information: Available to enlisted and company grade officers up to rank of captain who have either served one year active duty; are currently on active duty status; or have been active for at least five consecutive years and have been called to federal active duty for at least six months and be within 12 months after discharge date. Applied toward tuition and certain fees. Recipients may use award for eight semesters or 12 quarters (or the equivalent). Award amount varies. Deadlines: 10/1 for full year, 3/1 for second/third term, and 6/15 for summer term. Applications available from ISAC or National Guard units. Contact ISAC or National Guard units or visit Website for additional information.

Number of awards:	1,698
Total amount awarded:	$4,216,713

Contact:
Illinois Student Assistance Commission
ISAC College Zone Counselor
1755 Lake Cook Road
Deerfield, IL 60015
Phone: 800-899-ISAC
Web: www.collegezone.com

Illinois Veteran Grant (IVG) Program

Type of award: Scholarship, renewable.
Intended use: For undergraduate or graduate study at postsecondary institution.
Eligibility: Applicant must be U.S. citizen or permanent resident residing in Illinois. Applicant must be veteran. Must have been Illinois resident six months prior to entering service and must have returned to Illinois to reside within six months of leaving service. Must have served one year of federal active duty or have served in a foreign country in a time of hostilities in that country.
Application requirements: Proof of eligibility.
Additional information: Provides payment of tuition and mandatory fees to qualified Illinois veterans or military service members. Grant is available for equivalent of four academic years of full-time enrollment for undergraduate and graduate study. Recipient not required to enroll for minimum number of credit hours each term. One-time application only. See Website for additional information and application.

Amount of award:	Full tuition
Number of awards:	11,511
Total amount awarded:	$19,217,037

Contact:
Illinois Student Assistance Commission
ISAC College Zone Counselor
1755 Lake Cook Road
Deerfield, IL 60015
Phone: 800-899-ISAC
Web: www.collegezone.com

Merit Recognition Scholarship

Type of award: Scholarship.

Illinois Student Assistance Commission: Merit Recognition Scholarship

Intended use: For freshman study at postsecondary institution. Designated institutions: ISAC-approved institutions in Illinois or approved U.S. service academies.
Eligibility: Applicant must be high school senior. Applicant must be U.S. citizen or permanent resident residing in Illinois.
Basis for selection: Applicant must demonstrate high academic achievement.
Application requirements: Proof of eligibility.
Additional information: Applicant must rank in top five percent of Illinois high school class at end of third semester prior to graduation, or score in top five percent of Illinois students taking college entrance tests during designated time frame. Recipients must use award within one year of high school graduation and must be enrolled for undergraduate study at least half-time. High school counselors designate eligible students. Contact ISAC or high school counselor, or visit Website for additional information.
    Amount of award: $1,000
    Number of awards: 5,458
    Total amount awarded: $5,372,000
Contact:
Illinois Student Assistance Commission
ISAC College Zone Counselor
1755 Lake Cook Road
Deerfield, IL 60015
Phone: 800-899-ISAC
Web: www.collegezone.com

Minority Teachers of Illinois Scholarship

Type of award: Scholarship, renewable.
Intended use: For undergraduate or graduate study at postsecondary institution. Designated institutions: ISAC-approved institutions in Illinois.
Eligibility: Applicant must be Alaskan native, Asian American, African American, Mexican American, Hispanic American, Puerto Rican or American Indian. Applicant must be U.S. citizen or permanent resident residing in Illinois.
Basis for selection: Major/career interest in education, teacher or education.
Application requirements: Teacher Education Program application.
Additional information: Minimum 2.5 GPA. Applicant should be in course of study leading to teacher certification. Recipient must sign commitment to teach one year in Illinois for each year assistance is received. Must teach at nonprofit Illinois preschool, elementary school, or secondary school with at least 30 percent minority enrollment. If teaching commitment is not fulfilled, scholarship converts to loan, and entire amount, plus interest, must be paid. Contact ISAC or visit Website for additional information.
    Amount of award: $5,000
    Number of awards: 607
    Application deadline: March 1
    Total amount awarded: $2,817,073
Contact:
Illinois Student Assistance Commission
ISAC College Zone Counselor
1755 Lake Cook Road
Deerfield, IL 60015
Phone: 800-899-ISAC
Web: www.collegezone.com

Monetary Award Program (MAP)

Type of award: Scholarship, renewable.
Intended use: For undergraduate study at 2-year or 4-year institution. Designated institutions: ISAC/MAP-approved institutions in Illinois.
Eligibility: Applicant must be U.S. citizen or permanent resident residing in Illinois.
Basis for selection: Applicant must demonstrate financial need.
Application requirements: FAFSA.
Additional information: Must reapply every year for renewal. Contact ISAC or visit Website for application, deadlines, and additional information. Amount of award dependent on legislative action and available funding in any given year.
    Amount of award: $300-$4,968
    Number of applicants: 553,962
    Application deadline: September 30
    Total amount awarded: $330,328,687
Contact:
Illinois Student Assistance Commission
ISAC College Zone Counselor
1755 Lake Cook Road
Deerfield, IL 60015
Phone: 800-899-ISAC
Web: www.collegezone.com

Robert C. Byrd Honors Scholarship Program

Type of award: Scholarship, renewable.
Intended use: For full-time undergraduate study at accredited postsecondary institution in United States.
Eligibility: Applicant must be high school senior. Applicant must be U.S. citizen or permanent resident residing in Illinois.
Basis for selection: Applicant must demonstrate high academic achievement.
Additional information: Names of qualifying students submitted by high school guidance counselors. Student must be high school senior and enrolled, or accepted for enrollment, as full-time undergraduate. Eligibility based on standardized test scores, high school rank, and GPA.
    Amount of award: $1,500
    Number of awards: 1,074
    Total amount awarded: $1,589,986
Contact:
Illinois Student Assistance Commission
ISAC College Zone Counselor
1755 Lake Cook Road
Deerfield, IL 60015
Phone: 800-899-ISAC
Web: www.collegezone.com

Silas Purnell Illinois Incentive for Access

Type of award: Scholarship.
Intended use: For freshman study at postsecondary institution. Designated institutions: ISAC-approved institutions.
Eligibility: Applicant must be U.S. citizen or permanent resident residing in Illinois.
Basis for selection: Applicant must demonstrate financial need.
Application requirements: FAFSA.
Additional information: Applicant must have been determined by federal needs calculation to have an expected family contribution (EFC) of $0. Must meet Monetary Award Program eligibility requirements. Contact ISAC or visit Website for additional information.

Amount of award: $500
Number of applicants: 45,000
Contact:
Illinois Student Assistance Commission
ISAC College Zone Counselor
1755 Lake Cook Road
Deerfield, IL 60015
Phone: 800-899-ISAC
Web: www.collegezone.com

Special Education Teacher Tuition Waiver

Type of award: Scholarship, renewable.
Intended use: For undergraduate or graduate study at postsecondary institution in United States. Designated institutions: Eligible four-year institutions in Illinois: Chicago State University, Eastern Illinois University, Governors State University, Illinois State University, Northeastern Illinois University, Northern Illinois University, Southern Illinois University (Carbondale and Edwardsville), University of Illinois (Chicago, Springfield, Urbana), and Western Illinois University.
Eligibility: Applicant must be U.S. citizen or permanent resident residing in Illinois.
Basis for selection: Major/career interest in education, special.
Additional information: Must be Illinois high school graduate and rank in upper half of graduating class. Must not already hold valid teaching certificate in special education. Recipients must teach in Illinois for two years, or scholarship becomes loan. See Website for application and more details.

Amount of award: Full tuition
Number of awards: 250
Application deadline: March 1
Notification begins: July 1
Contact:
Illinois Student Assistance Commission
1755 Lake Cook Road
Deerfield, IL 60015-5209
Phone: 800-899-ISAC
Web: www.collegezone.com

Student-to-Student (STS) Program

Type of award: Scholarship, renewable.
Intended use: For undergraduate study at postsecondary institution. Designated institutions: Participating institutions in Illinois.
Eligibility: Applicant must be U.S. citizen or permanent resident residing in Illinois.
Basis for selection: Applicant must demonstrate financial need.
Additional information: Voluntary student contributions are matched, dollar for dollar, by ISAC, and paid to participating institutions. Need-based grants are then made available to students through procedures established by campus financial aid administrator and local student government. Deadline for application set by individual schools. Recipient must attend school on at least half-time basis. Must reapply for renewal. Contact college or university financial aid office, or visit ISAC Website for additional information.

Number of awards: 3,427
Total amount awarded: $949,576

Contact:
Illinois Student Assistance Commission
ISAC College Zone Counselor
1755 Lake Cook Road
Deerfield, IL 60015
Phone: 800-899-ISAC
Web: www.collegezone.com

Institute for Humane Studies

Humane Studies Fellowship

Type of award: Scholarship.
Intended use: For full-time junior, senior or graduate study.
Basis for selection: Applicant must demonstrate high academic achievement.
Application requirements: $25 application fee. Recommendations, essay, transcript. Test scores (GRE, LSAT, GMAT, SAT, ACT, etc.), resume and writing sample. Sample is typically draft dissertation or academic paper; 30 page maximum.
Additional information: Applicants should have demonstrated interest in the principles, practices, and institutions necessary to a free society. Amounts awarded take into account the cost of tuition at the recipient's institution and any other funds received. Number of fellowships awarded each year varies. IHS begins accepting applications online in September.

Amount of award: $2,000-$12,000
Number of awards: 120
Application deadline: December 31
Notification begins: April 20
Total amount awarded: $450,000

Contact:
Institute for Humane Studies at George Mason University
3301 N. Fairfax Drive
Suite 440
Arlington, VA 22201
Phone: 800-697-8799
Fax: 703-993-4890
Web: www.theihs.org

Institute of Environmental Sciences and Technology

Eugene Borson Memorial Scholarship

Type of award: Scholarship.
Intended use: For full-time undergraduate study at accredited 4-year institution.
Basis for selection: Major/career interest in science, general or engineering.
Application requirements: Recommendations, transcript. Essay, verification of relevant experience, copy of student ID, proof of full-time student status, address of school where award should be sent.
Additional information: Selection based on studies related to the environmental sciences in connection with controlled

Institute of Environmental Sciences and Technology: Eugene Borson Memorial Scholarship

environments, particularly through contamination control and nanotechnologies, in which products and equipment are manufactured, processed, or tested. Minimum 3.0 GPA in most recent semester. See Website for further information.

Amount of award:	$500
Number of awards:	1
Number of applicants:	1
Application deadline:	January 15
Notification begins:	March 26

Contact:
Institute of Environmental Sciences and Technology
Arlington Place One
2340 S. Arlington Rd., Ste. 100
Arlington Heights, IL 60005-4516
Phone: 847-891-0100
Fax: 847-981-4130
Web: www.iest.org

Park Espenschade Memorial Scholarship

Type of award: Scholarship.
Intended use: For full-time undergraduate study at accredited 4-year institution.
Basis for selection: Major/career interest in science, general or engineering.
Application requirements: Recommendations, transcript. Essay, verification of relevant experience, copy of student ID, address of school where award should be sent, proof of full-time student status.
Additional information: Selection based on original technical paper in a topic related to the environmental sciences. Minimum 3.0 GPA in most recent semester. See Website for further information.

Amount of award:	$500
Number of awards:	1
Number of applicants:	1
Application deadline:	January 15
Notification begins:	March 26

Contact:
Institute of Environmental Sciences and Technology
Arlington Place One
2340 S. Arlington Hts. Rd., Ste. 100
Arlington Heights, IL 60005-4516
Phone: 847-981-0100
Fax: 847-981-4130
Web: www.iest.org

Robert N. Hancock Memorial Scholarship

Type of award: Scholarship.
Intended use: For full-time sophomore, junior, senior or graduate study at accredited 4-year or graduate institution.
Basis for selection: Major/career interest in engineering or science, general.
Application requirements: Proof of full-time student status, copy of student ID, technical paper, biography, address of school where award should be sent.
Additional information: Awarded annually for best original science or engineering paper written by a student and published in the Journal of the IEST. Visit Website for more information.

Amount of award:	$500
Number of awards:	1
Number of applicants:	1
Application deadline:	January 15
Notification begins:	March 26

Contact:
Institute of Environmental Science and Technology
Arlington Place One
2340 S. Arlington Heights Rd., Ste. 100
Arlington Heights, IL 60005-4516
Phone: 847-981-0100
Fax: 847-981-4130
Web: www.iest.org

Institute of Food Technologists

Institute of Food Technologists Freshman Scholarship

Type of award: Scholarship, renewable.
Intended use: For full-time freshman study at 4-year institution in United States or Canada. Designated institutions: Educational institutions with approved programs in food science/technology.
Eligibility: Applicant must be high school senior.
Basis for selection: Major/career interest in food science/technology. Applicant must demonstrate high academic achievement.
Application requirements: Recommendations, essay, transcript. SAT/ACT report. Essay should be one page statement regarding applicant's desire to become food scientist/techonologist.
Additional information: IFT Scholarship recipients must be member of IFT student association. Applicant must be high school senior or high school graduate entering college for first time. Minimum 3.0 GPA required. Must have a well-rounded personality. Must enroll in IFT-approved program. Program descriptions and application available on Website. All inquiries and completed applications should be directed to department head of approved school.

Amount of award:	$1,000
Number of awards:	8
Application deadline:	February 15
Notification begins:	April 15
Total amount awarded:	$8,000

Contact:
Department head at approved school
Phone: 317-782-8424
Fax: 312-782-8348
Web: www.ift.org

Institute of Food Technologists Junior/Senior Scholarship

Type of award: Scholarship, renewable.
Intended use: For full-time sophomore, junior or senior study at 4-year institution in United States or Canada. Designated institutions: Educational institutions with approved programs in food science/technology.
Basis for selection: Major/career interest in food science/technology. Applicant must demonstrate high academic achievement.
Application requirements: Recommendations, transcript.
Additional information: Applicant must have minimum 3.0 GPA and must be enrolled in IFT-approved program. Program description and application available through Website or via fax. All other inquiries and completed applications should be

directed to department head of approved school. Previous scholarship recipients must be IFT members to reapply.

Amount of award:	$1,000-$2,500
Number of awards:	22
Application deadline:	February 1
Notification begins:	April 15
Total amount awarded:	$16,900

Contact:
Scholarship Department
Institute of Food Technologists
525 W. Van Buren, Suite 1000
Chicago, IL 60601
Phone: 312-782-8424
Fax: 312-782-8348
Web: www.ift.org

Institute of Food Technologists Sophomore Scholarship

Type of award: Scholarship, renewable.
Intended use: For full-time freshman study at 4-year institution in United States or Canada. Designated institutions: Educational institutions with approved programs in food science/technology. Essay must be 1 page statement regarding desire to continue studies in food science/tecnology. Non food majors must submit 1 page explaining desire to become food scientist/techonologist.
Basis for selection: Major/career interest in food science/technology. Applicant must demonstrate high academic achievement.
Application requirements: Recommendations, essay, transcript, proof of eligibility. SAT/ACT report.
Additional information: Applicant must be college freshman. Scholarship recipients must be member of IFT student association. Must have 3.0 GPA minimum. Must be enrolled in or plan to enroll in IFT-approved program. Program descriptions and application available through Website or via fax. All inquiries and completed applications should be directed to the department head of approved school. Previous scholarship recipients must be IFT members to reapply.

Amount of award:	$1,000
Number of awards:	8
Application deadline:	March 1
Notification begins:	April 15
Total amount awarded:	$8,000

Contact:
Institute of Food Technologists
Scholarship Department
525 West Van Buren, Suite 1000
Chicago, IL 60607
Phone: 312-782-8424
Fax: 312-782-8348
Web: www.ift.org

Institute of International Education

Freeman-ASIA Award Program

Type of award: Scholarship.
Intended use: For full-time undergraduate study at 2-year or 4-year institution in Cambodia, China, Hong Kong, Indonesia, Japan, Korea, Laos, Macao, Malaysia, Mongolia, Philippines, Singapore, Taiwan, Thailand, Vietnam.
Eligibility: Applicant must be U.S. citizen or permanent resident.
Basis for selection: Applicant must demonstrate financial need, high academic achievement, depth of character and service orientation.
Application requirements: Proof of eligibility. FAFSA, personal statement, service proposal.
Additional information: Applicants must have applied or been accepted to study abroad program in approved country. Program must be sponsored by U.S. accredited institution awarding college credit. Applicants must design projects to educate about and encourage study abroad in Asia upon returning to U.S. Priority given to students with limited experience in Asia. Applicant must currently receive need-based financial aid or demonstrate verifiable need to study abroad. Applicant must have at least one term of enrollment remaining at home institution following return from study in Asia. Award amounts range up to: $5,000 for fall or spring semester, $7,000 for academic year, $3,000 for summer term. See Website for application deadlines and additional eligibility requirements. Application must be filed electronically.

Contact:
Freeman-ASIA U.S. Student Programs Division
Institute of International Education
809 United Nations Plaza
New York, NY 10017-3580
Phone: 212-984-5542
Fax: 212-984-5325
Web: www.iie.org/Freeman-ASIA

Institute of Real Estate Management Foundation

George M. Brooker Collegiate Scholarship for Minorities

Type of award: Scholarship.
Intended use: For full-time junior, senior, master's or doctoral study at 4-year or graduate institution.
Eligibility: Applicant must be Alaskan native, Asian American, African American, Mexican American, Hispanic American, Puerto Rican or American Indian. Applicant must be U.S. citizen.
Basis for selection: Major/career interest in real estate; business or business/management/administration. Applicant must demonstrate high academic achievement, depth of character, leadership and seriousness of purpose.
Application requirements: Interview, recommendations, essay, transcript.
Additional information: Must have 3.0 GPA in major. Must intend to enter the field of real estate management. Undergraduate scholarships $1,000; graduate $2,500. Award notification is made on an ongoing basis.

Amount of award:	$1,000-$2,500
Number of awards:	3
Number of applicants:	5
Application deadline:	March 31
Total amount awarded:	$4,500

Institute of Real Estate Management Foundation: George M. Brooker Collegiate Scholarship for Minorities

Contact:
Institute of Real Estate Management Foundation
Foundation Administrator
430 North Michigan Avenue
Chicago, IL 60611
Phone: 312-329-6008
Web: www.irem.org

Insurance Scholarship Foundation of America

ISFA Education Foundation College Scholarship

Type of award: Scholarship.
Intended use: For junior, senior or graduate study at accredited 4-year or graduate institution.
Basis for selection: Major/career interest in insurance/actuarial science.
Application requirements: Essay, transcript. Three letters of recommendation.
Additional information: Applicant must be major or minor in insurance, risk management, or actuarial science with a minimum 3.0 GPA. Must have completed or be currently enrolled in two insurance, actuarial science, or risk-management-related courses, a minimum of three credit hours each. Application must be received by ISFA by Feb 15. Postmark dates have no bearing on the deadline. See Website to download form.

Amount of award:	$500-$4,000
Application deadline:	February 15

Contact:
NAIW Education Foundation
Insurance Scholarship Foundation of America
P.O. Box 866
Hendersonville, NC 28793-0866
Phone: 828-890-3328
Fax: 828-891-2667
Web: www.inssfa.org

International Association of Fire Fighters

W.H. McClennan Scholarship

Type of award: Scholarship, renewable.
Intended use: For full-time undergraduate study at accredited vocational, 2-year or 4-year institution.
Eligibility: Applicant or parent must be member/participant of International Association of Fire Fighters. Applicant's parent must have been killed or disabled in work-related accident as firefighter.
Basis for selection: Applicant must demonstrate financial need, high academic achievement, depth of character, seriousness of purpose and service orientation.
Application requirements: Recommendations, essay, transcript, proof of eligibility.
Additional information: Open to children of firefighters who were killed in the line of duty and were members in good standing of IAFF at the time of deaths. Minimum 2.0 GPA.

Amount of award:	$2,500
Number of awards:	28
Number of applicants:	28
Application deadline:	February 1
Notification begins:	August 1
Total amount awarded:	$65,000

Contact:
W. H. McClennan Scholarship, Office of the General President
International Association of Fire Fighters
1750 New York Avenue, NW
Washington, DC 20006
Phone: 202-824-1533
Fax: 202-737-8418
Web: www.iaff.org

International Buckskin Horse Association, Inc.

Buckskin Horse Association Scholarship

Type of award: Scholarship, renewable.
Intended use: For full-time undergraduate study at accredited postsecondary institution in United States.
Eligibility: Applicant or parent must be member/participant of International Buckskin Horse Association. Applicant must be high school senior. Applicant must be U.S. citizen.
Basis for selection: Applicant must demonstrate financial need, high academic achievement, depth of character, leadership and seriousness of purpose.
Application requirements: Portfolio, recommendations, proof of eligibility.
Additional information: Applicant must be association member for at least two years.

Amount of award:	$500-$1,500
Number of awards:	13
Number of applicants:	15
Application deadline:	February 1
Notification begins:	September 15
Total amount awarded:	$10,750

Contact:
International Buckskin Horse Association, Inc.
P.O. Box 268
Shelby, IN 46377
Web: www.ibha.net

International Executive Housekeepers Association

IEHA Educational Foundation Scholarship

Type of award: Scholarship.
Intended use: For undergraduate or non-degree study at accredited postsecondary institution.
Eligibility: Applicant or parent must be member/participant of International Executive Housekeepers Association.
Basis for selection: Major/career interest in hospitality administration/management.

Application requirements: Essay, transcript. Letter from school official verifying enrollment. Class schedule and coursework curriculum. Original and three copies of prepared manuscript on housekeeping (maximum 2,000 words, double-spaced). Photographs must be black-and-white glossy prints.
Additional information: Applicant must be member of IEHA. This scholarship will be awarded to student submitting best original manuscript on housekeeping within any industry segment (e.g., hospitality, healthcare, education, rehabilitation centers, government buildings). Other major/career interest: facilities management. Can be used for IEHA certification program. No set limit on number of awards granted.

Amount of award:	$800
Application deadline:	January 10
Notification begins:	June 1

Contact:
International Executive Housekeepers Association
Educational Foundation Scholarships
1001 Eastwind Drive, Suite 301
Westerville, OH 43081-3361
Phone: 800-200-6342
Fax: 614-895-1248
Web: www.ieha.org

International Foodservice Editorial Council

Foodservice Communicators Scholarship

Type of award: Scholarship.
Intended use: For full-time undergraduate or master's study at accredited postsecondary institution in United States.
Basis for selection: Major/career interest in food science/technology; food production/management/services; culinary arts or communications. Applicant must demonstrate financial need, high academic achievement, depth of character, leadership, seriousness of purpose and service orientation.
Application requirements: Recommendations, transcript, proof of eligibility.
Additional information: Applicant must work or pursue academic study in both culinary arts and communications. Applications may be requested by e-mail or downloaded from Website. Four to six awards granted each year for total of $8,000 to $15,000.

Amount of award:	$1,000-$3,750
Number of awards:	4
Number of applicants:	85
Application deadline:	March 15
Notification begins:	July 1
Total amount awarded:	$15,000

Contact:
International Foodservice Editorial Council (IFEC)
P.O. Box 491
Hyde Park, NY 12538
Phone: 845-229-6973
Fax: 845-229-6993
Web: www.ifeconline.com

International Furnishings and Design Association Educational Foundation

International Furnishings and Design Association Student Scholarships

Type of award: Scholarship.
Intended use: For full-time undergraduate or graduate study at accredited postsecondary institution in United States.
Basis for selection: Major/career interest in architecture or interior design. Applicant must demonstrate high academic achievement, depth of character, seriousness of purpose and service orientation.
Application requirements: Recommendations, essay, transcript. Two digital images of student work, four copies of each element of application.
Additional information: Full-time applicants must have completed four courses in interior design (or related field) at post-secondary level. Some scholarships require IFDA membership. Student membership fee is $25. Student scholarship requires recommendation from IFDA member. Applicants must have completed at least one semester of postsecondary school. Number and award amounts vary. Furniture design majors also eligible. See Website for further requirements and applications for Charles E. Mayo Student Scholarship, IFDA Student Scholarships, Vercille Voss Scholarship, Ruth Clark Scholarship, and Marketing Internship Grant.

Amount of award:	$2,000
Number of awards:	6
Number of applicants:	80
Application deadline:	March 31
Notification begins:	July 31
Total amount awarded:	$9,500

Contact:
IFDA Educational Foundation Joan Long
150 S. Warner Rd. Scholarships and Grants
Suite 156
King of Prussia, PA 19406
Web: www.ifdaef.org

Part-Time Student Scholarship

Type of award: Scholarship.
Intended use: For half-time undergraduate study.
Basis for selection: Major/career interest in interior design.
Application requirements: Portfolio, recommendations, transcript. Two photos of the student's original work; resume; 300-400 word essay explaining your long and short term goals, achievements, awards and accomplishments. Four copies of all application materials.
Additional information: Applicants must have completed four courses in interior design or related field. Must be currently enrolled in at least two interior design-related courses. Visit Website for application and additional information.

Amount of award:	$1,000
Application deadline:	March 31
Notification begins:	July 31

International Furnishings and Design Association Educational Foundation: Part-Time Student Scholarship

Contact:
IFDA Educational Foundation Joan Long
150 S. Warner Rd.
Suite 156
King of Prussia, PA 19406
Web: www.ifdeaf.org

Contact:
International Order of the King's Daughters and Sons
Director, North American Indian Dept.
P.O. Box 1040
Chautauqua, NY 14722-1040
Web: www.iokds.org

International Order of the King's Daughters and Sons

Health Career Scholarship

Type of award: Scholarship, renewable.
Intended use: For full-time junior, senior, master's or first professional study at accredited 4-year or graduate institution in United States or Canada.
Eligibility: Applicant must be U.S. citizen or Canadian citizen.
Basis for selection: Major/career interest in medicine; dentistry; pharmacy/pharmaceutics/pharmacology; nursing; health sciences; health-related professions; physical therapy or occupational therapy. Applicant must demonstrate financial need, high academic achievement, depth of character, leadership, seriousness of purpose and service orientation.
Application requirements: Recommendations, essay, transcript, proof of eligibility.
Additional information: To request application, student must write to director stating field and present level of study and include business-size SASE. Pre-med students not eligible. R.N., M.D. and D.D.S. students must have completed first year. Number of scholarships varies year to year.
    Amount of award: $1,000
    Application deadline: April 1
Contact:
International Order of the King's Daughters and Sons
Director, Health Careers Department
P.O. Box 1040
Chautauqua, NY 14722-1040
Web: www.iokds.org

North American Indian Scholarship

Type of award: Scholarship, renewable.
Intended use: For full-time undergraduate study at accredited 2-year or 4-year institution in United States.
Eligibility: Applicant must be American Indian. Applicant must be U.S. citizen.
Basis for selection: Applicant must demonstrate financial need, depth of character, leadership, seriousness of purpose and service orientation.
Application requirements: Recommendations, essay, transcript, proof of eligibility. Written documentation of tribal registration and other requirements.
Additional information: Offers scholarships with no restrictions as to tribal affiliations or Indian blood quantum. For more information, send SASE to director of North American Indian Department.
    Application deadline: April 1
    Notification begins: July 1
    Total amount awarded: $650

Intertribal Timber Council

Truman D. Picard Scholarship

Type of award: Scholarship, renewable.
Intended use: For full-time undergraduate or graduate study at accredited 2-year, 4-year or graduate institution in United States.
Eligibility: Applicant must be Alaskan native or American Indian. Must be enrolled member of a federally recognized tribe. Applicant must be U.S. citizen.
Basis for selection: Major/career interest in natural resources/conservation; forestry; wildlife/fisheries or agriculture. Applicant must demonstrate financial need, high academic achievement, depth of character, leadership, seriousness of purpose and service orientation.
Application requirements: Recommendations, transcript. Resume, and two-page (maximum) letter of application.
Additional information: Check Website for application acceptance dates.
    Amount of award: $1,500-$2,000
    Number of awards: 26
    Number of applicants: 70
    Notification begins: November 1
    Total amount awarded: $49,000
Contact:
Intertribal Timber Council
Education Committee
1112 NE 21st Avenue, Ste. 4
Portland, OR 97232-2114
Phone: 503-282-4296
Fax: 503-282-1274
Web: www.itcnet.org

Iowa College Student Aid Commission

Iowa Grant

Type of award: Scholarship, renewable.
Intended use: For undergraduate study at vocational, 2-year or 4-year institution.
Eligibility: Applicant must be U.S. citizen or permanent resident residing in Iowa.
Basis for selection: Applicant must demonstrate financial need.
Application requirements: FAFSA.
Additional information: Award amount adjusted for part-time study.
    Amount of award: $100-$1,000
    Notification begins: March 20
    Total amount awarded: $1,029,784

Contact:
Iowa College Student Aid Commission
200 Tenth Street, Fourth Floor
Des Moines, IA 50309-3609
Phone: 515-242-3344
Web: www.iowacollegeaid.org

Iowa National Guard Educational Assistance Program

Type of award: Scholarship, renewable.
Intended use: For undergraduate study.
Eligibility: Applicant must be U.S. citizen residing in Iowa. Applicant must be in military service in the Reserves/National Guard.
Application requirements: National Guard application.
Additional information: Applicant must be in military service in the Iowa Reserves/National Guard. Selection is based on National Guard designation. Award varies yearly and ranges from 50 to 100 percent of tuition for students at public institutions; for students at private institutions, award is equal to average tuition rate at Iowa Regents Universities. Must apply through National Guard unit.

Amount of award:	Full tuition
Application deadline:	August 31
Total amount awarded:	$3,725,000

Contact:
Iowa National Guard Headquarters
Military Personnel Office
77000 NW Beaver Drive
Johnston, IA 50131-1902
Web: www.iowacollegeaid.org

Iowa Robert C. Byrd Honor Scholarship

Type of award: Scholarship.
Intended use: For full-time undergraduate or graduate study at accredited 2-year or 4-year institution in United States.
Eligibility: Applicant must be high school senior. Applicant must be U.S. citizen or permanent resident residing in Iowa.
Basis for selection: Applicant must demonstrate high academic achievement, leadership and service orientation.
Application requirements: Recommendations, essay, transcript, proof of eligibility. AP scores.
Additional information: Eligible applicants must have completed three years of social studies, math (beyond general math and pre-Algebra) and science (beyond general science), two years of the same foreign language, and four years of English. Must have minimum 28 ACT or 1860 SAT, and 3.5 GPA. Must rank in top ten percent of class. Award amount varies; maximum is $1,500.

Amount of award:	$1,500
Application deadline:	February 1
Notification begins:	July 15
Total amount awarded:	$387,000

Contact:
Julie Leeper, Byrd Scholarship Competition
Iowa College Student Aid Commission
200 Tenth Street, Fourth Floor
Des Moines, IA 50309-3609
Phone: 515-242-3344
Fax: 515-242-3388
Web: www.iowacollegeaid.org

Iowa Tuition Grant

Type of award: Scholarship, renewable.
Intended use: For undergraduate study at accredited 2-year or 4-year institution. Designated institutions: Private colleges in Iowa.
Eligibility: Applicant must be U.S. citizen or permanent resident residing in Iowa.
Basis for selection: Applicant must demonstrate financial need.
Application requirements: Proof of eligibility. FAFSA.

Amount of award:	$4,000
Application deadline:	July 1
Total amount awarded:	$49,723,575

Contact:
Iowa College Student Aid Commission
200 Tenth Street, Fourth Floor
Des Moines, IA 50309-3609
Phone: 515-242-3344
Fax: 515-242-3388
Web: www.iowacollegeaid.org

Iowa Vocational-Technical Tuition Grant

Type of award: Scholarship, renewable.
Intended use: For undergraduate study at vocational or 2-year institution.
Eligibility: Applicant must be U.S. citizen or permanent resident residing in Iowa.
Basis for selection: Applicant must demonstrate financial need.
Application requirements: Proof of eligibility. FAFSA.
Additional information: Only vocational-technical career majors considered.

Amount of award:	$1,200
Number of awards:	5,129
Number of applicants:	20,261
Application deadline:	July 1
Total amount awarded:	$2,337,786

Contact:
Iowa College Student Aid Commission
200 Tenth Street, Fourth Floor
Des Moines, IA 50309-3609
Phone: 515-242-3344
Web: www.iowacollegeaid.org

Italian Catholic Federation

Italian Catholic Federation Scholarship

Type of award: Scholarship, renewable.
Intended use: For full-time freshman study at accredited 2-year or 4-year institution.
Eligibility: Applicant must be high school senior. Applicant must be Italian. Applicant must be Roman Catholic. Applicant must be U.S. citizen residing in California, Illinois, Arizona or Nevada.
Basis for selection: Applicant must demonstrate financial need and high academic achievement.
Application requirements: Recommendations, essay, transcript.

Italian Catholic Federation: Italian Catholic Federation Scholarship

Additional information: Applicants must live in Arizona, California, Illinois or Nevada, where branches of Federation are established. Minimum 3.2 GPA. Also open to non-Italian students whose parents or grandparents are members of Federation. First year's scholarship award is $400. Larger amounts available for advanced scholarships.

- **Amount of award:** $400-$1,000
- **Number of awards:** 200
- **Number of applicants:** 350
- **Application deadline:** March 15
- **Notification begins:** May 1
- **Total amount awarded:** $70,000

Contact:
Italian Catholic Federation
675 Hegenberger Road, #230
Oakland, CA 94621
Phone: 510-633-9058
Fax: 510-633-9758
Web: www.icf.org

IUE-CWA

Bruce van Ess Scholarship

Type of award: Scholarship.
Intended use: For full-time undergraduate study at accredited vocational, 2-year or 4-year institution.
Eligibility: Applicant or parent must be member/participant of International Union of EESMF Workers, AFL-CIO.
Basis for selection: Applicant must demonstrate depth of character, leadership, seriousness of purpose and service orientation.
Application requirements: Proof of GPA, short statement on civic contributions. 500-word essay on importance of labor movement.
Additional information: Available to children and grandchildren of all IUE-CWA members and employees (including retired or deceased members and employees). Apply online.

- **Amount of award:** $2,500
- **Number of awards:** 1
- **Application deadline:** March 31
- **Total amount awarded:** $2,500

Contact:
Trudy Humphrey IUE Department of Education
Int'l Union of EESMF Workers, ALF-CIO
1275 K Street, NW
Washington, DC 20005-4064
Web: www.iue-cwa.org

David J. Fitzmaurice Scholarship

Type of award: Scholarship.
Intended use: For full-time undergraduate study at accredited vocational, 2-year or 4-year institution.
Eligibility: Applicant or parent must be member/participant of International Union of EESMF Workers, AFL-CIO.
Basis for selection: Applicant must demonstrate depth of character, leadership, seriousness of purpose and service orientation.
Application requirements: Proof of GPA, 150 word essay on civic contributions, 500 word essay on importance of labor movement.
Additional information: Available to children and grandchildren of all IUE-CWA members and employees (including retired or deceased members and employees). Applicant must be in engineering program. Apply online.

- **Amount of award:** $2,000
- **Number of awards:** 1
- **Application deadline:** March 31
- **Total amount awarded:** $2,000

Contact:
Trudy Humphrey IUE Department of Education
Int'l Union of EESMF Workers, AFL-CIO
1275 K Street, NW
Washington, DC 20005-4064
Web: www.iue-cwa.org

James B. Carey Scholarship

Type of award: Scholarship.
Intended use: For full-time undergraduate study in United States.
Eligibility: Applicant or parent must be member/participant of International Union of EESMF Workers, AFL-CIO.
Basis for selection: Applicant must demonstrate depth of character, leadership, seriousness of purpose and service orientation.
Application requirements: Recommendations, transcript, proof of eligibility. 150 word essay on civic contributions, 500 word essay on importance of labor movement.
Additional information: Available to children and grandchildren of all IUE-CWA members and employees (including retired or deceased members and employees). Apply online.

- **Amount of award:** $1,000
- **Number of awards:** 9
- **Application deadline:** March 31
- **Total amount awarded:** $9,000

Contact:
Trudy Humphrey, IUE Department of Education
Int'l Union of EESMF Workers, AFL-CIO
1275 K Street, N.W.
Washington, DC 20005-4064
Web: www.iue-cwa.org

Paul Jennings Scholarship

Type of award: Scholarship.
Intended use: For full-time undergraduate study in United States.
Eligibility: Applicant or parent must be member/participant of International Union of EESMF Workers, AFL-CIO. Applicant must be high school senior.
Basis for selection: Applicant must demonstrate depth of character, leadership and service orientation.
Application requirements: Transcript, proof of eligibility. 150 word essay on civic contributions, 500 word essay on importance of labor movement.
Additional information: Award available to children and grandchildren of IUE-CWA members who are now or have been local union elected officials. Families of full-time union officers or employees not eligible. Must be accepted or enrolled in college, university, nursing school or technical school. Apply online.

- **Amount of award:** $3,000
- **Number of awards:** 1
- **Application deadline:** March 31
- **Total amount awarded:** $3,000

Contact:
Trudy Humphrey, IUE Department of Education
Int'l Union of EESMF Workers, AFL-CIO
1275 K Street, N.W.
Washington, DC 20005-4064
Web: www.iue-cwa.org

Robert L. Livingston Scholarship

Type of award: Scholarship.
Intended use: For full-time undergraduate study at accredited vocational, 2-year or 4-year institution.
Eligibility: Applicant or parent must be member/participant of International Union of EESMF Workers, AFL-CIO.
Basis for selection: Applicant must demonstrate depth of character, leadership, seriousness of purpose and service orientation.
Application requirements: Proof of GPA, 150-word essay on civic contributions, career objectives, and extracurricular activities.
Additional information: Open to dependents of IUE-CWA Automotive Conference Board members (active, retired or deceased). Dependents of IUE-CWA Division employees ineligible. Apply online.

Amount of award:	$1,500
Number of awards:	2
Application deadline:	March 31
Total amount awarded:	$3,000

Contact:
Trudy Humphrey IUE Department of Education
Int'l Union of EESMF Workers, ALF-CIO
1275 K Street, NW
Washington, DC 20005-4064
Web: www.iue-cwa.org

Sal Ingrassia Scholarship

Type of award: Scholarship.
Intended use: For full-time undergraduate study at accredited vocational, 2-year or 4-year institution.
Eligibility: Applicant or parent must be member/participant of International Union of EESMF Workers, AFL-CIO.
Basis for selection: Applicant must demonstrate depth of character, leadership, seriousness of purpose and service orientation.
Application requirements: Proof of GPA, 150 word essay on civic contributions, 500 word essay on relationship to labor movement.
Additional information: Available to children and grandchildren of all IUE-CWA members and employees (including retired or deceased members and employees). Apply online.

Amount of award:	$2,500
Number of awards:	1
Application deadline:	March 31
Total amount awarded:	$2,500

Contact:
Trudy Humphrey IUE Department of Education
Int'l Union of EESMF Workers, ALF-CIO
1275 K Street, NW
Washington, DC 20005-4064
Web: www.iue-cwa.org

Willie Rudd Scholarship

Type of award: Scholarship.
Intended use: For full-time undergraduate study at accredited vocational, 2-year or 4-year institution.
Eligibility: Applicant or parent must be member/participant of International Union of EESMF Workers, AFL-CIO.
Basis for selection: Applicant must demonstrate depth of character, leadership, seriousness of purpose and service orientation.
Application requirements: Proof of GPA, 150 word essay on civic contributions, 500 word essay on importance of labor movement.
Additional information: Available to children and grandchildren of all IUE-CWA members and employees (including retired or deceased members and employees). Apply online.

Amount of award:	$1,000
Number of awards:	1
Application deadline:	March 31
Total amount awarded:	$1,000

Contact:
Trudy Humphrey IUE Department of Education
Int'l Union of EESMF Workers, AFL-CIO
1275 K Street, NW
Washington, DC 20005-4064
Web: www.iue-cwa.org

Jackie Robinson Foundation

Education and Leadership Development Program

Type of award: Scholarship, renewable.
Intended use: For full-time undergraduate study at accredited 4-year institution in United States.
Eligibility: Applicant must be Alaskan native, Asian American, African American, Mexican American, Hispanic American, Puerto Rican or American Indian. Applicant must be high school senior. Applicant must be U.S. citizen.
Basis for selection: Applicant must demonstrate financial need, high academic achievement and leadership.
Application requirements: Interview, recommendations, essay, transcript.
Additional information: Applicants must have minimum SAT score of 1000 or ACT score of 21. Award amount varies up to $6,000. Applications available online and must be submitted via website.

Amount of award:	$3,000-$6,000
Application deadline:	March 31
Notification begins:	July 15
Total amount awarded:	$24,000

Contact:
Jackie Robinson Foundation
Attn: Scholarship Programs
3 West 35 Street, 11th Floor
New York, NY 10001-2204
Phone: 212-290-8600
Web: www.jackierobinson.org

James Beard Foundation

Allen Susser Scholarship

Type of award: Scholarship.

James Beard Foundation: Allen Susser Scholarship

Intended use: For undergraduate study. Designated institutions: Florida Culinary Institute, Johnson & Wales University, Florida International University, The School of Culinary Arts at The Art Institute of Florida.
Eligibility: Applicant must be high school senior. Applicant must be residing in Florida.
Basis for selection: Major/career interest in culinary arts; food production/management/services or food science/technology. Applicant must demonstrate financial need.
Application requirements: Recommendations, essay, transcript, proof of eligibility. Proof of residency, financial statement, resume.
Additional information: Applicants currently enrolled also eligible. Must be resident of Dade, Palm Beach, or Broward County.
    Amount of award: $1,500
    Number of awards: 1
    Application deadline: May 15
    Total amount awarded: $1,500
Contact:
Scholarship America
1 Scholarship Way
PO Box 297
St. Peter, MN 56082
Phone: 507-931-1682
Web: www.jamesbeard.org

American Restaurant Scholarship

Type of award: Scholarship.
Intended use: For undergraduate study. Designated institutions: Licensed or accredited culinary schools.
Eligibility: Applicant must be residing in Kansas, Pennsylvania, Missouri or Florida.
Application requirements: Proof of eligibility.
    Amount of award: $16,000
    Number of awards: 4
    Total amount awarded: $4,000
Contact:
Scholarship America
1 Scholarship Way
PO Box 297
St. Peter, MN 56082
Phone: 507-931-1682
Web: www.jamesbeard.org

Bern Laxer Memorial Scholarship

Type of award: Scholarship.
Intended use: For undergraduate study. Designated institutions: Licensed or accredited culinary schools.
Eligibility: Applicant must be residing in Florida.
Basis for selection: Major/career interest in culinary arts; hospitality administration/management or food science/technology. Applicant must demonstrate financial need.
Application requirements: Recommendations, essay, transcript, proof of eligibility. Proof of residency, financial statement, resume.
Additional information: Must have at least one year of culinary experience and have high school diploma or equivalent. Recipients who reapply will be given priority consideration over new applicants. May be received for a maximum of four years, but applicant must maintain a B- GPA.
    Amount of award: $2,500
    Number of awards: 3
    Application deadline: May 15
    Total amount awarded: $7,500

Contact:
Scholarship America
1 Scholarship Way
PO Box 297
St. Peter, MN 56082
Phone: 507-931-1682
Web: www.jamesbeard.org

Bryan Close Polo Grill Scholarship

Type of award: Scholarship.
Intended use: For undergraduate study. Designated institutions: Licensed or accredited culinary schools.
Eligibility: Applicant must be residing in Oklahoma.
Basis for selection: Major/career interest in culinary arts; food production/management/services or food science/technology. Applicant must demonstrate financial need.
Application requirements: Recommendations, essay, transcript, proof of eligibility. Proof of residency, financial statement, resume.
Additional information: Minimum one year culinary experience either as student or employee.
    Amount of award: $1,000
    Number of awards: 1
    Application deadline: May 15
    Total amount awarded: $1,000
Contact:
Scholarship America
1 Scholarship Way
PO Box 297
St. Peter, MN 56082
Phone: 507-931-1682
Web: www.jamesbeard.org

Chris Desens Scholarship

Type of award: Scholarship.
Intended use: For undergraduate study. Designated institutions: St. Louis Community College at Forest Park, L'Ecole Culinaire, East Central College, Belleview Area Community College.
Eligibility: Applicant must be residing in Missouri.
Basis for selection: Major/career interest in culinary arts; food production/management/services or food science/technology. Applicant must demonstrate financial need.
Application requirements: Recommendations, essay, transcript, proof of eligibility. Proof of residency, financial statement, resume.
Additional information: Must be resident of city of St. Louis or St. Louis county.
    Amount of award: $2,000
    Number of awards: 1
    Application deadline: May 15
Contact:
Scholarship America
1 Scholarship Way
PO Box 297
St. Peter, MN 56082
Phone: 507-931-1682
Web: www.jamesbeard.org

Christian Wolffer Scholarship

Type of award: Scholarship.
Intended use: For undergraduate study. Designated institutions: Licensed or accredited culinary schools.
Eligibility: Applicant must be residing in New York.

Basis for selection: Major/career interest in culinary arts; food production/management/services or food science/technology. Applicant must demonstrate high academic achievement.
Application requirements: Recommendations, essay, transcript, proof of eligibility. Proof of residency, financial statement, resume.
Additional information: Minimum 3.0 GPA. Must be enrolled or planning to enroll in accredited culinary or wine studies program.

Amount of award:	$5,000
Number of awards:	1
Application deadline:	May 15

Contact:
Scholarship America
1 Scholarship Way
PO Box 297
St. Peter, MN 56082
Phone: 507-931-1682
Web: www.jamesbeard.org

Clat Triplette Scholarship

Type of award: Scholarship.
Intended use: For undergraduate study.
Basis for selection: Major/career interest in culinary arts; food production/management/services or food science/technology. Applicant must demonstrate financial need.
Application requirements: Recommendations, transcript, proof of eligibility. Proof of residency, financial statement, resume, 250 word essay on James Beard.
Additional information: Applicants must be enrolled or planning to enroll in accredited baking or pastry studies program at licensed or accredited culinary school.

Amount of award:	$4,000
Number of awards:	4
Application deadline:	May 15
Total amount awarded:	$16,000

Contact:
Scholarship America
1 Scholarship Way
PO Box 297
St. Peter, MN 56082
Phone: 507-931-1682
Web: www.jamesbeard.org

Dana Campbell Memorial Scholarship

Type of award: Scholarship.
Intended use: For sophomore or junior study in United States.
Eligibility: Applicant must be residing in Texas, Arkansas, Delaware, Maryland, Louisiana, South Carolina, Georgia, Florida, Oklahoma, Virginia, West Virginia, Mississippi, Kentucky, Alabama, North Carolina or Missouri.
Basis for selection: Major/career interest in journalism; culinary arts; food production/management/services or food science/technology. Applicant must demonstrate financial need.
Application requirements: Recommendations, transcript, proof of eligibility. Proof of residency, financial statement, resume, 250-word essay about memorable dining experience or favorite restaurant.
Additional information: Scholarship recipient will be considered for Southern Living internship. Must have career interest in food journalism. Must be resident of southern state within Southern Living readership area.

Amount of award:	$3,000
Number of awards:	1
Application deadline:	May 15
Total amount awarded:	$3,000

Contact:
Scholarship America
1 Scholarship Way
PO Box 297
St. Peter, MN 56082
Phone: 507-931-1682
Web: www.jamesbeard.org

Deseo at the Westin Scholarship

Type of award: Scholarship.
Intended use: For undergraduate study.
Eligibility: Applicant must be residing in Arizona.
Basis for selection: Major/career interest in culinary arts; food production/management/services or food science/technology. Applicant must demonstrate financial need.
Application requirements: Recommendations, essay, transcript, proof of eligibility. Proof of residency, financial statement, resume.
Additional information: Applicants must have participated in Arizona Careers Through Culinary Arts program and be recommended by Arizona C-CAP.

Amount of award:	$3,125
Number of awards:	2
Application deadline:	May 15
Total amount awarded:	$6,250

Contact:
Scholarship America
1 Scholarship Way
PO Box 297
St. Peter, MN 56082
Phone: 507-931-1682
Web: www.jamesbeard.org

Gene Hovis Memorial Scholarship

Type of award: Scholarship.
Intended use: For undergraduate study. Designated institutions: Licensed or accredited culinary schools.
Eligibility: Applicant must be African American. Applicant must be female.
Basis for selection: Major/career interest in culinary arts; food production/management/services or food science/technology. Applicant must demonstrate financial need.
Application requirements: Recommendations, transcript, proof of eligibility. Proof of residency, financial statement, resume, and 500-word essay on culinary goals.

Amount of award:	$4,000
Number of awards:	1
Application deadline:	May 15
Total amount awarded:	$4,000

Contact:
Scholarship America
1 Scholarship Way
PO Box 297
St. Peter, MN 56082
Phone: 507-931-1682
Web: www.jamesbeard.org

James Beard General Scholarships

Type of award: Scholarship.
Intended use: For undergraduate study. Designated institutions: Licensed or accredited culinary institutions.

James Beard Foundation: James Beard General Scholarships

Basis for selection: Major/career interest in culinary arts; food production/management/services; food science/technology; hospitality administration/management or hotel/restaurant management. Applicant must demonstrate financial need, high academic achievement, leadership, seriousness of purpose and service orientation.
Application requirements: Recommendations, essay, transcript.
    Amount of award: $2,000
    Number of awards: 7
    Application deadline: May 15
    Total amount awarded: $14,000
Contact:
Scholarship America
1 Scholarship Way
PO Box 297
St. Peter, MN 56082
Phone: 507-931-1682
Web: www.jamesbeard.org

James Beard School Scholarships

Type of award: Scholarship.
Intended use: For undergraduate, graduate or non-degree study in or outside United States or Canada. Designated institutions: Apicius Culinary Institute of Florence, Art Institute of Colorado, Art Institute of Houston, Art Institute of Phoenix, Baltimore International College, Culinary Institute of America, French Culinary Institute, Institute of Culinary Education, Istanbul Culinary Institute, Johnson & Wales University, Le Cordon Bleu, The Natural Gourmet Institute for Health and Culinary Arts, New England Culinary Institute, Scottsdale Culinary Institute, Walnut Hill College, Western Culinary Institute.
Basis for selection: Major/career interest in culinary arts.
Application requirements: Recommendations, essay, transcript.
Additional information: Must meet eligibility requirements of participating schools. Visit Website for application and additional information.
    Amount of award: $1,500-$12,500
    Number of awards: 45
    Application deadline: May 15
    Total amount awarded: $114,000
Contact:
Scholarship America
1 Scholarship Way
PO Box 297
St. Peter, MN 56082
Phone: 507-931-1682
Web: www.jamesbeard.org

Jean-Louis Palladin Memorial Scholarship

Type of award: Scholarship.
Intended use: For undergraduate study.
Basis for selection: Major/career interest in culinary arts; food production/management/services; food science/technology; hospitality administration/management or hotel/restaurant management.
Application requirements: Recommendations, essay, transcript.
    Amount of award: $5,000
    Number of awards: 1
    Application deadline: May 15
Contact:
Scholarship America
One Scholarship Way
PO Box 297
St. Peter, MN 56082
Phone: 504-931-1682
Web: www.jamesbeard.org

La Toque Scholarship in Wine Studies

Type of award: Scholarship.
Intended use: For undergraduate study. Designated institutions: Licensed or accredited culinary schools.
Basis for selection: Major/career interest in culinary arts or food production/management/services. Applicant must demonstrate financial need.
Application requirements: Recommendations, essay, transcript, proof of eligibility. Proof of residency, financial statement, resume.
Additional information: Applicants must be enrolled in or be planning to enroll in an accredited wine studies program.
    Amount of award: $3,000
    Number of awards: 2
    Application deadline: May 15
Contact:
Scholarship America
1 Scholarship Way
PO Box 297
St. Peter, MN 56082
Phone: 507-931-1682
Web: www.jamesbeard.org

The Peter Cameron Scholarship

Type of award: Scholarship.
Intended use: For undergraduate study. Designated institutions: Licensed or accredited culinary schools.
Eligibility: Applicant must be high school senior.
Basis for selection: Major/career interest in culinary arts; food production/management/services or food science/technology. Applicant must demonstrate financial need and high academic achievement.
Application requirements: Recommendations, essay, transcript, proof of eligibility. Financial statement, resume.
Additional information: Minimum 3.0 GPA.
    Amount of award: $5,000
    Number of awards: 1
    Application deadline: May 15
    Total amount awarded: $5,000
Contact:
Scholarship America
1 Scholarship Way
PO Box 297
St. Peter, MN 56082
Phone: 507-931-1682
Web: www.jamesbeard.org

Peter Kump Memorial Scholarship

Type of award: Scholarship.
Intended use: For undergraduate study. Designated institutions: Licensed or accredited culinary schools.
Basis for selection: Major/career interest in culinary arts; food production/management/services or food science/technology. Applicant must demonstrate financial need and high academic achievement.

Application requirements: Recommendations, essay, transcript, proof of eligibility. Proof of residency, financial statement, resume.
Additional information: Minimum 3.0 GPA. Minimum one year substantiated culinary experience.
    Amount of award: $5,000
    Number of awards: 4
    Application deadline: May 15
    Total amount awarded: $5,000
Contact:
Scholarship America
1 Scholarship Way
PO Box 297
St. Peter, MN 56082
Phone: 507-931-1682
Web: www.jamesbeard.org

Taste America San Francisco Scholarship

Type of award: Scholarship.
Intended use: For undergraduate study.
Eligibility: Applicant must be U.S. citizen.
Basis for selection: Major/career interest in culinary arts; food production/management/services; food science/technology; hospitality administration/management or hotel/restaurant management.
Application requirements: Recommendations, essay, transcript.
    Amount of award: $1,200
    Number of awards: 1
    Application deadline: May 15
    Total amount awarded: $1,200
Contact:
Scholarship America
One Scholarship Way
PO Box 297
St. Peter, MN 56082
Phone: 504-931-1682
Web: www.sms.scholarshipamerica.org/jamesbeard/

Wally Joe (KC's) Scholarship

Type of award: Scholarship.
Intended use: For undergraduate study.
Eligibility: Applicant must be residing in Tennessee, Mississippi, Arkansas or Louisiana.
Basis for selection: Major/career interest in culinary arts; food production/management/services or food science/technology. Applicant must demonstrate financial need.
Application requirements: Recommendations, essay, transcript, proof of eligibility. Proof of residency, financial statement, resume.
    Amount of award: $2,000
    Number of awards: 1
    Application deadline: May 15
    Total amount awarded: $2,000
Contact:
Scholarship America
1 Scholarship Way
PO Box 297
St. Peter, MN 56082
Phone: 507-931-1682
Web: www.jamesbeard.org

James F. Byrnes Foundation

James F. Byrnes Scholarship

Type of award: Scholarship, renewable.
Intended use: For full-time freshman study at accredited 4-year institution.
Eligibility: Applicant must be high school senior. Applicant must be U.S. citizen residing in South Carolina.
Basis for selection: Applicant must demonstrate financial need, high academic achievement, depth of character, leadership, patriotism, seriousness of purpose and service orientation.
Application requirements: Interview, essay, transcript. SAT/ACT scores, photograph, autobiography (three typed pages maximum) describing home situation, death of parent/s, desire for college education, college ambitions, reasons financial assistance is needed, how college will be financed, etc. Two non-relative references (one from current guidance counselor or teacher).
Additional information: Applicant must be high school senior or college freshman. Applicant must have 2.5 GPA. One or both parents of applicant must be deceased. Visit Website for additional information.
    Amount of award: $3,250
    Number of awards: 6
    Number of applicants: 149
    Application deadline: February 15
    Notification begins: April 20
Contact:
James F. Byrnes Foundation
P.O. Box 6781
Columbia, SC 29260-6781
Phone: 803-254-9325
Fax: 803-254-9354
Web: www.byrnesscholars.org

Japanese American Association of New York

Japanese American General Scholarship

Type of award: Scholarship.
Intended use: For full-time freshman study at accredited 2-year or 4-year institution in United States.
Eligibility: Applicant must be Asian American. Applicant must be high school senior. Applicant must be Japanese. Applicant must be U.S. citizen or permanent resident residing in Connecticut, New York or New Jersey.
Basis for selection: Applicant must demonstrate financial need, high academic achievement and service orientation.
Application requirements: Essay, transcript. SAT scores, photograph. Letter of recommendation from a JAA member if no one in family is a member.
Additional information: Two awards given are need-based.
    Amount of award: $1,000-$5,000
    Number of awards: 11
    Number of applicants: 2,006
    Application deadline: May 2
    Notification begins: May 19
    Total amount awarded: $23,000

Japanese American Music Scholarship Competition

Type of award: Scholarship.
Intended use: For undergraduate or graduate study at postsecondary institution.
Eligibility: Applicant must be Asian American. Applicant must be Japanese. Applicant must be U.S. citizen, permanent resident or Japanese citizen.
Basis for selection: Competition/talent/interest in music performance/composition, based on string performance. Major/career interest in music.
Application requirements: Photograph.
Additional information: Open to Japanese students and students of Japanese descent. Please contact sponsor and/or visit Website for future competitions and deadlines.
    Amount of award: $1,500-$3,000
    Number of awards: 5
    Number of applicants: 2,006
    Total amount awarded: $10,500
Contact:
Japanese American Association of New York
15 West 44 Street
New York, NY 10036
Phone: 212-840-6942
Fax: 212-840-0616
Web: www.jaany.org

Jaycee War Memorial Fund

Charles R. Ford Scholarship

Type of award: Scholarship.
Intended use: For undergraduate study at postsecondary institution.
Eligibility: Applicant or parent must be member/participant of Jaycees. Applicant must be returning adult student. Applicant must be U.S. citizen.
Basis for selection: Applicant must demonstrate financial need, high academic achievement and leadership.
Application requirements: $10 application fee.
Additional information: Intended for active member who wishes to return to college or university to complete education. To receive application, send business-size SASE with application fee between July 1 and February 1. Make check or money order payable to the Jaycee War Memorial Fund. Visit Website for more information.
    Amount of award: $2,500
    Number of awards: 1
    Application deadline: February 1, March 1
    Notification begins: May 15
Contact:
Jaycee War Memorial Fund
Ford Scholarship
P.O. Box 7
Tulsa, OK 74102-0007
Phone: 918-584-2481 ext. 434
Fax: 918-584-4422
Web: www.usjaycees.org/other_scholarships.htm

Jaycee War Memorial Scholarship

Type of award: Scholarship.
Intended use: For full-time undergraduate study at accredited vocational, 2-year or 4-year institution.
Eligibility: Applicant must be U.S. citizen.
Basis for selection: Applicant must demonstrate financial need, high academic achievement and leadership.
Application requirements: $10 application fee.
Additional information: To receive application, send business-size SASE with application fee between July 1 and February 1. Make check or money order payable to the Jaycee War Memorial Fund. Visit Website for additional information.
    Amount of award: $1,000
    Number of awards: 10
    Application deadline: February 1, March 1
    Notification begins: May 15
    Total amount awarded: $25,000
Contact:
Jaycee War Memorial Scholarship
P.O. Box 7
Tulsa, OK 74102-0007
Phone: 918-584-2481 ext. 434
Fax: 918-584-4422
Web: www.usjaycees.org/other_scholarships.htm

Thomas Wood Baldridge Scholarship

Type of award: Scholarship.
Intended use: For full-time undergraduate study at accredited 2-year or 4-year institution.
Eligibility: Applicant or parent must be member/participant of Jaycees. Applicant must be U.S. citizen.
Basis for selection: Applicant must demonstrate financial need, high academic achievement and leadership.
Application requirements: $10 application fee.
Additional information: Applicant must be member or have immediate family as Jaycee member. To receive application, send business-size SASE along with application fee between July 1 and February 1. Make check or money order payable to the Jaycee War Memorial Fund. Visit Website for additional information.
    Amount of award: $3,000
    Number of awards: 1
    Application deadline: February 1, March 1
    Total amount awarded: $3,000
Contact:
Jaycee War Memorial Fund
Baldridge Scholarship
P.O. Box 7
Tulsa, OK 74102-0007
Phone: 918-584-2481 ext. 434
Fax: 918-584-4422
Web: www.usjaycees.org/other_scholarships.htm

Jeannette Rankin Foundation

Jeanette Rankin Foundation Scholarship

Type of award: Scholarship.
Intended use: For undergraduate study at accredited vocational, 2-year or 4-year institution in United States.
Eligibility: Applicant must be female, at least 35. Applicant must be U.S. citizen.
Basis for selection: Applicant must demonstrate financial need, high academic achievement, depth of character and seriousness of purpose.
Application requirements: Recommendations, essay.
Additional information: Applicant must be 35+ as of March 1 and meet low-income guidelines. Must display courage and attainable goals. Download application from Website from November through mid-February, or send SASE with application request.

Amount of award:	$2,000
Number of awards:	30
Number of applicants:	700
Application deadline:	March 1
Notification begins:	June 30
Total amount awarded:	$80,000

Contact:
Jeannette Rankin Foundation
P.O. Box 6653
Athens, GA 30604
Phone: 706-208-1211
Web: www.rankinfoundation.org

Jewish Vocational Service

JVS Jewish Community Scholarship Fund

Type of award: Scholarship, renewable.
Intended use: For full-time undergraduate or graduate study at accredited postsecondary institution in United States.
Eligibility: Applicant must be Jewish. Applicant must be U.S. citizen or permanent resident residing in California.
Basis for selection: Applicant must demonstrate financial need, seriousness of purpose and service orientation.
Application requirements: Recommendations, essay, transcript. FAFSA and tax returns.
Additional information: Minimum 2.7 GPA required. Must be Jewish and legal, permanent resident of Los Angeles County with verifiable financial need. Visit Website for electronic application.

Amount of award:	$500-$5,000
Number of applicants:	250
Application deadline:	March 14
Notification begins:	June 15
Total amount awarded:	$305,500

Contact:
JVS Scholarship Fund
c/o Hilary Mandel
6505 Wilshire Blvd., Suite 200
Los Angeles, CA 90048
Phone: 323-761-8888 ext. 8868
Fax: 323-761-8575
Web: www.jvsla.org

Jewish War Veterans of the United States of America

Jewish War Veterans of the United States of America Bernard Rotberg Memorial Scholarship

Type of award: Scholarship.
Intended use: For freshman study at accredited 4-year institution.
Eligibility: Applicant must be high school senior. Applicant must be Jewish.
Basis for selection: Major/career interest in nursing. Applicant must demonstrate financial need and high academic achievement.
Additional information: Applicant must be direct descendant of JWV member. Must be in upper 25 percent of high school class; must have participated in extracurricular activities in school as well as in Jewish community. SAT and recommendations encouraged. Visit Website for application and more information.

Amount of award:	$1,000
Number of awards:	1
Application deadline:	May 3

Contact:
Jewish War Veterans of the United States of America
National Scholarship Committee
1811 R Street NW
Washington, DC 20009
Phone: 202-265-6280
Fax: 202-234-5662
Web: www.jwv.org

Jewish War Veterans of the United States of America JWV Grant

Type of award: Research grant.
Intended use: For freshman study at accredited vocational or 4-year institution.
Eligibility: Applicant must be high school senior. Applicant must be Jewish.
Basis for selection: Major/career interest in nursing. Applicant must demonstrate financial need and high academic achievement.
Additional information: Applicant must be direct descendant of JWV member. Must be in upper 25 percent of high school class; must have participated in extracurricular activities in school as well as in Jewish community. SAT and recommendations encouraged. Visit Website for application and more information.

Amount of award:	$500
Number of awards:	1
Application deadline:	May 3

Contact:
Jewish War Veterans of the United States of America
National Scholarship Committee
1811 R Street NW
Washington, DC 20009
Phone: 202-265-6280
Fax: 202-234-5662
Web: www.jwv.org

Jewish War Veterans of the United States of America XX Olympiad Memorial Award

Type of award: Scholarship.
Intended use: For undergraduate study at accredited 4-year institution.
Eligibility: Applicant must be high school senior.
Basis for selection: Applicant must demonstrate high academic achievement, leadership and service orientation.
Application requirements: SAT scores.
Additional information: Selection based on merit with focus on athletic achievement. Application deadline March - May. Visit Website for application and more information.
    Amount of award: $1,000
    Number of awards: 1
Contact:
Jewish War Veterans of the United States of America
National Scholarship Committee
1811 R Street NW
Washington, DC 20009
Phone: 202-265-6280
Fax: 202-234-5662
Web: www.jwv.org

Louis S. Silvey Grant

Type of award: Research grant.
Intended use: For freshman study at accredited 4-year institution.
Eligibility: Applicant must be high school senior. Applicant must be Jewish.
Basis for selection: Major/career interest in nursing. Applicant must demonstrate financial need and high academic achievement.
Additional information: Applicant must be direct descendant of JWV member. Must be in upper 25 percent of high school class; must have participated in extracurricular activities in school as well as in Jewish community. SAT and recommendations encouraged. Visit Website for application and more information.
    Amount of award: $750
    Number of awards: 1
    Application deadline: May 3
Contact:
Jewish War Veterans of the United States of America
National Scholarship Committee
1811 R St. NW
Washington, DC 20009
Phone: 202-265-6280
Fax: 202-234-5662
Web: www.jwv.org

Kansas Board of Regents

Kansas Comprehensive Grant

Type of award: Scholarship, renewable.
Intended use: For full-time undergraduate study at accredited 4-year institution.
Eligibility: Applicant must be U.S. citizen or permanent resident residing in Kansas.
Basis for selection: Applicant must demonstrate financial need.
Application requirements: Proof of eligibility. FAFSA.
Additional information: Up to $1,100 for those attending public institutions; up to $3,000 for those attending private institutions.
    Number of awards: 9,593
    Number of applicants: 25,916
    Application deadline: April 1
    Notification begins: May 1
    Total amount awarded: $14,193,042
Contact:
Kansas Board of Regents
1000 SW Jackson St.
Suite 520
Topeka, KS 66612-1368
Phone: 785-296-3517
Fax: 785-296-0983
Web: www.kansasregents.org

Kansas Ethnic Minority Scholarship

Type of award: Scholarship, renewable.
Intended use: For full-time undergraduate study at postsecondary institution.
Eligibility: Applicant must be Alaskan native, Asian American, African American, Mexican American, Hispanic American, Puerto Rican or American Indian. Applicant must be U.S. citizen or permanent resident residing in Kansas.
Basis for selection: Applicant must demonstrate financial need and high academic achievement.
Application requirements: $10 application fee. Proof of eligibility, nomination. State of Kansas Student Aid Application. FAFSA.
Additional information: Minimum 3.0 GPA.
    Amount of award: $1,850
    Number of awards: 187
    Number of applicants: 651
    Application deadline: May 1
    Total amount awarded: $314,124
Contact:
Kansas Board of Regents
1000 SW Jackson St.
Suite 520
Topeka, KS 66612-1368
Phone: 785-296-3517
Fax: 785-296-0983
Web: www.kansasregents.org

Kansas Nursing Service Scholarship

Type of award: Scholarship, renewable.
Intended use: For full-time undergraduate study at postsecondary institution. Designated institutions: Kansas postsecondary schools with approved nursing programs.
Eligibility: Applicant must be U.S. citizen or permanent resident residing in Kansas.

Basis for selection: Major/career interest in nursing. Applicant must demonstrate financial need.
Application requirements: $10 application fee. State of Kansas Student Aid Application. FAFSA.
Additional information: Must obtain sponsorship from adult-care home licensed under the Adult Care Home Licensure Act; state agency that employs LPNs or RNs; or state-licensed medical care facility, psychiatric hospital, home health agency or local health department. Must agree to work in Kansas one year for each year that scholarship is received. If recipient does not meet obligation, award becomes loan.

Amount of award:	$2,500-$3,500
Number of awards:	170
Number of applicants:	278
Application deadline:	May 1
Total amount awarded:	$557,295

Contact:
Kansas Board of Regents
1000 SW Jackson St.
Suite 520
Topeka, KS 66612-1368
Phone: 785-296-3518
Fax: 785-296-0983
Web: www.kansasregents.org

Kansas ROTC Service Scholarship

Type of award: Scholarship.
Intended use: For full-time undergraduate study.
Eligibility: Applicant or parent must be member/participant of Reserve Officers Training Corps (ROTC). Applicant must be residing in Kansas.
Additional information: Applicant must be Kansas resident enrolled in Kansas ROTC program. Must be full-time undergraduate with at least 12 credit hours. Scholarship limited to eight semesters. Award amount may be up to tuition and costs of average four-year regents institution; average award is $1,650.

Number of awards:	11
Number of applicants:	11
Application deadline:	August 1
Total amount awarded:	$74,341

Contact:
Kansas Board of Regents
Director of Student Financial Assistance
1000 SW Jackson St., Suite 520
Topeka, KS 66612-1368
Phone: 785-296-3518
Fax: 785-296-0983
Web: www.kansasregents.org

Kansas State Scholarship

Type of award: Scholarship, renewable.
Intended use: For full-time undergraduate study at postsecondary institution.
Eligibility: Applicant must be residing in Kansas.
Basis for selection: Applicant must demonstrate financial need and high academic achievement.
Application requirements: $10 application fee. Proof of eligibility. FAFSA.
Additional information: Applicant must be Kansas resident, high school senior or undergraduate, and must be designated State Scholar in senior year of high school. Must have high GPA (average: 3.9) and ACT scores (average: 29).

Amount of award:	$1,000
Number of awards:	1,281
Number of applicants:	1,666
Application deadline:	May 1
Total amount awarded:	$1,038,137

Contact:
Kansas Board of Regents
1000 SW Jackson St.
Suite 520
Topeka, KS 66612-1368
Phone: 785-296-3517
Fax: 785-296-0983
Web: www.kansasregents.org

Kansas Teacher Service Scholarship

Type of award: Scholarship, renewable.
Intended use: For full-time undergraduate or post-bachelor's certificate study at 4-year or graduate institution.
Eligibility: Applicant must be residing in Kansas.
Basis for selection: Major/career interest in education, teacher or education, special. Applicant must demonstrate high academic achievement.
Application requirements: $10 application fee. Recommendations, transcript, proof of eligibility. FAFSA.
Additional information: Applicant must be Kansas resident enrolled in Kansas school that offers education degree. Must identify a "hard-to fill" or "underserved" area. Must not have teaching license. Scholarships are competitive; selection based on ACT score, GPA, high school rank, transcript and recommendation. Preference given to juniors and seniors, or currently licensed teachers pursuing licensure or endorsement in hard-to-fill disciplines.

Amount of award:	$5,000
Number of awards:	248
Number of applicants:	618
Application deadline:	May 1
Total amount awarded:	$873,466

Contact:
Kansas Board of Regents
1000 SW Jackson St.
Suite 520
Topeka, KS 66612-1368
Phone: 785-296-3517
Fax: 785-296-0983
Web: www.kansasregents.org

Kansas Vocational Education Scholarship

Type of award: Scholarship, renewable.
Intended use: For full-time undergraduate study at vocational or 2-year institution.
Eligibility: Applicant must be U.S. citizen or permanent resident residing in Kansas.
Application requirements: $10 application fee. Proof of eligibility.
Additional information: Applicant must be Kansas resident and graduate of Kansas high school. Must take vocational test given on first Saturday of November or March and complete Vocational Education application. Renewals awarded first; remaining scholarships offered to those with highest exam scores.

Kansas Board of Regents: Kansas Vocational Education Scholarship

Amount of award:	$500
Number of awards:	244
Number of applicants:	277
Application deadline:	May 1, February 1
Notification begins:	May 15
Total amount awarded:	$119,000

Contact:
Kansas Board of Regents
1000 SW Jackson St.
Suite 520
Topeka, KS 66612-0983
Phone: 785-296-3518
Fax: 785-296-0983
Web: www.kansasregents.org

National Guard Educational Assistance Program

Type of award: Scholarship, renewable.
Intended use: For undergraduate study.
Eligibility: Applicant must be U.S. citizen residing in Kansas.
Additional information: Award amount varies. Requires service obligation.

Number of awards:	281
Number of applicants:	296
Application deadline:	August 1
Total amount awarded:	$922,164

Contact:
Kansas Board of Regents
Att: Diane Lindeman
1000 SW Jackson St. Suite 520
Topeka, KS 66612-1368
Phone: 785-296-3518
Fax: 785-296-0983
Web: www.kansasregents.org

Kaplan, Inc.

Kaplan/Newsweek "My Turn" Essay Contest

Type of award: Scholarship.
Intended use: For full-time undergraduate study at 2-year or 4-year institution.
Eligibility: Applicant must be enrolled in high school. Applicant must be U.S. citizen or permanent resident.
Basis for selection: Competition/talent/interest in writing/journalism, based on effectiveness; creativity; insight; organization and development; consistent use of language; variety in sentence structure and vocabulary; and use of proper grammar, spelling and punctuation. Major/career interest in publishing.
Application requirements: Essay.
Additional information: Winning essays may be published by Newsweek. Call Kaplan for entry form including official rules. Completed entries may be sent to address listed. Essays must be original and factually accurate. Visit Website for more information.

Amount of award:	$1,000-$5,000
Number of awards:	10
Application deadline:	February 1
Notification begins:	June 15
Total amount awarded:	$15,000

Contact:
Kaplan, Inc.
Pre-College
1440 Broadway, 9th Floor
New York, NY 10018
Phone: 800-KAP-TEST
Web: www.kaptest.com/essay

Kappa Kappa Gamma Foundation

Kappa Kappa Gamma Scholarship

Type of award: Scholarship, renewable.
Intended use: For full-time undergraduate or graduate study at 4-year or graduate institution in United States.
Eligibility: Applicant or parent must be member/participant of Kappa Kappa Gamma.
Basis for selection: Applicant must demonstrate financial need and high academic achievement.
Application requirements: Two recommendations (one academic, one chapter). Send original and two copies of all application materials.
Additional information: Applicant must be active member in good standing of Kappa Kappa Gamma fraternity, with minimum 3.0 GPA. Must be U.S. citizen or permanent resident from Canada.

Amount of award:	$500-$3,000
Number of awards:	125
Number of applicants:	310
Application deadline:	February 1
Total amount awarded:	$4,222,404

Contact:
Kappa Kappa Gamma Foundation
P.O. Box 38
Columbus, OH 43216-0038
Phone: 614-228-6515
Fax: 614-228-6303
Web: www.kappa.org

KarMel Scholarship Committee

KarMel Scholarship

Type of award: Scholarship.
Intended use: For undergraduate or graduate study at postsecondary institution in United States.
Eligibility: Applicant must be high school senior. Applicant must be U.S. citizen.
Basis for selection: Competition/talent/interest in gay/lesbian, based on artistic or written ability on Gay/Lesbian subject. Applicant must demonstrate depth of character, leadership and seriousness of purpose.
Application requirements: Artistic work samples.
Additional information: Open to high school seniors, undergraduates, and graduate students. Applicant need not be gay/lesbian/bi to apply for scholarship, but must submit works that include gay/lesbian/bi content. Scholarship is divided into two categories: Best "Written" Gay/Lesbian/Bi Themed Work

and Best "Artistic" Gay/Lesbian/Bi Themed Work. Applicant may submit up to three works in both categories. Written work of any length will be accepted. All applicants may submit work via e-mail or postal mail. Visit Website for complete more information.

Amount of award: $200-$400
Number of awards: 2
Number of applicants: 1,300
Application deadline: March 31
Notification begins: July 31
Total amount awarded: $700

Contact:
KarMel Scholarship Committee
P.O. Box 70382
Sunnyvale, CA 94086
Web: www.karenandmelody.com

Kentucky Higher Education Assistance Authority (KHEAA)

Early Childhood Development Scholarship

Type of award: Scholarship.
Intended use: For half-time undergraduate study. Designated institutions: Approved Kentucky institutions.
Eligibility: Applicant must be U.S. citizen or permanent resident residing in Kentucky.
Basis for selection: Major/career interest in education, early childhood. Applicant must demonstrate financial need.
Application requirements: FAFSA.
Additional information: Part-time students working at least twenty hours in childcare facility eligible. Must agree to service commitment. To apply register through Zip Access on Website. Must reapply for each term. Deadlines: July 15 for fall, November 15 for spring, April 15 for summer.

Amount of award: $1,800
Number of awards: 1,115
Number of applicants: 1,690
Total amount awarded: $1,075,300

Contact:
Kentucky Higher Education Assistance Authority
P.O. Box 798
Frankfort, KY 40602-0798
Phone: 800-928-8926
Fax: 502-696-7373
Web: www.kheaa.com

Kentucky College Access Program Grant (CAP)

Type of award: Scholarship, renewable.
Intended use: For undergraduate study at postsecondary institution.
Eligibility: Applicant must be U.S. citizen or permanent resident residing in Kentucky.
Basis for selection: Applicant must demonstrate financial need.
Application requirements: Proof of eligibility. FAFSA.
Additional information: Applicant ineligible if family contribution exceeds $4,041. May be used at eligible schools. Visit Website for additional information.

Amount of award: $50-$1,900
Number of awards: 39,000
Number of applicants: 198,400
Notification begins: April 15
Total amount awarded: $59,600,000

Contact:
Kentucky Higher Education Assistance Authority (KHEAA)
Grant Programs
P.O. Box 798
Frankfort, KY 40602-0798
Phone: 800-928-8926
Fax: 502-696-7373
Web: www.kheaa.com

Kentucky Educational Excellence Scholarship (KEES)

Type of award: Scholarship, renewable.
Intended use: For undergraduate study at accredited vocational, 2-year or 4-year institution in United States. Designated institutions: Participating public and private postsecondary institutions in Kentucky and selected out-of-state institutions if program of study not offered in Kentucky.
Eligibility: Applicant must be enrolled in high school. Applicant must be U.S. citizen or permanent resident residing in Kentucky.
Basis for selection: Applicant must demonstrate high academic achievement.
Additional information: Scholarship is earned each year of high school. Minimum annual high school GPA of 2.5. Supplemental award is given for highest ACT score (or SAT equivalent) achieved by high school graduation, based on minimum ACT score of 15. Recipient must be enrolled in postsecondary program at least half-time. Visit Website or contact via e-mail for additional information.

Amount of award: $125-$2,500
Number of awards: 64,070
Number of applicants: 64,070
Total amount awarded: $88,441,100

Contact:
Kentucky Higher Education Assistance Authority (KHEAA)
P.O. Box 798
Frankfort, KY 40602-0798
Phone: 800-928-8926
Fax: 502-696-7373
Web: www.kheaa.com

Kentucky Teacher Scholarship

Type of award: Scholarship, renewable.
Intended use: For full-time undergraduate or graduate study at 2-year, 4-year or graduate institution.
Eligibility: Applicant must be U.S. citizen residing in Kentucky.
Basis for selection: Major/career interest in education, teacher; education, early childhood or education, special. Applicant must demonstrate financial need.
Application requirements: Proof of eligibility. FAFSA.
Additional information: Must enroll in course of study leading to initial Kentucky teacher certification. Loan forgiveness for teaching in Kentucky schools: one semester for each semester of financial assistance, two semesters if service is in teacher shortage area. Visit Website for application (see ZipAccess) and additional information.

Amount of award:	$300-$5,000
Number of awards:	840
Number of applicants:	1,300
Application deadline:	May 1
Notification begins:	May 30
Total amount awarded:	$2,712,400

Contact:
Kentucky Higher Education Assistance Authority (KHEAA)
Teacher Scholarship Program
P.O. Box 798
Frankfort, KY 40602-0798
Phone: 800-928-8926
Fax: 502-696-7373
Web: www.kheaa.com

Kentucky Tuition Grant

Type of award: Scholarship, renewable.
Intended use: For full-time undergraduate study at 2-year or 4-year institution. Designated institutions: Eligible private institutions in Kentucky.
Eligibility: Applicant must be U.S. citizen residing in Kentucky.
Basis for selection: Applicant must demonstrate financial need.
Application requirements: Proof of eligibility. FAFSA.
Additional information: Visit Website for additional information.

Amount of award:	$200-$2,900
Number of awards:	12,600
Number of applicants:	34,600
Notification begins:	April 15
Total amount awarded:	$31,300,000

Contact:
Kentucky Higher Education Assistance Authority
Grant Programs
P.O. Box 798
Frankfort, KY 40602-0798
Phone: 800-928-8926
Fax: 502-696-7373
Web: www.kheaa.com

Mary Jo Young Scholarship

Type of award: Scholarship.
Intended use: For freshman study.
Eligibility: Applicant must be enrolled in high school. Applicant must be residing in Kentucky.
Basis for selection: Applicant must demonstrate financial need.
Additional information: Provides college tuition assistance to disadvantaged high school students taking dual credit college courses and AP courses through the Kentucky Virtual High School. Eligibility for free or reduced lunch through high school required. Award amounts are: $350 per semester if taking one course; $575 per semester if taking two courses.

Number of awards:	907
Number of applicants:	1,300
Total amount awarded:	$327,800

Contact:
Kentucky Higher Education Assistance Authority (KHEAA)
P.O. Box 798
Frankfort, KY 40602-0798
Phone: 800-928-8926
Fax: 502-696-7373
Web: www.kheaa.com

Robert C. Byrd Honors Scholarship

Type of award: Scholarship, renewable.
Intended use: For undergraduate study at 2-year or 4-year institution in United States.
Eligibility: Applicant must be high school senior. Applicant must be U.S. citizen residing in Kentucky.
Basis for selection: Applicant must demonstrate high academic achievement.
Application requirements: Recommendation from school official or GED coordinator, which must certify eligibility on KHEAA Website.
Additional information: Must have minimum 3.5 GPA, and minimum 23 on ACT, 1060 on SAT, or 2700 on GED. Award amount varies; maximum is $1,500 per year, renewable for four years. See Website or school guidance counselor for more information. Apply through ZipAccess on Website.

Number of awards:	350
Number of applicants:	1,775
Application deadline:	February 15
Notification begins:	June 15
Total amount awarded:	$483,600

Contact:
Kentucky Higher Education Assistance Authority
P.O. Box 798
Frankfort, KY 40602-0798
Phone: 800-928-8926
Fax: 502-696-7373
Web: www.kheaa.com

KGO-TV/RTNDF

Pete Wilson Journalism Scholarship

Type of award: Scholarship.
Basis for selection: Major/career interest in journalism.
Additional information: Must have one full year of school left to be eligible. Must be San Francisco Bay Area resident.

Amount of award:	$4,000
Number of awards:	1
Application deadline:	May 12

Contact:
RTNDF
Attn: Melanie Lo
1025 F Street NW, 7th Floor
Washington, DC 20004
Phone: 202-437-5218
Web: www.rtndf.org

The Kim and Harold Louie Family Foundation

The Louie Foundation Scholarship

Type of award: Scholarship.
Intended use: For full-time undergraduate study at vocational, 2-year or 4-year institution.
Eligibility: Applicant must be U.S. citizen or permanent resident.
Basis for selection: Applicant must demonstrate financial need and high academic achievement.

Application requirements: Essay, transcript, proof of eligibility. Two recommendations (at least one academic), proof of acceptance to college, SAR, 500 word essay, proof of citizenship or legal residency.
Additional information: Minimum 3.5 GPA; SAT score of 1800. Special consideration will be noted for applicants whose parents did not attend college, whose parents are United States veterans, who have overcome significant adversity, or who are first-generation immigrants to the United States.

Number of awards:	31
Number of applicants:	60
Application deadline:	March 31
Total amount awarded:	$100,000

Contact:
The Kim and Harold Louie Family Foundation - Scholarship
102 Fey Drive
Burlingame, CA 94010
Phone: 650-491-3434
Fax: 650-490-3153

Knights of Columbus

Matthews/Swift Educational Trust - Military Dependants

Type of award: Scholarship, renewable.
Intended use: For full-time undergraduate study at 4-year institution in United States. Designated institutions: Catholic colleges and universities.
Eligibility: Applicant or parent must be member/participant of Knights of Columbus. Applicant must be Roman Catholic. Applicant must be veteran; or dependent of disabled veteran or deceased veteran who served in the Army, Air Force, Marines, Navy, Coast Guard or Reserves/National Guard during Korean War, Persian Gulf War, WW II or Vietnam. Veterans of Iraq, Afghanistan and Pakistan conflicts and their dependents are also eligible. Parent must have been active Knights of Columbus member who died or became totally disabled while serving in the military during hostile action.
Application requirements: Proof of eligibility.
Additional information: Application must be filed within two years of death or determination of disability. Award pays tuition up to $25,000 for bachelor's degree at Catholic college. No application deadline.

Amount of award:	$25,000
Number of awards:	10
Number of applicants:	10

Contact:
Knights of Columbus
Department of Scholarships
P.O. Box 1670
New Haven, CT 06507-0901
Phone: 203-752-4332
Fax: 203-752-4103

Matthews/Swift Educational Trust - Police/Firefighters

Type of award: Scholarship, renewable.
Intended use: For full-time undergraduate study at 4-year institution in United States. Designated institutions: Catholic colleges and universities.
Eligibility: Applicant or parent must be member/participant of Knights of Columbus. Applicant must be Roman Catholic. Applicant's parent must have been killed or disabled in work-related accident as firefighter or police officer.
Application requirements: Proof of eligibility.
Additional information: Parent must have been active Knights of Columbus member who died or became totally disabled as the result of criminal violence while performing duties as full-time firefighter or law enforcement officer. Application must be filed within two years of death or determination of disability. Award pays tuition up to $25,000 for bachelor's degree at Catholic college. No application deadline.

Amount of award:	Full tuition
Number of awards:	10
Number of applicants:	10

Contact:
Knights of Columbus
Department of Scholarships
P.O. Box 1670
New Haven, CT 06507-0901
Phone: 203-752-4332
Fax: 203-752-4103

Pro Deo/Pro Patria Scholarship

Type of award: Scholarship, renewable.
Intended use: For full-time undergraduate study at 4-year institution in United States. Designated institutions: Catholic colleges and universities.
Eligibility: Applicant or parent must be member/participant of Knights of Columbus. Applicant must be high school senior. Applicant must be Roman Catholic. Applicant must be U.S. citizen.
Basis for selection: Applicant must demonstrate high academic achievement.
Application requirements: Recommendations, essay, transcript, proof of eligibility.
Additional information: Must be Knights of Columbus member in good standing; child of such a member or deceased member; or member in good standing of Columbian Squires. There are 12 scholarships designated for students at the Catholic University of America in Washington, DC; 50 scholarships available to students entering other Catholic colleges in the United States. Scholarships are renewable for up to four years, pending satisfactory academic performance. Scholarship applications must be filed by March 1. Obtain application from Department of Scholarships, Knights of Columbus, in New Haven, CT.

Amount of award:	$1,500
Number of awards:	62
Number of applicants:	600
Application deadline:	March 1
Notification begins:	May 1
Total amount awarded:	$93,000

Contact:
Knights of Columbus
Department of Scholarships
P.O. Box 1670
New Haven, CT 06510-0901
Phone: 203-752-4332
Fax: 203-752-4103

Kosciuszko Foundation

Dr. Marie E. Zakrzewski Medical Scholarship

Type of award: Scholarship.
Intended use: For undergraduate study.
Eligibility: Applicant must be female. Applicant must be Polish. Applicant must be Must be woman of Polish ancestry attending first, second or or third year of medical school at an accredited U.S. institution. Applicant must be residing in Massachusetts.
Basis for selection: Major/career interest in medicine. Applicant must demonstrate high academic achievement.
Application requirements: Personal statement regarding academic goals, two photos, transcripts, recommendations, proof of Polish ancestry.
Additional information: Selection is based on academic excellence, the applicant's academic achievements, motivation, interest in Polish subjects and involvement in the Polish American community. Financial need is taken into consideration. First preference is given to residents of the state of Massachusetts. Qualified residents of New England are considered if no first preference candidates apply. Visit website for more details.

| Application deadline: | January 15 |
| Total amount awarded: | $3,500 |

Contact:
Kosciuszko Foundation
15th East 65th St
New York, NY 10065
Phone: 212-734-2130 ext. 210
Web: www.kosciuszkofoundation.org

Kosciuszko Foundation Tuition Scholarships

Type of award: Scholarship, renewable.
Intended use: For full-time graduate study at graduate institution in or outside United States.
Eligibility: Applicant must be Polish. Applicant must be U.S. citizen or permanent resident.
Basis for selection: Major/career interest in polish language/studies. Applicant must demonstrate financial need, high academic achievement, seriousness of purpose and service orientation.
Application requirements: $35 application fee. Essay, transcript, proof of eligibility. Proof of Polish descent, two letters of recommendation from professors, two passport photos 1.5"x1.5" with full name on reverse side of each. Graduates must submit copies of degree diplomas.
Additional information: Minimum 3.0 GPA. Only one member per immediate family awarded at once. Eligible applicants must be either U.S. citizens of Polish descent, Polish citizens with permanent residency status in U.S., or U.S. citizens pursuing Polish studies as major. Students of other nationalities doing work in Polish studies considered. Award can be used for graduate study in U.S. or 1 year master's program at Center of European Studies, Jagellonian University in Cracow or English Schools of Medicine in Poland. Student must reapply for renewal of award. Visit Website or call for application. Applications available from October 1 to December 30.

Amount of award:	$1,000-$7,000
Application deadline:	January 15
Notification begins:	May 15

Contact:
Kosciuszko Foundation
15 East 65 Street
New York, NY 10065
Phone: 212-734-2130 ext.210
Fax: 212-628-4552
Web: www.kosciuszkofoundation.org

Kosciuszko Foundation Year Abroad Program

Type of award: Scholarship, renewable.
Intended use: For sophomore, junior, senior or graduate study at 4-year or graduate institution in United States in Poland. Designated institutions: Jagiellonian University, Institute of Polish Diaspora and Ethnic Studies (formerly the Polonia Institute, Krakow).
Eligibility: Applicant must be U.S. citizen or permanent resident.
Basis for selection: Competition/talent/interest in study abroad. Major/career interest in polish language/studies. Applicant must demonstrate high academic achievement.
Application requirements: $50 application fee. Essay, transcript. Two letters of reference, certificate of proficiency in Polish, two passport-sized photos with full name on reverse side of each. Graduates must submit copies of degree diplomas, Polish Ministry of Education application completed in English.
Additional information: Must have interest in Polish subjects and/or involvement in Polish-American community. Scholarship covers tuition and stipend for housing and living expenses for one academic year or semester. Airfare not included. Minimum 3.0 GPA. Visit Website for more information and application. Applications available from October 1 to December 30.

| Amount of award: | Full tuition |
| Application deadline: | January 15 |

Contact:
Kosciuszko Foundation
Year Abroad Program
15 East 65th Street
New York, NY 10065
Phone: 212-734-2130 ext.210
Fax: 212-628-4552
Web: www.kosciuszkofoundation.org

Massachusetts Federation of Polish Women's Clubs Scholarships

Type of award: Scholarship.
Intended use: For full-time sophomore, junior or senior study at postsecondary institution in United States.
Eligibility: Applicant must be Polish. Applicant must be U.S. citizen or permanent resident.
Basis for selection: Applicant must demonstrate financial need and high academic achievement.
Application requirements: $35 application fee. Essay, transcript, proof of eligibility. Two letters of recommendation. Proof of Polish ancestry. Two passport-sized photos with full name printed on reverse side of each. SASE.
Additional information: Applicant must be member of Massachusetts Federation of Polish Women's Clubs. Children and grandchildren of federation members also eligible. Minimum 3.0 GPA. Selection based on academic excellence, motivation, and interest in Polish subjects or involvement in Polish-American community. Only one member per immediate

family may receive Massachusetts Federation of Polish Women's Scholarship during any given academic year. Visit Website for more information and application.

Amount of award:	$1,250
Application deadline:	January 15
Notification begins:	May 1

Contact:
Kosciuszko Foundation
15 East 65th Street
New York, NY 10065
Phone: 212-734-2130 ext.210
Fax: 212-628-4552
Web: www.kosciuszkofoundation.org

The Polish American Club of North Jersey Scholarships

Type of award: Scholarship, renewable.
Intended use: For full-time undergraduate or graduate study at accredited postsecondary institution in United States.
Eligibility: Applicant must be Polish. Applicant must be U.S. citizen or permanent resident.
Basis for selection: Applicant must demonstrate financial need and high academic achievement.
Application requirements: $35 application fee. Essay, transcript, proof of eligibility. Two letters of recommendation. Proof of Polish ancestry. Two passport-sized photos with full name printed on reverse side of each. SASE.
Additional information: Applicant must be an active member of Polish American Club of North Jersey. Children and grandchildren of Polish American Club of North Jersey members also eligible. Minimum 3.0 GPA. Only one member per immediate family may receive a Polish American Club of North Jersey Scholarship during any given academic year. Selection based on academic excellence, motivation, and interest in Polish subjects or involvement in the Polish-American community. Applications available October 1 through December 30. Visit Website for application and more information.

Amount of award:	$500-$2,000
Number of awards:	9
Application deadline:	January 15
Notification begins:	May 1
Total amount awarded:	$11,750

Contact:
Kosciuszko Foundation
15 East 65th Street
New York, NY 10065
Phone: 212-734-2130 ext.210
Fax: 212-628-4552
Web: www.kosciuszkofoundation.org

The Polish National Alliance of Brooklyn, USA, Inc. Scholarships

Type of award: Scholarship, renewable.
Intended use: For full-time undergraduate study at accredited postsecondary institution in United States.
Eligibility: Applicant or parent must be member/participant of Polish National Alliance of Brooklyn. Applicant must be Polish. Applicant must be U.S. citizen or permanent resident.
Basis for selection: Applicant must demonstrate financial need and high academic achievement.
Application requirements: $35 application fee. Essay, transcript, proof of eligibility. Two letters of recommendation. Proof of Polish ancestry. Two passport-sized photos with full name printed on reverse side of each. SASE.
Additional information: Applicant must be member in good standing of Polish National Alliance of Brooklyn, USA, Inc. Minimum 3.0 GPA. Only one member per immediate family may receive scholarship during any given academic year. Selection based on academic excellence, motivation, and interest in Polish subjects or involvement in the Polish-American community. Applications available October 1 through December 30. Visit Website for application and more information.

Amount of award:	$2,000
Number of awards:	3
Application deadline:	January 15
Notification begins:	May 15
Total amount awarded:	$6,000

Contact:
Kosciuszko Foundation
15 East 65th Street
New York, NY 10065
Phone: 212-734-2130 ext.210
Fax: 212-628-4552
Web: www.kosciuszkofoundation.org

The Lagrant Foundation

Lagrant Scholarships

Type of award: Scholarship.
Intended use: For full-time undergraduate or graduate study at accredited 4-year or graduate institution.
Eligibility: Applicant must be Alaskan native, Asian American, African American, Mexican American, Hispanic American, Puerto Rican or American Indian. Applicant must be U.S. citizen.
Basis for selection: Major/career interest in advertising; marketing or public relations.
Application requirements: Transcript. Resume. Two-page typed essay outlining career goals, accomplishments, reasons why he/she should be selected, and steps he/she will take to increase ethnic representation in this field. Include paragraph indicating how education is currently financed and why financing in coming year is needed, explaining college and community activities, describing any honors or awards received, and (if employed) indicating hours worked and responsibilities.
Additional information: Minimum 2.75 GPA. Chosen applicant must attend The Lagrant Foundation's career development workshop and awards reception to receive scholarship. In addition, recipient must make one-year commitment to maintain contact with TLF to receive professional guidance and academic support. Maximum award for undergraduates $5,000; maximum for graduate students $10,000.

Number of awards:	15
Application deadline:	February 28
Total amount awarded:	$100,000

Contact:
The Lagrant Foundation
626 Wilshire Boulevard, Suite 700
Los Angeles, CA 90017-2920
Phone: 323-469-8680
Fax: 323-469-8683
Web: www.lagrantfoundation.org

Lambda Alpha National Collegiate Honors Society for Anthropology

Senior Scholarship

Type of award: Scholarship.
Intended use: For senior study in United States.
Eligibility: Applicant or parent must be member/participant of Lambda Alpha. Applicant must be U.S. citizen or permanent resident.
Basis for selection: Major/career interest in anthropology. Applicant must demonstrate high academic achievement and seriousness of purpose.
Application requirements: Recommendations, transcript, nomination by faculty sponsor from department of anthropology. Curriculum vitae, writing sample.
Additional information: Institution must have a chartered Lambda Alpha chapter. Apply in senior year.

Amount of award:	$5,000
Number of awards:	1
Number of applicants:	16
Application deadline:	March 1
Notification begins:	April 1
Total amount awarded:	$5,000

Contact:
Lambda Alpha National Collegiate Honors Society for Anthropology
Department of Anthropology, Attn: B.K. Swartz
Ball State University
Muncie, IN 47306-0435
Phone: 765-285-1575
Web: www.lambdaalpha.com

Landscape Architecture Foundation

Courtland Paul Scholarship

Type of award: Scholarship.
Intended use: For junior or senior study. Designated institutions: Schools accredited by the Landscape Architecture Accreditation Board.
Eligibility: Applicant must be U.S. citizen.
Basis for selection: Major/career interest in landscape architecture. Applicant must demonstrate financial need and seriousness of purpose.
Application requirements: Cover sheet, personal profile, 500-word essay, two letters of recommendation.
Additional information: All application materials must be sent together in one email, except for the recommendation letters which must be sent by email from the author. Minimum 'C' GPA. Award must be used for tuition and/or books within the school year of the award.

Amount of award:	$1-$5,000
Number of applicants:	37
Application deadline:	February 15

Contact:
Landscape Architecture Foundation
818 18th Street, Suite 810
Washington, DC 20006
Phone: 202-331-7070
Web: www.lafoundation.org

David T. Woolsey Scholarship

Type of award: Scholarship.
Intended use: For full-time junior, senior or graduate study at accredited 4-year or graduate institution.
Eligibility: Applicant must be permanent resident residing in Hawaii.
Basis for selection: Major/career interest in landscape architecture. Applicant must demonstrate service orientation.
Application requirements: Portfolio, recommendations, essay, proof of eligibility. Photo. Cover Letter. Typed, double-spaced autobiography and statement of personal and professional goals (minimum 500 words); three 8 1/2x11 work samples as jpg or PDF; two letters of recommendation, including one from design instructor; personal profile; and proof of Hawaii residency.
Additional information: Applicant must be enrolled in landscape architecture program at accredited college or university. Visit Website for more information.

Amount of award:	$2,000
Number of awards:	1
Application deadline:	February 15

Contact:
Landscape Architecture Foundation
818 18th Street
Suite 810
Washington, DC 20006
Phone: 202-331-7070
Web: www.lafoundation.org

The EDSA Minority Scholarship

Type of award: Scholarship.
Intended use: For junior or senior study.
Eligibility: Applicant must be African American, Hispanic American or American Indian.
Basis for selection: Major/career interest in landscape architecture. Applicant must demonstrate financial need and seriousness of purpose.
Application requirements: Portfolio, recommendations, essay, transcript. Cover letter, personal profile, 500-word essay, three work samples (jpg or pdf), two letters of recommendation.
Additional information: Essay must describe a design or research effort and explain how it will contribute to the advancement of the profession and the applicant's ethnic heritage.

Amount of award:	$5,000
Number of awards:	1
Number of applicants:	7
Application deadline:	February 15

Contact:
Landscape Architecture Foundation
818 18th Street, Suite 810
Washington, DC 20006
Phone: 202-331-7070
Fax: 202-898-1185
Web: www.lafoundation.org

LAF/CLASS Fund (California Landscape Architectural Student Scholarship) University Scholarship Program

Type of award: Scholarship.
Intended use: For junior or senior study at accredited postsecondary institution in United States. Designated institutions: University of California, Davis; Cal Poly; Cal Poly Pomona; Cal Poly San Luis Obispo.
Eligibility: Applicant must be residing in California.
Basis for selection: Major/career interest in landscape architecture. Applicant must demonstrate financial need and service orientation.
Application requirements: Transcript. Photo, cover sheet, personal profile, 300-word statement on the profession; 100-word statement on intended use of funds. Two faculty recommendation letters. One confidential recommendation from department head.
Additional information: Two awards per institution. Visit Website for more information.
    Amount of award: $2,000
    Number of awards: 6
    Application deadline: February 15
Contact:
Landscape Architecture Foundation
818 18th Street
Suite 810
Washington, DC 20006
Phone: 202-331-7070
Web: www.lafoundation.org

LAF/CLASS Fund Landscape Architecture Program

Type of award: Scholarship.
Intended use: For full-time undergraduate study. Designated institutions: University of California, Berkeley; University of California, Los Angeles.
Eligibility: Applicant must be residing in California.
Basis for selection: Major/career interest in landscape architecture. Applicant must demonstrate financial need and service orientation.
Application requirements: Transcript. Photo. 300-word statement on the profession; 100-word statement on intended use of funds. Two faculty recommendation letters. One confidential recommendation from department head. Cover sheet and personal profile.
Additional information: Two awards per institution. Visit Website for more details.
    Amount of award: $1,000
    Number of awards: 4
    Application deadline: February 15
    Total amount awarded: $4,000
Contact:
Landscape Architecture Foundation
818 18th Street
Suite 810
Washington, DC 20006
Phone: 202-331-7070
Web: www.lafoundation.org

LAF/CLASS Fund Scholarship Ornamental Horticulture Program

Type of award: Scholarship.
Intended use: For junior or senior study at accredited postsecondary institution in United States. Designated institutions: University of California, Davis; Cal Poly Pomona; Cal Poly San Luis Obispo.
Eligibility: Applicant must be residing in California.
Basis for selection: Major/career interest in horticulture. Applicant must demonstrate service orientation.
Application requirements: Transcript. Photo. 300-word statement on profession; 100-word statement on intended use of funds; two faculty recommendation letters; one confidential recommendation from department head; cover sheet and personal profile.
Additional information: One award per institution. Faxed applications will not be accepted.
    Amount of award: $3,000
    Number of awards: 1
    Application deadline: February 15
    Total amount awarded: $3,000
Contact:
Landscape Architecture Foundation
818 18th Street
Suite 810
Washington, DC 20006
Phone: 202-331-7070
Web: www.lafoundation.org

Landscape Forms Design for People Scholarship

Type of award: Scholarship.
Intended use: For full-time senior study. Designated institutions: Schools with LAAB-accredited program.
Basis for selection: Major/career interest in landscape architecture. Applicant must demonstrate financial need and seriousness of purpose.
Application requirements: Portfolio, transcript. Cover sheet, personal profile, 300-word essay describing qualities essential to great and successful public spaces, three work samples (jpg or pdf), two letters of recommendation.
Additional information: Must show proven contribution to design of public spaces that promote social interaction.
    Amount of award: $3,000
    Number of awards: 1
    Number of applicants: 17
    Application deadline: February 15
Contact:
Landscape Architecture Foundation
818 18th Street, Suite 810
Washington, DC 20006
Phone: 202-331-7070
Fax: 202-898-1185
Web: www.lafoundation.org

Peridian International Inc./Rae L. Price FASLA Scholarship

Type of award: Scholarship.
Intended use: For junior or senior study. Designated institutions: UCLA.
Eligibility: Applicant must be U.S. citizen.

Landscape Architecture Foundation: Peridian International Inc./Rae L. Price FASLA Scholarship

Basis for selection: Major/career interest in landscape architecture. Applicant must demonstrate financial need and high academic achievement.
Application requirements: Two letters of recommendation from current professors, photo in jpg format, 500-word essay describing applicant's aspirations and need for financial assistance.
Additional information: Award restricted to tuition, books, and program required supplies. Applicants must have minimum grade point average of B.
    Amount of award: $5,000
    Application deadline: February 15
Contact:
Landscape Architecture Foundation
818 18th Street
Suite 810
Washington, DC 20006
Phone: 202-331-7070
Web: www.lafoundation.org

Rain Bird intelligent Use of Water Company Scholarship

Type of award: Scholarship.
Intended use: For full-time junior or senior study at accredited 4-year institution.
Basis for selection: Major/career interest in landscape architecture; horticulture; hydrology or urban planning. Applicant must demonstrate high academic achievement.
Application requirements: Photo, personal profile, 300-word essay stating career goals and expected contribution to landscape architecture; financial aid forms; cover letter; personal statement.
Additional information: Visit Website for more information.
    Amount of award: $2,500
    Number of awards: 1
    Number of applicants: 30
    Application deadline: February 15
Contact:
Landscape Architecture Foundation
818 18th Street
Suite 810
Washington, DC 20006
Phone: 202-331-7070
Web: www.lafoundation.org

Steven G. King Play Environments Scholarship

Type of award: Scholarship.
Intended use: For full-time junior, senior or graduate study. Designated institutions: LAAB-accredited schools.
Basis for selection: Major/career interest in landscape architecture. Applicant must demonstrate financial need and seriousness of purpose.
Application requirements: Transcript. Cover sheet, personal profile, 500-word essay explaining value of play and of integrating playgrounds into recreation environments, plan or details of play environment of applicant's design (jpg or pdf).
Additional information: Must have demonstrated interest in park and playground planning.
    Amount of award: $5,000
    Number of awards: 1
    Number of applicants: 9
    Application deadline: February 15

Contact:
Landscape Architecture Foundation
818 18th Street, Suite 810
Washington, DC 20006
Phone: 202-331-7070
Fax: 202-898-1185
Web: www.lafoundation.org

Latin American Educational Foundation

Latin American Educational Scholarship

Type of award: Scholarship, renewable.
Intended use: For full-time undergraduate, graduate or non-degree study at accredited postsecondary institution in United States.
Eligibility: Applicant must be Mexican American, Hispanic American or Puerto Rican. Applicant must be residing in Colorado.
Basis for selection: Applicant must demonstrate financial need, high academic achievement and service orientation.
Application requirements: Recommendations, essay, transcript, proof of eligibility. Previous year's tax return.
Additional information: Minimum 3.0 GPA. SAT/ACT scores required for high school seniors. Must be Hispanic American or actively involved in Hispanic American community. Recipients must fulfill ten hours of community service during the award year. Applicants must reapply each year.
    Amount of award: $750-$2,000
    Number of awards: 400
    Number of applicants: 200
    Application deadline: March 1
    Notification begins: June 15
    Total amount awarded: $200,000
Contact:
Latin American Education Foundation
561 Santa Fe Drive
Denver, CO 80204
Phone: 303-446-0541 ext. 12
Fax: 303-446-0526
Web: www.laef.org

League of United Latin American Citizens

GE Business/Engineering Scholarship for Minority Students

Type of award: Scholarship, renewable.
Intended use: For full-time sophomore study at accredited 2-year or 4-year institution in United States.
Eligibility: Applicant must be U.S. citizen or permanent resident.
Basis for selection: Major/career interest in business or engineering. Applicant must demonstrate high academic achievement, seriousness of purpose and service orientation.

Application requirements: Transcript, proof of eligibility. 300 word personal statement describing professional and career goals. Three reference letters (at least one being a college professor) addressed to GE/LULAC Scholarship Selection Committee, including telephone number and mailing address for each reference.
Additional information: Applicant must be minority student with minimum 3.25 GPA who is entering sophomore year in the fall. Recipients may be offered temporary summer or internship positions with GE businesses; however, the students are under no obligation to accept GE employment. Application available on Website.

Amount of award:	$5,000
Number of awards:	9
Application deadline:	July 15
Notification begins:	August 15
Total amount awarded:	$45,000

Contact:
League of United Latin American Citizens
Attn: GE Scholarship
2000 L Street NW, Suite 610
Washington, DC 20036
Phone: 202-833-6130
Web: www.lnesc.org

GM Engineering Scholarship For Minority Students

Type of award: Scholarship, renewable.
Intended use: For full-time undergraduate study at 4-year institution. Designated institutions: Colleges and Universities approved by LULAC and GM.
Eligibility: Applicant must be Alaskan native, African American, Mexican American, Hispanic American, Puerto Rican or American Indian.
Basis for selection: Major/career interest in engineering. Applicant must demonstrate high academic achievement, seriousness of purpose and service orientation.
Application requirements: Recommendations, transcript. Personal statement of no more than 300 words describing professional and career goals.
Additional information: Applicant must be a minority student pursuing a bachelor's degree in engineering. Minimum 3.2 college GPA, or 3.5 high school GPA for entering freshmen. Entering freshmen must have minimum 23 ACT score or 970 SAT score. Applicant must submit letters of reference from three adults (at least one being a teacher or professor) addressed to the GM/LULAC Scholarship Selection Committee. Include a complete telephone number and mailing address for each reference. Must maintain satisfactory academic progress to be eligible for renewal. See Website for application. Scholarship recipients may be offered temporary summer or internship positions with GM businesses; however students are not obligated to accept such offers.

Amount of award:	$2,000
Number of awards:	20
Application deadline:	July 15
Notification begins:	August 15
Total amount awarded:	$40,000

Contact:
Leage of United Latin American Citizens (LULAC)
GM/LULAC Scholarship Selection Committee
2000 L Street, NW, Suite 610
Washington, DC 20036
Phone: 202-833-6130
Web: www.lnesc.org

LULAC National Scholarship Fund Honors Awards

Type of award: Scholarship.
Intended use: For full-time undergraduate or graduate study at accredited 2-year, 4-year or graduate institution in United States.
Eligibility: Applicant must be Hispanic American. Applicant must be U.S. citizen or permanent resident.
Basis for selection: Applicant must demonstrate high academic achievement.
Application requirements: Transcript, proof of eligibility. Verification of admittance to institution. Personal essay of no more than 300 words, typed or neatly printed.
Additional information: Students are ineligible for scholarship if related to scholarship committee member, council president, or individual contributor to the local funds of the council. Minimum 3.25 GPA required. Entering freshmen must have scored at least 23 on ACT or 1100 on SAT. See Website for list of participating LULAC councils. Local LULAC council may require additional information and personal interview.

Amount of award:	$250-$1,000
Application deadline:	March 31
Notification begins:	May 15

Contact:
Contact local LULAC council for more information and application.
Phone: 202-833-6130
Web: www.lnesc.org

LULAC National Scholarship Fund National Scholastic Achievement Awards

Type of award: Scholarship.
Intended use: For full-time undergraduate or graduate study at accredited 2-year, 4-year or graduate institution in United States.
Eligibility: Applicant must be Hispanic American. Applicant must be U.S. citizen or permanent resident.
Basis for selection: Applicant must demonstrate high academic achievement.
Application requirements: Transcript, proof of eligibility. Verification of admittance to institution. Personal essay of no more than 300 words, typed or neatly printed.
Additional information: Students are ineligible for scholarship if related to scholarship committee member, council president, or individual contributor to the local funds of the council. Entering freshmen must have scored at least 29 on ACT or 1350 on SAT. Minimum 3.5 GPA required. Minimum amount of award is $1,000. See Website for list of participating LULAC councils. Local LULAC council may require additional information and personal interview.

Application deadline:	March 31
Notification begins:	May 15

Contact:
Contact local LULAC council for more information.
Phone: 202-833-6130
Web: www.lnesc.org

LULAC National Scholarshp Fund General Awards

Type of award: Scholarship.

League of United Latin American Citizens: LULAC National Scholarshp Fund General Awards

Intended use: For undergraduate or graduate study at accredited 2-year, 4-year or graduate institution in United States.
Eligibility: Applicant must be Hispanic American. Applicant must be U.S. citizen or permanent resident.
Basis for selection: Applicant must demonstrate financial need, high academic achievement, depth of character, leadership and service orientation.
Application requirements: Interview, transcript, proof of eligibility. Verification of admittance to institution. Personal essay of no more than 300 words, typed or neatly printed.
Additional information: Applicant must have applied to or be enrolled in college, university, or graduate school, including 2-year colleges and vocational schools. Academic performance considered, however motivation, sincerity, and integrity will also be considered in selection process. Students are ineligible for scholarship if related to scholarship committee member, council president, or individual contributor to the local funds of the council. See Website for list of participating LULAC councils. Local LULAC council may require additional information and personal interview.

Amount of award:	$250-$1,000
Application deadline:	March 31
Notification begins:	May 15
Total amount awarded:	$750,000

Contact:
Contact local LULAC council for more information.
Phone: 202-833-6130
Web: www.lnesc.org

Learning for Life

National Technical Investigators' Captain James J. Regan Memorial Scholarship

Type of award: Scholarship.
Intended use: For full-time undergraduate study.
Eligibility: Applicant or parent must be member/participant of Learning for Life. Applicant must be U.S. citizen or permanent resident.
Basis for selection: Major/career interest in criminal justice/law enforcement. Applicant must demonstrate high academic achievement, leadership and seriousness of purpose.
Application requirements: Essay, transcript, proof of eligibility. Certification from post advisor, head of participating organization, Learning for Life representative. Three letters of recommendation (two from outside of law enforcement). Additional essay (minimum of 250 words) on "How Will Technology Affect Law Enforcement in the 21st Century?" Black-and-white photo (preferably in uniform). Must submit original and four copies of all materials.
Additional information: Program open to Learning for Life's Law Enforcement Explorers. Visit Website for application and more information.

Amount of award:	$500
Number of awards:	2
Application deadline:	March 31
Total amount awarded:	$1,000

Contact:
National Law Enforcement Scholarships and Awards
1325 West Walnut Hill Lane
P.O. Box 152079
Irving, TX 75015-2079
Phone: 972-580-2433
Fax: 972-580-2502
Web: www.learning-for-life.org/exploring

Sheryl A. Horak Law Enforcement Explorer Scholarship

Type of award: Scholarship.
Intended use: For full-time undergraduate study at accredited 2-year or 4-year institution.
Eligibility: Applicant or parent must be member/participant of Learning for Life. Applicant must be high school senior. Applicant must be U.S. citizen or permanent resident.
Basis for selection: Major/career interest in criminal justice/law enforcement. Applicant must demonstrate high academic achievement, leadership and service orientation.
Application requirements: Transcript. Certification from post advisor, head of participating organization, Learning for Life representative. Three letters of recommendation (two from outside of law enforcement). Essay (500 words minimum) on "Why I Want to Pursue a Career in Law Enforcement." Black-and-white photo (preferably in uniform). Must submit original and two copies of all materials.
Additional information: Program open to Learning for Life's Law Enforcement Explorers. Award includes plaque and pin. Visit Website for application and more information.

Amount of award:	$1,000
Number of awards:	1
Application deadline:	March 31

Contact:
National Law Enforcement Scholarships and Awards
1325 West Walnut Hill Lane
P.O. Box 152079
Irving, TX 75015-2418
Phone: 972-580-2433
Fax: 972-580-2502
Web: www.learning-for-life.org/exploring

Life and Health Insurance Foundation for Education

LIFE Lessons Essay Contest

Type of award: Scholarship.
Intended use: For undergraduate study at postsecondary institution in United States.
Eligibility: Applicant must be at least 17, no older than 24. Applicant must be U.S. citizen or permanent resident.
Basis for selection: Competition/talent/interest in writing/journalism, based on 500-word essay describing how applicant has experienced personal and financial challenges caused by death of parent or legal guardian.
Application requirements: Essay, proof of eligibility. Essay of 500 words or 3-minute video describing personal and financial challenges caused by death of a parent.
Additional information: Applicant must be between 17 and 24 and have experienced the death of a parent or legal guardian. One grand prize of $5,000; four first-prize scholarships of $1,000; 14 second runner-up prizes of $500.

Video entries: five first prize scholarships of $1,000. One bonus prize of $4,000. Apply online or e-mail or call to receive paper application. Employees of Life and Health Insurance Foundation for Education ("LIFE" or "Sponsor"), Weber Shandwick, and their respective parents, affiliates, subsidiaries, and advertising, and promotion agencies, and any such employee's immediate family members and those living in their same households, whether or not related, are not eligible.

Amount of award:	$500-$5,000
Number of awards:	25
Number of applicants:	900
Application deadline:	April 18
Total amount awarded:	$25,000

Contact:
Life and Health Insurance Foundation for Education
Attn: Life Lessons Scholarship Essay Contest
1655 North Fort Meyer Drive, Suite 610
Arlington, VA 22209
Phone: 202-464-5000 ext. 4446
Fax: 202-464-5011
Web: www.lifehappens.org/scholarship

Liggett-Stashower, Inc.

David L. Stashower Scholarship

Type of award: Scholarship.
Intended use: For senior study at 4-year institution.
Eligibility: Applicant must be residing in Ohio.
Basis for selection: Major/career interest in advertising; graphic arts/design; public relations or communications. Applicant must demonstrate high academic achievement.
Application requirements: Recommendations, essay, transcript. Optional: Portfolio of work, writing samples, or other form of appropriate communication.
Additional information: Award includes trip to Cleveland in August for awards ceremony at Liggett-Stashower.

Amount of award:	$2,000
Number of awards:	2
Number of applicants:	23
Application deadline:	April 20
Total amount awarded:	$4,000

Contact:
Scholarship Award Committee Liggett-Stashower, Inc
1228 Euclid Ave.
Cleveland, OH 44115
Phone: 216-348-8500
Web: www.liggett.com

Lighthouse International

Christine H. Eidie Memorial Scholarship

Type of award: Scholarship.
Intended use: For full-time undergraduate or graduate study at accredited 4-year or graduate institution.
Application requirements: Essay, proof of eligibility. Proof of legal blindness.
Additional information: Applicant must be legally blind.

Amount of award:	$500-$1,000
Application deadline:	January 15, September 3

Contact:
Lighthouse International
111 East 59th Street
New York, NY 10022-1202
Phone: 212-821-9428
Fax: 212-821-9703
Web: www.lighthouse.org/education-services/eide

Lighthouse College-Bound Award

Type of award: Scholarship.
Intended use: For full-time freshman study at accredited 2-year or 4-year institution in United States.
Eligibility: Applicant must be visually impaired. Applicant must be high school senior. Applicant must be U.S. citizen residing in New York, Delaware, Massachusetts, Virginia, Connecticut, Vermont, Maine, Maryland, Pennsylvania, Florida, Georgia, South Carolina, District of Columbia, New Hampshire, West Virginia, New Jersey, North Carolina or Rhode Island.
Basis for selection: Applicant must demonstrate high academic achievement.
Application requirements: Recommendations, essay, transcript, proof of eligibility. Official documentation of legal blindness. Recommendations required from two people other than family members. Personal essay should be at least 500 words. Letter of acceptance to college.
Additional information: Applicant must be legally blind. College-bound high school seniors or recent high school graduates now planning to begin college may apply. Student must be blind or partially sighted.

Amount of award:	$5,000
Number of awards:	1
Application deadline:	March 1
Total amount awarded:	$5,000

Contact:
Lighthouse International
Scholarship Awards Program
111 East 59 Street
New York, NY 10022-1202
Phone: 212-821-9428
Fax: 212-821-9703
Web: www.lighthouse.org/scholarship_awards.htm

Lighthouse Graduate Award

Type of award: Scholarship.
Intended use: For full-time graduate study at graduate institution.
Eligibility: Applicant must be visually impaired. Applicant must be returning adult student. Applicant must be U.S. citizen residing in New York, Delaware, Massachusetts, Virginia, Connecticut, Vermont, Maine, Maryland, Pennsylvania, Florida, Georgia, South Carolina, District of Columbia, New Hampshire, West Virginia, New Jersey, North Carolina or Rhode Island.
Basis for selection: Applicant must demonstrate high academic achievement.
Application requirements: Recommendations, essay, transcript, proof of eligibility. Official documentation of legal blindness. Recommendations required from two people other than family members. Personal essay should be at least 500 words. Letter of acceptance from college.
Additional information: Applicant must be legally blind. Students may apply at any time immediately prior to, or during, their course of study. Visit Website for more information and to be placed on the mailing list for an application.

Lighthouse International: Lighthouse Graduate Award

Amount of award: $5,000
Number of awards: 1
Application deadline: February 28
Total amount awarded: $5,000
Contact:
Lighthouse International
Scholarship Awards Program
111 East 59 Street
New York, NY 10022-1202
Phone: 212-821-9428
Fax: 212-821-9703
Web: www.lighthouse.org/scholarship_awards.htm

Lighthouse Undergraduate Award

Type of award: Scholarship.
Intended use: For full-time undergraduate study at postsecondary institution.
Eligibility: Applicant must be visually impaired. Applicant must be U.S. citizen residing in New York, Delaware, Massachusetts, Virginia, Connecticut, Vermont, Maine, Maryland, Pennsylvania, Florida, Georgia, South Carolina, District of Columbia, New Hampshire, West Virginia, New Jersey, North Carolina or Rhode Island.
Basis for selection: Applicant must demonstrate high academic achievement.
Application requirements: Recommendations, essay, transcript, proof of eligibility. Official documentation of legal blindness. Recommendations required from two people other than family members. Personal essay should be at least 500 words.
Additional information: Applicant must be legally blind.
Amount of award: $5,000
Number of awards: 1
Application deadline: February 28
Total amount awarded: $5,000
Contact:
Lighthouse International
Scholarship Awards Program
111 East 59 Street
New York, NY 10022-1202
Phone: 212-821-9428
Fax: 212-821-9703
Web: www.lighthouse.org/scholarship_awards.htm

Los Padres Foundation

Los Padres Foundation Scholarships

Type of award: Scholarship, renewable.
Intended use: For full-time undergraduate or graduate study at 4-year or graduate institution in United States.
Eligibility: Applicant must be Hispanic American or Puerto Rican. Applicant must be high school senior. Applicant must be U.S. citizen or permanent resident.
Basis for selection: Applicant must demonstrate seriousness of purpose and service orientation.
Additional information: Applicant must have minimum 3.0 GPA and proof of low income. Applicant must be first generation in family to attend college. Award is renewable up to four years. Must complete 100 hours of community service by June 1st of first college year. Application available at financial aid office, high school counselor's office, and online.

Amount of award: $2,000
Number of applicants: 30
Application deadline: November 1
Notification begins: March 1
Contact:
Los Padres Foundation
CTA Program
658 Live Oak Drive
McLean, VA 22101
Phone: 877-843-7555
Fax: 866-810-1361
Web: www.lospadresfoundation.org

Louisiana Department of Veterans Affairs

Louisiana Veterans Affairs Educational Assistance for Dependent Children

Type of award: Scholarship, renewable.
Intended use: For full-time undergraduate, graduate or non-degree study at vocational, 2-year, 4-year or graduate institution.
Eligibility: Applicant must be at least 16, no older than 25. Applicant must be residing in Louisiana. Applicant must be dependent of disabled veteran or deceased veteran. Deceased veteran must have died of service-related disability.
Application requirements: Proof of eligibility. Certification of eligibility.
Additional information: Award is a tuition waiver at all Louisiana state-supported schools. Veteran must have been Louisiana resident for at least two years prior to entering service. Disability must be at least 90 percent as rated by U.S. Department of Veterans Affairs to qualify. Applicant also eligible if disability rating is 60 percent or more but employability rating is 100 percent unemployable. Award amounts vary and may be applied only toward state public schools.
Amount of award: Full tuition
Contact:
Louisiana Department of Veterans Affairs
P.O. Box 94095, Capitol Station
Baton Rouge, LA 70804-9095
Web: www.vetaffairs.com

Louisiana Veterans Affairs Educational Assistance for Surviving Spouse

Type of award: Scholarship, renewable.
Intended use: For full-time undergraduate, graduate or non-degree study at postsecondary institution.
Eligibility: Applicant must be single. Applicant must be residing in Louisiana. Applicant must be spouse of deceased veteran.
Application requirements: Proof of eligibility. Certification of eligibility.
Additional information: Award is tuition waiver at all Louisiana state-supported schools. Veteran must have been a Louisiana resident at least 12 months prior to entering service.
Amount of award: Full tuition

Contact:
Louisiana Department of Veterans Affairs
P.O. Box 94095, Capitol Station
Baton Rouge, LA 70804-9095
Web: www.vetaffairs.com

Louisiana Office of Student Financial Assistance

Louisiana Rockefeller Wildlife Scholarship

Type of award: Scholarship, renewable.
Intended use: For full-time undergraduate or graduate study at 4-year or graduate institution.
Eligibility: Applicant must be U.S. citizen residing in Louisiana.
Basis for selection: Major/career interest in wildlife/fisheries; forestry or oceanography/marine studies. Applicant must demonstrate high academic achievement.
Application requirements: FAFSA.
Additional information: Minimum 2.5 GPA for undergraduate students or 3.0 for graduate students.

Amount of award:	$1,000
Number of awards:	60
Number of applicants:	150
Application deadline:	July 31
Total amount awarded:	$60,000

Contact:
Louisiana Office of Student Financial Assistance
P.O. Box 91202
Baton Rouge, LA 70821-9202
Phone: 800-259-5626 ext. 1012
Fax: 225-922-0790
Web: www.osfa.state.la.us

Louisiana Tuition Opportunity Program for Students (TOPS) Award

Type of award: Scholarship, renewable.
Intended use: For full-time undergraduate study. Designated institutions: Eligible Louisiana postsecondary institutions.
Eligibility: Applicant must be U.S. citizen residing in Louisiana.
Basis for selection: Applicant must demonstrate high academic achievement.
Application requirements: FAFSA.
Additional information: Open to Louisiana residents who will be first-time, full-time freshmen at Louisiana public or LAICU private postsecondary institution no later than fall following first anniversary of high school graduation. Must be U.S. citizen with no criminal convictions. Must be registered with selective service (if necessary). Must have completed 17.5 units college-prep core curriculum. Individual requirements for awards below; please send one inquiry, only, for all award levels: TOPS OPPORTUNITY AWARD: Equal to tuition at public institution (or weighted average tuition at LAICU member institution). Must have minimum 2.5 GPA, minimum ACT score based on state's prior year average (never below 20) or minimum SAT of 940. TOPS PERFORMANCE AWARDS: Equal to tuition at public institution (or weighted average tuition at LAICU member institution) plus $400/yr stipend. Minimum 3.5 GPA, minimum ACT score of 23 or SAT score of 1060. TOPS HONORS AWARDS: Equal to tuition at public institution (or weighted average tuition at LAICU member institution) plus $800/yr stipend. Minimum 3.5 GPA, ACT score of 27 or SAT score of 1210. Contact Public Information Rep for more details.

Amount of award:	Full tuition
Application deadline:	July 1

Contact:
Louisiana Office of Student Financial Assistance
P.O. Box 91202
Baton Rouge, LA 70821-9202
Phone: 800-259-5626 ext. 1012
Fax: 225-922-0790
Web: www.osfa.state.la.us

Louisiana State Department of Education

Robert C. Byrd Honors Scholarship

Type of award: Scholarship, renewable.
Intended use: For full-time undergraduate study at vocational, 2-year or 4-year institution.
Eligibility: Applicant must be U.S. citizen or permanent resident residing in Louisiana.
Application requirements: Proof of eligibility. FAFSA.
Additional information: Minimum 3.5 GPA and ACT score of 23. Award amount varies; maximum is $1,500 per year, renewable for up to four years. Must be registered with the Selective Service, if required. Students at military academies not eligible. Award may be used for tuition for schools outside Louisiana.

Amount of award:	$1,500

Contact:
Louisiana State Department of Education
P.O. Box 94064
Baton Rouge, LA 70804
Phone: 225-342-2098 or 877-453-2721
Fax: 225-342-3432
Web: www.doe.state.la.us/lde/students.html

Luso-American Education Foundation

Dolores Nunes Lowry Scholarship

Type of award: Scholarship.
Intended use: For freshman study at vocational, 2-year or 4-year institution.
Eligibility: Applicant must be high school senior. Applicant must be U.S. citizen residing in California.
Basis for selection: Applicant must demonstrate high academic achievement.
Application requirements: 2 letters of recommendation, SAT scores.
Additional information: Applicant must be of Portuguese descent with a minimum 3.5 GPA or be studying Portuguese language in high school with a minimum of GPA of 3.0. If not currently enrolled in college or university, must plan to enroll

in the current academic year. Must be attending high school in San Jose/Santa Clara area.
- Amount of award: $500
- Number of awards: 1

Contact:
Luso-American Education Foundation
Scholarship Committee
PO Box 2967
Dublin, CA 94568
Phone: 925-828-3883
Fax: 925-828-3883
Web: www.luso-american.org

Eva Vieira Memorial Scholarship

Type of award: Scholarship, renewable.
Intended use: For full-time undergraduate study at accredited 4-year institution.
Eligibility: Applicant must be high school senior. Applicant must be U.S. citizen residing in California.
Basis for selection: Major/career interest in nursing. Applicant must demonstrate high academic achievement.
Application requirements: Recommendations, transcript. SAT or ACT scores.
Additional information: Applicant must be of Portuguese descent. Must have minimum 3.0 GPA beginning junior year of high school. Special consideration for first-generation college-bound students and students from farming families.
- Amount of award: $1,000
- Number of awards: 1
- Application deadline: March 1

Contact:
Secretary, Administrative Director
Luso-American Education Foundation
P.O. Box 2967
Dublin, CA 94568
Phone: 925-828-3883
Fax: 925-828-3883
Web: www.luso-american.org

Herbert Fernandes Scholarship

Type of award: Scholarship.
Intended use: For full-time sophomore, junior or senior study at 4-year institution.
Eligibility: Applicant must be U.S. citizen residing in California.
Basis for selection: Applicant must demonstrate high academic achievement.
Application requirements: Recommendations, transcript.
Additional information: Applicant must be of Portuguese descent. Must have taken or will enroll in Portuguese classes and be actively involved in Portuguese-American community. Minimum 3.0 GPA.
- Amount of award: $1,000
- Number of awards: 1
- Application deadline: March 1

Contact:
Secretary, Administrative Director
Luso-America Education Foundation
P.O. Box 2967
Dublin, CA 94568
Phone: 925-828-3883
Fax: 925-828-3883
Web: www.luso-american.org

Luso-American Education Foundation Scholarship

Type of award: Scholarship, renewable.
Intended use: For freshman study at accredited vocational, 2-year or 4-year institution.
Eligibility: Applicant or parent must be member/participant of Portuguese Continental Union. Applicant must be U.S. citizen or permanent resident residing in California.
Basis for selection: Applicant must demonstrate high academic achievement, depth of character, leadership and seriousness of purpose.
Application requirements: Recommendations, essay, transcript, proof of eligibility, nomination. 2 letters of recommendation, SAT scores, report from secondary school or college attended by student.
Additional information: Applicant must have been Luso-American Life Insurance Society member with at least one year in good standing. Applicant must be of Portuguese descent with a minimum 3.5 GPA or be studying Portuguese language in high school with a minimum of GPA of 3.0. If not currently enrolled in college or university, must plan to enroll in the current academic year. Award amount varies. Contact sponsor for more information.
- Amount of award: $500-$1,500
- Number of awards: 13
- Application deadline: March 1
- Notification begins: April 30

Contact:
Luso-American Education Foundation
Scholarship Committee
7 Hartwell Ave.
Lexington, MA 02421
Phone: 781-676-2002
Fax: 781-541-6191
Web: www.luso-american.org

Nicole Marie Goulart Memorial Scholarship

Type of award: Scholarship, renewable.
Intended use: For full-time sophomore, junior or senior study at 4-year institution in United States.
Eligibility: Applicant must be U.S. citizen or permanent resident.
Basis for selection: Major/career interest in medicine; health-related professions; neurology; nursing or pharmacy/pharmaceutics/pharmacology. Applicant must demonstrate high academic achievement.
Application requirements: Recommendations.
Additional information: Minimum 3.5 GPA. Award amount varies.
- Number of awards: 1
- Application deadline: March 1

Contact:
Secretary, Administrative Director
Luso-American Education Foundation
P.O. Box 2967
Dublin, CA 94568
Phone: 925-828-3883
Fax: 925-828-3883
Web: www.luso-american.org

Maine Department of Agriculture, Food and Rural Resources

Maine Rural Rehabilitation Fund

Type of award: Scholarship, renewable.
Intended use: For full-time undergraduate study at postsecondary institution.
Eligibility: Applicant must be residing in Maine.
Basis for selection: Major/career interest in agribusiness; agricultural economics; agricultural education; agriculture; animal sciences or engineering, agricultural. Applicant must demonstrate financial need and high academic achievement.
Additional information: Applicant must be Maine resident studying agriculture. Cumulative 2.7 GPA, or 3.0 GPA most recent semester. Amount of awards vary. Certain materials may be accepted after due date, if unavailable prior to deadline. Contact sponsor or visit Website for application and more information.
    Amount of award: $1,000-$3,000
    Number of awards: 4
    Application deadline: June 5
    Total amount awarded: $10,000
Contact:
Maine Department of Agriculture, Food and Rural Resources
28 State House Station
Augusta, ME 04333-4470
Phone: 207-287-3871
Fax: 207-287-7548
Web: www.maine.gov/agriculture

Maine Division of Veterans Services

Maine Veterans Services Dependents Educational Benefits

Type of award: Scholarship.
Intended use: For undergraduate or master's study at vocational, 2-year or 4-year institution.
Eligibility: Applicant must be at least 16, no older than 26. Applicant must be residing in Maine. Applicant must be dependent of disabled veteran, deceased veteran or POW/MIA; or spouse of disabled veteran or deceased veteran. Must apply for program prior to 22nd birthday, or before 26th birthday if applicant was enrolled in the U.S. Armed Forces. Age limits apply to child applicants only, not spouses.
Application requirements: Proof of eligibility. Proof of veteran's disability; child of veteran: birth certificate; stepchild of veteran: birth certificate and parent's marriage certificate to veteran; adopted child: birth certificate, adoption certificate; adopted child with natural parent as veteran: birth certificate and proof of paternity to natural parent; spouse: marriage certificate.
Additional information: Applicant must have graduated from high school and must be dependent upon deceased or permanently and totally disabled veteran. Parent or spouse must have been resident of Maine prior to enlistment or resident of Maine for five years preceding application for aid. Provides tuition at all branches of University of Maine system, all State of Maine vocational-technical colleges, and Maine Maritime Academy for eight semesters to be used within six years.
    Amount of award: Full tuition
Contact:
Maine Division of Veterans Services
117 State House Station
Augusta, ME 04333-0117
Phone: 207-626-4464
Fax: 207-626-4471
Web: www.mainebvs.org

Maine Innkeepers Association

Maine Innkeepers Association Scholarship

Type of award: Scholarship.
Intended use: For full-time undergraduate study at accredited vocational or 4-year institution in United States. Designated institutions: Institutions with fully accredited programs in hotel administration or culinary arts.
Eligibility: Applicant must be U.S. citizen or permanent resident residing in Maine.
Basis for selection: Major/career interest in culinary arts; hotel/restaurant management or hospitality administration/management. Applicant must demonstrate financial need and high academic achievement.
Application requirements: Recommendations, essay, transcript.
Additional information: Applicant must be Maine resident who is high school senior or college undergraduate.
    Amount of award: $250-$2,000
    Number of awards: 10
    Number of applicants: 30
    Application deadline: April 13
    Notification begins: January 1
    Total amount awarded: $8,500
Contact:
Maine Innkeepers Association
Scholarship Chairperson
304 US Route 1
Freeport, ME 04032
Phone: 207-865-6100
Fax: 207-865-6120
Web: www.maineinns.com

Maine Metal Products Association

Maine Metal Products Association Scholarship

Type of award: Scholarship.
Intended use: For undergraduate study at postsecondary institution.
Eligibility: Applicant must be permanent resident residing in Maine.

Basis for selection: Major/career interest in engineering or welding. Applicant must demonstrate financial need, high academic achievement, depth of character, leadership, seriousness of purpose and service orientation.
Application requirements: Recommendations, essay, transcript, proof of eligibility, nomination.
Additional information: Applicant must have career interest in Maine precision machining technology or manufacturing technology industry or related majors. Amount of award varies based on need and fund account. Visit Website for more information.

Number of awards:	12
Number of applicants:	30
Application deadline:	May 1
Total amount awarded:	$14,000

Contact:
Dorota Olaru, Marketing & Development Manager
Maine Metal Products Association
28 Stroudwater St. Suite #4
Westbrook, ME 04092
Phone: 207-854-2153
Fax: 207-854-3865
Web: www.mainemfg.org

Maine Recreation and Parks Association

Maine Recreation and Parks Association Scholarship

Type of award: Scholarship.
Intended use: For full-time undergraduate study. Designated institutions: Institutions with parks & recreation or leisure studies programs.
Eligibility: Applicant must be U.S. citizen.
Basis for selection: Major/career interest in parks/recreation. Applicant must demonstrate high academic achievement.
Application requirements: Recommendations, transcript. Three copies of requested materials.
Additional information: For parks and recreation or leisure studies majors only. Students who intend to study physical education, wildlife management, natural resources or law enforcement are not eligible. Out-of-state applicant must attend college in Maine; Maine residents may attend out-of-state college. One $500 award reserved for high school seniors; remaining awards are for enrolled undergraduates. Send SASE to receive application form.

Amount of award:	$500-$2,000
Number of awards:	2
Number of applicants:	6
Application deadline:	April 1

Contact:
Maine Recreation and Parks Association
c/o Caribou Parks & Recreation Dept.
55 Bennett Drive
Caribou, ME 04736
Phone: 207-493-4224
Fax: 207-493-4225
Web: www.merpa.org

Maine Restaurant Association

Russ Casey Scholarship

Type of award: Scholarship.
Intended use: For undergraduate or graduate study at accredited 2-year, 4-year or graduate institution. Designated institutions: New England colleges and universities.
Eligibility: Applicant must be U.S. citizen residing in Maine.
Basis for selection: Major/career interest in culinary arts. Applicant must demonstrate high academic achievement.
Application requirements: Transcript. Two recommendations from high school or college teachers, one from restaurant owner/manager or allied member of Maine Restaurant Association. Cover letter detailing applicant's interest in and connection to food service industry in 300 words or less.
Additional information: Open to Maine students pursuing career in food service industry.

Amount of award:	$1,000
Number of awards:	3
Number of applicants:	20
Application deadline:	May 1
Total amount awarded:	$3,000

Contact:
Chairman, Scholarship Committee Maine Restaurant Association
P.O. Box 5060
5 Wade St.
Augusta, ME 04332
Phone: 207-623-2178
Fax: 207-623-8377
Web: www.mainerestaurant.com

Maine Society of Professional Engineers

Maine Society of Professional Engineers Scholarship Program

Type of award: Scholarship.
Intended use: For freshman study at 2-year or 4-year institution in United States.
Eligibility: Applicant must be high school senior. Applicant must be permanent resident residing in Maine.
Basis for selection: Major/career interest in engineering or engineering, civil.
Application requirements: Recommendations, essay, transcript. SAT/ACT scores.
Additional information: Applicant must intend to earn a degree in engineering and to enter the practice of engineering after graduation.

Amount of award:	$1,500
Number of awards:	2
Application deadline:	March 1
Notification begins:	May 30

Contact:
Robert G. Martin, P.E. NSPE
Maine Society of Professional Engineers
1387 Augusta Road
Belgrade, ME 04917-3732
Phone: 207-495-2244

Maine State Society of Washington, DC

Maine State Society of Washington, DC, Foundation Scholarship Program

Type of award: Scholarship.
Intended use: For full-time sophomore, junior or senior study at accredited 4-year institution.
Eligibility: Applicant must be no older than 25. Applicant must be U.S. citizen residing in Maine.
Basis for selection: Applicant must demonstrate high academic achievement and seriousness of purpose.
Application requirements: Portfolio, essay, transcript, proof of eligibility.
Additional information: Applicant must have been born in Maine or have been legal resident of Maine for at least four years or have at least one parent who was born in Maine or who has been legal resident of Maine for at least four years. Applicant must currently attend college in Maine, with a minimum GPA of 3.0 for latest academic year. Requests for applications must include SASE. Applications may be downloaded at Website.

Amount of award:	$1,000-$2,000
Number of awards:	8
Number of applicants:	45
Application deadline:	April 1
Notification begins:	May 15
Total amount awarded:	$8,000

Contact:
Maine State Society Scholarship Foundation
3508 Wilson Street
Fairfax, VA 22030
Web: www.mainestatesociety.org

Manomet Center for Conservation Sciences

Kathleen S. Anderson Award

Type of award: Research grant.
Intended use: For junior, senior or graduate study in or outside United States. Designated institutions: Institutions in Western Hemisphere.
Basis for selection: Major/career interest in ornithology. Applicant must demonstrate leadership and seriousness of purpose.
Application requirements: Recommendations, research proposal.
Additional information: Research grant: Either one $1,000 award or two $500 awards. Kathleen Anderson is asked to choose winner from five finalists submitted by Manomet staff.

Amount of award:	$500-$1,000
Number of awards:	2
Number of applicants:	25
Application deadline:	December 1
Notification begins:	March 1
Total amount awarded:	$1,000

Contact:
Manomet Center for Conservation Sciences
Kathleen Anderson Award
81 Stage Point Road, P.O. Box 1770
Manomet, MA 02345
Phone: 508-224-6521
Fax: 508-224-9220
Web: www.manomet.org

Marin Community Foundation

Goldman Family Fund: New Leader Scholarship

Type of award: Scholarship, renewable.
Intended use: For full-time junior or senior study. Designated institutions: University of California, Berkeley; California State University East Bay; San Francisco State University; San Jose State University; Sonoma State University.
Eligibility: Applicant must be U.S. citizen or permanent resident residing in California.
Basis for selection: Major/career interest in psychology; medicine; political science/government; economics; Latin American studies; sociology or social work. Applicant must demonstrate financial need, high academic achievement, leadership and service orientation.
Application requirements: Interview, recommendations, essay, transcript. Financial statement.
Additional information: Preference given to recent immigrants and students of color. Applicants do not need to be Marin County residents to apply. Applicants should demonstrate commitment to giving back to their communities and plan to pursue career in public, legal, psychological, health, or social services. Graduate students may be considered if they have received scholarship as undergraduate and are attending CA public universities. See Website (www.goldmanfamilyfund.com) for more information. Minimum 3.5 GPA.

Amount of award:	$7,000
Number of awards:	10
Number of applicants:	55
Application deadline:	March 15
Total amount awarded:	$45,000

Contact:
Marin Education Fund
New Leader Scholarship of Goldman Family Fund
781 Lincoln Ave., Suite 140
San Rafael, CA 94901
Phone: 415-459-4240
Fax: 415-459-0527
Web: www.goldmanfamilyfund.org,
www.marineducationfund.org

Marine Corps Scholarship Foundation

Marine Corps Scholarship

Type of award: Scholarship, renewable.
Intended use: For undergraduate study at accredited vocational, 2-year or 4-year institution in United States.
Eligibility: Applicant must be high school senior. Applicant must be U.S. citizen. Applicant must be dependent of active service person or veteran in the Marines. Must be child of active Marine, Marine reservist, or Marine who has received honorable discharge.
Basis for selection: Applicant must demonstrate financial need.
Application requirements: Essay, transcript, proof of eligibility. FAFSA, Tax return.
Additional information: Gross family income must not exceed $77,000. Undergraduates attending post-high school vocational/technical institutions are also eligible. Deadline for high school seniors March 3; April 15 for all other applicants.

Amount of award:	$1,000-$10,000
Number of awards:	1,500
Number of applicants:	1,400
Application deadline:	March 3, April 15
Notification begins:	April 16, July 15
Total amount awarded:	$3,491,000

Contact:
Marine Corps Scholarship Foundation
P.O. Box 3008
Princeton, NJ 08543-3008
Phone: 800-292-7777
Fax: 609-452-2259
Web: www.mcsf.org

Maryland Higher Education Commission Office of Student Financial Assistance

Charles W. Riley Fire and Emergency Medical Services Tuition Reimbursement Program

Type of award: Scholarship, renewable.
Intended use: For undergraduate study.
Eligibility: Applicant must be U.S. citizen or permanent resident residing in Maryland.
Basis for selection: Major/career interest in fire science/technology or medical emergency.
Application requirements: Transcript, proof of eligibility.
Additional information: Applicant must be active career/volunteer firefighter or ambulance/rescue squad member serving the Maryland community while taking courses, and must agree to continue to serve for one year after completing courses. To renew award, student must maintain satisfactory academic progress and remain enrolled in eligible program.

Amount of award:	Full tuition
Number of awards:	147
Application deadline:	July 1
Total amount awarded:	$340,630

Contact:
Maryland Higher Ed. Commission Office of Student Financial Assistance
Reimbursement of Firefighters
839 Bestgate Road, Suite 400
Annapolis, MD 21401-3013
Phone: 800-974-1024
Fax: 410-260-3200
Web: www.mhec.state.md.us/financialaid/programdescriptions/prog_fire

Howard P. Rawlings Guaranteed Access Grant

Type of award: Scholarship, renewable.
Intended use: For full-time undergraduate study at accredited postsecondary institution.
Eligibility: Applicant must be high school senior. Applicant must be U.S. citizen or permanent resident residing in Maryland.
Basis for selection: Applicant must demonstrate financial need.
Application requirements: Proof of eligibility. FAFSA.
Additional information: Applicant must be high school senior who has completed college preparatory program or has graduated prior to the academic year who provides written documentation explaining why they were unable to attend college within one year of graduation from high school. Minimum 2.5 GPA. Must meet Guaranteed Access Family Grant income requirements; award equals 100% of student's financial need.

Amount of award:	$400-$14,800
Number of awards:	1,204
Application deadline:	March 1
Total amount awarded:	$10,740,516

Contact:
Maryland Higher Ed. Commission Office of Student Financial Assistance
Guaranteed Access Grant
839 Bestgate Road, Suite 400
Annapolis, MD 21401-3103
Phone: 800-974-1024
Fax: 410-260-3200
Web: www.mhec.state.md.us/financialaid/programdescriptions/prog_ga

Maryland Delegate Scholarship

Type of award: Scholarship, renewable.
Intended use: For undergraduate or graduate study at vocational, 2-year, 4-year or graduate institution.
Eligibility: Applicant must be U.S. citizen, permanent resident or eligible non-U.S. citizen. Applicant must be residing in Maryland.
Application requirements: Proof of eligibility, nomination by local state delegate. FAFSA.
Additional information: Applicant's parents (if applicant is dependent) must be Maryland residents. Rolling application deadline. Certain vocational programs eligible. Out-of-state institutions eligible only if major not offered in Maryland. Each state delegate makes awards to students. If OSFA makes awards for delegates, applicant must demonstrate financial need. Non-U.S. citizens living in Maryland may be eligible. Applicants

must reapply yearly for renewal and maintain satisfactory academic progress.

Amount of award:	$200-$19,000
Number of awards:	5,145
Application deadline:	March 1
Notification begins:	July 1
Total amount awarded:	$4,517,275

Contact:
Maryland Higher Ed. Commission Office of Student Financial Assistance
Delegate Scholarship
839 Bestgate Road, Suite 400
Annapolis, MD 21401-3013
Phone: 800-974-1024
Fax: 410-260-3200
Web: www.mhec.state.md.us

Maryland Distinguished Scholar: Achievement

Type of award: Scholarship, renewable.
Intended use: For full-time undergraduate study at 2-year or 4-year institution. Designated institutions: Eligible Maryland institutions.
Eligibility: Applicant must be high school junior. Applicant must be U.S. citizen or permanent resident residing in Maryland.
Basis for selection: Applicant must demonstrate high academic achievement.
Application requirements: Transcript, nomination. SAT scores from tests taken in January of junior year or earlier. PSAT or ACT scores may be submitted if student has not taken SAT 1.
Additional information: Applicant's parents (if applicant is dependent) must be Maryland residents. Applications must be submitted to high school guidance office in February of junior year. Guidance counselor submits talent nominations in March. Applicant must have minimum 3.7 GPA. Students not funded initially will be placed on waiting list; funds may not be available to award all eligible students. Award is automatically renewed up to three additional years if annual minimum 3.0 GPA and other eligibility requirements are maintained.

Amount of award:	$3,000
Number of awards:	1,271
Notification begins:	June 30
Total amount awarded:	$3,734,250

Contact:
Maryland Higher Ed. Commission Office of Student Financial Assistance
Distinguished Scholar Program
839 Bestgate Road, Suite 400
Annapolis, MD 21401-3013
Phone: 800-974-1024
Fax: 410-260-3200
Web: www.mhec.state.md.us/financialaid/programdescriptions/prog_ds

Maryland Distinguished Scholar: National Merit and National Achievement Finalists

Type of award: Scholarship, renewable.
Intended use: For full-time undergraduate study at 2-year or 4-year institution in United States. Designated institutions: Eligible Maryland institutions.
Eligibility: Applicant must be high school junior. Applicant must be U.S. citizen or permanent resident residing in Maryland.
Additional information: Applicant's parents (if applicant is dependent) must be Maryland residents. Applicant must be National Merit Finalist or National Achievement Finalist. Award automatically offered to students in these scholarship programs when they have been selected as finalists and indicate they will attend a Maryland institution. Award is automatically renewed up to three additional years if annual minimum 3.0 GPA and other eligibility requirements are maintained.

Amount of award:	$3,000
Number of awards:	1,271
Total amount awarded:	$3,734,250

Contact:
Maryland Higher Ed. Commission Office of Student Financial Assistance
Distinguished Scholar Program
839 Bestgate Road, Suite 400
Annapolis, MD 21401-3013
Phone: 800-735-2258
Fax: 410-260-3200
Web: www.mhec.state.md.us/financialaid/programdescriptions/prog_ds

Maryland Distinguished Scholar: Talent in the Arts

Type of award: Scholarship, renewable.
Intended use: For full-time undergraduate study at 2-year or 4-year institution. Designated institutions: Eligible Maryland schools.
Eligibility: Applicant must be high school junior. Applicant must be U.S. citizen or permanent resident residing in Maryland.
Basis for selection: Competition/talent/interest in performing arts. Major/career interest in performing arts; theater arts or music.
Application requirements: Audition, nomination by designated magnet high schools in spring of junior year. Audition or portfolio review.
Additional information: Awards for dance, drama, visual arts, and vocal and instrumental music. Winners determined by panel of judges. Applicant's parents (if applicant is dependent) must be Maryland residents. Students not funded initially will be placed on waiting list; funds may not be available to award all eligible students. Award is automatically renewed if annual minimum 3.0 GPA and other eligibility requirements are maintained.

Amount of award:	$3,000
Number of awards:	1,271
Total amount awarded:	$3,734,250

Contact:
Maryland Higher Ed. Commission Office of Student Financial Assistance
Distinguished Scholar Program
839 Bestgate Road, Suite 400
Annapolis, MD 21401-3013
Phone: 800-974-1024
Fax: 410-260-3200
Web: www.mhec.state.md.us/financialaid/programdescriptions/prog_ds

Maryland Educational Assistance Grant

Type of award: Scholarship, renewable.

Intended use: For full-time undergraduate study at 2-year or 4-year institution.
Eligibility: Applicant must be U.S. citizen or permanent resident residing in Maryland.
Basis for selection: Applicant must demonstrate financial need.
Application requirements: Proof of eligibility.
Additional information: Applicant's parents (if applicant is dependent) must be Maryland resident. Applicants are ranked by Expected Family Contribution (EFC); those with lowest EFC are awarded first. Award may be renewed if eligibility is maintained and FAFSA is submitted by March 1 each year. Funds may not be available to award all eligible students each year. Must file FAFSA before March 1.

Amount of award:	$400-$3,000
Number of awards:	24,506
Application deadline:	March 1
Notification begins:	April 15
Total amount awarded:	$48,519,829

Contact:
Maryland Higher Ed. Commission Office of Student Financial Assistance
Educational Assistance Grant
839 Bestgate Road, Suite 400
Annapolis, MD 21401-3013
Phone: 800-974-1024
Fax: 410-260-3200
Web: www.mhec.state.md.us/financialaid/programdescriptions/prog_ea

Maryland Edward T. Conroy Memorial Scholarship Program

Type of award: Scholarship, renewable.
Intended use: For undergraduate or graduate study at postsecondary institution. Designated institutions: Eligible Maryland institutions.
Eligibility: Applicant must be U.S. citizen. Applicant must be veteran or disabled while on active duty; or dependent of veteran, disabled veteran or deceased veteran; or spouse of disabled veteran, deceased veteran or POW/MIA who served in the Army during Vietnam. If applicant is dependent of disabled US Armed Forces veteran, the veteran must be declared 100% disabled as direct result of military service. Applicant may also be dependent or surviving spouse of victim of September 11, 2001, attack. Also open to dependent or surviving spouse (not remarried) of Maryland resident who was public safety employee or volunteer who died or was 100% disabled in the line of duty.
Additional information: The parent, veteran, POW, public safety employee, or volunteer specified above must have been resident of Maryland at time of death or when declared disabled. Amount of award may be equal to tuition and fees, but may not exceed $9,000. Visit Website for more information and application.

Amount of award:	$9,000
Number of awards:	89
Application deadline:	July 15
Total amount awarded:	$452,266

Contact:
Maryland Higher Ed. Commission Office of Student Financial Assistance
Edward T. Conroy Memorial Grant Program
839 Bestgate Road, Suite 400
Annapolis, MD 21401-3013
Phone: 800-974-1024
Fax: 410-260-3200
Web: www.mhec.state.md.us/financialaid/programdescriptions/prog_conroy

Maryland Jack F. Tolbert Memorial Grant

Type of award: Scholarship, renewable.
Intended use: For full-time undergraduate study at vocational institution. Designated institutions: Private career schools in Maryland.
Eligibility: Applicant must be U.S. citizen or permanent resident residing in Maryland.
Basis for selection: Applicant must demonstrate financial need.
Application requirements: Nomination by financial aid counselor at private career school. FAFSA.
Additional information: Applicant's parents (if applicant is dependent) must be Maryland residents. Applicant must enroll for minimum of eighteen hours per week. Award amount varies; maximum is $500.

Amount of award:	$500
Number of awards:	932
Application deadline:	March 1
Total amount awarded:	$279,900

Contact:
Maryland Higher Ed. Commission Office of Student Financial Assistance
Jack F. Tolbert Memorial Grant
839 Bestgate Road, Suite 400
Annapolis, MD 21401-3013
Phone: 800-974-1024
Fax: 410-260-3200
Web: www.mhec.state.md.us/financialaid/programdescriptions/prog_tolbert

Maryland Part-Time Grant Program

Type of award: Scholarship, renewable.
Intended use: For half-time undergraduate study.
Eligibility: Applicant must be enrolled in high school. Applicant must be residing in Maryland.
Basis for selection: Applicant must demonstrate financial need.
Additional information: Applicant's parents (if applicant is dependent) must be Maryland residents. Applicant must be taking 6 to 11 semester credit hours. Apply through financial aid office of Maryland institution. Applicants simultaneously enrolled in secondary school and an institution of higher education are also eligible. To renew award, student must maintain satisfactory academic progress and submit FAFSA by March 1 each year; may receive award up to eight years.

Amount of award:	$200-$2,000
Number of awards:	7,309
Application deadline:	March 1
Total amount awarded:	$4,670,007

Contact:
Maryland Higher Ed. Commission Office of Student Financial Assistance
Part-Time Grant Program
839 Bestgate Road, Suite 400
Annapolis, MD 21401-3013
Phone: 800-974-1024
Fax: 410-260-3200
Web: www.mhec.state.md.us/financialaid/programdescriptions/prog_ptgrant

Maryland Senatorial Scholarship

Type of award: Scholarship, renewable.
Intended use: For undergraduate or graduate study at postsecondary institution.
Eligibility: Applicant must be residing in Maryland.
Basis for selection: Applicant must demonstrate financial need.
Application requirements: Nomination by local state senator. FAFSA.
Additional information: Applicant and parents (if applicant is dependent) must be Maryland residents. SAT or ACT required for freshmen at four-year institutions unless applicant graduated from high school five years prior to aid application or has earned 24 college credit hours. Out-of-state institutions eligible only if major not offered in Maryland. Contact state senator's office for more information. Award will be automatically renewed if satisfactory academic progress is maintained. Full-time students may be awarded four years total, part-time students eight years total.
    Amount of award: $400-$9,000
    Number of awards: 6,567
    Application deadline: March 1
    Total amount awarded: $5,675,400
Contact:
Maryland Higher Ed. Commission Office of Student Financial Assistance
Senatorial Scholarship Program
839 Bestgate Road, Suite 400
Annapolis, MD 21401-3013
Phone: 800-974-1024
Fax: 410-260-3200
Web: www.mhec.state.md.us/financialaid/programdescriptions/prog_senatorial

Maryland Tuition Reduction for Non-Resident Nursing Students

Type of award: Scholarship, renewable.
Intended use: For undergraduate study at postsecondary institution.
Eligibility: Applicant must be U.S. citizen residing in Maryland.
Basis for selection: Major/career interest in nursing.
Additional information: Must be resident of state other than Maryland and accepted into Maryland degree-granting nursing program at two- or four-year public institution. Awardees fulfill service obligation in Maryland following graduation; two years for two-year program, four years for four-year program. Service must begin within six months of graduation. Award amount varies; college may reduce tuition so that non-residents pay tuition charged to Maryland resident.

Contact:
Maryland Higher Ed. Commission Office of Student Financial Assistance
Out-of-State Nursing Program
839 Bestgate Road, Suite 400
Annapolis, MD 21401-3013
Phone: 800-974-1024
Fax: 410-260-3200
Web: www.mhec.state.md.us/financialaid/programdescriptions/prog_nonresnurse

Tuition Waiver for Foster Care Recipients

Type of award: Scholarship, renewable.
Intended use: For undergraduate study at 2-year or 4-year institution. Designated institutions: Eligible Maryland public institutions.
Eligibility: Applicant must be no older than 21. Applicant must be residing in Maryland.
Application requirements: FAFSA.
Additional information: Applicant must have resided in Maryland foster care home at time of high school graduation or completion of GED. Also open to applicants who resided in Maryland foster care home on 14th birthday and were subsequently adopted. The Department of Human Resources must confirm applicant's eligibility. Applicant must be enrolled as a degree-seeking student before age of 21. Award renewal possible if satisfactory academic progress and enrollment in eligible program maintained.
    Amount of award: Full tuition
    Application deadline: March 1
Contact:
Maryland Higher Ed. Commission Office of Student Financial Assistance
839 Bestgate Road, Suite 400
Annapolis, MD 21401-3013
Phone: 800-974-1024
Fax: 410-260-3200
Web: www.mhec.state.md.us/financialaid/programdescriptions/prog_fostercare

Maryland Hospitality Education Foundation

The Erikka A. Hayes Foundation Scholarship

Type of award: Scholarship.
Intended use: For undergraduate study.
Eligibility: Applicant must be residing in Maryland.
Basis for selection: Major/career interest in hospitality administration/management. Applicant must demonstrate financial need.
Application requirements: Recommendations, essay, transcript. Must be Prince George's County resident with interest in hospitality industry career.
Additional information: Applicant must be Prince George's County resident. Must demonstrate financial need. Must be high school or college student or hospitality industry professional enrolled in a post secondary or professional development course. Applicant must be pursuing hospitality-related coursework in one of the following: Culinary Arts, Hospitality

Maryland Hospitality Education Foundation: The Erikka A. Hayes Foundation Scholarship

Management, Bartending Academy Program. Interviews may be required for finalists. Visit website for more details.

Application deadline: March 12

Contact:
Maryland Hospitality Education Foundation
6301 Hillside Ct
Columbia, MD 21046
Phone: 410-290-6800
Fax: 410-290-6882
Web: www.mhef.org

Letitia B. Carter Scholarship

Type of award: Scholarship.
Intended use: For undergraduate study in United States.
Eligibility: Applicant must be enrolled in high school. Applicant must be U.S. citizen residing in Maryland.
Basis for selection: Major/career interest in hospitality administration/management. Applicant must demonstrate high academic achievement.
Application requirements: Essay. Paystub from most recent employer providing industry related work, two letter of recommendation, two typed and double-spaced essays required. 1) Describe any personal skills and characteristics that will help you meet the future challenges of the food service/hospitality industry. 2) Which person was most influential in helping you choose a career in the food service/hospitality industry?
Additional information: Applicant must be a resident of Maryland and pursuing hospitality-related work. Applicant must have applied to an MHEF-recognized professional development program in hospitality or enrolled in a MHEF-recognized food service/hospitality program. Any high school or college student applying for scholarship must have a minimum cumulative grade point average of 3.0 and a minimum of 400 hours documented industry experience. Any teachers or instructors applying must have a minimum of 1,500 hours documented industry experience. Visit Website for more information.

Amount of award: $500-$2,000
Application deadline: April 13
Notification begins: May 11

Contact:
Maryland Hospitality Education Foundation
6301 Hillside Court
Columbia, MD 21046
Phone: 410-290-6800
Fax: 410-290-6882
Web: www.mhef.org

Marcia S. Harris Legacy Fund Scholarship

Type of award: Scholarship.
Intended use: For undergraduate study.
Eligibility: Applicant must be residing in Maryland.
Basis for selection: Major/career interest in culinary arts; food production/management/services; food science/technology; hospitality administration/management or hotel/restaurant management. Applicant must demonstrate financial need and high academic achievement.
Application requirements: Proof of employment in culinary or hospitality industry. Three essays.
Additional information: Selection based on grades in food service coursework, essays, work experience, and essays.

Application deadline: March 14

Contact:
Maryland Hospitality Education Foundation
6301 Hillside Court
Columbia, MD 21046
Phone: 410-290-6800 ext. 1015
Fax: 410-290-6882
Web: www.mhef.org

Massachusetts Board of Higher Education

Massachusetts Christian A. Herter Memorial Scholarship Program

Type of award: Scholarship, renewable.
Intended use: For full-time undergraduate study at accredited vocational, 2-year or 4-year institution.
Eligibility: Applicant must be high school sophomore or junior. Applicant must be U.S. citizen or permanent resident residing in Massachusetts.
Basis for selection: Applicant must demonstrate financial need, depth of character and seriousness of purpose.
Application requirements: Interview, recommendations, essay, transcript, nomination by high school principal, counselor, teacher, or social service agency.
Additional information: Program provides grant assistance for students from low income or disadvantaged backgrounds who have had to overcome adverse circumstances. Selection made during sophomore and junior years in high school. Award amount is up to half of student's demonstrated financial need. Minimum 2.5 GPA.

Amount of award: $15,000
Number of awards: 25
Number of applicants: 200
Application deadline: March 14
Total amount awarded: $900,000

Contact:
Office of Student Financial Assistance
Massachusetts Board of Higher Education
454 Broadway, Suite 200
Revere, MA 02151
Phone: 617-727-9420
Fax: 617-727-0667
Web: www.osfa.mass.edu

Massachusetts Gilbert Matching Student Grant

Type of award: Scholarship, renewable.
Intended use: For full-time undergraduate study at accredited 2-year or 4-year institution. Designated institutions: Independent colleges or hospital schools of nursing in Massachusetts.
Eligibility: Applicant must be U.S. citizen or permanent resident residing in Massachusetts.
Basis for selection: Applicant must demonstrate financial need.
Additional information: Deadline depends on institution. Applicant must be dependent of parent who has been a Massachusetts resident for at least 12 months prior to start of academic year.

Amount of award: $200-$2,500
Total amount awarded: $18,600,000

Contact:
Apply to college financial aid office.
Phone: 617-727-9420
Fax: 617-727-0667
Web: www.osfa.mass.edu

Massachusetts MASSgrant Program

Type of award: Scholarship, renewable.
Intended use: For full-time undergraduate study at accredited vocational, 2-year or 4-year institution. Designated institutions: Schools in Massachusetts, Connecticut, Maine, New Hampshire, Vermont, Rhode Island, Pennsylvania or Washington, DC.
Eligibility: Applicant must be U.S. citizen or permanent resident residing in Vermont, Maine, Pennsylvania, Massachusetts, District of Columbia, Connecticut, New Hampshire or Rhode Island.
Basis for selection: Applicant must demonstrate financial need.
Additional information: Applicant must have expected family contribution of $4,110 or less and be eligible for Title IV financial aid. Applicant must maintain satisfactory academic progress.

Amount of award:	$300-$2,400
Number of awards:	28,553
Number of applicants:	250,000
Application deadline:	May 1
Notification begins:	June 15
Total amount awarded:	$24,000,000

Contact:
Office of Student Financial Assistance
Massachusetts Board of Higher Education
454 Broadway, Suite 200
Revere, MA 02151
Phone: 617-727-9420
Fax: 617-727-0667
Web: www.osfa.mass.edu

Massachusetts Public Service Grant Program

Type of award: Scholarship, renewable.
Intended use: For full-time undergraduate study at accredited 2-year or 4-year institution.
Eligibility: Applicant must be U.S. citizen or permanent resident residing in Massachusetts. Applicant must be dependent of deceased veteran or POW/MIA. Applicant's parent must have been killed or disabled in work-related accident as firefighter, police officer or public safety officer.
Application requirements: Proof of eligibility.
Additional information: Award in form of entitlement grant. Death of veteran, POW/MIA, police officer or firefighter parent must have been service related or in line of duty for applicant to be eligible for program. Applicant must be resident of Massachusetts at least one year prior to start of school. For recipients attending Massachusetts public college or university, award shall equal cost of tuition. Recipients attending Massachusetts independent college or university, award will be equivalent to highest tuition amount paid to public institution.

Amount of award:	$800-$2,500
Application deadline:	May 1
Notification begins:	June 1
Total amount awarded:	$22,665

Contact:
Office of Student Financial Assistance
Massachusetts Board of Higher Education
454 Broadway, Suite 200
Revere, MA 02151
Phone: 617-727-9420
Fax: 617-727-0667
Web: www.osfa.mass.edu

Paul Tsongas Scholarship Program

Type of award: Scholarship.
Intended use: For undergraduate study.
Eligibility: Applicant must be U.S. citizen or permanent resident residing in Massachusetts.
Basis for selection: Applicant must demonstrate financial need.
Additional information: Minimum 3.75 GPA and SAT score of 1200. Tuition waiver for full tuition and related fees. For renewal, must maintain 3.3 GPA.

Amount of award:	Full tuition
Number of awards:	45

Contact:
Contact State College financial aid office.
Phone: 617-727-9420
Fax: 617-727-0667
Web: www.osfa.mass.edu

Massachusetts Democratic Party

John F. Kennedy Scholars Award

Type of award: Scholarship.
Intended use: For junior or senior study at 4-year institution.
Eligibility: Applicant must be at least 18, no older than 23. Applicant must be U.S. citizen or permanent resident residing in Massachusetts.
Basis for selection: Major/career interest in political science/government or public administration/service. Applicant must demonstrate financial need, high academic achievement, leadership, seriousness of purpose and service orientation.
Additional information: Awarded to one male and one female at Massachusetts Democratic State Convention. Preference given to registered Democrats and students with 3.0 GPA or higher. Visit Website or contact local chairperson for more information and important dates.

Amount of award:	$1,500
Number of awards:	2
Total amount awarded:	$3,000

Contact:
Massachusetts Democratic Party
DSC Office, Attn: Gloribell Mota
56 Roland St., Suite 203
Boston, MA 02129
Phone: 617-776-2676
Fax: 617-776-2579
Web: www.massdems.org

Massachusetts Department of Education

Massachusetts Robert C. Byrd Honors Scholarship

Type of award: Scholarship, renewable.
Intended use: For full-time undergraduate study at accredited postsecondary institution.
Eligibility: Applicant must be high school senior. Applicant must be residing in Massachusetts.
Basis for selection: Applicant must demonstrate high academic achievement, leadership and service orientation.
Application requirements: Nomination.
Additional information: Minimum 3.5 GPA or class rank in top five percent required. Students are nominated by high school. See guidance officer for additional information and application procedure. Number of awards varies.
  Amount of award: $1,500
  Number of applicants: 235
  Application deadline: June 1
Contact:
Massachusetts Department of Education
Sally Teixeira
350 Main Street
Malden, MA 02148-5023
Phone: 781-338-6304
Web: www.doe.mass.edu

McKee Scholars

John McKee Scholarship

Type of award: Scholarship, renewable.
Intended use: For undergraduate study at postsecondary institution.
Eligibility: Applicant must be male, high school senior. Applicant must be U.S. citizen residing in Pennsylvania.
Basis for selection: Applicant must demonstrate financial need and high academic achievement.
Application requirements: Interview, transcript. SAT/ACT scores.
Additional information: For male applicants whose father's are dead, missing, permanently absent or dysfunctional. Applicant must be a resident of Philadelphia, Bucks, Chester, Montgomery or Delaware counties. Award allotment after initial award year is based on upheld academic standards. Application available at Website.
  Amount of award: $1,000-$5,500
  Number of awards: 20
  Application deadline: February 1
  Total amount awarded: $320,000
Contact:
John McKee Scholarship Committee
c/o George S. Forde, Jr., Executive Secretary
2005 Market Street, 26th Floor
Philadelphia, PA 19103-7098
Fax: 215-242-1475
Web: www.mckeescholars.org

Menominee Indian Tribe of Wisconsin

Menominee Adult Vocational Training Grant

Type of award: Scholarship, renewable.
Intended use: For undergraduate or non-degree study at accredited vocational or 2-year institution in United States.
Eligibility: Applicant must be American Indian. Applicant must be enrolled member of Menominee Indian tribe of Wisconsin.
Basis for selection: Applicant must demonstrate financial need.
Application requirements: FAFSA and Menominee Tribal Grant Application.
Additional information: Award also applicable toward associate's degree. Must apply through college financial aid office.
  Amount of award: $550-$2,200
  Application deadline: October 30, March 1
Contact:
Menominee Indian Tribe of Wisconsin
P.O. Box 910
Keshena, WI 54135
Phone: 715-799-5118 or 715-799-5110
Fax: 715-799-5102
Web: www.menominee-nsn.gov/education/educationhome.asp

Menominee Higher Education Grant

Type of award: Scholarship, renewable.
Intended use: For undergraduate study at accredited 2-year or 4-year institution in United States.
Eligibility: Applicant must be American Indian. Applicant must be enrolled member of Menominee Indian tribe.
Basis for selection: Applicant must demonstrate financial need.
Application requirements: FAFSA and Menominee Tribal Grant Application.
Additional information: Applications and deadline dates available through Tribal Education office.
  Amount of award: $550-$2,200
  Number of awards: 97
  Application deadline: October 30, March 1
Contact:
Menominee Indian Tribe of Wisconsin
P.O. Box 910
Keshena, WI 54135
Phone: 715-799-5118 or 715-799-5110
Fax: 715-799-5102
Web: www.menominee-nsn.gov/education/educationhome.asp

The Merchants Exchange

The Merchants Exhange Scholarship Fund

Type of award: Scholarship, renewable.
Intended use: For sophomore, junior or senior study at postsecondary institution.

Basis for selection: Major/career interest in international relations. Applicant must demonstrate high academic achievement and depth of character.
Application requirements: Transcript. Signed letter of intent to attend as a student in a program related to maritime affairs/international trade.
Additional information: Scholarship is for students from the Pacific Northwest studying maritime affairs/international trade. Minimum 2.5 GPA. Financial need may be considered if all other factors are equal. Visit Website for application.

Amount of award:	$1,000
Number of awards:	2
Number of applicants:	4
Application deadline:	June 16
Total amount awarded:	$2,000

Contact:
The Merchants Exchange
200 SW Market, Suite 190
Portland, OR 97201
Web: www.pdxmex.com/bulletins/mex/scholarship.htm

Mercy Corps

Mercy Corps Global Action Awards

Type of award: Scholarship.
Intended use: For undergraduate study.
Eligibility: Applicant must be at least 14, no older than 18, enrolled in high school. Applicant must be permanent resident.
Basis for selection: Applicant must demonstrate leadership and service orientation.
Additional information: Applicant must have organized and led innovative project that has directly impacted people living in poor countries and/or has raised awareness about global poverty and related issues. Honorees will be chosen by panel of judges, based on the level of innovation, cooperation, leadership, inspiration, and impact displayed by their work. Issues addressed by projects should be global in nature and may include but are not limited to alleviating hunger; promoting human rights, children's rights, or gender equity; increasing access to clean drinking water, health care, or education; preventing and treating HIV/AIDS or other diseases; supporting sustainable environment. See Website to apply.

Amount of award:	$5,000
Number of awards:	5
Application deadline:	November 30
Total amount awarded:	$25,000

Contact:
Mercy Corps
75 Broad Street
Suite 2410
New York, NY 10004
Phone: 212-537-0500
Fax: 212-537-0501
Web: www.globalactionawards.org

Mexican American Grocers Association Foundation

Mexican American Grocers Association Scholarship

Type of award: Scholarship.
Intended use: For full-time sophomore, junior or senior study at accredited 4-year institution in United States.
Eligibility: Applicant must be Hispanic American.
Basis for selection: Major/career interest in business or business/management/administration. Applicant must demonstrate financial need and high academic achievement.
Application requirements: Essay, transcript.
Additional information: Minimum 2.5 GPA. Applications may be obtained beginning in April by sending a SASE. Completed application must be postmarked between June 1 and July 31. Awards presented in October or November.

Amount of award:	$500-$1,500
Number of awards:	25
Number of applicants:	1,000
Application deadline:	July 31
Notification begins:	August 15

Contact:
Mexican-American Grocers Association Foundation
Attn: Jackie Solis/Scholarship Coordinator
405 North San Fernando Road
Los Angeles, CA 90031
Phone: 323-227-1565

Michigan Higher Education Assistance Authority

Children of Veterans Tuiton Grant

Type of award: Scholarship, renewable.
Intended use: For undergraduate study.
Eligibility: Applicant must be U.S. citizen or permanent resident residing in Michigan. Applicant must be dependent of disabled veteran or deceased veteran; or spouse of disabled veteran or deceased veteran.

Amount of award:	$1,400-$2,800
Number of awards:	357
Total amount awarded:	$801,998

Contact:
Michigan Higher Education Assistance Authority
Office of Scholarships and Grants
P.O. Box 30462
Lansing, MI 48909-7962
Phone: 888-477-2687
Web: www.michigan.gov/osg

Michigan Adult Part-Time Grant

Type of award: Scholarship, renewable.
Intended use: For half-time undergraduate study at 2-year or 4-year institution.
Eligibility: Applicant must be U.S. citizen or permanent resident residing in Michigan.
Basis for selection: Applicant must demonstrate financial need.

Application requirements: Proof of eligibility. FAFSA.
Additional information: Number of awards varies. Apply to college financial aid office.
- **Amount of award:** $600
- **Number of awards:** 6,037
- **Total amount awarded:** $2,640,154

Contact:
College financial aid office
Web: www.michigan.gov/osg

Michigan Competitive Scholarship

Type of award: Scholarship, renewable.
Intended use: For undergraduate study at postsecondary institution.
Eligibility: Applicant must be U.S. citizen or permanent resident residing in Michigan.
Basis for selection: Applicant must demonstrate financial need.
Application requirements: FAFSA and qualifying ACT score.
- **Amount of award:** $100-$1,300
- **Number of awards:** 27,802
- **Application deadline:** March 1
- **Total amount awarded:** $37,030,387

Contact:
Michigan Higher Education Assistance Authority
Office of Scholarships and Grants
P.O. Box 30462
Lansing, MI 48909-7962
Phone: 888-477-2687
Web: www.michigan.gov/osg

Michigan Educational Opportunity Grant

Type of award: Scholarship, renewable.
Intended use: For undergraduate study at postsecondary institution.
Eligibility: Applicant must be U.S. citizen or permanent resident residing in Michigan.
Basis for selection: Applicant must demonstrate financial need.
Application requirements: Proof of eligibility. FAFSA.
Additional information: Applicant must be enrolled at least half-time.
- **Amount of award:** $1,000
- **Number of awards:** 4,299
- **Total amount awarded:** $2,080,560

Contact:
College financial aid office
Web: www.michigan.gov/osg

Michigan Nursing Scholarship

Type of award: Scholarship, renewable.
Intended use: For undergraduate or graduate study.
Eligibility: Applicant must be U.S. citizen or permanent resident residing in Michigan.
Basis for selection: Major/career interest in nursing.
Additional information: Apply through college financial aid office. One year work commitment for each year of award. Limited to students pursuing LPN, ADN, BSN, or MSN.
- **Amount of award:** $4,000
- **Number of awards:** 1,483
- **Total amount awarded:** $4,257,060

Contact:
Contact Institution's Financial Aid Office
Phone: 888-447-2687
Web: www.michigan.gov/osg

Michigan Promise Scholarship

Type of award: Scholarship.
Intended use: For undergraduate study at postsecondary institution. Designated institutions: Approved Michigan postsecondary institutions.
Eligibility: Applicant must be U.S. citizen or permanent resident residing in Michigan.
Additional information: Must take Michigan Merit Exam (MME).
- **Amount of award:** $4,000

Contact:
Michigan Higher Education Assistance Authority
Office of Scholarships and Grants
P.O. Box 30462
Lansing, MI 48909-7962
Phone: 888-477-2687
Web: www.michigan.gov/promise

Michigan Robert C. Byrd Honors Scholarship

Type of award: Scholarship, renewable.
Intended use: For full-time undergraduate study at accredited postsecondary institution in United States.
Eligibility: Applicant must be high school senior. Applicant must be U.S. citizen or permanent resident.
Basis for selection: Applicant must demonstrate high academic achievement.
Application requirements: Nomination by high school principal.
- **Amount of award:** $1,500
- **Total amount awarded:** $1,410,000

Contact:
Michigan Higher Education Assistance Authority
Office of Scholarships and Grants
P.O. Box 30462
Lansing, MI 48909-7962
Phone: 888-477-2687
Web: www.michigan.gov/osg

Michigan Tuition Grant

Type of award: Scholarship, renewable.
Intended use: For undergraduate, master's or doctoral study at 2-year, 4-year or graduate institution.
Eligibility: Applicant must be U.S. citizen or permanent resident residing in Michigan.
Basis for selection: Applicant must demonstrate financial need.
Application requirements: FAFSA.
- **Amount of award:** $100-$2,100
- **Number of awards:** 34,141
- **Application deadline:** July 1
- **Total amount awarded:** $50,961,457

Contact:
Michigan Higher Education Assistance Authority
Office of Scholarships and Grants
P.O. Box 30462
Lansing, MI 48909-7962
Phone: 888-477-2687
Web: www.michigan.gov/osg

Tuition Incentive Program

Type of award: Scholarship, renewable.
Intended use: For undergraduate study at postsecondary institution.
Eligibility: Applicant must be U.S. citizen or permanent resident residing in Michigan.
Basis for selection: Applicant must demonstrate financial need.
Application requirements: Proof of eligibility.
Additional information: Eligibility determined by Medicaid status. Provides tuition assistance for up to 24 semesters or 36 term credits for first two years. Up to $2,000 total assistance for third and fourth years.
   Number of awards: 10,462
   Total amount awarded: $17,600,277
Contact:
Michigan Higher Education Assistance Authority
Office of Scholarships and Grants
P.O. Box 30462
Lansing, MI 48909-7962
Phone: 888-477-2687
Web: www.michigan.gov/osg

Michigan Society of Professional Engineers

Michigan Society of Professional Engineers Scholarships

Type of award: Scholarship.
Intended use: For undergraduate study at accredited 4-year institution. Designated institutions: ABET-accredited schools in Michigan.
Eligibility: Applicant must be high school senior. Applicant must be U.S. citizen residing in Michigan.
Basis for selection: Major/career interest in engineering. Applicant must demonstrate high academic achievement, depth of character, leadership and service orientation.
Application requirements: Transcript. 500-word essay describing interest in engineering for undergraduates; two academic recommendations.
Additional information: Some scholarships for graduating high school seniors and some for undergraduates. Minimum 3.0 GPA, 26 ACT score for high school seniors. Second Monday in January deadline for high school seniors; second Monday in April deadline for undergraduates. Undergraduates must be members of MSPE. Contact guidance counselor or local MSPE chapter for application and specific eligibility requirements.
   Amount of award: $1,000-$3,000
   Number of awards: 42
   Application deadline: January 1, April 2
   Notification begins: April 1
Contact:
Scholarship Coordinator Michigan Society of Professional Engineers
P.O. Box 15276
Lansing, MI 48901-5276
Phone: 517-487-9388
Fax: 517-487-0635
Web: www.michiganspe.org

Microscopy Society of America

Microscopy Society of America Undergraduate Research Scholarship

Type of award: Research grant.
Intended use: For full-time junior or senior study.
Basis for selection: Major/career interest in science, general; biology; physics; chemistry; natural sciences or engineering, materials. Applicant must demonstrate seriousness of purpose.
Application requirements: Resume, budget, research proposal, letter from laboratory supervisor, two academic recommendations, letter from MSA member (may be same as supervisor or professor). Four copies of all application materials.
Additional information: Award for students interested in pursuing microscopy as career or major research tool. Applicant should be sponsored by MSA member. Must supply abstract of research project. Funds must be spent within year of award date, but in special cases may be extended to cover additional research during summer semester following graduation. Visit Website for more information and application.
   Amount of award: $3,500
   Number of awards: 6
   Number of applicants: 20
   Application deadline: December 31
   Notification begins: April 1
Contact:
Microscopy Society of America
Undergraduate Research Scholarship
230 East Ohio Street, Suite 400
Chicago, IL 60611
Phone: 800-538-3672 or 312-644-1527
Fax: 312-644-8557
Web: www.microscopy.org

Microsoft Corporation

Microsoft General Scholarship

Type of award: Scholarship.
Intended use: For full-time undergraduate study. Designated institutions: Colleges and universities in the United States, Canada, and Mexico.
Basis for selection: Major/career interest in computer/information sciences; engineering, computer; mathematics or physics. Applicant must demonstrate financial need and high academic achievement.
Application requirements: Recommendations, essay, transcript. Resume.
Additional information: Minimum 3.0 GPA. Scholarship will cover up to 100 percent of tuition for one academic year. All recipients required to complete salaried summer internship of 12 weeks or more at Microsoft in Redmond, Washington. Applicant must be enrolled in degree-granting program in computer science, computer engineering, or related technical discipline, with demonstrated interest in computer science. See Website for important dates, more information and application.

Microsoft Corporation: Microsoft General Scholarship

Application deadline: February 1
Notification begins: March 20
Total amount awarded: $500,000
Contact:
Microsoft Scholarship Program
Microsoft Corporation
One Microsoft Way
Redmond, WA 98052-8303
Web: www.microsoft.com/college/ss_overview.mspx

Microsoft Minority Technical Scholarship

Type of award: Scholarship.
Intended use: For full-time undergraduate study. Designated institutions: Colleges and universities in the United States, Canada, and Mexico.
Eligibility: Applicant must be African American, Mexican American, Hispanic American, Puerto Rican or American Indian.
Basis for selection: Major/career interest in computer/information sciences; engineering, computer; mathematics or physics. Applicant must demonstrate financial need and high academic achievement.
Application requirements: Recommendations, essay, transcript. Resume.
Additional information: Minimum 3.0 GPA. Scholarship will cover up to 100 percent of tuition for one academic year. All recipients required to complete salaried summer internship of 12 weeks or more at Microsoft in Redmond, Washington. Applicant must be enrolled in degree-granting program in computer science, computer engineering, or related technical discipline, with demonstrated interest in computer science. See Website for important dates, more information and application.

Application deadline: February 1
Notification begins: March 20
Total amount awarded: $500,000
Contact:
Microsoft Scholarship Program
Microsoft Corporation
One Microsoft Way
Redmond, WA 98052-8303
Web: www.microsoft.com/college/ss_overview.mspx

Microsoft Scholarship for Students with Disabilities

Type of award: Scholarship.
Intended use: For full-time undergraduate study at 4-year institution. Designated institutions: Colleges and universities in the United States, Canada and Mexico.
Eligibility: Applicant must be physically challenged.
Basis for selection: Major/career interest in computer/information sciences; engineering, computer; mathematics or physics. Applicant must demonstrate financial need and high academic achievement.
Application requirements: Recommendations, essay, transcript. Resume.
Additional information: Minimum 3.0 GPA. Scholarship will cover up to 100 percent of tuition for one academic year. All recipients required to complete salaried summer internship of 12 weeks or more at Microsoft in Redmond, Washington. Applicant must be enrolled in degree-granting program in computer science, computer engineering, or related technical discipline, with demonstrated interest in computer science. See Website for important dates, more information and application.

Amount of award: Full tuition
Application deadline: February 1
Notification begins: March 20
Total amount awarded: $500,000
Contact:
Microsoft Scholarship Program
Microsoft Corporation
One Mircosoft Way
Redmond, WA 98052-8303
Web: www.microsoft.com/college/ss_overview.mspx

Microsoft Women's Technical Scholarship

Type of award: Scholarship.
Intended use: For full-time undergraduate study. Designated institutions: Colleges and universities in the United States, Canada, and Mexico.
Eligibility: Applicant must be female.
Basis for selection: Major/career interest in computer/information sciences; engineering, computer; mathematics or physics. Applicant must demonstrate financial need and high academic achievement.
Application requirements: Recommendations, essay, transcript. Resume.
Additional information: Minimum 3.0 GPA. Scholarship will cover up to 100 percent of tuition for one academic year. All recipients required to complete salaried summer internship of 12 weeks or more at Microsoft in Redmond, Washington. Applicant must be enrolled in degree-granting program in computer science, computer engineering, or related technical discipline, with demonstrated interest in computer science. See Website for important dates, more information and application.

Application deadline: February 1
Notification begins: March 20
Total amount awarded: $500,000
Contact:
Microsoft Scholarship Program
Microsoft Corporation
One Microsoft Way
Redmond, WA 98052-8303
Web: www.microsoft.com/college/ss_overview.mspx

Midwestern Higher Education Compact

Midwest Student Exchange Program

Type of award: Scholarship, renewable.
Intended use: For full-time undergraduate, master's, doctoral or first professional study at accredited 2-year, 4-year or graduate institution in United States. Designated institutions: Participating institutions in Kansas, Michigan, Minnesota, Missouri, Nebraska, North Dakota, and Wisconsin.
Eligibility: Applicant must be residing in Wisconsin, Michigan, Minnesota, Kansas, Nebraska, Illinois, Missouri or North Dakota.
Application requirements: Proof of eligibility.
Additional information: Reduced tuition rate for Kansas, Michigan, Minnesota, Missouri, Nebraska, North Dakota, and Wisconsin residents attending participating out-of-state institutions in one of six other states in designated institutions or programs of study. For information, contact high school counselor or college admissions officer. For list of participating

institutions and programs, and for individual state contact information, visit Website.

    Number of applicants: 2,431
    Total amount awarded: $11,783,560

Contact:
Midwestern Higher Education Compact
Attn: Jennifer Dahlquist
1300 S. Second St., Suite 130
Minneapolis, MN 55454-1079
Phone: 612-626-1602
Fax: 612-626-8290
Web: msep.mhec.org

Military Officers Association of America

MOAA American Patriot Scholarship Program

Type of award: Scholarship, renewable.
Intended use: For undergraduate study.
Eligibility: Applicant must be dependent of disabled veteran or deceased veteran.
Basis for selection: Applicant must demonstrate financial need.
Additional information: Applicant must be under 24 and dependent of a uniformed service member who died or became severely disabled and received a purple heart while in active service. Military academy cadets are ineligible. Amount and number of awards given vary.

    Amount of award: $2,500-$5,000
    Number of awards: 48
    Application deadline: March 3

Contact:
MOAA Scholarship Fun
American Patriot Scholarships Department 889
201 North Washington Street
Alexandria, VA 22314-2529
Phone: 800-234-6622 ext. 169
Web: www.moaa.org/education

Military Order of the Purple Heart

Military Order of the Purple Heart Scholarship

Type of award: Scholarship, renewable.
Intended use: For full-time undergraduate or graduate study.
Eligibility: Applicant must be U.S. citizen. Applicant must be descendent of veteran or disabled while on active duty; or dependent of disabled veteran or deceased veteran; or spouse of disabled veteran or deceased veteran. Applicant must be either a recipient of the Purple Heart or a descendent, spouse or widow of a recipient of the Purple Heart, a veteran killed in action, or a veteran who died of wounds incurred during service.
Basis for selection: Applicant must demonstrate high academic achievement.
Application requirements: $10 application fee. Transcript, proof of eligibility. Official high school or college transcript, two letters of recommendation, 200-300 words or more essay explaining "What Americanism Means to Me," $10 application fee.
Additional information: Applicant must either be a recipient of the Purple Heart or descendent of recipient of the Purple Heart, or descendant or spouse of veteran killed in action or who died of wounds. Contact the Military Order of the Purple Heart for applications, deadline information, award amounts, and other details.

    Amount of award: $3,000
    Number of awards: 50
    Number of applicants: 700
    Application deadline: February 17
    Total amount awarded: $250,000

Contact:
Military Order of the Purple Heart
Scholarship Coordinator
5413-B Backlick Road
Springfield, VA 22151
Phone: 703-642-5360
Fax: 703-642-2054
Web: www.PurpleHeart.org

Milk Processor's Education Program

Scholar Athlete Milk Mustache of the Year Awards

Type of award: Scholarship.
Intended use: For undergraduate study.
Eligibility: Applicant must be high school senior.
Basis for selection: Competition/talent/interest in athletics/sports. Applicant must demonstrate high academic achievement, leadership and service orientation.
Application requirements: Essay. A description, in 75 words or less, of how drinking milk is part of applicant's life and training regimen.
Additional information: In addition to scholarship, winners receive spot in SAMMY Hall of Fame located in Milk House at Disney's Wide World of Sports and trip to Disney World to be honored in special ceremony. SAMMY award winners will be selected based on four criteria: academic performance, athletic excellence, leadership skills, and community service. Visit Website for application and more information.

    Amount of award: $7,500
    Number of awards: 25
    Number of applicants: 65,199
    Application deadline: March 8
    Total amount awarded: $187,500

Contact:
Visit Website for more information.
Web: www.bodybymilk.com

Minnesota Department of Veterans Affairs

Minnesota Educational Assistance for Veterans

Type of award: Scholarship.
Intended use: For undergraduate or graduate study at postsecondary institution. Designated institutions: Approved Minnesota institutions.
Eligibility: Applicant must be residing in Minnesota. Applicant must be veteran. Applicant must have been Minnesota resident at time of entry into active duty and for six months immediately preceding entry.
Application requirements: Proof of eligibility.
Additional information: Applicant must have exhausted eligible federal educational benefits prior to the delimiting date or within the eligibility period in which benefits were available. Grant is one-time award. Contact county veterans service officer or institution for more information.
   Amount of award: $750
Contact:
Minnesota Department of Veterans Affairs
Veterans Service Building, 2nd Floor
20 West 12 Street
St. Paul, MN 55155
Phone: 651-296-2562
Fax: 651-296-3954
Web: www.mdva.state.mn.us

Minnesota Educational Assistance for War Orphans

Type of award: Scholarship, renewable.
Intended use: For full-time undergraduate study at accredited vocational, 2-year or 4-year institution. Designated institutions: Approved Minnesota public institutions.
Eligibility: Applicant must be residing in Minnesota. Applicant must be dependent of deceased veteran. Parent must have been in Minnesota at time of entry on active duty (and for six months prior). Veteran's death must have been on active duty or service connected.
Application requirements: Proof of eligibility.
Additional information: All recipients also receive $750 stipend. Applicant must be resident of Minnesota for two years prior to application. Information also available from institution or county veterans service officer. Adopted children eligible. Step-children and foster children not eligible. Available until recipient obtains bachelor's degree or equivalent.
   Amount of award: Full tuition
Contact:
Minnesota Department of Veterans Affairs
Veterans Service Building, 2nd Floor
20 West 12 Street
St. Paul, MN 55155-2079
Phone: 651-296-2562
Fax: 651-296-3954
Web: www.mdva.state.mn.us

Minnesota Office of Higher Education

Minnesota GI Bill

Type of award: Scholarship, renewable.
Eligibility: Applicant must be U.S. citizen residing in Minnesota. Applicant must be in military service or veteran; or dependent of disabled veteran or deceased veteran; or spouse of disabled veteran or deceased veteran who serves or served in the Reserves/National Guard.
Additional information: Applicant must be Minnesota resident. Applicant must be a veteran, or spouse or child of military personnel who died or became permanently disabled since September 11, 2001. Applicant may also be non-veteran who has served a total of five years in reserve of Unites States military with any part of service occurring after September 11, 2001.
   Amount of award: $50-$2,000
   Number of applicants: 265
   Total amount awarded: $219,129
Contact:
Minnesota Office of Higher Education
1450 Energy Park Drive, Ste. 350
St. Paul, MN 80065
Phone: 800-657-3866
Web: www.getreadyforcollege.org

Minnesota Indian Scholarship Program

Type of award: Scholarship.
Intended use: For full-time undergraduate study at 4-year or graduate institution in United States.
Eligibility: Applicant must be American Indian. Applicant must be U.S. citizen.
Application requirements: Proof of one-fourth or more Indian ancestry.
Additional information: Applicant must have one-quarter Indian ancestry. Must be eligible for Pell grant or Minnesota state grant.
   Amount of award: $4,000-$6,000
   Number of awards: 500
   Number of applicants: 505
   Application deadline: June 30
   Total amount awarded: $1,875,000
Contact:
Minnesota Office of Higher Education
1450 Energy Park Dr., Ste. 350
St. Paul, MN 55108-5227
Phone: 800-657-3866
Web: www.getreadyforcollege.org

Minnesota Post-Secondary Child Care Grant

Type of award: Scholarship, renewable.
Intended use: For undergraduate study. Designated institutions: Eligible Minnesota schools.
Eligibility: Applicant must be U.S. citizen or permanent resident residing in Minnesota.
Basis for selection: Applicant must demonstrate financial need.

Additional information: Apply at college's financial aid office. Award amount prorated upon enrollment. Award based on family income and size. Eligibility limited to applicants with children 12 years or younger; maximum of $2,600 per eligible child per academic year. Applicant cannot be receiving Aid to Families With Dependent Children, Minnesota Family Investment Program, or tuition reciprocity, or be in default of loan. Those with bachelor's degree or eight semesters or 12 quarters of credit, or equivalent, are not eligible. Applicant must be enrolled at least half-time in nonsectarian program and must be in good academic standing. Deadlines established by individual institution.

 Amount of award: $2,600
 Number of awards: 2,832
 Number of applicants: 2,832
 Total amount awarded: $5,086,400

Contact:
Minnesota Office of Higher Education
1450 Energy Park Drive, Suite 350
St. Paul, MN 55108-5227
Phone: 800-657-3866
Web: www.getreadyforcollege.org

Minnesota Public Safety Officers Survivors Program

Type of award: Scholarship.
Intended use: For undergraduate or non-degree study at accredited postsecondary institution.
Eligibility: Applicant must be residing in Minnesota. Applicant's parent must have been killed or disabled in work-related accident as firefighter, police officer or public safety officer.
Application requirements: Proof of eligibility. Eligibility certificate.
Additional information: Must be enrolled in degree or certificate program at institution participating in State Grant Program. Must be child of police officer, fire fighter or other public service personnel whose death was work related. Also eligible if parent or spouse, not officially employed in public safety, was killed while assisting public safety officer or offering emergency medical assistance. Obtain eligibility certificate from Department of Public Safety, 211 Transportation Building, St. Paul, MN 55155. Apply through financial aid office. Award covers tuition and fees up to $9,838 at four-year college and $6,114 at two-year college.

 Number of awards: 16
 Number of applicants: 16
 Total amount awarded: $79,002

Contact:
Minnesota Office of Higher Education
1450 Energy Park Drive, Suite 350
St. Paul, MN 55108-5227
Phone: 800-657-3866
Web: www.getreadyforcollege.org

Minnesota State Grant Program

Type of award: Scholarship, renewable.
Intended use: For undergraduate study at accredited vocational, 2-year or 4-year institution.
Eligibility: Applicant must be U.S. citizen or permanent resident residing in Minnesota.
Basis for selection: Applicant must demonstrate financial need.
Application requirements: Proof of eligibility. FAFSA.

Additional information: Applicant must not have completed four years of college. If not Minnesota high school graduate and parents not residents of Minnesota, applicant must be resident of Minnesota for at least one year without being enrolled half-time or more. Cannot be in default on loans or delinquent on child-support payments. FAFSA used as application for Minnesota State Grant. Application deadline is 30 days from term start date.

 Amount of award: $100-$8,499
 Number of awards: 80,182
 Number of applicants: 80,182
 Total amount awarded: $156,096,165

Contact:
Minnesota Office of Higher Education
1450 Energy Park Drive, Suite 350
St. Paul, MN 55108-5227
Phone: 800-657-3866
Web: www.getreadyforcollege.org

Miss America Organization

Albert A. Marks Education Scholarship for Teacher Education

Type of award: Scholarship.
Intended use: For undergraduate study at postsecondary institution.
Eligibility: Applicant must be female.
Basis for selection: Major/career interest in education. Applicant must demonstrate financial need and high academic achievement.
Application requirements: Recommendations, essay, transcript, proof of eligibility.
Additional information: Must be pursuing a degree in education. Must have competed in Miss America system in local, state or national level after 1993.

 Application deadline: June 30
 Notification begins: September 1

Contact:
Miss America Organization ATTN: Scholarship Department
Two Ocean Way
Suite 1000
Atlantic City, NJ 08401
Phone: 609-345-7571 ext. 27
Fax: 609-347-6079
Web: www.missamerica.org

Allman Medical Scholarships

Type of award: Scholarship, renewable.
Intended use: For undergraduate or graduate study at postsecondary institution.
Eligibility: Applicant must be female.
Basis for selection: Major/career interest in medicine. Applicant must demonstrate financial need and high academic achievement.
Application requirements: Recommendations, essay, transcript, proof of eligibility. MCAT scores.
Additional information: Must be pursuing a degree in medicine. Must have competed in Miss America system at local, state or national level after 1996. Notification begins in August.

 Application deadline: June 30

Miss America Organization: Allman Medical Scholarships

Contact:
Miss America Organization ATTN: Scholarship Department
Miss America Way
Suite 1000
Atlantic City, NJ 08401
Phone: 609-345-7571 ext. 27
Fax: 609-347-6079
Web: www.missamerica.org

Eugenia Vellner Fischer Award for the Performing Arts

Type of award: Scholarship.
Intended use: For undergraduate or graduate study at postsecondary institution.
Eligibility: Applicant must be female.
Basis for selection: Major/career interest in performing arts. Applicant must demonstrate financial need and high academic achievement.
Application requirements: Recommendations, essay, transcript, proof of eligibility.
Additional information: Must be pursuing degree in the performing arts, such as dance or music. Must have competed in Miss America system in local, state or national level after 1996. Visit Website for more information.
   Application deadline: June 30
   Notification begins: September 1
Contact:
Miss America Organization ATTN: Scholarship Department
Miss America Way
Suite 1000
Atlantic City, NJ 08401
Phone: 609-345-7571 ext. 27
Fax: 609-347-6079
Web: www.missamerica.org

Leonard C. Horn Award for Legal Studies

Type of award: Scholarship, renewable.
Intended use: For undergraduate or graduate study at postsecondary institution.
Eligibility: Applicant must be female.
Basis for selection: Major/career interest in law.
Application requirements: Recommendations, essay, transcript, proof of eligibility. LSAT score.
Additional information: Must be pursuing degree in field of law. Must have competed within Miss America system at local, state or national level after 1993. Notification begins in September.
   Application deadline: June 30
Contact:
Miss America Organization ATTN: Scholarship Department
Two Ocean Way
Suite 1000
Atlantic City, NJ 08401
Phone: 609-345-7571 ext. 27
Fax: 609-347-6079
Web: www.missamerica.org

Miss America Competition Awards

Type of award: Scholarship.
Intended use: For undergraduate, graduate or non-degree study at accredited postsecondary institution.
Eligibility: Applicant must be single, female, at least 17, no older than 24. Applicant must be U.S. citizen.
Basis for selection: Competition/talent/interest in poise/talent/fitness. Applicant must demonstrate depth of character, leadership, patriotism, seriousness of purpose and service orientation.
Application requirements: Proof of eligibility.
Additional information: Local winners go on to compete at state level, and state winners compete for Miss America. Contestants will apply their talent, intelligence, and speaking ability, and demonstrate their commitment to community service. Cash and tuition-based scholarships available at every level of competition. Deadlines for local competitions vary. Contact the Miss America Organization for more information or visit Website.
   Amount of award: $3,000-$30,000
   Total amount awarded: $40,000,000
Contact:
Miss America Organization
Two Miss America Way
Suite 1000
Atlantic City, NJ 08401
Phone: 609-345-7571 ext. 27
Fax: 609-347-6079
Web: www.missamerica.org

Mississippi Office of Student Financial Aid

Gulf Coast Research Laboratory Minority Summer Grant

Type of award: Research grant.
Intended use: For undergraduate study.
Eligibility: Applicant must be Alaskan native, Asian American, African American, Mexican American, Hispanic American, Puerto Rican or American Indian. Applicant must be U.S. citizen or permanent resident residing in Mississippi.
Basis for selection: Major/career interest in oceanography/marine studies or environmental science.
Additional information: Program provides summer grants for minority students to attend classes or conduct independent study at Gulf Coast Research Laboratory in Gulf Coast Research Laboratory Summer Academic Institute. Four- to ten-week program. Award covers program tuition and stipend. College credit possible, depending on grant holder's educational institution. Number of awards depends upon availability of funds. Call 228-872-4200 for application. Preference given to early applicants.
   Application deadline: March 31
Contact:
Mississippi Office of Student Financial Aid
3825 Ridgewood Road
Jackson, MS 39211-6453
Phone: 800-327-2980
Fax: 601-432-6527
Web: www.ihl.state.ms.us/financialaid/gcrl.asp

Leveraging Educational Assistance Partnership Program (LEAP)

Type of award: Scholarship, renewable.
Intended use: For full-time undergraduate study at accredited 2-year or 4-year institution.

Eligibility: Applicant must be enrolled in high school. Applicant must be U.S. citizen or permanent resident residing in Mississippi.
Basis for selection: Applicant must demonstrate financial need and high academic achievement.
Application requirements: Recommendations, proof of eligibility. FAFSA.
Additional information: Must meet general requirements for participation in federal student aid program. Award amount varies. Apply to college financial aid office.
Contact:
Mississippi Student Financial Aid
3825 Ridgewood Road
Jackson, MS 39211-6453
Phone: 800-327-2980
Web: www.ihl.state.ms.us/financialaid/leap.asp

Mississippi Eminent Scholars Grant

Type of award: Scholarship, renewable.
Intended use: For full-time undergraduate study at accredited vocational, 2-year or 4-year institution. Designated institutions: Eligible Mississippi institutions.
Eligibility: Applicant must be high school senior. Applicant must be residing in Mississippi.
Basis for selection: Applicant must demonstrate high academic achievement.
Application requirements: Transcript. State of Mississippi tax return.
Additional information: Applicant may be high school senior and resident of Mississippi for at least one year. Must have minimum 3.5 GPA. Must have ACT of 29 or SAT of 1280, or be recognized as a semifinalist or finalist by the National Merit Scholarship Program or the National Achievement Scholarship Program.
   Amount of award: $2,500
   Application deadline: October 15
Contact:
Mississippi Student Financial Aid
3825 Ridgewood Road
Jackson, MS 39211-6453
Phone: 800-327-2980
Web: www.ihl.state.ms.us/financialaid/mesg.asp

Mississippi Higher Education Legislative Plan

Type of award: Scholarship, renewable.
Intended use: For full-time freshman or sophomore study at accredited 2-year or 4-year institution. Designated institutions: Eligible Mississippi institutions.
Eligibility: Applicant must be U.S. citizen residing in Mississippi.
Basis for selection: Applicant must demonstrate financial need.
Application requirements: FAFSA. Household verification form.
Additional information: Minimum 2.5 GPA and 20 on ACT. Must be legal resident of Mississippi for at least two years. Must have graduated from high school within two years of application. Preference given to early applicants. Covers tuition and fees up to ten semesters. Visit Website for application and more details.
   Application deadline: March 31

Contact:
Mississippi Office of Student Financial Aid
3825 Ridgewood Road
Jackson, MS 39211-6453
Phone: 800-327-2980
Web: www.ihl.state.ms.us/financialaid/help.asp

Mississippi Law Enforcement Officers & Firemen Scholarship

Type of award: Scholarship, renewable.
Intended use: For full-time undergraduate study at 2-year or 4-year institution.
Eligibility: Applicant must be residing in Mississippi. Applicant's parent must have been killed or disabled in work-related accident as firefighter, police officer or public safety officer.
Application requirements: Proof of eligibility.
Additional information: Award covers tuition, housing, and fees at Mississippi public institutions. Spouses also eligible.
   Amount of award: Full tuition
Contact:
Susan Eckels, Program Manager
Mississippi Office of Student Financial Aid
3825 Ridgewood Road
Jackson, MS 39211-6453
Phone: 800-327-2980
Fax: 601-432-6527
Web: www.ihl.state.ms.us/financialaid/law.asp

Mississippi Resident Tuition Assistance Grant

Type of award: Scholarship, renewable.
Intended use: For full-time undergraduate study at accredited vocational, 2-year or 4-year institution. Designated institutions: Eligible Mississippi institutions.
Eligibility: Applicant must be U.S. citizen residing in Mississippi.
Application requirements: FAFSA and Student Aid Report.
Additional information: Applicant must be resident of Mississippi for no less than one year. Must be receiving less than full Federal Pell Grant. High school seniors must have minimum 2.5 GPA and ACT score of 15 or 720 on SAT. Other first-time applicants must have 2.5 GPA. Award is up to $500 per year for freshmen and sophomores; up to $1,000 per year for juniors and seniors. Recipients must maintain 2.5 GPA to reapply. Applicants must not be in default on an educational loan. Apply online.
   Amount of award: $500-$1,000
   Application deadline: September 15
Contact:
Mississippi Student Financial Aid
3825 Ridgewood Road
Jackson, MS 39211-6453
Phone: 800-327-2980
Web: www.ihl.state.ms.us/financialaid/mtag.asp

Nissan Scholarship

Type of award: Scholarship, renewable.
Intended use: For full-time undergraduate study at 2-year or 4-year institution.
Eligibility: Applicant must be residing in Mississippi.
Basis for selection: Applicant must demonstrate financial need, high academic achievement, leadership, seriousness of purpose and service orientation.

Application requirements: FAFSA, 200-word essay.
Additional information: High school senior applicants must be graduating from Mississippi high school. Minimum 2.5 GPA and 20 ACT or 940 SAT. Visit Website for more information and online application.

Amount of award:	Full tuition
Application deadline:	March 1

Contact:
Mississippi Office of Student Financial Aid
3825 Ridgewood Road
Jackson, MS 39211-6453
Phone: 800-327-2980
Web: www.ihl.state.ms.us/financialaid/nissan.html

Missouri Department of Elementary and Secondary Education

Missouri Minority Teaching Scholarship

Type of award: Scholarship, renewable.
Intended use: For full-time undergraduate or master's study at accredited 2-year or 4-year institution in United States. Designated institutions: Missouri institutions with approved teacher education programs.
Eligibility: Applicant must be Alaskan native, Asian American, African American, Mexican American, Hispanic American, Puerto Rican or American Indian. Applicant must be returning adult student, high school senior. Applicant must be residing in Missouri.
Basis for selection: Major/career interest in education. Applicant must demonstrate high academic achievement.
Application requirements: Recommendations, essay, transcript, proof of eligibility.
Additional information: Must rank in top 25 percent of class or score in top 25 percent on ACT or SAT. If in college, may have 3.0 GPA at 30 hours to qualify. If college graduate, may receive award if returning to a master's level math or science education program. Upon graduation, recipient must teach for five years in Missouri public schools or scholarship becomes loan.

Amount of award:	$3,000
Number of awards:	100
Number of applicants:	50
Application deadline:	February 15
Notification begins:	April 15
Total amount awarded:	$200,000

Contact:
Missouri Department of Elementary and Secondary Education
Educator Recruitment and Retention
P.O. Box 480
Jefferson City, MO 65102
Phone: 573-751-1668
Fax: 573-526-3580
Web: www.dese.mo.gov

Missouri Robert C. Byrd Honors Scholarship

Type of award: Scholarship, renewable.
Intended use: For undergraduate study at accredited 4-year institution in United States. Designated institutions: Eligible Missouri institutions.
Eligibility: Applicant must be high school senior. Applicant must be U.S. citizen or permanent resident residing in Missouri.
Basis for selection: Applicant must demonstrate high academic achievement.
Application requirements: Seventh semester transcripts.
Additional information: Applicant must be completing high school or GED in year of application. Must score in 90th percentile on ACT. Final selection at each congressional district level based on SAT/ACT scores and GPA. Award amount varies; contact sponsor for more information. Applicant's high school guidance counselor must sign and verify application form. Applications may be renewed for total of four years.

Amount of award:	$1,500
Number of applicants:	700
Application deadline:	April 15
Notification begins:	October 1
Total amount awarded:	$750,000

Contact:
Missouri Department of Elementary and Secondary Education
Robert C. Byrd Honors Scholarship
P.O. Box 480
Jefferson City, MO 65102
Phone: 573-751-1668
Fax: 573-526-3580
Web: www.dese.mo.gov

Missouri Teacher Education Scholarship

Type of award: Scholarship.
Intended use: For full-time undergraduate study. Designated institutions: Accredited Missouri schools with approved teacher education programs.
Eligibility: Applicant must be U.S. citizen residing in Missouri.
Basis for selection: Major/career interest in education. Applicant must demonstrate high academic achievement.
Application requirements: Recommendations, essay, transcript, proof of eligibility. ACT/SAT scores and class rank.
Additional information: Applicant may be high school senior or college student who has ranked in top 15 percent of graduating class or scored in top 15 percent on ACT, SAT, or other standardized tests. Must teach in Missouri public school for five years after graduation or scholarship becomes a loan. Fifteen percent of awards set aside for minorities.

Amount of award:	$2,000
Number of awards:	240
Number of applicants:	400
Application deadline:	February 15
Notification begins:	April 15
Total amount awarded:	$240,000

Contact:
Missouri Department of Elementary and Secondary Education
Educator Recruitment and Retention
P.O. Box 480
Jefferson City, MO 65102
Phone: 573-751-1668
Fax: 573-526-3580
Web: www.dese.mo.gov

Urban Flight and Rural Needs Scholarship Program

Type of award: Scholarship.

Intended use: For freshman, sophomore or junior study at 2-year or 4-year institution.
Eligibility: Applicant must be returning adult student. Applicant must be U.S. citizen residing in Missouri.
Basis for selection: Major/career interest in education.
Application requirements: Transcript. FAFSA.
Additional information: Minimum 2.5 GPA. Recipients of award must enroll in fulltime four-year approved teacher education program and must agree to teach in Missouri eight years. If recipients do not complete teacher education program or eight-year teaching requirement, scholarship converts to loan and must be repaid. Repayment is reduced by one-eighth for each year of teaching experience in appropriate school.

Number of awards:	25
Number of applicants:	235
Application deadline:	April 15
Notification begins:	May 1
Total amount awarded:	$150,000

Contact:
Missouri Department of Elementary and Secondary Education
Teacher Quality and Urban Education
P.O. Box 480
Jefferson City, MO 65102-0480
Phone: 573-751-1191
Web: www.dese.mo.gov

Missouri Department of Higher Education

Access Missouri Financial Assistance Program

Type of award: Scholarship, renewable.
Eligibility: Applicant must be U.S. citizen or permanent resident residing in Missouri.
Basis for selection: Applicant must demonstrate financial need.
Application requirements: FAFSA.
Additional information: Must be used only toward first baccalaureate degree and may not be used towards theology or divinity studies. Eligibility based on EFC, with individuals with EFC of $12,000 or less eligible. Award amounts vary. No paper application. Students must apply for renewal each year.

Amount of award:	$300-$4,600
Number of awards:	37,054
Application deadline:	April 1
Total amount awarded:	$72,000,000

Contact:
Missouri Department of Higher Education
3515 Amazonas Dr.
Jefferson City, MO 65109
Phone: 800-473-6757
Fax: 573-751-6635
Web: www.dhe.mo.gov

Marguerite Ross Barnett Memorial Scholarship

Type of award: Scholarship, renewable.
Intended use: For half-time undergraduate study at accredited vocational, 2-year or 4-year institution in United States.
Designated institutions: Participating Missouri schools.
Eligibility: Applicant must be at least 18. Applicant must be U.S. citizen or permanent resident residing in Missouri.
Basis for selection: Applicant must demonstrate financial need.
Application requirements: Proof of eligibility. FAFSA.
Additional information: For students employed at least 20 hours per week while attending school part-time. Scholarship awarded on first-come, first-served basis. Maximum award is tuition charged at school of part-time enrollment; amount of tuition charged to Missouri undergraduate resident enrolled part-time in same class level at University of Missouri-Columbia; or demonstrated financial need. Employer must verify applicant's employment. Recipient may not be pursuing degree in theology or divinity.

Number of awards:	165
Number of applicants:	312
Application deadline:	April 1
Total amount awarded:	$418,519

Contact:
Missouri Department of Higher Education
3515 Amazonas Drive
Jefferson City, MO 65109
Phone: 800-473-6757
Fax: 573-751-6635
Web: www.dhe.mo.gov

Missouri Department of Higher Education Vietnam Veteran's Survivor Grant Program

Type of award: Scholarship, renewable.
Intended use: For full-time undergraduate study at accredited vocational, 2-year or 4-year institution in United States.
Eligibility: Applicant must be U.S. citizen or permanent resident residing in Missouri. Applicant must be dependent of deceased veteran; or spouse of deceased veteran.
Additional information: For children and spouses of Vietnam veterans whose death was attributed to or caused by exposure to toxic chemicals during Vietnam conflict. Applicant cannot pursue degree in theology or divinity. Applications accepted in January; end date based on fund availability. Amount of award varies. Maximum amount is the least of actual tuition charged at school where applicant is enrolled, or the average amount of tuition charged to undergraduate Missouri resident enrolled full-time in same class level and academic major at regional four-year public Missouri institutions.

Number of awards:	20
Number of applicants:	14
Total amount awarded:	$50,000

Contact:
Missouri Department of Higher Education
3515 Amazonas Drive
Jefferson City, MO 65109
Phone: 800-473-6757
Fax: 573-751-6635
Web: www.dhe.mo.gov

Missouri Higher Education "Bright Flight" Academic Scholarship

Type of award: Scholarship, renewable.
Intended use: For full-time undergraduate study at accredited vocational, 2-year or 4-year institution in United States.
Designated institutions: Approved Missouri public and private schools.

Missouri Department of Higher Education: Missouri Higher Education "Bright Flight" Academic Scholarship

Eligibility: Applicant must be U.S. citizen or permanent resident residing in Missouri.
Basis for selection: Applicant must demonstrate high academic achievement.
Application requirements: Proof of eligibility.
Additional information: May only be used for first baccalaureate degree. May not be used for theology or divinity studies. SAT/ACT scores required for determining academic achievement; composite scores must be in top three percent of state students. Must achieve qualifying scores by June assessment date of senior year. GED and home-schooled students may also qualify. Application deadline is June assessment date of senior year. No paper application needed. Check with high school counselor or financial aid administrator for additional information. Also see Website.

Amount of award:	$2,000
Number of awards:	8,179
Number of applicants:	16,921
Application deadline:	June 14
Total amount awarded:	$16,180,786

Contact:
Missouri Department of Higher Education
3515 Amazonas Drive
Jefferson City, MO 65109
Phone: 800-473-6757
Fax: 573-751-6635
Web: www.dhe.mo.gov

Missouri Public Service Survivor Grant

Type of award: Scholarship, renewable.
Intended use: For full-time undergraduate study at accredited vocational, 2-year or 4-year institution in United States. Designated institutions: Approved Missouri public and private schools.
Eligibility: Applicant must be U.S. citizen or permanent resident residing in Missouri. Applicant's parent must have been killed or disabled in work-related accident as firefighter, police officer or public safety officer.
Application requirements: Proof of eligibility.
Additional information: For spouses or children of Missouri public safety officers (including law enforcement, firefighters, corrections, water safety, and conservation officers) killed or totally and permanently disabled in the line of duty. Children or spouses of Missouri Department of Highway and Transportation employees also eligible if parent died during performance of job. May not be used for theology or divinity studies. Award amounts vary; contact sponsor for information. Estimated amount is based on 12 credit hours at chosen institution or no more than 12 hours at University of Missouri. Applications accepted in January; end date based on fund availability.

Number of awards:	14
Number of applicants:	14
Total amount awarded:	$55,375

Contact:
Missouri Department of Higher Education
3515 Amazonas Drive
Jefferson City, MO 65109
Phone: 800-473-6757
Fax: 573-751-6635
Web: www.dhe.mo.gov

Missouri League for Nursing

Erby Young Scholarship

Type of award: Scholarship, renewable.
Intended use: For full-time sophomore, junior or senior study at accredited 2-year or 4-year institution.
Eligibility: Applicant must be U.S. citizen residing in Missouri.
Basis for selection: Major/career interest in nursing. Applicant must demonstrate financial need and high academic achievement.
Application requirements: Recommendations.
Additional information: Minimum 3.0 GPA. Scholarship must be used for study in Missouri. Amount of award varies. Applications can be obtained from dean of nationally recognized accredited schools of nursing in Missouri. Must be an LPN enrolled in RN program approved by the Missouri Board of Nursing.

Amount of award:	$5,000
Application deadline:	November 15
Notification begins:	December 1

Contact:
Contact deans of school of nursing programs in Missouri.
Web: www.monursing.org

Missouri League for Nursing Scholarship

Type of award: Scholarship, renewable.
Intended use: For full-time sophomore, junior, senior or master's study.
Eligibility: Applicant must be U.S. citizen residing in Missouri.
Basis for selection: Major/career interest in nursing. Applicant must demonstrate financial need and high academic achievement.
Application requirements: Recommendations.
Additional information: Minimum 3.0 GPA. Scholarship must be used for study in Missouri. Amount of award varies. Applications can be obtained from dean of nationally recognized accredited schools of nursing in Missouri.

Amount of award:	$2,000
Number of awards:	3
Number of applicants:	60
Application deadline:	November 15
Notification begins:	December 1

Contact:
Contact deans of school of nursing programs in Missouri.
Web: www.monursing.org

Moneygram of New York

Hispanic Youth Leaders Scholarship

Type of award: Scholarship.
Intended use: For full-time undergraduate study at accredited 2-year or 4-year institution.
Eligibility: Applicant must be Hispanic American or Puerto Rican. Applicant must be high school senior. Applicant must be residing in New York.

Basis for selection: Applicant must demonstrate financial need, high academic achievement, depth of character, seriousness of purpose and service orientation.
Application requirements: Recommendations, transcript, proof of eligibility. Two page essay on community service. Verification of community service.
Additional information: Must be resident of the Bronx, Brooklyn, Manhattan, or Queens and attend a New York City public school.

    Amount of award: $2,000-$3,000
    Number of awards: 5
    Number of applicants: 35
    Application deadline: April 30
    Notification begins: May 15

Contact:
Moneygram of New York Youth Leader's Scholarship
Attn: Jacquie Medina
521 West 181 Street
New York, NY 10033
Phone: 212-740-1440 ext. 208

Montana Board of Regents of Higher Education

Governor's Postsecondary Scholarship

Type of award: Scholarship, renewable.
Intended use: For undergraduate study at 2-year or 4-year institution.
Eligibility: Applicant must be residing in Montana.
Basis for selection: Applicant must demonstrate financial need and high academic achievement.
Additional information: Applications available on Website.

    Amount of award: $1,000-$2,000
    Number of awards: 480
    Application deadline: March 31

Contact:
Governor's Scholarship
c/o MGSLP
P.O. Box 8010
Helena, MT 59604-8010
Phone: 406-444-1869
Fax: 406-444-0638
Web: www.mgslp.org

Montana Higher Education Grant

Type of award: Scholarship.
Intended use: For undergraduate study.
Eligibility: Applicant must be residing in Montana.
Basis for selection: Applicant must demonstrate financial need.
Application requirements: FAFSA.

    Total amount awarded: $591,305

Contact:
Contact college financial aid office for application information.
Web: www.mgslp.org

Montana State Fund Scholarship Program

Type of award: Scholarship, renewable.
Intended use: For undergraduate study. Designated institutions: Approved institutions.
Additional information: Spouses and children of workers insured by MSF who were killed on or after July 1, 1990, in compensable industrial accidents. Visit Website for more information.

    Amount of award: $2,000
    Application deadline: March 1, October 1

Contact:
Montana State Fund Scholarship Program
P.O. Box 203101
Helena, MT 59120-3101
Phone: 406-444-1869
Fax: 406-444-0638
Web: www.mgslp.org

Montana Tuition Fee Waiver for Veterans

Type of award: Scholarship.
Intended use: For undergraduate or graduate study. Designated institutions: Montana University system institutions.
Eligibility: Applicant must be permanent resident residing in Montana. Applicant must be veteran. Must have been honorably discharged person who served with the United States forces during wartime.
Application requirements: Proof of eligibility.
Additional information: Veterans who have served in the armed forces subsequent to the conflict in Vietnam are eligible for a fee waiver if the following conditions are met: 1) The veteran has been awarded an Armed Forces Expeditionary Medal for service in Lebanon, Grenada, or Panama or the veteran served in a combat theater in the Persian Gulf between August 2, 1990, and April 11, 1991, and received the Southwest Asia Service Medal; 2) The veteran is pursuing his or her initial undergraduate degree. Must have used up all federal veterans educational assistance benefits. Contact college financial aid office.

    Amount of award: Full tuition

Contact:
Montana University System
P.O. Box 203101
Helena, MT 59620-3101
Web: www.mgslp.org

Montana University System Community College Honor Scholarship

Type of award: Scholarship.
Intended use: For junior study at 4-year institution. Designated institutions: Montana University system institutions.
Eligibility: Applicant must be residing in Montana.
Basis for selection: Applicant must demonstrate high academic achievement.
Application requirements: Proof of eligibility. Recommendation from president/faculty of accredited Montana community college.
Additional information: Holder of scholarship must enter Montana University System within nine months after receiving associate degree. Award provides for tuition/fee waiver in any unit of Montana University System. The waiver will be valid through the completion of the first academic year (two semesters) of enrollment, exclusive of any credits earned prior to high school or community college graduation.

    Amount of award: Full tuition

Contact:
Financial aid office of community college.
Web: www.mgslp.org

Montana University System Honor Scholarship

Type of award: Scholarship, renewable.
Intended use: For freshman study at 4-year institution. Designated institutions: Campuses in Montana University system, as well as Dawson, Flathead Valley, and Miles community colleges.
Eligibility: Applicant must be high school senior. Applicant must be U.S. citizen residing in Montana.
Basis for selection: Applicant must demonstrate high academic achievement.
Application requirements: Recommendations, transcript, proof of eligibility. College acceptance letter.
Additional information: Recipients ranked based on GPA and ACT or SAT score, have minimum 3.4 GPA, and have met college preparatory requirements. Must submit completed application to high school guidance counselor. See Website for more details. former international exchange student.

Amount of award:	Full tuition
Number of awards:	200
Application deadline:	February 15

Contact:
Montana Board of Regents of Higher Education
P.O. Box 203101
Helena, MT 59620-3101
Web: www.mgslp.org

Montana Trappers Association

MTA Doug Slifka Memorial Scholarship

Type of award: Scholarship.
Intended use: For undergraduate study.
Eligibility: Applicant must be at least 15, no older than 25. Applicant must be residing in Montana.
Basis for selection: Major/career interest in environmental science; life sciences; natural resources/conservation or wildlife/fisheries. Applicant must demonstrate depth of character and seriousness of purpose.
Application requirements: Interview, transcript. Essay or story on trapping or conservation. Recommendations by MTA members, teachers, or other pertinent individuals. Endorsement of MTA District Director (or sub-director) where applicant resides. Student involvement in activities that include MTA programs, trapping, school programs, and community service.
Additional information: Applicant must be member of MTA for at least one year or minor dependent of MTA member. MTA member in question must have been member of Association for one year prior to application. MTA members out of state and their families also eligible to apply. For application, complete request form on Website or contact local director, officer or committee member.

Amount of award:	$500
Number of awards:	2
Application deadline:	June 1
Total amount awarded:	$1,000

Contact:
Montana Trappers Association MTA Scholarship Committee
C/O Gary VanHaele
P.O. Box 264
Hysham, MT 59038
Phone: 406-342-5552
Web: www.montanatrappers.org/programs/scholarship.htm

The Moody's Foundation

Moody's Mega Math "M3" Challenge

Type of award: Scholarship.
Intended use: For sophomore or junior study at 2-year or 4-year institution.
Eligibility: Applicant must be high school junior or senior. Applicant must be residing in New York.
Basis for selection: Competition/talent/interest in academics, based on responses to the assigned modeling problem.
Additional information: Applicant must be high school junior or senior residing in eligible counties in CT, DE, MA, NH, NJ, NY, PA, RI. Visit website for more information. Each school may enter up to two teams of three to five students. Team prizes range from $1,000 to $20,000. Entrants must attend the challenge weekend in New York in March. Deadlines vary; visit Website for details and to register.

Amount of award:	$1,000-$20,000
Number of awards:	11
Number of applicants:	172
Application deadline:	March 3
Notification begins:	April 30
Total amount awarded:	$65,000

Contact:
Society for Industrial and Applied Mathematics
3600 Market Street, 6th Floor
Philadelphia, PA 19104
Web: m3challenge.siam.org

Myasthenia Gravis Foundation

Myasthenia Gravis Foundation Nursing Research Fellowship

Type of award: Research grant.
Intended use: For full-time undergraduate or graduate study at accredited 4-year or graduate institution in United States.
Eligibility: Applicant must be U.S. citizen or permanent resident.
Basis for selection: Major/career interest in nursing.
Application requirements: Recommendations, research proposal. Four copies: cover letter, proposed budget, curriculum vitae of applicant and sponsoring preceptor, proposed work plan and budget.
Additional information: For nursing students or professionals interested in studying problems encountered by patients with myasthenia gravis or related neuromuscular conditions.

Amount of award:	$5,000

Contact:
Research Grant Committee
Myasthenia Gravis Foundation
1821 University Ave W, Suite S256
St. Paul, MN 55104
Phone: 800-541-5454
Fax: 651-917-1835
Web: www.myasthenia.org

Viets Medical Student/Graduate Student Fellowship

Type of award: Research grant.
Intended use: For full-time junior, senior or first professional study at accredited 4-year or graduate institution in United States.
Eligibility: Applicant must be U.S. citizen or permanent resident.
Basis for selection: Major/career interest in medicine.
Application requirements: Recommendations, proof of eligibility, research proposal. Recommendation and curriculum vitae from sponsoring preceptor, letter of interest, curriculum vitae of applicant, summary of research and its relation to myasthenia gravis, proposed budget.
Additional information: Focus of research must be myasthenia gravis or related field.
    Amount of award: $5,000
    Number of awards: 4
    Number of applicants: 10
    Application deadline: March 15
    Total amount awarded: $12,000
Contact:
Research Grant Committee
Myasthenia Gravis Foundation
1821 University Avenue W, Suite S256
St. Paul, MN 55104
Phone: 800-541-5454
Fax: 651-917-1835
Web: www.myasthenia.org

NAACP

Agnes Jones Jackson Scholarship

Type of award: Scholarship, renewable.
Intended use: For full-time undergraduate or graduate study at accredited 2-year, 4-year or graduate institution.
Eligibility: Applicant or parent must be member/participant of National Association for Advancement of Colored People. Applicant must be no older than 24. Applicant must be U.S. citizen.
Basis for selection: Applicant must demonstrate financial need.
Application requirements: Recommendations, essay, transcript, proof of eligibility. Financial aid forms or copies of parents' latest income tax forms. Send one personal reference, one academic reference, and one NAACP reference (from an officer). Proof of enrollment.
Additional information: Must be current regular member of NAACP. Minimum 2.5 GPA for undergraduates, 3.0 GPA for graduate students. Award amounts: $1,500 undergraduate, $2,500 graduate. Graduate students can be full-time or part-time. Applications may be requested after January 1; include business-sized SASE. Visit Website for application and more information.
    Amount of award: $1,500-$2,500
    Application deadline: April 11
    Notification begins: July 31
Contact:
United Negro College Fund: Scholarships and Grants Administration
Attn: Kimberly Hall
8260 Willow Oaks Corporate Drive
Fairfax, VA 22301
Phone: 800-331-2244
Web: www.naacp.org/youth/scholarships/information/naacp

Earl G. Graves Scholarship

Type of award: Scholarship.
Intended use: For full-time junior, senior or graduate study at accredited 4-year or graduate institution in United States.
Basis for selection: Major/career interest in business. Applicant must demonstrate high academic achievement.
Application requirements: Essay, transcript, proof of eligibility. One personal and two academic recommendations.
Additional information: Applicants must be in top 20 percent of their class. May apply during sophomore year. Visit Website for application and more information.
    Amount of award: $5,000
    Application deadline: April 11
    Notification begins: July 31
Contact:
United Negro College Fund: Scholarships and Grants Administration
Attn: Kimberly Hall
8260 Willow Oaks Corporate Drive
Fairfax, VA 22031
Phone: 800-331-2244
Web: www.naacp.org/youth/scholarships/information/naacp

Historically Black College and University Scholarship Fund

Type of award: Scholarship.
Intended use: For full-time freshman study at accredited 4-year institution in United States. Designated institutions: Historically Black Colleges and Universities.
Eligibility: Applicant must be U.S. citizen.
Basis for selection: Major/career interest in engineering; chemistry; biology or physics. Applicant must demonstrate financial need.
Application requirements: Essay, transcript. One personal, one academic and one letter of recommendation from NAACP officer. Proof of enrollment and financial documentation.
Additional information: Minimum 2.5 GPA required. NAACP membership and participation is highly desirable. Visit Website for application and more information.
    Amount of award: $2,000
    Application deadline: April 11
    Notification begins: July 31
Contact:
United Negro College Fund: Scholarships and Grants Administration
Attn: Kimberly Hall
8260 Willow Oaks Corporate Drive
Fairfax, VA 22031
Phone: 800-331-2244
Web: www.naacp.org/youth/scholarships/information/naacp

Hubertus W.V. Willems Scholarship for Male Students

Type of award: Scholarship, renewable.
Intended use: For full-time undergraduate or graduate study at accredited 2-year, 4-year or graduate institution in United States.
Eligibility: Applicant or parent must be member/participant of National Association for Advancement of Colored People. Applicant must be male. Applicant must be U.S. citizen.
Basis for selection: Major/career interest in engineering; chemistry; science, general or mathematics. Applicant must demonstrate financial need.
Application requirements: Essay, transcript, proof of eligibility. Two recommendations from teachers or professors in field of study. Financial aid forms. Proof of enrollment, application for admissions.
Additional information: Applications may be requested after January 1. Send 9x12 SASE. Minimum 2.5 GPA for undergraduates and 3.0 GPA for graduate students. Award is $2,000 for undergraduates, $3,000 for graduate students. Graduate students may be enrolled part-time. Visit Website for application and more information.

Amount of award:	$2,000-$3,000
Application deadline:	April 11
Notification begins:	July 31

Contact:
United Negro College Fund: Scholarships and Grants Administration
Attn: Kimberly Hall
8260 Willow Oaks Corporate Drive
Fairfax, VA 22031
Phone: 800-331-2244
Web: www.naacp.org/youth/scholarships/information/naacp

Lillian and Samuel Sutton Education Scholarship

Type of award: Scholarship, renewable.
Intended use: For full-time undergraduate or graduate study at accredited 2-year, 4-year or graduate institution in United States. Designated institutions: Historically Black Colleges and Universities.
Eligibility: Applicant or parent must be member/participant of National Association for Advancement of Colored People. Applicant must be U.S. citizen.
Basis for selection: Major/career interest in education. Applicant must demonstrate leadership.
Application requirements: Essay, transcript, proof of eligibility. Two recommendations from teachers or professors in major field of study. Proof of enrollment, acceptance letter from college or university. Financial aid forms.
Additional information: Undergraduates must have minimum 2.5 GPA, graduate students must have minimum 3.0 GPA. Applications available in January. Include business-sized SASE. Graduate students may be enrolled part-time. NAACP membership and participation highly desirable. Award $1,000 for undergraduates; $2,000 for graduates. Visit Website for application and more information.

Amount of award:	$1,000-$2,000
Application deadline:	April 11
Notification begins:	July 31

Contact:
United Negro College Fund: Scholarships and Grants Administration
Attn: Kimberly Hall
8260 Willow Oaks Corporate Drive
Fairfax, VA 22031
Phone: 800-331-2244
Web: www.naacp.org/youth/scholarships/information/naacp

Roy Wilkins Scholarship

Type of award: Scholarship.
Intended use: For full-time freshman study at accredited 2-year or 4-year institution in United States.
Eligibility: Applicant or parent must be member/participant of National Association for Advancement of Colored People. Applicant must be U.S. citizen.
Application requirements: Recommendations, essay, transcript, proof of eligibility. One personal and one academic recommendation. Send financial aid forms along with copy of letter of acceptance from college or university. Business-sized SASE.
Additional information: Must be entering college freshman. Minimum 2.5 GPA. Applications may be requested after January 1. Visit Website for application and more information.

Amount of award:	$1,000
Application deadline:	April 11
Notification begins:	July 31

Contact:
United Negro College Fund: Scholarships and Grants Administration
Attn: Kimberly Hall
8260 Willow Oaks Corporate Drive
Fairfax, VA 22031
Phone: 800-331-2244
Web: www.naacp.org/youth/scholarships/information/naacp

NAACP Legal Defense and Education Fund, Inc.

Herbert Lehman Educational Fund

Type of award: Scholarship, renewable.
Intended use: For full-time freshman study at accredited 4-year institution in United States.
Eligibility: Applicant must be African American. Applicant must be high school senior. Applicant must be U.S. citizen.
Basis for selection: Applicant must demonstrate financial need, high academic achievement, depth of character, leadership, seriousness of purpose and service orientation.
Application requirements: Recommendations, essay, transcript. Standardized test scores.
Additional information: For initial application, must be entering first year of college where African Americans are substantially underrepresented. Application request should be made in writing between November 1 and February 15 with statement of career and educational goals, reason why assistance is needed, and name of college to be attended. See Website for additional information.

Amount of award:	$2,000
Application deadline:	April 30
Notification begins:	August 1

Contact:
The Herbert Lehman Fund
NAACP Legal Defense and Educational Fund, Inc
99 Hudson Street Suite 1600
New York, NY 10013
Phone: 212-965-2200 or 212-965-2225
Fax: 212-219-1595
Web: www.naacpldf.org/content.aspx?article=32

NASA Alabama Space Grant Consortium

NASA Space Grant Undergraduate Scholarship

Type of award: Scholarship, renewable.
Intended use: For full-time junior or senior study at accredited 4-year institution. Designated institutions: Alabama Space Grant member universities: University of Alabama Huntsville, Alabama A&M, University of Alabama, University of Alabama Birmingham, University of South Alabama, Auburn University, Tuskegee University.
Eligibility: Applicant must be U.S. citizen residing in Alabama.
Basis for selection: Major/career interest in aerospace; engineering or science, general. Applicant must demonstrate high academic achievement.
Application requirements: Recommendations, essay, transcript, nomination by faculty advisor at Alabama Space Grant Consortium member institution. Resume.
Additional information: Applicants must have 3.0 or greater GPA and attend Alabama University. Must be in final term of sophomore year or later when applying. The Consortium actively encourages women, minority, and physically challenged students to apply, but others not excluded.

Amount of award:	$1,000
Number of awards:	35
Number of applicants:	45
Application deadline:	March 1
Notification begins:	April 15

Contact:
NASA Alabama Space Grant Consortium
University of Alabama in Huntsville
301 Sparkman Dr. Materials Science Bldg, 205
Huntsville, AL 35899
Phone: 256-824-6800
Fax: 256-824-6061
Web: www.uah.edu/ASGC/

NASA Arkansas Space Grant Consortium

NASA Space Grant Arkansas Undergraduate Scholarship

Type of award: Scholarship.
Intended use: For full-time undergraduate study in United States. Designated institutions: Arkansas Space Grant Consortium members: University of Arkansas at Little Rock, Arkansas State University, Arkansas Tech University, Harding University, Henderson State University, Hendrix College, Lyon College, Ouachita Baptist University, University of Arkansas at Fayetteville, University of Arkansas at Pine Bluff, University of Arkansas for Medical Sciences, University of Central Arkansas, University of the Ozarks, and University of Arkansas at Monticello.
Eligibility: Applicant must be U.S. citizen residing in Arkansas.
Basis for selection: Major/career interest in aerospace; astronomy; chemistry; engineering; physics or medicine. Applicant must demonstrate high academic achievement.
Application requirements: Research proposal. Recommendation from sponsoring faculty member or mentor.
Additional information: Awards must be used at Consortium Member institutions in Arkansas. For any space-related research. Applications usually accepted September through November; contact campus program office. Application deadlines vary by campus. Minimum 3.0 GPA preferred.

Amount of award:	$250-$5,000
Number of applicants:	200

Contact:
Contact local campus Space Grant representative.
Phone: 501-569-8212 or 501-569-8213
Fax: 501-569-8039
Web: asgc.ualr.edu

NASA Connecticut Space Grant Consortium

NASA Connecticut Space Grant Undergraduate Fellowship

Type of award: Research grant, renewable.
Intended use: For full-time undergraduate study at accredited 4-year institution in United States. Designated institutions: Connecticut Space Grant Consortium member institutions.
Eligibility: Applicant must be U.S. citizen.
Basis for selection: Major/career interest in aerospace; engineering or science, general.
Application requirements: Recommendations, transcript, proof of eligibility. Resume. Research proposal.
Additional information: Must be used at a Connecticut Consortium member institution. Consortium actively encourages women, minority, and disabled students to apply. Award amount varies; maximum is $4,000.

Amount of award:	$4,500
Number of awards:	8
Number of applicants:	20
Application deadline:	November 1, February 1
Total amount awarded:	$25,000

Contact:
NASA Connecticut Space Grant Consortium
University of Hartford
200 Bloomfield Ave.
West Hartford, CT 06117
Phone: 860-768-4813
Fax: 860-768-5073
Web: uhaweb.hartford.edu/ctspgrant

NASA Delaware Space Grant Consortium

Delaware Space Grant Undergraduate Summer Scholarship

Type of award: Scholarship, renewable.
Intended use: For full-time undergraduate study. Designated institutions: University of Delaware, Delaware Technical and Community College, Swarthmore College, Delaware State University at Dover, Villanova University, Wilmington College.
Eligibility: Applicant must be U.S. citizen.
Basis for selection: Major/career interest in aerospace; astronomy; engineering; physics; engineering, materials; oceanography/marine studies; geography or geology/earth sciences.
Application requirements: Recommendations, transcript. Applicant statement.
Additional information: Applicants must be college freshmen or above when applying to be eligible. Applicants must have proven interest in space science-related studies. Recipient must attend a Delaware Space Grant Consortium member institution. Contact Consortium office for deadlines and additional information.
Contact:
Delaware Space Grant Consortium Program Office
University of Delaware
106 Sharp Lab
Newark, DE 19716
Phone: 302-831-1094
Fax: 302-831-1843
Web: www.delspace.org

Delaware Space Grant Undergraduate Tuition Scholarship

Type of award: Scholarship, renewable.
Intended use: For full-time undergraduate study. Designated institutions: University of Delaware, Delaware Technical and Community College, Swarthmore College, Delaware State University at Dover, Villanova University, Wilmington College.
Eligibility: Applicant must be U.S. citizen.
Basis for selection: Major/career interest in aerospace; astronomy; communications; engineering; geography; geology/earth sciences; geophysics; physics or oceanography/marine studies.
Application requirements: Recommendations, transcript. Applicant statement; letter from Department Chairperson.
Additional information: Applicants must be undergraduate freshmen or above when applying to be eligible. Applicants must have proven interest in space-related studies. Recipient must currently attend Delaware Space Grant Consortium member institution. Award amounts vary and are available pending funding. Contact Consortium office for deadlines and additional information.

Amount of award:	$2,000-$3,000
Number of applicants:	22
Application deadline:	April 15

Contact:
Delaware Space Grant Consortium Program Office
University of Delaware
106 Sharp Lab
Newark, DE 19716
Phone: 302-831-1094
Fax: 302-831-1843
Web: www.delspace.org

NASA District of Columbia Space Grant Consortium

NASA District of Columbia Undergraduate Scholarship

Type of award: Scholarship, renewable.
Intended use: For full-time undergraduate or graduate study. Designated institutions: The American University, Catholic University, Gallaudet University, George Washington University, Georgetown University, Howard University, Southeastern University, Trinity University, University of District of Columbia.
Eligibility: Applicant must be U.S. citizen.
Basis for selection: Major/career interest in science, general; mathematics; engineering; aerospace; physical education; political science/government or engineering. Applicant must demonstrate high academic achievement.
Application requirements: Recommendations, transcript, proof of eligibility.
Additional information: Number of grants, amounts of funding, deadlines, and application requirements vary by year and by institutions. See Website for more information.
Contact:
DC Space Grant Consortium American University - Dept. of Physics
4400 Massachusetts Ave, NW
McKinley Building Suite 102
Washington, DC 20016-8058
Phone: 202-885-2755
Fax: 202-885-2723
Web: www.dcspacegrant.org

NASA Georgia Space Grant Consortium

NASA Space Grant Georgia Fellowship Program

Type of award: Scholarship, renewable.
Intended use: For full-time junior, senior, master's or doctoral study at accredited postsecondary institution in United States. Designated institutions: Albany State University, Armstrong Atlantic State University, Clark Atlanta University, Columbus State University, Fort Valley State University, Georgia Institute of Technology, Georgia Southern University, Georgia State University, Kennesaw State University, Mercer University, Morehouse College, Savannah State University, Spelman College, West Georgia State University, University of Georgia.
Eligibility: Applicant must be U.S. citizen residing in Georgia.

Basis for selection: Major/career interest in engineering; science, general; aerospace; physics; atmospheric sciences/meteorology; computer/information sciences; education or chemistry. Applicant must demonstrate seriousness of purpose and service orientation.
Application requirements: Interview, portfolio, recommendations, essay, transcript.
Additional information: Funding available for students in all areas of engineering and science, and many areas of social science.
   Amount of award: $300
Contact:
Georgia Space Grant Consortium
Georgia Tech-Aerospace and Engineering
Space Science and Technology Bldg., Room 210
Atlanta, GA 30332-0150
Phone: 404-894-0521
Fax: 404-894-9313
Web: www.ae.gatech.edu/research/gsgc

NASA Hawaii Space Grant Consortium

NASA Space Grant Hawaii Undergraduate Fellowship

Type of award: Scholarship.
Intended use: For full-time undergraduate study in United States. Designated institutions: Consortium member schools: University of Hawaii at Manoa and Hilo; Community Colleges; University of Maui.
Eligibility: Applicant must be U.S. citizen residing in Hawaii.
Basis for selection: Major/career interest in astronomy; geology/earth sciences; oceanography/marine studies; physics; zoology; engineering or geography.
Application requirements: Recommendations, transcript. Abstract, research proposal, budget, resume. Three copies of all application materials.
Additional information: Applicant must be resident of Hawaii or attend school at one of the designated institutions. Applicants must be sponsored by a faculty member willing to act as the student's mentor during the award period. Field of study must be relevant to NASA's goals, e.g. areas of math, science, engineering, computer science (concerned with utilizing or exploring space), and air transportation. Full-time undergraduates at Manoa, Hilo with major declared can apply for two-semester fellowships. Stipend of $3,000 per semester. Also up to $500 for supplies or travel. Recipients expected to work 10-15 hours per week on space-related projects. Women, under-represented minorities (specifically Native Hawaiians, Filipinos, other Pacific Islanders, Native Americans, Blacks, Hispanics), physically challenged students who have interest in space-related fields are particularly encouraged to apply. Freshmen and sophomores may also apply. Visit Website for more information and application.
   Amount of award: $3,000
   Number of awards: 20
   Number of applicants: 25
   Application deadline: June 15, December 1
Contact:
Hawaii Space Grant College
University of Hawaii
1680 East West Road, Post 501
Honolulu, HI 96822
Phone: 808-956-3138
Fax: 808-956-6322
Web: www.spacegrant.hawaii.edu

NASA Idaho Space Grant Consortium

NASA Idaho Space Grant Undergraduate Scholarship

Type of award: Scholarship, renewable.
Intended use: For full-time undergraduate study at accredited 4-year institution. Designated institutions: College of Idaho, Boise State University, College of Southern Idaho, Idaho State University, Lewis Clark State College, North Idaho College, Northwest Nazarene University, BYU-Idaho, and the University of Idaho.
Eligibility: Applicant must be U.S. citizen.
Basis for selection: Major/career interest in engineering; mathematics or science, general.
Application requirements: Recommendations, essay. High school and college transcripts.
Additional information: Applicants must attend Idaho Space Grant Consortium member institution in Idaho and maintain a 3.0 GPA. Application should include ACT/SAT scores, if available. Consortium actively encourages women, minority students, and disabled students to apply. Application essay should not exceed 500 words. Applications may be downloaded from Website.
   Amount of award: $500-$1,000
   Number of awards: 40
   Number of applicants: 100
   Application deadline: March 1
   Notification begins: May 1
   Total amount awarded: $40,000
Contact:
NASA Space Grant Idaho Space Grant Consortium
University of Idaho
P.O. Box 441011
Moscow, ID 83844-1011
Phone: 208-885-6438
Fax: 208-885-1399
Web: isgc.uidaho.edu

NASA Illinois Space Grant Consortium

NASA Space Grant Illinois Undergraduate Scholarship

Type of award: Scholarship, renewable.
Intended use: For full-time undergraduate study. Designated institutions: Illinois Space Grant Consortium member institutions.

Eligibility: Applicant must be U.S. citizen.
Basis for selection: Major/career interest in engineering or aerospace. Applicant must demonstrate high academic achievement.
Application requirements: Recommendations, essay, transcript.
Additional information: Minimum 2.5 GPA. Contact sponsor for deadline information. Recipient required to work on research or design project.

Amount of award:	$2,500
Number of awards:	20
Number of applicants:	20
Total amount awarded:	$50,000

Contact:
Associate Director/ Illinois Space Grant Consortium
U of Illinois-Urbana, 306 Talbot Lab
104 S. Wright St.
Urbana, IL 61801-2935
Phone: 217-244-8048
Fax: 217-244-0720
Web: www.ae.uiuc.edu/ISGC

NASA Indiana Space Grant Consortium

NASA Indiana Space Grant Consortium Undergraduate Scholarships

Type of award: Scholarship, renewable.
Intended use: For undergraduate study. Designated institutions: Indiana Space Grant Consortium member institutions: Purdue University at West Lafayette, Purdue University-Calumet in Hammond, Indiana University in Bloomington, Indiana State University in Terre Haute, Ball State University, Southern Indiana University, Taylor University, Valparaiso University, IUPUI, IPFW, University of Evansville, University of Souther Indiana.
Eligibility: Applicant must be U.S. citizen residing in Indiana.
Basis for selection: Major/career interest in science, general; mathematics; engineering or aerospace. Applicant must demonstrate high academic achievement.
Additional information: Number of grants, amount of funding, deadlines and application requirements vary by institution; contact sponsor for more information. Must be used at Indiana Space Grant Consortium member institution. Applicant must be studying to work in a NASA-related field. Preference given to applicants with permanent address in Indiana. Application can be obtained on Website.

Amount of award:	$2,500
Number of applicants:	23
Application deadline:	January 15
Notification begins:	March 1

Contact:
NASA: Indiana Space Grant Consortium
Purdue University, Mann Hall, Room 160
203 S. Martin Jischke Dr.
West Lafayette, IN 47907-2051
Phone: 765-494-5873
Web: www.insgc.org

NASA Kentucky Space Grant Consortium

NASA Space Grant Kentucky Undergraduate Scholarship

Type of award: Scholarship, renewable.
Intended use: For full-time undergraduate study at accredited 4-year institution in United States. Designated institutions: Consortium member institutions: Bellarmine University, Centre College, Eastern Kentucky University, Kentucky Center for Space Enterprise, Kentucky State University, Morehead State University, Murray State University, Northern Kentucky University, Thomas More College, Transylvania University, Tribo Flow Separations, University of Kentucky, University of Louisville, Western Kentucky University.
Eligibility: Applicant must be U.S. citizen residing in Kentucky.
Basis for selection: Major/career interest in aerospace; astronomy; education; engineering or physics. Applicant must demonstrate high academic achievement.
Application requirements: Interview, recommendations, essay, transcript, nomination by professor/mentor at participating institution. Research proposal, written with mentor.
Additional information: Preference given to schools that waive tuition for recipient. Consortium actively encourages women, minority students, and physically challenged students to apply. Deadline is in early April. Check Website for exact date. Applicants doing work related to space exploration may qualify for funding, whatever their field of study may be.

Amount of award:	$5,000
Number of awards:	2
Number of applicants:	4
Application deadline:	April 1

Contact:
NASA/Kentucky Space Grant Consortium
Department of Physics and Astronomy, TCCW246
1906 College Heights Boulevard #11077
Bowling Green, KY 42101-1077
Phone: 270-745-4156
Web: www.wku.edu/KSGC

NASA Maine Space Grant Consortium

NASA Space Grant Maine Consortium Annual Scholarship and Fellowship Program

Type of award: Research grant, renewable.
Intended use: For full-time undergraduate or graduate study at accredited 4-year or graduate institution. Designated institutions: University of Maine (Orono), University of Maine (Presque Isle), University of Southern Maine, University of New England, Maine Maritime Academy, College of the Atlantic, Bowdoin College, Colby College, Bates College.
Eligibility: Applicant must be U.S. citizen residing in Maine.
Basis for selection: Major/career interest in astronomy; geology/earth sciences; geophysics; engineering; aerospace; biology or medicine.

Additional information: Applicants from out of state who attend one of the designated institutions are eligible. Research project must be in an aerospace related field. Applications from academic institutions in Maine other than those designated will be reviewed for consideration. Visit Website for additional details.

Amount of award: $3,000-$6,000
Contact:
Maine Space Grant Consortium
87 Winthrop Street
Suite 200
Augusta, ME 04330
Phone: 877-397-7223
Fax: 207-622-4548
Web: www.msgc.org

NASA Michigan Space Grant Consortium

MSGC Undergraduate Underrepresented Minority Fellowship Program

Type of award: Research grant.
Intended use: For full-time undergraduate study at 4-year institution in United States. Designated institutions: Michigan Space Grant Consortium member institutions: Eastern Michigan University, Grand Valley State University, Hope College, Michigan State University, Michigan Technological University, Oakland University, Saginaw Valley State University, Wayne State University, Western Michigan University.
Eligibility: Applicant must be African American, Hispanic American, American Indian or Native Hawaiian/Pacific Islander. Applicant must be U.S. citizen residing in Michigan.
Basis for selection: Major/career interest in aerospace; engineering; science, general or mathematics. Applicant must demonstrate high academic achievement.
Application requirements: Transcript, research proposal. Two letters of recommendation; two page personal essay; description of project expectations and specifications; 150 word abstract.
Additional information: Offers support in form of undergraduate research and public service fellowships to students in aerospace, space science, Earth system science and other related science, engineering, or math fields. Students working on educational research topics in math, science, or technology also eligible to apply. Preference given to projects directly related to aerospace, space science, Earth system science, and directly related educational efforts. Only underrepresented minority students (African- American, Hispanic, Latino, Native American, and Pacific Islanders) at MSGC institutions eligible. Visit Website for more information.

Amount of award: $2,500
Application deadline: November 20
Notification begins: March 15
Total amount awarded: $14,000
Contact:
NASA Michigan Space Grant Consortium
University of Michigan
1320 Beal Ave. - 1216-C FXB
Ann Arbor, MI 48109-2140
Phone: 734-764-9508
Fax: 734-763-0437
Web: www.umich.edu/~msgc

NASA Space Grant Michigan Undergraduate Fellowship

Type of award: Research grant, renewable.
Intended use: For undergraduate study at accredited 4-year institution. Designated institutions: Michigan Space Grant Consortium member institutions: Eastern Michigan University, Grand Valley State University, Hope College, Michigan State University, Michigan Technological University, Oakland University, Saginaw Valley State University, Wayne State University, Western Michigan University.
Eligibility: Applicant must be U.S. citizen residing in Michigan.
Basis for selection: Major/career interest in aerospace; engineering; science, general or mathematics. Applicant must demonstrate high academic achievement.
Application requirements: Transcript. Two letters of recommendation; two-page personal essay; description of project expectations and specifications; 150 word abstract.
Additional information: Offers support in form of undergraduate research and public service fellowships to students in aerospace, space science, Earth system science and other related science, engineering, or math fields. Students working on educational research topics in math, science, or technology also eligible to apply. Preference given to projects directly related to aerospace, space science, Earth system science, and directly related educational efforts. Announcements for next funding interval can be found on Website.

Amount of award: $2,500
Application deadline: November 20
Notification begins: March 15
Total amount awarded: $100,000
Contact:
NASA Space Grant Michigan Space Grant Consortium
U of Michigan
1320 Beal Ave. - 1216-C FXB
Ann Arbor, MI 48109-2140
Phone: 734-764-9508
Fax: 734-763-0437
Web: www.umich.edu/~msgc

NASA Minnesota Space Grant Consortium

NASA Minnesota Space Grant Consortium Wide Scholarship

Type of award: Scholarship, renewable.
Intended use: For full-time undergraduate study at accredited 4-year institution in United States. Designated institutions: Augsburg College, Bethel University, Bemidji State University, Carleton College, Concordia College, College of St. Catherine, Fond du Lac Tribal and Community College, Leech Lake Tribal College, Macalester College, Southwest Minnesota State University, University of Minnesota - Duluth, University of Minnesota - Twin Cities, University of St. Thomas.
Eligibility: Applicant must be U.S. citizen.
Basis for selection: Major/career interest in aerospace; astronomy; atmospheric sciences/meteorology; mathematics; engineering, mechanical; chemistry; engineering, electrical/electronic; engineering, chemical; engineering, civil or engineering, computer.

Application requirements: Recommendations, transcript. Letter of intent.
Additional information: Minimum 3.2 GPA. Awardees must attend a Minnesota Space Grant Consortium member institution. The Consortium actively encourages women, minority, and physically challenged students to apply. Applicant must be attending a Minnesota Space Grant Consortium school but does not have to be a resident of the state. Visit Website for application.

Amount of award:	$500-$2,500
Number of awards:	15
Number of applicants:	40
Application deadline:	May 15

Contact:
NASA Minnesota Space Grant Consortium
University of Minnesota
Dept. of Aerospace Engineering & Mechanics
Minneapolis, MN 55455
Phone: 612-626-9295
Web: www.aem.umn.edu/mnsgc

NASA Mississippi Space Grant Consortium

Community College Graduates Scholarship Program

Type of award: Scholarship, renewable.
Intended use: For full-time undergraduate study at 4-year institution. Designated institutions: Mississippi Space Grant Consortium member institutions.
Eligibility: Applicant must be U.S. citizen residing in Mississippi.
Basis for selection: Major/career interest in science, general; computer/information sciences; engineering or mathematics.
Application requirements: Recommendations, essay, transcript. Statement of goals and plan of study.
Additional information: Must be enrolled or recently graduated from a Mississippi Community College and will be a full-time STEM (Science, Technology, Engineering and Math) student at one of the eight Mississippi Space Grant Universities. Minimum 3.0 GPA.

Amount of award:	$3,000
Number of awards:	10
Application deadline:	March 21
Total amount awarded:	$30,000

Contact:
NASA Mississippi Space Grant Consortium
308 Vardman Hall
P.O. Box 1848
University, MS 38677-1848
Phone: 662-915-1187
Fax: 662-915-3927
Web: www.olemiss.edu/programs/nasa/

NASA Space Grant Mississippi Undergraduate Scholarship

Type of award: Scholarship, renewable.
Intended use: For full-time undergraduate or graduate study in United States. Designated institutions: University of Mississippi, Jackson State University, University of Southern Mississippi, Mississippi State University, Alcorn State University, Delta State University, Mississippi University for Women, Mississippi Valley State University, Coahoma Community College, Hinds Community College-Utica Campus, Itawamba Community College, Meridian Community College, Mississippi Delta Community College, Mississippi Gulf Coast Community College, Northeast Mississippi Community College, and Pearl River Community College.
Eligibility: Applicant must be U.S. citizen residing in Mississippi.
Basis for selection: Major/career interest in engineering; mathematics; science, general or aerospace. Applicant must demonstrate high academic achievement, leadership and seriousness of purpose.
Application requirements: Nomination by faculty mentor at participating Mississippi Space Grant Consortium member institution.
Additional information: Award amounts per term vary; contact sponsor. Awardees must attend Mississippi Space Grant Consortium member institution. Selection criteria vary by institution; most consider GPA, field of study and written essay. Most awards require research or public service activity. List of campus contacts available online. Applicants from groups traditionally underrepresented in space-related fields encouraged.

Number of awards:	40
Number of applicants:	120

Contact:
NASA Mississippi Space Grant Consortium
308 Vardaman Hall
P.O. Box 1848
University, MS 38677-1848
Phone: 662-915-1187
Fax: 662-915-3927
Web: www.olemiss.edu/programs/nasa/

NASA Missouri Space Grant Consortium

NASA Missouri State Space Grant Undergraduate Scholarship

Type of award: Scholarship, renewable.
Intended use: For full-time undergraduate study at accredited 4-year institution in United States. Designated institutions: Missouri State University, University of Missouri - Columbia, Missouri University of Science and Technology, University of Missouri - St. Louis, and Washington University in St. Louis.
Eligibility: Applicant must be U.S. citizen residing in Missouri.
Basis for selection: Major/career interest in aerospace; astronomy; engineering; geology/earth sciences; physics; mathematics or engineering, mechanical.
Application requirements: Recommendations, essay, transcript.
Additional information: Program encourages applications from eligible space science students. Awardees must attend Missouri Space Grant Consortium affiliate institution. Women, minority students, and physically challenged students are actively encouraged to apply. Deadline varies but is usually the first week in April. Check sponsor for exact date. Awards normally granted sometime in May.

Amount of award: $1,500-$3,500
Number of awards: 45
Number of applicants: 43
Application deadline: April 20
Total amount awarded: $140,000

Contact:
NASA Missouri Space Grant Consortium
University of Missouri - Rolla
226 Mechanical. Eng. Bldg.
Rolla, MO 65401-0249
Phone: 573-341-4887
Fax: 573-341-4607
Web: www.mst.edu/~spaceg

NASA Montana Space Grant Consortium

NASA Space Grant Montana Undergraduate Scholarship Program

Type of award: Scholarship, renewable.
Intended use: For full-time undergraduate study at accredited 2-year or 4-year institution in United States. Designated institutions: Montana Space Grant Consortium member institutions.
Eligibility: Applicant must be U.S. citizen.
Basis for selection: Major/career interest in aerospace; biology; chemistry; geology/earth sciences; physics; astronomy; computer/information sciences; engineering, chemical; engineering, civil or engineering, electrical/electronic. Applicant must demonstrate depth of character and leadership.
Additional information: Awards for one year, renewable on a competitive basis. Visit Website for more information.
Amount of award: $1,000
Application deadline: April 1

Contact:
NASA Space Grant Montana Space Grant Consortium
Montana State University
P.O. Box 173835
Bozeman, MT 59717-3835
Phone: 406-994-4223
Fax: 406-994-4452
Web: www.spacegrant.montana.edu

NASA Nevada Space Grant Consortium

NASA Space Grant Nevada Undergraduate Scholarship

Type of award: Scholarship.
Intended use: For full-time undergraduate or graduate study at accredited postsecondary institution in United States. Designated institutions: Nevada System of Higher Education institutions.
Eligibility: Applicant must be U.S. citizen residing in Nevada.
Basis for selection: Major/career interest in science, general; engineering; education; economics; business; mathematics or computer/information sciences.
Application requirements: Essay. Proof of GPA. Career goal statement, including applicant's motivation toward aerospace career.
Additional information: Math, science, engineering, or majors in relevant fields eligible to apply. Applications available on Website. Contact institution of interest for more detailed information, deadlines, award amounts, and application requirements.
Amount of award: $2,500-$5,000
Application deadline: April 11
Total amount awarded: $155,000

Contact:
Nevada Space Grant Consortium Christian H. Fritsen, Ph.D.
Desert Research Institute
2215 Raggio Parkway
Reno, NV 89512
Phone: 775-673-7674
Fax: 775-673-7485
Web: www.nevadaspacegrant.com

NASA New Mexico Space Grant Consortium

NASA Space Grant New Mexico Undergraduate Scholarship

Type of award: Research grant, renewable.
Intended use: For full-time sophomore, junior, senior or graduate study at accredited 4-year institution in United States. Designated institutions: New Mexico Space Grant Consortium institutions.
Eligibility: Applicant must be U.S. citizen residing in New Mexico.
Basis for selection: Major/career interest in astronomy; biology; chemistry; computer/information sciences; engineering, chemical; engineering, civil; engineering, electrical/electronic; engineering, mechanical; physics or mathematics.
Application requirements: Transcript, research proposal, nomination by faculty mentor.
Additional information: Minimum 3.0 GPA. Preference given to applicants who can show nonfederal matching funds. Women, minority students, and physically challenged students encouraged to apply. Application and deadline details on Website.
Amount of award: $2,000-$5,000
Number of applicants: 20
Application deadline: March 15
Notification begins: March 30
Total amount awarded: $100,000

Contact:
NASA New Mexico Space Grant Consortium
Program Office, New Mexico State University
3050 Knox St., Sugarman Space Grant Building
Las Cruces, NM 88003-0001
Phone: 505-646-6414
Fax: 505-646-7791
Web: spacegrant.nmsu.edu

NASA North Carolina Space Grant Consortium

Undergraduate Research Scholarship

Type of award: Scholarship.
Intended use: For full-time sophomore, junior or senior study. Designated institutions: North Carolina Space Grant Consortium member institution, including Appalachian State University, Elizabeth City State University, North Carolina State University, North Carolina Central University, Duke University, North Carolina A&T State University, Winston-Salem State University, University of North Carolina at Asheville, University of North Carolina at Charlotte, University of North Carolina at Chapel Hill, and University of North Carolina at Pembroke.
Eligibility: Applicant must be returning adult student. Applicant must be U.S. citizen residing in North Carolina.
Basis for selection: Major/career interest in science, general; engineering or aerospace. Applicant must demonstrate high academic achievement and leadership.
Application requirements: Recommendations, transcript, research proposal.
Additional information: Visit Website for more information and application.
  Amount of award: $2,000-$4,000
  Number of awards: 15
  Number of applicants: 15
  Application deadline: February 15
  Notification begins: April 15
Contact:
NASA North Carolina Space Grant
NCSU Box 7515
Raleigh, NC 27695
Phone: 919-515-5937 or 919-515-4240
Fax: 919-515-5934
Web: www.ncspacegrant.org/fs/

Undergraduate Scholarship Program

Type of award: Scholarship, renewable.
Intended use: For full-time freshman, sophomore or junior study at 4-year institution. Designated institutions: North Carolina Space Grant Consortium Member Institutions.
Eligibility: Applicant must be U.S. citizen residing in North Carolina.
Basis for selection: Major/career interest in science, general; engineering or aerospace. Applicant must demonstrate high academic achievement and leadership.
Application requirements: Recommendations, essay, transcript.
Additional information: May be new or returning adult student. Visit Website for application and more information.
  Amount of award: $1,000
  Number of awards: 10
  Number of applicants: 10
  Application deadline: February 15
  Notification begins: April 15
Contact:
NASA North Carolina Space Grant
NCSU Box 7515
Raleigh, NC 27695
Phone: 919-515-5937 or 919-515-4240
Fax: 919-515-5934
Web: www.ncspacegrant.org/fs/

NASA North Dakota Space Grant Consortium

NASA Space Grant North Dakota Consortium Lillian Goettler Scholarship

Type of award: Scholarship.
Intended use: For full-time undergraduate study in United States. Designated institutions: North Dakota State University.
Eligibility: Applicant must be female. Applicant must be U.S. citizen residing in North Dakota.
Basis for selection: Major/career interest in engineering; mathematics or science, general.
Additional information: Awarded to female undergraduate science or mathematics student, ideally involved in research project of interest to NASA. Minimum 3.5 GPA. Contact coordinator for deadline information.
  Amount of award: $2,500
Contact:
North Dakota Space Grant Consortium
U of North Dakota, Space Studies Dept.
P.O. Box 9008
Grand Forks, ND 58202-9008
Phone: 701-777-4856
Web: www.space.edu/spacegrant

NASA Space Grant North Dakota Undergraduate Scholarship

Type of award: Scholarship, renewable.
Intended use: For full-time undergraduate study.
Eligibility: Applicant must be U.S. citizen residing in North Dakota.
Basis for selection: Major/career interest in biology; chemistry; engineering; geology/earth sciences; computer/information sciences or mathematics.
Application requirements: Recommendations, transcript, nomination by participating North Dakota Space Grant Consortium member institution.
Additional information: Awardees must attend North Dakota Space Grant Consortium member institution, but does not need to be a resident of North Dakota. Consortium actively encourages women, minority students, and physically challenged students to apply. Deadlines vary. Contact financial aid office at institutions directly.
  Amount of award: $500-$750
Contact:
NASA Space Grant North Dakota Space Grant Consortium
U of North Dakota, Space Studies Dept.
P.O. Box 9008
Grand Forks, ND 58202-9008
Phone: 701-777-4856
Fax: 701-777-3711
Web: www.nd.spacegrant.org

Pearl I. Young Scholarship

Type of award: Scholarship.
Intended use: For full-time undergraduate study in United States. Designated institutions: University of North Dakota.
Eligibility: Applicant must be female. Applicant must be U.S. citizen or permanent resident residing in North Dakota.
Basis for selection: Major/career interest in biology; chemistry; engineering; geology/earth sciences; computer/information sciences or mathematics.
Additional information: Awarded to female undergraduate science or mathematics student. Applicants must have minimum 3.5 GPA and ideally be involved in research project of interest to NASA. Contact coordinator for deadline information.

Amount of award:	$2,500
Number of awards:	1

Contact:
NASA Space Grant North Dakota Space Grant Consortium
U of North Dakota, Space Studies Dept.
P.O. Box 9008
Grand Forks, ND 58202-9008
Phone: 701-777-4856
Web: www.space.edu/spacegrant

NASA Ohio Space Grant Consortium

NASA Ohio Space Grant Junior/Senior Scholarship Program

Type of award: Scholarship, renewable.
Intended use: For full-time junior or senior study at accredited 4-year institution. Designated institutions: Ohio Space Grant Consortium members: Air Force Institute of Technology, Case Western Reserve University, Cedarville College, Central State University, Cleveland State University, Marietta College, Ohio Northern University, Ohio University, Ohio State University, University of Akron, University of Cincinnati, University of Dayton, University of Toledo, Wilberforce University, Wright State University, Miami University, and Youngstown State University.
Eligibility: Applicant must be U.S. citizen residing in Ohio.
Basis for selection: Major/career interest in science, general; engineering; aerospace or mathematics.
Application requirements: Recommendations, essay, transcript. Proposal of research project.
Additional information: Awards are $2,000 for juniors, $3,000 for seniors. Must attend a Consortium member institution.

Amount of award:	$2,000-$3,000
Number of awards:	50
Number of applicants:	150
Application deadline:	February 28
Notification begins:	April 30
Total amount awarded:	$130,000

Contact:
NASA Ohio Space Grant Consortium
OAI
22800 Cedar Point Road
Cleveland, OH 44142
Phone: 800-828-6742
Web: www.osgc.org

NASA Oregon Space Grant Consortium

NASA Space Grant Oregon Undergraduate Scholarship

Type of award: Scholarship.
Intended use: For full-time undergraduate study at accredited 2-year or 4-year institution in United States. Designated institutions: Oregon State University, University of Oregon, Portland State University, Eastern Oregon University, Southern Oregon University, Oregon Institute of Technology, Linfield College, Western Oregon University, George Fox University, Portland Community Colleges (Sylvania, Rock Creek and Cascades Campuses), Lane Community College.
Eligibility: Applicant must be U.S. citizen residing in Oregon.
Basis for selection: Major/career interest in science, general; engineering; aerospace; mathematics or physical sciences. Applicant must demonstrate high academic achievement.
Application requirements: Recommendations, essay, transcript.
Additional information: Must attend one of the designated institutions. Contact Space Grant Consortium representative on campus or see Website for application deadlines and more information.

Amount of award:	$500-$5,000
Number of awards:	30
Number of applicants:	75
Notification begins:	November 1
Total amount awarded:	$30,000

Contact:
Oregon NASA Space Grant Consortium
Oregon State University
92 Kerr Administration Bldg.
Corvallis, OR 97331-2103
Phone: 541-737-2414
Fax: 541-737-9946
Web: www.spacegrant.oregonstate.edu

NASA Pennsylvania Space Grant Consortium

NASA Pennsylvania Space Grant Undergraduate Scholarship

Type of award: Scholarship.
Intended use: For full-time junior or senior study at accredited 4-year institution in United States. Designated institutions: Pennsylvania State University, Carnegie Mellon University, Lincoln University, Abington College, Susquehanna University, Temple University, West Chester University, University of Pittsburgh, California University of Pennsylvania, Franklin and Marshall University, and Gettysburg College.
Eligibility: Applicant must be U.S. citizen residing in Pennsylvania.
Basis for selection: Major/career interest in science, general; mathematics; engineering; education; aerospace or astronomy. Applicant must demonstrate high academic achievement.
Application requirements: Recommendations, essay, transcript.

Additional information: Competitive scholarships provided for undergraduates at Pennsylvania Space Grant Consortium member institutions. Sylvia Stein Memorial Space Grant Scholarship at Penn State University (two one-year scholarships for $4,000 per year) awarded to outstanding undergraduate with extensive community service. Other awards and eligibility requirements vary with institution. Earth science students also eligible. Contact campus Space Grant Consortium representative for details. Consortium actively encourages women, minority, and physically challenged students to apply.

| Amount of award: | $500-$4,000 |

Contact:
NASA Pennsylvania Space Grant Consortium
Penn State, University Park
2217 Earth-Engineering Sciences Building
University Park, PA 16802
Phone: 814-865-2535
Fax: 814-863-8286
Web: www.psu.edu/spacegrant

NASA Rhode Island Space Grant Consortium

NASA Space Grant Rhode Island Summer Undergraduate Scholarship

Type of award: Scholarship.
Intended use: For sophomore, junior or senior study at postsecondary institution. Designated institutions: Rhode Island Space Grant Consortium member institutions: Brown University, Bryant College, Community College of Rhode Island, Providence College, Roger Williams University, Rhode Island College, Rhode Island School of Design, Salve Regina University, University of Rhode Island, Wheaton College.
Eligibility: Applicant must be U.S. citizen residing in Rhode Island.
Basis for selection: Major/career interest in physics; engineering; biology; geology/earth sciences or aerospace. Applicant must demonstrate high academic achievement.
Application requirements: Interview, recommendations, essay, transcript. Research proposal, resume.
Additional information: Awardees expected to work full-time with 75 percent of time devoted to research and the other 25 percent to science education outreach. Applications due in late February; call sponsor for exact dates. Number of awards may vary. Topics of study in space sciences also funded. Students should contact campus representative or the Rhode Island Space Grant office.

Amount of award:	$4,000
Number of awards:	4
Number of applicants:	15

Contact:
NASA Rhode Island Space Grant Consortium
Brown University
Box 1846
Providence, RI 02912
Phone: 401-863-2889
Fax: 401-863-3978
Web: www.planetary.brown.edu/RI_Space_Grant/

Undergraduate Research Scholarship

Type of award: Scholarship, renewable.
Intended use: For sophomore, junior or senior study at postsecondary institution. Designated institutions: Rhode Island Space Grant Consortium member institutions: Brown University, Bryant College, Community College of Rhode Island, Providence College, Roger Williams University, Rhode Island College, Rhode Island School of Design, Salve Regina University, University of Rhode Island, Wheaton College.
Eligibility: Applicant must be U.S. citizen residing in Rhode Island.
Basis for selection: Major/career interest in physics; engineering; biology; geology/earth sciences or aerospace. Applicant must demonstrate high academic achievement.
Application requirements: Interview, recommendations, essay, transcript. Research proposal, resume.
Additional information: Awardees expected to devote four hours per week to science education outreach. Application deadline in late February; call sponsor for exact dates. Number of awards may vary. Topics of study in space sciences also funded. Students should contact their campus representative or the Rhode Island Space Grant office.

Amount of award:	$4,000
Number of awards:	3
Number of applicants:	5

Contact:
NASA Rhode Island Space Grant Consortium
Brown University
Box 1846
Providence, RI 02912
Phone: 401-863-2889
Fax: 401-863-3978
Web: www.planetary.brown.edu/RI_Space_Grant/

NASA Rocky Mountain Space Grant Consortium

NASA Rocky Mountain Space Grant Consortium Undergraduate Scholarship

Type of award: Scholarship, renewable.
Intended use: For full-time undergraduate or graduate study in United States. Designated institutions: Utah State University, University of Utah, Brigham Young University, University of Denver, Weber State University, and Southern Utah University.
Eligibility: Applicant must be U.S. citizen.
Basis for selection: Major/career interest in science, general or engineering. Applicant must demonstrate high academic achievement.
Application requirements: Recommendations, transcript, research proposal. Resume.
Additional information: Award varies from year to year. Contact sponsor for deadline information. Must be used at Rocky Mountain Space Grant Consortium member institution. Award amounts are per month during academic year.

Amount of award:	$200-$1,500
Number of awards:	20
Number of applicants:	60

Contact:
Rocky Mountain NASA Space Grant Consortium
Utah State University
EL Building, Room 302
Logan, UT 84332-4140
Phone: 435-797-3666
Fax: 435-797-3382
Web: spacegrant.usu.edu

NASA South Carolina Space Grant Consortium

Kathryn D. Sullivan Science and Engineering Fellowship

Type of award: Scholarship, renewable.
Intended use: For full-time senior study at 4-year institution. Designated institutions: SCSGC member institutions: Benedict College, The Citadel, Claflin University, Clemson University, Coastal Carolina University, Francis Marion University, Furman University, Medical University of South Carolina, South Carolina State University, University of South Carolina, Wofford College.
Eligibility: Applicant must be high school senior. Applicant must be U.S. citizen residing in South Carolina.
Basis for selection: Major/career interest in science, general; engineering; mathematics or aerospace. Applicant must demonstrate high academic achievement.
Application requirements: Recommendations, essay, transcript. Faculty sponsorship.
Additional information: Applicants must attend South Carolina member institution. Applicants must have sponsorship from faculty advisor. The Consortium actively encourages women, minority, and disabled students to apply. Application deadline usually in January.

Amount of award:	$7,000
Number of awards:	1
Application deadline:	December 14

Contact:
NASA South Carolina Space Grant Consortium Tara B. Scozzaro, MPA
College of Charleston, Department of Geology
66 George St.
Charleston, SC 29424
Phone: 843-953-5463
Fax: 843-953-5446
Web: www.cofc.edu/~scsgrant/scholar/overview

NASA Space Grant South Carolina Undergraduate Academic Year Research Program

Type of award: Research grant, renewable.
Intended use: For full-time junior or senior study at accredited 4-year institution in United States. Designated institutions: SCSGC member institutions: Benedict College, The Citadel, Claflin University, Clemson University, Coastal Carolina University, Francis Marion University, Furman University, Medical University of South Carolina, South Carolina State University, University of South Carolina, Wofford College.
Eligibility: Applicant must be U.S. citizen residing in South Carolina.
Basis for selection: Major/career interest in mathematics; science, general; astronomy; aerospace; engineering, mechanical; geophysics or atmospheric sciences/meteorology. Applicant must demonstrate high academic achievement.
Application requirements: Recommendations, essay, transcript, research proposal. Faculty sponsorship.
Additional information: Applicants must attend South Carolina Space Grant Consortium member institution. Applicants must have sponsorship from a faculty advisor. Applicants may have a field of study or interest related to any NASA enterprise. Presentation and written report on project findings due within one year of completion. Consortium actively encourages women, minority, and disabled students to apply. Application deadline usually in January. See Website for application and more details.

Amount of award:	$5,000
Application deadline:	December 14

Contact:
NASA South Carolina Space Grant Consortium Tara B. Scozzaro MPA
College of Charleston, Department of Geology
66 George St.
Charleston, SC 29424
Phone: 843-953-5463
Fax: 843-953-5446
Web: www.cofc.edu/~scsgrant/scholar/overview

NASA Texas Space Grant Consortium

NASA Space Grant Texas Undergraduate Scholarship Program

Type of award: Scholarship.
Intended use: For full-time junior or senior study at accredited 4-year institution in United States. Designated institutions: Texas Space Grant member institutions.
Eligibility: Applicant must be U.S. citizen.
Basis for selection: Applicant must demonstrate high academic achievement and leadership.
Application requirements: Recommendations, essay, transcript, proof of eligibility.
Additional information: Awardees must be sophomores or juniors, or in second year at junior college at time of application. May be first or second year students at medical school. Must attend Texas Space Grant Consortium member institution. Online application.

Amount of award:	$1,000
Number of awards:	15
Number of applicants:	40
Application deadline:	March 10
Total amount awarded:	$15,000

Contact:
Texas Space Grant Consortium
3925 W. Braker Lane
Suite 200
Austin, TX 78759-5321
Phone: 800-248-8742
Web: www.tsgc.utexas.edu

NASA Vermont Space Grant Consortium

NASA Space Grant Vermont Consortium Undergraduate Scholarships

Type of award: Scholarship, renewable.
Intended use: For full-time undergraduate study in United States.
Eligibility: Applicant must be high school senior. Applicant must be U.S. citizen residing in Vermont.
Basis for selection: Major/career interest in science, general; engineering; mathematics; aerospace or physics.
Application requirements: Recommendations, essay, transcript.
Additional information: Open to high school seniors who intend to be enrolled full time in the following year. Applicant must be enrolled in program relevant to NASA's goals at a Vermont institution. Minimum 3.0 GPA. Out-of-state recipients qualify for in-state tuition. Three awards designated for Native American applicants; three scholarships designated for Burlington Technical Center Aviation & Technical Center, Aerospace Work Force Development, and Aviation Technical School. Can be used at any accredited Vermont institution of higher education.

Amount of award:	$2,000
Number of awards:	15
Number of applicants:	25
Application deadline:	March 1
Notification begins:	March 15
Total amount awarded:	$22,500

Contact:
Vermont Space Grant Consortium
Votey Hall, College of Engineering and Math
University of Vermont
Burlington, VT 05405-0156
Phone: 802-656-1429
Web: www.cems.uvm.edu/VSGC

NASA Virginia Space Grant Consortium

Aerospace Undergraduate Research Scholarship Program

Type of award: Scholarship.
Intended use: For full-time undergraduate study at accredited 4-year institution in United States. Designated institutions: Space Grant Consortium schools: College of William and Mary, Hampton University, Old Dominion University, University of Virginia, Virginia Tech.
Eligibility: Applicant must be U.S. citizen residing in Virginia.
Basis for selection: Major/career interest in aerospace; astronomy; chemistry; computer/information sciences; engineering; geology/earth sciences; mathematics or physics. Applicant must demonstrate high academic achievement.
Application requirements: Recommendations, essay, transcript, research proposal. Resume.
Additional information: Any undergraduate major that includes coursework related to an understanding of aerospace is eligible. Minimum 3.0 GPA. Awards can include $3,000 stipend plus $1,000 travel/research during the academic year, and $3,500 stipend plus $1,000 travel/research during the summer (ten weeks). Awardees must attend a Virginia Space Grant Consortium member institution. The consortium actively encourages women, minorities, and students with disabilities to apply.

Amount of award:	$3,000-$8,500
Application deadline:	February 11
Notification begins:	April 15

Contact:
Virginia Space Grant Consortium
Old Dominion University Peninsula Center
600 Butler Farm Road, Ste. 2253
Hampton, VA 23666
Phone: 757-766-5210
Fax: 757-766-5205
Web: www.vsgc.odu.edu

NASA Space Grant Teacher Education Scholarship

Type of award: Scholarship.
Intended use: For full-time undergraduate study in United States. Designated institutions: College of William and Mary, Hampton University, Old Dominion University, University of Virginia, Virginia Tech.
Eligibility: Applicant must be U.S. citizen.
Basis for selection: Major/career interest in education; computer/information sciences; mathematics or science, general.
Application requirements: Recommendations, essay, transcript.
Additional information: Applicants must be enrolled in course of study leading to precollege teacher certification. Priority given to technology education, mathematics, and earth/space/environmental science majors. Minimum 3.0 GPA. High school seniors eligible. See Website for application and additional information.

Amount of award:	$1,000
Application deadline:	February 28
Notification begins:	April 1
Total amount awarded:	$10,000

Contact:
Virginia Space Grant Consortium
Old Dominion University Peninsula Center
600 Butler Farm Road, Ste. 2253
Hampton, VA 23666
Phone: 757-766-5210
Fax: 757-766-5205
Web: www.vsgc.odu.edu

NASA Space Grant Virginia Community College Scholarship

Type of award: Scholarship.
Intended use: For sophomore study at accredited 2-year institution in United States. Designated institutions: Virginia community colleges.
Eligibility: Applicant must be U.S. citizen residing in Virginia.
Basis for selection: Major/career interest in aerospace; computer/information sciences; electronics; engineering; mathematics or science, general.
Application requirements: Recommendations, essay, transcript. Resume, photograph and biographical information.

Additional information: Awards are generally to full-time students (12 semester hours), but part-time students (six to nine hours) demonstrating academic achievements are also eligible. Minimum 3.0 GPA. Scholarship is open to students at all community colleges in Virginia. Application deadline may vary. Women, minorities, and students with disabilities are encouraged to apply. Visit Website for application.

Amount of award:	$1,500
Application deadline:	February 28
Notification begins:	April 1

Contact:
Virginia Space Grant Consortium
600 Butler Farm Road, Suite 2253
Hampton, VA 23666
Phone: 757-766-5210
Fax: 757-766-5205
Web: www.vsgc.odu.edu

NASA West Virginia Space Grant Consortium

NASA West Virginia Space Grant Undergraduate Research Fellowship

Type of award: Scholarship.
Intended use: For full-time undergraduate study at accredited 4-year institution in United States. Designated institutions: West Virginia University, Bethany College, Fairmont State College, Marshall University, Salem International University, Shepherd College, West Virginia University Institute of Technology, West Virginia State College, Wheeling-Jesuit University, West Liberty State College, and West Virginia Wesleyan College.
Eligibility: Applicant must be U.S. citizen residing in West Virginia.
Basis for selection: Major/career interest in aerospace; science, general; engineering or mathematics. Applicant must demonstrate high academic achievement and seriousness of purpose.
Application requirements: Research proposal. Letter of endorsement from faculty advisor. Proposal must include statement of purpose, methodology, expected results, and timeline.
Additional information: Visit Website for more information and to download application. Female and minority students encouraged to apply.

Amount of award:	$3,000-$5,000
Application deadline:	March 7
Notification begins:	April 1

Contact:
NASA West Virginia Space Grant Consortium
G-68 Engineering Sciences Building
P.O. Box 6070
Morgantown, WV 26506-6070
Phone: 304-293-4099 ext. 3738
Fax: 304-293-4970
Web: www.nasa.wvu.edu

NASA Wisconsin Space Grant Consortium

NASA Space Grant Wisconsin Consortium Undergraduate Research Program

Type of award: Research grant.
Intended use: For full-time undergraduate study at 2-year or 4-year institution. Designated institutions: WSGC colleges and universities.
Eligibility: Applicant must be U.S. citizen.
Basis for selection: Major/career interest in aerospace; astronomy; engineering; science, general; architecture; law; business or medicine. Applicant must demonstrate high academic achievement and seriousness of purpose.
Application requirements: Transcript, research proposal. Project proposal with budget. Two letters of recommendation.
Additional information: Funding for qualified students to create and implement a research project related to aerospace, space science, or other interdisciplinary space-related studies. For academic year or summer term use. Award up to $3,500; additional $500 for exceptional expenses. Minimum 3.0 GPA and above-average SAT/ACT scores required. Consortium encourages applications from women, minorities, and students with disabilities. For more information, see Website.

Application deadline:	February 4
Notification begins:	April 7
Total amount awarded:	$3,500

Contact:
Wisconsin Space Grant Consortium
Space Science and Engineering Center
1225 W. Dayton Street, Room 251
Madison, WI 53706-1280
Phone: 608-263-4206
Fax: 608-262-5974
Web: www.uwgb.edu/wsgc

NASA Space Grant Wisconsin Consortium Undergraduate Scholarship

Type of award: Scholarship, renewable.
Intended use: For full-time undergraduate study at accredited 4-year institution in United States. Designated institutions: WSGC colleges and universities.
Eligibility: Applicant must be U.S. citizen.
Basis for selection: Major/career interest in aerospace; astronomy; engineering; physics or science, general. Applicant must demonstrate high academic achievement.
Application requirements: Essay, transcript. Two letters of recommendation. One- to two-page statement of intent.
Additional information: Applicant must attend Wisconsin Space Grant Consortium member institution and reside in Wisconsin during school year. Minimum 3.0 GPA and above-average SAT/ACT scores required. Award amount varies; maximum is $1,500. Qualified students may also apply for summer session's Undergraduate Research Award. Consortium actively encourages women, minorities, and students with disabilities to apply. See Website for application and details.

Application deadline:	February 4
Notification begins:	April 7
Total amount awarded:	$1,500

Contact:
Associate Director for Fellowships, Wisconsin Space Grant Consortium
University of Wisconsin - Green Bay
2420 Nicolet Drive
Green Bay, WI 54311-7001
Phone: 920-465-2446
Fax: 920-465-2376
Web: www.uwgb.edu/WSGC

NASA Wyoming Space Grant Consortium

NASA Wyoming Space Grant Undergraduate Research Fellowships

Type of award: Research grant.
Intended use: For undergraduate study at accredited postsecondary institution in United States. Designated institutions: Eligible Wyoming institutions.
Eligibility: Applicant must be U.S. citizen.
Basis for selection: Major/career interest in aerospace; engineering; science, general; energy research or mathematics. Applicant must demonstrate high academic achievement.
Application requirements: Transcript, proof of eligibility, research proposal.
Additional information: Funding for research projects available through Wyoming Space Grant program. Contact Space Grant Office at the University of Wyoming. Proposals that cannot be funded from other sources given priority. Research expected to result in refereed publication. Underrepresented groups encouraged to apply. Contact sponsor for complete list of eligible Wyoming institutions. Deadline in mid-February; visit Website for more details.

Amount of award:	$5,000
Number of awards:	8
Number of applicants:	10
Total amount awarded:	$40,000

Contact:
Wyoming NASA Space Grant Consortium University of Wyoming
Dept. 3905
1000 East University Avenue
Laramie, WY 82071-3905
Phone: 307-766-2862
Web: wyomingspacegrant.uwyo.edu

National Academy for Nuclear Training

Scholarship Educational Assistance Program

Type of award: Scholarship, renewable.
Intended use: For full-time junior or senior study at accredited 4-year institution in United States.
Eligibility: Applicant must be U.S. citizen.
Basis for selection: Major/career interest in engineering, chemical; engineering, mechanical; engineering, electrical/electronic or engineering, nuclear. Applicant must demonstrate high academic achievement, depth of character, leadership, seriousness of purpose and service orientation.
Application requirements: Recommendations, transcript, proof of eligibility by INFO member utility.
Additional information: Minimum 3.0 GPA. Renewal for eligible students. Additional field of study: power generation health physics. Study of chemical engineering must include nuclear or power option. Applicant should be considering career in nuclear utility industry. For additional information and important dates, contact by e-mail or visit Website.

Amount of award:	$2,500
Number of awards:	60
Number of applicants:	120
Application deadline:	July 2
Notification begins:	August 1
Total amount awarded:	$150,000

Contact:
National Academy for Nuclear Training Scholarship Program
301 ACT Drive, P.O. Box 4030
Iowa City, IA 52243-4030
Phone: 800-294-7492
Web: www.nei.org/nantscholarships

National Amateur Baseball Federation, Inc.

National Amateur Baseball Federation Scholarship

Type of award: Scholarship, renewable.
Intended use: For undergraduate study in United States or Canada.
Eligibility: Applicant or parent must be member/participant of National Amateur Baseball Federation.
Basis for selection: Competition/talent/interest in athletics/sports. Major/career interest in athletic training. Applicant must demonstrate financial need and high academic achievement.
Application requirements: Recommendations, transcript, proof of eligibility, nomination. Written statement. Documentation of previous awards received from sponsoring association, nomination by president or director of franchised member team.
Additional information: Amount of award determined annually. Applicant must have participated in National Amateur Baseball Federation event in the current season and be sponsored by National Amateur Baseball Federation member association. Send SASE for application packet.

Amount of award:	$500-$1,000
Number of awards:	14
Number of applicants:	14
Application deadline:	October 1
Notification begins:	January 1

Contact:
National Amateur Baseball Federation
Attn: Chairman Awards Committee
P.O. Box 705
Bowie, MD 20718
Phone: 301-464-5460
Web: www.nabf.com

National Art Materials Trade Association

NAMTA Educational Assistance Award

Type of award: Scholarship.
Intended use: For undergraduate or graduate study at accredited vocational, 2-year, 4-year or graduate institution.
Eligibility: Applicant or parent must be member/participant of National Art Materials Trade Association.
Basis for selection: Applicant must demonstrate financial need and high academic achievement.
Application requirements: Essay, transcript. Proof of acceptance.
Additional information: Applicant must be employee or family member of employee of NAMTA member firm. Applicants must have graduated high school by July 1, 2008. All application materials must be mailed together.
- Amount of award: $1,000
- Number of awards: 3
- Application deadline: March 15

Contact:
National Art Materials Trade Association
15806 Brookway Drive, Suite 300
Huntersville, NC 28078
Phone: 704-892-6244
Fax: 704-892-6247
Web: www.namta.org

NAMTA Foundation Visual Arts Major Scholarship

Type of award: Scholarship.
Intended use: For undergraduate study at accredited postsecondary institution.
Eligibility: Applicant or parent must be member/participant of National Art Materials Trade Association.
Basis for selection: Major/career interest in arts, general; arts management or art/art history. Applicant must demonstrate financial need and high academic achievement.
Application requirements: Essay, transcript. Proof of acceptance, 3-6 examples of work via CD or email.
Additional information: Applicant must major in visual arts or visual arts education. Applicants judged on basis of financial need, GPA, extracurricular activities and special interests.
- Amount of award: $1,000
- Number of awards: 8
- Number of applicants: 83
- Application deadline: April 1
- Notification begins: June 15
- Total amount awarded: $8,000

Contact:
Karen Brown, National Art Materials Trade Association
15806 Brookway Drive
Suite 300
Huntersville, NC 28078
Phone: 704-892-6244
Fax: 704-892-6247
Web: www.namtafoundation.org

National Association for Equal Opporuntiy in Higher Education (NAFEO)

"Writers of Passage" Essay Contest

Type of award: Scholarship.
Intended use: For full-time undergraduate study. Designated institutions: Historically Black Colleges and Universities; Predominately Black Institutions.
Eligibility: Applicant must be African American.
Basis for selection: Competition/talent/interest in writing/journalism. Applicant must demonstrate financial need.
Application requirements: Transcript. FAFSA, SAR, federal tax forms, 500-word essay, telling compelling story about obstacles overcome.
Additional information: $5,000 award for student and $20,000 grant for school. Minimum 2.5 GPA.
- Number of awards: 4
- Number of applicants: 100
- Application deadline: February 15
- Notification begins: March 15
- Total amount awarded: $25,000

Contact:
The "Writers of Passage" Essay Contest (NAFEO)
209 Third Street, S.E.
Washington, DC 20003
Phone: 202-552-3300
Web: www.nafeo.org or www.salliemaefund.org

National Association of Black Accountants Inc.

NABA National Scholarship Program

Type of award: Scholarship.
Intended use: For full-time undergraduate or master's study at 4-year or graduate institution.
Eligibility: Applicant or parent must be member/participant of National Association of Black Accountants. Applicant must be Alaskan native, Asian American, African American, Mexican American, Hispanic American, Puerto Rican or American Indian.
Basis for selection: Major/career interest in accounting; business or finance/banking. Applicant must demonstrate depth of character, leadership and service orientation.
Application requirements: Essay, transcript, proof of eligibility. Autobiography discussing career objectives, leadership abilities, community activities and involvement with NABA (500 words or less). Resume and two letters of recommendation.
Additional information: Applicants must have minimum 2.5 GPA for some awards, 3.3 GPA for others. Applicants must join association by December 31.

Amount of award:	$1,000-$10,000
Number of awards:	70
Number of applicants:	400
Application deadline:	January 31
Notification begins:	September 1
Total amount awarded:	$7,100,000

Contact:
National Association of Black Accountants Inc.
National Scholarship Program
7249-A Hanover Parkway
Greenbelt, MD 20770
Phone: 301-474-6222
Fax: 301-474-3114
Web: www.nabainc.org

National Association of Black Journalists

Allison E. Fisher Scholarship

Type of award: Scholarship.
Intended use: For undergraduate or graduate study.
Eligibility: Applicant must be U.S. citizen, permanent resident or international student.
Basis for selection: Major/career interest in journalism.
Application requirements: Essay, transcript. Resumer, work samples. Must send four copies of all application materials.
Additional information: Minimum 3.0 GPA. Must be a print or broadcast journalism major and a member of NABJ.

Number of awards:	1
Application deadline:	March 17
Total amount awarded:	$2,500

Contact:
National Association of Black Journalists
University of Maryland
8701-A Adelphi Road
Adelphi, MD 20783-1716
Phone: 866-479-6225
Fax: 301-445-7101
Web: www.nabj.org

Carole Simpson Scholarship

Type of award: Scholarship.
Intended use: For undergraduate or graduate study at 4-year or graduate institution.
Eligibility: Applicant must be U.S. citizen, permanent resident or international student.
Basis for selection: Major/career interest in journalism.
Application requirements: Essay, transcript. Resume, work samples. Must send in four copies of all application materials.
Additional information: Minimum 2.5 GPA. Applicant must be member of NABJ and major in broadcast journalism.

Amount of award:	$2,500
Number of awards:	1
Application deadline:	March 17

Contact:
National Association of Black Journalists
University of Maryland
8701-A Adelphi Road
Adelphi, MD 20783-1716
Phone: 866-479-6225
Fax: 301-445-7101
Web: www.nabj.org

NABJ Scholarship

Type of award: Scholarship.
Intended use: For undergraduate or graduate study in United States.
Eligibility: Applicant must be African American.
Basis for selection: Major/career interest in journalism or radio/television/film. Applicant must demonstrate financial need.
Application requirements: Recommendations, essay, transcript, nomination. Essay must demonstrate why applicant wants to become a journalist. Resume, examples of work required. Four copies of all application materials (only one transcript need be official).
Additional information: Must be a student member of National Association of Black Journalists to apply for and participate in NABJ Mentor Program. Applicants of African descent from countries outside United States also eligible. Applicant must either be going into a journalism degree program, have position on their school newspaper or have position on campus TV station, radio station or Website. Applicant must maintain minimum 2.5 GPA and attend NABJ convention to work on convention student project.

Amount of award:	$2,500
Application deadline:	March 17
Total amount awarded:	$60,000

Contact:
NABJ Scholarship Programs
8701 Adelphi Road
Adelphi, MD 20783-1716
Phone: 301-445-7100 ext. 108
Fax: 301-445-7101
Web: www.nabj.org/programs/scholarships

National Association of Letter Carriers

Costas G. Lemonopoulos Scholarship

Type of award: Scholarship, renewable.
Intended use: For full-time undergraduate study at accredited 4-year institution. Designated institutions: St. Petersburg Junior College or four-year public Florida university.
Eligibility: Applicant or parent must be member/participant of National Association of Letter Carriers. Applicant must be high school senior.
Basis for selection: Applicant must demonstrate high academic achievement.
Application requirements: Transcript. SAT/ACT scores and NALC form.
Additional information: Applicant must be child of NALC member in good standing (active, retired, or deceased). Preliminary application available on Website; required for further details and primary application form. Notification published in March issue of Postal Record magazine.

Number of awards:	20
Application deadline:	June 1

Contact:
National Association of Letter Carriers
Costas G. Lemonopoulos Scholarship Trust
100 Indiana Avenue NW
Washington, DC 20001-2144
Phone: 202-393-4695
Fax: 202-737-1540
Web: www.nalc.org/nalc/members/scholarships.html

William C. Doherty - John T. Donelson Scholarships

Type of award: Scholarship, renewable.
Intended use: For full-time undergraduate study at accredited 4-year institution.
Eligibility: Applicant or parent must be member/participant of National Association of Letter Carriers. Applicant must be high school senior.
Basis for selection: Applicant must demonstrate financial need and high academic achievement.
Application requirements: Recommendations, essay, transcript, proof of eligibility. SAT/ACT scores.
Additional information: Applicant must be child of letter carrier NALC member in good standing (active, retired, or deceased). Preliminary application on Website due December 31; supporting materials due March 31. Notification published in July issue of Postal Record magazine.

Amount of award:	$1,000-$4,000
Number of awards:	5
Number of applicants:	5
Application deadline:	December 31, March 31
Total amount awarded:	$21,000

Contact:
National Association of Letter Carriers
Scholarship Committee
100 Indiana Avenue NW
Washington, DC 20001-2144
Phone: 202-393-4695
Fax: 202-393-4695
Web: www.nalc.org/nalc/members/scholarships.html

National Association of Water Companies (NJ Chapter)

Water Companies (NJ Chapter) Scholarship

Type of award: Scholarship.
Intended use: For freshman, sophomore, junior, senior or graduate study at accredited 2-year, 4-year or graduate institution in United States.
Eligibility: Applicant must be U.S. citizen residing in New Jersey.
Basis for selection: Major/career interest in hydrology; natural resources/conservation; science, general; engineering, environmental; finance/banking; communications; accounting; business; computer/information sciences or law. Applicant must demonstrate financial need, high academic achievement, depth of character, leadership, seriousness of purpose and service orientation.
Application requirements: Recommendations, essay, transcript. Essay must illustrate interest in water utility industry or related field.
Additional information: Applicant must have interest in fields of study related to water industry. Acceptable fields of study also include consumer affairs and human resources. At least five years residence in New Jersey required. Minimum 3.0 GPA.

Amount of award:	$2,500
Number of awards:	2
Number of applicants:	80
Application deadline:	April 1
Notification begins:	June 1
Total amount awarded:	$5,000

Contact:
Nat'l Assn. of Water Companies (NJ Chapter)
Gail P. Brady
49 Howell Drive
Verona, NJ 07044
Phone: 973-669-5807

National Association of Women in Construction

Women in Construction: Founders' Scholarship

Type of award: Scholarship.
Intended use: For full-time undergraduate study at accredited postsecondary institution in United States or Canada.
Eligibility: Applicant must be U.S. citizen.
Basis for selection: Major/career interest in construction; construction management; engineering, construction or architecture. Applicant must demonstrate financial need and high academic achievement.
Application requirements: Interview, recommendations, essay, transcript. Resume.
Additional information: Number and amount of awards vary. Interest in construction, extracurricular activities, and employment experience also taken into consideration. Applicants must have completed one term of study in construction-related field. Must have current GPA of 3.0 or higher. Only semifinalists will be interviewed. Visit Website for additional information and to download application.

Amount of award:	$1,000-$2,000
Number of awards:	16
Application deadline:	March 15
Notification begins:	April 1
Total amount awarded:	$25,000

Contact:
National Association of Women in Construction
327 South Adams Street
Fort Worth, TX 76104
Phone: 800-552-3506
Web: www.nawic.org

National Athletic Trainers' Association Research & Education Foundation

Athletic Trainers' Entry Level Scholarship

Type of award: Scholarship.
Intended use: For full-time junior, senior, master's or doctoral study at 4-year or graduate institution.
Eligibility: Applicant or parent must be member/participant of National Athletic Trainers Association.
Basis for selection: Major/career interest in athletic training. Applicant must demonstrate high academic achievement.
Application requirements: Recommendations, essay, transcript, proof of eligibility, nomination by BOC certified trainer. Must apply to become NATA member by November 1st.
Additional information: Minimum 3.2 GPA required. Intention to pursue the profession of athletic training as career required. Must be sponsored by a certified athletic trainer. See complete guidelines on Website.

Amount of award:	$2,000
Number of awards:	70
Number of applicants:	213
Application deadline:	February 10
Notification begins:	April 15
Total amount awarded:	$136,000

Contact:
National Athletic Trainers' Association
Research & Education Foundation
2952 Stemmons Freeway
Dallas, TX 75247
Phone: 214-637-6282 ext. 127
Fax: 214-637-2206
Web: www.natafoundation.org

Athletic Trainers' Student Writing Contest

Type of award: Scholarship.
Intended use: For undergraduate or graduate study at 2-year, 4-year or graduate institution.
Eligibility: Applicant or parent must be member/participant of National Athletic Trainers Association.
Basis for selection: Competition/talent/interest in writing/journalism. Major/career interest in athletic training. Applicant must demonstrate high academic achievement.
Application requirements: Essay, proof of eligibility.
Additional information: Applicants must submit one original and two copies of essay. Topic may be case report, literature review, experimental report, analysis of training room techniques, etc. Must not have been published or be under consideration for publication. Award varies depending on availability of funds. See NATA News bulletin for more information.

Number of awards:	1
Application deadline:	February 1
Notification begins:	April 15

Contact:
National Athletic Trainer's Association
2952 Stemmons Freeway
Dallas, TX 75247
Phone: 214-637-6282
Web: www.natafoundation.org

National Black Nurses Association

Black Nurses Scholarship

Type of award: Scholarship.
Intended use: For undergraduate or graduate study.
Eligibility: Applicant or parent must be member/participant of National Black Nurses' Association. Applicant must be African American.
Basis for selection: Major/career interest in nursing or nurse practitioner. Applicant must demonstrate leadership, seriousness of purpose and service orientation.
Application requirements: Transcript. Evidence of participation in both student nursing activities and the African-American community. Two-page double-spaced essay describing extracurricular activities, community involvement, how role as nurse can improve the health and/or social conditions of African Americans and statement about future goals in nursing. Two letters of recommendation from school of nursing and local chapter or nurse from local area. Full frontal picture.
Additional information: Applicants must be currently enrolled in a nursing program and have at least one full year of school left. Must be in good academic standing. Call association for current information on program.

Amount of award:	$1,000-$2,000
Number of awards:	10
Number of applicants:	50
Application deadline:	April 15
Notification begins:	July 1

Contact:
National Black Nurses Association
8630 Fenton Street
Silver Spring, MD 20910
Phone: 301-589-3200
Fax: 301-589-3223
Web: www.nbna.org

National Black Police Association

Alphonso Deal Scholarship

Type of award: Scholarship.
Intended use: For freshman study at 2-year or 4-year institution in United States.
Eligibility: Applicant must be enrolled in high school. Applicant must be U.S. citizen.
Basis for selection: Major/career interest in law or criminal justice/law enforcement. Applicant must demonstrate high academic achievement, depth of character, seriousness of purpose and service orientation.

Application requirements: Recommendations, essay, transcript. Photo of applicant required.
Additional information: Award provides higher education training for the betterment of the criminal justice system. Applicant must be accepted by a college or university prior to date of award.

Amount of award:	$500
Number of awards:	5
Number of applicants:	2,500
Application deadline:	June 1
Total amount awarded:	$2,500

Contact:
National Black Police Association Scholarship Award
30 Kennedy St.
Suite 101
Washington, DC 20011-2103
Phone: 202-986-2070
Fax: 202-986-0410
Web: www.blackpolice.org

National Center For Learning Disabilities

Anne Ford Scholarship

Type of award: Scholarship, renewable.
Intended use: For undergraduate study at 4-year institution.
Eligibility: Applicant must be high school senior. Applicant must be U.S. citizen.
Basis for selection: Applicant must demonstrate financial need, depth of character, leadership, seriousness of purpose and service orientation.
Application requirements: Essay, transcript, proof of eligibility. Personal statement may be written or recorded (audio or video). Financial statements, 3 letters of recommendation, SAT/ACT scores.
Additional information: Applicants must have identifiable learning disability. Minimum 3.0 GPA. Minorities encouraged to apply.

Amount of award:	$10,000
Number of awards:	1
Number of applicants:	400
Application deadline:	December 31
Notification begins:	April 1
Total amount awarded:	$10,000

Contact:
Anne Ford Scholarship
National Center for Learning Disabilities
381 Park Avenue South, Sutie 1401
New York, NY 10016-8806
Phone: 212-545-9665
Web: www.ncld.org

National Commission for Cooperative Education

National Co-op Scholarship

Type of award: Scholarship, renewable.
Intended use: For undergraduate study. Designated institutions: Drexel University, Johnson & Wales University, Kettering University, C. W. Post Campus of Long Island University, Northeastern University, Pace University, Rochester Institute of Technology, University of Cincinnati, University of Toledo, Wentworth Institute of Technology.
Eligibility: Applicant must be high school senior. Applicant must be residing in Washington or U.S. Territories.
Application requirements: One-page essay on decision to pursue a college cooperative education program.
Additional information: Applicants must be accepted to and attend one of the ten participating institutions. Minimum 3.5 GPA. Visit Website for more information and online application.

Amount of award:	$6,000
Number of awards:	185
Number of applicants:	2,251
Application deadline:	February 15
Total amount awarded:	$4,500,000

Contact:
National Commission for Cooperative Education
360 Huntington Avenue, 384 CP
Boston, MA 02115-5096
Phone: 617-373-3770
Fax: 617-373-3463
Web: www.co-op.edu

National Dairy Promotion and Research Board

Dairy Product Marketing Scholarships

Type of award: Scholarship, renewable.
Intended use: For full-time sophomore, junior or senior study at accredited 4-year institution.
Eligibility: Applicant must be U.S. citizen.
Basis for selection: Major/career interest in advertising; marketing; food production/management/services; food science/technology or dairy. Applicant must demonstrate high academic achievement, leadership and seriousness of purpose.
Application requirements: Recommendations, transcript.
Additional information: Applications available through food science department chairperson or financial aid officer of applicant's institution as well as online at Website listed below. Nineteen recipients receive $1,500 and one recipient receives $2,500. Student must have commitment to career in dairy.

Amount of award:	$1,500-$2,500
Number of awards:	20
Number of applicants:	30
Application deadline:	May 31
Notification begins:	July 30
Total amount awarded:	$7,500

Contact:
National Dairy Promotion and Research Board
c/o Marykate Ginter
10255 W Higgins Road, Suite 900
Rosemont, IL 60018-5615
Phone: 847-627-3252
Web: www.dairyinfo.com

National Dairy Shrine

Dairy Student Recognition Program

Type of award: Scholarship.
Intended use: For senior study.
Basis for selection: Major/career interest in dairy; food production/management/services or food science/technology. Applicant must demonstrate leadership.
Application requirements: Recommendations, essay, nomination by college or university dairy-science department.
Additional information: Cash awards for graduating seniors planning career in dairy cattle. Two candidates eligible per institution. First-place winner receives $1,500; second, $1,000; third through seventh, $500. National Dairy Shrine chooses final winners. Students who placed in top five in previous years not eligible for further competition.

Amount of award:	$500-$1,500
Number of awards:	10
Number of applicants:	20
Application deadline:	March 15
Notification begins:	June 10
Total amount awarded:	$6,000

Contact:
National Dairy Shrine
1224 Alton Darby Creek Road
Columbus, OH 43228-9792
Phone: 614-878-5333
Fax: 614-870-2622
Web: www.dairyshrine.org

Marshall E. McCullough Undergraduate Scholarship

Type of award: Scholarship.
Intended use: For full-time senior study at accredited 4-year institution in United States.
Eligibility: Applicant must be high school senior. Applicant must be U.S. citizen.
Basis for selection: Major/career interest in animal sciences; dairy; communications or journalism.
Application requirements: Recommendations, essay.
Additional information: Two awards: one for $2,500; one for $1,000. Must major in dairy/animal science with communications emphasis or agricultural journalism with dairy/animal science emphasis.

Amount of award:	$1,000-$2,500
Number of awards:	2
Number of applicants:	12
Application deadline:	March 15
Notification begins:	July 1
Total amount awarded:	$3,500

Contact:
National Dairy Shrine
1224 Alton Darby Creek Road
Columbus, OH 43228-9792
Phone: 614-878-5333
Fax: 614-870-9792
Web: www.dairyshrine.org

National Dairy Shrine Kildee Scholarship

Type of award: Scholarship.
Intended use: For undergraduate study.
Basis for selection: Major/career interest in food production/management/services; food science/technology or dairy.
Additional information: Applicant must have placed in top 25 in National 4-H, FFA or National Intercollegiate Judging Contests. Platinum winners from National Dairy Challenge are eligible to compete for graduate study scholarships. Up to two $3,000 scholarships for graduate study and one $2,000 scholarship for undergraduate study awarded. May request application from Website or National Dairy Shrine.

Amount of award:	$2,000-$3,000
Number of awards:	3
Number of applicants:	18
Application deadline:	March 15
Notification begins:	June 1
Total amount awarded:	$8,000

Contact:
National Dairy Shrine
1224 Alton Darby Creek
Columbus, OH 43228
Phone: 614-878-5333
Fax: 614-870-2622
Web: www.dairyshrine.org

National Dairy Shrine Klussendorf Scholarship

Type of award: Scholarship.
Intended use: For sophomore, junior or senior study.
Basis for selection: Major/career interest in food production/management/services; food science/technology or dairy.
Additional information: For dairy or animal science majors in second, third, or fourth year of college. May request application from Website or National Dairy Shrine.

Amount of award:	$1,500
Number of awards:	2
Number of applicants:	15
Application deadline:	March 15
Notification begins:	June 1
Total amount awarded:	$3,000

Contact:
National Dairy Shrine
1224 Alton Darby Creek
Columbus, OH 43228
Phone: 614-878-5333
Fax: 614-870-2622
Web: www.dairyshrine.org

National Dairy Shrine/Iager Dairy Scholarship

Type of award: Scholarship.
Intended use: For undergraduate study.
Basis for selection: Major/career interest in food production/management/services; food science/technology or dairy.
Additional information: Must be second-year college student in two-year agricultural college. May request application from Website or National Dairy Shrine.

Amount of award:	$1,000
Number of awards:	1
Number of applicants:	6
Application deadline:	July 1
Notification begins:	September 1
Total amount awarded:	$1,000

Contact:
National Dairy Shrine
1224 Alton Darby Creek
Columbus, OH 43228
Phone: 614-878-533
Fax: 614-870-2622
Web: www.dairyshrine.org

NOS/DMI Milk Marketing Scholarships

Type of award: Scholarship.
Intended use: For undergraduate study.
Additional information: Visit Website for more details.
   Amount of award: $1,000-$1,500
   Number of awards: 8
   Number of applicants: 20
   Application deadline: March 15
   Notification begins: June 1
   Total amount awarded: $9,500
Contact:
National Dairy Shrine
Att: Maurice E. Core
1224 Alton Darby Creek Road
Columbus, OH 43228-2622
Phone: 614-878-5333
Fax: 614-870-2622
Web: www.dairyshrine.org

National Environmental Health Association/ American Academy of Sanitarians

NEHA/AAS Scholarship

Type of award: Scholarship.
Intended use: For full-time junior, senior or graduate study at accredited 4-year or graduate institution.
Basis for selection: Major/career interest in environmental science or public health. Applicant must demonstrate financial need, high academic achievement and seriousness of purpose.
Application requirements: Transcript, proof of eligibility. Three letters of recommendation (one from active NEHA member, two from faculty members at applicant's school).
Additional information: Undergraduates must be enrolled in an Environmental Health Accreditation Council accredited school or National Environmental Health Association Institutional/Educational or sustaining member school (list available at sponsor Website). Graduates must be enrolled in environmental health science and/or public health program. Visit Website for further information and updates.
   Amount of award: $1,000-$1,500
   Number of awards: 3
   Number of applicants: 200
   Application deadline: February 1
Contact:
National Environmental Health Association
NEHA/AAS Scholarship
720 South Colorado Boulevard., 1000-N
Denver, CO 80246-1925
Phone: 303-756-9090
Fax: 303-691-9490
Web: www.neha.org

National Federation of the Blind

Charles and Melva T. Owen Memorial Scholarship

Type of award: Scholarship, renewable.
Intended use: For full-time undergraduate or graduate study at postsecondary institution.
Eligibility: Applicant must be visually impaired.
Basis for selection: Applicant must demonstrate financial need, high academic achievement and service orientation.
Application requirements: Transcript. Personal letter from applicant, letter from state officer of Federation, two letters of recommendation, score reports for all standardized tests taken for college admission (high school seniors only), proof of legal blindness.
Additional information: Applicant must be legally blind. Field of study should be directed toward attaining financial independence. Excludes study of religion and those seeking only to further general or cultural education. Recipients of Federation scholarships need not be members of National Federation of the Blind. Visit Website to download application. All applications must be filed in hard copy by mail.
   Amount of award: $10,000
   Number of awards: 1
   Application deadline: March 31
   Notification begins: June 1
Contact:
National Federation of the Blind Scholarship Committee
1800 Johnson St.
Baltimore, MD 21230
Phone: 404-371-1000
Web: www.nfb.org/scholarships

Computer Science Scholarship

Type of award: Scholarship, renewable.
Intended use: For full-time undergraduate or graduate study at postsecondary institution.
Eligibility: Applicant must be visually impaired.
Basis for selection: Major/career interest in computer/information sciences; engineering, computer or computer graphics. Applicant must demonstrate financial need, high academic achievement and service orientation.
Application requirements: Transcript. Personal letter from applicant, letter from state officer of Federation, two letters of recommendation, score reports for all standardized tests taken for college admission (high school seniors only), proof of legal blindness.
Additional information: Applicant must be legally blind. Recipients of Federation scholarships need not be members of National Federation of the Blind. Visit Website to download application. All applications must be filed in hard copy by mail.

National Federation of the Blind: Computer Science Scholarship

Amount of award:	$3,000
Number of awards:	1
Application deadline:	March 31
Notification begins:	June 1
Total amount awarded:	$3,000

Contact:
National Federation of the Blind Scholarship Committee
1800 Johnson St.
Baltimore, MD 21230
Phone: 404-371-1000
Web: www.nfb.org/scholarships

E.U. Parker Memorial Scholarship

Type of award: Scholarship, renewable.
Intended use: For full-time undergraduate or graduate study at postsecondary institution.
Eligibility: Applicant must be visually impaired.
Basis for selection: Applicant must demonstrate financial need, high academic achievement and service orientation.
Application requirements: Transcript. Personal letter from applicant, letter from state officer of Federation, two letters of recommendation, score reports for all standardized tests taken for college admission (high school seniors only), proof of legal blindness.
Additional information: Applicant must be legally blind. Recipients of Federation scholarships need not be members of National Federation of the Blind. Visit Website to download application. All applications must be filed in hardcopy by mail.

Amount of award:	$3,000
Number of awards:	1
Application deadline:	March 31
Notification begins:	June 1
Total amount awarded:	$3,000

Contact:
National Federation of the Blind Scholarship Committee
1800 Johnson St.
Baltimore, MD 21230
Phone: 404-371-1000
Web: www.nfb.org/scholarships

Hank LeBonne Scholarship

Type of award: Scholarship.
Intended use: For full-time undergraduate or graduate study at postsecondary institution in United States.
Eligibility: Applicant must be visually impaired.
Basis for selection: Applicant must demonstrate financial need, high academic achievement and service orientation.
Application requirements: Transcript. Personal letter from applicant, letter from state officer of Federation, two letters of recommendation, score reports for all standardized tests (high school seniors only), proof of legal blindness.
Additional information: Applicant must be legally blind. Recipients of scholarships need not be members of Federation. Visit Website to download application. All applications must be filed in hard copy by mail.

Amount of award:	$5,000
Application deadline:	March 31

Contact:
National Federation for the Blind
1800 Johnson St.
Baltimore, MD 21230
Phone: 404-371-1000
Web: www.nfb.org/scholarships

Hermione Grant Calhoun Scholarship

Type of award: Scholarship, renewable.
Intended use: For full-time undergraduate or graduate study at postsecondary institution.
Eligibility: Applicant must be visually impaired. Applicant must be female.
Basis for selection: Applicant must demonstrate financial need, high academic achievement and service orientation.
Application requirements: Transcript. Personal letter from applicant, letter from state officer of Federation, two letters of recommendation, score reports for all standardized tests taken for college admission (high school seniors only), proof of legal blindness.
Additional information: Applicant must be a legally blind woman. Recipients of Federation scholarships need not be members of National Federation of the Blind. Visit Website to download application. All applications must be filed in hard copy by mail.

Amount of award:	$3,000
Number of awards:	1
Application deadline:	March 31
Notification begins:	June 1
Total amount awarded:	$3,000

Contact:
National Federation of the Blind Scholarship Committee
1800 Johnson St.
Baltimore, MD 21230
Phone: 404-371-1000
Web: www.nfb.org/scholarship

Howard Brown Rickard Scholarship

Type of award: Scholarship, renewable.
Intended use: For full-time undergraduate or graduate study at postsecondary institution.
Eligibility: Applicant must be visually impaired.
Basis for selection: Major/career interest in law; medicine; engineering; architecture or natural sciences. Applicant must demonstrate financial need, high academic achievement and service orientation.
Application requirements: Transcript. Personal letter from applicant, letter from state officer of Federation, two letters of recommendation, score reports for all standardized tests taken for college admission (high school seniors only), proof of legal blindness.
Additional information: Applicant must be legally blind. Recipients of Federation scholarships need not be members of National Federation of the Blind. Visit Website to download application. All applications must be filed in hard copy by mail.

Amount of award:	$3,000
Number of awards:	1
Application deadline:	March 31
Notification begins:	June 1
Total amount awarded:	$3,000

Contact:
National Federation of the Blind Scholarship Committee
1800 Johnson St.
Baltimore, MD 21230
Phone: 404-371-1000
Web: www.nfb.org/scholarships

Jennica Ferguson Memorial Scholarship

Type of award: Scholarship, renewable.

Intended use: For full-time undergraduate or graduate study at postsecondary institution.
Eligibility: Applicant must be visually impaired.
Basis for selection: Applicant must demonstrate financial need, high academic achievement and service orientation.
Application requirements: Transcript. Personal letter from applicant, letter from state officer of Federation, two letters of recommendation, score reports for all standardized tests taken for college admission (high school seniors only).
Additional information: Applicant must be legally blind. Recipients of Federation scholarships need not be members of National Federation of the Blind. Visit Website to download application. Applications should be filed in hard copy and by mail.
 Amount of award: $5,000
 Number of awards: 1
 Application deadline: March 31
 Notification begins: June 1
 Total amount awarded: $5,000
Contact:
National Federation of the Blind Scholarship Committee
Mrs. Peggy Elliott, Chairman
805 Fifth Avenue
Grinnell, IA 50112
Phone: 641-236-3366
Web: www.nfb.org

Kenneth Jernigan Memorial Scholarship

Type of award: Scholarship, renewable.
Intended use: For full-time undergraduate or graduate study.
Eligibility: Applicant must be visually impaired.
Basis for selection: Applicant must demonstrate financial need, high academic achievement and service orientation.
Application requirements: Transcript. Personal letter from applicant, letter from state officer of Federation, two letters of recommendation, score reports for all standardized tests taken for college admission (high school seniors only), proof of blindness.
Additional information: Applicant must be legally blind. Recipients of Federation scholarships need not be members of Federation. Visit Website to download application. All applications must be filed in hard copy by mail.
 Amount of award: $12,000
 Number of awards: 1
 Application deadline: March 31
 Notification begins: June 1
 Total amount awarded: $12,000
Contact:
National Federation of the Blind Scholarship Committee
1800 Johnson St.
Baltimore, MD 21230
Phone: 404-371-1000
Web: www.nfb.org/scholarships

Kuchler-Killian Memorial Scholarship

Type of award: Scholarship, renewable.
Intended use: For full-time undergraduate or graduate study at postsecondary institution.
Eligibility: Applicant must be visually impaired.
Basis for selection: Applicant must demonstrate financial need, high academic achievement and service orientation.
Application requirements: Transcript. Personal letter from applicant, letter from state officer of Federation, two letters of recommendation, score reports for all standardized tests taken for college admission (high school seniors only), proof of legal blindness.
Additional information: Applicant must be legally blind. Recipients of Federation scholarships need not be members of National Federation of the Blind. Visit Website to download application. All applications must be filed in hard copy by mail.
 Amount of award: $3,000
 Number of awards: 1
 Application deadline: March 31
 Notification begins: June 1
 Total amount awarded: $3,000
Contact:
National Federation of the Blind Scholarship Committee
1800 Johnson St.
Baltimore, MD 21230
Phone: 404-371-1000
Web: www.nfb.org/scholarships

Michael and Marie Marucci Scholarship

Type of award: Scholarship, renewable.
Intended use: For full-time undergraduate or graduate study at postsecondary institution.
Eligibility: Applicant must be visually impaired.
Basis for selection: Major/career interest in foreign languages; literature; history; geography; political science/government; international studies or international relations. Applicant must demonstrate financial need, high academic achievement and service orientation.
Application requirements: Transcript. Personal letter from applicant, letter from state officer of Federation, two letters of recommendation, score reports for all standardized tests taken for college admission (high school seniors only), proof of legal blindness.
Additional information: Applicant must be legally blind. Applicant must be studying foreign language or comparative literature; pursuing degree in history, geography, or political science with concentration in international studies; or majoring in any discipline that involves study abroad. Must also show evidence of competence in foreign language. Recipients of Federation scholarships need not be members of National Federation of the Blind. Visit Website to download application. All applications must be filed in hard copy by mail.
 Amount of award: $5,000
 Number of awards: 1
 Application deadline: March 31
 Notification begins: June 1
Contact:
National Federation of the Blind Scholarship Committee
1800 Johnson St.
Baltimore, MD 21230
Phone: 404-371-1000
Web: www.nfb.org/scholarships

National Federation of the Blind Educator of Tomorrow Award

Type of award: Scholarship, renewable.
Intended use: For full-time undergraduate or graduate study at postsecondary institution.
Eligibility: Applicant must be visually impaired.
Basis for selection: Major/career interest in education, teacher or education. Applicant must demonstrate financial need, high academic achievement and service orientation.

National Federation of the Blind: National Federation of the Blind Educator of Tomorrow Award

Application requirements: Transcript. Personal letter from applicant, letter from state officer of Federation, two letters of recommendation, score reports for all standardized tests taken for college admission (high school seniors only), proof of legal blindness.
Additional information: Applicant must be legally blind. Must be planning career in elementary, secondary, or postsecondary teaching. Recipients of Federation scholarships need not be members of National Federation of the Blind. Visit Website to download application. All applications must be filed in hard copy by mail.

Amount of award:	$3,000
Number of awards:	1
Application deadline:	March 31
Notification begins:	June 1
Total amount awarded:	$3,000

Contact:
National Federation of the Blind Scholarship Committee
1800 Johnson St.
Baltimore, MD 21230
Phone: 404-371-1000
Web: www.nfb.org/scholarships

National Federation of the Blind Scholarships

Type of award: Scholarship, renewable.
Intended use: For full-time undergraduate or graduate study at postsecondary institution.
Eligibility: Applicant must be visually impaired.
Basis for selection: Major/career interest in humanities/liberal arts. Applicant must demonstrate financial need, high academic achievement and service orientation.
Application requirements: Transcript. Personal letter from applicant, letter from state officer of Federation, two letters of recommendation, score reports for all standardized tests taken for college admission (high school seniors only), proof of legal blindness.
Additional information: Applicant must be legally blind. Recipients of Federation scholarships need not be members of National Federation of the Blind. Visit Website to download application. All applications should be filed in hard copy by mail.

Amount of award:	$3,000-$7,000
Number of awards:	15
Application deadline:	March 31
Notification begins:	June 1

Contact:
National Federation of the Blind Scholarship Committee
1800 Johnson St.
Baltimore, MD 21230
Phone: 404-371-1000
Web: www.nfb.org/scholarships

National Foster Parent Association

Youth Scholarship

Type of award: Scholarship.
Intended use: For undergraduate or non-degree study at postsecondary institution.
Eligibility: Applicant or parent must be member/participant of National Foster Parent Association. Applicant must be high school senior.
Basis for selection: Applicant must demonstrate financial need.
Application requirements: Recommendations, essay, transcript. Photograph, list of extracurricular activities.
Additional information: For postsecondary education in both degree- and non-degree-granting institutions. Consideration to applicants with physical disability, handicap or other special needs. Foster children, adoptive children and birth children of licensed, approved foster parents who are members of NFPA are eligible. Applications accepted year-round.

Amount of award:	$1,000
Number of awards:	6
Number of applicants:	55
Application deadline:	March 31
Notification begins:	May 31
Total amount awarded:	$5,000

Contact:
NFPA Scholarship
7512 Stanich Lane #6
Gig Harbor, WA 98335
Phone: 800-557-5238
Fax: 253-853-4001
Web: www.nfpainc.org

National Future Farmers of America

National FFA Organization Scholarship Program

Type of award: Scholarship.
Intended use: For undergraduate study.
Additional information: Open to FFA members as well as a small number of qualifying non-members. Visit Website for more information and application.

Amount of award:	$1,000-$10,000
Application deadline:	February 15
Notification begins:	June 1
Total amount awarded:	$2,000,000

Contact:
The National FFA
Attn. Scholarship Office
P.O. Box 68960
Indianapolis, IN 46268-0960
Web: www.ffa.org

National Ground Water Research and Education Foundation

NGWREF Len Assante Scholarship Fund

Type of award: Scholarship.

Intended use: For full-time undergraduate study at accredited 2-year or 4-year institution.
Basis for selection: Applicant must demonstrate financial need, high academic achievement, depth of character, leadership, patriotism, seriousness of purpose and service orientation.
Application requirements: Essay, transcript, proof of eligibility. Essay should be one-page biography.
Additional information: Applicant must be studying in a ground water-related field. Students in two-year well drilling associate degree program also eligible. Minimum 2.5 GPA. Amount and number of awards vary annually. Application available on Website.
   Number of awards: 6
   Number of applicants: 14
   Application deadline: April 1
Contact:
NGWREF: Len Assante Scholarship Fund
601 Dempsey Road
Westerville, OH 43081
Phone: 800-551-7379
Fax: 614-898-7786
Web: www.ngwa.org

National Inventors Hall of Fame

Collegiate Inventors Competition

Type of award: Scholarship.
Intended use: For full-time undergraduate or graduate study in United States or Canada.
Basis for selection: Competition/talent/interest in science project, based on invention's potential for society and scope of use.
Application requirements: Advisor letter, 500 words maximum; four copies of application and three copies of any supplementary material; diagrams, illustrations, photos, slides or videos of invention; 1500-word essay describing invention, including a title page and one-paragraph overview of invention.
Additional information: Amount of awards vary. Entry must include summary of current literature and patent search, test data and invention's benefit. Competition accepts individual and team entries. Students must be (or have been) enrolled full-time at least part of 12-month period prior to date entry submitted. For teams, at least one member must meet full-time eligibility criteria. Other team members must have been enrolled on part-time basis (at minimum) sometime during 24-month period prior to date entry submitted. See Website for more information.
   Amount of award: $15,000-$25,000
   Number of awards: 3
   Application deadline: May 16
Contact:
The Collegiate Inventors Competition
The National Inventors Hall of Fame
221 South Broadway St.
Akron, OH 44308-1595
Phone: 800-968-4332 ext. 5
Web: www.invent.org/collegiate

National Italian American Foundation

Emanuele and Emilia Inglese Memorial Scholarship

Type of award: Scholarship.
Intended use: For undergraduate study at accredited postsecondary institution.
Eligibility: Applicant must be U.S. citizen or permanent resident.
Basis for selection: Applicant must demonstrate financial need and high academic achievement.
Application requirements: Transcript. Teacher Evaluation Form, Student Aid Report from FAFSA.
Additional information: Applicant must be first-generation of family to attend college. Must be able to trace lineage to Lombardy region in Italy. Minimum 3.0 GPA. Applications must be submitted online. See Website for details and application.
   Amount of award: $2,500
   Number of awards: 1
Contact:
The Inglese Memorial Scholarship c/o NIAF
1860 19th Street NW
Washington, DC 20009
Web: www.niaf.org/scholarships/index.asp

National Italian American Foundation Scholarship Program

Type of award: Scholarship.
Intended use: For full-time undergraduate or graduate study at accredited 4-year or graduate institution in United States.
Eligibility: Applicant must be U.S. citizen or permanent resident.
Basis for selection: Applicant must demonstrate high academic achievement, depth of character, leadership, seriousness of purpose and service orientation.
Application requirements: Transcript. FAFSA (optional).
Additional information: Completed application submitted online. One teacher evaluation may be filed online using student's file number established when application created. Changes to online application may be made up until date of deadline. "Italian-American" defined as having at least one ancestor who emigrated from Italy. Awards in two categories. General Category I Awards: Open to Italian-American students who demonstrate outstanding potential and high academic achievement who wish to pursue any area of study. General Category II Awards: Open to those students from any ethnic background majoring or minoring in Italian Language, Italian studies, Italian American Studies, or related fields. Awards are given based on academic performance, field of study, career objectives, and the potential, commitment, and demonstrated ability to make significant contributions to chosen field of study. Recipients are awarded money for one academic year only, but are encouraged to reapply in subsequent years. Awards not applicable for summer study. Minimum 3.5 GPA.
   Amount of award: $2,500-$10,000
   Number of awards: 150
   Number of applicants: 4,000

Contact:
The National Italian American Foundation
1860 19th Street NW
Washington, DC 20009
Web: www.niaf.org/scholarships/index.asp

National Jewish Committee on Scouting, Boy Scouts of America

Chester M. Vernon Memorial Eagle Scout Scholarship

Type of award: Scholarship, renewable.
Intended use: For full-time undergraduate study at accredited 2-year or 4-year institution.
Eligibility: Applicant or parent must be member/participant of Boy Scouts of America, Eagle Scouts. Applicant must be male, high school senior. Applicant must be Jewish. Applicant must be U.S. citizen or permanent resident.
Basis for selection: Applicant must demonstrate financial need, depth of character, leadership and service orientation.
Application requirements: Recommendation from a volunteer or professional scout leader.. FAFSA.
Additional information: Award renewable for four years. Applicant must be registered, active member of a Boy Scout troop, Varsity Scout team, or Venturing crew. Must have received Eagle Scout Award. Must be active member of synagogue and have received Ner Tamid or Etz Chaim emblem. Contact National Jewish Committee on Scouting to request application form. Visit Website for more information.

Amount of award:	$1,000
Number of awards:	1
Application deadline:	February 28
Notification begins:	May 1
Total amount awarded:	$1,000

Contact:
National Jewish Committee on Scouting, BSA
1325 W. Walnut Hill Lane
P.O. Box 152079
Irving, TX 75015-2079
Phone: 972-580-2119
Fax: 972-580-2535
Web: www.jewishscouting.org

Frank L. Weil Memorial Eagle Scout Scholarship

Type of award: Scholarship.
Intended use: For full-time undergraduate study at accredited 2-year or 4-year institution.
Eligibility: Applicant or parent must be member/participant of Boy Scouts of America, Eagle Scouts. Applicant must be male, high school senior. Applicant must be Jewish. Applicant must be U.S. citizen or permanent resident.
Basis for selection: Applicant must demonstrate depth of character, leadership and service orientation.
Application requirements: Recommendation from volunteer or professional scout leader. FAFSA.
Additional information: Recipient of scholarship receives $1,000. Two $500 second-place scholarship awards also given. Applicant must be registered, active member of a Boy Scout troop, Varsity Scout team, or Venturing crew. Must have received Eagle Scout Award. Must be active member of synagogue and have received Ner Tamid or Etz Chaim emblem. Contact National Jewish Committee on Scouting to request application form. Visit Website for more information.

Amount of award:	$500-$1,000
Number of awards:	3
Application deadline:	February 28
Notification begins:	May 1
Total amount awarded:	$2,000

Contact:
National Jewish Committee on Scouting, BSA
1325 West Walnut Hill Lane
P.O. Box 152079
Irving, TX 75015-2079
Phone: 972-580-2119
Fax: 972-580-2535
Web: www.jewishscouting.org

National Merit Scholarship Corporation

National Achievement Scholarships

Type of award: Scholarship.
Intended use: For full-time undergraduate study in United States.
Eligibility: Applicant must be African American. Applicant must be enrolled in high school. Applicant must be U.S. citizen or permanent resident.
Basis for selection: Applicant must demonstrate high academic achievement and leadership.
Application requirements: Recommendations, essay.
Additional information: A privately financed academic competition for black American high school students. To enter, students must meet published participation requirements and request consideration in program when they take PSAT/NMSQT and enter National Merit Program. Entry requirements published each year in PSAT/NMSQT Official Student Guide, sent to schools for distribution to students before October test administration, and on NMSC's Website. Some 1,600 of highest scoring participants named Semifinalists on regional representation basis. Semifinalists must meet additional requirements and advance to Finalist standing to compete for about 800 National Achievement Scholarships offered annually. There are 700 National Achievement $2,500 Scholarships for which all Finalists compete and about 100 corporate-sponsored scholarships for Finalists who meet specified criteria of sponsoring organization.

Number of awards:	800
Number of applicants:	150,000
Notification begins:	February 15
Total amount awarded:	$2,500,000

Contact:
National Achievement Scholarship Program
1560 Sherman Avenue
Suite 200
Evanston, IL 60201-4897
Web: www.nationalmerit.org

National Merit Scholarships

Type of award: Scholarship.

Intended use: For full-time undergraduate study in United States.
Eligibility: Applicant must be enrolled in high school. Applicant must be U.S. citizen or permanent resident.
Basis for selection: Applicant must demonstrate high academic achievement and leadership.
Application requirements: Recommendations, essay.
Additional information: Open to U.S. high school students who take PSAT/NMQST in specified year in high school and meet other entry requirements. Entry requirements published each year in PSAT/NMQST Official Student Guide, sent to schools for distribution to students before October test administration, and on NMSC's Website. Some 16,000 high-scoring participants designated Semifinalists on state representational basis. Applications sent to students through their schools. Semifinalists must meet additional requirements and advance to Finalist standing to be considered for National Merit Scholarships. About 8,200 awards of three types offered annually: 2,500 National Merit $2,500 Scholarships for which all Finalists compete; about 1,100 corporate-sponsored Merit Scholarship awards for Finalists who meet criteria of sponsoring corporate organization; and 4,600 college-sponsored Merit Scholarship awards for Finalists who will attend sponsor college/university. Corporate organizations also provide about 1,600 Special Scholarships for other high performers in competition who are not Finalists. Permanent residents eligible if in process of becoming U.S. citizen.

Number of awards:	9,700
Number of applicants:	1,500,000
Notification begins:	March 1
Total amount awarded:	$46,000,000

Contact:
National Merit Scholarship Program
1560 Sherman Avenue
Suite 200
Evanston, IL 60201-4897
Web: www.nationalmerit.org

National Poultry & Food Distributors Association

NPFDA Scholarship

Type of award: Scholarship, renewable.
Intended use: For full-time junior or senior study at 4-year institution in United States.
Basis for selection: Major/career interest in dietetics/nutrition; agriculture; agricultural economics; agribusiness or food science/technology. Applicant must demonstrate high academic achievement.
Application requirements: Essay, transcript, proof of eligibility. Recommendation by dean. One-page statement about applicant's goals and aspirations.
Additional information: Poultry science, animal science, or related agricultural business majors also eligible.

Amount of award:	$1,500
Number of awards:	4
Number of applicants:	80
Application deadline:	May 31
Notification begins:	January 1
Total amount awarded:	$6,500

Contact:
National Poultry & Food Distributors Association
958 McEver Road Ext., Unit B-8
Gainesville, GA 30504
Phone: 770-535-9901
Fax: 770-535-7385
Web: www.npfda.org

National Press Photographers Foundation

Bob Baxter Scholarship

Type of award: Scholarship.
Intended use: For full-time undergraduate study in United States or Canada.
Basis for selection: Major/career interest in journalism. Applicant must demonstrate financial need.
Application requirements: Recommendations, essay. Portfolio of six to twenty slides (digital formats also accepted), statement of financial need.
Additional information: Applicants must be studying photojournalism. Visit Website for more information and application.

Amount of award:	$1,000
Number of awards:	1
Application deadline:	March 1

Contact:
Danielle Richards
The Record - Photo Department
150 River St.
Hackensack, NJ 07601
Phone: 201-646-4130
Web: www.nppa.org/professional_development/students/scholarships/baxter

Bob East Scholarship Fund

Type of award: Scholarship.
Intended use: For undergraduate study in United States or Canada.
Eligibility: Applicant must be U.S. citizen or permanent resident residing in Florida.
Basis for selection: Major/career interest in journalism. Applicant must demonstrate financial need.
Application requirements: Portfolio, recommendations, essay. Portfolio must include at least five single images in addition to picture story. Digital portfolios accepted; see Website for instructions.
Additional information: Open to students studying photojournalism for newspapers. Must be undergraduate in first three and one half years of college, or be planning to pursue postgraduate work and offer indication of acceptance in such program.

Amount of award:	$2,000
Application deadline:	March 1
Total amount awarded:	$2,000

National Press Photographers Foundation: Bob East Scholarship Fund

Contact:
The Miami Herald
Attn: Chuck Fadely
One Herald Plaza
Miami, FL 33132
Phone: 305-376-2015
Web: www.nppa.org/professional_development/students/scholarships/east

College Photographer of the Year Competition

Type of award: Scholarship.
Intended use: For undergraduate study at 4-year institution in United States or Canada.
Basis for selection: Major/career interest in journalism. Applicant must demonstrate financial need and high academic achievement.
Application requirements: Portfolio, recommendations, proof of eligibility. Portfolio must include five single images in addition to picture story. Digital portfolios accepted; see Website for instructions.
Additional information: Contest recognizes outstanding work of student photojournalists. NPPF Booster club provides $1,000 Col. William Lookadoo Award and $500 Milton Frier Award.

Amount of award:	$500-$1,000
Number of awards:	2
Application deadline:	October 1
Total amount awarded:	$1,500

Contact:
University of Missouri School of Journalism
David Rees, CPOY Dir.
106 Lee Hills Hall
Columbia, MO 65211
Phone: 573-882-4442
Web: www.nppa.org/professional_development/students/scholarships/copy

National Press Photographers Foundation Still Scholarship

Type of award: Scholarship.
Intended use: For sophomore, junior or senior study at 4-year institution in United States or Canada.
Basis for selection: Major/career interest in journalism. Applicant must demonstrate financial need and high academic achievement.
Application requirements: Portfolio, proof of eligibility. Portfolio must include five single images in addition to picture story. Digital portfolios accepted; see Website for instructions.
Additional information: Awards aimed at those with journalism potential, but with little opportunity and great need. Must have completed one year at recognized four-year college or university with courses in photojournalism. Must be continuing in program leading to bachelor's degree.

Amount of award:	$2,000
Number of awards:	1
Application deadline:	March 1
Total amount awarded:	$2,000

Contact:
Bill Sanders
Ashville Citizen-Times
P.O. Box 2090
Ashville, NC 28802
Web: www.nppa.org/professional_development/students/scholarships/still

National Press Photographers Foundation Television News Scholarship

Type of award: Scholarship.
Intended use: For junior or senior study at 4-year institution in United States or Canada.
Basis for selection: Major/career interest in radio/television/film or journalism. Applicant must demonstrate financial need and high academic achievement.
Application requirements: Portfolio, recommendations, essay. Videotape containing no more than three complete stories no longer than six minutes total with voice narration and natural sound. One-page biographical sketch including personal statement addressing professional goals.
Additional information: Must be enrolled in recognized four-year college or university with courses in TV news photojournalism. Must be continuing program leading to bachelor's degree.

Amount of award:	$1,000
Number of awards:	1
Application deadline:	March 1
Total amount awarded:	$1,000

Contact:
Ed Dooks
5 Mohawk Drive
Lexington, MA 02421-6217
Phone: 781-861-6062
Web: www.nppa.org/professional_development/students/scholarships/tv

Reid Blackburn Scholarship

Type of award: Scholarship.
Intended use: For sophomore, junior or senior study at 4-year institution in United States or Canada.
Basis for selection: Major/career interest in journalism. Applicant must demonstrate financial need, high academic achievement and seriousness of purpose.
Application requirements: Portfolio, essay, proof of eligibility. Statement of philosophy and goals. Portfolio must include at least five single images in addition to picture story. Digital portfolios accepted; see Website for instructions.
Additional information: Must have completed at least one year at recognized four-year college or university with courses in photojournalism and must have at least half-year of undergraduate schooling remaining at time of award. Program must be leading to bachelor's degree.

Number of awards:	1
Application deadline:	March 1
Total amount awarded:	$2,000

Contact:
The Columbian
Attn: Fay Blackburn
PO Box 180
Vancouver, WA 98666
Phone: 360-759-8027
Web: www.nppa.org/professional_development/students/scholarships/blackburn

National Restaurant Association Educational Foundation

Academic Scholarship for High School Seniors

Type of award: Scholarship.
Intended use: For undergraduate study at vocational, 2-year or 4-year institution.
Eligibility: Applicant must be high school senior. Applicant must be U.S. citizen or permanent resident.
Basis for selection: Major/career interest in food science/technology; hotel/restaurant management; food science/technology; culinary arts or marketing.
Application requirements: Transcript. One to three letters of recommendation, preferably on business letterhead, from current or previous employer in the restaurant or food service industry.
Additional information: Must be accepted into accredited restaurant/food-service-related postsecondary program and plan to enroll in minimum of two terms for following school year. Minimum 2.75 high school GPA required. Must have minimum 250 hours of food-service-related work experience. To apply, visit Website.

Amount of award:	$2,000
Application deadline:	May 16

Contact:
National Restaurant Association Educational Foundation
Scholarships and Mentoring Initiative
175 W. Jackson Blvd., Suite 1500
Chicago, IL 60604-2814
Phone: 312-715-1010 ext. 738
Fax: 312-566-9733
Web: www.nraef.org/scholarships

Academic Scholarship for Undergraduate Students

Type of award: Scholarship.
Intended use: For undergraduate or post-bachelor's certificate study at accredited vocational, 2-year or 4-year institution in United States.
Eligibility: Applicant must be U.S. citizen or permanent resident.
Basis for selection: Major/career interest in food production/management/services; culinary arts; hotel/restaurant management; hospitality administration/management; food science/technology or food science/technology. Applicant must demonstrate high academic achievement.
Application requirements: Essay, transcript. One to three letters of recommendation, preferably on business letterhead, from a current or previous employer in the restaurant or food service industry, paychecks or paystubs verifying restaurant employment.
Additional information: Applicant must have completed at least one term of two- or four-year degree program. Must have performed minimum 750 hours foodservice-related work. Minimum 2.75 GPA. For application and more information, visit Website.

Amount of award:	$2,000
Application deadline:	July 31, October 31

Contact:
National Restaurant Assn. Educational Foundation
Scholarships and Mentoring Initiative
175 West Jackson Boulevard, Suite 1500
Chicago, IL 60604-2814
Phone: 312-715-1010 ext. 738
Fax: 312-566-9733
Web: www.nraef.org/scholarships

ProStart National Certificate of Achievement Scholarship

Type of award: Scholarship.
Intended use: For undergraduate study at accredited 2-year or 4-year institution in United States.
Eligibility: Applicant must be high school senior. Applicant must be U.S. citizen or permanent resident.
Basis for selection: Major/career interest in food production/management/services; food science/technology; culinary arts or hotel/restaurant management.
Application requirements: Essay, transcript. 300 word case study. Letter of intent or acceptance. Copy of ProStart Certification.
Additional information: Minimum 2.75 GPA. Applicant must earn ProStart National Certificate of Achievement by August 15, 2008. Must have applied and gained acceptance to a college with an accredited restaurant- and/or foodservice-related post-secondary program.

Amount of award:	$2,000
Application deadline:	August 15
Notification begins:	September 7

Contact:
National Restaurant Association Educational Foundation
Scholarships and Mentoring Initiative
175 W. Jackson Blvd., Suite 1500
Chicago, IL 60604-2814
Phone: 312-715-1010 ext. 738
Fax: 312-566-9726
Web: www.nraef.org/scholarships

National Rifle Association

Jeanne E. Bray Law Enforcement Dependents Scholarship

Type of award: Scholarship.
Intended use: For full-time undergraduate or graduate study at accredited 2-year, 4-year or graduate institution in United States.
Eligibility: Applicant or parent must be member/participant of National Rifle Association. Applicant must be U.S. citizen. Applicant's parent must have been killed or disabled in work-related accident as police officer.
Basis for selection: Applicant must demonstrate high academic achievement and service orientation.
Application requirements: Transcript, proof of eligibility. 3 letters of recommendation; letter from employing law enforcement agency; 500-700 word essay on the 2nd Amendment.
Additional information: Number of awards varies. Parent must be active, disabled, deceased, discharged, or retired peace officer and member of National Rifle Association. Applicant must also be NRA member. Minimum 2.5 GPA, SAT score of 950 or ACT score of 25. Award given for up to four years or

National Rifle Association: Jeanne E. Bray Law Enforcement Dependents Scholarship

until applicable monetary cap is reached, as long as student maintains eligibility. Applications accepted on continuous basis.
- Amount of award: $500-$2,000
- Application deadline: November 15
- Notification begins: February 15

Contact:
National Rifle Association, Attn: Sandy S. Elkin
Jeanne E. Bray Memorial Scholarship
11250 Waples Mill Road
Fairfax, VA 22030
Phone: 703-267-1131
Fax: 703-267-1083
Web: www.nrahq.org

Women's Wildlife Management/Conservation Scholarship

Type of award: Scholarship, renewable.
Intended use: For full-time junior or senior study at 4-year institution.
Eligibility: Applicant must be female.
Basis for selection: Major/career interest in wildlife/fisheries. Applicant must demonstrate service orientation.
Application requirements: Recommendations, transcript, proof of eligibility. 300-word essay on topic "Is hunting a valid wildlife management /conservation tool?"
Additional information: Minimum 3.0 GPA. Open to wildlife management/conservation majors. Relatives of NRA Women's Policies Committee not eligible. Visit Website for application and further information.
- Amount of award: $1,000
- Application deadline: February 15

Contact:
The NRA Foundation
Attn: Women's Scholarship
11250 Waples Mill Road
Fairfax, VA 22030
Phone: 800-423-6894
Fax: 703-267-3985
Web: www.nrafoundation.org

National Science Teachers Association

Toshiba/NSTA ExploraVision Award

Type of award: Scholarship.
Intended use: For undergraduate or non-degree study in United States or Canada.
Eligibility: Applicant must be enrolled in high school.
Basis for selection: Competition/talent/interest in science project, based on scientific accuracy, creativity, communication and feasibility of vision. Major/career interest in science, general.
Application requirements: Essay. Written description of research and design project, five graphics simulating Web pages.
Additional information: Applicant must attend public, private or home school. Must be full-time student, no older than 21. Technology study project. Open to grades K-12. Each student member of first-place team receives $10,000 savings bond, each student member of second-place team receives $5,000 savings bond, and regional winners receive notebook computers.

Contact sponsor for entry kit, and visit Website to download application.
- Amount of award: $5,000-$10,000
- Application deadline: January 29
- Notification begins: March 1
- Total amount awarded: $340,000

Contact:
Toshiba/NSTA ExploraVision Awards
1840 Wilson Boulevard
Arlington, VA 22201-3000
Phone: 800-EXPLOR9
Web: www.exploravision.org

National Sculpture Society

Sculpture Society Scholarship

Type of award: Scholarship.
Intended use: For undergraduate, master's or doctoral study at postsecondary institution in United States.
Eligibility: Applicant must be U.S. citizen or permanent resident.
Basis for selection: Competition/talent/interest in visual arts, based on slides or photos of figurative or representational sculpture created by applicant. Major/career interest in arts, general. Applicant must demonstrate financial need.
Application requirements: Portfolio, essay, proof of eligibility. Brief letter of application or biography explaining background in sculpture; 8-10 photographs of at least three works submitted on CD; proof of financial need; two recommendation letters. SASE.
Additional information: Must be studying figurative or representational sculpture. Number of awards varies. Deadline is in April.
- Amount of award: $2,000
- Application deadline: May 31

Contact:
National Sculpture Society
237 Park Avenue, Ground Floor
New York, NY 10017
Phone: 212-764-5645
Fax: 212-764-5651
Web: www.nationalsculpture.org

National Security Agency

National Security Agency Stokes Educational Scholarship Program

Type of award: Scholarship, renewable.
Intended use: For full-time undergraduate study in United States.
Eligibility: Applicant must be high school senior. Applicant must be U.S. citizen.
Basis for selection: Major/career interest in computer/information sciences; mathematics; engineering, computer; engineering, electrical/electronic or foreign languages. Applicant must demonstrate high academic achievement, depth of character, leadership, patriotism, seriousness of purpose and service orientation.

Application requirements: Interview, recommendations, transcript, proof of eligibility. Resume.
Additional information: Current applications available after September 1 of each year. Must have minimum 3.0 GPA, SAT score of 1600 and/or ACT score of 25. Must undergo polygraph and security screening. Freshmen must major in computer science or electric or computer engineering. College sophomores eligible if majoring in mathematics, Arabic or Farsi, or majors leading to careers in intelligence analysis. See Website for current program information.

Amount of award:	Full tuition
Number of awards:	20
Number of applicants:	700
Application deadline:	November 30
Notification begins:	April 1

Contact:
National Security Agency Stokes Scholars Program
9800 Savage Road
Suite 6779
Fort Meade, MD 20755-6779
Phone: 410-854-4725 or 866-NSA-HIRE
Fax: 410-854-3002
Web: www.nsa.gov

National Society of Accountants Scholarship Foundation

National Society of Accountants Scholarship

Type of award: Scholarship.
Intended use: For undergraduate study at accredited vocational, 2-year or 4-year institution in United States.
Eligibility: Applicant must be U.S. citizen or Canadian citizen.
Basis for selection: Major/career interest in accounting. Applicant must demonstrate financial need, high academic achievement and leadership.
Application requirements: Transcript. Appraisal form.
Additional information: Minimum 3.0 GPA. Competition's most outstanding student receives additional stipend. Visit Website for more information and application.

Amount of award:	$500-$2,000
Number of awards:	32
Number of applicants:	1,200
Application deadline:	March 10
Total amount awarded:	$40,000

Contact:
National Society of Accountants
Scholarship Foundation
1010 North Fairfax Street
Alexandria, VA 22314-1574
Phone: 800-966-6679
Fax: 703-549-2984
Web: www.nsacct.org

National Society of Black Engineers

Fulfilling the Legacy Scholarship

Type of award: Scholarship.
Intended use: For full-time undergraduate or graduate study at accredited postsecondary institution.
Eligibility: Applicant or parent must be member/participant of National Society of Black Engineers.
Basis for selection: Major/career interest in engineering. Applicant must demonstrate high academic achievement, depth of character, leadership, seriousness of purpose and service orientation.
Application requirements: Essay, transcript, proof of eligibility. Resume.
Additional information: Number of awards and amount depend on total contributions made by members and others. NSBE membership required. Society does not provide paper application. All eligible applicants must apply online through their membership account.

Amount of award:	$1,000
Number of awards:	15
Number of applicants:	6,990
Application deadline:	January 18
Notification begins:	February 1
Total amount awarded:	$15,000

Contact:
National Society of Black Engineers
205 Daingerfield Road
Alexandria, VA 22314
Phone: 703-549-2207
Fax: 703-683-5312
Web: www.nsbe.org

GE Lloyd Trotter African American Forum Scholarship

Type of award: Scholarship.
Intended use: For junior or senior study at accredited postsecondary institution in United States. Designated institutions: Universities located East of the Mississippi River (Regions I-IV).
Eligibility: Applicant or parent must be member/participant of National Society of Black Engineers. Applicant must be African American. Applicant must be U.S. citizen or permanent resident.
Basis for selection: Major/career interest in engineering; engineering, electrical/electronic; engineering, mechanical; information systems or computer/information sciences. Applicant must demonstrate high academic achievement, depth of character and service orientation.
Application requirements: Essay, transcript, proof of eligibility. Resume.
Additional information: Minimum 3.0 GPA required. Service to NSBE and/or other professional, campus, and community activities considered when selecting awardees. NSBE membership required. All eligible applicants must apply online through their membership account.

Amount of award:	$2,500
Number of awards:	16
Number of applicants:	1,231
Application deadline:	January 18
Notification begins:	February 1
Total amount awarded:	$40,000

National Society of Black Engineers Corporate Scholarships Program

Type of award: Scholarship.
Intended use: For sophomore, junior or senior study at 4-year institution.
Eligibility: Applicant or parent must be member/participant of National Society of Black Engineers.
Basis for selection: Major/career interest in engineering, chemical; engineering, petroleum or engineering, mechanical.
Application requirements: Essay, transcript. Resume.
Additional information: NSBE membership required; general information available on Website. All eligible applicants must apply online through their membership account. Minimum 3.0 GPA.

Amount of award:	$3,000-$5,000
Number of awards:	80
Number of applicants:	1,035
Application deadline:	January 18
Notification begins:	February 1

Contact:
National Society of Black Engineers
205 Daingerfield Road
Alexandria, VA 22314
Phone: 703-549-2207
Fax: 703-683-5312
Web: www.nsbe.org

National Society of Black Engineers Golden Torch Awards

Type of award: Scholarship, renewable.
Intended use: For full-time undergraduate study at accredited 4-year institution.
Eligibility: Applicant or parent must be member/participant of National Society of Black Engineers. Applicant must be high school senior.
Basis for selection: Major/career interest in engineering; computer/information sciences or mathematics. Applicant must demonstrate depth of character, leadership and service orientation.
Application requirements: Transcript. Three letters of recommendation. Essay about how applicant will continue legacy of NSBE and serve as a role model after college.
Additional information: Minimum 3.0 GPA required. NSBE Jr. membership required. All eligible applicants must apply online through their membership account. Renewable over four years; must maintain minimum 2.75 GPA in engineering/technology program. Award amount may vary.

Amount of award:	$1,000
Number of awards:	7
Number of applicants:	495
Application deadline:	January 18
Notification begins:	February 1
Total amount awarded:	$7,000

Contact:
GTA Scholarship PCI
National Society of Black Engineers
205 Daingerfield Road
Alexandria, VA 22314
Phone: 703-549-2207
Fax: 703-683-5312
Web: www.nsbe.org

National Society of Black Engineers Leroy Callendar Award Program

Type of award: Scholarship.
Intended use: For undergraduate study at 4-year institution.
Eligibility: Applicant or parent must be member/participant of National Society of Black Engineers. Applicant must be African American. Applicant must be high school senior.
Basis for selection: Applicant must demonstrate high academic achievement and service orientation.
Application requirements: Recommendations, transcript.
Additional information: Applicants must reside in the Host Region Six of NSBE National Convention. NSBE Jr. membership required. All eligible applicants must apply online through their membership account.

Amount of award:	$500
Number of awards:	2
Number of applicants:	357
Application deadline:	January 18
Notification begins:	February 1
Total amount awarded:	$1,000

Contact:
Leroy Callendar Award PCI Programs
National Society of Black Engineers
205 Daingerfield Road
Alexandria, VA 22314
Phone: 703-549-2207
Fax: 703-683-5312
Web: www.nsbe.org

NSBE Fellows Scholarship

Type of award: Scholarship.
Intended use: For full-time undergraduate or graduate study at accredited 4-year or graduate institution in United States or Canada in the West Indies.
Eligibility: Applicant or parent must be member/participant of National Society of Black Engineers.
Basis for selection: Major/career interest in engineering. Applicant must demonstrate high academic achievement, depth of character, leadership, seriousness of purpose and service orientation.
Application requirements: Essay, transcript, proof of eligibility. Resume.
Additional information: Minimum 2.7 GPA. Intended for applicants dedicated to Society's cause and other community organizations, who show promise in their studies and professional pursuits. Recipients receive $500 travel stipend for travel to annual NSBE convention in Las Vegas, Nevada. NSBE membership required. Society does not provide paper application. All eligible applicants must apply online through their membership account.

Amount of award:	$1,000-$3,000
Number of awards:	100
Number of applicants:	5,858
Application deadline:	January 18
Notification begins:	February 1

Contact:
National Society of Black Engineers
205 Daingerfield Road
Alexandria, VA 22314
Phone: 703-549-2207
Fax: 703-683-5312
Web: www.nsbe.org

National Society of the Sons of the American Revolution

Arthur M. and Berdena King Eagle Scout Scholarship

Type of award: Scholarship.
Intended use: For undergraduate study.
Eligibility: Applicant or parent must be member/participant of Eagle Scouts. Applicant must be male, no older than 18.
Basis for selection: Applicant must demonstrate depth of character, leadership and patriotism.
Application requirements: Essay, proof of eligibility. Essay should be 500 words on Revolutionary War, subject of applicant's choice. Four generations ancestor chart.
Additional information: Open to all Eagle Scouts currently registered in active unit who have not reached 19th birthday during year of application. Competition conducted in three phases: Chapter (local), Society (state), and National. Applicants need only apply at Chapter level. Winners at local level entered into state competition; state winners used in National contest. Number of awards varies. Awards may also be available at chapter and state level. For more information, contact State Eagle Scout Chairman. See Website for more information and application.

    Amount of award: $2,000-$8,000
    Number of awards: 3
    Application deadline: December 31
    Total amount awarded: $14,000

Contact:
National Society of the Sons of the American Revolution
1000 S. Fourth St.
Louisville, KY 40203
Phone: 502-589-1776
Web: www.sar.org

National Speakers Association

National Speakers Association Scholarship

Type of award: Scholarship.
Intended use: For full-time junior, senior or graduate study at 4-year or graduate institution.
Basis for selection: Major/career interest in communications. Applicant must demonstrate financial need, high academic achievement, leadership and seriousness of purpose.
Application requirements: Recommendations, essay, transcript.
Additional information: Applicant must have an above-average academic record and major or minor in speech or communication-related studies. Application available on Website.

    Amount of award: $5,000
    Number of awards: 4
    Application deadline: June 1
    Notification begins: September 1
    Total amount awarded: $20,000

Contact:
National Speakers Association
1500 South Priest Drive
Tempe, AZ 85281
Phone: 480-968-2552
Fax: 480-968-0911
Web: www.nsaspeaker.org

National Stone, Sand & Gravel Association

Barry K. Wendt Commitment Award and Scholarship

Type of award: Scholarship.
Intended use: For full-time undergraduate study in United States. Designated institutions: Engineering schools.
Eligibility: Applicant must be U.S. citizen or permanent resident.
Basis for selection: Major/career interest in engineering. Applicant must demonstrate high academic achievement.
Application requirements: Essay. Recommendation from faculty adviser. Essay should be 300-500 words on applicant's plans for career in aggregate industry.
Additional information: Visit Website for details and application.

    Number of awards: 1
    Application deadline: June 2

Contact:
Wendt Memorial Scholarship Committee
c/o NSSGA
1605 King Street
Alexandria, VA 22314
Phone: 800-342-1415
Fax: 703-525-7782
Web: www.nssga.org/careerscholarships/scholarships.cfm

Jennifer Curtis Byler Scholarship Fund for the Study of Public Affairs

Type of award: Scholarship.
Intended use: For full-time undergraduate study in United States.
Basis for selection: Major/career interest in public administration/service. Applicant must demonstrate high academic achievement, seriousness of purpose and service orientation.
Application requirements: Essay. Essay should be 300-500 words on applicant's plans for career in public affairs. Recommendation from faculty adviser, or from employer if applicant has work experience in public affairs though summer job, internship, or co-op program.

Additional information: Applicant must be graduating high school senior or student already enrolled in public affairs program in college. Must be child of aggregate company employee. Must demonstrate commitment to career in public affairs. Visit Website for details and application.

 Number of awards: 1
 Application deadline: May 31
Contact:
Jennifer Curtis Byler Scholarship
c/o NSSGA
1605 King Street
Alexandria, VA 22314
Phone: 800-342-1415
Fax: 703-525-7782
Web: www.nssga.org/careerscholarships/scholarships.cfm

Native Daughters of the Golden West

Native Daughters of the Golden West Scholarship

Type of award: Scholarship, renewable.
Intended use: For full-time undergraduate or graduate study at accredited postsecondary institution in United States.
Eligibility: Applicant or parent must be member/participant of Native Daughters of the Golden West. Applicant must be U.S. citizen residing in California. Applicant must be veteran; or dependent of active service person or veteran.
Basis for selection: Major/career interest in business; education; social work or nursing. Applicant must demonstrate financial need, high academic achievement, depth of character, leadership, patriotism, seriousness of purpose and service orientation.
Application requirements: Recommendations, essay, transcript, nomination by local club or parlor.
Additional information: High school seniors and college freshmen may apply. Must be nominated by local parlor. Applicant must have been born in California. Requirements vary for different awards; contact Grand Parlor Office for more information. Minimum amount of scholarship $900.

 Application deadline: April 15
 Notification begins: May 15
Contact:
Native Daughters of the Golden West
543 Baker Street
San Francisco, CA 94117-1405
Phone: 415-563-9091
Fax: 415-563-5230
Web: www.ndgw.org

Navy Supply Corps Foundation

Navy Supply Corps Foundation Scholarship

Type of award: Scholarship, renewable.
Intended use: For full-time undergraduate study at accredited 2-year or 4-year institution.
Eligibility: Applicant must be U.S. citizen. Applicant must be dependent of veteran who served in the Navy. Applicant must be spouse, child or grandchild of Supply Corps Officer/Warrant Officer and associated supply enlisted rating on active duty, prior service in Supply Corps, in the Selected Reserve or Individual Ready Reserve, retired with pay, or deceased eligible to apply. Associated ratings are AK, SK, MS, DK, SH, LI and PC.
Basis for selection: Applicant must demonstrate financial need, high academic achievement, depth of character, leadership and service orientation.
Application requirements: Transcript, proof of eligibility.
Additional information: Minimum 2.5 GPA required. Any family member of Foundation member or enlisted member (active duty, reservist, or retired) is eligible for consideration. Number of awards varies. Visit Website for application and further information.

 Amount of award: $1,000-$10,000
 Number of awards: 60
 Number of applicants: 200
 Application deadline: April 18
 Notification begins: April 30
Contact:
Navy Supply Corps Foundation
Navy Supply Corps School
1425 Prince Avenue
Athens, GA 30606-2205
Phone: 706-354-4111
Web: www.usnscf.com/scholarship.html

Navy-Marine Corps Relief Society

Dependents of Deceased Service Members Scholarship Program

Type of award: Scholarship, renewable.
Intended use: For undergraduate study.
Eligibility: Applicant must be dependent of deceased veteran who served in the Marines or Navy. Dependents of deceased service members who died on active duty, in combat situation or after retirement.
Basis for selection: Applicant must demonstrate financial need.
Application requirements: Current military dependent ID card; DD214 and death certificate or DD1300.
Additional information: Minimum 2.0 GPA. Visit Website for more information and application.

 Amount of award: $500-$3,000
 Number of awards: 44
 Number of applicants: 50
 Application deadline: March 1
 Total amount awarded: $132,000
Contact:
Navy-Marine Corps Relief Society
875 North Randolph Street, Suite 225
Arlington, VA 22203-1977
Phone: 703-696-4960
Fax: 730-696-0144
Web: www.nmcrs.org/education

NCAA

The Freedom Forum/NCAA Sports Journalism Scholarship

Type of award: Scholarship.
Intended use: For full-time junior study. Designated institutions: NCAA member institutions.
Basis for selection: Major/career interest in journalism.
Application requirements: Portfolio, recommendations, transcript. Three examples of sports journalism work, such as newspaper articles, program copy, published photographs, editorials, television, and/or radio scripts. VHS tapes, CDs and DVDs accepted.
Additional information: Students must apply during junior year of college. Eight scholarships awarded at NCAA member institutions. Applications available in September. Application available on Website.

Amount of award:	$3,000
Number of awards:	8
Total amount awarded:	$24,000

Contact:
Sports Journalism Scholarship Committee
NCAA Leadership Advisory Board
P.O. Box 6222
Indianapolis, IN 46206-6222
Phone: 317-917-6477
Web: www.ncaa.org/about/scholarships

NCAA Division I Degree-Completion Award Program

Type of award: Scholarship.
Intended use: For senior study at 4-year institution. Designated institutions: Colleges in Division I of the NCAA.
Basis for selection: Competition/talent/interest in athletics/sports. Major/career interest in athletic training. Applicant must demonstrate financial need, depth of character, leadership and service orientation.
Application requirements: Recommendations, essay, transcript. Endorsement and signature from dean of college or head of department and director of athletics; statement and signature from financial aid office. Official tax forms.
Additional information: Applicants must have received athletics-related grant-in-aid at NCAA Division I institution. Must have less than 30 semester hours or 45 quarter hours remaining to complete degree and be attainable within two semesters or three-quarters. Must be entering at least sixth year of postsecondary education. Application materials available at office of Director of Athletics on member school campuses. Must also submit IRS forms. Awards will not exceed full athletics-related grant-in-aid as defined by institution and is renewable for second term, given completion of 12 hours with 2.0 GPA or better.

Number of applicants:	313
Application deadline:	September 21
Total amount awarded:	$950,000

Contact:
NCAA Division I Degree-Completion Program
Karen Cooper
P.O. Box 6222
Indianapolis, IN 46206-6222
Phone: 317-917-6307
Fax: 317-917-6364
Web: www.ncaa.org/about/scholarships

Nebraska State Department of Education

Nebraska Robert C. Byrd Honors Scholarship

Type of award: Scholarship, renewable.
Intended use: For full-time freshman study at accredited postsecondary institution in United States.
Eligibility: Applicant must be high school senior. Applicant must be U.S. citizen or permanent resident residing in Nebraska.
Basis for selection: Applicant must demonstrate high academic achievement.
Application requirements: Transcript. ACT scores.
Additional information: Renewable up to four years with good academic standing. Minimum ACT score of 30. Applications mailed to counselors at all Nebraska high schools in January. Award not available to students of U.S. military academies.

Amount of award:	$1,500
Number of awards:	38
Number of applicants:	38
Application deadline:	March 15
Total amount awarded:	$231,000

Contact:
Nebraska State Department of Education
Robert C. Byrd Scholarship
P.O. Box 94987
Lincoln, NE 68509-4987
Phone: 402-471-3962
Web: www.nde.state.ne.us/byrd

Nevada Department of Education

Nevada Robert C. Byrd Honors Scholarship

Type of award: Scholarship, renewable.
Intended use: For undergraduate study at postsecondary institution.
Eligibility: Applicant must be high school senior. Applicant must be U.S. citizen or permanent resident residing in Nevada.
Basis for selection: Applicant must demonstrate high academic achievement, depth of character and seriousness of purpose.
Additional information: Applicant must be Nevada High School Scholar. Minimum 3.5 GPA and SAT score of 1100 or ACT score of 25 required. Renewable for up to 4 years.

Amount of award:	$1,500
Number of awards:	40
Number of applicants:	1,300
Notification begins:	May 1

Nevada Student Incentive Grant

Type of award: Scholarship.
Intended use: For undergraduate or graduate study at vocational, 2-year, 4-year or graduate institution.
Eligibility: Applicant must be U.S. citizen or permanent resident residing in Nevada.
Basis for selection: Applicant must demonstrate financial need.
Application requirements: FAFSA.
Additional information: Must apply through post-secondary financial aid office. Deadlines vary by institution. Maximum award is $5,000.

Amount of award:	$5,000
Number of awards:	826
Number of applicants:	19,123
Notification begins:	July 1
Total amount awarded:	$494,774

Contact:
Nevada Department of Education
700 East Fifth Street
Capital Complex
Carson City, NV 87910
Phone: 775-687-9150
Fax: 775-687-9113

New England Board of Higher Education

New England Board of Higher Education's Regional Student Program

Type of award: Scholarship.
Intended use: For undergraduate or graduate study in United States. Designated institutions: New England public colleges and universities.
Eligibility: Applicant must be permanent resident residing in Vermont, New Hampshire, Connecticut, Maine, Massachusetts or Rhode Island.
Additional information: Regional Student Program provides New England residents with a tuition discount when they study approved majors not offered at public institutions in their own state at out-of-state public colleges in New England. Must be enrolling in approved major listed in annual catalog.

Contact:
New England Board of Higher Education
45 Temple Place
Boston, MA 02111
Phone: 617-357-9620
Web: www.nebhe.org

New England Employee Benefits Council

NEEBC Scholarship

Type of award: Scholarship, renewable.
Intended use: For undergraduate or graduate study at accredited postsecondary institution.
Basis for selection: Major/career interest in business/management/administration; human resources or insurance/actuarial science. Applicant must demonstrate high academic achievement, depth of character, leadership, seriousness of purpose and service orientation.
Application requirements: Recommendations, transcript. 500 word essay, minimum of two references from college professors, NEEBC members or other benefits professionals.
Additional information: Applicants must aspire towards career in employee benefits. Applicants must reside or attend college in New England.

Amount of award:	$5,000
Number of applicants:	2
Application deadline:	April 1
Notification begins:	May 1

Contact:
New England Benefits Council
440 Totten Pond Road
Waltham, MA 02451
Phone: 781-684-8700
Web: www.neebc.org

New Hampshire Postsecondary Education Commission

New Hampshire Incentive Program

Type of award: Scholarship, renewable.
Intended use: For undergraduate study at accredited vocational, 2-year or 4-year institution. Designated institutions: Eligible institutions in New England.
Eligibility: Applicant must be U.S. citizen or permanent resident residing in New Hampshire.
Basis for selection: Applicant must demonstrate financial need.
Application requirements: Proof of eligibility. FAFSA.
Additional information: Application online at www.fafsa.org.

Amount of award:	$125-$1,000
Number of awards:	2,858
Application deadline:	May 1
Total amount awarded:	$1,496,894

Contact:
New Hampshire Postsecondary Education Commission
Sherrie Tucker
3 Barrell Court, Suite 300
Concord, NH 03301-8543
Phone: 603-271-2555 ext. 355
Fax: 603-271-2696
Web: www.nh.gov/postsecondary

New Hampshire Scholarship for Orphans of Veterans

Type of award: Scholarship, renewable.
Intended use: For full-time undergraduate or graduate study at vocational, 2-year or 4-year institution.
Eligibility: Applicant must be at least 16, no older than 25. Applicant must be U.S. citizen residing in New Hampshire. Applicant must be dependent of veteran, disabled veteran or deceased veteran during Korean War, WW I, WW II or Vietnam. Dependents of veterans of Gulf War or veterans awarded an armed forces expeditionary medal.
Application requirements: Proof of eligibility.
Additional information: Parent must have been legal resident of New Hampshire at time of service-related death.
   Amount of award: $2,500
Contact:
New Hampshire Postsecondary Education Commission
Judith Knapp
3 Barrell Court, Suite 300
Concord, NH 03301-8543
Phone: 603-271-2555 ext. 352
Fax: 603-271-2696
Web: www.nh.gov/postsecondary

New Jersey Commission on Higher Education

New Jersey Educational Opportunity Fund Grant

Type of award: Scholarship, renewable.
Intended use: For full-time undergraduate or graduate study at accredited 2-year or 4-year institution. Designated institutions: Participating New Jersey community colleges, four-year colleges and universities.
Eligibility: Applicant must be U.S. citizen or permanent resident residing in New Jersey.
Basis for selection: Applicant must demonstrate financial need.
Application requirements: FAFSA.
Additional information: For students from educationally disadvantaged backgrounds with demonstrated financial need. Must be New Jersey resident for at least 12 consecutive months prior to enrollment. Students are admitted into EOF program by college. Program includes summer sessions, tutoring, counseling, and student leadership development. Award amounts vary; undergraduate $200-$2,500, graduate $200-$4,350. Contact EOF director at institution for specific application requirements.
   Number of awards: 19,224
   Application deadline: October 1
   Notification begins: April 1
   Total amount awarded: $25,885,906
Contact:
New Jersey Commission on Higher Education
P.O. Box 542
Trenton, NJ 08625-0542
Phone: 609-984-2709
Fax: 609-633-8420
Web: www.state.nj.us/highereducation/eof.htm

New Jersey Department of Military and Veterans Affairs

New Jersey POW/MIA Program

Type of award: Scholarship, renewable.
Intended use: For full-time undergraduate study at accredited 4-year institution in United States.
Eligibility: Applicant must be residing in New Jersey. Applicant must be dependent of active service person or POW/MIA. Parent must have been officially declared Prisoner of War or Missing in Action after January 1, 1960.
Application requirements: Proof of eligibility. Copy of DD 1300.
Additional information: Award is full-tuition waiver (no room, board or expenses) at eligible institution.
   Amount of award: Full tuition
   Number of awards: 1
Contact:
New Jersey Department of Military and Veterans Affairs
DVP
P.O. Box 340
Trenton, NJ 08625-7005
Phone: 609-530-6854
Fax: 609-530-6970
Web: www.state.nj.us/military

New Jersey War Orphans Tuition Credit Program

Type of award: Scholarship, renewable.
Intended use: For undergraduate or graduate study at postsecondary institution in United States.
Eligibility: Applicant must be residing in New Jersey. Applicant must be veteran who served in the Army, Air Force, Marines, Navy, Coast Guard or Reserves/National Guard during Vietnam. Child of service personnel who died due to service-connected disabilities or who is officially listed as Missing In Action. Veteran must have been New Jersey resident.
Application requirements: Proof of eligibility.
Additional information: Must have been New Jersey resident for one year prior to application.
   Amount of award: $500
   Number of applicants: 1
Contact:
New Jersey Department of Military and Veterans Affairs
DVP
P.O. Box 340
Trenton, NJ 08625-7005
Phone: 609-530-6854
Fax: 609-530-6970
Web: www.state.nj.us/military

New Jersey Higher Education Student Assistance Authority

Dana Christmas Scholarship for Heroism

Type of award: Scholarship.
Intended use: For undergraduate or graduate study.
Eligibility: Applicant must be enrolled in high school. Applicant must be residing in New Jersey.
Additional information: Honors young New Jersey residents for acts of heroism. Students must be age 21 or younger at time of act of heroism. Applicant must be resident of New Jersey at time act of heroism was performed and application submitted. Application can be obtained by calling HESAA or by visiting Website.

    Amount of award: $10,000
    Number of awards: 5
    Number of applicants: 19
    Application deadline: October 15
    Notification begins: December 1
    Total amount awarded: $50,000

Contact:
New Jersey Higher Education Student Assistance Authority
P.O. Box 540
Trenton, NJ 08625
Phone: 800-792-8670
Web: www.hesaa.org

Educational Opportunity Fund (EOF)

Type of award: Scholarship, renewable.
Intended use: For undergraduate or graduate study. Designated institutions: Eligible New Jersey institutions.
Eligibility: Applicant must be U.S. citizen or permanent resident residing in New Jersey.
Basis for selection: Applicant must demonstrate financial need.
Application requirements: FAFSA.
Additional information: Must be permanent New Jersey resident for at least 12 months prior to application. Provides financial aid to eligible students from educationally and economically disadvantaged backgrounds at participating in-state institutions. Household income cannot exceed guidelines. Contact campus EOF director to apply.

    Amount of award: $200-$2,500
    Application deadline: October 1, March 1

Contact:
New Jersey Higher Education Assistance Authority
P.O. Box 540
Trenton, NJ 08625
Phone: 800-792-8670
Web: www.hesaa.org

New Jeresy Student Tuition Assistance Reward Scholarship (NJSTARS)

Type of award: Scholarship, renewable.
Intended use: For full-time undergraduate study at 2-year institution.
Eligibility: Applicant must be residing in New Jersey.
Application requirements: FAFSA.
Additional information: Must be resident of NJ for 12 months prior to enrollment. Provides tuition and approved fees for up to five semesters at a county college for students graduating in top 20 percent of high school class. To be eligible for renewal, students must have minimum GPA of 3.0.

    Application deadline: June 1, October 1

Contact:
New Jersey Higher Education Student Assistance Authority
P.O. Box 540
Trenton, NJ 08625
Phone: 800-792-8670
Web: www.hesaa.org

New Jersey Edward J. Bloustein Distinguished Scholars

Type of award: Scholarship, renewable.
Intended use: For full-time undergraduate study at accredited 2-year or 4-year institution. Designated institutions: Approved NJ colleges, universities, and degree-granting proprietary institutions.
Eligibility: Applicant must be high school senior. Applicant must be U.S. citizen or permanent resident residing in New Jersey.
Basis for selection: Applicant must demonstrate high academic achievement.
Application requirements: Transcript, nomination by high school. SAT scores, junior year class rank.
Additional information: Students may not apply directly to this program. Candidates will be selected for consideration by their secondary schools based upon standard of academic criteria. Must be a New Jersey resident for at least 12 consecutive months prior to receiving the award. Candidates are nominated for consideration by high schools and are notified in fall of senior year. See guidance counselor for more information.

    Amount of award: $1,000

Contact:
New Jersey Higher Education Student Assistance Authority
4 Quakerbridge Plaza, P.O. Box 540
Trenton, NJ 08625-0540
Phone: 800-792-8670
Web: www.hesaa.org

New Jersey STARS II

Type of award: Scholarship, renewable.
Intended use: For full-time undergraduate study at accredited 4-year institution in United States.
Eligibility: Applicant must be residing in Vermont, New Hampshire, Connecticut, Maine, Massachusetts or Rhode Island.
Basis for selection: Applicant must demonstrate financial need and high academic achievement.
Application requirements: FAFSA.
Additional information: Must be successful NJSTARS scholar receiving associate's degree with a minimum 3.0 GPA. Provides for tuition and fees for up to 18 credits per semester for four semesters at a New Jersey public four-year institution.

    Amount of award: Full tuition
    Application deadline: June 1, October 1

Contact:
New Jersey Higher Education Student Assistance Authority
P.O. Box 540
Trenton, NJ 08625
Phone: 800-792-8670
Fax: 609-588-3266
Web: www.hesaa.org

New Jersey Survivor Tuition Benefits Program

Type of award: Scholarship, renewable.
Intended use: For undergraduate study. Designated institutions: Approved NJ colleges, universities, and degree-granting institutions.
Eligibility: Applicant's parent must have been killed or disabled in work-related accident as firefighter, police officer or public safety officer.
Application requirements: Proof of eligibility.
Additional information: Parent or spouse must have been New Jersey firefighter, law enforcement or emergency service personnel killed in line of duty. Applications available on agency's website or toll-free hotline. Grants pay cost of tuition up to highest tuition charged at a New Jersey public postsecondary school.
   Amount of award: Full tuition
   Application deadline: October 1, March 1
Contact:
New Jersey Higher Education Student Assistance Authority
4 Quakerbridge Plaza, P.O. Box 540
Trenton, NJ 08625-0540
Phone: 800-792-8670
Fax: 609-588-3266
Web: www.hesaa.org

New Jersey Tuition Aid Grants (TAG)

Type of award: Scholarship, renewable.
Intended use: For full-time undergraduate study in United States. Designated institutions: Approved New Jersey colleges, universities, and degree-granting proprietary institutions.
Eligibility: Applicant must be U.S. citizen or permanent resident residing in New Jersey.
Basis for selection: Applicant must demonstrate financial need.
Application requirements: FAFSA.
Additional information: Students must demonstrate financial need and maintain satisfactory academic progress. Deadline for fall and spring awards: June 1 for renewal students; October 1 for new applicants who did not receive Tuition Aid Grant in the prior academic year.
   Amount of award: $962-$10,236
   Application deadline: June 1, October 1
Contact:
New Jersey Higher Education Student Assistance Authority
4 Quakerbridge Plaza, P.O. Box 540
Trenton, NJ 08625-0540
Phone: 800-792-8670
Fax: 609-558-2228
Web: www.hesaa.org

New Jersey Urban Scholars

Type of award: Scholarship, renewable.
Intended use: For full-time undergraduate study at accredited 2-year institution in United States. Designated institutions: Approved New Jersey colleges, universities, and degree-granting institutions.
Eligibility: Applicant must be U.S. citizen or permanent resident residing in New Jersey.
Basis for selection: Applicant must demonstrate high academic achievement.
Application requirements: Nomination by high school. Class rank and GPA.
Additional information: Students may not apply directly for award. Open to students in top 10 percent of their high school class, with minimum 3.0 GPA or equivalent, attending high schools in New Jersey's urban and economically distressed areas. Candidates nominated for consideration by high schools will receive notification by fall of senior year. See guidance counselors for more information.
   Amount of award: $1,000
Contact:
New Jersey Higher Education Student Assistance Authority
4 Quakerbridge Plaza
P.O. Box 540
Trenton, NJ 08625-0540
Phone: 800-792-8670
Fax: 609-588-2228
Web: www.hesaa.org

New Jersey World Trade Center Scholarship

Type of award: Scholarship, renewable.
Eligibility: Applicant must be residing in New Jersey.
Additional information: Must be spouse or dependent of New Jersey resident who was killed or presumed dead as a result of the terrorist attacks of September 11, 2001. This includes first responders and rescue workers who died as a result of illness caused by attack sites.
   Amount of award: $6,500
   Number of awards: 67
   Number of applicants: 67
   Application deadline: October 15
   Total amount awarded: $370,668
Contact:
New Jersey Higher Education Student Assistance Authority
P.O. Box 540
Trenton, NJ 08625
Phone: 800-792-8670
Fax: 609-588-2228
Web: www.hesaa.org

Part-Time Tuition Aid Grant for County Colleges

Type of award: Scholarship, renewable.
Intended use: For half-time undergraduate study at postsecondary institution. Designated institutions: Participating New Jersey county colleges.
Eligibility: Applicant must be U.S. citizen or permanent resident residing in New Jersey.
Basis for selection: Applicant must demonstrate financial need.
Application requirements: FAFSA.
Additional information: Must be enrolled part-time (9-11 credits). Must be NJ resident for at least 12 months prior to enrollment. Must maintain satisfactory academic progress. Renewals due June 1. New applications due October 1. Application and additional information can be obtained on Website.

Amount of award: $205-$715
Application deadline: June 1, October 1
Contact:
New Jersey Higher Education Student Assistance Authority
P.O. Box 540
Trenton, NJ 08625
Phone: 800-792-8670
Fax: 609-588-2228
Web: www.hesaa.org

New Jersey State Golf Association

Caddie Scholarship

Type of award: Scholarship, renewable.
Intended use: For full-time undergraduate study at accredited 2-year or 4-year institution in United States. Designated institutions: Accredited members of Association of American Colleges and Universities.
Basis for selection: Applicant must demonstrate financial need and high academic achievement.
Application requirements: Proof of eligibility. Recommendation from golf club.
Additional information: Applicants must caddie at least two seasons at a member club of New Jersey State Golf Association. Must be in top half of class and have minimum 900 SAT and 2.5 GPA. Awards renewable for up to four years. Foundation also offers one full scholarship award at Rutgers University.
Amount of award: $2,000-$4,000
Number of awards: 50
Number of applicants: 120
Application deadline: May 1
Notification begins: June 15
Total amount awarded: $530,000
Contact:
New Jersey State Golf Association
Caddie Scholarship Foundation
P.O. Box 6947
Freehold, NJ 07728
Phone: 973-338-8334
Web: www.njsga.org

New Mexico Commission on Higher Education

New Mexico Competitive Scholarships

Type of award: Scholarship.
Intended use: For undergraduate study at postsecondary institution in United States. Designated institutions: Public New Mexico institutions.
Eligibility: Applicant must be residing in New Mexico.
Basis for selection: Applicant must demonstrate high academic achievement.
Additional information: Awards to encourage out-of-state students who have demonstrated high academic achievement in high school to enroll in public institutions in New Mexico. Recipients of at least $100 in competitive scholarships per semester eligible for resident tuition and fees. Applicants must meet GPA/ACT score requirements, which vary by institution. Contact financial aid office of any New Mexico postsecondary institution or see Website.
Contact:
New Mexico Commission on Higher Education
Financial Aid and Student Services
1068 Cerrillos Road
Santa Fe, NM 87505
Phone: 800-279-9777
Web: www.hed.state.nm.us

New Mexico Legislative Endowment Program

Type of award: Scholarship, renewable.
Intended use: For undergraduate study at accredited postsecondary institution.
Eligibility: Applicant must be U.S. citizen or permanent resident residing in New Mexico.
Basis for selection: Applicant must demonstrate financial need.
Application requirements: FAFSA.
Additional information: Contact financial aid office of any public postsecondary institution in New Mexico. Four-year public institutions may award up to $2,500 per student per academic year. Two-year public institutions may award up to $1,000 per student per year. Part-time students eligible for prorated awards. Deadlines set by institution.
Amount of award: $1,000-$2,500
Contact:
New Mexico Commission on Higher Education
Financial Aid and Student Services
1068 Cerrillos Road
Santa Fe, NM 87505
Phone: 800-279-9777
Web: www.hed.state.nm.us

New Mexico Legislative Lottery Scholarship

Type of award: Scholarship.
Intended use: For full-time undergraduate study at postsecondary institution. Designated institutions: Eligible New Mexico public colleges and universities.
Eligibility: Applicant must be high school senior. Applicant must be residing in New Mexico.
Additional information: Must be enrolled full-time and complete 12 graded credit hours at eligible New Mexico public college or university in the first regular semester immediately following graduation from New Mexico high school. Must obtain 2.5 GPA during first college semester. Deadlines vary according to institution; see Website or apply through financial aid office.
Amount of award: Full tuition
Contact:
New Mexico Commission on Higher Education
Financial Aid and Student Services
1068 Cerrillos Road
Santa Fe, NM 87505
Phone: 800-279-9777
Web: www.hed.state.nm.us

New Mexico Scholars Program

Type of award: Scholarship, renewable.

Intended use: For undergraduate study at accredited 2-year or 4-year institution. Designated institutions: Public institutions in New Mexico or the following private institutions: College of Santa Fe, St. John's College, College of the Southwest.
Eligibility: Applicant must be no older than 21. Applicant must be U.S. citizen or permanent resident residing in New Mexico.
Basis for selection: Applicant must demonstrate financial need and high academic achievement.
Application requirements: FAFSA.
Additional information: Tuition waiver (tuition, books, and required fees). Number of awards based on availability of funds. Must be graduate of New Mexico high school. Must score at least 25 on ACT or rank in top five percent of high school graduating class and have family income no greater than $30,000 per year or $40,000 if two or more family members are enrolled at post-secondary institution. Contact financial aid office of New Mexico postsecondary institution of choice for information and application. Application deadlines set by institution.
Contact:
New Mexico Commission on Higher Education
Financial Aid and Student Services
1068 Cerrillos Road
Santa Fe, NM 87505
Phone: 800-279-9777
Web: www.hed.state.nm.us

New Mexico Student Choice Program

Type of award: Scholarship, renewable.
Intended use: For undergraduate study at postsecondary institution. Designated institutions: St. John's College, College of Southwest, College of Santa Fe.
Eligibility: Applicant must be U.S. citizen or permanent resident residing in New Mexico.
Basis for selection: Applicant must demonstrate financial need.
Application requirements: FAFSA.
Additional information: Award varies, with maximum based on highest tuition at New Mexico public university. Apply to financial aid office at one of three private non-profit colleges where award may be used. Must be enrolled in eligible institution as undergraduate. Part-time students eligible for pro-rated awards.
Contact:
New Mexico Commission on Higher Education
Financial Aid and Student Services
1068 Cerrillos Road
Santa Fe, NM 87505
Phone: 800-279-9777
Web: www.hed.state.nm.us

New Mexico Student Incentive Grant

Type of award: Scholarship, renewable.
Intended use: For undergraduate study at accredited postsecondary institution. Designated institutions: Public and selected private nonprofit New Mexico postsecondary institutions.
Eligibility: Applicant must be U.S. citizen or permanent resident residing in New Mexico.
Basis for selection: Applicant must demonstrate financial need.
Application requirements: FAFSA.

Additional information: Must demonstrate exceptional financial need. Contact financial aid office of New Mexico public postsecondary institutions or eligible private nonprofits for information, application and deadline. Part-time students eligible for pro-rated awards.
Amount of award: $200-$2,500
Contact:
New Mexico Commission on Higher Education
Financial Aid and Student Services
1068 Cerrillos Road
Santa Fe, NM 87505
Phone: 800-279-9777
Web: www.hed.state.nm.us

New Mexico Vietnam Veteran's Scholarship

Type of award: Scholarship, renewable.
Intended use: For undergraduate or graduate study at postsecondary institution. Designated institutions: Public and selected private non-profit institutions in New Mexico.
Eligibility: Applicant must be U.S. citizen residing in New Mexico. Applicant must be veteran during Vietnam.
Application requirements: Proof of eligibility.
Additional information: Maximum award provides tuition/fees and book allowance on first come, first served basis. Eligibility must be certified by New Mexico Veterans Service Commission. Contact financial aid office of any New Mexico public postsecondary institution for information, deadline, and application. Coursework must be certified by New Mexico Veterans' Service Commission.
Amount of award: Full tuition
Contact:
New Mexico Veteran's Service Commission
P.O. Box 2324
Santa Fe, NM 87505
Phone: 505-827-6300
Web: www.hed.state.nm.us

New York Lottery

Leaders of Tomorrow Scholarship

Type of award: Scholarship.
Intended use: For full-time undergraduate study at accredited vocational, 2-year or 4-year institution in United States. Designated institutions: Eligible New York State postsecondary institutions.
Eligibility: Applicant must be high school senior. Applicant must be residing in New York.
Basis for selection: Applicant must demonstrate high academic achievement, leadership and service orientation.
Application requirements: Transcript, proof of eligibility.
Additional information: $5,000 scholarship paid over four years, at $1,250 per year. One student from every participating public and private high school in New York State is awarded scholarship. Student must plan to attend New York State-accredited college, university, trade school, or community college; should have at least B average based on seven semesters of high school. Student must complete studies within five years of high school graduation. Deadline in March; check Website for exact date. Students with parents/guardians employed by New York State Lottery or its contractors are not eligible.

Amount of award: $1,250
Number of awards: 1,200
Number of applicants: 2,010
Application deadline: March 26
Notification begins: May 31
Total amount awarded: $1,033,000
Contact:
CASDA-LOT
University of Albany - East Campus
Five University Pl. - A409
Rensselear, NY 12144
Phone: 518-525-2686
Fax: 518-525-2689
Web: www.nylottery.org

New York State Education Department

New York State Higher Education Opportunity Program (HEOP)

Type of award: Scholarship.
Intended use: For undergraduate study at 2-year or 4-year institution. Designated institutions: Independent New York State colleges and universities.
Eligibility: Applicant must be residing in New York.
Basis for selection: Applicant must demonstrate financial need.
Additional information: Applicant must be resident of New York State for one year preceding entry into HEOP and be academically and economically disadvantaged. Contact college or university of interest for application and additional information, and apply at time of admission. Support services include presession summer program and tutoring, counseling, and special coursework during academic year. Award amounts vary; contact sponsor for information.
Contact:
Contact Financial Aid Office
Phone: 518-474-5313
Fax: 518-486-5221
Web: www.highered.nysed.gov

New York State Readers Aid Program

Type of award: Scholarship, renewable.
Intended use: For undergraduate, master's or doctoral study at 2-year, 4-year or graduate institution.
Eligibility: Applicant must be visually impaired or hearing impaired. Applicant must be residing in New York.
Application requirements: Proof of eligibility.
Additional information: Number of awards varies. Applications available at degree-granting institutions. For deaf or blind students, award provides funds for note-takers, readers, or interpreters. Applicants must be New York residents; may be attending out of state institution.
Amount of award: $1,000
Number of applicants: 411
Total amount awarded: $300,000
Contact:
Office of Vocational and Ed. Services for People with Disabilities
Readers Aid Program
One Commerce Plaza, room 1623
Albany, NY 12234
Phone: 518-474-5652
Fax: 518-473-5769
Web: www.vesid.nysed.gov

New York State Robert C. Byrd Federal Honors Scholarship

Type of award: Scholarship, renewable.
Intended use: For full-time undergraduate study at accredited 2-year or 4-year institution in United States.
Eligibility: Applicant must be high school senior. Applicant must be U.S. citizen or permanent resident residing in New York.
Basis for selection: Applicant must demonstrate high academic achievement.
Application requirements: Nomination by high school.
Additional information: Must have 1875 SAT score, minimum 95 average or 410 GED score. Applicants will be ranked within county of legal residence based on final ranking score composed of 75 percent GPA and 25 percent SAT score. Applications available in early fall at student's high school.
Amount of award: $1,500
Number of awards: 400
Number of applicants: 5,000
Application deadline: March 1
Contact:
New York State Education Department
Scholarships Unit
Room 1078 EBA
Albany, NY 12234
Phone: 518-486-1319
Fax: 518-486-5346
Web: www.highered.nysed.gov

New York State Grange

Caroline Kark Scholarship

Type of award: Scholarship.
Intended use: For undergraduate study.
Eligibility: Applicant must be residing in New York.
Basis for selection: Major/career interest in deafness studies.
Additional information: Award available to Grange members preparing for a career working with the deaf or hearing impaired and to non-members who are deaf and want to further their education beyond high school. Hearing applicants must have been a Grange member for one year prior to applying. Deaf applicants must show sufficient hearing loss to receive full-time amplification.
Application deadline: April 15
Contact:
New York State Grange
100 Grange Place
Cortland, NY 13045
Phone: 607-756-7553
Fax: 607-756-7557
Web: www.nysgrange.com

Grange Denise Scholarship

Type of award: Scholarship, renewable.
Intended use: For full-time undergraduate study at 2-year or 4-year institution.
Eligibility: Applicant must be residing in New York.
Basis for selection: Major/career interest in agriculture; agribusiness; agricultural education; agricultural economics or natural resources/conservation. Applicant must demonstrate financial need.
Application requirements: Recommendations, transcript.
Additional information: Send SASE for application.
    Amount of award: $1,000
    Number of awards: 6
    Number of applicants: 20
    Application deadline: April 15
    Notification begins: June 15
    Total amount awarded: $6,000
Contact:
New York State Grange
100 Grange Place
Cortland, NY 13045
Phone: 607-756-7553

Grange Susan W. Freestone Education Award

Type of award: Scholarship, renewable.
Intended use: For full-time undergraduate or graduate study at 2-year or 4-year institution in United States.
Eligibility: Applicant or parent must be member/participant of New York State Grange. Applicant must be residing in New York.
Basis for selection: Applicant must demonstrate financial need, depth of character and service orientation.
Additional information: Applicant must be current Grange member in New York state to qualify for grant. Must have been Junior Grange member to qualify for maximum award. Send SASE for application. Award granted by scholarship committee, based on many factors.
    Amount of award: $500-$1,000
    Number of awards: 2
    Number of applicants: 5
    Application deadline: April 15
    Notification begins: June 15
    Total amount awarded: $2,000
Contact:
New York State Grange
100 Grange Place
Cortland, NY 13045
Phone: 607-756-7553

June Gill Nursing Scholarship

Type of award: Scholarship.
Intended use: For undergraduate study.
Eligibility: Applicant must be residing in New York.
Basis for selection: Major/career interest in nursing. Applicant must demonstrate financial need and high academic achievement.
Application requirements: Career statement.
Additional information: Applicant must be a member of the New York State Grange. Award amounts vary.
    Application deadline: April 15
    Notification begins: June 1
Contact:
New York State Grange
100 Grange Place
Cortland, NY 13045
Phone: 607-756-7553
Fax: 607-756-7557
Web: www.nysgrange.com

New York State Higher Education Services Corporation

City University Seek/College Discovery Program

Type of award: Scholarship.
Intended use: For undergraduate study at 2-year or 4-year institution. Designated institutions: City University of New York campuses.
Eligibility: Applicant must be U.S. citizen or permanent resident residing in New York.
Basis for selection: Applicant must demonstrate financial need.
Application requirements: Proof of eligibility. FAFSA; TAP.
Additional information: Applicant must be both academically and economically disadvantaged. Available at CUNY and community college campuses. Apply to CUNY financial aid office. For Seek, student must have resided in New York State for at least one year; for College Discovery, student must have resided in New York City for at least one year.
Contact:
City University of New York
Office of Admission Services
1114 Ave. of the Americas
New York, NY 10036
Phone: 212-997-CUNY
Web: www.cuny.edu

Flight 587 Memorial Scholarships

Type of award: Scholarship, renewable.
Intended use: For full-time undergraduate study.
Eligibility: Applicant must be residing in New York.
Application requirements: FAFSA. TAP. Scholarship supplement. Proof of applicant's relationship to the deceased (birth certificate, marriage license, etc).
Additional information: Provides financial aid to children, spouses and financial dependents of individuals killed as a direct result of American Airlines Flight 587's crash in the Belle Harbor neighborhood of Queens, New York, on the morning of November 12, 2001. Program aids the 266 families who lost loved ones cover the cost of attending college in New York State. Award is full tuition for students attending public colleges and universities in New York State, and the monetary equivalent for students attending private New York schools.
    Application deadline: May 1
Contact:
New York State Higher Education Services Corporation
HESC Scholarship Unit
99 Washington Ave, Room 1430A
Albany, NY 12255
Phone: 888-NYS-HESC
Web: www.hesc.com

Military Service Recognition Scholarship (MSRS)

Type of award: Scholarship, renewable.
Intended use: For full-time undergraduate study at 2-year or 4-year institution. Designated institutions: Approved New York State institutions.
Eligibility: Applicant must be residing in New York. Applicant must be disabled while on active duty; or dependent of disabled veteran, deceased veteran or POW/MIA; or spouse of disabled veteran, deceased veteran or POW/MIA. Must be child, spouse, or financial dependent of members of the U.S. armed forces or state-organized militia who, at any time after August 2, 1990, while New York State residents, (1) died or became permanently disabled as a result of injury or illness in a combat theater or combat zone or during military training operations in preparation for duty in a combat theater or (2) are classified as MIA in a combat theater or combat zone of operations.
Application requirements: FAFSA, TAP application.
Additional information: At public colleges and universities (CUNY or SUNY), award covers actual tuition and mandatory educational fees; actual room and board for living on campus (or an allowance for commuters); and allowances for books, supplies, and transportation. At private institutions, award amount equals SUNY four-year college tuition and fees and allowances for room and board, books, supplies, and transportation. New York State resident family members who were enrolled in undergraduate programs at U.S. colleges or universities outside of New York State on September 11, 2001, are also eligible. See Website for more details.
   Application deadline: May 1
Contact:
New York State Higher Education Services Corporation
Scholarships and Grants
99 Washington Ave.
Albany, NY 12255
Phone: 888-NYS-HESC
Web: www.hesc.com

New York State Aid for Part-time Study Program

Type of award: Scholarship, renewable.
Intended use: For half-time undergraduate study at postsecondary institution. Designated institutions: Participating New York postsecondary institutions.
Eligibility: Applicant must be U.S. citizen or permanent resident residing in New York.
Basis for selection: Applicant must demonstrate financial need.
Application requirements: Proof of eligibility.
Additional information: Must fall within income limits. Campus-based program; recipients selected and award amount determined by school. Apply to financial aid office of institution. Maximum award is $2,000. Must not have used up TAP eligibility or be in default on Federal Family Education Loan. Student must maintain minimum 2.0 GPA. Visit Website for additional information.
   Amount of award: $2,000
Contact:
New York State Higher Education Services Corporation
Grants and Scholarships
99 Washington Avenue
Albany, NY 12255
Phone: 888-NYS-HESC
Web: www.hesc.com

New York State Memorial Scholarship for Families of Deceased Police/Volunteer Firefighters/Peace Officers and Emergency Medical Service Workers

Type of award: Scholarship, renewable.
Intended use: For full-time undergraduate study at 2-year or 4-year institution. Designated institutions: Approved New York institutions.
Eligibility: Applicant must be U.S. citizen residing in New York. Applicant's parent must have been killed or disabled in work-related accident as firefighter, police officer or public safety officer.
Application requirements: Proof of eligibility. Memorial Scholarship Supplement, FAFSA, and Express TAP Application.
Additional information: Spouse and/or children of police officer/firefighter/peace officer/EMS worker who died as result of injuries sustained in line of duty in service to New York State are eligible. Award will equal applicant's actual tuition cost or SUNY undergraduate tuition cost, whichever is less. Also provides funds to meet non-tuition costs, such as room and board, books, supplies and transportation. Visit Website for additional information.
   Application deadline: May 1
Contact:
New York State Higher Education Services Corporation
Grants and Scholarships
99 Washington Avenue
Albany, NY 12255
Phone: 888-NYS-HESC
Web: www.hesc.com

New York State Regents Awards for Children of Deceased and Disabled Veterans

Type of award: Scholarship.
Intended use: For full-time undergraduate or non-degree study at 2-year or 4-year institution.
Eligibility: Applicant must be residing in New York. Applicant must be dependent of veteran, disabled veteran or deceased veteran during Korean War, Persian Gulf War, WW I, WW II or Vietnam. Student's parent must have been disabled or deceased veteran or POW, or classified as MIA. Students whose parent(s) have been recipient of Armed Forces, Navy, or Marine Corps expeditionary medal for participation in operations in Lebanon, Grenada, and Panama also eligible. Also eligible are students born with spina bifida whose parent(s) served in Vietnam between 12/22/61 and 5/7/75.
Application requirements: Proof of eligibility. FAFSA and Express TAP Application.
Additional information: Student must initially establish eligibility by submitting a Child of Veteran Award Supplement before applying. Visit Website for additional information.
   Amount of award: $450
   Application deadline: May 1
Contact:
New York State Higher Education Services Corporation
Grants and Scholarships
99 Washington Avenue
Albany, NY 12255
Phone: 888-NYS-HESC
Web: www.hesc.com

New York State Tuition Assistance Program

Type of award: Scholarship, renewable.
Intended use: For undergraduate or graduate study at accredited postsecondary institution in United States. Designated institutions: TAP-eligible postsecondary schools in New York.
Eligibility: Applicant must be U.S. citizen or permanent resident residing in New York.
Basis for selection: Applicant must demonstrate financial need.
Application requirements: Proof of eligibility. FAFSA.
Additional information: Must fall within income limits. Submit FAFSA and receive prefilled Express TAP Application (ETA) to review, sign and return. Institution must be approved by New York State Education Department to offer TAP-eligible programs of study. Award subject to budget appropriations. Must maintain at least C average. Must not be in default on a HESC-guaranteed loan. Part-time first-time freshmen attending CUNY, SUNY, or not-for-profit independent degree-granting college also eligible. Visit Website for additional information.
   Amount of award: $5,000
   Application deadline: May 1
Contact:
New York State Higher Education Services Corporation
Grants and Scholarships
99 Washington Avenue
Albany, NY 12255
Phone: 888-NYS-HESC
Web: www.hesc.com

New York State Veterans Tuition Award

Type of award: Scholarship, renewable.
Intended use: For undergraduate or graduate study at accredited vocational, 2-year, 4-year or graduate institution in United States. Designated institutions: Approved postsecondary schools in New York.
Eligibility: Applicant must be returning adult student. Applicant must be U.S. citizen or permanent resident residing in New York. Applicant must be veteran during Persian Gulf War or Vietnam. Must have served in armed forces in hostilities in Indochina between December 1961 and May 1975, or in Persian Gulf starting August 2, 1990. Veterans of the conflict in Afghanistan also eligible. Must have other than dishonorable charge for either.
Application requirements: Proof of eligibility. FAFSA. Express Tap Application (ETA). Documentation of Indochina, Persian Gulf, or Afghanistan service.
Additional information: Maximum award is $2,000 annually for full-time students; $1,000 annually for part-time students. Students must have also applied for TAP and Federal Pell Grant awards. Visit Website for additional information.
   Amount of award: $1,000-$2,000
   Application deadline: May 1
Contact:
New York State Higher Education Services Corporation
Grants and Scholarships
99 Washington Avenue
Albany, NY 12255
Phone: 888-NYS-HESC
Web: www.hesc.com

New York State Volunteer Recruitment Service Scholarship

Type of award: Scholarship, renewable.
Intended use: For undergraduate study. Designated institutions: Approved New York State schools within 50 miles of volunteer firefighter or ambulance worker organization. If no college is available within 50-mile limit, must be attending the nearest college/institution.
Eligibility: Applicant must be residing in New York.
Application requirements: FAFSA.
Additional information: Scholarship for volunteer firefighters and ambulance workers. If applicant is 23 or older, should have less than six months of volunteer service at time of initial award. If under 23, no minimum or maximum time of service is required at time of initial award. Applicant must be pursuing his/her first bachelor's degree. Must have applied for state and federal aid. Must have been New York State resident for at least one year at time of application. Must maintain C average or better and maintain status as an active volunteer in order to renew scholarship. Award amount and deadline vary; see Website or contact volunteer company official for details.
   Application deadline: May 1
Contact:
Contact volunteer company official for application.
Phone: 888-697-4372
Web: www.hesc.com

New York State World Trade Center Memorial Scholarship

Type of award: Scholarship, renewable.
Intended use: For full-time undergraduate study at 2-year or 4-year institution. Designated institutions: Approved New York colleges and universities.
Application requirements: Proof of eligibility. FAFSA, Express TAP Application.
Additional information: Must be child, spouse, or financial dependent of persons who died or became severely and permanently disabled due to the September 11th attacks or rescue and recovery operation. Survivors of the attack who are severely and permanently disabled as a result of injuries sustained during the attacks or rescue and recovery operation are also eligible. At public colleges and universities (CUNY or SUNY), award covers actual tuition and mandatory educational fees; actual room and board for living on campus (or an allowance for commuters); and allowances for books, supplies and transportation. At private institutions, award amount equals SUNY four-year college tuition and fees and allowances for room and board, books, supplies and transportation. New York State resident family members who were enrolled in undergraduate programs at U.S. colleges or universities outside of New York State on September 11, 2001, are also eligible. See Website for details.
   Amount of award: Full tuition
Contact:
New York State Higher Education Services Corporation
Grants and Scholarships
99 Washington Ave.
Albany, NY 12255
Phone: 888-NYS-HESC
Web: www.hesc.com

New York State Native American Education Unit

New York State Native American Student Aid Program

Type of award: Scholarship, renewable.
Intended use: For undergraduate study at accredited vocational, 2-year or 4-year institution.
Eligibility: Applicant must be American Indian. Must be on official tribal roll of New York State tribe or be a child of enrolled member. Applicant must be residing in New York.
Application requirements: Transcript, proof of eligibility. Tribal certification form, documentation of high school graduation, college acceptance letter.
Additional information: Must reapply to renew award each semester. Minimum 2.0 semester GPA required. Summer application deadline May 20. Students taking 12 or more credits receive $1,000; under 12 credits, $85 per credit hour.
   Amount of award: $2,000
   Application deadline: July 15, December 31
Contact:
New York State Native American Education Unit
New York State Education Department
Room 374, Education Building Annex
Albany, NY 12234
Phone: 518-474-0537
Fax: 518-474-3666

New York Women in Communications Foundation

New York Women in Communications Foundation Scholarship

Type of award: Scholarship, renewable.
Intended use: For undergraduate or graduate study at accredited postsecondary institution.
Eligibility: Applicant must be residing in Connecticut, New York, New Jersey or Pennsylvania.
Basis for selection: Applicant must demonstrate financial need, high academic achievement, leadership and service orientation.
Application requirements: Interview, recommendations, essay, transcript, proof of eligibility. Resume.
Additional information: Minimum 3.2 GPA. Applicant must be majoring in a communications-related field or a high school senior intending to declare a major in a communications-related field. Recipients will be selected on the basis of academic achievement, need, demonstrated leadership, participation in school and community-service activities, honors and other awards or recognition, work experience, statement of goals and aspirations, and unusual personal and/or family circumstances. Finalists will be required to attend an in-person interview in New York City on a date in February. Visit Website for application and additional requirements.
   Amount of award: $2,500-$10,000
   Number of awards: 18
   Number of applicants: 300
   Application deadline: January 22
   Notification begins: April 1
   Total amount awarded: $100,000
Contact:
New York Women in Communications Foundation Scholarship Program
355 Lexington Avenue, 15th Floor
New York, NY 10017-6603
Web: www.nywici.org

Nisei Student Relocation Commemorative Fund

Nisei Student Relocation Commemorative Fund

Type of award: Scholarship.
Intended use: For freshman study at vocational, 2-year or 4-year institution in United States.
Eligibility: Applicant must be Southeast Asian (Vietnamese, Cambodian, Hmong, Laotian, Amerasian) refugee or immigrant. Applicant must be high school senior.
Basis for selection: Applicant must demonstrate financial need and high academic achievement.
Application requirements: Recommendations, essay, transcript.
Additional information: Applicant must be high school senior living in city/area/region of the U.S. where scholarships awarded as determined annually by organization's board of directors. Location changes yearly; contact group for information. Number of awards varies.
   Amount of award: $500-$2,000
   Number of applicants: 80
   Application deadline: March 31
   Total amount awarded: $37,500
Contact:
Nisei Student Relocation Commemorative Fund
c/o Y. Kobayashi or J. Hibino
19 Scenic Drive
Portland, CT 06480
Phone: 860-342-1731

Non Commissioned Officers Association

Non Commissioned Officers Association Scholarship for Children of Members

Type of award: Scholarship, renewable.
Intended use: For full-time undergraduate study in United States.
Eligibility: Applicant's parent must be member of Non Commissioned Officers Association.
Application requirements: Transcript. Autobiography, ACT/SAT scores, and minimum 200-word essay on Americanism.

Include two recommendation letters from school and one personal recommendation letter from adult who is not a relative.
Additional information: Applicant must be dependent of member of Non Commissioned Officers Association.
> **Amount of award:** $900-$1,000
> **Number of awards:** 16
> **Number of applicants:** 250
> **Application deadline:** March 31
> **Notification begins:** June 1
> **Total amount awarded:** $52,500

Contact:
Non Commissioned Officers Association
P.O. Box 33790
San Antonio, TX 78265
Phone: 210-653-6161
Fax: 210-637-3337
Web: www.ncoausa.org

Non Commissioned Officers Association Scholarship for Spouses

Type of award: Scholarship, renewable.
Intended use: For full-time undergraduate study in United States.
Eligibility: Applicant must be U.S. citizen. Must be spouse of member of Non Commissioned Officers Association. Recipient must apply for auxiliary membership in Non Commissioned Officers Association.
Application requirements: Transcript. Copy of high school diploma or GED, brief biographical background, and certificates for any training courses completed. Letter of intent describing degree course of study, plans for completion of program, and a closing paragraph on "What a College Degree Means to Me."
> **Amount of award:** $900
> **Number of awards:** 4
> **Number of applicants:** 30
> **Application deadline:** March 31
> **Notification begins:** June 1

Contact:
Non Commissioned Officers Association
P.O. Box 33790
San Antonio, TX 78265
Phone: 210-653-6161
Fax: 210-637-3337
Web: www.ncoausa.org

North American Limousin Foundation

Limouselle Scholarship

Type of award: Scholarship.
Intended use: For undergraduate or graduate study at 2-year or 4-year institution.
Eligibility: Applicant or parent must be member/participant of North American Limousin Junior Association.
Basis for selection: Applicant must demonstrate financial need, high academic achievement, depth of character, leadership, patriotism, seriousness of purpose and service orientation.
Application requirements: Transcript, proof of eligibility. Recent photo. One of the three recommendations must be from active NALF member other than relative or guardian; 4H and FFA work.
Additional information: Must rank in top third of class.
> **Amount of award:** $500
> **Number of awards:** 2
> **Application deadline:** May 15

Contact:
North American Limousin Foundation
Attn: Donna Etherton
8961 Oak Crest Road
Dawson, IL 62520
Web: www.nalf.org

National Limouselle Financial Assistance Grant

Type of award: Scholarship.
Intended use: For undergraduate study at vocational, 2-year or 4-year institution.
Eligibility: Applicant or parent must be member/participant of North American Limousin Junior Association.
Basis for selection: Major/career interest in agriculture. Applicant must demonstrate financial need, high academic achievement, depth of character, leadership, patriotism, seriousness of purpose and service orientation.
Application requirements: Recommendations, proof of eligibility. Recent photo. One of the three recommendations must be from active NALF other than relative or guardian; two must be from the following: school superintendent, school principal, minister, 4-H leader, FFA instructor, county agent or teacher.
Additional information: Experience with Limousin cattle preferred. Proven excellence in Limousin activities as well as leadership skills demonstrated in NALJA, 4-H, and FFA.
> **Amount of award:** $500
> **Application deadline:** May 15

Contact:
North American Limousin Junior Association
Attn: Donna Etherton
8961 Oak Crest Road
Dawson, IL 62520
Web: www.nalf.org

North Carolina Bar Association

North Carolina Law Enforcement Dependents Scholarship

Type of award: Scholarship, renewable.
Intended use: For full-time undergraduate, master's, doctoral or first professional study at accredited postsecondary institution.
Eligibility: Applicant must be no older than 27. Applicant's parent must have been killed or disabled in work-related accident as police officer.
Application requirements: Essay, transcript, proof of eligibility. Photo.
Additional information: Applicant's parent must have been working as North Carolina Law Enforcement Officer at time of death or permanent disablement. Amount awarded depends on available funding, number of applicants and cost of institution.

Number of applicants: 17
Application deadline: April 1
Notification begins: June 30
Contact:
North Carolina Bar Association
Young Lawyers Division Scholarship Committee
P. O. Box 3688
Cary, NC 27519
Phone: 919-677-0561
Fax: 919-677-0761
Web: www.ncbar.org

North Carolina Community Colleges Foundation

North Carolina Community Colleges Wachovia Technical Scholarship

Type of award: Scholarship.
Intended use: For full-time sophomore study at vocational or 2-year institution.
Eligibility: Applicant must be residing in North Carolina.
Basis for selection: Applicant must demonstrate financial need and high academic achievement.
Additional information: Must be enrolled in two-year education/technical program. Apply through financial aid office of institution where enrolled. Scholarships distributed through the 58 community colleges in the system.
Amount of award: $500
Number of awards: 58
Contact:
North Carolina Community Colleges Foundation
5016 Mail Service Center
Raleigh, NC 27699-5016
Phone: 919-807-6962
Fax: 919-807-7164
Web: www.ncccs.cc.nc.us

Ray Jeffries Scholarship

Type of award: Scholarship.
Intended use: For undergraduate study at 2-year institution.
Eligibility: Applicant must be residing in North Carolina.
Basis for selection: Applicant must demonstrate leadership.
Application requirements: Written statement from Student Government Association advisor and/or dean verifying applicant's position in the North Carolina Comprehensive Student Government Association.
Additional information: Scholarship awarded to president of the North Carolina Comprehensive Student Government Association. Fall deadline October 1, spring deadline March 1.
Amount of award: $1,000
Number of awards: 1
Application deadline: October 1, March 1
Contact:
North Carolina Community Colleges Foundation
5016 Mail Service Center
Raleigh, NC 2799-5016
Phone: 919-807-6962
Fax: 919-807-7164
Web: www.ncccs.cc.nc.us

Rodney E. Powell Memorial Scholarship

Type of award: Scholarship.
Intended use: For full-time undergraduate study at 2-year institution. Designated institutions: Community colleges in Progress Energy's service area.
Eligibility: Applicant must be residing in North Carolina.
Basis for selection: Major/career interest in engineering, electrical/electronic or electronics. Applicant must demonstrate financial need and high academic achievement.
Additional information: Minimum 3.0 GPA. Scholarship for students of electronic technology. Applicant must be enrolled full time or must intend to enroll as new student at designated institution. Number of awards varies.
Application deadline: March 1, October 1
Contact:
North Carolina Department of Community Colleges
Attn: Lee McCollum
410 S. Wilmington St. PEB 8A1
Raleigh, NC 27601
Phone: 919-546-7585
Fax: 919-546-6005
Web: www.ncccs.cc.nc.us

North Carolina Division of Veterans Affairs

North Carolina Scholarships for Children of War Veterans

Type of award: Scholarship, renewable.
Intended use: For undergraduate or graduate study at accredited postsecondary institution.
Eligibility: Applicant must be no older than 25. Applicant must be residing in North Carolina. Applicant must be dependent of disabled veteran, deceased veteran or POW/MIA who served in the Army, Air Force, Marines, Navy or Coast Guard. Parent must have served during a period of war.
Basis for selection: Applicant must demonstrate financial need.
Application requirements: Interview, transcript, proof of eligibility. Birth certificate.
Additional information: For state schools, award is tuition waiver plus maximum of $2,200 room and board allowance for up to four years. For private schools, award is up to $4,500 per year. Parent must have been North Carolina resident at time of enlistment or child must have been born in and reside permanently in North Carolina. See website for deadline information.
Amount of award: Full tuition
Number of applicants: 555
Contact:
North Carolina Division of Veterans Affairs
1315 Mail Service Center
Albemarle Building, Suite 1065
Raleigh, NC 27699-1315
Web: www.doa.state.nc.us/vets/benefits-scholarships.htm

North Carolina Division of Vocational Rehabilitation Services

North Carolina Vocational Rehabilitation Award

Type of award: Scholarship, renewable.
Intended use: For full-time undergraduate study at accredited vocational, 2-year or 4-year institution.
Eligibility: Applicant must be physically challenged or learning disabled. Applicant must be residing in North Carolina.
Basis for selection: Applicant must demonstrate financial need.
Application requirements: Interview, proof of eligibility. Proof of mental, physical, or learning disability that is an impediment to employment.
Additional information: This program provides educational assistance for individuals who meet eligibility requirements and require training to reach their vocational goals.
   Amount of award: $2,670
Contact:
North Carolina Division of Vocational Rehabilitation Services
2801 Mail Service Center
Raleigh, NC 27699-2801
Phone: 919-855-3500
Fax: 919-715-0616
Web: dvr.dhhs.state.nc.us

North Carolina State Board of Refrigeration Examiners

North Carolina State Board of Refrigeration Examiners Scholarship

Type of award: Scholarship.
Intended use: For undergraduate study at 2-year institution.
Eligibility: Applicant must be residing in North Carolina.
Basis for selection: Major/career interest in air conditioning/heating/refrigeration technology. Applicant must demonstrate financial need and high academic achievement.
Application requirements: Essay.
Additional information: Number of awards varies.
   Number of awards: 2
   Application deadline: January 1
Contact:
North Carolina State Board of Refrigeration Examiners
Suite 208
893 Highway 70 W
Garner, NC 27529
Web: www.refrigerationboard.org/wp/

North Carolina State Education Assistance Authority

GlaxoSmithKline Opportunity Scholarship

Type of award: Scholarship.
Intended use: For undergraduate study at vocational, 2-year or 4-year institution in United States.
Eligibility: Applicant must be residing in North Carolina.
Basis for selection: Applicant must demonstrate depth of character and seriousness of purpose.
Additional information: Applicant must have been a permanent resident of Chatham, Durham, Orange, or Wake county for one year prior to application. GlaxoSmithKline and Triangle Community Foundation employees or their families not eligible. Apply online at www.trianglecf.org/static/compschols.shtml.
   Amount of award: $5,000
   Number of awards: 5
   Application deadline: March 15
Contact:
Triangle Community Foundation Scholarship Program
Attn: Libby Long
324 Blackwell St., Ste. 1220
Durham, NC 27701
Phone: 919-474-8370
Fax: 919-941-9208
Web: www.ncseea.edu

Golden LEAF Scholars Program - Two-Year Colleges

Type of award: Scholarship.
Intended use: For undergraduate study at 2-year institution. Designated institutions: Member institutions of North Carolina Community College system.
Eligibility: Applicant must be residing in North Carolina.
Basis for selection: Applicant must demonstrate financial need, high academic achievement, depth of character, leadership and service orientation.
Application requirements: Disclosure of other financial aid awards.
Additional information: Applicant must demonstrate need under federal TRIO formula. Award is up to $750 per semester (including summer) for curriculum students; up to $250 per semester for occupational education students. Finalist will undergo merit competition and be judged on academics, leadership, community service and the effect of the tobacco industry's and economy's decline on his/her family. Applicant must be permanent resident of one of 73 eligible counties. Visit Website for more information. Contact financial aid office for application.
   Amount of award: $500-$1,500
Contact:
Contact financial aid office at local community college.
Phone: 800-700-1775 ext. 624
Fax: 919-549-8481
Web: www.ncseaa.edu or www.nccs.cc.nc.us

Golden LEAF Scholarship - Four-Year University Program

Type of award: Scholarship, renewable.
Intended use: For freshman study at 4-year institution. Designated institutions: Public universities.
Eligibility: Applicant must be high school senior. Applicant must be residing in North Carolina.
Basis for selection: Applicant must demonstrate financial need.
Application requirements: Nomination. FAFSA.
Additional information: Must be incoming freshman, transfer student from a North Carolina community college, or previous recipient applying for renewal. Must reapply for renewal and submit FAFSA by March 15. New applicants must be permanent resident of economically distressed and/or tobacco-dependent rural county. Recipients of other aid amounting to 75 percent or more of total education costs will be given low priority. Visit Website for application and more information.
    Amount of award: $3,000
    Number of awards: 500
    Application deadline: March 17
Contact:
North Carolina State Education Assistance Authority
P.O. Box 14103
Research Triangle Park, NC 27709
Phone: 919-549-8614
Web: www.ncseaa.edu

Latino Diamante Scholarship Fund

Type of award: Scholarship.
Intended use: For freshman or sophomore study.
Eligibility: Applicant must be Hispanic American. Applicant must be residing in North Carolina.
Application requirements: Recommendations, essay, transcript.
Additional information: Minimum 2.5 GPA. Visit Website for application and more information.
    Number of awards: 2
    Application deadline: August 15
    Notification begins: September 15
    Total amount awarded: $500
Contact:
Diamante, Inc.
106 Lockwood East Dr.
Cary, NC 27511
Phone: 919-852-0075
Web: www.ncseaa.edu or www.diamanteinc.org/index_files/Page417.htm

NC Sherrif's Association Criminal Justice Scholarship

Type of award: Scholarship.
Intended use: For full-time undergraduate study in United States. Designated institutions: Appalachian State University, East Carolina University, Elizabeth City State University, Fayetteville State University, North Carolina Central University, North Carolina State University, the University of North Carolina at Charlotte, the University of North Carolina at Pembroke, the University of North Carolina at Wilmington, Western Carolina University.
Eligibility: Applicant must be residing in North Carolina.
Basis for selection: Major/career interest in criminal justice/law enforcement.
Application requirements: Recommendations, essay, transcript.
Additional information: Application available at financial aid offices of UNC Charlotte, UNC Pembroke, UNC Wilmington, Western Carolina University, NC State University, NC Central University, Fayetteville State University, Elizabeth City State University, East Carolina University, and Appalachian State University.
    Amount of award: $2,000
    Number of awards: 10
    Number of applicants: 50
    Total amount awarded: $20,000
Contact:
North Carolina State Education Assistance Authority
P.O. Box 14103
Research Triangle Park, NC 27709-3663
Phone: 800-700-1775 ext. 673
Web: www.ncseaa.edu

North Carolina Aubrey Lee Brooks Scholarship

Type of award: Scholarship, renewable.
Intended use: For full-time undergraduate study at 4-year institution in United States. Designated institutions: North Carolina State University, University of North Carolina at Chapel Hill, University of North Carolina at Greensboro.
Eligibility: Applicant must be high school senior. Applicant must be U.S. citizen residing in North Carolina.
Basis for selection: Applicant must demonstrate financial need, depth of character, leadership and seriousness of purpose.
Application requirements: Proof of eligibility.
Additional information: Scholarship awards vary; maximum $8,000 per year, plus one-time computer award up to $3,000. Scholarship pays additional amounts for approved summer study or internships. Applications available through high school. Applicants must reside in one of the following counties: Alamance, Bertie, Caswell, Durham, Forsyth, Granville, Guilford, Orange, Person, Rockingham, Stokes, Surry, Swain or Warren. One additional scholarship awarded to student from cities of Greensboro and High Point and to eligible senior at North Carolina School of Science and Mathematics.
    Amount of award: $8,000
    Number of awards: 17
    Application deadline: February 1
Contact:
North Carolina State Education Assistance Authority
P.O. Box 14103
Research Triangle Park, NC 27709-3663
Phone: 800-700-1775 ext 650
Web: www.cfnc.org

North Carolina Legislative Tuition Grant

Type of award: Scholarship, renewable.
Intended use: For undergraduate study at accredited 2-year or 4-year institution. Designated institutions: Eligible North Carolina private institutions.
Eligibility: Applicant must be U.S. citizen or permanent resident residing in North Carolina.
Additional information: Award not applicable for theology, divinity or religious education programs. Applicants should contact NC private institution they attend or North Carolina State Education Assistance Authority. Award amount determined by North Carolina General Assembly. Applications available from eligible institutions' financial aid offices.

Amount of award: $1,950
Number of awards: 24,078
Total amount awarded: $43,911,790
Contact:
North Carolina State Education Assistance Authority
P.O. Box 14103
Research Triangle Park, NC 27709-3663
Phone: 800-700-1775 ext. 650
Web: www.cfnc.org

State Contractual Scholarship Fund

Type of award: Scholarship, renewable.
Intended use: For undergraduate study at accredited 2-year or 4-year institution. Designated institutions: Private institutions in North Carolina.
Eligibility: Applicant must be U.S. citizen or permanent resident residing in North Carolina.
Basis for selection: Applicant must demonstrate financial need.
Application requirements: Proof of eligibility.
Additional information: Theology and divinity students not eligible. Contact school's financial aid office or NCSEAA for more information. Must be enrolled in degree-seeking program. Award amount varies; check with private institution's financial aid office for current award amount.
Amount of award: $1,350
Contact:
North Carolina State Education Assistance Authority
P.O. Box 14103
Research Triangle Park, NC 27709-3663
Phone: 800-700-1775 ext. 650
Web: www.cfnc.org

Teacher Assistant Scholarship Fund

Type of award: Scholarship, renewable.
Intended use: For undergraduate study at 2-year or 4-year institution in United States. Designated institutions: North Carolina institutions offering teacher licensure programs (visit Website for list).
Eligibility: Applicant must be residing in North Carolina.
Basis for selection: Major/career interest in education, teacher. Applicant must demonstrate financial need.
Application requirements: FAFSA.
Additional information: Applicant must be full-time teacher assistant for at least one year at public or federal school in North Carolina. Must be enrolled in program leading toward initial teacher licensure. Minimum 3.0 GPA. Must maintain 2.8 GPA to renew. Students at two-year schools receive up to $1,800 per year; those at four-year schools receive up to $3,600 per year. Students cannot receive more than $25,200 in total aid over time. Must not be in default on a student loan.
Amount of award: $3,600
Application deadline: April 15
Contact:
North Carolina State Education Assistance Authority
P.O. Box 13663
Research Triangle Park, NC 27709-3663

North Dakota University System

North Dakota Indian Scholarship Program

Type of award: Scholarship, renewable.
Intended use: For full-time undergraduate or graduate study at vocational, 2-year or 4-year institution.
Eligibility: Applicant must be American Indian. Must be enrolled member of Indian tribe. Applicant must be U.S. citizen residing in North Dakota.
Basis for selection: Applicant must demonstrate financial need.
Application requirements: Transcript, proof of eligibility. Budget completed by financial aid officer at institution student is attending/will attend.
Additional information: Minimum 2.0 GPA. Priority given to full-time undergraduates with cumulative GPA of 3.5 or higher.
Amount of award: $500-$2,000
Number of awards: 175
Number of applicants: 400
Application deadline: July 15
Total amount awarded: $102,000
Contact:
North Dakota University System
Indian Scholarship Program
919 S. 7th Street, Suite 310
Bismarck, ND 58504-5881
Phone: 701-328-9661
Web: www.ndus.nodak.edu

North Dakota Scholars Program

Type of award: Scholarship, renewable.
Intended use: For full-time undergraduate study at postsecondary institution.
Eligibility: Applicant must be high school senior. Applicant must be residing in North Dakota.
Basis for selection: Applicant must demonstrate high academic achievement.
Application requirements: Proof of eligibility.
Additional information: Applicant must take ACT between October and June of junior year and score in upper five percentile of all North Dakota ACT test-takers. Numeric sum of English, math, reading and science reasoning scores may be considered. Award is full-tuition scholarship for students attending ND's public and tribal colleges; equal to NDSU/UND tuition for students attending private institutions. Recipients must maintain 3.5 GPA for renewal. Contact sponsor for more information and deadline.
Number of awards: 50
Number of applicants: 400
Contact:
North Dakota University System
600 East Boulevard
Dept. 215
Bismarck, ND 58505-0230
Phone: 701-328-4114
Web: www.ndus.nodak.edu

North Dakota State Student Incentive Grant

Type of award: Scholarship, renewable.
Intended use: For full-time undergraduate study at vocational, 2-year or 4-year institution.
Eligibility: Applicant must be U.S. citizen or permanent resident residing in North Dakota.
Basis for selection: Applicant must demonstrate financial need.
Application requirements: Proof of eligibility. FAFSA.
Additional information: Application automatic with FAFSA. Applicant must be first-time undergraduate student. Must not be in default on any federal loans or owe refund on any Title IV grants or loans.

Amount of award:	$600-$1,000
Number of awards:	2,500
Number of applicants:	28,000
Application deadline:	March 15
Total amount awarded:	$2,220,000

Contact:
North Dakota University System
Student Financial Assistance Program
600 East Boulevard - Dept. 215
Bismarck, ND 58505-0230
Phone: 701-328-4114
Web: www.ndus.nodak.edu

Northern Cheyenne Tribal Education Department

Northern Cheyenne Higher Education Program

Type of award: Scholarship, renewable.
Intended use: For undergraduate study at postsecondary institution.
Eligibility: Applicant must be American Indian. Must be enrolled with Northern Cheyenne Tribe. Applicant must be U.S. citizen.
Basis for selection: Applicant must demonstrate financial need.
Application requirements: Recommendations, essay, transcript, proof of eligibility. FAFSA.
Additional information: Award amount varies, depends on unmet need. Deadlines: October 1 for spring, April 1 for summer, and March 1 for fall.

Amount of award:	$175-$6,000
Number of awards:	84
Number of applicants:	82
Application deadline:	March 1
Notification begins:	August 1, November 1
Total amount awarded:	$282,000

Contact:
Northern Cheyenne Tribal Education Department
Attn: Norma Bixby
Box 307
Lame Deer, MT 59043
Phone: 406-477-6602
Fax: 406-477-8150

Northwest Danish Foundation

The Inger and Jens Bruun Scholarship for Study in Denmark

Type of award: Scholarship.
Application requirements: Essay on why you wish to study in Denmark, written statement on what has prepared you to take full advantage of your study experience, two references.
Additional information: Open to any person 18 years or older who is currently a resident of WA/OR or who is a student currently registered in a school, university, or institution of learning in WA/OR and who wishes to study in Denmark.

Amount of award:	$5,000
Number of awards:	1
Application deadline:	March 31

Contact:
Northwest Danish Foundation
1833 North 105 St.
Suite 203
Seattle, WA 98133-8973
Phone: 800-564-7736
Fax: 206-729-6997
Web: www.northwestdanishfoundation.org

The Kaj Christensen Scholarship for Vocational Training

Type of award: Scholarship, renewable.
Intended use: For undergraduate or graduate study at postsecondary institution in or outside United States.
Eligibility: Applicant must be Danish. Applicant must be U.S. citizen or permanent resident residing in Oregon or Washington.
Basis for selection: Applicant must demonstrate depth of character and service orientation.
Application requirements: Recommendations, transcript. Personal essay on educational goals. Recommendations, transcripts, two references.
Additional information: Applicant must be under 18 and demonstrate some connection to Denmark via life experience, travel, heritage, etc. Applicant must be a U.S. citizen residing in OR, WA. Must have interest in vocational training.

Amount of award:	$500
Number of awards:	5
Number of applicants:	40
Application deadline:	March 31
Notification begins:	May 1

Contact:
Northwest Danish Foundation
1833 North 105th Street
Suite 203
Seattle, WA 98133-8973
Phone: 800-564-7736
Fax: 206-729-6997
Web: www.northwestdanishfoundation.org

Oak Ridge Institute for Science and Education

National Oceanic and Atmospheric Administration Educational Partnership Program with Minority Serving Institutions Undergraduate Scholarship

Type of award: Scholarship.
Intended use: For junior or senior study at 4-year institution. Designated institutions: Minority-serving institutions, including Hispanic-serving institutions, historically black colleges and universities, and tribal colleges and universities. Internship assignments at NOAA sites.
Eligibility: Applicant must be U.S. citizen.
Basis for selection: Major/career interest in science, general; biology; cartography; chemistry; computer/information sciences; engineering; environmental science; geography; mathematics or physics.
Additional information: Provides scholarships and internships for students pursuing degrees in fields related to the National Oceanic and Atmospheric Administration. Application deadline in January. Award is tuition and fees up to $4,000. Internship pays weekly stipend of $650. Weekly housing allowance during internship. See Website for application and more information.

Amount of award:	$4,000
Number of awards:	15
Application deadline:	February 15

Contact:
Oak Ridge Institute for Science and Education
P.O. Box 117
Oak Ridge, TN 37831-0117
Phone: 865-576-9279
Web: www.orau.gov/orise/educ.htm

Ohio Board of Regents

Ohio Academic Scholarship

Type of award: Scholarship, renewable.
Intended use: For full-time undergraduate study at accredited 2-year or 4-year institution.
Eligibility: Applicant must be high school senior. Applicant must be U.S. citizen or permanent resident residing in Ohio.
Basis for selection: Applicant must demonstrate high academic achievement.
Application requirements: ACT scores.
Additional information: Contact high school guidance counselors.

Amount of award:	$2,205
Number of awards:	1,000
Number of applicants:	5,500
Application deadline:	February 23
Notification begins:	March 1
Total amount awarded:	$7,800,000

Contact:
Jathiya Abdullah-Simmons, Program Administrator
Ohio Board of Regents
30 E. Broad St., 36th Floor
Columbus, OH 43215-3414
Phone: 888-833-1133 ext. 29528
Fax: 614-752-5903
Web: www.regents.ohio.gov

Ohio College Opportunity Grant

Type of award: Scholarship, renewable.
Intended use: For freshman study at accredited 2-year or 4-year institution. Designated institutions: Ohio and select Pennsylvania schools.
Eligibility: Applicant must be residing in Ohio.
Basis for selection: Applicant must demonstrate financial need.
Application requirements: FAFSA.
Additional information: Awards are based on Expected Family Contribution (EFC). Maximum award for public institutions is $2,496 (subject to change); proprietary institutions, $3,996; private institutions, $4,992. Any student enrolled prior to 2006-07 award year will have eligibility determined for Ohio Instructional Grant.

Amount of award:	$4,992
Number of applicants:	25,570
Application deadline:	October 1
Total amount awarded:	$49,500,000

Contact:
Ohio Board of Regents
30 E. Broad St., 36th Floor
Columbus, OH 43215
Phone: 888-833-1133 ext 88862
Fax: 614-752-5903
Web: www.regents.ohio.gov/sgs

Ohio Instructional Grant

Type of award: Scholarship.
Intended use: For full-time undergraduate study at accredited 2-year or 4-year institution. Designated institutions: Ohio schools and select Pennsylvania schools.
Eligibility: Applicant must be U.S. citizen or permanent resident residing in Ohio.
Basis for selection: Applicant must demonstrate financial need.
Application requirements: FAFSA.
Additional information: Theology students not eligible. FAFSA serves as application. Number of awards varies. Max award amounts (subject to change) for public institutions are $2,190; proprietary institutions, $4,632; private institutions, $5,466.

Amount of award:	$5,466
Number of applicants:	83,933
Application deadline:	October 1
Total amount awarded:	$119,000,000

Contact:
Ohio Board of Regents
Tamika Braswell, Program Administrator
30 E. Broad St., 36th Floor
Columbus, OH 43215-3414
Phone: 888-833-1133, ext.88862
Fax: 614-752-5903
Web: www.regents.ohio.gov

Ohio Safety Officers College Memorial Fund

Type of award: Scholarship, renewable.
Intended use: For undergraduate study at vocational, 2-year or 4-year institution.
Eligibility: Applicant must be U.S. citizen or permanent resident residing in Ohio. Applicant's parent must have been killed or disabled in work-related accident as firefighter, police officer or public safety officer.
Application requirements: Proof of eligibility.
Additional information: Award pays full tuition at public institutions and part of tuition at private institutions. Number of awards varies. Apply at college financial aid office. Applicant's parent must have been killed in the line of duty as a firefighter, police officer, public safety officer.

| Number of applicants: | 54 |
| Total amount awarded: | $121,068 |

Contact:
Barbara Thoma, Program Administrator
Ohio Board of Regents
30 E. Broad St., 36th Floor
Columbus, OH 43215-3414
Phone: 888-833-1133 ext. 29535
Fax: 614-752-5903
Web: www.regents.ohio.gov

Ohio Student Choice Grant

Type of award: Scholarship, renewable.
Intended use: For full-time undergraduate study at 4-year institution. Designated institutions: Private non-profit colleges and universities in Ohio.
Eligibility: Applicant must be U.S. citizen or permanent resident residing in Ohio.
Additional information: Number of awards varies. Apply at college financial aid office.

Amount of award:	$660
Number of applicants:	54,000
Total amount awarded:	$24,200,000

Contact:
Barbara Thoma, Program Administrator
Ohio Board of Regents
30 E. Broad St., 36th Floor
Columbus, OH 43215-3414
Phone: 888-833-1133 ext. 29535
Fax: 614-752-5903
Web: www.regents.ohio.gov

Ohio War Orphans Scholarship

Type of award: Scholarship, renewable.
Intended use: For full-time undergraduate study at accredited 2-year or 4-year institution.
Eligibility: Applicant must be at least 16, no older than 25. Applicant must be U.S. citizen or permanent resident residing in Ohio. Applicant must be dependent of veteran, disabled veteran, deceased veteran or POW/MIA.
Application requirements: Proof of eligibility.
Additional information: Award covers full tuition at public institutions, $5,100 at private institutions.

Number of applicants:	248
Application deadline:	July 1, November 1
Notification begins:	August 1
Total amount awarded:	$4,672,320

Contact:
Jathiya Abdullah-Simmons, Program Administrator
Ohio Board of Regents
30 E. Broad St., 36th Floor
Columbus, OH 43215-3414
Phone: 888-833-1133 ext. 29528
Fax: 614-752-5903
Web: www.regents.ohio.gov

Part-time Student Instructional Grant Program

Type of award: Scholarship, renewable.
Intended use: For half-time undergraduate study at 2-year or 4-year institution. Designated institutions: Eligible Ohio institutions.
Eligibility: Applicant must be U.S. citizen residing in Ohio.
Basis for selection: Applicant must demonstrate financial need.
Additional information: Number of awards varies. Contact college financial aid office for application and deadline information.

| Number of applicants: | 26,000 |
| Total amount awarded: | $10,000,000 |

Contact:
Barbara Thoma, Program Administrator
Ohio Board of Regents
30 E. Broad St., 36th Floor
Columbus, OH 43215-3414
Phone: 888-833-1133 ext. 29535
Fax: 614-752-5903
Web: www.regents.ohio.gov

Ohio National Guard

Ohio National Guard Scholarship Program

Type of award: Scholarship, renewable.
Intended use: For undergraduate study at accredited postsecondary institution. Designated institutions: Degree-granting institutions in Ohio approved by Ohio Board of Regents.
Eligibility: Applicant or parent must be member/participant of Ohio National Guard. Applicant must be residing in Ohio. Applicant must be in military service in the Reserves/National Guard. Must enlist, reenlist, or extend current enlistment to equal six years with Ohio National Guard. Must remain in good standing.
Application requirements: Proof of eligibility.
Additional information: Minimum six credit hours per semester or quarter. Award covers 100 percent instructional and general fee for state-assisted institutions; average of state-assisted university fees for proprietary institutions. Application deadlines: fall-July 1, winter quarter/spring semester-November 1, spring quarter-February 1, summer-April 1. Must not already possess bachelor's degree. Lifetime maximum of 12 full-time quarters or 8 full-time semesters. Number of awards available fluctuates with season; Fall/Winter, 3500; Spring, 2345; Summer, 800.

Amount of award:	Full tuition
Number of awards:	6,645
Number of applicants:	5,000

Contact:
Adjutant General's Department
Ohio National Guard Scholarship Program
2825 West Dublin Granville Road
Columbus, OH 43235
Phone: 888-400-6484
Web: www.ongsp.org or www.ohionationalguard.com

Ohio Newspapers Foundation

Harold K. Douthit Scholarship

Type of award: Scholarship.
Intended use: For freshman study.
Eligibility: Applicant must be high school senior. Applicant must be U.S. citizen residing in Ohio.
Basis for selection: Major/career interest in journalism. Applicant must demonstrate financial need and high academic achievement.
Application requirements: Essay, transcript. Two letters of recommendation from faculty members.
Additional information: Applicant must be resident of one of the following Ohio counties: Cuyahoga, Lorain, Huron, Erie, Wood, Geauga, Sandusky, Ottawa or Lucas. Minimum 3.0 GPA. Student may provide up to two published writing samples.

Amount of award:	$1,000
Number of awards:	1
Number of applicants:	14
Application deadline:	March 31
Notification begins:	May 15
Total amount awarded:	$1,500

Contact:
Ohio Newspapers Foundation
1335 Dublin Road
Suite 216-B
Columbus, OH 43215
Phone: 614-486-6677
Fax: 614-486-4940
Web: www.ohionews.org

Ohio Newspaper Women's Scholarship

Type of award: Scholarship.
Intended use: For junior or senior study.
Eligibility: Applicant must be residing in Ohio.
Basis for selection: Major/career interest in journalism.
Application requirements: Recommendations, transcript. Three or four newspaper clippings pasted on 8.5- by 11-inch paper. Answer to questions: Who or what was your inspiration to get involved in the field of journalism and why did you select print journalism as your area of interest? Why do you need a scholarship? What do you think qualifies you for a scholarship? What do you hope to accomplish during your career as a professional journalist?

Amount of award:	$1,500
Number of awards:	1
Application deadline:	March 31

Contact:
Ohio Newspapers Foundation
1335 Dublin Road
Suite 216-B
Columbus, OH 43215
Phone: 614-486-6677
Fax: 614-486-4940
Web: www.ohionews.org

Ohio Newspapers Minority Scholarship

Type of award: Scholarship.
Intended use: For full-time freshman study.
Eligibility: Applicant must be Alaskan native, Asian American, African American, Mexican American, Hispanic American, Puerto Rican, American Indian or Native Hawaiian/Pacific Islander. Applicant must be residing in Ohio.
Basis for selection: Major/career interest in journalism. Applicant must demonstrate high academic achievement.
Application requirements: Recommendations, essay, transcript, proof of eligibility. Up to two writing samples or published articles.
Additional information: Minimum 2.5 GPA.

Amount of award:	$1,500
Number of awards:	3
Number of applicants:	8
Application deadline:	March 31
Notification begins:	May 15
Total amount awarded:	$4,500

Contact:
Ohio Newspapers Foundation
1335 Dublin Road
Suite 216-B
Columbus, OH 43215
Phone: 614-486-6677
Fax: 614-486-4940
Web: www.ohionews.org

University Journalism Scholarship

Type of award: Scholarship.
Intended use: For sophomore, junior or senior study at 2-year or 4-year institution.
Eligibility: Applicant must be enrolled in high school. Applicant must be residing in Ohio.
Basis for selection: Major/career interest in journalism.
Application requirements: Essay, transcript. Two letters of recommendation from faculty members and any published writing samples.
Additional information: Minimum 2.5 GPA.

Amount of award:	$1,500
Number of awards:	1
Number of applicants:	6
Application deadline:	March 31
Notification begins:	May 15

Contact:
Ohio Newspaper Foundation
1335 Dublin Road
Suite 216-B
Columbus, OH 43215
Phone: 614-486-6677
Fax: 614-486-4940
Web: www.ohionews.org

Oklahoma Engineering Foundation

Oklahoma Engineering Foundation Scholarship

Type of award: Scholarship, renewable.
Intended use: For undergraduate study at accredited 4-year institution in United States. Designated institutions: Oklahoma Christian University of Science & Arts, Oklahoma State University, University of Oklahoma, Oral Roberts University, University of Tulsa.
Eligibility: Applicant must be high school senior. Applicant must be U.S. citizen residing in Oklahoma.
Basis for selection: Major/career interest in engineering. Applicant must demonstrate depth of character, leadership and service orientation.
Application requirements: Interview, essay, transcript.
Additional information: Minimum 3.0 GPA, ACT composite score of 24-29, and ACT Math component score of 28 or above. Applicants eligible for National Merit or Oklahoma Regents Scholarships not eligible for this award. Contact office for more information.

Amount of award:	$500-$1,000
Number of awards:	12
Number of applicants:	52
Application deadline:	February 10
Notification begins:	May 1
Total amount awarded:	$12,000

Contact:
Executive Director
201 Northeast 27th St.
Room 125
Oklahoma City, OK 73105
Phone: 405-528-1435
Web: www.ospe.org

Oklahoma State Department of Education Professional Services Division

Robert C. Byrd Honors Scholarship Program

Type of award: Scholarship, renewable.
Intended use: For full-time undergraduate study at postsecondary institution.
Eligibility: Applicant must be high school senior. Applicant must be U.S. citizen or permanent resident residing in Oklahoma.
Basis for selection: Applicant must demonstrate high academic achievement.
Application requirements: Recommendations, essay, transcript.
Additional information: Students receive award for first year of study at eligible postsecondary institutions. Scholarships renewable up to three additional years of study provided students continue to meet eligibility requirements as defined by the institution they are attending. Award amount varies based on funding. Deadlines vary, check Website for details. Must have minimum ACT composite score of 32 and/or minimum SAT combined score of 2130 or GED score of 700.

Application deadline: April 11
Contact:
Oklahoma State Department of Education
Oliver Hodge Building
2500 N. Lincoln Boulevard, Room 212
Oklahoma City, OK 73105-4599
Phone: 405-521-2808
Web: www.sde.state.ok.us

Oklahoma State Regents for Higher Education

Academic Scholars Program

Type of award: Scholarship, renewable.
Intended use: For full-time undergraduate study at postsecondary institution in United States.
Eligibility: Applicant must be residing in Oklahoma.
Basis for selection: Applicant must demonstrate high academic achievement.
Application requirements: Transcript, proof of eligibility, nomination by institution.
Additional information: Applicant must be National Merit Scholar or Finalist; Presidential Scholar; have SAT/ACT in 99.5 percentile for Oklahoma residents. Scholarships awarded to students with high academic performance who plan to attend Oklahoma public or private universities. Application deadline varies.

Amount of award: $1,800-$5,500
Contact:
Oklahoma State Regents for Higher Education
P.O. Box 108850
Oklahoma City, OK 73101-8850
Phone: 800-858-1840
Fax: 405-225-9230
Web: www.okhighered.org

Future Teachers Scholarship

Type of award: Scholarship, renewable.
Intended use: For undergraduate or graduate study at accredited 2-year or 4-year institution.
Eligibility: Applicant must be U.S. citizen or permanent resident residing in Oklahoma.
Basis for selection: Major/career interest in education, early childhood or education, special. Applicant must demonstrate high academic achievement.
Application requirements: Essay, transcript, proof of eligibility, nomination by college. SAT/ACT scores.
Additional information: Science education majors also eligible. Application deadline varies. Visit Website for more information. Priority given to full-time students. Minimum 2.5 GPA. Recipient must agree to teach in shortage area in Oklahoma public schools for at least three years after graduation and licensure. Must apply for renewal.

Amount of award:	$500-$1,500
Number of awards:	85

Contact:
Oklahoma State Regents For Higher Education
P.O. Box 108850
Oklahoma City, OK 73101-8850
Phone: 800-858-1840
Fax: 405-225-9230
Web: www.okhighered.org

Heartland Scholarship Fund

Type of award: Scholarship.
Intended use: For full-time undergraduate study at accredited 2-year or 4-year institution.
Eligibility: Applicant must be residing in Oklahoma.
Application requirements: Proof of eligibility.
Additional information: Applicant must be dependent child of individual killed as a result of the April 19, 1995 bombing of Alfred P. Murrah Federal Building in Oklahoma City. Award applicable to cost of tuition, fees, books, and room and board. For details, contact Oklahoma State Regents for Higher Education.
   Amount of award: $3,500-$5,500
Contact:
Oklahoma State Regents for Higher Education
P.O. Box 108850
Oklahoma City, OK 73101-8500
Phone: 800-858-1840 or 405-225-9239
Fax: 405-225-9230
Web: www.okhighered.org

Independent Living Act (Department of Human Services Tuition Waiver)

Type of award: Scholarship.
Intended use: For undergraduate study at postsecondary institution.
Eligibility: Applicant must be no older than 21. Applicant must be residing in Oklahoma.
Application requirements: Proof of eligibility.
Additional information: Awards tuition waivers to eligible individuals who have been or are in the Oklahoma Department of Human Services foster care program. Within last three years, applicant must have graduated from State Board of Education-accredited high school, the Oklahoma School of Science and Mathematics, or approved school in a bordering state, or have attained GED.
   Amount of award: Full tuition
Contact:
Oklahoma State Regents for Higher Education
P.O. Box 108850
Oklahoma City, OK 73101
Phone: 800-858-1840
Fax: 405-225-9230
Web: www.okhighered.org

National Guard Tuition Waiver

Type of award: Scholarship.
Intended use: For undergraduate study at 2-year or 4-year institution.
Eligibility: Applicant must be residing in Oklahoma. Applicant must be bona fide member in good standing of Oklahoma National Guard.
Application requirements: Proof of eligibility. Statement of Understanding and Certificate of Basic Eligibility.
Additional information: Applicant must be enrolled in degree-granting program. Waivers not awarded for certificate-granting courses, continuing education courses or career technology courses.
   Amount of award: Full tuition
Contact:
Oklahoma National Guard
P.O. Box 108850
Oklahoma City, OK 73101
Phone: 800-858-1840 or 800-464-8273
Fax: 405-225-9230
Web: www.okhighered.org or www.ok.ngb.army.mil

Oklahoma Tuition Aid Grant

Type of award: Scholarship, renewable.
Intended use: For undergraduate study at vocational, 2-year or 4-year institution. Designated institutions: Approved Oklahoma institutions.
Eligibility: Applicant must be U.S. citizen or permanent resident residing in Oklahoma.
Basis for selection: Applicant must demonstrate financial need.
Application requirements: Proof of eligibility. FAFSA.
Additional information: Award is $1,000 for public schools and $1,300 for private non-profit institutions. Applications accepted through June 30. For best consideration, apply by April 15.
   Amount of award: $1,000-$1,300
   Number of awards: 22,000
   Number of applicants: 50,000
   Total amount awarded: $18,900,000
Contact:
Oklahoma Tuition Aid Grant Program
P.O. Box 108850
Oklahoma City, OK 73101-8850
Phone: 877-662-6231
Fax: 405-225-9392
Web: www.okhighered.org

Oklahoma's Promise - OHLAP (Oklahoma Higher Learning Access Program)

Type of award: Scholarship.
Intended use: For undergraduate study at 2-year or 4-year institution.
Eligibility: Applicant must be residing in Oklahoma.
Basis for selection: Applicant must demonstrate financial need, high academic achievement and seriousness of purpose.
Additional information: Scholarship for students in families earning less than $50,000 per year. Student must enroll in the program in eighth, ninth, or tenth grade and demonstrate commitment to academic success in high school. Minimum 2.5 GPA. Award amount varies; full tuition at public institutions or portion of tuition at private institutions in OK. See counselor or visit Website for details.
   Application deadline: June 30
Contact:
Oklahoma State Regents for Higher Education
P.O. Box 108850
Oklahoma City, OK 73101
Phone: 800-858-1840
Fax: 405-225-9230
Web: www.okpromise.org

Regional University Baccalaureate Scholarship

Type of award: Scholarship.
Intended use: For full-time undergraduate study at postsecondary institution.
Eligibility: Applicant must be residing in Oklahoma.
Basis for selection: Applicant must demonstrate high academic achievement.
Additional information: These scholarships are awarded based on the academic merit of Oklahoma residents who plan to attend an Oklahoma regional university. Must have ACT score of at least 30 or be National Merit Semifinalist or Commended Student. Award is $3,000 plus resident tuition waver. Application deadlines vary by institution.
    Amount of award: $3,000
Contact:
Oklahoma State Regents for Higher Education
P.O. Box 108850
Oklahoma City, OK 73101
Phone: 800-858-1840
Fax: 405-225-9230
Web: www.okhighered.org

OMNE/Nursing Leaders of Maine

OMNE/Nursing Leaders of Maine Scholarship

Type of award: Scholarship.
Intended use: For undergraduate study at accredited 4-year or graduate institution.
Eligibility: Applicant must be U.S. citizen residing in Maine.
Basis for selection: Major/career interest in nursing. Applicant must demonstrate high academic achievement, seriousness of purpose and service orientation.
Application requirements: Recommendations, transcript, proof of eligibility.
Additional information: Applicant must be enrolled in baccalaureate nursing program.
    Amount of award: $500
    Number of awards: 2
    Number of applicants: 14
    Application deadline: May 1
    Notification begins: June 30
    Total amount awarded: $500
Contact:
Sherry Rogers, RN, MS
Redington Fairview General Hospital
P.O. Box 468
Skowhegan, ME 04976
Phone: 207-474-5121
Fax: 207-474-2670
Web: www.omne.org

ONS Foundation

Oncology Nursing Certification Corporation Bachelor's Scholarships

Type of award: Scholarship.
Intended use: For undergraduate study in United States. Designated institutions: Schools accredited by National League for Nursing or Commission on Collegiate Nursing Education.
Basis for selection: Major/career interest in nursing or oncology. Applicant must demonstrate high academic achievement, depth of character, leadership and service orientation.
Application requirements: $5 application fee. Essay, transcript, proof of eligibility.
Additional information: Must be currently enrolled in bachelor's nursing degree program. At the end of each year of scholarship participation, recipient shall submit a summary of education activities in which he/she participated.
    Amount of award: $2,000
    Application deadline: February 1
    Notification begins: March 15
Contact:
ONS Foundation
125 Enterprise Drive
Pittsburgh, PA 15275-1214
Phone: 412-859-6100
Fax: 412-859-6163
Web: www.nursingawards.org

Roberta Pierce Scofield Bachelor's Scholarships

Type of award: Scholarship.
Intended use: For undergraduate study. Designated institutions: Schools accredited by National League for Nursing or Commission on Collegiate Nursing Education.
Basis for selection: Major/career interest in nursing or oncology. Applicant must demonstrate high academic achievement, depth of character, leadership and service orientation.
Application requirements: $5 application fee. Essay, transcript, proof of eligibility.
Additional information: Must have current license to practice as registered nurse or practical (vocational) nurse and must be currently enrolled in bachelor's degree nursing program. At the end of each year of scholarship participation, recipient shall submit a summary of education activities in which he/she participated.
    Amount of award: $5,000
    Number of awards: 1
    Application deadline: February 1
    Notification begins: March 15
Contact:
ONS Foundation
125 Enterprise Drive
Pittsburgh, PA 15275-1214
Phone: 412-859-6100
Fax: 412-859-6163
Web: www.nursingawards.org

OP Loftbed

OP Loftbed $500 Scholarship Award

Type of award: Scholarship.
Intended use: For undergraduate or graduate study at accredited postsecondary institution in United States.
Eligibility: Applicant must be U.S. citizen.
Basis for selection: Competition/talent/interest in writing/journalism, based on creativity of answers to a given set of questions.
Application requirements: Transcript. Applications must be submitted on Website, which includes set of questions that must be answered and judged.
Additional information: Faxed or mailed entries not accepted. Applications first accepted January-February. Guidelines and additional information available online.
    Amount of award: $500
    Number of awards: 1
    Number of applicants: 1
    Application deadline: July 31
Contact:
Visit Website for entry form and additional information.
Web: www.oploftbed.com

Oregon Student Assistance Commission

Ahmad-Sehar Saleha Ahmad and Abrahim Ekramullah Zafar Foundation

Type of award: Scholarship, renewable.
Intended use: For undergraduate study at accredited 4-year institution in United States.
Eligibility: Applicant must be high school senior. Applicant must be U.S. citizen or permanent resident residing in Oregon.
Basis for selection: Major/career interest in English.
Application requirements: Essay, transcript. FAFSA.
Additional information: Must be graduate of an Oregon high school. Minimum 3.5 GPA. Female students given preference. Visit Website for details and application. For those with disabilities: TYY 541-687-7395 (voice), 800-452-8807 ext. 7395.
    Application deadline: March 1
Contact:
Oregon Student Assistance Commission
Grants and Scholarship Division
1500 Valley River Drive, Suite 100
Eugene, OR 97401-2146
Phone: 800-452-8807
Web: www.osac.state.or.us

Albina Fuel Company Scholarship

Type of award: Scholarship.
Intended use: For undergraduate study in United States.
Eligibility: Applicant must be residing in Oregon or Washington.
Application requirements: Transcript.
Additional information: Applicant must be dependent child of current Albina Fuel Company employee who has been employed by Albina for at least one year by October 1 prior to scholarship deadline. Early bird deadline Feb 15. Visit Website for more details.
    Application deadline: March 1
Contact:
Oregon Student Assistance Commission
1500 Valley River Drive, Suite 100
Eugene, OR 97401-2148
Phone: 800-452-8807
Web: www.osac.state.or.us

Allcott/Hunt Share It Now II Scholarship

Type of award: Scholarship.
Intended use: For undergraduate study in United States.
Eligibility: Applicant must be residing in Oregon.
Basis for selection: Applicant must demonstrate financial need.
Application requirements: Transcript. Names, addresses, and phone numbers of two community or school references. Essay (250-350 words): Describe why you might be the best candidate for the Share It Now II Scholarship and your experience living or working in diverse environments.
Additional information: Preference given to first- or second-generation immigrants to the U.S. Early bird deadline Feb 15. Visit Website for details.
    Application deadline: March 1
Contact:
Oregon Student Assistance Commission
1500 Valley River Drive, Suite 100
Eugene, OR 97401-2148
Phone: 800-452-8807
Web: www.osac.state.or.us

Alpha Delta Kappa/Harriet Simmons Scholarship

Type of award: Scholarship, renewable.
Intended use: For full-time senior or graduate study at accredited postsecondary institution in United States.
Eligibility: Applicant must be U.S. citizen or permanent resident residing in Oregon.
Basis for selection: Major/career interest in education or education, teacher. Applicant must demonstrate financial need and high academic achievement.
Application requirements: Transcript. FAFSA. Two essays required.
Additional information: Applicants must be elementary or secondary education majors. Visit Website for details and application. For those with disabilities: TYY 541-687-7395 (voice), 800-452-8807 ext. 7395.
    Amount of award: $500
    Application deadline: March 1
Contact:
Oregon Student Assistance Commission
Grants and Scholarship Division
1500 Valley River Drive, Suite 100
Eugene, OR 97401-2146
Phone: 800-452-8807
Web: www.osac.state.or.us

American Council of Engineering Companies of Oregon Scholarship

Type of award: Scholarship, renewable.
Intended use: For freshman study at 4-year institution. Designated institutions: Oregon four-year colleges offering ABET-accredited programs.
Eligibility: Applicant must be U.S. citizen or permanent resident residing in Oregon.
Basis for selection: Major/career interest in engineering, chemical; engineering, civil; engineering, electrical/electronic or engineering, mechanical.
Application requirements: Transcript. FAFSA. Essay: Describe why you are interested in a career in consulting engineering and how you expect your career to contribute to society.
Additional information: Applicant must be graduating high school senior or have had no previous college education. Visit Website for details and application. For those with disabilities: TYY 542-687-7395 (voice), 800-452-8807 ext. 7395.
   Application deadline: March 1
Contact:
Oregon Student Assistance Commission
Grants and Scholarship Division
1500 Valley River Drive, Suite 100
Eugene, OR 97401-2146
Phone: 800-452-8807
Web: www.osac.state.or.us

American Ex-Prisoner of War, Peter Connacher Memorial Scholarship

Type of award: Scholarship, renewable.
Intended use: For full-time undergraduate or graduate study at postsecondary institution in United States.
Eligibility: Applicant must be U.S. citizen or permanent resident residing in Oregon. Must be American former prisoner of war or descendant.
Basis for selection: Applicant must demonstrate financial need and high academic achievement.
Application requirements: Transcript, proof of eligibility. FAFSA, two essays, copy of POW's military discharge papers and proof of POW status. State relationship to POW on supporting documents.
Additional information: Visit Website for details and application. For those with disabilities: TYY 542-687-7395 (voice), 800-452-8807 ext. 7395.
   Amount of award: $500
   Application deadline: March 1
Contact:
Oregon Student Assistance Commission
Grants and Scholarship Division
1500 Valley River Drive, Suite 100
Eugene, OR 97401-2146
Phone: 800-452-8807
Web: www.osac.state.or.us

American Federation of State, County, and Municipal Employees (AFSCME) Oregon Council # 75

Type of award: Scholarship, renewable.
Intended use: For undergraduate or graduate study at 4-year or graduate institution in United States.
Eligibility: Applicant must be U.S. citizen or permanent resident residing in Oregon.
Application requirements: Transcript. FAFSA. Essay: What is the importance of organizing political action and contract bargaining for workers?
Additional information: Applicant, spouse, parent, or grandparent must be member (active, laid-off, retired or disabled) of Oregon AFSCME Council. Must have been member for at least one year prior to scholarship deadline or for one year prior to death, layoff, disability, or retirement. Part-time enrollment (minimum 6 credit hours) considered for active members and spouses, or laid-off members. Visit Website for application and details. For those with disabilities: TYY 541-687-7395 (voice), 800-452-8807 x7395.
   Application deadline: March 1
Contact:
Oregon Student Assistance Commission
Grants and Scholarship Division
1500 Valley Road Drive, Suite 100
Eugene, OR 97401-2146
Phone: 800-452-8807
Web: www.osac.state.or.us

American Society for Training and Development -- Cascadia Chapter Scholarship

Type of award: Scholarship.
Intended use: For full-time undergraduate or graduate study. Designated institutions: Colleges in Oregon and southwestern Washington.
Eligibility: Applicant must be residing in Oregon or Washington.
Basis for selection: Major/career interest in education.
Application requirements: Transcript.
Additional information: Scholarship for students seeking certificate or degree in training and development, organizational development, instructional design, or related field. Early bird deadline Feb 15. Visit Website for details.
   Application deadline: March 1
Contact:
Oregon Student Assistance Commission
1500 Valley River Drive, Suite 100
Eugene, OR 97401-2148
Phone: 800-452-8807
Web: www.osac.state.or.us

Bandon Submarine Cable Council Scholarship

Type of award: Scholarship, renewable.
Intended use: For freshman study in United States.
Eligibility: Applicant must be residing in Oregon.
Basis for selection: Applicant must demonstrate financial need.
Application requirements: Transcript. One-page essay: What are the pros and cons of processor (buyer) shares in an individual quota system?
Additional information: Applicant must not be matriculated in postsecondary studies at time of application. First preference given to members of the Bandon Submarine Cable Council or their dependent children. Second preference given to commercial fishermen or their family members residing in Coos County. Third preference given to any commercial fishermen or family member. Fourth preference given to postsecondary students residing in Clatsop, Coos, Curry, Lane, Lincoln or Tillamook County. Visit Website for details. Early bird deadline February 15.

Application deadline: March 1
Contact:
Oregon Student Assistance Commission
1500 Valley River Drive, Suite 100
Eugene, OR 97401-2148
Phone: 800-452-8807
Web: www.osac.state.or.us

Bank of the Cascades Scholarship

Type of award: Scholarship.
Intended use: For undergraduate study at postsecondary institution.
Eligibility: Applicant must be at least 17, no older than 25. Applicant must be residing in Oregon.
Additional information: Age requirements apply only to children of employees. Applicant must be employee or child or stepchild of Bank of the Cascades employee. Employee must have been continuously employed for at least one year at 20 hours or more per week at the deadline. Children of members of the Cascades Board of Directors ineligible. Minimum 3.0 GPA. Early bird deadline February 15. Visit Website for more details.
   Application deadline: March 1
Contact:
Oregon Student Assistance Commission
1500 Valley River Drive, Suite 100
Eugene, OR 97401-2148
Phone: 800-452-8807
Web: www.osac.state.or.us

Ben Selling Scholarship

Type of award: Scholarship, renewable.
Intended use: For full-time sophomore, junior or senior study at postsecondary institution in United States.
Eligibility: Applicant must be U.S. citizen or permanent resident residing in Oregon.
Basis for selection: Applicant must demonstrate financial need and high academic achievement.
Application requirements: Essay, transcript. FAFSA.
Additional information: Minimum 3.5 GPA. Visit Website for details and application. For those with disabilities: TYY 541-687-7395 (voice), 800-452-8807 ext. 7395.
   Amount of award: $500
   Application deadline: March 1
Contact:
Oregon Student Assistance Commission
Grants and Scholarship Division
1500 Valley River Drive, Suite 100
Eugene, OR 97401-2146
Phone: 800-452-8807
Web: www.osac.state.or.us

Benjamin Franklin/Edith Green Scholarship

Type of award: Scholarship.
Intended use: For full-time undergraduate study at accredited 4-year institution. Designated institutions: Oregon public colleges.
Eligibility: Applicant must be high school senior. Applicant must be U.S. citizen or permanent resident residing in Oregon.
Basis for selection: Applicant must demonstrate financial need and high academic achievement.
Application requirements: Essay, transcript. FAFSA.
Additional information: Minimum 2.5 GPA. Must show improvements in grades from freshman year. Must be graduating senior from an OR high school and planning to attend an OR college or university. Visit Website for details and application. For those with disabilities: TYY 542-687-7395 (voice), 800-452-8807 ext. 7395.
   Amount of award: $500
   Application deadline: March 1
Contact:
Oregon Student Assistance Commission
Grants and Scholarship Division
1500 Valley River Drive, Suite 100
Eugene, OR 97401-2146
Phone: 800-452-8807
Web: www.osac.state.or.us

Bertha P. Singer Scholarship

Type of award: Scholarship, renewable.
Intended use: For full-time undergraduate or graduate study at accredited postsecondary institution.
Eligibility: Applicant must be U.S. citizen or permanent resident residing in Oregon.
Basis for selection: Major/career interest in nursing.
Application requirements: Essay, transcript, proof of eligibility. FAFSA. Documentation of enrollment in third year of four-year nursing degree program or second year of two-year associate degree nursing program.
Additional information: Employees of U.S. Bank, their children or near relatives not eligible. Minimum 3.0 GPA. Visit Website for details and application. For those with disabilities: TYY 541-687-7395 (voice), 800-452-8807 ext. 7395.
   Amount of award: $500
   Application deadline: March 1
Contact:
Oregon Student Assistance Commission
Grants and Scholarship Division
1500 Valley River Drive, Suite 100
Eugene, OR 97401-2146
Phone: 800-452-8807
Web: www.osac.state.or.us

Chafee Education and Training Scholarship

Type of award: Scholarship.
Intended use: For undergraduate or graduate study in United States.
Eligibility: Applicant must be at least 14, no older than 20. Applicant must be residing in Oregon.
Basis for selection: Applicant must demonstrate financial need and service orientation.
Application requirements: Transcript. Two essays.
Additional information: Applicant must be currently in foster care placement with the Oregon Department of Human Services or federally recognized Oregon Tribes; be a former foster youth with 180 days of substitute care after age 14 with Oregon DHS or an Oregon Tribe; or be adopted from DHS foster care system after age 16. Deadline for fall, March 1; spring, February 1; summer, May 1; winter, November 1. Students may continue receiving award until age 23, but first-time recipients must be no older than 20. May apply for fall after deadline, but all funds may already be allocated. Visit Website for details and supplemental information form.
   Amount of award: $5,000
   Application deadline: March 1, May 1

Contact:
Oregon Student Assistance Commission
1500 Valley River Drive, Suite 100
Eugene, OR 97401-2148
Phone: 800-452-8807
Web: www.osac.state.or.us/chafeetv.html

Crowley Family Scholarship

Type of award: Scholarship, renewable.
Intended use: For full-time undergraduate study at postsecondary institution in United States.
Eligibility: Applicant must be U.S. citizen or permanent resident residing in Oregon.
Basis for selection: Major/career interest in education. Applicant must demonstrate seriousness of purpose and service orientation.
Application requirements: Essay, transcript. FAFSA.
Additional information: For graduates of Medford, Oregon, high schools. Preference given to female students demonstrating strong work ethic and interest in community service. Applicants returning to school to pursue education as a career encouraged to apply. Visit Website for details and application. For those with disabilities: TYY 541-687-7395 (voice), 800-452-8807 ext. 7395.
    Application deadline: March 1
Contact:
Oregon Student Assistance Commission
Grants and Scholarship Division
1500 Valley River Drive, Suite 100
Eugene, OR 97401-2146
Phone: 800-452-8807
Web: www.osac.state.or.us

David Family Scholarship

Type of award: Scholarship, renewable.
Intended use: For sophomore, junior, senior or graduate study at postsecondary institution in United States.
Eligibility: Applicant must be U.S. citizen or permanent resident residing in Oregon.
Basis for selection: Applicant must demonstrate financial need and high academic achievement.
Application requirements: Essay, transcript. FAFSA.
Additional information: Minimum 2.5 GPA. Intended for residents of Benton, Clackamas, Lane, Multnomah and Washington counties. Preference given to applicants enrolling at least half-time in upper-division or graduate health- or education-related programs at four-year colleges. Visit Website for details and application. For those with disabilities: TYY 542-687-7395 (voice), 800-452-8807 ext. 7395.
    Amount of award: $500
    Application deadline: March 1
Contact:
Oregon Student Assistance Commission
Grants and Scholarship Division
1500 Valley River Drive, Suite 100
Eugene, OR 97401-2146
Phone: 800-452-8807
Web: www.osac.state.or.us

Dorothy Campbell Memorial Scholarship

Type of award: Scholarship, renewable.
Intended use: For full-time undergraduate study at accredited 4-year institution.
Eligibility: Applicant must be female, high school senior. Applicant must be U.S. citizen or permanent resident residing in Oregon.
Basis for selection: Applicant must demonstrate financial need and high academic achievement.
Application requirements: Transcript. FAFSA. Two essays required. Additional essay: one page describing strong and continuing interest in golf and contribution the sport has made to applicant's development.
Additional information: Minimum 2.75 GPA. Must be female graduating senior of any Oregon high school. Visit Website for details and application. For those with disabilities: TYY 541-687-7395 (voice), 800-452-8807 ext. 7395.
    Amount of award: $500
    Application deadline: March 1
Contact:
Oregon Student Assistance Commission
Grants and Scholarship Division
1500 Valley River Drive, Suite l00
Eugene, OR 97401-2146
Phone: 800-452-8807
Web: www.osac.state.or.us

Eugene Bennet Visual Arts Scholarship

Type of award: Scholarship.
Intended use: For undergraduate or graduate study in United States.
Eligibility: Applicant must be residing in Oregon.
Basis for selection: Major/career interest in arts, general. Applicant must demonstrate financial need.
Application requirements: Interview, transcript.
Additional information: Applicants must be graduates of a Jackson County high school or GED recipients or home-schooled graduates from Jackson County. Minimum 2.75 GPA. Students selected as semifinalists will be called for an interview to which they should bring 5-8 pieces of original art work. Early bird deadline February 15. Visit Website for details.
    Application deadline: March 1
Contact:
Oregon Student Assistance Commission
1500 Valley River Drive, Suite 100
Eugene 97401-2148
Phone: 800-452-8807
Web: www.osac.state.or.us

Fashion Group International of Portland Scholarship

Type of award: Scholarship.
Intended use: For sophomore, junior or senior study at postsecondary institution in United States.
Eligibility: Applicant must be U.S. citizen or permanent resident residing in California, Oregon, Idaho or Washington.
Basis for selection: Major/career interest in fashion/fashion design/modeling.
Application requirements: Interview, transcript. FAFSA and two essays.
Additional information: Minimum 3.0 GPA. See Website for details and application. For those with disabilities: TYY 541-687-7395 (voice), 800-452-8807 ext. 7395.
    Application deadline: March 1

Contact:
Oregon Student Assistance Commission
Grants and Scholarship Division
1500 Valley River Drive, Suite 100
Eugene, OR 97401-2146
Phone: 800-452-8807
Web: www.osac.state.or.us

Ford Opportunity Program

Type of award: Scholarship, renewable.
Intended use: For full-time undergraduate study at accredited 2-year or 4-year institution.
Eligibility: Applicant must be U.S. citizen or permanent resident residing in Oregon.
Basis for selection: Applicant must demonstrate financial need and high academic achievement.
Application requirements: Essay, transcript. FAFSA.
Additional information: Minimum 3.0 GPA or 2650 GED score, unless application is accompanied by Special Recommendation Form from counselor or OSAC. Must be single head of household with custody of dependent child/children. Interviews required of all semifinalists. Visit Website for details and application. For those with disabilities: TYY 541-687-7395 (voice), 800-452-8807 ext. 7395. Counselors who wish to intervene on behalf of applicant who does not meet minimum requirements should check Financial Aid Handbook for recommendation form or call 800-452-8807 ext. 7388.

   Number of awards: 30
   Application deadline: March 1

Contact:
Oregon Student Assistance Commission
Grants and Scholarship Division
1500 Valley River Drive, Suite 100
Eugene, OR 97401-2146
Phone: 800-452-8807
Web: www.osac.state.or.us

Ford Scholars Program

Type of award: Scholarship, renewable.
Intended use: For full-time undergraduate study at accredited 2-year or 4-year institution.
Eligibility: Applicant must be U.S. citizen or permanent resident residing in Oregon.
Basis for selection: Applicant must demonstrate financial need and high academic achievement.
Application requirements: Interview, essay, transcript. FAFSA.
Additional information: Minimum 3.0 GPA or 2650 GED score, unless application accompanied by Special Recommendation Form from counselor or OSAC. Intended for high school graduates who have not yet been full-time undergraduates, or for individuals who have completed two years at Oregon community college and are entering junior year at Oregon four-year college. Visit Website for details and application. For those with disabilities: TYY 541-687-7395 (voice), 800-452-8807 ext. 7395. Counselors who wish to intervene on behalf of applicant who does not meet minimum requirements should check Financial Aid Handbook for recommendation form or call 800-452-8807 ext. 7388.

   Amount of award: $500
   Application deadline: March 1

Contact:
Oregon Student Assistance Commission
Grants and Scholarship Division
1500 Valley River Drive, Suite 100
Eugene, OR 97401-2146
Phone: 800-452-8807
Web: www.osac.state.or.us

Glenn Jackson Scholars

Type of award: Scholarship, renewable.
Intended use: For full-time undergraduate study at postsecondary institution in United States.
Eligibility: Applicant or parent must be employed by Oregon Department of Transportation/Parks and Recreation Dept. Applicant must be high school senior. Applicant must be U.S. citizen or permanent resident residing in Oregon.
Application requirements: Essay, transcript. FAFSA. Two additional one-page essays: (1) "How do you plan to finance your college education?" and (2) "If you could have a personal meeting with the Governor of Oregon, what would you talk about and why?"
Additional information: Must be dependent of employee or retiree of Oregon Department of Transportation or Parks and Recreation Department. Employees must have been employed by their department at least three years. Visit Website for details and application. For those with disabilities: TYY 541-687-7395 (voice), 800-452-8807 ext. 7395.

   Amount of award: $500
   Application deadline: March 1

Contact:
Oregon Student Assistance Commission
Grants and Scholarship Division
1500 Valley River Drive, Suite 100
Eugene, OR 97401-2146
Phone: 800-452-8807
Web: www.osac.state.or.us

Homestead Capital Housing Scholarship

Type of award: Scholarship.
Intended use: For junior or senior study at 4-year institution.
Eligibility: Applicant must be U.S. citizen or permanent resident residing in Oregon or Washington.
Basis for selection: Major/career interest in accounting; architecture; construction management; finance/banking; real estate; engineering, civil; engineering, environmental or engineering, structural. Applicant must demonstrate financial need.
Application requirements: Transcript. FAFSA. Essay: "How this scholarship and my applied discipline will contribute to affordable housing and community development."
Additional information: Applicant must be graduate of Oregon high school. Minimum 3.0 GPA. Visit Website for details and application. For those with disabilities: TYY 542-687-7395 (voice), 800-452-8807 ext. 7395.

   Application deadline: March 1

Contact:
Oregon Student Assistance Commission
Grants and Scholarship Division
1500 Valley River Drive, Suite 100
Eugene, OR 97401-2146
Phone: 800-452-8807
Web: www.osac.state.or.us

Howard Vollum American Indian Scholarship

Type of award: Scholarship, renewable.
Intended use: For undergraduate study at postsecondary institution in United States.
Eligibility: Applicant must be American Indian. Applicant must be U.S. citizen or permanent resident residing in Oregon or Washington.
Basis for selection: Major/career interest in science, general; computer/information sciences; mathematics; engineering or engineering, computer. Applicant must demonstrate high academic achievement and service orientation.
Application requirements: Essay, transcript, proof of eligibility. FAFSA. Additional essay topic: "How do you view your cultural heritage and its importance to you?" Submit certification of tribal enrollment or American Indian ancestry: photocopy of (1) tribal enrollment card that includes enrollment number and/or blood quantum, (2) Johnson O'Malley student eligibility form, or (3) letter from tribe stating blood quantum and/or enrollment number of parent or grandparent.
Additional information: Preference given to applicants with demonstrated commitment to the American Indian community. Must be resident of Clackamas, Multnomah or Washington County in Oregon, or Clark County, Washington. Visit Website for details and application. For those with disabilities: TYY 541-687-7395 (voice), 800-452-8807 ext. 7395.
   Application deadline: March 1
Contact:
Oregon Student Assistance Commission
Grants and Scholarship Division
1500 Valley River Drive, Suite 100
Eugene, OR 97401-2146
Phone: 800-452-8807
Web: www.osac.state.or.us

Ida M. Crawford Scholarship

Type of award: Scholarship, renewable.
Intended use: For full-time undergraduate study at accredited postsecondary institution in United States.
Eligibility: Applicant must be U.S. citizen or permanent resident residing in Oregon.
Basis for selection: Applicant must demonstrate financial need and high academic achievement.
Application requirements: Essay, transcript, proof of eligibility. FAFSA. Proof of birth in U.S.
Additional information: Minimum 3.5 GPA. Must be graduate of accredited Oregon high school. Not available to students majoring in law, medicine, music, theology, or teaching. U.S. Bank employees, their children and near relatives not eligible. Visit Website for details and application. For those with disabilities: TYY 541-687-7395 (voice), 800-452-8807 ext. 7395.
   Amount of award: $500
   Application deadline: March 1
Contact:
Oregon Student Assistance Commission
Grants and Scholarship Division
1500 Valley River Drive, Suite 100
Eugene, OR 97401-2146
Phone: 800-452-8807
Web: www.osac.state.or.us

Jackson Foundation Journalism Scholarship

Type of award: Scholarship, renewable.
Intended use: For full-time undergraduate study at postsecondary institution.
Eligibility: Applicant must be U.S. citizen or permanent resident residing in Oregon.
Basis for selection: Major/career interest in journalism. Applicant must demonstrate financial need and high academic achievement.
Application requirements: Essay, transcript. FAFSA.
Additional information: Must be graduate of an Oregon high school. Visit Website for details and application. For those with disabilities: TYY 541-687-7395 (voice), 800-452-8807 ext. 7395.
   Amount of award: $500
   Application deadline: March 1
Contact:
Oregon Student Assistance Commission
Grants and Scholarship Division
1500 Valley River Drive, Suite 100
Eugene, OR 97401-2146
Phone: 800-452-8807
Web: www.ossc.state.or.us

James Carlson Memorial Scholarship

Type of award: Scholarship.
Intended use: For full-time senior or graduate study at accredited 4-year institution in United States.
Eligibility: Applicant must be U.S. citizen or permanent resident residing in Oregon.
Basis for selection: Major/career interest in education; education, teacher; education, special or education, early childhood. Applicant must demonstrate financial need and high academic achievement.
Application requirements: Essay, transcript. FAFSA.
Additional information: Available to elementary or secondary education majors entering senior year or fifth year of study, or to graduate students in fifth year for elementary or secondary certificate. Preference given to students with experience living or working in diverse environments (250-350-word essay describing this experience required for applicants qualifying under this preference); dependents of Oregon Education Association members; and students committed to teach autistic children. Visit Website for details and application. For those with disabilities: TYY 541-687-7395 (voice), 800-452-8807 ext. 7395.
   Amount of award: $500
   Application deadline: March 1
Contact:
Oregon Student Assistance Commission
Grants and Scholarship Division
1500 Valley River Drive, Suite 100
Eugene, OR 97401-2146
Phone: 800-452-8807
Web: www.osac.state.or.us

Jerome B. Steinbach Scholarship

Type of award: Scholarship.
Intended use: For full-time sophomore, junior or senior study at accredited postsecondary institution in United States.
Eligibility: Applicant must be U.S. citizen residing in Oregon.

Basis for selection: Applicant must demonstrate financial need and high academic achievement.
Application requirements: Essay, transcript. FAFSA. Proof of U.S. birth.
Additional information: Minimum 3.5 GPA required. U.S. Bank employees, their children and near relatives not eligible. Visit Website for details and application. For those with disabilities: TYY 542-687-7395 (voice), 800-452-8807 ext. 7395.

Amount of award:	$500
Application deadline:	March 1

Contact:
Oregon Student Assistance Commission
Grants and Scholarship Division
1500 Valley River Drive, Suite 100
Eugene, OR 97401-2146
Phone: 800-452-8807
Web: www.osac.state.or.us

Jose D. Garcia Migrant Education Scholarship

Type of award: Scholarship.
Intended use: For freshman study at postsecondary institution in United States.
Eligibility: Applicant must be U.S. citizen or permanent resident residing in Oregon.
Application requirements: Essay, transcript. FAFSA.
Additional information: Applicant must be high school graduate or GED recipient participating in Oregon Migrant Education Program. Must indicate parents' names on application. Visit Website for details and application. For those with disabilities: TYY 541-687-7395 (voice), 800-452-8807 ext. 7395.

Amount of award:	$500
Application deadline:	March 1

Contact:
Oregon Student Assistance Commission
Grants and Scholarship Division
1500 Valley River Drive, Suite 100
Eugene, OR 97401-2146
Phone: 800-452-8807
Web: www.osac.state.or.us

Kaiser-Permanente Dental Assistant Scholarship

Type of award: Scholarship.
Intended use: For full-time undergraduate certificate study. Designated institutions: Accredited dental assistant programs at Blue Mountain Community College, Central Oregon College, Chemeketa Community College, Concorde Career Institute, Lane Community College, Linn-Benton Community College and Portland Community College.
Eligibility: Applicant must be U.S. citizen or permanent resident residing in Oregon or Washington.
Basis for selection: Major/career interest in dental assistant. Applicant must demonstrate financial need.
Application requirements: Essay, transcript. FAFSA.
Additional information: Visit Website for details and application. For those with disabilities: TYY 541-687-7395 (voice), 800-452-8807 ext. 7395.

Amount of award:	$500
Application deadline:	March 1

Contact:
Oregon Student Assistance Commission
Grants and Scholarship Division
1500 Valley River Drive, Suite 100
Eugene, OR 97401-2146
Phone: 800-452-8807
Web: www.osac.state.or.us

Laurence R. Foster Memorial Scholarship

Type of award: Scholarship, renewable.
Intended use: For undergraduate or graduate study at accredited 4-year institution in United States.
Eligibility: Applicant must be U.S. citizen or permanent resident residing in Oregon.
Basis for selection: Major/career interest in nursing; medical specialties/research; physician assistant; public health; medical assistant; health-related professions; bioengineering; engineering, biomedical or nurse practitioner. Applicant must demonstrate financial need and service orientation.
Application requirements: Essay, transcript. FAFSA. Additional two-page essay describing applicant's views on public health and his/her suitability for the public health field.
Additional information: Applicant must be seeking career in public health, not private practice. General preference given to applicants of diverse cultures. Preference also given to graduate students majoring in public health and to undergraduates entering junior/senior-year health programs. Visit Website for details and application. For those with disabilities: TYY 541-687-7395 (voice), 800-452-8807 ext. 7395.

Amount of award:	$500
Application deadline:	March 1

Contact:
Oregon Student Assistance Commission
Grants and Scholarship Division
1500 Valley River Drive, Suite 100
Eugene, OR 97401-2146
Phone: 800-452-8807
Web: www.osac.state.or.us

Maria C. Jackson-General George A. White Scholarship

Type of award: Scholarship, renewable.
Intended use: For full-time undergraduate or graduate study at postsecondary institution.
Eligibility: Applicant must be U.S. citizen or permanent resident residing in Oregon. Applicant must have served, or applicant's parent must serve or have served, in U.S. Armed Forces and resided in Oregon at time of enlistment.
Basis for selection: Applicant must demonstrate financial need and high academic achievement.
Application requirements: Essay, transcript, proof of eligibility. FAFSA. Provide documentation (DD93, DD214, discharge papers).
Additional information: Minimum 3.75 GPA for undergraduates; no GPA requirement for graduate students or students at technical schools. U.S. Bank employees, children, and near relatives not eligible. Visit Website for details and application. For those with disabilities: TYY 541-687-7395 (voice), 800-452-8807 ext. 7395.

Application deadline:	March 1

Contact:
Oregon Student Assistance Commission
Grants and Scholarship Division
1500 Valley River Drive, Suite 100
Eugene, OR 97401-2146
Phone: 800-452-8807
Web: www.osac.state.or.us

Oregon Collectors Association Bob Hasson Memorial Scholarship Fund Essay

Type of award: Scholarship.
Intended use: For full-time freshman study at postsecondary institution.
Eligibility: Applicant must be high school senior. Applicant must be U.S. citizen or permanent resident residing in Oregon.
Application requirements: Transcript. FAFSA. Three- to four-page essay: "Credit in the 21st Century." Applicant's name/address/social security number, parent name/telephone number, high school name/telephone number, and name of intended college must appear on first page of essay.
Additional information: Must enroll in Oregon college within 12 months of high school graduation. Children and grandchildren of owners and officers of collection agencies in Oregon not eligible. Finalists must read their essays at Association's annual spring meeting. Essays may be printed/published at discretion of Oregon Collectors Association. Apply only by mailing essays or submitting online. Visit Website for details and application. For those with disabilities: TYY 541-687-7395 (voice), 800-452-8807 ext. 7395.
    Amount of award: $1,500-$3,000
    Application deadline: March 1
Contact:
ORCA Scholarship Fund
P.O. Box 42409
Portland, OR 97242
Phone: 800-452-8807
Web: www.orcascholarshipfund.com

Oregon Dungeness Crab Commission

Type of award: Scholarship.
Intended use: For full-time undergraduate study at postsecondary institution in United States.
Eligibility: Applicant or parent must be employed by Oregon Dungeness Crab Fishermen. Applicant must be no older than 23. Applicant must be U.S. citizen or permanent resident residing in Oregon.
Basis for selection: Major/career interest in wildlife/fisheries or environmental science. Applicant must demonstrate financial need and high academic achievement.
Application requirements: Essay, transcript. FAFSA. Identify name of vessel in place of "worksite" on item 16 of application.
Additional information: Major/career interest restrictions do not apply to high school seniors. For dependents of licensed Oregon Dungeness Crab fishermen or crew. Visit Website for details and application. For those with disabilities: TYY 541-687-7395 (voice), 800-452-8807 ext. 7395.
    Amount of award: $500
    Application deadline: March 1

Contact:
Oregon Student Assistance Commission
Grants and Scholarship Division
1500 Valley River Drive, Suite 100
Eugene, OR 97401-2146
Phone: 800-452-8807
Web: www.osac.state.or.us

Oregon Foundation for Blacktail Deer Outdoor & Wildlife Scholarship

Type of award: Scholarship.
Intended use: For undergraduate study.
Eligibility: Applicant must be residing in Oregon.
Basis for selection: Major/career interest in forestry; biology; wildlife/fisheries or zoology. Applicant must demonstrate financial need.
Application requirements: Transcript. Essay (250 words) discussing the challenges of wildlife management in the coming ten years. Copy of previous year's hunting license.
Additional information: Must have serious commitment to career in wildlife management. Early bird deadline February 15. Visit Website for details.
    Application deadline: March 1
Contact:
Oregon Student Assistance Commission
1500 Valley River Drive, Suite 100
Eugene, OR 97401-2148
Phone: 800-452-8807
Web: www.osac.state.or.us

Oregon Occupational Safety and Health Division Workers Memorial Scholarship

Type of award: Scholarship, renewable.
Intended use: For full-time undergraduate or graduate study at postsecondary institution in United States.
Eligibility: Applicant must be U.S. citizen or permanent resident residing in Oregon. Applicant's parent must have been killed or disabled in work-related accident as public safety officer.
Basis for selection: Applicant must demonstrate financial need and high academic achievement.
Application requirements: Essay, transcript, proof of eligibility. FAFSA. Additional 500-word essay: "How has the injury or death of your parent or spouse affected or influenced your decision to further your education?" Must provide name, social security number, or workers compensation claim number of worker permanently disabled or fatally injured; date of death or injury; location of incident; and exact relationship to disabled or fatally injured worker.
Additional information: Must be high school graduate or GED recipient. Must be dependent or spouse of Oregon worker permanently disabled on the job or be the recipient of fatality benefits as dependent or spouse of worker fatally injured in Oregon. Visit Website for details and application. For those with disabilities: TYY 541-687-7395 (voice), 800-452-8807 ext. 7395.
    Amount of award: $500
    Application deadline: March 1

Contact:
Oregon Student Assistance Commission
Grants and Scholarship Division
1500 Valley River Drive, Suite 100
Eugene, OR 97401-2146
Phone: 800-452-8807
Web: www.osac.state.or.us

Oregon Robert C. Byrd Honors Scholarship

Type of award: Scholarship, renewable.
Intended use: For full-time undergraduate study at accredited postsecondary institution in United States.
Eligibility: Applicant must be high school senior. Applicant must be U.S. citizen or permanent resident residing in Oregon.
Basis for selection: Applicant must demonstrate high academic achievement.
Application requirements: Essay, transcript. FAFSA.
Additional information: Minimum 3.85 GPA or Oregon GED of 3300. Minimum 1300 on SAT (Math and Reading) or 29 on ACT. Must be graduating senior of Oregon high school. Fifteen recipients per federal congressional district. Visit Website for details and application. For those with disabilities: TYY 542-687-7395 (voice), 800-452-8807 ext. 7395.

Amount of award:	$1,500
Number of awards:	60
Application deadline:	March 1

Contact:
Oregon Student Assistance Commission
Grants and Scholarship Division
1500 Valley River Drive, Suite 100
Eugene, OR 97401-2146
Phone: 800-452-8807
Web: www.osac.state.or.us

Oregon Scholarship Fund Community College Student

Type of award: Scholarship, renewable.
Intended use: For full-time undergraduate study at accredited postsecondary institution.
Eligibility: Applicant must be high school senior. Applicant must be U.S. citizen or permanent resident residing in Oregon.
Basis for selection: Applicant must demonstrate high academic achievement.
Application requirements: Transcript. FAFSA and two essays.
Additional information: Visit Website for details and application. For those with disabilities: TYY 541-687-7395 (voice), 800-452-8807 ext. 7395.

Amount of award:	$500
Application deadline:	March 1

Contact:
Oregon Student Assistance Commission
Grants and Scholarship Division
1500 Valley River Drive, Suite 100
Eugene, OR 97401
Phone: 800-452-8807 ext. 7395
Web: www.osac.state.or.us

Professional Land Surveyors of Oregon Scholarship

Type of award: Scholarship, renewable.
Intended use: For full-time undergraduate study at postsecondary institution.
Eligibility: Applicant must be U.S. citizen or permanent resident residing in Oregon.
Basis for selection: Major/career interest in surveying/mapping.
Application requirements: Essay, transcript. FAFSA. One additional essay: brief statement of education/career goals relating to land surveying. Names, addresses, and phone numbers of two references (do not submit letters).
Additional information: Students must be enrolled in curricula leading to land-surveying career. Community college applicants must intend to transfer to eligible four-year schools. Four-year applicants must intend to take Fundamentals of Land Surveying (FLS) exam. Maximum award based on year in school. Visit Website for details and application. For those with disabilities: TYY 541-687-7395 (voice), 800-452-8807 ext. 7395.

Application deadline:	March 1

Contact:
Oregon Student Assistance Commission
Grants and Scholarship Division
1500 Valley River Drive, Suite 100
Eugene, OR 97401-2146
Phone: 800-452-8807
Web: www.osac.state.or.us

Richard F. Brentano Memorial Scholarship

Type of award: Scholarship, renewable.
Intended use: For full-time undergraduate study at postsecondary institution in United States.
Eligibility: Applicant or parent must be employed by Waste Control Systems, Inc. Applicant must be no older than 24. Applicant must be U.S. citizen or permanent resident residing in Oregon.
Basis for selection: Applicant must demonstrate high academic achievement.
Application requirements: Essay, transcript. FAFSA.
Additional information: Age extended to maximum 26 for applicants who entered U.S. Armed Forces directly from high school. Intended for children or IRS-legal dependents of employees of Waste Control Systems, Inc., and subsidiaries. Employees must have been employed by Waste Control Systems one year as of deadline. Visit Website for details and application. For those with disabilities: TYY 541-687-7395 (voice), 800-452-8807 ext. 7395.

Amount of award:	$500
Application deadline:	March 1

Contact:
Oregon Student Assistance Commission
Grants and Scholarship Division
1500 Valley Drive, Suite 100
Eugene, OR 97401-2146
Phone: 800-452-8807
Web: www.osac.state.or.us

Roger W. Emmons Memorial Scholarship

Type of award: Scholarship, renewable.
Intended use: For full-time undergraduate study at accredited postsecondary institution in United States.
Eligibility: Applicant or parent must be employed by Oregon Refuse & Recycling Association. Applicant must be high school senior. Applicant must be U.S. citizen or permanent resident residing in Oregon.

Basis for selection: Applicant must demonstrate high academic achievement.
Application requirements: Essay, transcript, proof of eligibility. FAFSA.
Additional information: Must be graduating senior of an Oregon high school. Parent(s) or grandparent(s) must have been solid waste company owner(s) or employees (for at least three years) and members of Oregon Refuse & Recycling Association. Visit Website for details and application. For those with disabilities: TYY 542-687-7395 (voice), 800-452-8807 ext. 7395.

   Amount of award: $500
   Application deadline: March 1
Contact:
Oregon Student Assistance Commission
Grants and Scholarship Division
1500 Valley River Drive, Suite l00
Eugene, OR 97401-2146
Phone: 800-452-8807
Web: www.osac.state.or.us

Teamsters Clyde C. Crosby/Joseph M. Edgar Memorial Scholarship

Type of award: Scholarship, renewable.
Intended use: For full-time undergraduate study at postsecondary institution in United States.
Eligibility: Applicant must be high school senior. Applicant must be U.S. citizen or permanent resident residing in Oregon.
Basis for selection: Applicant must demonstrate financial need and high academic achievement.
Application requirements: Essay, transcript. FAFSA.
Additional information: Minimum 3.0 cumulative GPA. Must be child or dependent stepchild of active, retired, disabled, or deceased member of local unions affiliated with Joint Council of Teamsters #37. Qualifying members must have been active at least one year. Visit Website for details and application. For those with disabilities: TYY 541-687-7395 (voice), 800-452-8807 ext. 7395.

   Amount of award: $500
   Application deadline: March 1
Contact:
Oregon Student Assistance Commission
Grants and Scholarship Division
1500 Valley River Drive, Suite 100
Eugene, OR 97401-2146
Phone: 800-452-8807
Web: www.osac.state.or.us

Teamsters Council #37 Federal Credit Union Scholarship

Type of award: Scholarship.
Intended use: For undergraduate or graduate study at postsecondary institution in United States.
Eligibility: Applicant must be U.S. citizen or permanent resident residing in Oregon.
Basis for selection: Applicant must demonstrate financial need and high academic achievement.
Application requirements: Essay, transcript. FAFSA. Additional essay topic: "The Importance of Preserving the Right to Strike in a Free Enterprise System."
Additional information: For members (or dependents) of Council #37 credit union. Members must have been active in local affiliated with the Joint Council of Teamsters #37 at least one year. Applicant must have cumulative GPA between 2.0 and 3.0 and be enrolled or intend to enroll at least half-time in college. Visit Website for details and application. For those with disabilities: TYY 541-687-7395 (voice), 800-452-8807 ext. 7395.

   Amount of award: $500
   Application deadline: March 1
Contact:
Oregon Student Assistance Commission
Grants and Scholarship Division
1500 Valley River Drive, Suite 100
Eugene, OR 97401-2146
Phone: 800-452-8807
Web: www.osac.state.or.us

Teamsters Local 305 Scholarship

Type of award: Scholarship, renewable.
Intended use: For full-time undergraduate study at postsecondary institution in United States.
Eligibility: Applicant must be high school senior. Applicant must be U.S. citizen or permanent resident residing in Oregon.
Basis for selection: Applicant must demonstrate high academic achievement.
Application requirements: Essay, transcript. FAFSA.
Additional information: Must be child or dependent stepchild of active, retired, disabled, or deceased member of Local 305 of the Joint Council of Teamsters #37. Member must have been active at least one year. Visit Website for details and application. For those with disabilities: TYY 541-687-7395 (voice), 800-452-8807 ext. 7395.

   Amount of award: $500
   Application deadline: March 1
Contact:
Oregon Student Assistance Commission
Grants and Scholarship Division
1500 Valley River Drive, Suite 100
Eugene, OR 97401-2146
Phone: 800-452-8807
Web: www.osac.state.or.us

Walter and Marie Schmidt Scholarship

Type of award: Scholarship, renewable.
Intended use: For undergraduate study at postsecondary institution in United States.
Eligibility: Applicant must be U.S. citizen or permanent resident residing in Oregon.
Basis for selection: Major/career interest in nursing or gerontology. Applicant must demonstrate financial need and high academic achievement.
Application requirements: Essay, transcript. FAFSA. Additional essay describing desire to pursue nursing career in geriatric health care.
Additional information: Available to students enrolling in programs to become registered nurses and intending to pursue careers in geriatric healthcare. Priority given to students from Lane County. U.S. Bank employees, children, and near relatives not eligible. Visit Website for details and application. For those with disabilities: TYY 542-687-7395 (voice), 800-452-8807 ext. 7395.

   Amount of award: $500
   Application deadline: March 1

Contact:
Oregon Student Assistance Commission
Grants and Scholarship Division
1500 Valley River Drive, Suite 100
Eugene, OR 97401-2146
Phone: 800-452-8807
Web: www.osac.state.or.us

Organization of Chinese Americans

OCA-AXA Achievement Scholarship

Type of award: Scholarship.
Intended use: For freshman study.
Eligibility: Applicant must be Asian American or Native Hawaiian/Pacific Islander. Applicant must be U.S. citizen or permanent resident.
Basis for selection: Applicant must demonstrate high academic achievement, leadership and service orientation.
Additional information: Applicant must be entering freshman in the fall. Minimum 3.0 GPA. Visit Website for more information.

Amount of award:	$2,000
Number of awards:	8
Application deadline:	April 18

Contact:
OCA-AXA Scholarship
1001 Connecticut Ave., NW
Suite 601
Washington, DC 20036
Phone: 202-223-5500
Fax: 202-296-0540
Web: www.ocanatl.org

OCA/UPS Foundation Gold Mountain College Scholarship

Type of award: Scholarship.
Intended use: For full-time undergraduate study.
Eligibility: Applicant must be Asian American. Applicant must be U.S. citizen or permanent resident.
Basis for selection: Applicant must demonstrate financial need.
Application requirements: Recommendations, essay. FAFSA.
Additional information: Minimum 3.0 GPA. Applicant must be entering college freshman and first person in family to go to college.

Amount of award:	$2,000
Number of awards:	12
Number of applicants:	250
Application deadline:	April 18
Total amount awarded:	$24,000

Contact:
Organization of Chinese Americans
1001 Connecticut Avenue NW, #601
Washington, DC 20036
Phone: 202-223-5500
Fax: 202-296-0540
Web: www.ocanatl.org

OCA/Verizon Foundation College Scholarship

Type of award: Scholarship.
Intended use: For full-time freshman study.
Eligibility: Applicant must be Asian American. Applicant must be U.S. citizen or permanent resident.
Basis for selection: Applicant must demonstrate financial need.
Application requirements: Recommendations, essay. FAFSA.
Additional information: Minimum 3.0 GPA. Contact sponsor for more information.

Amount of award:	$2,000
Number of awards:	25
Application deadline:	April 18
Total amount awarded:	$50,000

Contact:
Organization of Chinese Americans
1001 Connecticut Ave., NW
#601
Washington, DC 20036
Phone: 202-223-5500
Fax: 202-296-0540
Web: www.ocanatl.org

The Orthotic and Prosthetic Education and Development Fund

Chester Haddan Scholarship Program

Type of award: Scholarship.
Intended use: For undergraduate study at accredited 2-year or 4-year institution in United States.
Eligibility: Applicant must be U.S. citizen.
Basis for selection: Major/career interest in orthotics/prosthetics or medical specialties/research. Applicant must demonstrate financial need, depth of character, leadership, seriousness of purpose and service orientation.
Application requirements: Recommendations, transcript. A 200-word essay on why student wants to work in orthotics or prosthetics.
Additional information: Students may apply directly or professors may nominate them. Applicants must be willing to contribute financially to their own education.

Amount of award:	$1,000
Application deadline:	January 31
Notification begins:	March 3
Total amount awarded:	$1,000

Contact:
The Academy, Orthotic and Prosthetic Education and Development Fund
526 King Street
Suite 201
Alexandria, VA 22314
Phone: 703-836-0788 ext. 206
Web: www.oandp.org/education

Dan McKeever Scholarship Program

Type of award: Scholarship.

The Orthotic and Prosthetic Education and Development Fund: Dan McKeever Scholarship Program

Intended use: For senior study at accredited 2-year or 4-year institution in United States.
Eligibility: Applicant must be U.S. citizen.
Basis for selection: Major/career interest in orthotics/prosthetics or medical specialties/research. Applicant must demonstrate financial need, leadership, seriousness of purpose and service orientation.
Application requirements: Recommendations, transcript. 200-word essay on why student wants to work in orthotics or prosthetics.
Additional information: Students may apply directly or professors may nominate them. Must maintain minimum 3.0 GPA. Applicants must be willing to contribute financially to their own education.

Amount of award:	$1,000
Number of awards:	3
Application deadline:	May 31
Notification begins:	March 3
Total amount awarded:	$1,000

Contact:
The Academy, Orthotic and Prosthetic Education and Development Fund
526 King Street
Suite 201
Alexandria, VA 22314
Phone: 703-836-0788 ext. 206
Web: www.oandp.org/education

Ken Chagnon Scholarship

Type of award: Scholarship.
Intended use: For undergraduate study at accredited 2-year or 4-year institution in United States.
Eligibility: Applicant must be U.S. citizen.
Basis for selection: Major/career interest in orthotics/prosthetics or medical specialties/research. Applicant must demonstrate financial need, leadership and seriousness of purpose.
Application requirements: Recommendations, transcript. 200-word essay on why student wants to work in orthotics or prosthetics.
Additional information: Students may apply directly for the scholarship or professors may nominate them. Applicants must be willing to contribute financially to their education. Must show exceptional technical aptitude.

Amount of award:	$500
Number of awards:	1
Application deadline:	January 31
Notification begins:	March 3
Total amount awarded:	$500

Contact:
The Academy, Orthotic and Prosthetic Education and Development Fund
526 King Street
Suite 201
Alexandria, VA 22314
Phone: 703-836-0788 ext. 206
Web: www.oandp.org/education

Osage Tribal Education Committee

Osage Tribal Education Scholarship

Type of award: Scholarship, renewable.
Intended use: For undergraduate or graduate study at accredited postsecondary institution in United States.
Eligibility: Applicant must be American Indian. Must be a member of the Osage Nation. Applicant must be U.S. citizen.
Application requirements: Proof of Osage Indian blood.
Additional information: Must maintain 2.0 GPA. July 1 deadline for fall semester; December 31 for spring. Award amount varies.

Application deadline:	July 1, December 31

Contact:
Osage Tribal Education Committee
Oklahoma Area Education Office
200 Northwest 4th, Suite 4049
Oklahoma City, OK 73102
Phone: 405-605-6051 ext. 304
Fax: 405-605-6057

Outdoor Writers Association of America, Inc.

Bodie McDowell Scholarship

Type of award: Scholarship.
Intended use: For full-time junior, senior or graduate study at accredited 2-year or 4-year institution in United States. Designated institutions: Schools of journalism and mass communication registered with OWAA as scholarship program participants.
Basis for selection: Major/career interest in journalism; communications; film/video; arts, general or public relations.
Application requirements: Recommendations, essay, transcript. Examples of work in outdoor communications.
Additional information: Candidate should have career goal in outdoor communications. Award amount varies.

Number of awards:	6
Number of applicants:	15
Application deadline:	March 1
Notification begins:	July 1
Total amount awarded:	$14,600

Contact:
Outdoor Writers Association of America, Inc.
121 Hickory St.
Suite 1
Missoula, MT 59801
Phone: 406-728-7434
Web: www.owaa.org

Papercheck.com

Papercheck.com Charles Shafae' Scholarship Fund

Type of award: Scholarship.
Intended use: For undergraduate study at accredited postsecondary institution in United States.
Eligibility: Applicant must be U.S. citizen or permanent resident.
Basis for selection: Competition/talent/interest in writing/journalism. Applicant must demonstrate high academic achievement.
Application requirements: Transcript. Minimum 1,000-word essay in MLA format. Include works cited page with at least two sources.
Additional information: Minimum 3.2 GPA. Applicant must be in good standing at institution. Visit Website for essay questions, guidelines and deadlines. Complete entry form online. Contact via e-mail.
    Amount of award: $500
    Number of awards: 2
Contact:
Visit Website for application and more information.
Phone: 866-693-EDIT
Web: www.papercheck.com

Par Aide

Par Aide's Joseph S. Garske Collegiate Grant Program

Type of award: Scholarship, renewable.
Intended use: For undergraduate study at postsecondary institution.
Eligibility: Applicant must be high school senior.
Basis for selection: Applicant must demonstrate leadership.
Application requirements: Transcript. A 500-word essay evaluating a significant experience, achievement or risk and its impact on the student.
Additional information: Minimum 2.0 GPA. Applicant's parent or stepparent must be GCSAA member for five or more consecutive years and must be active GCSAA member in one of the following classifications: A, Superintendent Member, C, Retired-A, Retired-B, or AA life. Children or stepchildren of deceased members eligible if member was active for five years at time of death. Children of Par Aide employees, the Environmental Institute for Golf's Board of Trustees, the GCSAA Board of Directors, and GCSAA staff not eligible.
    Amount of award: $2,500
    Number of awards: 2
    Application deadline: March 15
    Notification begins: May 15
Contact:
Golf Course Superintendents Association of America
Garske Grant Program
1421 Research Park Drive
Lawrence, KS 66049-3859
Phone: 785-841-2240
Web: www.gcsaa.org

Parapsychology Foundation

Eileen J. Garrett Scholarship

Type of award: Scholarship.
Intended use: For undergraduate study.
Application requirements: Letters of reference from three individuals familiar with applicant's work and/or studies in parapsychology.
    Amount of award: $3,000
    Application deadline: July 15
Contact:
Parapsychology Foundation
P.O. Box 1562
New York, NY 10021
Phone: 212-628-1550
Fax: 212-628-1559
Web: www.parapsychology.org

Patient Advocate Foundation

Scholarships for Survivors

Type of award: Scholarship.
Intended use: For full-time undergraduate or graduate study at accredited 2-year, 4-year or graduate institution.
Eligibility: Applicant must be no older than 25.
Basis for selection: Applicant must demonstrate financial need, depth of character and leadership.
Application requirements: Recommendations, essay, transcript, proof of eligibility. Previous year's tax returns. Written documentation from physician stating medical history.
Additional information: Applicants must pursue course of study that renders them immediately employable after graduation. Must be survivor of life-threatening, chronic or debilitating disease. Must maintain overall 3.0 GPA. Must complete 20 hours of community service in year scholarship will be dispensed.
    Amount of award: $3,000
    Number of awards: 10
    Application deadline: April 15
    Notification begins: July 7
    Total amount awarded: $30,000
Contact:
Patient Advocate Foundation
700 Thimble Shoals Blvd., Suite 200
Newport News, VA 23606
Web: www.patientadvocate.org

Paul Loeffler

Masonic Range Science Scholarship

Type of award: Scholarship.
Intended use: For full-time freshman or sophomore study. Designated institutions: Colleges or universities with range-science programs.

Paul Loeffler: Masonic Range Science Scholarship

Basis for selection: Major/career interest in range science. Applicant must demonstrate high academic achievement and leadership.
Application requirements: Recommendations, essay, transcript. SAT/ACT scores.
Additional information: Must be sponsored by member of Society for Range Management, National Association of Conservation Districts, or Soil and Water Conservation Society. Award amount varies. Maximum eight semesters. Student must maintain 2.5 GPA first two semesters, 3.0 GPA any subsequent semester. Visit Website for more information and application. Applications should be mailed to: Paul Loeffler, Texas General Land Office, 500 W. Ave H, Box 2, Alpine, TX 79830-6008.

Number of awards:	1
Application deadline:	January 15
Notification begins:	March 1

Contact:
Texas General Land Office
500 West Ave H, Suite 101, Box 2
Alpine, TX 79830-6008
Phone: 303-986-3309
Web: www.rangelands.org

Peacock Productions, Inc.

The Audria M. Edwards Scholarship Fund

Type of award: Scholarship, renewable.
Intended use: For full-time undergraduate study at accredited vocational, 2-year or 4-year institution in United States.
Eligibility: Applicant must be U.S. citizen residing in Oregon or Washington.
Basis for selection: Major/career interest in arts, general. Applicant must demonstrate financial need, depth of character and leadership.
Application requirements: Proof of eligibility.
Additional information: Applicant must be gay, lesbian or transgendered, or the child of gay, lesbian or transgendered parents. Applicant must be pursuing degree in academic field, trade, vocation or the arts. Applicants living in Washington must reside in Clark, Cowlitz, Lewis, Pacific, Skamania or Wahkiakum counties. Please visit Website for application information.

Number of awards:	10
Number of applicants:	25
Application deadline:	May 1
Total amount awarded:	$18,000

Contact:
Peacock Productions, Inc.
Audria M. Edwards Scholarship Fund
P.O. Box 8854
Portland, OR 97207-8854
Web: www.peacockinthepark.com/scholarship.shtm

Penguin Putnam, Inc.

Signet Classic Student Scholarship Essay Contest

Type of award: Scholarship.
Intended use: For undergraduate study.
Eligibility: Applicant must be high school junior or senior. Applicant must be U.S. citizen or permanent resident.
Basis for selection: Competition/talent/interest in writing/journalism, based on style, content, grammar and originality; judges look for clear, concise writing that is articulate, logically organized and well supported. Major/career interest in English or literature.
Application requirements: Proof of eligibility, nomination by high school English teacher. Entrant must read designated book and answer one of several book-related questions in two- to three-page essay. Essay must be submitted by high school English teacher on behalf of student, along with cover letter on school letterhead. Parent or legal guardian must submit essay for home-schooled students.
Additional information: Home-schooled entrants must be between ages 16 and 18. Immediate relatives of employees and employees of Penguin Group (USA) Inc. and its affiliates ineligible. Visit Website for details and application, or contact high school English department. Winner also receives Signet Classic library for school (or for public library in the case of home-schooled winner).

Amount of award:	$1,000
Number of awards:	5
Number of applicants:	1,000
Application deadline:	April 15
Notification begins:	June 15
Total amount awarded:	$5,000

Contact:
Penguin Group Signet Classic Student Scholarship Essay Contest
Academic Marketing Department
375 Hudson Street
New York, NY 10014
Phone: 212-366-2377
Web: www.penguinputnam.com/scessay

Pennsylvania Higher Education Assistance Agency

Pennsylvania Robert C. Byrd Honors Scholarship

Type of award: Scholarship, renewable.
Intended use: For full-time freshman study at accredited postsecondary institution in United States.
Eligibility: Applicant must be high school senior. Applicant must be U.S. citizen or permanent resident residing in Pennsylvania.
Basis for selection: Applicant must demonstrate high academic achievement.
Application requirements: Transcript. SAT/ACT or GED scores.

Additional information: Applicant must rank in top five percent of class, have minimum 3.5 GPA, 1150 SAT (Math and Reading) or 25 ACT, or 355 GED. Must graduate from high school same year scholarship is awarded. Information available from high school guidance office.
   Application deadline: May 1
Contact:
Pennsylvania Higher Education Assistance Agency
Robert C. Byrd Scholarship
P.O. Box 8114
Harrisburg, PA 17105-8114
Phone: 800-692-7392
Web: www.pheaa.org

Pennsylvania State Grant Program

Type of award: Scholarship, renewable.
Intended use: For undergraduate study at accredited vocational, 2-year or 4-year institution in United States.
Eligibility: Applicant must be residing in Pennsylvania.
Basis for selection: Applicant must demonstrate financial need.
Application requirements: Proof of eligibility. FAFSA.
Additional information: Applicant must be high school graduate or GED recipient enrolled in PHEAA-approved program. Applicant must not already have four-year undergraduate degree. Grants are portable to approved institutions in other states. Number and amount of awards vary. Deadlines: August 1 for first-time applicants in business, trade, technical, or nursing schools or terminal two-year programs; May 1 for other applicants.
   Amount of award: $300-$3,300
   Application deadline: May 1, August 1
Contact:
Pennsylvania Higher Education Assistance Agency
State Grant and Special Programs Division
1200 North Seventh Street
Harrisburg, PA 17102-1444
Phone: 800-692-7392
Web: www.pheaa.org

Pennsylvania Work-Study Program

Type of award: Scholarship, renewable.
Intended use: For undergraduate, master's, doctoral or first professional study at accredited postsecondary institution. Designated institutions: PHEAA-approved institutions.
Eligibility: Applicant must be U.S. citizen or permanent resident residing in Pennsylvania.
Basis for selection: Applicant must demonstrate financial need.
Application requirements: Interview, proof of eligibility. Proof of state grant or subsidized Stafford loan.
Additional information: Student must demonstrate ability to benefit from career-related high-tech or community service work experience. Funds earned must be used to pay school costs. Applicant must be state grant or subsidized federal loan recipient and not owe state grant refund or be in default on student loan. Recipient must secure a job with PHEAA-approved on or off-campus SWSP employer. Amount and number of awards vary. Deadlines: Fall and entire year, October 1; spring term only, January 15; summer, May 15.
   Number of applicants: 3,400
   Application deadline: October 1, January 1

Contact:
Pennsylvania Higher Education Assistance Agency
State Grant and Special Programs Division
1200 North Seventh Street
Harrisburg, PA 17102
Phone: 800-692-7392
Web: www.pheaa.org

PHEAA Academic Excellence Scholarship Award Program

Type of award: Scholarship.
Intended use: For full-time freshman study at accredited postsecondary institution in United States. Designated institutions: PHEAA-approved Pennsylvania institutions.
Eligibility: Applicant must be high school senior. Applicant must be U.S. citizen residing in Pennsylvania.
Basis for selection: Applicant must demonstrate high academic achievement.
Additional information: Award is given to students who applied and qualified for but did not receive the Robert C. Byrd Honors Scholarship. There is no separate application. Application available from high school guidance counselor/school authority. Must be Pennsylvania State Grant recipient for at least one term during freshman year. Applicant must rank in top five percent of class, have 3.5 GPA, 1150 SAT or 25 ACT, or 355 GED. Renewal based on full-time enrollment and maintenance of satisfactory academic progress.
   Application deadline: May 1
Contact:
State Grant and Special Programs
P.O. Box 8114
Harrisburg, PA 17105-8114
Phone: 800-692-7392
Web: www.pheaa.org

SciTech Scholarship

Type of award: Scholarship, renewable.
Intended use: For full-time sophomore, junior or senior study at 4-year institution in United States. Designated institutions: Approved Pennsylvania institutions.
Eligibility: Applicant must be residing in Pennsylvania.
Additional information: Applicant must be pursuing a bachelor's degree in an approved science or technology field. Must apply for Federal Pell and Pennsylvania State Grant. Minimum 3.0 GPA at time of application; must maintain GPA to be eligible for renewal. Must complete approved internship or relevant work experience with Pennsylvania company prior to graduation. Must begin employment in state within one year of graduation--one year for each year scholarship was awarded. Must provide employment verification every six months. Students pursuing full-time graduate study within one year of receiving bachelor's may request deferment of work obligation. Award is renewable for maximum of three years (some exceptions made for approved five-year programs). Scholarship converts to loan if student fails to satisfy work obligation.
   Amount of award: $3,000
Contact:
PHEAA State Grant and Special Programs
1200 North Seventh Street
Harrisburg, PA 17102-1444
Phone: 800-692-7392
Web: www.pheaa.org

Technology Scholarship

Type of award: Scholarship, renewable.

Intended use: For undergraduate study at vocational, 2-year or 4-year institution. Designated institutions: PHEAA-approved institutions.
Eligibility: Applicant must be residing in Pennsylvania.
Additional information: Applicant must apply for Federal Pell Grant and Pennsylvania State Grant. Minimum 3.0 GPA. Applicant must begin employment in Pennsylvania within one year of graduation--one year for each year scholarship was awarded. Employment verification must be provided every six months. Deferment of work obligation possible if student begins full-time graduate study within one month of receiving bachelor's. Scholarship converts to loan if student fails to satisfy work obligation.

   Amount of award: $1,000
   Application deadline: December 31
Contact:
PHEAA State Grant and Special Programs
1200 North Seventh Street
Harrisburg, PA 17102-1444
Phone: 800-692-7392
Web: www.pheaa.org

Pennsylvania State System of Higher Education Foundation, Inc.

Dr. & Mrs. Arthur William Phillips Scholarship

Type of award: Scholarship.
Intended use: For full-time undergraduate study at 4-year institution in United States. Designated institutions: PASSHE Universities: Bloomsburg University of Pennsylvania, California University of Pennsylvania, Cheyney University of Pennsylvania, Clarion University of Pennsylvania, Edinboro University of Pennsylvania, East Stroudsburg University of Pennsylvania, Indiana University of Pennsylvania, Kutztown University of Pennsylvania, Lock Haven University of Pennsylvania, Mansfield University of Pennsylvania, Millersville University of Pennsylvania, Shippensburg University of Pennsylvania, Slippery Rock University of Pennsylvania, West Chester University of Pennsylvania.
Eligibility: Applicant must be residing in Pennsylvania.
Basis for selection: Applicant must demonstrate financial need and high academic achievement.
Additional information: Applicant must be resident of Butler, Clarion, Forest, Jefferson, Lawrence, Mercer or Venango Counties. Visit Website for deadlines and other information.

   Amount of award: $500-$1,000
   Notification begins: May 31
Contact:
Pennsylvania State System of Higher Education Foundation, Inc.
2896 N. 2nd Street
Harrisburg, PA 17110
Phone: 717-720-4065
Fax: 717-720-7082
Web: www.thepafoundation.org/scholarships

George Griffiths/Ada Jakubic Scholarship

Type of award: Scholarship.
Intended use: For full-time undergraduate study. Designated institutions: PASSHE Universities: Bloomsburg University of Pennsylvania, California University of Pennsylvania, Cheyney University of Pennsylvania, Clarion University of Pennsylvania, Edinboro University of Pennsylvania, East Stroudsburg University of Pennsylvania, Indiana University of Pennsylvania, Kutztown University of Pennsylvania, Lock Haven University of Pennsylvania, Mansfield University of Pennsylvania, Millersville University of Pennsylvania, Shippensburg University of Pennsylvania, Slippery Rock University of Pennsylvania, West Chester University of Pennsylvania.
Eligibility: Applicant must be residing in Pennsylvania.
Additional information: Parent of applicant must be member of Union of Needletrades, Industrial and Textile Employees, AFL-CIO (UNITE). Students interested in this scholarship should contact their parent's UNITE representative.

   Amount of award: $1,000
Contact:
Pennsylvania State System of Higher Education Foundation, Inc.
2986 N. 2nd St.
Harrisburg, PA 17110
Phone: 717-720-4086
Fax: 717-720-7082
Web: www.thepafoundation.org/scholarships

James Hughes Memorial Scholarship Fund

Type of award: Scholarship, renewable.
Intended use: For full-time undergraduate study at postsecondary institution in United States. Designated institutions: PASSHE Universities.
Eligibility: Applicant must be residing in Pennsylvania.
Basis for selection: Applicant must demonstrate financial need and high academic achievement.
Application requirements: Recommendations, essay, transcript.
Additional information: Applicants must have graduated from any public or charter school in the School District of Philadelphia. Minimum 2.0 GPA required for renewals. Application available at Website.

   Amount of award: $750-$1,500
   Number of awards: 27
   Application deadline: March 31
   Notification begins: May 1
Contact:
Pennsylvania State System of Higher Education Foundation, Inc.
2986 N. 2nd St.
Harrisburg, PA 17110
Phone: 717-720-4065
Fax: 717-720-7082
Web: www.thapafoundation.org

Minnie Patton Stayman Scholarship

Type of award: Scholarship, renewable.
Intended use: For full-time undergraduate study in United States. Designated institutions: PASSHE Universities: Bloomsburg University of Pennsylvania, California University of Pennsylvania, Cheyney University of Pennsylvania, Clarion University of Pennsylvania, Edinboro University of

Pennsylvania, East Stroudsburg University of Pennsylvania, Indiana University of Pennsylvania, Kutztown University of Pennsylvania, Lock Haven University of Pennsylvania, Mansfield University of Pennsylvania, Millersville University of Pennsylvania, Shippensburg University of Pennsylvania, Slippery Rock University of Pennsylvania, West Chester University of Pennsylvania.
Eligibility: Applicant must be residing in Pennsylvania.
Additional information: Applicant must be resident of Altoona, PA.

   Amount of award: $1,000
Contact:
Pennsylvania State System of Higher Education Foundation, Inc.
2986 N. Second St.
Harrisburg, PA 17110
Phone: 717-720-4065
Fax: 717-720-7082
Web: www.thepafoundation.org

Robert Noyce Scholarship Program

Type of award: Scholarship, renewable.
Intended use: For full-time junior or senior study at 4-year or graduate institution in United States.
Eligibility: Applicant must be residing in Pennsylvania.
Basis for selection: Major/career interest in education; mathematics; engineering; technology or science, general. Applicant must demonstrate high academic achievement.
Application requirements: Recommendations, essay, transcript.
Additional information: For STEM majors and STEM professionals with a commitment to becoming mathematics and science teachers. Each semester awarded requires one year of teaching in Pennsylvania high needs school. Minimum 3.0 GPA. Transfer students or post-baccalaureates must complete semester or more of coursework at a State System university to establish qualifying GPA. Terms and responsibilities of recipients available on Website.

   Amount of award: $7,500-$10,000
   Application deadline: April 20
Contact:
Noyce Scholarship Program
Dixon University Center
2986 N. 2nd St.
Harrisburg, PA 17110
Phone: 717-720-4065
Web: www.cetp-pa.iup.edu/noyce.htm

Wayne G. Failor Scholarship

Type of award: Scholarship.
Intended use: For full-time freshman study at postsecondary institution in United States. Designated institutions: PASSHE Universities: Bloomsburg University of Pennsylvania, California University of Pennsylvania, Cheyney University of Pennsylvania, Clarion University of Pennsylvania, Edinboro University of Pennsylvania, East Stroudsburg University of Pennsylvania, Indiana University of Pennsylvania, Kutztown University of Pennsylvania, Lock Haven University of Pennsylvania, Mansfield University of Pennsylvania, Millersville University of Pennsylvania, Shippensburg University of Pennsylvania, Slippery Rock University of Pennsylvania, West Chester University of Pennsylvania.
Eligibility: Applicant must be high school senior. Applicant must be residing in Pennsylvania.
Basis for selection: Major/career interest in business. Applicant must demonstrate financial need and high academic achievement.
Application requirements: PHEAA grant.
Additional information: Award amount and number varies yearly. Applicants must be graduating from a West Shore School District high school and plan to attend State System University. Must have "B" average or better by the end of junior year. Visit Website for deadlines and other information.

   Application deadline: May 1
Contact:
Pennsylvania State System of Higher Education, Inc.
2986 N. 2nd St.
Harrisburg, PA 17110
Phone: 717-720-4065
Fax: 717-720-7082
Web: www.thepafoundation.org

The Persian Scholarship Foundation

The Persian Scholarship Recognition Award

Type of award: Scholarship.
Intended use: For undergraduate or graduate study in United States.
Application requirements: Transcript. Cover letter, digital copy of valid student ID, scanned copy of published article, MS Word copy of article, scanned copy of official transcript.
Additional information: Applicant must be of Iranian descent. Applicant must have published an essay or article in a school, local or national newspaper discussing the positive achievements of Iranian people and society. All documents must be emailed to applications@persianscholarship.org. One winner each will be selected from high school, undergraduate, and graduate levels.

   Amount of award: $500-$1,000
   Number of awards: 3
   Application deadline: December 14
   Notification begins: March 1
   Total amount awarded: $2,500
Contact:
The Persian Scholarship Foundation
1434 Westwood Boulevard, #5
Los Angeles, CA 90024
Web: www.persianscholarship.org

PFLAG National Office

PFLAG National Scholarship Program

Type of award: Scholarship.
Intended use: For full-time freshman study at 2-year or 4-year institution.
Eligibility: Applicant must be high school senior.
Basis for selection: Applicant must demonstrate financial need, high academic achievement and service orientation.

PFLAG National Office: PFLAG National Scholarship Program

Additional information: Minimum 3.0 GPA. Must self-identify as gay, lesbian, bisexual, transgender, or supporter of GLBF people. Applications and full details available online in December.

Amount of award:	$1,000-$5,000
Number of awards:	16
Number of applicants:	220
Application deadline:	March 15
Total amount awarded:	$35,000

Contact:
PFLAG National Office
1726 M Street, NW, Suite 400
Washington, DC 20036
Phone: 202-467-8180 ext. 219
Web: www.pflag.org/Scholarships.122.0.html

Phi Delta Kappa International

Phi Delta Kappa Scholarship for Prospective Educators

Type of award: Scholarship.
Intended use: For full-time undergraduate study at accredited postsecondary institution in or outside United States.
Basis for selection: Major/career interest in education. Applicant must demonstrate high academic achievement, leadership, seriousness of purpose and service orientation.
Application requirements: Recommendations, essay, transcript.
Additional information: Applicant must be high school senior or current undergraduate member of PDK, child/grandchild of Kappan in good standing, or who have letter written by Kappan in good standing. No minimum GPA required. One scholarship is renewable for $1,250 per year; another for $1,000 per year. Send application to local chapter.

Amount of award:	$1,000-$5,000
Number of awards:	30
Number of applicants:	800
Application deadline:	February 1
Notification begins:	June 1
Total amount awarded:	$30,000

Contact:
Phi Delta Kappa International
Scholarship Program
Box 789, 408 N. Union Street
Bloomington, IN 47402-0789
Phone: 800-766-1156
Fax: 812-339-0018
Web: www.pdkintl.org

The Phillips Foundation

Ronald Reagan College Leaders Scholarship Program

Type of award: Scholarship, renewable.
Intended use: For full-time sophomore or junior study at accredited 4-year institution in United States.
Eligibility: Applicant must be U.S. citizen.

Basis for selection: Applicant must demonstrate high academic achievement, depth of character, leadership, patriotism, seriousness of purpose and service orientation.
Application requirements: Recommendations, essay. 500- to 750-word essay describing background, career objective, and scope of participation in leadership activities promoting freedom, American values and constitutional principles. Proof of full-time enrollment in good standing; proof of leadership activities.
Additional information: Award amounts are $1,000, $2,500, $5,000, $7,500, and $10,000. Number of awards varies based on merit. Recipients will be notified in late March/early April. Visit Website for application and more information.

Number of awards:	90
Number of applicants:	430
Application deadline:	January 15
Total amount awarded:	$303,500

Contact:
The Phillips Foundation
Attn: Jeff Hollingsworth
1 Massachusetts Ave NW, Suite 620
Washington, DC 20001
Phone: 202-842-2002
Web: www.thephillipsfoundation.org

Physician Assistant Foundation

Physician Assistant Scholarship

Type of award: Scholarship.
Intended use: For undergraduate study. Designated institutions: Any physician assistant program accredited by Committee on Allied Health Education and Accreditation/Commission on Accreditation of Allied Health Education Programs.
Eligibility: Applicant or parent must be member/participant of American Academy of Physician Assistants.
Basis for selection: Applicant must demonstrate financial need, high academic achievement, seriousness of purpose and service orientation.
Application requirements: Transcript, proof of eligibility. Financial aid statements, standard student budget. Three copies of all paperwork required. Two passport photos.
Additional information: Applicant must have completed first semester of P.A. program. Must be student member of American Academy of Physician Assistants at time of application. Number of awards varies.

Amount of award:	$2,000
Application deadline:	January 15
Notification begins:	May 15

Contact:
Susan Hoefling, Foundation Manager
Physician Assistant Foundation
950 North Washington Street
Alexandria, VA 22314
Phone: 703-519-5686
Fax: 703-684-1924
Web: www.aapa.org/paf/app-scholarship.html

Playtex Products, Inc.

Playtex Scholarship

Type of award: Scholarship, renewable.
Intended use: For full-time freshman study at accredited 4-year institution in United States or Canada.
Eligibility: Applicant or parent must be employed by Playtex Products, Inc. and subsidiaries. Applicant must be high school senior. Applicant must be U.S. citizen, permanent resident or Canadian and Puerto Rican citizens.
Basis for selection: Applicant must demonstrate high academic achievement, depth of character, leadership, seriousness of purpose and service orientation.
Application requirements: Recommendations, essay, transcript, proof of eligibility.
Additional information: Parent or guardian must have completed one year of continuous service with Playtex by time of application. Two scholarships given in most recent year, six renewed.

Amount of award:	$5,000
Number of applicants:	11
Application deadline:	November 30
Notification begins:	May 1
Total amount awarded:	$40,000

Contact:
Playtex Products Scholarship Program
50 N. Dupont Highway
Dover, DE 19903
Web: www.playtexproducts.com

Plumbing-Heating-Cooling Contractors - National Assoc. Educational Foundation

American Standard Scholarship

Type of award: Scholarship.
Intended use: For full-time undergraduate study at accredited 2-year or 4-year institution in United States.
Eligibility: Applicant must be U.S. citizen or Canadian citizen.
Basis for selection: Major/career interest in engineering, mechanical; business/management/administration or construction management.
Application requirements: Recommendations, essay, transcript. List of extracurricular activities. SAT/ACT scores.
Additional information: Students enrolled or planning to enroll in PHCC-approved apprenticeship program also eligible. Other eligible majors include mechanical CAD design, plumbing or HVACR installation and others directly related to the plumbing-heating-cooling profession. Visit Website for details and application.

Amount of award:	$2,500
Number of awards:	4
Application deadline:	May 1

Contact:
American Standard Scholarship Program
180 South Washington Street
P.O. Box 6808
Falls Church, VA 22046
Phone: 800-533-7694
Fax: 703-237-7442
Web: www.foundation.phccweb.org/Scholarships

A.O. Smith Water Heaters Scholarship

Type of award: Scholarship.
Intended use: For full-time undergraduate or post-bachelor's certificate study at accredited vocational, 2-year or 4-year institution in United States.
Eligibility: Applicant must be U.S. citizen or Canadian citizen.
Basis for selection: Major/career interest in business/management/administration; construction management or engineering, mechanical.
Application requirements: Recommendations, essay, transcript. SAT/ACT scores. List of extracurricular activities.
Additional information: Students enrolled or planning to enroll in PHCC-approved apprenticeship program also eligible. Other eligible majors include mechanical CAD design, plumbing or HVACR installation and others directly related to the plumbing-heating-cooling profession. Visit Website for details and application.

Amount of award:	$2,500
Number of awards:	2
Application deadline:	May 1

Contact:
A.O. Smith Scholarship Program
180 South Washington Street
P.O. Box 6808
Falls Church, VA 22046
Phone: 800-533-7694
Fax: 703-237-7442
Web: www.foundation.phccweb.org/Scholarships

Bradford White Scholarship

Type of award: Scholarship.
Intended use: For full-time undergraduate study at accredited vocational or 2-year institution in United States.
Eligibility: Applicant must be U.S. citizen or Canadian citizen.
Basis for selection: Major/career interest in business/management/administration or construction management.
Application requirements: Recommendations, essay, transcript. SAT/ACT scores. List of extracurricular activities.
Additional information: Students enrolled or planning to enroll in PHCC-approved apprenticeship program also eligible. Other eligible majors include mechanical CAD design, plumbing or HVACR installation and others directly related to the plumbing-heating-cooling profession. Visit Website for details and application.

Amount of award:	$2,500
Number of awards:	3
Application deadline:	May 1

Contact:
Bradford White Scholarship Program
180 South Washington St.
P.O. Box 6808
Falls Church, VA 22046
Phone: 800-533-7694
Fax: 703-237-7442
Web: www.foundation.phccweb.org/Scholarships

Delta Faucet Company Scholarship

Type of award: Scholarship.
Intended use: For full-time undergraduate study at accredited vocational, 2-year or 4-year institution in United States or Canada.
Eligibility: Applicant must be U.S. citizen or Canadian citizen.
Basis for selection: Major/career interest in air conditioning/heating/refrigeration technology; architecture; business; engineering, construction or construction management.
Application requirements: Recommendations, essay, transcript.
Additional information: Applicants must pursue studies in major related to plumbing-heating-cooling industry or apprentice in a PHCC-approved program. Must be sponsored by active member of PHCC National Association. Funds provided by Delta Faucet Company and administered by PHCC Educational Foundation. Submit SAT/ACT scores.
    Amount of award: $2,500
    Number of awards: 6
    Number of applicants: 45
    Application deadline: May 1
    Total amount awarded: $15,000
Contact:
Delta Faucet Scholarship Program
180 S. Washington Street
P.O. Box 6808
Falls Church, VA 22046
Phone: 800-533-7694
Fax: 703-237-7442
Web: www.phccweb.org/Scholarships

PHCC Auxiliary of Massachusetts Scholarship

Type of award: Scholarship.
Intended use: For full-time undergraduate study at accredited 4-year institution in United States.
Eligibility: Applicant must be high school senior. Applicant must be U.S. citizen residing in Massachusetts.
Application requirements: Recommendations, essay, transcript. SAT/ACT scores. List of extracurricular activities.
Additional information: Visit Website for details and application.
    Amount of award: $1,500
    Number of awards: 1
    Application deadline: May 1
Contact:
PHCC Auxiliary of Massachusetts Scholarship Program
180 South Washington St.
P.O. Box 6808
Falls Church, VA 22046
Phone: 800-533-7694
Fax: 703-237-7442
Web: www.foundation.phccweb.org/Scholarships

PHCC Educational Foundation Need-Based Scholarship

Type of award: Scholarship.
Intended use: For full-time undergraduate study at accredited vocational, 2-year or 4-year institution in United States.
Eligibility: Applicant must be U.S. citizen or Canadian citizen.
Basis for selection: Major/career interest in business/management/administration; construction management or engineering, mechanical. Applicant must demonstrate financial need.
Application requirements: Recommendations, essay, transcript. SAT/ACT scores. List of extracurricular activities.
Additional information: Students enrolled or planning to enroll in PHCC-approved apprenticeship program also eligible. Other eligible majors include mechanical CAD design, plumbing or HVACR installation and others directly related to the plumbing-heating-cooling profession. Visit Website for details and application.
    Amount of award: $2,500
    Number of awards: 1
    Application deadline: May 1
Contact:
PHCC Educational Foundation Need-Based Scholarship Program
180 South Washington St.
P.O. Box 6808
Falls Church, VA 22046
Phone: 800-533-7694
Fax: 703-237-7442
Web: www.foundation.phccweb.org/Scholarships

Plumbing-Heating-Cooling Contractors - National Association Educational Foundation Scholarship

Type of award: Scholarship, renewable.
Intended use: For full-time undergraduate study at accredited postsecondary institution in United States.
Eligibility: Applicant must be U.S. citizen or Canadian citizen.
Basis for selection: Major/career interest in air conditioning/heating/refrigeration technology; architecture; business; engineering, construction or construction management. Applicant must demonstrate high academic achievement.
Application requirements: Recommendations, transcript.
Additional information: Applicants must pursue studies in major related to plumbing-heating-cooling industry or apprentice in a PHCC-approved program. Must be sponsored by active member of PHCC National Association. Award for four-year students is $12,000 ($3,000 per year for up to four years), and award for two-year students is $3,000 ($1,500 per year for up to two years). Applicant must maintain 2.0 GPA.
    Amount of award: $3,000-$12,000
    Number of awards: 5
    Application deadline: May 1
    Notification begins: August 1
    Total amount awarded: $48,000
Contact:
PHCC Educational Foundation Scholarship Program
180 S. Washington St.
P.O. Box 6808
Falls Church, VA 22046
Phone: 800-533-7694
Fax: 703-237-7442
Web: www.phccweb.org

The Point Foundation

Point Scholarship

Type of award: Scholarship.
Intended use: For undergraduate or graduate study in United States.

Basis for selection: Applicant must demonstrate financial need, high academic achievement, depth of character, leadership, seriousness of purpose and service orientation.
Application requirements: Transcript. Two or three letters of recommendation, with two of them from a teacher or professor. Applicants who have been out of school five years or more may substitute a reference from a supervisor for one letter.
Additional information: Applicant's sexuality is not a factor, but applicants should have a history of leadership in the lesbian, gay, bisexual, and transgendered community and plan to be an LGBT leader in the future. Award amount varies based on available funds. Scholars must maintain a 3.5 GPA, be willing to speak publicly about Foundation events, provide the Foundation with transcripts, remain in contact with Foundation Trustees, and do an individual project with the LGBT community. Applicants selected as semi-finalists will be notified within 60 days of deadline. Visit Website for application.

Amount of award:	$13,600
Number of awards:	38
Number of applicants:	3,000
Application deadline:	March 1
Notification begins:	May 15

Contact:
The Point Foundation
Office Box 565
Genoa, NV 89411
Phone: 775-782-5659
Fax: 775-782-5690
Web: www.pointfoundation.org

Presbyterian Church (USA)

National Presbyterian Scholarship

Type of award: Scholarship, renewable.
Intended use: For full-time undergraduate study in United States. Designated institutions: Presbyterian-related institutions.
Eligibility: Applicant must be high school senior. Applicant must be Presbyterian. Applicant must be U.S. citizen or permanent resident.
Basis for selection: Applicant must demonstrate financial need and high academic achievement.
Application requirements: Transcript. Recommendation from church pastor, biographical questionnaire, and record from high school guidance counselor.
Additional information: SAT/ACT must be taken no later than December 15 of senior year of high school. Must be preparing to enter participating college related to the Presbyterian Church (USA).

Amount of award:	$500-$1,400
Number of awards:	440
Number of applicants:	206
Application deadline:	January 31
Notification begins:	March 1

Contact:
Presbyterian Church (USA)
Financial Aid for Studies
100 Witherspoon Street
Louisville, KY 40202-1396
Phone: 888-728-7228 ext. 5776
Fax: 502-569-8766
Web: www.pcusa.org/financialaid

Presbyterian Student Opportunity Scholarship

Type of award: Scholarship.
Intended use: For full-time undergraduate study at accredited 4-year institution in United States.
Eligibility: Applicant must be high school senior. Applicant must be Presbyterian. Applicant must be U.S. citizen or permanent resident.
Basis for selection: Applicant must demonstrate financial need.
Application requirements: Recommendations, transcript, proof of eligibility.
Additional information: Preference given to students of African American, Asian American, Hispanic American, Alaska Native, and Native American descent. Applications available after February 1. Minimum GPA 2.5. Must reapply annually for renewal.

Amount of award:	$200-$3,000
Number of awards:	156
Number of applicants:	156
Application deadline:	June 15
Notification begins:	August 1
Total amount awarded:	$175,000

Contact:
Presbyterian Church (USA)
Financial Aid for Studies
100 Witherspoon Street
Louisville, KY 40202-1396
Phone: 888-728-7228 ext. 5745
Fax: 502-569-8766
Web: www.pcusa.org/financialaid

Samuel Robinson Award

Type of award: Scholarship.
Intended use: For full-time junior or senior study at 4-year institution. Designated institutions: One of 69 colleges related to Presbyterian Church (USA).
Eligibility: Applicant must be Presbyterian. Applicant must be U.S. citizen or permanent resident.
Application requirements: A 2,000-word essay on assigned topic related to the Catechism.
Additional information: One-time award. Applicant must successfully recite answers of the Westminster Shorter Catechism. Amount of award based on annual funds.

Amount of award:	$200-$2,500
Application deadline:	April 1
Notification begins:	May 15

Contact:
Presbyterian Church (USA)
Financial Aid for Studies
100 Witherspoon Street
Louisville, KY 40202-1396
Phone: 888-728-7228 ext. 5776
Fax: 502-569-8766
Web: www.pcusa.org/financialaid

Press Club of Houston Educational Foundation

Press Club of Houston Scholarship

Type of award: Scholarship.
Intended use: For full-time junior or senior study at accredited 4-year institution in United States.
Eligibility: Applicant must be U.S. citizen.
Basis for selection: Major/career interest in journalism; radio/television/film or communications. Applicant must demonstrate financial need and high academic achievement.
Application requirements: Interview, recommendations, transcript. Writing samples, statement from college financial aid office about current financial aid package, personal statement outlining career goal and reasons behind that goal.
Additional information: Applicant must be student at college in Greater Houston Area (Harris, Brazoria, Chambers, Fort Bend, Galveston, Liberty, Montgomery, and Waller Counties) or resident of Greater Houston Area attending college anywhere. Applications available after January 1. Total amount available for awards depends on proceeds from annual Gridiron Show. Deadlines vary; visit Website for details and application.

   Amount of award: $500-$3,000
   Application deadline: December 12

Contact:
Press Club of Houston Educational Foundation
Scholarship Chairman
P.O. Box 541038
Houston, TX 77254-1038
Phone: 713-743-1822
Web: www.houstonpressclub.com

Pride of the Greater Lehigh Valley

Rainbow Scholarship

Type of award: Scholarship.
Intended use: For undergraduate study.
Eligibility: Applicant must be residing in Pennsylvania.
Application requirements: Recommendations, transcript.
Additional information: Three awards available to students who identify as gay, lesbian, bisexual, transgender, or intersex: Queer Student of the Year, awarded to a queer teen who is a positive force in the GBLTI community through involvement and participation in community activities; Rainbow Award, awarded to a queer teen for academic excellence; Diversity Essay Contest, open to all college-bound youth, regardless of sexual orientation or gender identity. Must live in Berks, Bucks, Carbon, Lehigh, Monroe, Montgomery, Northampton, Schuylkill, or Warren county. Visit Website for more information and application.

   Amount of award: $200-$1,200
   Number of awards: 3
   Number of applicants: 2
   Application deadline: June 1

Contact:
The Rainbow Scholarship
c/o Pride-GLV
1101 West Hamilton St.
Allentown, PA 18101-1043
Phone: 610-770-6200
Web: www.prideglv.org

The Princess Grace Foundation USA

Princess Grace Award for Dance

Type of award: Scholarship.
Intended use: For undergraduate or graduate study in United States. Designated institutions: Non-profit institutions.
Eligibility: Applicant must be U.S. citizen or permanent resident.
Application requirements: Nomination by dean or department head.
Additional information: Scholarships for dance students who have completed at least one year of professional training, undergraduate, or graduate work at a non-profit institution. Award amount varies.

   Number of awards: 6
   Application deadline: April 30
   Notification begins: July 21

Contact:
Princess Grace Foundation USA
150 E. 58th Street
25th Floor
New York, NY 10155
Phone: 212-317-1470
Fax: 212-317-1473
Web: www.pgfusa.org

Princess Grace Award For Film

Type of award: Scholarship.
Intended use: For senior or graduate study at accredited 4-year or graduate institution. Designated institutions: Eligible film schools.
Eligibility: Applicant must be U.S. citizen or permanent resident.
Basis for selection: Major/career interest in film/video.
Application requirements: Nomination by dean or department head.
Additional information: Award amount varies. Film scholarships available to help undergraduate seniors or graduate students produce thesis projects. Only invited film schools are eligible to apply.

   Number of awards: 6
   Application deadline: June 2
   Notification begins: July 21

Contact:
The Princess Grace Foundation USA
150 E. 58th Street
25th Floor
New York, NY 10155
Phone: 212-317-1470
Fax: 212-317-1473
Web: www.pgfusa.org

Princess Grace Award For Playwriting

Type of award: Scholarship.
Intended use: For undergraduate study in United States.
Eligibility: Applicant must be U.S. citizen or permanent resident.
Basis for selection: Major/career interest in playwriting/screen writing.
Application requirements: One unproduced play.
Additional information: Award given directly to individual through residency at New Dramatists, Inc. in New York. Playwrights may submit applications independently; they do not have to be nominated. Applicant must not have had any professional productions--readings, workshops, and Equity showcases are admissible. See Website for application.
    Amount of award: $7,500
    Number of awards: 1
    Application deadline: March 31
Contact:
The Princess Grace Foundation USA
150 E. 58th Street
25th Floor
New York, NY 10155
Phone: 212-317-1470
Fax: 212-317-1473
Web: www.pgfusa.org

Princess Grace Award For Theater

Type of award: Scholarship.
Intended use: For senior or master's study at accredited 4-year or graduate institution.
Eligibility: Applicant must be U.S. citizen or permanent resident.
Basis for selection: Major/career interest in arts, general.
Application requirements: Nomination by dean or department head.
Additional information: Scholarships awarded to students for their last year (undergraduate or graduate) of professional training in acting, directing, scenic, lighting, sound or costume design. Award amount varies.
    Number of awards: 6
    Application deadline: March 31
Contact:
The Princess Grace Foundation USA
150 E. 58th Street
25th Floor
New York, NY 10155
Phone: 212-317-1470
Fax: 212-317-1473
Web: www.pgfusa.org

Print and Graphics Scholarship Foundation

PGSF Annual Scholarship Competition

Type of award: Scholarship, renewable.
Intended use: For full-time undergraduate study at 2-year or 4-year institution.
Eligibility: Applicant must be U.S. citizen.
Basis for selection: Major/career interest in graphic arts/design; printing or publishing. Applicant must demonstrate high academic achievement.
Application requirements: Recommendations, transcript. Biographical information including extracurricular activities and academic honors. Photocopy of intended course of study. High school students must submit SAT scores.
Additional information: To renew, recipients must maintain 3.0 GPA and continue as graphic arts/printing technology major. Application deadline March 1 for high school seniors and high school graduates not currently attending college and April 1 for current undergraduates. Recipients granted membership in the Graphic Arts Technical Foundation. Application requirements and criteria may vary by trust fund member institution. Contact sponsor for application or download from Website.
    Amount of award: $500-$5,000
    Number of awards: 240
    Number of applicants: 1,600
    Application deadline: March 1, April 1
    Notification begins: June 30
Contact:
Print and Graphics Scholarship Foundation
200 Deer Run Road
Sewickley, PA 15143-2600
Phone: 412-259-1740
Fax: 412-741-2311
Web: www.pgsf.org

Professional Association of Georgia Educators Foundation, Inc.

PAGE Foundation Scholarships

Type of award: Scholarship.
Intended use: For junior, senior or post-bachelor's certificate study at accredited postsecondary institution in United States.
Eligibility: Applicant must be U.S. citizen or permanent resident residing in Georgia.
Basis for selection: Major/career interest in education. Applicant must demonstrate high academic achievement and service orientation.
Application requirements: Recommendations, essay, transcript.
Additional information: Minimum 3.0 GPA. Must be PAGE or SPAGE member. Intended for future teachers and certified teachers seeking advanced degrees. Must agree to teach in Georgia for three years. Applications available from September to April. Visit Website for additional information, deadlines, and application procedures.
    Amount of award: $1,000
    Number of awards: 15
    Number of applicants: 125
    Application deadline: April 30
    Notification begins: July 1
    Total amount awarded: $15,000
Contact:
PAGE Foundation
P.O. Box 942270
Atlanta, GA 31141-2270
Phone: 800-334-6861
Fax: 770-216-9672
Web: www.pagefoundation.org

Quill and Scroll Foundation

Edward J. Nell Memorial Scholarship

Type of award: Scholarship.
Intended use: For full-time freshman study at accredited 2-year or 4-year institution in United States.
Eligibility: Applicant must be high school senior. Applicant must be U.S. citizen.
Basis for selection: Major/career interest in journalism. Applicant must demonstrate seriousness of purpose.
Application requirements: Recommendations, essay, transcript. Statement of intent to major in journalism. Five selections of student's published work.
Additional information: Open only to winners of Quill and Scroll Annual National Yearbook Excellence or International Writing/Photo Contests at any time during high school career.
    Amount of award: $500-$1,500
    Number of awards: 10
    Number of applicants: 43
    Application deadline: May 10
    Notification begins: May 20
Contact:
Quill and Scroll Foundation
School of Journalism and Mass Communication
University of Iowa
Iowa City, IA 52242-1401
Phone: 319-335-3457
Web: www.uiowa.edu/~quill-sc

Radio and Television News Directors Foundation

Carole Simpson Scholarship

Type of award: Scholarship.
Intended use: For full-time sophomore, junior or senior study at 4-year institution.
Basis for selection: Major/career interest in journalism; radio/television/film or communications. Applicant must demonstrate depth of character and seriousness of purpose.
Application requirements: Recommendations, essay, proof of eligibility. Audio or video tape of one to three work samples, maximum 15 minutes, with accompanying scripts. Statement explaining reasons for seeking career in broadcast or cable journalism, and specific career preferences in radio or television of reporting, producing, or news management. Dean or faculty sponsor letter of reference certifying eligibility.
Additional information: Must have at least one full year of school remaining. Previous Radio and Television News Directors Foundation scholarship or internship winners not eligible. Preference given to minority students.
    Amount of award: $2,000
    Number of awards: 1
    Number of applicants: 20
    Application deadline: May 12
    Notification begins: July 15
    Total amount awarded: $2,000
Contact:
Radio and Television News Directors Foundation
1600 K Street NW
Suite 700
Washington, DC 20036
Phone: 202-467-5218
Fax: 202-223-4007
Web: www.rtndf.org

Ed Bradley Scholarship

Type of award: Scholarship.
Intended use: For full-time sophomore, junior, senior or graduate study at 4-year institution.
Basis for selection: Major/career interest in journalism; radio/television/film or communications. Applicant must demonstrate seriousness of purpose.
Application requirements: Recommendations, proof of eligibility. Audio or video tape of one to three work samples, maximum length 15 minutes total, with accompanying scripts. Essay explaining reasons for seeking career in broadcast or cable journalism, and specific career preferences in radio or television of reporting, producing, or news management. Dean or faculty sponsor endorsement letter certifying eligibility.
Additional information: Must have at least one full year of school remaining. Previous Radio and Television News Directors Foundation scholarship or internship winners not eligible. Preference given to minority undergraduates.
    Amount of award: $10,000
    Number of awards: 1
    Number of applicants: 47
    Application deadline: May 12
    Notification begins: July 15
    Total amount awarded: $10,000
Contact:
Radio and Television News Directors Foundation
1600 K Street NW
Suite 700
Washington, DC 20006
Phone: 202-467-5218
Fax: 202-223-4007
Web: www.rtndf.org

The George Foreman Tribute to Lyndon B. Johnson Scholarship

Type of award: Scholarship.
Intended use: For full-time sophomore, junior or senior study at 4-year institution in United States. Designated institutions: University of Texas at Austin.
Eligibility: Applicant must be U.S. citizen or permanent resident residing in Texas.
Basis for selection: Major/career interest in journalism.
Additional information: This award was developed by George Foreman, television commentator and former heavyweight champion, for a broadcast journalism student at the University of Texas-Austin. For more information and application requirements, visit Website.
    Amount of award: $6,000
    Number of awards: 1
    Number of applicants: 9
    Application deadline: May 12
    Notification begins: July 15
    Total amount awarded: $6,000

Contact:
Radio and Television News Directors Foundation
1600 K St., NW Suite 700
Washington, DC 20006
Phone: 202-467-5218
Fax: 202-223-4007
Web: www.rtnda.org

Ken Kashiwahara Scholarship

Type of award: Scholarship.
Intended use: For full-time sophomore, junior or senior study at postsecondary institution in United States.
Eligibility: Applicant must be Alaskan native, Asian American, African American, Mexican American, Hispanic American, Puerto Rican, American Indian or Native Hawaiian/Pacific Islander. Applicant must be U.S. citizen or permanent resident.
Basis for selection: Major/career interest in journalism.
Application requirements: Recommendations, essay. Resume, taped examples of work.
Additional information: Applicant must be in good standing and majoring in broadcast or electronic journalism.

Amount of award:	$2,500
Number of awards:	1
Number of applicants:	27
Application deadline:	May 12
Notification begins:	July 15
Total amount awarded:	$2,500

Contact:
Radio and Television News Directors Foundation
1600 K Street NW
Suite 700
Washington, DC 20006
Phone: 202-467-5218
Fax: 202-223-4007
Web: www.rtnda.org

Lou and Carole Prato Sports Reporting Scholarship

Type of award: Scholarship.
Intended use: For full-time sophomore, junior or senior study.
Basis for selection: Major/career interest in radio/television/film; journalism or sports/sports administration.
Application requirements: Portfolio, recommendations, essay, proof of eligibility. Resume. One to three samples (audio or video cassettes) showing journalistic skills, accompanied by script.
Additional information: Award is for student planning career as sports reporter in television or radio. Applicant must have one or more years of school remaining and can be enrolled in any major as long as career intent is radio or television news. Visit Website for more information.

Amount of award:	$1,000
Number of awards:	1
Number of applicants:	15
Application deadline:	May 12
Notification begins:	July 15
Total amount awarded:	$1,000

Contact:
RTNDF Scholarships
1600 K Street NW
Suite 700
Washington, DC 20006
Phone: 202-467-5218
Fax: 202-223-4007
Web: www.rtndf.org

Mike Reynolds Scholarship

Type of award: Scholarship.
Intended use: For full-time sophomore, junior or senior study in United States.
Basis for selection: Major/career interest in communications; film/video or journalism. Applicant must demonstrate financial need.
Application requirements: Portfolio, recommendations, essay, proof of eligibility. Resume. One to three samples (audio or video cassettes) showing journalistic skills, accompanied by script.
Additional information: Applicant should indicate media-related jobs held and contribution made to funding of education. Applicant must have one or more years of school remaining. Visit Website for more information.

Number of awards:	1
Number of applicants:	13
Application deadline:	May 12
Notification begins:	July 15
Total amount awarded:	$1,000

Contact:
RTNDF Scholarships
1600 K Street NW
Suite 700
Washington, DC 20006
Phone: 202-467-5218
Fax: 202-223-4007
Web: www.rtndf.org

Pete Wilson Journalism Scholarship

Type of award: Scholarship.
Intended use: For full-time undergraduate or graduate study at 4-year or graduate institution. Designated institutions: San Francisco Bay area accredited Insitutions.
Eligibility: Applicant must be residing in California.
Basis for selection: Major/career interest in journalism.
Application requirements: Recommendations, essay.
Additional information: Applicant must be student in San Francisco Bay area.

Amount of award:	$4,000
Application deadline:	May 12
Notification begins:	July 15

Contact:
Radio and Television News Directors Foundation
1600 K Street NW
Suite 700
Washington, DC 20006
Phone: 202-467-5218
Fax: 202-223-4007
Web: www.rtndf.org

Presidents' $2,500 Scholarships

Type of award: Scholarship.
Intended use: For full-time sophomore, junior or senior study at 2-year or 4-year institution.
Basis for selection: Major/career interest in journalism; communications or radio/television/film. Applicant must demonstrate high academic achievement and seriousness of purpose.
Application requirements: Recommendations, essay. One to three samples showing reporting or producing skills on audio or video tape, accompanied by scripts. Letter of endorsement from dean or faculty adviser certifying proof of eligibility.
Additional information: Previous winners not eligible. Must have at least one full year of school remaining. Applicant may

Radio and Television News Directors Foundation: Presidents' $2,500 Scholarships

be enrolled in any major so long as career intent is television or radio news.

Amount of award:	$2,500
Number of awards:	2
Number of applicants:	79
Application deadline:	May 12
Notification begins:	July 15
Total amount awarded:	$2,500

Contact:
Radio and Television News Directors Foundation
RTNDF Scholarships
1600 K Street NW, Suite 700
Washington, DC 2006
Phone: 202-467-5218
Fax: 202-223-4007
Web: www.rtndf.org

Recording for the Blind and Dyslexic

Marion Huber Learning Through Listening Award

Type of award: Scholarship.
Intended use: For undergraduate study at vocational, 2-year or 4-year institution.
Eligibility: Applicant or parent must be member/participant of Recording for the Blind & Dyslexic. Applicant must be learning disabled. Applicant must be high school senior.
Basis for selection: Applicant must demonstrate high academic achievement, leadership and service orientation.
Application requirements: Essay, transcript. Two teacher/school administrator referrals.
Additional information: Applicant must be registered member of Recording for the Blind and Dyslexic for at least one year prior to application deadline. Must have 3.0 GPA or better in grades 10-12.

Amount of award:	$2,000-$6,000
Number of awards:	6
Application deadline:	March 1
Total amount awarded:	$24,000

Contact:
Recording for the Blind and Dyslexic
Strategic Communications Department
20 Roszel Road
Princeton, NJ 08540
Phone: 609-520-8044
Fax: 609-452-2585
Web: www.rfbd.org

Mary P. Oenslager Scholastic Achievement Award

Type of award: Scholarship.
Intended use: For undergraduate study.
Eligibility: Applicant or parent must be member/participant of Recording for the Blind & Dyslexic. Applicant must be visually impaired.
Basis for selection: Applicant must demonstrate high academic achievement, leadership and service orientation.
Application requirements: Essay, transcript. Two professor/college administrator report forms must be completed.
Additional information: Applicant must be legally blind or visually impaired and must receive a bachelor's degree from an accredited four-year college or university in the U.S. or its territories during the current year. Must have minimum 3.0 GPA on 4.0 scale or equivalent. Must be registered member of Recording for the Blind and Dyslexic for at least one year prior to application deadline. Continuing education beyond bachelor's degree not required.

Amount of award:	$1,000-$6,000
Number of awards:	9
Application deadline:	March 2
Total amount awarded:	$30,000

Contact:
Recording for the Blind and Dyslexic
Strategic Communications Department
20 Roszel Road
Princeton, NJ 08540
Phone: 609-520-8044
Fax: 609-452-2585
Web: www.rfbd.org

Red River Valley Fighter Pilots Association

Red River Valley Fighter Pilots Association (RRVA) Scholarship Program

Type of award: Scholarship, renewable.
Intended use: For undergraduate or graduate study at accredited 2-year, 4-year or graduate institution in United States.
Eligibility: Applicant must be U.S. citizen. Applicant must be dependent of deceased veteran or POW/MIA; or spouse of deceased veteran or POW/MIA. Must be spouse or child of member of any branch of the U.S. Armed Forces listed as KIA or MIA since August 1964, including those lost in the World Trade Center and Pentagon events of 9/11/01. Immediate dependents of military aircrew members killed in combat or non-combat military missions and dependents or spouses of current or deceased RRVA members in good standing also eligible.
Basis for selection: Applicant must demonstrate financial need.
Application requirements: Transcript, proof of eligibility.
Additional information: Award funds sent directly to school to be used for tuition, books, and other academic expenditures, including room and board for full-time students. See Website for application and more information.

Amount of award:	$500-$3,500
Number of awards:	32
Number of applicants:	42
Application deadline:	May 15
Total amount awarded:	$67,000

Contact:
Red River Valley Fighter Pilots Association
P.O. Box 1553
Front Royal, VA 22630
Phone: 540-636-9798
Fax: 540-636-9776
Web: www.river-rats.org

Reserve Officers Association

Henry J. Reilly Memorial College Scholarship

Type of award: Scholarship, renewable.
Intended use: For full-time undergraduate study at accredited 4-year institution in United States.
Eligibility: Applicant or parent must be member/participant of Reserve Officers Association or ROAL. Applicant must be U.S. citizen.
Basis for selection: Applicant must demonstrate high academic achievement, depth of character, leadership and seriousness of purpose.
Application requirements: Essay, transcript, proof of eligibility.
Additional information: Applicant, parent, or grandparent must be member of either Reserve Officers Association or ROAL. Must meet minimum SAT/ACT score requirements. Minimum 3.0 GPA. Must have registered for the draft if eligible. Visit Website for more information.

Amount of award:	$500
Number of awards:	60
Number of applicants:	85
Application deadline:	April 10
Notification begins:	June 15

Contact:
Reserve Officers Association
Ms. Betsy Allen
One Constitution Avenue, NE
Washington, DC 20002-5655
Phone: 800-809-9448
Fax: 202-646-7762
Web: www.roa.org

Rhode Island Higher Education Assistance Authority

College Bound Fund Academic Promise Scholarship

Type of award: Scholarship, renewable.
Intended use: For full-time undergraduate study at vocational, 2-year or 4-year institution. Designated institutions: Institutions participating in at least one Title IV financial aid program.
Eligibility: Applicant must be U.S. citizen or permanent resident residing in Rhode Island.
Basis for selection: Applicant must demonstrate financial need and high academic achievement.
Application requirements: FAFSA. SAT or ACT.
Additional information: Initial eligibility based on SAT/ACT scores and expected family contribution; renewal subject to maintenance of specified GPA. Dependent applicant's parent must reside in Rhode Island.

Amount of award:	$2,500
Number of awards:	100
Number of applicants:	1,450
Application deadline:	March 1
Total amount awarded:	$1,000,000

Contact:
Rhode Island Higher Education Assistance Authority
560 Jefferson Blvd.
Warwick, RI 02886
Phone: 401-736-1171
Fax: 401-732-3541
Web: www.riheaa.org

Rhode Island State Grant

Type of award: Scholarship, renewable.
Intended use: For undergraduate study at vocational, 2-year or 4-year institution in or outside United States or Canada. Designated institutions: U.S., Canadian, or Mexican institutions that participate in at least one federal financial aid program.
Eligibility: Applicant must be U.S. citizen or permanent resident residing in Rhode Island.
Basis for selection: Applicant must demonstrate financial need.
Application requirements: FAFSA.
Additional information: Must meet all Title IV eligibility requirements. Dependent applicant's parent must reside in Rhode Island.

Amount of award:	$300-$1,400
Number of awards:	13,000
Number of applicants:	45,734
Application deadline:	March 1
Total amount awarded:	$14,000,000

Contact:
Rhode Island Higher Education Assistance Authority
560 Jefferson Boulevard
Warwick, RI 02886
Phone: 401-736-1171
Fax: 401-736-1178
Web: www.riheaa.org

Rocky Mountain Coal Mining Institute

Rocky Mountain Coal Mining Scholarship

Type of award: Scholarship, renewable.
Intended use: For full-time junior or senior study in United States. Designated institutions: Mining schools approved by Rocky Mountain Coal Mining Institute.
Eligibility: Applicant must be U.S. citizen residing in Wyoming, Utah, Texas, Montana, New Mexico, Colorado, Arizona or North Dakota.
Basis for selection: Major/career interest in engineering; engineering, mining or geology/earth sciences. Applicant must demonstrate high academic achievement.
Application requirements: Interview, recommendations.
Additional information: Must have career interest in western coal mining. Recommended GPA of 3.0 or above. One new award per Rocky Mountain Coal Mining Institute member state per year. Can be renewed as senior or post-graduate. Money paid directly to school as tuition reimbursement. Applications available after September 1.

Rocky Mountain Coal Mining Institute: Rocky Mountain Coal Mining Scholarship

Amount of award:	$2,000
Number of awards:	16
Number of applicants:	30
Application deadline:	February 1
Notification begins:	March 1
Total amount awarded:	$32,000

Contact:
Rocky Mountain Coal Mining Institute
8057 S. Yukon Way
Littletown, CO 80128-5510
Phone: 303-948-3300
Fax: 303-948-1132
Web: www.rmcmi.org

Roger Von Amelunxen Foundation

Roger Von Amelunxen Scholarship

Type of award: Scholarship, renewable.
Intended use: For full-time undergraduate study.
Eligibility: Applicant must be no older than 21.
Basis for selection: Applicant must demonstrate high academic achievement, depth of character, leadership, seriousness of purpose and service orientation.
Application requirements: Recommendations, transcript. Copy of high school diploma, class rank, college acceptance letter, SAT scores, personal statement.
Additional information: Number and amount of awards vary. Scholarship available only to minor children of Immigration and Customs Enforcement or Customs and Border Protection employees. Current college students must have 3.0 GPA.

Amount of award:	$1,000-$4,000
Number of awards:	88,000
Application deadline:	July 1
Notification begins:	August 31

Contact:
Roger Von Amelunxen Foundation
104-15 100 St.
Ozone Park, NY 11417
Phone: 718-641-4800
Web: www.rogerfoundation.org

Ronald McDonald House Charities

RMHC National Scholarship Programs

Type of award: Scholarship.
Intended use: For full-time undergraduate study at accredited vocational, 2-year or 4-year institution.
Eligibility: Applicant must be high school senior. Applicant must be U.S. citizen or permanent resident.
Basis for selection: Applicant must demonstrate leadership and service orientation.
Application requirements: Recommendations, essay, transcript, proof of eligibility. IRS Form 1040.
Additional information: Intended for those who live in geographic boundaries of a chapter that offers scholarships. Geographic areas listed on Website. Some requirements include--RMHC/ASIA: Applicant must have at least one parent of Asian heritage. RMHC/Future Achievers: Applicant must have at least one parent of African American or Black/Caribbean heritage. RMHC/HACER: Applicant must have at least one parent of Hispanic heritage. RMHC/Scholars: No race restrictions. See Website for contact information, deadlines and application.

Application deadline:	February 15
Total amount awarded:	$100,000

Contact:
Ronald McDonald House Charities Scholarship Program Administrators
One Kroc Drive
Oak Brook, IL 60523
Phone: 630-623-7048
Fax: 630-623-7488
Web: www.rmhc.org

The Rotary Foundation

Academic-Year Ambassadorial Scholarship

Type of award: Scholarship.
Intended use: For junior, senior or graduate study in proposed host country where there are active Rotary Clubs.
Eligibility: Applicant must be citizen of country that has Rotary Clubs.
Basis for selection: Competition/talent/interest in study abroad. Applicant must demonstrate high academic achievement, leadership, seriousness of purpose and service orientation.
Application requirements: Interview, recommendations, essay, transcript, proof of eligibility. Proof of language ability.
Additional information: Deadlines set by the local Rotary Clubs and fall between March and August of year prior to when studies begin. Applicant must have interest in international understanding and peace. Scholarship provides funding for one academic year of study in another country. Covers tuition, room and board, round-trip transportation and one month of language training (if necessary). Need not be current student but must have completed two years of postsecondary work or have equivalent professional experience and be proficient in the language of the proposed host country. Number of awards varies from year to year. Spouses or descendants of Rotarians ineligible. Visit Website or check with local Rotary Club for more information and scholarship availability.

Amount of award:	$11,500

Contact:
The Rotary Foundation
One Rotary Center
1560 Sherman Avenue
Evanston, IL 60201-3698
Phone: 847-866-4459
Web: www.rotary.org

Cultural Ambassadorial Scholarship

Type of award: Scholarship.
Intended use: For junior, senior or non-degree study in a Rotary-designated language institution outside the U.S.
Eligibility: Applicant must be citizen of country that has Rotary Clubs.

Basis for selection: Competition/talent/interest in study abroad. Major/career interest in foreign languages. Applicant must demonstrate leadership, seriousness of purpose and service orientation.
Application requirements: Interview, recommendations, essay, transcript, proof of eligibility.
Additional information: Deadlines set by local Rotary Clubs and fall between March and August of year prior to when studies begin. Scholarship for three or six months of intensive language study in foreign country at a Rotary-designated language institution. Applicant need not be current student but must have completed at least one year of university-level course work in proposed language. Spouses or descendants of Rotarians ineligible. Funding covers tuition, round-trip transportation and homestay expenses (not to exceed $12,000 for three-month study; $19,000 for six-month study). Applications will be considered for those interested in studying English, French, German, Hebrew, Japanese, Italian, Mandarin Chinese, Polish, Russian, Portuguese, Spanish, Swahili and Swedish. Other languages considered if scholar submits a valid proposal of study institution and country. Number of awards varies. Check with local Rotary Club for more information and scholarship availability.
Contact:
The Rotary Foundation
One Rotary Center
1560 Sherman Avenue
Evanston, IL 60201-3698
Phone: 847-866-4459
Web: www.rotary.org

Multi-Year Ambassadorial Scholarship

Type of award: Scholarship.
Intended use: For junior, senior, master's or doctoral study at postsecondary institution in proposed host country where there are active Rotary Clubs.
Eligibility: Applicant must be citizen of country that has Rotary Clubs.
Basis for selection: Competition/talent/interest in study abroad. Applicant must demonstrate leadership, seriousness of purpose and service orientation.
Application requirements: Interview, recommendations, essay, transcript, proof of eligibility. Proof of language ability.
Additional information: Deadlines set by local Rotary Clubs and fall between March and August of year prior to when studies begin. Provides flat grant of $11,500 each year for two years of degree-oriented study abroad. Applicant need not be current student, but must have completed two years of university-level education or have equivalent professional experience and be proficient in the language of proposed host country. Spouses or descendants of Rotarians ineligible. Check with local Rotary Club for more information and scholarship availability.
   Amount of award: $11,500
Contact:
The Rotary Foundation
One Rotary Center
1560 Sherman Avenue
Evanston, IL 60201-3698
Phone: 847-866-4459
Web: www.rotary.org

ROTC/Air Force

ROTC/Air Force Four-Year Scholarship (Types 1, 2, and 7)

Type of award: Scholarship.
Intended use: For freshman study at accredited 4-year institution in United States.
Eligibility: Applicant must be at least 17, no older than 25. Applicant must be U.S. citizen. Recipients agree to serve four years' active duty.
Basis for selection: Applicant must demonstrate high academic achievement.
Application requirements: Interview, recommendations, transcript.
Additional information: Minimum 3.0 GPA. At least 24 ACT or 1100 SAT. Opportunities available in any major. Applicants must not be enrolled in college full-time prior to application. Type 1 provides full tuition, fees, textbook allowance without restriction, and $250-400 monthly stipend during academic year. Type 2 provides tuition, fees up to $15,000 per year, and $250-450 monthly stipend. Type 7 provides tuition and fees at institutions with tuition of $9,000 or less, and $250-400 monthly stipend. Scholarship board decides which type is offered. For all scholarships, amount of stipend is based on student's academic year.
   Amount of award: Full tuition
   Application deadline: December 1
Contact:
Contact local ROTC recruiter.
Phone: 866-4AF-ROTC
Fax: 334-953-6167
Web: www.afrotc.com

ROTC/Air Force Three-Year Scholarship (Types 2 and Targeted)

Type of award: Scholarship.
Intended use: For sophomore study at accredited 4-year institution in United States.
Eligibility: Applicant must be at least 17, no older than 30. Applicant must be U.S. citizen. Recipients agree to serve four years' active duty.
Basis for selection: Applicant must demonstrate high academic achievement.
Application requirements: Interview, recommendations, transcript.
Additional information: Minimum 2.5 GPA. Minimum 24 ACT or 1100 SAT. Opportunities available in any major. Type 2 provides tuition, fees up to $15,000 per year, and $250-400 monthly stipend during academic year. Targeted scholarships provide full tuition and fees at "low cost" schools (mostly state institutions), and $250-450 monthly stipend. ROTC scholarship board decides which type is offered.
   Amount of award: Full tuition
Contact:
HQ/Air Force ROTC/RROO
551 East Maxwell Boulevard
Maxwell AFB, AL 36112
Phone: 866-4AF-ROTC
Fax: 334-953-6167
Web: www.afrotc.com

ROTC/United States Army

ROTC/United States Army Four-Year Historically Black College/University Scholarship

Type of award: Scholarship.
Intended use: For freshman study at accredited 4-year institution in United States. Designated institutions: Alabama A&M, Tuskegee, University of Arkansas-Pine Bluff, Howard, Florida A&M, Fort Valley St., Grambling St., Southern University, A&M College, Bowie St., Morgan St., Alcorn St., Jackson St., Lincoln University, Elizabeth City St., North Carolina A&T St., St. Augustine's, Central St. (OH), South Carolina St., Prairie View A&M University, Hampton University, Norfolk St., West Virginia St.
Eligibility: Applicant must be at least 17, no older than 26, high school senior. Applicant must be U.S. citizen.
Basis for selection: Applicant must demonstrate high academic achievement and depth of character.
Application requirements: Interview, transcript. Class rank. SAT/ACT score. Applicant must complete item 11 on first page of application and will also be considered for national Four-Year Scholarship program.
Additional information: Minimum 920 SAT (Math and Reading) or 19 ACT. Minimum college GPA of 2.5 on 4.0 scale. Scholarships offered at different levels, providing college tuition and educational fees. Same requirements as Army ROTC Four-Year Scholarship. Limited number of scholarships for attendance at historically Black college or university (HBCU). Tax-free sustenance allowance (increasing each year) for up to ten months each year of scholarship, plus allowance for books and other educational items. Scholarships do not pay flight fees. First school choice must be one of the schools identified in the list of HBCUs, if not, application will not be considered for dedicated HBCU scholarships. Contact local ROTC recruiter for more information.
   Amount of award: Full tuition
   Application deadline: January 1
Contact:
Army ROTC Scholarship
Fort Monroe
VA 23651-5238
Phone: 800-USA-ROTC
Web: www.goarmy.com/rotc or www.rotc.monroe.army.mil

United States Army Four-Year Nursing Scholarship

Type of award: Scholarship.
Intended use: For freshman study at accredited 4-year institution in United States.
Eligibility: Applicant must be at least 17, no older than 26. Applicant must be U.S. citizen.
Basis for selection: Major/career interest in military science or nursing. Applicant must demonstrate high academic achievement and depth of character.
Application requirements: Interview, transcript. Individuals applying for nurse program scholarships must indicate "JXX" as choice of major in item four of page eight of the four-year scholarship application; item three should include approved institution applicant wishes to attend.
Additional information: Minimum 920 SAT (Math and Reading) or 19 ACT. Minimum college GPA of 2.5 on 4.0 scale. Scholarships offered at different levels, providing college tuition and educational fees. All applicants considered for each level. Tax-free subsistence allowance (increasing each year) for up to ten months each year of scholarship, plus allowance for books and other educational items. Scholarships do not pay flight fees. Limited numbers of three- and two-year scholarships available once a student is on campus. Applicants should check with school's professor of military science or contact local Army ROTC recruiter.
   Amount of award: Full tuition
   Application deadline: January 1
Contact:
Army ROTC Scholarship
Fort Monroe
VA 23651-5238
Phone: 800-USA-ROTC
Web: www.goarmy.com/rotc or www.rotc.monroe.army.mil

United States Army Four-Year Scholarship

Type of award: Scholarship, renewable.
Intended use: For freshman study at accredited 4-year institution in United States.
Eligibility: Applicant must be at least 17, no older than 26. Applicant must be U.S. citizen. Must enlist in Army on active duty, or in Army Reserve or Army National Guard for minimum eight years.
Basis for selection: Major/career interest in military science. Applicant must demonstrate high academic achievement and depth of character.
Application requirements: Interview, recommendations, transcript. SAT/ACT scores. Proof of high school class rank.
Additional information: Recipient receives tax-free subsistence allowance (increasing each year) for up to ten months for each year of scholarship, plus allowance for books and other educational items. Minimum 920 SAT (Math and Reading) or 19 ACT. Must have minimum 2.5 GPA on 4.0 scale. Limited numbers of three- and two-year scholarships available once student is on campus; students should check with professor of military science once they are attending classes. Contact local Army ROTC recruiter.
   Amount of award: Full tuition
   Application deadline: December 1
Contact:
Army ROTC Scholarship
Fort Monroe
VA 23651-5238
Phone: 800-USA-ROTC
Web: www.goarmy.com/rotc or www.rotc.monroe.army.mil

Royce Builders

RoyceBuilders.com Foundation for Youth Scholarship

Type of award: Scholarship, renewable.
Intended use: For undergraduate study at postsecondary institution.
Eligibility: Applicant must be residing in Texas.
Basis for selection: Applicant must demonstrate financial need, high academic achievement and service orientation.
Application requirements: Recommendations, transcript. One-page essay: How can one person make a difference?

Additional information: For students graduating from school districts within the Houston Gulf Coast area. Graduating high school seniors also eligible. Deadline and number of awards varies. Visit Website for details.

Amount of award:	$2,500
Number of awards:	50
Application deadline:	April 11

Contact:
Royce Builders
Foundation for Youth
7850 North Sam Houston Parkway West
Houston, TX 77064
Phone: 281-569-1185
Web: www.rbffy.com

Sachs Foundation

Sachs Foundation Undergraduate Grant

Type of award: Scholarship, renewable.
Intended use: For full-time undergraduate study at accredited 2-year or 4-year institution.
Eligibility: Applicant must be African American. Applicant must be high school senior. Applicant must be U.S. citizen or permanent resident residing in Colorado.
Basis for selection: Applicant must demonstrate financial need, depth of character and leadership.
Application requirements: Interview, recommendations, transcript, proof of eligibility. Financial statement and parents' tax returns. Small recent photo.
Additional information: Must be resident of Colorado for more than five years. Must maintain at least 2.5 GPA throughout college for renewal consideration.

Amount of award:	$4,000
Number of awards:	45
Number of applicants:	200
Application deadline:	March 1
Notification begins:	March 1
Total amount awarded:	$1,000,000

Contact:
Sachs Foundation
90 South Cascade Avenue
Suite 1410
Colorado Springs, CO 80903
Phone: 719-633-2353
Web: www.sachsfoundation.org

Sallie Mae Fund

911 Education Fund Scholarship Program

Type of award: Scholarship, renewable.
Intended use: For full-time undergraduate study at 2-year or 4-year institution.
Eligibility: Applicant's parent must have been killed or disabled in work-related accident as firefighter, police officer or public safety officer.
Basis for selection: Applicant must demonstrate financial need.
Application requirements: Proof of eligibility. Insurance determination letter or referral letter from family member verifying death of parent. Application must be submitted to and verified by Financial Aid Administrator.
Additional information: Applicant must be child of police, fire safety or medical personnel victim of September 11, 2001 attacks. Visit Website for application.

Amount of award:	$2,500
Application deadline:	May 15, July 1
Notification begins:	September 1

Contact:
The Sallie Mae 911 Education Fund Scholarship Program
CFNCR
1201 15th Street, NW, Suite 420
Washington, DC 20005
Web: www.wiredscholar.com

Unmet Need Scholarship Program

Type of award: Scholarship.
Intended use: For full-time undergraduate study at accredited postsecondary institution in or outside United States. Designated institutions: Title IV eligible institutions in United States and Puerto Rico.
Eligibility: Applicant must be U.S. citizen or permanent resident.
Basis for selection: Applicant must demonstrate financial need.
Application requirements: Transcript. SAR, FAFSA, financial aid award letter from institution.
Additional information: Family's adjusted gross income must be $30,000 or less. Minimum 2.5 GPA or GED score of 42. Visit Website for more information and application.

Amount of award:	$1,000-$3,800
Application deadline:	May 31

Contact:
The Sallie Mae Fund Unmet Need Scholarship Fund
Scholarship America
One Scholarship Way, P.O. Box 297
Saint Peter, MN 56082
Phone: 507-931-1682
Web: www.salliemaefund.org

Salute to Education, Inc.

Salute to Education Scholarship

Type of award: Scholarship.
Intended use: For undergraduate study at postsecondary institution.
Eligibility: Applicant must be high school senior. Applicant must be U.S. citizen residing in Florida.
Basis for selection: Applicant must demonstrate high academic achievement, depth of character, leadership, seriousness of purpose and service orientation.
Application requirements: Responses to four essay questions. Application must be accessed online at www.stescholarships.org.
Additional information: Applicants must demonstrate weighted academic average of 3.0 or above and participation in at least one school organization/activity or one area of community service. Financial need also taken into consideration. Application available in September. Deadline in January. Number of awards varies from 200 to 250 per year.

Applicant must be a resident of Miami-Dade or Broward County.

Amount of award:	$1,000
Number of awards:	220
Number of applicants:	1,200
Application deadline:	January 28
Total amount awarded:	$220,000

Contact:
Salute to Education, Inc.
2600 Douglas Rd., Suite 610
Coral Gables, FL 33134
Phone: 305-476-7709
Fax: 305-476-7710
Web: www.stescholarships.org

Scarlett Family Foundation

Scarlett Family Foundation Scholarship

Type of award: Scholarship.
Intended use: For undergraduate study.
Basis for selection: Major/career interest in business. Applicant must demonstrate financial need.

Amount of award:	$2,500
Application deadline:	April 30

Contact:
Scarlett Family Foundation
Phone: 615-320-3149
Web: www.scholarshipadministrators.net

Scholarship Chicago

College Bound Scholarship

Type of award: Scholarship, renewable.
Intended use: For freshman study.
Eligibility: Applicant must be high school junior. Applicant must be residing in Illinois.
Basis for selection: Applicant must demonstrate financial need.
Additional information: Applicant must live or go to high school within Chicago city limits. Award provides five years' support, including a year of college prep, up to $10,000 in "gap" scholarships, and internship opportunities. Visit Website for more details.

Amount of award:	$1,500-$2,500
Number of awards:	200
Number of applicants:	350
Application deadline:	March 15
Total amount awarded:	$250,000

Contact:
Scholarship Chicago
333 W. Wacker, 33rd Floor
Chicago, IL 60606
Web: www.scholarshipchicago.com

Screen Actors Guild Foundation

John L. Dales Standard Scholarship

Type of award: Scholarship, renewable.
Intended use: For full-time undergraduate or graduate study at accredited 2-year, 4-year or graduate institution in United States.
Eligibility: Applicant or parent must be member/participant of Screen Actor's Guild.
Basis for selection: Applicant must demonstrate financial need.
Application requirements: Recommendations, essay, transcript, proof of eligibility. Most recent federal income tax return and additional financial information. SAT/ACT scores.
Additional information: Must be member of Guild for five years with lifetime earnings of $30,000 or child of ten-year Guild member with lifetime earnings of $100,000. Guild employees, scholarship committee members, and Foundation directors and their relatives not eligible. Consult office or visit Website for more information. Number and amount of awards vary.

Number of awards:	88
Number of applicants:	136
Application deadline:	March 14
Notification begins:	July 7
Total amount awarded:	$340,000

Contact:
Screen Actors Guild Foundation
John L. Dales Scholarship Fund
5757 Wilshire Boulevard, Suite 124
Los Angeles, CA 90036
Phone: 323-549-6649
Fax: 323-549-6710
Web: www.sagfoundation.org

John L. Dales Transitional Scholarship

Type of award: Scholarship, renewable.
Intended use: For full-time undergraduate or graduate study at accredited postsecondary institution in United States.
Basis for selection: Applicant must demonstrate financial need.
Application requirements: Recommendations, essay, transcript, proof of eligibility. Most recent federal income tax return and additional financial information. SAT/ACT scores.
Additional information: Applicant must be Guild member for at least ten years and have lifetime earnings of $60,000. Guild employees, scholarship committee members, Foundation directors, Foundation staff, and their families not eligible. Amount and number of awards varies from year to year.

Number of awards:	12
Number of applicants:	16
Notification begins:	July 7
Total amount awarded:	$60,000

Contact:
Screen Actors Guild Foundation
John L. Dales Scholarship Fund
5757 Wilshire Boulevard, Suite 124
Los Angeles, CA 90036
Phone: 323-549-6649
Fax: 323-549-6710
Web: www.sagfoundation.org

Seabee Memorial Scholarship Association, Inc.

Seabee Memorial Scholarship

Type of award: Scholarship, renewable.
Intended use: For full-time undergraduate study in United States.
Eligibility: Applicant must be U.S. citizen. Applicant must be descendant of veteran who served in the Navy. Applicant must be child or grandchild of a current, honorably discharged, deceased or enlisted member of Naval Construction FROCE (Seabees) or Navy CEC (Civil Engineer Corps).
Basis for selection: Applicant must demonstrate financial need, high academic achievement, depth of character, leadership, patriotism, seriousness of purpose and service orientation.
Application requirements: Essay, transcript, proof of eligibility. IRS Form 1040. Official document (DD214, reenlistment certificate, transfer orders, etc.) that verifies rate/rank of sponsor.
Additional information: Award is renewable for up to four years. Download application from Website.

Amount of award:	$1,000-$5,000
Number of applicants:	350
Application deadline:	April 15
Notification begins:	June 15

Contact:
Scholarship Committee
P.O. Box 6574
Silver Spring, MD 20916
Phone: 301-570-2850
Fax: 301-570-2873
Web: www.seabee.org

Seattle Jaycees

Seattle Jaycees Scholarship

Type of award: Scholarship, renewable.
Intended use: For undergraduate or graduate study at accredited postsecondary institution.
Eligibility: Applicant must be residing in Washington.
Basis for selection: Applicant must demonstrate depth of character and service orientation.
Application requirements: $5 application fee. Transcript. Community-service resume.
Additional information: Scholarships granted for exemplary civic involvement, volunteerism, and community service. Visit Website for application and more information. Deadline first workday in April.

Amount of award:	$1,000
Number of awards:	20
Number of applicants:	480
Application deadline:	April 1

Contact:
Seattle Jaycees
Scholarship Committee
109 West Mercer Street
Seattle, WA 98119
Phone: 206-286-2014
Fax: 206-286-4459
Web: www.seattlejaycees.org

Second Marine Division Association Memorial Scholarship Fund

Second Marine Division Scholarship

Type of award: Scholarship, renewable.
Intended use: For full-time undergraduate study at accredited vocational, 2-year or 4-year institution.
Eligibility: Applicant must be descendant of veteran who served in the Marines. Must be child or grandchild of person who serves or served in Second Marine Division, U.S. Marine Corps, or unit attached to the division.
Basis for selection: Applicant must demonstrate financial need.
Application requirements: Recommendations, essay, transcript, proof of eligibility.
Additional information: Family's adjusted gross income should not exceed $57,000 for the taxable year prior to application. Exceptions may be made for larger families. Minimum 2.75 GPA. Must reapply for renewal. Include SASE when requesting application. Parent or grandparent who served in the Second Marine Division must join SMDA, if not already a member, once scholarship is awarded.

Amount of award:	$1,000
Application deadline:	April 1, July 1
Notification begins:	September 30
Total amount awarded:	$32,000

Contact:
Second Marine Division Association Memorial Scholarship Fund
P.O. Box 8180
Camp Lejeune, NC 28547

SEG Foundation

SEG Foundation Scholarship

Type of award: Scholarship, renewable.
Intended use: For undergraduate or graduate study in or outside United States.
Basis for selection: Major/career interest in physics; mathematics; geology/earth sciences or geophysics. Applicant must demonstrate high academic achievement and seriousness of purpose.
Application requirements: Recommendations, essay, transcript, proof of eligibility.
Additional information: Results of aptitude tests, college entrance exams, National Merit Scholarship competition, etc., not required but should be furnished if taken. Applicant must

pursue college course directed toward career in geophysics or a closely related field and must possess an interest in and aptitude for physics, mathematics and geology. Amount and number of awards vary. Visit Website for more information and to download application.

Amount of award:	$500
Number of awards:	172
Number of applicants:	600
Application deadline:	February 1
Notification begins:	September 1
Total amount awarded:	$448,350

Contact:
SEG Foundation
P.O. Box 702740
Tulsa, OK 74170-2740
Phone: 918-497-5586
Fax: 918-497-5560
Web: www.seg.org

Senator George J. Mitchell Scholarship Research Institute

Senator George J. Mitchell Scholarship

Type of award: Scholarship, renewable.
Intended use: For freshman study at accredited 2-year or 4-year institution in United States.
Eligibility: Applicant must be high school senior. Applicant must be U.S. citizen residing in Maine.
Basis for selection: Applicant must demonstrate financial need, seriousness of purpose and service orientation.
Application requirements: Essay, transcript, proof of eligibility. Letter from guidance counselor, SAR, copy of financial aid award from college student plans to attend.
Additional information: One award made to graduating senior from every public high school in Maine. Renewable for up to four years. Starting in 2006, four-year award total is $5,000 -- $1,250 per year for four years. Current Mitchell Scholars will continue to receive $1,000 per year. Scholarship to be applied to spring semester bill. Application due first Monday in April, supporting materials due May 1.

Amount of award:	$6,000
Number of awards:	130
Number of applicants:	1,000
Application deadline:	April 1
Notification begins:	June 1

Contact:
Senator George J. Mitchell Scholarship Research Institute
22 Monument Square
Suite 200
Portland, ME 04101
Phone: 207-773-7700
Fax: 207-773-1133
Web: www.mitchellinstitute.org

Seneca Nation and BIA

Seneca Nation Higher Education Program

Type of award: Scholarship, renewable.
Intended use: For undergraduate or graduate study at accredited 2-year, 4-year or graduate institution.
Eligibility: Applicant must be American Indian. Must be an enrolled member of Seneca Nation of Indians. Applicant must be U.S. citizen.
Basis for selection: Applicant must demonstrate financial need.
Application requirements: Essay, transcript, proof of eligibility. Proof of tribal enrollment, letter of reference from non-relative.
Additional information: Amount and number of awards vary. Residency requirements: Level 1- New York State residents living on reservation; Level 2- New York State residents living in New York; Level 3- enrolled members living outside New York. Applicants of any age can apply. Application deadlines: fall, July 1; spring, December 1; summer, May 1. Contact sponsor or see Website for more information.

Contact:
Seneca Nation of Indians
Higher Education Program
P.O. Box 231
Salamanca, NY 14779
Phone: 716-945-1790 ext. 3013
Fax: 716-945-7170
Web: www.sni.org

Sertoma International

Sertoma Scholarships for Hearing-Impaired Students

Type of award: Scholarship, renewable.
Intended use: For full-time undergraduate study at 4-year institution in United States.
Eligibility: Applicant must be hearing impaired. Applicant must be U.S. citizen or permanent resident.
Basis for selection: Applicant must demonstrate high academic achievement, depth of character and seriousness of purpose.
Application requirements: Recommendations, transcript, proof of eligibility. Statement of purpose, letter of acceptance from college or university, documentation of hearing impairment in form of recent audiogram or signed statement by hearing-health professional.
Additional information: Minimum 3.2 GPA. May reapply for up to four years. Winners notified in June. Visit Website for application and more information.

Amount of award:	$1,000
Number of awards:	40
Number of applicants:	250
Application deadline:	May 1
Total amount awarded:	$40,000

Contact:
Sertoma International
Scholarships for Hearing-Impaired Students
1912 East Meyer Boulevard
Kansas City, MO 64132-1174
Web: www.sertoma.org

Service Employees International Union, California State Council

Charles Hardy Memorial Scholarship

Type of award: Scholarship, renewable.
Intended use: For full-time freshman study at accredited 2-year or 4-year institution in United States.
Eligibility: Applicant or parent must be member/participant of Service Employees International Union. Applicant must be high school senior. Applicant must be residing in California.
Application requirements: Recommendations, essay, transcript.
Additional information: Visit Website for more information, including application and online test.
    Amount of award: $1,000
    Number of awards: 4
    Application deadline: March 15
    Total amount awarded: $4,000
Contact:
Service Employees International Union, California State Council
1007 7th Street
4th Floor
Sacramento, CA 95814-3407
Phone: 916-442-3838
Fax: 916-442-0976
Web: www.seiu.org

Shoshone Tribe

Shoshone Tribal Scholarship

Type of award: Scholarship, renewable.
Intended use: For undergraduate or graduate study at accredited vocational, 2-year or 4-year institution in United States.
Eligibility: Applicant must be American Indian. Must be enrolled member of Eastern Shoshone Tribe.
Basis for selection: Applicant must demonstrate financial need.
Application requirements: Transcript, proof of eligibility.
Additional information: Must first apply for Pell Grant and appropriate campus-based aid. Minimum 2.5 GPA required. Award renewable for maximum ten semesters. Application deadline for summer is April 15. Number of awards varies.
    Amount of award: $50-$5,000
    Number of awards: 60
    Number of applicants: 100
    Application deadline: June 1, November 15
    Total amount awarded: $300,000
Contact:
Eastern Shoshone Tribe
PL102-447 Program
104 Washakie Street, P.O. Box 1210
Fort Washakie, WY 82514
Phone: 307-332-8052
Fax: 307-332-9932

Sid Richardson Memorial Fund

Sid Richardson Scholarship

Type of award: Scholarship, renewable.
Intended use: For full-time undergraduate or graduate study at accredited postsecondary institution.
Basis for selection: Major/career interest in humanities/liberal arts. Applicant must demonstrate financial need and high academic achievement.
Application requirements: Essay, transcript, proof of eligibility. SAT or ACT scores.
Additional information: Must be child or grandchild of person presently employed (or retired) with a minimum of three years' full-time service at a Sid Bass/Richardson company or its subsidiaries. Also eligible are descendents of those who retired on or before 2/28/06 from Sid Richardson Energy Services or Richardson Energy Marketing, Ltd. Direct requests for applications to Peggy Laskoski, Sid Richardson Memorial Fund, and include name, social security number, place and approximate dates of employment of qualifying employee.
    Amount of award: $500-$6,000
    Number of awards: 62
    Number of applicants: 84
    Application deadline: March 31
    Notification begins: May 15
    Total amount awarded: $232,500
Contact:
Sid Richardson Memorial Fund
309 Main Street
Fort Worth, TX 76102
Phone: 817-336-0494
Fax: 817-332-2176

Siemens Foundation

Siemens Awards for Advanced Placement

Type of award: Scholarship.
Intended use: For full-time freshman study at accredited 4-year institution.
Eligibility: Applicant must be enrolled in high school. Applicant must be U.S. citizen or permanent resident.
Basis for selection: Competition/talent/interest in academics, based on the most five scores on AP tests among eight subjects: Calculus BC, Computer Science AB, Statistics, Chemistry, Biology, Environmental Science, Physics C: Mechanics, and Physics C: Electricity. Applicant must demonstrate high academic achievement.

Siemens Foundation: Siemens Awards for Advanced Placement

Additional information: A $2,000 college scholarship awarded each spring to up to one male and one female student from each of the 50 states. No application for award. Two additional national winners (one male, one female) will be awarded $5,000 college scholarship. Students must still be in high school in the spring when the award is announced. Must attain a score of 5 on at least two of the aforementioned exams. Composite exams used as tiebreaker if multiple students attain same number of 5s. All U.S. high school students who have taken an AP exam in year prior to applying are eligible, as well as homeschooled students. Students may be awarded state or national award only once, but state winners may be considered for national award in subsequent years. See Website for more details.

Amount of award:	$2,000-$5,000
Number of awards:	102
Total amount awarded:	$210,000

Contact:
The College Board
Attn: Siemens Awards for AP
11911 Freedom Drive, Suite 300
Reston, VA 20190
Phone: 800-626-9795
Fax: 703-935-7795
Web: www.collegeboard.com/siemens or www.siemens-foundation.org

Siemens Competition in Math, Science and Technology

Type of award: Scholarship.
Intended use: For full-time undergraduate or graduate study at accredited 4-year or graduate institution.
Eligibility: Applicant must be enrolled in high school. Applicant must be U.S. citizen or permanent resident.
Basis for selection: Competition/talent/interest in science project, based on research project displaying originality, scientific importance, validity, creativity, academic rigor, clarity of expression, comprehensiveness, experimental work, field knowledge. Major/career interest in biology; chemistry; engineering; environmental science; materials science; mathematics; physics; computer/information sciences or medicine.
Application requirements: Proof of eligibility, research proposal. A 20-page (maximum) research report followed by poster and oral presentations for Regional Finalists. Confirmation page signed by school principal. Completed Supplemental Form and Project Advisor or Mentor Comments Form.
Additional information: Competition to encourage students to do research in math, science, or technology, giving young scientists the opportunity to present their research to leading scientists in their field. Regional Finalists awarded trip to compete at one of six regional competitions. At regional event, after presenting a poster, giving an oral presentation, and participating in Q&A session, the student or team of students will qualify for $1,000 or $3,000 scholarship. National Finalists qualify for $10,000 to $100,000 scholarship. Solo applicants must be seniors; team applicants may be freshmen, sophomores, juniors, or seniors. Register at Website.

Amount of award:	$1,000-$100,000
Number of awards:	60
Number of applicants:	1,361
Application deadline:	October 1
Notification begins:	October 24
Total amount awarded:	$450,000

Contact:
Siemens Competition Program Manager
c/o The College Board
11911 Freedom Drive, Suite 300
Reston, VA 20190
Phone: 800-626-9795 ext. 5849
Fax: 703-935-7795
Web: www.collegeboard.com/siemens

Slovak Gymnastic Union Sokol, USA

Milan Getting Scholarship

Type of award: Scholarship, renewable.
Intended use: For full-time undergraduate study at accredited 4-year institution.
Eligibility: Applicant or parent must be member/participant of Slovak Gymnastic Union Sokol, USA. Applicant must be high school junior or senior. Applicant must be U.S. citizen.
Basis for selection: Applicant must demonstrate high academic achievement, depth of character, leadership, patriotism and seriousness of purpose.
Application requirements: Recommendations, transcript.
Additional information: Applicant must be member of Slovak Gymnastic Union Sokol, USA, in good standing for at least three years. Minimum scholastic average of C+ or equivalent required. Award renewable for four years. Number of awards varies. Write sponsor for application form.

Amount of award:	$500
Application deadline:	March 1

Contact:
Slovak Gymnastic Union Sokol, USA
P.O. Box 189
East Orange, NJ 07019
Phone: 973-676-0280

Slovenian Women's Union of America

Slovenian Women's Union Scholarship

Type of award: Scholarship.
Intended use: For full-time undergraduate study at accredited 2-year or 4-year institution in United States.
Eligibility: Applicant or parent must be member/participant of Slovenian Women's Union of America.
Basis for selection: Applicant must demonstrate financial need, depth of character, leadership and service orientation.
Application requirements: Recommendations, transcript. FAFSA, resume, personal statement/autobiography and photograph.
Additional information: Applicant must be member of Slovenian Women's Union or active participant of organization's activities for three years. Open to women and men with interest in promoting Slovene culture. Recommendation must be from SWUA branch officer and instructor. Number of awards varies. Contact Mary Turvey for more information.

Amount of award:	$1,000-$3,000
Number of awards:	5
Number of applicants:	15
Application deadline:	March 1
Notification begins:	April 1
Total amount awarded:	$7,000

Contact:
Slovenian Women's Union of America
Scholarship Director
4 Lawrence Dr.
Marquette, MI 49855
Phone: 906-249-4288
Web: www.swua.org/scholarships

Slovenian Women's Union Scholarship For Returning Adults

Type of award: Scholarship.
Intended use: For undergraduate certificate or non-degree study at vocational, 2-year or 4-year institution in United States.
Eligibility: Applicant or parent must be member/participant of Slovenian Women's Union of America. Applicant must be returning adult student.
Basis for selection: Applicant must demonstrate financial need, depth of character, leadership and service orientation.
Application requirements: Resume and/or personal statement or autobiography.
Additional information: Applicant must be member of Slovenian Women's Union or active participant of organization's activities for three years. Open to men and women with interest in promoting Slovene culture. Contact Mary Turvey for more information.

Amount of award:	$500
Number of awards:	2
Number of applicants:	1
Application deadline:	March 1
Total amount awarded:	$1,000

Contact:
Slovenian Women's Union of America
Scholarship Director
4 Lawrence Dr.
Marquette, MI 49855
Phone: 906-249-4288
Web: www.swua.org/scholarships

SNM

Nuclear Medicine Student Fellowship Award

Type of award: Research grant.
Intended use: For undergraduate, master's, doctoral or first professional study at postsecondary institution.
Basis for selection: Major/career interest in nuclear medicine.
Application requirements: Research proposal. Resume. Letters of support from nuclear medicine faculty advisor and at least one (preferably two) others. Preceptor form.
Additional information: Major/career interest may include molecular imaging. Minimum two-month summer research internship assisting in clinical and basic research activities in nuclear medicine. Competence in physical and/or biological aspects of radioactivity essential. Total amount awarded varies. Recipients must give foundation 1,000-word resume of activities before receiving final monthly allocation. Preceptor for project: either nuclear medicine physician or nuclear medicine scientist.

Amount of award:	$3,000
Application deadline:	January 25

Contact:
Renee Bergen
SNM Development Office
1850 Samuel Morse Drive
Reston, VA 20190-5316
Phone: 703-708-9000 ext. 1255
Web: snm.org/grants

SNM Technologist Section

Paul Cole Scholarship

Type of award: Scholarship.
Intended use: For undergraduate study at accredited 2-year or 4-year institution. Designated institutions: Schools accredited by the Joint Review Committee on Educational Programs in Nuclear Medicine Technology (JRCNMT).
Basis for selection: Major/career interest in nuclear medicine. Applicant must demonstrate financial need and high academic achievement.
Application requirements: Recommendations, essay, transcript. Proof of acceptance or enrollment in nuclear medicine technology program. Application must be signed by director of nuclear medicine technology program.
Additional information: Minimum 2.5 GPA. Special consideration will be given to applicants who are not only academically capable but who might be financially unable to attend training program without the scholarship. Visit Website for more information.

Amount of award:	$1,000
Number of awards:	32
Number of applicants:	125
Application deadline:	October 17
Notification begins:	February 1
Total amount awarded:	$30,000

Contact:
SNM Development Office
Attn: Renee Bergen
1850 Samuel Morse Drive
Reston, VA 20190-5316
Phone: 703-708-9000 ext. 1255
Web: www.snm.org/grants

Sociedad Honoraria Hispanica

Joseph S. Adams Scholarship

Type of award: Scholarship.
Intended use: For full-time freshman study in United States.
Eligibility: Applicant or parent must be member/participant of Sociedad Honoraria Hispanica. Applicant must be high school senior.
Basis for selection: Major/career interest in Latin American studies or foreign languages. Applicant must demonstrate high academic achievement, depth of character, leadership, patriotism, seriousness of purpose and service orientation.

Sociedad Honoraria Hispanica: Joseph S. Adams Scholarship

Application requirements: Recommendations, essay, transcript, proof of eligibility, nomination by local high-school chapter sponsor.
Additional information: Applicant must be active senior member of the honor society. Applicant must be presently enrolled in high school Spanish or Portuguese class. SHH members should contact their sponsor, not the national director, regarding application. All majors eligible; strong interest in Latin American Studies, Spanish, Portuguese preferred. Contact high school sponsor of Sociedad Honoraria Hispanica for official application before December 31. One member per chapter may apply; scholarship is not renewable.

Amount of award:	$1,000-$2,000
Number of awards:	52
Number of applicants:	200
Application deadline:	February 15
Notification begins:	April 15
Total amount awarded:	$64,000

Contact:
Contact high school sponsor of Sociedad Honoraria Hispanica
Phone: 847-550-0455
Fax: 847-550-0460
Web: www.sociedadhonorariahispanica.org

Society for Science and the Public

Intel International Science and Engineering Fair

Type of award: Scholarship.
Intended use: For undergraduate study.
Eligibility: Applicant must be enrolled in high school.
Basis for selection: Competition/talent/interest in science project, based on merit at Intel ISEF-affiliated regional or state fair. Major/career interest in science, general or engineering.
Additional information: World's largest precollege science competition. Students compete at Intel ISEF-affiliated regional or state fair; winners advance to Intel ISEF. Individual and team projects eligible if entry requirements met. All paperwork must be received by SSP within 12 days after regional or state fair is held. Students in U.S. and other countries with science service-affiliated fairs eligible. Please consult Website for full details.

Amount of award:	$100-$50,000
Number of applicants:	1,500
Total amount awarded:	$3,000,000

Contact:
Intel ISEF
Society for Science and the Public
1719 N Street NW
Washington, DC 20036
Phone: 202-785-2255
Fax: 202-785-1243
Web: www.societyforscience.org

Intel Science Talent Search

Type of award: Scholarship.
Intended use: For undergraduate study.
Eligibility: Applicant must be high school senior.
Basis for selection: Competition/talent/interest in science project, based on creative thinking and scientific originality of individual research reports in science, math, or engineering. Major/career interest in biology; science, general; physics or mathematics.
Application requirements: Recommendations, transcript, proof of eligibility. Three recommendations; 20-page research paper on independent research in science, math, or engineering; standardized test scores.
Additional information: Highly competitive program for college-bound students. Open only to high school seniors meeting all entry requirements. Consult Website for full details and deadline dates.

Amount of award:	$1,000-$100,000
Number of awards:	340
Number of applicants:	1,600
Application deadline:	November 15
Notification begins:	January 16
Total amount awarded:	$1,250,000

Contact:
Intel Science Talent Search
Society for Science and the Public
1719 N Street NW
Washington, DC 20036
Phone: 202-785-2255
Fax: 202-785-1243
Web: www.societyforscience.org

Society for Technical Communication

Society for Technical Communication Scholarship Program

Type of award: Scholarship.
Intended use: For full-time sophomore, junior or graduate study at accredited 4-year or graduate institution.
Basis for selection: Major/career interest in graphic arts/design; communications or computer/information sciences. Applicant must demonstrate high academic achievement.
Application requirements: Recommendations, essay, transcript.
Additional information: Two awards for undergraduates, two for graduate students. Must have completed at least one year of postsecondary education, have major/career interest in technical communication and have potential to contribute to the profession.

Amount of award:	$1,500
Number of awards:	4
Application deadline:	February 15
Notification begins:	April 15
Total amount awarded:	$6,000

Contact:
Society for Technical Communication Attn: Scholarships
901 North Stuart Street
Suite 904
Arlington, VA 22203-1822
Phone: 845-339-4927 or 703-522-4114
Web: www.stc.org

Society of Actuaries/ Casualty Actuarial Society

Joint CAS/SOA Minority Scholarships for Actuarial Students

Type of award: Scholarship, renewable.
Intended use: For full-time undergraduate or graduate study at accredited 4-year or graduate institution.
Eligibility: Applicant must be Alaskan native, African American, Mexican American, Hispanic American, Puerto Rican, American Indian or Native Hawaiian/Pacific Islander. Applicant must be U.S. citizen, permanent resident or international student.
Basis for selection: Major/career interest in insurance/actuarial science or mathematics. Applicant must demonstrate financial need and high academic achievement.
Application requirements: Recommendations, transcript, proof of eligibility, nomination by faculty members or actuarial supervisors. SAT/ACT scores. Financial statement and Student Aid Report.
Additional information: Scholarship intended for minority groups underrepresented in actuarial profession. Applicant must be admitted to institution offering actuarial science program or courses that will prepare student for actuarial career. Award amount varies. Minimum 3.0 GPA. International students must have F1 visa. Visit Website for application and more information.

- Number of awards: 15
- Application deadline: April 18
- Notification begins: June 15
- Total amount awarded: $24,375

Contact:
Society of Actuaries/Casualty Actuarial Society
Minority Scholarship Coordinator
475 North Martingale Road, Suite 600
Schaumburg, IL 60173-2226
Phone: 847-706-3501
Fax: 847-706-3599
Web: www.beanactuary.org

Society of Automotive Engineers

BMW/Society of Automotive Engineers (SAE) Engineering Scholarships

Type of award: Scholarship.
Intended use: For full-time freshman study at accredited 4-year institution in United States. Designated institutions: ABET-accredited institutions.
Eligibility: Applicant must be high school senior. Applicant must be U.S. citizen.
Basis for selection: Major/career interest in engineering. Applicant must demonstrate high academic achievement, depth of character and leadership.
Application requirements: $5 application fee. Essay, transcript.
Additional information: Must have 3.75 GPA and rank in 90th percentile on ACT composite or SAT I (Math and Reading). Must maintain 3.0 GPA to renew scholarship. Renewable for four years. Visit Website for more information.

- Amount of award: $1,500
- Number of awards: 1
- Application deadline: December 15
- Total amount awarded: $6,000

Contact:
Society of Automotive Engineers
Customer Service
400 Commonwealth Drive
Warrendale, PA 15096-0001
Phone: 877-606-7323
Web: www.sae.org/students/engschlr.htm

Detroit Section SAE Technical Scholarship

Type of award: Scholarship, renewable.
Intended use: For freshman study at accredited 2-year or 4-year institution.
Eligibility: Applicant must be high school senior. Applicant must be U.S. citizen.
Basis for selection: Major/career interest in engineering or computer/information sciences. Applicant must demonstrate financial need.
Application requirements: FAFSA.
Additional information: Applicant must be child or grandchild of current SAE Detroit Section member. Minimum 3.0 GPA and 1200 SAT (exclusive of Writing) or 28 ACT. Must maintain 2.5 GPA to renew scholarship. Renewable and transferable up to four consecutive years.

- Amount of award: $3,500
- Number of awards: 1
- Application deadline: December 15
- Notification begins: June 30

Contact:
Society of Automotive Engineers
Customer Service
400 Commonwealth Drive
Warrendale, PA 15096
Phone: 724-776-4970
Web: www.sae.org/students/scholarships

Edward D. Hendrickson/SAE Scholarship

Type of award: Scholarship, renewable.
Intended use: For undergraduate study at accredited postsecondary institution. Designated institutions: ABET-accredited institutions.
Eligibility: Applicant must be high school senior. Applicant must be U.S. citizen.
Basis for selection: Major/career interest in engineering. Applicant must demonstrate high academic achievement.
Additional information: Minimum 3.75 GPA. Must rank in 90th percentile on SAT (Math and Reading) or on composite ACT. Award renewable for four years if student maintains 3.0 GPA.

- Amount of award: $1,000
- Number of awards: 1
- Application deadline: December 15
- Notification begins: June 30
- Total amount awarded: $4,000

Contact:
Society of Automotive Engineers
Customer Service
400 Commonwealth Drive
Warrendale, PA 15096
Phone: 724-776-4970
Web: www.sae.org/students/scholarships

Fred M. Young Sr./SAE Engineering Scholarship

Type of award: Scholarship.
Intended use: For undergraduate study at accredited postsecondary institution. Designated institutions: ABET-accredited institutions.
Eligibility: Applicant must be high school senior. Applicant must be U.S. citizen.
Basis for selection: Major/career interest in engineering.
Additional information: Minimum 3.75 GPA. Applicants must rank in the 90th percentile on SAT (Math and Reading) or on ACT. Award renewable for four years if student maintains 3.0 GPA.
    Amount of award: $1,000
    Number of awards: 1
    Application deadline: December 15
    Notification begins: June 30
    Total amount awarded: $4,000
Contact:
Society of Automotive Engineers
Customer Service
400 Commonwealth Drive
Warrendale, PA 15096
Phone: 724-776-4970
Web: www.sae.org/students/scholarships

SAE Women Engineers Committee Scholarship

Type of award: Scholarship.
Intended use: For freshman study. Designated institutions: ABET-accredited engineering schools.
Eligibility: Applicant must be female, high school senior. Applicant must be U.S. citizen.
Additional information: Minimum 3.0 GPA.
    Amount of award: $2,000
    Number of awards: 1
    Application deadline: December 15
    Notification begins: June 30
Contact:
Society of Automotive Engineers
400 Commonwealth Drive
Warrendale, PA 15096
Phone: 724-776-4970
Web: www.sae.org/students/scholarships

Society of Automotive Engineers (SAE) Longterm Member Sponsored Scholarship

Type of award: Scholarship.
Intended use: For full-time senior study at 4-year institution.
Eligibility: Applicant or parent must be member/participant of Society of Automotive Engineers.
Basis for selection: Major/career interest in engineering. Applicant must demonstrate leadership.
Application requirements: Recommendations, proof of eligibility.
Additional information: Applicant must be active SAE student member. Must demonstrate support for SAE activities and programs. Must be junior in college at time of application. Number of awards varies. Apply online.
    Amount of award: $1,000
    Application deadline: April 1
    Notification begins: July 30
Contact:
Society of Automotive Engineers
Customer Service
400 Commonwealth Drive
Warrendale, PA 15096-0001
Phone: 724-776-4970
Web: www.sae.org/students/scholarships

Society of Automotive Engineers (SAE) Yanmar Scholarship

Type of award: Scholarship, renewable.
Intended use: For full-time senior or graduate study at 4-year institution.
Eligibility: Applicant must be U.S. citizen or Canadian or Mexican citizen.
Basis for selection: Major/career interest in engineering. Applicant must demonstrate high academic achievement and leadership.
Application requirements: Essay, transcript, proof of eligibility.
Additional information: Must pursue course of study or research related to conservation of energy in transportation, agriculture, construction or power generation. Emphasis placed on research or study related to internal combustion engine. Must be junior in college at time of application.
    Amount of award: $1,000
    Number of awards: 2
    Application deadline: April 1
    Notification begins: June 1
    Total amount awarded: $2,000
Contact:
Society of Automotive Engineers
Customer Service
400 Commonwealth Drive
Warrendale, PA 15096-0001
Phone: 724-776-4970
Web: www.sae.org/students/scholarships

Tau Beta Pi/SAE Engineering Scholarship

Type of award: Scholarship.
Intended use: For freshman study at accredited postsecondary institution. Designated institutions: ABET-accredited institutions.
Eligibility: Applicant must be high school senior. Applicant must be U.S. citizen.
Basis for selection: Major/career interest in engineering. Applicant must demonstrate high academic achievement.
Additional information: Minimum 3.75 GPA. Applicant must rank in 90th percentile on SAT (Math and Reading) or on composite ACT.
    Amount of award: $1,000
    Number of awards: 6
    Application deadline: December 15
    Notification begins: June 30

Contact:
Society of Automotive Engineers
Customer Service
400 Commonwealth Drive
Warrendale, PA 15096
Phone: 724-776-4970
Web: www.sae.org/students/scholarships

TMC/SAE Donald D. Dawson Technical Scholarship

Type of award: Scholarship, renewable.
Intended use: For freshman study. Designated institutions: ABET-accredited engineering schools.
Eligibility: Applicant must be high school senior. Applicant must be U.S. citizen.
Basis for selection: Major/career interest in engineering.
Application requirements: Essay showing evidence of hands-on automotive experience or activity.
Additional information: Graduating high school seniors must have minimum 3.25 GPA, 600 SAT (Math) and 550 SAT (Reading) 27 ACT. Transfer students from four-year schools with 3.0 GPA, and students/graduates from technical/vocational schools with 3.5 GPA also eligible. Award renewable for four years as long as a 3.0 GPA maintained.

Amount of award:	$1,500
Number of awards:	1
Application deadline:	December 15
Notification begins:	June 30

Contact:
Society of Automotive Engineers
400 Commonwealth Drive
Warrendale, PA 15096
Phone: 724-776-4970
Web: www.sae.org/students/scholarships

Society of Exploration Geophysicists

Society of Exploration Geophysicists Scholarship

Type of award: Scholarship, renewable.
Intended use: For full-time undergraduate or graduate study at accredited 4-year or graduate institution in United States.
Basis for selection: Major/career interest in geophysics; geology/earth sciences or physics. Applicant must demonstrate high academic achievement.
Application requirements: Recommendations, essay, transcript, proof of eligibility.
Additional information: Graduating high school seniors eligible. Number of scholarships available yearly depends on the number of sponsors and the amount they contribute. Applicants must intend to pursue career in exploration geophysics (graduate students in operations, teaching, or research). Visit Website for more information.

Amount of award:	$500-$14,000
Number of awards:	172
Application deadline:	February 18
Total amount awarded:	$448,350

Contact:
SEG Foundation
P.O. Box 702740
Tulsa, OK 74170-2740
Web: www.seg.org

Society of Manufacturing Engineers Education Foundation

Albert E. Wischmeyer Memorial Scholarship Award

Type of award: Scholarship, renewable.
Intended use: For undergraduate study at accredited 4-year institution.
Eligibility: Applicant must be U.S. citizen or permanent resident residing in New York.
Basis for selection: Major/career interest in manufacturing; engineering or technology. Applicant must demonstrate high academic achievement.
Application requirements: Recommendations, essay, transcript. Student statement, resume, and five copies of application materials.
Additional information: Applicants must reside in New York State west of Interstate 81. Applicant must be graduating high school senior or current undergraduate student. Minimum GPA 2.5. Must reapply for renewal. Financial need considered only between two otherwise equal applicants. Award amount may increase depending on endowment funds. Application available on Website.

Amount of award:	$2,000
Number of awards:	2
Application deadline:	February 1
Total amount awarded:	$4,000

Contact:
Society of Manufacturing Engineers
Scholarship Review Committee
One SME Drive, P.O. Box 930
Dearborn, MI 48121-0930
Phone: 313-425-3300
Web: www.sme.org/foundation

Arthur and Gladys Cervenka Scholarship

Type of award: Scholarship, renewable.
Intended use: For full-time sophomore, junior or senior study at accredited 4-year institution in United States or Canada.
Basis for selection: Major/career interest in manufacturing or engineering. Applicant must demonstrate high academic achievement.
Application requirements: Recommendations, essay, transcript. Student statement, resume.
Additional information: Applicant must have completed minimum of 30 college credit hours. Minimum GPA 3.0. Preference given to students attending institutions in Florida.

Amount of award:	$2,000
Number of awards:	1
Application deadline:	February 1

Society of Manufacturing Engineers Education Foundation: Arthur and Gladys Cervenka Scholarship

Contact:
Society of Manufacturing Engineers
Scholarship Review Committee
One SME Drive, P.O. Box 930
Dearborn, MI 48121-0930
Phone: 313-425-3300
Web: www.sme.org/foundation

Caterpillar Scholars Award

Type of award: Scholarship, renewable.
Intended use: For full-time undergraduate study at 4-year institution in United States or Canada.
Basis for selection: Major/career interest in manufacturing or engineering. Applicant must demonstrate high academic achievement.
Application requirements: Recommendations, essay, transcript. Statement letter. Resume. One original and five copies of application materials. Name of intended college or university.
Additional information: Freshmen must supply SAT scores. Applicants must be enrolled in manufacturing engineering degree program and must have completed minimum 30 college credit hours. Minority applicants may apply as incoming freshmen. Minimum 3.0 GPA. Applicants must reapply for renewal. Summer internships may be offered to select Caterpillar scholars. Financial need considered only between two otherwise equal applicants. Application available on Website.

Amount of award:	$2,000
Number of awards:	5
Application deadline:	February 1
Total amount awarded:	$10,000

Contact:
Society of Manufacturing Engineers
Scholarship Review Committee
One SME Drive, P.O. Box 930
Dearborn, MI 48121-0930
Phone: 313-425-3300
Web: www.sme.org/foundation

Chapter 17 St. Louis Scholarship

Type of award: Scholarship.
Intended use: For full-time freshman, sophomore or junior study at accredited 2-year or 4-year institution.
Eligibility: Applicant or parent must be member/participant of Society of Manufacturing Engineers.
Basis for selection: Major/career interest in manufacturing; engineering or engineering, mechanical. Applicant must demonstrate high academic achievement, depth of character and seriousness of purpose.
Application requirements: Recommendations, essay, transcript. Student statement, resume, one original and five copies of application materials, name of intended college/university.
Additional information: Applicants must be enrolled in manufacturing engineering or related degree program. Preference given to applicants residing in boundaries of St. Louis Chapter 17. Second preference given to applicants living in Missouri. Minimum 2.5 GPA at application; 3.0 GPA must be maintained. Must reapply for renewal. Financial need considered only between two otherwise equal applicants. Application available on Website.

Amount of award:	$1,500
Number of awards:	2
Application deadline:	February 1
Total amount awarded:	$3,000

Contact:
Society of Manufacturing Engineers
Scholarship Review Committee
One SME Drive, P.O. Box 930
Dearborn, MI 48121-0930
Phone: 313-425-3300
Web: www.sme.org/foundation

Chapter 198 - Downriver Detroit Scholarship

Type of award: Scholarship.
Intended use: For full-time undergraduate or graduate study at accredited 2-year, 4-year or graduate institution.
Basis for selection: Major/career interest in manufacturing; engineering, mechanical or engineering.
Application requirements: Recommendations, essay, transcript.
Additional information: First preference given to children or grandchildren of current SME Downriver Chapter 198 members. Second preference given to members of student SME chapters sponsored by Chapter 198. Third preference given to residents of Michigan. Fourth preference given to applicants planning to attend college/university in Michigan. Minimum 2.5 GPA.

Amount of award:	$1,200
Number of awards:	1
Application deadline:	February 1

Contact:
Society of Manufacturing Engineers Education Foundation
Scholarship Review Committee
One SME Drive, P.O. Box 930
Dearborn, MI 48121-0930
Phone: 313-425-3300
Web: www.sme.org/foundation

Chapter 4 - Lawrence A. Wacker Memorial Scholarship

Type of award: Scholarship, renewable.
Intended use: For undergraduate study at accredited 4-year institution in United States or Canada.
Eligibility: Applicant must be high school senior. Applicant must be U.S. citizen or permanent resident residing in Wisconsin.
Basis for selection: Major/career interest in manufacturing; engineering or engineering, mechanical. Applicant must demonstrate high academic achievement.
Application requirements: Recommendations, essay, transcript. Student statement, resume, one original and five copies of application materials, name of intended college/university.
Additional information: Applicants must be seeking bachelor's degree in manufacturing, mechanical, or industrial engineering. Minimum 3.0 GPA. One scholarship granted to graduating high school senior, one to current undergraduate. First preference given to SME Chapter 4 members or spouses, children or grandchildren of members. Second preference given to residents of Milwaukee, Ozaukee, Washington and Waukesha counties. Third preference given to Wisconsin residents. Applicants must reapply for renewal. Financial need considered only between two otherwise equal applicants. Application available on Website.

Amount of award:	$1,500
Number of awards:	2
Application deadline:	February 1
Total amount awarded:	$3,000

Contact:
Society of Manufacturing Engineers
Scholarship Review Committee
One SME Drive, P.O. Box 930
Dearborn, MI 48121-0930
Phone: 313-425-3300
Web: www.sme.org/foundation

Chapter 52 - Wichita Scholarship

Type of award: Scholarship.
Intended use: For undergraduate or graduate study at accredited 2-year, 4-year or graduate institution in United States.
Eligibility: Applicant must be residing in Oklahoma, Kansas or Missouri.
Basis for selection: Major/career interest in engineering or engineering, mechanical.
Application requirements: Recommendations, essay, transcript.
Additional information: First preference given to children, grandchildren, or other relatives of current SME Wichita Chapter 52 members. Second preference given to residents of Kansas, Oklahoma, and Missouri. Third preference given to applicants attending college or university in Kansas. Minimum GPA 2.5.
   Amount of award: $2,000
   Number of awards: 1
   Application deadline: February 1
Contact:
Society of Manufacturing Engineers Education Foundation
Scholarship Review Committee
One SME Drive, P.O. Box 930
Dearborn, MI 48121-0930
Phone: 313-425-3300
Web: www.sme.org/foundation

Chapter 56 - Fort Wayne Scholarship

Type of award: Scholarship.
Intended use: For undergraduate or graduate study at 2-year, 4-year or graduate institution.
Eligibility: Applicant must be residing in Indiana.
Basis for selection: Major/career interest in engineering or engineering, mechanical.
Application requirements: Recommendations, essay, transcript.
Additional information: First preference given to children or grandchildren of current member of SME Fort Wayne Chapter 56. Second preference given to members of SME student chapters sponsored by Chapter 56. Third preference given to residents of Indiana. Fourth preference given to applicants attending or planning to attend Indiana institutions. Minimum GPA 2.5.
   Amount of award: $2,000
   Number of awards: 3
   Application deadline: February 1
Contact:
Society of Manufacturing Engineers Education Foundation
Scholarship Review Committee
One SME Drive, P.O. Box 930
Dearborn, MI 48121-0930
Phone: 313-425-3300
Web: www.sme.org/foundation

Chapter 6 - Fairfield County Scholarship

Type of award: Scholarship.
Intended use: For full-time undergraduate study in United States or Canada.
Basis for selection: Major/career interest in engineering or manufacturing.
Application requirements: Recommendations, essay, transcript.
Additional information: Minimum 3.0 GPA. Preference given to residents of the eastern United States.
   Amount of award: $1,500
   Number of awards: 1
   Application deadline: February 1
Contact:
Society of Manufacturing Engineers Education Foundation
Scholarship Review Committee
One SME Drive, P.O. Box 930
Dearborn, MI 48121-0930
Phone: 313-425-3300
Web: www.sme.org/foundation

Chapter 67 - Phoenix Scholarship

Type of award: Scholarship, renewable.
Intended use: For full-time undergraduate study.
Eligibility: Applicant must be residing in Arizona.
Basis for selection: Major/career interest in engineering or manufacturing.
Application requirements: Recommendations, essay, transcript.
Additional information: Minimum 2.5 GPA overall; 3.0 in manufacturing courses. Graduating high school seniors eligible.
   Amount of award: $2,000
   Number of awards: 2
   Application deadline: February 1
Contact:
Society of Manufacturing Engineers Education Foundation
Scholarship Review Committee
One SME Drive, P.O. Box 930
Dearborn, MI 48121-0930
Phone: 313-425-3300
Web: www.sme.org/foundation

The Clarence & Josephine Myers Scholarship

Type of award: Scholarship.
Intended use: For undergraduate or graduate study at 2-year, 4-year or graduate institution.
Eligibility: Applicant must be residing in Indiana.
Basis for selection: Major/career interest in engineering, mechanical; engineering or manufacturing.
Additional information: Preference given to students planning to or currently attending college or university in Indiana; students who attend Arsenal Technological High School in Indianapolis; members of SME student chapters sponsored by SME Chapter 37; and children or grandchildren of current SME Chapter 37 member. Minimum 3.0 GPA.
   Amount of award: $1,200
   Number of awards: 1
   Application deadline: February 1
   Total amount awarded: $1,200

Society of Manufacturing Engineers Education Foundation: The Clarence & Josephine Myers Scholarship

Contact:
Society of Manufacturing Engineers Education Foundation
Scholarship Review Committee
One SME Drive, P.O. Box 930
Dearborn, MI 48121-0930
Phone: 313-425-3300
Web: www.sme.org/foundation

Clinton J. Helton Manufacturing Scholarship Award

Type of award: Scholarship.
Intended use: For full-time sophomore, junior or senior study at accredited 4-year institution. Designated institutions: Colorado State University and all University of Colorado campuses.
Eligibility: Applicant must be residing in Colorado.
Basis for selection: Major/career interest in manufacturing or engineering. Applicant must demonstrate high academic achievement and depth of character.
Application requirements: Recommendations, essay, transcript. Student statement, resume, one original and five copies of application materials, name of intended college/university.
Additional information: Applicants must be enrolled in manufacturing engineering or technology degree program and must have completed at least 30 credit hours. Minimum 3.0 GPA. Applicants must reapply for renewal. Financial need considered only between two otherwise equal applicants. Application available on Website.

Amount of award:	$3,000
Number of awards:	2
Application deadline:	February 1
Total amount awarded:	$6,000

Contact:
Society of Manufacturing Engineers Education Foundation
Scholarship Review Committee
One SME Drive, P.O. Box 930
Dearborn, MI 48121-0930
Phone: 313-425-3300
Web: www.sme.org/foundation

Connie and Robert T. Gunter Scholarship

Type of award: Scholarship.
Intended use: For full-time sophomore, junior or senior study at accredited 4-year institution. Designated institutions: Georgia Institute of Technology, Georgia Southern College and Southern College of Technology.
Basis for selection: Major/career interest in manufacturing or engineering. Applicant must demonstrate high academic achievement, depth of character and seriousness of purpose.
Application requirements: Recommendations, essay, transcript. Student statement, resume, one original and five copies of application materials, name of intended college/university.
Additional information: Applicants must be enrolled in manufacturing engineering degree program and must have completed at least 30 credit hours. Minimum 3.5 GPA. Applicants must reapply for renewal. Financial need considered only between two otherwise equal applicants. Application available on Website.

Amount of award:	$1,200
Number of awards:	1
Application deadline:	February 1
Total amount awarded:	$1,200

Contact:
Society of Manufacturing Engineers Education Foundation
Scholarship Review Committee
One SME Drive, P.O. Box 930
Dearborn, MI 48121-0930
Phone: 313-425-3300
Web: www.sme.org/foundation

Detroit Chapter One - Founding Chapter Scholarship Award

Type of award: Scholarship, renewable.
Intended use: For undergraduate or graduate study at accredited 2-year, 4-year or graduate institution. Designated institutions: Wayne State University, Lawrence Technological University, University of Detroit Mercy, Focus: HOPE Center for Advanced Technologies, Henry Ford Community College, Macomb Community College, University of Michigan.
Eligibility: Applicant or parent must be member/participant of Society of Manufacturing Engineers.
Basis for selection: Major/career interest in manufacturing or engineering. Applicant must demonstrate high academic achievement, depth of character and leadership.
Application requirements: Recommendations, essay, transcript. Student statement, resume. One original and five copies of application materials. Name of intended college or university.
Additional information: Awarded to one student each at associate, baccalaureate and graduate levels. Applicants must be enrolled in manufacturing engineering, manufacturing engineering technology or closely related degree or certificate program. Award $2,000 for undergraduates; $3,000 for graduate students. Applicants must be involved in SME student chapter at one of listed schools and have overall minimum GPA of 3.0. Applicants must reapply for renewal. Financial need considered only between two otherwise equal applicants. Application available on Website.

Amount of award:	$2,000-$3,000
Number of awards:	3
Application deadline:	February 1
Total amount awarded:	$7,000

Contact:
Society of Manufacturing Engineers Education Foundation
Scholarship Review Committee
One SME Drive, P.O. Box 930
Dearborn, MI 48121-0930
Phone: 313-425-3300
Web: www.sme.org/foundation

Directors Scholarship

Type of award: Scholarship, renewable.
Intended use: For full-time sophomore, junior or senior study at accredited 4-year institution in United States or Canada.
Basis for selection: Major/career interest in manufacturing. Applicant must demonstrate high academic achievement and leadership.
Application requirements: Recommendations, essay, transcript. Student statement, resume, one original and five copies of application materials, name of intended college/university.
Additional information: Applicants must have completed minimum 30 college credit hours. Minimum 3.5 GPA. Applicants must reapply for renewal. Financial need considered only between two otherwise equal applicants. Application available on Website.

Society of Manufacturing Engineers Education Foundation: E. Wayne Kay Scholarship

Amount of award:	$5,000
Number of awards:	2
Application deadline:	February 1
Total amount awarded:	$10,000

Contact:
Society of Manufacturing Engineers
Scholarship Review Committee
One SME Drive, P.O. Box 930
Dearborn, MI 48121-0930
Phone: 313-425-3300
Web: www.sme.org/foundation

E. Wayne Kay Co-op Scholarship

Type of award: Scholarship, renewable.
Intended use: For full-time sophomore, junior or senior study in United States or Canada.
Basis for selection: Major/career interest in manufacturing or engineering. Applicant must demonstrate high academic achievement.
Application requirements: Essay, transcript, proof of eligibility. Name of intended college or university. Two letters of recommendation from employers and letter of support from faculty member at college or university. Must provide evidence of demonstrated excellence related to manufacturing engineering or technology that may include project completed for employer.
Additional information: Applicants must be enrolled in manufacturing engineering or technology degree program and working through co-op program in a manufacturing-related environment. Applicants must have completed minimum 30 college credit hours. Minimum GPA 3.0. Applicants must reapply for renewal. Financial need considered only between two otherwise equal applicants. Application available on Website.

Amount of award:	$2,500
Number of awards:	2
Application deadline:	February 1
Total amount awarded:	$5,000

Contact:
Society of Manufacturing Engineers
Scholarship Review Committee
One SME Drive, P.O. Box 930
Dearborn, MI 48121-0930
Phone: 313-425-3300
Web: www.sme.org/foundation

E. Wayne Kay Community College Scholarship

Type of award: Scholarship, renewable.
Intended use: For full-time freshman or sophomore study at accredited vocational or 2-year institution in United States or Canada.
Basis for selection: Major/career interest in manufacturing. Applicant must demonstrate high academic achievement.
Application requirements: Recommendations, essay, transcript. Student statement, resume, one original and five copies of application materials, name of intended college/university.
Additional information: Applicants must be enrolled in manufacturing engineering or closely related degree program and must have completed less than 60 college credit hours. Minimum 3.0 GPA. Must reapply for renewal. Financial need considered only between two otherwise equal applicants. Application available on Website.

Amount of award:	$1,000
Number of awards:	3
Application deadline:	February 1
Total amount awarded:	$3,000

Contact:
Society of Manufacturing Engineers
Scholarship Review Committee
One SME Drive, P.O. Box 930
Dearborn, MI 48121-0930
Phone: 313-425-3300
Web: www.sme.org/foundation

E. Wayne Kay High School Scholarship

Type of award: Scholarship, renewable.
Intended use: For full-time freshman study at accredited 4-year institution in United States or Canada.
Eligibility: Applicant must be high school senior.
Basis for selection: Major/career interest in manufacturing or engineering. Applicant must demonstrate high academic achievement.
Application requirements: Recommendations, essay, transcript. Student statement, resume, one original and five copies of application materials, name of intended college/university.
Additional information: Applicant must commit to enrolling in manufacturing engineering degree or technology program. Minimum 3.0 GPA. Award is $1,000 for first year, renewable for $1,500 for second year based on recipient's academic excellence and career path. Financial need considered only between two otherwise equal applicants. Application available on Website.

Amount of award:	$2,500
Number of awards:	2
Application deadline:	February 1
Total amount awarded:	$5,000

Contact:
Society of Manufacturing Engineers
Scholarship Review Committee
One SME Drive, P.O. Box 930
Dearborn, MI 48121-0930
Phone: 313-425-3300
Web: www.sme.org/foundation

E. Wayne Kay Scholarship

Type of award: Scholarship, renewable.
Intended use: For full-time sophomore, junior or senior study at accredited 4-year institution in United States or Canada.
Basis for selection: Major/career interest in manufacturing or engineering. Applicant must demonstrate high academic achievement.
Application requirements: Recommendations, essay, transcript. Student statement, resume, one original and five copies of application materials, name of intended college/university.
Additional information: Applicants must be enrolled in manufacturing engineering or technology degree program and have completed less than 60 credit hours. Minimum 3.0 GPA. Must reapply for renewal. Financial need considered only between two otherwise equal applicants. Application available on Website.

Amount of award:	$2,500
Number of awards:	2
Application deadline:	February 1
Total amount awarded:	$25,000

Society of Manufacturing Engineers Education Foundation: E. Wayne Kay Scholarship

Contact:
Society of Manufacturing Engineers
Scholarship Review Committee
One SME Drive, P.O. Box 930
Dearborn, MI 48121-0930
Phone: 313-425-3300
Web: www.sme.org/foundation

Edward S. Roth Manufacturing Engineering

Type of award: Scholarship, renewable.
Intended use: For full-time undergraduate or graduate study at accredited 4-year institution in United States. Designated institutions: California Polytechnic State University, California State Polytechnic University, University of Miami, Bradley University, Central State University, Miami University (OH), Boston University, Worcester Polytechnic Institute, University of Massachusetts, St. Cloud State University, University of Texas-Pan American, Brigham Young University and Utah State University.
Eligibility: Applicant must be U.S. citizen.
Basis for selection: Major/career interest in manufacturing or engineering. Applicant must demonstrate high academic achievement, depth of character and seriousness of purpose.
Application requirements: Recommendations, essay, transcript. Student statement, resume, one original and five copies of application materials, name of intended college/university.
Additional information: Applicants must be enrolled in manufacturing engineering degree program. Minimum 3.0 GPA. Preference given to students demonstrating financial need, minority students and students participating in co-op program. Must reapply for renewal. Application available on Website.

Amount of award:	$2,500
Number of awards:	1
Application deadline:	February 1
Total amount awarded:	$2,500

Contact:
Society of Manufacturing Engineers Education Foundation
Scholarship Review Committee
One SME Drive, P.O. Box 930
Dearborn, MI 48121-0930
Phone: 313-425-3300
Web: www.sme.org/foundation

Future Leaders of Manufacturing Scholarships

Type of award: Scholarship.
Intended use: For full-time undergraduate or graduate study.
Basis for selection: Major/career interest in manufacturing or engineering.
Application requirements: Recommendations, transcript, nomination by SME student chapter faculty advisors. Resume.
Additional information: Applicant must be current SME student member. Visit Website for nomination form.

Amount of award:	$1,000
Number of awards:	10
Application deadline:	February 1

Contact:
Society of Manufacturing Engineers Education Foundation
Scholarship Review Committee
One SME Drive, P.O. Box 930
Dearborn, MI 48121-0930
Phone: 313-425-3300
Web: www.sme.org/foundation

Giuliano Mazzetti Scholarship

Type of award: Scholarship, renewable.
Intended use: For full-time sophomore, junior or senior study at accredited 4-year institution in United States or Canada.
Basis for selection: Major/career interest in manufacturing or engineering. Applicant must demonstrate high academic achievement.
Application requirements: Recommendations, essay, transcript. Student statement, resume, one original and five copies of application materials, name of intended college/university.
Additional information: Applicants must be enrolled in manufacturing engineering, technology or closely related field degree program and must have completed minimum 30 college credit hours. Minimum GPA 3.0. Must reapply for renewal. Financial need considered only between two otherwise equal applicants. Application available on Website.

Amount of award:	$2,000
Number of awards:	3
Application deadline:	February 1
Total amount awarded:	$6,000

Contact:
Society of Manufacturing Engineers
Scholarship Review Committee
One SME Drive, P.O. Box 930
Dearborn, MI 48121-0930
Phone: 313-425-3300
Web: www.sme.org/foundation

Lucile B. Kaufman Women's Scholarship

Type of award: Scholarship, renewable.
Intended use: For full-time sophomore, junior or senior study at 4-year institution in United States or Canada.
Eligibility: Applicant must be female.
Basis for selection: Major/career interest in manufacturing or engineering. Applicant must demonstrate high academic achievement.
Application requirements: Recommendations, essay, transcript. Statement letter. Resume. One original and five copies of application materials. Name of intended college or university.
Additional information: Applicants must be enrolled in manufacturing engineering or manufacturing engineering technology degree program and must have completed minimum 30 credits. Minimum 3.0 GPA. Must reapply for renewal. Financial need considered only between two otherwise equal applicants. Application available on Website.

Amount of award:	$1,500
Number of awards:	2
Application deadline:	February 1
Total amount awarded:	$3,000

Contact:
Society of Manufacturing Engineers
Scholarship Review Committee
One SME Drive, P.O. Box 930
Dearborn, MI 48121-0930
Phone: 313-425-3300
Web: www.sme.org/foundation

Myrtle and Earl Walker Scholarship

Type of award: Scholarship, renewable.
Intended use: For full-time undergraduate study at accredited 4-year institution in United States or Canada.

Basis for selection: Major/career interest in manufacturing or engineering. Applicant must demonstrate high academic achievement.
Application requirements: Recommendations, essay, transcript. Student statement, resume, one original and five copies of application materials, name of intended college/university.
Additional information: Applicants must be enrolled in manufacturing engineering degree or technology program and must have completed minimum 15 credits. Minimum 3.0 GPA. Must reapply for renewal. Financial need considered only between two otherwise equal applicants. Application available on Website.

    Amount of award: $2,000
    Number of awards: 20
    Application deadline: February 1
    Total amount awarded: $40,000
Contact:
Society of Manufacturing Engineers
Scholarship Review Committee
One SME Drive, P.O. Box 930
Dearborn, MI 48121-0930
Phone: 313-425-3300
Web: www.sme.org/foundation

North Central Region Scholarship

Type of award: Scholarship.
Intended use: For full-time undergraduate study at 2-year or 4-year institution.
Eligibility: Applicant must be residing in Michigan, Wisconsin, Iowa, South Dakota, Minnesota, Nebraska or North Dakota.
Basis for selection: Major/career interest in manufacturing; engineering or engineering, mechanical.
Application requirements: Recommendations, essay, transcript.
Additional information: First preference given to applicants from the North Central Region who are SME members, spouses of members, or children or grandchildren of members. Second preference given to residents of Iowa, Minnesota, Nebraska, North Dakota, South Dakota, Wisconsin and the upper peninsula of Michigan. Minimum 3.0 GPA.

    Amount of award: $1,250
    Number of awards: 1
    Application deadline: February 1
Contact:
Society of Manufacturing Engineers Education Foundation
Scholarship Review Committee
One SME Drive, P.O. Box 930
Dearborn, MI 48121-0930
Phone: 313-425-3300
Web: www.sme.org/foundation

SME Education Foundation Family Scholarship

Type of award: Scholarship.
Intended use: For full-time freshman or sophomore study in United States or Canada.
Eligibility: Applicant or parent must be member/participant of Society of Manufacturing Engineers.
Basis for selection: Major/career interest in engineering. Applicant must demonstrate high academic achievement, leadership and seriousness of purpose.
Application requirements: Recommendations, essay, transcript, proof of eligibility. Resume, SAT/ACT scores.

Additional information: Applicant must have parent or grandparent who has been SME member in good standing for at least two years. Graduating high school seniors and current undergraduates with fewer than 30 credit hours are eligible. Minimum GPA 3.0. Minimum 1000 SAT or 21 ACT. Three scholarships awarded: two one-year scholarships, minimum $5,000; one $80,000 scholarship payable as $20,000 per year over four years.

    Amount of award: $5,000-$20,000
    Number of awards: 3
    Application deadline: February 1
Contact:
Society of Manufacturing Engineers Education Foundation
Scholarship Review Committee
One SME Drive, P.O. Box 930
Dearborn, MI 48121-0930
Phone: 313-425-3300
Web: www.sme.org/foundation

Walt Bartram Memorial Education Award (Region 12 and Chapter 119)

Type of award: Scholarship, renewable.
Intended use: For full-time undergraduate study at accredited 2-year or 4-year institution. Designated institutions: Schools with manufacturing engineering programs within Desert Pacific Region 12 (Arizona, New Mexico, Southern California).
Eligibility: Applicant or parent must be member/participant of Society of Manufacturing Engineers. Applicant must be high school senior. Applicant must be residing in California, New Mexico or Arizona.
Basis for selection: Major/career interest in manufacturing or engineering. Applicant must demonstrate high academic achievement, depth of character and seriousness of purpose.
Application requirements: Recommendations, essay, transcript. Student statement, resume, one original and five copies of application materials, name of intended college/university.
Additional information: Applicants must reside within Desert Pacific Region 12, and, unless high school senior, must be member of SME. Applicants must be enrolled in manufacturing engineering or closely related degree program. Minimum 3.5 GPA. Financial need considered only between two otherwise equal applicants. Application available on Website.

    Amount of award: $1,500
    Number of awards: 1
    Application deadline: February 1
    Total amount awarded: $1,500
Contact:
Society of Manufacturing Engineers
Scholarship Review Committee
One SME Drive, P.O. Box 930
Dearborn, MI 48121-0930
Phone: 313-425-3300
Web: www.sme.org/foundation

William E. Weisel Scholarship

Type of award: Scholarship, renewable.
Intended use: For full-time sophomore, junior or senior study at 4-year institution in United States or Canada.
Eligibility: Applicant must be U.S. citizen or Canadian citizen.
Basis for selection: Major/career interest in manufacturing; engineering or robotics. Applicant must demonstrate high academic achievement.
Application requirements: Recommendations, essay, transcript. Student statement, resume, one original and five

copies of application materials, name of intended college/university.
Additional information: Applicant must be enrolled in manufacturing engineering degree program and must have completed minimum 30 credits. Must be seeking career in robotics or automated systems used in manufacturing, or robotics used in medical field. Minimum 3.0 GPA. Applicants must reapply for renewal. Financial need considered only between two otherwise equal applicants. Application available on Website.

Amount of award:	$2,000
Number of awards:	1
Application deadline:	February 1
Total amount awarded:	$2,000

Contact:
Society of Manufacturing Engineers
Scholarship Review Committee
One SME Drive, P.O. Box 930
Dearborn, MI 48121-0930
Phone: 313-425-3300
Web: www.sme.org/foundation

Society of Physics Students

Society of Physics Students Leadership Scholarship

Type of award: Scholarship.
Intended use: For full-time junior or senior study at 2-year or 4-year institution.
Eligibility: Applicant or parent must be member/participant of Society of Physics Students.
Basis for selection: Major/career interest in physics. Applicant must demonstrate high academic achievement and seriousness of purpose.
Application requirements: Transcript. Letters from at least two full-time faculty members.
Additional information: Awards payable in equal installments at the beginning of each semester or quarter of full-time study in final year of study leading to a baccalaureate degree. Applicants in two-year schools should apply after completing one semester of physics. Must be active participant in Society of Physics Students. Must show intention for continued scholastic development in physics. Number of awards varies. Obtain application from Website or SPS Chapter Advisers.

Amount of award:	$2,000-$5,000
Number of awards:	18
Application deadline:	February 15
Notification begins:	April 1

Contact:
SPS Scholarships Committee
One Physics Ellipse
College Park, MD 20740
Phone: 301-209-3007
Fax: 301-204-0839
Web: www.spsnational.org

Society of Plastics Engineers

Extrusion Division/Lew Erwin Memorial Scholarship

Type of award: Scholarship.
Intended use: For full-time senior or graduate study at vocational, 2-year, 4-year or graduate institution.
Basis for selection: Major/career interest in chemistry; engineering; engineering, chemical; engineering, materials; engineering, mechanical or physics. Applicant must demonstrate financial need.
Application requirements: Research proposal. One- to two-page typed statement explaining reasons for application, qualifications and educational/career goals in the plastics industry. Recommendation letter from faculty adviser associated with project.
Additional information: All applicants must be in good academic standing and have a demonstrated or expressed interest in the plastics industry. Applicants must be working on senior or MS research project in polymer extrusion that the scholarship will help support. The project must be described in writing, including background, objective and proposed experiments. Recipient will be expected to furnish final research summary report. Visit Website for more information.

Amount of award:	$2,500
Number of awards:	1
Number of applicants:	1
Application deadline:	March 1
Total amount awarded:	$2,500

Contact:
Society of Plastics Engineers
14 Fairfield Drive
P.O. Box 403
Brookfield, CT 06804-0403
Phone: 203-740-5447
Fax: 203-775-1157
Web: www.4spe.org

Fleming/Blaszcak Scholarship

Type of award: Scholarship.
Intended use: For full-time undergraduate or graduate study at 4-year or graduate institution.
Basis for selection: Major/career interest in chemistry; engineering; engineering, chemical; engineering, materials; engineering, mechanical or physics. Applicant must demonstrate financial need.
Application requirements: Transcript. One- to two-page typed statement explaining reasons for application, qualifications and educational/career goals in the plastics industry. Three recommendation letters: two from teachers or school officials and one from an employer or non-relative.
Additional information: Applicant must be of Mexican heritage, a Mexican citizen, or a legal resident of the United States. All applicants must be in good standing and have a demonstrated or expressed interest in the plastics industry. Visit Website for more information.

Amount of award:	$2,000
Number of awards:	1
Number of applicants:	1
Application deadline:	January 15
Total amount awarded:	$2,000

Contact:
Society of Plastics Engineers
14 Fairfield Drive
P.O. Box 403
Brookfield, CT 06804-0403
Phone: 203-740-5447
Fax: 203-775-1157
Web: www.4spe.org

Society of Plastics Engineers General Scholarships

Type of award: Scholarship, renewable.
Intended use: For full-time undergraduate study at vocational, 2-year or 4-year institution.
Basis for selection: Major/career interest in chemistry; engineering; engineering, chemical; engineering, mechanical; engineering, materials or physics. Applicant must demonstrate financial need and seriousness of purpose.
Application requirements: Transcript. One- to two-page typed statement explaining reasons for application, qualifications and educational/career goals in the plastics industry. Three recommendation letters: two from teachers or school officials and one from an employer or non-relative.
Additional information: Scholarships awarded for one year only, but applicants may apply to be re-awarded for up to three additional years. All applicants must be in good standing with their colleges and must have a demonstrated or expressed interest in the plastics industry. Visit Website for more information.

Amount of award:	$4,000
Number of applicants:	15
Application deadline:	January 15
Total amount awarded:	$48,000

Contact:
Society of Plastics Engineers
14 Fairfield Drive
P.O. Box 403
Brookfield, CT 06804-0403
Phone: 203-740-5447
Fax: 203-775-1157
Web: www.4spe.org

The SPE Foundation Blow Molding Division Memorial Scholarships

Type of award: Scholarship.
Intended use: For sophomore study at 4-year institution.
Basis for selection: Major/career interest in engineering. Applicant must demonstrate financial need.
Application requirements: Recommendations, transcript. Essay on the importance of blow molding to the technical parts and packing industries.
Additional information: Applicants must be members of a Society of Plastics Engineers Student Chapter and be in second year of four-year undergraduate plastics engineering program. Award is $8,000 payable over two years.

Amount of award:	$4,000
Number of awards:	2
Number of applicants:	1
Application deadline:	January 15

Contact:
Society of Plastics Engineers
14 Fairfield Drive
P.O. Box 403
Brookfield, CT 06804-0403
Phone: 203-740-5447
Fax: 203-775-1157
Web: www.4spe.org

Thermoforming Division Memorial Scholarships

Type of award: Scholarship.
Intended use: For full-time undergraduate or graduate study at vocational, 2-year, 4-year or graduate institution.
Basis for selection: Major/career interest in chemistry; engineering; engineering, chemical; engineering, materials; engineering, mechanical or physics. Applicant must demonstrate financial need.
Application requirements: Transcript. One- to two-page typed statement explaining reasons for application, qualifications and educational/career goals. Statement detailing exposure to the thermostat industry, including courses, research conducted or jobs held. Three recommendation letters: two from teachers or school officials, and one from an employer or other non-relative.
Additional information: All applicants must be in good standing and have a demonstrated or expressed interest in the plastics industry. Visit Website for more information.

Amount of award:	$7,500
Number of awards:	2
Number of applicants:	2
Application deadline:	January 15

Contact:
Society of Plastics Engineers
14 Fairfield Drive
P.O. Box 403
Brookfield, CT 06084-0403
Phone: 203-740-5447
Fax: 203-775-1157
Web: www.4spe.org

Thermoset Division/James I. MacKenzie Memorial Scholarship

Type of award: Scholarship.
Intended use: For full-time undergraduate or graduate study at vocational, 2-year or 4-year institution.
Basis for selection: Major/career interest in chemistry; engineering; engineering, chemical; engineering, materials; engineering, mechanical or physics. Applicant must demonstrate financial need.
Application requirements: Transcript. One- to two-page typed statement explaining reasons for application, qualifications, and educational/ career goals. Statement detailing exposure to the thermoset industry. Three recommendation letters: two from teachers or school officials and one from an employer or non-relative.
Additional information: All applicants must be in good academic standing and have a demonstrated or expressed interest in the plastics industry. Must have experience in the thermoset industry, such as courses taken, research conducted, or jobs held. Visit Website for more information.

Amount of award:	$2,500
Number of awards:	2
Application deadline:	January 15

Contact:
Society of Plastics Engineers
14 Fairfield Drive
P.O. Box 403
Brookfield, CT 06084-0403
Phone: 203-740-5447
Fax: 203-775-1157
Web: www.4spe.org

Society of Professional Journalists, Greater Los Angeles Professional Chapter

Bill Farr Scholarship

Type of award: Scholarship, renewable.
Intended use: For full-time junior, senior or graduate study at accredited 4-year institution in United States.
Eligibility: Applicant must be U.S. citizen.
Basis for selection: Major/career interest in journalism.
Application requirements: Essay, proof of eligibility. Proof of enrollment in journalism program. Resume, clips, samples of work. References.
Additional information: Applicant must be resident of or attending university in Los Angeles, Ventura or Orange counties. Scholarship awarded based on accomplishments and potential. Financial need considered in making selection between equally qualified applicants. Must reapply for renewal. Visit Website for details and application.
    Amount of award: $500-$1,000
    Application deadline: April 15
Contact:
SPJ/LA Scholarships Department of Journalism
California State University, Long Beach
1250 Bellflower
Long Beach, CA 90840
Web: www.spj.org/losangeles

Carl Greenberg Scholarship

Type of award: Scholarship, renewable.
Intended use: For full-time junior, senior or graduate study at accredited 4-year institution in United States.
Basis for selection: Major/career interest in journalism.
Application requirements: Essay, proof of eligibility. Proof of enrollment in journalism program. Resume, clips, samples of work. References.
Additional information: Award for investigative or political reporting. Applicant must be resident of or attending university in Los Angeles, Ventura or Orange counties. Scholarship awarded based on applicant's accomplishments and potential. Financial need considered in making selections between equally qualified candidates. Must reapply for renewal. Visit Website for details and application.
    Amount of award: $1,000
    Application deadline: April 15

Contact:
SPJ/LA Scholarships Department of Journalism
California State University, Long Beach
18111 Nordhoff St. Mail Drop 8311
Northridge, CA 91330-8311
Web: www.spj.org/losangeles

Helen Johnson Scholarship

Type of award: Scholarship, renewable.
Intended use: For full-time junior, senior or graduate study at accredited 4-year institution in United States.
Basis for selection: Major/career interest in journalism.
Application requirements: Essay, proof of eligibility. Proof of enrollment in journalism program. Resume, samples of work, references.
Additional information: Award for broadcast journalism students. Applicant must be resident of or attending university in Los Angeles, Ventura or Orange counties. Scholarship awarded based on applicant's accomplishments; financial need considered in making selections between equally qualified applicants. Must reapply for renewal. Visit Website for details and application.
    Amount of award: $500-$1,000
    Application deadline: April 15
Contact:
SPJ/LA Scholarships Department of Journalism
California State University, Northridge
18111 Nordoff St. Mail Drop 8311
Northridge, CA 91330-8311
Web: www.spj.org/losangeles

Ken Inouye Scholarship

Type of award: Scholarship, renewable.
Intended use: For full-time junior, senior or graduate study at accredited 4-year institution in United States.
Eligibility: Applicant must be Alaskan native, Asian American, African American, Mexican American, Hispanic American, Puerto Rican, American Indian or Native Hawaiian/Pacific Islander. Applicant must be U.S. citizen.
Basis for selection: Major/career interest in journalism.
Application requirements: Essay, proof of eligibility. Proof of enrollment in journalism program. Resume, clips, samples of work. References.
Additional information: Applicant must be resident of or attending university in Los Angeles, Ventura or Orange counties. Scholarship award based on applicant's accomplishments and potential. Financial need considered in making selections between equally qualified applicants. Must reapply for renewal. Visit Website for details and application.
    Amount of award: $500-$1,000
    Application deadline: April 15
Contact:
SPJ/LA Scholarships Department of Journalism
California State University, Northridge
18111 Nordoff St. Mail Drop 8311
Northridge, CA 91330-8311
Web: www.spj.org/losangeles

Society of Women Engineers

Ada I. Pressman Memorial Scholarship

Type of award: Scholarship.
Intended use: For full-time sophomore, junior, senior or graduate study at accredited 4-year institution.
Eligibility: Applicant must be female. Applicant must be U.S. citizen.
Basis for selection: Major/career interest in engineering. Applicant must demonstrate high academic achievement.
Application requirements: Recommendations, essay, transcript, proof of eligibility.
Additional information: Applicants must be enrolled or plan to be enrolled in ABET- or CSAB-accredited program. Minimum 3.0 GPA. Application forms available through deans of engineering at eligible schools, through SWE sections, SWE student sections, SWE Headquarters, or on Website. Applicants considered for all scholarships for which they are eligible and need submit only one application package.

Amount of award:	$5,000
Number of awards:	5
Application deadline:	February 15
Notification begins:	May 15
Total amount awarded:	$25,000

Contact:
Society of Women Engineers
World Headquarters
230 E. Ohio Street, Suite 400
Chicago, IL 60611-3265
Phone: 312-596-5223
Fax: 312-596-5252
Web: www.swe.org

ADC Communications and Foundation Scholarship

Type of award: Scholarship.
Intended use: For full-time junior or senior study at accredited 4-year institution in United States.
Eligibility: Applicant must be female. Applicant must be U.S. citizen or international student.
Basis for selection: Major/career interest in engineering, computer or engineering, electrical/electronic.
Application requirements: Recommendations, essay, transcript, proof of eligibility.
Additional information: Minimum 3.0 GPA. Applicant must be SWE student member. Applicants must be enrolled or plan to be enrolled in ABET- or CSAB-accredited program. Application forms available through deans of engineering at eligible schools, through SWE sections, SWE student sections, SWE Headquarters, or on Website. Include SASE with requests for hard copy from SWE Headquarters. Applicants considered for all scholarships for which they are eligible and need submit only one application package. International students must have work authorization.

Amount of award:	$2,250
Number of awards:	4
Application deadline:	February 15

Contact:
Society of Women Engineers
230 E. Ohio Street
Suite 400
Chicago, IL 60611-3265
Phone: 312-596-5223
Fax: 312-596-5252
Web: www.swe.org

Admiral Grace Murray Hopper Scholarship

Type of award: Scholarship.
Intended use: For full-time freshman study at accredited 4-year institution in United States.
Eligibility: Applicant must be female, high school senior. Applicant must be U.S. citizen or permanent resident.
Basis for selection: Major/career interest in engineering. Applicant must demonstrate high academic achievement.
Application requirements: Recommendations, essay, transcript, proof of eligibility.
Additional information: Applicants must be enrolled or plan to be enrolled in ABET- or CSAB-accredited program or SWE-approved school. Preference given to computer-related engineering majors. Application forms available through deans of engineering at eligible schools, through SWE sections, SWE student sections, SWE Headquarters, or on Website. Include SASE with requests for hard copy from SWE Headquarters. Applicants considered for all scholarships for which they are eligible and need submit only one application package.

Amount of award:	$1,500
Number of awards:	5
Application deadline:	May 15
Notification begins:	September 15
Total amount awarded:	$7,500

Contact:
Society of Women Engineers
Scholarship Selection Committee
230 E. Ohio Street, Suite 400
Chicago, IL 60611-3265
Phone: 312-596-5223
Fax: 312-596-5252
Web: www.swe.org

Adobe Systems Computer Science Scholarships

Type of award: Scholarship.
Intended use: For full-time junior or senior study at accredited 4-year institution in United States. Designated institutions: SWE-approved schools.
Eligibility: Applicant must be female. Applicant must be U.S. citizen or permanent resident.
Basis for selection: Major/career interest in computer/information sciences. Applicant must demonstrate high academic achievement.
Application requirements: Recommendations, essay, transcript, proof of eligibility.
Additional information: Preference given to students attending selected San Francisco Bay Area schools and those majoring in computer science. Applicants must be enrolled or plan to be enrolled in an ABET- or CSAB-accredited program. Minimum 3.0 GPA. Application forms available through deans of engineering at eligible schools, through SWE sections, SWE student sections, SWE Headquarters, or on Website. Include SASE with requests for hard copy from SWE Headquarters.

Amount of award:	$1,500-$2,000
Number of awards:	2
Application deadline:	February 15
Notification begins:	June 15
Total amount awarded:	$3,500

Contact:
Society of Women Engineers
World Headquarters
230 E. Ohio Street, Suite 400
Chicago, IL 60611-3265
Phone: 312-596-5223
Fax: 312-596-5252
Web: www.swe.org

Anne Maureen Whitney Barrow Memorial

Type of award: Scholarship.
Intended use: For full-time undergraduate study at accredited 4-year institution in United States. Designated institutions: SWE-approved schools.
Eligibility: Applicant must be female, high school senior. Applicant must be U.S. citizen or permanent resident.
Basis for selection: Major/career interest in engineering.
Application requirements: Recommendations, essay, transcript, proof of eligibility.
Additional information: Minimum 3.0 GPA. Applicants must be enrolled or plan to be enrolled in an ABET- or CSAB-accredited program. Application forms available through deans of engineering at eligible schools, through SWE sections, SWE student sections, SWE Headquarters, or on Website. Include SASE with requests for hard copy from SWE Headquarters. Applicants considered for all scholarships for which they are eligible and need submit only one application package.

Amount of award:	$5,000
Number of awards:	1
Application deadline:	February 15, May 15
Notification begins:	June 15, September 15

Contact:
Society of Women Engineers
230 E. Ohio Street
Suite 400
Chicago, IL 60611-3265
Phone: 312-596-5223
Fax: 312-596-5252
Web: www.swe.org

B. J. Harrod Scholarships

Type of award: Scholarship.
Intended use: For full-time freshman study at accredited 4-year institution in United States.
Eligibility: Applicant must be female, high school senior. Applicant must be U.S. citizen or permanent resident.
Basis for selection: Major/career interest in engineering. Applicant must demonstrate high academic achievement.
Application requirements: Essay, transcript, proof of eligibility. Two letters of reference: one from a high school teacher, one from a person who knows the applicant, but not a family member.
Additional information: Applicants must be enrolled or plan to be enrolled in an ABET- or CSAB-accredited program. Application forms available through deans of engineering at eligible schools, through SWE sections, SWE student sections, SWE Headquarters, or on Website. Include SASE with requests for hard copy from SWE Headquarters. Applicants considered for all scholarships for which they are eligible and need submit only one application package.

Amount of award:	$4,000
Number of awards:	2
Application deadline:	May 15
Notification begins:	September 15
Total amount awarded:	$2,000

Contact:
Society of Women Engineers
World Headquarters
230 E. Ohio Street, Suite 400
Chicago, IL 60611-3265
Phone: 312-596-5223
Fax: 312-644-8557
Web: www.swe.org

B. K. Krenzer Reentry Scholarship

Type of award: Scholarship.
Intended use: For undergraduate or graduate study at accredited 4-year or graduate institution in United States.
Eligibility: Applicant must be female, returning adult student. Applicant must be U.S. citizen or permanent resident.
Basis for selection: Major/career interest in engineering. Applicant must demonstrate high academic achievement.
Application requirements: Recommendations, essay, transcript, proof of eligibility.
Additional information: Eligibility restricted to women who have been out of school for at least two years prior to reentry. Also open to women who have been out of engineering workforce and school at least two years. Preference given to degreed engineers. Applicants must be enrolled or plan to be enrolled in an ABET- or CSAB-accredited program. Application forms available through deans of engineering at eligible schools, through SWE sections, SWE student sections, SWE Headquarters, or on Website. Include SASE with requests for hard copy from SWE Headquarters. Applicants considered for all scholarships for which they are eligible and need submit only one application package.

Amount of award:	$2,000
Number of awards:	1
Application deadline:	February 15
Notification begins:	June 15
Total amount awarded:	$2,000

Contact:
Society of Women Engineers
World Headquarters
230 E. Ohio Street, Suite 400
Chicago, IL 60611-3265
Phone: 312-596-5223
Fax: 312-596-5252
Web: www.swe.org

Bechtel Foundation Scholarship

Type of award: Scholarship.
Intended use: For full-time sophomore, junior or senior study at accredited 4-year institution in United States.
Eligibility: Applicant or parent must be member/participant of Society of Women Engineers. Applicant must be female. Applicant must be U.S. citizen or permanent resident.
Basis for selection: Major/career interest in engineering, chemical; engineering, electrical/electronic; engineering, environmental; engineering, mechanical; engineering or architecture. Applicant must demonstrate high academic achievement.
Application requirements: Recommendations, essay, transcript, proof of eligibility.

Additional information: Architectural engineering majors also eligible to apply. Applicants must be enrolled or plan to be enrolled in an ABET- or CSAB-accredited program. Minimum 3.0 GPA. Application forms available through deans of engineering at eligible schools, through SWE sections, SWE student sections, SWE Headquarters, or on Website. Include SASE with requests for hard copy from SWE Headquarters. Applicants considered for all scholarships for which they are eligible and need submit only one application package.

Amount of award:	$1,400
Number of awards:	2
Application deadline:	February 15
Notification begins:	June 15
Total amount awarded:	$2,800

Contact:
Society of Women Engineers
World Headquarters
230 E. Ohio Street, Suite 400
Chicago, IL 60611-3265
Phone: 312-596-5223
Fax: 312-596-5252
Web: www.swe.org

Bertha Lamme Memorial Scholarship

Type of award: Scholarship.
Intended use: For full-time freshman study at 4-year institution in United States.
Eligibility: Applicant must be female. Applicant must be U.S. citizen.
Basis for selection: Major/career interest in engineering, electrical/electronic.
Additional information: Applicants must be enrolled or plan to be enrolled in an ABET- or CSAB-accredited program. Application forms available through deans of engineering at eligible schools, through SWE sections, SWE student sections, SWE Headquarters, or on Website. Include SASE with requests for hard copy from SWE Headquarters. Applicants considered for all scholarships for which they are eligible and need submit only one application package.

Amount of award:	$1,200
Number of awards:	1
Application deadline:	May 15
Notification begins:	September 15

Contact:
Society of Women Engineers
230 E. Ohio Street
Suite 400
Chicago, IL 60611-3265
Phone: 312-596-5223
Fax: 312-596-5252
Web: www.swe.org

Boston Scientific Scholarship

Type of award: Scholarship.
Intended use: For full-time senior study at 4-year institution in United States. Designated institutions: SWE-approved schools.
Eligibility: Applicant must be female. Applicant must be U.S. citizen or permanent resident.
Basis for selection: Major/career interest in engineering, chemical; computer/information sciences; engineering, electrical/electronic; engineering, mechanical or engineering, materials. Applicant must demonstrate high academic achievement.
Application requirements: Recommendations, essay, transcript, proof of eligibility.
Additional information: Minimum 3.5 GPA. Applicants must be enrolled or plan to be enrolled in an ABET- or CSAB-accredited program. Application forms available through deans of engineering at eligible schools, through SWE sections, SWE student sections, SWE Headquarters, or on Website. Include SASE with requests for hard copy from SWE headquarters. Applicants considered for all scholarships for which they are eligible and need submit only one application package.

Amount of award:	$5,000
Number of awards:	2
Application deadline:	February 15
Notification begins:	June 15

Contact:
Society of Women Engineers
230 E. Ohio Street
Suite 400
Chicago, IL 60611-3265
Phone: 312-596-5223
Fax: 312-596-5252
Web: www.swe.org

Caterpillar Inc. Scholarship

Type of award: Scholarship.
Intended use: For full-time undergraduate or graduate study at 4-year or graduate institution in United States. Designated institutions: SWE region C, D, H, or I schools (see Website for details).
Eligibility: Applicant must be female. Applicant must be U.S. citizen, permanent resident or international student.
Basis for selection: Major/career interest in engineering.
Application requirements: Recommendations, essay, transcript, proof of eligibility.
Additional information: Minimum 2.8 GPA. Applicants must be enrolled in or plan to be enrolled in ABET- or CSAB-accredited program. Application forms available through deans of engineering at eligible schools, through SWE sections, SWE student sections, SWE Headquarters, or on Website. Include SASE with requests for hard copy from SWE headquarters. International students must have work authorization. Applicants considered for all scholarships for which they are eligible and need submit only one application package.

Amount of award:	$2,400
Number of awards:	3
Application deadline:	February 15
Notification begins:	June 15

Contact:
Society of Women Engineers
230 E. Ohio Street
Suite 400
Chicago, IL 60611-3265
Phone: 312-596-5223
Fax: 312-596-5252
Web: www.swe.org

Central New Mexico Scholarship

Type of award: Scholarship, renewable.
Intended use: For sophomore, junior or senior study at 4-year institution.
Eligibility: Applicant must be female. Applicant must be residing in New Mexico.
Basis for selection: Major/career interest in engineering.
Additional information: Applicants re-entering school after two-year-plus absence eligible. Applicants must be enrolled in or plan to be enrolled in ABET- or CSAB-accredited program.

Application forms available through deans of engineering at eligible schools, through SWE sections, SWE student sections, SWE Headquarters, or on Website. Include SASE with requests for hard copy from SWE headquarters. Applicants considered for all scholarships for which they are eligible and need submit only one application package.

Amount of award:	$1,250
Number of awards:	2
Application deadline:	February 15

Contact:
Society of Women Engineers
230 E. Ohio Street
Suite 400
Chicago, IL 60611-3265
Phone: 312-596-5228
Fax: 312-596-5252
Web: www.swe.org/scholarships

Chevron Corporation Scholarships

Type of award: Scholarship.
Intended use: For full-time sophomore or junior study at accredited 4-year institution in United States.
Eligibility: Applicant or parent must be member/participant of Society of Women Engineers. Applicant must be female.
Basis for selection: Major/career interest in engineering, civil; engineering, chemical; engineering, petroleum; engineering, mechanical; engineering, electrical/electronic or computer/information sciences. Applicant must demonstrate high academic achievement.
Application requirements: Recommendations, essay, transcript, proof of eligibility.
Additional information: Applicant must be active SWE student member. Applicants must be enrolled or plan to be enrolled in ABET- or CSAB-accredited program. Minimum 3.5 GPA. Application forms available through deans of engineering at eligible schools, through SWE sections, SWE student sections, SWE Headquarters, or on Website. Include SASE with requests for hard copy from SWE Headquarters. Applicants considered for all scholarships for which they are eligible and need submit only one application package.

Amount of award:	$2,000
Number of awards:	8
Application deadline:	February 15
Notification begins:	June 15
Total amount awarded:	$16,000

Contact:
Society of Women Engineers
World Headquarters
230 E. Ohio Street, Suite 400
Chicago, IL 60611-3265
Phone: 312-596-5223
Fax: 312-596-5252
Web: www.swe.org

DaimlerChrysler Corporation Fund Scholarships

Type of award: Scholarship, renewable.
Intended use: For full-time sophomore study at accredited 4-year institution in United States.
Eligibility: Applicant must be female. Applicant must be U.S. citizen or permanent resident.
Basis for selection: Major/career interest in engineering, electrical/electronic or engineering, mechanical. Applicant must demonstrate high academic achievement.

Application requirements: Recommendations, essay, transcript, proof of eligibility.
Additional information: Applicants must be enrolled or plan to be enrolled in ABET- or CSAB-accredited program. Minimum 3.0 GPA. Application forms available through deans of engineering at eligible schools, through SWE sections, SWE student sections, SWE Headquarters, or on Website. Include SASE with requests for hard copy from SWE Headquarters. Applicants considered for all scholarships for which they are eligible and need submit only one application package.

Amount of award:	$2,000
Number of awards:	1
Application deadline:	February 15
Notification begins:	June 15

Contact:
Society of Women Engineers
World Headquarters
230 E. Ohio Street, Suite 400
Chicago, IL 60611-3265
Phone: 312-596-5223
Fax: 312-596-5252
Web: www.swe.org

Dell Inc. Scholarship

Type of award: Scholarship.
Intended use: For full-time junior or senior study at 4-year institution in United States or Canada.
Eligibility: Applicant must be female. Applicant must be U.S. citizen or permanent resident.
Basis for selection: Major/career interest in engineering, electrical/electronic; engineering, computer; engineering, mechanical or computer/information sciences. Applicant must demonstrate financial need.
Application requirements: Recommendations, essay, transcript, proof of eligibility.
Additional information: Minimum 3.0 GPA. Applicants must be enrolled or plan to be enrolled in an ABET- or CSAB-accredited program. Application forms available through deans of engineering at eligible schools, through SWE sections, SWE student sections, SWE Headquarters, or on Website. Include SASE with requests for hard copy from SWE Headquarters. Applicants considered for all scholarships for which they are eligible and need submit only one application package.

Amount of award:	$2,250
Number of awards:	2
Application deadline:	February 15
Notification begins:	June 15

Contact:
Society of Women Engineers
230 E. Ohio Street
Suite 400
Chicago, IL 60611-3265
Phone: 312-596-5223
Fax: 312-596-5252
Web: www.swe.org

Dorothy Lemke Howarth Scholarships

Type of award: Scholarship.
Intended use: For full-time sophomore study at accredited 4-year institution.
Eligibility: Applicant must be female. Applicant must be U.S. citizen.
Basis for selection: Major/career interest in engineering. Applicant must demonstrate high academic achievement.

Application requirements: Recommendations, essay, transcript, proof of eligibility.
Additional information: Applicants must be enrolled or plan to be enrolled in ABET- or CSAB-accredited program. Minimum 3.0 GPA. Application forms available through deans of engineering at eligible schools, through SWE sections, SWE student sections, SWE Headquarters, or on Website. Include SASE with requests for hard copy from SWE Headquarters. Applicants considered for all scholarships for which they are eligible and need submit only one application package.

Amount of award:	$2,500
Number of awards:	5
Application deadline:	February 15
Notification begins:	June 15
Total amount awarded:	$12,500

Contact:
Society of Women Engineers
World Headquarters
230 E. Ohio Street, Suite 400
Chicago, IL 60611-3265
Phone: 312-596-5223
Fax: 312-596-5252
Web: www.swe.org

Dorothy M. & Earl S. Hoffman Scholarships

Type of award: Scholarship, renewable.
Intended use: For full-time freshman study at accredited 4-year institution in United States. Designated institutions: Bucknell University and Rensselaer Polytechnic University.
Eligibility: Applicant must be female, high school senior. Applicant must be U.S. citizen or permanent resident.
Basis for selection: Major/career interest in engineering. Applicant must demonstrate high academic achievement.
Application requirements: Recommendations, essay, transcript, proof of eligibility.
Additional information: Applicants must be enrolled or plan to be enrolled in ABET- or CSAB-accredited program. Application forms available through deans of engineering at eligible schools, through SWE sections, SWE student sections, SWE Headquarters, or on Website. Include SASE with requests for hard copy from SWE headquarters. Applicants considered for all scholarships for which they are eligible and need submit only one application package.

Amount of award:	$3,000
Number of awards:	5
Application deadline:	May 15
Notification begins:	September 15

Contact:
Society of Women Engineers
World Headquarters
230 E. Ohio Street, Suite 400
Chicago, IL 60611-3265
Phone: 312-596-5223
Fax: 312-644-8557
Web: www.swe.org

Dorothy P. Morris Scholarship

Type of award: Scholarship.
Intended use: For full-time sophomore, junior or senior study at 4-year institution in United States.
Eligibility: Applicant must be female. Applicant must be U.S. citizen.
Basis for selection: Major/career interest in engineering.
Application requirements: Recommendations, essay, transcript, proof of eligibility.
Additional information: Minimum 3.0 GPA. Applicants must be enrolled or plan to be enrolled in an ABET- or CSAB-accredited program. Application forms available through deans of engineering at eligible schools, through SWE sections, SWE student sections, SWE Headquarters, or on Website. Include SASE with requests for hard copy from SWE Headquarters. Applicants considered for all scholarships for which they are eligible and need submit only one application package.

Amount of award:	$1,000
Number of awards:	1
Application deadline:	February 15
Notification begins:	June 15

Contact:
Society of Women Engineers
230 E. Ohio Street
Suite 400
Chicago, IL 60611-3265
Phone: 312-596-5223
Fax: 312-596-5252
Web: www.swe.org

DuPont Company Scholarship

Type of award: Scholarship.
Intended use: For full-time sophomore, junior or senior study at 4-year institution in United States. Designated institutions: Eastern U.S. institutions.
Eligibility: Applicant must be female. Applicant must be U.S. citizen or permanent resident.
Basis for selection: Major/career interest in engineering, chemical or engineering, mechanical.
Additional information: Minimum 3.0 GPA. Applicants must be enrolled or plan to be enrolled in ABET- or CSAB-accredited program. Application forms available through deans of engineering at eligible schools, through SWE sections, SWE student sections, SWE Headquarters, or on Website. Include SASE with requests for hard copy from SWE headquarters. Applicants considered for all scholarships for which they are eligible and need submit only one application package.

Amount of award:	$1,000
Number of awards:	2
Application deadline:	February 15
Notification begins:	June 15

Contact:
Society of Women Engineers
230 E. Ohio Street
Suite 400
Chicago, IL 60611-3265
Phone: 312-596-5223
Fax: 312-596-5252
Web: www.swe.org

Electronics for Imaging Scholarship

Type of award: Scholarship.
Intended use: For sophomore, junior, senior or graduate study at 4-year or graduate institution in United States. Designated institutions: Approved institutions (visit Website for list).
Eligibility: Applicant must be female.
Basis for selection: Major/career interest in engineering.
Additional information: Minimum 3.0 GPA. Application forms available through deans of engineering at eligible schools, through SWE sections, SWE student sections, SWE Headquarters, or on Website. Include SASE with requests for hard copy from SWE headquarters. Applicants considered for

all scholarships for which they are eligible and need submit only one application package.

Amount of award:	$4,000
Number of awards:	4
Application deadline:	February 15

Contact:
Society of Women Engineers
230 E. Ohio St
Suite 400
Chicago, IL 60611
Phone: 312-596-5223
Fax: 312-596-5252
Web: www.swe.org/scholarships

Elizabeth McLean Memorial Scholarship

Type of award: Scholarship.
Intended use: For sophomore, junior or senior study at accredited 4-year institution in United States.
Eligibility: Applicant must be female.
Basis for selection: Major/career interest in engineering, civil.
Additional information: Minimum 3.0 GPA. Application forms available through deans of engineering at eligible schools, through SWE sections, SWE student sections, SWE Headquarters, or on Website. Include SASE with requests for hard copy from SWE headquarters. Applicants considered for all scholarships for which they are eligible and need submit only one application package.

Amount of award:	$1,000
Number of awards:	1
Application deadline:	February 15

Contact:
Society of Women Engineers
230 East Ohio St
Suite 400
Chicago, IL 60611
Phone: 312-596-5223
Fax: 312-596-5252
Web: www.swe.org/scholarships

Exelon Scholarship

Type of award: Scholarship.
Intended use: For full-time freshman study at 4-year institution in United States or Canada.
Eligibility: Applicant must be female, high school senior. Applicant must be U.S. citizen or permanent resident.
Basis for selection: Major/career interest in engineering.
Additional information: Applicants must be enrolled or plan to be enrolled in an ABET- or CSAB-accredited program. Application forms available through deans of engineering at eligible schools, through SWE sections, SWE student sections, SWE Headquarters, or on Website. Include SASE with requests for hard copy from SWE headquarters. Applicants considered for all scholarships for which they are eligible and need submit only one application package.

Amount of award:	$1,000
Number of awards:	5
Application deadline:	May 15
Notification begins:	September 15

Contact:
Society of Women Engineers
230 E. Ohio Street
Suite 400
Chicago, IL 60611-3265
Phone: 312-596-5223
Fax: 312-596-5252
Web: www.swe.org

Ford Motor Company Scholarship

Type of award: Scholarship.
Intended use: For sophomore or junior study at accredited 4-year or graduate institution.
Eligibility: Applicant must be female.
Basis for selection: Major/career interest in engineering, electrical/electronic; engineering, mechanical; automotive technology or manufacturing. Applicant must demonstrate leadership.
Additional information: Minimum 3.5 GPA. Applicants must be enrolled or plan to be enrolled in ABET- or CSAB-accredited program. Application forms available through deans of engineering at eligible schools, through SWE sections, SWE student sections, SWE Headquarters, or on Website. Include SASE with requests for hard copy from SWE headquarters. Applicants considered for all scholarships for which they are eligible and need submit only one application package.

Amount of award:	$1,000
Number of awards:	2
Application deadline:	February 15
Notification begins:	June 15

Contact:
Society of Women Engineers
230 E. Ohio Street
Suite 400
Chicago, IL 60611
Phone: 312-596-5223
Fax: 312-644-8557
Web: www.swe.org

General Electric Foundation Scholarship

Type of award: Scholarship.
Intended use: For full-time freshman study at 4-year institution in United States or Canada.
Eligibility: Applicant must be female, high school senior. Applicant must be U.S. citizen.
Basis for selection: Major/career interest in engineering.
Additional information: Applicants must be enrolled or plan to be enrolled in an ABET- or CSAB-accredited program. Scholarship includes travel grant for SWE National Conference. Application forms available through deans of engineering at eligible schools, through SWE sections, SWE student sections, SWE Headquarters, or on Website. Include SASE with requests for hard copy from SWE headquarters. Applicants considered for all scholarships for which they are eligible and need submit only one application package.

Amount of award:	$1,250
Number of awards:	3
Application deadline:	May 15
Notification begins:	September 15

Contact:
Society of Women Engineers
230 E. Ohio Street
Suite 400
Chicago, IL 60611-3265
Phone: 312-596-5223
Fax: 312-596-5252
Web: www.swe.org

General Electric Women's Network Scholarship

Type of award: Scholarship.
Intended use: For sophomore, junior or senior study at accredited 4-year institution in United States. Designated institutions: SWE-approved schools.
Eligibility: Applicant must be female. Applicant must be U.S. citizen.
Basis for selection: Major/career interest in engineering.
Additional information: Minimum 3.0 GPA. Application forms available through deans of engineering at eligible schools, through SWE sections, SWE student sections, SWE Headquarters, or on Website. Include SASE with requests for hard copy from SWE headquarters. Applicants considered for all scholarships for which they are eligible and need submit only one application package.

Amount of award:	$2,425
Number of awards:	13
Application deadline:	February 15

Contact:
Society of Women Engineers
230 East Ohio St.
Suite 400
Chicago, IL 60611
Phone: 312-596-5223
Fax: 312-596-5252
Web: www.swe.org/scholarships

General Motors Foundation Scholarships

Type of award: Scholarship, renewable.
Intended use: For full-time sophomore or junior study at accredited 4-year institution in United States. Designated institutions: SWE-approved schools.
Eligibility: Applicant must be female. Applicant must be U.S. citizen or permanent resident.
Basis for selection: Major/career interest in engineering; automotive technology; engineering, electrical/electronic; engineering, mechanical; engineering, chemical; engineering, materials or manufacturing. Applicant must demonstrate financial need, high academic achievement and leadership.
Application requirements: Recommendations, essay, transcript, proof of eligibility.
Additional information: Industrial engineering and manufacturing engineering majors also eligible to apply. Applicants must be enrolled or plan to be enrolled in ABET- or CSAB-accredited program. Applicants should have career interest in automotive industry or manufacturing. Foundation provides travel grant to attend SWE National Convention and Student Conference. Minimum 3.5 GPA. Application forms available through deans of engineering at eligible schools, through SWE sections, SWE student sections, SWE Headquarters, or on Website. Include SASE with requests for hard copy from SWE headquarters. Applicants considered for all scholarships for which they are eligible and need submit only one application package.

Amount of award:	$1,225-$3,000
Number of awards:	2
Application deadline:	February 15
Notification begins:	June 15

Contact:
Society of Women Engineers
World Headquarters
230 E. Ohio Street, Suite 400
Chicago, IL 60611-3265
Phone: 312-596-5223
Fax: 312-644-8557
Web: www.swe.org

Goldman, Sachs and Co. Scholarship

Type of award: Scholarship.
Intended use: For junior or senior study at accredited 4-year institution in United States.
Eligibility: Applicant or parent must be member/participant of Society of Women Engineers. Applicant must be female.
Basis for selection: Major/career interest in engineering, computer; engineering, electrical/electronic or computer/information sciences.
Additional information: Minimum 3.2 GPA. Applicants must be enrolled in or plan to be enrolled in ABET- or CSAB-accredited program. Application forms available through deans of engineering at eligible schools, through SWE sections, SWE student sections, SWE Headquarters, or on Website. Include SASE with requests for hard copy from SWE headquarters. Applicants considered for all scholarships for which they are eligible and need submit only one application package.

Amount of award:	$2,000
Number of awards:	4
Application deadline:	February 15

Contact:
Society of Women Engineers
230 East Ohio St.
Suite 400
Chicago, IL 60611
Phone: 312-596-5223
Fax: 312-596-5252
Web: www.swe.org/scholarships

Honeywell International Inc. Scholarship

Type of award: Scholarship.
Intended use: For sophomore or junior study at accredited 4-year institution in United States.
Eligibility: Applicant must be female. Applicant must be U.S. citizen.
Basis for selection: Major/career interest in engineering, chemical; engineering, computer; engineering, electrical/electronic; engineering, mechanical; engineering, materials; computer/information sciences; aerospace; architecture or manufacturing. Applicant must demonstrate financial need.
Additional information: Minimum 3.0 GPA. Architectural, industrial, and manufacturing engineering majors also eligible. Applicants must be enrolled in or plan to be enrolled in ABET- or CSAB-accredited program. Application forms available through deans of engineering at eligible schools, through SWE sections, SWE student sections, SWE Headquarters, or on Website. Include SASE with requests for hard copy from SWE headquarters. Applicants considered for all scholarships for which they are eligible and need submit only one application package.

Society of Women Engineers: Honeywell International Inc. Scholarship

Amount of award: $5,000
Number of awards: 2
Application deadline: February 15
Contact:
Society of Women Engineers
230 East Ohio St.
Suite 400
Chicago, IL 60611
Phone: 312-596-5223
Fax: 312-596-5252
Web: www.swe.org/scholarships

IBM Corporation Scholarship

Type of award: Scholarship.
Intended use: For sophomore or junior study at accredited 4-year institution in United States.
Eligibility: Applicant must be female. Applicant must be U.S. citizen, permanent resident or international student.
Basis for selection: Major/career interest in engineering, electrical/electronic; engineering, computer or computer/information sciences.
Additional information: Applicants must be enrolled or plan to be enrolled in ABET- or CSAB-accredited program. Minimum 3.4 GPA. Application forms available through deans of engineering at eligible schools, through SWE sections, SWE student sections, SWE Headquarters, or on Website. Applicants considered for all scholarships for which they are eligible and need submit only one application package. International students must have work authorization.

Amount of award: $1,000
Number of awards: 4
Application deadline: February 15
Contact:
Society of Women Engineers
230 East Ohio St.
Suite 400
Chicago, IL 60611
Phone: 312-596-5223
Fax: 312-596-5252
Web: www.swe.org/scholarships

Ivy Parker Memorial Scholarship

Type of award: Scholarship.
Intended use: For full-time junior or senior study at accredited 4-year institution in United States.
Eligibility: Applicant must be female. Applicant must be U.S. citizen or permanent resident.
Basis for selection: Major/career interest in engineering. Applicant must demonstrate financial need and high academic achievement.
Application requirements: Recommendations, essay, transcript, proof of eligibility.
Additional information: Applicants must be enrolled or plan to be enrolled in ABET- or CSAB-accredited program. Minimum 3.0 GPA. Application forms available through deans of engineering at eligible schools, through SWE sections, SWE student sections, SWE Headquarters, or on Website. Include SASE with requests for hard copy from SWE headquarters. Applicants considered for all scholarships for which they are eligible and need submit only one application package.

Amount of award: $2,500
Number of awards: 1
Application deadline: February 15
Notification begins: June 15
Total amount awarded: $2,500

Contact:
Society of Women Engineers
World Headquarters
230 E. Ohio Street, Suite 400
Chicago, IL 60611-3265
Phone: 312-596-5223
Fax: 312-596-5252
Web: www.swe.org

Jill S. Tietjen P.E. Scholarship

Type of award: Scholarship.
Intended use: For sophomore, junior or senior study at accredited 4-year institution in United States.
Eligibility: Applicant must be female. Applicant must be U.S. citizen.
Basis for selection: Major/career interest in engineering.
Additional information: Applicants must be enrolled or plan to be enrolled in ABET- or CSAB-accredited program. All engineering majors eligible. Minimum 3.0 GPA. Application forms available through deans of engineering at eligible schools, through SWE sections, SWE student sections, SWE Headquarters, or on Website. Include SASE with requests for hard copy from SWE headquarters. Applicants considered for all scholarships for which they are eligible and need submit only one application package.

Amount of award: $1,500
Number of awards: 1
Application deadline: February 15
Contact:
Society of Women Engineers
230 East Ohio St.
Suite 400
Chicago, IL 60611
Phone: 312-596-5223
Fax: 312-596-5252
Web: www.swe.org/scholarships

Judith Resnik Memorial Scholarship

Type of award: Scholarship.
Intended use: For full-time junior or senior study at accredited 4-year institution.
Eligibility: Applicant or parent must be member/participant of Society of Women Engineers. Applicant must be female. Applicant must be U.S. citizen or permanent resident.
Basis for selection: Major/career interest in engineering or aerospace. Applicant must demonstrate high academic achievement.
Application requirements: Recommendations, essay, transcript, proof of eligibility.
Additional information: Must be aeronautical/aerospace engineering or astronautical engineering major. Applicants must be enrolled or plan to be enrolled in ABET- or CSAB-accredited program. Applicant must be SWE student member. Minimum 3.0 GPA. Application forms available through deans of engineering at eligible schools, through SWE sections, SWE student sections, SWE Headquarters, or on Website. Include SASE with requests for hard copy from SWE headquarters. Applicants considered for all scholarships for which they are eligible and need submit only one application package.

Amount of award: $2,500
Number of awards: 1
Application deadline: February 15
Notification begins: June 15
Total amount awarded: $2,500

Contact:
Society of Women Engineers
World Headquarters
230 E. Ohio Street, Suite 400
Chicago, IL 60611-3265
Phone: 312-596-5223
Fax: 312-596-5252
Web: www.swe.org

Lillian Moller Gilbreth Scholarship

Type of award: Scholarship.
Intended use: For full-time junior or senior study at accredited 4-year institution in United States.
Eligibility: Applicant must be female. Applicant must be U.S. citizen or permanent resident.
Basis for selection: Major/career interest in engineering. Applicant must demonstrate high academic achievement.
Application requirements: Recommendations, essay, transcript, proof of eligibility.
Additional information: Applicants must be enrolled or plan to be enrolled in ABET- or CSAB-accredited program. Minimum 3.0 GPA. Application forms available through deans of engineering at eligible schools, through SWE sections, SWE student sections, SWE Headquarters, or on Website. Include SASE with requests for hard copy from SWE headquarters. Applicants considered for all scholarships for which they are eligible and need submit only one application package.

Amount of award:	$10,000
Number of awards:	1
Application deadline:	February 15
Notification begins:	June 15
Total amount awarded:	$10,000

Contact:
Society of Women Engineers
World Headquarters
230 E. Ohio Street, Suite 400
Chicago, IL 60611-3265
Phone: 312-596-5223
Fax: 312-596-5252
Web: www.swe.org

Lockheed Martin Aeronautics Company Scholarships

Type of award: Scholarship.
Intended use: For full-time junior study at accredited 4-year institution in United States.
Eligibility: Applicant must be female. Applicant must be U.S. citizen or permanent resident.
Basis for selection: Major/career interest in engineering, electrical/electronic or engineering, mechanical. Applicant must demonstrate high academic achievement.
Application requirements: Recommendations, essay, transcript, proof of eligibility.
Additional information: Awards given to one student in each of above majors. Applicants must be enrolled or plan to be enrolled in an ABET- or CSAB-accredited program. Minimum 3.5 GPA. Application forms available through deans of engineering at eligible schools, through SWE sections, SWE student sections, SWE Headquarters, or on Website. Include SASE with requests for hard copy from SWE headquarters. Applicants considered for all scholarships for which they are eligible and need submit only one application package.

Amount of award:	$1,500
Number of awards:	2
Application deadline:	February 15
Notification begins:	June 15
Total amount awarded:	$3,000

Contact:
Society of Women Engineers
World Headquarters
230 E. Ohio Street, Suite 400
Chicago, IL 60611-3265
Phone: 312-596-5223
Fax: 312-596-5252
Web: www.swe.org

Lockheed Martin Foundation Scholarships

Type of award: Scholarship.
Intended use: For full-time freshman study at accredited 4-year institution in United States.
Eligibility: Applicant must be female, high school senior. Applicant must be U.S. citizen or permanent resident.
Basis for selection: Major/career interest in engineering. Applicant must demonstrate high academic achievement.
Application requirements: Recommendations, essay, transcript, proof of eligibility.
Additional information: Includes travel grant for SWE National Conference. Applicants must be enrolled or plan to be enrolled in an ABET- or CSAB-accredited program. Application forms available through deans of engineering at eligible schools, through SWE sections, SWE student sections, SWE Headquarters, or on Website. Include SASE with requests for hard copy from SWE headquarters. Applicants considered for all scholarships for which they are eligible and need only submit one application package.

Amount of award:	$3,000
Number of awards:	2
Application deadline:	May 15
Notification begins:	September 15
Total amount awarded:	$6,000

Contact:
Society of Women Engineers
World Headquarters
230 E. Ohio Street, Suite 400
Chicago, IL 60611-3265
Phone: 312-596-5223
Fax: 312-596-5252
Web: www.swe.org

MASWE Scholarships

Type of award: Scholarship.
Intended use: For full-time sophomore, junior or senior study at accredited 4-year institution in United States.
Eligibility: Applicant must be female. Applicant must be U.S. citizen or permanent resident.
Basis for selection: Major/career interest in engineering. Applicant must demonstrate financial need and high academic achievement.
Application requirements: Recommendations, essay, transcript, proof of eligibility.
Additional information: Applicants must be enrolled or plan to be enrolled in ABET- or CSAB-accredited program. Minimum 3.0 GPA. Application forms available through deans of engineering at eligible schools, through SWE sections, SWE student sections, SWE Headquarters, or on Website. Include SASE with requests for hard copy from SWE headquarters.

Society of Women Engineers: MASWE Scholarships

Applicants considered for all scholarships for which they are eligible and need submit only one application package.
- **Amount of award:** $2,000
- **Number of awards:** 4
- **Application deadline:** February 15
- **Notification begins:** June 15
- **Total amount awarded:** $8,000

Contact:
Society of Women Engineers
World Headquarters
230 E. Ohio Street, Suite 400
Chicago, IL 60611-3265
Phone: 312-596-5223
Fax: 312-596-5252
Web: www.swe.org

Meridith Thoms Memorial Scholarships

Type of award: Scholarship.
Intended use: For full-time sophomore, junior or senior study at accredited 4-year institution in United States.
Eligibility: Applicant must be female. Applicant must be U.S. citizen or permanent resident.
Basis for selection: Major/career interest in engineering. Applicant must demonstrate high academic achievement.
Application requirements: Recommendations, essay, transcript, proof of eligibility.
Additional information: Minimum GPA 3.0. Applicants must be enrolled or plan to be enrolled in an ABET- or CSAB-accredited program. Application forms available through deans of engineering at eligible schools, through SWE sections, SWE student sections, SWE Headquarters, or on Website. Include SASE with requests for hard copy from SWE headquarters. Applicants considered for all scholarships for which they are eligible and need submit only one application package.
- **Amount of award:** $2,000
- **Number of awards:** 6
- **Application deadline:** February 15
- **Notification begins:** June 15
- **Total amount awarded:** $12,000

Contact:
Society of Women Engineers
World Headquarters
230 E. Ohio Street, Suite 400
Chicago, IL 60611-3265
Phone: 312-596-5223
Fax: 312-596-5252
Web: www.swe.org

Microsoft Corporation Scholarships

Type of award: Scholarship.
Intended use: For full-time sophomore, junior, senior or master's study at accredited 4-year institution in United States.
Eligibility: Applicant must be female. Applicant must be U.S. citizen or permanent resident.
Basis for selection: Major/career interest in engineering, computer or computer/information sciences. Applicant must demonstrate high academic achievement.
Application requirements: Recommendations, essay, transcript, proof of eligibility.
Additional information: Master's students eligible only in first year. Applicants must be enrolled or plan to be enrolled in an ABET- or CSAB-accredited program. Minimum 3.5 GPA. Application forms available through deans of engineering at eligible schools, through SWE sections, SWE student sections, SWE Headquarters, or on Website. Include SASE with requests for hard copy from SWE headquarters. Applicants considered for all scholarships for which they are eligible and need submit only one application package.
- **Amount of award:** $2,500
- **Number of awards:** 2
- **Application deadline:** February 15
- **Notification begins:** June 15
- **Total amount awarded:** $5,000

Contact:
Society of Women Engineers
World Headquarters
230 E. Ohio Street, Suite 400
Chicago, IL 60611-3265
Phone: 312-596-5223
Fax: 312-644-8557
Web: www.swe.org

New Jersey Scholarship

Type of award: Scholarship.
Intended use: For full-time freshman study at accredited 4-year institution in United States.
Eligibility: Applicant must be female, high school senior. Applicant must be U.S. citizen or permanent resident residing in New Jersey.
Basis for selection: Major/career interest in engineering. Applicant must demonstrate high academic achievement.
Application requirements: Recommendations, essay, transcript, proof of eligibility.
Additional information: Applicants must be enrolled or plan to be enrolled in an ABET- or CSAB-accredited program. Application forms available through deans of engineering at eligible schools, through SWE sections, SWE student sections, SWE Headquarters, or on Website. Include SASE with requests for hard copy from SWE headquarters. Applicants considered for all scholarships for which they are eligible and need submit only one application package.
- **Amount of award:** $1,500
- **Number of awards:** 1
- **Application deadline:** May 15
- **Notification begins:** September 15
- **Total amount awarded:** $1,500

Contact:
Society of Women Engineers
World Headquarters
230 E. Ohio Street, Suite 400
Chicago, IL 60611-3265
Phone: 312-596-5223
Fax: 312-644-8557
Web: www.swe.org

Northrop Grumman Corporation Scholarship

Type of award: Scholarship.
Intended use: For full-time freshman study at accredited 4-year institution in United States.
Eligibility: Applicant must be female. Applicant must be U.S. citizen or permanent resident.
Basis for selection: Major/career interest in engineering, materials; engineering, chemical; engineering, computer; computer/information sciences or engineering, electrical/electronic. Applicant must demonstrate high academic achievement.
Application requirements: Recommendations, essay, transcript, proof of eligibility.

Additional information: Minimum 3.0 GPA. Applicants must be enrolled or plan to be enrolled in ABET- or CSAB-accredited program. Application forms available through deans of engineering at eligible schools, through SWE sections, SWE student sections, SWE Headquarters, or on Website. Include SASE with requests for hard copy from SWE headquarters. Applicants considered for all scholarships for which they are eligible and need submit only one application package.

Amount of award:	$5,000
Number of awards:	3
Application deadline:	May 15
Notification begins:	September 15

Contact:
Society of Women Engineers
230 E. Ohio Street
Suite 400
Chicago, IL 60611-3265
Phone: 312-596-5223
Fax: 312-596-5252
Web: www.swe.org

Olive Lynn Salembier Reentry Scholarship

Type of award: Scholarship.
Intended use: For undergraduate or graduate study at accredited 4-year or graduate institution in United States.
Eligibility: Applicant must be female, returning adult student. Applicant must be U.S. citizen or permanent resident.
Basis for selection: Major/career interest in engineering.
Application requirements: Recommendations, essay, transcript, proof of eligibility.
Additional information: Must have been out of school or engineering workforce at least two years prior to reentry. Applicants must be enrolled or plan to be enrolled in ABET- or CSAB-accredited program. Minimum 3.0 GPA after first year of reentry. Application forms available through deans of engineering at eligible schools, through SWE sections, SWE student sections, SWE Headquarters, or on Website. Include SASE with requests for hard copy from SWE headquarters. Applicants considered for all scholarships for which they are eligible and need submit only one application package.

Amount of award:	$2,000
Number of awards:	1
Application deadline:	February 15
Notification begins:	June 15
Total amount awarded:	$2,000

Contact:
Society of Women Engineers
World Headquarters
230 E. Ohio Street, Suite 400
Chicago, IL 60611-3265
Phone: 312-596-5223
Fax: 312-644-8557
Web: www.swe.org

Past Presidents Scholarships

Type of award: Scholarship.
Intended use: For full-time undergraduate or graduate study at accredited 4-year or graduate institution in United States.
Eligibility: Applicant must be female. Applicant must be U.S. citizen.
Basis for selection: Major/career interest in engineering. Applicant must demonstrate high academic achievement.
Application requirements: Recommendations, essay, transcript, proof of eligibility.

Additional information: Minimum 3.0 GPA. Applicants must be enrolled or plan to be enrolled in an ABET- or CSAB-accredited program. Application forms available through deans of engineering at eligible schools, through SWE sections, SWE student sections, SWE Headquarters, or on Website. Include SASE with requests for hard copy from SWE headquarters. Applicants considered for all scholarships for which they are eligible therefore need only submit one application package.

Amount of award:	$2,000
Number of awards:	2
Application deadline:	February 15
Notification begins:	June 15
Total amount awarded:	$4,000

Contact:
Society of Women Engineers
World Headquarters
230 E. Ohio Street, Suite 400
Chicago, IL 60611-3265
Phone: 312-596-5223
Fax: 312-644-8557
Web: www.swe.org

Phoenix Section Scholarship

Type of award: Scholarship.
Intended use: For full-time freshman study at accredited 4-year institution in United States.
Eligibility: Applicant must be high school senior. Applicant must be U.S. citizen or permanent resident residing in Arizona.
Basis for selection: Major/career interest in engineering. Applicant must demonstrate high academic achievement.
Application requirements: Recommendations, essay, transcript, proof of eligibility.
Additional information: Must be Arizona resident or attending school in Arizona. Applicants must be enrolled or plan to be enrolled in an ABET- or CSAB-accredited program. Application forms available through deans of engineering at eligible schools, through SWE sections, SWE student sections, SWE Headquarters, or on Website. Include SASE with requests for hard copy from SWE headquarters. Applicants considered for all scholarships for which they are eligible and need submit only one application package.

Amount of award:	$1,000
Number of awards:	2
Application deadline:	May 15
Notification begins:	September 15

Contact:
Society of Women Engineers
230 E. Ohio Street
Suite 400
Chicago, IL 60611-3265
Phone: 312-596-5223
Fax: 312-596-5252
Web: www.swe.org

Rockwell Automation Scholarships

Type of award: Scholarship.
Intended use: For full-time junior or senior study at accredited 4-year institution in United States. Designated institutions: SWE-approved schools.
Eligibility: Applicant must be female. Applicant must be U.S. citizen or permanent resident.
Basis for selection: Major/career interest in engineering; engineering, computer; engineering, electrical/electronic; engineering, mechanical; computer/information sciences or manufacturing. Applicant must demonstrate leadership.

Application requirements: Recommendations, essay, transcript, proof of eligibility.
Additional information: Applicants must be enrolled or plan to be enrolled in ABET- or CSAB-accredited program. Minimum 3.0 GPA. Application forms available through deans of engineering at eligible schools, through SWE sections, SWE student sections, SWE Headquarters, or on Website. Include SASE with requests for hard copy from SWE headquarters. Applicants considered for all scholarships for which they are eligible and need submit only one application package.

Amount of award:	$2,500
Number of awards:	2
Application deadline:	February 15
Notification begins:	June 15
Total amount awarded:	$5,000

Contact:
Society of Women Engineers
World Headquarters
230 E. Ohio Street, Suite 400
Chicago, IL 60611-3265
Phone: 312-596-5223
Fax: 312-596-5252
Web: www.swe.org

Susan Miszkowitz Memorial Scholarship

Type of award: Scholarship.
Intended use: For full-time sophomore, junior, senior or graduate study at accredited 4-year institution in United States.
Eligibility: Applicant must be female. Applicant must be U.S. citizen or permanent resident.
Basis for selection: Major/career interest in engineering. Applicant must demonstrate high academic achievement.
Additional information: Minimum 3.0 GPA. Applicants must be enrolled or plan to be enrolled in an ABET- or CSAB-accredited program. Application forms available through deans of engineering at eligible schools, through SWE sections, SWE student sections, SWE Headquarters, or on Website. Include SASE with requests for hard copy from SWE headquarters. Applicants considered for all scholarships for which they are eligible and need submit only one application package.

Amount of award:	$1,500
Number of awards:	1
Application deadline:	February 15
Notification begins:	June 15

Contact:
Society of Women Engineers
230 E. Ohio Street
Suite 400
Chicago, IL 60611-3265
Phone: 312-596-5223
Fax: 312-596-5252
Web: www.swe.org

Soil and Water Conservation Society

Donald A. Williams Soil Conservation Scholarship

Type of award: Scholarship.
Intended use: For undergraduate study.
Basis for selection: Major/career interest in natural resources/conservation. Applicant must demonstrate financial need, depth of character and seriousness of purpose.
Additional information: Applicant must have been member of Soil and Water Conservation Society for at least one year at time of application. Must demonstrate competence in line of work. Must have completed at least one year of full-time employment and be currently employed in a natural resource conservation endeavor. Send SASE or visit Website for application.

Amount of award:	$1,500
Number of awards:	1
Number of applicants:	3
Application deadline:	February 13
Total amount awarded:	$1,500

Contact:
Soil and Water Conservation Society
945 SW Ankeny Road
Ankeny, IA 50021
Phone: 515-289-2331
Fax: 515-289-1227
Web: www.swcs.org

Sons of Italy Foundation

Henry Salvatori Scholarship

Type of award: Scholarship.
Intended use: For full-time undergraduate study.
Eligibility: Applicant must be high school senior. Applicant must be Italian. Applicant must be U.S. citizen.
Basis for selection: Applicant must demonstrate high academic achievement, depth of character, leadership, patriotism, seriousness of purpose and service orientation.
Application requirements: $30 application fee. Transcript, proof of eligibility. SAT/ACT report; two letters of recommendation from public figures who have demonstrated the ideals of liberty, freedom, and equality in their work; cover letter; and 750-1,000 word essay discussing the relevance of the Declaration of Independence, the Constitution, and the Bill of Rights to the principles of liberty, freedom, and equality in the U.S. today.
Additional information: Visit Website for application.

Amount of award:	$5,000
Number of awards:	1
Number of applicants:	100
Application deadline:	February 28
Notification begins:	April 15
Total amount awarded:	$5,000

Contact:
Order of Sons of Italy in America
219 E Street NE
Washington, DC 20002
Phone: 202-547-5106
Web: www.osia.org

Sons of Italy National Leadership Grant

Type of award: Scholarship.
Intended use: For full-time undergraduate, master's, doctoral or first professional study at accredited 4-year or graduate institution in United States.

Eligibility: Applicant must be Italian. Applicant must be U.S. citizen.
Basis for selection: Applicant must demonstrate high academic achievement, depth of character, leadership, seriousness of purpose and service orientation.
Application requirements: $30 application fee. Recommendations, essay, transcript, proof of eligibility. SAT/ACT scores, resume.
Additional information: Amount and number of awards vary. Visit Website for application.

Amount of award:	$5,000-$25,000
Number of awards:	7
Number of applicants:	600
Application deadline:	February 28
Notification begins:	April 15

Contact:
Order of Sons of Italy in America
219 E Street NE
Washington, DC 20002
Phone: 202-547-5106
Web: www.osia.org

Sons of Norway Foundation

Astrid G. Cates Scholarship Fund and Myrtle Beinhauer Scholarship

Type of award: Scholarship.
Intended use: For undergraduate study at postsecondary institution.
Eligibility: Applicant or parent must be member/participant of Sons of Norway. Applicant must be U.S. citizen.
Basis for selection: Applicant must demonstrate financial need, high academic achievement, depth of character and service orientation.
Application requirements: Recommendations, transcript, proof of eligibility.
Additional information: Applicant, parent, or grandparent must be current member of Sons of Norway. Student must include the following information with application: GPA, what type of study is intended, where and when. Related fees must be specified as well as long-term career goals, Sons of Norway involvement, extracurricular activities and financial need. The Cates Scholarship is $1,000; Beinhauer Scholarship awards $3,000 to the most qualified of all candidates. Student can be awarded maximum two scholarships within five-year period. Visit Website for application.

Amount of award:	$1,000-$3,000
Number of awards:	8
Number of applicants:	99
Application deadline:	March 1
Notification begins:	May 1

Contact:
Sons of Norway Foundation
1455 West Lake Street
Minneapolis, MN 55408
Web: www.sonsofnorway.com/foundation

King Olav V Norwegian-American Heritage Fund

Type of award: Scholarship.
Intended use: For full-time undergraduate or graduate study at accredited postsecondary institution in United States.
Eligibility: Applicant must be at least 18.
Basis for selection: Major/career interest in Scandinavian studies/research. Applicant must demonstrate financial need, high academic achievement, depth of character, leadership and service orientation.
Application requirements: Recommendations, transcript, proof of eligibility. Essay of maximum 500 words about reasons for application; course of study to be pursued; length of the course; name, tuition and cost of institution; amount of financial assistance required; and how the applicant's course of study will benefit his or her community and accord with the goals and objectives of the Sons of Norway Foundation.
Additional information: Open to Americans who have demonstrated keen and sincere interest in Norwegian heritage or Norwegians who have demonstrated interest in American heritage and have desire to further study their heritage (arts, crafts, literature, history, music, folklore, etc.) at recognized educational institution. Number and amount of awards varies. Visit Website for application.

Amount of award:	$1,000-$5,000
Number of awards:	7
Number of applicants:	100
Application deadline:	March 1
Notification begins:	May 1

Contact:
Sons of Norway Foundation
1455 West Lake Street
Minneapolis, MN 55408
Web: www.sonsofnorway.com/foundation

Nancy Lorraine Jensen Memorial Scholarship

Type of award: Scholarship, renewable.
Intended use: For full-time freshman, sophomore, junior or senior study.
Eligibility: Applicant or parent must be member/participant of Sons of Norway. Applicant must be female, at least 17, no older than 35. Applicant must be U.S. citizen.
Basis for selection: Major/career interest in chemistry; physics; engineering, electrical/electronic; engineering, mechanical or engineering, chemical. Applicant must demonstrate high academic achievement, depth of character and seriousness of purpose.
Application requirements: Recommendations, essay, transcript, proof of eligibility. SAT/ACT report.
Additional information: Applicant or applicant's parent or grandparent must have been a member of Sons of Norway for at least three years. Must have completed at least one semester of undergraduate study in current program. Award is no less than 50 percent of one semester's tuition and no more than full tuition for one year. Minimum 1800 SAT (or at least 600 Math) or 26 ACT. Must apply each year. Visit Website for application.

Number of awards:	6
Application deadline:	April 1

Contact:
Sons of Norway Foundation
1455 West Lake Street
Minneapolis, MN 55408-2666
Web: www.sonsofnorway.com/foundation

South Carolina Commission on Higher Education

LIFE Scholarship Program

Type of award: Scholarship, renewable.
Intended use: For full-time undergraduate study at vocational, 2-year or 4-year institution. Designated institutions: Eligible public and private institutions in South Carolina.
Eligibility: Applicant must be U.S. citizen or permanent resident residing in South Carolina.
Basis for selection: Applicant must demonstrate high academic achievement.
Application requirements: Transcript.
Additional information: First-time entering freshmen at four-year institutions must meet two of three criteria: 3.0 high school GPA on UGP; minimum 1100 SAT or 24 ACT; rank in top 30 percent of graduating class. First-time entering freshmen at two-year institution must have 3.0 high school GPA on UGP. Students should contact institution's financial aid office. No application required. Applicant must graduate from high school as South Carolina resident. College/university will determine eligibility based on transcript and will notify students directly. Maximum award $5,000 for four-year schools, average in-state tuition for two-year schools and up to full in-state tuition at technical schools.

Amount of award:	$5,000
Number of awards:	29,838
Total amount awarded:	$134,337,002

Contact:
South Carolina Commission on Higher Education
1333 Main Street, Suite 200
Columbia, SC 29201
Phone: 803-737-2260
Fax: 803-737-2297
Web: www.che.sc.gov

Lottery Tuition Assistance Program

Type of award: Scholarship, renewable.
Intended use: For undergraduate study at 2-year institution. Designated institutions: Eligible South Carolina institutions.
Eligibility: Applicant must be residing in South Carolina.
Application requirements: FAFSA.
Additional information: Award may not exceed cost of tuition. Award based on lottery revenue and number of applicants; hence, amounts vary by semester. All federal grants and need-based grants must be awarded first before determining amount for which student is eligible. Student must be degree-seeking and enrolled in minimum six credit hours. Institution will notify student of award amount based on number of eligible recipients and available funding. Student must fill out FAFSA or FAFSA waiver. See Website for further information.

Number of awards:	26,408
Number of applicants:	40,708
Total amount awarded:	$48,712,469

Contact:
South Carolina Commission on Higher Education
1333 Main Street, Suite 200
Columbia, SC 29201
Phone: 803-737-2260
Fax: 803-737-2297
Web: www.che.sc.gov

Palmetto Fellows Scholarship Program

Type of award: Scholarship, renewable.
Intended use: For full-time undergraduate study at 4-year institution. Designated institutions: Eligible South Carolina public and private institutions.
Eligibility: Applicant must be high school senior. Applicant must be U.S. citizen or permanent resident residing in South Carolina.
Basis for selection: Applicant must demonstrate high academic achievement.
Application requirements: Transcript.
Additional information: Applicant must have minimum 1200 SAT (Math and Reading) or 27 ACT, 3.5 GPA, and rank in top six percent of class. Class ranking requirement waived for students with 1400 SAT (Math and Reading) or 32 ACT and 4.0 GPA. High school graduates or students who have completed home-school program as prescribed by law may be eligible. For more information, contact guidance counselor or S.C. Commission.

Amount of award:	$6,700
Number of awards:	4,846
Application deadline:	December 15
Notification begins:	February 15
Total amount awarded:	$10,037,889

Contact:
South Carolina Commission on Higher Education
1333 Main Street, Suite 200
Columbia, SC 29201
Phone: 877-349-7183
Fax: 803-737-2297
Web: www.che.sc.gov

South Carolina HOPE Scholarships

Type of award: Scholarship.
Intended use: For freshman study at 4-year institution. Designated institutions: Eligible South Carolina public and independent institutions.
Eligibility: Applicant must be U.S. citizen or permanent resident residing in South Carolina.
Basis for selection: Applicant must demonstrate high academic achievement.
Application requirements: Transcript, proof of eligibility.
Additional information: No application necessary. College or university will determine eligibility based upon official high school transcript and will notify students directly. Student must earn cumulative 3.0 GPA upon high school graduation. Student must certify that he/she has not been convicted of any felonies or any second drug/alcohol misdemeanors within past academic year. Contact institution's financial aid office for more information.

Amount of award:	$2,800
Number of awards:	2,605
Total amount awarded:	$6,295,751

Contact:
South Carolina Commission on Higher Education
1333 Main St., Suite 200
Columbia, SC 29201
Phone: 803-737-2260
Fax: 803-737-2297
Web: www.che.sc.gov

South Carolina Need-Based Grants Program

Type of award: Scholarship.
Intended use: For undergraduate study at 2-year or 4-year institution.
Eligibility: Applicant must be U.S. citizen or permanent resident residing in South Carolina.
Basis for selection: Applicant must demonstrate financial need.
Application requirements: FAFSA.
Additional information: Award amount information is for public institutions. Need-based dollars are given as lump sum to another agency administering grants at independent institutions. May receive award for maximum eight full-time equivalent terms or until degree is earned, whichever is less. Must enroll in at least 12 credit hours per semester if full-time or six if part-time. Requires FAFSA or FAFSA waiver.

Amount of award:	$1,250-$2,500
Number of awards:	26,730
Number of applicants:	27,186
Total amount awarded:	$24,406,354

Contact:
Institution's financial aid office or
South Carolina Commission on Higher Education
1333 Main Street, Suite 200
Columbia, SC 29201
Phone: 877-349-7183
Fax: 803-737-2297
Web: www.che.sc.gov

South Carolina Higher Education Tuition Grants Commission

South Carolina Tuition Grants

Type of award: Scholarship, renewable.
Intended use: For full-time undergraduate study at accredited 2-year or 4-year institution in United States. Designated institutions: SACS-accredited South Carolina private, nonprofit institutions.
Eligibility: Applicant must be U.S. citizen residing in South Carolina.
Basis for selection: Applicant must demonstrate financial need.
Application requirements: FAFSA.
Additional information: Award amount varies. Recipient may reapply for up to four years. Incoming freshmen must score 900 SAT (Math and Reading) or 19 ACT, graduate in top three-fourths of high school class, or graduate from South Carolina high school with 2.0 GPA. Upperclassmen must complete 24 semester hours and meet college's satisfactory progress requirements. Application is automatic with FAFSA; submit to federal processor and list eligible college in college choice section. All eligible applicants funded if deadline is met. Contact campus financial aid office for details.

Number of awards:	11,735
Number of applicants:	25,747
Application deadline:	June 30
Total amount awarded:	$31,071,094

Contact:
South Carolina Higher Education Tuition Grants Commission
101 Business Park Blvd., Suite 2100
Columbia, SC 29203-9498
Phone: 803-896-1120
Fax: 803-896-1126
Web: www.sctuitiongrants.com

South Dakota Board of Regents

South Dakota Annis I. Fowler/Kaden Scholarship

Type of award: Scholarship.
Intended use: For freshman study. Designated institutions: University of South Dakota, Black Hills State University, Dakota State University, and Northern State University.
Eligibility: Applicant must be U.S. citizen residing in South Dakota.
Basis for selection: Major/career interest in education. Applicant must demonstrate high academic achievement, depth of character, leadership, seriousness of purpose and service orientation.
Application requirements: Recommendations, essay, transcript, proof of eligibility. Copy of applicant's ACT scores.
Additional information: Open to high school seniors who have a cumulative GPA of 3.0 after three years. Applicants must select elementary education as major field. Special consideration given to applicants with demonstrated motivation or disability, or who are self-supporting. Transcript must include class rank, cumulative GPA, and list of courses to be taken during senior year.

Amount of award:	$1,000
Number of awards:	2
Number of applicants:	30
Application deadline:	February 15
Notification begins:	April 15

Contact:
South Dakota Board of Regents
Scholarship Committee
306 E. Capitol Avenue, Suite 200
Pierre, SD 57501-3159
Phone: 605-773-3455
Web: www.ris.sdbor.edu

South Dakota Ardell Bjugstad Scholarship

Type of award: Scholarship.
Intended use: For freshman study at postsecondary institution in United States.
Eligibility: Applicant must be American Indian. Member of federally recognized Indian tribe whose reservation is in North Dakota or South Dakota. Applicant must be high school senior. Applicant must be U.S. citizen residing in South Dakota or North Dakota.
Basis for selection: Major/career interest in agribusiness; agriculture; natural resources/conservation or environmental science. Applicant must demonstrate high academic achievement, depth of character, leadership and seriousness of purpose.

Application requirements: Recommendations, transcript, proof of eligibility. Verification of tribal enrollment.
Additional information: Transcript must include class rank and cumulative GPA.

Amount of award:	$500
Number of awards:	1
Number of applicants:	3
Application deadline:	February 15
Notification begins:	April 15

Contact:
South Dakota Board of Regents
Scholarship Committee
306 E. Capitol Avenue, Suite 200
Pierre, SD 57502-3159
Phone: 605-773-3455
Web: www.ris.sdbor.edu

South Dakota Haines Memorial Scholarship

Type of award: Scholarship.
Intended use: For full-time sophomore, junior or senior study at accredited 4-year institution in United States.
Eligibility: Applicant must be residing in South Dakota.
Basis for selection: Major/career interest in education. Applicant must demonstrate depth of character, leadership, seriousness of purpose and service orientation.
Application requirements: Proof of eligibility. Resume. Two two-page essays: one describing personal philosophy and another describing philosophy of education.
Additional information: Minimum 2.5 GPA.

Amount of award:	$2,150
Number of awards:	1
Number of applicants:	20
Application deadline:	February 15
Notification begins:	April 15

Contact:
South Dakota Board of Regents Scholarship Committee
306 E. Capitol, Suite 200
Pierre, SD 57501-3159
Phone: 605-773-3455
Web: www.ris.sdbor.edu

South Dakota Marlin R. Scarborough Memorial Scholarship

Type of award: Scholarship.
Intended use: For full-time junior study at accredited 4-year institution in United States.
Eligibility: Applicant must be residing in South Dakota.
Basis for selection: Applicant must demonstrate high academic achievement, depth of character, leadership, seriousness of purpose and service orientation.
Application requirements: Nomination by participating South Dakota public university. Essay explaining leadership and academic qualities, career plans, and educational interests.
Additional information: Must be sophomore at time of application. Apply through school financial aid office. Minimum 3.5 GPA. Must have completed three full semesters at same university. Call or e-mail sponsor for deadlines and application. Each South Dakota public university may nominate one student.

Amount of award:	$1,000
Number of awards:	1
Application deadline:	February 15
Notification begins:	April 15

Contact:
South Dakota Board of Regents Scholarship Committee
306 East Capitol, Suite 200
Pierre, SD 57501-3159
Phone: 605-773-3455
Web: www.ris.sdbor.edu

South Dakota Department of Education

South Dakota Robert C. Byrd Honors Scholarship

Type of award: Scholarship, renewable.
Intended use: For full-time undergraduate study in United States.
Eligibility: Applicant must be high school senior. Applicant must be U.S. citizen or permanent resident residing in South Dakota.
Basis for selection: Applicant must demonstrate high academic achievement.
Application requirements: Transcript.
Additional information: Must have minimum 3.5 GPA. Must have at least 30 ACT.

Amount of award:	$1,500
Number of awards:	74
Number of applicants:	124
Application deadline:	May 1
Notification begins:	March 1
Total amount awarded:	$108,000

Contact:
South Dakota Department of Education
700 Governors Drive
Pierre, SD 57501-2291
Phone: 605-773-3248
Fax: 605-773-6139
Web: www.state.sd.us/deca

South Dakota Department of Military and Veterans Affairs

South Dakota National Guard Tuition Assistance

Type of award: Scholarship, renewable.
Intended use: For undergraduate study at vocational or 4-year institution.
Eligibility: Applicant or parent must be member/participant of South Dakota National Guard. Applicant must be residing in South Dakota.
Application requirements: Proof of eligibility.
Additional information: Provides tuition/fee waiver of 50 percent.

Number of awards:	500
Number of applicants:	500
Total amount awarded:	$125,000

Contact:
SDNG Unit or South Dakota Department of Military and Veterans Affairs
Soldiers and Sailors Building
500 East Capitol Avenue
Pierre, SD 57501-5070
Phone: 605-773-3269

Southern Nursery Organization

Southern Nursery Organization Sidney B. Meadows Scholarship

Type of award: Scholarship.
Intended use: For full-time junior, senior, master's or doctoral study at accredited 4-year or graduate institution.
Eligibility: Applicant must be U.S. citizen.
Basis for selection: Major/career interest in horticulture.
Additional information: Must be enrolled in ornamental horticulture or related discipline in good standing. Minimum 2.25 GPA for undergraduates, 3.0 for graduates. Must be resident of one of 16 states in Southern Nursery Organization, but matriculation in these states is not mandatory. For list of states, application, and additional information, visit Website.

Amount of award:	$2,500
Number of awards:	7
Application deadline:	May 31
Total amount awarded:	$17,500

Contact:
Southern Nursery Organization
1827 Power Ferry Road SE
Building 4, Suite 100
Atlanta, GA 30339
Web: www.sna.org/education

SPIE - The International Society for Optical Engineering

SPIE Educational Scholarship in Optical Science and Engineering

Type of award: Scholarship, renewable.
Intended use: For full-time undergraduate, graduate or non-degree study in or outside United States.
Basis for selection: Major/career interest in engineering or physics. Applicant must demonstrate seriousness of purpose.
Application requirements: Recommendations, essay.
Additional information: Open only to SPIE student members; nonmembers may submit SPIE student membership application and dues with scholarship application. High school and pre-university students may receive one-year complimentary membership. Applicant must be enrolled full-time in optics, photonics, imaging, optoelectronics, or related program at accredited institution for year in which award will be used (unless high school student). Award amount varies. Students must reapply for renewal. See Website for application.

Amount of award:	$1,000-$11,000
Application deadline:	January 11

Contact:
SPIE Scholarship Committee
P.O. Box 10
Bellingham, WA 98227-0010
Phone: 360-676-3290 ext. 659
Fax: 360-647-1445
Web: www.spie.org/scholarships

Spina Bifida Association

Spina Bifida Association Four-Year Scholarship

Type of award: Scholarship, renewable.
Intended use: For full-time undergraduate study at postsecondary institution in United States.
Basis for selection: Applicant must demonstrate financial need, high academic achievement, leadership, seriousness of purpose and service orientation.
Application requirements: Recommendations, essay, transcript, proof of eligibility. SAT/ACT scores. Statement from physician verifying disability. Verification of high school diploma or GED; verification of acceptance at school/college. Financial aid forms.
Additional information: Open to all persons with spina bifida. May be used for any postsecondary four-year study. Number of awards varies. Award is up to $5,000 a year for four years.

Amount of award:	$5,000
Number of awards:	6
Application deadline:	March 7
Notification begins:	November 1

Contact:
Scholarship Committee
4590 MacArthur Boulevard NW
Suite 250
Washington, DC 20007-4226
Phone: 202-944-3285
Fax: 202-944-3295
Web: www.sbaa.org

Spina Bifida Association One-Year Scholarship

Type of award: Scholarship.
Intended use: For undergraduate study at postsecondary institution in United States.
Basis for selection: Applicant must demonstrate financial need, high academic achievement, leadership, seriousness of purpose and service orientation.
Application requirements: Recommendations, essay, transcript, proof of eligibility. SAT/ACT scores. Statement verifying disability from physician. Verification of high school diploma or GED; verification of acceptance at school/college. Financial aid forms.
Additional information: Open to all persons with spina bifida. Applicant must be high school graduate or GED recipient. Applicant must be enrolled in/accepted by college, junior college, graduate program, or approved trade or vocational program. Number of awards varies. Visit Website for more information.

Spina Bifida Association: Spina Bifida Association One-Year Scholarship

Amount of award:	$2,000
Number of awards:	5
Application deadline:	March 7

Contact:
Scholarship Committee
4590 MacArthur Boulevard, NW
Suite 250
Washington, DC 20007-4226
Phone: 202-944-3285
Fax: 202-944-3295
Web: www.sbaa.org

Staples

Staples Associates Annual Scholarships Plan

Type of award: Scholarship, renewable.
Intended use: For undergraduate, graduate or non-degree study at vocational, 2-year, 4-year or graduate institution.
Eligibility: Applicant or parent must be employed by Staples.
Application requirements: Proof of eligibility.
Additional information: Applicants must have worked at Staples for 90 days, averaging at least 18 hours per week. Award may be used for tuition, books, fees and CLEP (College Level Examination Program) exams. Contact Human Resources for complete details and application. Number of awards granted depends on funding.

Amount of award:	$750-$2,000
Number of applicants:	2,600
Application deadline:	September 30
Notification begins:	November 15
Total amount awarded:	$2,000,000

Contact:
Staples
500 Staples Dr.
Framingham, MA 01702

State Council of Higher Education for Virginia

Virginia Academic Common Market

Type of award: Scholarship.
Intended use: For full-time undergraduate or graduate study at 4-year or graduate institution. Designated institutions: Eligible public institutions outside of Virginia.
Eligibility: Applicant must be permanent resident residing in Virginia.
Additional information: Awards Virginia residents in-state tuition at participating non-Virginia institutions in 15 states in the South. Institution must offer programs unavailable in Virginia public institutions. Applicant must be domiciled in Virginia.

Number of awards:	100

Contact:
Academic Common Market/SCHEV
James Monroe Building
101 North Fourteenth Street
Richmond, VA 23219
Phone: 804-225-2632
Fax: 804-225-2604
Web: www.schev.edu

Virginia Tuition Assistance Grant

Type of award: Scholarship, renewable.
Intended use: For full-time undergraduate, master's, doctoral or first professional study at accredited postsecondary institution. Designated institutions: Private, nonprofit institutions in Virginia.
Eligibility: Applicant must be residing in Virginia.
Application requirements: Proof of eligibility.
Additional information: Non-need-based award. Applicant must be in eligible degree program in participating Virginia private college. Applicant must be domiciled in Virginia and enrolled full-time. Must provide proof of domicile. Theology and divinity majors not eligible. If funding is insufficient, priority given first to renewals, then to new applicants who apply prior to deadline. Interested students should contact financial aid office of qualifying postsecondary institution.

Amount of award:	$3,200
Number of awards:	20,000
Application deadline:	July 31
Total amount awarded:	$60,000,000

Contact:
Financial aid office of qualifying postsecondary institution.
Web: www.schev.edu

State of Alabama

Alabama Scholarship for Dependents of Blind Parents

Type of award: Scholarship, renewable.
Intended use: For undergraduate study at vocational, 2-year or 4-year institution.
Eligibility: Parent must be visually impaired. Applicant must be U.S. citizen or permanent resident residing in Alabama.
Basis for selection: Applicant must demonstrate financial need.
Application requirements: Proof of eligibility.
Additional information: Award waives instructional fees and tuition costs at Alabama public institutions of higher education and pays for portion of books. Parent must be head of household and legally blind and family income must be at or below 1.3% of federal poverty guidelines. Applicant must have been Alabama resident for five years prior to application. Must reapply for renewal.

Amount of award:	Full tuition
Number of awards:	21
Application deadline:	June 30, September 30

Contact:
Alabama Department of Rehabilitation Services
7 Bemiston Ave
Talladega, AL 35160
Phone: 334-613-2248
Fax: 334-613-3444

State Student Assistance Commission of Indiana

Frank O'Bannon Grant

Type of award: Scholarship, renewable.
Intended use: For full-time undergraduate study at 2-year or 4-year institution. Designated institutions: Eligible Indiana schools.
Eligibility: Applicant must be U.S. citizen or permanent resident residing in Indiana.
Basis for selection: Applicant must demonstrate financial need.
Application requirements: FAFSA.
Additional information: May also be Title IV eligible non-citizen. All eligible students offered an award. Renewal recipients must maintain satisfactory academic progress. Summer work-study program available to recipients.
    Amount of award: $200-$10,272
    Number of awards: 45,924
    Application deadline: March 10
    Notification begins: July 1
    Total amount awarded: $145,518,190
Contact:
State Student Assistance Commission of Indiana
150 West Market Street, Suite 500
Indianapolis, IN 46204
Web: www.in.gov/ssaci

Hoosier Scholar Award

Type of award: Scholarship.
Intended use: For full-time freshman study at accredited vocational, 2-year or 4-year institution. Designated institutions: Eligible Indiana postsecondary schools.
Eligibility: Applicant must be high school senior. Applicant must be U.S. citizen or permanent resident residing in Indiana.
Basis for selection: Applicant must demonstrate high academic achievement.
Application requirements: Proof of eligibility, nomination by high school guidance counselor.
Additional information: List of eligible Indiana colleges provided with application. Applicant must be in top 20 percent of high school class. Nomination forms must be submitted by March 1.
    Amount of award: $500
    Number of awards: 689
    Number of applicants: 689
    Application deadline: March 1
    Notification begins: April 15
    Total amount awarded: $344,500
Contact:
Contact high school guidance counselor for further information.
Web: www.in.gov/ssaci

Indiana Minority Teacher & Special Education Services Scholarship

Type of award: Scholarship, renewable.
Intended use: For full-time undergraduate or graduate study at accredited 4-year or graduate institution.
Eligibility: Applicant must be African American, Mexican American, Hispanic American or Puerto Rican. Applicant must be U.S. citizen or permanent resident residing in Indiana.
Basis for selection: Major/career interest in education; education, special; occupational therapy or physical therapy. Applicant must demonstrate high academic achievement.
Application requirements: Proof of eligibility. FAFSA.
Additional information: Minimum 2.0 GPA. Applicant must be black or Latino, unless applicant is entering field of special education, occupational or physical therapy. Contact college financial aid office for more information.
    Amount of award: $1,000-$4,000
    Number of awards: 269
    Number of applicants: 269
    Total amount awarded: $413,759
Contact:
Contact financial aid office of applicant's chosen college.
Phone: 317-232-2350
Fax: 317-232-3260
Web: www.in.gov/ssaci

Indiana National Guard Supplemental Grant

Type of award: Scholarship, renewable.
Intended use: For undergraduate study at 2-year or 4-year institution.
Eligibility: Applicant must be residing in Indiana. Member of Indiana Air and Army National Guard. Applicant must be in active drilling status and be certified by Indiana National Guard (ING).
Application requirements: FAFSA.
Additional information: Applicant must apply for the Frank O'Bannon Grant and meet requirements for Indiana Higher Education Grant. Applicant must maintain satisfactory academic progress.
    Amount of award: $200-$7,460
    Number of awards: 903
    Number of applicants: 903
    Application deadline: March 10
    Notification begins: September 1
    Total amount awarded: $2,740,499
Contact:
State Student Assistance Commission of Indiana
150 West Market St.
Suite 500
Indianapolis, IN 46204
Web: www.in.gov/ssaci

Indiana Nursing Scholarship

Type of award: Scholarship, renewable.
Intended use: For undergraduate study at accredited vocational, 2-year or 4-year institution. Designated institutions: Eligible Indiana schools.
Eligibility: Applicant must be U.S. citizen residing in Indiana.
Basis for selection: Major/career interest in nursing. Applicant must demonstrate financial need and high academic achievement.
Application requirements: Proof of eligibility. FASFA.
Additional information: Minimum 2.0 GPA. Must be admitted to eligible Indiana school. Must commit to work two years as nurse in any Indiana health care setting. Contact financial aid office of institution for application or e-mail State Student Assistance Commission of Indiana. Deadline varies by institution.
    Amount of award: $50-$5,000
    Number of awards: 448
    Number of applicants: 448
    Total amount awarded: $336,305

Indiana Robert C. Byrd Honors Scholarship

Type of award: Scholarship, renewable.
Intended use: For full-time undergraduate study at accredited 2-year or 4-year institution in United States.
Eligibility: Applicant must be high school senior. Applicant must be U.S. citizen residing in Indiana.
Basis for selection: Applicant must demonstrate high academic achievement.
Application requirements: Transcript, proof of eligibility.
Additional information: Must have minimum 1300 SAt, 29 ACT, or 65 GED. Must have 3.0 GPA. Cannot be in debt to federal government or have been sentenced for drug offense. Award cannot exceed $6,000 over four years.

Amount of award:	$1,500
Number of awards:	580
Number of applicants:	580
Application deadline:	April 26
Notification begins:	June 1
Total amount awarded:	$829,881

Contact:
Contact high school guidance counselor for information.
Web: www.in.gov/ssaci

Indiana Twenty-First Century Scholars Program

Type of award: Scholarship.
Intended use: For full-time undergraduate study at accredited 2-year or 4-year institution. Designated institutions: Participating Indiana schools.
Eligibility: Applicant must be high school senior. Applicant must be U.S. citizen or permanent resident residing in Indiana.
Basis for selection: Applicant must demonstrate financial need.
Application requirements: Proof of eligibility. FAFSA.
Additional information: Minimum 2.0 high school GPA. Must enroll in 7th or 8th grade by taking pledge to remain drug, alcohol, and crime free. Must file affirmation that pledge was fulfilled in high school senior year. Full tuition waiver up to $7,460 after other financial aid applied.

Amount of award:	$7,460
Number of awards:	8,945
Number of applicants:	8,945
Application deadline:	March 10
Notification begins:	July 1
Total amount awarded:	$19,925,482

Contact:
State Student Assistance Commission of Indiana
150 West Market Street, Suite 500
Indianapolis, IN 46204
Phone: 317-233-2100
Fax: 317-232-3260

Stephen T. Marchello Scholarship Foundation

Legacy of Hope

Type of award: Scholarship.
Intended use: For undergraduate study at accredited vocational, 2-year or 4-year institution in United States.
Eligibility: Applicant must be high school senior. Applicant must be U.S. citizen residing in California, Montana, Colorado or Arizona.
Application requirements: Interview, recommendations, essay, transcript, proof of eligibility.
Additional information: One award is renewable each semester for up to four years. All others are one-time grants. Applicant must be survivor of childhood cancer. Visit Website for more information. Submit application online or send SASE to address below. Number of awards varies. Submit SAT/ACT scores when available.

Amount of award:	$5,000-$30,000
Number of awards:	8
Number of applicants:	30
Application deadline:	March 15
Total amount awarded:	$2,000

Contact:
Stephen T. Marchello Scholarship Foundation
1170 E. Long Place
Centennial, CO 80122
Phone: 303-886-5018
Web: www.stmfoundation.org

Studio Art Centers International

Anna K. Meredith Fund Scholarship

Type of award: Scholarship.
Intended use: For undergraduate study in Florence, Italy. Designated institutions: Studio Art Centers International (SACI).
Basis for selection: Competition/talent/interest in study abroad. Major/career interest in arts, general or art/art history. Applicant must demonstrate financial need and high academic achievement.
Application requirements: Portfolio of 20 labeled slides of own work (CD format accepted); at least two art history writing samples must be submitted in lieu of portfolio for students seeking scholarships in non-studio study. SAR, FAFSA.
Additional information: Number of awards offered varies according to budget.

Amount of award:	$500-$2,000
Application deadline:	March 15, October 1
Notification begins:	April 15, November 1

Contact:
Studio Art Centers International
Institute of International Education
809 United Nations Plaza
New York, NY 10017-3580
Phone: 212-984-5548
Fax: 212-984-5325
Web: www.saci-florence.org

Clare Brett Smith Scholarship

Type of award: Scholarship.
Intended use: For undergraduate or graduate study in Florence, Italy. Designated institutions: Studio Art Centers International (SACI).
Basis for selection: Competition/talent/interest in study abroad. Major/career interest in arts, general.
Application requirements: Portfolio of 20 labeled slides of own work (CD format accepted) or two short papers. SAR, FAFSA.
Additional information: Applicant must be studying photography. Number of awards varies yearly according to budget.
    Amount of award: $1,000
    Application deadline: March 15, October 1
    Notification begins: April 15, November 1
Contact:
Studio Art Centers International
Institute of International Education
809 United Nations Plaza
New York, NY 10017-3580
Phone: 212-984-5548
Fax: 212-984-5325
Web: www.saci-florence.org

Elizabeth A. Sackler Museum Educational Trust

Type of award: Scholarship.
Intended use: For undergraduate study.
Eligibility: Applicant must be female.
Basis for selection: Major/career interest in arts, general or art/art history. Applicant must demonstrate financial need and high academic achievement.
Application requirements: FAFSA, SAR, statement of intent, six passport-sized photos, two letters of recommendation, portfolio on CD or set of twenty labeled slides (name, medium, size, date) presented in slide portfolio sleeve.
Additional information: Amount varies from year to year and includes full tuition, roundtrip airfare, housing, activity and materials fees. Must exhibit exceptional artistic excellence in painting, drawing, printmaking, sculpture, ceramics, photography, or art conservation and intend to pursue career in one of these fields. Visit Website for application and more information.
    Amount of award: $30,000
    Number of awards: 1
    Number of applicants: 112
    Application deadline: March 15
    Notification begins: May 1
    Total amount awarded: $30,000
Contact:
Studio Art Centers International
Institute of International Education
809 United Nations Plaza
New York, NY 10017-3580
Web: www.saci-florence.org/admissions/sackler.htm

International Incentive Awards

Type of award: Scholarship.
Intended use: For sophomore, junior or senior study in Florence, Italy. Designated institutions: Studio Art Centers International (SACI).
Basis for selection: Competition/talent/interest in study abroad. Major/career interest in arts, general or art/art history. Applicant must demonstrate financial need and high academic achievement.
Application requirements: Portfolio of 20 labeled slides of own work (CD format accepted). SAR, FAFSA.
Additional information: Must be at least sophomore with minimum 3.0 GPA. Special efforts made to encourage applications from minorities and underrepresented groups.
    Amount of award: $1,500
    Number of awards: 2
    Application deadline: March 15, October 1
    Notification begins: April 15, November 1
Contact:
Studio Art Centers International
Institute of International Education
809 United Nations Plaza
New York, NY 10017-3580
Phone: 212-984-5548
Fax: 212-984-5325

Jules Maidoff Scholarship

Type of award: Scholarship.
Intended use: For undergraduate or graduate study in Florence, Italy. Designated institutions: Studio Art Centers International (SACI).
Basis for selection: Competition/talent/interest in study abroad. Major/career interest in arts, general or art/art history. Applicant must demonstrate financial need.
Application requirements: Portfolio. FAFSA.
Additional information: Awarded to students exhibiting both exceptional artistic talent and financial need.
    Amount of award: $2,500
    Number of awards: 2
    Application deadline: March 15, October 1
    Notification begins: April 15, November 1
Contact:
Studio Art Centers International
Institute of International Education
809 United Nations Plaza
New York, NY 10017-3580
Phone: 212-984-5548
Fax: 212-984-5325
Web: www.saci-florence.org

Lele Cassin Scholarship

Type of award: Scholarship.
Intended use: For undergraduate or graduate study in Florence, Italy. Designated institutions: Studio Art Centers International (SACI).
Basis for selection: Competition/talent/interest in study abroad. Major/career interest in film/video.
Application requirements: Video (no longer than 15 minutes) of own work. SAR, FAFSA.
Additional information: For video/film-making student. Number of awards offered varies yearly according to budget.
    Amount of award: $1,000
    Application deadline: March 15, October 1
    Notification begins: April 15, November 1
Contact:
Studio Art Centers International
Institute of International Education
809 United Nations Plaza
New York, NY 10017-3580
Phone: 212-984-5548
Fax: 212-984-5325
Web: www.saci-florence.org

SACI Consortium Scholarship

Type of award: Scholarship.
Intended use: For undergraduate or graduate study in Florence, Italy. Designated institutions: Studio Art Centers International (SACI) consortium institution--see Website for list.
Basis for selection: Competition/talent/interest in study abroad. Major/career interest in arts, general or art/art history.
Application requirements: Portfolio, nomination by SACI consortium school. FAFSA.
Additional information: Each consortium school may submit one nominee. Award provides full tuition for one semester. Include SASE. See Website for details.

Amount of award:	Full tuition
Number of awards:	2
Application deadline:	March 15, October 1
Notification begins:	April 15, November 1

Contact:
Studio Art Centers International
c/o Institute of International Education
809 United Nations Plaza
New York, NY 10017-3580
Phone: 212-984-5548
Fax: 212-984-5325
Web: www.saci-florence.org

Scholarships for Children of SACI Alumni

Type of award: Scholarship.
Intended use: For undergraduate or graduate study in Florence, Italy. Designated institutions: Studio Art Centers International (SACI).
Basis for selection: Major/career interest in arts, general or art/art history. Applicant must demonstrate financial need and high academic achievement.
Application requirements: A CD or set of twenty labeled slides in a slide portfolio sleeve. Students seeking scholarships in non-studio study must submit two art history writing samples. FAFSA. Must also submit a statement indicating the name of parent who attended SACI and dates of attendance.
Additional information: Applicant must have a parent who attended SACI. Applicants for late spring or summer terms must submit materials by the admissions deadline of the term they wish to enroll. Fall and spring deadlines are March 15 and October 1, respectively.

Amount of award:	$500-$2,500
Application deadline:	March 15, October 1

Contact:
Studio Art Centers International
Institute of International Education
809 United Nations Plaza
New York, NY 10017-3580
Phone: 212-984-5548
Fax: 212-984-5325
Web: www.saci-florence.com

Sunkist Growers

A.W. Bodine Sunkist Memorial Scholarship

Type of award: Scholarship, renewable.
Intended use: For full-time undergraduate study at accredited 2-year or 4-year institution.
Eligibility: Applicant must be residing in California or Arizona.
Basis for selection: Applicant must demonstrate financial need, high academic achievement, depth of character, leadership, seriousness of purpose and service orientation.
Application requirements: Recommendations, essay, transcript, proof of eligibility. Tax return (or parents' tax return for applicants younger than 21).
Additional information: Applicant or someone in immediate family must have derived majority of income from California- or Arizona-based agriculture. All majors eligible. Award renewable up to four years based on annual review. Must maintain 2.7 GPA and carry 12 credits per semester to qualify for renewal.

Amount of award:	$2,000
Number of awards:	22
Number of applicants:	300
Application deadline:	April 30

Contact:
A.W. Bodine Sunkist Memorial Scholarship
Sunkist Growers
P.O. Box 7888
Van Nuys, CA 91409-7888
Phone: 818-986-4800
Web: www.sunkist.com/about/bodine_scholarship.asp

Supreme Guardian Council, International Center for Job's Daughters

The Grottos Scholarships

Type of award: Scholarship.
Intended use: For full-time undergraduate study at 2-year or 4-year institution.
Eligibility: Applicant or parent must be member/participant of International Order of Job's Daughters. Applicant must be single, female, no older than 30.
Basis for selection: Major/career interest in dentistry. Applicant must demonstrate financial need, high academic achievement, depth of character, leadership and seriousness of purpose.
Application requirements: Recommendations, transcript, proof of eligibility. Personal letter.
Additional information: Job's Daughters activities, financial self-help, and achievements outside of Job's Daughters are also factors in awarding scholarships. Training in the handicapped field is preferred. Visit Website for more information.

Amount of award:	$1,500
Application deadline:	April 30

Contact:
International Center for Job's Daughters
233 W. 6th Street
Papillion, NE 68046-2210
Phone: 402-592-7987
Fax: 402-592-2177
Web: www.iojd.org

Supreme Guardian Council, International Order of Job's Daughters

Supreme Guardian Council, International Order of Job's Daughters Scholarship

Type of award: Scholarship.
Intended use: For undergraduate study at vocational, 2-year or 4-year institution.
Eligibility: Applicant or parent must be member/participant of International Order of Job's Daughters. Applicant must be single, female, no older than 30.
Basis for selection: Applicant must demonstrate financial need, high academic achievement, depth of character, leadership, seriousness of purpose and service orientation.
Application requirements: Recommendations, transcript, proof of eligibility. Personal letter. Recommendation by Executive Bethel Guardian Council. Recommendation by school faculty.
Additional information: High school seniors eligible to apply. Job's Daughters activities, applicant's financial self-help, and achievements outside of Job's Daughters are also factors evaluated in awarding scholarships. Visit Website for more information.
   Amount of award: $750
   Number of applicants: 100
   Application deadline: April 30
Contact:
Supreme Guardian Council
International Order of Job's Daughters
233 West 6 Street
Papillion, NE 68046
Phone: 402-592-7987
Fax: 402-592-2177
Web: www.iojd.org

Susie Holmes Memorial Scholarship

Type of award: Scholarship.
Intended use: For full-time undergraduate study at 2-year or 4-year institution.
Eligibility: Applicant or parent must be member/participant of International Order of Job's Daughters. Applicant must be single, female, no older than 30.
Basis for selection: Applicant must demonstrate financial need, depth of character and seriousness of purpose.
Application requirements: Recommendations, transcript, proof of eligibility. Personal letter.
Additional information: Applicant must be high school graduate with 2.5 GPA; show dedicated, continuous, joyful service to Job's Daughters; and regularly attend Grand and/or Supreme Session with participation in competitions at Grand and/or Supreme Session. Job's Daughter's activities, applicant's financial self-help, and achievements outside of Job's Daughters are also factors in awarding scholarships. Visit Website for more details.
   Amount of award: $1,000
   Application deadline: April 30

Contact:
International Center for Job's Daughters
233 W. 6th Street
Papillion, NE 68046-2210
Phone: 402-592-7987
Fax: 402-592-2177
Web: www.iojd.org

Swiss Benevolent Society of New York

Sonia Streuli Maguire Outstanding Scholastic Achievement Award

Type of award: Scholarship.
Intended use: For full-time senior, post-bachelor's certificate, master's, doctoral or first professional study at accredited 4-year or graduate institution in United States.
Eligibility: Applicant must be Swiss. Applicant must be permanent resident residing in New York, Connecticut, Delaware, New Jersey or Pennsylvania.
Basis for selection: Applicant must demonstrate high academic achievement.
Application requirements: Recommendations, transcript, proof of eligibility. SAT/GRE results.
Additional information: Applicant or parent must be Swiss citizen. Must have minimum 3.8 GPA. See Website for application.
   Amount of award: $2,500-$5,000
   Number of awards: 2
   Application deadline: March 31
   Notification begins: June 1
   Total amount awarded: $5,000
Contact:
Swiss Benevolent Society
500 Fifth Avenue
Room 1800
New York, NY 10110
Web: www.swissbenevolentny.com/scholarships.htm

Swiss Benevolent Society Medicus Student Exchange

Type of award: Scholarship.
Intended use: For full-time junior, senior, post-bachelor's certificate, master's, doctoral or first professional study at accredited 4-year or graduate institution in universities and polytechnic institutes in Switzerland.
Eligibility: Applicant must be Swiss. Applicant must be U.S. citizen, permanent resident or Swiss citizen.
Basis for selection: Competition/talent/interest in study abroad. Applicant must demonstrate high academic achievement.
Application requirements: Recommendations, transcript, proof of eligibility. Statement of funding. Proof of fluency in language of instruction.
Additional information: Provides partial financial support for U.S. students accepted to Swiss post-secondary institutions. Applicant or parent must be Swiss national.
   Application deadline: March 31
   Notification begins: June 1

Contact:
Swiss Benevolent Society
500 Fifth Avenue
Room 1800
New York, NY 10110
Phone: 212-246-0655
Fax: 212-246-1366
Web: www.swissbenevolentny.com/scholarships.htm

Swiss Benevolent Society Pellegrini Scholarship

Type of award: Scholarship, renewable.
Intended use: For undergraduate, graduate or non-degree study at accredited postsecondary institution in United States.
Eligibility: Applicant must be Swiss. Applicant must be permanent resident residing in New York, Connecticut, Delaware, New Jersey or Pennsylvania.
Basis for selection: Applicant must demonstrate financial need and high academic achievement.
Application requirements: Recommendations, transcript, proof of eligibility. Proof of Swiss parentage and tax return. Copy of bursar's bill. Incoming freshmen should provide figures of anticipated cost.
Additional information: Applicant or parent must be a Swiss national. Minimum 3.0 GPA required. Scholarship paid directly to school. See Website for application.

Amount of award:	$500-$4,000
Number of awards:	55
Number of applicants:	61
Application deadline:	March 31
Notification begins:	June 1
Total amount awarded:	$95,550

Contact:
Swiss Benevolent Society
500 Fifth Avenue
Room 1800
New York, NY 10110
Web: www.swissbenevolentny.com/scholarships.htm

Taglit-Birthright Israel

Taglit-Birthright Israel Gift

Type of award: Scholarship.
Intended use: For undergraduate study.
Eligibility: Applicant must be at least 18, no older than 26. Applicant must be Jewish.
Application requirements: Proof of eligibility.
Additional information: Applicant must be out of high school. All eligible applicants receive free trip to Israel under the auspices of Aish HaTorah, Hillel and other organizations. Round-trip airfare and ten days of program activity funded. Must not have visited Israel previously on an educational peer-group trip or study program. Must not have lived in Israel past age 12. Visit Website or contact sponsor for current offerings.

Number of awards:	20,000

Contact:
Phone: 888-99-ISRAEL
Web: www.birthrightisrael.com

Technology Association of Georgia

Web Challenge Contest

Type of award: Scholarship.
Intended use: For full-time undergraduate study.
Eligibility: Applicant must be enrolled in high school. Applicant must be U.S. citizen or permanent resident residing in Georgia.
Basis for selection: Competition/talent/interest in web-site design, based on originality, creativity, and sophistication in Website design. Major/career interest in computer/information sciences or computer graphics. Applicant must demonstrate seriousness of purpose.
Application requirements: Proof of eligibility.
Additional information: Applicants must assemble team of at least two participants to design and build a Website; team must be sponsored by faculty advisor. Total amount awarded varies. Visit Website for registration information, contest information and theme.

Number of awards:	15
Number of applicants:	100
Application deadline:	April 15
Notification begins:	April 23
Total amount awarded:	$30,000

Contact:
Technology Association of Georgia
75 Fifth Street, NW
Suite 310
Atlanta, GA 30308
Phone: 770-374-4223
Web: www.tagonline.org/webchallenge.php

Tekmark Global Solutions

TGS Scholarship

Type of award: Scholarship.
Intended use: For full-time. Designated institutions: Rider University, Monmouth University, Rutgers University.
Eligibility: Applicant must be U.S. citizen residing in New Jersey.
Basis for selection: Major/career interest in engineering or computer/information sciences. Applicant must demonstrate high academic achievement, leadership and service orientation.
Application requirements: Recommendations, essay, transcript. Two reference letters. List of significant achievements, academic awards, volunteer or community work, extracurricular activities, etc.
Additional information: Awarded to students who demonstrate ambition and drive, determination to set and reach goals, and show leadership potential. Must be working towards a bachelor's degree in engineering/engineering technology, computer science/MIS, or telecommunications/information technology. Must have a high school GPA of 3.0 and must have minimum 1200 SAT (Math and Reading). Write scholarship@tekmarkinc.com for the application and further information.

Amount of award:	$500
Number of awards:	6
Application deadline:	April 1
Notification begins:	May 1
Total amount awarded:	$3,000

Contact:
Tekmark Global Solutions, LLC
100 Metroplex Drive, Suite 102
Edison, NJ 08817
Phone: 732-572-9600
Fax: 732-572-7117
Web: www.tekmarkinc.com

Tennessee Student Assistance Corporation

HOPE-Aspire Award

Type of award: Scholarship.
Intended use: For freshman or sophomore study. Designated institutions: Eligible Tennessee institutions.
Eligibility: Applicant must be residing in Tennessee.
Application requirements: FAFSA.
Additional information: Applicant must be eligible for HOPE. Entering freshman must have a minimum 21 ACT or 980 SAT or 3.0 GPA. Parent's or student's income must be $36,000 or less.

Amount of award:	$1,500
Application deadline:	September 1
Notification begins:	January 1

Contact:
Tennessee Student Assistance Corporation
Parkway Towers, Suite 1510
404 James Robertson Parkway
Nashville, TN 37243-0820
Phone: 800-342-1663
Fax: 615-741-6101
Web: www.collegepaystn.com

Hope-General Assembly Merit Scholarship

Type of award: Scholarship, renewable.
Intended use: For undergraduate study. Designated institutions: Eligible Tennessee institutions.
Eligibility: Applicant must be residing in Tennessee.
Application requirements: FAFSA.
Additional information: Supplement to the HOPE Scholarship. Entering freshman must have minimum 3.75 weighted GPA, 29 ACT or 1280 SAT.

Amount of award:	$1,000
Number of applicants:	284,700
Application deadline:	September 1
Notification begins:	January 1

Contact:
Tennessee Student Assistance Corporation
Parkway Towers, Suite 1510
404 James Robertson Parkway
Nashville, TN 37243-0820
Phone: 800-342-1663
Fax: 614-741-6101
Web: www.collegepaystn.com

Tennessee Christa McAuliffe Scholarship Program

Type of award: Scholarship.
Intended use: For full-time senior study. Designated institutions: Eligible Tennessee institutions.
Eligibility: Applicant must be residing in Tennessee.
Basis for selection: Major/career interest in education, teacher; education; education, early childhood or education, special. Applicant must demonstrate high academic achievement, depth of character, leadership, seriousness of purpose and service orientation.
Application requirements: Transcript. Written statement of intent to teach in a Tennessee elementary or secondary school.
Additional information: To be eligible, applicant must be enrolled full-time in an accredited teacher education program. Applicant must have completed first semester of junior year with a cumulative GPA of 3.5 or higher and ACT or SAT score that meets or exceeds national norm. Amount of award based on funding.

Amount of award:	$500
Number of awards:	1
Number of applicants:	10
Application deadline:	April 1
Total amount awarded:	$500

Contact:
Tennessee Student Assistance Corporation
Parkway Towers, Suite 1510
404 James Robertson Parkway
Nashville, TN 37243-0820
Phone: 800-342-1663
Fax: 615-741-6101
Web: www.collegepaystn.com

Tennessee Dependent Children Scholarship Program

Type of award: Scholarship, renewable.
Intended use: For full-time undergraduate study at accredited postsecondary institution.
Eligibility: Applicant must be U.S. citizen residing in Tennessee. Applicant's parent must have been killed or disabled in work-related accident as firefighter or police officer.
Basis for selection: Applicant must demonstrate financial need.
Application requirements: Proof of eligibility. FAFSA.
Additional information: Applicant must be enrolled full-time in a degree-granting program. Applicant's parent may also be emergency medical technician killed or disabled in work-related accident. Award based on student's financial aid package.

Amount of award:	Full tuition
Number of awards:	28
Number of applicants:	57
Application deadline:	July 15
Total amount awarded:	$138,191

Contact:
Tennessee Student Assistance Corporation
Parkway Towers, Suite 1510
404 James Robertson Parkway
Nashville, TN 37243-0820
Phone: 800-342-1663
Fax: 615-741-6101
Web: www.collegepaystn.com

Tennessee HOPE Access Grant

Type of award: Scholarship.

Intended use: For freshman study at 2-year or 4-year institution. Designated institutions: Eligible Tennessee institutions.
Eligibility: Applicant must be residing in Tennessee.
Application requirements: FAFSA.
Additional information: Award amount varies: $2,750 for four-year institutions, $1,750 for two-year institutions. Minimum 2.75 GPA. Minimum 18 ACT, 860 SAT. Parents' or independent student's and spouse's adjusted gross income must be $36,000 or less on IRS tax form.

Amount of award:	$1,750-$2,750
Application deadline:	September 1
Notification begins:	January 1
Total amount awarded:	$490,294

Contact:
Tennessee Student Assistance Corporation
Parkway Towers, Suite 1510
404 James Robertson Parkway
Nashville, TN 37243-0820
Phone: 800-342-1663
Fax: 615-741-6101
Web: www.collegepaystn.com

Tennessee HOPE Scholarship

Type of award: Scholarship.
Intended use: For full-time undergraduate study. Designated institutions: Eligible Tennessee institutions.
Eligibility: Applicant must be residing in Tennessee.
Application requirements: FAFSA.
Additional information: Award amount varies: $4,000 for four-year institutions, $2,000 for two-year institutions. Minimum 3.0 GPA. Minimum ACT 21, 980 SAT.

Amount of award:	$1,900-$3,800
Application deadline:	September 1
Notification begins:	January 1

Contact:
Tennessee Student Assistance Corporation
Parkway Towers, Suite 1510
404 James Robertson Parkway
Nashville, TN 37243-0820
Phone: 800-342-1663
Fax: 615-741-6101
Web: www.collegepaystn.com

Tennessee Ned McWherter Scholars Program

Type of award: Scholarship, renewable.
Intended use: For full-time freshman study at accredited 2-year or 4-year institution.
Eligibility: Applicant must be high school senior. Applicant must be U.S. citizen residing in Tennessee.
Basis for selection: Applicant must demonstrate high academic achievement and leadership.
Application requirements: Transcript, proof of eligibility. List of leadership activities.
Additional information: Applicant must score at 95th percentile on ACT/SAT. Minimum 3.5 GPA through seven semesters. Difficulty level of high school courses considered. Applicant must provide transcript, proof of eligibility, and list of leadership activities.

Amount of award:	$6,000
Number of awards:	179
Number of applicants:	980
Application deadline:	February 15
Total amount awarded:	$523,500

Contact:
Tennessee Student Assistance Corporation
Parkway Towers, Suite 1510
404 James Robertson Parkway
Nashville, TN 37243-0820
Phone: 800-342-1663
Fax: 615-741-6101
Web: www.collegepaystn.com

Tennessee Robert C. Byrd Honors Scholarship Program

Type of award: Scholarship, renewable.
Intended use: For full-time freshman study at accredited vocational, 2-year or 4-year institution in United States.
Eligibility: Applicant must be high school senior. Applicant must be U.S. citizen or permanent resident residing in Tennessee.
Application requirements: Transcript, proof of eligibility.
Additional information: Minimum 3.5 GPA. May also qualify with 3.0 GPA and 24 ACT or 1090 SAT. At least 570 GED also accepted.

Amount of award:	$1,500
Number of awards:	531
Number of applicants:	4,419
Application deadline:	March 1
Total amount awarded:	$763,292

Contact:
Tennessee Student Assistance Corporation
Parkway Towers, Suite 1510
404 James Robertson Parkway
Nashville, TN 37243-0820
Phone: 800-342-1663
Fax: 615-741-6101
Web: www.collegepaystn.com

Tennessee Student Assistance Award Program

Type of award: Scholarship, renewable.
Intended use: For undergraduate study.
Eligibility: Applicant must be U.S. citizen residing in Tennessee.
Basis for selection: Applicant must demonstrate financial need.
Application requirements: FAFSA by application deadline.
Additional information: Applicant's expected family contribution must be $2,100 or less. Award is up to $4,644 for private institutions; up to $2,322 for public, based on funding.

Amount of award:	$2,322-$4,644
Number of awards:	19,838
Number of applicants:	296,296
Application deadline:	March 1
Total amount awarded:	$42,407,728

Contact:
Tennessee Student Assistance Corporation
Parkway Towers, Suite 1510
404 James Robertson Parkway
Nashville, TN 37243-0820
Phone: 800-342-1663
Fax: 615-741-6101
Web: www.collegepaystn.com

Wilder-Naifeh Technical Skills Grant

Type of award: Scholarship.

Intended use: For freshman or sophomore study at vocational institution. Designated institutions: Tennessee Technology Centers.
Eligibility: Applicant must be residing in Tennessee.
Application requirements: FAFSA.
   Amount of award: $2,000
   Notification begins: January 1
Contact:
Tennessee Student Assistance Corporation
Parkway Towers, Suite 1510
404 James Robertson Parkway
Nashville, TN 37243-0820
Phone: 800-342-1663
Fax: 615-741-6101
Web: www.collegepaystn.com

Texas Higher Education Coordinating Board

Educational Aide Exemption

Type of award: Scholarship.
Intended use: For undergraduate or graduate study at postsecondary institution in United States.
Eligibility: Applicant must be U.S. citizen or permanent resident residing in Texas.
Basis for selection: Applicant must demonstrate financial need.
Application requirements: Proof of certification by Texas Board of Teacher Certification as a Certified Aide. FAFSA.
Additional information: Assists educational aides by exempting them from payment of tuition and fees (other than lab or class fees). Applicant must have applied for financial aid through college of attendance, including filing FAFSA or qualifying based on income. Applicant must have worked as educational aide (includes library, computer lab and P.E. aides) for at least one year out of last five years or as substitute teacher for 180 days of the past five school years. Applicant must also be working, in some capacity, in Texas public school during semester for which exemption is applied and must be enrolled in classes toward teacher certification. Must maintain good academic standing. The deadlines for applying are: fall, June 1 through February 1; spring, November 1 through July 1. Visit Website or call for application.
   Number of awards: 4,000
Contact:
Texas Higher Education Coordinating Board
Student Services Division
P.O. Box 12788
Austin, TX 78711-2788
Phone: 800-242-3062 ext. 6387
Fax: 512-427-6420
Web: www.collegefortexans.com

Exemption for Peace Officers Disabled in the Line of Duty

Type of award: Scholarship.
Intended use: For undergraduate study at postsecondary institution in United States.
Eligibility: Applicant must be residing in Texas.
Application requirements: Proof of eligibility. Satisfactory evidence of status as a disabled peace officer as required by that institution.
Additional information: Award for persons injured in the line of duty while serving as peace officers in Texas. Must enroll in classes for which college receives tax support. Maximum award is exemption from payment of tuition and fees for not more than 12 semesters or sessions. Contact college for additional information.
   Amount of award: Full tuition
Contact:
Texas Higher Education Coordinating Board
Student Services Division
P. O. Box 12788
Austin, TX 78711-2788
Phone: 800-242-3062
Fax: 512-427-6420
Web: www.collegefortexans.com

Exemption for the Surviving Spouse and Dependent Children of Certain Deceased Public Servants (Employees)

Type of award: Scholarship.
Intended use: For full-time undergraduate study at postsecondary institution in United States.
Eligibility: Applicant must be residing in Texas.
Application requirements: Proof of eligibility.
Additional information: Exemption for surviving spouse and/or dependent children of certain public employees (defined by Texas Government Code 615.003) killed in the line of duty. Public employee must have died on or after September 1, 2000. Program provides free tuition and fees, free textbooks, and possibly free room and board. Contact registrar's office at college/university for information on claiming this exemption.
   Amount of award: Full tuition
Contact:
Texas Higher Education Coordinating Board
Student Services Division
P. O. Box 12788
Austin, TX 78711-2788
Phone: 800-242-3062
Fax: 512-427-6420
Web: www.collegefortexans.com

License Plate Insignia Scholarship

Type of award: Scholarship.
Intended use: For undergraduate or graduate study at accredited 2-year or 4-year institution. Designated institutions: Eligible Texas institutions; see Website for list.
Basis for selection: Applicant must demonstrate financial need.
Application requirements: FAFSA.
Additional information: Award amount varies but may not exceed student's financial need. Deadlines vary. Contact financial aid office at college or university for more information.
Contact:
Apply through school's financial aid office.
Phone: 800-242-3062
Web: www.collegefortexans.com

Reduction in Tuition Charges for Students Taking 15 or More Semester Credit Hours Per Term

Type of award: Scholarship.

Intended use: For full-time undergraduate study at postsecondary institution.
Eligibility: Applicant must be residing in Texas.
Application requirements: Proof of eligibility.
Additional information: Applicant must be enrolled in at least 15 credit hours at institution during semester/term for which reduction is offered. Must be enrolled in and making satisfactory progress toward completion of a degree program. Contact registrar's office at college/university to inquire whether the college offers reduction.
Contact:
Texas Higher Education Coordinating Board
Student Services Division
P. O. Box 12788
Austin, TX 78711-2788
Phone: 800-242-3062
Fax: 512-427-6420
Web: www.collegefortexans.com

Robert C. Byrd Honors Scholarship

Type of award: Scholarship, renewable.
Intended use: For undergraduate study at vocational, 2-year or 4-year institution.
Eligibility: Applicant must be high school senior. Applicant must be U.S. citizen or permanent resident residing in Texas.
Basis for selection: Applicant must demonstrate high academic achievement.
Application requirements: Transcript, nomination by high school guidance counselor or GED-center director.
Additional information: Average award $1,330. Those completing GED eligible to receive initial award. Must be in top 10 percent of class. High school guidance officer or GED center director will submit applications of top candidates to Texas Higher Education Coordinating Board. Students attending a U.S. Military Academy not eligible.

Amount of award:	$1,500
Number of awards:	3,839
Application deadline:	March 15

Contact:
High school guidance office or GED center director.
Phone: 800-242-3062
Fax: 512-427-6420
Web: www.collegefortexans.com

Senior Citizen, 65 or Older, Free Tuition for Up to 6 Credit Hours

Type of award: Scholarship.
Intended use: For half-time undergraduate or graduate study at 2-year or 4-year institution in United States. Designated institutions: Participating Texas public colleges and universities.
Eligibility: Applicant must be at least 65, returning adult student. Applicant must be U.S. citizen, permanent resident or international student.
Application requirements: Proof of eligibility.
Additional information: Program allows senior citizens to take up to 6 credit hours per semester, tuition-free. Texas institutions not required to offer program; applicants should check with registrar. Classes must not already be filled with students paying at full price and must use tax support for some of their cost. Contact college for additional information.

Number of awards:	2,316

Contact:
Texas Higher Education Coordinating Board
Student Services Division
P.O. Box 12788
Austin, TX 78711-2788
Phone: 800-242-3062
Fax: 512-427-6420
Web: www.collegefortexans.com

TANF (Temporary Assistance to Needy Families) Exemption

Type of award: Scholarship.
Intended use: For undergraduate certificate or freshman study at accredited 2-year or 4-year institution in United States.
Eligibility: Applicant must be no older than 22. Applicant must be U.S. citizen or permanent resident residing in Texas.
Application requirements: Proof of eligibility. Proof that a parent received TANF (Temporary Assistance to Needy Families) on their behalf for at least six months of their senior year of high school.
Additional information: Award includes tuition and fees for student's first academic year. Must enroll within two years of graduation from Texas public high school. Must enroll in classes for which college receives state tax support. Contact financial aid office at college or university for more information.

Number of awards:	128

Contact:
Contact college/university financial aid office to apply.
Phone: 800-242-3062
Fax: 512-427-6420
Web: www.collegefortexans.com

Texas College Work-Study Program

Type of award: Scholarship.
Intended use: For undergraduate, graduate or non-degree study at accredited 2-year, 4-year or graduate institution.
Eligibility: Applicant must be U.S. citizen or permanent resident residing in Texas.
Basis for selection: Applicant must demonstrate financial need.
Application requirements: FAFSA.
Additional information: Candidate must be enrolled at least half-time. Award amount based on financial need. Must register for Selective Service or sign statement of exemption. Number of hours of part-time work based on need. May reapply. Contact financial aid office at college or university for more information.

Number of awards:	5,179
Total amount awarded:	$2,547,719

Contact:
Contact school's financial aid office.
Phone: 800-242-3062
Fax: 512-427-6420
Web: www.collegefortexans.com

Texas Early High School Graduation Scholarship

Type of award: Scholarship, renewable.
Intended use: For undergraduate study at accredited postsecondary institution in United States.
Eligibility: Applicant must be U.S. citizen or permanent resident residing in Texas.
Application requirements: Proof of eligibility.

Additional information: Applicant must have completed recommended high school curriculum at Texas public high school in less than 36 months. Must register for selective service unless exempt. If award is to be used at private institution, college must provide matching scholarship. Visit Website for application.
    Amount of award: $500-$3,000
    Number of awards: 5,959
    Application deadline: September 1
Contact:
Contact college/university financial aid office to apply.
Phone: 800-242-3062
Fax: 512-427-6420
Web: www.collegefortexans.com

Texas Fifth-Year Accounting Student Scholarship Program

Type of award: Scholarship.
Intended use: For senior, post-bachelor's certificate or master's study at accredited postsecondary institution in United States.
Eligibility: Applicant must be residing in Texas.
Basis for selection: Major/career interest in accounting. Applicant must demonstrate financial need.
Application requirements: Proof of eligibility. Signed statement of intent to take CPA exam in Texas. FAFSA.
Additional information: Must be enrolled as fifth-year accounting student who has completed at least 120 credit hours, including 15 hours of accounting.
    Amount of award: $5,000
    Number of awards: 328
    Total amount awarded: $655,878
Contact:
Contact college financial aid office for application.
Phone: 800-242-3062
Web: www.collegefortexans.com

Texas Foster Care Students Exemption

Type of award: Scholarship, renewable.
Intended use: For undergraduate or graduate study at accredited vocational, 2-year or 4-year institution in United States.
Eligibility: Applicant must be no older than 21. Applicant must be U.S. citizen or permanent resident residing in Texas.
Application requirements: Proof of eligibility from the Department of Protective and Regulatory Services.
Additional information: Applicants must have been either in the care or conservatorship of Texas Department of Family and Protective Services on the day before their 18th birthday, the day of their graduation from high school, or the day of receipt of GED; or in the care or conservatorship of the TDFS on 14th birthday and then adopted. Must enroll in college before third anniversary of discharge from foster care. Program awards tuition and fees; once student determined eligible for the benefit, it continues indefinitely. Contact college's financial aid office for application.
    Amount of award: Full tuition
Contact:
Contact college/university financial aid office to apply.
Phone: 800-242-3062
Fax: 512-427-6420
Web: www.collegefortexans.com

Texas Good Neighbor Scholarship

Type of award: Scholarship.
Intended use: For undergraduate or graduate study at accredited 2-year, 4-year or graduate institution in United States.
Eligibility: Applicant must be native-born citizen of any Western Hemisphere country other than Cuba. Applicant must be residing in Texas.
Application requirements: Proof of eligibility.
Additional information: Must be current resident of country of citizenship. Must reside in Texas but plan to return to native country. Award amount is one year of tuition. Contact institution's financial aid office or the international student affairs office for application.
    Amount of award: Full tuition
    Number of awards: 235
    Application deadline: March 15
Contact:
Contact college/university financial aid office/int'l student office.
Phone: 800-242-3062
Fax: 512-427-6420
Web: www.collegefortexans.com

TEXAS Grant (Toward Excellence, Access, and Success)

Type of award: Scholarship, renewable.
Intended use: For undergraduate study at vocational, 2-year or 4-year institution.
Eligibility: Applicant must be U.S. citizen or permanent resident residing in Texas.
Basis for selection: Applicant must demonstrate financial need and high academic achievement.
Application requirements: Selective Service registration or exemption from requirement. FAFSA.
Additional information: Applicant must have completed Recommended High School Program or Distinguished Achievement Program and enroll in college at least 3/4-time (unless granted hardship waiver) within 16 months of high school graduation and must receive first award prior to completing 30 hours on campus. Also eligible are students with associate degrees from public technical state or community colleges in Texas, who enroll in public Texas university within 12 months of receiving associate's. Minimum 2.5 GPA. Applicant must not have been convicted of felony or crime involving controlled substance. No awards given for more than student's need or public institution tuition and fees. Contact financial aid office at specific college/university for application deadlines and procedures.
    Number of awards: 18,162
Contact:
Financial aid office at college/university
Phone: 800-242-3062
Fax: 512-427-6420
Web: www.collegefortexans.com

Texas Hazlewood Act Tuition Exemption: Veterans

Type of award: Scholarship, renewable.
Intended use: For undergraduate or graduate study at accredited 2-year, 4-year or graduate institution.
Eligibility: Applicant must be U.S. citizen residing in Texas. Applicant must be veteran; or dependent of deceased veteran. Must have served at least 181 days of active military duty,

excluding basic training. Must have received honorable discharge or general discharge under honorable conditions.
Application requirements: Proof of eligibility.
Additional information: Must have tuition and fee charges that exceed all federal education benefits. Veteran must have been resident of Texas prior to enlistment. Award amount includes all dues, fees, and charges, excluding property deposit, student services, and lodging/board/clothing fees. Must be enrolled in courses receiving state tax support. Applicants should contact specific school's financial aid office for more information.
Contact:
Contact college/university financial aid office to apply.
Phone: 800-242-3062
Fax: 512-427-6420
Web: www.collegefortexans.com

Texas Highest Ranking High School Graduate Tuition Exemption

Type of award: Scholarship.
Intended use: For freshman study at accredited postsecondary institution.
Eligibility: Applicant must be U.S. citizen, permanent resident or international student residing in Texas.
Basis for selection: Applicant must demonstrate high academic achievement.
Application requirements: Proof of eligibility. Valedictorian certificate issued by Texas Education Agency.
Additional information: Must be highest-ranking graduate of accredited public or private Texas high school. Award covers tuition during both semesters of first regular session immediately following the student's high school graduation; fees not included. Deadline varies.
   Amount of award: Full tuition
   Number of awards: 1,000
Contact:
Contact college/university financial aid office to apply.
Phone: 800-242-3062
Web: www.collegefortexans.com

Texas National Guard Tuition Assistance Program

Type of award: Scholarship.
Intended use: For undergraduate study at postsecondary institution in United States.
Eligibility: Applicant must be residing in Texas.
Application requirements: Proof of eligibility.
Additional information: Program provides tuition exemption to certain members of Texas National Guard, Texas Air Guard, or State Guard. Must be registered for Selective Service or exempt from this requirement. Awards at public colleges/universities are for student's tuition charges up to 12 credit hours per semester. Awards for private, non-profit institutions are based on public university tuition charges for 12 credit hours. For more information, visit Texas National Guard Website at www.agd.state.tx.us. Applicants may also contact the unit commander of their National Air Guard or State Guard unit or the Education Officer, State Adjutant General's Office, P.O. Box 5218/AGTX-PAE, Austin TX 78763-5218 or at 512-465-5001. The Education Office will provide instructions.
   Number of awards: 2,297

Contact:
Texas Higher Education Coordinating Board
Student Services Division
P.O. Box 12788
Austin, TX 78711-2788
Phone: 800-242-3062
Fax: 512-427-6420
Web: www.collegefortexans.com

Texas Public Educational Grant

Type of award: Scholarship.
Intended use: For undergraduate or graduate study at accredited vocational, 2-year or 4-year institution.
Eligibility: Applicant must be U.S. citizen, permanent resident or international student residing in Texas.
Basis for selection: Applicant must demonstrate financial need.
Application requirements: FAFSA.
Additional information: Award amount varies; may not exceed student's financial need. Deadlines vary. Contact financial aid office at college/university for more information. Applicant must register for Selective Service, unless exempt.
   Number of awards: 100,000
Contact:
Contact financial aid office at college/university.
Phone: 800-242-3062 or 877-782-7322
Web: www.collegefortexans.com

Texas Scholarships for Nursing Students

Type of award: Scholarship.
Intended use: For undergraduate or graduate study at accredited vocational, 2-year, 4-year or graduate institution.
Eligibility: Applicant must be U.S. citizen or permanent resident residing in Texas.
Basis for selection: Major/career interest in nursing or health-related professions. Applicant must demonstrate financial need.
Application requirements: Proof of eligibility.
Additional information: A variety of scholarships for vocational or professional nursing students. Based on academic promise and financial need. Award amount varies; maximum is $3,000. Contact institutional financial aid office to apply. Must register for the Selective Service (unless exempt).
Contact:
Contact the college/university financial aid office to apply.
Phone: 800-242-3062
Fax: 512-427-6420
Web: www.collegefortexans.com

Texas Tuition Exemption for Blind or Deaf Students

Type of award: Scholarship, renewable.
Intended use: For undergraduate or graduate study at accredited 2-year or 4-year institution in United States.
Eligibility: Applicant must be visually impaired or hearing impaired. Applicant must be U.S. citizen or permanent resident residing in Texas.
Basis for selection: Applicant must demonstrate depth of character.
Application requirements: Recommendations, transcript, proof of eligibility. Certification of disability. FAFSA. Written statement indicating which certificate, degree program, or professional enhancement applicant intends to pursue.

Additional information: Must be certified by relevant Texas vocational rehabilitation agency and have high school diploma or equivalent. Applicant must enroll in classes for which the college receives tax support. Award amount and deadlines vary. Contact financial aid office at college/university for more information.
Contact:
Financial aid office at college/university.
Phone: 800-242-3062
Fax: 512-427-6420
Web: www.collegefortexans.com

Tuition Equalization Grant (TEG)

Type of award: Scholarship.
Intended use: For undergraduate or graduate study at accredited 2-year or 4-year institution in United States. Designated institutions: Private, non-profit Texas colleges and universities.
Eligibility: Applicant must be U.S. citizen or permanent resident residing in Texas.
Basis for selection: Applicant must demonstrate financial need.
Application requirements: Proof of eligibility. Selective Service registration or exemption from requirement. FAFSA.
Additional information: Applicant must be Texas resident or non-resident National Merit Finalist. Not open to athletic scholarship recipients. Award cannot exceed difference between applicant's tuition at private institution and what applicant would pay at public institution. Award amount varies; maximum is $3,331, but students with exceptional need may receive up to $4,996.50. Students must be enrolled on at least a half-time basis. Applicants should contact the financial aid office at the Texas private college/university they plan to attend for more information.
   Number of awards: 28,000
Contact:
Financial aid office at college or university.
Phone: 800-242-3062
Web: www.collegefortexans.com

Tuition Exemption for Children of Disabled or Deceased Firefighters, Peace Officers, Game Wardens, and Employees of Correctional Institutions

Type of award: Scholarship, renewable.
Intended use: For undergraduate or graduate study at 2-year or 4-year institution in United States.
Eligibility: Applicant must be no older than 21. Applicant must be residing in Texas. Applicant's parent must have been killed or disabled in work-related accident as firefighter, police officer or public safety officer.
Application requirements: Proof of eligibility.
Additional information: Applicant must be child of paid or volunteer firefighter; paid municipal, county or state peace officer; custodial employee of Department of Corrections; or game warden disabled or killed in Texas in the line of duty. Persons eligible to participate in a school district's special education program under section 29.003 at age 22 may also apply. Applicant must enroll in courses that use tax support to cover some of their cost. Applicant must obtain certification form from Texas Higher Education Coordinating Board, have parent's former employer complete form, and submit form back to Texas Higher Education Coordinating Board. The Board will notify applicant's institution of eligibility. Students may be exempted from tuition and fees for the first 120 semester credits or until age 26, whichever comes first.
Contact:
Texas Higher Education Coordinating Board
Student Services Division
P.O. Box 12788
Austin, TX 78711-2788.
Phone: 800-242-3062
Web: www.collegefortexans.com

Tuition Exemption for Children of U.S. Military POW/MIAs from Texas

Type of award: Scholarship, renewable.
Intended use: For undergraduate study at accredited 2-year or 4-year institution.
Eligibility: Applicant must be no older than 25. Applicant must be U.S. citizen or permanent resident residing in Texas. Applicant must be dependent of POW/MIA.
Application requirements: Proof of eligibility. Documentation from Department of Defense that a parent, classified as Texas resident, is MIA or a POW. Completed FAFSA.
Additional information: Applicants 22 to 25 years of age must receive most of their support from a parent. Applicant must enroll in courses that use tax support to cover some of their cost. Maximum award is tuition and fees. Applicants should contact the registrar at the college/university they plan to attend for more information.
Contact:
Financial aid office at college/university.
Phone: 800-242-3062
Web: www.collegefortexans.com

Tuition Rebate for Certain Undergraduates

Type of award: Scholarship.
Intended use: For undergraduate study at postsecondary institution in United States.
Eligibility: Applicant must be residing in Texas.
Additional information: Program provides tuition rebates for students who efficiently acquire their bachelor's degrees. Students must graduate in a timely manner to receive rebate: within four years for four-year degree, five years for five-year degree. Student must have taken all coursework at Texas public institutions, and must have been entitled to pay in-state tuition at all times while pursuing degree. Student must complete bachelor's degree with no more than 3 hours in excess of degree plan, excluding up to 9 hours of credit by examination. Students must apply for tuition rebate prior to receiving bachelor's degree. Contact business office at college/university for more information.
   Amount of award: $1,000
Contact:
Texas Higher Education Coordinating Board
Student Services Division
P.O. Box 12788
Austin, TX 78711-2788
Phone: 800-242-3062
Fax: 512-427-6420
Web: www.collegefortexans.com

Third Marine Division Association

Third Marine Division Memorial Scholarship Fund

Type of award: Scholarship, renewable.
Intended use: For undergraduate study at accredited 2-year or 4-year institution in United States.
Eligibility: Applicant or parent must be member/participant of Third Marine Division Association. Applicant must be at least 16, no older than 24. Applicant must be U.S. citizen. Applicant must be dependent of active service person. Must be dependent of active duty Marines or Navy Corpsmen who are serving or who have served in Third Marine division. Parent must be a member of Third Marine Division Association for at least two years.
Basis for selection: Applicant must demonstrate financial need.
Application requirements: Proof of eligibility. Financial aid form.
Additional information: Number of awards varies. Must maintain 2.0 GPA. Eligible dependent children automatically receive renewal application forms upon submission of copies of grade reports.

Amount of award:	$500-$1,500
Number of awards:	12
Number of applicants:	13
Application deadline:	April 15

Contact:
MGySgt James G. Kyser USMC
Secretary, Memorial Scholarship Fund
15727 Vista Drive
Dumfries, VA 22025-1810

Thurgood Marshall College Fund

Thurgood Marshall Scholarship Award

Type of award: Scholarship, renewable.
Intended use: For full-time undergraduate or graduate study at 4-year or graduate institution in United States. Designated institutions: One of 47 designated historically black public universities. Download list from Website.
Eligibility: Applicant must be U.S. citizen.
Basis for selection: Applicant must demonstrate financial need, high academic achievement and service orientation.
Application requirements: Recommendations, essay, transcript. Resume. Headshot or personal photograph.
Additional information: Must be admitted to college and university before applying. Must have high school or current GPA of 3.0 or higher; must maintain 3.0 GPA throughout duration of scholarship. Must have minimum 1600 SAT or 25 ACT. Awards made directly to applicant's university. Award is $2,200 per semester. Contact university's Thurgood Marshall College Fund campus coordinator directly for more information.

Amount of award:	$4,400
Number of awards:	1,000
Number of applicants:	3,000
Application deadline:	July 1
Total amount awarded:	$2,500,000

Contact:
Thurgood Marshall College Fund,
80 Maiden Lane
Suite 2204
New York, NY 10038
Phone: 212-573-8888
Web: www.thurgoodmarshallfund.org

Tourism Cares

Canada Scholarship

Type of award: Scholarship.
Intended use: For senior or graduate study at accredited 2-year or 4-year institution in United States or Canada. Designated institutions: Accredited two- or four-year colleges in the United States or Canada; three-year schools in Quebec.
Eligibility: Applicant must be permanent resident of Canada.
Basis for selection: Major/career interest in tourism/travel.
Application requirements: Transcript. Resume. Copy of Canadian driver's license. One recommendation from tourism-related faculty, one from a professional in the tourism industry. Two-page essay addressing one of the following topics: future of international inbound tourism, impact of technology on distribution channels, challenges to group travel of changing demographics and lifestyles, impact of mass tourism on visited communities, sustainable tourism, niche marketing, culture and heritage tourism, or learning and enrichment travel.
Additional information: Minimum 3.0 GPA. Open to undergraduates enrolled in a tourism-specific program or hospitality program with focus on travel/tourism; also open to graduate students who can demonstrate focus and commitment to tourism.

Amount of award:	$1,000
Number of awards:	1
Application deadline:	April 1

Contact:
Carolyn Viles, CTC, Program Director
Tourism Cares
585 Washington Street
Canton, MA 02021
Web: www.tourismcares.org

Kathy LeTarte Scholarship

Type of award: Scholarship.
Intended use: For junior or senior study in United States or Canada.
Eligibility: Applicant must be residing in Michigan.
Basis for selection: Major/career interest in tourism/travel.
Application requirements: Transcript. Resume. Copy of Michigan driver's license. One recommendation from tourism-related faculty and one from a professional in tourism industry. Two-page essay on niche markets with an emphasis on student markets.
Additional information: Minimum 3.0 GPA. Must be a permanent resident of Michigan.

Amount of award:	$1,000
Number of awards:	1
Application deadline:	April 1

Contact:
Carolyn Viles, CTC, Program Director
Tourism Cares
585 Washington Street
Canton, MA 02021
Web: www.tourismcares.org

LaMacchia Family Scholarship

Type of award: Scholarship.
Intended use: For full-time junior or senior study at 4-year institution.
Eligibility: Applicant must be residing in Wisconsin.
Basis for selection: Major/career interest in tourism/travel.
Application requirements: Transcript. Resume. Two letters of recommendation (one from tourism-related faculty member, one from tourism professional). Two page essay on why you have chosen to pursue a career in tourism/hospitality.
Additional information: Must have minimum 3.0 GPA. Application available on Website. Open to undergraduate students enrolled in tourism-specific programs or hospitality programs with focus on travel/tourism.
    Amount of award: $1,000
    Number of awards: 1
    Application deadline: April 1
Contact:
Tourism Cares
585 Washington Street
Canton, MA 02021
Web: www.tourismcares.org

Quebec Scholarship

Type of award: Scholarship.
Intended use: For senior or graduate study at accredited 4-year institution in United States or Canada. Designated institutions: Accredited four-year schools in Canada or the US; three-year schools in Quebec.
Eligibility: Applicant must be permanent resident of Quebec.
Basis for selection: Major/career interest in tourism/travel.
Application requirements: Transcript. Transcript should be sent directly from school. Resume. Copy of Quebec driver's license. One recommendation from tourism-related faculty, one from a professional in the tourism industry. Two-page essay addressing one of the following topics; future of international inbound tourism, impact of technology on distribution channels, challenges to group travel of changing demographics and lifestyles, impact of mass tourism on visited communities, sustainable tourism, niche marketing, culture and heritage tourism, or learning and enrichment travel.
Additional information: Minimum 3.0 GPA.
    Amount of award: $1,500
    Number of awards: 1
    Application deadline: April 1
Contact:
Carolyn Viles, CTC, Program Director
Tourism Cares
585 Washington Street
Canton, MA 02021
Web: www.tourismcares.org

Rene Campbell Memorial Scholarship

Type of award: Scholarship.
Intended use: For junior or senior study at accredited 4-year institution in United States or Canada.
Eligibility: Applicant must be residing in North Carolina.
Basis for selection: Major/career interest in tourism/travel.
Application requirements: Recommendations, essay, transcript. Resume. Two letters of recommendation (one from tourism-related faculty member, one from tourism professional). Copy of North Carolina driver's license. Two page personal essay on why you have chosen to pursue a career in tourism/hospitality industry.
Additional information: Minimum 3.0 GPA. Applicant must be NC resident, but may attend school anywhere in the U.S. or Canada. Open to undergraduate students enrolled in tourism-specific program or hospitality program with focus on travel/tourism.
    Amount of award: $1,000
    Number of awards: 1
    Application deadline: April 1
Contact:
Tourism Cares
585 Washington Street
Canton, MA 02021
Web: www.tourismcares.org

Yellow Ribbon Scholarship

Type of award: Scholarship.
Intended use: For undergraduate study at accredited postsecondary institution in United States or Canada.
Eligibility: Applicant must be visually impaired, hearing impaired or physically challenged.
Basis for selection: Major/career interest in tourism/travel or hotel/restaurant management. Applicant must demonstrate high academic achievement.
Application requirements: Transcript, proof of eligibility. Two recommendation letters (one from tourism-related faculty members (one from tourism industry professional). Copy of U.S./Canadian driver's license. Letter from an accredited physician attesting to applicant's disability. Resume. Typed, signed, and referenced essay (minimum 500 words) explaining how education will be used in making career in travel/tourism.
Additional information: Available to students with physical or sensory disability. Minimum 3.0 GPA for students entering postsecondary institution; minimum 2.5 GPA at college level. Visit Website for updates and more information.
    Amount of award: $5,000
    Number of awards: 1
    Application deadline: April 1
    Total amount awarded: $5,000
Contact:
Tourism Cares
585 Washington Street
Canton, MA 02021
Phone: 781-821-5990
Fax: 781-821-8949
Web: www.tourismcares.org

Transportation Clubs International

Alice Glaisyer Warfield Memorial Scholarship

Type of award: Scholarship.
Intended use: For sophomore, junior, senior or graduate study at accredited postsecondary institution.

Transportation Clubs International: Alice Glaisyer Warfield Memorial Scholarship

Basis for selection: Major/career interest in transportation. Applicant must demonstrate financial need, high academic achievement and depth of character.
Application requirements: Recommendations, essay, transcript. Small photograph (for publication).
- Amount of award: $1,000
- Number of awards: 1
- Application deadline: April 30
- Total amount awarded: $1,000

Contact:
Transportation Clubs International
Attention: Bill Blair
15710 JFK Boulevard
Houston, TX 77032
Web: www.transportationclubsinternational.com

Charlotte Woods Memorial Scholarship

Type of award: Scholarship.
Intended use: For undergraduate or graduate study.
Eligibility: Applicant or parent must be member/participant of Transportation Clubs International.
Basis for selection: Major/career interest in transportation. Applicant must demonstrate financial need, high academic achievement and depth of character.
Application requirements: Recommendations, essay, transcript. Small photograph (for publication).
- Amount of award: $1,000
- Number of awards: 1
- Application deadline: April 30
- Total amount awarded: $1,000

Contact:
Transportation Clubs International, Attention: Bill Blair
15710 JFK Boulevard
Houston, TX 77032
Web: www.transportationclubsinternational.com

Denny Lydic Scholarship

Type of award: Scholarship.
Intended use: For sophomore, junior, senior or graduate study.
Basis for selection: Major/career interest in transportation. Applicant must demonstrate financial need, high academic achievement and depth of character.
Application requirements: Recommendations, essay, transcript. Small photograph (for publication).
- Amount of award: $500
- Number of awards: 1
- Application deadline: April 30
- Total amount awarded: $500

Contact:
Transportation Clubs International
Attention: Bill Blair
15710 JFK Boulevard
Houston, TX 77032
Web: www.transportationclubsinternational.com

Ginger and Fred Deines Canada Scholarship

Type of award: Scholarship.
Intended use: For sophomore, junior, senior or graduate study in United States or Canada.
Eligibility: Applicant must be Canadian citizen.
Basis for selection: Major/career interest in transportation. Applicant must demonstrate financial need, high academic achievement and depth of character.
Application requirements: Recommendations, essay, transcript. Small photograph (for publication).
- Amount of award: $1,500
- Number of awards: 1
- Application deadline: April 30
- Total amount awarded: $1,500

Contact:
Transportation Clubs International
Attention: Bill Blair
15710 JFK Boulevard
Houston, TX 77032
Web: www.transportationclubinternational.com

Ginger and Fred Deines Mexico Scholarship

Type of award: Scholarship.
Intended use: For sophomore, junior, senior or graduate study.
Designated institutions: Institutions in U.S. or Mexico.
Eligibility: Applicant must be Mexican citizen.
Basis for selection: Major/career interest in transportation. Applicant must demonstrate financial need, high academic achievement and depth of character.
Application requirements: Recommendations, essay, transcript. Small photograph (for publication).
- Amount of award: $1,500
- Number of awards: 1
- Application deadline: April 30
- Total amount awarded: $1,500

Contact:
Transportation Clubs International
Attention: Bill Blair
15710 JFK Boulevard
Houston, TX 77032
Web: www.transportationclubsinternational.com

Hooper Memorial Scholarship

Type of award: Scholarship.
Intended use: For sophomore, junior, senior or graduate study.
Basis for selection: Major/career interest in transportation. Applicant must demonstrate financial need, high academic achievement and depth of character.
Application requirements: Recommendations, essay, transcript. Small photograph (for publication).
- Amount of award: $1,500
- Number of awards: 1
- Application deadline: April 30
- Total amount awarded: $1,500

Contact:
Transportation Clubs International
Attention: Bill Blair
15710 JFK Boulevard
Houston, TX 77032
Web: www.transportationclubsinternational.com

Texas Transportation Scholarship

Type of award: Scholarship.
Intended use: For sophomore, junior, senior or graduate study.
Basis for selection: Major/career interest in transportation. Applicant must demonstrate financial need, high academic achievement and depth of character.
Application requirements: Recommendations, essay, transcript. Small photograph (for publication).

Additional information: Applicant must have been enrolled in a Texas school for some phase of elementary through high school education.

    Amount of award: $1,000
    Number of awards: 1
    Application deadline: April 30
    Total amount awarded: $1,000

Contact:
Transportation Clubs International
Attention: Bill Blair
15710 JFK Boulevard
Houston, TX 77032
Web: www.transportationclubsinternational.com

Travel and Tourism Research Association

J. Desmond Slattery Award: Student

Type of award: Scholarship.
Intended use: For undergraduate study at postsecondary institution.
Basis for selection: Competition/talent/interest in research paper, based on originality, creativity, quality of research, relationship to travel/tourism, usefulness/applicability, and quality of presentation. Major/career interest in tourism/travel.
Application requirements: Original research paper and 500- to 1,000-word abstract.
Additional information: Must be in degree-granting program. Winner also receives plaque, one-year student TTRA membership, $300 travel allowance and complimentary registration at TTRA annual conference. Winner notified end of May. Download application from Website.

    Amount of award: $700
    Application deadline: March 31

Contact:
Travel and Tourism Research Association
P.O. Box 2133
Boise, ID 83701
Phone: 208-429-9511
Fax: 208-429-9512
Web: www.ttra.com

Travel Research Grant

Type of award: Research grant.
Intended use: For undergraduate, graduate or non-degree study.
Basis for selection: Competition/talent/interest in research paper, based on ability to improve measurement, decrease costs, and improve information for better application and understanding. Major/career interest in tourism/travel.
Application requirements: Research proposal.
Additional information: Grant recipient has three years to complete project. Material must be submitted in English; project must show significant benefits to travel/tourism industry. Winner also receives plaque, $300 travel allowance, and complimentary registration at TTRA annual conference. Download application from Website. No entries accepted for this award in 2008; will resume in 2009.

    Amount of award: $4,000
    Number of awards: 1
    Application deadline: March 31

Contact:
Travel and Tourism Research Association
P.O. Box 2133
Boise, ID 83701
Phone: 208-429-9511
Fax: 208-429-9512
Web: www.ttra.com

Treacy Company

Treacy Company Scholarship

Type of award: Scholarship, renewable.
Intended use: For full-time freshman or sophomore study at postsecondary institution.
Eligibility: Applicant must be residing in South Dakota, Montana, Idaho or North Dakota.
Basis for selection: Applicant must demonstrate financial need, leadership, seriousness of purpose and service orientation.
Application requirements: Transcript. Letter stating reason for applying, including personal information.
Additional information: Student may attend school outside of ND, ID and MT. Must write for application; applications available from January to end of May.

    Amount of award: $1,000
    Number of awards: 70
    Number of applicants: 350
    Application deadline: June 15
    Notification begins: July 31
    Total amount awarded: $28,000

Contact:
Treacy Company
P.O. Box 1479
Helena, MT 59624

Trinity Episcopal Church

Shannon Scholarship

Type of award: Scholarship, renewable.
Intended use: For undergraduate study.
Eligibility: Applicant must be female. Applicant must be Episcopal. Applicant must be residing in Pennsylvania.
Basis for selection: Applicant must demonstrate financial need.
Application requirements: Proof of eligibility.
Additional information: Only open to daughters of Episcopal clergy in state of Pennsylvania. Must apply for state and federal financial assistance first. Previous recipients may reapply. Number of awards varies. For more information, contact church office.

    Amount of award: $1,000-$7,000
    Application deadline: April 30

Contact:
Trinity Episcopal Church
200 South Second Street
Pottsville, PA 17901
Phone: 570-622-8720

Troy Douglass Carr Scholarship Fund

Troy Douglas Carr Scholarship for Criminal Justice

Type of award: Scholarship.
Intended use: For undergraduate study.
Eligibility: Applicant must be residing in North Carolina.
Basis for selection: Major/career interest in criminal justice/law enforcement.
Additional information: Visit Website for more details and for application.
   Amount of award: $2,000
   Number of awards: 2
   Application deadline: April 30
   Total amount awarded: $1,000
Contact:
275 McLendon Hills Dr.
West End, NC 27376
Phone: 910-673-4951
Fax: 910-673-8326
Web: www.troycarr.org

Two Ten Footwear Foundation

Two Ten Footwear Design Scholarship

Type of award: Scholarship, renewable.
Intended use: For in or outside United States.
Eligibility: Applicant must be U.S. citizen or permanent resident.
Basis for selection: Applicant must demonstrate financial need.
Application requirements: Portfolio, recommendations, transcript, proof of eligibility.
Additional information: Rolling deadline. Must major in and be committed to career in footwear design.
   Amount of award: $2,500-$5,000
Contact:
Two Ten Footwear Foundation
Scholarship Department
1466 Main Street
Waltham, MA 02451
Phone: 800-346-3210 ext. 1503
Web: www.twoten.org

Two Ten Footwear Foundation Scholarship

Type of award: Scholarship, renewable.
Intended use: For undergraduate study at accredited vocational, 2-year or 4-year institution.
Eligibility: Applicant or parent must be employed by Footwear/Leather Industry. Applicant must be U.S. citizen.
Basis for selection: Applicant must demonstrate financial need and high academic achievement.
Application requirements: Recommendations, essay, transcript, proof of eligibility.
Additional information: Applicant must have worked 500 hours in footwear or leather industries or have parent currently employed in this field for at least two years. Top-ranking applicant is candidate for $15,000 super-scholarship, renewable up to four years. Additional information and application available on website.
   Amount of award: $200-$15,000
   Application deadline: February 15
   Notification begins: June 15
   Total amount awarded: $650,000
Contact:
Two Ten Footwear Foundation
Attn: Scholarship Department
1466 Main Street
Waltham, MA 02451-1623
Phone: 800-346-3210 ext 1503
Web: www.twoten.org

UCB Pharma Inc.

Keppra Family Epilepsy Scholarship Program

Type of award: Scholarship.
Intended use: For undergraduate study at postsecondary institution in United States.
Eligibility: Applicant must be U.S. citizen or permanent resident.
Basis for selection: Applicant must demonstrate high academic achievement, leadership and service orientation.
Application requirements: Transcript. Essay or artistic presentation explaining why applicant should be selected for scholarship (awards received, community involvement, etc.) and how epilepsy has impacted his or her life. Photograph. Three letters of recommendation: one from a school official, one from a community member, and one from applicant's epilepsy healthcare team.
Additional information: Twenty scholarships awarded to epilepsy patients, ten to caregivers and family members of epilepsy patients. Application available from Website.
   Amount of award: $5,000
   Number of awards: 30
   Application deadline: May 25
Contact:
Keppra Scholarship Program
c/o S&R Communications Group
2511 Old Cornwallis Road, Suite 200
Durham, NC 27713
Phone: 888-275-7928
Web: www.keppra.com

Ukrainian Fraternal Association

Eugene and Elinor Kotur Scholarship

Type of award: Scholarship, renewable.

Intended use: For full-time sophomore, junior, senior or graduate study at accredited 4-year institution. Designated institutions: Brown, Caltech, Carnegie Mellon, Connecticut University, Cornell, Dartmouth, Duke, George Washington University (St. Louis), Harvard, Haverford, Indiana University, John Hopkins University, MIT, McGill University (Montreal), Michigan State, Notre Dame, Oberlin, Purdue, Princeton, Rochester University, Swarthmore, Tulane, University of California (Berkeley or LA), University of Chicago, University of Michigan, University of Pennsylvania, University of Toronto, University of Washington (Seattle), University of Wisconsin (Madison), Vanderbilt, Williams, Yale.
Eligibility: Applicant must be Ukrainian.
Basis for selection: Applicant must demonstrate financial need, high academic achievement and depth of character.
Application requirements: Transcript, proof of eligibility. Autobiographical statement containing information regarding Ukrainian roots. Small photograph.
Additional information: Must have completed first year of undergraduate studies. Membership in the Ukrainian Fraternal Association is not required for application but is required for renewal.

Amount of award:	$1,000-$3,000
Number of applicants:	7
Application deadline:	June 1

Contact:
Ukrainian Fraternal Association Scholarship Coordinator
371 N. 9th Ave.
Scranton, PA 18504
Phone: 570-342-0937
Fax: 570-347-5649
Web: www.members.tripod.com/UFA_home/

Ukrainian Fraternal Association Scholarship

Type of award: Scholarship, renewable.
Intended use: For full-time sophomore, junior or senior study.
Eligibility: Applicant or parent must be member/participant of Ukrainian Fraternal Association. Applicant must be Ukrainian.
Basis for selection: Applicant must demonstrate financial need and high academic achievement.
Application requirements: Transcript. Photo and autobiography.
Additional information: Applicant must be member of Ukrainian Fraternal Association. Must have completed first year of undergraduate study.

Amount of award:	$300
Number of applicants:	20
Application deadline:	June 1

Contact:
Ukrainian Fraternal Association Scholarship Coordinator
371 N 9th Ave.
Scranton, PA 18504
Phone: 570-342-0937
Fax: 570-347-5649
Web: www.members.tripod.com/UFA_home/

Unico Foundation, Inc.

Alphonse A. Miele Scholarship

Type of award: Scholarship.
Intended use: For undergraduate study.
Eligibility: Applicant must be high school senior. Applicant must be Italian.
Basis for selection: Applicant must demonstrate financial need, high academic achievement, depth of character and leadership.
Application requirements: Recommendations, essay, transcript, proof of eligibility. SAT/ACT scores.
Additional information: Must reside in corporate limits of city with active chapter of Unico National. Award is $1,500 per year for four years. Student must be Italian.

Amount of award:	$6,000
Number of awards:	1
Application deadline:	April 15

Contact:
Unico Foundation, Inc.
271 US Highway, 46 West
Suite A-108
Fairfield, NJ 07004
Phone: 973-808-0035
Web: www.unico.org

Major Don S. Gentile Scholarship

Type of award: Scholarship.
Intended use: For undergraduate study.
Eligibility: Applicant must be high school senior. Applicant must be Italian.
Basis for selection: Applicant must demonstrate financial need, high academic achievement, depth of character and leadership.
Application requirements: Recommendations, essay, transcript, proof of eligibility.
Additional information: Must reside in corporate limits of city with active chapter of Unico National. Award distributed in four annual installments of $1,500.

Amount of award:	$6,000
Number of awards:	1
Application deadline:	April 15

Contact:
Unico Foundation, Inc.
271 US Highway 46 #A108
Fairfield, NJ 07004-2458
Phone: 973-808-0035
Web: www.unico.org

Theodore Mazza Scholarship

Type of award: Scholarship.
Intended use: For undergraduate study.
Eligibility: Applicant must be high school senior. Applicant must be Italian.
Basis for selection: Major/career interest in art/art history; music or theater arts. Applicant must demonstrate financial need, high academic achievement, depth of character and leadership.
Application requirements: Recommendations, essay, transcript, proof of eligibility.
Additional information: Must reside in corporate limits of city with active chapter of Unico National. Award distributed in four annual installments of $1,500.

Amount of award:	$6,000
Number of awards:	1
Application deadline:	April 15

Contact:
Unico Foundation, Inc.
271 US Highway 46 #A108
Fairfield, NJ 07004-2458
Web: www.unico.org

William C. Davini Scholarship

Type of award: Scholarship.
Intended use: For undergraduate study.
Eligibility: Applicant must be high school senior. Applicant must be Italian.
Basis for selection: Applicant must demonstrate financial need, high academic achievement, depth of character and leadership.
Application requirements: Recommendations, essay, transcript, proof of eligibility.
Additional information: Must reside in corporate limits of city with active chapter of Unico National. Award distributed in four annual installments of $1,500.

Amount of award:	$6,000
Number of awards:	1
Application deadline:	April 15

Contact:
Unico Foundation, Inc.
271 US Highway 46 #A108
Fairfield, NJ 07004-2458
Web: www.unico.org

Unitarian Universalist Association

Stanfield and D'Orlando Art Scholarship

Type of award: Scholarship.
Intended use: For full-time undergraduate or first professional study in United States.
Eligibility: Applicant must be at least 16. Applicant must be Unitarian Universalist.
Basis for selection: Major/career interest in arts, general or art/art history. Applicant must demonstrate financial need, depth of character and service orientation.
Application requirements: Portfolio, recommendations, essay, transcript, proof of eligibility.
Additional information: Number of awards varies; on average, five are given. Applicant must be preparing for fine arts career in fields such as painting, drawing, sculpture, or photography. Art therapy and performing arts majors not eligible. Returning adult students also eligible. See Website for application and more information.

Amount of award:	$1,000-$6,000
Number of awards:	6
Number of applicants:	15
Application deadline:	February 15, March 1
Notification begins:	March 31
Total amount awarded:	$20,000

Contact:
Unitarian Universalist Funding Program
P.O. Box 301149
Jamaica Plain, MA 02130
Phone: 617-971-9600
Fax: 617-971-0029
Web: www.uua.org/awards/stanfield

United Food and Commercial Workers International Union

United Food and Commercial Workers International Union Scholarship Program

Type of award: Scholarship.
Intended use: For full-time undergraduate study at accredited postsecondary institution.
Eligibility: Applicant or parent must be member/participant of United Food and Commerical Workers. Applicant must be high school senior.
Basis for selection: Applicant must demonstrate high academic achievement and service orientation.
Application requirements: Essay, transcript. Complete biographical questionnaire. Personal essay. Transcript.
Additional information: Open to current and prospective high school graduates and to GED recipients. Applicant or applicant's parent must be member of United Food and Commercial Workers International Union for one year prior to application. Dependents of members must be under the age of 20. Must include personal essay, transcript, and completed biographical questionnaire with application.

Amount of award:	$8,000
Number of awards:	16
Number of applicants:	4,500
Application deadline:	March 15
Total amount awarded:	$112,000

Contact:
United Food and Commercial Workers International Union
1775 K Street, N.W.
Washington, DC 20006
Phone: 202-223-3111
Web: www.ufcw.org/scholarship

United Methodist Church General Education Board of Higher Education and Ministry

United Methodist Scholarships

Type of award: Scholarship, renewable.
Intended use: For full-time undergraduate or graduate study at accredited 2-year, 4-year or graduate institution in United States.
Eligibility: Applicant must be United Methodist. Applicant must be U.S. citizen or permanent resident.
Basis for selection: Applicant must demonstrate seriousness of purpose.
Application requirements: Transcript.
Additional information: Sponsor administers more than 60 scholarship programs. All recipients must be full active member of United Methodist Church for minimum of one year prior to application and maintain minimum 2.5 GPA. Deadlines vary.

Some scholarships are renewable. Visit Website for more information.
Contact:
United Methodist Church General Board of Higher Education and Ministry
Office of Loans and Scholarships
P.O. Box 340007
Nashville, TN 37203-0007
Phone: 614-340-7344
Web: www.gbhem.org

United Methodist Communications

Leonard M. Perryman Communications Scholarship

Type of award: Scholarship.
Intended use: For junior or senior study.
Basis for selection: Major/career interest in religion/theology or journalism.
Application requirements: Candidates must be in junior or senior year to qualify.
Additional information: $2,500 scholarship for undergrad study in religion journalism/mass communications. Candidates must be in junior or senior year to qualify.

Number of awards:	1
Number of applicants:	15
Application deadline:	March 15
Total amount awarded:	$2,500

Contact:
United Methodist Communications
P.O. Box 320
810 12th Avenue South
Nashville, TN 31202-0320
Phone: 888-CRT-4UMC
Web: www.umcom.org/scholarships

Leonard M. Perryman Communications Scholarship for Ethnic Minority Students

Type of award: Scholarship.
Intended use: For full-time junior or senior study at accredited 4-year institution in United States.
Eligibility: Applicant must be Alaskan native, Asian American, African American, Mexican American, Hispanic American, Puerto Rican, American Indian or Native Hawaiian/Pacific Islander. Applicant must be United Methodist.
Basis for selection: Major/career interest in journalism; communications; radio/television/film or religion/theology. Applicant must demonstrate seriousness of purpose.
Application requirements: Recommendations, essay, transcript. Three examples of journalistic work in any medium; statement of interest in religious journalism and planned course of study; photograph (appropriate for publicity purposes).
Additional information: Must plan to pursue career in religious journalism or religious communication. Application forms available October 1 and may be downloaded from Website.

Amount of award:	$2,500
Number of awards:	1
Number of applicants:	6
Application deadline:	March 15
Total amount awarded:	$2,500

Contact:
United Methodist Communications
Scholarship Committee
P.O. Box 320
Nashville, TN 37202-0320
Phone: 888-278-4862
Web: www.umcom.org

Stoody-West Fellowship

Type of award: Scholarship.
Intended use: For postgraduate study.
Basis for selection: Major/career interest in religion/theology or journalism.
Application requirements: Must be post-grad. Must be pursuing career in religion journalism.
Additional information: $6,000 award for students in post-graduate study at an accredited U.S. college or university who intend on pursuing a career in religion journalism.

Number of awards:	1
Number of applicants:	12
Application deadline:	March 15
Total amount awarded:	$6,000

Contact:
United Methodist Communications
P.O. Box 320
810 12th Avenue South
Nashville, TN 37202-0320
Phone: 888-CRT-4UMC
Web: www.umcom.org/scholarships

United Negro College Fund

Abercrombie & Fitch Scholarship Program

Type of award: Scholarship, renewable.
Intended use: For full-time freshman study at accredited 4-year institution in United States.
Eligibility: Applicant must be Alaskan native, Asian American, African American, Mexican American, Hispanic American, Puerto Rican, American Indian or Native Hawaiian/Pacific Islander. Applicant must be U.S. citizen or permanent resident.
Basis for selection: Applicant must demonstrate financial need and high academic achievement.
Application requirements: Recommendations, essay, transcript, proof of eligibility. FAFSA and photograph.
Additional information: Minimum 3.0 GPA. Visit Website or contact financial aid office of member institution for application, deadlines, award amount, and details.

Amount of award:	$3,000
Number of awards:	22
Application deadline:	October 13

United Negro College Fund: Abercrombie & Fitch Scholarship Program

Contact:
United Negro College Fund
8260 Willow Oaks Corporate Drive
P.O. Box 10444
Fairfax, VA 22031
Phone: 800-331-2244
Web: www.uncf.org

Alfred R. Chisholm Memorial Scholarship

Type of award: Scholarship, renewable.
Intended use: For full-time undergraduate study at accredited 4-year institution in United States. Designated institutions: Historically Black Colleges and Universities (HBCU) schools in California, New Jersey, Illinois, Ohio, Georgia, Wisconsin, Michigan, Texas, Florida, Alabama, South Carolina, Louisiana, North Carolina, and West Virginia.
Eligibility: Applicant must be African American. Applicant must be U.S. citizen or permanent resident residing in New Jersey.
Basis for selection: Major/career interest in computer/information sciences; engineering; chemistry or mathematics. Applicant must demonstrate high academic achievement and service orientation.
Application requirements: Recommendations, essay, transcript, proof of eligibility. FAFSA, photographs.
Additional information: Minimum 2.7 GPA. Applicant must have one relative employed by BASF - The Chemical Company.

Amount of award:	$5,000
Number of awards:	1
Application deadline:	July 10

Contact:
United Negro College Fund
8260 Willow Oaks Corporate Drive
P.O. Box 10444
Fairfax, VA 22031-8044
Phone: 800-331-2244
Web: www.uncf.org

Alton R. Higgins, MD, and Dorothy Higgins Scholarship

Type of award: Scholarship, renewable.
Intended use: For full-time junior, senior or first professional study at accredited 4-year or graduate institution in United States. Designated institutions: Dillard University, Fisk University, Morehouse College, Oakwood College, Spelman College, Talladega College, Tougaloo College, Tuskegee University, Xavier University.
Eligibility: Applicant must be African American. Applicant must be U.S. citizen or permanent resident.
Basis for selection: Major/career interest in medicine. Applicant must demonstrate financial need.
Application requirements: Recommendations, essay, transcript, proof of eligibility. FAFSA, photographs.
Additional information: Minimum 3.0 GPA. Undergraduates eligible for $5,000 award, renewable in senior year. Graduate award is $7,500 - $10,000.

Amount of award:	$5,000-$10,000
Number of applicants:	13
Application deadline:	June 4
Notification begins:	August 27

Contact:
United Negro College Fund
8260 Willow Oaks Corporate Drive
P.O. Box 10444
Fairfax, VA 22031-8044
Phone: 800-331-2244
Web: www.uncf.org

Berbeco Senior Research Fellowship

Type of award: Scholarship.
Intended use: For full-time junior or senior study at accredited 4-year institution in United States. Designated institutions: UNCF member institutions.
Eligibility: Applicant must be Alaskan native, Asian American, African American, Mexican American, Hispanic American, Puerto Rican, American Indian or Native Hawaiian/Pacific Islander. Applicant must be U.S. citizen or permanent resident.
Application requirements: Essay, proof of eligibility. One-page letter of intent outlining research project and summer research objectives.
Additional information: The Berbeco Senior Research Fellowship is intended to encourage study abroad, through an established program or under the guidance of faculty member at a foreign university. Applicant must have a senior project/thesis as graduation requirement. Minimum 2.5 GPA. Visit Website for deadlines and additional information.

Application deadline:	November 28

Contact:
United Negro College Fund
8260 Willow Oaks Corporate Drive
P.O. Box 10444
Fairfax, VA 22031-8044
Phone: 800-331-2244
Web: www.uncf.org

Cargill Scholarship Program

Type of award: Scholarship.
Intended use: For full-time freshman, sophomore or junior study at accredited 2-year or 4-year institution. Designated institutions: UNCF member institutions and Kansas State University, University of Illinois, University of Minnesota, Iowa State University, North Carolina A&T State University, and University of Wisconsin-Madison.
Eligibility: Applicant must be Alaskan native, Asian American, African American, Mexican American, Hispanic American, Puerto Rican, American Indian or Native Hawaiian/Pacific Islander. Applicant must be U.S. citizen or permanent resident.
Basis for selection: Major/career interest in accounting; finance/banking; computer/information sciences; chemistry; biochemistry; microbiology; engineering, chemical or engineering, mechanical. Applicant must demonstrate financial need and high academic achievement.
Application requirements: Recommendations, transcript. FAFSA, resume, 250-word essay about applicant, selected major, career goals and how they might be fulfilled at Cargill.
Additional information: Minimum 3.0 GPA. Internship opportunities may become available. Cargill will also consider food sciences majors. Deadlines vary, visit Website for details.

Amount of award:	$5,000

Contact:
United Negro College Fund Program Services
8260 Willow Oaks Corporate Drive
P.O. Box 10444
Fairfax, VA 22031-8044
Phone: 800-331-2244
Web: www.uncf.org

ChevronTexaco Scholars Program

Type of award: Scholarship, renewable.
Intended use: For full-time sophomore or junior study at accredited 4-year institution in United States. Designated institutions: Clark Atlanta University, Morehouse College, Spelman College, Tuskegee University.
Eligibility: Applicant must be Alaskan native, Asian American, African American, Mexican American, Hispanic American, Puerto Rican, American Indian or Native Hawaiian/Pacific Islander.
Basis for selection: Major/career interest in engineering, civil; engineering, mechanical or engineering, petroleum. Applicant must demonstrate financial need, high academic achievement, leadership and service orientation.
Application requirements: Recommendations, essay, transcript. FAFSA, resume, two personal reference letters, one-page personal statement of career interest, photograph.
Additional information: Minimum 2.5 GPA. Residents of Texas, Florida, or California preferred. Funds from this scholarship may be used toward tuition and room/board or to repay federal student loans.
   Amount of award: $3,000
   Number of awards: 80
   Application deadline: February 18
Contact:
United Negro College Fund
8260 Willow Oaks Corporate Drive
P.O. Box 10444
Fairfax, VA 22031-8044
Phone: 800-331-2244
Web: www.uncf.org

Cisco/UNCF Scholars Program

Type of award: Scholarship, renewable.
Intended use: For full-time sophomore study at accredited 4-year institution in United States. Designated institutions: Claflin University, Clark Atlanta University, Dillard University, Jarvis Christian College, Johnson C. Smith University, Livingstone College, Morehouse College, Morgan State University, Paul Quinn College, Rust College, Saint Augustine's College, Shaw University, Spelman College, Wiley College, Xavier University.
Eligibility: Applicant must be Alaskan native, Asian American, African American, Mexican American, Hispanic American, Puerto Rican, American Indian or Native Hawaiian/Pacific Islander. Applicant must be female. Applicant must be U.S. citizen or permanent resident.
Basis for selection: Major/career interest in computer/information sciences or engineering, electrical/electronic. Applicant must demonstrate financial need, high academic achievement and service orientation.
Application requirements: Recommendations, essay, transcript, proof of eligibility. Resume, financial need statement.
Additional information: Minimum 3.2 GPA. Application available online.
   Amount of award: $4,000
   Number of awards: 10
   Application deadline: April 15
Contact:
United Negro College Fund
8260 Willow Oaks Corporate Drive
P.O. Box 10444
Fairfax, VA 22031-8044
Phone: 800-331-2244
Web: www.uncf.org

Earl & Patricia Armstrong Scholarship

Type of award: Scholarship.
Intended use: For full-time undergraduate or graduate study at accredited 4-year institution in United States. Designated institutions: UNCF member institutions.
Eligibility: Applicant must be Alaskan native, Asian American, African American, Mexican American, Hispanic American, Puerto Rican, American Indian or Native Hawaiian/Pacific Islander. Applicant must be U.S. citizen or permanent resident.
Basis for selection: Major/career interest in medicine; biology or health sciences. Applicant must demonstrate financial need and high academic achievement.
Application requirements: Recommendations, essay, transcript, proof of eligibility. FAFSA and SAR.
Additional information: Minimum 3.0 GPA. Visit Website for application.
   Amount of award: $3,000
   Notification begins: March 1
Contact:
United Negro College Fund
8260 Willow Oaks Corporate Drive
P.O. Box 10444
Fairfax, VA 22031-8044
Phone: 800-331-2244
Web: www.uncf.org

Gates Millennium Scholars Program

Type of award: Scholarship, renewable.
Intended use: For full-time freshman or graduate study at accredited 4-year or graduate institution.
Eligibility: Applicant must be Alaskan native, Asian American, African American, Mexican American, Hispanic American, Puerto Rican, American Indian or Native Hawaiian/Pacific Islander.
Basis for selection: Applicant must demonstrate financial need, high academic achievement, leadership and service orientation.
Application requirements: Recommendations, transcript, nomination by high school principal, teacher or counselor or college president, professor or dean. Nominee Personal Information Form, FAFSA, GMS information sheet, admission letters.
Additional information: Must be Pell Grant eligible. Must participate in community service, volunteer work or extracurricular activities. Minimum 3.0 GPA required. Scholarship provides tuition, room, materials, and board not covered by existing financial aid. Eliminates loans, work-study, and outside jobs for scholarship recipients. All majors accepted for undergraduate scholarships; graduate students must be enrolled in degree program in engineering, mathematics, science, education, or library science. Funded by Bill and Melinda Gates Foundation.
   Number of awards: 4,000
   Application deadline: January 11
   Total amount awarded: $50,000,000
Contact:
United Negro College Fund Program Services
8260 Willow Oaks Corporate Drive
P. O. Box 10444
Fairfax, VA 22031-8044
Phone: 800-331-2244 or 877-690-4677
Web: www.uncf.org or www.gmsp.org

Janet Jackson Rhythm Nation Scholarships

Type of award: Scholarship, renewable.
Intended use: For full-time undergraduate study at accredited 4-year institution in United States. Designated institutions: UNCF member institutions.
Eligibility: Applicant must be Alaskan native, Asian American, African American, Mexican American, Hispanic American, Puerto Rican, American Indian or Native Hawaiian/Pacific Islander.
Basis for selection: Major/career interest in communications; performing arts; English or music.
Application requirements: Recommendations, essay, proof of eligibility. FAFSA, resume, photograph, and SAR must be sent to school's financial aid office.
Additional information: Minimum 3.0 GPA. Fine arts majors also eligible. Awards are made annually and may be used for tuition costs, room and board, or to repay federal student loans. For more information and application, see Website.
  Amount of award: $2,000
Contact:
United Negro College Fund
8260 Willow Oaks Corporate Deive
P. O. Box 10444
Fairfax, VA 22031-8044
Phone: 800-331-2244
Web: www.uncf.org

John Lennon Scholarship Fund

Type of award: Scholarship, renewable.
Intended use: For full-time undergraduate study at accredited 4-year institution in United States. Designated institutions: UNCF member institutions.
Eligibility: Applicant must be Alaskan native, Asian American, African American, Mexican American, Hispanic American, Puerto Rican, American Indian or Native Hawaiian/Pacific Islander.
Basis for selection: Major/career interest in performing arts or communications. Applicant must demonstrate financial need and high academic achievement.
Application requirements: Recommendations, essay, transcript, proof of eligibility. FAFSA and photograph.
Additional information: Minimum 3.0 GPA. Visit Website for additional information. Contact financial aid office of member institution for application and deadlines.
  Amount of award: $5,000
  Application deadline: February 16
Contact:
United Negro College Fund
8260 Willow Oaks Corporate Drive
P. O. Box 10444
Fairfax, VA 22031-8044
Phone: 800-331-2244
Web: www.uncf.org

John W. Anderson Foundation Scholarship

Type of award: Scholarship, renewable.
Intended use: For full-time undergraduate study at accredited 4-year institution in United States. Designated institutions: UNCF member institutions.
Eligibility: Applicant must be Alaskan native, Asian American, African American, Mexican American, Hispanic American, Puerto Rican, American Indian or Native Hawaiian/Pacific Islander. Applicant must be U.S. citizen or permanent resident residing in Indiana.
Basis for selection: Applicant must demonstrate financial need and high academic achievement.
Application requirements: FAFSA and SAR.
Additional information: Minimum 2.5 GPA. See Website for more information.
  Amount of award: $3,000
Contact:
United Negro College Fund
8260 Willow Oaks Corporate Drive
P.O. Box 10444
Fairfax, VA 22031-8044
Phone: 800-331-2244
Web: www.uncf.org

Malcolm X Scholarship for Exceptional Courage

Type of award: Scholarship, renewable.
Intended use: For full-time junior study at accredited 4-year institution in United States. Designated institutions: UNCF member institutions.
Eligibility: Applicant must be Alaskan native, Asian American, African American, Mexican American, Hispanic American, Puerto Rican, American Indian or Native Hawaiian/Pacific Islander.
Basis for selection: Applicant must demonstrate financial need, high academic achievement, leadership and seriousness of purpose.
Application requirements: Recommendations, essay, transcript, proof of eligibility.
Additional information: Minimum 2.5 GPA. Application and list of colleges available online. Renewable each year until graduation. Scholarship is awarded to students who demonstrate exceptional courage. Deadlines vary, visit Website for details. FAFSA and SAR must be sent to school's financial aid office.
  Amount of award: $4,000
Contact:
United Negro College Fund Attn: William Dunham
8260 Willow Oaks Corporate Drive
P. O. Box 10444
Fairfax, VA 22031-8044
Phone: 800-331-2244
Web: www.uncf.org

Maya Angelou/Vivian Baxter Scholarship

Type of award: Scholarship, renewable.
Intended use: For full-time undergraduate study at accredited 4-year institution in United States. Designated institutions: UNCF member institutions.
Eligibility: Applicant must be Alaskan native, Asian American, African American, Mexican American, Hispanic American, Puerto Rican, American Indian or Native Hawaiian/Pacific Islander. Applicant must be residing in North Carolina.
Basis for selection: Applicant must demonstrate financial need, high academic achievement, leadership and service orientation.
Application requirements: FAFSA and SAR.
Additional information: Minimum 2.5 GPA. Visit Website for details.
  Amount of award: $2,500

Contact:
United Negro College Fund
8260 Willow Oaks Corporate Drive
P. O. Box 10444
Fairfax, VA 22031-8044
Phone: 800-331-2244
Web: www.uncf.org

Michael Jackson Scholarships

Type of award: Scholarship, renewable.
Intended use: For undergraduate study at accredited 4-year institution in United States. Designated institutions: UNCF member institutions.
Eligibility: Applicant must be Alaskan native, Asian American, African American, Mexican American, Hispanic American, Puerto Rican, American Indian or Native Hawaiian/Pacific Islander.
Basis for selection: Major/career interest in performing arts; communications or English. Applicant must demonstrate financial need and high academic achievement.
Application requirements: Recommendations, essay, transcript, proof of eligibility. FAFSA, photographs. SAR must be sent to school's financial aid office.
Additional information: Minimum 3.0 GPA. Funds may be used for tuition, room and board, and books, or to repay federal student loans. Visit Website for deadline information.
   Amount of award: $4,000
Contact:
United Negro College Fund
8260 Willow Oaks Corporate Drive
P. O. Box 10444
Fairfax, VA 22031-8044
Phone: 800-331-2244
Web: www.uncf.org

Reader's Digest Foundation Scholarship Program

Type of award: Scholarship, renewable.
Intended use: For full-time junior or senior study at accredited 4-year institution in United States. Designated institutions: UNCF member institutions.
Eligibility: Applicant must be Alaskan native, Asian American, African American, Mexican American, Hispanic American, Puerto Rican or American Indian.
Basis for selection: Major/career interest in journalism; communications or English. Applicant must demonstrate financial need and high academic achievement.
Application requirements: Essay, transcript, proof of eligibility. Published writing sample, photograph, FAFSA, personal statement on background and career goals, recommendation from professor of journalism, communications, or English.
Additional information: Minimum 3.0 GPA. Scholarship designed for students demonstrating interest in print journalism. Funds from this scholarship may be used for tuition, room/board, and books, or to repay a federal student loan. Renewable only if eligibility requirements met and funds available. Contact sponsor for application or visit Website.

Amount of award:	$5,000
Number of awards:	6
Application deadline:	February 15
Total amount awarded:	$30,000

Contact:
United Negro College Fund Program Services
8260 Willow Oaks Corparate Drive
P.O. Box 10444
Fairfax, VA 22031-8044
Phone: 800-331-2244
Web: www.uncf.org

Richmond Scholarship

Type of award: Scholarship.
Intended use: For undergraduate study in United States. Designated institutions: UNCF member institutions.
Eligibility: Applicant must be Alaskan native, Asian American, African American, Mexican American, Hispanic American, Puerto Rican, American Indian or Native Hawaiian/Pacific Islander. Applicant must be U.S. citizen or permanent resident residing in Virginia.
Basis for selection: Applicant must demonstrate financial need and high academic achievement.
Application requirements: Recommendations, essay, transcript, proof of eligibility. FAFSA and photograph.
Additional information: Minimum 2.5 GPA. Visit Website for additional information. Must be resident of Richmond, Virginia area. Contact financial aid office of member institution for application, deadlines, award amount, and details. Funds provided by Richmond Scholarship Committee.
   Amount of award: $2,000
Contact:
United Negro College Fund
8260 Willow Oaks Corporate Drive
P.O. Box 10444
Fairfax, VA 22031-8044
Phone: 800-331-2244
Web: www.uncf.org

Sallie Mae Fund American Dream Scholarship

Type of award: Scholarship.
Intended use: For full-time undergraduate study at accredited 2-year or 4-year institution in United States. Designated institutions: Title IV-accredited colleges and universities in the United States or Puerto Rico.
Eligibility: Applicant must be African American. Applicant must be U.S. citizen or permanent resident.
Basis for selection: Applicant must demonstrate financial need and high academic achievement.
Application requirements: Recommendations, essay, transcript. FAFSA.
Additional information: Applicant must be eligible for Federal Pell Grant. Minimum 2.5 GPA. Visit Website for list of member colleges and universities.

Amount of award:	$500-$5,000
Application deadline:	April 15
Notification begins:	June 1

Contact:
United Negro College Fund
8260 Willow Oaks Corporate Drive
P.O. Box 10444
Fairfax, VA 22031-8044
Phone: 800-331-2244
Web: www.uncf.org

UBS/PaineWebber Scholarships

Type of award: Scholarship, renewable.

United Negro College Fund: UBS/PaineWebber Scholarships

Intended use: For full-time sophomore or junior study at accredited 4-year institution. Designated institutions: UNCF member institutions.
Eligibility: Applicant must be Alaskan native; Asian American, African American, Mexican American, Hispanic American, Puerto Rican, American Indian or Native Hawaiian/Pacific Islander.
Basis for selection: Major/career interest in business; economics; business/management/administration or finance/banking.
Application requirements: Recommendations, essay, transcript, proof of eligibility. FAFSA and photograph.
Additional information: Minimum 3.0 GPA. Applicant with career interest in sales also eligible. Visit Website for additional information. Contact financial aid office of member institution for application, deadlines, award amount, and details.
   Amount of award: $8,000
   Application deadline: November 27
Contact:
United Negro College Fund
8260 Willow Oaks Corporate Drive
P.O. Box 10444
Fairfax, VA 22031-8044
Phone: 800-331-2244
Web: www.uncf.org

United States Association of Blind Athletes

Arthur E. Copeland Scholarship for Males

Type of award: Scholarship.
Intended use: For full-time undergraduate study at postsecondary institution.
Eligibility: Applicant or parent must be member/participant of United States Association of Blind Athletes. Applicant must be visually impaired. Applicant must be male, high school senior. Applicant must be U.S. citizen.
Application requirements: Transcript, proof of eligibility. Autobiographical sketch outlining USABA involvement and academic goals. References.
Additional information: Applicants must be legally blind. Must be current USABA member. Open to all majors.
   Amount of award: $500
   Number of awards: 1
   Application deadline: August 15
   Notification begins: November 1
Contact:
USABA Scholarship Director
33 North Institute St.
Colorado Springs, CO 80903
Web: www.usaba.org

Helen Copeland Scholarship for Females

Type of award: Scholarship.
Intended use: For undergraduate study.
Eligibility: Applicant must be visually impaired. Applicant must be female. Applicant must be U.S. citizen.
Application requirements: Transcript, proof of eligibility. Autobiographical sketch outlining USABA involvement, academic goals and objective for which scholarship funds will be used.
Additional information: Applicants must be legally blind and a participant in USABA sports programs. Must be current USABA member.
   Amount of award: $500
   Number of awards: 1
   Application deadline: August 15
   Notification begins: November 1
   Total amount awarded: $500
Contact:
U.S. Association of Blind Athletes
33 North Institute Street
Colorado Springs, CO 80903
Phone: 719-630-0422
Fax: 719-630-0616
Web: www.usaba.org

United States Institute of Peace

National Peace Essay Contest

Type of award: Scholarship.
Intended use: For undergraduate or graduate study.
Eligibility: Applicant must be enrolled in high school. Applicant must be U.S. citizen.
Basis for selection: Competition/talent/interest in writing/journalism. Major/career interest in journalism or international relations.
Application requirements: Three-part maximum 1500-word essay on topic chosen by the Institute. Applicant must submit essay to contest coordinator before deadline; the coordinator will submit essay to the Institute. Student form and coordinator form must accompany essay submission.
Additional information: Homeschooled students or those enrolled in correspondence programs also eligible. State-level winners receive $1,000 for their college or university studies and will compete for national awards of $10,000, $5,000, and $2,500 (national amount includes state award). Also invited to attend awards dinner in Washington, DC. Visit Website for more information.
   Number of awards: 53
   Number of applicants: 1,000
   Application deadline: February 1
   Notification begins: May 1
   Total amount awarded: $67,500
Contact:
United States Institute of Peace
1200 17th St. NW
Suite 200
Washington, DC 20036-3011
Phone: 202-429-3854
Fax: 202-429-6063
Web: www.usip.org/npec

United Transportation Union Insurance Association

United Transportation Union Insurance Association Scholarship

Type of award: Scholarship, renewable.
Intended use: For full-time undergraduate study at accredited vocational, 2-year or 4-year institution in or outside United States.
Eligibility: Applicant or parent must be member/participant of United Transportation Union. Applicant must be no older than 25. Applicant must be permanent resident.
Application requirements: Proof of eligibility.
Additional information: Applicant must be accepted to or enrolled in an eligible institution. Members and direct descendants of living or deceased members eligible. Members of the United Transportation Union Insurance Association also eligible. Scholarships awarded by lottery. Notification takes place prior to fall enrollment.

Amount of award:	$500
Number of awards:	50
Number of applicants:	1,600
Application deadline:	March 31

Contact:
United Transportation Union Insurance Association
14600 Detroit Ave.
Cleveland, OH 44107-4250
Phone: 216-228-9400
Fax: 216-228-0411
Web: www.utu.org

University Film and Video Association

Carole Fielding Video Grant

Type of award: Research grant.
Intended use: For undergraduate or graduate study at accredited 2-year or 4-year institution.
Basis for selection: Major/career interest in film/video.
Application requirements: Resume, budget, research/production proposal. Five collated and stapled copies of completed application.
Additional information: Project categories include narrative, documentary, experimental, multimedia/installation, animation, and research. Applicant must be sponsored by faculty member who is active member of University Film and Video Association. Number of awards varies.

Amount of award:	$1,000-$4,000
Number of awards:	3
Number of applicants:	86
Application deadline:	December 15
Notification begins:	March 31
Total amount awarded:	$5,000

Contact:
Professor Robert Johnson, Jr., Grants Chair
Framingham State College, Commun. Arts Dept.
100 State Street
Framingham, MA 01701
Phone: 508-626-4684
Web: www.ufva.org

University of New Mexico Health Sciences Center

UNM Hospital Nursing Scholarship

Type of award: Scholarship.
Basis for selection: Major/career interest in nursing.
Application requirements: Recommendations, essay, proof of eligibility. Resume. Proof of acceptance in an accredited BSN or ASN program. Transcript.
Additional information: Applicant must make 2-year commitment to University of New Mexico Hospital upon graduation. See Website for application.

Amount of award:	$3,500-$4,000
Application deadline:	May 30

Contact:
UNM Hospitals Recruitment Department
1650 University Blvd NE, Suite 200
Albuquerque, NM 87102
Phone: 505-272-0489
Web: http://hospitals.unm.edu/Careers/Scholarships.shtml

Upakar

Indian American Scholarship

Type of award: Scholarship, renewable.
Intended use: For freshman study.
Eligibility: Applicant must be U.S. citizen or permanent resident.
Basis for selection: Applicant must demonstrate financial need and high academic achievement.
Application requirements: Recommendations, essay.
Additional information: Applicant must have either been born or have one grandparent/parent born in the Republic of India. Applicant must have a cumulative unadjusted GPA over 3.6. Applicant's family must have Adjusted Gross Income of less than $75,000.

Amount of award:	$3,000
Number of awards:	20
Number of applicants:	250
Application deadline:	April 28
Notification begins:	June 1
Total amount awarded:	$60,000

Contact:
Upakar
c/o M. Mukunda
10237 Nolan Drive
Rockville, MD 20850
Web: www.upakar.org

UPS

UPS Earn and Learn Program Grant

Type of award: Scholarship, renewable.
Intended use: For undergraduate study at accredited vocational, 2-year or 4-year institution in United States.
Eligibility: Applicant or parent must be employed by United Parcel Service (UPS).
Application requirements: Proof of eligibility.
Additional information: Employees attending college part-time qualify for up to $1,500 per semester. Visit Website for current list of participating locations and more information.
Contact:
UPS
55 Glenlake Parkway N.E.
Atlanta, GA 30328
Phone: 888-WORK-UPS
Web: www.upsjobs.com

U.S. Army Recruiting Command

Montgomery GI Bill (MGIB)

Type of award: Scholarship.
Intended use: For undergraduate or graduate study at accredited postsecondary institution in United States.
Eligibility: Applicant must be at least 18, no older than 34. Applicant must be U.S. citizen. Applicant must be in military service in the Army. Must enlist for minimum two years active duty service.
Basis for selection: Applicant must demonstrate depth of character, leadership, patriotism, seriousness of purpose and service orientation.
Application requirements: Interview. Armed Services Vocational Aptitude Battery.
Additional information: Award amount varies.
Contact:
U.S. Army Recruiting Command
P.O. Box 3219
Warminster, PA 18974-9844
Phone: 800-USA-ARMY
Web: www.goarmy.com

Montgomery GI Bill Plus Army College Fund

Type of award: Scholarship.
Intended use: For undergraduate or graduate study at accredited postsecondary institution.
Eligibility: Applicant must be at least 18, no older than 34, returning adult student. Applicant must be U.S. citizen. Applicant must be in military service in the Army. Must enlist in Army for two to six years for active duty service in eligible ACF Military Occupational Specialty.
Basis for selection: Applicant must demonstrate depth of character, leadership, patriotism, seriousness of purpose and service orientation.
Application requirements: Interview.
Additional information: Applicant must have high school diploma or 15 college semester hours. Enrollment in colleges outside U.S. must be approved by Veterans Administration. Award amount depends on length of enlistment. Minimum score of 50 on Armed Services Vocational Aptitude Battery.
    Amount of award: $30,000-$72,900
Contact:
U.S. Army Recruiting Command
P.O. Box 3219
Warminster, PA 18974-9844
Phone: 800-USA-ARMY
Web: www.goarmy.com

Selected Reserve Montgomery GI Bill

Type of award: Scholarship.
Intended use: For undergraduate or graduate study at accredited postsecondary institution.
Eligibility: Applicant must be at least 17, no older than 34. Applicant must be U.S. citizen. Applicant must be veteran who served in the Army or Reserves/National Guard. Must have six-year obligation to serve in the Selected Reserve signed after June 30, 1985. Officers must have agreed to serve six years in addition to original obligation. For some types of training, must have six-year commitment that begins after September 30, 1990. Must remain in good standing while serving.
Basis for selection: Applicant must demonstrate depth of character, leadership, patriotism, seriousness of purpose and service orientation.
Application requirements: Interview. Armed Services Vocational Aptitude Battery.
Additional information: Award amount varies.
Contact:
U.S. Army
P.O. Box 3219
Warminster, PA 18974-9844
Phone: 800-USA-ARMY
Web: www.goarmy.com

U.S. Bank Student Banking Division

U.S. Bank Internet Scholarship Program

Type of award: Scholarship.
Intended use: For full-time undergraduate study at accredited 2-year or 4-year institution in United States.
Eligibility: Applicant must be high school senior. Applicant must be U.S. citizen or permanent resident.
Basis for selection: Applicant must demonstrate depth of character.
Additional information: Scholarship awarded based on random drawing. Visit Website from October through February to apply. Must apply online; no paper application available.
    Amount of award: $1,000
    Number of awards: 30
    Notification begins: April 1
    Total amount awarded: $30,000
Contact:
Phone: 800-242-1200
Web: www.usbank.com/studentbanking

U.S. Department of Agriculture

USDA/1890 National Scholars Program

Type of award: Scholarship.
Intended use: For full-time undergraduate study at 4-year institution in United States. Designated institutions: One of the 1890 Historically Black Land-Grant Institutions: Alabama A&M University, Alcorn State University (MS), Delaware State University, Florida A&M University, Fort Valley State University (GA), Kentucky State University, Lincoln University (MO), Langston University (OK), North Carolina A&T University, Prairie View A&M University (TX), South Carolina State University, Southern University (LA), Tennessee State University, Tuskegee University (AL), University of Arkansas at Pine Bluff, University of Maryland at Eastern Shore, Virginia State University, and West Virginia State University.
Eligibility: Applicant must be U.S. citizen.
Basis for selection: Major/career interest in agriculture; agribusiness; agricultural education; agricultural economics; animal sciences; botany; food science/technology; wildlife/fisheries; forestry or horticulture. Applicant must demonstrate high academic achievement, leadership and service orientation.
Application requirements: Recommendations, transcript.
Additional information: For entering freshman at designated universities who are seeking bachelor's degrees in agriculture, food, natural resource sciences, and related disciplines. Scholarship covers full tuition and fees, plus room and board, for four years. Upon completion of academic degree program, recipient has obligation of one year of service to USDA for each year of financial support. Number of awards varies depending on funding. Minimum 1000 SAT (Math and Reading; 1500 Math/Reading/Writing) or minimum 21 ACT and 3.0 GPA.
   Amount of award: Full tuition
   Application deadline: February 1
Contact:
U.S. Department of Agriculture
USDA/1890 National Scholars Program Manager
STOP 9478, 1400 Independence Ave., SW 3038-SB
Washington, DC 20250
Phone: 202-205-5692
Fax: 202-205-2641
Web: www.1890scholarsprogram.usda.gov

U.S. Department of Education

Federal Pell Grant Program

Type of award: Scholarship, renewable.
Intended use: For undergraduate study at 2-year or 4-year institution.
Eligibility: Applicant must be U.S. citizen or permanent resident.
Basis for selection: Applicant must demonstrate financial need.
Application requirements: Proof of eligibility. FAFSA.
Additional information: Federal Pell Grant does not have to be repaid. Grant based on financial need, costs to attend school, and enrollment status. Must not have previously earned baccalaureate or professional degree. Amount of award varies.
   Amount of award: $4,731
   Application deadline: June 30
Contact:
Federal Student Aid Programs
P.O. Box 84
Washington, DC 20044-0084
Phone: 800-4-FED-AID or 800-730-8913
Web: www.studentaid.ed.gov

Federal Supplemental Educational Opportunity Grant Program

Type of award: Scholarship, renewable.
Intended use: For undergraduate study at accredited vocational, 2-year or 4-year institution in United States.
Eligibility: Applicant must be U.S. citizen or permanent resident.
Basis for selection: Applicant must demonstrate financial need.
Application requirements: Proof of eligibility. FAFSA.
Additional information: Priority given to Federal Pell Grant recipients with exceptional financial need. Must not have defaulted on federal grant or educational loan. Awards not generally made to students enrolled less than half-time. Unlike Pell Grants, availability of FSEOG awards not federally guaranteed, but depends on availability of funds at student's institution. Check with institution's financial aid office for deadline.
   Amount of award: $100-$4,000
Contact:
Federal Student Aid Programs
P.O. Box 84
Washington, DC 20044-0084
Phone: 800-4-FED-AID
Web: www.studentaid.ed.gov

Federal Work-Study Program

Type of award: Scholarship.
Intended use: For undergraduate or graduate study at accredited postsecondary institution in United States.
Eligibility: Applicant must be U.S. citizen or permanent resident.
Basis for selection: Applicant must demonstrate financial need.
Application requirements: Proof of eligibility. FAFSA.
Additional information: Part-time on-campus and off-campus jobs based on class schedule and academic progress. Students earn at least minimum wage.
   Application deadline: June 30
Contact:
Federal Student Aid Programs
P.O. Box 84
Washington, DC 20044-0084
Phone: 800-4-FED-AID
Web: www.studentaid.ed.gov

Robert C. Byrd Honors Scholarship Program

Type of award: Scholarship, renewable.
Intended use: For undergraduate study at postsecondary institution in United States.

U.S. Department of Education: Robert C. Byrd Honors Scholarship Program

Eligibility: Applicant must be high school senior. Applicant must be U.S. citizen or permanent resident.
Basis for selection: Applicant must demonstrate high academic achievement.
Application requirements: Proof of eligibility.
Additional information: Merit-based. Renewable up to three years. Selections by state education agencies (SEAs) supervising public elementary/secondary schools. Awards made in all 50 states, District of Columbia, Puerto Rico, and insular areas. Application deadlines are set forth by the respective SEA. Contact high school guidance counselor for details, or call number listed for contact information of appropriate SEA.
Amount of award: $1,500
Contact:
Federal Student Aid Programs
P.O. Box 84
Washington, DC 20044
Phone: 800-4-FED-AID
Web: www.studentaid.ed.gov

U.S. Department of Education Rehabilitation Services Administration

Vocational Rehabilitation Assistance

Type of award: Scholarship, renewable.
Intended use: For undergraduate or graduate study at postsecondary institution in United States.
Additional information: Students apply to individual institution, not Rehabilitation Services Administration. Number of awards varies; amounts vary depending on institution. Award applicable to many fields/majors, but must be consistent with applicant's abilities, interest, and informed choice. See Website for more information.
Contact:
Rehabilitation Services Administration
400 Maryland Ave SW
PCP Room 5014
Washington, DC 20202-2800
Web: www.ed.gov/about/offices/list/osers/rsa/index.html or www.jan.wvu.edu/SBSES/VOCREHAB.HTM

U.S. Department of Health and Human Services

National Health Service Corps Scholarship

Type of award: Scholarship.
Intended use: For full-time undergraduate or graduate study at accredited 4-year or graduate institution in United States.
Eligibility: Applicant must be U.S. citizen.
Basis for selection: Major/career interest in dentistry; nursing; nurse practitioner; physician assistant or midwifery. Applicant must demonstrate depth of character, seriousness of purpose and service orientation.
Application requirements: Interview, proof of eligibility.

Additional information: Scholarship is for students pursuing allopathic (MD) and osteopathic (DO) medicine; nurse midwifery; dentistry; family nurse practitioner; and physician assistant education. Doctorate nurse training and premedical students ineligible. Awardees commit to providing health-care services in underserved communities anywhere in the U.S. One year of service owed for every year of scholarship support. Minimum service commitment two years; maximum four years. Award includes monthly stipend. Must be in training program.
Amount of award: Full tuition
Number of awards: 100
Number of applicants: 1,400
Application deadline: March 30
Notification begins: August 1
Contact:
United States Department of Health and Human Services
c/o Discovery Logic
1375 Piccard Drive, Suite 325
Rockville, MD 20850
Phone: 800-638-0824
Web: nhsc.bhpr.hrsa.gov

U.S. Department of Interior-Bureau of Indian Affairs

Indians Higher Education Grant Program

Type of award: Scholarship.
Intended use: For full-time undergraduate study at accredited 2-year or 4-year institution.
Eligibility: Applicant must be Alaskan native or American Indian. Must be member (or at least one-quarter degree Indian blood descendant of member) of American Indian tribe eligible for special programs and services provided by United States through Bureau of Indian Affairs. Applicant must be U.S. citizen.
Basis for selection: Applicant must demonstrate financial need.
Application requirements: Proof of eligibility.
Additional information: Deadlines vary. Contact education officer of affiliated tribe for application.
Contact:
U.S. Department of Interior-Bureau of Indian Affairs
Office of Education Programs MS 3512- MIB
1849 C Street, NW
Washington, DC 20240
Web: www.oiep.bia.edu

U.S. Environmental Protection Agency

EPA National Network for Environmental Management Studies Fellowship

Type of award: Research grant.
Intended use: For undergraduate or graduate study.

Eligibility: Applicant must be U.S. citizen or permanent resident.
Basis for selection: Major/career interest in environmental science; public relations; communications; computer/information sciences or law.
Application requirements: Transcript. Resume. One-page work-plan proposal. Letter of reference from faculty member or department head familiar with student's work and qualifications; letter must state how research project will benefit student's academic studies.
Additional information: Program provides students with research opportunities and experience at EPA locations nationwide. NNEMS develops and distributes annual catalog listing available research opportunities for coming year. Selected students receive stipend for performing research project. Projects also available in environmental management/administration and environmental policy, regulation, and law. Undergraduate applicants must: 1) be enrolled in program directly related to pollution control or environmental protection; 2) have 3.0 GPA; 3) have already completed four courses related to environmental field. Seniors who graduate prior to completion of advertised NNEMS fellowship period ineligible unless admitted to graduate school with submittable verification.

    Amount of award: $6,900-$11,000
    Number of awards: 65
    Application deadline: January 22
Contact:
NNEMS Fellowship Program
Tetratech EM Inc.
1881 Campus Common Drive, Suite 200
Reston, VA 20191
Phone: 800-358-8769
Web: www.epa.gov/enviroed/students.html

Greater Research Opportunities Undergraduate Student Fellowships

Type of award: Scholarship.
Intended use: For full-time junior or senior study at accredited 4-year institution in United States.
Eligibility: Applicant must be U.S. citizen or permanent resident.
Basis for selection: Major/career interest in life sciences; environmental science; engineering; social/behavioral sciences; physical sciences; mathematics; computer/information sciences or economics. Applicant must demonstrate financial need, high academic achievement and seriousness of purpose.
Application requirements: Recommendations, essay, transcript, proof of eligibility. Pre-application form. Resident Aliens must include green card number. EPA may verify number with the Immigration and Naturalization Service.
Additional information: Award provides funding for last two years of four-year education. Students must apply before beginning of junior year. Applicant must attend a four-year institution or be in the second year at a two-year school at the time of applying, with the intent of transferring to a four-year institution. Minimum 3.0 GPA. Fellowship provides up to $17,000 per year for two years to cover tuition and fees as well as $7,500 of internship support for a three month period. Stipends and expense allowance also provided. Recipient must complete summer internship at EPA facility between funded junior and senior years. Preference given to applicants attending minority academic institutions. Applicants must submit preapplication form first; following a merit review, top-ranked applicants will be asked to submit formal application. See Website for details and list of eligible schools. Applications available beginning in mid-August.

    Number of awards: 20
    Application deadline: November 3
Contact:
U.S. Environmental Protection Agency
Peer Review Division (8703R), Ariel Rios Bldg
1200 Pennsylvania Avenue, NW
Washington, DC 20460
Web: www.epa.gov/ncer

U.S. Navy/Marine NROTC College Scholarship Program

ROTC/Navy Nurse Corps Scholarship Program

Type of award: Scholarship.
Intended use: For full-time undergraduate study at accredited 4-year institution in United States. Designated institutions: NROTC-approved nursing schools.
Eligibility: Applicant must be at least 17, no older than 23. Applicant must be U.S. citizen.
Basis for selection: Major/career interest in nursing. Applicant must demonstrate high academic achievement and leadership.
Application requirements: Interview, recommendations, transcript, proof of eligibility.
Additional information: Scholarships pay for college tuition, fees, books, uniforms, and offer $250 monthly allowance, which increases yearly. Electronic application is first step in application process. Number of awards varies. Applicant must be medically qualified for the NROTC Scholarship Program. SAT 530 (Reading), 520 (Math); 22 ACT (English), 22 ACT (Math). SAT/ACT scores must be received by December 31. Participation in extracurricular activities and work experience. Applicants must have fewer than 30 hours college credit. Contact local recruiter for further details.

    Amount of award: Full tuition
    Number of applicants: 200
    Application deadline: January 15
Contact:
Contact your local recruitment officer.
Phone: 800-NAV-ROTC
Web: www.nrotc.navy.mil

ROTC/Navy/Marine Four-Year Scholarship

Type of award: Scholarship.
Intended use: For freshman study at accredited 4-year institution in United States. Designated institutions: Colleges and universities hosting NROTC program.
Eligibility: Applicant must be at least 17, no older than 23. Applicant must be U.S. citizen.
Basis for selection: Applicant must demonstrate high academic achievement.
Application requirements: Interview, recommendations, transcript.
Additional information: Scholarships are highly competitive and based on individual merit. Provide full tuition, fees, book allowance, and $250 monthly allowance, which increases annually. Number of awards varies. Applicant must be medically qualified for NROTC Scholarship. Contact nearest

NROTC unit for more information or visit Website. SAT 530 (Reading), 520 (Math); 22 ACT (English), 22 ACT (Math). SAT/ACT scores must be received by December 31. Participation in extracurricular activities and work experience. Applicant must have fewer than 30 hours college credit.

Amount of award:	Full tuition
Number of applicants:	4,000
Application deadline:	January 15

Contact:
Contact your local recruitment officer.
Phone: 800-NAV-ROTC
Web: www.nrotc.navy.mil

ROTC/Navy/Marine Two-Year Scholarship

Type of award: Scholarship.
Intended use: For full-time junior or senior study at 4-year institution in United States. Designated institutions: Colleges and universities hosting NROTC programs.
Eligibility: Applicant or parent must be member/participant of Reserve Officers Training Corps (ROTC). Applicant must be at least 17, no older than 22. Applicant must be U.S. citizen. Total military service obligation is eight years, four of which must be active duty.
Basis for selection: Applicant must demonstrate high academic achievement and leadership.
Application requirements: Interview, recommendations, transcript, proof of eligibility.
Additional information: Scholarships open to students who have completed sophomore year, or third year in a five-year curriculum. NROTC scholarships pay for college tuition, fees, book allowance, uniforms, and $250 monthly allowance, which increases annually. SAT 530 (Reading), 520 (Math); 22 ACT (English), 22 ACT (Math). Participation in extracurricular activities and work experience.

Amount of award:	Full tuition
Number of applicants:	100
Application deadline:	March 15

Contact:
Contact your local recruitment officer.
Phone: 800-USA-NAVY
Web: www.nrotc.navy.mil

USTA Tennis and Education Foundation

USTA Scholarships

Type of award: Scholarship, renewable.
Intended use: For full-time undergraduate study at accredited 2-year or 4-year institution.
Eligibility: Applicant must be high school senior.
Basis for selection: Major/career interest in sports/sports administration. Applicant must demonstrate financial need, high academic achievement, leadership and seriousness of purpose.
Application requirements: Interview, recommendations, essay, transcript. Three recommendations (coach, teacher, personal), photograph, FAFSA, ACT/SAT reports.
Additional information: The USTA offers seven different scholarship programs. Amounts and numbers of awards vary. Applications available online and must be mailed to local USTA Section office. Applicants must be involved in organized community tennis program. Deadlines vary, visit Website for details.

Amount of award:	$500-$15,000
Number of awards:	76
Application deadline:	February 9
Notification begins:	April 1
Total amount awarded:	$379,000

Contact:
United States Tennis Association
4 West Red Oak Lane, Suite 300
White Plains, NY 10604
Phone: 914-696-7000
Web: www.usta.com

Utah Higher Education Assistance Authority (UHEAA)

Leveraging Educational Assistance Partnership (LEAP)

Type of award: Scholarship, renewable.
Intended use: For undergraduate study in United States. Designated institutions: Participating Utah state institutions.
Eligibility: Applicant must be residing in Utah.
Basis for selection: Applicant must demonstrate financial need.
Application requirements: FAFSA.
Additional information: Awards made by individual institutions from allotments sent by UHEAA as part of campus-based financial packaging. Contact institution for deadline.

Amount of award:	$300-$2,500
Number of awards:	3,894
Number of applicants:	3,886
Total amount awarded:	$1,988,531

Contact:
Contact institution's financial aid office.

UHEAA Grant

Type of award: Scholarship, renewable.
Intended use: For undergraduate or graduate study at 4-year or graduate institution in United States. Designated institutions: Participating Utah institutions.
Eligibility: Applicant must be residing in Utah.
Basis for selection: Applicant must demonstrate financial need.
Application requirements: Nomination by financial aid director.
Additional information: Awards range from $300 to $2,800 for undergraduates; $300 to $4,500 for graduates. Awards are made by individual institutions from allotments from UHEAA as part of campus-based financial aid. Contact institution for deadlines.

Amount of award:	$300-$4,500
Number of awards:	1,423
Number of applicants:	2,988
Total amount awarded:	$1,230,754

Contact:
Contact participating institution for eligibility and application.

Utah Centennial Opportunity Program for Education (UCOPE)

Type of award: Scholarship, renewable.
Intended use: For undergraduate study.
Eligibility: Applicant must be residing in Utah.
Basis for selection: Applicant must demonstrate financial need.
Application requirements: FAFSA.
Additional information: Awards are made by individual institutions from allotments sent to them by UHEAA as part of campus-based financial packaging. Award available through school's financial aid office. Applicants must be Utah residents and demonstrate substantial need. Contact school for deadline.
   Amount of award: $300-$5,000
   Number of awards: 5,183
   Total amount awarded: $4,146,019
Contact:
Contact institution's financial aid office.

Utah State Office of Education

Utah Robert C. Byrd Honors Scholarship

Type of award: Scholarship, renewable.
Intended use: For full-time undergraduate study.
Eligibility: Applicant must be high school senior. Applicant must be permanent resident residing in Utah.
Basis for selection: Applicant must demonstrate high academic achievement.
Application requirements: Transcript.
Additional information: Minimum 3.5 GPA. Contact high school counselor or financial aid adviser for application after January, or see Website.
   Amount of award: $1,500
   Number of awards: 62
   Number of applicants: 500
   Application deadline: March 30
   Notification begins: May 15
   Total amount awarded: $384,000
Contact:
High school counselor or financial aid adviser.
Web: www.usoe.k12.ut.us/cert

The Vegetarian Resource Group

The Vegetarian Resource Group College Scholarships

Type of award: Scholarship.
Intended use: For freshman study at postsecondary institution in United States.
Eligibility: Applicant must be high school senior. Applicant must be U.S. citizen.
Application requirements: Essay.
Additional information: Award for graduating high school students who have promoted vegetarianism or veganism in their schools or communities. Students will be judged on having shown compassion, courage and a strong commitment to promoting a peaceful world through a vegetarian or vegan diet/lifestyle. Visit Website for application information.
   Amount of award: $5,000
   Number of awards: 2
   Number of applicants: 2
   Application deadline: February 20
   Total amount awarded: $10,000
Contact:
The Vegetarian Resource Group
P.O. Box 1463
Baltimore, MD 21203
Phone: 410-366-8343
Web: www.vrg.org

Ventura County Japanese-American Citizens League

Ventura County Japanese-American Citizens League Scholarships

Type of award: Scholarship.
Intended use: For freshman study at vocational, 2-year, 4-year or graduate institution in United States.
Eligibility: Applicant must be high school senior. Applicant must be Japanese. Applicant must be U.S. citizen residing in California.
Application requirements: Recommendations, essay, transcript, proof of eligibility.
Additional information: Must be member of JACL, or child of member. Applicant must be resident of Ventura County.
   Number of awards: 11
   Application deadline: April 1
   Total amount awarded: $10,000
Contact:
Ventura County JACL Continuing Education Program
P.O. Box 1092
Camarillo, CA 93011
Phone: 805-373-4536
Web: www.vcjacl.org/scholarship.htm

Vermont Golf Association Scholarship Fund, Inc.

Vermont Golf Association Scholarship

Type of award: Scholarship, renewable.
Intended use: For full-time undergraduate study at 2-year or 4-year institution.
Eligibility: Applicant must be high school senior. Applicant must be permanent resident residing in Vermont.
Application requirements: Interview, recommendations, transcript. FAFSA.
Additional information: Must be graduate of Vermont high school and in top 40 percent of class or have GPA of 3.0 and

1500 SAT. Students of Hanover High School, NH, Riverdell Interstate School District, NH, and Grandville High School, NY, are also eligible. Applicant must have valid connection to golf. Can renew scholarship up to four years.
- **Amount of award:** $1,000
- **Number of awards:** 10
- **Number of applicants:** 38
- **Application deadline:** April 20
- **Total amount awarded:** $10,000

Contact:
Vermont Golf Association Scholarship Fund
P.O. Box 1612
Station A
Rutland, VT 05701
Phone: 800-924-0418
Fax: 802-773-7182
Web: www.vtga.org

Vermont Student Assistance Corporation

Champlain Valley Kennel Club Scholarship

Type of award: Scholarship.
Intended use: For undergraduate or graduate study at accredited postsecondary institution. Designated institutions: Institutions approved for federal Title IV funding.
Eligibility: Applicant must be residing in Vermont.
Basis for selection: Major/career interest in veterinary medicine. Applicant must demonstrate financial need and high academic achievement.
Application requirements: Recommendations, essay.
Additional information: Graduating high school seniors also eligible. Applicant must have been Vermont resident for at least five years at time of application.
- **Amount of award:** $500
- **Number of awards:** 1
- **Number of applicants:** 20
- **Application deadline:** May 10

Contact:
VSAC Scholarships Program
10 East Allen St
P.O. Box 2000
Winooski, VT 05404
Phone: 888-253-4819
Fax: 802-654-3765
Web: www.vsac.org

Chittenden Bank Scholarship

Type of award: Scholarship, renewable.
Intended use: For freshman study at accredited 2-year or 4-year institution in United States. Designated institutions: Accredited Vermont postsecondary schools approved for federal Title IV funding.
Eligibility: Applicant must be high school senior. Applicant must be residing in Vermont.
Basis for selection: Applicant must demonstrate financial need, high academic achievement and service orientation.
Application requirements: Recommendations, essay.

- **Amount of award:** $2,500
- **Number of awards:** 2
- **Number of applicants:** 220
- **Application deadline:** April 10

Contact:
Vermont Student Assistance Corporation Scholarships Program
10 East Allen St
P.O. Box 2000
Winooski, VT 05404
Phone: 888-253-4819
Fax: 802-654-3765
Web: www.vsac.org

Emily Lester Vermont Opportunity Scholarship

Type of award: Scholarship, renewable.
Intended use: For undergraduate or graduate study at accredited postsecondary institution. Designated institutions: Vermont postsecondary schools approved for federal Title IV funding.
Eligibility: Applicant must be residing in Vermont.
Basis for selection: Applicant must demonstrate financial need.
Application requirements: Proof of eligibility.
Additional information: Applicant must be under the custody of the Vermont commissioner of social and rehabilitation services or be between the ages of 18 and 24 and have been under the custody of the commissioner of social and rehabilitation services for at least six months when between ages 16 and 18. Graduating high school seniors also eligible.
- **Amount of award:** $1,000-$3,000
- **Application deadline:** July 15
- **Total amount awarded:** $22,500

Contact:
VSAC Scholarship Program
10 East Allen St.
P.O. Box 2000
Winooski, VT 05404
Phone: 888-253-4819
Fax: 802-654-3765
Web: www.vsac.org

Green Mountain Dog Club Scholarship

Type of award: Scholarship.
Intended use: For undergraduate or graduate study at accredited postsecondary institution. Designated institutions: Institutions approved for federal Title IV funding.
Eligibility: Applicant must be residing in Vermont.
Basis for selection: Major/career interest in veterinary medicine or animal sciences. Applicant must demonstrate financial need and high academic achievement.
Application requirements: Recommendations, essay.
Additional information: Applicant must intend to work with animals to improve their quality of health/life. Minimum 2.5 GPA. Graduating high school seniors eligible.
- **Amount of award:** $500
- **Number of awards:** 1
- **Number of applicants:** 33
- **Application deadline:** July 5

Contact:
VSAC Scholarships Program
10 East Allen St
P.O. Box 2000
Winooski, VT 05404
Phone: 888-253-4819
Fax: 802-654-3765
Web: www.vsac.org

Jebidiah Zabrosky Scholarship

Type of award: Scholarship.
Intended use: For undergraduate study at 2-year or 4-year institution in United States.
Eligibility: Applicant must be residing in Vermont.
Basis for selection: Major/career interest in business or education. Applicant must demonstrate financial need, high academic achievement and service orientation.
Application requirements: Recommendations, essay.
Additional information: Minimum 2.5 GPA. Applicant must be employed at time of application working minimum ten hours per week.

Amount of award:	$2,000
Number of awards:	1
Number of applicants:	7
Application deadline:	April 20

Contact:
VSAC Scholarship Porgrams
10 East Allen St
P.O. Box 2000
Winooski, VT 05404
Phone: 888-253-4819
Fax: 802-654-3765
Web: www.vsac.org

Michael and Deborah Weinberg Scholarship

Type of award: Scholarship.
Intended use: For full-time undergraduate study at accredited postsecondary institution. Designated institutions: Institutions approved for federal Title IV funding.
Eligibility: Applicant must be residing in Vermont.
Basis for selection: Applicant must demonstrate financial need and high academic achievement.
Application requirements: Essay.
Additional information: Applicant's parents must have volunteered with a Vermont rescue squad and/or fire department for five years at time of application. Graduating high school seniors eligible.

Amount of award:	$2,000
Number of awards:	1
Number of applicants:	68
Application deadline:	May 5

Contact:
VSAC Scholarships Program
10 East Allen St
P.O. Box 2000
Winooski, VT 05404
Phone: 888-253-4819
Fax: 802-654-3765
Web: www.vsac.org

National Association of Women in Construction Scholarship

Type of award: Scholarship.
Intended use: For undergraduate or graduate study at postsecondary institution.
Eligibility: Applicant must be female. Applicant must be residing in Vermont.
Basis for selection: Major/career interest in construction or construction management. Applicant must demonstrate financial need and high academic achievement.
Application requirements: Recommendations, essay.
Additional information: Applicant must seek education or training in a field related to construction. Graduating high school seniors eligible.

Amount of award:	$500
Number of awards:	1
Number of applicants:	7
Application deadline:	April 1

Contact:
VSAC Scholarships Program
10 East Allen St
P.O. Box 2000
Winooski, VT 05404
Phone: 888-253-4819
Fax: 802-654-3765
Web: www.vsac.org

Philip and Alice Angell Eastern Star Scholarship

Type of award: Scholarship.
Intended use: For undergraduate study at accredited postsecondary institution. Designated institutions: Postsecondary institutions approved for federal Title IV funding.
Eligibility: Applicant must be residing in Vermont.
Basis for selection: Major/career interest in business or education. Applicant must demonstrate financial need and high academic achievement.
Application requirements: Recommendations, essay.
Additional information: Minimum 3.5 GPA. Graduating high school seniors eligible.

Amount of award:	$350-$500
Number of awards:	1
Number of applicants:	78
Application deadline:	April 10

Contact:
VSAC Scholarships Program
10 East Allen St
P.O. Box 2000
Winooski, VT 05404
Phone: 888-253-4819
Fax: 802-654-3765
Web: www.sae.org

Samara Foundation of Vermont Scholarship

Type of award: Scholarship.
Intended use: For undergraduate study at vocational, 2-year or 4-year institution.
Eligibility: Applicant must be high school senior. Applicant must be residing in Vermont.
Application requirements: Recommendations, essay.
Additional information: Applicant must demonstrate, through personal experience and/or public commitment, dedication to the interests of the gay, lesbian, bisexual, transgendered, and questioning community. Recipients will have option of public or non-public recognition of the award.

Vermont Student Assistance Corporation: Samara Foundation of Vermont Scholarship

Number of awards:	3
Number of applicants:	15
Application deadline:	April 1
Total amount awarded:	$4,000

Contact:
VSAC Scholarship Programs
10 East Allen St, P.O. Box 2000
Winooski, VT 05404
Phone: 888-253-4819
Fax: 802-654-3765
Web: www.vsac.org/scholarships

Vermont Incentive Grant

Type of award: Scholarship.
Intended use: For full-time undergraduate study in United States.
Eligibility: Applicant must be U.S. citizen or permanent resident residing in Vermont.
Basis for selection: Applicant must demonstrate financial need.
Application requirements: Proof of eligibility. FAFSA.
Additional information: Open to Vermont residents who plan to attend college full-time and who do not yet have bachelor's degree. Application may be completed online. FAFSA required.

Amount of award:	$500-$10,600
Number of applicants:	15,825
Total amount awarded:	$16,521,900

Contact:
Grant Department
Vermont Student Assistance Corporation
P.O. Box 2000
Winooski, VT 05404-2601
Phone: 888-253-4819
Fax: 802-654-3765
Web: www.vsac.org

Vermont Non-Degree Program

Type of award: Scholarship.
Intended use: For non-degree study at postsecondary institution in United States.
Eligibility: Applicant must be permanent resident residing in Vermont.
Basis for selection: Applicant must demonstrate financial need.
Application requirements: Proof of eligibility.
Additional information: Award varies; maximum amount is $885 for one course per semester. Available to any Vermont resident enrolled in non-degree course that will improve employability or encourage further study. Applications available at Vermont Department of Employment and Training offices, schools and vocation centers, and VSAC.

Number of applicants:	1,290
Total amount awarded:	$645,732

Contact:
Grant Department
Vermont Student Assistance Corporation
P.O. Box 2000
Winooski, VT 05404-2601
Phone: 888-253-4819
Fax: 802-654-3765
Web: www.vsac.org

Vermont Part-Time Grant

Type of award: Scholarship.
Intended use: For half-time undergraduate study at vocational, 2-year or 4-year institution in United States.
Eligibility: Applicant must be permanent resident residing in Vermont.
Basis for selection: Applicant must demonstrate financial need.
Application requirements: Proof of eligibility. FAFSA.
Additional information: Must be taking fewer than 12 credits and not yet received bachelor's degree. Award amounts vary according to number of credits.

Number of applicants:	3,743
Total amount awarded:	$1,016,909

Contact:
Grant Department
Vermont Student Assistance Corporation
P.O. Box 2000
Winooski, VT 05404-2601
Phone: 888-253-4819
Fax: 802-654-3765
Web: www.vsac.org

Veterans of Foreign Wars

Voice of Democracy Scholarship

Type of award: Scholarship.
Intended use: For undergraduate or graduate study at postsecondary institution in United States.
Eligibility: Applicant must be no older than 19, enrolled in high school.
Application requirements: Audiotape or CD of essay. Participants are judged by tape or CD, not written essay script.
Additional information: Must apply through high school or local Veterans of Foreign Wars post. Not all VFW posts participate in program. Any entry submitted to VFW National Headquarters will be returned to sender. Selection based on interpretation of assigned patriotic theme, content, and presentation of recorded 3-5 minute audio-essay. Visit Website for additional information and application form. Award is non-renewable.

Amount of award:	$1,000-$30,000
Number of awards:	60
Number of applicants:	80,000
Application deadline:	November 1
Total amount awarded:	$146,000

Contact:
Veterans of Foreign Wars National Headquarters
Voice of Democracy Program
406 West 34 Street
Kansas City, MO 64111
Phone: 816-968-1117
Fax: 816-968-1149
Web: www.vfw.org

Virgin Islands Board of Education

Virgin Islands Leveraging Educational Assistance Partnership Program

Type of award: Scholarship, renewable.
Intended use: For full-time undergraduate or graduate study at postsecondary institution.
Eligibility: Applicant must be U.S. citizen or permanent resident residing in Virgin Islands.
Basis for selection: Applicant must demonstrate financial need and high academic achievement.
Application requirements: Transcript. Acceptance letter from institution for first-time applicants or transfer students.
Additional information: Minimum 2.0 GPA required. Number of awards and applicants varies.

Amount of award:	$500-$3,000
Number of awards:	36
Number of applicants:	47
Application deadline:	May 1

Contact:
Virgin Islands Board of Education-Financial Aid Office
P.O. Box 11900
St. Thomas, VI 00801
Phone: 340-774-4546

Virgin Islands Music Scholarship

Type of award: Scholarship, renewable.
Intended use: For full-time undergraduate study at accredited 2-year or 4-year institution in United States.
Eligibility: Applicant must be high school senior. Applicant must be U.S. citizen or permanent resident residing in Virgin Islands.
Basis for selection: Major/career interest in music. Applicant must demonstrate financial need.
Application requirements: Transcript.
Additional information: Minimum 2.0 GPA. Number of awards varies.

Amount of award:	$2,000
Number of awards:	8
Number of applicants:	12
Application deadline:	May 1

Contact:
Virgin Islands Board of Education-Financial Aid Office
P.O. Box 11900
St. Thomas, VI 00801
Phone: 340-774-4546

Virginia Department of Education

Virginia Lee-Jackson Scholarship

Type of award: Scholarship.
Intended use: For full-time freshman study at accredited 4-year institution in United States.
Eligibility: Applicant must be high school junior or senior. Applicant must be residing in Virginia.
Basis for selection: Competition/talent/interest in writing/journalism.
Application requirements: Essay demonstrating appreciation for virtues exemplified by General Robert E. Lee or General "Stonewall" Jackson. Students must submit essay and application form to high school principal or guidance counselor.
Additional information: Three $1,000 awards in each of Virginia's eight public high school regions. Three $1,000 awards for best essays by private school or home-schooled students. Additional awards for exceptional essays. Application deadline is generally in December. See Website for more information.

Amount of award:	$1,000-$10,000
Number of awards:	37
Application deadline:	December 15
Total amount awarded:	$60,000

Contact:
High school guidance counselor or principal.
Phone: 434-977-1861
Web: www.lee-jackson.org

Virginia Robert C. Byrd Honors Scholarship

Type of award: Scholarship, renewable.
Intended use: For full-time undergraduate study at accredited postsecondary institution in United States.
Eligibility: Applicant must be high school senior. Applicant must be U.S. citizen or permanent resident residing in Virginia.
Basis for selection: Applicant must demonstrate high academic achievement and service orientation.
Application requirements: Recommendations, transcript, nomination by high school. SAT/ACT scores.
Additional information: Application and information sent to principals of public and private high schools in February. Number of awards varies. Award renewable for three years during first four years of higher education.

Amount of award:	$1,500
Application deadline:	April 11

Contact:
High school principal or guidance counselor or
Dr. Willie Stroble
James Monroe Building
101 North 14th St., VA 23219
Phone: 804-786-9377
Fax: 804-786-5466
Web: www.pen.k12.va.us

Virginia Department of Health

Mary Marshall Nursing Scholarship

Type of award: Scholarship.
Intended use: For full-time undergraduate study. Designated institutions: Virginia nursing schools.
Eligibility: Applicant must be U.S. citizen or permanent resident residing in Virginia.
Basis for selection: Major/career interest in nursing. Applicant must demonstrate financial need.
Application requirements: Transcript. FAFSA.
Additional information: Award amount varies. Provides awards to students who agree to work in nursing profession in Virginia at rate of one month for every $100 of aid received.

Virginia Department of Health: Mary Marshall Nursing Scholarship

Must reside in Virginia at least one year prior to application. Recipient may reapply for up to four succeeding years. Applications and guidelines available from dean or financial aid office at applicant's nursing school or from below address.

> **Number of awards:** 91
> **Application deadline:** June 30

Contact:
Virginia Dept. of Health Office of Health Policy and Planning
P.O. Box 2448
Richmond, VA 23218
Phone: 804-864-7433

Nurse Pracitioner Nurse Midwife Scholarship

Type of award: Scholarship.
Intended use: For full-time undergraduate study at postsecondary institution. Designated institutions: Institutions in Virginia or nearby state.
Eligibility: Applicant must be residing in Virginia.
Basis for selection: Major/career interest in nurse practitioner. Applicant must demonstrate high academic achievement and depth of character.
Application requirements: Transcript. Two reference letters.
Additional information: Applicant must commit to post-graduate employment in a medically underserved area of Virginia, in a setting that provides services to persons unable to pay for service and participates in all government-sponsored insurance programs designed to assure access to medical care services for covered persons. Employment must last for a number of years equal to the number of annual scholarships received. If work commitment is not fulfilled or student does not complete studies, the award amount converts to loan. Preference for the scholarship given to 1) residents of the Commonwealth, 2) minority students, 3) students enrolled in family practice, obstetrics and gynecology, pediatric, adult health and geriatric nurse practitioner programs, 4) residents of medically underserved areas of Virginia, as determined by the Board of Health. Minimum 3.0 GPA. Award amount and number of awards varies.

> **Amount of award:** $5,000
> **Number of awards:** 4
> **Application deadline:** June 30

Contact:
Virginia Department of Health, Office of Health Policy and Planning
P.O. Box 2448
Richmond, VA 23218
Phone: 804-864-7433

Virginia Department of Rehabilitative Services

Virginia Rehabilitative Services College Program

Type of award: Scholarship.
Intended use: For undergraduate study at postsecondary institution.
Eligibility: Applicant must be visually impaired, hearing impaired, physically challenged or learning disabled. Applicant must be residing in Virginia.
Basis for selection: Applicant must demonstrate financial need.
Application requirements: Proof of eligibility. Proof must be furnished at least 60 days before start of school or educational program.
Additional information: Applicant must have a disability and an employment goal. Funding is available to eligible individuals only if need remains after other federal, state, and private sources are used. Program provides vocational rehabilitation and related services to Virginians with disabilities in order to foster the skills necessary to achieve greater self-sufficiency, independence, and employment. Contact nearest Department of Rehabilitative Services office or visit Website for numbers.

Contact:
Phone: 800-552-5019
Web: www.vadrs.org

Virginia Museum of Fine Arts

Virginia Museum of Fine Arts Fellowship

Type of award: Scholarship, renewable.
Intended use: For full-time undergraduate or graduate study at accredited 4-year or graduate institution.
Eligibility: Applicant must be U.S. citizen residing in Virginia.
Basis for selection: Major/career interest in arts, general; film/video or art/art history. Applicant must demonstrate financial need.
Application requirements: Portfolio, transcript. Ten 35mm slides representing recent work or three of the following: 16mm or video format films, videos, DVD, research papers, or published articles. References.
Additional information: May apply in one of the following categories on the undergraduate or graduate level: crafts, drawing, sculpture, filmmaking, painting, photography, printmaking, video. Candidates in art history may apply on the graduate level only. Visit Website for guidelines and application.

> **Amount of award:** $4,000-$6,000
> **Number of awards:** 18
> **Number of applicants:** 400
> **Application deadline:** November 15
> **Notification begins:** February 1
> **Total amount awarded:** $80,000

Contact:
Virginia Museum of Fine Arts Fellowships
Education and Outreach Division
200 N. Boulevard
Richmond, VA 23220-4007
Phone: 804-204-2661
Web: www.vmfa.museum

Wal-Mart Foundation

Higher REACH Scholarship

Type of award: Scholarship.
Intended use: For undergraduate study.

Eligibility: Applicant or parent must be employed by Wal-Mart Stores, Inc.
Basis for selection: Applicant must demonstrate financial need.
Application requirements: Essay, transcript. Job performance appraisal.
Additional information: Awarded to nontraditional students who have been employed by Wal-Mart Stores, Inc. for at least one year. Award amount varies depending on part-time or full-time enrollment; maximum is $2,000. Applicants must be out of high school for one year. Applications available in November from personnel office. Deadlines vary, visit Website for more information.
    Application deadline: January 14
    Notification begins: April 25
    Total amount awarded: $1,000
Contact:
Higher Reach Scholarship
c/o Scholarship Program Administrators, Inc.
P.O. Box 22492
Nashville, TN 37202
Phone: 866-524-7385
Fax: 615-320-3151
Web: www.walmartfoundation.org

Sam Walton Community Scholarship

Type of award: Scholarship.
Intended use: For full-time freshman study at accredited 2-year or 4-year institution in United States. Designated institutions: Institutions approved by the Wal-Mart Foundation.
Eligibility: Applicant must be high school senior. Applicant must be U.S. citizen or permanent resident.
Basis for selection: Applicant must demonstrate financial need and high academic achievement.
Application requirements: Transcript, proof of eligibility. ACT/SAT scores, list of community/extracurricular involvement and work experience.
Additional information: Applicant must not be an employee of Wal-Mart Stores, Inc., or child/dependent of an employee. Applications available first week of November. Application available on Website. Minimum 2.5 GPA. Student must have his/her local Sam's Club or Wal-Mart store's 4-digit location number to apply. Deadlines vary, visit Website for details.
    Amount of award: $1,000
    Number of awards: 4,617
    Number of applicants: 42,564
    Application deadline: January 14
    Notification begins: April 25
Contact:
Sam Walton Community Scholarship
c/o Scholarship Program Administrators, Inc.
P.O. Box 22117
Nashville, TN 37202-2117
Phone: 866-851-3372
Fax: 615-523-7100
Web: www.walmartfoundation.org

Wal-Mart Associate Scholarship

Type of award: Scholarship.
Intended use: For full-time undergraduate study at accredited 2-year or 4-year institution in United States.
Eligibility: Applicant or parent must be employed by Wal-Mart Stores, Inc. Applicant must be high school senior.
Basis for selection: Applicant must demonstrate financial need and high academic achievement.
Application requirements: Transcript, proof of eligibility. SAT/ACT scores and financial data.
Additional information: Award for Wal-Mart employees and their dependents who are not eligible for the Walton Foundation Scholarship. Applications available starting November. Minimum 18 ACT or 800 SAT. Visit Wal-Mart/Sam's Club personnel department for applications and deadline information.
    Amount of award: $2,000
    Application deadline: January 14
    Notification begins: April 25
Contact:
Wal-Mart Associate Scholarship
c/o Scholarship Program Administrators, Inc.
P.O. Box 22492
Nashville, TN 37202
Phone: 866-524-7385
Fax: 615-320-7160
Web: www.walmartfoundation.org

Walton Family Foundation Scholarship

Type of award: Scholarship.
Intended use: For full-time undergraduate study at accredited 2-year or 4-year institution.
Eligibility: Applicant or parent must be employed by Wal-Mart Stores, Inc. Applicant must be high school senior.
Basis for selection: Applicant must demonstrate financial need and high academic achievement.
Application requirements: Transcript, proof of eligibility. SAT/ACT scores and financial data.
Additional information: Award is $10,000 scholarship payable over four years. Applicant's parent or guardian must have been employed with Wal-Mart full-time (32 hours/week) at least one year as of April 25, 2008. Minimum 22 ACT or 1030 SAT. Visit Wal-Mart/Sam's Club personnel department for applications and deadlines.
    Amount of award: $10,000
    Number of awards: 150
    Number of applicants: 2,000
    Application deadline: January 14
    Notification begins: April 25
    Total amount awarded: $960,000
Contact:
Walton Family Foundation Scholarship
c/o Scholarship Program Administrators, Inc.
P.O. Box 22492
Nashville, TN 37202
Phone: 866-524-7385
Fax: 615-320-3151
Web: www.walmartfoundation.org

Washington Crossing Foundation

Washington Crossing Foundation Scholarship

Type of award: Scholarship.
Intended use: For full-time undergraduate study at accredited 4-year institution.

Eligibility: Applicant must be high school senior. Applicant must be U.S. citizen.
Basis for selection: Major/career interest in political science/government or public administration/service. Applicant must demonstrate high academic achievement, depth of character, leadership, patriotism, seriousness of purpose and service orientation.
Application requirements: Recommendations, transcript. Essay on why student plans a career in government service, including any inspiration to be derived from Washington's famous crossing of the Delaware. SAT/ACT scores.
Additional information: Applicants must pursue course of study related to public service of any kind. One award is reserved for Pennsylvania's five southeastern counties; one for the state. Number of awards varies.

Amount of award:	$500-$5,000
Number of awards:	27
Number of applicants:	350
Application deadline:	January 15
Notification begins:	April 15

Contact:
Washington Crossing Foundation
Attn: Vice Chairman
P.O. Box 503
Levittown, PA 19058
Phone: 215-949-8841
Web: www.gwcf.org

Washington State Higher Education Coordinating Board

Washington State American Indian Endowed Scholarship

Type of award: Scholarship.
Intended use: For full-time undergraduate or graduate study at accredited vocational, 2-year, 4-year or graduate institution.
Eligibility: Applicant must be U.S. citizen residing in Washington.
Basis for selection: Applicant must demonstrate financial need, high academic achievement and service orientation.
Application requirements: Recommendations, essay, transcript, proof of eligibility. FAFSA.
Additional information: Must have close social and cultural ties to American Indian community within Washington State and strong commitment to return service to state's American Indian community. Applicants pursuing degree in theology not eligible.

Amount of award:	$500-$2,000
Number of awards:	15
Application deadline:	February 1

Contact:
Washington State Higher Education Coordinating Board
917 Lakeridge Way SW
P.O. Box 43430
Olympia, WA 98504-3430
Phone: 360-753-7843
Web: www.hecb.wa.gov

Washington State Educational Opportunity Grant

Type of award: Scholarship, renewable.
Intended use: For full-time junior or senior study at accredited 4-year institution. Designated institutions: Eligible postsecondary institutions in Washington.
Eligibility: Applicant must be U.S. citizen or permanent resident residing in Washington.
Basis for selection: Applicant must demonstrate financial need.
Application requirements: Essay, proof of eligibility. FAFSA.
Additional information: Must be "place-bound," i.e. having family, work, health, financial need, or similar concerns making it difficult to continue education at a four-year college. Place-bound students either have to relocate or are unable to relocate for college due to personal barriers. Applicant must be a transfer student--cannot receive award at current school Application deadlines vary. Contact financial aid office of institution for details and to initiate an application. Must not be pursuing a degree in religion, theology, or seminarian studies. Application deadlines: for Fall semester, 10/1; Winter, 2/1; Spring, 4/1; Summer, 6/1.

Amount of award:	$5,000
Number of awards:	400
Total amount awarded:	$1,500,000

Contact:
Washington State Higher Education Coordinating Board
917 Lakeridge Way SW
P.O. Box 43430
Olympia, WA 98504-3430
Phone: 360-753-7846
Web: www.hecb.wa.gov

Washington State Need Grant

Type of award: Scholarship, renewable.
Intended use: For undergraduate study at accredited vocational, 2-year or 4-year institution. Designated institutions: Eligible postsecondary institutions in Washington.
Eligibility: Applicant must be U.S. citizen or permanent resident residing in Washington.
Basis for selection: Applicant must demonstrate financial need.
Application requirements: Proof of eligibility. FAFSA.
Additional information: Grants are given only to students from low-income families. Must meet qualifications every year for renewal, up to five years. Contact institution's financial aid office for additional requirements and deadlines. Must not be studying theology.

Number of awards:	53,000
Total amount awarded:	$104,000,000

Contact:
Washington State Higher Education Coordinating Board
917 Lakeridge Way SW
P.O. Box 43430
Olympia, WA 98504-3430
Phone: 360-753-7850
Fax: 360-753-7808
Web: www.hecb.wa.gov

Washington State Scholars Program

Type of award: Scholarship.

Intended use: For undergraduate study at accredited vocational, 2-year or 4-year institution. Designated institutions: Eligible colleges and universities in Washington State.
Eligibility: Applicant must be high school senior. Applicant must be U.S. citizen or permanent resident residing in Washington.
Basis for selection: Applicant must demonstrate high academic achievement, depth of character, leadership, seriousness of purpose and service orientation.
Application requirements: Nomination by high school principal or guidance counselor. SAT/ACT scores.
Additional information: Four-year award based on tuition, which may be prorated. Must rank in top one percent of class. May not defer enrollment. Eligible high school seniors should contact their high school counselors for more information. Must not pursue a degree in theology.

Number of awards:	420
Total amount awarded:	$2,300,000

Contact:
Washington State Higher Education Coordinating Board
917 Lakeridge Way SW
P.O. Box 43430
Olympia, WA 98504-3430
Phone: 360-753-7843
Fax: 360-704-6243
Web: www.hecb.wa.gov

Washington State PTA

Washington State PTA Financial Grant Program

Type of award: Scholarship.
Intended use: For full-time freshman study at accredited vocational, 2-year or 4-year institution.
Eligibility: Applicant must be residing in Washington.
Basis for selection: Applicant must demonstrate financial need, high academic achievement, depth of character, leadership, seriousness of purpose and service orientation.
Application requirements: Recommendations, essay, transcript, proof of eligibility.
Additional information: Applicant must be graduate of a Washington State public high school. Grant administered according to college's determination. Not transferable to another institution if already enrolled in classes. Visit Website for additional information and application.

Amount of award:	$1,000-$2,000
Number of awards:	60
Number of applicants:	2,000
Application deadline:	March 31
Notification begins:	May 1
Total amount awarded:	$65,000

Contact:
Washington State PTA Financial Grant Program
2003 65 Avenue West
Tacoma, WA 98466-6215
Phone: 253-565-2153
Fax: 253-565-7753
Web: www.wastatepta.org

Wells Fargo

CollegeSTEPS Program

Type of award: Scholarship.
Intended use: For undergraduate study.
Eligibility: Applicant must be high school senior. Applicant must be U.S. citizen.
Additional information: Tuition prizes and educational electronic postcards on college-preparatory topics offered. Visit Website to apply. High school freshmen, sophomores, and juniors can also sign up to receive postcards. Employees of Wells Fargo and immediate family members not eligible for tuition prize.

Amount of award:	$1,000
Number of awards:	20
Total amount awarded:	$20,000

Contact:
Education Financial Services
Wells Fargo
P.O. Box 5185
Sioux Falls, SD 57117-5185
Phone: 888-511-7302
Fax: 800-456-0561
Web: www.wellsfargo.com/collegesteps

Welsh Society of Philadelphia

Welsh Heritage Scholarship

Type of award: Scholarship, renewable.
Intended use: For full-time undergraduate study at accredited postsecondary institution.
Eligibility: Applicant must be Welsh.
Basis for selection: Applicant must demonstrate high academic achievement and seriousness of purpose.
Application requirements: Recommendations, essay, transcript. Statement of purpose.
Additional information: Applicant must live or attend college within 150 miles of Philadelphia. Participation in Welsh organizations or events preferred.

Amount of award:	$1,000
Number of awards:	5
Number of applicants:	50
Application deadline:	March 1
Notification begins:	May 1
Total amount awarded:	$5,000

Contact:
Welsh Society of Philadelphia
Scholarship Committee Chairman
P.O. Box 7287
St. David's, PA 19087-7287

West Pharmaceutical Services, Inc.

Herman O. West Foundation Scholarship Program

Type of award: Scholarship, renewable.
Intended use: For full-time undergraduate study at accredited 2-year or 4-year institution.
Eligibility: Applicant or parent must be employed by West Pharmaceutical Services, Inc. Applicant must be high school senior. Applicant must be U.S. citizen.
Basis for selection: Applicant must demonstrate high academic achievement.
Application requirements: Recommendations, essay, transcript, proof of eligibility. List of extracurricular activities.
Additional information: Parent must be employee of West Pharmaceutical Services, Inc. Award is renewable annually for maximum of four years.

Amount of award:	$2,500
Number of awards:	7
Number of applicants:	26
Application deadline:	February 28
Notification begins:	May 1
Total amount awarded:	$50,000

Contact:
H.O. West Foundation
101 Gordon Drive
Lionville, PA 19341
Phone: 610-594-2945

West Virginia Division of Veterans Affairs

West Virginia War Orphans Educational Assistance

Type of award: Scholarship, renewable.
Intended use: For undergraduate, graduate or non-degree study in United States.
Eligibility: Applicant must be at least 16, no older than 25. Applicant must be U.S. citizen residing in Wisconsin. Applicant must be dependent of deceased veteran who served in the Army, Air Force, Marines, Navy, Coast Guard or Reserves/National Guard. Applicant's parent must be veteran who was killed while on active duty during wartime or who died of injury or illness resulting from wartime service.
Application requirements: Proof of eligibility.
Additional information: Award is waiver of tuition and registration fees for West Virginia residents attending a West Virginia school. If attending a private school in West Virginia or out of state college, may only receive a maximum of $2,000. Non West Virginia residents exempt.

Amount of award:	Full tuition
Number of awards:	23
Number of applicants:	23
Application deadline:	July 1, December 1
Notification begins:	July 15, December 15

Contact:
West Virginia Division of Veterans Affairs
1321 Plaza East, Suite 101
Charleston, WV 25301-1400
Phone: 888-838-2332
Fax: 304-558-3662
Web: www.state.wv.us

West Virginia Higher Education Policy Commission

PROMISE Scholarship

Type of award: Scholarship, renewable.
Intended use: For undergraduate study.
Eligibility: Applicant must be U.S. citizen or permanent resident residing in West Virginia.
Additional information: Merit-based scholarship; all eligible applicants will receive award. Minimum 22 composite ACT, with scores of at least 20 in math, science, English, and reading, or 1020 SAT (Math and Reading) with minimum 480 Math and 490 Reading. Minimum 3.0 GPA. Tuition waiver only for public institutions. Students attending private institutions will receive $4,098 in tuition assistance--equivalent of public college tuition and fees. See Website for more information.

Amount of award:	$4,098
Number of awards:	10,000
Number of applicants:	8,000
Application deadline:	March 1
Total amount awarded:	$30,000,000

Contact:
West Virginia Higher Education Policy Commission
1018 Kanawha Boulevard East
Suite 700
Charleston, WV 25301
Phone: 877-987-7664
Fax: 304-558-3264
Web: www.promisescholarships.org

West Virginia Engineering, Science and Technology Scholarship

Type of award: Scholarship, renewable.
Intended use: For full-time undergraduate study at postsecondary institution in United States. Designated institutions: Eligible West Virginia institutions.
Eligibility: Applicant must be U.S. citizen or permanent resident residing in West Virginia.
Basis for selection: Major/career interest in science, general; engineering; engineering, civil; engineering, computer; engineering, electrical/electronic; engineering, mechanical; computer/information sciences; life sciences; physical sciences or natural sciences. Applicant must demonstrate high academic achievement and seriousness of purpose.
Additional information: Recipients should obtain degree/certificate in engineering, science, or technology and pursue career in West Virginia. Recipient must, within one year after ceasing to be a full-time student, work full-time in engineering, science, or technology field in West Virginia, or begin a program of community service relating to these fields in West Virginia for a duration of one year for each year scholarship was received. If work requirement fails to be met, recipient

must repay scholarship plus interest and any required collection fees. Interested high school students should apply through high school counselor; currently enrolled college/university students should apply through their institution. Minimum 3.0 GPA.

Amount of award: $3,000
Number of awards: 290
Number of applicants: 350
Application deadline: March 1
Total amount awarded: $500,000

Contact:
West Virginia Higher Education Policy Commission
Engineering, Science and Technology Program
1018 Kanawha Boulevard East, Suite 700
Charleston, WV 25301-2827
Phone: 304-558-4618
Fax: 304-558-4622
Web: www.hepc.wvnet.edu

West Virginia Higher Education Adult Part-time Student (HEAPS) Grant Program

Type of award: Scholarship, renewable.
Intended use: For half-time undergraduate study at postsecondary institution.
Eligibility: Applicant must be returning adult student. Applicant must be U.S. citizen or permanent resident residing in West Virginia.
Basis for selection: Applicant must demonstrate financial need.
Application requirements: FAFSA and any supplemental materials required by individual institutions.
Additional information: Applicant must be out of high school for at least two years and plan to continue education on part-time basis. Must either be enrolled in college with cumulative 2.0 GPA (for renewal applicants), or be accepted for enrollment by intended institution (for first-time applicants); must have complied with Military Selective Service Act; must qualify as independent student according to federal financial aid criteria; must not be in default on higher education loan; and must not be incarcerated in correctional facility. At public colleges/universities, award is actual amount of tuition and fees. At independent colleges/universities and vocational/technical schools, award is based upon average per credit/term hours tuition and fee charges assessed by all public undergraduate institutions. Contact school's financial aid office, or visit Website for additional information.

Contact:
West Virginia Higher Education Policy Commission
Judy Kee
1018 Kanawha Boulevard, Fifth Floor
Charleston, WV 25301
Phone: 304-558-4618
Web: www.hepc.wvnet.edu

West Virginia Higher Education Grant

Type of award: Scholarship, renewable.
Intended use: For full-time undergraduate study at accredited 2-year or 4-year institution.
Eligibility: Applicant must be U.S. citizen residing in West Virginia or Pennsylvania.
Basis for selection: Applicant must demonstrate financial need and high academic achievement.
Application requirements: Transcript. FAFSA. ACT/SAT scores.
Additional information: Applicants must fill out common application for state-level financial aid programs.

Amount of award: $375-$3,358
Number of awards: 13,000
Number of applicants: 60,833
Application deadline: March 1
Notification begins: April 1
Total amount awarded: $27,000,000

Contact:
West Virginia Higher Education Grant Program
Office of Financial Aid and Outreach Services
1018 Kanawha Boulevard East, Suite 700
Charleston, WV 25301-2827
Phone: 888-825-5707
Web: www.hepc.wvnet.edu

West Virginia Robert C. Byrd Honors Scholarship

Type of award: Scholarship, renewable.
Intended use: For full-time freshman study at vocational, 2-year or 4-year institution in United States.
Eligibility: Applicant must be high school senior. Applicant must be U.S. citizen or permanent resident residing in West Virginia.
Basis for selection: Applicant must demonstrate high academic achievement.
Application requirements: Transcript, proof of eligibility, nomination by high school. SAT or ACT scores.
Additional information: Because of limited funding, high schools with senior class enrollment of 1-199 may submit one application for consideration and high schools with senior class of 200+ may submit two applications for consideration.

Amount of award: $1,500
Number of awards: 35
Number of applicants: 164
Application deadline: March 1
Notification begins: April 1
Total amount awarded: $216,000

Contact:
West Virginia Higher Education Policy Commission
Robert C. Byrd Honors Scholarship Program
1018 Kanawha Boulevard East, Suite 700
Charleston, WV 25301-2827
Phone: 304-558-4618
Fax: 304-558-4622
Web: www.hepc.wvnet.edu

Western European Architecture Foundation

Gabriel Prize

Type of award: Research grant.
Intended use: For non-degree study.
Eligibility: Applicant must be U.S. citizen.
Basis for selection: Major/career interest in architecture. Applicant must demonstrate seriousness of purpose.
Application requirements: Portfolio, recommendations, research proposal. Resume.
Additional information: To encourage personal investigative and critical studies of French architectural compositions

Western European Architecture Foundation: Gabriel Prize

completed between 1630 and 1830. Work is expected to be executed in France under supervision of foundation's European representative. Winner is required to begin studies in France by May 1, keep a traveling sketchbook, and prepare three large colored drawings within three months. Must use stipend for travel and study. Send SASE for return of materials. Visit Website for deadlines and application.

Amount of award:	$17,500
Number of awards:	1
Number of applicants:	24
Application deadline:	December 31
Notification begins:	February 22
Total amount awarded:	$17,500

Contact:
Western European Architecture Foundation
306 West Sunset Road, Suite 119
San Antonio, TX 78209
Phone: 210-829-4040
Web: www.gabrielprize.org

Western Golf Association/Evans Scholars Foundation

Chick Evans Caddie Scholarship

Type of award: Scholarship, renewable.
Intended use: For full-time undergraduate study at accredited 4-year institution in United States.
Eligibility: Applicant must be high school senior.
Basis for selection: Competition/talent/interest in athletics/sports, based on consistent caddie record at Western Golf Association-affiliated club. Applicant must demonstrate financial need, high academic achievement, depth of character and leadership.
Application requirements: Recommendations, transcript, proof of eligibility. Tax returns, financial aid profile.
Additional information: Scholarship for full tuition, plus housing where applicable. Must have caddied minimum two years at Western Golf Association-affiliated club and maintain at least B average in college prep classes. Must have strong caddie record and work at sponsoring club during summer of application. Most recipients attend one of 14 universities where Evans Scholars Foundation owns and operates chapter house. Approximately 200 new Evans Scholarships awarded each year. Renewable up to four years. See Website for designated institutions.

Amount of award:	Full tuition
Number of awards:	200
Application deadline:	September 30

Contact:
Scholarship Committee
Western Golf Assoc./Evans Scholars Foundation
1 Briar Road
Golf, IL 60029
Phone: 847-724-4600
Fax: 847-724-7133
Web: www.evansscholarsfoundation.com

William Randolph Hearst Foundation

Hearst Journalism Award

Type of award: Scholarship.
Intended use: For undergraduate study at accredited 4-year institution. Designated institutions: Institutions accredited by Accrediting Council on Education in Journalism and Mass Communication.
Basis for selection: Competition/talent/interest in writing/journalism, based on newsworthiness, research, excellence of journalistic writing, photojournalism, or broadcast news. Major/career interest in journalism; radio/television/film or communications.
Additional information: Field of study may also include photojournalism or broadcast news. Applicants must submit work that has been published or aired. Competition consists of monthly contests and one championship. Scholarships awarded to student winners with matching grants awarded to their departments of journalism. Entries must be submitted by journalism department. For additional information, applicants should contact journalism department chair or visit Website.

Amount of award:	$500-$2,000
Number of awards:	12
Total amount awarded:	$500,000

Contact:
Hearst Journalism Awards Program
90 New Montgomery Street
Suite 1212
San Francisco, CA 94105-4504
Phone: 415-543-6033
Fax: 415-348-0887
Web: www.hearstfdn.org

United States Senate Youth Program

Type of award: Scholarship.
Intended use: For undergraduate study at accredited 2-year or 4-year institution in United States.
Eligibility: Applicant must be high school junior or senior. Applicant must be U.S. citizen or permanent resident.
Basis for selection: Applicant must demonstrate leadership and service orientation.
Application requirements: Nomination by high school principal.
Additional information: Applicant must be permanent resident and currently enrolled in public or private secondary school located in the state (including District of Columbia) in which parent or guardian legally resides. Must be currently serving in elected capacity as student body officer; class officer; student council representative; or student representative to district, regional, or state-level civic or educational organization. Selection process managed by state-level department of education. Scholarship includes all-expenses-paid week in Washington, D.C., in March. Application deadline is in early fall for most states; application available from high school principal. Visit Website for more information.

Amount of award:	$5,000
Number of awards:	104
Total amount awarded:	$520,000

Wilson Ornithological Society

George A. Hall/Harold F. Mayfield Award

Type of award: Research grant.
Intended use: For non-degree study.
Basis for selection: Major/career interest in ornithology.
Application requirements: Recommendations, research proposal. Budget. Research proposal must be no longer than three pages.
Additional information: Award restricted to amateur researchers, including high school students, without access to funds and facilities of academic institutions or governmental agencies. Willingness to report research results as oral or poster paper is condition of award. Applicants whose first language is not English may submit proposal in their first language. See Website for contact information.

Amount of award:	$1,000
Number of awards:	1
Application deadline:	February 1
Total amount awarded:	$1,000

Contact:
Web: www.ummz.lsa.umich.edu/birds/wosawards.html

Paul A. Stewart Award

Type of award: Research grant.
Intended use: For undergraduate, master's, doctoral, postgraduate or non-degree study at graduate institution.
Basis for selection: Major/career interest in ornithology.
Application requirements: Recommendations, research proposal. Research budget.
Additional information: Preference given to proposals studying bird movements based on banding, analysis of recoveries, and returns of banded birds, with an emphasis on economic ornithology. Willingness to report research results as oral or poster paper is condition of award. Multiple awards given annually. Applicants whose first language is not English may submit proposal in their first language. See Website for contact information.

Amount of award:	$500
Number of awards:	6
Application deadline:	February 1
Total amount awarded:	$2,000

Contact:
Web: www.ummz.lsa.umich.edu/birds/wosawards.html

Wisconsin Department of Veterans Affairs

Wisconsin Veterans Affairs Retraining Grant

Type of award: Scholarship.
Intended use: For undergraduate study at accredited vocational institution.
Eligibility: Applicant must be residing in Wisconsin. Applicant must be veteran. Must have served two years of continuous active duty during peacetime or 90 days of active duty during designated wartime period. Applicant must be recently unemployed or underemployed veteran and registered for or enrolled in education program that will lead to reemployment and be completed within two years.
Basis for selection: Applicant must demonstrate financial need.
Additional information: Must have been involuntarily laid off within a period beginning one year before WDVA receives application. Must have been employed for six consecutive months with same employer or in the same or similar occupation. Must have been a resident of Wisconsin on entry into military service or a continuous resident of Wisconsin for at least five years after separation from military service. Certification and counseling is provided at accredited Wisconsin schools. Training at other schools does not qualify. Apply year-round at local county Veterans Service Office to establish eligibility.

Amount of award:	$3,000

Contact:
Wisconsin Department of Veterans Affairs
P.O. Box 7843
30 West Mifflin Street
Madison, WI 53707-7843
Phone: 800-947-8387
Web: www.dva.state.wi.us

Wisconsin Veterans Education Tuition and Fee Reimbursement Grant

Type of award: Scholarship, renewable.
Intended use: For undergraduate study at postsecondary institution. Designated institutions: Approved Wisconsin postsecondary schools.
Eligibility: Applicant must be residing in Wisconsin. Applicant must be veteran.
Basis for selection: Applicant must demonstrate financial need.
Application requirements: Proof of eligibility. Federal tax return or proof of annual income.
Additional information: Family income limit of $50,000. Limit increases by $1,000 for each dependent child. Veterans may receive up to 100 percent reimbursement of cost of tuition and fees. May receive reimbursement for up to eight semesters of full-time study. Courses must be taken within ten years of separation from active military service.

Contact:
Wisconsin Department of Veterans Affairs
P.O. Box 7843
30 West Mifflin Street
Madison, WI 53707-7843
Phone: 800-947-8387
Web: www.dva.state.wi.us

Wisconsin Higher Educational Aids Board

Wisconsin Academic Excellence Scholarship

Type of award: Scholarship, renewable.
Intended use: For full-time undergraduate study at vocational, 2-year or 4-year institution.
Eligibility: Applicant must be high school senior. Applicant must be residing in Wisconsin.
Basis for selection: Applicant must demonstrate high academic achievement.
Application requirements: Nomination by high school guidance counselor.
Additional information: Awarded to Wisconsin high school seniors who have the highest grade point average in each public and private high school throughout Wisconsin. 3.0 GPA must be maintained for renewal. Awards range from $2,250 to full tuition and fees.
   Number of awards: 2,670
   Application deadline: February 15
   Total amount awarded: $2,894,469
Contact:
Higher Educational Aids Board
Attn: Alice Winters
131 West Wilson
Madison, WI 53707
Phone: 608-267-2213
Web: www.heab.state.wi.us/programs.html

Wisconsin Hearing & Visually Handicapped Student Grant

Type of award: Scholarship, renewable.
Intended use: For undergraduate study.
Eligibility: Applicant must be visually impaired or hearing impaired. Applicant must be residing in Wisconsin.
Basis for selection: Applicant must demonstrate financial need.
Application requirements: Proof of eligibility. FAFSA.
   Amount of award: $250-$1,800
   Number of awards: 54
   Total amount awarded: $85,910
Contact:
Higher Educational Aids Board
Attn: Sandy Thomas
131 West Wilson
Madison, WI 53707-7885
Phone: 608-266-0888

Wisconsin Higher Education Grant

Type of award: Scholarship, renewable.
Intended use: For undergraduate study at vocational or 4-year institution. Designated institutions: University of Wisconsin, Wisconsin Technical College, Tribal institutions.
Eligibility: Applicant must be residing in Wisconsin.
Basis for selection: Applicant must demonstrate financial need.
Application requirements: Proof of eligibility.
Additional information: Apply with FAFSA through high school guidance counselor or financial aid office of institution.
   Amount of award: $250-$3,000
   Number of awards: 37,172
   Total amount awarded: $35,060,586
Contact:
Higher Educational Aids Board
Attn: Sandra Thomas
131 West Wilson
Madison, WI 53707
Phone: 608-266-0888

Wisconsin Indian Student Assistance Grant

Type of award: Scholarship, renewable.
Intended use: For undergraduate or graduate study.
Eligibility: Applicant must be American Indian. Must be at least one-quarter Native American. Applicant must be residing in Wisconsin.
Basis for selection: Major/career interest in humanities/liberal arts. Applicant must demonstrate financial need.
Application requirements: Proof of eligibility. FAFSA.
   Amount of award: $250-$1,100
   Number of awards: 837
   Total amount awarded: $784,857
Contact:
Higher Educational Aids Board
Attn: Sandra Thomas
131 West Wilson
Madison, WI 53707
Phone: 608-267-2206
Web: www.heab.state.wi.us

Wisconsin Minority Undergraduate Retention Grant

Type of award: Scholarship, renewable.
Intended use: For sophomore, junior or senior study at vocational, 2-year or 4-year institution.
Eligibility: Applicant must be African American, Hispanic American or American Indian. Asian American applicants must be former citizens or children of former citizens of Laos, Vietnam, or Cambodia admitted to United States after 12/31/75. Applicant must be residing in Wisconsin.
Basis for selection: Applicant must demonstrate financial need.
Application requirements: Nomination. FAFSA and nomination by Financial Aid Office.
   Amount of award: $250-$2,500
   Number of awards: 913
   Number of applicants: 915
   Total amount awarded: $687,596

Contact:
Higher Educational Aids Board
Attn: May Lou Kuzdas
131 West Wilson
Wisconsin, WI 53707
Phone: 608-267-2212
Fax: 608-267-2808
Web: www.heab.state.wi.us

Wisconsin Talent Incentive Program Grant

Type of award: Scholarship, renewable.
Intended use: For undergraduate study at postsecondary institution.
Eligibility: Applicant must be residing in Wisconsin.
Basis for selection: Major/career interest in humanities/liberal arts. Applicant must demonstrate financial need.
Application requirements: Nomination by financial aid department or WEOP. FAFSA.
Additional information: Eligibility cannot exceed ten semesters.
    Amount of award: $250-$1,800
    Number of awards: 4,146
    Total amount awarded: $5,489,498
Contact:
Higher Educational Aids Board
Attn: John Whitt
131 West Wilson
Madison, WI 53707
Phone: 608-266-1665
Web: www.heab.state.wi.us/programs.html

Wisconsin Tuition Grant

Type of award: Scholarship, renewable.
Intended use: For undergraduate study. Designated institutions: Independent, nonprofit institutions in Wisconsin.
Eligibility: Applicant must be residing in Wisconsin.
Basis for selection: Applicant must demonstrate financial need.
Application requirements: FAFSA.
Additional information: Minimum award $250; maximum award amount set annually by HEAB.
    Number of awards: 12,343
    Total amount awarded: $23,247,820
Contact:
Higher Educational Aids Board
Attn: Mary Lou Kuzdas
131 West Wilson
Madison, WI 53707
Phone: 608-267-2212
Web: www.heab.state.wi.us

Women Grocers of America

Mary Macey Scholarship

Type of award: Scholarship, renewable.
Intended use: For sophomore, junior, senior or graduate study at accredited 2-year, 4-year or graduate institution in United States.
Basis for selection: Major/career interest in food production/management/services.
Application requirements: Recommendations, essay, transcript.
Additional information: Must plan on a career in the independent sector of the grocery industry. Majors in public health and hotel management are not eligible. Minimum 2.0 GPA. Minimum of two awards each year.
    Amount of award: $1,000-$1,500
    Number of awards: 7
    Number of applicants: 18
    Application deadline: May 15
    Notification begins: July 1
    Total amount awarded: $7,000
Contact:
Women Grocers of America
1005 North Glebe Road
Suite 250
Arlington, VA 22201-5758
Phone: 703-516-0700
Fax: 703-516-0115
Web: www.nationalgrocers.org

Women of the Evangelical Lutheran Church in America

Laywomen Scholarships

Type of award: Scholarship.
Intended use: For undergraduate or graduate study.
Eligibility: Applicant must be female, at least 21, returning adult student. Applicant must be Lutheran. Applicant must be U.S. citizen.
Basis for selection: Applicant must demonstrate financial need, high academic achievement and service orientation.
Application requirements: Essay, transcript, proof of eligibility. Academic and personal references. Reference from pastor or, if pastor is a relative, from chairperson or vice-chairperson of congregation.
Additional information: Must be member of Evangelical Lutheran Church in America. Must have interrupted education since high school for at least two years. Must show clear educational goals. Cannot be studying for ordination, diaconate, or church-certified professions. Must be laywoman. Applicants may reapply and receive assistance for maximum of two years. Award varies; maximum is $2,000. Visit Website or write to address below for more information and to request application.
    Number of applicants: 100
    Application deadline: February 15
    Notification begins: May 25
Contact:
Women of the ELCA Scholarship Program
8765 W. Higgins Road
Chicago, IL 60631-4189
Web: www.womenoftheelca.org

Women's Western Golf Foundation

Women's Western Golf Foundation Scholarship

Type of award: Scholarship, renewable.
Intended use: For full-time freshman study at accredited 4-year institution in United States.
Eligibility: Applicant must be female, high school senior. Applicant must be U.S. citizen.
Basis for selection: Competition/talent/interest in athletics/sports. Applicant must demonstrate financial need, high academic achievement, depth of character, leadership and seriousness of purpose.
Application requirements: Essay, transcript, proof of eligibility. SAT/ACT scores, FAFSA. Personal recommendation required from high school teacher or counselor. List of high school activities.
Additional information: Must be in top 15 percent of class. 3.5 GPA is recommended. Must demonstrate involvement in golf, but skill not criterion. Deadline to request application is March 1; SASE required. Awards renew for each of four years, assuming scholarship terms are fulfilled (financial need, GPA above 3.0). About 20 new awards each year, plus 50 renewals.

Amount of award:	$2,000
Number of awards:	22
Number of applicants:	500
Application deadline:	April 5
Notification begins:	May 20
Total amount awarded:	$150,000

Contact:
Director of Scholarship
Women's Western Golf Foundation
393 Ramsay Road
Deerfield, IL 60015

Woodrow Wilson National Fellowship Foundation

Thomas R. Pickering Foreign Affairs Fellowship

Type of award: Scholarship.
Intended use: For full-time sophomore study at accredited 4-year institution in United States. Designated institutions: Institutions affiliated with Association of Professional Schools of International Affairs (graduate portion of fellowship).
Eligibility: Applicant must be U.S. citizen.
Basis for selection: Major/career interest in international relations. Applicant must demonstrate financial need, high academic achievement, depth of character, leadership, seriousness of purpose and service orientation.
Application requirements: Recommendations, essay, transcript, proof of eligibility.
Additional information: Undergrads must apply as sophomore; applicants for graduate fellowship must be seeking admission to graduate school for the following academic year. Must have interest in career as Foreign Service officer. Number of fellowships determined by available funding. Finalists will attend interview session in Princeton, NJ, or Washington, DC; transportation to interview site paid. Orientation in Washington, D.C. Medical and security clearances required for program participation. Applicants must have minimum 3.2 GPA at time of application and maintain GPA throughout fellowship. Women and members of minority groups historically underrepresented in the Foreign Service encouraged to apply. Successful applicants obligated to a minimum of four and a half years service as a Foreign Service officer. Deadline varies, visit Website for details.

Amount of award:	Full tuition
Application deadline:	February 8
Notification begins:	April 1

Contact:
Dr. Richard Hope, Director Foreign Affairs Fellowship Program
Woodrow Wilson National Fellowship Foundation
P.O. Box 2437
Princeton, NJ 08543-2437
Phone: 609-452-7007
Web: www.woodrow.org

Working in Support of Education (WISE)

Quality of Life Research Competition

Type of award: Scholarship.
Intended use: For undergraduate study at accredited 4-year institution.
Eligibility: Applicant must be enrolled in high school. Applicant must be U.S. citizen or permanent resident residing in New York.
Basis for selection: Competition/talent/interest in research paper, based on research methods and research-based practice recommendation.
Application requirements: A 6-15 page research paper with recommendations on improving the quality of life in New York City.
Additional information: Applicant must be resident of New York City. Entry forms due in December, research papers due in March. Semi-finalists announced in April. Finalists invited to present to panel of judges in late April/early May. Scholarships awarded in late May/early June. All students submitting proposals will receive a certificate signed by the Mayor of New York City. Students must contact WISE through the designated representative at their respective high schools.

Number of awards:	4
Number of applicants:	900
Application deadline:	March 28

Contact:
WISE
Quality of Life Competition
227 E. 56th Street, Suite 201
New York, NY 10022
Phone: 212-421-2700
Web: www.qlcompetition.org

Worldstudio Foundation

Worldstudio AIGA Scholarship

Type of award: Scholarship.
Intended use: For full-time undergraduate or graduate study at accredited postsecondary institution in United States.
Eligibility: Applicant must be U.S. citizen or permanent resident.
Basis for selection: Major/career interest in arts, general or design. Applicant must demonstrate financial need, seriousness of purpose and service orientation.
Application requirements: Recommendations, transcript. Portfolio in digital format. Short autobiography, statement of purpose, and self-portrait.
Additional information: The foundation's primary aim is to increase diversity in the creative professions and to foster social and environmental responsibility in the artists, designers, and studios of tomorrow. Awards are paid directly to college or university to be applied toward student's tuition. Applicants must be enrolled in courses related to or planning a career in design arts professions, and must demonstrate a social agenda in their work. Students with minority status given preference. Minimum 2.0 GPA. Visit Website to download guidelines and application, or send SASE to receive application by mail. Deadline in mid-April; exact date varies. Applicants will be notified by e-mail in late June.

Amount of award:	$2,000-$6,000
Number of awards:	25
Number of applicants:	600
Application deadline:	April 18
Notification begins:	June 1
Total amount awarded:	$60,000

Contact:
Worldstudio Foundation
c/o AIGA
164 Fifth Ave
New York, NY 10010
Phone: 212-807-1990
Fax: 212-807-1799
Web: www.worldstudio.org or www.aiga.org

Xerox

Technical Minority Scholarship

Type of award: Scholarship.
Intended use: For undergraduate study in United States.
Eligibility: Applicant must be Alaskan native, Asian American, African American, Mexican American, Hispanic American, Puerto Rican, American Indian or Native Hawaiian/Pacific Islander. Applicant must be U.S. citizen or permanent resident.
Basis for selection: Major/career interest in chemistry; engineering; science, general; information systems; physics or computer/information sciences. Applicant must demonstrate high academic achievement, leadership, patriotism and seriousness of purpose.
Application requirements: Resume and cover letter.
Additional information: Minimum 3.0 GPA. Spouses and children of Xerox employees not eligible. Visit Website for application and more information.

Amount of award:	$1,000-$10,000
Number of awards:	119
Application deadline:	September 30
Notification begins:	December 31

Contact:
Xerox
Xerox Technical Minority Scholarship Program
150 State St., 4th Floor
Rochester, NY 14614
Web: www.xerox.com

Yakama Nation Higher Education Program

Yakama Nation Tribal Scholarship

Type of award: Scholarship.
Intended use: For undergraduate, master's or doctoral study at accredited 2-year, 4-year or graduate institution.
Eligibility: Must be enrolled member of Yakama Nation.
Application requirements: Transcript. High school or GED scoresheet. Tribal ID card copy. Enrollment verification, FAFSA, college acceptance letter.
Additional information: Amount of awards varies from year to year. Recipients notified two weeks prior to the start of semester to which aid will be applied.

Amount of award:	$2,000
Number of awards:	262
Number of applicants:	285
Application deadline:	July 1
Notification begins:	July 10
Total amount awarded:	$200,000

Contact:
Yakama Nation Higher Education Program
P.O. Box 151
Toppenish, WA 98948
Phone: 509-865-5121
Fax: 509-865-6994

Internships

Academy of Television Arts & Sciences Foundation

Academy of Television Arts & Sciences Foundation Student Internship Program

Type of award: Internship.
Intended use: For full-time undergraduate or graduate study in United States.
Eligibility: Applicant must be U.S. citizen or permanent resident.
Basis for selection: Major/career interest in film/video.
Application requirements: Essay, transcript. Resume and cover letter. Two letters of recommendation.
Additional information: Designed to expose students to professional TV production facilities, techniques, and practices. Opportunities available in many fields. See Website for categories and special requirements; students must have current information in order to apply. Most internships start in late June and end eight weeks after start date. Interns responsible for housing, transportation, and living expenses. Interns must have car for transportation in Los Angeles.

    Amount of award: $4,000
    Number of awards: 35
    Number of applicants: 830
    Application deadline: March 15
    Notification begins: May 1

Contact:
Academy of Television Arts & Sciences Foundation
Internships
5220 Lankershim Boulevard
North Hollywood, CA 91601-3109
Phone: 818-754-2800
Fax: 818-509-2266
Web: www.emmysfoundation.org

Accuracy in Media/ American Journalism Center

Accuracy in Media Internships

Type of award: Internship.
Intended use: For undergraduate or graduate study.
Basis for selection: Major/career interest in journalism; marketing or public relations.
Application requirements: Cover letter and resume. Writing sample.
Additional information: Accuracy in Media is a nonprofit media watchdog group that reports on media bias. Internships open to applicants from all majors, though some positions require experience in a particular field. Internships pay $50 per day. High school students may apply, as well as recent college graduates. Applications are processed on rolling basis; send early for best chance and to allow for find housing. Deadlines: April 15 for summer, August 15 for fall, January 15 for spring. See Website for application and more information.

    Amount of award: $3,000
    Number of awards: 24
    Application deadline: April 15, August 15

Contact:
Accuracy in Media/American Journalism Center
Internship Coordinator
4455 Connecticut Avenue, NW, Suite 330
Washington, DC 20008
Phone: 202-364-4401 ext. 110
Fax: 202-364-4098
Web: www.aimajc.org

Allstate

Allstate Internships

Type of award: Internship, renewable.
Intended use: For full-time undergraduate study at accredited 4-year institution.
Basis for selection: Major/career interest in insurance/actuarial science; accounting; marketing; business; business/management/administration; computer/information sciences; finance/banking; mathematics or statistics. Applicant must demonstrate high academic achievement.
Application requirements: Resume and cover letter.
Additional information: In addition to salary, eligible interns receive subsidized transportation to and from Allstate Home Office in Northbrook, IL, at the beginning and end of internship; daily transportation; and subsidized housing. Please respond directly to position as posted on Website.

Contact:
Allstate Insurance Company
2775 Sanders Rd., Suite A-1
Northbrook, IL 60062
Fax: 800-526-4831
Web: www.allstate.com/careers

American Association of Advertising Agencies

Multicultural Advertising Intern Program

Type of award: Internship, renewable.
Intended use: For full-time senior or graduate study at accredited 4-year or graduate institution.
Eligibility: Applicant must be Asian American, African American, Mexican American, Hispanic American, Puerto

Rican, American Indian or Native Hawaiian/Pacific Islander. Applicant must be U.S. citizen or permanent resident.
Basis for selection: Major/career interest in advertising; communications; marketing or humanities/liberal arts.
Application requirements: Interview, recommendations, transcript. Resume, creative samples (if applying for creative department, please see assignment on application). Must submit two copies of application and supporting materials.
Additional information: Applicants must have completed at least junior year of college and have strong interest in advertising. Minimum 3.0 GPA required. Applicants with lower GPA (2.7-2.9) must complete essay question on application. Students are placed in member agency offices for ten weeks during the summer. Salary minimum $350 per week. AAAA covers 70 percent of housing and travel costs (if applicable). Can apply for following departments: account management, creative, interactive technologies, media, production, traffic, or strategic planning. Agency professionals interview semifinalists before selection. See Website for more information.

Number of awards:	100
Application deadline:	December 7

Contact:
American Association of Advertising Agencies
Manager of Diversity Programs
405 Lexington Avenue, 18th Floor
New York, NY 10174-1801
Phone: 800-676-9333
Fax: 212-682-2028
Web: www.aaaa-maip.org

American Bar Foundation

Summer Research Diversity Fellowships in Law and Social Sciences for Undergraduate Students

Type of award: Internship.
Intended use: For sophomore or junior study.
Eligibility: Applicant must be U.S. citizen or permanent resident.
Basis for selection: Major/career interest in law; social/behavioral sciences; criminal justice/law enforcement; public administration/service or humanities/liberal arts. Applicant must demonstrate high academic achievement.
Application requirements: Recommendations, essay, transcript.
Additional information: Interns work eight 35-hour weeks as research assistants at American Bar Foundation in Chicago and receive $3,600 stipend. Fellowships are intended for, but not limited to, persons who are African American, Hispanic/Latino, Native American or Puerto Rican. Applicants must have minimum 3.0 GPA and intend to pursue academic major in social sciences or humanities.

Amount of award:	$3,600
Number of awards:	4
Application deadline:	February 15
Notification begins:	April 1

Contact:
American Bar Foundation
750 North Lake Shore Drive, Fourth Floor
Chicago, IL 60611
Phone: 312-988-6560
Web: www.americanbarfoundation.org

American Conservatory Theater

American Conservatory Theater Production Internships

Type of award: Internship.
Intended use: For undergraduate or graduate study.
Eligibility: Applicant must be U.S. citizen or permanent resident.
Basis for selection: Major/career interest in performing arts; theater arts or theater/production/technical. Applicant must demonstrate high academic achievement.
Application requirements: Interview, portfolio, recommendations, essay. Work permit. Resume. Three confidential letters of recommendation. Writing sample, if required by specific internship.
Additional information: Provides intern with practical experience in many areas of theater production. Departments include costume rentals, costume shop, lighting design, properties, sound design, stage management, technical design, wig construction/makeup, production. A small weekly stipend is available for full-time seasonal internships. Visit Website for more information.

Number of awards:	10
Number of applicants:	70
Notification begins:	May 30

Contact:
American Conservatory Theater
Internship Coordinator
30 Grant Avenue, 6th Floor
San Francisco, CA 94108
Phone: 415-834-3200
Web: www.act-sf.org

Artistic and Administrative Internships

Type of award: Internship.
Intended use: For undergraduate or graduate study at 2-year, 4-year or graduate institution.
Eligibility: Applicant must be U.S. citizen or permanent resident.
Basis for selection: Major/career interest in theater arts; theater/production/technical; arts management; arts, general; public relations; marketing; English; English literature; literature or performing arts. Applicant must demonstrate high academic achievement.
Application requirements: Interview, portfolio, recommendations, essay. Work permit. Writing/art samples if required by specific internship.
Additional information: Provides intern with opportunity to work in artistic, literary/publications, management, development, and marketing/public relations departments. A weekly stipend is available. If intern needs paying employment, ACT will adjust hours. Different departments have available

positions at different times of year. Visit Website for more information.
- **Number of awards:** 6
- **Number of applicants:** 75
- **Notification begins:** May 30

Contact:
American Conservatory Theater
Internship Coordinator
30 Grant Avenue, 6th Floor
San Francisco, CA 94108
Phone: 415-834-3200
Web: www.act-sf.org

American Museum of Natural History

Anthropology Internship Program

Type of award: Internship.
Intended use: For undergraduate or graduate study.
Basis for selection: Major/career interest in anthropology; archaeology or museum studies.
Application requirements: Essay, transcript. Resume, one page essay, contact information of academic advisor.
Additional information: Must specify whether applying for paid, credit-granting, or unpaid internship. Deadline for summer internship: April 1; for fall: August 27; for spring: December 1. Internships may range from three months to one year.
- **Application deadline:** April 1, December 1

Contact:
Chair, Division of Anthropology
American Museum of Natural History
Central Park West at 79th Street
New York, NY 10024
Phone: 212-769-5638
Web: anthro.amnh.org/anthro.html

Research Experiences for Undergraduates in Systematics and Evolutionary Biology

Type of award: Internship.
Intended use: For undergraduate study at accredited postsecondary institution in United States.
Eligibility: Applicant must be U.S. citizen or permanent resident.
Basis for selection: Major/career interest in science, general; biology or microbiology. Applicant must demonstrate high academic achievement and seriousness of purpose.
Application requirements: Essay. List of courses. List of references. Ranking of first two choices among summer projects listed on Website and explanation of why applicant chose them. Send original and two copies of all application materials.
Additional information: Applicant must have strong scientific background. Stipend is $3,600 plus $520 for relocation; $2,075 for accommodations in NYC; $300 for local travel; $1,500 for living allowance; and $875 for research materials and supplies. Internship lasts from beginning of June to mid-August. College seniors may not apply. See Website for detailed descriptions of summer projects.
- **Amount of award:** $8,870
- **Number of awards:** 8
- **Application deadline:** February 15

Contact:
Mark E. Siddall Office of Grants and Fellowships
REU, American Museum of Natural History
Central Park West at 79th Street
New York, NY 10024-5192
Phone: 212-769-5638
Web: www.research.amnh.org/grants/EvoREU.html

Research Experiences for Undergraduates in the Physical Sciences

Type of award: Internship.
Intended use: For undergraduate study at 4-year institution.
Eligibility: Applicant must be U.S. citizen.
Basis for selection: Major/career interest in physical sciences; astronomy or geophysics.
Application requirements: Recommendations, essay, transcript. Two letters of recommendation; 600 word personal statement.
Additional information: Nearby university dormitory housing provided, as well as travel to and from New York City, as per need. Visit Website for updated list of projects offered and application. Contact Dr. James Webster (jdw@amnh.org) for more information on the Earth and Planetary Science program or Dr. Charles Liu (cliu@amnh.org) for the Astrophysics program.
- **Amount of award:** $4,000
- **Application deadline:** February 15

Contact:
The Office of Grants and Fellowships REU Program in Physical Science
American Museum of Natural History
Central Park West and 79th Street
New York, NY 10024
Phone: 212-769-5638
Web: research.amnh.org/earthplan

American Society of International Law

American Society of International Law Internships

Type of award: Internship.
Intended use: For undergraduate or graduate study at accredited postsecondary institution.
Basis for selection: Major/career interest in law; international relations; public administration/service; journalism or communications.
Application requirements: Cover letter, resume, writing samples, and a list of three references with contact information.
Additional information: Positions require a minimum commitment of 15 hours per week during fall and winter semesters, and 20 hours per week during summer semester. All internships unpaid; students may arrange academic credit. Some positions for graduate students only. Deadlines: December 1 for spring semester, April 1 for summer semester, August 1 for fall semester. See Website for more information.
- **Application deadline:** April 1, August 1

Contact:
American Society of International Law
Internship Coordinator
2223 Massachusetts Avenue, NW
Washington, DC 20008
Fax: 202-797-7133
Web: www.asil.org/careers/internships.html

Americans for the Arts

Arts Action Fund Internship

Type of award: Internship.
Intended use: For undergraduate or graduate study.
Basis for selection: Major/career interest in arts management; communications; marketing or political science/government.
Application requirements: Cover letter with brief personal statement outlining career goals and telling how internship will help achieve goals, resume, and three academic or professional references.
Additional information: Intern may also be recent college graduate. Positions available part-time for winter/spring and fall and full-time for summer. Application deadlines are 4/1 for summer, 7/31 for fall, and 12/1 for winter/spring. Internship not always available for all seasons. All interns receive stipend. Must have experience/interest in politics, advocacy, campaigning, nonprofit administration and/or cultural policy. Must write and communicate well, be organized, be able to prioritize and multitask, be able to manage Websites, know Outlook and MS Office, be able to work independently or as part of a team, and be committed to advancing arts in the U.S. Check Website for more details. E-mail submission is preferred.
Number of awards: 1
Application deadline: April 1, July 31
Contact:
Michael Tyburczy Human Resources
Americans for the Arts
1000 Vermont Avenue NW, 6th Floor
Washington, DC 20005
Phone: 202-371-2830
Fax: 202-371-0424
Web: www.AmericansForTheArts.org

Executive Office Intern

Type of award: Internship.
Intended use: For undergraduate or graduate study.
Basis for selection: Major/career interest in communications; public relations; art/art history; business; arts management; human resources or nonprofit administration.
Application requirements: Cover letter with brief personal statement outlining career goals and telling how internship will help achieve goals, resume, and three academic or professional references.
Additional information: Also for those majoring/interested in organizational development and program/project management. Internship positions are available on a part-time basis for the winter/spring and fall terms and on a full-time basis for summer. Application deadlines are 4/1 for summer, 7/31 for fall, and 12/1 for winter/spring. Internship not always available for all seasons. All interns receive stipend. Must know Windows and MS Office, be organized, and preferably have experience in comparative research. Check Website for details. E-mail submission is preferred.
Number of awards: 1
Application deadline: April 1, July 31
Contact:
Michael Tyburczy Human Resources
Americans for the Arts
1000 Vermont Avenue, NW 6th Floor
Washington, DC 20005
Phone: 202-371-2830
Fax: 202-371-0424
Web: www.americansforthearts.org

Field Services Internship

Type of award: Internship.
Intended use: For undergraduate or graduate study.
Basis for selection: Major/career interest in arts management or marketing.
Application requirements: Cover letter with brief personal statement outlining career goals and telling how internship will help achieve goals; resume; and three academic or professional references.
Additional information: Recent college graduates may apply. Major/career interest may include project/program management, arts education, and public art. Positions available part-time for winter/spring and fall and full-time for summer. All receive stipend. Application deadline is 4/1 for summer, 7/31 for fall, and 12/1 for winter/spring. Internship not always available for all seasons. Check Website for details. Must know MS Office and have good communication. Experience with arts-based community development preferred. E-mail submission preferred.
Number of awards: 1
Application deadline: April 1, July 31
Contact:
Michael Tyburczy Human Resources
Americans for the Arts
1000 Vermont Avenue NW, 6th Floor
Washington, DC 20005
Phone: 202-371-2830
Fax: 202-371-0424
Web: www.AmericansForTheArts.org

Government and Public Affairs Internship

Type of award: Internship.
Intended use: For undergraduate or graduate study.
Basis for selection: Major/career interest in arts management; arts, general; education; governmental public relations or public administration/service.
Application requirements: Cover letter with brief personal statement outlining career goals and telling how internship will help achieve goals; resume; and three academic or professional references.
Additional information: Recent college graduates may apply. Major/career interest may include advocacy. Positions available part-time for winter/spring and fall and full-time for summer. Application deadlines are 4/1 for summer, 7/31 for fall, and 12/1 for winter/spring. Internship not always available for all seasons. Check Website for details. All interns receive stipend. Must know MS Office and HTML editing and have good communication skills. E-mail submission preferred.
Number of awards: 1
Application deadline: April 1, July 31

Contact:
Michael Tyburczy Human Resources
Americans for the Arts
1000 Vermont Avenue NW, 6th Floor
Washington, DC 20005
Phone: 202-371-2830
Fax: 202-371-0424
Web: www.AmericansForTheArts.org

Leadership Alliances and Development Internship

Type of award: Internship.
Intended use: For undergraduate or graduate study.
Application requirements: Cover letter with brief personal statement outlining career goals and telling how internship will help achieve goals; resume; and three academic or professional references.
Additional information: Recent college graduates may apply. Major/career interest may include fundraising and development. Positions available part-time for winter/spring and fall and full-time for summer. Application deadlines are 4/1 for summer, 7/31 for fall, and 12/1 for winter/spring. Internship not always available for all seasons. Check Website for details. All interns receive stipend. Must know Word, Excel, especially mail merge and data sorting. Good communication skills and gregarious personality preferred. E-mail submission preferred.
   Number of awards: 1
   Application deadline: April 1, July 31
Contact:
Michael Tyburczy Human Resources
Americans for the Arts
1000 Vermont Avenue NW, 6th Floor
Washington, DC 20005
Phone: 202-371-2830
Fax: 202-371-0424
Web: www.AmericansForTheArts.org

Policy and Research Internship

Type of award: Internship.
Intended use: For undergraduate or graduate study.
Basis for selection: Major/career interest in arts management or arts, general.
Application requirements: Cover letter with brief personal statement outlining career goals and telling how internship will help achieve goals; resume; and three academic or professional references.
Additional information: Recent college graduates may apply. Positions available part-time for winter/spring and fall and full-time for summer. Application deadlines are 4/1 for summer, 7/31 for fall, and 12/1 for winter/spring. Internship not always available for all seasons. Check Website for details. All interns receive stipend. Must know MS office, be independent, detailed, have qualitative research skills, and commitment to nonprofit arts. E-mail submission preferred.
   Number of awards: 1
   Application deadline: April 1, July 31
Contact:
Michael Tyburczy Human Resources
Americans for the Arts
1000 Vermont Avenue NW, 6th Floor
Washington, DC 20005
Phone: 202-371-2830
Fax: 202-371-0424
Web: www.AmericansForTheArts.org

Private-Sector Affairs Internship

Type of award: Internship.
Intended use: For undergraduate or graduate study.
Basis for selection: Major/career interest in business or arts, general.
Application requirements: Cover letter with brief personal statement outlining career goals and telling how internship will help achieve goals; resume; and three academic or professional references.
Additional information: Recent college graduates may apply. Major/career interest may include program/project management and research and development. Positions available part-time for winter/spring and fall and full-time for summer. Application deadlines are 4/1 for summer, 7/31 for fall, and 12/1 for winter/spring. Internship not always available for all seasons. Check Website for details. All interns receive stipend. Must have excellent writing and research skills, know Excel, and have interest in the business value of the arts. E-mail submission preferred.
   Number of awards: 1
   Application deadline: April 1, July 31
Contact:
Michael Tyburczy Human Resources
Americans for the Arts
1000 Vermont Avenue NW, 6th Floor
Washington, DC 20005
Phone: 202-371-2830
Fax: 202-371-0424
Web: www.AmericansForTheArts.org

Sales and Marketing Internship

Type of award: Internship.
Intended use: For undergraduate or graduate study.
Basis for selection: Major/career interest in public relations; marketing or communications.
Application requirements: Cover letter with brief personal statement outlining career goals and telling how internship will help achieve goals; resume; and three academic or professional references.
Additional information: Recent college graduates may apply. Positions available part-time for winter/spring and fall and full-time for summer. Application deadlines are 4/1 for summer, 7/31 for fall, and 12/1 for winter/spring. Internship not always available for all seasons. Check Website for details. All interns receive stipend. Must know MS Office, have good communication skills. Preferable if applicant has experience with database software, HTML, and proofreading/editing. E-mail submission preferred.
   Number of awards: 1
   Application deadline: April 1, July 31
Contact:
Americans for the Arts
1000 Vermont Avenue
6th Floor
Washington, DC 20005
Phone: 202-371-2830
Fax: 202-371-0424
Web: www.AmericansForTheArts.org

Web and Technology Internship

Type of award: Internship.
Intended use: For undergraduate or graduate study.
Basis for selection: Major/career interest in information systems or arts management.

Application requirements: Cover letter with brief personal statement outlining career goals and telling how internship will help achieve goals; resume; and three academic or professional references.
Additional information: Recent college graduates may apply. Positions available part-time for winter/spring and fall and full-time for summer. Application deadlines are 4/1 for summer, 7/31 for fall, and 12/1 for winter/spring. Internship not always available for all seasons. Check Website for details. All interns receive stipend. Must know Windows, Macintosh, MS Office. Must be able to teach about software use. E-mail submission preferred.
   Number of awards: 1
   Application deadline: April 1, July 31
Contact:
Michael Tyburczy Human Resources
Americans for the Arts
1000 Vermont Avenue NW, 6th Floor
Washington, DC 20005
Phone: 202-371-2830
Fax: 202-371-0424
Web: www.AmericansForTheArts.org

Applied Arts

Applied Arts Internships

Type of award: Internship.
Intended use: For undergraduate study.
Basis for selection: Major/career interest in art/art history; public administration/service; marketing or education.
Application requirements: Resume, cover letter.
Additional information: Internships are for college credit and are open to all high school graduates and college students and graduates. Internships allow students to see working artists enriching and supporting the artist community. Interns are expected to understand the workings of an art institution by assisting in office management, classes, school events and general studio maintenance. Task assignments are given by the staff according to the student's interest, desire to learn, and ability level. The internship has a rolling application deadline and open duration. E-mail applications preferred.
   Number of awards: 10
   Number of applicants: 100
Contact:
Applied Arts Attn: Internship Coordinator
P.O. Box 1336
Amagansett, NY 11930
Phone: 631-267-2787
Fax: 631-267-3428
Web: www.appliedartsschool.com/internships.html

Elizabeth Dow Ltd. Internships

Type of award: Internship.
Intended use: For undergraduate or graduate study.
Basis for selection: Major/career interest in art/art history; interior design or marketing.
Application requirements: Recommendations. Resume, cover letter.
Additional information: This internship offers fine arts and design students the chance to hone their skills and apply their craft in a working environment. It also offers positions in marketing and managerial fields. Internship is unpaid, but college credit is available. Program has rolling admission; duration of internship is flexible.
   Number of awards: 30
   Number of applicants: 100
Contact:
Applied Arts Attn: Internship Coordinator
P.O. Box 2310
Amagansett, NY 11930
Phone: 631-267-3401
Fax: 631-267-3408
Web: www.appliedartsschool.com/internships.html

Applied Materials

Applied Materials Internships and Co-ops

Type of award: Internship.
Intended use: For undergraduate or graduate study.
Basis for selection: Major/career interest in engineering or business. Applicant must demonstrate high academic achievement.
Application requirements: Resume.
Additional information: Applicant should have interest in the semi-conductor industry and should be pursuing a degree. Paid internships and co-op positions based in Texas and California. Summer and year-round positions. Resumes can be sent via mail to the attention of College Programs. Visit Website for additional addresses, to submit resume, and to find out when internship interviews will be held at college campuses. Minimum 3.0 GPA.
   Number of awards: 400
Contact:
Applied Materials -- Attn: College Programs
3195 Kifer Road
M/S 2963
Santa Clara, CA 95051
Web: www.appliedmaterials.com/careers/intern_coop_prog.html

Arts and Business Council of New York

Arts Management Internship Program

Type of award: Internship.
Intended use: For junior or senior study.
Basis for selection: Major/career interest in arts management.
Application requirements: Interview, recommendations, essay, transcript. Resume.
Additional information: Interns spend 10 weeks (June to August) working full time at a New York City arts organization. Preference given to African-American, Asian-American, Latino/a, and Native American students. Must have 2.5 GPA and should have taken arts, business, or marketing courses or been involved in similar extracurricular activities. Students who will graduate right before start of internship are eligible but must explain how internship relates to career goals. Application available online.

Amount of award:	$2,500
Number of awards:	11
Number of applicants:	104
Application deadline:	February 15
Notification begins:	May 1

Contact:
Arts and Business Council of New York Janet Wong
520 8th Avenue, 3rd Floor
Suite 319
New York, NY 10018-8906
Phone: 212-279-5910 ext. 1126
Fax: 212-279-5915
Web: www.artsandbusiness-ny.org

Asian American Journalists Association

Siani Lee Broadcast Internship

Type of award: Internship.
Intended use: For undergraduate study at postsecondary institution.
Eligibility: Applicant must be at least 18.
Basis for selection: Major/career interest in journalism.
Application requirements: Essay, transcript. Work samples. Resume. Advisor's verification form and internship agreement downloaded from kyw.com/jobs. Must submit three copies of all application materials.
Additional information: Summer internship at CBS affiliate KYW-TV in Philadelphia. Must be enrolled in postsecondary program that offers academic credit for internships. Must be 18 by application deadline. Must be seriously considering career in broadcast journalism. Must be AAJA student member. Minimum 2.7 GPA overall. Minimum 3.0 GPA in major courses. Application may be downloaded from Website.

Amount of award:	$2,500
Number of awards:	1
Number of applicants:	20
Application deadline:	April 25

Contact:
Siani Lee Broadcast Internship
Asian American Journalists Association
1182 Market Street, Suite 320
San Francisco, CA 94102
Phone: 415-346-2051 ext. 102
Fax: 415-346-6343
Web: www.aaja.org

Stanford Chen Internship Grant

Type of award: Internship.
Intended use: For junior or senior study at 4-year institution.
Basis for selection: Major/career interest in journalism. Applicant must demonstrate financial need.
Application requirements: Recommendations, essay. Resume, statement of financial need, and internship verification. Three copies of all application materials.
Additional information: Applicant must be intern or have been accepted into a journalism internship program with small- to medium-size media company. Daily circulation for print companies must be under 100,000. For broadcast, markets must be 50 to 100. One of three grants will be awarded to resident of the Pacific Northwest. Application may be downloaded from Website. AAJA membership is recommended for all finalists and required for selected internship recipients.

Amount of award:	$1,500
Number of awards:	3
Number of applicants:	9
Application deadline:	April 25
Total amount awarded:	$4,500

Contact:
Asian American Journalists Association
Stanford Chen Internship Grant
1182 Market Street, Suite 320
San Francisco, CA 94102
Phone: 415-346-2051 ext. 102
Fax: 415-346-6343
Web: www.aaja.org

Baxter International Inc.

Baxter International Inc. Internships

Type of award: Internship.
Intended use: For undergraduate study at accredited 4-year institution.
Eligibility: Applicant must be U.S. citizen or permanent resident.
Basis for selection: Major/career interest in finance/banking; engineering or marketing. Applicant must demonstrate high academic achievement.
Additional information: Paid intern positions offered on as-needed basis. Visit Website for additional information and to apply. If unable to find intern position online, can fill in online profile for future. May apply for less than one year of post-graduation full-time work experience. Must have academic or work experience relevant to position.

Contact:
Web: www.baxter.com/about_baxter/careers/development_programs/index.html

Bernstein-Rein Advertising

Advertising Internship (Summer Only)

Type of award: Internship.
Intended use: For junior or senior study.
Basis for selection: Major/career interest in advertising; journalism; marketing or communications.
Application requirements: Interview, recommendations, essay, proof of eligibility. Resume, cover letter, three reference names. Essay is one-page writing sample.
Additional information: Applicant must be second-semester junior or first-semester senior (will graduate in one to two semesters after summer). Pay is $10/hour.

Number of awards:	7
Number of applicants:	150
Application deadline:	February 1
Total amount awarded:	$27,000

Bernstein-Rein Advertising: Advertising Internship (Summer Only)

Contact:
Bernstein-Rein Advertising
Human Resources
4600 Madison, Suite 1500
Kansas City, MO 64112
Phone: 816-960-5299
Fax: 816-399-6299
Web: www.bradv.com

Black & Veatch Corporation

Black & Veatch Internships, Co-op, and Summer Employment

Type of award: Internship.
Intended use: For full-time sophomore, junior or senior study in United States.
Eligibility: Applicant must be U.S. citizen or permanent resident.
Basis for selection: Major/career interest in engineering; construction or architecture. Applicant must demonstrate high academic achievement.
Application requirements: Transcript. Resume submitted online.
Additional information: Internship compensation varies on discipline and major. Seniors will be asked to give presentation, five minutes in length, at final Lunch-n-Learn sessions in August. Minimum 2.75 GPA. Positions offered across the U.S. Black & Veatch is an Equal Opportunity Employer M/F/D/V.
Contact:
Black & Veatch Job Code CB00 Job Code: CB00
Web: www.bv.com/careers

BMI Foundation, Inc.

Pete Carpenter Fellowship

Type of award: Internship.
Intended use: For undergraduate study.
Eligibility: Applicant must be no older than 35.
Basis for selection: Competition/talent/interest in music performance/composition, based on original one- to three-minute composition or selection from score appropriate for theatrical or TV film or series theme music. Major/career interest in music or radio/television/film.
Application requirements: One- to three-minute composition in CD format.
Additional information: Application can be found on the Website. It must be complete and notarized. Application deadline last week of January. See Website for exact date. Applicant must be under age of 35 at deadline. Winner of competition will work for four to five weeks in Los Angeles on day-to-day basis with distinguished TV/film composer Mike Post. Includes $3,000 for travel and living expenses.
    Amount of award: $3,000
    Number of awards: 1

Contact:
BMI Foundation, Inc. Linda Livingston
8730 Sunset Boulevard
3rd Floor West
Los Angeles, CA 90069
Web: www.bmi.com/bmifoundation

Board of Governors of the Federal Reserve System

Economic Research Division Project Internships

Type of award: Internship, renewable.
Intended use: For undergraduate or graduate study.
Basis for selection: Major/career interest in economics; statistics; computer/information sciences; mathematics or finance/banking. Applicant must demonstrate high academic achievement.
Application requirements: Interview, recommendations, transcript. Resume and cover letter sent via e-mail. Unpaid internship applicants must submit letter validating receipt of college credit.
Additional information: Project internships last from June to September. Application deadline is 4/1. Unpaid internships available for 10 to 12 weeks year-round. Application deadlines for unpaid internships are 4/1 and 11/15.
    Application deadline: April 1, November 15
Contact:
Board of Governors of the Federal Reserve System
Lori Carrington, Mail Stop 65
20th St. and Constitution Avenue, NW
Washington, DC 20551
Phone: 202-452-3374
Fax: 202-736-1919
Web: www.federalreserve.gov/careers/intern_research.htm

Boeing Company

Boeing Internship Program

Type of award: Internship.
Intended use: For undergraduate or graduate study in United States. Designated institutions: Boeing sites in Seattle, WA; Arizona; Florida; Southern California; St. Louis, MO; Texas; Philadelphia, PA; Huntsville, AL; Washington, D.C.; Chicago, IL; and Wichita, KS.
Eligibility: Applicant must be U.S. citizen or permanent resident.
Basis for selection: Major/career interest in aerospace; computer/information sciences; finance/banking; human resources; manufacturing; marketing; public relations; engineering; mathematics or business.
Application requirements: Recommendations, transcript, proof of eligibility. Resume.
Additional information: See Website for detailed information on available positions and to submit resume. Applicant must apply online. Deadlines, eligibility requirements, major/interest fields, and compensation vary from location to location; contact sponsor for more information.

Contact:
Web: www.boeing.com/collegecareers

Boston Globe

Boston Globe Summer Internship

Type of award: Internship.
Intended use: For junior, senior or graduate study at 4-year or graduate institution.
Basis for selection: Major/career interest in journalism.
Application requirements: Interview, recommendations. Writing samples and clips.
Additional information: Award is for 12 weeks full-time summer employment at approximately $600/week. Application available online in September.
  Number of awards: 10
  Number of applicants: 500
  Application deadline: November 1
  Notification begins: January 1
Contact:
The Boston Globe
P.O. Box 55819
Boston, MA 02205-5819
Phone: 617-929-3120
Web: www.bostonglobe.com/aboutus/careerops/internscoops

Brown and Caldwell

The Minority Scholarship

Type of award: Scholarship.
Intended use: For full-time junior or senior study at accredited 4-year institution in United States.
Eligibility: Applicant must be Alaskan native, Asian American, African American, Mexican American, Hispanic American, Puerto Rican, American Indian or Native Hawaiian/Pacific Islander. Applicant must be U.S. citizen or permanent resident.
Basis for selection: Major/career interest in engineering, civil; engineering, chemical; engineering, environmental or environmental science.
Application requirements: Transcript. Two written recommendations, at least one from university official. Essay (250 words or less) on "My future career goals in environmental science."
Additional information: Applicant must participate in summer internship at Brown and Caldwell office; must have cumulative GPA of at least 3.0 (on 4.0 point scale); and must be member of minority group as defined by the EEOC.
  Amount of award: $1,000
  Number of awards: 3
  Application deadline: March 1
  Total amount awarded: $3,000
Contact:
Brown and Caldwell
201 N. Civic Drive
Suite 115
Walnut Creek, CA 94598
Phone: 800-727-2224
Web: http://brownandcaldwell.com/MinorApp.pdf

Chevron Corporation

Chevron Internship Program

Type of award: Internship.
Intended use: For full-time junior, senior or master's study.
Eligibility: Applicant must be U.S. citizen, permanent resident or international student.
Basis for selection: Major/career interest in science, general; engineering; finance/banking; information systems; computer/information sciences; human resources; business; accounting or marketing.
Application requirements: Transcript. Resume and cover letter.
Additional information: Major/career interest may also include earth science. Masters students should be in first or second year of MBA program. Paid full-time internships, terms vary. International students must be qualified to work in U.S. Openings available in many fields. Visit Website for more details and information about on-campus recruiting dates and special events. Apply through a college recruiting event or national convention recruiting event or for those attending nonrecruited schools, apply for internships posted online.
Contact:
See Website for college recruiting events and convention dates.
Web: careers.chevron.com/students/

Citizens for Global Solutions

Citizens for Global Solutions Internship

Type of award: Internship, renewable.
Intended use: For undergraduate study.
Basis for selection: Major/career interest in international relations or international studies.
Application requirements: Resume and cover letter. Three to five page writing sample.
Additional information: Internship includes a $10 per day stipend per intern. Visit Website for more information.
Contact:
Citizens for Global Solutions
418 7th Street, SE
Washington, DC 20003-2796
Phone: 202-546-3950
Web: www.globalsolutions.org/about/work_for_us

Congressional Hispanic Caucus Institute

CHCI Congressional Internship Program

Type of award: Internship.
Intended use: For full-time sophomore, junior or senior study at accredited 2-year or 4-year institution.

Eligibility: Applicant must be Mexican American, Hispanic American or Puerto Rican. Applicant must be U.S. citizen or permanent resident.
Basis for selection: Applicant must demonstrate high academic achievement, depth of character, leadership, seriousness of purpose and service orientation.
Application requirements: Recommendations, essay, transcript. Resume.
Additional information: Applicant must have completed one year of college by start of program. Two month internship in Washington, D.C. congressional offices. Transportation, summer housing, and $2,000 stipend provided. Must have excellent writing and communications skills and an active interest in community affairs. Interns assigned to congressional offices regardless of political affiliation. Work experience is complemented by leadership development sessions. Minimum 3.0 GPA. Application available on Website.
   Amount of award: $2,000
   Number of awards: 34
   Application deadline: January 31
Contact:
CHCI Internship Program
911 Second Street, NE
Washington, DC 20002
Phone: 202-543-1771
Fax: 202-546-2143
Web: www.chciyouth.org

Congressional Institute, Inc.

Congressional Institute Internships

Type of award: Internship.
Intended use: For undergraduate study at accredited 2-year or 4-year institution in United States.
Eligibility: Applicant must be U.S. citizen.
Basis for selection: Major/career interest in political science/government; public administration/service; law or communications. Applicant must demonstrate high academic achievement.
Application requirements: Recommendations. Resume and writing samples.
Additional information: Paid internships available throughout the year on flexible terms. Must be undergraduate with interest in public policy or legislative policy issues. For application and additional information, visit Website.
Contact:
Congressional Institute, Inc.
1001 N. Fairfax St.
#410
Alexandria, VA 22314
Phone: 703-837-8812
Fax: 703-837-8817
Web: www.conginst.org

Creede Repertory Theatre

CRT Internship Program

Type of award: Internship.
Intended use: For undergraduate study.
Eligibility: Applicant must be at least 18.
Basis for selection: Major/career interest in business; design; humanities/liberal arts; performing arts; theater arts; theater/production/technical; education or marketing.
Application requirements: Recommendations. Statement of intent. Resume.
Additional information: Potential internship and apprenticeship positions available depending on seasons' needs/limitations: wardrobe, prop assistant, stage management, actors, box office/front of house, or business/marketing. Interns receive $150 weekly and free housing. See Website for more information or e-mail with questions.
   Application deadline: March 1
Contact:
CRT Internship Program Attn: Renee Stynchula
Creede Repertory Theatre
P.O. Box 269
Creede, CO 81130
Phone: 719-658-2540 ext. 21
Web: www.creederep.org

Cushman School

Cushman School Internship

Type of award: Internship, renewable.
Intended use: For undergraduate or graduate study. Designated institutions: Cushman School.
Eligibility: Applicant must be U.S. citizen, permanent resident or international student.
Basis for selection: Major/career interest in education. Applicant must demonstrate depth of character.
Application requirements: Resume, cover letter.
Additional information: 17-week internships on Cushman School campus for fall and spring semesters. Interns assist staff in grading papers, supervising students, and performing administrative work. Internships are full-time, 8 a.m. to 3 p.m., Monday to Friday. Stipend of $2,000 for U.S. students and $3,000 for international students awarded each semester. Students may also participate in Education Camp for six weeks during summer. International students must have J1 visa. For details, contact Cheryl Rogers at 305-757-1966 after 7 p.m. EST.
   Amount of award: $2,000-$3,000
Contact:
Cushman School
592 Northeast 60th St.
Miami, FL 33137
Phone: 305-754-3729 or 305-757-1966
Fax: 305-757-1632
Web: www.cushmanschool.org

Deloitte and Touche

Deloitte and Touche Internship Program

Type of award: Internship.
Intended use: For full-time sophomore, junior or senior study at accredited 4-year institution.
Eligibility: Applicant must be U.S. citizen, permanent resident or international student.

Basis for selection: Major/career interest in accounting; business/management/administration; engineering or finance/banking. Applicant must demonstrate high academic achievement, depth of character and seriousness of purpose.
Application requirements: Interview. Resume, cover letter.
Additional information: Internships in more than 40 offices nationwide. Interns also attend annual conference and receive laptop computer for use during internship. Interns are required to complete two-day orientation. Visit Website to submit resume online. Check with school career center to find out when Deloitte & Touche will be visiting campus. International students must be eligible to work in the U.S.
Contact:
Deloitte and Touche
Web: careers.deloitte.com

Denver Rescue Mission

Denver Rescue Mission Center for Mission Studies Interns

Type of award: Internship.
Intended use: For undergraduate or graduate study at postsecondary institution in United States.
Basis for selection: Major/career interest in social work; religion/theology; ministry; nonprofit administration; health services administration; public relations; marketing; animal sciences or information systems. Applicant must demonstrate service orientation.
Additional information: Denver Rescue Mission is a nondenominational charity offering internships in the following areas: Servant Corps, animal science, child development, family studies, human services, management information systems, medical office administration, public relations/marketing, and social work. Internships vary in length, and some may have gender, age, level-of-study, or other specific restrictions or requirements. Actual number of internships granted varies. See Website for details, and check with sponsor for pay, college credit opportunity, current openings, and job qualifications. Apply online.

Number of awards:	68
Number of applicants:	130

Contact:
Denver Rescue Mission
P.O. Box 5206
Denver, CO 80217
Phone: 303-953-3956
Web: www.denverrescuemission.org/internships

Dow Jones Newspaper Fund

Business Reporting Intern Program

Type of award: Internship.
Intended use: For full-time sophomore, junior or senior study at 2-year or 4-year institution.
Eligibility: Applicant must be U.S. citizen, permanent resident or international student.
Basis for selection: Major/career interest in journalism or business. Applicant must demonstrate high academic achievement and seriousness of purpose.
Application requirements: Essay, transcript, proof of eligibility. Resume, three to five recently published clips, list of courses with grades, and 500-word essay. Must also take a reporting test.
Additional information: May have any major, but must plan to pursue journalism career. Special interest in business a plus. Applications available August to October 30. Finalists notified mid-January. All applicants notified by January 31. Reporting test administered by designated professor on applicant's campus. Telephone interview required for finalists. Paid summer internships as business reporters at daily newspapers last at least 10 to 12 weeks. Interns returning to school receive scholarship at end of summer to apply toward following year. All interns attend pre-internship training that lasts one week. International students must have work visa.

Amount of award:	$1,000
Number of awards:	12
Application deadline:	November 1
Notification begins:	December 15
Total amount awarded:	$12,000

Contact:
Dow Jones Newspaper Fund
Business Reporting Intern Program
P.O. Box 300
Princeton, NJ 08543-0300
Phone: 609-452-2820
Web: www.newspaperfund.org

General News Copy Editing Internship

Type of award: Internship.
Intended use: For full-time junior, senior or graduate study at 4-year or graduate institution in United States.
Eligibility: Applicant must be U.S. citizen, permanent resident or international student.
Basis for selection: Major/career interest in journalism. Applicant must demonstrate high academic achievement and seriousness of purpose.
Application requirements: Essay, transcript. Resume, list of courses with grades, 500-word essay. Editing test.
Additional information: May have any major but must plan to pursue journalism career. Applications available August to October 30. Finalists notified mid-December. All applicants notified by December 31. Applicants may apply for sports, online, and/or general copy editing programs using common application. Editing test administered by designated professor on applicant's campus. Telephone interview required for finalists. Paid summer internships, as editors at daily newspapers, online newspapers, or real-time financial news services, last ten to 12 weeks. Interns returning to school receive scholarship at end of summer to apply toward following year. All interns attend pre-internship training that lasts one to two weeks. International students must have work visa.

Amount of award:	$1,000
Number of awards:	100
Number of applicants:	600
Application deadline:	November 1
Notification begins:	December 15
Total amount awarded:	$70,000

Dow Jones Newspaper Fund: General News Copy Editing Internship

Contact:
Dow Jones Newspaper Fund
General News Copy Editing Intern Program
P.O. Box 300
Princeton, NJ 08543-0300
Phone: 609-452-2820
Web: www.newspaperfund.org

Sports Copy Editing Program

Type of award: Internship.
Intended use: For full-time undergraduate or graduate study.
Eligibility: Applicant must be U.S. citizen, permanent resident or international student.
Basis for selection: Major/career interest in journalism.
Application requirements: Essay, transcript. List of courses with grades, 500-word essay. Editing exam.
Additional information: Applicants may have any major but must plan to pursue career in journalism. Interns will work on sports copy desks at daily newspapers and attend training at the University of Nebraska at Lincoln, taught by Dr. Charlyne Berens. The seminars last two weeks. Applicants may apply for sports, online, and/or news copy editing programs using common application form. International students must have work visa.

Amount of award:	$1,000
Number of awards:	12
Application deadline:	November 1
Notification begins:	December 15
Total amount awarded:	$12,000

Contact:
Dow Jones Newspaper Fund
P.O. Box 300
Princeton, NJ 08543-0300
Phone: 609-452-2820
Web: www.newspaperfund.org

Dow Jones Newspaper Fund and Yahoo! News

Online Intern Program

Type of award: Internship.
Intended use: For full-time junior, senior or graduate study at 4-year or graduate institution in United States.
Eligibility: Applicant must be U.S. citizen, permanent resident or international student.
Basis for selection: Major/career interest in journalism. Applicant must demonstrate high academic achievement and seriousness of purpose.
Application requirements: Essay, transcript. Resume, list of courses with grades.
Additional information: May have any major but must intend to pursue journalism career. Applications available August through October 30. Must take editing test administered by designated professor on applicant's campus. Finalists undergo telephone interview. Paid 10 to 12-week summer internships as editors at daily newspapers, online newspapers, or real-time financial news services. Must attend one-week pre-internship training. Interns returning to school receive scholarship. International students must have work visa.

Amount of award:	$1,000
Number of awards:	12
Number of applicants:	600
Application deadline:	November 1
Notification begins:	December 15
Total amount awarded:	$12,000

Contact:
Dow Jones Newspaper Fund
Newspaper Editing Intern Program
P.O. Box 300
Princeton, NJ 08543-0300
Phone: 609-452-2820
Web: www.newspaperfund.org

E. I. du Pont de Nemours and Company

DuPont Cooperative Education Program

Type of award: Internship.
Intended use: For full-time sophomore, junior or senior study at accredited 4-year institution in United States.
Eligibility: Applicant must be U.S. citizen or permanent resident.
Basis for selection: Major/career interest in engineering, chemical; engineering, mechanical; engineering, electrical/electronic; science, general; biology; chemistry; information systems; business; accounting or materials science.
Application requirements: Resume and cover letter.
Additional information: Internships available at DuPont company sites throughout U.S. Participants alternate work assignments and academic terms. Applicants can start no earlier than after completion of freshman year and work a minimum of three industrial work periods. Preference given to juniors and seniors. Must be registered with school's co-op office. Internships and co-ops offer competitive compensation. Must have minimum 3.0 GPA. Contact school co-op office or visit Website to apply.

Contact:
Web: www.dupont.com/careers

DuPont Internships

Type of award: Internship.
Intended use: For full-time junior or senior study at accredited 4-year institution in United States.
Eligibility: Applicant must be U.S. citizen or permanent resident.
Basis for selection: Major/career interest in engineering, chemical; engineering, mechanical; engineering, electrical/electronic; science, general; biology; chemistry; information systems; business; accounting or computer/information sciences.
Application requirements: Resume and cover letter.
Additional information: Positions available for summer, fall and winter/spring at DuPont company sites throughout U.S. Preference given to juniors and seniors. May apply for extended internship (summer and fall semester). Must have minimum 3.0 GPA. Number and amount of awards vary. Must apply through Website.

Contact:
Web: www.dupont.com/careers

Eastman Kodak Company

Eastman Kodak Cooperative Internship Programs

Type of award: Internship.
Intended use: For full-time sophomore, junior, senior or graduate study.
Eligibility: Applicant must be U.S. citizen or permanent resident.
Basis for selection: Major/career interest in computer/information sciences; engineering; science, general; physics; mathematics; manufacturing; chemistry or business.
Application requirements: Resume and cover letter.
Additional information: Internship must be minimum of ten consecutive weeks anytime during year (most occur in the summer). Most positions are technical in nature. Internship includes competitive salary based upon discipline and education level, travel expenses, and assistance in locating housing. Applicant must be drug-screened as condition of employment. Minimum 3.0 GPA highly desired. Apply online at www.kodak.com/go/careers.
Contact:
Eastman Kodak Company
Talent Acquisition
343 State Street
Rochester, NY 14650-1139
Fax: 585-724-9416
Web: www.kodak.com/go/careers

Elizabeth Dow Ltd.

Elizabeth Dow Internship Program

Type of award: Internship.
Intended use: For undergraduate or graduate study.
Basis for selection: Major/career interest in interior design; arts, general; design or marketing. Applicant must demonstrate seriousness of purpose.
Application requirements: Interview, recommendations. Resume and cover letter.
Additional information: High school students, undergraduates, and graduate students are eligible. Duration of internship is flexible. Generally, positions are unpaid, though limited paid positions available. Candidates should have ability to work independently and with others, oral communication skills, personal interest in the field, and self-motivation. Application deadline is rolling, but apply as early as possible for summer. Academic credit available. Visit Website for more information.
   Number of awards: 30
   Number of applicants: 100
Contact:
Elizabeth Dow Ltd. Internship Coordinator
P.O. Box 2310
11 Indian Wells Highway
Amagansett, NY 11930
Phone: 631-267-3401
Fax: 631-267-3408
Web: www.elizabethdow.com

EMC

EMC Summer Internship Program and Co-ops

Type of award: Internship.
Intended use: For full-time undergraduate study at accredited 4-year institution.
Basis for selection: Major/career interest in accounting; engineering; finance/banking; human resources; manufacturing; marketing; computer/information sciences or engineering, computer. Applicant must demonstrate high academic achievement.
Additional information: Offering both co-op and summer internship positions, EMC's program is designed to provide a challenging learning experience. Paid three- and six-month co-op positions available throughout year for eligible students. Must be committed to the duration of the assignment. Minimum 3.0 GPA. Summer intern program begins in June and runs through August. Submit resume at www.emc.com/college. Visit Website for more information.
Contact:
EMC University Relations
176 South Street
Hopkinton, MA 01748
Phone: 508-435-1000
Web: www.emc.com

Entergy

Entergy Jumpstart Co-ops and Internships

Type of award: Internship, renewable.
Intended use: For full-time undergraduate or graduate study at accredited 4-year or graduate institution in United States.
Eligibility: Applicant must be U.S. citizen or permanent resident.
Basis for selection: Major/career interest in engineering, civil; business; accounting; computer/information sciences; human resources; engineering, electrical/electronic; engineering, mechanical; engineering, nuclear; information systems or finance/banking. Applicant must demonstrate high academic achievement and depth of character.
Additional information: Paid undergraduate and graduate co-ops and internships available. Minimum 3.0 GPA. Apply online. Visit Website for application deadline, list of targeted campuses in the South, recruiting schedule, and current openings. Must have work experience and give graduation date.
Contact:
Phone: 504-576-4000
Web: www.entergy.com/careers/collegeopps.aspx

Entertainment Weekly

Entertainment Weekly Internship Program

Type of award: Internship.

Intended use: For junior, senior or graduate study at postsecondary institution.
Basis for selection: Major/career interest in journalism or publishing. Applicant must demonstrate seriousness of purpose.
Application requirements: Resume, cover letter and five clips/writing samples.
Additional information: Opportunities to work in editorial department. Internship lasts 12-18 weeks and pays $10/hour. Overtime available. Summer internships open to rising seniors and recent graduates. Summer deadline is February 15. Fall and spring internships for recent college graduates only. Fall deadline is June 15. Spring deadline is October 15.

Number of awards:	2
Number of applicants:	230
Application deadline:	February 15, June 15

Contact:
Entertainment Weekly Internship Coordinator
1675 Broadway
New York, NY 10019
Phone: 212-522-5600
Fax: 212-522-6104
Web: www.ew.com

ESPN Inc.

ESPN Internship

Type of award: Internship.
Intended use: For full-time junior, senior or graduate study.
Eligibility: Applicant must be U.S. citizen.
Basis for selection: Major/career interest in journalism; communications; radio/television/film; graphic arts/design; marketing; accounting; business; computer/information sciences or sports/sports administration. Applicant must demonstrate high academic achievement.
Application requirements: Resume and cover letter; submit at espn.com/joinourteam.
Additional information: Sports knowledge/interest/participation highly desirable. ESPN will assist interns in finding housing. Undergraduate interns receive $9 per hour, graduates $13. Application deadlines: March 1 for summer; June 1 for fall; November 1 for spring. See Website for specific application details.

Number of awards:	220
Number of applicants:	5,000
Application deadline:	March 1

Contact:
ESPN Inc.
Phone: 860-766-2000
Web: www.espn.com/joinourteam

Essence Magazine

Essence Summer Internship

Type of award: Internship, renewable.
Intended use: For senior study at 2-year or 4-year institution in United States.
Eligibility: Applicant must be African American. Applicant must be U.S. citizen.
Basis for selection: Major/career interest in publishing; marketing; advertising; graphic arts/design; public relations; business or fashion/fashion design/modeling. Applicant must demonstrate depth of character.
Application requirements: Resume and writing sample or digital portfolio.
Additional information: Nine-week summer internship open to college seniors. Internships available in several departments: sales and marketing, Essence.com, fashion and beauty, graphic arts/design/photography, public relations, business, or editorial. Interns responsible for travel, housing, food, and personal expenses. Will receive a bi-weekly stipend. Must write well, be organized, have research skills, be interested in African American culture. Must be motivated, detailed, and a good multitasker. Visit Website for application and more information. Submit application and material by mail.

Application deadline:	December 31
Notification begins:	April 1

Contact:
Essence Magazine
Internship Coordinator
135 West 50th Street, 4th Floor
New York, NY 10020
Phone: 212-522-1212
Fax: 212-467-2357
Web: www.essence.com

fahrenHEIGHT360

fahrenHEIGHT 360 Intern Placement

Type of award: Internship.
Intended use: For undergraduate or graduate study at accredited 4-year institution.
Eligibility: Applicant must be U.S. citizen or permanent resident.
Basis for selection: Major/career interest in accounting; business/management/administration; finance/banking; computer/information sciences; communications; marketing; engineering or health-related professions. Applicant must demonstrate high academic achievement.
Additional information: FahrenHEIGHT360 is an intern placement service for placements in St. Paul/Minneapolis, MN. Not a scholarship. Wages are competitive. Visit Website to register.
Contact:
FahrenHEIGHT360
800 Transfer Road
Suite 30
St. Paul, MN 55114
Phone: 651-894-6360
Web: www.fahrenheight360.com

Federal Bureau of Investigation

Honors Internship Program

Type of award: Internship, renewable.
Intended use: For junior, senior or graduate study at accredited 4-year or graduate institution in United States.

Eligibility: Applicant must be U.S. citizen.
Basis for selection: Major/career interest in criminal justice/law enforcement; law; engineering; computer/information sciences; finance/banking; accounting or foreign languages. Applicant must demonstrate high academic achievement, depth of character, leadership and seriousness of purpose.
Application requirements: Interview, recommendations, essay, transcript, proof of eligibility. Background survey. Two current professional photographs and program term acknowledgment.
Additional information: All students must return to their respective schools for at least one semester immediately following internship. Graduate students must be attending school full-time. Positions available in Washington, D.C., Virginia and Maryland. Deadline for application submission is October 10, but application process must start in July for necessary vetting. Individuals selected based on how their specific skills and educational background meet current FBI needs. Must have minimum 3.0 GPA. Must be able to pass extensive background check and drug test. Visit Website for application package. Students must turn application package into field office closest to their university.
   Amount of award: $6,350
   Application deadline: October 10
Contact:
Federal Bureau of Investigation
Contact local field office
Web: www.fbijobs.gov/intern.asp

Federal Reserve Bank of New York

Federal Reserve Undergraduate Summer Analyst Program

Type of award: Internship.
Intended use: For full-time undergraduate study.
Eligibility: Applicant must be U.S. citizen, permanent resident or international student.
Basis for selection: Major/career interest in finance/banking; economics; business; computer/information sciences; accounting or mathematics. Applicant must demonstrate high academic achievement.
Application requirements: Interview, transcript. Cover letter, resume, and writing sample.
Additional information: Paid internships begin in May/June. Applicants should have completed junior year of college before beginning internship. Opportunities available in bank supervision and regulation, domestic and international research, information technology services, markets, and operations. Applicants must be available for in-bank interviews in March/April. Housing not provided. International students must be legally authorized to work in U.S. on a multi-year basis for other than practical training purposes. Further restrictions may apply.
   Application deadline: January 31
Contact:
Federal Reserve Bank of New York
Summer Internship Coordinator
33 Liberty Street, Floor 2M
New York, NY 10045
Phone: 212-720-5000
Web: www.ny.frb.org/careers/summerintern.html

Federated Department Stores, Inc.

Federated Department Stores Internships

Type of award: Internship, renewable.
Intended use: For full-time undergraduate study.
Basis for selection: Applicant must demonstrate high academic achievement.
Application requirements: Resume.
Additional information: Students from all majors are considered, though paid internships generally focus on marketing, business, and retailing/merchandising. May apply online. Visit Website for additional information and campus recruiting schedule.
Contact:
Federated Department Stores, Inc.
7 West Seventh Street
Cincinnatti, OH 45202
Web: www.macysjobs.com/college/internships

Feminist Majority Foundation

Feminism & Leadership Internship

Type of award: Internship.
Intended use: For undergraduate study at accredited 4-year institution.
Basis for selection: Major/career interest in law; public relations; social/behavioral sciences; women's studies or political science/government. Applicant must demonstrate leadership.
Application requirements: Resume, cover letter.
Additional information: Full-time internships for a minimum of two months available year-round in the Washington, DC, area and Los Angeles. Part-time internships also available in spring and fall. Interns have various responsibilities, such as monitoring press conferences and public hearings, researching, writing, analyzing policies, and organizing events and demonstrations. Internships unpaid, but students may be able to earn small stipend in exchange for administrative work. Applicants with experience working on women's issues preferred. People of color, people with disabilities, and math/science majors encouraged to apply. Applications processed on rolling basis. See Website for more information.
Contact:
Feminist Majority Foundation
1600 Wilson Boulevard, Suite 801
Arlington, VA 22209
Phone: 703-522-2214
Fax: 703-522-2219
Web: www.feminist.org/intern

Feminist Web Internship

Type of award: Internship.
Intended use: For undergraduate study.

Basis for selection: Major/career interest in women's studies; computer graphics; public administration/service or computer/information sciences. Applicant must demonstrate leadership.
Application requirements: Resume and cover letter. Samples of writing and Web work.
Additional information: Full-time internships for minimum of two months available year-round in the Washington, DC, area. Part-time internships also available in spring and fall. Interns learn about online activism strategies and contribute to organization's online presence. Internships unpaid, but students may be able to earn small stipend in exchange for administrative work. Applicants with experience in women's issues and Website design or online activism preferred. People of color, people with disabilities, and math/science majors encouraged to apply. Applications processed on rolling basis. Visit Website for more information.
Contact:
Feminist Majority Foundation
Information Technology Director
1600 Wilson Boulevard, Suite 801
Arlington, VA 22209
Phone: 703-522-2214
Fax: 703-522-2219
Web: www.feminist.org/intern

Filoli Center

Filoli Center Garden Internships and Apprenticeships

Type of award: Internship.
Intended use: For undergraduate, graduate or non-degree study. Designated institutions: Filoli Center.
Basis for selection: Major/career interest in horticulture; landscape architecture or botany. Applicant must demonstrate depth of character, leadership and seriousness of purpose.
Application requirements: Interview, recommendations, transcript. Resume and cover letter outlining interests. Three letters of recommendation.
Additional information: Also for students pursuing careers in public garden management and landscape maintenance. Students paid $8 per hour and may earn college credit for ten-week internship program or six-month apprenticeship program. Applicants must have at least 15 units of horticulture classes and 3.0 GPA. Ability to work well with public and work teams essential. Maximum five students per internship. Visit Website for deadlines and application.
   Amount of award: $3,200-$8,320
   Number of awards: 12
Contact:
Filoli Center
Filoli Garden Internships
86 Cañada Road
Woodside, CA 94062
Phone: 650-364-8300 ext. 214
Fax: 650-366-7836
Web: www.filoli.org/garden_intern.htm

Florida Department of Education

Florida Work Experience Program

Type of award: Internship, renewable.
Intended use: For undergraduate study at 2-year or 4-year institution. Designated institutions: Eligible Florida postsecondary institutions.
Eligibility: Applicant must be U.S. citizen or permanent resident residing in Florida.
Basis for selection: Applicant must demonstrate financial need.
Application requirements: Proof of eligibility. FAFSA.
Additional information: Minimum 2.0 GPA. Provides students with opportunity to be employed off campus in jobs related to their academic major or area of career interest. Applications available from participating universities' financial aid offices. Amount of award determined by institution's financial aid office, and may not exceed student's financial need.
Contact:
Florida Department of Education
Office of Student Financial Assistance
1940 North Monroe Street, Suite 70
Tallahassee, FL 32303-4759
Phone: 888-827-2004
Web: www.FloridaStudentFinancialAid.org

Florida Power & Light Company

Florida Power & Light Co-op Program

Type of award: Internship, renewable.
Intended use: For full-time undergraduate or graduate study at accredited 4-year or graduate institution in United States.
Eligibility: Applicant must be U.S. citizen or permanent resident.
Basis for selection: Major/career interest in engineering; engineering, nuclear; engineering, mechanical; engineering, electrical/electronic or engineering, civil. Applicant must demonstrate high academic achievement.
Application requirements: Resume.
Additional information: Industrial engineering majors also eligible. Co-op positions are paid. For more information on co-op recruitment, contact designated institution's Cooperative Education Coordinator or check Website's campus calendar.
Contact:
Florida Power & Light Company
College Coordinator
P. O. Box 14000, HRR/JB
Juno Beach, FL 33408-0420
Web: www.fplcareers.com/recruiting/contents/co-op_program.shtml

Franklin D. Roosevelt Library

Franklin D. Roosevelt Library/ Roosevelt Summer Internship

Type of award: Internship.
Intended use: For undergraduate or graduate study.
Basis for selection: Major/career interest in education; computer/information sciences; museum studies; history or political science/government.
Application requirements: Transcript. Resume.
Additional information: Interns work at FDR library with other interns and staff organizing archival materials, making indices, finding aids and databases, digitizing documents and photographs, and assisting with other projects. Internships also available in the fields of museum, education, and public affairs. Internship can last up to eight weeks and must take place during summer break (mid-May through end of August). FDR Library is in Hyde Park, NY, 80 miles north of NYC. Housing not provided. Work Monday through Friday, 9 am to 5 pm. Stipend of $300/week for summer interns, academic credit for fall and spring. Number of awards depends on funding. Familiarity with FDR presidency helpful. Application may be downloaded from Website.
   Application deadline: April 15
Contact:
Franklin D. Roosevelt Library
Attn: Cliff Laube
4079 Albany Post Road
Hyde Park, NY 12538
Phone: 845-486-7745
Fax: 845-486-1981
Web: www.fdrlibrary.marist.edu/intern.html

Garden Club of America

GCA Internship in Garden History and Design

Type of award: Internship.
Intended use: For undergraduate or graduate study.
Basis for selection: Major/career interest in horticulture; landscape architecture or botany.
Application requirements: Recommendations, essay, transcript. Two letters of recommendation (one from professor in major, one from advisor).
Additional information: May apply to Archives of American Gardens in Washington, DC or at other eligible institutions (contact sponsor to verify). Interns at Archives of American Gardens, Smithsonian Institutes work for 10 to 16 weeks and receive stipends: $360/week for undergraduates, $420 for graduate students.
   Amount of award: $2,000
   Application deadline: January 15
Contact:
GCA Internship Award in Garden History and Design
Garden Club of America
14 East 60th Street
New York, NY 10022
Phone: 212-753-8287
Fax: 212-753-0134
Web: www.gcamerica.org

Genentech, Inc.

Genentech Internship Program

Type of award: Internship, renewable.
Intended use: For full-time junior or senior study at accredited 4-year institution.
Eligibility: Applicant must be U.S. citizen, permanent resident or international student.
Basis for selection: Major/career interest in biology; chemistry; engineering, chemical; computer/information sciences or life sciences. Applicant must demonstrate high academic achievement.
Application requirements: Resume and cover letter.
Additional information: Summer internships last 10-12 weeks and are available in various research and business areas. Internships paid by competitive monthly stipend and membership at health club. Students majoring in biochemical engineering also eligible. Co-op positions also available. International students must have work authorization. Apply online or send resume and cover letter by mail.
   Number of awards: 165
Contact:
Genentech College Programs
1 DNA Way MS 39A
South San Francisco, CA 94080
Phone: 650-225-1000
Web: www.gene.com

General Mills

General Mills Summer Internship

Type of award: Internship, renewable.
Intended use: For sophomore, junior or senior study.
Eligibility: Applicant must be U.S. citizen.
Basis for selection: Major/career interest in marketing; advertising; food science/technology; engineering; economics; finance/banking or business/management/administration.
Application requirements: Interview. Resume.
Additional information: Paid internships available in various departments and locations. Visit Website for more information and to submit resume.
Contact:
Internship Coordinator
P.O. Box 9452
Minneapolis, MN 55440
Phone: 763-764-2505
Web: www.generalmills.com/corporate/careers

General Motors North America

General Motors Corporation Talent Acquisition Internship

Type of award: Internship, renewable.
Intended use: For full-time sophomore, junior, senior or master's study at accredited 4-year or graduate institution.
Basis for selection: Major/career interest in engineering or business. Applicant must demonstrate high academic achievement and leadership.
Application requirements: Interview, transcript. Resume.
Additional information: Co-ops and paid internships available. Salary varies with job, skills and degree/program of study. Temporary, full-time positions during semester break, three months in summer. Visit Website for details or to submit resume. In most cases, applicant must have completed freshman year of study to be eligible.
Contact:
General Motors North America
200 Renaissance Center
MC: 482-BO9-D46
Detroit, MI 48265
Web: www.gm.com/company/careers/student_center.jsp

Georgia-Pacific Corporation

Georgia-Pacific Internships and Co-ops

Type of award: Internship.
Intended use: For undergraduate study in United States.
Eligibility: Applicant must be U.S. citizen or permanent resident.
Basis for selection: Major/career interest in accounting; computer/information sciences; communications; engineering; forestry; human resources or marketing. Applicant must demonstrate high academic achievement.
Application requirements: Transcript, proof of eligibility.
Additional information: Internships and co-ops are paid, and number awarded varies. Requirements vary by department. Submit resume through Website form or by using "job search" feature.
Contact:
Georgia Pacific Corporation
Attn: College Relations
133 Peachtree Street, NE, Floor 14
Atlanta, GA 30303
Phone: 404-652-5463
Fax: 404-584-1481
Web: www.gp.com/careers/collegerel/

Hannaford Bros Co.

Hannaford Internships

Type of award: Internship.
Intended use: For undergraduate or master's study.
Eligibility: Applicant must be U.S. citizen, permanent resident or international student.
Basis for selection: Major/career interest in pharmacy/pharmaceutics/pharmacology.
Application requirements: Cover letter and resume.
Additional information: Ten week summer internship, beginning early June. Interns at Hannaford are exposed to a multicultural organization with support systems and training opportunities. Internships available at Hannaford's corporate office, distribution centers, and retail locations. Inquire at campus placement office to schedule recruiting interview or e-mail for additional information. Minimum 3.0 GPA. Must be legally authorized to work in United States. Amount of payment or course credit awarded varies. International students must have work authorization. Visit Website for more information.
Application deadline: February 15
Contact:
Hannaford Brothers Company Employment Department
P.O. Box 1000
Mail Sort #7800
Portland, ME 04104
Phone: 800-442-6049
Fax: 207-885-2859
Web: www.hannaford.com

Hispanic Association of Colleges and Universities

HACU National Internship Program

Type of award: Internship.
Intended use: For sophomore, junior, senior or graduate study at 2-year, 4-year or graduate institution. Designated institutions: Institutions with significant number of Hispanic students.
Eligibility: Applicant must be U.S. citizen or permanent resident.
Basis for selection: Applicant must demonstrate high academic achievement and service orientation.
Application requirements: Essay, transcript. Resume, certificate of enrollment and class level, 250- to 500-word essay.
Additional information: Paid internships provide opportunities for students from institutions with significant numbers of Hispanic students to explore potential careers with federal agencies and private corporations. Interns work in Washington, DC, area and field sites throughout country. Some internships require U.S. citizenship to participate. Applicants must have 3.0 GPA and have completed freshman year of college before internship begins. Weekly pay varies according to class level: $450 for sophomores and juniors, $480 for seniors and $570 for graduates. Must be active in college and community service. Fall and spring internships last 15 weeks; summer internships last ten weeks. Deadlines: November 1 for spring, February 23 for summer, June 14 for fall. Visit Website for more information.
Application deadline: November 1, February 23

Contact:
Hispanic Association of Colleges and Universities
One Dupont Circle, NW
Suite 430
Washington, DC 20036
Phone: 202-467-0893
Fax: 202-496-9177
Web: www.hnip.net

Historic Bok Sanctuary

Historic Bok Sanctuary Conservation Program Internship

Type of award: Internship.
Intended use: For full-time undergraduate or graduate study at 4-year or graduate institution. Designated institutions: Historic Bok Sanctuary.
Basis for selection: Major/career interest in botany; biology or ecology.
Application requirements: Interview, recommendations, transcript. Resume, three references, and letter outlining interests.
Additional information: Experience in biological surveying, monitoring with GPS unit, plant propagation, or working with Florida ecosystems is highly desirable. Good written and oral communication skills and good data collection abilities necessary. Paid internship entirely grant funded; onsite housing may be available. Interns receive $12.00 per hour, full time, no benefits. Intern must have own vehicle and be willing to make field visits (mileage will be reimbursed). Write or call for application.

Number of awards:	1
Number of applicants:	1
Application deadline:	May 31

Contact:
Historic Bok Sanctuary
Attn: Human resources
1151 Tower Boulevard
Lake Wales, FL 33853-3412
Phone: 863-676-1408
Fax: 863-676-6770
Web: www.boksanctuary.org

Hoffman-La Roche Inc.

Hoffman-La Roche Inc. Student Internship

Type of award: Internship.
Intended use: For full-time freshman, sophomore, junior or graduate study. Designated institutions: Howard, Fuqua, Johnson School, Rutgers, Yale.
Basis for selection: Major/career interest in pharmacy/pharmaceutics/pharmacology; engineering; computer/information sciences; science, general; business; business/management/administration; biology; chemistry or biochemistry.
Application requirements: Interview. Cover letter, resume.
Additional information: Applicant must be authorized to work in the United States. Internship fields, topics, and amount of compensation vary. Send materials to address provided. If deadline is missed, application will be considered after those students who have met deadline.

Application deadline:	February 15
Notification begins:	April 16

Contact:
University Relations Department Hoffman-La Roche, Inc.
340 Kingsland Street
Nutley, NJ 07110-1199
Phone: 973-235-4035 or 973-235-5000
Web: www.rocheusa.com

IBM

IBM Co-op and Intern Program

Type of award: Internship.
Intended use: For full-time undergraduate or graduate study at accredited 4-year or graduate institution in United States.
Basis for selection: Major/career interest in computer/information sciences; engineering, computer; engineering, electrical/electronic; information systems; accounting or finance/banking. Applicant must demonstrate high academic achievement and leadership.
Application requirements: Interview.
Additional information: Applicants chosen on competitive basis, based on relevant work or research experience, communication, and team skills, high evaluation during interview process. Competitive salary based on number of credits completed towards degree. Applicants hired on semester basis. Must submit resume via IBM Website.

Contact:
IBM Co-op and Intern Program
7029 Albert Pick Rd.
Greensboro, NC 27409-9538
Web: www-03.ibm.com/employment/us/

The Indianapolis Star, a Gannett Newspaper

Pulliam Journalism Fellowship

Type of award: Internship.
Intended use: For undergraduate or postgraduate study.
Basis for selection: Competition/talent/interest in writing/journalism. Major/career interest in humanities/liberal arts or journalism. Applicant must demonstrate high academic achievement, depth of character, leadership and seriousness of purpose.
Application requirements: Portfolio, recommendations, essay, transcript, proof of eligibility. Writing samples. Photograph. Three letters of recommendation.
Additional information: Fellowship lasts ten weeks during summer. Ten recipients work for The Indianapolis Star, ten for The Arizona Republic in Phoenix. Applicants must be college students. Early deadline in November; final postmark deadline in March. Go to Website for application and more information.

Amount of award:	$6,500
Number of awards:	25
Number of applicants:	200
Application deadline:	November 1
Notification begins:	January 15

The Indianapolis Star, a Gannett Newspaper: Pulliam Journalism Fellowship

Contact:
Russell B. Pulliam, Director
The Pulliam Fellowship
P.O. Box 145
Indianapolis, IN 46206-0145
Phone: 317-444-6001
Web: www.indystar.com/pjf

INROADS, Inc.

INROADS Internship

Type of award: Internship, renewable.
Intended use: For full-time freshman or sophomore study.
Eligibility: Applicant must be Alaskan native, Asian American, African American, Mexican American, Hispanic American, Puerto Rican or American Indian. Applicant must be high school senior. Applicant must be U.S. citizen or permanent resident.
Basis for selection: Major/career interest in engineering; business; computer/information sciences; communications; retailing/merchandising or health-related professions. Applicant must demonstrate high academic achievement, leadership and service orientation.
Application requirements: Interview, transcript. Resume. National College Component Application.
Additional information: Applicant must have minimum high school 3.0 GPA or college 2.8 GPA; minimum 1000 SAT or 20 ACT. Internship duration and compensation varies, and deadlines vary according to local affiliate office. Visit Website for additional information.
  Number of awards: 6,600
  Number of applicants: 30,000
  Application deadline: March 31
Contact:
INROADS, Inc.
10 S. Broadway
Suite 300
St. Louis, MO 63102
Phone: 314-241-7488
Fax: 314-241-9325
Web: www.inroads.org

International Radio and Television Society Foundation

International Radio and Television Society Foundation

Type of award: Internship.
Intended use: For junior, senior or graduate study.
Basis for selection: Major/career interest in communications.
Additional information: Nine week internship. Applicants must have prior internship experience and demonstrated interest in the field of communications. Fellows are awarded travel and housing expenses and small stipend. Please visit Website for deadlines, information, and application.
  Number of awards: 25

Contact:
International Radio and Television Society Foundation
420 Lexington Avenue, Suite 1601
New York, NY 10170
Phone: 212-867-6650 ext. 303
Fax: 212-867-6653
Web: www.irts.org

J. Paul Getty Trust

Multicultural Undergraduate Summer Internships at the Getty Center

Type of award: Internship.
Intended use: For full-time undergraduate study at 4-year institution.
Eligibility: Applicant must be Asian American, African American, Mexican American, Hispanic American, Puerto Rican, American Indian or Native Hawaiian/Pacific Islander.
Basis for selection: Major/career interest in arts management; communications; humanities/liberal arts; architecture; museum studies/administration or art/art history.
Application requirements: Interview. Two letters of recommendation, supplemental application (plus three copies), all official transcripts (plus three copies), and SASE.
Additional information: Ten-week internship in specific departments of Getty Museum and other programs located at the Getty Center in Los Angeles. Interns receive $3500 stipend. Limited to students attending school in or residing in Los Angeles County. Intended for outstanding students who are members of groups currently underrepresented in museum professions and fields related to visual arts and humanities. Applicants must have completed at least one semester of college by June and not be graduating before December. Housing and transportation not included. Applications accepted in December, and applicants notified of acceptance in early May.
  Amount of award: $3,500
  Number of awards: 20
  Number of applicants: 124
  Application deadline: March 1
Contact:
Multicultural Undergraduate Internships at the Getty Center
The Getty Foundation
1200 Getty Center Dr., Suite 800
Los Angeles, CA 90049-1685
Phone: 310-440-7320
Fax: 310-440-7703
Web: www.getty.edu/grants/education

Jeppesen Dataplan

Jeppesen Meterology Internship

Type of award: Internship.
Intended use: For full-time junior or senior study at accredited 4-year institution.
Basis for selection: Major/career interest in geography; atmospheric sciences/meteorology or aviation.
Application requirements: Resume.

Additional information: All available internships posted online. Must have 2.5 to 3.0 GPA. Part-time internship available all year, up to 20 hours per week. Salary $8 to $10 per hour. Must be enrolled in accredited degree program. Number of awards granted varies. Visit Website for application.
Contact:
Jeppesen Dataplan
225 West Santa Clara Street
Suite 1600
San Jose, CA 95113
Phone: 408-961-2280
Web: www.jeppesen.com

John Deere

John Deere Student Training Programs

Type of award: Internship.
Intended use: For full-time sophomore, junior, senior or graduate study at accredited 2-year, 4-year or graduate institution.
Eligibility: Applicant must be U.S. citizen or permanent resident.
Basis for selection: Major/career interest in accounting; finance/banking; human resources; health services administration; engineering; information systems or marketing. Applicant must demonstrate high academic achievement.
Application requirements: Recommendations.
Additional information: Deere and Company offers paid internships, course credit, and academic scholarships through Student Training Program. Applicants may also be interested/ majoring in supply management and credit. Open to undergraduates; graduate students may also be eligible. Minimum 3.0 GPA. Apply through Career Section on Website. Co-op applicants must be enrolled undergraduates and meet academic requirement. Number and amount of awards vary. For co-ops, students must apply through and be recommended by Cooperative Education Office at college or university.
Contact:
Recruitment Coordinator
Deere and Company
One John Deere Place
Moline, IL 61265
Phone: 309-765-8000
Web: www.deere.com

The John F. Kennedy Center for the Performing Arts

Kennedy Center Arts Management Internship

Type of award: Internship.
Intended use: For junior, senior or post-bachelor's certificate study at accredited 4-year or graduate institution.
Basis for selection: Major/career interest in arts management.
Application requirements: Interview, transcript. Cover letter stating career goals. Two letters of recommendation. Resume and writing sample.
Additional information: Interns receive $225 stipend per week to defray housing and transportation costs. College credit may be available. Interns attend weekly sessions led by executives of Kennedy Center and other major arts institutions in Washington, D.C., Interns may attend performances, workshops, classes and courses presented by center, free of charge (space available), during their internship. Application deadline for fall, June 15; winter/spring, October 25; summer, March 1. Visit Website for application and more information.
   Number of awards: 20
   Number of applicants: 800
   Application deadline: June 15, October 25
Contact:
Vilar Institute for Arts Management/Internships
2700 F Street N.W
Washington, DC 20566
Phone: 202-416-8821
Fax: 202-416-8853
Web: www.kennedy-center.org/vilarinstitute/internships

John F. Kennedy Library Foundation

Kennedy Library Archival Internship

Type of award: Internship.
Intended use: For undergraduate study. Designated institutions: John F. Kennedy Presidential Library.
Eligibility: Applicant must be U.S. citizen or permanent resident.
Basis for selection: Major/career interest in history; political science/government; library science; English; journalism; communications or museum studies. Applicant must demonstrate high academic achievement.
Application requirements: Interview, recommendations, transcript.
Additional information: Minimum 12 hours per week, $12.50 per hour. Provides intern with opportunity to work on projects such as preservation of papers of Kennedy and his administration. Interns given career-relevant archival experience. Limited number of additional internships may open up during fall, winter, and spring. Library considers proposals for unpaid internships, independent study, work-study, and internships undertaken for academic credit. See Website for application and more information.
   Application deadline: February 25
   Notification begins: April 1
Contact:
Archival Internships c/o Intern Coordinator
John F. Kennedy Presidential Library & Museum
Columbia Point
Boston, MA 02125-3313
Phone: 617-514-1624
Fax: 617-514-1625
Web: www.jfklibrary.org

John Wiley and Sons, Inc.

John Wiley and Sons, Inc. Internship Program

Type of award: Internship.
Intended use: For junior or senior study at 4-year institution.
Basis for selection: Major/career interest in marketing; publishing; information systems or public relations.
Application requirements: Resume. Letter addressing why applicant would like to be selected for the program and listing areas of interest.
Additional information: Summer internship programs available for students who have completed junior year; program runs from mid-June through mid-August. Internships available in marketing, editorial, production, information technology, new media, and publicity; based at corporate offices in Hoboken and Somerset in New Jersey, and San Francisco. Interns receive weekly stipend. Those interested in interning in Somerset, NJ, San Francisco, CA, Indianapolis, IN, and Malden, MA should visit www.wiley.com for more information.
   Application deadline: April 1
Contact:
John Wiley and Sons, Inc. Attn: Internship Program
Human Resources Department
111 River Street
Hoboken, NJ 07030
Fax: 201-748-6049
Web: www.wiley.com

Johnson Controls

Johnson Controls Co-op and Internship Programs

Type of award: Internship, renewable.
Intended use: For full-time undergraduate or graduate study at accredited 4-year institution in United States.
Basis for selection: Major/career interest in engineering; law; business/management/administration; manufacturing or automotive technology. Applicant must demonstrate high academic achievement.
Application requirements: Proof of eligibility. Resume, cover letter.
Additional information: Johnson Controls offers several co-op and internship programs in locations throughout the U.S. and abroad. The Engineering Co-op Program develops and trains students in all aspects of the Automotive Systems Group at Johnson Controls. Over a period of two to five years, mechanical and design engineering students alternate between work terms at Johnson Controls and school terms at college or university. Paid summer internships and positions in most other company divisions also available. Visit Website for complete program descriptions and application.
Contact:
Johnson Controls Human Resources
5757 N. Green Bay Ave.
P.O. Box 591
Milwaukee, WI 53201
Phone: 414-524-1200
Web: www.johnsoncontrols.com/hr/coops.htm

J.W. Saxe Memorial Fund

J.W. Saxe Memorial Prize

Type of award: Internship.
Intended use: For undergraduate, graduate or non-degree study.
Basis for selection: Major/career interest in public administration/service. Applicant must demonstrate financial need, depth of character, leadership, seriousness of purpose and service orientation.
Application requirements: Resume, letter of support from faculty member, three recommendations, and an essay on short- and long-term goals.
Additional information: Award enables public-service-minded college or university students to gain practical experience working no-pay or low-pay public service job or internship during summer or other term. Preference given to applicants who have already found public service-oriented position, but require additional funds. Interns receive $1500 stipend. Number of awards varies.
   Amount of award: $2,000
   Number of awards: 10
   Number of applicants: 200
   Application deadline: March 15
   Notification begins: May 1
   Total amount awarded: $24,000
Contact:
J.W. Saxe Memorial Fund
1524 31 St. N.W.
Washington, DC 20007-3074
Web: www.jwsaxefund.org

Kentucky Higher Education Assistance Authority (KHEAA)

Kentucky Work-Study Program

Type of award: Internship, renewable.
Intended use: For undergraduate, master's, doctoral, first professional or postgraduate study at vocational, 2-year, 4-year or graduate institution.
Eligibility: Applicant must be U.S. citizen residing in Kentucky.
Application requirements: Interview, proof of eligibility.
Additional information: Job must be related to major course of study. Work-study wage is at least federal minimum wage. May also be enrolled in technical schools. Visit Website for additional information.
   Number of awards: 1,140
   Number of applicants: 1,140
   Total amount awarded: $809,500
Contact:
Kentucky Higher Education Assistance Authority (KHEAA)
KHEAA Work-Study Program
P.O. Box 798
Frankfort, KY 40602-0798
Phone: 800-928-8926
Fax: 502-696-7373
Web: www.kheaa.com

KIMT

KIMT Weather/News Internships

Type of award: Internship.
Intended use: For undergraduate study.
Eligibility: Applicant must be at least 18.
Basis for selection: Major/career interest in atmospheric sciences/meteorology; journalism; radio/television/film or sports/sports administration.
Application requirements: Interview. Resume.
Additional information: Applicant must be majoring in field directly related to the department of internship. All internships for college credit only. Student must arrange to receive college credit. Internships available year-round. Hours are flexible.
    Number of applicants: 3
Contact:
KIMT
Attn: Human Resources Coordinator
112 North Pennsylvania
Mason City, IA 50401
Phone: 641-423-2540

Landscape Architecture Foundation

LAF/CLASS Fund Internship Program

Type of award: Internship.
Intended use: For full-time junior or senior study. Designated institutions: University of California, Davis; Cal Polytechnic (Pomona and San Luis Obispo campuses).
Eligibility: Applicant must be residing in California.
Basis for selection: Major/career interest in landscape architecture. Applicant must demonstrate financial need and service orientation.
Application requirements: Transcript. Photo. 300-word statement on the profession; 100-word statement on intended use of funds. Two faculty recommendation letters. One confidential recommendation from department head. Cover sheet and personal profile.
Additional information: Award consists of $3,000 scholarship and nine-week summer internship in selected field within the green industry. Firm/office sponsoring internship provides participant with an additional $12 per hour. Visit Website for more details.
    Amount of award: $3,000
    Number of awards: 1
    Application deadline: February 15
    Total amount awarded: $3,000
Contact:
Landscape Architecture Foundation
818 18th Street
Suite 810
Washington, DC 20006
Phone: 202-331-7070
Web: www.lafoundation.org

Library of Congress

Library of Congress Hispanic Division Junior Fellows Internship

Type of award: Internship.
Intended use: For senior study at accredited 4-year or graduate institution. Designated institutions: Library of Congress.
Eligibility: Applicant must be U.S. citizen or permanent resident.
Basis for selection: Major/career interest in library science or Latin American studies. Applicant must demonstrate seriousness of purpose.
Application requirements: Interview, recommendations, transcript. Resume and cover letter including contact information and interview availability.
Additional information: Fellowships last approximately eight weeks during the summer, where fellows will be required to work full-time (40 hours per week) in the Hispanic Division of the Library of Congress. Fellows receive stipend of $1200 per month. Women, minorities, and people with disabilities encouraged to apply. Applicant must be fluent in Spanish. Visit Website to download application. Fax completed applications to 202-707-2005.
    Amount of award: $1,200
    Number of awards: 2
    Number of applicants: 10
    Application deadline: April 20
    Total amount awarded: $2,400
Contact:
Library of Congress
Chief of Hispanic Division
Washington, DC 20540-4850
Phone: 202-707-5400
Fax: 202-707-2005
Web: www.loc.gov/rr/hispanic

Louis Carr Internship Foundation (LCIF)

Louis Carr Summer Internship

Type of award: Internship.
Intended use: For full-time freshman, sophomore or junior study in United States.
Eligibility: Applicant must be Alaskan native, Asian American, African American, Mexican American, Hispanic American, Puerto Rican, American Indian or Native Hawaiian/Pacific Islander. Applicant must be U.S. citizen.
Basis for selection: Major/career interest in advertising; marketing or communications. Applicant must demonstrate high academic achievement, depth of character, leadership and seriousness of purpose.
Application requirements: Recommendations, essay, transcript. Resume.
Additional information: Paid, ten-week summer internship in New York, Chicago, Detroit, or Washington D.C.

Louis Carr Internship Foundation (LCIF): Louis Carr Summer Internship

Amount of award:	$4,000
Number of awards:	15
Number of applicants:	21
Application deadline:	March 1
Notification begins:	April 20
Total amount awarded:	$84,000

Contact:
Louis Carr Internship Foundation
P.O. Box 81859
Chicago, IL 60681-0589
Phone: 800-524-3740
Web: www.nabj.org or www.louiscarrfoundation.org

Makovsky & Company Inc.

Public Relations Internship

Type of award: Internship.
Intended use: For junior or senior study at 4-year institution in United States or Canada.
Basis for selection: Major/career interest in public relations or communications. Applicant must demonstrate high academic achievement.
Application requirements: Interview. Resume, cover letter, writing sample.
Additional information: One full- or part-time (20 hours minimum) paid position offered in spring and fall. Two full-time paid positions offered in summer. Compensation $10/hr. Applicant must be responsible, diligent, and energetic. Provides opportunity to receive hands-on experience in all facets of public relations under direction of forums staff. Deadlines: April 15 for summer; August 15 for fall; December 15 for spring. Submit resume to vrupeka@makovsky.com.

Number of awards:	4
Number of applicants:	150

Contact:
Makovsky & Company, Inc. Internship Coordinator
New York, NY
Phone: 212-508-9639
Fax: 212-751-9710
Web: www.makovsky.com

Massachusetts Democratic Party

John Joseph Moakely Democratic Internship

Type of award: Internship.
Intended use: For junior or senior study at accredited 4-year institution.
Eligibility: Applicant must be at least 18, no older than 23. Applicant must be U.S. citizen or permanent resident residing in Massachusetts.
Basis for selection: Major/career interest in political science/government or public administration/service. Applicant must demonstrate financial need, high academic achievement, leadership, seriousness of purpose and service orientation.
Additional information: Preference given to registered Democrats and students with 3.0 GPA or higher. Eight week, summer internship (with stipend) at Massachusetts Democratic State Convention Headquarters. Interns receive $2500 stipend. Visit Website for more program information and important dates.

Amount of award:	$2,000
Number of awards:	1

Contact:
Massachusetts Democratic Party
DSC Office, Attn: Gloribell Mota
56 Roland St., Suite 203
Boston, MA 02129
Phone: 617-776-2676
Fax: 617-776-2579
Web: www.massdems.org

MCC Theater

MCC Theater Internships

Type of award: Internship.
Intended use: For undergraduate study at vocational institution.
Eligibility: Applicant must be residing in New York.
Basis for selection: Major/career interest in theater arts; theater/production/technical; performing arts; design; business/management/administration or arts management.
Application requirements: Resume.
Additional information: Rolling application deadlines, negotiable schedule. Internships available in general management/theater administration, development, marketing, production, and literary and arts education. College credit available. E-mail resume to apply.

Contact:
MCC Theater
311 West 43rd Street, Suite 206
New York, NY 10036
Phone: 212-727-7722
Fax: 212-727-7780
Web: www.mcctheater.org/jobs

Metropolitan Museum of Art

The Cloisters Summer Internship Program

Type of award: Internship.
Intended use: For undergraduate study. Designated institutions: Metropolitan Museum of Art: The Cloisters.
Basis for selection: Major/career interest in art/art history; history; museum studies or museum studies/administration.
Application requirements: Recommendations, essay, transcript. Resume and list of art history courses taken.
Additional information: Must be currently enrolled college student at time of internship. First- and second-year students especially encouraged to apply. Interns receive $2,750 stipend. Interest in medieval history appreciated. Nine-week full-time internship from mid-June to mid-August. Five-day, 35-hour work week.

Amount of award: $2,750
Application deadline: January 18
Contact:
The Cloisters
College Internship Program
Fort Tryon Park
New York, NY 10040
Phone: 212-650-2280
Web: www.metmuseum.org/education/er_internship.asp

Six-Month Internship

Type of award: Internship.
Intended use: For senior, graduate or non-degree study at 4-year or graduate institution.
Eligibility: Applicant must be U.S. citizen or international student.
Basis for selection: Major/career interest in art/art history; museum studies or history.
Application requirements: Recommendations, transcript, proof of eligibility. Resume. List of art history and other relevant courses taken and foreign languages spoken. 500-word essay describing career goals, interest in museum work, specific areas of interest within the museum, and reasons for applying to the program.
Additional information: Interns work full time from early June to early December and participate in summer orientation program. Interns receive $11,000 stipend. International students must have permission to earn stipend in U.S. Visit Website for more information.
Amount of award: $11,000
Application deadline: January 4
Contact:
Metropolitan Museum of Art
1000 Fifth Avenue
New York, NY 10028-0198
Phone: 212-570-3710
Web: www.metmuseum.org/education/er_internship.asp

Summer Internship Program

Type of award: Internship.
Intended use: For junior, senior, graduate or non-degree study at postsecondary institution.
Eligibility: Applicant must be U.S. citizen or international student.
Basis for selection: Major/career interest in art/art history; arts management or museum studies/administration. Applicant must demonstrate seriousness of purpose.
Application requirements: Typed paper indicating desired internship and include name, home and school addresses and phone numbers. Resume. Two academic recommendations. Transcripts. Separate list with art history or relevant courses taken and knowledge of foreign languages. 500-word (maximum) essay describing career goals, interest in museum work, specific areas of interest within the museum, and reason for applying.
Additional information: Ten-week program for college students, recent college graduates who have not yet entered graduate school, and graduate students who have completed at least one year of graduate work in art history or related field. Interns work full-time. International students must have permission to work in U.S. Applicants should have broad background in art history. Program begins in June with two-week orientation, ends in August, and includes $3,250 honorarium for college interns and recent graduates and $3,500 for graduate interns. Visit Website for more information.

Amount of award: $3,250-$3,500
Application deadline: January 4
Contact:
Attn: Internship Programs
Metropolitan Museum of Art
1000 Fifth Avenue
New York, NY 10028-0198
Phone: 212-570-3710
Web: www.metmuseum.org/education/er_internship.asp

Michigan Higher Education Assistance Authority

Michigan Work-Study Program

Type of award: Internship, renewable.
Intended use: For undergraduate or graduate study at 2-year, 4-year or graduate institution.
Eligibility: Applicant must be U.S. citizen or permanent resident residing in Michigan.
Basis for selection: Applicant must demonstrate financial need.
Application requirements: Proof of eligibility. FAFSA.
Additional information: Program pays students with financial need to work in school-related jobs while enrolled.
Number of awards: 4,938
Total amount awarded: $6,930,902
Contact:
College financial aid office
Web: www.michigan.gov/osg

Minnesota Office of Higher Education

Minnesota Work-Study Program

Type of award: Internship.
Intended use: For undergraduate or graduate study.
Eligibility: Applicant must be U.S. citizen or permanent resident residing in Minnesota.
Basis for selection: Applicant must demonstrate financial need.
Application requirements: Interview.
Additional information: This is a work-study program, but it may be applied to internships. Work placement must be approved by school or nonprofit agency. Must be used at Minnesota college or for internship with nonprofit or private sector employer located in Minnesota. Apply to financial aid office of school. Award maximum set at cost of attendance minus EFC and other financial aid.
Number of awards: 11,922
Number of applicants: 11,922
Total amount awarded: $14,768,353
Contact:
Minnesota Office of Higher Education
1450 Energy Park Drive, Suite 350
St. Paul, MN 55108-5227
Phone: 800-657-3866
Web: www.getreadyforcollege.org

Morris Arboretum of the University of Pennsylvania

Arboriculture Internship

Type of award: Internship.
Intended use: For undergraduate or graduate study.
Basis for selection: Major/career interest in horticulture; forestry or landscape architecture.
Application requirements: Transcript. Letter of intent, resume, three recommendations.
Additional information: Applicant should have interest in arboriculture. Internships train students in most up-to-date tree care techniques. Interns work 40 hrs/week at hourly rate of $9.18 for full year. Intern works with Chief Arborist in all aspects of tree care, including tree assessment, pruning, cabling, and removal. Safety-conscious techniques are emphasized, and recent innovations in climbing and rigging are demonstrated and put into practice. Other opportunities include assisting with outreach activities including workshops and off-site consulting. Benefits include health insurance and dental plan. Must have solid academic background in arboriculture and horticulture. Tree climbing ability helpful. Driver's license required. Academic credit given.

Application deadline: February 15
Contact:
Morris Arboretum of the University of Pennsylvania
Internship Coordinator
100 Northwestern Ave.
Philadelphia, PA 19118
Phone: 215-247-5777 ext. 156
Web: www.upenn.edu/arboretum

Flora of Pennsylvania Internship

Type of award: Internship.
Intended use: For undergraduate or graduate study.
Basis for selection: Major/career interest in horticulture; biology or botany. Applicant must demonstrate seriousness of purpose.
Application requirements: Transcript. Letter of intent, resume, three recommendations.
Additional information: Interns work 40 hours/week at $9.18/hour for full year. Benefits include health insurance, dental plan, and tuition benefits. May require travel. Academic credit given. Interns receive training in all aspects of management collections in a major herborium. Must have undergraduate degree in botany or in biology with coursework in botany.

Application deadline: February 15
Contact:
Morris Arboretum of the University of Pennsylvania
Internship Coordinator
100 Northwestern Ave.
Philadelphia, PA 19118
Phone: 215-247-5777 ext. 156
Web: www.upenn.edu/arboretum

Morris Arboretum Education Internship

Type of award: Internship.
Intended use: For undergraduate or graduate study.
Basis for selection: Major/career interest in education; botany; horticulture; ecology or education, teacher.
Application requirements: Transcript. Letter of intent, resume, three recommendations.
Additional information: Interns work 40 hours/week at hourly wage of $9.18 for full year. Interns develop workshops for experienced guides, training sessions for new guides, occasionally lead tours. Other responsibilities include supervising the school tour program, running special programs for the public, helping to prepare the adult education course brochure, and writing promotional copy including a newsletter for volunteer guides. Benefits include insurance, a dental plan, and tuition benefits. Academic background or experience in education or educational programming preferred. Knowledge of plant-related subjects helpful. Strong writing and interpersonal skills essential. Academic credit given.

Application deadline: February 15
Contact:
Morris Arboretum of the University of Pennsylvania
Internship Coordinator
100 Northwestern Ave.
Philadelphia, PA 19118
Phone: 215-247-5777 ext. 156
Web: www.upenn.edu/arboretum

Morris Arboretum Horticulture Internship

Type of award: Internship.
Intended use: For undergraduate or graduate study.
Basis for selection: Major/career interest in horticulture.
Application requirements: Transcript. Letter of intent, resume, three recommendations.
Additional information: Intern assists in all phases of garden development and care of collections. Specific emphasis on refining practical horticultural skills. Supervisory skills are developed by directing activities of volunteers and part-time staff. Other activities include developing Integrated Pest Management skills, arboricultural techniques, and the operation and maintenance of garden machinery. Special projects will be assigned to develop individual skills in garden planning and management. Must have strong academic background in horticulture or closely related field. Interns work 40 hours/week at hourly wage of $9.18 for full year. Benefits include health insurance, a dental plan, and tuition benefits. Some internships require travel. Driver's license is required. Academic credit given.

Application deadline: February 15
Contact:
Morris Arboretum of the University of Pennsylvania
Internship Coordinator
100 Northwestern Ave.
Philadelphia, PA 19118
Phone: 215-247-5777 ext. 156
Web: www.upenn.edu/arboretum

Plant Propagation Internship

Type of award: Internship.
Intended use: For undergraduate or graduate study.
Basis for selection: Major/career interest in botany or horticulture.
Application requirements: Transcript. Letter of intent, resume, three recommendations.
Additional information: Strong background in woody landscape plants, plant propagation, nursery management, and plant physiology required. Interns work 40 hours/week at hourly rate of $9.18 for full year. Benefits include health insurance, a dental plan, and tuition benefits. Academic credit

given. Intern assists Propagator in the development of plant propagation and production schemes for arboretum. Emphasis is placed on the refinement of skills in traditional methods of plant propagation, nursery production, and greenhouse management. Other duties include management of the field nursery and data collection for ongoing research projects.

Application deadline: February 15
Contact:
Morris Arboretum of the University of Pennsylvania
Internship Coordinator
100 Northwestern Ave.
Philadelphia, PA 19118
Phone: 215-247-5777 ext. 156
Web: www.upenn.edu/arboretum

Plant Protection Internship

Type of award: Internship.
Intended use: For undergraduate or graduate study.
Basis for selection: Major/career interest in horticulture; entomology or botany.
Application requirements: Transcript. Letter of intent, resume, three recommendations.
Additional information: Interns work 40 hours/week at hourly wage of $9.18 for full year. Course work in entomology or plant pathology required. Intern assists arboretum's plant pathologist with the Integrated Pest Management program, which includes regular monitoring of the living collection and communicating information on pests and diseases to staff members. Related projects include establishing threshold levels for specific plant pests and evaluating the effectiveness of control measures. Modern laboratory facilities are available for identifying plant pests and pathogens. Intern also participates in Plant Clinic's daily operations, providing diagnostic services to the public about horticultural problems. Benefits include health insurance, a dental plan, and tuition benefits. Strong writing skills essential. Academic credit given.

Application deadline: February 15
Contact:
Morris Arboretum of the University of Pennsylvania
Internship Coordinator
100 Northwestern Ave.
Philadelphia, PA 19118
Phone: 215-247-5777 ext. 156
Web: www.upenn.edu/arboretum

Rose and Flower Garden Internship

Type of award: Internship.
Intended use: For undergraduate or graduate study.
Basis for selection: Major/career interest in horticulture. Applicant must demonstrate seriousness of purpose.
Application requirements: Transcript. Letter of intent, resume, three recommendations.
Additional information: Intern assists Rosarian in garden development, management, and care of collections. Emphasis on mastering skills used in the culture of modern and antique roses, developing pest management skills, and refining horticulture skills including formal garden maintenance. Other duties include plant record keeping, support for volunteer gardeners, operation of garden machinery, and supervision of part-time staff. Interns work 40-hour week at hourly rate of $9.18 for full year. Benefits include health insurance, dental plan, and tuition benefits. Applicant should have strong academic background in horticulture with course work in herbaceous and woody landscape plants. Driver's license required. Academic credit given.

Application deadline: February 15

Contact:
Morris Arboretum of the University of Pennsylvania
Internship Coordinator
100 Northwestern Ave.
Philadelphia, PA 19118
Phone: 215-247-5777 ext. 156
Web: www.upenn.edu/arboretum

Urban Forestry Internship

Type of award: Internship.
Intended use: For undergraduate study.
Basis for selection: Major/career interest in forestry; horticulture; landscape architecture or ecology.
Application requirements: Transcript. Letter of intent, resume, three recommendations.
Additional information: Intern will engage in urban forestry and natural resources programs and strategies for public gardens, government agencies, and educational and community organizations; learn and teach stewardship concepts and practical applications through riparian and woodland restoration projects; develop community partnership, urban vegetation analysis, and management planning skills. Forty hours/week at hourly wage of $9.18 for full year. Benefits include health insurance, a dental plan, and tuition benefits. Academic background in urban forestry, horticulture, landscape design, or related field. Communication skills essential. Car required; mileage reimbursed. Academic credit given.

Application deadline: February 15
Contact:
Morris Arboretum of the University of Pennsylvania
Internship Coordinator
100 Northwestern Ave.
Philadelphia, PA 19118
Phone: 215-247-5777 ext. 156
Web: www.upenn.edu/arboretum

Mother Jones

Mother Jones Magazine Editorial Internship

Type of award: Internship.
Intended use: For junior, senior, graduate or non-degree study.
Basis for selection: Major/career interest in political science/government; communications; journalism or publishing. Applicant must demonstrate high academic achievement.
Application requirements: Interview, recommendations. Resume with cover letter; contact information for two references; writing samples.
Additional information: Deadlines are rolling. Internships are full time and run four months with $150/month travel stipend, five day vacation allowance, and possible $700 cost of living scholarship. After four months, interns are reviewed for fellowship program which also runs four months with $1,380/month stipend. Hours vary according to magazine production schedule. No course credit offered. Reporting, writing, and research skills preferred. See Website for more information.

Contact:
Mother Jones
c/o Elizabeth Gettelman, Research Editor
222 Sutter Street, Suite 600
San Francisco, CA 94108
Web: www.motherjones.com/about/admin/internships

Mother JonesPhoto/Art Internship

Type of award: Internship.
Intended use: For junior, senior, graduate or non-degree study.
Basis for selection: Major/career interest in journalism or publishing. Applicant must demonstrate high academic achievement.
Application requirements: Interview, recommendations. Resume with cover letter; contact information for two references.
Additional information: Intern will assist Photo Editor. Deadlines are rolling. Internships are full-time and run four months with $150/month stipend, five vacation days, and possible cost of living scholarship. After four months, interns are reviewed for fellowship program which runs 15 hours/week for eight months with $552.50/month stipend. Reporting, writing, and research skills preferred. No course credit offered. See Website for more information.
Contact:
Mother Jones
c/o Emma Pierce, HR Manager
222 Sutter Street, Suite 600
San Francisco, CA 94108
Web: www.motherjones.com/about/admin/internship

Museum of Modern Art

Museum of Modern Art Internship

Type of award: Internship.
Intended use: For junior, senior or graduate study.
Basis for selection: Major/career interest in arts management; museum studies/administration; arts, general or art/art history.
Application requirements: Interview, essay, transcript. Resume and two recommendations.
Additional information: Course credit available. Fall, spring, summer, and 12-month internships. Summer internship pays $3,000 depending on available funds. Twelve-month internships are paid, full-time programs for recent college graduates. Fall and spring are part-time and unpaid. Fields of study encompass broad spectrum of topics. Visit Website for complete list of departments, applications, and deadline information.
    Number of awards: 100
    Number of applicants: 1,600
Contact:
The Museum of Modern Art
Internship Coordinator, Dept. of Education
11 W. 53rd St.
New York, NY 10019
Phone: 212-408-8440
Web: www.moma.org

NASA Arizona Space Grant Consortium

NASA Space Grant Arizona Undergraduate Research Internship

Type of award: Internship, renewable.
Intended use: For full-time sophomore, junior or senior study at accredited 2-year or 4-year institution in United States. Designated institutions: Arizona Space Grant Consortium (AZSGC) Colleges and Universities.
Eligibility: Applicant must be U.S. citizen residing in Arizona.
Basis for selection: Major/career interest in aerospace; astronomy; engineering; physics; geology/earth sciences; science, general; journalism or education.
Additional information: Approximately 100 full-time undergraduate students will be employed for 10-20 hours per week for the academic year in research programs, working alongside upper-level graduate students and practicing scientists. Hourly wage offered. Awardees must attend Arizona Space Grant Consortium member institution. Availability of internships varies. Some internships are renewable. Current announcements/application posted on Website.
    Number of applicants: 350
    Application deadline: June 30
Contact:
NASA Space Grant Arizona Space Grant Consortium
Lunar and Planetary Laboratory, Room 349
U of Arizona, 1629 E. University Blvd.
Tucson, AZ 85721-0092
Phone: 520-621-8556
Web: spacegrant.arizona.edu

NASA Hawaii Space Grant Consortium

NASA Hawaii Undergraduate Traineeship

Type of award: Internship.
Intended use: For full-time freshman or sophomore study in United States. Designated institutions: Consortium member schools: University of Hawaii at Manoa and Hilo, Community Colleges, and University of Guam.
Eligibility: Applicant must be U.S. citizen residing in Hawaii.
Basis for selection: Major/career interest in science, general; mathematics or engineering.
Application requirements: Recommendations, transcript. Two-page research proposal, budget, resume.
Additional information: This is a training program providing practical experience in any space-related field of science, engineering or math that covers one or two semesters, plus up to $250 for travel and supplies. Student must have faculty mentor. Contact sponsor for application details. Women, minority and physically challenged students who have interest in space-related fields encouraged to apply. Visit Website for more information and application.
    Amount of award: $250-$1,000
    Application deadline: June 15, December 1
Contact:
Hawaii Space Grant College
University of Hawaii
1680 East West Road
Honolulu, HI 96822
Phone: 808-956-3138
Fax: 808-956-6322
Web: www.spacegrant.hawaii.edu

NASA Massachusetts Space Grant Consortium

NASA Massachusetts Space Grant Summer Jobs for Students

Type of award: Internship, renewable.
Intended use: For undergraduate or graduate study in United States. Designated institutions: Massachusetts Space Grant Consortium members: Boston University, Harvard University, Holy Cross, Massachusetts Institute of Technology, Mount Holyoke, Tufts University, University of Massachusetts, Wellesley College, Worcester Polytechnic Institute, The Five College Astronomy Department.
Eligibility: Applicant must be U.S. citizen or permanent resident.
Basis for selection: Major/career interest in aerospace; astronomy; physics; engineering; engineering, electrical/electronic or engineering, computer.
Application requirements: Interview. Resume.
Additional information: The Space Grant Summer Jobs program is designed to give college students a practical learning experience in industry. Students with space-related majors are eligible. Each summer 20-30 students are placed in space-related technical positions. Must attend Massachusetts Space Grant Consortium member institution. Deadline in mid-December; call coordinator for exact date.
Contact:
NASA Massachusetts Space Grant Consortium
MIT, Aeronautics & Astronautics
77 Massachusetts Ave., Bldg. 33, Rm. 208
Cambridge, MA 02139
Phone: 617-258-5546
Fax: 617-253-0823
Web: www.maspacegrant.org

NASA New Jersey Space Grant Consortium

Undergraduate Fellowships in Engineering and Science

Type of award: Internship, renewable.
Intended use: For junior or senior study at accredited 4-year institution in United States. Designated institutions: New Jersey Institute of Technology, Princeton University, Rutgers University, Stevens Institute of Technology, University of Medicine and Dentistry of NJ.
Eligibility: Applicant must be U.S. citizen.
Basis for selection: Major/career interest in aerospace; biology; computer/information sciences; engineering, computer; engineering, chemical; engineering, electrical/electronic; engineering, mechanical; materials science; natural sciences or physical sciences.
Application requirements: Recommendations, essay. Biographical sketch, statement that describes career goals and what applicant hopes to accomplish as Space Grant Fellow, plan for immediate future and reference letter from faculty advisor.
Additional information: Applicants must have completed at least two but preferably three years of college. Consortium actively encourages women, minority students, and physically challenged students to apply. Awardees must attend NJSGC member institution. Academic year ($12,000 stipend) and summer fellowships ($5,000 stipend) offered. Visit Website for important dates and additional information.
   Amount of award: $5,000-$12,000
   Number of awards: 10
   Number of applicants: 6
   Total amount awarded: $68,000
Contact:
Program Director
New Jersey Space Grant Consortium
Stevens Institute of Technology
Hoboken, NJ 07030-5991
Phone: 201-216-8964
Fax: 201-216-8929
Web: www.njsgc.org

NASA Pennsylvania Space Grant Consortium

NASA Academy Internship

Type of award: Internship.
Intended use: For full-time junior or senior study at accredited 4-year or graduate institution in United States. Designated institutions: Pennsylvania colleges and universities.
Eligibility: Applicant must be U.S. citizen or permanent resident residing in Pennsylvania.
Basis for selection: Major/career interest in engineering; science, general; mathematics; aerospace or astronomy. Applicant must demonstrate high academic achievement and leadership.
Application requirements: Recommendations, essay, transcript.
Additional information: Awards are for ten-week internships at participating NASA centers. Stipend, plus room and board and travel expenses. Applicants should be juniors, seniors, or first year graduate students. Earth science students also eligible. Awardees must attend Pennsylvania institution or be a full-time resident. Interns receive $4,000 stipend. Consortium actively encourages women, minority, and physically challenged students to apply. Visit the NASA Academy Website for application information.
   Amount of award: $4,000
   Application deadline: January 16
Contact:
NASA Pennsylvania Space Grant Consortium
Penn State, University Park
2217 Earth-Engineering Sciences Building
University Park, PA 16802
Phone: 814-865-2535
Fax: 814-863-8286
Web: www.academy.nasa.gov

National Association of Black Journalists

NABJ Internships

Type of award: Internship.
Intended use: For full-time undergraduate study.
Eligibility: Applicant must be African American.
Basis for selection: Major/career interest in journalism.
Application requirements: Portfolio, essay. Print and online applicants must submit minimum of six samples of published work. Broadcast applicants must send resume tape of no longer than ten minutes. TV off-air applicants must submit two stories or edited version of newscast or program produced, directed, shot or edited by applicant. Radio applicants must submit three on-air reports, stories, interviews or newscasts or an edited version of a program written, broadcast, directed or produced by applicant.
Additional information: Ten-week paid internship in print, broadcast, online, sports, or photo journalism. Applicants must have prior experience. Applicant must be member of NABJ. Weekly stipend varies between $400 and $600. Visit Website for more information.
   Application deadline: December 1
Contact:
Irving Washington Program Coordinator
NABJ
8701 Adelphi Road
Adelphi, MD 20783-7101
Phone: 301-445-7100 ext. 108
Web: www.nabj.org/programs/internships/index.html

Newhouse Foundation Scholarship

Type of award: Internship, renewable.
Intended use: For undergraduate study.
Eligibility: Applicant must be U.S. citizen, permanent resident or international student.
Basis for selection: Major/career interest in journalism.
Application requirements: Essay, transcript. Resume, works samples. Must provide 4 copies of all application materials.
Additional information: Minimum 3.0 GPA. Must be member of NABJ and work for campus newspaper. Must major in print journalism.
   Amount of award: $5,000
   Application deadline: March 17
Contact:
National Association of Black Journalists
University of Maryland
8701-A Adelphi Road
Adelphi, MD 20783-1716
Phone: 866-479-6885
Fax: 301-445-7101
Web: www.nabj.org

National Association of Latino Elected and Appointed Officials (NALEO)

Shell Legislative Internship Program

Type of award: Internship.
Intended use: For full-time junior, senior or graduate study at accredited 4-year institution in United States.
Eligibility: Applicant must be Mexican American, Hispanic American or Puerto Rican. Applicant must be U.S. citizen or permanent resident residing in California, New York, Texas, New Mexico, Illinois, Colorado, Arizona or Florida.
Basis for selection: Major/career interest in social work; public administration/service; political science/government; sociology; psychology; public relations; urban planning or Latin American studies. Applicant must demonstrate high academic achievement, depth of character, leadership and service orientation.
Application requirements: Recommendations, essay, transcript. Resume and legislative analysis.
Additional information: Interns work for a state or federal elected official. Stipend of $1,500. Must possess sense of commitment to Latino community. Contact sponsor for additional information.
Contact:
National Association of Latino Elected and Appointed Officials (NALEO)
Attn: Cielo Castro
1122 Washington Blvd., 3rd Floor
Los Angeles, CA 90015
Phone: 213-747-7606
Fax: 213-747-7664
Web: www.naleo.org

National Basketball Association

NBA Internship Program

Type of award: Internship.
Intended use: For sophomore or junior study.
Basis for selection: Major/career interest in sports/sports administration; marketing; theater/production/technical; public relations; finance/banking or computer/information sciences.
Application requirements: Resume and cover letter.
Additional information: Internship opportunities are available throughout the year and are in various areas including television production, broadcast operations, finance, design, global merchandising, international public relations, corporate communications, human resources, and events and attractions. For more information, visit Website and click on "Internships" link.

Contact:
National Basketball Association
Internship Coordinator
645 Fifth Ave.
New York, NY 10022
Web: nbateamjobs.teamworkonline.com

National Geographic Society

Geography Students Internship

Type of award: Internship.
Intended use: For junior, senior or master's study at 4-year or graduate institution in United States.
Basis for selection: Major/career interest in geography or cartography.
Application requirements: Recommendations, essay, transcript. Resume.
Additional information: Spring, summer, and fall internships for 14 to 16 weeks in Washington, D.C., at $325/week. Emphasis on editorial and cartographic research. Students should contact their school's geography department chair or call internship hotline for more information.
  Number of awards: 30
  Number of applicants: 100
Contact:
National Geographic Society
Robert E. Dulli
1145 17 Street, NW
Washington, DC 20036-4688
Phone: 202-857-7134
Web: www.nationalgeographic.com

National Museum of the American Indian

National Museum of the American Indian Internship

Type of award: Internship.
Intended use: For undergraduate, graduate or non-degree study.
Basis for selection: Major/career interest in museum studies.
Application requirements: Transcript. Resume.
Additional information: Provides educational work/research experience for students in museum practice and related programming using resources of museum and other Smithsonian offices. Internships available at NMAI in Suitland, MD; Washington, DC; and New York City. Applicants must have minimum 3.0 GPA. Four 10-week internships, deadlines as follows: February 6 for summer; July 12 for fall; October 10 for winter; and November 20 for spring. Selection based on professional and educational goals of student; needs of museum. Students receiving stipends must work full-time; other interns must work at least 20 hours/week. Museum will grant academic credit if student makes arrangements with school. Visit Website or contact via e-mail for more information.
  Number of awards: 20
  Number of applicants: 40

Contact:
Internship Program, National Museum of the American Indian
Cultural Resources Center- Community Services
4220 Silver Hill Road
Suitland, MD 20746-2863
Phone: 301-238-1541
Fax: 301-238-3200
Web: www.nmai.si.edu

National Museum of Women in the Arts

Museum Coca-Cola Internship

Type of award: Internship.
Intended use: For junior, senior, graduate or non-degree study in United States. Designated institutions: National Museum of Women in the Arts.
Basis for selection: Major/career interest in public relations; advertising; library science; journalism; museum studies; art/art history; museum studies/administration; accounting; education or retailing/merchandising. Applicant must demonstrate high academic achievement and seriousness of purpose.
Application requirements: Transcript. One personal and one academic recommendation. Resume, cover letter, and one- to two-page writing sample.
Additional information: Internship available to students interested in pursuing careers in museum environments. Minimum 3.25 GPA. Interns receive $1500 stipend. Full-time internship lasts 12 weeks; application deadline for spring is October 15; summer is March 15; fall is June 15.
  Amount of award: $1,500
  Number of awards: 3
  Number of applicants: 50
  Total amount awarded: $1,500
Contact:
Manager of Public Programs National Museum of Women in the Arts
1250 New York Ave. NW
Washington, DC 20005-3970
Phone: 202-783-7982
Fax: 202-393-3234
Web: www.nmwa.org

Southern California Council Endowed Internship

Type of award: Internship, renewable.
Intended use: For junior, senior or graduate study. Designated institutions: Art and design institutions in Los Angeles County area.
Eligibility: Applicant must be residing in California.
Basis for selection: Major/career interest in art/art history; arts management; arts, general; museum studies or museum studies/administration.
Application requirements: Recommendations, essay, transcript. Cover letter, brief writing sample, resume.
Additional information: Full-time, twelve-week internship. $2,000 stipend. Applicants must be resident of Los Angeles County. Minimum 3.25 GPA.

Amount of award: $2,000
Number of awards: 1
Number of applicants: 10
Application deadline: March 15
Total amount awarded: $2,000

Contact:
Manager of Public Programs Education Department
National Museum of Women in the Arts
1250 New York Avenue, NW
Washington, DC 20005-3970
Phone: 202-783-7982
Fax: 202-393-3234
Web: www.nmwa.org

National Science Foundation

Research Experiences for Undergraduates - Maria Mitchell Observatory

Type of award: Internship.
Intended use: For undergraduate study at 4-year institution. Designated institutions: Maria Mitchell Observatory, Nantucket, MA.
Eligibility: Applicant must be U.S. citizen or permanent resident.
Basis for selection: Major/career interest in astronomy. Applicant must demonstrate high academic achievement.
Application requirements: Essay, transcript. Minimum 2 recommendations.
Additional information: Positions provide chance for students to conduct independent research and to participate in common project. Students expected to develop their ability to communicate with the public. Furnished housing is available at no cost. Partial travel funds available. Internship runs from June through August, with $1,400 monthly stipend. Applicant must demonstrate motivation in research. Minimum of one year undergraduate physics required.

Number of awards: 6
Number of applicants: 100
Application deadline: February 15
Notification begins: March 1

Contact:
Maria Mitchell Observatory
Attn: Vladimir Strelnitski
4 Vestal Street
Nantucket, MA 02554
Phone: 508-228-9273
Fax: 508-228-1031
Web: www.mmo.org

NCR Corporation

NCR Summer Internships

Type of award: Internship.
Intended use: For full-time undergraduate study at accredited 4-year institution.
Eligibility: Applicant must be residing in District of Columbia, California, Ohio, South Carolina or Georgia.
Basis for selection: Major/career interest in computer/information sciences; engineering, computer; marketing; information systems; finance/banking; accounting or human resources.
Application requirements: Interview, proof of eligibility. Resume.
Additional information: Minimum 3.0 GPA required. Interns paid hourly wage. Applicants must complete personal profile, including resume, on Website before applying for positions. Applicants encouraged to visit Website frequently during spring to review newly added offerings and important information.
Contact:
Visit Website for further information.
Web: www.ncr.com/careers

New Dramatists

New Dramatists Internship

Type of award: Internship.
Intended use: For undergraduate or graduate study.
Basis for selection: Major/career interest in theater arts; performing arts or arts management.
Application requirements: Interview, essay. Two letters of recommendation, resume.
Additional information: Must have passion for new plays and playwrights. Twelve- to twenty-week internships, three to five days per week. Internships run September to December, January to May, and June to August. Stipend $25/week for three days, $50/week for five days. College credit may be available. Computer and writing skills essential. Applications must be filled out online.
Contact:
New Dramatists
Internship Coordinator
424 West 44th Street
New York, NY 10036
Web: www.newdramatists.org

New Mexico Commission on Higher Education

New Mexico Work-Study Program

Type of award: Internship, renewable.
Intended use: For undergraduate study at postsecondary institution. Designated institutions: Public and approved private non-profit postsecondary institutions in New Mexico.
Eligibility: Applicant must be U.S. citizen or permanent resident residing in New Mexico.
Basis for selection: Applicant must demonstrate financial need.
Application requirements: FAFSA.
Additional information: Awards vary. Limit of 20 hrs/wk, on-campus or off-campus in federal, state, or local public agency. New Mexico residents receive state portion of funding. Contact financial aid office of New Mexico public postsecondary institutions for information, deadlines, and application.

Contact:
New Mexico Commission on Higher Education
Financial Aid and Student Services
1068 Cerrillos Road
Santa Fe, NM 87505
Phone: 800-279-9777
Web: www.hed.state.nm.us

The New Republic

The New Republic Internship

Type of award: Internship.
Intended use: For undergraduate, graduate or non-degree study.
Eligibility: Applicant must be U.S. citizen.
Basis for selection: Major/career interest in journalism. Applicant must demonstrate depth of character and seriousness of purpose.
Application requirements: Cover letter, resume, two writing samples (one showing reporting ability, other showing opinion writing ability), plus one 750-word critique of "Politics of the World" section of recent New Republic issue.
Additional information: Year-long full-time internship for college graduates and soon-to-be college graduates with journalism experience. Must be fluent with LexisNexis and other research tools. Payment is $280 (including overtime) per week plus health benefits. Provides intern with opportunity to gain editorial experience at leading opinion magazine. Must have excellent organizational skills, research ability, and experience writing news and opinion. Position starts in August or September. No calls or snail mail.
    Number of awards: 3
    Number of applicants: 100
    Application deadline: February 15
Contact:
The New Republic
1331 H Street NW
Suite 700
Washington, DC 20005
Phone: 202-508-4444
Web: www.tnr.com

New York State Assembly

New York State Assembly Session Internship Program

Type of award: Internship, renewable.
Intended use: For full-time junior, senior or graduate study in United States.
Basis for selection: Applicant must demonstrate high academic achievement.
Application requirements: Recommendations, essay, transcript, proof of eligibility. Two recommendations. Writing sample. Letter from college endorsing candidate and outlining course credit arrangements.
Additional information: All majors eligible. Interns assigned to work with assembly members or assembly staff. Program runs from January to May. Undergraduate interns receive $4,140 stipend. Applications accepted on an ongoing basis until deadline. Extensions granted upon request. Housing not provided, but assistance in finding apartments and roommates is. Visit Website for deadline information.
    Amount of award: $4,140-$11,500
    Number of awards: 150
    Application deadline: November 1
Contact:
Kathleen McCarty, Director New York State Assembly
Assembly Intern Committee
Legislative Office Building, Room 104A
Albany, NY 12248
Phone: 518-455-4704
Fax: 518-455-4705
Web: www.assembly.state.ny.us/internship/

New York Times

New York Times Summer Internship Program

Type of award: Internship.
Intended use: For senior, graduate or non-degree study.
Basis for selection: Major/career interest in journalism. Applicant must demonstrate seriousness of purpose.
Application requirements: Portfolio. Cover letter, resume, eight to ten writing samples.
Additional information: Program open to all applicants, regardless of race or ethnicity. Salary is $904 per week for 10 weeks, plus housing allowance. Editing applicants must have Dow Jones training. All applicants must have had at least one previous internship, preferably on a daily newspaper. All queries by mail or e-mail (rulesh@nytimes.com).
    Application deadline: November 15
Contact:
The New York Times
Sheila Rule, Senior Editor
620 8th Ave.
New York, NY 10018
Web: www.nytco.com/internships

Oak Ridge Institute for Science and Education

Department of Commerce Internship for Postsecondary Students

Type of award: Internship.
Intended use: For undergraduate or graduate study at 4-year or graduate institution in United States. Designated institutions: Department of Commerce headquarters, division offices and field centers.
Eligibility: Applicant must be U.S. citizen.
Basis for selection: Major/career interest in computer/information sciences; engineering; life sciences; physical sciences or business.
Additional information: Provides opportunities to participate in hands-on education and training related to Department of Commerce mission. Ten-week internship in summer; 16-week

internship for fall or spring semesters. Weekly stipend of $450 for undergraduates, $550 for graduate students; dislocation allowance of $125 per week based on appointment location; limited travel reimbursement; accidental medical expense coverage provided. Summer deadline third Tuesday in January. Number of awards varies.

Application deadline: July 30, December 31
Contact:
Web: www.orau.gov/orise/educ.htm

Department of Energy Special Emphasis Program

Type of award: Internship.
Intended use: For undergraduate or graduate study at 2-year, 4-year or graduate institution in United States. Designated institutions: Germantown, MD, and participating facilities.
Eligibility: Applicant must be U.S. citizen.
Basis for selection: Major/career interest in computer/information sciences; economics; engineering; finance/banking; law; mathematics; business or science, general.
Additional information: Provides opportunities to participate in ongoing research and related activities at the U.S. Department of Energy Office of Science. Program lasts ten weeks; some part-time appointments. Weekly stipend of $500 to $550. Limited travel reimbursement (round-trip transportation expenses between facility and home or campus). Number of awards granted varies. Deadline third Tuesday in January. See Website for application and more information.
Contact:
Web: www.orau.gov/orise/educ.htm

DOE Pre-Service Teacher Internships

Type of award: Internship.
Intended use: For undergraduate or graduate study. Designated institutions: Oak Ridge National Laboratory (Oak Ridge, TN).
Eligibility: Applicant must be at least 18. Applicant must be U.S. citizen or permanent resident.
Basis for selection: Major/career interest in science, general; mathematics or education. Applicant must demonstrate high academic achievement.
Application requirements: Recommendations, transcript. List of courses, research paper.
Additional information: Minimum 3.0 GPA. Provides opportunities to participate in educational training and research relating to preparation for teaching K-12 science, math, and technology. Ten-week summer program. Bi-weekly stipend with limited travel reimbursement and limited housing allowance. Must have health insurance and must have completed a minimum of two math classes above college algebra or at least two laboratory science classes. Application available online. Visit www.scied.science.doe.gov for deadline.

Application deadline: February 1
Notification begins: April 1
Contact:
Web: www.orau.gov/orise/educ.htm or www.scied.science.doe.gov

Energy Student Achievement Program

Type of award: Internship.
Intended use: For undergraduate or graduate study.
Eligibility: Applicant must be U.S. citizen.
Basis for selection: Major/career interest in computer/information sciences; economics; engineering; physical sciences; law; mathematics or international relations.
Additional information: Ten-week internship introduces students to operational functions and specialized areas pertaining to the Department of Energy. Weekly stipend of $550 to $600, and limited travel reimbursement.

Application deadline: January 31
Contact:
Web: www.orau.gov/orise/educ.htm

Great Lakes Colleges Association/Associated Colleges of the Midwest Oak Ridge Science Semester

Type of award: Internship.
Intended use: For full-time undergraduate study at accredited 4-year institution in United States. Designated institutions: Oak Ridge National Laboratory (Oak Ridge, TN).
Basis for selection: Major/career interest in computer/information sciences; engineering; life sciences; mathematics; physical sciences or health sciences.
Additional information: Applicant must be undergraduate at institutions belonging to the Great Lakes Colleges Association or the Associated Colleges of the Midwest. Provides opportunities to join ongoing investigations at the Oak Ridge National Laboratory (ORNL) in research areas relating to energy production, use, conservation, and societal implications. Program is 16 weeks in the fall (late August through mid-December). See Website for application deadline, www.denison.edu/oakridge. Weekly stipend; limited travel reimbursement; housing; academic credit offered for combination of research, coursework, and seminar series.

Total amount awarded: $7,800
Contact:
Web: www.orau.gov/orise/educ.htm or www.denison.edu/oakridge

Internship Program for Laboratory Technology

Type of award: Internship.
Intended use: For undergraduate or graduate study. Designated institutions: Metals & Ceramics Division of Oak Ridge National Laboratory (Oak Ridge, TN).
Eligibility: Applicant must be U.S. citizen or permanent resident.
Basis for selection: Major/career interest in engineering or engineering, mechanical.
Additional information: Provides opportunity to receive hands-on experience in technical areas via long-term assignment. Internship duration varies with academic level; full-time or part-time appointments of up to one year, renewable up to two additional years. Applications accepted year-round. Stipend available; amount based on academic level or degree. Interns also receive benefits of full-time or part-time employees.
Contact:
Web: www.orau.gov/orise/educ.htm

ORISE Community College Institute

Type of award: Internship.
Intended use: For full-time undergraduate study at accredited 2-year institution in United States. Designated institutions: Oak Ridge National Laboratory (Oak Ridge, TN).

Eligibility: Applicant must be at least 18. Applicant must be U.S. citizen or permanent resident.
Basis for selection: Major/career interest in computer/information sciences; science, general; engineering; environmental science; life sciences; mathematics or physical sciences.
Application requirements: Recommendations.
Additional information: Applicant must be student at community college. Provides opportunities to participate in educational training and research relating to energy production, use, conservation, and societal implications. Applicant must have passed at least 12 credit hours of coursework toward a degree (with at least six credit hours in science, math, engineering, or technology courses) at community college. Ten-week summer internship. Bi-weekly stipend. Limited travel reimbursement and limited housing allowance. Student must have health insurance. Visit Website for application and deadlines.
   Application deadline: February 1
   Notification begins: April 1
Contact:
Web: www.orau.gov/orise/educ.htm or www.scied.science.doe.gov

ORISE Higher Education Research Experiences at Oak Ridge National Laboratory

Type of award: Internship.
Intended use: For undergraduate or graduate study in United States. Designated institutions: Oak Ridge National Laboratory (Oak Ridge, TN).
Eligibility: Applicant must be at least 18. Applicant must be U.S. citizen or permanent resident.
Basis for selection: Major/career interest in chemistry; environmental science; geology/earth sciences; hydrology; engineering, chemical; engineering, civil; engineering, environmental; engineering, mechanical; computer/information sciences or mathematics.
Application requirements: Recommendations. Two academic references.
Additional information: Provides opportunities to participate in energy-related research. Terms vary with academic level; full- or part-time positions available. Minimum 3.0 GPA. Weekly stipend varies with academic level. One round-trip travel reimbursement and housing allowance. Number of awards varies. Deadlines for undergraduates: February 1 for summer, June 1 for fall, and October 1 for spring. Deadline for freshmen is February 1. See Website for application and more information.
Contact:
Web: www.orau.gov/hereatornl

ORISE National Oceanic and Atmospheric Administration Faculty and Student Intern Research Participation

Type of award: Internship.
Intended use: For undergraduate or graduate study at 2-year, 4-year or graduate institution in United States. Designated institutions: NOAA headquarters and field centers.
Eligibility: Applicant must be U.S. citizen.
Basis for selection: Major/career interest in computer/information sciences; life sciences; engineering; physical sciences or business.
Additional information: Provides opportunities to participate in research and development relating to science, math, and engineering. Ten-week summer internship. Weekly stipend of $440 to $1200, depending on academic classification; limited travel reimbursement (round-trip transportation expenses between facility and home or campus). Applications accepted on year-round basis. Number of internships varies.
Contact:
Web: www.orau.gov/orise/educ.htm

ORISE Professional Internship Program for National Energy Technology Laboratory

Type of award: Internship, renewable.
Intended use: For undergraduate or graduate study at accredited 2-year, 4-year or graduate institution in United States. Designated institutions: National Energy Technology Laboratory (Pittsburgh, PA, Albany, OR, and Morgantown, WV).
Eligibility: Applicant must be at least 18. Applicant must be U.S. citizen or permanent resident.
Basis for selection: Major/career interest in chemistry; computer/information sciences; engineering; environmental science; geology/earth sciences; mathematics; physics; physical sciences or statistics.
Application requirements: Transcript. Proof of health insurance. Two references; at least one academic reference.
Additional information: Provides opportunities to participate in fossil energy-related research. Three to 24 consecutive months, full-time or part-time appointments. Weekly stipend. Limited travel reimbursement (round-trip transportation expenses between facility and home or campus). Off-campus tuition and fees may be paid. Deadline for summer is February 15. Number of awards varies. Minimum 2.5 GPA.
   Number of awards: 20
   Number of applicants: 80
   Application deadline: June 1, October 1
Contact:
Web: www.orau.gov/orise/educ.htm

ORISE Student Environmental Management Participation at the U.S. Army Environmental Center

Type of award: Internship, renewable.
Intended use: For undergraduate or graduate study at 2-year, 4-year or graduate institution. Designated institutions: U.S. Army Environmental Center (Aberdeen Proving Ground, MD) and other approved locations.
Eligibility: Applicant must be U.S. citizen.
Basis for selection: Major/career interest in forestry; archaeology; biology; chemistry; computer/information sciences; zoology; ecology; engineering; entomology or environmental science.
Additional information: Provides opportunities to participate in research in environmental programs involving cultural and natural resources, restoration, compliance, conservation, pollution prevention, validation, demonstration, technology transfer, quality assurance and quality control, training, information management and reporting, and related programs. Up to one year; full-time or part-time appointments. Stipend

based on research area and academic classification. Applications accepted year-round. Number of awards varies.
Contact:
Web: www.orau.gov/orise/educ.htm

ORISE Student Internship at the Office of Water

Type of award: Internship, renewable.
Intended use: For graduate study in United States. Designated institutions: Office of Water (Cincinnati, Ohio, and Washington, D.C.).
Eligibility: Applicant must be U.S. citizen.
Basis for selection: Major/career interest in engineering; environmental science or physical sciences.
Application requirements: Recommendations, transcript. Resume.
Additional information: Provides opportunities to participate in studies related to development and implementation of drinking water regulations. Internships last one year. Number of awards varies. Stipend based on research area and academic classification; limited reimbursement for inbound travel and moving. Applications accepted year-round. See Website for application and more information.
Contact:
Web: www.orau.gov/orise/educ.htm

ORISE Student Internship at the U.S. Army Center for Health Promotion and Preventive Medicine

Type of award: Internship, renewable.
Intended use: For undergraduate or graduate study at postsecondary institution in United States. Designated institutions: U.S. Army Center for Health Promotion and Preventive Medicine (Aberdeen Proving Ground, MD) and other approved locations.
Eligibility: Applicant must be U.S. citizen.
Basis for selection: Major/career interest in biology; chemistry; entomology; engineering; environmental science; physical sciences; science, general or health sciences.
Additional information: Provides opportunities to participate in applied clinical research in areas such as occupational and environmental health engineering, entomology, ionizing and nonionizing radiation, health promotion, industrial hygiene and worksite hazards, ergonomics, environmental sanitation and hygiene, laboratory science, chemistry, biology, toxicology, health physics, environmental health risk assessment and risk communication, and related projects. Up to one year; full-time or part-time appointments. Stipend based on research area and academic classification. Number of awards varies. Applications accepted year-round.
Contact:
Phone: 410-306-9206
Web: www.orau.gov/orise/educ.htm

ORISE Student Research - National Center for Toxicological Research

Type of award: Internship, renewable.
Intended use: For undergraduate or graduate study at accredited 2-year, 4-year or graduate institution in United States. Designated institutions: National Center for Toxicological Research (Jefferson, AK).
Eligibility: Applicant must be U.S. citizen.
Basis for selection: Major/career interest in biology; chemistry; computer/information sciences; mathematics; pharmacy/pharmaceutics/pharmacology; science, general or medicine.
Additional information: Provides opportunities to participate in research on biological effects of potentially toxic chemicals and solutions to toxicology problems that have a major impact on human health and the environment. One month to one year; full-time or part-time appointments. Stipend based on research area and academic classification. Summer deadline is March 15; applications accepted year-round for academic year appointments. Number of awards varies.

Number of awards:	40
Number of applicants:	100
Application deadline:	March 15
Notification begins:	April 1

Contact:
Web: www.orau.gov/orise/educ.htm

ORISE Student Research at the Centers for Disease Control and Prevention

Type of award: Internship.
Intended use: For undergraduate or graduate study at accredited 2-year, 4-year or graduate institution in United States. Designated institutions: Centers for Disease Control and Prevention (Atlanta, GA, and other domestic and international locations).
Basis for selection: Major/career interest in epidemiology; health sciences; environmental science; communications; economics; science, general; life sciences; medicine or physical sciences.
Additional information: Provides opportunities to participate in research on infectious diseases, environmental health, epidemiology, or occupational safety and health. One month to one year; full-time or part-time appointments. Stipend based on research area(s) and academic classification. Applications accepted year-round, available on Website.
Contact:
Phone: 865-576-1089
Web: www.orau.gov/cdc

ORISE Student Research Participation at the U.S. Army Medical Research Institute of Chemical Defense

Type of award: Internship, renewable.
Intended use: For undergraduate or graduate study at 2-year, 4-year or graduate institution in United States. Designated institutions: U.S. Army Medical Research Institute of Chemical Defense (Aberdeen Proving Ground, MD).
Eligibility: Applicant must be U.S. citizen.
Basis for selection: Major/career interest in biochemistry; biology; medicine or physical sciences.
Additional information: Minimum 2.5 GPA. Provides opportunities to participate in development of medical countermeasures to chemical warfare agents. Internship lasts up to one year; full- and part-time appointments available. Stipend based on research area and academic classification. Number of awards varies. Applications accepted year-round. See Website for application and more details.
Contact:
Web: www.orau.gov/orise/educ.htm

ORISE Student Research Participation at U.S. Army Research Laboratory

Type of award: Internship.
Intended use: For undergraduate or graduate study at 2-year, 4-year or graduate institution in United States. Designated institutions: U.S. Army Research Laboratory (Adelphi and Aberdeen Proving Ground, MD) and other approved locations.
Eligibility: Applicant must be U.S. citizen.
Basis for selection: Major/career interest in biology; medicine; physical sciences; computer/information sciences; materials science or engineering.
Additional information: Provides opportunities to participate in research and technology development in areas such as engineering, mechanics, chemistry, computational modeling, science, and materials research related to enhancing the lethality and survivability of America's ground forces. Internship lasts up to one year; up to a total of three years; full- or part-time appointments available. Stipend based on research area and classification. Number of awards varies. Applications accepted year-round. See Website for application packet.
Contact:
Web: www.orau.gov/orise/educ.htm

ORISE U.S. Nuclear Regulatory Commission Historically Black Colleges and Universities Student Research Participation

Type of award: Internship.
Intended use: For undergraduate or graduate study at accredited postsecondary institution in United States. Designated institutions: Laboratories conducting NRC research; some appointments on HBCU campuses; some appointments at host universities under the guidance of principal investigators who have NRC research grants.
Eligibility: Applicant must be U.S. citizen or permanent resident.
Basis for selection: Major/career interest in computer/information sciences; engineering; biology; mathematics; geophysics; physics; materials science; physical sciences or health sciences.
Additional information: Provides opportunities for students from historically black colleges to participate in ongoing NRC research and development. Ten to 12 weeks during the summer; some part-time appointments of one year. Weekly stipend of $500 to $600. Limited travel reimbursement (round-trip transportation expenses between facility and home or campus). Funded by U.S. Nuclear Regulatory Commission.
Contact:
Oak Ridge Associated Universities OAB-44
ATTN: Alicia Wells
P.O. Box 117, Mail Stop 36
Oak Ridge, TN 37831-0117
Phone: 865-576-3409
Fax: 865-241-5220
Web: www.orau.gov/orise/educ.htm

Savannah River Site Professional Internship Program

Type of award: Internship.
Intended use: For undergraduate or graduate study at 2-year, 4-year or graduate institution in United States.
Eligibility: Applicant must be U.S. citizen.
Basis for selection: Major/career interest in environmental science; chemistry; engineering; geology/earth sciences; physics or computer/information sciences.
Additional information: Provides opportunities to participate in energy-related and environmental research. Three to 24 consecutive months; full-time or part-time appointments. Weekly stipend; limited travel reimbursement (round-trip transportation expenses between facility and home or campus). Summer deadline February 15. Funded by Westinghouse Savannah River Company.
Application deadline: June 1, October 1
Contact:
Web: www.orau.gov/orise/educ.htm

Science Undergraduate Laboratory Internships

Type of award: Internship.
Intended use: For undergraduate study. Designated institutions: Oak Ridge National Laboratory (Oak Ridge, TN).
Eligibility: Applicant must be U.S. citizen or permanent resident.
Basis for selection: Major/career interest in computer/information sciences; physical sciences; mathematics; life sciences; engineering; science, general; environmental science or health sciences.
Additional information: Internship program provides opportunity to participate in research relating to energy production, use, conservation, and societal implications. Bi-weekly stipend; limited travel reimbursement and housing allowance. Internship lasts ten weeks in the summer; 16 weeks during semester. See Website for more information and deadlines.
Contact:
Web: www.orau.gov/orise/edu/ornl/doeprog/

Student Research Participation at the Federal Bureau of Investigation Counterterrorism/Forensic Science Research Unit

Type of award: Internship.
Intended use: For undergraduate or graduate study at accredited 2-year or 4-year institution in United States. Designated institutions: FBI Academy (Quantico, VA).
Eligibility: Applicant must be U.S. citizen.
Basis for selection: Major/career interest in forensics; chemistry; biology; physical sciences; health sciences or life sciences.
Additional information: Opportunities to participate in advancement of forensic science for the FBI Laboratory as well as federal, state, and local law enforcement agencies. Award number varies. Applications accepted on year-round basis. Stipend based on academic classification. Appointments range from ten weeks to one year.
Contact:
Web: www.orau.gov/orise/educ.html

U.S. Department of Homeland Security Scholarship and Fellowship Program

Type of award: Internship.

Intended use: For full-time sophomore study at accredited 4-year or graduate institution in United States.
Eligibility: Applicant must be U.S. citizen.
Basis for selection: Major/career interest in biology; engineering; social/behavioral sciences; physical sciences; mathematics; computer/information sciences; life sciences or physical sciences. Applicant must demonstrate high academic achievement.
Application requirements: Recommendations, transcript.
Additional information: Opportunity to participate in educational program intended to ensure diverse and highly talented science and technology human resource base to meet mission, goals, and objectives of U.S. Department of Homeland Security. Appointments are two years for undergraduates and three years for graduate students, given satisfactory progress. Successful applicants will receive full-tuition scholarship and monthly stipend. Minimum 3.3 GPA. Visit Website for application and more information.

   Number of awards: 28
   Number of applicants: 609
   Application deadline: January 7
   Notification begins: April 15
Contact:
Web: www.orau.gov/dhsed

Ohio Newspapers Foundation

Ohio Newspaper Association Publications/Public Relations Internship

Type of award: Internship.
Intended use: For sophomore, junior or senior study.
Eligibility: Applicant must be residing in Ohio.
Basis for selection: Major/career interest in journalism.
Application requirements: Resume, writing samples, and cover letter.
Additional information: Ten-week internship at this trade association, which represents 84 daily and 87 weekly newspapers in Ohio. Duties include writing and assisting in production of newsletter, miscellaneous flyers, and mailings, meeting planning, research. Start date negotiable after June 1. Salary of $350 per week. Finalists will be contacted for interviews.

   Application deadline: March 31
Contact:
Ohio Newspapers Foundation
1335 Dublin Road
Suite 216-B
Columbus, OH 43215
Phone: 614-486-6677
Fax: 611-486-4940
Web: www.ohionews.org

Ohio Newspaper Services, Inc. Advertising Internship

Type of award: Internship.
Intended use: For junior or senior study.
Eligibility: Applicant must be residing in Ohio.
Basis for selection: Major/career interest in journalism or advertising.
Application requirements: Resume, writing samples, and cover letter.
Additional information: Ten-week internship in Columbus office of this trade association, which represents 84 daily and 87 weekly newspapers in Ohio. Duties include writing and layout for sales presentation sheets and client mailings, assistance with newspaper ad bid sheets, newspaper tear sheets, research. Start date is negotiable after June 1. Salary is $350 per week. Finalists will be contacted for interviews.

   Application deadline: March 31
Contact:
Ohio Newspapers Foundation
1335 Dublin Road
Suite 216-B
Columbus, OH 43215
Phone: 614-486-6677
Fax: 614-486-4940
Web: www.ohionews.org

Owens Corning

Owens Corning Internships

Type of award: Internship.
Intended use: For full-time junior or senior study at accredited 4-year institution.
Eligibility: Applicant must be U.S. citizen or permanent resident.
Basis for selection: Major/career interest in engineering; accounting; human resources; information systems; marketing; materials science; communications or finance/banking. Applicant must demonstrate high academic achievement and leadership.
Application requirements: Proof of eligibility.
Additional information: Summer internship with housing assistance, competitive salary. Summer program lasts ten to twelve weeks. Most positions in Toledo, Ohio. See Website for more information.
Contact:
Owens Corning
One Owens Corning Parkway
Toledo, OH 43659
Web: www.owenscorningcareers.com

Pacific Gas and Electric Company

Pacific Gas and Electric Summer Intern Program

Type of award: Internship.
Intended use: For full-time undergraduate or graduate study in United States.
Eligibility: Applicant must be U.S. citizen or permanent resident.
Basis for selection: Applicant must demonstrate high academic achievement and seriousness of purpose.
Application requirements: Interview. Resume, cover letter.
Additional information: Internships available throughout northern and central California, many in San Francisco.

Deadline is rolling, but early applications are encouraged. Resume may be submitted online; format specifications available online. Visit Website or call sponsor for openings and campus recruitment dates. Must be eligible to work in the United States. Number and amount of awards vary. Most internships are summer only and typically last 10-12 weeks.
Contact:
Pacific Gas and Electric Company
College Relations/CHP
P.O. Box 770000, Mail Code N14G
San Francisco, CA 94177
Phone: 415-817-8237
Web: www.pge.com/jobs

PBS

PBS Internships

Type of award: Internship.
Intended use: For undergraduate study.
Application requirements: Resume and cover letter.
Additional information: Various paid internships are available in different departments. Internships change on a semester basis. Visit Website for internship listings, application forms, and more information.
Contact:
PBS Internship Program
2100 Crystal Dr.
Arlington, VA 22202
Phone: 703-739-5400
Web: www.pbs.org/jobs

PGA Tour

PGA Tour Diversity Intern Program

Type of award: Internship.
Intended use: For sophomore, junior, senior or master's study.
Eligibility: Applicant must be U.S. citizen.
Basis for selection: Major/career interest in marketing; business/management/administration; communications; information systems; journalism; radio/television/film; sports/sports administration or public relations. Applicant must demonstrate high academic achievement, depth of character, leadership, seriousness of purpose and service orientation.
Application requirements: Interview, recommendations, essay, transcript.
Additional information: Internship lasts ten weeks at $440/week with $200/month deducted for housing (if needed). Site locations include California, Florida, Georgia, Maryland, Massachusetts, and New York. Minimum 2.8 GPA. Visit Website to apply.

Amount of award:	$4,400
Number of awards:	40
Number of applicants:	900
Application deadline:	February 16
Notification begins:	May 11

Contact:
PGA Tour Diversity Intern Program
Attn: Mike Cooney
100 PGA Tour Blvd.
Ponte Vedra Beach, FL 32082
Phone: 904-273-3520
Fax: 904-273-3588
Web: www.pgatour.com/company/internships.html

Phipps Conservatory and Botanical Gardens

Phipps Conservatory and Botanical Gardens Internships

Type of award: Internship.
Intended use: For full-time junior, senior or graduate study at accredited postsecondary institution.
Eligibility: Applicant must be U.S. citizen.
Basis for selection: Major/career interest in horticulture; landscape architecture; environmental science or botany. Applicant must demonstrate high academic achievement.
Additional information: Contact sponsor or visit Website for more information.

Number of awards:	6
Application deadline:	March 31

Contact:
Human Resources
Phipps Conservatory and Botanical Gardens
1059 Shady Ave.
Pittsburgh, PA 15232
Phone: 412-441-4442
Fax: 412-622-7363
Web: www.conservatory.org

Princeton Plasma Physics Laboratory

Plasma Physics National Undergraduate Fellowship Program

Type of award: Internship.
Intended use: For junior study.
Eligibility: Applicant must be U.S. citizen or permanent resident.
Basis for selection: Major/career interest in engineering; physics; mathematics or computer/information sciences. Applicant must demonstrate high academic achievement, depth of character, leadership, seriousness of purpose and service orientation.
Application requirements: Recommendations, essay, transcript.
Additional information: Minimum 3.5 GPA. Internship is ten weeks in the summer. Application due in mid-February.

Amount of award:	$4,800
Number of awards:	25
Number of applicants:	100
Application deadline:	February 28
Notification begins:	March 15

Princeton Plasma Physics Laboratory: Plasma Physics National Undergraduate Fellowship Program

Contact:
Princeton Plasma Physics Laboratory
P.O. Box 451, MS-40
Princeton, NJ 08543-0451
Phone: 609-243-2116
Web: www.pppl.gov

Random House

Random House Summer Internship Program

Type of award: Internship.
Intended use: For junior study at 4-year institution.
Basis for selection: Major/career interest in publishing. Applicant must demonstrate seriousness of purpose.
Application requirements: Resume, cover letter.
Additional information: Ten-week internship beginning in early June open to rising college seniors. All majors encouraged to apply. Apply in spring semester of junior year for New York program; Westminster program open to all undergrads. $450 per week stipend. Application accepted beginning online from January 1 to March 15. If invited, applicant must travel to New York City or Westminster, Maryland, at own expense for interview in late February through mid-April. See Website for application and more information.

Number of awards:	65
Number of applicants:	2,400
Application deadline:	March 15
Notification begins:	April 1

Contact:
Random House Internship Coordinator
Human Resources, 19th Floor
1745 Broadway
New York, NY 10019
Web: www.careers.randomhouse.com

Rhode Island State Government

Rhode Island State Government Internship Program

Type of award: Internship.
Intended use: For undergraduate or postgraduate study.
Basis for selection: Major/career interest in governmental public relations or public administration/service. Applicant must demonstrate high academic achievement, depth of character, leadership, seriousness of purpose and service orientation.
Application requirements: Interview, recommendations, transcript, proof of eligibility. Writing sample required (for law students only).
Additional information: Minimum 2.5 GPA. Summer program lasts eight weeks; spring and fall programs last entire semester. Fall application deadline is rolling. Compensation for summer interns only, at $100 per week. Spring and fall interns earn academic credit or work-study, if eligible. All placements in Rhode Island.

Number of awards:	243
Number of applicants:	450
Application deadline:	May 15, November 15

Contact:
Rhode Island State Government
State Capitol, Rm. 8AA
Providence, RI 02903
Phone: 401-222-6782
Fax: 401-222-4447

Seventeen Magazine

Seventeen Magazine Internship

Type of award: Internship.
Intended use: For undergraduate study at postsecondary institution.
Basis for selection: Major/career interest in journalism or design.
Application requirements: Portfolio, recommendations. Resume, cover letter. Student should submit writing samples, photos, layouts, or other work samples appropriate to the department in which he/she wishes to intern.
Additional information: Non-paying internship. Course credit is necessary. Spring (February-May) deadline is 11/15. Summer (June-August) deadline is 3/15. Fall (September-January) deadline is 7/15. Applicants with interest in photography also encouraged to apply. Please mail all resumes. Applicants should specify which one area of the magazine they wish to intern in (design, features, fashion, etc).

Number of applicants:	1,000

Contact:
Seventeen Magazine
Internship Coordinator
300 West 57th St., 17th Floor
New York, NY 10019
Phone: 646-280-1064

SGI (Silicon Graphics)

SGI (Silicon Graphics) Internship/Co-op Program

Type of award: Internship.
Intended use: For undergraduate or graduate study.
Basis for selection: Major/career interest in computer/information sciences; engineering, computer; engineering, electrical/electronic; mathematics; information systems; human resources; business or marketing.
Application requirements: Resume and cover letter.
Additional information: Positions, locations, and awards vary. Visit Website for internship descriptions and application deadlines, and to submit resume. Interns receive competitive salaries and paid holidays. Programs run for 10-12 weeks, from May to August or from June to September.

Number of awards:	10

Contact:
SGI (Silicon Graphics)
Internship Program
1140 E. Arquez Ave.
Sunnyvale, CA 94085
Web: www.sgi.com/employment

Simon and Schuster Inc.

Simon and Schuster Summer Internship Program

Type of award: Internship, renewable.
Intended use: For full-time junior or senior study at accredited vocational or 4-year institution.
Basis for selection: Major/career interest in publishing. Applicant must demonstrate high academic achievement.
Application requirements: Interview. Resume. Cover letter. Letter of interest.
Additional information: This is a nine-week, full-time program. Interns are paid $11 per hour. It runs from early June through early August, and is designed to train and recruit a diverse group of students interested in exploring careers in publishing. Applicants must have well-rounded extracurricular interests and work experience. Deadline is in the first week of April. This company also offers fall/spring internships for college credit only.
   Application deadline: April 1
Contact:
Simon and Schuster, Inc.
HR Department/Internship Program
1230 Avenue of the Americas
New York, NY 10020
Web: www.simonandschuster.com

Smithsonian Environmental Research Center

Smithsonian Environmental Research Center Internship Program

Type of award: Internship, renewable.
Intended use: For undergraduate or graduate study at 4-year or graduate institution. Designated institutions: Smithsonian Environmental Research Center in Edgewater, Maryland.
Basis for selection: Major/career interest in biology; chemistry; environmental science; engineering, environmental; physics; mathematics or education. Applicant must demonstrate seriousness of purpose.
Application requirements: Recommendations, essay, transcript.
Additional information: Projects are 40 hours per week, lasting from 10 to 16 weeks. Stipends are $400 per week and available during spring and summer months. Dorm space is available for $75 per week on limited basis. Several application deadlines: spring, November 15; summer, February 1; fall, June 1. Applicants should demonstrate academic credentials, relevant experience, and the congruence of student's expressed goals with those of Internship Program.

Number of awards: 25
Number of applicants: 250
Notification begins: March 15, December 15
Total amount awarded: $60,000
Contact:
Smithsonian Environmental Research Center
Internship Program
647 Contees Wharf Road
Edgewater, MD 21037
Phone: 443-428-2217
Fax: 443-428-2380
Web: www.serc.si.edu/pro_training

Smithsonian Institution

James E. Webb Internship Program for Minority Undergraduate Seniors and Graduate Students in Business and Public Administration

Type of award: Internship.
Intended use: For senior or graduate study at 4-year or graduate institution. Designated institutions: Smithsonian Institution.
Eligibility: Applicant must be African American, Puerto Rican or American Indian. Applicant must be U.S. citizen or permanent resident.
Basis for selection: Major/career interest in business/ management/administration or public administration/service. Applicant must demonstrate high academic achievement.
Application requirements: Recommendations, essay, transcript. Resume, cover sheets.
Additional information: Minimum 3.0 GPA. Applicant must be minority student enrolled as undergraduate senior or graduate student in business or public administration program. Selection based on relevance of internship at the Smithsonian to student's academic and career goals. Internships are full-time, 40 hours per week. Stipend is $500/week, with additional travel allowances offered in some cases. Contact sponsor or visit Website for more information and application.
   Application deadline: February 1, October 1
Contact:
Smithsonian Institution Office of Research Training and Services
470 L'Enfant Plaza, SW, Suite 7102, MRC 902
P.O. Box 37012
Washington, DC 20013-7012
Phone: 202-633-7070
Web: www.si.edu/research+study

Smithsonian Minority Internship

Type of award: Internship.
Intended use: For undergraduate or graduate study. Designated institutions: Smithsonian Institution.
Basis for selection: Major/career interest in anthropology; archaeology; ecology; environmental science; art/art history; museum studies; zoology or natural sciences.
Additional information: Research internships at Smithsonian Institution in anthropology/archaeology; astrophysics; earth sciences/paleontology; ecology; environmental, behavioral (tropical animals), evolutionary, and systematic biology; history of science and technology; history of art (including American

contemporary, African, Asian); 20th-century American crafts; social and cultural history and folk life of America. Applicants must have major/career interest in research or museum-related activity pursued by the Smithsonian Institution. Stipend of $500 a week for ten weeks. February 1 deadline for summer session and for fall; October 1 deadline for spring. U.S. minority students encouraged to apply. Contact Office of Research Training and Services for application procedures or visit Website.

   Application deadline: February 1, October 1
Contact:
Smithsonian Institution Office of Research Training and Services
470 L'Enfant Plaza, SW, Suite 7102, MRC 902
P.O. Box 37012
Washington, DC 20013-7012
Phone: 202-633-7070
Web: www.si.edu/research+study

Smithsonian Native American Internship

Type of award: Internship.
Intended use: For undergraduate or graduate study. Designated institutions: Smithsonian Institution.
Basis for selection: Major/career interest in Native American studies.
Additional information: Internship at Smithsonian Institution in research or museum activities related to Native American studies. Stipend of $500 a week for ten weeks. Deadline for summer and fall is February 1; spring is October 1. American Indian students encouraged to apply. Contact Office of Research Training and Services for application procedures or visit Website.

   Application deadline: February 1, October 1
Contact:
Smithsonian Institution Office of Research Training and Services
470 L'Enfant Plaza, SW, Suite 7102, MRC 902
P.O. Box 37012
Washington, DC 20013-7012
Phone: 202-633-7070
Web: www.si.edu/research+study

Society of Physics Students

Society of Physics Students Summer Internship Program

Type of award: Internship.
Intended use: For full-time undergraduate study.
Eligibility: Applicant or parent must be member/participant of Society of Physics Students.
Basis for selection: Major/career interest in physics. Applicant must demonstrate high academic achievement.
Application requirements: Recommendations, transcript. Resume and cover letter. Two letters of recommendation (one should be written by SPS advisor).
Additional information: Offers eight-week internships in science policy and research for undergraduate physics majors. Internships include $3,200 stipend, paid housing, and transportation supplement. Internships are based in Washington, DC. Applicants must be active SPS members with excellent scholastic record and experience in science outreach events or science research. See Website for application and deadline.

   Amount of award: $3,700
   Number of awards: 8
   Number of applicants: 40
   Application deadline: February 1
   Notification begins: March 15
Contact:
SPS Summer Internship Program
One Physics Ellipse
College Park, MD 20740
Phone: 301-209-3034
Fax: 301-209-0839
Web: www.spsnational.org/programs/interns.htm

Solomon R. Guggenheim Museum

Guggenheim Museum Internship

Type of award: Internship.
Intended use: For junior, senior or graduate study.
Eligibility: Applicant must be U.S. citizen, permanent resident or international student.
Basis for selection: Major/career interest in arts management; art/art history; arts, general; film/video; museum studies or museum studies/administration. Applicant must demonstrate high academic achievement.
Application requirements: Interview, recommendations, essay, transcript. Cover letter, resume. Separate list of relevant coursework and foreign languages. All official academic transcripts with official seal of universities. Essay should be 500 words and indicate interest in program and museum work, with reason for applying.
Additional information: International students must have J-1 visa. Applicant must have taken at least one modern art course. Summer application deadline is January 10. Fall deadline is May 1. Spring and fall internships are full- or part-time, with a minimum commitment of 15 hours/week for six months. Summer internships are full-time. See Website for list of individual programs and departments.

   Number of applicants: 300
   Application deadline: January 10, May 1
Contact:
Solomon R. Guggenheim Museum
Internship Coordinator
1071 Fifth Avenue
New York, NY 10128
Phone: 212-423-3526
Web: www.guggenheim.org

Peggy Guggenheim Internship

Type of award: Internship.
Intended use: For undergraduate or graduate study.
Basis for selection: Major/career interest in arts, general; art/art history or museum studies. Applicant must demonstrate high academic achievement, depth of character, leadership and seriousness of purpose.
Application requirements: Recommendations, essay, transcript. Resume.
Additional information: One- to three-month internship at Peggy Guggenheim Collection in Venice, Italy. Two deadlines: October 15 for internships between January and April;

December 1 for internships in May-December. Must be fluent in English with knowledge of spoken Italian. Interns receive a monthly stipend. Internships may be arranged for any one-, two-, or three-month period. Request further information and application forms from the Peggy Guggenheim Collection. Visit Website for details.

Number of awards:	139
Number of applicants:	800
Application deadline:	October 15, December 1
Notification begins:	December 1, February 15

Contact:
Peggy Guggenheim Collection Internship Coodinator
Palazzo Venier dei Leoni
701 Dorsoduro, 30123 Venice, Italy
Phone: 39-041-2405-401
Web: www.guggenheim.org

Sony Music Entertainment

Sony Credited Internship

Type of award: Internship.
Intended use: For undergraduate or graduate study at accredited postsecondary institution.
Basis for selection: Major/career interest in business; accounting; finance/banking; computer/information sciences; law; music; music management or marketing.
Application requirements: Interview, transcript, proof of eligibility. Resume and cover letter.
Additional information: Unpaid internship. Applicant must be available to work at least two full days a week. Internships are available in various departments throughout company. See Website for details. Deadlines for spring and fall are rolling. When applying, specify which semester you are applying for. Applicant must be enrolled at accredited university and provide verification of course credit. Send resume and cover letter in envelope clearly marked Sony Credited Internship.

Number of awards:	60
Number of applicants:	200

Contact:
Sony Music Entertainment
Internship Program Sky Lobby
550 Madison Avenue, 2nd Floor
New York, NY 10022-3211
Phone: 212-833-7980
Fax: 212-833-5774
Web: www.sonybmg.com

Southern Progress Corporation

Southern Progress Corporation Internship Program

Type of award: Internship.
Intended use: For junior, senior or graduate study.
Basis for selection: Major/career interest in journalism; graphic arts/design; marketing; advertising; accounting; information systems; landscape architecture or horticulture.

Application requirements: Recommendations, transcript. Cover letter, resume and writing/design samples (for editorial internships only).
Additional information: Summer and six-month internships in editorial, graphic design, market research, advertising, accounting, IT, and test kitchen departments. Internship available at Birmingham location only. Application deadlines: September 26 for first term (January-June), March 5 for second term (July-December), and February 6 for summer internships. Salary is $10/hour. Minimum 3.0 GPA. Recent graduates who received their bachelor's degree no more than one year prior to beginning of internship also eligible. Visit Website for details.

Number of awards:	90
Number of applicants:	500

Contact:
Meg Dedmon, Student Intern Coordinator
Southern Progress Corporation
2100 Lakeshore Drive
Birmingham, AL 35209
Web: www.southernprogress.com

Southface Energy Institute

Southface Internship

Type of award: Internship.
Intended use: For undergraduate or graduate study at accredited 2-year, 4-year or graduate institution in United States.
Eligibility: Applicant must be U.S. citizen, permanent resident or international student.
Basis for selection: Major/career interest in architecture; environmental science; engineering, environmental; urban planning; landscape architecture or business/management/administration. Applicant must demonstrate high academic achievement.
Application requirements: Statement of intent. Names of references with contact information.
Additional information: Internships cover variety of interests; sustainable building, community design, water-efficient landscaping, smart growth, environmental event planning, energy policy and tech assistance, non-profit marketing, and public relations. Six- to twelve-month positions available. Students work 40 hours per week; weekly stipend of $100. Shared housing is available if space permits. Transportation assistance available. Some part-time positions may be available. Applications accepted year-round. International students must have work authorization.

Contact:
Southface Energy Institute
241 Pine Street, NE
Atlanta, GA 30308
Phone: 404-872-3549
Fax: 404-872-5009
Web: www.southface.org

Spoleto Festival USA

Spoleto Festival Apprenticeship Program

Type of award: Internship, renewable.
Intended use: For undergraduate, graduate or non-degree study in United States.
Basis for selection: Major/career interest in arts management; arts, general; music; public relations or theater/production/technical. Applicant must demonstrate seriousness of purpose.
Additional information: Four-week apprenticeship with arts professionals producing and operating international arts festival. Posts available in media relations, special events, finance, box office, production, merchandising, orchestra management, education, artist services, and office administration. Weekly stipend, housing and travel allowance provided. See Website for details and deadlines.
   Number of awards: 50
Contact:
Spoleto Festival USA
Apprentice Program
14 George St.
Charleston, SC 29401
Web: www.spoletousa.org

Sports Journalism Institute

Aspiring Sports Journalist Internship

Type of award: Internship.
Intended use: For sophomore, junior or senior study.
Basis for selection: Major/career interest in journalism. Applicant must demonstrate high academic achievement and seriousness of purpose.
Application requirements: Recommendations, essay, transcript. Professional-style photo, up to seven writing samples, 500-word essay.
Additional information: The Sports Journalist Institute is a nine-week, summer training and internship program for undergraduate interested in sports journalism, followed by an eight-week paid internship at newspapers (to be determined individually). Applicants need not be journalism majors. Visit Website for more information and application.
   Amount of award: $500
   Number of awards: 10
   Application deadline: December 5
Contact:
Leon Carter
New York Daily News/sports
450 West 33rd Street
New York, NY 10001
Web: www.sportsjournalisminstitute.org or www.apse.dallasnews.com

Student Conservation Association

SCA Conservation Internships

Type of award: Internship, renewable.
Intended use: For undergraduate or graduate study at accredited postsecondary institution in United States.
Eligibility: Applicant must be U.S. citizen.
Basis for selection: Major/career interest in archaeology; ecology; forestry; natural resources/conservation; history; education; wildlife/fisheries; biology or communications.
Application requirements: Interview, recommendations.
Additional information: Internships include expenses such as food, travel, housing, and insurance. Positions at various locations in United States. Applicants are advised to apply three months prior to position start date. Rolling admissions process -- seven application deadlines per year. Applications received on or before February 1 may be considered for early selection. Applicants with interest in environmental education, interpretation, marine biology, and wilderness preservation also eligible. See Website for application.
   Amount of award: $4,725
Contact:
Admissions Department Student Conservation Association
P.O. Box 550
Charlestown, NH 03603
Phone: 603-543-1700
Fax: 603-543-1828
Web: www.thesca.org

Sun Microsystems

Sun Microsystems Student Intern and Co-op Program

Type of award: Internship.
Intended use: For full-time sophomore, junior, senior or graduate study at accredited 4-year or graduate institution in United States.
Eligibility: Applicant must be U.S. citizen, permanent resident or international student.
Basis for selection: Major/career interest in computer/information sciences; engineering, electrical/electronic; engineering, computer; engineering, mechanical; information systems; marketing; finance/banking; human resources or business/management/administration. Applicant must demonstrate high academic achievement.
Additional information: Foreign student must have unrestricted permission to work in United States. Students enrolled in industrial engineering degree program also eligible to apply. Must maintain GPA of 3.0 or higher. Visit Website to submit resume and sign up to search for current openings. Internships last 10 to 12 weeks but can be repeated. Best-qualified students contacted within two weeks. Most internships take place in San Francisco Bay Area (Broomfield and Burlington campuses) and in San Diego, Los Angeles, and Austin. Occasional positions elsewhere in United States.
Contact:
Apply through Website.
M/S UPAL01-471
Web: www.sun.com/studentzone

Tourism Cares

Mayflower Tours Patrick Murphy Internship

Type of award: Internship.
Intended use: For sophomore, junior, senior or graduate study in United States or Canada.
Basis for selection: Major/career interest in tourism/travel or hospitality administration/management. Applicant must demonstrate high academic achievement.
Application requirements: Essay, transcript. Resume.
Additional information: Intern will be assigned to work at office of Stephen Richer, National Tour Association Public Affairs Advocate. Internship lasts from September to December. $2,000 stipend. Must have excellent written, oral, and interpersonal skills. Check Website for updated information.
    Amount of award: $2,000
    Number of awards: 1
    Application deadline: April 1
    Total amount awarded: $2,000
Contact:
Toursim Cares
585 Washington Street
Canton, MA 02021
Phone: 781-821-5990
Fax: 781-821-8949
Web: www.tourismcares.org

Pat & Jim Host Internship/Scholarship

Type of award: Internship.
Intended use: For full-time undergraduate or graduate study at 4-year institution. Designated institutions: Eastern Kentucky University, Transylvania University, University of Kentucky.
Eligibility: Applicant must be residing in Kentucky.
Basis for selection: Major/career interest in tourism/travel; hotel/restaurant management or hospitality administration/management. Applicant must demonstrate high academic achievement.
Application requirements: Recommendations, essay, transcript. Copy of Kentucky driver's license. For returning students only: two letters of recommendation (one from tourism-related faculty member; other from tourism industry professional). Must also submit typewritten, referenced, and signed two- to five-page essay on why they have chosen to pursue a career in the hospitality/tourism industry.
Additional information: Minimum 3.0 GPA. Must be graduate of Kentucky High school. Scholarship includes an internship for the Alltech FEI World Equestrian Games 2010. Must demonstrate a clear focus on and commitment to tourism.
    Amount of award: $1,000
    Number of awards: 1
    Application deadline: April 1
    Notification begins: May 1
Contact:
Tourism Cares
585 Washington Street
Canton, MA 02021
Web: www.tourismcares.org

Twentieth Century Fox

Twentieth Century Fox Internship

Type of award: Internship.
Intended use: For full-time sophomore, junior, senior or graduate study at accredited 4-year or graduate institution in United States.
Eligibility: Applicant must be U.S. citizen, permanent resident or international student eligible to work in United States.
Basis for selection: Major/career interest in theater/production/technical; communications or film/video.
Application requirements: Resume and cover letter that includes areas of interest.
Additional information: Ten-week summer internships in many divisions of Fox Filmed Entertainment. Interns are eligible to participate in program for maximum of two semesters. Applicants must apply via Website.
Contact:
Twentieth Century Fox
Personnel Dept.
P.O. Box 900
Beverly Hills, CA 90123
Web: www.foxcareers.com

Tyson Foods, Inc.

Tyson Foods Intern Program

Type of award: Internship.
Intended use: For full-time undergraduate study at accredited vocational, 2-year or 4-year institution.
Basis for selection: Major/career interest in computer/information sciences; food science/technology or engineering, agricultural. Applicant must demonstrate high academic achievement.
Application requirements: Proof of eligibility. Resume and cover letter.
Additional information: Paid summer internships in computer programming, industrial engineering, livestock (pork) procurement, quality assurance, carcass sales, and production. Program locations across the United States. Must be eligible to work in the country. Visit Website for job descriptions and list of campus recruiting events, or to submit resume and cover letter. Deadline for Summer is 4/15, but year-round internships w/ rolling deadlines are offered as well.
    Number of awards: 120
    Application deadline: April 15
Contact:
College Relations Representative
Tyson Foods, Inc.
2210 West Oaklawn Drive (CP 425)
Springdale, AR 72762-6999
Fax: 479-290-4000
Web: www.tysonfoodsinc.com

United Negro College Fund

Oracle Scholars Internship Program

Type of award: Internship.
Intended use: For junior or senior study at 4-year institution in United States. Designated institutions: UNCF member institutions; HBCU schools.
Eligibility: Applicant must be African American. Applicant must be residing in Virginia or California.
Basis for selection: Major/career interest in business; marketing; finance/banking; engineering; human resources; computer/information sciences or accounting. Applicant must demonstrate high academic achievement.
Application requirements: Recommendations, transcript. Resume, statement of career interests, and financial need statement.
Additional information: Minimum 3.0 GPA. Award is an 8-week paid summer internship at an Oracle location, which includes a $4,000 monthly salary; housing accommodations or monthly housing allowance; and round-trip transportation from school to internship location and local transportation to and from internship site. There is also a $10,000 scholarship available upon successful completion of the internship. Completed applications with all supporting documentation should be forwarded to UNCF/Oracle Scholars Internship Program. Once applications are submitted, UNCF will identify the top-ranked candidates; these candidates will be sent to Oracle for review and final selection.
   Application deadline: February 1
Contact:
UNCF/Oracle Scholarship Interns Program Attn: Marquis Miller
8260 Willow Oaks Corporate Drive
P.O. Box 1044
Fairfax, VA 22031-8044
Phone: 800-331-2244
Web: www.uncf.org

United States Holocaust Memorial Museum

United States Holocaust Memorial Museum Internship

Type of award: Internship, renewable.
Intended use: For sophomore, junior, senior or graduate study.
Eligibility: Applicant must be U.S. citizen, permanent resident or international student.
Basis for selection: Major/career interest in museum studies/administration; history; English; foreign languages; communications; geography; graphic arts/design; communications or law.
Application requirements: Interview, recommendations, transcript. Resume, cover letter, brief personal statement.
Additional information: Semester-long internships available during summer, fall, and spring in Holocaust research and museum studies. Phone interviews conducted with top qualified candidates. Not all positions paid. Applicants interested in German or Eastern European studies also eligible. Application deadline is March 15 for summer; July 1 for fall; October 15 for spring. Apply online. All applicants subject to criminal background check. International students must have work authorization.
Contact:
Internship Coordinator, Office of Volunteer and Intern Services
United States Holocaust Memorial Museum
100 Raoul Wallenburg Place, SW
Washington, DC 20024-2150
Phone: 202-479-9737
Fax: 202-488-6568
Web: www.ushmm.org

United States Senate

United States Senate Member Internships

Type of award: Internship.
Intended use: For full-time undergraduate study at accredited 4-year institution.
Eligibility: Applicant must be U.S. citizen or permanent resident.
Basis for selection: Major/career interest in political science/government; law; communications; public relations; public administration/service or economics. Applicant must demonstrate high academic achievement.
Application requirements: Resume, cover letter, writing sample.
Additional information: Senators administer their own internship programs complete with unique and more specific guidelines. Senate member interns generally reside or attend college in senator's state. Positions available in Washington, D.C., or member's state. Internships may be unpaid or (less frequently) paid, but generally offer assistance obtaining college credit. Term of service, eligibility vary. Some internships restricted to upper-level undergraduates. Contact individual senator's office directly. Visit Website for complete links to member sites, e-mail addresses, and telephone contact numbers.
Contact:
Office of (Name of Senator)
United States Senate
Washington, DC 20510
Web: www.senate.gov

U.S. Department of Agriculture

USDA Summer Intern Program

Type of award: Internship.
Intended use: For undergraduate or graduate study.
Eligibility: Applicant must be U.S. citizen.
Application requirements: Transcript. Resume, U.S. government forms.
Additional information: Internships last approximately four months (May to August). Stipends are based on level of education, prior experience, and position. Various internships available, at different agencies. Open to undergraduates and high school graduates entering college. Applications available in late December. All majors encouraged to apply. Deadline varies. See Website for more information.

Notification begins: May 31
Contact:
Contact individual agencies or see Website.
Web: www.usda.gov

U.S. Department of Energy

Student Research at the U.S. Army Edgewood Chemical Biological Center

Type of award: Internship, renewable.
Intended use: For undergraduate or graduate study at accredited 4-year or graduate institution in United States. Designated institutions: U.S. Army Edgewood Chemical Biological Center (Aberdeen Proving Ground, MD) and other approved locations.
Eligibility: Applicant must be U.S. citizen.
Basis for selection: Major/career interest in biology; computer/information sciences; engineering; environmental science; physical sciences or science, general.
Additional information: Provides opportunities to participate in research and development in support of military missions. Three months to one year; full-time or part-time appointments. Stipend based on research area and academic classification. Applications accepted year-round. Funded by U.S. Army Edgewood Chemical Biological Center through interagency agreement with U.S. Department of Energy.
Contact:
Web: www.orau.gov/orise/educ.htm

U.S. Department of State

U.S. Department of State Internship

Type of award: Internship.
Intended use: For junior, senior or graduate study at accredited 4-year or graduate institution.
Eligibility: Applicant must be U.S. citizen.
Basis for selection: Major/career interest in political science/government; foreign languages; governmental public relations; business; public administration/service; social work; economics; information systems; journalism or science, general. Applicant must demonstrate high academic achievement.
Application requirements: Transcript. Statement of interest.
Additional information: Applicant must be continuing student. Provides opportunities working in varied administrative branches of the Department of State, both abroad and in Washington, D.C. Internships are generally unpaid, but many institutions provide academic credit and/or financial assistance for overseas assignments. Paid internships primarily granted to students in financial need. Must be able to work a minimum of ten weeks. Selected students must undergo background investigation to receive security clearance. Deadlines: November 1 for summer, March 1 for fall, July 1 for spring. Contact intern coordinator or visit Website for further details.
Application deadline: March 1, July 1

Contact:
Intern Coordinator
U.S. Department of State
2401 E Street, NW, Room H518
Washington, DC 20522
Web: www.state.gov

U.S. House of Representatives

House Member Internships

Type of award: Internship, renewable.
Intended use: For full-time undergraduate study.
Eligibility: Applicant must be U.S. citizen or permanent resident.
Basis for selection: Major/career interest in political science/government; public administration/service; public relations or communications. Applicant must demonstrate high academic achievement.
Additional information: Members of the United Stated House of Representatives use undergraduate interns for a variety of jobs including constituent contact, research and correspondence. Positions are based in Congressional District Offices and in Washington, DC. Internships generally facilitate course credit, but offer no stipend. Some paid internships are funded through private nonprofit organizations. Information about the individual House member intern programs can usually be found online. A complete set of links to representatives' sites is available at www.house.gov. In general, applicants residing in the member's home district and enrolled in the same political party are favored. Typically, many Washington, D.C.-based internships are filled by students from outside the member district. Applicants may also be interested in working for congressperson serving on committee (i.e. Agriculture, Financial Services) relevant to their major. Interested parties should contact the representative with whom they are interested in working.
Contact:
Contact individual congressman/congresswoman's office
Phone: 202-224-3121
Web: www.house.gov/house/MemberWWW.html

U.S. National Arboretum

U.S. National Arboretum Internship

Type of award: Internship.
Intended use: For undergraduate or graduate study at postsecondary institution.
Eligibility: Applicant must be U.S. citizen.
Basis for selection: Major/career interest in horticulture; botany; agriculture or forestry.
Application requirements: Transcript. Resume and cover letter.
Additional information: Internships pay stipend of $10.94/hr. Average workday for most interns: Monday through Friday, 7am to 3:30pm. Provides opportunity to gain experience in plant research in premier horticultural collection. Applicants need to have completed coursework or have acquired practical experience in horticulture or related field. Basic gardening or

U.S. National Arboretum: U.S. National Arboretum Internship

laboratory skills, interest in plants, strong communication skills, and ability to work independently preferred. Course credit may be arranged. See Website for deadlines, application requirements, and more information.
   Number of awards: 7
   Number of applicants: 30
Contact:
Internship Coordinator
U.S. National Arboretum
3501 New York Avenue, NE
Washington, DC 20002-1958
Phone: 202-245-2708
Fax: 202-245-4575
Web: www.usna.usda.gov

Wachovia

Finance Undergraduate Internships

Type of award: Internship.
Intended use: For full-time junior or senior study at accredited 4-year institution.
Eligibility: Applicant must be U.S. citizen or permanent resident.
Basis for selection: Major/career interest in finance/banking; accounting; business/management/administration or economics. Applicant must demonstrate high academic achievement and leadership.
Application requirements: Resume and cover letter.
Additional information: Ten-week program that consists of work assignments and professional development opportunities. Annual start date is on or around June 1. Number of awards varies; most positions located in Charlotte, North Carolina. Visit Website to apply online. Graduate program also offered. Minimum 3.0 GPA.
Contact:
Apply through Wachovia Website.
Web: www.wachovia.com/college

Wall Street Journal

Wall Street Journal Internship

Type of award: Internship.
Intended use: For undergraduate or graduate study.
Basis for selection: Major/career interest in journalism.
Application requirements: Cover letter, resume and 12 bylined clips (letter- or legal-sized).
Additional information: Full-time summer internship lasts ten weeks. Previous journalism or college newspaper experience required. Interns paid $700 a week. All majors encouraged to apply. Currently enrolled students only.
   Number of awards: 18
   Number of applicants: 328
   Application deadline: November 1
   Notification begins: February 28
   Total amount awarded: $7,000

Contact:
WSJ Intern Application Cathy Panagoulias Asst. Managing Editor
The Wall Street Journal
200 Liberty Street
New York, NY 10281
Web: www.dowjones.com/Careers/Careers.htm

The Walt Disney Company

Disney Professional Internships

Type of award: Internship.
Intended use: For junior or senior study at 2-year or 4-year institution in United States. Designated institutions: Walt Disney World, Disneyland, Walt Disney Imagineering.
Eligibility: Applicant must be U.S. citizen, permanent resident or international student.
Basis for selection: Major/career interest in architecture; construction management; engineering; finance/banking; food production/management/services; human resources; marketing; hospitality administration/management; science, general or computer/information sciences. Applicant must demonstrate high academic achievement, seriousness of purpose and service orientation.
Application requirements: Interview. Resume and cover letter.
Additional information: Program open to students participating in the Disney College Program. Pay rates and schedules vary by location. Must have valid driver's license. Housing may be available. International students must have valid student visa. Please visit Website for more information and application deadline. Visit www.disneycareers.com to search for openings.
   Number of awards: 300
Contact:
Disney Professional Recruiting
P.O. Box 10000
Lake Buena Vista, FL 32830
Phone: 800-722-2930
Web: www.disneyinterns.com

Walt Disney World and Disneyland

Disney College Program

Type of award: Internship.
Intended use: For undergraduate study.
Eligibility: Applicant must be U.S. citizen, permanent resident or international student.
Basis for selection: Based on strong communication skills, understanding of Guest Service principles, ability to work independently and/or with a large team. Major/career interest in animal sciences or communications.
Application requirements: Interview, recommendations. Online application, interview (for Disneyland, additional web-based interview also required).
Additional information: Applicant must have completed one semester at college or university. Must view Disney College Program presentation (online or on campus) to interview for

program. Students participate in college-level coursework, and may be able to earn college credit. Students placed at Walt Disney World (Orlando, FL) are guaranteed a minimum of 30-45 hours per week with additional hours during peak periods. Starting pay range is $6.79-8.14/hour. Company-sponsored housing is available. Students placed at Disneyland (Anaheim, CA) must live in Southern California or arrange for own housing. Disneyland schedules and pay rates vary by role. See Website for application and more information.
   Number of awards: 10,000
   Application deadline: April 15, November 15
Contact:
Walt Disney World College Recruiting
P.O. Box 10090
Lake Buena Vista, FL 32830
Phone: 800-722-2930
Web: www.disneycollegeprogram.com

Washington Internships for Students of Engineering

Washington Internships for Students of Engineering

Type of award: Internship.
Intended use: For junior, senior or graduate study.
Eligibility: Applicant must be U.S. citizen or permanent resident.
Basis for selection: Major/career interest in engineering or computer/information sciences.
Application requirements: Recommendations, transcript. Reference forms.
Additional information: Ten-week summer internship available to students who have completed three years of study. Interns write required research paper as part of process. Fare card for Washington metro system supplied. Lodging expenses covered. Must be member of ANS, ASCE, ASME, or IEEE. IEEE will sponsor computer science majors.
   Amount of award: $2,100
   Number of awards: 3
   Application deadline: February 10
Contact:
Washington Internships for Students of Engineering
c/o IEEE - USA
1828 L St. NW Suite 1202
Washington, DC 20036
Phone: 202-785-0017
Fax: 202-785-0835
Web: www.wise-intern.org

Wilhelmina Models

Wilhelmina Models Internship

Type of award: Internship.
Intended use: For undergraduate or graduate study.
Eligibility: Applicant must be U.S. citizen or permanent resident.
Basis for selection: Major/career interest in fashion/fashion design/modeling. Applicant must demonstrate seriousness of purpose and service orientation.
Application requirements: Recommendations. Cover letter, resume.
Additional information: Internships available in New York City. Stipend of $35 a day to cover lunch and travel expenses. High school graduates, undergraduates, recent college graduates and graduate students eligible. Interns assist booking agents in men's, women's, children's, and marketing divisions.
   Number of applicants: 1,000
Contact:
Internship Coordinator
Dawn Messinger
300 Park Ave. S.
New York, NY 10010
Web: www.wilhelmina.com

Wolf Trap Foundation for the Performing Arts

Wolf Trap Foundation for the Performing Arts Internship

Type of award: Internship.
Intended use: For sophomore, junior, senior or graduate study in United States.
Eligibility: Applicant must be U.S. citizen, permanent resident or international student.
Basis for selection: Major/career interest in performing arts or arts management. Applicant must demonstrate seriousness of purpose.
Application requirements: Recommendations, essay. Cover letter outlining career goals and specifying internship desired; resume; two letters of recommendation. Two writing samples (except technical, scenic painting, costuming, stage management, accounting, graphic design, photography, or information systems applicants). Graphic design applicants must submit three design samples.
Additional information: Deadline for full-time summer internships is March 1; deadline for part-time fall internships is July 1; deadline for part-time spring internships is November 1. Stipend ($210/week in summer, $126/week in fall and spring) provided to help offset housing and travel expenses. College credit available. Applicant must have own transportation. Internships available in the following areas: opera (directing, administrative, stage management, technical, costume, scenic/prop painting); education; development; communications and marketing (advertising, marketing, graphic design, publications, media relations, photography, Web design, multimedia); human resources; ticket services; information systems; intellectual property; arts education; accounting; and special events. Notification begins approximately one month following application deadline. International students must meet INS I-9 requirement. Visit Website for internship descriptions.
   Number of awards: 35
   Application deadline: March 1

Contact:
Wolf Trap Foundation for the Performing Arts
Internship Program
1645 Trap Road
Vienna, VA 22182
Phone: 800-404-8461
Fax: 703-255-1924
Web: www.wolftrap.org

Women's Sports Foundation

Women's Sports Foundation Internship

Type of award: Internship, renewable.
Intended use: For undergraduate or graduate study in United States.
Basis for selection: Major/career interest in sports/sports administration. Applicant must demonstrate high academic achievement.
Application requirements: Interview. Resume and two letters of recommendation.
Additional information: Internship set up to provide sports management students with exposure to sports industry. Open to students or women in career change. Stipend is $800 to $900 per month, with minimum six-month term and a maximum length of one year. Internships available in two sessions: January to June and June to December. Download application from Website.

- **Number of awards:** 6
- **Number of applicants:** 50

Contact:
Women's Sports Foundation
Eisenhower Park
East Meadow, NY 11554
Phone: 800-227-3988
Web: www.womenssportsfoundation.org

World Security Institute

World Security Institute Internship

Type of award: Internship.
Intended use: For undergraduate or graduate study.
Basis for selection: Major/career interest in political science/government; military science; international relations; communications or computer/information sciences. Applicant must demonstrate high academic achievement, depth of character, leadership, seriousness of purpose and service orientation.
Application requirements: Recommendations, essay, transcript. Resume and cover letter stating interests and reasons for wanting to work at WSI. Writing sample of 3-5 pages long. Two letters of recommendation.
Additional information: Intended for graduates and highly qualified undergraduates. Students must work full time for internship's duration (three to five months) to receive monthly stipend of $1,000. Internships divided into three sections: research, television, and Web design/software support. Deadlines are March 1, July 1, and October 1 for the summer, fall, and spring semesters, respectively. Notification begins on April 1, August 1, and November 1. Check Website for latest information.

- **Amount of award:** $3,000-$5,000
- **Number of awards:** 12
- **Number of applicants:** 100
- **Application deadline:** May 1, September 1
- **Notification begins:** July 22, November 7

Contact:
World Security Institute
1779 Massachusetts Avenue, NW
Washington, DC 20036
Phone: 202-332-0600
Fax: 202-462-4559
Web: www.worldsecurityinstitute.org/jobs.cfm

Loans

Alaska Commission on Postsecondary Education

Alaska Family Education Loan

Type of award: Loan, renewable.
Intended use: For full-time undergraduate or graduate study at postsecondary institution. Designated institutions: College/universities or career education programs at least two years in operation that complete a program participation agreement with the Alaska Commission on Postsecondary Education.
Eligibility: Applicant must be U.S. citizen or permanent resident residing in Alaska.
Application requirements: Proof of eligibility.
Additional information: Borrower may apply for 5 percent loan on behalf of family member if the borrower is an AK resident of at least one year, is credit-worthy or has a cosigner, does not have status at time of loan that would prevent repayment. Both borrower and student may not or ever have been delinquent in child support, must comply with selective service, may not have had student loan written off unless discharged in bankruptcy in the last five years, and may not have been delinquent or defaulted on prior student loans. Must apply annually. Award amounts: $6,500/year for career education program; $8,500 for undergraduate; $9,500 for graduate. Maximum for undergraduate is $42,500; graduate student, $47,500. Total per student: $60,000; total per borrower: $102,000.
   Amount of award: $6,500-$9,500
Contact:
Alaska Commission on Postsecondary Education
Alaska Student Loan
P.O. Box 110505
Juneau, AK 99811-0505
Phone: 800-441-2962
Fax: 907-465-5316
Web: www.alaskadvantage.state.ak.us

Alaska Teacher Education Loan

Type of award: Loan, renewable.
Intended use: For full-time undergraduate study at accredited 4-year institution. Designated institutions: Institutions that complete program participation agreement with the Alaska Commission on Postsecondary Education.
Eligibility: Applicant must be U.S. citizen or permanent resident residing in Alaska.
Basis for selection: Major/career interest in education, teacher or education, early childhood.
Application requirements: Recommendations, proof of eligibility, nomination by school districts, preference given to rural districts. Application for nomination obtained from local school board. Statement of intent for teaching career.
Additional information: Must be in program to be elementary or secondary school teacher. May borrow up to $37,500 in total. Must reapply each year. Applicant must meet requirements for teachers set by student's local school board. Must be graduate of AK high school. May not have past-due child support or status at application that will prevent repayment. Must be credit-worthy or have cosigner. Must comply with selective service. Eligible for forgiveness of percentage of loan and interest in each of first five years borrower teaches in rural AK elementary or secondary school: 15 percent for years one to three; 25 percent for year four; and 30 percent for over four years.
   Amount of award: $7,500
   Application deadline: July 1
Contact:
Alaska Commission on Postsecondary Education
Alaska Teacher Education Loan
P.O. Box 110505
Juneau, AK 99811-0505
Phone: 800-441-2962
Fax: 907-465-5316
Web: www.alaskadvantage.state.ak.us

Alaska Winn Brindle (W.B.) Memorial Education Loan Program

Type of award: Loan, renewable.
Intended use: For full-time undergraduate or graduate study at accredited postsecondary institution. Designated institutions: Institutions that complete program participation agreement with the Alaska Commission on Postsecondary Education.
Eligibility: Applicant must be U.S. citizen or permanent resident residing in Alaska.
Basis for selection: Major/career interest in wildlife/fisheries.
Application requirements: Proof of eligibility.
Additional information: Five percent-interest loan may not exceed tuition, fees, books and supplies, room and board, and limited transportation. Loan may not be for more than eight years of undergraduate/graduate study. Availability of loans is subject to annual funding levels. Preference to applicants nominated by private donors to memorial education loan account. Recipients qualify for forgiveness up to 10 percent of loan for each of first five years employed in fishery-related field. Must be current in repayment. No past-due child support. Must be creditworthy or have cosigner. Must comply with selective service.
Contact:
Alaska Commission on Postsecondary Education
Winn Brindle Memorial Education Loan
P.O. Box 110505
Juneau, AK 99811-0505
Phone: 800-441-2962
Fax: 907-465-5316
Web: www.alaskadvantage.state.ak.us

American Legion Kentucky Auxiliary

Mary Barrett Marshall Student Loan Fund

Type of award: Loan, renewable.
Intended use: For undergraduate study at vocational, 2-year or 4-year institution. Designated institutions: Eligible postsecondary institutions in Kentucky.
Eligibility: Applicant must be female. Applicant must be residing in Kentucky. Applicant must be descendant of veteran; or dependent of veteran; or spouse of veteran or deceased veteran.
Basis for selection: Applicant must demonstrate financial need.
Application requirements: SASE.
Additional information: Maximum $800 per year, payable monthly without interest after graduation or upon securing employment; 6% interest after five years.
   Amount of award: $800
   Application deadline: April 1
Contact:
American Legion Auxiliary, Department of Kentucky
Chairman Velma Greenleaf
1448 Leafdale Rd.
Hodgenville, KY 42748-9379
Phone: 720-358-3341

American Legion South Dakota

American Legion South Dakota Educational Loan

Type of award: Loan, renewable.
Intended use: For undergraduate study at vocational, 2-year or 4-year institution.
Eligibility: Applicant must be residing in South Dakota. Applicant must be dependent of veteran.
Additional information: Up to $1,500 per year; $3,000 maximum; 3% interest on unpaid balance.
   Amount of award: $1,500-$3,000
   Application deadline: November 1, May 1
Contact:
American Legion South Dakota
Department Adjutant
P.O. Box 67
Watertown, SD 57201-0067
Phone: 605-886-3604

American Society of Mechanical Engineers

ASME Student Loan Program

Type of award: Loan, renewable.
Intended use: For full-time undergraduate or graduate study in United States or Canada.
Eligibility: Applicant or parent must be member/participant of American Society of Mechanical Engineers.
Basis for selection: Major/career interest in engineering, mechanical. Applicant must demonstrate financial need.
Application requirements: Recommendations.
Additional information: Applicant must be member of ASME in United States, Canada or Mexico, and enrolled in mechanical engineering or mechanical engineering technology program/courses. Minimum 2.2 GPA for undergraduates; minimum 3.2 GPA for graduates. Award is $3,000 per year; $9,000 maximum for undergraduate degree. Download application from Website.
   Amount of award: $3,000
   Application deadline: April 15
Contact:
American Society of Mechanical Engineers
Three Park Avenue
New York, NY 10016-5990
Phone: 212-591-8131
Fax: 212-591-7856
Web: www.asme.org/education/college/financialaid

American Society of Mechanical Engineers Auxiliary

ASME Auxiliary Student Loan

Type of award: Loan.
Intended use: For junior, senior or graduate study at accredited 4-year or graduate institution in United States. Designated institutions: ABET-accredited institutions with mechanical engineering or engineering technology curricula.
Eligibility: Applicant or parent must be member/participant of American Society of Mechanical Engineers. Applicant must be U.S. citizen.
Basis for selection: Major/career interest in engineering, mechanical. Applicant must demonstrate financial need, high academic achievement and depth of character.
Application requirements: References. Financial statement.
Additional information: Loans are interest-free until graduation. No application deadline. Must be ASME member. Visit Website for information and to download application or send SASE to address.
   Amount of award: $5,000
   Number of awards: 5
   Number of applicants: 7
Contact:
Susan Hawthorne
Whitehorse Village, S. #121
535 Gradyville Road
Newtown Square, PA 19073-2814
Phone: 610-688-4826
Web: www.asme.org/auxiliary

Arkansas Department of Higher Education

Arkansas Department of Higher Education Teacher Assistance Resource (STAR) Program

Type of award: Loan, renewable.
Intended use: For full-time sophomore, junior or senior study.
Eligibility: Applicant must be U.S. citizen or permanent resident residing in Arkansas.
Basis for selection: Major/career interest in education, teacher; education, special or education. Applicant must demonstrate financial need.
Additional information: Applicant must have been AR resident for at least six months. Must agree to teach in geographical teacher shortage area or subject shortage area of math, science, foreign language, or special education. Minimum 2.75 GPA. Recipients required to teach one year for every year loan received in order to have loan forgiven. Possibility of equal amount of federal loan forgiveness. If not enrolled in Associates of Art in Teaching program, must have passed Praxis I examination and declared teacher education major.

Amount of award:	$3,000-$6,000
Application deadline:	June 1
Total amount awarded:	$1,500,000

Contact:
Arkansas Department of Higher Education
114 E. Capitol Street
Little Rock, AR 72201
Phone: 800-54-STUDY
Fax: 501-371-2001
Web: www.adhe.edu/star.html

Arkansas Minority Teachers Scholarship Program

Type of award: Loan, renewable.
Intended use: For full-time junior or senior study at accredited 4-year institution.
Eligibility: Applicant must be Asian American, African American, Mexican American, Hispanic American, Puerto Rican or American Indian. Applicant must be U.S. citizen or permanent resident residing in Arkansas.
Basis for selection: Major/career interest in education, teacher.
Application requirements: Transcript.
Additional information: Applicant must have completed at least 60 credit hours, intend to teach in Arkansas public schools, and have minimum 2.5 GPA. If not in teacher licensure program, must have passed Praxis I examination. Loan forgiveness 20% per year for teaching in Arkansas public schools or 33% per year in Arkansas teacher shortage area (the Delta Region; math, science, or foreign language; or African-American male elementary school teachers). Must reside in Arkansas six months before application. Award for up to four semesters. Visit Website or call 501-371-2050 or 800-54-STUDY for application.

Amount of award:	$5,000
Number of awards:	100
Application deadline:	June 1
Total amount awarded:	$500,000

Contact:
Arkansas Department of Higher Education
114 E. Capitol Street
Little Rock, AR 72201-3818
Phone: 800-547-8839
Web: www.adhe.edu/mteachers.html

California Student Aid Commission

California Assumption Program of Loans for Education (APLE)

Type of award: Loan, renewable.
Intended use: For junior, senior or graduate study at accredited postsecondary institution. Designated institutions: California postsecondary institutions with Commission on Teacher Credentialing-approved programs.
Eligibility: Applicant must be U.S. citizen residing in California.
Basis for selection: Major/career interest in education, teacher or education, special. Applicant must demonstrate financial need and high academic achievement.
Application requirements: Proof of eligibility, nomination by participating institution.
Additional information: June 30th is priority deadline. Must have outstanding educational loans in good status. Participants receive awards after providing eligible teaching service with a credential in designated teacher-shortage area. Loans assumed for up to four years: up to $2,000 for first year, and up to $3,000 for second, third, and fourth years of consecutive service. Those who agree to teach math, science, or special education may receive up to $1,000 of additional loan assumption benefits each year. Another annual $1,000 of benefits may be received by those teaching math, science, or education specialist instruction in schools ranked in API lowest 20 percentile for a maximum of $19,000. Applicants must be pursuing teaching credentials for K-12.

Amount of award:	$19,000
Number of awards:	7,400
Number of applicants:	50,000
Application deadline:	June 30

Contact:
California Student Aid Commission
Specialized Programs Operations Branch
P.O. Box 419029
Rancho Cordova, CA 95741-9029
Phone: 888-224-7268
Fax: 916-526-7977
Web: www.csac.ca.gov

Connecticut Higher Education Supplemental Loan Authority

Connecticut Family Education Loan Program (CT FELP)

Type of award: Loan.
Intended use: For undergraduate or graduate study in United States. Designated institutions: Non-profit institutions (non-residents must attend Connecticut non-profit institution to be eligible).
Eligibility: Applicant must be residing in Connecticut.
Application requirements: Alien registration receipt card (I-151 or I-551) for non-citizens.
Additional information: Visit Website for online application.
   Amount of award: $2,000
   Number of applicants: 1,668
   Total amount awarded: $25,564,009
Contact:
Connecticut Higher Education Supplemental Loan Authority (CHESLA)
342 North Main Street
Suite 202
West Hartford, CT 06117
Phone: 800-252-FELP (CT) 860-236-1400 (out of state)
Web: www.chesla.org

Delaware Higher Education Commission

Christa McAuliffe Teacher Incentive Program

Type of award: Loan, renewable.
Intended use: For undergraduate study at accredited 4-year institution.
Eligibility: Applicant must be U.S. citizen or permanent resident residing in Delaware.
Basis for selection: Major/career interest in education, teacher. Applicant must demonstrate high academic achievement.
Application requirements: Essay, transcript.
Additional information: Applicant must be high school senior with a combined score of 1570 on the SAT and rank in top half of class, or undergraduate with minimum 2.75 GPA. Preference given to applicants planning to teach in critical need area as defined by DE Department of Education. Though award is for full-time students, it may be prorated for part-time students in a qualifying program. Loan not to exceed cost of tuition, fees, and other direct educational expenses. Loan forgiveness provision at rate of one year of teaching in a DE public school for one year of loan. Visit Website for deadline information.
   Number of applicants: 108
   Notification begins: June 15
Contact:
Delaware Higher Education Commission
820 North French Street
Wilmington, DE 19801
Phone: 302-577-5240
Fax: 302-577-6765
Web: www.doe.k12.de.us/programs/dhec/how_to_apply/financial_aid

Delaware Nursing Incentive Program

Type of award: Loan, renewable.
Intended use: For undergraduate study at accredited vocational, 2-year or 4-year institution in United States. Designated institutions: Colleges with accredited nursing programs that lead to RN, LPN, or BSN certification.
Eligibility: Applicant must be U.S. citizen or permanent resident residing in Delaware.
Basis for selection: Major/career interest in nursing. Applicant must demonstrate high academic achievement.
Application requirements: Essay, transcript.
Additional information: Loan-forgiveness for practicing nursing at state-owned hospital or clinic, one year for each year of loan. High school seniors must rank in top half of class and have at least 2.5 GPA. Though award generally for full-time students who are residents of DE, current state employees do not have to be DE residents and may be considered for part-time enrollment. RNs with five or more years of state service may enroll in BSN program full or part time. Loan not to exceed cost of tuition, fees, and other direct educational expenses. Visit Website for deadline information.
   Number of applicants: 53
   Notification begins: June 15
Contact:
Delaware Higher Education Commission
820 North French Street
Wilmington, DE 19801
Phone: 302-577-5240
Fax: 302-577-6765
Web: www.doe.k12.de.us/programs/dhec/how_to_apply/financial_aid

Florida Department of Education

Critical Teacher Shortage Student Loan Forgiveness Program

Type of award: Loan, renewable.
Intended use: For undergraduate certificate or post-bachelor's certificate study at 4-year or graduate institution in United States.
Eligibility: Applicant must be U.S. citizen or permanent resident residing in Florida.
Basis for selection: Major/career interest in education, teacher; education, special or education.
Additional information: Must be full-time teacher in critical teacher shortage subject area in Florida public or developmental research school. Must have graduated from undergraduate or graduate teacher preparation program and have been certified in critical teacher shortage subject area. Applicants must apply within 12 months of certification and teach full-time in critical

subject area for at least 90 days. Loan must be repaid by teaching in Florida public school or in cash. Visit Website for application and more information. Applications may also be obtained from public school district office or Florida Department of Education, Office of Student Financial Assistance.

    Amount of award: $2,500-$10,000
    Application deadline: July 15

Contact:
Florida Department of Education
Office of Student Financial Assistance
1940 North Monroe Street, Suite 70
Tallahassee, FL 32303-4759
Phone: 888-827-2004
Web: www.FloridaStudentFinancialAid.org

Franklin Lindsay Student Aid Fund

Franklin Lindsay Student Aid Loan

Type of award: Loan, renewable.
Intended use: For full-time sophomore, junior, senior or graduate study at accredited postsecondary institution in United States. Designated institutions: Texas institutions approved by Southern Association of Accredited Schools.
Eligibility: Applicant must be U.S. citizen residing in Texas.
Basis for selection: Applicant must demonstrate financial need, depth of character, seriousness of purpose and service orientation.
Application requirements: Interview.
Additional information: Must have 2.0 GPA for undergraduates and 3.0 for graduates. Full-time study requires 12 credit hours undergraduate, nine credit hours graduate. Must have completed 24 credits before applying. Upon graduation or termination from school, loan goes to repayment structure at four percent, with maximum payment term of seven years. Visit Website for more information.

    Amount of award: $7,000
    Number of applicants: 248

Contact:
Franklin Lindsay Student Aid Fund
JPMorgan Chase Bank, N.A.
P.O. Box 227237
Dallas, TX 75222-7237
Phone: 866-300-6222
Fax: 214-965-2921
Web: www.franklinlindsay.org

Georgia Student Finance Commission

Georgia Promise Teacher Scholarship

Type of award: Loan, renewable.
Intended use: For junior or senior study at accredited 4-year institution. Designated institutions: Public or private colleges/universities in Georgia offering teacher-education programs approved by Georgia Professional Standards Commission.
Eligibility: Applicant must be U.S. citizen or permanent resident residing in Georgia.
Basis for selection: Major/career interest in education, teacher or education. Applicant must demonstrate high academic achievement and seriousness of purpose.
Application requirements: Transcript, proof of eligibility.
Additional information: Provides cancelable loans. Recipient must commit to teach one year in Georgia public school for each $1,500 awarded. Must teach at preschool, elementary, middle, or secondary level. Out-of-state residents attending accredited Georgia teacher-education programs also eligible. Applicant must have minimum 3.0 GPA; be academically classified as junior; have declared education as major; and/or be accepted for enrollment into teacher-education program leading to initial certification. Must obtain signatures from institution's Department of Education teacher-certification official and financial aid office.

    Amount of award: $1,500-$6,000
    Number of awards: 1,626
    Total amount awarded: $4,435,823

Contact:
Scholarship Committee
2082 East Exchange Place
Suite 100
Tucker, GA 30084
Phone: 800-505-4732
Fax: 770-724-9004
Web: www.gacollege411.org

Georgia Scholarship for Engineering Education

Type of award: Loan, renewable.
Intended use: For full-time undergraduate study at accredited postsecondary institution in United States. Designated institutions: GSFA-approved postsecondary private schools offering programs of study accredited by the Engineering Accreditation Commission.
Eligibility: Applicant must be U.S. citizen or permanent resident residing in Georgia.
Basis for selection: Major/career interest in engineering; engineering, civil or engineering, construction.
Application requirements: Transcript. Signed promissory note.
Additional information: Sophomores, juniors and seniors must maintain 2.5 GPA. Must work in Georgia in engineering field one year for each $3,500 received or repay within six years.

    Amount of award: $3,500-$17,500
    Number of awards: 199
    Total amount awarded: $666,373

Contact:
Georgia Student Finance Commission
2082 East Exchange Place
Suite 100
Tucker, GA 30084
Phone: 800-505-4732
Fax: 770-724-9004
Web: www.gacollege411.org

Grand Encampment of Knights Templar of the USA

Knights Templar Educational Foundation Loan

Type of award: Loan, renewable.
Intended use: For junior, senior, master's, doctoral, first professional or postgraduate study at accredited vocational, 4-year or graduate institution in United States.
Eligibility: Applicant must be U.S. citizen.
Basis for selection: Applicant must demonstrate high academic achievement and depth of character.
Application requirements: Recommendations.
Additional information: Student should request application from Grand Encampment of Knights Templar of U.S.A. in state of residence. Personal dependability important. Send SASE for application. Available loan amount varies by state division.
Contact:
Grand Encampment of Knights Templar of the USA
5909 West Loop South
Suite 495
Belaire, TX 77401
Phone: 713-349-8700
Web: www.knightstemplar.org

Hattie M. Strong Foundation

Strong Foundation Interest-Free Student Loan

Type of award: Loan.
Intended use: For full-time senior or graduate study at accredited 4-year or graduate institution.
Eligibility: Applicant must be U.S. citizen or permanent resident.
Basis for selection: Applicant must demonstrate financial need, high academic achievement, depth of character, leadership, seriousness of purpose and service orientation.
Application requirements: Recommendations, proof of eligibility.
Additional information: Must be entering final year of baccalaureate or graduate degree program. Terms of repayment are based upon monthly income after graduation. Students should write between January 1 and March 31, giving brief personal history and identification of educational institution attended, the subject studied, date expected to complete studies, and amount of funds needed. Enclose SASE with application.

Amount of award:	$5,000
Number of awards:	100
Number of applicants:	250
Application deadline:	March 31
Notification begins:	July 1
Total amount awarded:	$480,000

Contact:
Hattie M. Strong Foundation
1620 Eye Street, NW
Suite 700
Washington, DC 20006-4005
Phone: 202-331-1619
Fax: 202-466-2894
Web: www.hmstrongfoundation.org

Idaho State Board of Education

Idaho Education Incentive Loan Forgiveness Program

Type of award: Loan, renewable.
Intended use: For full-time undergraduate study.
Eligibility: Applicant must be residing in Idaho.
Basis for selection: Major/career interest in education, teacher or nursing.
Additional information: Loan forgiveness for teaching or nursing service in Idaho. Minimum 3.0 GPA. Must pursue license for teaching or nursing and pursue career within Idaho for a minimum of two years. Contact financial aid office of postsecondary Idaho public institutions for application materials and information.
Contact:
Financial aid office at designated institution.
Web: www.boardofed.idaho.gov

Jewish Family and Children's Services (JFCS)

JFCS Scholarship Fund

Type of award: Scholarship.
Intended use: For undergraduate or graduate study.
Eligibility: Applicant must be Jewish. Applicant must be residing in California.
Basis for selection: Applicant must demonstrate financial need and high academic achievement.
Additional information: Minimum 3.0 GPA for grants. High school seniors, undergraduates, and graduate students may apply. Applicants may also be high school students traveling to Israel and/or students studying about the Holocaust to teach future generations. Grants available for residents of Sonoma, Marin, San Francisco, San Mateo, or Northern Santa Clara counties; loans available for all nine Bay area counties. Total aid to any applicant will be $6,000; average grant award $1,000-$1,500. Bulk of grant awards given to applicants under 26. Deadline is for consideration for school year; applicants for Israel travel, Holocaust study, and vocational study may apply any time. Organization has several scholarships and loans; see Website for more details.

Amount of award:	$500-$6,000
Number of awards:	160
Application deadline:	September 1

Contact:
Jewish Family and Children's Services
Attn: Eric Singer
2150 Post Street
San Francisco, CA 94115
Phone: 415-449-1226
Fax: 415-449-1229
Web: www.jfcs.org

Contact:
Office of Student Financial Assistance
Massachusetts Board of Higher Education
454 Broadway, Suite 200
Revere, MA 02151
Phone: 617-727-9420
Fax: 617-727-0667
Web: www.osfa.mass.edu

Maine Educational Loan Authority

The Maine Loan

Type of award: Loan.
Intended use: For undergraduate or graduate study at accredited vocational, 2-year, 4-year or graduate institution in United States or Canada.
Application requirements: Proof of eligibility. Income information/credit analysis.
Additional information: Loans available to Maine residents attending approved schools and out-of-state students attending Maine schools. May borrow full cost of education minus other financial aid. May be used to pay prior balance up to one academic year. Applicant has 4-20 years to repay, depending on amount owed. See Website for interest rates, payment options, and additional information. Applications accepted year round. Minimum loan amount is $1,000.

    Number of applicants: 2,510
    Total amount awarded: $30,000,000

Contact:
Maine Educational Loan Authority
131 Presumpscot Street
Portland, ME 04103
Phone: 800-922-6352
Fax: 207-791-3616
Web: www.mela.net

Massachusetts Board of Higher Education

Massachusetts No Interest Loan

Type of award: Loan.
Intended use: For full-time undergraduate study at accredited vocational, 2-year or 4-year institution.
Eligibility: Applicant must be U.S. citizen or permanent resident residing in Massachusetts.
Basis for selection: Applicant must demonstrate financial need.
Application requirements: FAFSA.
Additional information: No Interest Loan (NIL) Program offers no interest loans to those who meet requirements; students have 10 years to repay NIL loans and a borrowing limit of $20,000 ($4,000/year).

    Amount of award: $1,000-$4,000
    Number of applicants: 2,200
    Application deadline: March 1
    Total amount awarded: $6,000,000

Michigan Higher Education Student Loan Authority

Michigan Alternative Student Loan (MI-LOAN)

Type of award: Loan.
Intended use: For undergraduate or graduate study.
Eligibility: Applicant must be U.S. citizen or permanent resident residing in Michigan.
Basis for selection: Applicant must demonstrate financial need.
Application requirements: Proof of eligibility.
Additional information: Students or parents/guardians may apply. Must be accepted for enrollment at a Michigan school or attending one currently. Applicant cannot be in default on any student loans. Cosigner may be required. Students can be attending less than half-time. Repayment terms: 25 years with maximum of 5 years of forbearance of either principal only or principal and interest. Applications accepted up to three months prior to loan period and deadline up to last day of loan period. Award will not exceed cost of attendance minus other aid received.

    Amount of award: $500-$50,511
    Number of applicants: 8,280
    Total amount awarded: $76,431,379

Contact:
Michigan Higher Education Student Loan Authority
MI-LOAN Program
P.O. Box 30051
Lansing, MI 48909
Phone: 888-643-7521
Fax: 517-335-6699
Web: www.miloanprogram.com

Military Officers Association of America

MOAA Interest-Free Loan and Grant Program

Type of award: Loan, renewable.
Intended use: For full-time undergraduate study at accredited 2-year or 4-year institution in United States.
Eligibility: Applicant must be no older than 24. Applicant must be U.S. citizen. Applicant must be dependent of active service person, veteran or deceased veteran who serves or served in the Army, Air Force, Marines, Navy, Coast Guard or Reserves/National Guard. Applicant must be child of MOAA

member or active-duty, Reserve, National Guard, or retired enlisted military personnel.
Basis for selection: Applicant must demonstrate financial need, high academic achievement, depth of character, leadership, patriotism, seriousness of purpose and service orientation.
Application requirements: Essay, transcript, proof of eligibility. SAT/ACT score. Parent or sponsor's military status and/or MOAA number.
Additional information: Minimum 3.0 GPA. Applicant must be child of MOAA member and/or child of active-duty or retired enlisted personnel. Must be under 24; however, if applicant served in Uniformed Service before completing college, maximum age for eligibility increases by number of years served, up to five years. Parent must sign promissory note before funds can be disbursed. Application available on Website.

    Amount of award: $4,000-$5,500
    Number of applicants: 2,000
    Application deadline: March 1
    Notification begins: June 1
Contact:
MOAA Scholarship Fund
Educational Assistance Program
201 North Washington Street
Alexandria, VA 22314-2529
Phone: 800-234-6622
Web: www.moaa.org/education

Minnesota Office of Higher Education

Minnesota Student Educational Loan Fund (SELF)

Type of award: Loan.
Intended use: For undergraduate or graduate study at vocational, 2-year, 4-year or graduate institution. Designated institutions: Minnesota and eligible out-of-state institutions.
Eligibility: Applicant must be residing in Minnesota.
Additional information: Applicant must be enrolled at least half-time in eligible Minnesota school, or be Minnesota resident enrolled in eligible school outside Minnesota. Must seek aid from certain other sources before applying, except federal unsubsidized and subsidized Stafford loans, National Direct Student loans, HEAL loans, and other private loans. Institution must approve application. Maximum award for undergraduates is $6,000; juniors, seniors, and fifth-year students, $7,500; graduate students, $9,000. Must have a creditworthy cosigner.

    Amount of award: $500-$9,000
    Number of applicants: 33,000
    Total amount awarded: $134,000,000
Contact:
Minnesota Office of Higher Education
1450 Energy Park Drive, Suite 350
St. Paul, MN 55108-5227
Phone: 800-657-3866
Web: www.selfloan.org

Mississippi Office of Student Financial Aid

Critical Needs Alternative Route Teacher Loan/Scholarship

Type of award: Loan, renewable.
Intended use: For junior or senior study at 4-year institution in United States.
Eligibility: Applicant must be U.S. citizen residing in Mississippi.
Basis for selection: Major/career interest in education, teacher.
Application requirements: Signed CNTP Rules and Regulations.
Additional information: Minimum 2.5 GPA. Must have passed Praxis I or have minimum composite score of 21 on ACT, 18 minimum on subscores. Must be enrolled in program of study leading to Class "A" teacher educator license. Must agree to full-time employment in Mississippi public school located in critical teacher shortage or subject area. Must participate in Entrance Counseling. Award covers tuition, fees and housing plus book allowance. Students at private institutions receive award equivalent to costs at nearest comparable public institution. Interested non-Mississippi residents may apply if they have been accepted to Mississippi school. See Website for application and more information.

    Application deadline: March 31
Contact:
Mississippi Student Financial Aid
3825 Ridgewood Road
Jackson, MS 39211-6453
Phone: 800-327-2980
Web: www.ihl.state.ms.us/financialaid/cnar.asp

Mississippi Health Care Professions Loan/Scholarship

Type of award: Loan, renewable.
Intended use: For full-time junior, senior or graduate study at accredited postsecondary institution.
Eligibility: Applicant must be residing in Mississippi.
Basis for selection: Major/career interest in physical therapy; occupational therapy; speech pathology/audiology or psychology. Applicant must demonstrate high academic achievement.
Application requirements: Proof of eligibility.
Additional information: Undergrads receive up to $1,500; graduate students receive up to $3,000. Loan forgiveness for service in Mississippi health care institution: one year for each year of financial assistance, with a maximum of two years. Visit Website for application and further information.

    Amount of award: $1,500-$3,000
    Application deadline: March 31
    Notification begins: August 1
Contact:
Susan Eckels, Program Manager
Mississippi Office of Student Financial Aid
3825 Ridgewood Road
Jackson, MS 39211-6453
Phone: 800-327-2980
Fax: 601-432-6527
Web: www.ihl.state.ms.us/financialaid/hep.asp

Mississippi Nursing Education Loan/Scholarship

Type of award: Loan, renewable.
Intended use: For junior or senior study at accredited 4-year or graduate institution.
Eligibility: Applicant must be U.S. citizen residing in Mississippi.
Basis for selection: Major/career interest in nursing; nurse practitioner; pediatric nurse practitioner; health education or health-related professions. Applicant must demonstrate high academic achievement.
Application requirements: Transcript, proof of eligibility. State of Mississippi tax return.
Additional information: Loan forgiveness for nursing service in Mississippi, one year for each year of financial assistance, for a maximum of two years. Undergraduate awards for RN to BSN study. Apply online.
   Amount of award: $4,000
   Application deadline: March 31
   Notification begins: August 1
Contact:
Mississippi Office of Student Financial Aid
3825 Ridgewood Road
Jackson, MS 39211-6453
Phone: 800-327-2980
Web: www.ihl.state.ms.us/financialaid/nels-bsn.html

Mississippi William Winter Teacher Scholar Loan Program

Type of award: Loan, renewable.
Intended use: For full-time junior or senior study at postsecondary institution.
Eligibility: Applicant must be U.S. citizen residing in Mississippi.
Basis for selection: Major/career interest in education, teacher. Applicant must demonstrate high academic achievement.
Application requirements: Proof of eligibility.
Additional information: Must be studying towards a Class A teacher educator license. Must have 2.5 GPA, 21 ACT, and passing scores on Praxis 1. Loan forgiveness for teaching service in Mississippi public school or public school district: one year for each year of financial assistance, for a maximum of two years. Apply online.
   Amount of award: $4,000
   Application deadline: March 31
   Notification begins: August 1
   Total amount awarded: $3,416,831
Contact:
Mississippi Student Financial Aid
3825 Ridgewood Road
Jackson, MS 39211-6453
Phone: 800-327-2980
Fax: 601-432-6527
Web: www.ihl.state.ms.us/financialaid/wwts.asp

Navy-Marine Corps Relief Society

Vice Admiral E.P. Travers Loan

Type of award: Loan, renewable.
Intended use: For full-time undergraduate study.
Eligibility: Applicant must be U.S. citizen. Applicant must be dependent of active service person or veteran; or spouse of active service person in the Marines or Navy.
Basis for selection: Applicant must demonstrate financial need.
Application requirements: Proof of eligibility. Current military ID of dependent and service member.
Additional information: Minimum 2.0 GPA. Applicant must be dependent child or spouse of an active duty or retired service member of Navy or Marine Corp (including Reservists on active duty). Loan must be repaid in allotments over 24-month period (minimum monthly repayment is $50). Must reapply to renew.
   Amount of award: $500-$3,000
   Number of applicants: 1,200
   Application deadline: March 1
   Total amount awarded: $800,000
Contact:
Navy-Marine Corps Relief Society
875 North Randolph Street, Suite 225
Arlington, VA 22203
Phone: 703-696-4960
Fax: 703-696-0144
Web: www.nmcrs.org/education

New Hampshire Higher Education Assistance Foundation (NHHEAF)

Leaf Loan Program

Type of award: Loan, renewable.
Intended use: For undergraduate or graduate study at postsecondary institution.
Eligibility: Applicant must be at least 18. Applicant must be U.S. citizen or permanent resident residing in New Hampshire.
Additional information: Must be New Hampshire resident enrolled in U.S. institution or non-resident enrolled in New Hampshire institution. Fee of up to eight percent of principal borrowed charged upon disbursement. Interest rate adjusted monthly. Award ranges from $500 to entire cost less financial aid received. Visit Website for more information.
   Amount of award: $500-$10,000
Contact:
New Hampshire Higher Education Loan Corporation
4 Barrell Court
P.O. Box 2097
Concord, NH 03302
Phone: 800-525-2577
Fax: 603-224-2581
Web: www.nhheaf.org

New Hampshire Postsecondary Education Commission

Workforce Incentive Program

Type of award: Loan, renewable.
Intended use: For full-time undergraduate or graduate study at accredited 2-year, 4-year or graduate institution.
Eligibility: Applicant must be U.S. citizen or permanent resident residing in New Hampshire.
Basis for selection: Major/career interest in education, special; foreign languages or nursing. Applicant must demonstrate financial need.
Additional information: Program assists in loan repayment. Contact financial aid office at New Hampshire institution or Melanie Deshaies at New Hampshire Postsecondary Education Commission. Maximum $10,000 over five years. Visit Website for more information.
   Number of awards: 50
   Number of applicants: 60
   Application deadline: June 1, October 31
Contact:
Postsecondary Education Commission WIP Repayment Program
3 Barrell Court
Suite 300
Concord, NH 03301-8543
Phone: 603-271-2555 ext. 352
Fax: 603-271-2696
Web: www.nh.gov/postsecondary

New Jersey Higher Education Student Assistance Authority

Federal Family Education Loan Program

Type of award: Loan.
Intended use: For half-time undergraduate study at postsecondary institution in United States. Designated institutions: Participating postsecondary institutions.
Eligibility: Applicant must be residing in New Jersey.
Application requirements: FAFSA.
Additional information: Program offers highly affordable loans available to students and their parents. Student loans require guarantor. Application and more information can be obtained on Website.
Contact:
New Jersey Higher Education Student Assistance Authority
P.O. Box 540
Trenton, NY 08625
Phone: 800-792-8670
Web: www.hesaa.org

New Jersey Class Loan Program

Type of award: Loan.
Intended use: For undergraduate or graduate study at accredited vocational, 2-year, 4-year or graduate institution in United States. Designated institutions: Approved institutions. Proprietary institutions also eligible.
Eligibility: Applicant must be U.S. citizen or permanent resident residing in New Jersey.
Application requirements: Proof of eligibility. Income and credit history; FAFSA.
Additional information: All New Jersey residents may apply, as may out-of-state students attending Must demonstrate credit-worthiness or provide co-signer. Parent or other eligible family member may borrow on behalf of student. Maximum loan amount may not exceed education cost less all other financial aid. Minimum loan amount $500. Low fixed interest rate loans available for both undergraduate and graduate students. Two percent administrative fee deducted from approved loan amount. Apply online for instant credit approval.
   Amount of award: $500
   Number of applicants: 30,000
   Total amount awarded: $235,000,000
Contact:
New Jersey Higher Education Student Assistance Authority
4 Quakerbridge Plaza, P.O. Box 538
Trenton, NJ 08625-0538
Phone: 800-792-8670
Web: www.hesaa.org

New Mexico Commission on Higher Education

New Mexico Allied Health Student Loan-for-Service Program

Type of award: Loan, renewable.
Intended use: For undergraduate or graduate study at accredited postsecondary institution.
Eligibility: Applicant must be U.S. citizen or permanent resident residing in New Mexico.
Basis for selection: Major/career interest in health-related professions; occupational therapy; mental health/therapy; physical therapy; pharmacy/pharmaceutics/pharmacology; dietetics/nutrition or speech pathology/audiology. Applicant must demonstrate financial need.
Application requirements: FAFSA.
Additional information: Loan forgiveness offered to those who practice in medically underserved areas in New Mexico. Must be accepted by or enrolled in approved programs at accredited New Mexico public postsecondary institution. Call sponsor number or visit Website for application and more information.
   Amount of award: $12,000
   Application deadline: July 1
Contact:
New Mexico Higher Education Department
Financial Aid and Student Services
1068 Cerrillos Road
Santa Fe, NM 87505
Phone: 800-279-9777
Web: www.hed.state.nm.us

New Mexico Medical Student Loan-for-Service

Type of award: Loan, renewable.
Intended use: For undergraduate or first professional study in United States.
Eligibility: Applicant must be U.S. citizen or permanent resident residing in New Mexico.
Basis for selection: Major/career interest in medicine or physician assistant. Applicant must demonstrate financial need.
Application requirements: FAFSA.
Additional information: Loan forgiveness for New Mexico residents to practice in medically underserved areas in New Mexico. Loan amount dependent upon financial need. Part-time students eligible for prorated awards. Preference given to students accepted for enrollment at the UNM School of Medicine.
    Amount of award: $12,000
    Application deadline: July 1
Contact:
New Mexico Commission on Higher Education
Financial Aid and Student Services
1068 Cerrillos Road
Santa Fe, NM 87505
Phone: 800-279-9777
Web: www.hed.state.nm.us

New Mexico Nursing Student Loan-for-Service

Type of award: Loan, renewable.
Intended use: For undergraduate or graduate study at accredited 2-year or 4-year institution.
Eligibility: Applicant must be U.S. citizen or permanent resident residing in New Mexico.
Basis for selection: Major/career interest in nursing. Applicant must demonstrate financial need.
Application requirements: FAFSA.
Additional information: Loan forgiveness for New Mexico resident to practice in medically underserved areas in New Mexico. Part-time students eligible for prorated awards.
    Amount of award: $12,000
    Application deadline: July 1
Contact:
New Mexico Commission on Higher Education
Financial Aid and Student Services
1068 Cerrillos Road
Santa Fe, NM 87505
Phone: 800-279-9777
Web: www.hed.state.nm.us

New Mexico Teacher's Loan-for-Service

Type of award: Loan.
Intended use: For undergraduate or post-bachelor's certificate study at accredited postsecondary institution.
Eligibility: Applicant must be physically challenged. Applicant must be U.S. citizen or permanent resident residing in New Mexico.
Basis for selection: Major/career interest in education, teacher. Applicant must demonstrate financial need.
Application requirements: FAFSA.
Additional information: Applicant must be from Lea, Chaves, Otero, Eddy, or Roosevelt counties. Must be accepted by undergraduate, graduate, or alternative licensure teacher preparation program approved by State Board of Education. Must provide one year of teaching service for each year of award at a public school in New Mexico.
    Amount of award: $4,000
    Application deadline: July 1
Contact:
New Mexico Commission on Higher Education
Financial Aid and Student Services
1068 Cerrillos Road
Santa Fe, NM 87505
Phone: 800-279-9777
Web: www.hed.state.nm.us

New York State Grange

Grange Student Loan Fund

Type of award: Loan, renewable.
Intended use: For full-time undergraduate or graduate study at postsecondary institution.
Eligibility: Applicant or parent must be member/participant of New York State Grange. Applicant must be residing in New York.
Basis for selection: Applicant must demonstrate financial need.
Additional information: Must send SASE for application. May apply for less than the maximum award. Loan repayment at five percent annual interest.
    Amount of award: $2,000
    Number of awards: 11
    Number of applicants: 11
    Application deadline: April 15
    Notification begins: June 15
    Total amount awarded: $22,000
Contact:
New York State Grange
100 Grange Place
Cortland, NY 13045
Phone: 607-756-7553

North Carolina Community Colleges Foundation

Community College Grant & Loan

Type of award: Loan.
Intended use: For undergraduate study at 2-year institution.
Eligibility: Applicant must be residing in North Carolina.
Basis for selection: Applicant must demonstrate financial need.
Application requirements: FAFSA.
Additional information: Value of grants and loans vary. Applicant must qualify for Federal Pell Grant. Provides financial assistance to credit and occupational extension students who enroll in low-enrollment programs that prepare students for high-demand occupations.

North Carolina Community Colleges Foundation: Community College Grant & Loan

Contact:
North Carolina Community Colleges Foundation
5016 Mail Service Center
Raleigh, NC 27699
Phone: 919-807-6962
Fax: 919-807-7164
Web: www.ncccs.cc.nc.us

North Carolina State Education Assistance Authority

North Carolina Nurse Scholars Program

Type of award: Loan, renewable.
Intended use: For full-time undergraduate study at accredited postsecondary institution.
Eligibility: Applicant must be U.S. citizen residing in North Carolina.
Basis for selection: Major/career interest in nursing. Applicant must demonstrate high academic achievement, leadership and service orientation.
Application requirements: Recommendations, essay, transcript, proof of eligibility.
Additional information: 3.0 GPA required. Applicant must be North Carolina resident for tuition purposes. Candidates for associate's degree in nursing and hospital diploma in nursing will receive $3,000. Candidates for bachelor's in nursing will receive $5,000 or $3,000 per year. Also, $2,500 per year scholarship/loan is available for a RN seeking a BSN degree. Loan-forgiveness for nursing service in North Carolina.
    Amount of award: $2,500-$5,000
    Number of awards: 450
    Application deadline: March 7, May 3
Contact:
North Carolina Nurse Scholars Program
P.O. Box 14223
Research Triangle Park, NC 27709-4223
Phone: 800-700-1775 ext. 313
Web: www.cfnc.org

North Carolina Student Loans for Health/Science/Mathematics

Type of award: Loan, renewable.
Intended use: For full-time undergraduate or graduate study at accredited postsecondary institution in United States. Designated institutions: North Carolina postsecondary institutions and eligible out-of-state schools.
Eligibility: Applicant must be U.S. citizen residing in North Carolina.
Basis for selection: Major/career interest in health-related professions; mathematics; science, general; dentistry; optometry/ophthalmology; social work or nursing. Applicant must demonstrate financial need.
Application requirements: Transcript, proof of eligibility. FAFSA.
Additional information: Loan obligation may be forgiven through approved employment within the state of North Carolina, provided the recipient works in the field for which he/she was funded. Application available on Website.

    Amount of award: $3,000-$8,500
    Application deadline: June 1
Contact:
North Carolina Student Loan Program
Health, Science and Mathematics
P.O. Box 14223
Research Triangle Park, NC 27709-4223
Phone: 919-549-8614
Web: www.cfnc.org/HSM

Ohio Board of Regents

Ohio Nurse Education Assistance Loan Program

Type of award: Loan, renewable.
Intended use: For undergraduate, post-bachelor's certificate or master's study at postsecondary institution. Designated institutions: Eligible Ohio institutions.
Eligibility: Applicant must be U.S. citizen or permanent resident residing in Ohio.
Basis for selection: Major/career interest in nursing. Applicant must demonstrate financial need and high academic achievement.
Application requirements: Proof of eligibility. FAFSA.
Additional information: Must be accepted to or enrolled in approved pre- or post-licensure LPN or RN education program. Maximum $3,000 award for pre-licensure applicants; $5,000 for post-licensure applicants. Debt cancellation at rate of 20 percent per year (for maximum of five years) for pre-licensure applicants, 25 percent per year for post-licensure applicants if borrower is employed in full-time practice of nursing in Ohio after graduation. Must not be in default or owe refund to any federal financial aid programs. Apply online.
    Number of applicants: 150
    Application deadline: June 1
    Notification begins: July 15
Contact:
Carlos Bing
Ohio Board of Regents
30 E. Broad St., 36th Floor
Columbus, OH 43215-3414
Phone: 888-833-1133 ext. 64818
Fax: 614-752-5903
Web: www.regents.state.oh.us/sgs/nealp.htm

Pickett and Hatcher Educational Fund, Inc.

Pickett and Hatcher Educational Loan

Type of award: Loan, renewable.
Intended use: For full-time undergraduate study at 4-year institution.
Eligibility: Applicant must be U.S. citizen.
Basis for selection: Applicant must demonstrate financial need and high academic achievement.

Additional information: Not available to law, medicine, or ministry students. Loans renewed up to $22,000. Applications accepted year-round.

Amount of award:	$1,000-$5,500
Number of awards:	550
Number of applicants:	539
Total amount awarded:	$2,869,434

Contact:
Pickett and Hatcher Educational Fund, Inc.
Loan Program
P.O. Box 8169
Columbus, GA 31908-8169
Phone: 706-327-6586
Fax: 706-324-6788
Web: www.phef.org

Presbyterian Church (USA)

Presbyterian Undergraduate and Graduate Loan

Type of award: Loan, renewable.
Intended use: For full-time undergraduate or graduate study at accredited 2-year, 4-year or graduate institution in United States.
Eligibility: Applicant must be Presbyterian. Applicant must be U.S. citizen or permanent resident.
Basis for selection: Applicant must demonstrate financial need and high academic achievement.
Additional information: Must establish and maintain minimum 2.0 GPA. Contact office for current interest rates and deferment policies. Must give evidence of financial reliability. Undergraduates and graduates can apply for up to $15,000 spread out over undergraduate and graduate studies.

Amount of award:	$200-$15,000
Number of awards:	100
Number of applicants:	112
Application deadline:	July 30
Notification begins:	August 15

Contact:
Presbyterian Church (USA)
Financial Aid for Studies
100 Witherspoon Street
Louisville, KY 40202-1396
Phone: 888-728-7228 ext. 5735
Fax: 502-569-8766
Web: www.pcusa.org/financialaid

South Carolina Student Loan Corporation

South Carolina Teacher Loans

Type of award: Loan, renewable.
Intended use: For undergraduate or graduate study at accredited 2-year, 4-year or graduate institution.
Eligibility: Applicant must be U.S. citizen residing in South Carolina.
Basis for selection: Major/career interest in education. Applicant must demonstrate high academic achievement.

Additional information: Freshmen and sophomores may borrow up to $2,500 per year; juniors, seniors, and graduate students may borrow up to $5,000 per year. Graduate study eligible only if required for initial teacher certification. Entering freshmen must have SAT score equal to South Carolina state average for year of high school graduation, and rank in top 40 percent of high school class. Undergraduate and entering graduate applicants must have 2.75 GPA and have passed PRAXIS1 Examination. Graduate applicants who have completed at least one semester must have 3.5 GPA. Loan forgiveness for service in teacher shortage area in South Carolina public schools: 20 percent for each year of service, 33 percent if service in geographic and subject shortage area.

Amount of award:	$2,500-$5,000
Number of awards:	1,597
Application deadline:	June 1
Notification begins:	July 15
Total amount awarded:	$5,556,496

Contact:
South Carolina Student Loan Corporation
P.O. Box 21487
Columbia, SC 29221
Phone: 803-798-0916
Web: www.scstudentloan.org

Student Aid Foundation

Student Aid Foundation Loan

Type of award: Loan, renewable.
Intended use: For full-time undergraduate, master's, doctoral or first professional study at accredited vocational, 2-year, 4-year or graduate institution in United States.
Eligibility: Applicant must be female. Applicant must be U.S. citizen residing in Georgia.
Basis for selection: Applicant must demonstrate financial need, high academic achievement and seriousness of purpose.
Application requirements: Recommendations, essay, transcript.
Additional information: Non-Georgia residents attending Georgia institutions can qualify. Loan not forgivable. Must have financially responsible endorser. Minimum 2.5 GPA. Send SASE with request for application, or download it from Website.

Amount of award:	$3,500-$7,500
Number of awards:	40
Number of applicants:	89
Application deadline:	April 15
Notification begins:	June 1

Contact:
Student Aid Foundation
2520 East Piedmont Road
Suite F, PMB 180
Marietta, GA 30062
Phone: 770-973-7077
Fax: 770-973-2220
Web: www.studentaidfoundation.org

Tennessee Student Assistance Corporation

Tennessee Minority Teaching Fellows Program

Type of award: Loan, renewable.
Intended use: For full-time undergraduate study at accredited 2-year or 4-year institution.
Eligibility: Applicant must be Alaskan native, Asian American, African American, Hispanic American, American Indian or Native Hawaiian/Pacific Islander. Applicant must be U.S. citizen residing in Tennessee.
Basis for selection: Applicant must demonstrate high academic achievement.
Application requirements: Recommendations, essay, transcript. List of extracurricular activities.
Additional information: Entering freshmen applicants have priority and must have a minimum 2.75 GPA, rank in top 25 percent of class, or score at least 18 on ACT (860 SAT). Undergraduate applicants must have a minimum 2.5 college GPA. Must make commitment to teaching. Loan can be forgiven by teaching in Tennessee public pre K-12 schools, one year for each year of funding.

Amount of award:	$5,000
Number of awards:	111
Number of applicants:	164
Application deadline:	April 15
Total amount awarded:	$530,227

Contact:
Tennessee Student Assistance Corporation
Parkway Towers, Suite 1950
404 James Robertson Parkway
Nashville, TN 37243-0820
Phone: 800-342-1663
Fax: 615-741-6101
Web: www.collegepaystn.com

Tennessee Student Assistance Corporation/Math And Science Teachers Loan Forgiveness Program

Type of award: Loan, renewable.
Intended use: For postgraduate study.
Eligibility: Applicant must be U.S. citizen residing in Tennessee.
Basis for selection: Major/career interest in mathematics or science, general.
Application requirements: Applicant must be TN resident, U.S. citizen, must be admitted to post-secondary institution seeking advanced degree in math/science, must teach math/science in TN school for two years.
Additional information: Applicant must be TN resident, U.S. citizen, must be admitted to post-secondary institution seeking advanced degree in math/science, must teach math/science in TN school for two years. The application deadline is September 1 for students beginning the academic year in the fall, February 1 for students who begin the academic year in the spring, and May 1 for students who begin the academic year in the summer.

Total amount awarded:	$2,000

Contact:
Tennessee Student Assistance Corporation
404 James Robertson Parkway
Suite 1510, Parkway Towers
Nashville, TN 37243-0820
Phone: 800-342-1663
Web: www.collegepaystn.com

Tennessee Teaching Scholars Program

Type of award: Loan, renewable.
Intended use: For junior, senior, post-bachelor's certificate or master's study at accredited graduate institution.
Eligibility: Applicant must be U.S. citizen residing in Tennessee.
Basis for selection: Major/career interest in education; education, teacher; education, special or education, early childhood. Applicant must demonstrate high academic achievement.
Application requirements: Recommendations, transcript, proof of eligibility. Verification of standardized test score and be accepted into Teacher Licensure Program.
Additional information: Loan can be forgiven for teaching in Tennessee public schools, K-12. Minimum 2.75 cumulative GPA and a standardized test score adequate for admission to the Teacher Education Program in Tennessee schools. Amount of award based on funding.

Amount of award:	$4,500
Number of awards:	189
Number of applicants:	219
Application deadline:	April 15
Total amount awarded:	$746,412

Contact:
Tennessee Student Assistance Corporation
Parkway Towers, Suite 1510
404 James Robertson Parkway
Nashville, TN 37243-0820
Phone: 800-342-1663
Fax: 615-741-6101
Web: www.collegepaystn.com

Texas Higher Education Coordinating Board

Hinson-Hazlewood College Access Loan (CAL)

Type of award: Loan.
Intended use: For undergraduate or graduate study at 2-year, 4-year or graduate institution in United States.
Eligibility: Applicant must be U.S. citizen or permanent resident residing in Texas.
Additional information: Texas colleges and universities have a limited number of CAL loans. Applicants need not show financial need. The loan may be used to cover the family's expected contribution (EFC). Cosigners must have good credit and meet other program criteria. Apply online.

Contact:
Texas Higher Education Coordinating Board
Student Services Division
P.O. Box 12788
Austin, TX 12788-2788
Phone: 800-242-3062
Fax: 512-427-6420
Web: www.collegefortexans.com

United Methodist Church

United Methodist Loan Program

Type of award: Loan, renewable.
Intended use: For undergraduate or graduate study at accredited postsecondary institution in United States.
Eligibility: Applicant must be United Methodist. Applicant must be U.S. citizen or permanent resident.
Additional information: Must be active member of United Methodist Church one year prior to application. Must maintain "C" average. May reapply for loan to maximum of $15,000. Interest rate 6 percent; cosigner required. Ten years permitted to repay loan after graduation or withdrawal from school. Qualified applicants are chosen on a first come, first served basis.
   Amount of award: $2,500
Contact:
United Methodist Church/Board of Higher Education and Ministry
Office of Loans and Scholarships
P.O. Box 340007
Nashville, TN 37203-0007
Phone: 615-340-7346
Web: www.gbhem.org

UPS

United Parcel Service Earn & Learn Program Loans

Type of award: Loan.
Intended use: For undergraduate study at accredited vocational, 2-year or 4-year institution in United States.
Eligibility: Applicant or parent must be employed by United Parcel Service (UPS).
Application requirements: Proof of eligibility.
Additional information: Award is $3,000 per year in forgivable student loans with $15,000 lifetime maximum. For part-time management employees, award is upped to $4,000 with a $20,000 lifetime guarantee. UPS pays back percentage of loan as long as student remains employed by UPS. Visit Website for specifics.
Contact:
UPS
55 Glenlake Parkway N.E.
Atlanta, GA 30328
Phone: 888-WORK-UPS
Web: www.upsjobs.com

U.S. Department of Education

Federal Direct Stafford Loans

Type of award: Loan, renewable.
Intended use: For undergraduate or graduate study at postsecondary institution.
Eligibility: Applicant must be U.S. citizen or permanent resident.
Basis for selection: Applicant must demonstrate financial need.
Application requirements: Proof of eligibility. FAFSA and promissory note.
Additional information: Maximum interest rate 8.25 percent. Some loans subsidized, based on need eligibility. Loan amount depends on grade level in school and student type. Telecommunications Device for the Deaf at 800-730-8913. FAFSA available online.
   Amount of award: $3,500-$20,500
   Application deadline: June 30
Contact:
Federal Student Aid Programs
P.O. Box 84
Washington, DC 20044-0084
Phone: 800-4-FED-AID
Web: www.studentaid.ed.gov

Federal Family Education Loan Program (FFEL)

Type of award: Loan, renewable.
Intended use: For undergraduate or graduate study at accredited postsecondary institution in or outside United States or Canada. Designated institutions: Schools approved by the U.S. Department of Education.
Eligibility: Applicant must be U.S. citizen or permanent resident.
Basis for selection: Applicant must demonstrate financial need.
Application requirements: Proof of eligibility. FAFSA.
Additional information: Subsidized and unsubsidized loans. If school participates in FFEL program, private lender provides funds for loan, although federal government guarantees loan funds. First-year dependent undergraduates eligible for up to $3,500; independent first-year undergraduates eligible for $7,500 (only $3,500 can come from subsidized loans). Maximum interest rate 8.25 percent.
   Application deadline: June 30
Contact:
Federal Student Aid Programs
P.O. Box 84
Washington, DC 20044-0084
Phone: 800-4-FED-AID
Web: www.studentaid.ed.gov

Federal Perkins Loan

Type of award: Loan, renewable.
Intended use: For undergraduate or graduate study at accredited postsecondary institution in United States.
Eligibility: Applicant must be U.S. citizen or permanent resident.
Basis for selection: Applicant must demonstrate financial need.

Application requirements: Proof of eligibility. FAFSA.
Additional information: Maximum annual loan amount: $4,000 for undergraduates, $6,000 for graduates. Five percent interest rate. Applicant must demonstrate exceptional financial need. Repayment begins nine months after graduation, leaving school, or dropping below half-time status.
Application deadline: June 30
Contact:
Federal Student Aid Programs
P.O. Box 84
Washington, DC 20044-0084
Phone: 800-4-FED AID
Web: www.studentaid.ed.gov

Federal Plus Loan

Type of award: Loan.
Intended use: For undergraduate or graduate study at accredited postsecondary institution in or outside United States or Canada. Designated institutions: Schools approved by the U.S. Department of Education.
Eligibility: Applicant must be U.S. citizen or permanent resident.
Basis for selection: Applicant must demonstrate financial need.
Application requirements: PLUS loan application and promissory note. FAFSA.
Additional information: Unsubsidized loans for parents of student. Must pass credit check. Interest rate is flexible, but capped at nine percent annually. Award amount varies. Loan is equal to cost of attendance minus any other financial aid. Generally, repayment must begin 60 days after the loan is fully disbursed.
Application deadline: June 30
Contact:
Federal Student Aid Programs
P.O. Box 84
Washington, DC 20044-0084
Phone: 800-4-FED-AID
Web: www.studentaid.ed.gov

Utah State Office of Education

Utah Career Teaching Scholarship/ T.H. Bell Teaching Incentive Loan

Type of award: Loan, renewable.
Intended use: For full-time undergraduate study at accredited postsecondary institution.
Eligibility: Applicant must be high school senior. Applicant must be U.S. citizen residing in Utah.
Basis for selection: Major/career interest in education, teacher; education; education, early childhood or education, special.
Application requirements: Transcript. SAT/ACT scores.
Additional information: Provides tuition waiver with additional awards to limited number of qualified recipients. Loan forgiveness for teaching in Utah public schools. Application available after January 15. Eligible are high school seniors and juniors who have completed requirements for Early Graduation Program (including ACT).

Number of awards: 25
Number of applicants: 320
Application deadline: March 28
Notification begins: May 15
Contact:
High school counselor or financial aid officer.
Web: www.usoe.k12.ut.us/cert

Vermont Student Assistance Corporation

VSAC Advantage Loan

Type of award: Loan.
Intended use: For undergraduate or graduate study at vocational, 2-year, 4-year or graduate institution in or outside United States.
Eligibility: Applicant must be U.S. citizen or permanent resident residing in Vermont.
Basis for selection: Applicant must demonstrate financial need.
Application requirements: FAFSA. Must be credit approved or applying with credit approved co-signer.
Additional information: Applicant must be eligible for federal aid and borrowing maximum for Stafford Loan. Must be enrolled or reenrolling at least half-time at an eligible postsecondary school. Interest rate changes quarterly.
Contact:
Vermont Student Assistance Corporation
Education Loan Finance Department
P.O. Box 2000
Winooski, VT 05404
Phone: 800-307-8722
Web: www.vsac.org

Virgin Islands Board of Education

Virgin Islands Territorial Grants/ Loans Program

Type of award: Loan, renewable.
Intended use: For full-time undergraduate or graduate study at accredited postsecondary institution.
Eligibility: Applicant must be high school senior. Applicant must be U.S. citizen or permanent resident residing in Virgin Islands.
Basis for selection: Applicant must demonstrate financial need.
Application requirements: Transcript. Acceptance letter from institution for first-time applicants or transfer students.
Additional information: Combined loan and grant program to assist Virgin Islands residents. Minimum 2.0 GPA. Must agree to accept employment in Virgin Islands government one year for every year of award upon completion of studies. Number and amount of awards vary. Six percent interest on repayment, additional 2 percent if delinquent.

Amount of award:	$500-$2,500
Number of awards:	597
Number of applicants:	763
Application deadline:	May 1

Contact:
Scholarship Committee
Virgin Islands Board of Education
P.O. Box 11900
St. Thomas, VI 00801
Phone: 340-774-4546

West Virginia Higher Education Policy Commission

West Virginia Underwood-Smith Teacher Scholarship

Type of award: Loan, renewable.
Intended use: For full-time junior, senior or graduate study at 4-year or graduate institution.
Eligibility: Applicant must be U.S. citizen or permanent resident residing in West Virginia.
Basis for selection: Major/career interest in education, teacher. Applicant must demonstrate high academic achievement.
Application requirements: Essay, proof of eligibility.
Additional information: Undergraduate applicants must be juniors or seniors majoring in education with cumulative 3.25 GPA; graduate students must rank in top 10 percent of class or have GPA of 3.5 or above. Must be permanent resident of West Virginia. Number of applicants varies. Recipients must agree to teach at the public school level in West Virginia for two years for each year the scholarship is received or be willing to repay the scholarship on a pro rata basis.

Amount of award:	$5,000
Number of awards:	54
Application deadline:	March 1
Notification begins:	July 1
Total amount awarded:	$150,000

Contact:
West Virginia Higher Education Policy Commission
Underwood-Smith Teacher Scholarship Program
1018 Kanawha Boulevard East, Suite 700
Charleston, WV 25301-2827
Phone: 304-558-4618 or 888-825-5707
Fax: 304-558-4622
Web: www.hepc.wvnet.edu

Wisconsin Department of Veterans Affairs

Wisconsin Veterans Affairs Personal Loan Program

Type of award: Loan.
Intended use: For undergraduate or graduate study at postsecondary institution in United States.
Eligibility: Applicant must be residing in Wisconsin. Applicant must be veteran; or dependent of veteran or deceased veteran; or spouse of veteran or deceased veteran. Must meet WDVA service requirements. Must have 90 days of active duty during wartime and/or two years of continuous active duty.
Additional information: Applicant must have been a resident of Wisconsin upon entry into military service or a continuous resident of Wisconsin for at least one year immediately preceding the application date. Loan amount up to $5,000 annually. Subsidized annual interest rate varies; loan has ten-year term. Apply to local county veterans service officer to establish eligibility.

Contact:
Wisconsin Department of Veterans Affairs
P.O. Box 7843
30 West Mifflin Street
Madison, WI 53707-7843
Phone: 800-947-8387
Web: www.dva.state.wi.us

Wisconsin Higher Educational Aids Board

Wisconsin Minority Teacher Loan Program

Type of award: Loan, renewable.
Intended use: For junior or senior study at accredited 4-year institution.
Eligibility: Applicant must be Asian American, African American, Mexican American, Hispanic American, Puerto Rican or American Indian. Asian American applicants must be either former citizens or descendants of former citizens of Laos, Vietnam, or Cambodia admitted to the U.S. after 12/31/1975. Applicant must be residing in Wisconsin.
Basis for selection: Major/career interest in education; education, special or education, teacher. Applicant must demonstrate financial need.
Application requirements: Nomination by Student Financial Aid Department. FAFSA.
Additional information: Recipient must agree to teach in Wisconsin school district where minority students constitute at least 29 percent of enrollment or in school district participating in the inter-district pupil transfer (Chapter 220) program. For each year student teaches in eligible district, 25 percent of loan is forgiven; otherwise loan must be repaid at interest rate of 5 percent.

Amount of award:	$250-$2,500
Number of awards:	109
Total amount awarded:	$238,662

Contact:
Higher Educational Aids Board
Attn: Mary Lou Kuzdas
131 West Wilson
Madison, WI 53707
Phone: 608-267-2212
Web: www.heab.state.wi.us

Sponsor Index

1199 National Benefit Fund, 75
Abbie Sargent Memorial Scholarship Fund, 75
Academy of Television Arts & Sciences Foundation, 75
Academy of Television Arts & Sciences Foundation, 527
Accuracy in Media/American Journalism Center, 527
ACFE Foundation, 76
The Actuarial Foundation, 76
ADA Foundation, 76
ADHA Institute for Oral Health, 77
AFCEA Educational Foundation, 80
AFSA Scholarship Programs, 81
AGC of Maine Education Foundation, 81
AHEPA Educational Foundation, 81
Air Force Aid Society, 81
Air Traffic Control Association, Inc., 82
Aircraft Electronics Association Educational Foundation, 83
Aircraft Owners and Pilots Association (AOPA), 86
Akademos, Inc., 86
Alabama Commission on Higher Education, 86
Alabama Department of Education, 87
Alabama Department of Postsecondary Education, 87
Alabama Department of Veterans Affairs, 88
Alaska Commission on Postsecondary Education, 577
Alcoa Foundation, 88
Alexander Graham Bell Association for the Deaf and Hard of Hearing, 88
Alexia Foundation, 89
Alliance for Young Artists and Writers, 89
All-Ink.com, 89
Allstate, 527
Alpha Beta Gamma International, Inc., 90
Alpha Mu Gamma, the National Collegiate Foreign Language Honor Society, 91
Alumnae Panhellenic Association of Washington, DC, 91
A.M. Castle & Co., 91
AMBUCS, 91
American Alpine Club, 92
American Architectural Foundation, 92
American Association for Cancer Research, 93
American Association of Advertising Agencies, 527
American Association of Airport Executives, 93
American Association of Critical Care Nurses, 94
American Bar Foundation, 528
American Board of Funeral Service Education, 94
American Cancer Society Great Lakes Division Foundation, 95
American Center of Oriental Research, 95
American Chemical Society, 95
American Classical League/National Junior Classical League, 95
American College of Musicians/National Guild of Piano Teachers, 96
American Congress on Surveying and Mapping, 97
American Conservatory Theater, 528
American Council of Engineering Companies, 99
American Council of the Blind, 100
American Dental Assistants Association/Oral B Laboratories, 100
American Dietetic Association Foundation, 100
American Electroplaters and Surface Finishers Foundation, 101
American Federation of State, County and Municipal Employees, 101
American Floral Endowment, 102
American Foundation for Aging Research, 104
American Foundation for Pharmaceutical Education, 104
American Foundation for the Blind, 104
American Ground Water Trust, 106
American Heart Association Western States Affiliate, 106
American Helicopter Society, Inc., 107
American Hotel & Lodging Educational Foundation, 107
American Indian College Fund, 108
American Indian Science & Engineering Society, 109
American Institute For Foreign Study, 109
American Institute of Aeronautics and Astronautics, 110
American Institute of Architects New Jersey Scholarship Foundation, Inc., 111
American Institute of Architects New York Chapter, 111
American Institute of Certified Public Accountants, 111
American Institute of Polish Culture, 112
American Legion Alabama, 112
American Legion Alabama Auxiliary, 113
American Legion Alaska, 113
American Legion Alaska Auxiliary, 113
American Legion Arizona, 114
American Legion Arizona Auxiliary, 114
American Legion Arkansas, 115
American Legion Arkansas Auxiliary, 115
American Legion California, 115
American Legion California Auxiliary, 116
American Legion Colorado, 116
American Legion Colorado Auxiliary, 117
American Legion Connecticut, 117
American Legion Connecticut Auxiliary, 117
American Legion Delaware Auxiliary, 118
American Legion District of Columbia, 118
American Legion Florida, 118
American Legion Florida Auxiliary, 119
American Legion Georgia Auxiliary, 119
American Legion Hawaii, 120
American Legion Idaho, 120
American Legion Idaho Auxiliary, 120
American Legion Illinois, 121
American Legion Illinois Auxiliary, 121
American Legion Indiana, 122
American Legion Indiana Auxiliary, 123
American Legion Iowa, 124
American Legion Iowa Auxiliary, 124
American Legion Kansas, 125
American Legion Kansas Auxiliary, 127
American Legion Kentucky, 127
American Legion Kentucky Auxiliary, 127
American Legion Kentucky Auxiliary, 578
American Legion Maine, 128
American Legion Maine Auxiliary, 128
American Legion Maryland, 129
American Legion Maryland Auxiliary, 129
American Legion Massachusetts, 130
American Legion Massachusetts Auxiliary, 130

Sponsor Index

American Legion Michigan, 131
American Legion Michigan Auxiliary, 131
American Legion Minnesota, 132
American Legion Minnesota Auxiliary, 133
American Legion Mississippi Auxiliary, 133
American Legion Missouri, 133
American Legion Missouri Auxiliary, 134
American Legion Montana Auxiliary, 135
American Legion National Headquarters, 135
American Legion Nebraska, 137
American Legion Nebraska Auxiliary, 137
American Legion Nevada, 139
American Legion Nevada Auxiliary, 139
American Legion New Hampshire, 140
American Legion New Hampshire Auxiliary, 141
American Legion New Jersey, 141
American Legion New Jersey Auxiliary, 142
American Legion New Mexico Auxiliary, 143
American Legion New York, 143
American Legion New York Auxiliary, 144
American Legion North Dakota, 144
American Legion North Dakota Auxiliary, 145
American Legion Ohio, 145
American Legion Ohio Auxiliary, 145
American Legion Oregon, 146
American Legion Oregon Auxiliary, 146
American Legion Pennsylvania, 147
American Legion Pennsylvania Auxiliary, 147
American Legion Puerto Rico Auxiliary, 147
American Legion South Carolina, 148
American Legion South Carolina Auxiliary, 148
American Legion South Dakota, 148
American Legion South Dakota, 578
American Legion South Dakota Auxiliary, 148
American Legion Tennessee, 149
American Legion Tennessee Auxiliary, 150
American Legion Texas, 150
American Legion Texas Auxiliary, 150
American Legion Utah Auxiliary, 151
American Legion Vermont, 151
American Legion Virginia, 152
American Legion Virginia Auxiliary, 152
American Legion Washington, 152
American Legion Washington Auxiliary, 153

American Legion West Virginia, 153
American Legion West Virginia Auxiliary, 154
American Legion Wisconsin, 154
American Legion Wisconsin Auxiliary, 155
American Legion Wyoming, 156
American Legion Wyoming Auxiliary, 156
American Medical Technologists, 156
American Meteorological Society, 157
American Morgan Horse Institute, 158
American Museum of Natural History, 158
American Museum of Natural History, 529
American Nuclear Society, 159
American Physical Society, 161
American Quarter Horse Foundation, 162
American Radio Relay League (ARRL) Foundation, Inc., 162
American Respiratory Care Foundation, 169
American Society for Enology and Viticulture, 170
American Society for Microbiology, 171
American Society of Civil Engineers, 171
American Society of Heating, Refrigerating and Air-Conditioning Engineers, 172
American Society of Heating, Refrigerating, and Air-Conditioning Engineers, Inc., 172
American Society of Interior Designers Foundation, 175
American Society of International Law, 529
American Society of Mechanical Engineers, 175
American Society of Mechanical Engineers, 578
American Society of Mechanical Engineers Auxiliary, 178
American Society of Mechanical Engineers Auxiliary, 578
American Society of Naval Engineers, 179
American Society of Travel Agents Foundation, 179
American Water Ski Educational Foundation, 182
American Welding Society Foundation, Inc., 182
Americans for the Arts, 530
America's Junior Miss, Inc., 92
Annie's Homegrown, 186
AOPA Air Safety Foundation, 187
Appaloosa Youth Foundation, 187
Applied Arts, 532
Applied Materials, 532
Arizona Board of Regents, 187
Arkansas Department of Higher Education, 188

Arkansas Department of Higher Education, 579
Armed Forces Communications and Electronics Association, 190
Armenian General Benevolent Union, 192
ARMY Emergency Relief, 192
The Art Institutes, 192
Arthur and Doreen Parrett Scholarship Trust Fund, 193
Arts and Business Council of New York, 532
The ASCAP Foundation, 193
Asian American Journalists Association, 193
Asian American Journalists Association, 533
Asian American Journalists Association, Texas Chapter, 194
ASM Materials Education Foundation, 194
Associated Builders and Contractors, Inc., 196
Associated General Contractors Education and Research Foundation, 196
Associated Press, 197
Association for Library and Information Science Foundation, 197
Association for Women in Architecture Foundation, 198
Association for Women in Communications, 199
Association of American Geographers, 199
The Association of Insurance Compliance Professionals, 199
Association of State Dam Safety Officials, 200
Astraea Lesbian Foundation for Justice, 200
Atlanta Association of Black Journalists, 200
Automotive Hall of Fame, 200
AXA Achievement Scholarship, 201
Ayn Rand Institute, 201
Barry M. Goldwater Scholarship and Excellence In Education Foundation, 202
Baxter International Inc., 533
Bay Area Family of Funds, 202
Bemis Company Foundation, 202
Bernstein-Rein Advertising, 533
Best Buy, 203
Bethesda Lutheran Homes and Services, Inc., 203
Bill and Melinda Gates Foundation, 203
Biocommunications Association, Inc., 204
Black & Veatch Corporation, 534
BlackNews.com, 204
Blinded Veterans Association, 204
BMI Foundation, Inc., 204
BMI Foundation, Inc., 534

Sponsor Index

Board of Governors of the Federal Reserve System, 534
Boeing Company, 205
Boeing Company, 534
Books and Scholarships LLC, 205
Boston Globe, 535
Boy Scouts of America, 205
Boys and Girls Clubs of Greater San Diego, 206
Broadcast Education Association, 206
Brown and Caldwell, 208
Brown and Caldwell, 535
Brown Foundation for Educational Equality, Excellence and Research, 208
Building Industry Association, 208
Bureau of Indian Affairs, 209
Bureau of Indian Affairs-Oklahoma Area Education Office, 209
Business and Professional Women's Foundation, 209
Butler Manufacturing Company Foundation, 209
California Association of Realtors Scholarship Foundation, 210
California Farm Bureau, 210
California Masonic Foundation, 210
California Student Aid Commission, 211
California Student Aid Commission, 579
California Teachers Association, 213
California's Junior Miss Program, 211
CAP Charitable Foundation, 214
Carl's Jr. Restaurants, 214
Catching the Dream, 215
Catholic Aid Association, 216
CCNMA, 216
Center for Education Solutions, 216
Central Intelligence Agency, 216
C.G. Fuller Foundation, 217
ChairScholars Foundation, Inc., 217
Charles & Lucille King Family Foundation, Inc., 217
The Charles A. and Anne Morrow Lindbergh Foundation, 218
Charleston Women in International Trade, 218
Charter Fund, 218
Chesapeake Corporation Foundation, 218
Chesterfield Federal Credit Union, 219
Chevron Corporation, 535
Choctaw Nation of Oklahoma, 219
Christian Record Services, 219
The Christophers, 219
Citizens for Global Solutions, 535
City University of New York, 220
Clinique Nursing Scholarship Program, 220
The Coca-Cola Foundation, 220
The College Board, 221
College Foundation of North Carolina, 221
Colorado Commission on Higher Education, 222

Colorado Masons Benevolent Fund Association, 222
Colorado Society of CPAs Educational Foundation, 222
Columbus Citizens Foundation, Inc., 223
Cone Mills Corporation, 223
Congressional Black Caucus Foundation, Inc., 224
Congressional Hispanic Caucus Institute, 224
Congressional Hispanic Caucus Institute, 535
Congressional Institute, Inc., 536
Connecticut Building Congress Scholarship Fund, 225
Connecticut Department of Higher Education, 225
Connecticut Higher Education Supplemental Loan Authority, 580
Connecticut League for Nursing, 227
Consortium of Information and Telecommunication Executives, Inc., 227
Costume Society of America, 228
Council on International Educational Exchange, 228
Courage Center Vocational Services-United Way Organization, 230
Creede Repertory Theatre, 536
Cushman School, 536
Cymdeithas Gymreig/Philadelphia, 230
The Cynthia E. Morgan Memorial Scholarship Fund, 230
Cystic Fibrosis Foundation, 230
Dairy Management, Inc., 231
The Dallas Foundation, 231
Data Processing Management Association/Portland Chapter, 232
Datatel Scholars Foundation, 232
Daughters of Penelope, 233
Daughters of Union Veterans of the Civil War 1861-1865, Inc., 235
Davidson Institute, 235
Davis-Roberts Scholarship Fund, 236
DEED, 236
Delaware Higher Education Commission, 236
Delaware Higher Education Commission, 580
Deloitte and Touche, 536
Delta Delta Delta Foundation, 238
Denver Rescue Mission, 537
Department For The Blind & Vision Impaired, 238
Descendants of the Signers of the Declaration of Independence, Inc., 238
Discover Financial Services, Inc., 239
District of Columbia Office of Post Secondar Education, 239
District of Columbia Office of Postsecondary Education, 239
Dolphin Scholarship Foundation, 240
Dow Jones Newspaper Fund, 537

Dow Jones Newspaper Fund and Yahoo! News, 538
E. I. du Pont de Nemours and Company, 538
Eastern Orthodox Committee on Scouting, 240
Eastman Kodak Company, 539
Edmund F. Maxwell Foundation, 241
Elder & Leemaur Publishers, 241
Elie Wiesel Foundation for Humanity, 241
Elizabeth Dow Ltd., 539
Elizabeth Greenshields Foundation, 241
Elks National Foundation, 242
EMC, 539
Engineers Foundation of Ohio, 242
Entergy, 539
Entertainment Weekly, 539
The Entomological Foundation, 242
Epilepsy Foundation of America, 243
Epilepsy Foundation of San Diego County, 243
EqualityMaine Foundation, 244
ESA Foundation, 244
ESPN Inc., 540
Essence Magazine, 540
Executive Women International, 244
Experimental Aircraft Association, Inc., 244
Explorers Club, 245
fahrenHEIGHT360, 540
Federal Bureau of Investigation, 540
Federal Employee Education and Assistance Fund, 245
Federal Reserve Bank of New York, 541
Federated Department Stores, Inc., 541
Feminist Majority Foundation, 541
Filoli Center, 542
Finance Authority of Maine, 245
First Catholic Slovak Ladies Association, 246
First Marine Division Association, Inc., 246
Fisher Communications, Inc., 246
Florida Department of Education, 247
Florida Department of Education, 542
Florida Department of Education, 580
Florida Division of Blind Services, 249
Florida Power & Light Company, 542
The Food Allergy & Anaphylaxis Network, 250
Foundation for Surgical Technology, 250
Foundation of Research and Education of the Am. Health Information Mgmt Assoc., 250
Foundation of the National Student Nurses Association, Inc., 250
Francis Ouimet Scholarship Fund, 251
Franklin D. Roosevelt Library, 543
Franklin Lindsay Student Aid Fund, 581
Fred G. Zahn Foundation, 251

597

Sponsor Index

Freedom From Religion Foundation, 251
The Gallup Organization, 252
Garden Club of America, 252
Garden Club of America, 543
Genentech, Inc., 543
General Mills, 543
General Motors North America, 544
Georgia Student Finance Commission, 254
Georgia Student Finance Commission, 581
Georgia-Pacific Corporation, 544
Glamour Magazine, 256
Golden Key International Honor Society, 256
Golf Course Superintendents Association of America, 259
Grand Encampment of Knights Templar of the USA, 582
Grange Insurance Association, 260
Greater Kanawha Valley Foundation, 260
Greenhouse Partners, 260
Hannaford Bros Co., 544
Harness Tracks of America, 260
Harry S. Truman Scholarship Foundation, 261
Hattie M. Strong Foundation, 582
Havana National Bank, 261
Hawaii Community Foundation, 261
Helicopter Association International, 276
Henkel Corporation, 276
Herschel C. Price Educational Foundation, 276
Hispanic Association of Colleges and Universities, 544
Hispanic College Fund, 277
Hispanic Engineer National Achievement Awards Conference, 278
Hispanic Heritage Foundation, 278
Hispanic Scholarship Fund, 278
Historic Bok Sanctuary, 545
Hoffman-La Roche Inc., 545
Hopi Tribe Grants and Scholarship Program, 279
Horatio Alger Association, 280
Horizons Foundation, 286
Horticultural Research Institute, 287
Houston Livestock Show and Rodeo, 288
IBM, 545
ICMA Retirement Corporation, 288
Idaho State Board of Education, 289
Idaho State Board of Education, 582
Illinois Student Assistance Commission, 290
The Indianapolis Star, a Gannett Newspaper, 545
INROADS, Inc., 546
Institute for Humane Studies, 293
Institute of Environmental Sciences and Technology, 293
Institute of Food Technologists, 294

Institute of International Education, 295
Institute of Real Estate Management Foundation, 295
Insurance Scholarship Foundation of America, 296
International Association of Fire Fighters, 296
International Buckskin Horse Association, Inc., 296
International Executive Housekeepers Association, 296
International Foodservice Editorial Council, 297
International Furnishings and Design Association Educational Foundation, 297
International Order of the King's Daughters and Sons, 298
International Radio and Television Society Foundation, 546
Intertribal Timber Council, 298
Iowa College Student Aid Commission, 298
Italian Catholic Federation, 299
IUE-CWA, 300
J. Paul Getty Trust, 546
Jackie Robinson Foundation, 301
James Beard Foundation, 301
James F. Byrnes Foundation, 305
Japanese American Association of New York, 305
Jaycee War Memorial Fund, 306
Jeannette Rankin Foundation, 307
Jeppesen Dataplan, 546
Jewish Family and Children's Services (JFCS), 582
Jewish Vocational Service, 307
Jewish War Veterans of the United States of America, 307
John Deere, 547
The John F. Kennedy Center for the Performing Arts, 547
John F. Kennedy Library Foundation, 547
John Wiley and Sons, Inc., 548
Johnson Controls, 548
J.W. Saxe Memorial Fund, 548
Kansas Board of Regents, 308
Kaplan, Inc., 310
Kappa Kappa Gamma Foundation, 310
KarMel Scholarship Committee, 310
Kentucky Higher Education Assistance Authority (KHEAA), 311
Kentucky Higher Education Assistance Authority (KHEAA), 548
KGO-TV/RTNDF, 312
The Kim and Harold Louie Family Foundation, 312
KIMT, 549
Knights of Columbus, 313
Kosciuszko Foundation, 314
The Lagrant Foundation, 315

Lambda Alpha National Collegiate Honors Society for Anthropology, 316
Landscape Architecture Foundation, 316
Landscape Architecture Foundation, 549
Latin American Educational Foundation, 318
League of United Latin American Citizens, 318
Learning for Life, 320
Library of Congress, 549
Life and Health Insurance Foundation for Education, 320
Liggett-Stashower, Inc., 321
Lighthouse International, 321
Los Padres Foundation, 322
Louis Carr Internship Foundation (LCIF), 549
Louisiana Department of Veterans Affairs, 322
Louisiana Office of Student Financial Assistance, 323
Louisiana State Department of Education, 323
Luso-American Education Foundation, 323
Maine Department of Agriculture, Food and Rural Resources, 325
Maine Division of Veterans Services, 325
Maine Educational Loan Authority, 583
Maine Innkeepers Association, 325
Maine Metal Products Association, 325
Maine Recreation and Parks Association, 326
Maine Restaurant Association, 326
Maine Society of Professional Engineers, 326
Maine State Society of Washington, DC, 327
Makovsky & Company Inc., 550
Manomet Center for Conservation Sciences, 327
Marin Community Foundation, 327
Marine Corps Scholarship Foundation, 328
Maryland Higher Education Commission Office of Student Financial Assistance, 328
Maryland Hospitality Education Foundation, 331
Massachusetts Board of Higher Education, 332
Massachusetts Board of Higher Education, 583
Massachusetts Democratic Party, 333
Massachusetts Democratic Party, 550
Massachusetts Department of Education, 334
MCC Theater, 550
McKee Scholars, 334
Menominee Indian Tribe of Wisconsin, 334

Sponsor Index

The Merchants Exchange, 334
Mercy Corps, 335
Metropolitan Museum of Art, 550
Mexican American Grocers Association Foundation, 335
Michigan Higher Education Assistance Authority, 335
Michigan Higher Education Assistance Authority, 551
Michigan Higher Education Student Loan Authority, 583
Michigan Society of Professional Engineers, 337
Microscopy Society of America, 337
Microsoft Corporation, 337
Midwestern Higher Education Compact, 338
Military Officers Association of America, 339
Military Officers Association of America, 583
Military Order of the Purple Heart, 339
Milk Processor's Education Program, 339
Minnesota Department of Veterans Affairs, 340
Minnesota Office of Higher Education, 340
Minnesota Office of Higher Education, 551
Minnesota Office of Higher Education, 584
Miss America Organization, 341
Mississippi Office of Student Financial Aid, 342
Mississippi Office of Student Financial Aid, 584
Missouri Department of Elementary and Secondary Education, 344
Missouri Department of Higher Education, 345
Missouri League for Nursing, 346
Moneygram of New York, 346
Montana Board of Regents of Higher Education, 347
Montana Trappers Association, 348
The Moody's Foundation, 348
Morris Arboretum of the University of Pennsylvania, 552
Mother Jones, 553
Museum of Modern Art, 554
Myasthenia Gravis Foundation, 348
NAACP, 349
NAACP Legal Defense and Education Fund, Inc., 350
NASA Alabama Space Grant Consortium, 351
NASA Arizona Space Grant Consortium, 554
NASA Arkansas Space Grant Consortium, 351
NASA Connecticut Space Grant Consortium, 351
NASA Delaware Space Grant Consortium, 352

NASA District of Columbia Space Grant Consortium, 352
NASA Georgia Space Grant Consortium, 352
NASA Hawaii Space Grant Consortium, 353
NASA Hawaii Space Grant Consortium, 554
NASA Idaho Space Grant Consortium, 353
NASA Illinois Space Grant Consortium, 353
NASA Indiana Space Grant Consortium, 354
NASA Kentucky Space Grant Consortium, 354
NASA Maine Space Grant Consortium, 354
NASA Massachusetts Space Grant Consortium, 555
NASA Michigan Space Grant Consortium, 355
NASA Minnesota Space Grant Consortium, 355
NASA Mississippi Space Grant Consortium, 356
NASA Missouri Space Grant Consortium, 356
NASA Montana Space Grant Consortium, 357
NASA Nevada Space Grant Consortium, 357
NASA New Jersey Space Grant Consortium, 555
NASA New Mexico Space Grant Consortium, 357
NASA North Carolina Space Grant Consortium, 358
NASA North Dakota Space Grant Consortium, 358
NASA Ohio Space Grant Consortium, 359
NASA Oregon Space Grant Consortium, 359
NASA Pennsylvania Space Grant Consortium, 359
NASA Pennsylvania Space Grant Consortium, 555
NASA Rhode Island Space Grant Consortium, 360
NASA Rocky Mountain Space Grant Consortium, 360
NASA South Carolina Space Grant Consortium, 361
NASA Texas Space Grant Consortium, 361
NASA Vermont Space Grant Consortium, 362
NASA Virginia Space Grant Consortium, 362
NASA West Virginia Space Grant Consortium, 363
NASA Wisconsin Space Grant Consortium, 363
NASA Wyoming Space Grant Consortium, 364

National Academy for Nuclear Training, 364
National Amateur Baseball Federation, Inc., 364
National Art Materials Trade Association, 365
National Association for Equal Opporuntiy in Higher Education (NAFEO), 365
National Association of Black Accountants Inc., 365
National Association of Black Journalists, 366
National Association of Black Journalists, 556
National Association of Latino Elected and Appointed Officials (NALEO), 556
National Association of Letter Carriers, 366
National Association of Water Companies (NJ Chapter), 367
National Association of Women in Construction, 367
National Athletic Trainers' Association Research & Education Foundation, 368
National Basketball Association, 556
National Black Nurses Association, 368
National Black Police Association, 368
National Center For Learning Disabilities, 369
National Commission for Cooperative Education, 369
National Dairy Promotion and Research Board, 369
National Dairy Shrine, 370
National Environmental Health Association/ American Academy of Sanitarians, 371
National Federation of the Blind, 371
National Foster Parent Association, 374
National Future Farmers of America, 374
National Geographic Society, 557
National Ground Water Research and Education Foundation, 374
National Inventors Hall of Fame, 375
National Italian American Foundation, 375
National Jewish Committee on Scouting, Boy Scouts of America, 376
National Merit Scholarship Corporation, 376
National Museum of the American Indian, 557
National Museum of Women in the Arts, 557
National Poultry & Food Distributors Association, 377
National Press Photographers Foundation, 377

Sponsor Index

National Restaurant Association Educational Foundation, 379
National Rifle Association, 379
National Science Foundation, 558
National Science Teachers Association, 380
National Sculpture Society, 380
National Security Agency, 380
National Society of Accountants Scholarship Foundation, 381
National Society of Black Engineers, 381
National Society of the Sons of the American Revolution, 383
National Speakers Association, 383
National Stone, Sand & Gravel Association, 383
Native Daughters of the Golden West, 384
Navy Supply Corps Foundation, 384
Navy-Marine Corps Relief Society, 384
Navy-Marine Corps Relief Society, 585
NCAA, 385
NCR Corporation, 558
Nebraska State Department of Education, 385
Nevada Department of Education, 385
New Dramatists, 558
New England Board of Higher Education, 386
New England Employee Benefits Council, 386
New Hampshire Higher Education Assistance Foundation (NHHEAF), 585
New Hampshire Postsecondary Education Commission, 386
New Hampshire Postsecondary Education Commission, 586
New Jersey Commission on Higher Education, 387
New Jersey Department of Military and Veterans Affairs, 387
New Jersey Higher Education Student Assistance Authority, 388
New Jersey Higher Education Student Assistance Authority, 586
New Jersey State Golf Association, 390
New Mexico Commission on Higher Education, 390
New Mexico Commission on Higher Education, 558
New Mexico Commission on Higher Education, 586
The New Republic, 559
New York Lottery, 391
New York State Assembly, 559
New York State Education Department, 392
New York State Grange, 392
New York State Grange, 587
New York State Higher Education Services Corporation, 393

New York State Native American Education Unit, 396
New York Times, 559
New York Women in Communications Foundation, 396
Nisei Student Relocation Commemorative Fund, 396
Non Commissioned Officers Association, 396
North American Limousin Foundation, 397
North Carolina Bar Association, 397
North Carolina Community Colleges Foundation, 398
North Carolina Community Colleges Foundation, 587
North Carolina Division of Veterans Affairs, 398
North Carolina Division of Vocational Rehabilitation Services, 399
North Carolina State Board of Refrigeration Examiners, 399
North Carolina State Education Assistance Authority, 399
North Carolina State Education Assistance Authority, 588
North Dakota University System, 401
Northern Cheyenne Tribal Education Department, 402
Northwest Danish Foundation, 402
Oak Ridge Institute for Science and Education, 403
Oak Ridge Institute for Science and Education, 559
Ohio Board of Regents, 403
Ohio Board of Regents, 588
Ohio National Guard, 404
Ohio Newspapers Foundation, 405
Ohio Newspapers Foundation, 564
Oklahoma Engineering Foundation, 406
Oklahoma State Department of Education Professional Services Division, 406
Oklahoma State Regents for Higher Education, 406
OMNE/Nursing Leaders of Maine, 408
ONS Foundation, 408
OP Loftbed, 409
Oregon Student Assistance Commission, 409
Organization of Chinese Americans, 419
The Orthotic and Prosthetic Education and Development Fund, 419
Osage Tribal Education Committee, 420
Outdoor Writers Association of America, Inc., 420
Owens Corning, 564
Pacific Gas and Electric Company, 564
Papercheck.com, 421
Par Aide, 421
Parapsychology Foundation, 421
Patient Advocate Foundation, 421

Paul Loeffler, 421
PBS, 565
Peacock Productions, Inc., 422
Penguin Putnam, Inc., 422
Pennsylvania Higher Education Assistance Agency, 422
Pennsylvania State System of Higher Education Foundation, Inc., 424
The Persian Scholarship Foundation, 425
PFLAG National Office, 425
PGA Tour, 565
Phi Delta Kappa International, 426
The Phillips Foundation, 426
Phipps Conservatory and Botanical Gardens, 565
Physician Assistant Foundation, 426
Pickett and Hatcher Educational Fund, Inc., 588
Playtex Products, Inc., 427
Plumbing-Heating-Cooling Contractors - National Assoc. Educational Foundation, 427
The Point Foundation, 428
Presbyterian Church (USA), 429
Presbyterian Church (USA), 589
Press Club of Houston Educational Foundation, 430
Pride of the Greater Lehigh Valley, 430
The Princess Grace Foundation USA, 430
Princeton Plasma Physics Laboratory, 565
Print and Graphics Scholarship Foundation, 431
Professional Association of Georgia Educators Foundation, Inc., 431
Quill and Scroll Foundation, 432
Radio and Television News Directors Foundation, 432
Random House, 566
Recording for the Blind and Dyslexic, 434
Red River Valley Fighter Pilots Association, 434
Reserve Officers Association, 435
Rhode Island Higher Education Assistance Authority, 435
Rhode Island State Government, 566
Rocky Mountain Coal Mining Institute, 435
Roger Von Amelunxen Foundation, 436
Ronald McDonald House Charities, 436
The Rotary Foundation, 436
ROTC/Air Force, 437
ROTC/United States Army, 438
Royce Builders, 438
Sachs Foundation, 439
Sallie Mae Fund, 439
Salute to Education, Inc., 439
Scarlett Family Foundation, 440
Scholarship Chicago, 440
Screen Actors Guild Foundation, 440

Sponsor Index

Seabee Memorial Scholarship Association, Inc., 441
Seattle Jaycees, 441
Second Marine Division Association Memorial Scholarship Fund, 441
SEG Foundation, 441
Senator George J. Mitchell Scholarship Research Institute, 442
Seneca Nation and BIA, 442
Sertoma International, 442
Service Employees International Union, California State Council, 443
Seventeen Magazine, 566
SGI (Silicon Graphics), 566
Shoshone Tribe, 443
Sid Richardson Memorial Fund, 443
Siemens Foundation, 443
Simon and Schuster Inc., 567
Slovak Gymnastic Union Sokol, USA, 444
Slovenian Women's Union of America, 444
Smithsonian Environmental Research Center, 567
Smithsonian Institution, 567
SNM, 445
SNM Technologist Section, 445
Sociedad Honoraria Hispanica, 445
Society for Science and the Public, 446
Society for Technical Communication, 446
Society of Actuaries/Casualty Actuarial Society, 447
Society of Automotive Engineers, 447
Society of Exploration Geophysicists, 449
Society of Manufacturing Engineers Education Foundation, 449
Society of Physics Students, 456
Society of Physics Students, 568
Society of Plastics Engineers, 456
Society of Professional Journalists, Greater Los Angeles Professional Chapter, 458
Society of Women Engineers, 459
Soil and Water Conservation Society, 470
Solomon R. Guggenheim Museum, 568
Sons of Italy Foundation, 470
Sons of Norway Foundation, 471
Sony Music Entertainment, 569
South Carolina Commission on Higher Education, 472
South Carolina Higher Education Tuition Grants Commission, 473
South Carolina Student Loan Corporation, 589
South Dakota Board of Regents, 473
South Dakota Department of Education, 474
South Dakota Department of Military and Veterans Affairs, 474
Southern Nursery Organization, 475
Southern Progress Corporation, 569

Southface Energy Institute, 569
SPIE - The International Society for Optical Engineering, 475
Spina Bifida Association, 475
Spoleto Festival USA, 570
Sports Journalism Institute, 570
Staples, 476
State Council of Higher Education for Virginia, 476
State of Alabama, 476
State Student Assistance Commission of Indiana, 477
Stephen T. Marchello Scholarship Foundation, 478
Student Aid Foundation, 589
Student Conservation Association, 570
Studio Art Centers International, 478
Sun Microsystems, 570
Sunkist Growers, 480
Supreme Guardian Council, International Center for Job's Daughters, 480
Supreme Guardian Council, International Order of Job's Daughters, 481
Swiss Benevolent Society of New York, 481
Taglit-Birthright Israel, 482
Technology Association of Georgia, 482
Tekmark Global Solutions, 482
Tennessee Student Assistance Corporation, 483
Tennessee Student Assistance Corporation, 590
Texas Higher Education Coordinating Board, 485
Texas Higher Education Coordinating Board, 590
Third Marine Division Association, 490
Thurgood Marshall College Fund, 490
Tourism Cares, 490
Tourism Cares, 571
Transportation Clubs International, 491
Travel and Tourism Research Association, 493
Treacy Company, 493
Trinity Episcopal Church, 493
Troy Douglass Carr Scholarship Fund, 494
Twentieth Century Fox, 571
Two Ten Footwear Foundation, 494
Tyson Foods, Inc., 571
UCB Pharma Inc., 494
Ukrainian Fraternal Association, 494
Unico Foundation, Inc., 495
Unitarian Universalist Association, 496
United Food and Commercial Workers International Union, 496
United Methodist Church, 591
United Methodist Church General Education Board of Higher Education and Ministry, 496

United Methodist Communications, 497
United Negro College Fund, 497
United Negro College Fund, 572
United States Association of Blind Athletes, 502
United States Holocaust Memorial Museum, 572
United States Institute of Peace, 502
United States Senate, 572
United Transportation Union Insurance Association, 503
University Film and Video Association, 503
University of New Mexico Health Sciences Center, 503
Upakar, 503
UPS, 504
UPS, 591
U.S. Army Recruiting Command, 504
U.S. Bank Student Banking Division, 504
U.S. Department of Agriculture, 505
U.S. Department of Agriculture, 572
U.S. Department of Education, 505
U.S. Department of Education, 591
U.S. Department of Education Rehabilitation Services Administration, 506
U.S. Department of Energy, 573
U.S. Department of Health and Human Services, 506
U.S. Department of Interior-Bureau of Indian Affairs, 506
U.S. Department of State, 573
U.S. Environmental Protection Agency, 506
U.S. House of Representatives, 573
U.S. National Arboretum, 573
U.S. Navy/Marine NROTC College Scholarship Program, 507
USTA Tennis and Education Foundation, 508
Utah Higher Education Assistance Authority (UHEAA), 508
Utah State Office of Education, 509
Utah State Office of Education, 592
The Vegetarian Resource Group, 509
Ventura County Japanese-American Citizens League, 509
Vermont Golf Association Scholarship Fund, Inc., 509
Vermont Student Assistance Corporation, 510
Vermont Student Assistance Corporation, 592
Veterans of Foreign Wars, 512
Virgin Islands Board of Education, 513
Virgin Islands Board of Education, 592
Virginia Department of Education, 513
Virginia Department of Health, 513
Virginia Department of Rehabilitative Services, 514
Virginia Museum of Fine Arts, 514

Sponsor Index

Wachovia, 574
Wall Street Journal, 574
Wal-Mart Foundation, 514
The Walt Disney Company, 574
Walt Disney World and Disneyland, 574
Washington Crossing Foundation, 515
Washington Internships for Students of Engineering, 575
Washington State Higher Education Coordinating Board, 516
Washington State PTA, 517
Wells Fargo, 517
Welsh Society of Philadelphia, 517
West Pharmaceutical Services, Inc., 518
West Virginia Division of Veterans Affairs, 518
West Virginia Higher Education Policy Commission, 518
West Virginia Higher Education Policy Commission, 593
Western European Architecture Foundation, 519
Western Golf Association/Evans Scholars Foundation, 520
Wilhelmina Models, 575
William Randolph Hearst Foundation, 520
Wilson Ornithological Society, 521
Wisconsin Department of Veterans Affairs, 521
Wisconsin Department of Veterans Affairs, 593
Wisconsin Higher Educational Aids Board, 522
Wisconsin Higher Educational Aids Board, 593
Wolf Trap Foundation for the Performing Arts, 575
Women Grocers of America, 523
Women of the Evangelical Lutheran Church in America, 523
Women's Sports Foundation, 576
Women's Western Golf Foundation, 524
Woodrow Wilson National Fellowship Foundation, 524
Working in Support of Education (WISE), 524
World Security Institute, 576
Worldstudio Foundation, 525
Xerox, 525
Yakama Nation Higher Education Program, 525

Program Index

911 Education Fund Scholarship Program, 439
A. Patrick Charnon Memorial Scholarship, 216
AAGS Joseph F. Dracup Scholarship Award, 97
AAJA Texas Scholarship, 194
AAJA/Chicago Tribune Internship Grant, 193
Abbie Sargent Memorial Scholarship, 75
Abe Voron Scholarship, 206
Abercrombie & Fitch Scholarship Program, 497
Academic Challenge Scholarship, 188
Academic Scholars Program, 406
Academic Scholarship for High School Seniors, 379
Academic Scholarship for Undergraduate Students, 379
Academic-Year Ambassadorial Scholarship, 436
Academy of Television Arts & Sciences Foundation Student Internship Program, 527
Accel Program Grant, 254
Access Missouri Financial Assistance Program, 345
Access to Better Learning and Education Grant Program (ABLE), 247
Accuracy in Media Internships, 527
ACSM Fellows Scholarship, 97
Ada I. Pressman Memorial Scholarship, 459
Ada Mucklestone Memorial Scholarship, 121
ADC Communications and Foundation Scholarship, 459
Adele Filene Travel Award, 228
ADHA Institute for Oral Health Part-Time Scholarship, 77
ADHA Institute General Scholarships, 77
ADHA Institute Merit Scholarships, 78
Adler Science and Math Scholarship, 129
Admiral Grace Murray Hopper Scholarship, 459
Adobe Systems Computer Science Scholarships, 459
Advertising Internship (Summer Only), 533
Aeronautics and Astronautics Undergraduate Scholarship, 110
Aerospace Undergraduate Research Scholarship Program, 362
AFCEA General Emmett Paige Scholarship, 190

AFCEA General John A. Wickham Scholarship, 190
AFCEA Professional Part-Time Scholarship, 190
AFCEA ROTC Scholarships, 190
AFCEA Scholarships for Math and Science Teachers, 80
AFCEA Sgt. Jeannette L. Winters, USMC Memorial Scholarship, 191
AFCEA/Lockheed Martin IT Scholarship, 191
AFPE "Gateway to Research" Scholarship, 104
AFSCME Family Scholarship, 101
AG Bell College Scholarship Awards, 88
AGC Education and Research Undergraduate Scholarship, 196
AGC of Maine Scholarship Program, 81
Agnes Jones Jackson Scholarship, 349
Agnes Malakate Kezios Scholarship, 178
AHEPA Educational Foundation Scholarships, 81
Ahmad-Sehar Saleha Ahmad and Abrahim Ekramullah Zafar Foundation, 409
AIA New Jersey Scholarship Foundation, Inc., 111
AIA/AAF Minority/Disadvantaged Scholarship, 92
AICP Heartland Chapter Scholarship, 199
AICP Scholarship, 199
Aiea General Hospital Association Scholarship, 261
Air Force Aid Society Education Grant, 81
Air Force Sergeants Association, Airmen Memorial Foundation, and Chief Master Sergeants of the Air Force Scholarship Programs, 81
Air Traffic Control Children of Specialists Scholarship, 82
Air Traffic Control Full-Time Employee Student Scholarship, 82
Air Traffic Control Half- to Full-Time Student Scholarship, 82
Airgas-Jerry Baker Scholarship, 182
Airgas-Terry Jarvis Memorial Scholarship, 182
A.J. "Andy" Spielman Travel Agents Scholarship, 179
Akademos, Inc. TextbookX.com Scholarship, 86
Alabama GI Dependents Educational Benefit, 88
Alabama Junior/Community College Athletic Scholarship, 87

Alabama National Guard Educational Assistance Award, 86
Alabama Robert C. Byrd Honors Scholarship, 87
Alabama Scholarship for Dependents of Blind Parents, 476
Alabama Student Assistance Program, 87
Alabama Student Grant, 87
Alaska Family Education Loan, 577
Alaska Teacher Education Loan, 577
Alaska Winn Brindle (W.B.) Memorial Education Loan Program, 577
Albert A. Marks Education Scholarship for Teacher Education, 341
Albert E. Wischmeyer Memorial Scholarship Award, 449
Albert M. Lappin Scholarship, 125
Albert T. Marcoux Memorial Scholarship, 140
Albina Fuel Company Scholarship, 409
Albuquerque ARC/Toby Cross Scholarship, 162
Alcoa Foundation Sons and Daughters Scholarship Program, 88
Alexander M. Tanger Scholarship, 206
Alexandra A. Sonenfeld Award, 233
Alexia Foundation Grant and Scholarship, 89
Alfred R. Chisholm Memorial Scholarship, 498
Alice Glaisyer Warfield Memorial Scholarship, 491
ALISE Bodhan S. Wynar Research Paper Competition, 197
ALISE Research Grant Award, 198
All-Arizona Academic Team, 187
Allcott/Hunt Share It Now II Scholarship, 409
Allen J. Baldwin Scholarship, 178
Allen Susser Scholarship, 301
Allied Dental Scholarship for Dental Assisting Students, 76
Allied Dental Scholarship for Dental Hygiene Students, 77
Allied Dental Scholarship for Dental Laboratory Technology Students, 77
All-Ink.com College Scholarship Program, 89
Allison E. Fisher Scholarship, 366
Allman Medical Scholarships, 341
Allstate Internships, 527
Alma White-Delta Kappa Gamma Scholarship, 262
Aloha Scholarship, 135
ALPFA Scholarship Program, 277
Alpha Beta Gamma International Scholarship, 90

Program Index

Alpha Delta Kappa/Harriet Simmons Scholarship, 409
Alpha Mu Gamma National Scholarship, 91
Alphonse A. Miele Scholarship, 495
Alphonso Deal Scholarship, 368
Alpine Club A.K. Gilkey and Putnam/Bedayn Research Grant, 92
Alton R. Higgins, MD, and Dorothy Higgins Scholarship, 498
Alumnae Panhellenic Association Women's Scholarship, 91
Alwin B. Newton Scholarship, 172
Ambassador Minerva Jean Falcon Hawaii Scholarship, 262
AMBUCS Scholars-Scholarship for Therapists, 91
American Association of Airport Executives Foundation Scholarship, 93
American Association of Airport Executives Foundation Scholarship for Native Americans, 93
American Association of Airport Executives Scholarship for Accredited Airport Executives (A.A.E.), 94
American Board of Funeral Service Education National Scholarship, 94
American Chemical Society Scholars Program, 95
American College of Musicians $200 Scholarship, 96
American College of Musicians Piano Composition Contest, 97
American Conservatory Theater Production Internships, 528
American Council of Engineering Companies of Oregon Scholarship, 410
American Council of Engineering Companies-Alaska Scholarship, 99
American Electroplaters and Surface Finishers Foundation Scholarship, 101
American Express Scholarship Competition, 107
American Express Travel Scholarship, 179
American Ex-Prisoner of War, Peter Connacher Memorial Scholarship, 410
American Federation of State, County, and Municipal Employees (AFSCME) Oregon Council # 75, 410
American Foundation for Aging Research Fellowship, 104
American Heart Association Undergraduate Student Research Program, 106
American Hotel & Lodging Educational Foundation Incoming Freshman Scholarship Competition, 107
American Legion Alabama Auxiliary Scholarship, 113

American Legion Alabama Oratorical Contest, 112
American Legion Alabama Scholarship, 112
American Legion Alaska Auxiliary Scholarship, 113
American Legion Alaska Auxiliary Western District Scholarship, 113
American Legion Alaska Oratorical Contest, 113
American Legion Americanism and Government Test, 122
American Legion Arizona Auxiliary Health Care Occupation Scholarship, 114
American Legion Arizona Auxiliary Nurses' Scholarship, 114
American Legion Arizona Oratorical Contest, 114
American Legion Arkansas Auxiliary Scholarships, 115
American Legion Arkansas Oratorical Contest, 115
American Legion Arkansas Scholarship, 115
American Legion Auxiliary National President's Scholarship, 135
American Legion Baseball Scholarship, 154
American Legion California Auxiliary General Scholarships, 116
American Legion California Oratorical Contest, 115
American Legion Department Oratorical Awards, 127
American Legion Department Oratorical Contest, 146
American Legion Department Oratorical Contest, 152
American Legion Eagle Scout of the Year, 135
American Legion Eagle Scout of the Year, 151
American Legion Family Scholarship, 122
American Legion Florida Auxiliary Memorial Scholarship, 119
American Legion Florida Auxiliary Scholarships, 119
American Legion Florida General Scholarship, 118
American Legion Georgia Auxiliary Scholarship, 119
American Legion Idaho Auxiliary Nurse's Scholarship, 120
American Legion Idaho Scholarships, 120
American Legion Illinois Boy Scout Scholarship, 121
American Legion Illinois Oratorical Contest, 121
American Legion Illinois Scholarships, 121
American Legion Indiana Oratorical Contest, 123
American Legion Iowa Oratorical Contest, 124

American Legion Kansas Auxiliary Department Scholarships, 127
American Legion Kentucky Auxiliary Mary Barrett Marshall Scholarship, 127
American Legion Legacy Scholarship, 136
American Legion Maine Auxiliary Scholarship, 128
American Legion Maryland Auxiliary Scholarship, 129
American Legion Maryland Boys State Scholarship, 129
American Legion Maryland Oratorical Contest, 129
American Legion Maryland Scholarship, 129
American Legion Massachusetts Auxiliary Scholarship, 130
American Legion Massachusetts General and Nursing Scholarships, 130
American Legion Michigan Auxiliary Memorial Scholarship, 131
American Legion Michigan Oratorical Contest, 131
American Legion Minnesota Auxiliary Department Scholarship, 133
American Legion Minnesota Legionnaire Insurance Trust Scholarship, 132
American Legion Minnesota Oratorical Contest, 132
American Legion Mississippi Auxiliary Scholarship, 133
American Legion Missouri Auxiliary Scholarship, 134
American Legion Montana Auxiliary Scholarships (1), 135
American Legion Montana Auxiliary Scholarships (2), 135
American Legion Music Scholarship, 125
American Legion National High School Oratorical Contest, 136
American Legion Nebraska Oratorical Contest, 137
American Legion Nebraska President's Scholarship, 137
American Legion Nevada Oratorical Contest, 139
American Legion New Hampshire Boys State Scholarship, 140
American Legion New Hampshire Oratorical Contest, 140
American Legion New Jersey Auxiliary Department Scholarships, 142
American Legion New Jersey Oratorical Contest, 141
American Legion New York Auxiliary Scholarship, 144
American Legion New York Oratorical Contest, 143
American Legion North Dakota Auxiliary Scholarships, 145

American Legion North Dakota Oratorical Contest, 144
American Legion Ohio Auxiliary Past President's Parley Nurse's Scholarship, 145
American Legion Ohio Auxiliary Scholarship, 146
American Legion Ohio Scholarships, 145
American Legion Oratorical Contest, 120
American Legion Oratorical Contest, 125
American Legion Oregon Auxiliary Department Nurses Scholarship, 146
American Legion Press Club of New Jersey and Post 170--Arthur Dehardt Memorial Scholarship, 142
American Legion Puerto Rico Auxiliary Nursing Scholarships, 147
American Legion South Carolina Auxiliary Scholarship, 148
American Legion South Carolina Department Oratorical Contest, 148
American Legion South Dakota Auxiliary Nurse's Scholarship, 148
American Legion South Dakota Auxiliary Scholarships, 149
American Legion South Dakota Educational Loan, 578
American Legion South Dakota Oratorical Contest, 148
American Legion Tennessee Oratorical Contest, 149
American Legion Texas Auxiliary General Education Scholarship, 150
American Legion Texas Auxiliary Medical Scholarship, 150
American Legion Utah Auxiliary National President's Scholarship, 151
American Legion Vermont Scholarship, 151
American Legion Vermont Scholarship Program, 151
American Legion Virginia Oratorical Contest, 152
American Legion Washington Auxiliary Scholarships, 153
American Legion Washington Scholarships, 153
American Legion West Virginia Auxiliary Scholarship, 154
American Legion West Virginia Oratorical Contest, 153
American Legion Western District Postsecondary Scholarship, 113
American Legion Wisconsin Auxiliary Department President's Scholarship, 155
American Legion Wisconsin Auxiliary H.S. and Angeline Lewis Scholarships, 155

American Legion Wisconsin Auxiliary Merit and Memorial Scholarship, 155
American Legion Wisconsin Auxiliary Past Presidents Parley Scholarship, 155
American Legion Wisconsin Eagle Scout of the Year Scholarship, 154
American Legion Wyoming Auxiliary Past Presidents' Parley Scholarship, 156
American Legion Wyoming E.A. Blackmore Memorial Scholarship, 156
American Legion Wyoming Oratorical Contest, 156
American Meteorological Society Undergraduate Scholarships, 157
American Meteorological Society/Industry Minority Scholarship, 157
American Quarter Horse Foundation Scholarships, 162
American Restaurant Scholarship, 302
American Savings Bank Scholars Program, 262
American Society for Training and Development -- Cascadia Chapter Scholarship, 410
American Society of International Law Internships, 529
American Society of Mechanical Engineers Foundation Scholarship, 175
American Standard Scholarship, 427
American Water Ski Educational Foundation Scholarship, 182
American Welding Society District Scholarship, 183
Americanism Essay Contest Scholarship, 121
AMHI Educational Scholarships, 158
AMHI van Schaik Dressage Scholarship, 158
Amtrol Scholarship, 106
Angelfire Scholarship, 232
Angelo S. Bisesti Scholarship, 159
Anna Gear Junior Scholarship, 152
Anna K. Meredith Fund Scholarship, 478
Anne Ford Scholarship, 369
Anne Maureen Whitney Barrow Memorial, 460
Anne U. White Fund, 199
Annie's Homegrown Sustainable Agriculture Scholarships, 186
ANS Undergraduate Scholarships, 159
"Anthem" Essay Contest, 201
Anthropology Internship Program, 529
A.O. Smith Water Heaters Scholarship, 427
AOPA Air Safety Foundation/McAllister Memorial Scholarship, 86
Appaloosa Youth Foundation Educational Scholarships, 187

Applied Arts Internships, 532
Applied Materials Internships and Co-ops, 532
Arboriculture Internship, 552
Area Go Texan Scholarships, 288
Arizona Chapter Dependent Scholarship Fund, 180
Arizona Chapter Gold Scholarship, 180
Arizona Tuition Scholarships for Children/Spouses of Slain Public Servants, 187
Arizona Tuition Scholarships for Residents, 188
Arkansas Department of Higher Education Teacher Assistance Resource (STAR) Program, 579
Arkansas Law Enforcement Officers' Dependents Scholarship, 188
Arkansas Minority Teachers Scholarship Program, 579
Armenian General Benevolent Union International Scholarship Program, 192
ARRL Earl I. Anderson Scholarship, 162
ARRL Scholarship Honoring Senator Barry Goldwater, K7UGA, 162
Arsham Amirikian Engineering Scholarship, 183
Arthur and Doreen Parrett Scholarship, 193
Arthur and Gladys Cervenka Scholarship, 449
Arthur E. Copeland Scholarship for Males, 502
Arthur M. and Berdena King Eagle Scout Scholarship, 383
Artistic and Administrative Internships, 528
Arts Action Fund Internship, 530
Arts Management Internship Program, 532
ASCAP Morton Gould Young Composers Award, 193
ASHRAE J. Richard Mehalick Scholarship, 172
ASHRAE Memorial Scholarship, 173
ASHRAE Region IV Benny Bootle Scholarship, 173
ASHRAE Region VIII Scholarship, 173
ASHRAE Scholarships, 173
Asian American Journalists Association Scholarships, 194
ASM Outstanding Scholars Awards, 194
ASME Auxiliary Student Loan, 578
ASME Student Loan Program, 578
ASME/FIRST Robotics Competition Scholarship, 175
Aspiring Sports Journalist Internship, 570
Associate Degree Engineering Technology Scholarship, 173
Associated General Contractors James L. Allhands Essay Competition, 197

Program Index

Associated Press/APTRA-CLETE Roberts Memorial Journalism Scholarship, 197
Association for Women in Communications Scholarship, 199
Astrid G. Cates Scholarship Fund and Myrtle Beinhauer Scholarship, 471
A.T. Anderson Memorial Scholarship, 109
Athletic Trainers' Entry Level Scholarship, 368
Athletic Trainers' Student Writing Contest, 368
Atlas Shrugged Essay Contest, 201
The Audria M. Edwards Scholarship Fund, 422
Automotive Educational Fund Scholarship, 200
Averyl Elaine Keriakedes Memorial Scholarship, 138
Aviation Maintenance Technician Scholarship Award, 276
A.W. Bodine Sunkist Memorial Scholarship, 480
Award in Desest Studies, 252
AXA Achievement Scholarship in Association with U.S. News & World Report, 201
B. Bradford Barnes Scholarship, 236
B. J. Harrod Scholarships, 460
B. K. Krenzer Reentry Scholarship, 460
Bachelor Degree Engineering Technology Scholarship, 174
Bal Dasa Scholarship Fund, 262
Bandon Submarine Cable Council Scholarship, 410
Bank of the Cascades Scholarship, 411
Baroid Scholarship, 106
Barry K. Wendt Commitment Award and Scholarship, 383
Barry M. Goldwater Scholarship, 202
Baxter International Inc. Internships, 533
Bay Area Council Scholarship Program, 202
Bechtel Foundation Scholarship, 460
Behavioral Sciences Student Fellowship, 243
Bemis Company Foundation Scholarship, 202
Ben Selling Scholarship, 411
Benjamin Franklin/Edith Green Scholarship, 411
Berbeco Senior Research Fellowship, 498
Bern Laxer Memorial Scholarship, 302
Berna Lou Cartwright Scholarship, 178
Berntsen International Scholarship in Surveying, 97
Berntsen International Scholarship in Surveying Technology, 97
Bertha Lamme Memorial Scholarship, 461
Bertha P. Singer Scholarship, 411

Best Buy Scholarship Program, 203
Best Teen Chef Culinary Scholarship Competition, 192
BIA North County Division Scholarship, 208
Bill Farr Scholarship, 458
Biocommunications Association Inc. Scholarship, 204
Black & Veatch Internships, Co-op, and Summer Employment, 534
Black Nurses Scholarship, 368
The BlackNews.com Scholarship, 204
Blanche Fearn Memorial Award, 251
Blossom Kalama Evans Memorial Scholarship, 262
BMW/Society of Automotive Engineers (SAE) Engineering Scholarships, 447
Bob Baxter Scholarship, 377
Bob East Scholarship Fund, 377
Bodie McDowell Scholarship, 420
The Boeing Company Undergraduate Scholarships, 205
Boeing Internship Program, 534
Bonus Incentive Grant (BIG), 290
Boston Globe Summer Internship, 535
Boston Scientific Scholarship, 461
Boy and Girl Scouts Scholarship, 240
Boy Scout of the Year Scholarship, 124
Bradford White Scholarship, 427
Broadcast Internship Grant, 194
Brown Foundation Academic Scholarships, 208
Bruce van Ess Scholarship, 300
Bryan Close Polo Grill Scholarship, 302
Buckingham Memorial Scholarship, 82
Buckskin Horse Association Scholarship, 296
Bud Glover Memorial Scholarship, 83
Bureau of Indian Affairs-Osage Tribal Education Committee Award, 209
Burlington Northern Santa Fe Foundation Scholarship, 109
Business Achievement Awards, 256
Business and Professional Women's Career Advancement Scholarship, 209
Business Reporting Intern Program, 537
Butler Manufacturing Company Foundation Scholarship, 209
Cadbury Adams Community Outreach Scholarships, 78
Caddie Scholarship, 390
Cady McDonnell Memorial Scholarship, 98
CaGIS Scholarship Award, 98
Cal Grant A & B Entitlement Award Program, 211
Cal Grant C Award Program, 211
California Association of Realtors Scholarship, 210
California Assumption Program of Loans for Education (APLE), 579

California Chafee Grant Program, 211
California Child Development Grant Program, 212
California Farm Bureau Scholarship, 210
California Law Enforcement Personnel Dependents Grant Program, 212
California Masonic Foundation Scholarship, 210
California Robert C. Byrd Honors Scholarship, 212
California Teachers Association Martin Luther King, Jr., Memorial Scholarship, 213
California's Junior Miss Competition, 211
Camille C. Chidiac Fund, 263
Canada Scholarship, 490
Candon Consulting Group Scholarship Fund, 263
Cargill Scholarship Program, 498
Carl Greenberg Scholarship, 458
Carl N. & Margaret Karcher Founders' Scholarship, 214
Carole Fielding Video Grant, 503
Carole Simpson Scholarship, 366
Carole Simpson Scholarship, 432
Caroline Kark Scholarship, 392
Caroline Thorn Kissel Summer Environmental Studies Scholarship, 253
Carville M. Akehurst Memorial Scholarship, 287
Castle & Cooke Mililani Technology Park Scholarship Fund, 263
Caterpillar Inc. Scholarship, 461
Caterpillar Scholars Award, 450
Catholic Aid Association Scholarship, 216
Cayetano Foundation Scholarship, 263
The CBC Spouses Cheerios Brand Health Initiative Scholarship, 224
The CBC Spouses Education Scholarship, 224
The CBC Spouses Performing Arts Scholarship, 224
The CBC Spouse's Visual Arts Scholarship, 224
CCNMA Scholarship, 216
Central New Mexico Scholarship, 461
Certified Public Accountants Minorities Scholarship, 111
C.G. Fuller Foundation Scholarship, 217
Chafee Education and Training Scholarship, 411
ChairScholars Scholarship, 217
The Challenge Met Scholarship, 163
Champlain Valley Kennel Club Scholarship, 510
Chapter 17 St. Louis Scholarship, 450
Chapter 198 - Downriver Detroit Scholarship, 450
Chapter 4 - Lawrence A. Wacker Memorial Scholarship, 450
Chapter 52 - Wichita Scholarship, 451

Chapter 56 - Fort Wayne Scholarship, 451
Chapter 6 - Fairfield County Scholarship, 451
Chapter 67 - Phoenix Scholarship, 451
Charles & Lucille King Family Foundation Scholarships, 217
Charles and Annette Hill Scholarship, 126
Charles and Melva T. Owen Memorial Scholarship, 371
Charles B. Scharp Scholarship, 178
Charles Clarke Cordle Memorial Scholarship, 163
Charles Hardy Memorial Scholarship, 443
Charles L. Bacon Memorial Scholarship, 133
Charles L. Hebner Memorial Scholarship, 236
Charles N. Fisher Memorial Scholarship, 163
Charles R. Ford Scholarship, 306
Charles R. Quaiff, Sr. Memorial Scholarship, 219
Charles (Tommy) Thomas Memorial Scholarship, 159
Charles W. Riley Fire and Emergency Medical Services Tuition Reimbursement Program, 328
Charleston Women in International Trade Scholarship, 218
Charlotte Woods Memorial Scholarship, 492
Charter Fund Scholarship, 218
CHCI Congressional Internship Program, 535
Chesapeake Corporation Scholarship, 218
Chester Haddan Scholarship Program, 419
Chester M. Vernon Memorial Eagle Scout Scholarship, 376
Chevron Corporation Scholarships, 462
Chevron Internship Program, 535
ChevronTexaco Scholars Program, 499
The Chicago FM Club Scholarships, 163
Chick Evans Caddie Scholarship, 520
Children and Youth Scholarships, 128
Children of Veterans Tuiton Grant, 335
Chittenden Bank Scholarship, 510
Choctaw Nation Higher Education Program, 219
Chris Desens Scholarship, 302
Christa McAuliffe Memorial Scholarship, 140
Christa McAuliffe Teacher Incentive Program, 580
Christian Record Services Scholarship, 219
Christian Wolffer Scholarship, 302
Christine H. Eidie Memorial Scholarship, 321

The Christophers Video Contest for College Students, 219
Chuck Fulgham Scholarship Fund, 231
CIA Undergraduate Scholarship, 216
CIEE International Study Programs (CIEE-ISP) Scholarships, 228
Cisco/UNCF Scholars Program, 499
CITE-NY Association Scholarship, 227
Citizens for Global Solutions Internship, 535
City University Seek/College Discovery Program, 393
Claire Oliphant Memorial Scholarship, 142
Clare Brett Smith Scholarship, 479
The Clarence & Josephine Myers Scholarship, 451
Clat Triplette Scholarship, 303
Clinique Nursing Scholarship, 220
Clinton J. Helton Manufacturing Scholarship Award, 452
The Cloisters Summer Internship Program, 550
Coca-Cola Scholars Program, 220
Coca-Cola Two-Year Colleges Scholarship, 220
Colgate "Bright Smiles, Bright Futures" Minority Scholarships, 78
College Bound Fund Academic Promise Scholarship, 435
College Bound Scholarship, 440
College Photographer of the Year Competition, 378
College Scholarship Fund, 278
College Television Award, 75
CollegeSTEPS Program, 517
Collegiate Inventors Competition, 375
Colorado Masons Scholarship, 222
Colorado Society of CPAs General Scholarship, 222
Colorado Student Grant, 222
Colorado Supplemental Leveraging Educational Assistance Partnership Program, 222
Colorado Work-Study Program, 222
Columbus Citizens Foundation College Scholarship Program, 223
Community College Graduates Scholarship Program, 356
Community College Grant & Loan, 587
Community Scholarship Fund, 264
Competitive Cal Grant A and B Award Programs, 213
Computer Science Scholarship, 371
Cone Mills Scholarship Program, 223
Congressional Hispanic Caucus Institute Scholarship Awards, 224
Congressional Institute Internships, 536
Connecticut Aid for Public College Students, 225
Connecticut Aid to Dependents of Deceased/Disabled/MIA Veterans, 225

Connecticut Building Congress Scholarship, 225
Connecticut Capitol Scholarship Program, 225
Connecticut Family Education Loan Program (CT FELP), 580
Connecticut Independent College Student Grant, 226
Connecticut Minority Teacher Incentive Grant, 226
Connecticut Nursing Scholarship, 227
Connecticut Robert C. Byrd Honors Scholarship, 226
Connecticut Tuition Set Aside Aid, 226
Connecticut Tuition Waiver for Senior Citizens, 226
Connecticut Tuition Waiver for Veterans, 227
Connecticut Tuition Waiver for Vietnam MIA/POW Dependents, 227
Connie and Robert T. Gunter Scholarship, 452
Continuing or Re-entry Student Scholarship, 116
Cora Aguda Manayan Fund, 264
Costas G. Lemonopoulos Scholarship, 366
Courtland Paul Scholarship, 316
Critical Care Nurses Education Advancement Scholarship, 94
Critical Needs Alternative Route Teacher Loan/Scholarship, 584
Critical Teacher Shortage Student Loan Forgiveness Program, 580
Crowley Family Scholarship, 412
CRT Internship Program, 536
CTA Scholarship for Dependent Children, 213
CTA Scholarships for Members, 213
Cultural Ambassadorial Scholarship, 436
Cushman School Internship, 536
CW Scholarships, 246
Cymdeithas Gymreig (Welsh Society) Philadelphia Scholarship, 230
The Cynthia E. Morgan Memorial Scholarship Fund, 230
Cystic Fibrosis Student Traineeship, 230
DaimlerChrysler Corporation Fund Scholarships, 462
Dairy Product Marketing Scholarships, 369
Dairy Student Recognition Program, 370
Dallas Architectural Foundation - Arch Swank, Jr. Fellowship in the Craft of Architecture, 231
Dam Safety Officials Scholarship, 200
Dan McKeever Scholarship Program, 419
Dana Campbell Memorial Scholarship, 303
Dana Christmas Scholarship for Heroism, 388

Program Index

Daniel E. Lambert Memorial Scholarship, 128
Datatel Scholars Foundation Scholarship, 233
Daughters of Penelope Past Grand Presidents' Award, 234
David Arver Memorial Scholarship, 83
David C. Goodwin Scholarship, 142
David Family Scholarship, 412
David J. Fitzmaurice Scholarship, 300
David L. Irons Memorial Scholarship Fund, 264
David L. Stashower Scholarship, 321
David T. Woolsey Scholarship, 316
Davidson Fellows Scholarship, 235
Davis-Roberts Scholarship, 236
The Dayton Amateur Radio Association Scholarships, 163
DC Adoption Scholarship, 239
DC Tuition Assistance Grant Program, 239
Decommissioning, Decontamination and Reutilization Scholarship, 159
Delaware Legislative Essay Scholarship, 237
Delaware Nursing Incentive Program, 580
Delaware Scholarship Incentive Program, 237
Delaware Space Grant Undergraduate Summer Scholarship, 352
Delaware Space Grant Undergraduate Tuition Scholarship, 352
Delayed Education Scholarship for Women, 159
Dell Inc. Scholarship, 462
Della Van Deuren Memorial Scholarship, 155
Deloitte and Touche Internship Program, 536
Delta Delta Delta Undergraduate Scholarship, 238
Delta Faucet Company Scholarship, 428
Delta Gamma Foundation Memorial Scholarship, 104
Demonstration of Energy-Efficient Developments Program Scholarship, 236
Denny Lydic Scholarship, 492
Denver Rescue Mission Center for Mission Studies Interns, 537
Department of Commerce Internship for Postsecondary Students, 559
Department of Energy Special Emphasis Program, 560
Department of Iowa Scholarships, 124
Department of Massachusetts Oratorical Contest, 130
Department of New Hampshire Scholarship, 140
Department Oratorical Awards, 145
Department President's Scholarship, 117
Department President's Scholarship for Junior Auxiliary Members, 117

Department Vocational Scholarship, 140
Dependents of Deceased Service Members Scholarship Program, 384
Descendants of the Signers of the Declaration of Independence Scholarship, 238
Deseo at the Westin Scholarship, 303
Detroit Chapter One - Founding Chapter Scholarship Award, 452
Detroit Section SAE Technical Scholarship, 447
Developmental Disabilities Nursing Scholastic Achievement Scholarship, 203
Developmental Disability Scholastic Achievement Scholarship, 203
Dialog/ALISE Methodology Paper Competition, 198
Diamond State Scholarship, 237
Directors Scholarship, 452
Discover Scholarship Program, 239
Disney College Program, 574
Disney Professional Internships, 574
Distance-Learning/On-Line Programs Scholarship, 191
District of Columbia Leveraging Educational Assistance Partnership Program, 240
DOE Pre-Service Teacher Internships, 560
Dolly Ching Scholarship Fund, 264
Dolores Nunes Lowry Scholarship, 323
Dolphin Scholarship, 240
Donald A. Williams Soil Conservation Scholarship, 470
Donald and Shirley Hastings National Scholarship, 183
Donald Burnside Memorial Scholarship, 187
Donald F. Hastings Scholarship, 183
The Donald Riebhoff Memorial Scholarship, 164
Doris & Clarence Glick Classical Music Scholarship, 265
Dorothy Campbell Memorial Scholarship, 412
Dorothy Lemke Howarth Scholarships, 462
Dorothy M. & Earl S. Hoffman Scholarships, 463
Dorothy P. Morris Scholarship, 463
Dosatron International Scholarship, 102
Douglas Haskell Awards for Student Journalism, 111
DPMA/PC Scholarship, 232
Dr. & Mrs. Arthur William Phillips Scholarship, 424
Dr. Alfred C. Fones Scholarship, 78
Dr. Alvin and Monica Saake Scholarship, 265
Dr. Click Cowger Scholarship, 126
Dr. Don and Rose Marie Benton Scholarship, 231

Dr. Hannah K. Vuolo Memorial Scholarship, 143
Dr. Hans & Clara Zimmerman Foundation Education Scholarship, 265
Dr. Hans and Clara Zimmerman Foundation Health Scholarship, 265
Dr. Harold Hillenbrand Scholarship, 78
Dr. James L. Lawson Memorial Scholarship, 164
Dr. Kate Waller Barrett Grant, 152
Dr. Marie E. Zakrzewski Medical Scholarship, 314
Dr. W. Wes Eckenfelder Jr. Scholarship, 208
Duane Hanson Scholarship, 174
Duck Brand Duct Tape Stuck at Prom Scholarship Contest, 276
DuPont Company Scholarship, 463
DuPont Cooperative Education Program, 538
DuPont Internships, 538
Dutch and Ginger Arver Scholarship, 83
E. Wayne Kay Community College Scholarship, 453
E. Wayne Kay Co-op Scholarship, 453
E. Wayne Kay High School Scholarship, 453
E. Wayne Kay Scholarship, 453
Eagle Scout Academic Scholarships, 205
Eagle Scout of the Year, 119
Eagle Scout of the Year Scholarship, 123
Eagle Scout of the Year Scholarship, 150
Earl & Patricia Armstrong Scholarship, 499
Earl Dedman Memorial Scholarship, 102
Earl G. Graves Scholarship, 349
Early Childhood Development Scholarship, 311
Eastman Kodak Cooperative Internship Programs, 539
Ecolab Scholarship Competition, 107
Economic Research Division Project Internships, 534
Ed Bradley Scholarship, 432
Ed Markham International Scholarship, 102
Edgar J. Boschult Memorial Scholarship, 137
Edmond A. Metzger Scholarship, 164
Edmund F. Maxwell Foundation Scholarship, 241
Edna M. Barcus Memorial Scholarship and Hoosier Scholarship, 123
The EDSA Minority Scholarship, 316
Education Achievement Awards, 257
Education Advancement Scholarship, 94
Education and Leadership Development Program, 301

Program Index

Educational Aide Exemption, 485
Educational Benefits for Children of Deceased Veterans and Others, 237
Educational Opportunity Fund (EOF), 388
Edward and Norma Doty Scholarship, 266
Edward D. Hendrickson/SAE Scholarship, 447
Edward J. Brady Memorial Scholarship, 183
Edward J. Dulis Scholarship, 195
Edward J. Nell Memorial Scholarship, 432
Edward Payson and Bernice Pi'ilani Irwin Scholarship Trust Fund, 266
Edward S. Roth Manufacturing Engineering, 454
E.E. Black Scholarship, 266
Eight and Forty Lung and Respiratory Nursing Scholarship Fund, 136
Eileen J. Garrett Scholarship, 421
Electronics for Imaging Scholarship, 463
Elie Wiesel Prize in Ethics, 241
Elizabeth A. Sackler Museum Educational Trust, 479
Elizabeth Dow Internship Program, 539
Elizabeth Dow Ltd. Internships, 532
The Elizabeth Greenshields Grant, 241
Elizabeth McLean Memorial Scholarship, 464
Elks Most Valuable Student Scholarship, 242
Elks National Foundation Legacy Awards, 242
Ellison Onizuka Memorial Scholarship, 266
Elwood Grimes Literary Scholarship, 205
Emanuele and Emilia Inglese Memorial Scholarship, 375
EMC Summer Internship Program and Co-ops, 539
Emily Lester Vermont Opportunity Scholarship, 510
Energy Student Achievement Program, 560
Engineering/Technology Achievement Awards, 257
Engineers Foundation of Ohio Scholarships, 242
Enology and Viticulture Scholarship, 170
Entergy Jumpstart Co-ops and Internships, 539
Entertainment Weekly Internship Program, 539
The Entomological Foundation BioQuip Undergraduate Scholarship, 242
Eos #1 Mother Lodge Chapter Award, 234
EPA National Network for Environmental Management Studies Fellowship, 506

Epilepsy Foundation of San Diego County Scholarship, 243
Erby Young Scholarship, 346
The Erikka A. Hayes Foundation Scholarship, 331
Erman W. Taylor Memorial Scholarship, 133
ESA Foundation Scholarship Program, 244
ESPN Internship, 540
Essence Summer Internship, 540
Esther Kanagawa Memorial Art Scholarship, 267
Ethics in Business Scholarship, 247
E.U. Parker Memorial Scholarship, 372
Eugene and Elinor Kotur Scholarship, 494
Eugene Bennet Visual Arts Scholarship, 412
Eugene Borson Memorial Scholarship, 293
Eugene C. Figg Jr. Civil Engineering Scholarship, 171
The Eugene "Gene" Sallee, W4YFR Memorial Scholarship, 164
Eugenia Vellner Fischer Award for the Performing Arts, 342
Eva Vieira Memorial Scholarship, 324
Executive Office Intern, 530
Executive Women International Scholarship, 244
Exelon Scholarship, 464
Exemption for Peace Officers Disabled in the Line of Duty, 485
Exemption for the Surviving Spouse and Dependent Children of Certain Deceased Public Servants (Employees), 485
Explorers Club Youth Activity Fund, 245
Extrusion Division/Lew Erwin Memorial Scholarship, 456
fahrenHEIGHT 360 Intern Placement, 540
Fashion Group International of Portland Scholarship, 412
Federal Direct Stafford Loans, 591
Federal Employee Education and Assistance Fund Scholarship, 245
Federal Family Education Loan Program, 586
Federal Family Education Loan Program (FFEL), 591
Federal Pell Grant Program, 505
Federal Perkins Loan, 591
Federal Plus Loan, 592
Federal Reserve Undergraduate Summer Analyst Program, 541
Federal Supplemental Educational Opportunity Grant Program, 505
Federal Work-Study Program, 505
Federated Department Stores Internships, 541
Feminism & Leadership Internship, 541
Feminist Web Internship, 541

Ferdinand Torres Scholarship, 105
FFRF Student Activist Award, 252
Field Aviation Co., Inc. Scholarship, 83
Field Botany Scholarships, 253
Field Services Internship, 530
The Filipino Nurses' Organization of Hawaii Scholarship, 267
Filoli Center Garden Internships and Apprenticeships, 542
Finance Undergraduate Internships, 574
Financial Women International Scholarship, 267
First Catholic Slovak Ladies Association Fraternal Scholarship, 246
First Generation Scholarship Program, 221
First Marine Division Association Scholarship, 246
Fisher Broadcasting Scholarship for Minorities, 246
Fleming/Blaszcak Scholarship, 456
Fletcher & Fritzi Hoffmann Education Fund, 267
Flight 587 Memorial Scholarships, 393
Flora of Pennsylvania Internship, 552
Florence Lemcke Memorial Scholarship, 153
Florida Academic Scholars Award, 247
Florida Educational Assistance for the Blind, 249
Florida Gold Seal Vocational Scholars Award, 247
Florida Medallion Scholars Award, 247
Florida Power & Light Co-op Program, 542
Florida Robert C. Byrd Honors Scholarship, 248
Florida Student Assistance Grant Program, 248
Florida Work Experience Program, 542
Floyd Qualls Memorial Scholarship, 100
The Food Allergy & Anaphylaxis Network College Scholarship Essay Contest, 250
Foodservice Communicators Scholarship, 297
Ford Motor Company Scholarship, 464
Ford Motor Company/American Indian College Fund Corporate Scholars Program, 108
Ford Opportunity Program, 413
Ford Scholars Program, 413
FORE Undergraduate Scholarship, 250
Foreign Study/Diversity Scholarship, 109
Foundation for Surgical Technology Scholarship Fund, 250

609

The Fountainhead Essay Contest, 201
Fran Johnson Non-Traditional Scholarship, 102
Francis M. Peacock Native Bird Habitat Scholarship, 253
Francis Ouimet Scholarship, 251
Frank D. Visceglia Memorial Scholarship, 205
Frank L. Weil Memorial Eagle Scout Scholarship, 376
Frank M. Coda Scholarship, 174
Frank M. McHale Memorial Scholarship, 123
Frank O'Bannon Grant, 477
Frank William and Dorothy Given Miller Mechanical Engineering Scholarship, 176
Franklin D. Roosevelt Library/Roosevelt Summer Internship, 543
Franklin Lindsay Student Aid Loan, 581
Fred G. Zahn Foundation Scholarship, 251
Fred M. Young Sr./SAE Engineering Scholarship, 448
Fred R. McDaniel Memorial Scholarship, 164
The Fred Rogers Memorial Scholarship, 75
The Freedom Forum/NCAA Sports Journalism Scholarship, 385
Freeman Fellowship, 172
Freeman-ASIA Award Program, 295
Freshman Undergraduate Scholarship Program, 157
Friends of Hawaii Public Housing Scholarship, 267
Fulfilling the Legacy Scholarship, 381
Future Leaders of Manufacturing Scholarships, 454
Future Teachers Scholarship, 406
F.W. "Beich" Beichley Scholarship, 176
Gabriel A. Hartl Scholarship, 83
Gabriel Prize, 519
The Gallup Management Development Scholarship 2,500 Award$, 252
Garden Club of America Summer Environmental Awards, 253
Garland Duncan Mechanical Engineering Scholarship, 176
Garmin Scholarship, 84
The Gates Millenium Scholarship, 203
Gates Millennium Scholars Program, 499
GCA Internship in Garden History and Design, 543
GCSAA Legacy Awards, 259
GCSAA Scholars Competition, 259
GCSAA Student Essay Contest, 259
GE Business/Engineering Scholarship for Minority Students, 318
GE Lloyd Trotter African American Forum Scholarship, 381
GEICO Life Scholarship, 257

Gene Hovis Memorial Scholarship, 303
Genentech Internship Program, 543
General Electric Foundation Scholarship, 464
General Electric Women's Network Scholarship, 465
The General Fund Scholarships, 165
General Mills Summer Internship, 543
General Motors Corporation Talent Acquisition Internship, 544
General Motors Engineering Scholarship, 109
General Motors Foundation Scholarships, 465
General News Copy Editing Internship, 537
Geography Students Internship, 557
George A. Hall/Harold F. Mayfield Award, 521
George A. Roberts Scholarships, 195
The George Foreman Tribute to Lyndon B. Johnson Scholarship, 432
George Griffiths/Ada Jakubic Scholarship, 424
George M. Brooker Collegiate Scholarship for Minorities, 295
George Mason Business Scholarship Fund, 268
George Reinke Scholarships, 180
Georgia Governor's Scholarship, 254
Georgia Hope Grant - GED Recipient, 254
Georgia Hope Grant - Public Technical Institution, 254
Georgia Hope Scholarship - Private Institution, 255
Georgia Hope Scholarship - Public College or University, 255
Georgia Law Enforcement Personnel Dependents Grant, 255
Georgia LEAP Grant, 255
Georgia Promise Teacher Scholarship, 581
Georgia Robert C. Byrd Scholarship, 255
Georgia Scholarship for Engineering Education, 581
Georgia Tuition Equalization Grant, 256
Georgia-Pacific Internships and Co-ops, 544
Gerrit R. Ludwig Scholarship, 268
Ginger and Fred Deines Canada Scholarship, 492
Ginger and Fred Deines Mexico Scholarship, 492
Girl Scout Achievement Award, 136
Giuliano Mazzetti Scholarship, 454
GlaxoSmithKline Opportunity Scholarship, 399
Glenn Jackson Scholars, 413
GM Engineering Scholarship For Minority Students, 319
Golden Key Research Grants, 257
Golden Key Service Award, 257

Golden Key Study Abroad Scholarships, 258
Golden LEAF Scholars Program - Two-Year Colleges, 399
Golden LEAF Scholarship - Four-Year University Program, 400
Goldman Family Fund: New Leader Scholarship, 327
Goldman, Sachs and Co. Scholarship, 465
Google Hispanic College Fund Scholarship Program, 277
Government and Public Affairs Internship, 530
Governor's Postsecondary Scholarship, 347
Governor's Scholars Program, 189
Grace S. High Memorial Child Welfare Scholarship Fund, 141
Graduate, Baccalaureate or Coordinated Program Scholarships, 100
Graduate Scholarship, 138
Grand Army of the Republic Living Memorial Scholarship, 235
Grange Denise Scholarship, 393
Grange Insurance Scholarship, 260
Grange Student Loan Fund, 587
Grange Susan W. Freestone Education Award, 393
Grant Program for Dependents of Correctional Officers, 290
Grant Program for Dependents of Police or Fire Officers, 291
Great Lakes Colleges Association/Associated Colleges of the Midwest Oak Ridge Science Semester, 560
Greater Kanawha Valley Scholarship Program, 260
Greater Research Opportunities Undergraduate Student Fellowships, 507
Green Mountain Dog Club Scholarship, 510
Greenhouse Scholars, 260
The Grottos Scholarships, 480
Grow Your Own Teacher Scholarship Program, 289
Guggenheim Museum Internship, 568
Guide Dogs for the Blind Dorthea and Roland Bohde Personal Achievement Scholarship, 105
Gulf Coast Research Laboratory Minority Summer Grant, 342
Guy M. Wilson Scholarship, 131
HACU National Internship Program, 544
Hall/McElwain Merit Scholarships, 206
Hank LeBonne Scholarship, 372
Hannaford Internships, 544
Hansen Scholarship, 244
Harness Tracks of America Scholarship Fund, 260
Harold Bettinger Memorial Scholarship, 102

Harold E. Fellows Scholarship, 207
Harold K. Douthit Scholarship, 405
Harriet Hoffman Memorial Scholarship, 125
Harriet Irsay Scholarship, 112
Harry S. Truman Scholarship, 261
HCF Scholarship Program, 277
Health Career Scholarship, 298
Healy Scholarship, 180
Hearst Journalism Award, 520
Heartland Scholarship Fund, 407
Helen Copeland Scholarship for Females, 502
Helen J. Sioussat/Fay Wells Scholarship, 207
Helen Johnson Scholarship, 458
HENAAC Scholars Program, 278
Henry A. Zuberano Scholarship, 268
Henry Adams Scholarship, 174
The Henry Broughton, K2AE Memorial Scholarship, 165
Henry J. Reilly Memorial College Scholarship, 435
Henry Salvatori Scholarship, 470
Herbert Fernandes Scholarship, 324
Herbert Lehman Educational Fund, 350
Herman M. Holloway, Sr., Memorial Scholarship, 237
Herman O. West Foundation Scholarship Program, 518
Hermione Grant Calhoun Scholarship, 372
Herschel C. Price Educational Scholarship, 276
High Honors Endorsement Tuition Scholarship, 188
High School Oratorical Contest, 119
Higher Education Grant Program, 209
Higher REACH Scholarship, 514
Hinson-Hazlewood College Access Loan (CAL), 590
Hispanic Heritage Youth Awards Program, 278
Hispanic Youth Leaders Scholarship, 346
Historic Bok Sanctuary Conservation Program Internship, 545
Historically Black College and University Scholarship Fund, 349
Historically Black Colleges and Minority Institutions Scholarships, 205
HKS/John Humphries Minority Scholarship, 231
Hoffman-La Roche Inc. Student Internship, 545
Holland America Line-Westours, Inc., Scholarship, 180
Homestead Capital Housing Scholarship, 413
Honeywell Avionics Scholarship, 84
Honeywell International Inc. Scholarship, 465
Honors Internship Program, 540
Hooper Memorial Scholarship, 492
Hoosier Scholar Award, 477

HOPE-Aspire Award, 483
Hope-General Assembly Merit Scholarship, 483
Hopi BIA Higher Education Grant, 279
Hopi Education Award, 279
Hopi Tribal Priority Award, 280
Horatio Alger Ak-Sar-Ben Scholarship Program, 280
Horatio Alger Alabama Scholarship Program, 280
Horatio Alger California Scholarship Program, 280
Horatio Alger Delaware Scholarship Program, 280
Horatio Alger District of Columbia, Maryland and Virgina Scholarship Program, 281
Horatio Alger Florida Scholarship Program, 281
Horatio Alger Franklin Scholarship, 281
Horatio Alger Georgia Scholarship Program, 281
Horatio Alger Hormel Scholarship Program, 282
Horatio Alger Idaho Scholarship Program, 282
Horatio Alger Illinois Scholarship Program, 282
Horatio Alger Indiana Scholarship Program, 282
Horatio Alger Iowa Scholarship Program, 282
Horatio Alger Kentucky Scholarship Program, 283
Horatio Alger Louisiana Scholarship Program, 283
Horatio Alger Minnesota Scholarship Program, 283
Horatio Alger Mississippi Scholarship Program, 283
Horatio Alger Missouri Scholarship Program, 283
Horatio Alger Montana Scholarship Program, 284
Horatio Alger National Scholarship, 284
Horatio Alger New Jersey Scholarship Program, 284
Horatio Alger New York Scholarship Program, 284
Horatio Alger North Dakota Scholarship Program, 284
Horatio Alger Oregon Scholarship Program, 285
Horatio Alger Pennsylvania Scholarship Program, 285
Horatio Alger South Dakota Scholarship Program, 285
Horatio Alger Texas Ft. Worth Scholarship Program, 285
Horatio Alger Texas Scholarship Program, 285
Horatio Alger Utah Scholarship Program, 286

Horatio Alger Washington Scholarship Program, 286
Horatio Alger Wyoming Scholarship Program, 286
Horizons Scholarship of Women in Defense, 286
Horticultural Research Institute Spring Meadow Scholarship, 287
House Member Internships, 573
Howard Brown Rickard Scholarship, 372
Howard E. and Wilma J. Adkins Memorial Scholarship, 184
Howard P. Rawlings Guaranteed Access Grant, 328
Howard Vollum American Indian Scholarship, 414
Hubertus W.V. Willems Scholarship for Male Students, 350
Hu-Friedy/Esther Wilkins Instrument Scholarships, 79
Hugh A. Smith Scholarship, 126
Humane Studies Fellowship, 293
The Hyatt Hotels Fund for Minority Lodging Management Students Competition, 108
IBM Co-op and Intern Program, 545
IBM Corporation Scholarship, 466
Ida M. Crawford Scholarship, 414
Idaho Education Incentive Loan Forgiveness Program, 582
Idaho Governor's Cup Scholarship, 289
Idaho Minority/"At-Risk" Scholarship, 289
Idaho Robert C. Byrd Scholarship, 289
Idaho Robert R. Lee Category A Promise Scholarship, 289
Idaho Robert R. Lee Category B Promise Scholarship, 290
IEHA Educational Foundation Scholarship, 296
Illinois Future Teacher Corps, 291
Illinois National Guard Grant, 291
Illinois Veteran Grant (IVG) Program, 291
Independent Living Act (Department of Human Services Tuition Waiver), 407
Indian American Scholarship, 503
Indiana Minority Teacher & Special Education Services Scholarship, 477
Indiana National Guard Supplemental Grant, 477
Indiana Nursing Scholarship, 477
Indiana Robert C. Byrd Honors Scholarship, 478
Indiana Twenty-First Century Scholars Program, 478
Indians Higher Education Grant Program, 506
The Inger and Jens Bruun Scholarship for Study in Denmark, 402
INROADS Internship, 546

Program Index

Institute of Food Technologists Freshman Scholarship, 294
Institute of Food Technologists Junior/Senior Scholarship, 294
Institute of Food Technologists Sophomore Scholarship, 295
Institutional Scholarship Waivers, 88
Intel International Science and Engineering Fair, 446
Intel Science Talent Search, 446
International Furnishings and Design Association Student Scholarships, 297
International Gas Turbine Institute Scholarship, 176
International Incentive Awards, 479
International Radio and Television Society Foundation, 546
International Semester Scholarship, 110
Internship Program for Laboratory Technology, 560
Iowa Grant, 298
Iowa National Guard Educational Assistance Program, 299
Iowa Robert C. Byrd Honor Scholarship, 299
Iowa Tuition Grant, 299
Iowa Vocational-Technical Tuition Grant, 299
Irene E. Newman Scholarship, 79
Irving W. Cook, WAOCGS Scholarship, 165
ISFA Education Foundation College Scholarship, 296
Italian Catholic Federation Scholarship, 299
ITW Welding Companies Scholarship, 184
Ivy Parker Memorial Scholarship, 466
J. Desmond Slattery Award: Student, 493
Jack R. Barckhoff Welding Management Scholarship, 184
Jackson Foundation Journalism Scholarship, 414
Jacob Van Namen Marketing Scholarship, 103
Jagannathan Scholarship, 221
James A. Turner, Jr., Memorial Scholarship, 184
James B. Carey Scholarship, 300
James Beard General Scholarships, 303
James Beard School Scholarships, 304
James Carlson Memorial Scholarship, 414
James E. Webb Internship Program for Minority Undergraduate Seniors and Graduate Students in Business and Public Administration, 567
James F. Byrnes Scholarship, 305
James Hughes Memorial Scholarship Fund, 424
James V. Day Scholarship, 128
Janet Jackson Rhythm Nation Scholarships, 500

Japanese American General Scholarship, 305
Japanese American Music Scholarship Competition, 306
Jaycee War Memorial Scholarship, 306
Jean Cebik Memorial Scholarship, 165
Jean Fitzgerald Scholarship Fund, 268
Jeanette Rankin Foundation Scholarship, 307
Jean-Louis Palladin Memorial Scholarship, 304
Jeanne E. Bray Law Enforcement Dependents Scholarship, 379
Jebidiah Zabrosky Scholarship, 511
Jennica Ferguson Memorial Scholarship, 372
Jennifer C. Groot Fellowship, 95
Jennifer Curtis Byler Scholarship Fund for the Study of Public Affairs, 383
Jennifer Ritzmann Scholarship for Studies in Tropical Biology, 228
Jeppesen Meterology Internship, 546
Jere W. Thompson, Jr., Scholarship Fund, 232
Jerome B. Steinbach Scholarship, 414
Jerry Clark Memorial Scholarship, 101
Jerry Robinson-Inweld Corporation Scholarship, 184
Jewish War Veterans of the United States of America Bernard Rotberg Memorial Scholarship, 307
Jewish War Veterans of the United States of America JWV Grant, 307
Jewish War Veterans of the United States of America XX Olympiad Memorial Award, 308
JFCS Scholarship Fund, 582
Jill S. Tietjen P.E. Scholarship, 466
Jimmy A. Young Memorial Education Recognition Award, 169
J.K. Rathmell, Jr., Memorial for Work/Study Abroad, 103
Joel Polsky Academic Achievement Award, 175
John and Elsa Gracik Mechanical Engineering Scholarship, 177
John and Geraldine Hobble Licensed Practical Nursing Scholarship, 126
John and Muriel Landis Scholarship, 160
John C. Lincoln Memorial Scholarship, 185
John Dawe Dental Education Fund, 269
John Deere Student Training Programs, 547
John E. Bowman Travel Grants, 229
John F. Kennedy Scholars Award, 333
John Joseph Moakely Democratic Internship, 550
John L. Dales Standard Scholarship, 440
John L. Dales Transitional Scholarship, 440

John Lennon Scholarship, 204
John Lennon Scholarship Fund, 500
John M. Haniak Scholarship, 195
John M. Simpson Memorial Scholarship, 91
John McKee Scholarship, 334
John R. Lamarsh Scholarship, 160
John Ross Foundation, 269
John W. Anderson Foundation Scholarship, 500
John Wiley and Sons, Inc. Internship Program, 548
Johnny Davis Memorial Scholarship, 84
Johnson Controls Co-op and Internship Programs, 548
Joint CAS/SOA Minority Scholarships for Actuarial Students, 447
Jose D. Garcia Migrant Education Scholarship, 415
Jose Marti Scholarship Challenge Grant, 248
Joseph P. Gavenonis Scholarship, 147
Joseph R. Dietrich Scholarship, 160
Joseph R. Stone Scholarship, 181
Joseph S. Adams Scholarship, 445
Joseph Tauber Scholarship, 75
Judith Resnik Memorial Scholarship, 466
Jules Maidoff Scholarship, 479
Juliette A. Southard/Oral B Laboratories Scholarship, 100
Juliette M. Atherton Scholarship, 269
June Gill Nursing Scholarship, 393
Junior Member Scholarship, 138
Junior Miss Scholarship, 92
JVS Jewish Community Scholarship Fund, 307
J.W. Saxe Memorial Prize, 548
The K2TEO Martin J. Green, Sr. Memorial Scholarship, 165
Ka'a'awa Community Fund, 270
Kaiser Permanente College to Caring Program, 277
Kaiser-Permanente Dental Assistant Scholarship, 415
Ka'iulani Home for Girls Trust Scholarship, 269
The Kaj Christensen Scholarship for Vocational Training, 402
Kansas Comprehensive Grant, 308
Kansas Ethnic Minority Scholarship, 308
Kansas Nursing Service Scholarship, 308
Kansas ROTC Service Scholarship, 309
Kansas State Scholarship, 309
Kansas Teacher Service Scholarship, 309
Kansas Vocational Education Scholarship, 309
Kaplan/Newsweek "My Turn" Essay Contest, 310
Kapolei Community & Business Scholarship, 270

Kappa Kappa Gamma Scholarship, 310
KarMel Scholarship, 310
Katharine M. Grosscup Scholarship, 253
Katherine F. Gruber Scholarship Program, 204
Kathleen S. Anderson Award, 327
Kathryn D. Sullivan Science and Engineering Fellowship, 361
Kathy LeTarte Scholarship, 490
Kawasaki-McGaha Scholarship Fund, 270
Ken Chagnon Scholarship, 420
Ken Inouye Scholarship, 458
Ken Kashiwahara Scholarship, 433
Kennedy Center Arts Management Internship, 547
Kennedy Library Archival Internship, 547
Kenneth Andrew Roe Mechanical Engineering Scholarship, 177
Kenneth Jernigan Memorial Scholarship, 373
Kentucky College Access Program Grant (CAP), 311
Kentucky Educational Excellence Scholarship (KEES), 311
Kentucky Teacher Scholarship, 311
Kentucky Tuition Grant, 312
Kentucky Work-Study Program, 548
Keppra Family Epilepsy Scholarship Program, 494
KIMT Weather/News Internships, 549
King Kekaulike High School Scholarship, 270
King Olav V Norwegian-American Heritage Fund, 471
K.M. Hatano Scholarship, 270
Knights Templar Educational Foundation Loan, 582
Kohala Ditch Education Fund, 271
Koloa Scholarship, 271
Kosciuszko Foundation Tuition Scholarships, 314
Kosciuszko Foundation Year Abroad Program, 314
Kottis Family Award, 234
Kuchler-Killian Memorial Scholarship, 373
Kurt W. Schneider Memorial Scholarship Fund, 271
L. Gordon Bittle Memorial Scholarship for Student CTA, 214
L. Phil Wicker Scholarship, 166
L-3 Avionics Systems Scholarship, 84
La Toque Scholarship in Wine Studies, 304
LAF/CLASS Fund (California Landscape Architectural Student Scholarship) University Scholarship Program, 317
LAF/CLASS Fund Internship Program, 549
LAF/CLASS Fund Landscape Architecture Program, 317

LAF/CLASS Fund Scholarship Ornamental Horticulture Program, 317
Lagrant Scholarships, 315
LaMacchia Family Scholarship, 491
Landscape Forms Design for People Scholarship, 317
Latin American Educational Scholarship, 318
Latin Honor Society Scholarship, 95
Latino Diamante Scholarship Fund, 400
Laura Blackburn Memorial Scholarship, 127
Laura N. Dowsett Fund, 271
Laurence R. Foster Memorial Scholarship, 415
Lawrence Luterman Memorial Scholarships, 142
Laywomen Scholarships, 523
Leaders of Tomorrow Scholarship, 391
Leadership Alliances and Development Internship, 531
Leaf Loan Program, 585
Lee Tarbox Memorial Scholarship, 84
Legacy of Hope, 478
Lele Cassin Scholarship, 479
Leon Harris/Les Nichols Memorial to Spartan School of Aeronautics, 85
Leonard Bettinger Memorial Vocational Scholarship, 103
Leonard C. Horn Award for Legal Studies, 342
Leonard M. Perryman Communications Scholarship, 497
Leonard M. Perryman Communications Scholarship for Ethnic Minority Students, 497
Letitia B. Carter Scholarship, 332
Leveraging Educational Assistance Partnership (LEAP), 508
Leveraging Educational Assistance Partnership Program (LEAP), 342
Leveraging Educational Assistance State Partnership Program (LEAP), 290
Library of Congress Hispanic Division Junior Fellows Internship, 549
License Plate Insignia Scholarship, 485
LIFE Lessons Essay Contest, 320
LIFE Scholarship Program, 472
Lighthouse College-Bound Award, 321
Lighthouse Graduate Award, 321
Lighthouse Undergraduate Award, 322
Lillian and Samuel Sutton Education Scholarship, 350
Lillian Moller Gilbreth Scholarship, 467
Lillie Lois Ford Boys' Scholarship, 134
Lillie Lois Ford Girls' Scholarship, 134
Limouselle Scholarship, 397
Lindbergh Grant, 218

Literary Achievement Awards, 258
Lockheed Martin Aeronautics Company Scholarships, 467
Lockheed Martin Foundation Scholarships, 467
Lockheed Martin Scholarship Program, 278
Los Padres Foundation Scholarships, 322
Lottery Tuition Assistance Program, 472
Lou and Carole Prato Sports Reporting Scholarship, 433
The Louie Foundation Scholarship, 312
Louis Carr Summer Internship, 549
Louis S. Silvey Grant, 308
The Louisiana Memorial Scholarship, 166
Louisiana Rockefeller Wildlife Scholarship, 323
Louisiana Tuition Opportunity Program for Students (TOPS) Award, 323
Louisiana Veterans Affairs Educational Assistance for Dependent Children, 322
Louisiana Veterans Affairs Educational Assistance for Surviving Spouse, 322
Lowell Gaylor Memorial Scholarship, 85
The Lowell H. and Dorothy Loving Undergraduate Scholarship, 98
The Loy McCandless Marks Scholarship, 253
Lucile B. Kaufman Women's Scholarship, 454
Lucille & Charles A. Wert Scholarship, 195
LULAC National Scholarship Fund Honors Awards, 319
LULAC National Scholarship Fund National Scholastic Achievement Awards, 319
LULAC National Scholarshp Fund General Awards, 319
Luso-American Education Foundation Scholarship, 324
Maine Innkeepers Association Scholarship, 325
The Maine Loan, 583
Maine Metal Products Association Scholarship, 325
Maine Recreation and Parks Association Scholarship, 326
Maine Robert C. Byrd Honors Scholarship, 245
Maine Rural Rehabilitation Fund, 325
Maine Society of Professional Engineers Scholarship Program, 326
Maine State Society of Washington, DC, Foundation Scholarship Program, 327
Maine Veterans Services Dependents Educational Benefits, 325

Major Don S. Gentile Scholarship, 495
Malcolm X Scholarship for Exceptional Courage, 500
Marathon Oil Corporation College Scholarship, 279
Marcia S. Harris Legacy Fund Scholarship, 332
Margaret E. Swanson Scholarship, 79
Margaret Jones Memorial Nursing Scholarship, 272
Margarite McAlpin Nurse's Scholarship, 153
Margot Karle Scholarship, 200
Marguerite Ross Barnett Memorial Scholarship, 345
Maria C. Jackson-General George A. White Scholarship, 415
Marie Sheehe Trade School Scholarship, 122
Marine Corps Scholarship, 328
Marion Huber Learning Through Listening Award, 434
Marion J. Bagley Scholarship, 141
Marion Maccarrell Scott Scholarship, 272
Mark J. Smith Scholarship, 223
Marshall E. McCullough Undergraduate Scholarship, 370
Mary Barrett Marshall Student Loan Fund, 578
Mary Jo Young Scholarship, 312
Mary Josephine Bloder Scholarship, 272
Mary Lou Brown Scholarship, 166
Mary M. Verges Award, 234
Mary Macey Scholarship, 523
Mary Marshall Nursing Scholarship, 513
Mary McLeod Bethune Scholarship, 248
Mary P. Oenslager Scholastic Achievement Award, 434
Mary Virginia Macrea Memorial Scholarship, 125
Maryland Delegate Scholarship, 328
Maryland Distinguished Scholar: Achievement, 329
Maryland Distinguished Scholar: National Merit and National Achievement Finalists, 329
Maryland Distinguished Scholar: Talent in the Arts, 329
Maryland Educational Assistance Grant, 329
Maryland Edward T. Conroy Memorial Scholarship Program, 330
Maryland Jack F. Tolbert Memorial Grant, 330
Maryland Part-Time Grant Program, 330
Maryland Senatorial Scholarship, 331
Maryland Tuition Reduction for Non-Resident Nursing Students, 331
Masonic Range Science Scholarship, 421

Massachusetts Christian A. Herter Memorial Scholarship Program, 332
Massachusetts Federation of Polish Women's Clubs Scholarships, 314
Massachusetts Gilbert Matching Student Grant, 332
Massachusetts MASSgrant Program, 333
Massachusetts No Interest Loan, 583
Massachusetts Public Service Grant Program, 333
Massachusetts Robert C. Byrd Honors Scholarship, 334
MASWE Scholarships, 467
Matsuo Bridge Company Ltd of Japan Scholarship, 185
Matthews/Swift Educational Trust - Military Dependants, 313
Matthews/Swift Educational Trust - Police/Firefighters, 313
Maureen V. O'Donnell Memorial Teacher Training Award, 96
Maya Angelou/Vivian Baxter Scholarship, 500
Mayflower Tours Patrick Murphy Internship, 571
Maynard Jensen American Legion Memorial Scholarship, 137
MCC Theater Internships, 550
McFarland Charitable Foundation Scholarship, 261
McKinlay Summer Award, 96
M.D. "Jack" Murphy Memorial Nurses Training Fund, 134
Medical Career Scholarships, 131
Medical Technologists Student Scholarship, 156
Melvin R. Green Scholarship, 177
Memorial Education Grant, 117
Menominee Adult Vocational Training Grant, 334
Menominee Higher Education Grant, 334
The Merchants Exhange Scholarship Fund, 334
Mercy Corps Global Action Awards, 335
Meridith Thoms Memorial Scholarships, 468
Merit Recognition Scholarship, 291
MESBEC Scholarships, 215
Meteorological Society Father James B. Macelwane Annual Award, 157
Mexican American Grocers Association Scholarship, 335
MG James Ursano Scholarship Fund, 192
Michael and Deborah Weinberg Scholarship, 511
Michael and Marie Marucci Scholarship, 373
Michael Hakeem Memorial Award, 252
Michael Jackson Scholarships, 501
Michigan Adult Part-Time Grant, 335
Michigan Alternative Student Loan (MI-LOAN), 583

Michigan Competitive Scholarship, 336
Michigan Educational Opportunity Grant, 336
Michigan Nursing Scholarship, 336
Michigan Promise Scholarship, 336
Michigan Robert C. Byrd Honors Scholarship, 336
Michigan Society of Professional Engineers Scholarships, 337
Michigan Tuition Grant, 336
Michigan Work-Study Program, 551
Microbiology Undergraduate Research Fellowship (MURF), 171
Microscopy Society of America Undergraduate Research Scholarship, 337
Microsoft Corporation Scholarships, 468
Microsoft General Scholarship, 337
Microsoft Minority Technical Scholarship, 338
Microsoft Scholarship for Students with Disabilities, 338
Microsoft Women's Technical Scholarship, 338
Mid-Continent Instrument Scholarship, 85
Midwest Student Exchange Program, 338
Mike Reynolds Scholarship, 433
Milan Getting Scholarship, 444
Mildred R. Knoles Opportunity Scholarship, 122
Mildred Towle Scholarship - Study Abroad, 272
Mildred Towle Scholarship for African-Americans, 273
Military Dependents Scholarship Program, 189
Military Order of the Purple Heart Scholarship, 339
Military Service Recognition Scholarship (MSRS), 394
Miller Electric Manufacturing Company Ivic Scholarship, 185
The Minnesota American Legion Memorial Scholarship, 132
Minnesota Educational Assistance for Veterans, 340
Minnesota Educational Assistance for War Orphans, 340
Minnesota GI Bill, 340
Minnesota Indian Scholarship Program, 340
Minnesota Post-Secondary Child Care Grant, 340
Minnesota Public Safety Officers Survivors Program, 341
Minnesota State Grant Program, 341
Minnesota Student Educational Loan Fund (SELF), 584
Minnesota Work-Study Program, 551
Minnie Patton Stayman Scholarship, 424
The Minority Scholarship, 535

Minority Teachers of Illinois Scholarship, 292
Miss America Competition Awards, 342
Mississippi Eminent Scholars Grant, 343
Mississippi Health Care Professions Loan/Scholarship, 584
Mississippi Higher Education Legislative Plan, 343
Mississippi Law Enforcement Officers & Firemen Scholarship, 343
Mississippi Nursing Education Loan/Scholarship, 585
Mississippi Resident Tuition Assistance Grant, 343
The Mississippi Scholarship, 166
Mississippi William Winter Teacher Scholar Loan Program, 585
Missouri Department of Higher Education Vietnam Veteran's Survivor Grant Program, 345
Missouri Higher Education "Bright Flight" Academic Scholarship, 345
Missouri League for Nursing Scholarship, 346
Missouri Minority Teaching Scholarship, 344
Missouri Public Service Survivor Grant, 346
Missouri Robert C. Byrd Honors Scholarship, 344
Missouri Teacher Education Scholarship, 344
MOAA American Patriot Scholarship Program, 339
MOAA Interest-Free Loan and Grant Program, 583
Monetary Award Program (MAP), 292
Montana Higher Education Grant, 347
Montana State Fund Scholarship Program, 347
Montana Tuition Fee Waiver for Veterans, 347
Montana University System Community College Honor Scholarship, 347
Montana University System Honor Scholarship, 348
Monte R. Mitchell Global Scholarship, 85
Montgomery GI Bill (MGIB), 504
Montgomery GI Bill Plus Army College Fund, 504
Moody's Mega Math "M3" Challenge, 348
Morris Arboretum Education Internship, 552
Morris Arboretum Horticulture Internship, 552
Morton B. Duggan, Jr. Memorial Education Recognition Award, 170
Mother Jones Magazine Editorial Internship, 553
Mother Jones Photo/Art Internship, 554

MSGC Undergraduate Underrepresented Minority Fellowship Program, 355
MTA Doug Slifka Memorial Scholarship, 348
Multicultural Advertising Intern Program, 527
Multicultural Undergraduate Summer Internships at the Getty Center, 546
Multi-Year Ambassadorial Scholarship, 437
Museum Coca-Cola Internship, 557
Museum of Modern Art Internship, 554
Myasthenia Gravis Foundation Nursing Research Fellowship, 348
Myrtle and Earl Walker Scholarship, 454
NABA National Scholarship Program, 365
NABJ Internships, 556
NABJ Scholarship, 366
NAMTA Educational Assistance Award, 365
NAMTA Foundation Visual Arts Major Scholarship, 365
Nancy Goodhue Lynch Scholarship, 233
Nancy Lorraine Jensen Memorial Scholarship, 471
NASA Academy Internship, 555
NASA Connecticut Space Grant Undergraduate Fellowship, 351
NASA District of Columbia Undergraduate Scholarship, 352
NASA Hawaii Undergraduate Traineeship, 554
NASA Idaho Space Grant Undergraduate Scholarship, 353
NASA Indiana Space Grant Consortium Undergraduate Scholarships, 354
NASA Massachusetts Space Grant Summer Jobs for Students, 555
NASA Minnesota Space Grant Consortium Wide Scholarship, 355
NASA Missouri State Space Grant Undergraduate Scholarship, 356
NASA Ohio Space Grant Junior/Senior Scholarship Program, 359
NASA Pennsylvania Space Grant Undergraduate Scholarship, 359
NASA Rocky Mountain Space Grant Consortium Undergraduate Scholarship, 360
NASA Space Grant Arizona Undergraduate Research Internship, 554
NASA Space Grant Arkansas Undergraduate Scholarship, 351
NASA Space Grant Georgia Fellowship Program, 352
NASA Space Grant Hawaii Undergraduate Fellowship, 353
NASA Space Grant Illinois Undergraduate Scholarship, 353

NASA Space Grant Kentucky Undergraduate Scholarship, 354
NASA Space Grant Maine Consortium Annual Scholarship and Fellowship Program, 354
NASA Space Grant Michigan Undergraduate Fellowship, 355
NASA Space Grant Mississippi Undergraduate Scholarship, 356
NASA Space Grant Montana Undergraduate Scholarship Program, 357
NASA Space Grant Nevada Undergraduate Scholarship, 357
NASA Space Grant New Mexico Undergraduate Scholarship, 357
NASA Space Grant North Dakota Consortium Lillian Goettler Scholarship, 358
NASA Space Grant North Dakota Undergraduate Scholarship, 358
NASA Space Grant Oregon Undergraduate Scholarship, 359
NASA Space Grant Rhode Island Summer Undergraduate Scholarship, 360
NASA Space Grant South Carolina Undergraduate Academic Year Research Program, 361
NASA Space Grant Teacher Education Scholarship, 362
NASA Space Grant Texas Undergraduate Scholarship Program, 361
NASA Space Grant Undergraduate Scholarship, 351
NASA Space Grant Vermont Consortium Undergraduate Scholarships, 362
NASA Space Grant Virginia Community College Scholarship, 362
NASA Space Grant Wisconsin Consortium Undergraduate Research Program, 363
NASA Space Grant Wisconsin Consortium Undergraduate Scholarship, 363
NASA West Virginia Space Grant Undergraduate Research Fellowship, 363
NASA Wyoming Space Grant Undergraduate Research Fellowships, 364
National Achievement Scholarships, 376
National Amateur Baseball Federation Scholarship, 364
National Association of Women in Construction Scholarship, 511
National Co-op Scholarship, 369
National Dairy Shrine Kildee Scholarship, 370
National Dairy Shrine Klussendorf Scholarship, 370
National Dairy Shrine/Iager Dairy Scholarship, 370

Program Index

National Federation of the Blind Educator of Tomorrow Award, 373
National Federation of the Blind Scholarships, 374
National FFA Organization Scholarship Program, 374
National Guard Educational Assistance Program, 310
National Guard Tuition Waiver, 407
National Health Service Corps Scholarship, 506
National High School Oratorical Contest, 116
National High School Oratorical Contest, 117
National High School Oratorical Contest, 118
National High School Oratorical Contest, 151
National Italian American Foundation Scholarship Program, 375
National Junior Classical League Scholarship, 96
National Limouselle Financial Assistance Grant, 397
National Merit Scholarships, 376
National Museum of the American Indian Internship, 557
National Oceanic and Atmospheric Administration Educational Partnership Program with Minority Serving Institutions Undergraduate Scholarship, 403
National Peace Essay Contest, 502
National Presbyterian Scholarship, 429
National President's Scholarship, 132
National President's Scholarship, 146
National Press Photographers Foundation Still Scholarship, 378
National Press Photographers Foundation Television News Scholarship, 378
National Security Agency Stokes Educational Scholarship Program, 380
National Society of Accountants Scholarship, 381
National Society of Black Engineers Corporate Scholarships Program, 382
National Society of Black Engineers Golden Torch Awards, 382
National Society of Black Engineers Leroy Callendar Award Program, 382
National Speakers Association Scholarship, 383
National Student Nurses Association Scholarship, 250
National Technical Investigators' Captain James J. Regan Memorial Scholarship, 320
Native American Leadership in Education Scholarship, 215
Native Daughters of the Golden West Scholarship, 384

Naval Engineers Scholarship, 179
Navy Supply Corps Foundation Scholarship, 384
NBA Internship Program, 556
NBRC/AMP Robert M. Lawrence, MD Education Recognition Award, 170
NBRC/AMP William W. Burgin, Jr. MD Education Recognition Award, 170
NC Sherrif's Association Criminal Justice Scholarship, 400
NCAA Division I Degree-Completion Award Program, 385
The NCDXF Scholarship, 166
NCR Summer Internships, 558
NDS/DMI Milk Marketing Scholarship, 231
Nebraska Robert C. Byrd Honors Scholarship, 385
NEEBC Scholarship, 386
NEHA/AAS Scholarship, 371
The NEMAL Electronics Scholarship, 167
Nettie Dracup Memorial Scholarship, 98
Nevada Robert C. Byrd Honors Scholarship, 385
Nevada Student Incentive Grant, 386
New Dramatists Internship, 558
New England Board of Higher Education's Regional Student Program, 386
The New England FEMARA Scholarship, 167
New Hampshire Incentive Program, 386
New Hampshire Scholarship for Orphans of Veterans, 387
New Jeresy Student Tuition Assistance Reward Scholarship (NJSTARS), 388
New Jersey Class Loan Program, 586
New Jersey Educational Opportunity Fund Grant, 387
New Jersey Edward J. Bloustein Distinguished Scholars, 388
New Jersey POW/MIA Program, 387
New Jersey Scholarship, 468
New Jersey STARS II, 388
New Jersey Survivor Tuition Benefits Program, 389
New Jersey Tuition Aid Grants (TAG), 389
New Jersey Urban Scholars, 389
New Jersey War Orphans Tuition Credit Program, 387
New Jersey World Trade Center Scholarship, 389
New Mexico Allied Health Student Loan-for-Service Program, 586
New Mexico Competitive Scholarships, 390
New Mexico Legislative Endowment Program, 390
New Mexico Legislative Lottery Scholarship, 390

New Mexico Medical Student Loan-for-Service, 587
New Mexico Nursing Student Loan-for-Service, 587
New Mexico Scholars Program, 390
New Mexico Student Choice Program, 391
New Mexico Student Incentive Grant, 391
New Mexico Teacher's Loan-for-Service, 587
New Mexico Vietnam Veteran's Scholarship, 391
New Mexico Work-Study Program, 558
The New Republic Internship, 559
New York American Legion Press Association Scholarship, 144
New York State Aid for Part-time Study Program, 394
New York State Assembly Session Internship Program, 559
New York State Higher Education Opportunity Program (HEOP), 392
New York State Memorial Scholarship for Families of Deceased Police/Volunteer Firefighters/Peace Officers and Emergency Medical Service Workers, 394
New York State Native American Student Aid Program, 396
New York State Readers Aid Program, 392
New York State Regents Awards for Children of Deceased and Disabled Veterans, 394
New York State Robert C. Byrd Federal Honors Scholarship, 392
New York State Tuition Assistance Program, 395
New York State Veterans Tuition Award, 395
New York State Volunteer Recruitment Service Scholarship, 395
New York State World Trade Center Memorial Scholarship, 395
New York Times James B. Reston Writing Portfolio Award, 89
New York Times Summer Internship Program, 559
New York Women in Communications Foundation Scholarship, 396
Newhouse Foundation Scholarship, 556
NGWREF Len Assante Scholarship Fund, 374
Nicholas J. Grant Scholarship, 196
Nick Van Pernis Scholarship, 273
Nicole Marie Goulart Memorial Scholarship, 324
Nisei Student Relocation Commemorative Fund, 396
Nissan Community College Transfer Scholarship, 279
Nissan Scholarship, 343

Non Commissioned Officers Association Scholarship for Children of Members, 396
Non Commissioned Officers Association Scholarship for Spouses, 397
North American Indian Scholarship, 298
North Carolina Aubrey Lee Brooks Scholarship, 400
North Carolina Community Colleges Wachovia Technical Scholarship, 398
North Carolina Law Enforcement Dependents Scholarship, 397
North Carolina Legislative Tuition Grant, 400
North Carolina Nurse Scholars Program, 588
North Carolina Scholarships for Children of War Veterans, 398
North Carolina State Board of Refrigeration Examiners Scholarship, 399
North Carolina Student Incentive Grant, 221
North Carolina Student Loans for Health/Science/Mathematics, 588
North Carolina Vocational Rehabilitation Award, 399
North Central Region Scholarship, 455
North Dakota Indian Scholarship Program, 401
North Dakota Scholars Program, 401
North Dakota State Student Incentive Grant, 402
Northern California Chapter/Richard Epping Scholarship, 181
Northern Cheyenne Higher Education Program, 402
Northrop Grumman Corporation Scholarship, 468
NOS/DMI Milk Marketing Scholarships, 371
NPFDA Scholarship, 377
NSBE Fellows Scholarship, 382
NSPS Board of Governors Scholarship, 98
NSPS Scholarships, 99
Nuclear Medicine Student Fellowship Award, 445
Nurse Gift Tuition Scholarships, 138
Nurse Practitioner Nurse Midwife Scholarship, 514
OCA-AXA Achievement Scholarship, 419
OCA/UPS Foundation Gold Mountain College Scholarship, 419
OCA/Verizon Foundation College Scholarship, 419
Ohio Academic Scholarship, 403
Ohio College Opportunity Grant, 403
Ohio Instructional Grant, 403
Ohio National Guard Scholarship Program, 404

Ohio Newspaper Association Publications/Public Relations Internship, 564
Ohio Newspaper Services, Inc. Advertising Internship, 564
Ohio Newspaper Women's Scholarship, 405
Ohio Newspapers Minority Scholarship, 405
Ohio Nurse Education Assistance Loan Program, 588
Ohio Safety Officers College Memorial Fund, 404
Ohio Student Choice Grant, 404
Ohio War Orphans Scholarship, 404
Oklahoma Engineering Foundation Scholarship, 406
Oklahoma Tuition Aid Grant, 407
Oklahoma's Promise - OHLAP (Oklahoma Higher Learning Access Program), 407
Olive Lynn Salembier Reentry Scholarship, 469
OMNE/Nursing Leaders of Maine Scholarship, 408
Oncology Nursing Certification Corporation Bachelor's Scholarships, 408
Online Intern Program, 538
OP Loftbed $500 Scholarship Award, 409
Operations and Power Division Scholarship, 160
Opportunity Scholarship, 288
Oracle Scholars Internship Program, 572
Oral-B Laboratories Dental Hygiene Scholarship, 79
Oratorical Contest, 120
Oratorical Contest Scholarships, 154
Oregon Collectors Association Bob Hasson Memorial Scholarship Fund Essay, 416
Oregon Dungeness Crab Commission, 416
Oregon Foundation for Blacktail Deer Outdoor & Wildlife Scholarship, 416
Oregon Occupational Safety and Health Division Workers Memorial Scholarship, 416
Oregon Robert C. Byrd Honors Scholarship, 417
Oregon Scholarship Fund Community College Student, 417
ORISE Community College Institute, 560
ORISE Higher Education Research Experiences at Oak Ridge National Laboratory, 561
ORISE National Oceanic and Atmospheric Administration Faculty and Student Intern Research Participation, 561
ORISE Professional Internship Program for National Energy Technology Laboratory, 561

ORISE Student Environmental Management Participation at the U.S. Army Environmental Center, 561
ORISE Student Internship at the Office of Water, 562
ORISE Student Internship at the U.S. Army Center for Health Promotion and Preventive Medicine, 562
ORISE Student Research - National Center for Toxicological Research, 562
ORISE Student Research at the Centers for Disease Control and Prevention, 562
ORISE Student Research Participation at the U.S. Army Medical Research Institute of Chemical Defense, 562
ORISE Student Research Participation at U.S. Army Research Laboratory, 563
ORISE U.S. Nuclear Regulatory Commission Historically Black Colleges and Universities Student Research Participation, 563
Osage Tribal Education Scholarship, 420
Oscar and Rosetta Fish Fund, 273
Outstanding Citizen of Boys State Scholarship, 124
Outstanding Senior Baseball Player Scholarship, 124
Owens Corning Internships, 564
Pacific Gas and Electric Summer Intern Program, 564
PAGE Foundation Scholarships, 431
Palmetto Fellows Scholarship Program, 472
Papercheck.com Charles Shafae' Scholarship Fund, 421
Par Aide's Joseph S. Garske Collegiate Grant Program, 421
Paris Fracasso Production Floriculture Scholarship, 103
Park Espenschade Memorial Scholarship, 294
Part-time Student Instructional Grant Program, 404
Part-Time Student Scholarship, 297
Part-Time Tuition Aid Grant for County Colleges, 389
Past Department Presidents' Junior Scholarship, 116
Past Grand Presidents' Memorial Award, 235
Past President's Parley Education Grant, 118
Past President's Parley Health Care Scholarship, 133
Past President's Parley Nurse's Scholarship, 117
Past President's Parley Nurses Scholarship, 120
Past President's Parley Nurses' Scholarship, 139
Past President's Parley Nurses' Scholarship, 141

Program Index

Past President's Parley Nurses' Scholarship, 143
Past Presidents' Parley Nursing Scholarship, 116
Past President's Parley Nursing Scholarship, 118
Past President's Parley Nursing Scholarship, 123
Past President's Parley Scholarship, 130
Past President's Parley Scholarship, 130
Past President's Parley Scholarship, 134
Past President's Parley Scholarship, 145
Past President's Parley Student Nurses Scholarship for Girls or Boys, 144
Past President's Scholarship, 125
Past Presidents Scholarship, 185
Past Presidents Scholarships, 469
Pat & Jim Host Internship/Scholarship, 571
Paul A. Stewart Award, 521
Paul and Ellen Ruckes Scholarship, 105
Paul and Helen L. Grauer Scholarship, 167
Paul Cole Scholarship, 445
Paul Jennings Scholarship, 300
Paul Tsongas Scholarship Program, 333
Payzer Scholarship, 245
PBS Internships, 565
Pearl I. Young Scholarship, 359
Peggy Guggenheim Internship, 568
Pennsylvania Robert C. Byrd Honors Scholarship, 422
Pennsylvania State Grant Program, 423
Pennsylvania Work-Study Program, 423
Peridian International Inc./Rae L. Price FASLA Scholarship, 317
The Persian Scholarship Recognition Award, 425
Pete Carpenter Fellowship, 534
Pete Wilson Journalism Scholarship, 312
Pete Wilson Journalism Scholarship, 433
The Peter Cameron Scholarship, 304
Peter F. Vallone Academic Scholarship, 220
Peter Kump Memorial Scholarship, 304
Peter Wollitzer Scholarships for Study in Asia, 229
Pfizer Inc. Scholarships, 80
PFLAG National Scholarship Program, 425
PGA Tour Diversity Intern Program, 565
PGSF Annual Scholarship Competition, 431
PHCC Auxiliary of Massachusetts Scholarship, 428

PHCC Educational Foundation Need-Based Scholarship, 428
The PHD ARA Scholarship, 167
PHEAA Academic Excellence Scholarship Award Program, 423
Phi Delta Kappa Scholarship for Prospective Educators, 426
Philip and Alice Angell Eastern Star Scholarship, 511
Phipps Conservatory and Botanical Gardens Internships, 565
Phoenix Section Scholarship, 469
Physician Assistant Scholarship, 426
Pickett and Hatcher Educational Loan, 588
Pittsburgh Local Section Scholarship, 160
Plane & Pilot Magazine/Garmin Scholarship, 86
Plant Propagation Internship, 552
Plant Protection Internship, 553
Plasma Physics National Undergraduate Fellowship Program, 565
Playtex Scholarship, 427
Plumbing-Heating-Cooling Contractors - National Association Educational Foundation Scholarship, 428
Point Scholarship, 428
Police/Firefighters' Survivors Educational Assistance Program, 87
Policy and Research Internship, 531
The Polish American Club of North Jersey Scholarships, 315
The Polish National Alliance of Brooklyn, USA, Inc. Scholarships, 315
Practical Nurse Scholarship, 138
Praxair International Scholarship, 185
Presbyterian Student Opportunity Scholarship, 429
Presbyterian Undergraduate and Graduate Loan, 589
Presidents' $2,500 Scholarships, 433
President's Parley Nursing Scholarship, 128
President's Parley Scholarship for Teachers of Exceptional Children, 143
President's Scholarship and Junior Scholarship, 139
Press Club of Houston Scholarship, 430
Princess Cruises and Princess Tours Scholarship, 181
Princess Grace Award for Dance, 430
Princess Grace Award For Film, 430
Princess Grace Award For Playwriting, 431
Princess Grace Award For Theater, 431
Private-Sector Affairs Internship, 531
Pro Deo/Pro Patria Scholarship, 313
Professional Land Surveyors of Oregon Scholarship, 417
PROMISE Scholarship, 518

ProStart National Certificate of Achievement Scholarship, 379
PRSA-Hawaii/Roy Leffingwell Public Relations Scholarship, 273
Public Relations Internship, 550
Pulliam Journalism Fellowship, 545
Quality of Life Research Competition, 524
Quebec Scholarship, 491
Rain Bird intelligent Use of Water Company Scholarship, 318
Rainbow Scholarship, 430
Random House Summer Internship Program, 566
Ray Jeffries Scholarship, 398
Raymond DiSalvo Scholarship, 161
Reader's Digest Foundation Scholarship Program, 501
Red River Valley Fighter Pilots Association (RRVA) Scholarship Program, 434
Reduction in Tuition Charges for Students Taking 15 or More Semester Credit Hours Per Term, 485
Regional University Baccalaureate Scholarship, 408
Reid Blackburn Scholarship, 378
Rene Campbell Memorial Scholarship, 491
Research Experiences for Undergraduates - Maria Mitchell Observatory, 558
Research Experiences for Undergraduates in Systematics and Evolutionary Biology, 529
Research Experiences for Undergraduates in the Physical Sciences, 529
Reuben Trane Scholarships, 174
Rhode Island State Government Internship Program, 566
Rhode Island State Grant, 435
Richard F. Brentano Memorial Scholarship, 417
The Richard W. Bendicksen Memorial Scholarship, 167
Richmond Scholarship, 501
Ritchie-Jennings Memorial Scholarship, 76
R.L. Gillette Scholarship, 105
RMHC National Scholarship Programs, 436
Robert B. Bailey Scholarship, 229
Robert C. Byrd Honors Scholarship, 238
Robert C. Byrd Honors Scholarship, 312
Robert C. Byrd Honors Scholarship, 323
Robert C. Byrd Honors Scholarship, 486
Robert C. Byrd Honors Scholarship Program, 292
Robert C. Byrd Honors Scholarship Program, 406

Program Index

Robert C. Byrd Honors Scholarship Program, 505
Robert G. Lacy Scholarship, 161
Robert L. Livingston Scholarship, 301
Robert L. Peaslee-Detroit Brazing and Soldering Division Scholarship, 186
Robert N. Hancock Memorial Scholarship, 294
Robert Noyce Scholarship Program, 425
Robert T. (Bob) Liner Scholarship, 161
Robert W. Valimont Endowment Fund Scholarship, 147
Roberta Marie Stretch Memorial Scholarship, 138
Roberta Pierce Scofield Bachelor's Scholarships, 408
Rockwell Automation Scholarships, 469
Rocky Mountain Chapter-Donald Estey Scholarship Fund, 181
Rocky Mountain Coal Mining Scholarship, 435
Rodney E. Powell Memorial Scholarship, 398
Roger Von Amelunxen Scholarship, 436
Roger W. Emmons Memorial Scholarship, 417
Ron Bright Scholarship, 273
The Ron Brown Scholar Program, 214
Ronald Reagan College Leaders Scholarship Program, 426
Rose and Flower Garden Internship, 553
Rosedale Post 346 Scholarship, 126
Rosemary & Nellie Ebrie Fund, 274
Rosewood Family Scholarship Program, 249
ROTC/Air Force Four-Year Scholarship (Types 1, 2, and 7), 437
ROTC/Air Force Three-Year Scholarship (Types 2 and Targeted), 437
ROTC/Navy Nurse Corps Scholarship Program, 507
ROTC/Navy/Marine Four-Year Scholarship, 507
ROTC/Navy/Marine Two-Year Scholarship, 508
ROTC/United States Army Four-Year Historically Black College/University Scholarship, 438
Roy Wilkins Scholarship, 350
RoyceBuilders.com Foundation for Youth Scholarship, 438
RTKL Traveling Fellowship, 92
Ruby Paul Campaign Fund Scholarship, 139
Rudolf Nissim Prize, 193
Rudolph Dillman Memorial Scholarship, 105
Russ Casey Scholarship, 326
Russ Griffith Memorial Scholarship, 233
RWMA Scholarship, 186

Sachs Foundation Undergraduate Grant, 439
SACI Consortium Scholarship, 480
SAE Women Engineers Committee Scholarship, 448
Sal Ingrassia Scholarship, 301
Sales and Marketing Internship, 531
Sallie Mae Fund American Dream Scholarship, 501
Salute to Education Scholarship, 439
Sam Walton Community Scholarship, 515
Samara Foundation of Vermont Scholarship, 511
Samsung American Legion Scholarship, 136
Samuel Fletcher Tapman ASCE Student Chapter Scholarship, 172
Samuel Robinson Award, 429
Savannah River Site Professional Internship Program, 563
SCA Conservation Internships, 570
Scarlett Family Foundation Scholarship, 440
Scholar Athlete Milk Mustache of the Year Awards, 339
Scholarship Educational Assistance Program, 364
Scholarship for Children of Deceased or Totally Disabled Veterans, 147
Scholarship for Children of Living Veterans, 147
Scholarship for College or Vocational, 149
Scholarship for Minority Undergraduate Physics Majors, 161
Scholarship for People with Disabilities, 230
Scholarships for Children and Spouses of Deceased or Disabled Veterans and Servicemembers, 249
Scholarships for Children of SACI Alumni, 480
Scholarships for Survivors, 421
Scholastic Art Portfolio Gold Award, 89
Scholastic Art Portfolio Silver Award, 90
Scholastic Photography Portfolio Gold Award, 90
Scholastic Photography Portfolio Silver Award, 90
Scholastic Writing Portfolio Gold Award, 90
Schonstedt Scholarships in Surveying, 99
Science Undergraduate Laboratory Internships, 563
SciTech Scholarship, 423
Scotts Company Scholars Program, 259
Sculpture Society Scholarship, 380
Seabee Memorial Scholarship, 441
Seattle Jaycees Scholarship, 441
Second Effort Scholarship, 189
Second Marine Division Scholarship, 441

SEG Foundation Scholarship, 441
Selected Reserve Montgomery GI Bill, 504
Senator George J. Mitchell Scholarship, 442
Senator Joel Abromson Memorial Scholarship Fund, 244
Seneca Nation Higher Education Program, 442
Senior Citizen, 65 or Older, Free Tuition for Up to 6 Credit Hours, 486
Senior Scholarship, 316
Sertoma Scholarships for Hearing-Impaired Students, 442
Seth Horen, K1LOM, Memorial Scholarship, 168
Seventeen Magazine Internship, 566
SGI (Silicon Graphics) Internship/Co-op Program, 566
Shannon Scholarship, 493
Shell Legislative Internship Program, 556
Sheryl A. Horak Law Enforcement Explorer Scholarship, 320
Shirley McKown Scholarship Fund, 274
Shoshone Tribal Scholarship, 443
Shuichi, Katsu and Itsuyo Suga Scholarship, 274
Siani Lee Broadcast Internship, 533
Sid Richardson Scholarship, 443
Siemens Awards for Advanced Placement, 443
Siemens Competition in Math, Science and Technology, 444
Sigma Phi Alpha Undergraduate Scholarship, 80
Signet Classic Student Scholarship Essay Contest, 422
Silas Purnell Illinois Incentive for Access, 292
Silver Eagle Indian Scholarship, 139
Simon and Schuster Summer Internship Program, 567
The Six Meter Club of Chicago Scholarship, 168
Six-Month Internship, 551
Slovenian Women's Union Scholarship, 444
Slovenian Women's Union Scholarship For Returning Adults, 445
SME Education Foundation Family Scholarship, 455
Smithsonian Environmental Research Center Internship Program, 567
Smithsonian Minority Internship, 567
Smithsonian Native American Internship, 568
Society for Technical Communication Scholarship Program, 446
Society of Automotive Engineers (SAE) Longterm Member Sponsored Scholarship, 448
Society of Automotive Engineers (SAE) Yanmar Scholarship, 448

619

Program Index

Society of Exploration Geophysicists Scholarship, 449
Society of Physics Students Leadership Scholarship, 456
Society of Physics Students Summer Internship Program, 568
Society of Plastics Engineers General Scholarships, 457
Sonia Streuli Maguire Outstanding Scholastic Achievement Award, 481
Sons of Italy National Leadership Grant, 470
Sony Credited Internship, 569
South Carolina HOPE Scholarships, 472
South Carolina Need-Based Grants Program, 473
South Carolina Teacher Loans, 589
South Carolina Tuition Grants, 473
South Dakota Annis I. Fowler/Kaden Scholarship, 473
South Dakota Ardell Bjugstad Scholarship, 473
South Dakota Haines Memorial Scholarship, 474
South Dakota Marlin R. Scarborough Memorial Scholarship, 474
South Dakota National Guard Tuition Assistance, 474
South Dakota Robert C. Byrd Honors Scholarship, 474
Southern California Chapter/Pleasant Hawaiian Holidays Scholarship, 182
Southern California Council Endowed Internship, 557
Southern Nursery Organization Sidney B. Meadows Scholarship, 475
Southern Progress Corporation Internship Program, 569
Southface Internship, 569
The SPE Foundation Blow Molding Division Memorial Scholarships, 457
Special Education Teacher Tuition Waiver, 293
Special Education Teaching Scholarships, 122
Spence Reese Scholarship, 206
SPIE Educational Scholarship in Optical Science and Engineering, 475
Spina Bifida Association Four-Year Scholarship, 475
Spina Bifida Association One-Year Scholarship, 475
Spirit of Youth Scholarship, 146
Spirit of Youth Scholarship for Junior Members, 137
Spoleto Festival Apprenticeship Program, 570
Sports Copy Editing Program, 538
Stan Beck Fellowship, 243
Stanfield and D'Orlando Art Scholarship, 496
Stanford Chen Internship Grant, 533

Staples Associates Annual Scholarships Plan, 476
State Contractual Scholarship Fund, 401
Stella Blum Research Grant, 228
Steve Hymans Extended Stay Scholarship, 108
Steven G. King Play Environments Scholarship, 318
Stoody-West Fellowship, 497
Strong Foundation Interest-Free Student Loan, 582
Student Aid Foundation Loan, 589
Student Aid Grant or Vocational Technical Scholarship, 139
Student Leader Award, 258
Student Nurse Scholarship, 122
Student Research at the U.S. Army Edgewood Chemical Biological Center, 573
Student Research Participation at the Federal Bureau of Investigation Counterterrorism/Forensic Science Research Unit, 563
Student-to-Student (STS) Program, 293
Stutz Memorial Scholarship, 142
Summer Internship Program, 551
Summer Research Diversity Fellowships in Law and Social Sciences for Undergraduate Students, 528
Sun Microsystems Student Intern and Co-op Program, 570
Supreme Guardian Council, International Order of Job's Daughters Scholarship, 481
Susan Burdett Scholarship, 153
Susan Miszkowitz Memorial Scholarship, 470
Susie Holmes Memorial Scholarship, 481
Swiss Benevolent Society Medicus Student Exchange, 481
Swiss Benevolent Society Pellegrini Scholarship, 482
Sylvia W. Farny Scholarship, 178
Taglit-Birthright Israel Gift, 482
TANF (Temporary Assistance to Needy Families) Exemption, 486
Taste America San Francisco Scholarship, 305
Tau Beta Pi/SAE Engineering Scholarship, 448
Teacher Assistant Scholarship Fund, 401
Teamsters Clyde C. Crosby/Joseph M. Edgar Memorial Scholarship, 418
Teamsters Council #37 Federal Credit Union Scholarship, 418
Teamsters Local 305 Scholarship, 418
Technical Minority Scholarship, 525
Technology Scholarship, 423
Ted and Nora Anderson Scholarship, 126
Tennessee Christa McAuliffe Scholarship Program, 483

Tennessee Dependent Children Scholarship Program, 483
Tennessee HOPE Access Grant, 483
Tennessee HOPE Scholarship, 484
Tennessee Minority Teaching Fellows Program, 590
Tennessee Ned McWherter Scholars Program, 484
Tennessee Robert C. Byrd Honors Scholarship Program, 484
Tennessee Student Assistance Award Program, 484
Tennessee Student Assistance Corporation/Math And Science Teachers Loan Forgiveness Program, 590
Tennessee Teaching Scholars Program, 590
Texas College Work-Study Program, 486
Texas Early High School Graduation Scholarship, 486
Texas Fifth-Year Accounting Student Scholarship Program, 487
Texas Foster Care Students Exemption, 487
Texas Good Neighbor Scholarship, 487
TEXAS Grant (Toward Excellence, Access, and Success), 487
Texas Hazlewood Act Tuition Exemption: Veterans, 487
Texas Highest Ranking High School Graduate Tuition Exemption, 488
Texas Legion Oratorical Contest, 150
Texas National Guard Tuition Assistance Program, 488
Texas Public Educational Grant, 488
Texas Scholarships for Nursing Students, 488
Texas Transportation Scholarship, 492
Texas Tuition Exemption for Blind or Deaf Students, 488
TGS Scholarship, 482
Thelma Foster Junior American Legion Auxiliary Members Scholarship, 149
Thelma Foster Senior American Legion Auxiliary Member Scholarship, 149
Theodore Mazza Scholarship, 495
Thermoforming Division Memorial Scholarships, 457
Thermoset Division/James I. MacKenzie Memorial Scholarship, 457
Third Marine Division Memorial Scholarship Fund, 490
Thomas J. Bardos Science Education Awards for Undergraduate Students, 93
Thomas M. Stetson Scholarship, 106
Thomas R. Pickering Foreign Affairs Fellowship, 524
Thomas Wood Baldridge Scholarship, 306

Thurgood Marshall Scholarship Award, 490
Thz Fo Farm Fund, 274
Timothy Bigelow Scholarship, 287
TMC/SAE Donald D. Dawson Technical Scholarship, 449
Tom and Judith Comstock Scholarship, 168
Tommy Lee Memorial Scholarship Fund, 275
Top 10 College Women Competition, 256
Toraji & Toki Yoshinaga Scholarship, 275
Toshiba/NSTA ExploraVision Award, 380
Travel Research Grant, 493
Treacy Company Scholarship, 493
Tribal Business Management Scholarship, 215
Trimmer Education Foundation ABC Student Chapter Scholarship Program, 196
Tri-State Surveying & Photogrammetry Kris M. Kunze Scholarship, 99
Troy Douglas Carr Scholarship for Criminal Justice, 494
Truman D. Picard Scholarship, 298
Tuition Equalization Grant (TEG), 489
Tuition Exemption for Children of Disabled or Deceased Firefighters, Peace Officers, Game Wardens, and Employees of Correctional Institutions, 489
Tuition Exemption for Children of U.S. Military POW/MIAs from Texas, 489
Tuition Incentive Program, 337
Tuition Rebate for Certain Undergraduates, 489
Tuition Waiver for Foster Care Recipients, 331
Twentieth Century Fox Internship, 571
Two Ten Footwear Design Scholarship, 494
Two Ten Footwear Foundation Scholarship, 494
Two Year Community College BEA Award, 207
Tyson Foods Intern Program, 571
UBS/PaineWebber Scholarships, 501
UHEAA Grant, 508
Ukrainian Fraternal Association Scholarship, 495
Undergraduate Fellowships in Engineering and Science, 555
Undergraduate Research Fellowship (URF), 171
Undergraduate Research Scholarship, 358
Undergraduate Research Scholarship, 360
Undergraduate Scholarship Program, 358
Union Plus Scholarship, 101

United Food and Commercial Workers International Union Scholarship Program, 496
United Methodist Loan Program, 591
United Methodist Scholarships, 496
United Parcel Service Earn & Learn Program Loans, 591
United States Army Four-Year Nursing Scholarship, 438
United States Army Four-Year Scholarship, 438
United States Holocaust Memorial Museum Internship, 572
United States Senate Member Internships, 572
United States Senate Youth Program, 520
United Transportation Union Insurance Association Scholarship, 503
University Journalism Scholarship, 405
University Writing Scholarship Program, 241
UNM Hospital Nursing Scholarship, 503
Unmet Need Scholarship Program, 439
UPS Earn and Learn Program Grant, 504
Urban Flight and Rural Needs Scholarship Program, 344
Urban Forestry Internship, 553
U.S. Bank Internet Scholarship Program, 504
U.S. Department of Education Fulbright-Hays Project Abroad Scholarship for Programs in China, 229
U.S. Department of Homeland Security Scholarship and Fellowship Program, 563
U.S. Department of State Internship, 573
U.S. National Arboretum Internship, 573
USDA Summer Intern Program, 572
USDA/1890 National Scholars Program, 505
Usrey Family Scholarship, 287
USTA Scholarships, 508
Utah Career Teaching Scholarship/T.H. Bell Teaching Incentive Loan, 592
Utah Centennial Opportunity Program for Education (UCOPE), 509
Utah Robert C. Byrd Honors Scholarship, 509
Vantagepoint Public Employee Memorial Scholarship Fund, 288
Vara Gray Scholarship Fund, 150
The Vegetarian Resource Group College Scholarships, 509
Ventura County Japanese-American Citizens League Scholarships, 509
Vermont Golf Association Scholarship, 509

Vermont Incentive Grant, 512
Vermont Non-Degree Program, 512
Vermont Part-Time Grant, 512
Vertical Flight Foundation Scholarship, 107
Vice Admiral E.P. Travers Loan, 585
Vice Admiral Jerry O. Tuttle, USN (Ret.), and Mrs. Barbara A. Tuttle Science and Technology Scholarship, 191
Vicki Willder Scholarship Fund, 275
Viets Medical Student/Graduate Student Fellowship, 349
Vincent T. Wasilewski Scholarship, 207
Virgin Islands Leveraging Educational Assistance Partnership Program, 513
Virgin Islands Music Scholarship, 513
Virgin Islands Territorial Grants/Loans Program, 592
Virginia Academic Common Market, 476
Virginia Lee-Jackson Scholarship, 513
Virginia Museum of Fine Arts Fellowship, 514
Virginia Rehabilitative Services College Program, 514
Virginia Robert C. Byrd Honors Scholarship, 513
Virginia Tuition Assistance Grant, 476
Virginia Vocational Rehabilitation Program Education Sponsorship, 238
Visual and Performing Arts Achievement Award, 258
Vocational Rehabilitation Assistance, 506
Vogt Radiochemistry Scholarship, 161
Voice of Democracy Scholarship, 512
VSAC Advantage Loan, 592
Wall Street Journal Internship, 574
Wally Joe (KC's) Scholarship, 305
Wal-Mart Associate Scholarship, 515
Walt Bartram Memorial Education Award (Region 12 and Chapter 119), 455
Walter and Marie Schmidt Scholarship, 418
Walter H. Kupau Memorial Fund, 275
Walter S. Patterson Scholarship, 207
Walton Family Foundation Scholarship, 515
Washington Crossing Foundation Scholarship, 515
Washington Internships for Students of Engineering, 575
Washington State American Indian Endowed Scholarship, 516
Washington State Educational Opportunity Grant, 516
Washington State Need Grant, 516
Washington State PTA Financial Grant Program, 517
Washington State Scholars Program, 516

Water Companies (NJ Chapter) Scholarship, 367
Wayne G. Failor Scholarship, 425
Web and Technology Internship, 531
Web Challenge Contest, 482
Weisman Scholarship, 227
Welsh Heritage Scholarship, 517
Wendy Ella Guilford Scholarship Fund, 232
West Kauai Scholarship, 275
West Virginia Engineering, Science and Technology Scholarship, 518
West Virginia Higher Education Adult Part-time Student (HEAPS) Grant Program, 519
West Virginia Higher Education Grant, 519
West Virginia Robert C. Byrd Honors Scholarship, 519
West Virginia Underwood-Smith Teacher Scholarship, 593
West Virginia War Orphans Educational Assistance, 518
W.H. McClennan Scholarship, 296
Wilder-Naifeh Technical Skills Grant, 484
Wilhelmina Models Internship, 575
William A. and Ann M. Brothers Scholarship, 186
William B. Howell Memorial Scholarship, 186
William C. Davini Scholarship, 496
William C. Doherty - John T. Donelson Scholarships, 367
William D. & Jewell W. Brewer Scholarship Trusts, 131
William E. Weisel Scholarship, 455
William J. and Marijane E. Adams, Jr., Mechanical Engineering Scholarship, 177
William James & Dorothy Bading Lanquist Fund, 276
William L. Boyd, IV, Florida Resident Access Grant, 249
William Park Woodside Founder's Scholarship, 196
William R. Goldfarb Memorial Scholarship, 168
Willie Rudd Scholarship, 301
Willis H. Carrier Scholarships, 175
Wilma D. Hoyal/Maxine Chilton Memorial Scholarship, 114
Wilma Motley Memorial California Merit Scholarship, 80
Wisconsin Academic Excellence Scholarship, 522
Wisconsin Hearing & Visually Handicapped Student Grant, 522
Wisconsin Higher Education Grant, 522
Wisconsin Indian Student Assistance Grant, 522
Wisconsin Minority Teacher Loan Program, 593
Wisconsin Minority Undergraduate Retention Grant, 522
Wisconsin Talent Incentive Program Grant, 523
Wisconsin Tuition Grant, 523
Wisconsin Veterans Affairs Personal Loan Program, 593
Wisconsin Veterans Affairs Retraining Grant, 521
Wisconsin Veterans Education Tuition and Fee Reimbursement Grant, 521
Wolf Trap Foundation for the Performing Arts Internship, 575
Women in Architecture Scholarship, 198
Women in Construction: Founders' Scholarship, 367
Women's Architectural Auxiliary Eleanor Allwork Scholarship Grants, 111
Women's Sports Foundation Internship, 576
Women's Western Golf Foundation Scholarship, 524
Women's Wildlife Management/Conservation Scholarship, 380
Wooddy Scholarship, 76
Workforce Improvement Grant, 189
Workforce Incentive Program, 586
World Security Institute Internship, 576
Worldstudio AIGA Scholarship, 525
"Writers of Passage" Essay Contest, 365
Xernona Clayton Scholarship, 200
Yakama Nation Tribal Scholarship, 525
Yale R. Burge Competition, 175
Yankee Clipper Contest Club, Inc. Youth Scholarship, 168
The Yasme Foundation Scholarship, 169
Yellow Ribbon Scholarship, 491
Young Epidemiology Scholars Student Competition, 221
The Young Naturalist Awards Scholarship Program, 158
Young Survivor Scholarship, 95
Youth Scholarship, 374
"You've Got a Friend in Pennsylvania", 169
The Zachary Taylor Stevens Memorial Scholarship, 169
Zeller Summer Scholarship in Medicinal Botany, 254

Financial Aid EasyPlanner

Paying for your college education is no small undertaking. There are many questions to consider: what will it cost, how much can you save, how much can you and your family afford to pay, how much should you borrow, and what scholarships are available to you.

Not sure where to start? The College Board's Financial Aid EasyPlanner is a **FREE resource** that can help you:

- Find out what college will cost.
- Learn how savings can help you meet college costs.
- Figure out how much you can pay.
- Search for scholarships.
- Understand your loan options.
- Compare your aid awards.

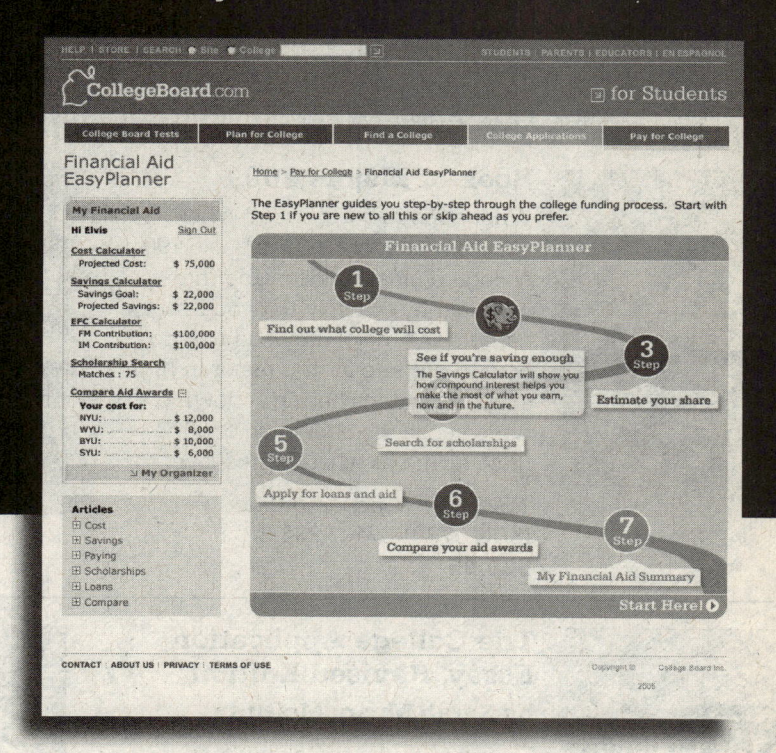

www.collegeboard.com/finaidplanner

CollegeBoard
connect to college success™

Also Available from the College Board

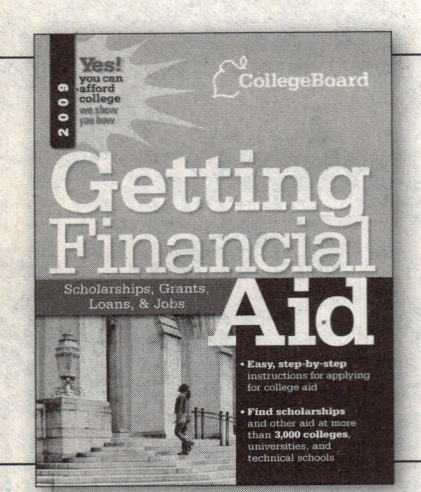

Getting Financial Aid 2009

This step-by-step guide tells you how to get aid, when to apply, and what kinds of aid to expect from colleges. Includes a planning calendar, tips from college financial aid officers, and indexes showing which colleges offer merit scholarships for your interests.

1,008 pages, paperbound
ISBN 978-0-87447-825-9
$19.95

Book of Majors 2009

What's the major for you? Where can you study it? In this book, 190 college professors describe the majors they teach: what you'll study, careers the major can lead to, and how to prepare for the major in high school. Includes listings showing which colleges offer each of 900 majors, and at what degree level.

1,328 pages, paperbound
ISBN 978-0-87447-824-2
$25.95

College Handbook 2009

Get instant access to crucial information on every accredited college in the United States. Completely updated and verified for 2009, this handbook contains detailed descriptions of 3,800 colleges, universities, and technical schools.

2,172 pages, paperbound
ISBN 978-0-87447-823-5
$29.95

The College Application Essay, Revised Edition
by Sarah Myers McGinty

Trying to find a topic for your application essay? Former admissions dean Sarah Myers McGinty shares strategies that will help you stand out from the crowd. Includes critiqued sample essays written by real students, jump starts for writer's block, and a chapter for your parents that explains their role in the process.

176 pages, paperbound
ISBN 978-0-87447-711-5
$15.95

Get It Together for College

Applying to college? Don't get overwhelmed—get organized with expert tips from the #1 college planning Web site, www.collegeboard.com. This easy-to-use planner will walk you through the forms, tests, and applications and keep you on track for each deadline. Includes insider tips, tracking charts, checklists, easy-to-follow timelines, and a junior–senior year calendar that pulls it all together.

224 pages, paperbound
ISBN 978-0-87447-829-7
$14.95

CollegeBoard
connect to college success™

Available wherever books are sold.
Distributed by Macmillan